IRB International Rugby Yearbook 2003–04

John Griffiths
Mick Cleary

CollinsWillow
An Imprint of HarperCollins*Publishers*

First published in Great Britain in 2003 by
CollinsWillow an imprint of
HarperCollins*Publishers* London

1 3 5 7 9 8 6 4 2

A CIP catalogue record for this book is available from the British Library

The HarperCollins website address is:
www.harpercollins.co.uk

ISBN 0 00 714047-9

Typeset by Letterpart Ltd, Reigate, Surrey

Printed and bound Clays Ltd, St Ives plc

Picture acknowledgements

All photographs courtesy of Allsport

CONTENTS

ABBREVIATIONS USED IN THIS YEARBOOK

International Teams

A – Australia; Arg – Argentina; AU – Australian Universities; AW – Anglo-Welsh; B – British Forces and Home Unions teams; Bb – Barbarians; Be – Belgium; BI – British/Irish teams; Bu – Bulgaria; C – Canada; Ch – Chile; Cr – Croatia; Cv – New Zealand Cavaliers; CT – Chinese Taipei; Cz – Czechoslovakia; E – England; F – France; Fj – Fiji; Gg – Georgia; H – Netherlands; HK – Hong Kong; I – Ireland; It – Italy; Iv – Ivory Coast; J – Japan; K – New Zealand Services; M – Maoris; Mo – Morocco; NAm – North America; Nm – Namibia; NZ – New Zealand; NZA – New Zealand Army; P – President's XV; Pg – Paraguay; Po – Poland; Pt – Portugal; R – Romania; Ru – Russia; S – Scotland; SA – South Africa; SAm – South America; SK – South Korea; Sm – Samoa; Sp – Spain; Tg – Tonga; U – Uruguay; US – United States; W – Wales; Wld – World Invitation XV; WS – Western Samoa; Y – Yugoslavia; Z – Zimbabwe.

Other Abbreviations used in the International Listings

(R) – Replacement or substitute; (t) – temporary replacement; [ ] – Rugby World Cup appearances.

NB: When a series has taken place, figures are used to denote the particular matches in which players have featured. Thus NZ 1,3, would indicate that a player has appeared in the First and Third Tests of the relevant series against New Zealand.

Irish Clubs

CIYMS – Church of Ireland Young Men's Society; KCH – King's College Hospital; NIFC – North of Ireland Football Club.

French Clubs

ASF – Association Sportive Française; BEC – Bordeaux Etudiants Club; CASG – Club Athlétique des Sports Generaux; PUC – Paris Université Club; RCF – Racing Club de France; SB – Stade Bordelais; SBUC – Stade Bordelais Université; SCUF – Sporting Club Universitaire de France; SF – Stade Français; SOE – Stade Olympien des Etudiants; TOEC – Toulouse Olympique Employés Club.

South African Provinces

BB – Blue Bulls; Bol – Boland; Bor – Border; EP – Eastern Province; FSC– Free State Cheetahs; GL – Gauteng Lions; GW – Griqualand West; Mp – Mpumulanga N – Natal; NT – Northern Transvaal; OFS – Free State; R – Rhodesia; SET – South-East Transvaal; SWA – South-West Africa; SWD – South-West Districts; Tvl – Transvaal; WP – Western Province; WT – Western Transvaal; Z–R – Zimbabwe–Rhodesia.

Australian States

ACT – Australian Capital Territory; NSW – New South Wales; Q – Queensland; V – Victoria; WA – Western Australia.

Competitions

CL – Celtic League; F – Final; HC – Heineken Cup; PC – Powergen Cup (English Clubs); PC – Principality Cup (Welsh Clubs); PPC – Parker Pen Cup; PPS – Parker Pen Shield; QF – Quarter Final; SF – Semi Final; SPC – Scottish Pro Championship; WP – Welsh Premiership; ZP – Zurich Premiership; ZW – Zurich Wildcard.

The authors and publishers wish to confirm that the views expressed in this Yearbook are not necessarily those of the International Rugby Board.

PREFACE

The third volume of the *IRB International Rugby Yearbook* is a special preview edition for the fifth Rugby World Cup. The eyes of rugby's global following will focus on Australia for six weeks in October and November as the 20 leading nations jostle for the title of world champion. Who better, then, than Nick Farr-Jones, captain of the Wallabies when they lifted the 1991 World Cup in England, to set the scene for our special preview?

In a lively article Nick reflects on what it means to Australians to have a major world tournament staged on home soil, and gives some fascinating insights into the support enjoyed by his successful squad. Few would dispute the World Cup thoughts of his coach Bob Dwyer, who said, 'To win we need to ensure that we have five players who would pick themselves in a World XV, five on the fringe of such a team and five tried and true Test performers.' Nick chooses New Zealand and England as the stand-out favourites for this year's tournament.

Dwyer's maxim clearly holds on the form shown by the two sides in the past six months. Our panel of experts also saw nominating the IRB Five Players of the Year as black and white. Jonny Wilkinson and Martin Johnson were the linchpins of England's outstanding form in the lead-up to the World Cup and the same could be said of their New Zealand counterparts Carlos Spencer and Chris Jack. Joe Rokocoko, the fifth nominee, enjoyed such a fairytale debut season in senior rugby that many have already compared him to fellow New Zealander Jonah Lomu, the player of the tournament in South Africa eight years ago.

It is with sadness that we record the passing of IRB Chairman Vernon Pugh, the man whose vision, intellect and energy did so much to raise the profile of rugby union as a worldwide sport. He was also an enthusiastic supporter of the Yearbook and felt very strongly that the sport deserved an annual chronicle. Our obituary pays tribute to a man who will be greatly missed.

Once again we extend thanks to Geoff Miller, the official IRB statistician for the southern hemisphere, Chris Rhys, Matthew Alvarez, Brian Newth, Michel Breton, Walter Pigatto, Matteo Silini, Doug Sturrock, Kobus Smit and Frankie Deges for preparing the records, while Jeremy Duxbury put at our disposal the fruits of his magnificent research into Fiji's Test history.

We should also like to pay tribute to the cheerful efficiency of the IRB's Michelle Treacy and to Chris Thau, whose extensive knowledge of the European Nations Cup brings authority to our coverage of the growing number of international tournaments that rely on the Board for support. Finally thanks to the in-house team of Michael Doggart and Tarda Davison-Aitkins at Collins Willow and Chris Leggatt at Letterpart. They have performed wonders behind the scenes to ensure that this edition is available before the Rugby World Cup kicks off. Let the Games begin.

London, 30th September 2003 Mick Cleary & John Griffiths

OBITUARY: VERNON PUGH

A Man for All Seasons

Mick Cleary

It was the most significant conversion in the history of rugby union, the terse announcement delivered by Vernon Pugh at the Ambassador Hotel along the Boulevard Haussmann one mid-August day in 1995 that signalled a momentous change in status of the game from amateur to professional. The declaration marked down Pugh as one of the sport's boldest and most forthright administrators, a man with respect for tradition but not ensnared by it. Pugh's death from cancer at the age of 57 on 24 April 2003 has left an imposing empty chair along rugby's corridors of power.

Born into a mining family in Carmarthenshire's Amman Valley, Pugh rose via Aberystwyth and Cambridge Universities to become a Queen's Counsel. He never forgot his socialist roots and endeavoured to encompass views at either end of the spectrum. Pugh's self-educated father once took his three sons down the pit and on reaching the surface turned to them and said: 'I never want to see you near this place again.'

For all his approachability and good fellowship, Pugh was not a trimmer or ditherer, nor one ready to compromise his opinion and settle for the safe middle ground. He fought hard to impose his view on proceedings, just as he fought hard to fend off the kidney tumour that was detected in the summer of 2002. He relinquished his chairmanship of the International Rugby Board (IRB), a post he had held since 1996, in order to recuperate. With typical disregard for overwhelming odds, he was at Chepstow Races two days before he died, determined to enjoy the moment.

Pugh did not seek high office but was quite at home in the surroundings. His first dealings with the labyrinthine, often murky, invariably fractious, world of rugby committees came in 1989 when he was asked to investigate the shady activities of those Welsh players and committee men who had taken part in a rebel tour of South Africa, a country still ostracised by the sporting community over apartheid but which had retained its old-school-tie links with rugby union. Pugh presented a damning critique of those who had sold their souls for a few rand.

Pugh's rise was swift. He became chairman of the Welsh Rugby Union in 1993, a position he held until 1997. By that time Pugh had been elected as the first independent chairman of the IRB, assuming leadership of the sport's governing body in 1996. It was as chairman of its amateurism committee the year before that Pugh had persuaded the many sceptics and traditionalists that rugby had no option but to turn its back on the noble amateur way and go professional. Pugh recognised that if the IRB did not establish control of the sport and reward players financially, then outside entrepreneurs surely would.

Under his guidance the sport embraced professionalism, about a century too late according to those in the northern union whose desire to see working men paid for labour led to the breakaway of 1893 and the formation of rugby league.

'If we had not taken the decision when we did, I have no doubt that the game would have disintegrated,' said Pugh. 'It seemed to me that the special ethos of rugby was not irrefutably linked to the non-payment of players. It just could not be proven. We had to acknowledge the changes which had taken place. The southern hemisphere had put building blocks in place for professionalism. There was no point fiddling about. It was too late for evolution.'

Pugh was both a modernist and a sentimentalist. He loved the grass-roots of the game as much as he enjoyed rubbing shoulders with the powerbrokers of the sporting world. He was a decent centre-threequarter who began his club career with Amman United, and from there enjoyed stints with Leicester, Pontypridd, St Peter's and Cardiff High School Old Boys. He was an enthusiastic coach, gladly swapping committee suit and tie to help out with Welsh student sides.

One of his cherished ambitions was to see rugby union recognised once again as an Olympic Sport. The founding father of the modern Olympic movement, Baron Pierre de Coubertin, was a supporter, a rugby referee to boot. The 1924 Olympics was the last time rugby featured in the Games. Pugh lobbied assiduously to have the sport readmitted. His last public function came at the Commonwealth Games in Manchester last summer when he hosted the recently-appointed president of the International Olympic Committee, Jacques Rogge, himself a former Belgian international back-row forward. The entreaties had some success. Rugby is now officially recognised as a contender for Olympic inclusion, although its claims for inclusion in the 2008 Beijing Games were rejected last autumn.

Under Pugh's chairmanship, IRB membership has doubled. Nearly 100 countries are now affiliated worldwide, many of them leading a parlous financial existence. Pugh recognised that Olympic membership would enable them to lay claim to government funding in their respective countries. In spreading the base, Pugh might have been guilty of diluting monies available. He was aware of the problem and had pressed hard for a charity match between the northern and southern hemispheres to take place last December in an effort to raise funds for the less-developed nations. The project was aborted after objections from leading players about a supposed lack of consultation and remuneration.

Pugh was also a driving force behind Italy's admission to the Five Nations championship in 2000. 'Vernon was always a *persona grata* in Italy,' said Giancarlo Dondi, the president of the Italian federation.

Pugh became a director of Rugby World Cup in 1996 and was influential in the setting-up of the European Cup in 1996, a cross-borders competition for clubs and provinces. All this while holding down a day job as a barrister specialising in planning and environmental law at Gray's Inn.

Like many in his position, there were times when Pugh was perhaps guilty of corralling too much power and influence. Everything had to pass his scrutiny. He made enemies, within Wales and worldwide. He was furious with the Rugby Football Union for brokering a unilateral deal with BSkyB television in 1996, a stance that saw England temporarily expelled from the Five Nations. Pugh was very suspicious if not downright hostile towards the new breed of millionaire owners that came into the English game in the wake of professionalism, men such as Sir John Hall and boxing promoter Frank Warren. Pugh and the English clubs were never bosom-buddies.

He was all too aware of the charge that the IRB lacked teeth and under his stewardship he was keen to ensure that it exercised its authority properly. It had to. For if it didn't, others would usurp its place.

'We had to show who was in charge,' said Pugh a few years ago. 'Professionalism brings problems. There is a danger of rugby's ethos being polluted and that is why we must have strong managers. We have to stand up to aggressive commercial concerns who want to put money solely in the pockets of the few. The great thing about rugby is that it has respect for itself. Because of the nature of the game there is also respect for individuals, from unglamorous prop to high-profile try-scorer.'

There was an acrimonious falling-out with the New Zealand Rugby Union when Pugh stripped them of their co-host status alongside Australia for this year's World Cup for failing to comply with certain commercial strictures. It was a messy business and the easy thing would have been to fudge the matter. Pugh had many close friends in New Zealand. Instead he did what was right. Pugh didn't enjoy those fights but he was prepared to fight them.

The tributes to him from round the world reflected not just his stature but also the warmth of his character and the strength of his convictions

'Vernon was the greatest administrator Wales has produced,' said former WRU secretary, Denis Gethin. 'There has been no-one better in the world game in my time, but I suspect he would have given it all up to be coach of Wales.'

From across the Channel came equally generous thoughts and appraisals. 'Vernon's name will forever be associated with the evolution of professional rugby which, as a rugby visionary, he helped develop while respecting the true values of the sport,' said chairman of the French federation, Bernard Lapasset.

The chairman of the Six Nations, Jacques Laurans, echoed those sentiments. 'Vernon was an enormous character in our game, a man that possessed not only warmth but also intellect. He was a great friend to the

French. It was Vernon that managed to professionalise the International Board and transform it into a truly global federation.'

It was hard to find a dissenting voice among the game's administrators as they evaluated Pugh's impact. 'I think it will be a very long time before rugby comes across a man of such breadth,' said Marcel Martin, an IRB colleague for many years. 'He had a brilliant mind and ensured that the International Board measured up to such quality.'

From Scotland, appreciative words too. 'Vernon's was a voice of calm in the aftermath of the game going open in 1995,' said Scottish Rugby Union president, Allan Hosie. 'He brought stability and wisdom to difficult situations. Without his leadership, guidance and vision, I'm not sure our game globally would be in such robust health'.

He is survived by his wife, Dorinda, and three daughters, Non, Nerys and Nia.

EDITORIAL

World Cup set to Capture Hearts and Minds as Australia Reaches out to Embrace Global Audience

Mick Cleary

Blink and you might have missed the last World Cup. Rugby fans had to scour the streets of Cardiff to unearth as much as an A4 poster pinned to the wall of a pub confirming that the show was coming to town. Australians will not be giving October's shindig a wide berth through apathy born of a lack of information.

All indications are that this Rugby World Cup will equal if not surpass the extravaganza held in South Africa eight years ago when, by supreme irony given that country's tarnished past, sport and politics fused as one to ignite the country and excite the interest of the world. Nelson is still with us, God Bless Him. Perhaps he might fancy a repeat gig in Sydney.

That would be a marketing stunt too far even for the go-ahead Aussies. They have not missed a trick in their projection of the tournament. Where Wales employed a staff of three people to get the promotional and logistical act together, Australia has some 200 on the case. It will be brash, at times over-the-top, but at least it is happening. It will engage the hearts and minds of the Aussies, and that takes some doing in a country where rugby union is some way down the pecking order. But the Australians are big into events and big into themselves. They like to show off what they've got to offer. And why not? They did it to splendid effect during the Sydney Games. They love an event and the Rugby World Cup looks like being the event of the year.

It's no use pretending, however, that all the flip-charts and glitzy marketing slogans will make or break this fifth World Cup. They won't. The stories on the field will do that. New heroes and old warriors are what people are interested in. 1995 had Lomu and Mandela, not a bad double act. Four years ago the wonderful topsy-turvy semi-final between New Zealand and France almost rescued the tournament from a mess of mediocrity and bungling. Almost but not quite. Given that the rugby itself was ordinary all the other factors came into play.

The teams themselves have no duty to entertain. But they have a duty to reach into themselves and push themselves to their outer limits. This is the moment to play rugby as it should be played. This is the stage on which to perform. It doesn't mean that caution should be thrown to the winds. All the teams have the right to pursue victory by whatever means. Well, perhaps not all means. The thuggish South African approach at Twickenham in November 2002 has no place in the game. It was brutal and it was also self-defeating as the Springboks shipped 53 points, winning neither the match nor friends.

But what all 20 teams in this World Cup must ensure is that they show the world just what rugby union can offer as a sport. There is every chance that will happen. There have never been more teams in with a shout of the ultimate recognition. England are genuine contenders for the first time ever. Even when they reached the final in 1991 there was always the sense that it was on a wing and a prayer rather than through real, sustained merit. This time there can be no argument about their status. Even David Campese rates them. Well, sort of.

And we can look forward also with real relish to see how the likes of Argentina, Italy, Canada and the Pacific Islanders shape up. The second tier countries, if we can be so patronising, are going to put some dents into the reputations of the supposedly senior sides.

For all the upbeat vibes, there are some misgivings and concerns. The tournament is about a week too long. In an effort to spread exposure right through the group stages and to give teams a proper break in the knockout rounds, the organisers have stretched the schedule to 44 days. Will the world sustain its watching brief? The soccer World Cup lasts a month, the Olympic Games just over a fortnight. The media attention span is not long. It means that the rugby will have to really assault the senses if the focus is not to wane.

There must be a worry too that the temperature for games in Queensland might prove too taxing. Even though the vast majority of games have evening kick-offs, the mercury could still be around 30°C. At the very least there has to be leniency on the use of water-carriers.

It's also to be hoped that the decision to broadcast warts-and-all replays, complete with refereeing howlers on the giant screens in the ground does not back-fire. It is only 12 months since a fat fool by the name of Pieter van Zyl was fined a derisory £600 for attacking Irish referee David McHugh during the Tri Nations game between South Africa and New Zealand in Durban.

The positives far outweigh the negatives. The organisers were handed a trump card for this tournament by the crass practices of the New Zealand union. Their dithering and naivety was to eventually cost them their role as sub-hosts to Australia. New Zealand's demise was Rugby World Cup's opportunity. It would have been heartening if the lessons gleaned from this World Cup had had the chance to impact on the voting process for the right to host the 2007 event. That decision has already been made with France getting a very decisive nod over England, winning by 18 votes to 3. No gripes with the right of France to host the tournament. There is no more uplifting place to follow rugby than in the passionate heartlands of south-west France.

But why oh why did they have to compromise the beauty and appeal of their bid by farming out three games apiece to Wales, Ireland and Scotland?

Well, we know why they did – to garner votes. The IRB needs to introduce some protocol to prevent this horse-trading. It may be the realpolitik of the world game. But it is not very edifying.

England put forward a slick, detailed bid. They also came up with the radical notion of holding a second-tier competition, the Rugby World Nations Cup, for the developing countries. They originally envisaged 32 countries taking part in this tournament that would run parallel to the elite 16-team event. They adjusted the number back to 20 teams on their revised bid. Both France and England were obliged to resubmit their bids after their initial presentations to the Board in November. France simply hadn't put enough flesh on bones. England perhaps had too much flesh for the liking of some.

The English bullish strategy rankled in some quarters. There weren't many quarters that didn't get to hear of the benefits that England reckoned they could bring to the world game as a three-man RFU delegation – Francis Baron, Graeme Cattermole and Paul Vaughan – set off on a lobbying mission visiting eight countries in the space of a couple of weeks. The trip cost in the region of £500,000 and only resulted in one vote – that of Canada's – to go with their two votes. Not what you would call value for money.

The RFU claimed they would generate 50% more revenue than France, looking to bring in some £150 million from the event. They also proposed a compensation package of £20 million to offset the losses incurred by the staging of the World Cup.

The RFU over-reached themselves and alienated many in the process. In order to boost their own credentials they claimed at one point that the IRB would run out of cash within five years, a suggestion angrily rejected by the Board.

'We've identified a cash-flow problem in the IRB reserves and estimate that they will have run out of money by 2008-09 and could well be in a negative position by the time of the 2007 World Cup,' said RFU chairman, Graeme Cattermole. 'We are at the stage where some unions have to wonder whether they can afford to participate in a World Cup. There is a real need for more robust forward-thinking by the IRB.'

These claims were dismissed out of hand. 'These comments are preposterous and naïve,' said IRB acting chairman, Syd Millar. 'The IRB are not going to run out of cash by spending more money than they have.'

The IRB have cash reserves of £40 million held back to cover extreme circumstances such as the cancellation of a Rugby World Cup, the game's only major revenue source. The IRB did have to swallow hard and cancel one of its events, the Northern versus Southern Hemisphere game due to be staged on 30 November. The project was dreamt up by the late Vernon Pugh in the summer of 2001 as a means of raising funds to help the ailing countries such as the Pacific Islands. The project was worthy but never found support among the players. They used the proposed game as a symbolic power-tussle with the IRB, flexing their collective muscle for the first time. In that sense they won, for the game was called off. However, the player unions went about the matter in the wrong way and came over as solely self-interested.

That said, the whole project was too hastily put together. There needs to be a concerted, mutually-inspired development programme. Some administrators may baulk at the thought of players having so much influence and input but that is the reality of the modern game. There has to be a partnership and the IRB needs to consider accepting a player representative on to the Board itself. It is the only sensible way forward.

The World Cup itself was under supposed threat at one point from a player boycott with the participation agreement at issue. The Australian Player Association took the ARU to court in Sydney only for the matter to be resolved at the eleventh hour. Deals need to be cut with more formality and dignity. Player representation is the only way to achieve this.

The IRB is aware of the need to streamline its operations, all the more so in the wake of the untimely death of its chairman and driving force, Vernon Pugh. The man who sanctioned professionalism in August 1995 and who had been at the helm of so many initiatives over the last decade died in April after a battle against cancer at the age of 57. He became the IRB's first elected chairman in 1996. A fuller appreciation appears elsewhere. Syd Millar stepped into the breach as chairman.

It was a grim year for rugby with several tragic, premature deaths. The most abrupt and shocking was that of 21-year-old England and Harlequins scrum-half Nick Duncombe who died on the eve of the Six Nations opener between England and France. If Duncombe had not been injured he would have been part of the England squad that week. As it was, he took himself off to Lanzarote with Quins team-mate Nathan Williams for some warm-weather training. That and a few beers. The innocence of the trip was blown asunder when Duncombe fell ill on the Thursday evening. On Friday afternoon he was pronounced dead from sepsis.

Saracens' chief executive Peter Deakin, the man who brought the dancing girls to rugby and put more bums on seats in the process than the fledgling professional game could have dared hope for, passed away in February after a long illness. Former Bristol captain Dave Tyler, a man who worked tirelessly for the clubs, died suddenly.

There are others who should be acknowledged too. The RFU lost some of its great servants: three former presidents, Sir Peter Yarranton, England lock in 1954-55; Ron Jacobs, a great bulwark of the England front-row between 1956 and 1964; and from an earlier era Dudley Kemp, who played for England in 1935. England's senior surviving player, Cliff Harrison, passed away at the age of 92, and Jack Wright, a lock in 1934, died aged 93. Lewis Cannell, Jeff Butterfield's partner in the England midfield, also died.

Scotland mourned the loss of several former players: Laurie Duff, flanker in the 1938 Triple Crown side; Ralph Sampson, hooker either side of the Second World War; Major David Gilbert-Smith and scrum-half Dallas Allardice.

Ireland gave tribute to Robin Thompson, captain of the outstanding 1955 British & Irish Lions in South Africa, and Wales to Ken Harris, a stalwart IRB figure whose custody of the WRU finances helped create the foundations from which the National Stadium rose. Bob Evans, Newport flanker, helped Wales to the Grand Slam in 1950 and played all six Tests for Karl Mullen's Lions in the same year. Kingsley Jones, Lions, Wales and Cardiff prop, died as did Bill Samuel, the games master who inspired the young Gareth Edwards.

In New Zealand there were countless tributes to the legendary Don Clarke, the world record holder for most points in Tests accumulated in an eight-year span between 1956 and 1964. During the Tri Nations came news of the deaths of Bob McMaster, a prop with the 1947-48 Wallabies, and the 1931-32 Springbok centre, J C van der Westhuizen, who was in his 98th year.

Two giants of the media passed away as the Yearbook went to press. Peter West covered international rugby as a broadcaster and journalist for nearly 40 years, and Colin Elsey – Big C to all his friends – inspired a generation of sports photographers with his innovative action shots of top-class rugby.

If those were the real low spots for the families concerned, then the game itself had its own disturbing moments. The RFU was rocked in December by allegations that a conspiracy had taken place between the 12 Premiership clubs and Rotherham to keep the Yorkshire club out of the top flight the previous year. As it was, their candidacy was rebuffed by the RFU after Rotherham failed to meet the entry criteria. The claims were made by Worcester owner Cecil Duckworth who might be said to have a vested interest in the affair given that his club had failed four years running to go up. 'I have absolutely no doubt that there was a conspiracy and worse still they have agreed to do it all over again this season,' said Duckworth.

Duckworth claimed that the Premiership clubs had agreed to contribute £60,000 each (£720,000 in total) as a slush fund payment to Rotherham. It took the RFU five months and a few hundred thousand pounds to decide that there was no real substance in the claims. An independent inquiry was overseen by Anthony Arlidge, QC.

RFU disciplinary officer Jeff Blackett, who took over from Robert Horner when he acceded to the presidency towards the end of the drawn-out saga, was scathing in his report. 'There is no cogent evidence to support the allegation that Rotherham RUFC was actually paid any money other than approved parachute payments . . . There is *prima facie* evidence that some members of the board of Premier Rugby did discuss the possibility of some payments additional to the parachute payments . . . Mr Tom Walkinshaw and Mr Charles Jillings, successive chairmen of PRL, encouraged and allowed these discussions . . . I will write to these people warning them as to their future conduct . . . This whole affair has been caused because some . . . are motivated solely by self-interest.'

There were reprimands too for Duckworth as well as Rotherham owner, Mike Yarlett. PRL were ordered to pay £90,000 costs and Worcester

£10,000. It was a tawdry affair. Rotherham, the only body to co-operate fully with the investigations, came under enormous scrutiny. It didn't affect their playing standards as they once again won promotion. Their place in National One went to Bristol whose own future was placed in considerable doubt when owner Malcolm Pearce threatened to quit in the New Year. There was fevered talk of a merger with Bath at a time when both clubs were threatened with relegation. It didn't come about but relegation did, as it will this year too.

There was a fuss at the other end of the table as well when Gloucester were comprehensively beaten 39-3 in the Zurich Premiership Grand Final at Twickenham in late May. No quibble with Wasps' right to wear the crown on the day. They out-thought and out-fought their opponents. But Gloucester had won the league itself by 15 points and had not laced a boot in anger for three weeks. The winner-takes-all, contrived and approved by the clubs, has yet to convince a wider, more sceptical audience of its merit.

Gloucester did at least have some silverware in the cabinet after winning the Powergen Cup by beating Northampton 40-22. Wasps had a fine end to the season, also winning the Parker Pen Challenge Cup, beating Bath 48-30 in the final of the successfully revamped competition. The first single-country Heineken Cup final was won by Stade Toulousain who beat Perpignan, 22-17.

France held sway on the administrative front with Jacques Laurans becoming the first French chairman in the history of the Six Nations, succeeding Allan Hosie. Former England Grand Slam captain Bill Beaumont was elected chairman of the British and Irish Lions.

England won the bragging rights on the European playing field. They won their first Grand Slam under Clive Woodward in emphatic style. How ironic that Woodward's one-time assistant, John Mitchell, should be nailing down his own Grand Slam as the All Blacks swept all before them in the Tri Nations. It was a good year for New Zealand rugby as it looked to compensate for the loss of World Cup hosting status by the only means possible – dominating the rest of the world out where it matters most. New Zealand once again won the IRB Sevens title although England came with a late gallop. The Under 21 World Cup, held in England, also went the way of New Zealand. With Auckland Blues winning the Super 12, New Zealand's only blemishes came with defeat by England in Wellington in June and a loss to South Africa in the final of the under 19 World Cup.

England are also in good fettle. They won all ten Tests played through the season, beginning and finishing with wins over the Tri Nations countries. The only blot on their copybook came in the August 2003 World Cup warm-up match in Marseilles where France scraped home by a point against one of Clive Woodward's experimental fifteens.

Attendances at English club games rose once again, reaching an average of 8,439. The season also saw the largest ever crowd for a Premiership game, 20,739 turning up at Ashton Gate in ghoulish fashion to see the west-country derby between relegation-threatened Bristol and Bath. Bristol won that skirmish but lost the war. Since the last World Cup in 1999, gates at club games in England have risen 53%.

If only things were so rosy across the whole landscape of European rugby. Two clubs in France, Bourgoin and Bordeaux, faced serious financial problems. In Wales, the whole parlous matter came to an acrimonious head with the compression of the clubs into five new provincial set-ups. Nothing is ever straightforward in Welsh rugby and two of the new outfits, Cardiff and Llanelli, retain their name and identity. No such reprieve for famous names such as Newport, Swansea, Neath, Pontypridd and Bridgend. The latter had some sort of last laugh by winning the last ever major club league title.

Llanelli won the Principality Cup. How different things are for neighbours and old rivals, Swansea, who were forced to seek administration. A once proud club was on its knees.

The whole of Welsh rugby has spent too long in the supine position. The desperate state of affairs was somehow captured in the farce surrounding the departure for Australia and New Zealand. A protracted wrangle over new contracts caused the squad to miss their flight. Another no show by Wales. There have been too many of them. WRU chairman Glanmor Griffiths will have to cope with it no longer as he announced his retirement after 20 years of service.

Scotland have taken a step forward with the appointment of their first foreign coach, Matt Williams. The Australian has done significant things with Leinster, taking them to the Celtic League title. Williams succeeds Ian McGeechan who in turn steps into the Director of Rugby office occupied by Jim Telfer, who has retired. Telfer deserves a few hurrahs before he leaves rugby's stage. Edinburgh won the Bank of Scotland Pro Cup.

The Irish provinces continue to make their presence felt in the Heineken Cup. At one point there was hope of an all-Ireland final, which would certainly have filled Dublin never mind Lansdowne Road. As it was both Munster and Leinster fell at the semi-final stages.

The IRB continues to foster the game worldwide. The Superpowers Cup, an innovation dreamt up by Vernon Pugh to tap into the vast potential of the Chinese market, was won by Russia although the competition was undermined by the withdrawal of China owing to the SARS epidemic. Portugal had a heartening year, claiming their own Grand Slam ahead of Romania in the European Six Nations Cup.

Domestic competition will take place during the Rugby World Cup. Attendances actually stood up very well during the last World Cup.

The World Cup has that sort of effect. It reaches all parts as one of the sport's leading sponsors might say. Let's hope so.

Enough said.

IRB FIVE PLAYERS OF THE YEAR

Outstanding Candidates are Black and White

Mick Cleary

Joe Rokocoko (New Zealand)

The conveyor belt didn't even stutter. As one great wing shuffled off the end, another was hopping enthusiastically on to the production line. We all hope that the stricken Jonah Lomu manages one day to overcome the kidney ailment that has blighted both his life and, latterly, his rugby career.

But New Zealand rugby already has a new star to admire and applaud. 20-year-old Fijian-born Joe Rokocoko has made as big an impact on international rugby as Lomu did in the mid-nineties. He became the youngest All Black since Lomu in 1994 when selected for the squad to face England a week before his 20th birthday, and raced to ten Test tries in only five appearances, a new world record.

He is a different build to Lomu – less bulky but sharper on his feet – but the end result is the same. He has already scored two hat-tricks of tries in his opening season of test rugby, first against France and then Australia.

Rokocoko was born in Nadi but his family moved to New Zealand when he was five years old. He is a cousin of former All Black wing Joel Vidiri. Rokocoko has played through all the age groups for New Zealand and was a key member of the Sevens squad that won the IRB World Series in 2002. He scored 27 tries in six international Sevens tournaments that year but missed out on the Manchester Commonwealth Games after breaking a leg in the Under-21 World Cup in South Africa.

Carlos Spencer (New Zealand)

The maverick has finally won over the doubters. No-one has ever disputed the outrageous natural talent of Carlos Spencer. That much was evident even to a British audience when he first appeared for the New Zealand Barbarians against England in 1997.

That was the year that he made his Test debut for the All Blacks, scoring 33 points against Argentina. He was soon past the century mark, taking only five Tests to share the world record for reaching that landmark with countrymen Simon Culhane and Andrew Mehrtens. But it was Mehrtens who was to eclipse Spencer for so many years. As the Canterbury fly-half collected caps, Spencer had to make do with intermittent appearances. There was a two-year gap between his 12th and 13th caps, Spencer being out of the frame after playing against Italy in Genoa in 2000 until his international recall against England at Twickenham in November 2002.

Joe Rokocoko (New Zealand) playing against Australia at Sydney in 2003 when he became the first player to score a hat-trick of tries in a Tri Nations match.

It was always felt that he was too inconsistent, as liable to cost a side a game as win it. However talent will out. It was the inspirational Spencer that was to the forefront of the Auckland Blues' march to the Super 12 title in 2003. He scored over a century of points for the Blues in this year's tournament, passing 500 career points during the victory over the Crusaders in the final.

Jonny Wilkinson (England)

They keep on coming and he keeps on knocking them down. There have been a whole host of players who fancy that they might be able to smash Jonny Wilkinson aside. Few have managed to do so. Not all of these attempts have been legitimate.

An ethically-dubious barometer of Wilkinson's worth to England is that some sides have tried to illegally take him out of the game. Springbok lock Jannes Labuschange was sent off at Twickenham for a late, high lunge at Wilkinson. Despite the dismissal, the blows kept coming at Wilkinson and he was eventually forced off.

His coaches have tried to persuade him to step back from the firing line but it's something of a lost cause. Even so, Wilkinson himself recognises that he can get suckered into a macho slugging contest. He did against France in 2002 when flanker Serge Betsen came looking for him. Wilkinson admits that he allowed himself to get distracted in trying to out-thump Betsen in the tackle. It is this ability to learn and adapt that has kept Wilkinson right at the top of the world rankings. For all his success he never takes anything for granted. His attention to detail is legendary, his desire to practise brooking no interference.

Wilkinson has broken through all record barriers for England. He has already scored 704 points in his 46 Tests. His importance to the England cause cannot be underestimated. Clive Woodward has made great play of the fact that he wants England to be able to cope without Wilkinson. And to that end, they have proved that they can still win matches. However, without him the threat is not as potent. Remember too that while Spencer was having a bad night with the boot in Wellington, Wilkinson was knocking them over. It was to prove the difference.

Martin Johnson (England)

No more than just a big bruiser? Martin Johnson has knocked that sweeping generalisation into a cocked hat this past year. Sure, Johnson does his fair share of bruising but his greatest asset has been his ability to move with the times. It's easy to see Johnson as no more than the enforcer in the England team, a solid, unflappable hunk that binds the side together in moments of crisis. He does all that and that is no mean achievement. Would England have survived the Goal Line Stand against New Zealand in Wellington, coped with a series of scrums on their own line when reduced to six men, if

Carlos Spencer (New Zealand) makes a typically determined break against England in Wellington in June. England won the match 15-13.

Three more points for Jonny Wilkinson in England's 25-14 victory against Australia in Melbourne in June.

Johnson had not been there? Probably not. But to truly appreciate his significance you have to move beyond even that. Johnson is, and continues to be an outstanding athlete and second-row forward. One glance of the tape of England's victory over the Wallabies in Melbourne will show you that. In the build-up to the first England try scored by Will Greenwood, Johnson handled no fewer than four times in the 13-phase sequence. His speciality used to be the set-piece: a rock in the scrum and a banker at the front of the line-out. Johnson has moved on, recognizing that a second-row forward has to contribute all round the field. Johnson, twice Lions captain, is getting more influential with each passing season.

Chris Jack (New Zealand)

If Johnson is the proven item of second-row play, then Chris Jack has made a very decent fist of revealing his own credentials over the course of the past year. The 25-year-old Canterbury lock was voted New Zealand Player of the Year last season for his consistent contributions to both the New Zealand and Canterbury Crusaders' cause. He scored a try barely ten minutes after coming on in his debut Test against Argentina at Christchurch's Jade Stadium in 2001, a sign of the agility and ball-carrying skill that has been much in evidence on the international scene ever since. Second-row play runs in the blood. Jack's father locked the Taranaki scrum in the late 50s while elder brother, Graham, made his way into the Canterbury and Crusaders pack ahead of him.

Jack broke through himself in the late nineties, winning back-to-back Super 12 titles with the Crusaders in 1999 and 2000. The tall, angular figure had already come to the attention of the All Black hierarchy as he passed through the various age groups to New Zealand Colts and New Zealand A. Even though he is at home in open play, his deft hands and pace making him an invaluable asset round the field, Jack has also proved himself a reliable operator at the set-piece. His line-out work has been a key part of the All Black success this season, his ability to spoil opposition ball and guarantee his own providing the solid base on which Carlos Spencer and his mates can flourish.

Martin Johnson, the England captain, is tackled by David Giffin and Nathan Grey during England's defeat of Australia in June.

Chris Jack of New Zealand on the charge during the Tri-Nations match between South Africa and New Zealand on July 19, 2003 at Loftus Versfeld in Pretoria, South Africa.

RUGBY WORLD CUP VIEWPOINT

The World Cup Comes Down Under

Nick Farr-Jones

Nick Farr-Jones, who captained Australia 36 times and led the side that won the 1991 Rugby World Cup staged in Britain, Ireland and France, looks forward to this year's event.

As we enter the serious countdown for the kick off of Rugby World Cup 2003, the great debate continues as to who are the likely contenders as teams eye each other off and the slide rule is run over the form of the heavyweights in the last 12 months or so. Many players are acutely aware that from their individual perspective this World Cup will be their final throw of the dice and pressures to secure rugby's greatest prize will continue to mount.

And to some extent it is somewhat a throw of the dice as three of the victorious teams to date have had their fair share of luck and the bounce of the ball on the way through. Only the mighty All Black team that secured the inaugural trophy way back in 1987 could claim that they ran first and daylight came second. But more as to the current likely pecking order a bit later. How will Australia and its people embrace the tournament, and what sort of momentum has grown to date?

It should be remembered that rugby union competes in our winter months for player participation, crowd support and the all-important sponsorship dollar against three other sports. On the east coast of Australia rugby league is immensely popular. In the southern and western states Australian Rules literally rules and in recent years has also infiltrated into the east coast states. Finally, as a participation sport soccer remains extremely popular especially amongst junior players – if only we could qualify for FIFA's World Cup finals!

But there is something to be said for the huge level of support that we Aussies will give when one of our own (and they can be inherited as is often the case in a new country) goes out into an international sporting arena with green and gold on their back. You don't need to understand the rules – a Godsend for the complex and sometimes convoluted game of rugby – but give an Aussie a fight on a major international stage and we get somewhat carried away in the emotion of it all. You only have to go back to 1983 when a boat named Australia II came back against insurmountable odds to unbolt the Americas Cup for the first time to appreciate this. Even our then Prime

Minister, Bob Hawke, emotionally declared that if any boss sacked someone for not turning up to work that day they were a bum. And this was a boat race!

And as I write this article I am hearing confirmation that our great runner Cathy Freeman has just announced her retirement. Australians will never ever forget the feeling that September night in 2000 at the Olympic Stadium in Sydney when our country literally stopped. Every Australian will remember where they were and how they felt as she braced the tape and forever became 'Our Cathy'.

But for rugby and the World Cup it didn't start this way. I well recall playing in an amazing semi-final in 1987 where the lead changed five times in the second half, the French eventually gaining the ascendancy in the final minutes after a last-gasp try by the mercurial Serge Blanco. The French would later describe the match as the game of the century; however, at the lonely and unloved Concord Oval in Sydney's inner west, only a little over 18,000 people turned up to take in the spectacle. It was a combination of the new Concord Oval being unloved by the traditional rugby die-hards but also that Australians really hadn't been taken by the concept of a global tournament then in its embryonic stages.

That all changed dramatically in 1991 when the stage moved to the northern hemisphere. Despite the fact that far fewer tries would be scored on the heavier and slower pitches, the Australian people took to it like kangaroos to a grassy pasture. From a distance, as our team continued to advance, sometimes in dramatic circumstances like the great escape against the Irish at Lansdowne Road, the more local fans sat up in the wee hours of the morning fascinated and captured by the event and the progress of their Wallabies.

And it wasn't just in the typical rugby strongholds of Sydney and Brisbane. Unbelievably to us players, in states where rugby was virtually unknown television ratings were revealing amazing statistics as to how many people were sitting up glued to their sets. The word spread and as we reached the final to be played at Twickenham parties all across the country had been organised as Aussies planned how they would ensure they were awake come 1am in the morning on that fateful day in early November.

Then there were the faxes that came pouring into our London Hotel when six machines had to be installed to cope with the demand. One couple in Melbourne of all places had just named their newly-born daughter after two of the Wallabies' players. Then there was the fax from a lady in Adelaide who went to great effort to explain that she knew nothing about the game but had been absorbed watching our progress. Her last sentence was a promise of sexual favours for the scorer of the first try in the final versus England. Sadly the only try that day came as our two prop forwards crashed over the English line seemingly joined by the ball – we never did hear back from the Adelaide fan! Then finally a street parade in Sydney that I tried to have cancelled for fear of a lack of interest. To our amazement more than 100,000 fans lined the streets of George Street to welcome back their team – how much things had changed.

Australians have continued to embrace the Wallabies especially since the recent Rod Macqueen-coached, John Eales-captained team achieved unprecedented success in winning the 1999 World Cup, Bledisloe and Tri Nations trophies and finally got the monkey off the back in beating the impressive Bristish Lions in 2001. Perhaps the only downside for the ever growing band of supporters is that with the recent success comes a growing expectation that George Gregan's Wallabies can become the first team to defend the title. Quite simply, the Wallabies have become victims of their own success.

In 2000 Australians embraced the Olympic Games. But that was a 15-day event in just one city. What is exciting sporting fans here in Australia is that Rugby World Cup will last for over five weeks and be played right across the country in 12 different towns and cities. Down in the little Tasmanian town of Launceston, October temperatures will be to the liking of most combatants; however, thousands of kilometres north in the tropical Queensland city of Townsville temperatures are likely to be stifling. Let's hope the French, who are due to play in the north, don't take a lesson from the Irish. Back in 1995 when preparing to play their pool matches on South Africa's veldt at 6,000 feet they spent their last week preparing in Kilkenny – officially 27 feet below sea level!

Back in the amateur days of rugby I was of the view that it was a potential disadvantage to play a major rugby event at home. Australia co-hosted the inaugural World Cup and there was great pressure on players to continue their day jobs. It was understandable that employers wanted their pound of flesh, especially when you were residing in your own city. But now the rugby unions are the employers and players can focus all their energies and attention on one thing – producing the best rugby they are capable of. As such it should be a huge advantage in 2003 for the Wallabies to be playing in front of full houses, the majority of whom should be locals. Ever since British Lions supporters in 2001 painted the Brisbane stadium red and their team proceeded to bash the Wallabies in the first Test, Australian supporters and administrators have been conscious of showing maximum support for the home team. We can expect stadiums to be awash with gold and I suspect the support will have a positive impact for the Wallabies, especially in the knockout stages of the tournament.

But that does not mean we will not embrace the overseas visitors. We love the goodwill and spirit that they bring – some with great expectation that their team will bubble to the surface, others just to join in the party. Since retirement I have discovered one of the great joys of rugby is what the French describe as *Le Troisième Mistemps* or third half. In a nutshell it is the party that goes on either side of the 80 minutes of action. In late spring here in Australia visitors from the northern hemisphere will be going to matches in summer clothes and you can be assured that the beer sponsors Heineken will be chasing their tails trying to keep up with the demand.

The stand-out favourites for me are England and New Zealand. For the All Blacks it has been an extraordinarily long time since their only title back in 1987. Their unforgiving supporters expect nothing but victory. As for the English, for most of their ageing team this is their swansong. They will either be a side remembered for reaching their potential or falling at the final hurdle. For a team that has historically excelled between World Cups, there will be immense pressure on them. The Wallabies are not yet settled with their personnel and have shown inconsistent form domestically, but with local support only the foolhardy would write them off. The French are the French and will enjoy their underdog status while the Springboks have only played to date in a dozen World Cup matches but at full time have never been behind. The pride in their traditions will carry them a long way. And if the Irish get some rub of the green they are always capable of springing major upsets – it just so happens that with the quality of their team their victories these days do not come as major shocks.

As we analyse our team's chances I think it is worth deliberating for a moment on what my 1991 coach said to me some 10 months before that season's World Cup commenced. 'To win Nick we need to ensure that we have five players who would pick themselves in a World XV, five on the fringe of such a team and five tried and true Test performers.' As I look back on the four previous World Cup champions each of those teams would meet this criteria. But whatever happens on the paddock we are bound to have five fun-filled, exhilarating weeks as the Rugby World Cup comes Down Under – bring it on and may our collective cups fill till they overflow.

RUGBY WORLD CUP PREVIEW

No Antidote as World Cup Fever Takes Hold

Mick Cleary

Wallaby coach Eddie Jones had no doubt about it. 'Mate, the French are holding something back, I'm telling you. They're not showing us their full hand,' said Jones as he crossed a hotel lobby in Rome early one morning.

The chance meeting took place way back in March. The paranoia sets in early these days as teams prepare for the World Cup. Not one of the coaches is content with thinking in the square. They are all to be found hugging the left side of the field as they look to out-fox their opposite numbers. A dummy here, a shimmy there, a contrived selection this way, a midfield scissors that way.

Do we buy the Jones looking-over-the-shoulder routine? Or are they all actually playing it straight? Bluff and double-bluff. You pays your money. It's all part of the fascination of the build-up to this fifth World Cup, one that promises to be the most closely-contested of all. It also promises to be a slick, professional operation, in contrast to the 1999 event in Britain, Ireland and France which was a disappointment. That event was divided between five countries and suffered as a result. There was no focus, no clear sense of identity and no tangible effort to promote the tournament and bring it to a wider audience. Perhaps as a result of those failings, the organisers this time have spent much time, effort as well as money to ensure that the World Cup reaches all corners of both that big sunny land Down Under as well as all other interested parts of the globe.

That the World Cup has come to be in one country has happened by default rather than design. New Zealand dithered and dissembled so much that Rugby World Cup eventually lost patience and removed their sub-host status. It was a savage blow to that country, both to its pride as well as to its economy. There will be many envious glances across the Tasman this October and November. It was a monumental cock-up on their part. The World Cup must go to that country alone one day. Never mind the commercial and logistical limitations. Rugby has obligations to its past as well as its future.

New Zealand's misfortune is Australia's opportunity. And, boy, do they seem to have realised that. There is an energy and enthusiasm about the venture – adventure would be a more fitting description – that has proved infectious. There is not one person encountered in recent months – player, administrators, fan, man-in-the-street-who-normally-doesn't-give-a-two-penny-stuff-for-rugby – who is not looking forward to the big kick-off on 10 October. The hard proof of that subjective assessment lies in ticket sales.

The Australians have done a terrific job in pushing their own quota. Gone are the days when a World Cup semi-final doesn't sell out in Australia, as happened in 1987 when the Concord Oval didn't reach its miserly capacity of 19,000 for what turned out to be one of the sport's greatest ever games; France, inspired by the magic of Serge Blanco, edging out the Wallabies in the dying moments.

Try these figures. Four months before the tournament begins the Australians were reporting that their allocation of tickets for games involving Ireland had already sold out – that is, 10,000 for the opening match against Romania at Gosford, an amazing 30,000 for the game against Namibia at Aussie Stadium in Sydney, over 18,000 for the Argentina game in Adelaide and 32,000 for that juicy-looking encounter between Australia and Ireland in Melbourne.

And who will win? Who cares might we say from this objective corner of the land, one of the few non-partisan parts of the planet. There are more genuine contenders for this World Cup than any of its predecessors. Take your pick from New Zealand, Australia, England, France or South Africa, despite their poor form of late. There are likely to be upsets along the way, too. Or perhaps not upsets, just a re-working of the old world order. Italy and Canada and even Tonga will push Wales all the way in Pool D; Argentina will cause similar mischief in Pool A where Australia and Ireland will be looking for a quiet life.

It's all shaping up wonderfully well. Enjoy.

The Teams

Pool A: Australia, Argentina, Ireland, Namibia, Romania

Australia

The defending champions will not give up their crown easily in front of their own supporters. Home advantage, however, is a double-edged sword. The support can intimidate as much as it can inspire. If things run smoothly, then the crowd does undoubtedly lift a side to even greater heights. But if the ride should get a little bumpy, the pressure of expectation as well as the critical sniping from the sidelines can weigh heavily on a team's morale. The Wallabies have not had the smoothest build-up. Their losses in Europe last year, to Ireland and England, suggested that the strength-in-depth of the squad is not a bottomless mine. Australia have always been adept, however, at maximising resources and there is little doubt that if they can get all their front-line troops in action then they are well-placed to become the first side to retain the Webb Ellis trophy. For that to happen their forward pack needs to move up at least three levels. It was underpowered earlier in the season, providing no sort of platform for George Gregan to work off. The line-out has been a constant source of attention for coach Eddie Jones. He knows if he can rectify these ailments then he has the firepower in Joe Roff, Wendell Sailor and Lote Tuqiri to do some real damage.

Argentina

The Pumas have always been proud participants in Rugby World Cups, playing with a passion that makes them troublesome opponents for any side, even if they did somehow contrive to lose all three pool matches in 1995. They made up for that failing when beating Ireland, 28-24, in the quarter-final play-off in Lens four years later. No more will the Pumas be seen as spirited underdogs. They have a track record that demands serious attention, a fact that was more than adequately proven only a few months ago. France were beaten twice on successive June weekends in Buenos Aires and just to prove that was no fluke, Argentina then travelled to Port Elizabeth where they were denied a landmark first-ever victory by a last-minute penalty from Springbok fly-half Louis Koen. That one-point defeat, ironically, made people more aware of the Pumas' potential for this World Cup than their two home victories. Argentina have always been a handful in Buenos Aires. Now we have evidence that they can do some damage on the road as well. And they did it without the inspirational direction of injured scrum-half Agustin Pichot. We know all about the power of the Pumas pack. But in wing José-Nuñez Piossek and full-back Juan-Martin Hernández they have players who can twinkle and threaten too.

Ireland

The warm glow of an immensely successful season was dissipated somewhat by consecutive games at either end of the globe. First England did a comprehensive number on Ireland in the Grand Slam showdown at Lansdowne Road at the end of March. That 42-6 victory blew away any notions that Ireland had the right to dine at the top table. True, they had provided a few tasty titbits of their own throughout a very productive year, winning a record 10 games in succession. But when it came to the crunch they were found wanting. Good but not yet good enough. The detail of their 45-16 defeat by the Wallabies in Perth was further evidence of this. Ireland, without a few front-ranking players, were blown away in the exchanges round the fringes, falling off tackles and failing to impose themselves. The squad regrouped well to come away with two commendable victories in the Pacific Islands, beating Tonga 40-19 and Samoa 40-14, Ronan O'Gara contributing a record 32 points to that win in Apia. Ireland, despite their limitations, will be the stronger for all these experiences.

Romania

The woes and pitfalls of Romanian rugby over the past decade have been many. The humbling 134-0 defeat by England two years ago was the lowest point of all for this once proud and productive rugby nation. If adversity doesn't break you, it will make you. And from the depths of that Twickenham debacle Romania have slowly pulled themselves together. Former flanker, Octavian Morariu, stepped into the breach, taking over as president of the Union. Former French under 19 coach, Bernard Charreyre, was brought in to oversee coaching. The double appointments paid dividends,

Romania winning the 2002 European Nations Cup and qualifying for the World Cup with some encouraging performances in defeat to Ireland (39-8 in a friendly) and Italy (25-17). Spain were comfortably beaten 67-6. Romania won six of its ten matches played in 2002 and finished as runners up in their 'away' leg of this season's European Nations Cup. The blooding of young players such as hooker Marius Tincu has helped galvanise Romanian forward play, a traditional source of strength. For the third time in succession Romania find themselves in the same pool as Australia.

Namibia

Much will depend on Namibia's ability to secure full and total release of all their players, many of whom are contracted in South Africa, as well as to a lesser extent France and England. They have struggled down the years to put out their best team. 'It's a terrible situation,' said coach, New Zealander Dave Waterston, who knows only too well the difficulty of gathering players from far-flung places having coached Tonga at the last World Cup. The Namibians are used to harsh environments, in life and so in rugby. Their union was only formally recognised in 1990 and they draw from a small base of just 19 clubs. Waterston, who has also worked with the Springboks and the All Blacks, will ensure that his side will be no soft touch. He will want to improve on their performance in qualifying where they only just scraped though the African group by dint of scoring one try more than Tunisia. The two countries finished level on match points after the home and away legs, points for and against were also equal, so the deciding factor went to tries.

Pool B: France, Scotland, Fiji, Japan and United States

France

Do we buy into the Eddie Jones line that they are hiding something? If you do, then it's bankrupt currency you're trading in. France have had a dreadfully muddled year and it's easy to see where the conspiracy theory arose from. However, the simple truth of the matter is that they would dearly love to have a settled side, in the groove and trusting each other. As it is, coach Bernard Laporte has had cause several times this year to launch a withering blast at his players, the last of which came in Argentina after successive defeats to the Pumas. Laporte pledged then that certain players would not be going to the World Cup. He was true to his strident word. In the 30-man group named at the beginning of July there was no place for established players such as Thomas Castaignède, Vincent Clerc or David Bory, who did not tour but who might have expected a call-up. Laporte has opted for the versatile South African-born Brian Liebenberg. There is another foreign national in the French squad, New Zealander Tony Marsh, who has made a heartening recovery from testicular cancer. South African-born prop Pieter de Villiers, who had rehabilitated himself from a drug scandal earlier in the year, withdrew from the World Cup squad owing to a training camp injury. France, for all the meanderings of form, are still very dangerous.

Scotland

The future of Scottish rugby has been secured with the appointment of Australian Matt Williams to succeed Ian McGeechan. But what sort of legacy will be passed down to the former Leinster coach? Will it be a glorious farewell for the highly-respected McGeechan or yet another tale of valiant but rather inevitable failure. McGeechan is unlikely to bow out on a low note. He is a past master at getting the best from not very much and the showing of his team in South Africa in June suggests that Scotland will be competitive. They will need, however, to improve their points-scoring strike-rate. In three of this year's Six Nations games they failed to reach double figures. Even though they managed two victories, against Italy and Wales, they still finished with the lowest tally of points scored in the entire Six Nations with a return of 81 points from five matches, one fewer than bottom-placed Wales. The problems with goal-kicking do at least seem to have been rectified now that Chris Paterson has stepped up to the mark.

Fiji

Glamour boys or serious items? No-one who has seen Fiji on the Sevens circuit has any doubts about their ability to both thrill and deliver the goods. However, those innate yet carefully-honed skills in the shorter game have never quite transferred to the big stage at World Cups. Yet there are signs that Fiji now recognises the value to be found in performing consistently in the 15-a-side version. At the last World Cup they were denied a place in the quarter-final proper when poor refereeing decisions cost them victory over France in Toulouse, the home side going through 28-19 meaning Fiji had to travel to Twickenham to play England in the play-off. Defeat was inevitable. Coach Brad Johnstone brought more vigour and organisation to Fijian forward play, a legacy that new coach Mac McCallion is determined not to waste. Fiji qualified top of their group, winning in Samoa, and had cause for hope after their short tour to Australia in June where they beat Queensland 31-24 and only narrowly lost to the Brumbies, 26-25. They finally sharpened their wits for the World Cup with a whistle-stop tour of South America where they met Argentina and Chile.

Hooker and captain Greg Smith ensures that his forward pack keep to the straight and narrow while the new sensation of Super Twelve, Auckland Blues wing Rupeni Caucaunibuca, is set to be a star of this World Cup. The Fijians will be the best suited of this group to the taxing high temperatures of the Queensland coast.

Japan

The Japanese have always made the most of market opportunities. As with their economy, so with their rugby. They have lived with their lack of indigenous size on a rugby field for generations and have simply bought in overseas talent to help rectify the shortfall. Once again their squad has a sprinkling of overseas talent with four New Zealanders in their 30-man group. Given that France has two overseas players in its squad and Scotland has long since pored over the ancestry rights of many a Kiwi, then the pots and kettles symphony had best remain mute. The Kiwi brigade comprises fly-half Andrew Miller, centres Reuben Parkinson and George Konia and lock Adam Parker.

Japan have not had an encouraging build-up. They did poorly on their tour of Australia in March, only winning one of four matches against club sides, and then suffered a heavy defeat by 69-27 in May in the inaugural Superpowers Cup to the United States, one of their pool opponents. A 43-34 loss to Russia followed in May.

Japan at least managed to keep hold of the coat-tails of the England second string that arrived there in early July on the way back from Canada. Four days later, however, the national side succumbed to the power of the English losing by 55-20 at the Municipal Stadium in Tokyo.

Japan easily won its World Cup qualifying group with one-sided home and away victories over Korea and Chinese Taipei, with an aggregate of 420 points from their four games. They have taken part in all four World Cups and have registered one win in their 12 matches, against Zimbabwe, 52-8, in 1991.

United States

The USA Eagles will not be content with also-ran status in this group. They have serious ambitions to claim at least one major scalp and have prepared themselves accordingly. Coach Tom Billups, the former Eagles and Harlequins hooker, has worked hard on his team's conditioning programme, the benefits of which were to be seen in the Churchill Cup in June. The United States beat their long-standing rivals Canada 16-11 in Vancouver, only their third ever victory over the higher-ranked Canucks on Canadian soil. That victory put them through to play England A in the final of the newly-created tournament. England A won 43-6, but the experience will stand Billups's men in good stead. 'We studied hard and prepared well as a team,' said Billups of the Churchill Cup venture. The win over Canada was the Eagles' fourth consecutive victory of the year, a new national record.

The UK experience of the likes of Dan Lyle, Dave Hodges, Luke Gross and Jason Keyter will ensure that the Eagles tend well to the basics. Such optimism is a far cry from the days of the qualifying process when they lost 21-13 to Chile in Santiago and then 10-9 to Uruguay in Montevideo, defeats which forced the Eagles to take a circuitous route through the repechage.

Pool C: England, South Africa, Georgia, Samoa, Uruguay

England

England have nothing to fear but fear itself. If they for one moment get fazed by their recent elevation to the top of the world rankings, then either the anxiety of expectation or the arrogance of presumptuousness could be their undoing. Happily for England followers, there is no evidence to suggest that any fault lines across their psychological landscape are likely to crumble during the World Cup.

England have acquitted themselves well on every front over the past 18 months. They have managed to conquer opposition teams out where it counts on the field and also succeeded in casting a few inner demons to the winds. The team finally landed the Grand Slam after three last-match failures. Their first clean sweep in the six-year reign of Clive Woodward was achieved in some style, too, a gutsy Ireland being eventually overrun 42-6 at Lansdowne Road in March. The Tri Nations sides fared little better. New Zealand, Australia and South Africa were beaten on successive Saturdays at Twickenham in November, a dose repeated for two of them, the All Blacks and the Wallabies, seven months later in their own back yard. England won all 10 matches in the season, their best return in almost half a century. The side is settled under the leadership of Martin Johnson. He and a few of his ageing mates such as Neil Back and Jason Leonard would dearly love to sign off with a World Cup triumph. England have put themselves in the best possible position to do just that.

South Africa

Will the real South Africa please stand up to be counted? It's been impossible to judge the true potential of those that will wear the famous green-and-gold Springbok shirt at the World Cup for the simple reason that there have been so many figures pulling the jersey over the heads in various changing rooms these last few months. Coach Rudolph Straeuli has chopped and changed throughout the season, making numerous alterations from game to game. Straeuli may insist that the mere ability to do this indicates the strength in depth of South African rugby. His critics, and they are growing in number, see it as a sign of desperation. Even when victories have been recorded, the murmurs of discontent have not been silenced. Scotland were beaten twice, followed by Argentina, yet most neutrals felt that the 'Boks were lucky to get away with one win let alone three. After their disappointing form in the Tri Nations tournament, South Africa will have to dig deep and summon up those famous reserves of cussedness to make a success of this tournament.

Georgia

Georgia will be on everyone's mind in this group. The big-hitters, England and South Africa, know that they will beat Georgia but they also know that they will have to be on their mettle to do so, particularly up-front. Georgian rugby has made great advances in the last decade, largely as a result of the appointment of Claude Saurel as head coach in 1999. The former Béziers hard-man flanker of the 1970s was an advisor before then and it was on his recommendation and help that some 70 or so Georgian players found placements in French club rugby. That experience has been instrumental in helping Georgia put together a side that can cause a few problems and one that certainly does the basics very well. They won the second-tier Six Nations, the European Nations Cup, two years ago. Georgia clinched their place in Australia by dint of beating arch-rivals, Russia, 17-13. The 40,000 packed into the Boris Paichadze National Stadium in Tbilisi enjoyed that.

Samoa

Manu Samoa have a distinguished record at World Cups. Just ask any Welsh fan. Any hopes Wales had of going the distance in the 1991 tournament were rudely smashed aside by the 16-13 defeat inflicted on them by Manu Samoa in their very first match. And just to prove that victory was no fluke the Samoans showed exactly the same lack of servitude eight years later when they beat Wales again, this time winning 38-31. That generation had several world-class performers to call on such as Pat Lam and Va'aiga Tuigamala. Those men have now retired but their spirit lives on. Samoa have had mixed fortunes in their build-up but are sure to be a handful come the day.

Uruguay

They're getting used to the big stage. And pretty decent performers on it they are too. Uruguay were an unknown quantity at the 1999 World Cup and there were fears that they might be over-run. They were not and even had the morale-boosting satisfaction of a win over fellow novice World Cup travellers, Spain, 27-15. Uruguay fronted up against the big fellows too, only going down 43-12 to Scotland and 39-3 to the Springboks. The South Americans have not wasted that legacy.

Uruguay finished the qualifying process strongly. They won three successive games in Montevideo to consign the United States to the repechage, deservedly so too given that Uruguay recorded their first ever wins over the Eagles as well as Canada in those qualifiers. One of the strong men of the Uruguyan game, No 8 Diego Ormaechea, who was 40 when he played in the 1999 tournament, has now taken over as coach. His forward pack will be based around the formidable figure of prop Pablo Lemoine, a well-known and respected figure on the European circuit after stints with Bristol and Stade Français. Centre Diego Aguirre will keep the back line honest and threatening.

Pool D: New Zealand, Wales, Canada, Italy, Tonga

New Zealand

Even the mighty All Blacks may have had a shiver or two when they saw the make-up of this group, one which has banana skins strewn about. Or, perhaps, they looked at the schedule in a far more positive light, figuring that each of the pool opponents would give them a damn good work-out and therefore leave them in better shape to face the rigours of the knockout phase. The All Blacks ought to qualify as pool leaders. For all the tricky obstacles that much seems assured. Despite the blips over the last 12 months, the All Blacks still have more natural talent to call on than any other country, even if a few of their young bolters have roots in other countries. The Fijian-born wing Joe Rokocoko showed in New Zealand's recent Tri Nations success that he is set to be a star of the show. His first-half hat-trick of tries in the 31-23 victory over France and another hat-trick – the first ever in Tri Nations matches – against Australia spoke of similar feats to come. New Zealand coach John Mitchell has plenty of options, even with the likes of Taine Randell, Christian Cullen and Andrew Mehrtens all failing to find favour this season. Mitchell, and his team, mean business.

Wales

It's been an easy slight on Wales in recent under-achieving times to say that they failed to show up. For their tour to Australia and New Zealand, they almost literally failed to show up. Last-minute haggling over contracts caused them to miss their Heathrow flight, a minor inconvenience in itself but somehow a raw symbol of the mess that Welsh rugby continues to find itself in. If the team managed to consistently show as much fighting spirit as some of the bickering officials in Wales, then every game would be an even contest. As it is, Wales do occasionally step up to the plate and deliver, notably against England in the Six Nations and even in defeat to Australia. The scoreline, 30-10, may have looked damning but Wales gave as good as they got for long stretches. However grim reality soon returned with the record 55-3 loss to New Zealand, Wales's 15th defeat in 19 games. Coach Steve Hansen is all too well aware of his side's limitations. 'One day we will get there,' said Hansen after the summer tour. 'But it's going to take time and along the way we will encounter a lot of pain.'

Canada

The Canucks have a proud track record to extend at the World Cup but have not had the best of starts to their lead-in. They were desperately disappointed with their showing in the Churchill Cup where they lost to England 43-7 and then to the USA Eagles. That 16-11 defeat meant they then had to watch their arch rivals contest the final on their own home turf in Vancouver.

Canada, though, have had a streamlined programme of games to get them in the best possible shape to contest this group in which they would fancy themselves to cause an upset by qualifying, evoking shades of 1991 when they gave such a spirited show before being beaten at the quarter-final stage by New Zealand in Lille. Despite losing both of the Test matches to the visiting NZ Maori in July, that mini-series and the Pan American Championship in August were perfect tests of their resources prior to taking on the All Blacks as well as Tonga in the World Cup. Canada can call on a bevy of experienced players, from the likes of scrum-half Morgan Williams to Stade Français lock Mike James. They will be hoping to redraft a few more pages in those history books.

Italy

Coach John Kirwan was quite right to complain long and hard about the ludicrously lop-sided schedule of this pool, one that seriously disadvantages his team. Italy are obliged to play their four pool games in 14 days, giving them little respite or recovery time. New Zealand have 23 days in which to play their games, Wales 22. The Italian federation even threatened to boycott the tournament but that would have been a protest too far. Kirwan got on with the business of steeling his men for what lay before them by organising a five-match tour of New Zealand, with all the games played in a fortnight. Three of the five matches were lost, to Southland, Bay of Plenty and Waikato, but the benefits will come down the line.

Italy were boosted by only their second ever win in the Six Nations, their 30-22 win over Wales their first in the Championship since that glorious debut against Scotland in 2000. That they managed 100 points in their five games shows that they know their way to the try-line.

Tonga

Tonga derived little benefit from the last stages of their qualifying process, except fine-tuning their sense of direction towards the try-line. The 194-0 aggregate in the repechage play-offs against Korea was no preparation for what awaits them in this group. However, Tonga have been busy since then, taking on sides both home and away. Results were mixed. A 12-point margin of victory over Queensland A was matched exactly by the margin of defeat against the ACT Brumbies. Tonga didn't fare too well on their trip to New Zealand, losing 47-12 to the Maori before drawing 10-10 with a NZ Development XV. They might have hoped to get closer to Ireland as well, especially in the heat of Nuku'Alofa, but went down 40-19. Tonga are now coached by former Maori assistant and back-row forward, Jim Love, who is sure to do a good job at knocking them into shape. A narrow 34-31 away loss followed by a 23-22 win back in Nuku'alofa to share a two-Test series with Fiji suggests that the process is already well under way.

RUGBY WORLD CUP 2003

How they Qualified

John Griffiths

After Ireland, Georgia, Italy, Romania and Namibia had claimed the last of the regional qualifying places last October, a further 11 World Cup matches were staged before and after the New Year to decide the final two repechage places. Regional play-offs took place between October and December 2002 to determine which nations would compete in the final home-and-away repechages in March and April.

The process was not without controversy. In Europe, Spain and Russia met to decide which nation would go forward to a play-off with Tunisia. The Russians, bolstered by their South African contingent, Johan Hendriks, Werner Pieterse and Reiner Volshenck, demolished the Spaniards 36-3 in Madrid before losing 22-38 at home in Krasnodar. They had done enough, however, in Madrid to win through on superior points difference. Or so they thought.

The Russians it transpired had fielded ineligible players. The Spaniards complained and an investigation headed by Tim Gresson of New Zealand was conducted. At length, the claims that the players in question had grandparents of Russian nationality could not be reliably confirmed. The IRB Appeals Committee ruled that Spain be reinstated and the Russians expelled, adding a hefty £75,000 fine on the Russian federation.

The Spaniards lived to fight another battle, but the Russians at least had the consolation of hearing that their fine was suspended for three years. The IRB statement read: 'The Committee has shown both determination to stamp out abuse of the regulations, and compassion for the financial circumstances of one of our most important developing unions.'

Owing to Spain and Tunisia's congested international schedules, the convention of deciding qualifiers through home-and-away legs was abandoned. They met on neutral territory at Valence in France in March, the fired up Tunisians taking a 13-3 interval lead before experienced Spain captain Alvaro Enciso inspired a second-half revival. The Spaniards rattled up four tries and their full-back Manuel Cascara contributed 13 points to a 33-16 win that took the Europeans into a play-off against the United States for the last place in the World Cup's Pool B. Meanwhile Tonga had comfortably beaten Papua New Guinea (conquerors of the Cook Islands) to face Korea in the play-off for a place in Pool D.

Tonga coasted to two landslide victories over the Koreans, winning 75-0 in Seoul and 119-0 in Nuku'alofa a week later to line up alongside New Zealand, Wales, Canada and Italy in the Finals. The 20th and final place in

Australia went in April to the United States, 62-13 winners against Spain in Madrid and 58-13 victors a fortnight later at Fort Lauderdale.

Rugby World Cup 2003 qualifying results

EUROPE

Round One Pool One: Monaco 15, Moldova 17 (Menton); Belgium 24, Slovenia 10 (Brussels); Slovenia 19, Lithuania 19 (Ljubljana); Moldova 58, Malta 8 (Chisinau); Malta 0, Belgium 26 (Marsa); Monaco 8, Slovenija 13 (Monte Carlo); Malta 3, Monaco 9 (Marsa); Monaco 12, Belgium 18 (St Laurent du Var); Belgium 26, Moldova 10 (Brussels); Slovenia 30, Moldova 15 (Ljubljana); Malta 11, Lithuania 39 (Marsa); Belgium 29, Lithuania 20 (Laakdal); Slovenia 45, Malta 5 (Ljubljana); Lithuania 33, Monaco 10 (Vilnius); Moldova 20, Lithuania 16 (Chisinau)

Belgium qualify for Round Two

Round One Pool Two: Bosnia 13, Hungary 12 (Zenica); Switzerland 43, Bosnia 6 (Geneva); Andorra 12, Yugoslavia 9 (Andorra); Bulgaria 9, Switzerland 90 (Pernik); Hungary 27, Andorra 21 (Szazhalombatta); Yugoslavia 46, Bulgaria 6 (Dimitrovgrad); Yugoslavia 25, Hungary 10 (Dimitrovgrad); Switzerland 38, Andorra 25 (Lausanne); Bulgaria 30, Bosnia 8 (Pernik); Switzerland 61, Hungary 23 (Basle); Bosnia 23, Yugoslavia 13 (Zenica); Andorra 59, Bulgaria 10 (Andorra); Hungary 46, Bulgaria 7 (Szazhalombatta); Yugoslavia 13, Switzerland 10 (Gornji); Andorra 23, Bosnia 13 (Andorra)

Switzerland qualify for Round Two

Round One Pool Three: Norway 9, Luxembourg 41 (Stavanger); Austria 10, Sweden 42 (Vienna); Latvia 24, Luxembourg 19 (Riga); Sweden 44, Norway 3 (Enköping); Latvia 38, Austria 12 (Riga); Luxembourg 3, Israel 62 (Cessange); Israel 3, Latvia 21 (Herzliyya); Israel 43, Norway 3 (Tel Aviv); Luxembourg 3, Sweden 116 (Cessange); Austria 77, Luxembourg 0 (Vienna); Sweden 35, Israel 20 (Växjö); Latvia 37, Norway 0 (Riga); Austria 21, Israel 6 (Vienna); Norway 7, Austria 51 (Horten); Sweden 17, Latvia 10 (Enköping)

Sweden and Latvia (Best runners-up) qualify for Round Two

Round Two Pool A: Czech Republic 46, Belgium 3; Switzerland 6, Czech Republic 32; Ukraine 21, Belgium 10; Croatia 5, Czech Republic 13; Uukraine 41, Croatia 7; Belgium 15, Switzerland 22; Czech Republic 26, Ukraine 8; Croatia 18, Switzerland 16; Belgium 0, Croatia 26; Switzerland 11, Ukraine 30

Czech Republic advance to Round Three

Round Two Pool B: Latvia 18, Poland 60; Poland 10, Sweden 3; Sweden 37, Latvia 12; Sweden 32, Germany 10; Denmark 33, Sweden 21; Denmark 19, Poland 26; Germany 34, Denmark 24; Germany 44, Latvia 0; Latvia 8, Denmark 32; Poland 20, Germany 12

Poland win and advance to Round Three

Round Three Pool A: Czech Republic 18, Russia 37; Holland 12, Czech Republic 54; Russia 65, Holland 3

Russia win and advance to Round Four

Round Three Pool B: Poland 27, Spain 15; Portugal 39, Poland 26; Spain 34, Portugal 21

Spain win and advance to Round Four

Round Four Pool A: Russia 3, Ireland 35 (Krasnoyarsk); Ireland 63, Georgia 14 (Dublin); Georgia 17, Russia 13 (Tbilisi)

Ireland and Georgia qualify; Russia qualify for Round Five

Round Four Pool B: Spain 3, Italy 50 (Valladolid); Italy 25, Romania 17 (Parma); Romania 67, Spain 6 (Iasi)

Italy and Romania qualify; Spain qualify for Round Five

Round Five: Spain 3, Russia 36 (Madrid); Russia 22, Spain 38 (Krasnodar)

Russia win but are subsequently disqualified for fielding ineligible players; Spain qualify for repechage

OCEANIA

Eastern Zone Pool: Cook Islands 86, Tahiti 0; (Rarotonga); Tahiti 6, Niue Island 41 (Papeete); Niue Island 8, Cook Islands 28 (Paliati)

Cook Islands qualify for Round Three

Round One Western Zone Pool: Papua New Guinea 32, Solomon Islands 10 (Port Moresby); Vanuatu 10, Papua New Guinea 32 (Port Vila); Solomon Islands 11, Vanuatu 3 (Honiara)

Papua New Guinea qualify for Round Three

Round Two: Samoa 16, Fiji 17 (Apia); Tonga 22, Fiji 47 (Nuku'alofa); Tonga 16, Samoa 25 (Nuku'alofa); Fiji 12, Samoa 22 (Nadi); Samoa 31, Tonga 13 (Apia); Fiji 47, Tonga 20 (Nadi)

Fiji and Samoa qualify; Tonga qualify for Round Four

Round Three: Papua New Guinea 29, Cook Islands 14 (Port Moresby); Cook Islands 21, Papua New Guinea 16 (Rarotonga)

Papua New Guinea qualify for Round Four

Round Four: Papua New Guinea 14, Tonga 47 (Port Moresby); Tonga 84, Papua New Guinea 12 (Nuku'alofa)

Tonga qualify for repechage

AFRICA

Round One Pool A: Zambia 25, Cameroon 24; Uganda 21, Zambia 12; Cameroon 17, Uganda 0

Round One Pool B: Botswana 13, Swaziland 3; Madagascar 33, Botswana 11; Swaziland 21, Madagascar 26

Round Two: Madagascar 27, Kenya 20; Cameroon 24, Madagascar 30; Kenya 40, Cameroon 15

Round Three North: Tunisia 27, Morocco 26; Ivory Coast 8, Tunisia 13; Morocco 23, Ivory Coast 21

Round Three South: Madagascar 3, Zimbabwe 52; Namibia 116, Madagascar 0; Zimbabwe 30, Namibia 42

Round Four: Namibia 26, Tunisia 19 (Windhoek); Tunisia 24, Namibia 17 (Tunis)

Namibia qualify on superior try-count; Tunisia qualify for repechage

AMERICAS

Round One: Venezuela 55, Colombia 0; Venezuela 46, Peru 19; Brazil 51, Peru 9; Colombia 12, Brazil 47; Brazil 14, Venezuela 3; Peru 31, Colombia 10

Round Two: Trinidad & Tobago 51, Jamaica 5; Cayman Islands 32, Guyana 13; Barbados 25, Bahamas 18; Barbados 5, Bermuda 13; Trinidad & Tobago 12, Cayman Islands 8; Bermuda 12, Trinidad & Tobago 23; Trinidad & Tobago 10, Brazil 11; Brazil 9, Trinidad & Tobago 0

Round Three: Brazil 6, Chile 46; Paraguay 14, Brazil 3; Chile 57, Paraguay 5

Round Four: Canada 26, United States 9; United States 13, Canada 36; Chile 10, Uruguay 6; United States 28, Uruguay 24; United States 35, Chile 22; Canada 51, Uruguay 16; Canada 27, Chile 6; Uruguay 25, Canada 23; Chile 21, United States 13; Uruguay 10, United States 9; Chile 11, Canada 29; Uruguay 34, Chile 23

Canada and Uruguay qualify. United States qualify for repechage.

ASIA

Round One: Malaysia 3, Chinese Taipei 57; Singapore 34, Malaysia 5; Chinese Taipei w/o Singapore; Arabian Gulf 40, Thailand 20; Thailand 8, Hong Kong 15; Hong Kong 17, Arabian Gulf 7; Sri Lanka 9, China 7; China 24, Kazakstan 10; Kazakstan 20, Sri Lanka 14

China, Chinese Taipei and Hong Kong qualify for Round Two

Round Two: Chinese Taipei 20, Hong Kong 15; China 21, Chinese Taipei 29; Hong Kong 34, China 7

Chinese Taipei and Hong Kong qualify for Round Three

Round Three: Japan 90, Korea 24; Chinese Taipei 31, Hong Kong 54; Korea 119, Chinese Taipei 7; Japan 155, Chinese Taipei 3; Korea 17, Japan 55; Chinese Taipei 3, Japan 120

Japan qualify. Korea qualify for repechage.

REPECHAGE

Preliminary Repechage: Tunisia 16, Spain 33 (Valence, France)

Spain qualify for repechage finals

Repechage Finals: Korea 0, Tonga 75 (Seoul); Tonga 119, Korea 0 (Nuku'alofa); Spain 13, United States 62 (Madrid); United States 58, Spain 13 (Fort Lauderdale)

Tonga and United States qualify

RUGBY WORLD CUP RECORDS

(Final stages only)

Overall Records

Most overall points in final stages

227	A G Hastings	Scotland	1987-95
195	M P Lynagh	Australia	1987-95
170	G J Fox	New Zealand	1987-91

Most overall tries in final stages

15	J T Lomu	New Zealand	1995-99
11	R Underwood	England	1987-95
10	D I Campese	Australia	1987-95

Leading Scorers

Most points in one competition

126	G J Fox	New Zealand	1987
112	T Lacroix	France	1995
104	A G Hastings	Scotland	1995
102	G Quesada	Argentina	1999
101	M Burke	Australia	1999

Most tries in one competition

8	J T Lomu	New Zealand	1999
7	M C G Ellis	New Zealand	1995
7	J T Lomu	New Zealand	1995

Most conversions in one competition

30	G J Fox	New Zealand	1987
20	S D Culhane	New Zealand	1995
20	M P Lynagh	Australia	1987

Most penalty goals in one competition

31	G Quesada	Argentina	1999
26	T Lacroix	France	1995
21	G J Fox	New Zealand	1987
20	C R Andrew	England	1995

Most dropped goals in one competition

6	J H de Beer	South Africa	1999
3	G P J Townsend	Scotland	1999
3	A P Mehrtens	New Zealand	1995
3	J T Stransky	South Africa	1995
3	C R Andrew	England	1995
3	J Davies	Wales	1987

Match Records

Most Points in a Match

by a team

145	New Zealand v Japan	1995
101	New Zealand v Italy	1999
101	England v Tonga	1999
89	Scotland v Ivory Coast	1995
74	New Zealand v Fiji	1987
72	Canada v Namibia	1999

by a player

45	S D Culhane	New Zealand v Japan	1995
44	A G Hastings	Scotland v Ivory Coast	1995
36	T E Brown	New Zealand v Italy	1999
36	P J Grayson	England v Tonga	1999
34	J H de Beer	South Africa v England	1999
32	J P Wilkinson	England v Italy	1999

Most Tries in a Match

by a team

21	New Zealand v Japan	1995
14	New Zealand v Italy	1999
13	England v Tonga	1999
13	Scotland v Ivory Coast	1995
13	France v Zimbabwe	1987

by a player

6	M C G Ellis	New Zealand v Japan	1995
4	K G M Wood	Ireland v United States	1999
4	A G Hastings	Scotland v Ivory Coast	1995
4	C M Williams	South Africa v Western Samoa	1995
4	J T Lomu	New Zealand v England	1995
4	B F Robinson	Ireland v Zimbabwe	1991
4	I C Evans	Wales v Canada	1987
4	C I Green	New Zealand v Fiji	1987
4	J A Gallagher	New Zealand v Fiji	1987

Most Conversions in a Match

by a team

20	New Zealand v Japan	1995
12	England v Tonga	1999
11	New Zealand v Italy	1999
10	New Zealand v Fiji	1987
9	Canada v Namibia	1999
9	Scotland v Ivory Coast	1995
9	France v Zimbabwe	1987

by a player

20	S D Culhane	New Zealand v Japan	1995
12	P J Grayson	England v Tonga	1999
11	T E Brown	New Zealand v Italy	1999
10	G J Fox	New Zealand v Fiji	1987
9	G L Rees	Canada v Namibia	1999
9	A G Hastings	Scotland v Ivory Coast	1995
9	D Camberabero	France v Zimbabwe	1987

Most Penalty Goals in a Match

by a team

8	Australia v South Africa	1999
8	Argentina v Samoa	1999
8	Scotland v Tonga	1995
8	France v Ireland	1995

by a player

8	M Burke	Australia v South Africa	1999
8	G Quesada	Argentina v Samoa	1999
8	A G Hastings	Scotland v Tonga	1995
8	T Lacroix	France v Ireland	1995

Most Dropped Goals in a Match

by a team

5	South Africa v England	1999
3	Fiji v Romania	1991

by a player

5	J H de Beer	South Africa v England	1999
2	P C Montgomery	South Africa v New Zealand	1999
2	C Lamaison	France v New Zealand	1999
2	J T Stransky	South Africa v New Zealand	1995
2	C R Andrew	England v Argentina	1995
2	T Rabaka	Fiji v Romania	1991
2	L Arbizu	Argentina v Australia	1991
2	J Davies	Wales v Ireland	1987

Rugby World Cup Tournaments: 1987 To 1999

First Tournament: 1987 In Australia & New Zealand

Pool 1

Australia	19	England	6
USA	21	Japan	18
England	60	Japan	7
Australia	47	USA	12
England	34	USA	6
Australia	42	Japan	23

	P	*W*	*D*	*L*	*F*	*A*	*Pts*
Australia	3	3	0	0	108	41	6
England	3	2	0	1	100	32	4
USA	3	1	0	2	39	99	2
Japan	3	0	0	3	48	123	0

Pool 2

Canada	37	Tonga	4
Wales	13	Ireland	6
Wales	29	Tonga	16
Ireland	46	Canada	19
Wales	40	Canada	9
Ireland	32	Tonga	9

	P	*W*	*D*	*L*	*F*	*A*	*Pts*
Wales	3	3	0	0	82	31	6
Ireland	3	2	0	1	84	41	4
Canada	3	1	0	2	65	90	2
Tonga	3	0	0	3	29	98	0

Pool 3

New Zealand	70	Italy	6
Fiji	28	Argentina	9
New Zealand	74	Fiji	13
Argentina	25	Italy	16
Italy	18	Fiji	15
New Zealand	46	Argentina	15

	P	*W*	*D*	*L*	*F*	*A*	*Pts*
New Zealand	3	3	0	0	190	34	6
Fiji	3	1	0	2	56	101	2
Argentina	3	1	0	2	49	90	2
Italy	3	1	0	2	40	110	2

Pool 4

Romania	21	Zimbabwe	20
France	20	Scotland	20
France	55	Romania	12
Scotland	60	Zimbabwe	21
France	70	Zimbabwe	12
Scotland	55	Romania	28

	P	*W*	*D*	*L*	*F*	*A*	*Pts*
France	3	2	1	0	145	44	5
Scotland	3	2	1	0	135	69	5
Romania	3	1	0	2	61	130	2
Zimbabwe	3	0	0	3	53	151	0

Quarter-finals

New Zealand	30	Scotland	3
France	31	Fiji	16
Australia	33	Ireland	15
Wales	16	England	3

Semi-finals

France	30	Australia	24
New Zealand	49	Wales	6

Third Place match

Wales	22	Australia	21

First World Cup Final, Eden Park, Auckland, 20 June 1987
New Zealand 29 (1G 4PG 1DG 2T) France 9 (1G 1PG)

NEW ZEALAND: J A Gallagher; J J Kirwan, J T Stanley, W T Taylor, C I Green; G J Fox, D E Kirk (*captain*); S C McDowell, S B T Fitzpatrick, J A Drake, M J Pierce, G W Whetton, A J Whetton, W T Shelford, M N Jones

Scorers *Tries:* Jones, Kirk, Kirwan *Conversion:* Fox *Penalty Goals:* Fox (4) *Drop Goal:* Fox

FRANCE: S Blanco; D Camberabero, P Sella, D Charvet, P Lagisquet; F Mesnel, P Berbizier; P Ondarts, D Dubroca (*captain*), J-P Garuet, A Lorieux, J Condom, E Champ, L Rodriguez, D Erbani

Scorers *Try:* Berbizier *Conversion:* Camberabero *Penalty Goal:* Camberabero

Referee K V J Fitzgerald (Australia)

Attendance: 48,350

Second Tournament: 1991 In Britain, Ireland & France

Pool 1

New Zealand	18	England	12
Italy	30	USA	9
New Zealand	46	USA	6
England	36	Italy	6
England	37	USA	9
New Zealand	31	Italy	21

	P	*W*	*D*	*L*	*F*	*A*	*Pts*
New Zealand	3	3	0	0	95	39	9
England	3	2	0	1	85	33	7
Italy	3	1	0	2	57	76	5
USA	3	0	0	3	24	113	3

Pool 2

Scotland	47	Japan	9
Ireland	55	Zimbabwe	11
Ireland	32	Japan	16
Scotland	51	Zimbabwe	12
Scotland	24	Ireland	15
Japan	52	Zimbabwe	8

	P	W	D	L	F	A	Pts
Scotland	3	3	0	0	122	36	9
Ireland	3	2	0	1	102	51	7
Japan	3	1	0	2	77	87	5
Zimbabwe	3	0	0	3	31	158	3

Pool 3

Australia	32	Argentina	19
Western Samoa	16	Wales	13
Australia	9	Western Samoa	3
Wales	16	Argentina	7
Australia	38	Wales	3
Western Samoa	35	Argentina	12

	P	W	D	L	F	A	Pts
Australia	3	3	0	0	79	25	9
Western Samoa	3	2	0	1	54	34	7
Wales	3	1	0	2	32	61	5
Argentina	3	0	0	3	38	83	3

Pool 4

France	30	Romania	3
Canada	13	Fiji	3
France	33	Fiji	9
Canada	19	Romania	11
Romania	17	Fiji	15
France	19	Canada	13

	P	W	D	L	F	A	Pts
France	3	3	0	0	82	25	9
Canada	3	2	0	1	45	33	7
Romania	3	1	0	2	31	64	5
Fiji	3	0	0	3	27	63	3

Quarter-finals

England	19	France	10
Scotland	28	Western Samoa	6
Australia	19	Ireland	18
New Zealand	29	Canada	13

Semi-finals

England	9	Scotland	6
Australia	16	New Zealand	6

Third Place match

New Zealand	13	Scotland	6

Second World Cup Final, Twickenham, 2 November 1991
Australia 12 (1G 2PG) **England 6** (2PG)

AUSTRALIA: M C Roebuck; D I Campese, J S Little, T J Horan, R H Egerton; M P Lynagh, N C Farr-Jones (*captain*); A J Daly, P N Kearns, E J A McKenzie, R J McCall, J A Eales, S P Poidevin, T Coker, V Ofahengaue

Scorers *Try:* Daly *Conversion:* Lynagh *Penalty Goals:* Lynagh (2)

ENGLAND: J M Webb; S J Halliday, W D C Carling (*captain*), J C Guscott, R Underwood; C R Andrew, R J Hill; J Leonard, B C Moore, J A Probyn, P J Ackford, W A Dooley, M G Skinner, M C Teague, P J Winterbottom

Scorer *Penalty Goals:* Webb (2)

Referee W D Bevan (Wales)

Attendance: 56,208

Third Tournament: 1995 In South Africa

Pool A

South Africa	27	Australia	18
Canada	34	Romania	3
South Africa	21	Romania	8
Australia	27	Canada	11
Australia	42	Romania	3
South Africa	20	Canada	0

	P	*W*	*D*	*L*	*F*	*A*	*Pts*
South Africa	3	3	0	0	68	26	9
Australia	3	2	0	1	87	41	7
Canada	3	1	0	2	45	50	5
Romania	3	0	0	3	14	97	3

Pool B

Western Samoa	42	Italy	18
England	24	Argentina	18
Western Samoa	32	Argentina	26
England	27	Italy	20
Italy	31	Argentina	25
England	44	Western Samoa	22

	P	*W*	*D*	*L*	*F*	*A*	*Pts*
England	3	3	0	0	95	60	9
Western Samoa	3	2	0	1	96	88	7
Italy	3	1	0	2	69	94	5
Argentina	3	0	0	3	69	87	3

Pool C

Wales	57	Japan	10
New Zealand	43	Ireland	19
Ireland	50	Japan	28
New Zealand	34	Wales	9
New Zealand	145	Japan	17
Ireland	24	Wales	23

	P	*W*	*D*	*L*	*F*	*A*	*Pts*
New Zealand	3	3	0	0	222	45	9
Ireland	3	2	0	1	93	94	7
Wales	3	1	0	2	89	68	5
Japan	3	0	0	3	55	252	3

Pool D

Scotland	89	Ivory Coast	0
France	38	Tonga	10
France	54	Ivory Coast	18
Scotland	41	Tonga	5
Tonga	29	Ivory Coast	11
France	22	Scotland	19

	P	*W*	*D*	*L*	*F*	*A*	*Pts*
France	3	3	0	0	114	47	9
Scotland	3	2	0	1	149	27	7
Tonga	3	1	0	2	44	90	5
Ivory Coast	3	0	0	3	29	172	3

Quarter-finals

France	36	Ireland	12
South Africa	42	Western Samoa	14
England	25	Australia	22
New Zealand	48	Scotland	30

Semi-finals

South Africa	19	France	15
New Zealand	45	England	29

Third Place match

France	19	England	9

Third World Cup Final, Ellis Park, Johannesburg, 24 June 1995
South Africa 15 (3PG 2DG) **New Zealand 12** (3PG 1DG)*

SOUTH AFRICA: A J Joubert; J T Small, J C Mulder, H P Le Roux, C M Williams; J T Stransky, J H van der Westhuizen; J P du Randt, C L C Rossouw, I S Swart, J J Wiese, J J Strydom, J F Pienaar (*captain*),

M G Andrews, R J Kruger *Substitutions:* G L Pagel for Swart (68 mins); R A W Straeuli for Andrews (90 mins); B Venter for Small (97 mins)

Scorer *Penalty Goals:* Stransky (3) *Drop Goals:* Stransky (2)

NEW ZEALAND: G M Osborne; J W Wilson, F E Bunce, W K Little, J T Lomu; A P Mehrtens, G T M Bachop; C W Dowd, S B T Fitzpatrick (*captain*), O M Brown, I D Jones, R M Brooke, M R Brewer, Z V Brooke, J A Kronfeld *Substitutions:* J W Joseph for Brewer (40 mins); M C G Ellis for Wilson (55 mins); R W Loe for Dowd (83 mins); A D Strachan for Bachop (temp 66 to 71 mins)

Scorer *Penalty Goals:* Mehrtens (3) *Drop Goal:* Mehrtens

Referee E F Morrison (England)

Attendance: 63,000

* *after extra time: 9-9 after normal time*

Fourth Tournament: 1999 In Britain, Ireland & France

Pool A

Spain	15	Uruguay	27
South Africa	46	Scotland	29
Scotland	43	Uruguay	12
South Africa	47	Spain	3
South Africa	39	Uruguay	3
Scotland	48	Spain	0

	P	*W*	*D*	*L*	*F*	*A*	*Pts*
South Africa	3	3	0	0	132	35	9
Scotland	3	2	0	1	120	58	7
Uruguay	3	1	0	2	42	97	5
Spain	3	0	0	3	18	122	3

Pool B

England	67	Italy	7
New Zealand	45	Tonga	9
England	16	New Zealand	30
Italy	25	Tonga	28
New Zealand	101	Italy	3
England	101	Tonga	10

	P	*W*	*D*	*L*	*F*	*A*	*Pts*
New Zealand	3	3	0	0	176	28	9
England	3	2	0	1	184	47	7
Tonga	3	1	0	2	47	171	5
Italy	3	0	0	3	35	196	3

Pool C

Fiji	67	Namibia	18
France	33	Canada	20
France	47	Namibia	13
Fiji	38	Canada	22
Canada	72	Namibia	11
France	28	Fiji	19

	P	*W*	*D*	*L*	*F*	*A*	*Pts*
France	3	3	0	0	108	52	9
Fiji	3	2	0	1	124	68	7
Canada	3	1	0	2	114	82	5
Namibia	3	0	0	3	42	186	3

Pool D

Wales	23	Argentina	18
Samoa	43	Japan	9
Wales	64	Japan	15
Argentina	32	Samoa	16
Wales	31	Samoa	38
Argentina	33	Japan	12

	P	*W*	*D*	*L*	*F*	*A*	*Pts*
Wales	3	2	0	1	118	71	7
Samoa	3	2	0	1	97	72	7
Argentina	3	2	0	1	83	51	7
Japan	3	0	0	3	36	140	3

Pool E

Ireland	53	United States	8
Australia	57	Romania	9
United States	25	Romania	27
Ireland	3	Australia	23
Australia	55	United States	19
Ireland	44	Romania	14

	P	*W*	*D*	*L*	*F*	*A*	*Pts*
Australia	3	3	0	0	135	31	9
Ireland	3	2	0	1	100	45	7
Romania	3	1	0	2	50	126	5
United States	3	0	0	3	52	135	3

Play-offs for quarter-final places

England	45	Fiji	24
Scotland	35	Samoa	20
Ireland	24	Argentina	28

Quarter-finals

Wales	9	Australia	24
South Africa	44	England	21
France	47	Argentina	26
Scotland	18	New Zealand	30

Semi-finals

South Africa	21	Australia	27
New Zealand	31	France	43

Third Place match

South Africa	22	New Zealand	18

Fourth World Cup Final, Millennium Stadium, Cardiff Arms Park, 6 November 1999
AUSTRALIA 35 (2G 7PG) **FRANCE 12** (4PG)

AUSTRALIA: M Burke; B N Tune, D J Herbert, T J Horan, J W Roff; S J Larkham, G M Gregan; R L L Harry, M A Foley, A T Blades, D T Giffin, J A Eales (*captain*), M J Cockbain, R S T Kefu, D J Wilson *Substitutions* J S Little for Herbert (46 mins); O D A Finegan for Cockbain (52 mins); M R Connors for Wilson (73 mins); D J Crowley for Harry (75 mins); J A Paul for Foley (85 mins); C J Whitaker for Gregan (86 mins); N P Grey for Horan (86 mins)

Scorers *Tries:* Tune, Finegan *Conversions:* Burke (2) *Penalty Goals:* Burke (7)

FRANCE: X Garbajosa; P Bernat Salles, R Dourthe, E Ntamack, C Dominici; C Lamaison, F Galthié; C Soulette, R Ibañez (*captain*), F Tournaire, A Benazzi, F Pelous, M Lièvremont, C Juillet, O Magne *Substitutions* O Brouzet for Juillet (HT); P de Villiers for Soulette (47 mins); A Costes for Magne (temp 19 to 22 mins) and for Lièvremont (67 mins); U Mola for Garbajosa (67 mins); S Glas for Dourthe (temp 49 to 55 mins and from 74 mins); S Castaignède for Galthié (76 mins); M Dal Maso for Ibañez (79 mins)

Scorer *Penalty Goals:* Lamaison (4)

Referee A Watson (South Africa)

Attendance: 72,500

RUGBY WORLD CUP WARM-UP MATCHES

Murphy's Law Sours Ireland's Preparations

Mick Cleary

Try telling Geordan Murphy that these matches counted for nothing. It's unlikely that anything could compound the misery of the Leicester player beyond the profound depth it has already reached. To even hint to him that each and every rugby fan round the globe will have largely erased all memory of these games from the moment New Zealand referee Paul Honiss blows his whistle to signal the start of the World Cup itself will surely cause the black cloud to descend once more.

You would have to be a hard-hearted type not to feel for Murphy. His World Cup dreams were shattered in the early stages of the game between Scotland and Ireland at Murrayfield. Murphy suffered a compound fracture of the tibia when caught in a double tackle by Scotland's Ben Blair and Andy Craig. The physical pain was matched by the searing emotional agony of realising that all Murphy had worked for over the previous few months lay in ruins.

The Irish fans empathised. Ireland were the only unbeaten team in this mini-Six Nations, but the supporters knew that their team's chances of an upset victory over Australia in their Pool A match had diminished. Murphy, the delightful rugby maverick who can charm his way past defenders with his outrageous talent, was Ireland's trump card. Without him, and even allowing for the genius of Brian O'Driscoll, Ireland's attacking edge lacks sharpness.

Such was the chilling backdrop of this sequence of games. No player can afford to go into any match worrying about injury. Well, he may not go into it feeling that way, but he certainly came out of it breathing a sigh of relief. Murphy was the only serious high-profile casualty of these games. The goal of every coach was to fine-tune their squads through these matches, filtering names to arrive at the final 30-man party, and also to avoid injury.

'Our aim was to win but to also come through intact,' said England head coach Clive Woodward shortly after his side's 45-14 victory over France at Twickenham. Woodward lost one of his men, Wasps' fly-half Alex King withdrawing just before that last game after a long-standing knee injury was aggravated in the opening game against Wales at the Millennium Stadium. England won that match with ease, 43-9, even though they were fielding a second team against the best that Wales could offer. Woodward only played his full-strength side in the last of England's three games, the French encounter at Twickenham. His prime focus was to find which players in his 43-man squad could really cope with the pressures of Test rugby.

He was even prepared to put England's record run of 14 successive Test victories on the line when going to Marseilles with an under-strength team.

France won 17-16 but Woodward felt that he prospered in defeat. Within 48 hours he was cutting eight players – Steve Borthwick, Alex Sanderson, Andy Titterrell, Will Green, Dave Walder, Jamie Noon, Andy Hazell and Dan Scarbrough.

France also had a decent run-out from their games. They had different aims from Woodward, given that their World Cup squad was already selected. As much as anything after a deflating tour to Argentina in the summer, their morale needed massaging. Egos were duly soothed and confidence bolstered by the win in Marseilles.

The same could not be said for Scotland and Wales. Both countries had a bumpy approach to the World Cup. Wales were dreadful against England yet pulled themselves up by beating Scotland, 23-9 in Cardiff.

Scotland saw off Italy, who themselves had a disturbing run of defeats against the home unions and an impressive 31-22 victory over Georgia, but were well beaten by both Wales and Ireland. If muscles were supposed to be flexed in these games, then Scotland, Wales and Italy will need to reach for Popeye's spinach before setting off to Australia.

At least their 30-man squads will make the plane. The same was not true for Geordan Murphy.

Teams and Results

16 August, Lansdowne Road, Dublin
Ireland 35 (5G) **Wales 12** (1G 1T)

Ireland: G E A Murphy; T G Howe, B G O'Driscoll, K M Maggs, A P Horgan; D G Humphreys, P A Stringer; R Corrigan, K G M Wood (*captain*), S J Best, M E O'Kelly, P J O'Connell, A Quinlan, A G Foley, K D Gleeson *Substitutions:* D P Wallace for Quinlan (temp 31 mins to 40 mins) and for Foley (40 mins); G T Dempsey for Humphreys (61 mins); J M Fitzpatrick for Best (61 mins); J S Byrne for Wood (67 mins); D O'Callaghan for O'Kelly (67 mins); G Easterby for Stringer (76 mins); G M D'Arcy for Howe (76 mins)

Scorers *Tries:* O'Connell (2), Quinlan, Wallace, O'Kelly *Conversions:* Humphreys (4), Murphy

Wales: N J Robinson; G R Evans, J P Robinson, I R Harris, G Thomas (*captain*); C Sweeney, D Peel; Duncan Jones, Mefin Davies, B R Evans, M Owen, G O Llewellyn, R Oakley, A Popham, R Parks *Substitutions:* G Jenkins for B Evans (50 mins); V Cooper for Owen (65 mins); H Bennett for Mefin Davies (68 mins)

Scorers *Tries:* G Evans, G Thomas *Conversion:* Harris

Referee J Dumé (France)

22 August, Stade Felix Bollaert, Lens
France 56 (8G) **Romania 8** (1PG 1T)

France: P Elhorga; A Rougerie, Y Jauzion, D Traille, C Dominici; F Michalak, F Galthié (*captain*); J-J Crenca, Y Bru, S Marconnet, F Pelous, J Thion, S Betsen, I Harinordoquy, O Magne *Substitutions:* B Liebenberg for Elhorga (40 mins); C Labit for Harinordoquy (40 mins); R Ibañez for Bru (47 mins); D Yachvili for

Galthié (62 mins); D Auradou for Pelous (62 mins); O Milloud for Marconnet (62 mins); G Merceron for Michalak (71 mins)

Scorers *Tries:* Traille, Rougerie, Harinordoquy, Betsen, Crenca, Jauzion, Liebenberg, Magne *Conversions:* Michalak (7), Merceron

Romania: D Dumbrava; C Sauan, V Maftei, R Gontineac (*captain*), G Brezoianu; I Tofan, L Sirbu; P Balan, M Tincu, M Socaciu, S Socol, C Petre, G Chiriac, O Tonita, C Mersoiu *Substitutions:* P Toderasc for Socaciu (51 mins); A Petrichei for Petre (54 mins); C Podea for Sirbu (57 mins); M Vioreanu for Tofan (62 mins); M Tudori for Chiriac (62 mins); C Popescu for Chiriac (temp 18 to 28 mins) and for Tincu (76 mins)

Scorers *Try:* Brezoianu *Penalty Goal:* Dumbrava

Referee G de Santis (Italy)

23 August, Millennium Stadium, Cardiff Arms Park
Wales 9 (3PG) England 43 (3G 3PG 1DG 2T)

Wales: G R Williams; G Thomas, M Taylor, S Parker, M A Jones; S M Jones (*captain*), G J Cooper; I D Thomas, R C McBryde, G Jenkins, R Sidoli, C P Wyatt, C L Charvis, D R Jones, M E Williams *Substitutions:* G J Williams for McBryde (61 mins); J Thomas for Wyatt (62 mins); A Jones for Jenkins (72 mins); Gavin Thomas for D R Jones (72 mins)

Scorer *Penalty Goals:* S Jones (3)

England: D Scarbrough; D D Luger, J Noon, S Abbott, J Simpson-Daniel; A D King, A C T Gomarsall; J Leonard (*captain*), M P Regan, J White, D J Grewcock, S D Shaw, M E Corry, J P R Worsley, L W Moody *Substitutions:* D E West for Regan (37 mins); O J Smith for Luger (57 mins); A Sanderson for Moody (62 mins); D J H Walder for King (71 mins); W R Green for White (72 mins); S W Borthwick for Shaw (temp 11 to 16 mins)

Scorers *Tries:* Moody, Luger, Worsley, Abbott, West *Conversions:* King (2), Walder *Penalty Goals:* King (3) *Dropped Goal:* King

Referee P C Deluca (Argentina)

23 August, Murrayfield
Scotland 47 (4G 3PG 2T) Italy 15 (1G 1PG 1T)

Scotland: B G Hinshelwood; S C J Danielli, J G McLaren, A R Henderson, K M Logan; G Ross, M R L Blair; T J Smith, R R Russell, B A F Douglas, S Murray (*captain*), N J Hines, J P R White, S M Taylor, J M Petrie *Substitutions:* C D Paterson for Logan (2 mins); G C Bulloch for Russell (35 mins); B J Laney for Henderson (61 mins); M D Leslie for White (62 mins); G R McIlwham for Douglas (68 mins); I A Fullarton for Hines (68 mins)

Scorers *Tries:* White, McLaren, Blair, Ross, Danielli, Laney *Conversions:* Ross (2), Paterson (2) *Penalty Goals:* Ross (3)

Italy: G Peens; N Mazzucato, A Masi, C Stoica, Mirco Bergamasco; R Pez, A Troncon (*captain*); A Lo Cicero, C Festuccia, S Perugini, S Dellape, M Bortolami, M Zaffiri, M Phillips, S Palmer *Substitutions:* Mauro Bergamasco for Zaffiri (51 mins); S Parisse for Zaffiri (51 mins); G Canale for Peens (temp 22 to 28 mins and 58 mins); F Mazzariol for Mazzucato (66 mins); R Martinez-Frugoni for Perugini (66 mins); F Ongaro for Festuccia (66 mins)

Scorers *Tries:* Palmer, Mazzucato *Conversion:* Pez *Penalty Goal:* Pez

Referee D Courtney (Ireland)

27 August, Racecourse Football Ground, Wrexham
Wales 54 (6G 4PG) Romania 8 (1PG 1T)

Wales: G L Henson; N Brew, M J Watkins, A W N Marinos, S M Williams; N J Robinson, M Phillips; P James, Mefin Davies (*captain*), B R Evans, I M Gough, B Cockbain, J Thomas, A Popham, Gavin Thomas *Substitutions:* A Williams for Phillips (51 mins); D L Jones for Gough (60 mins); J Bater for Popham (67 mins); G Wyatt for Watkins (72 mins); J Bryant for Marinos (75 mins); C T Anthony for Evans (78 mins); P Young for Davies (78 mins)

Scorers *Tries:* S M Williams (2), Phillips, Popham, Brew, Gavin Thomas *Conversions:* Henson (6) *Penalty Goals:* Henson (4)

Romania: D Dumbrava; C Sauan, V Maftei, R Gontineac (*captain*), G Brezoianu; I Tofan, L Sirbu; P Balan, M Tincu, M Socaciu, S Socol, C Petre, G Chiriac, O Tonita, C Mersoiu *Substitutions:* A Petrichei for Socol (40 mins); I Teodorescu for Tofan (40 mins); P Toderasc for Socaciu (47 mins); C Popescu for Chiriac (temp 58 to 66 mins) and for Tincu (66 mins); M Tudori for Mersoiu (66 mins); D Tudosa for Chiriac (temp 52 to 57 mins) and for Balan (73 mins); I Andrei for Sirbu (75 mins)

Scorers *Try:* Balan *Penalty Goal:* Dumbrava

Referee A D Turner (South Africa)

30 August, Millennium Stadium, Cardiff Arms Park
Wales 23 (5PG 1DG 1T) Scotland 9 (3PG)

Wales: G R Evans; J P Robinson, T Shanklin, I R Harris, M J Watkins; C Sweeney, D Peel; Duncan Jones, R C McBryde, A Jones, V Cooper, M Owen, C L Charvis (*captain*), A Popham, R Parks *Substitutions:* R Oakley for Popham (23 mins); G O Llewellyn for Cooper (51 mins); H Bennett for McBryde (78 mins); H Luscombe for Watkins (83 mins)

Scorers *Try:* Owen *Penalty Goals:* Harris (5) *Dropped Goal:* Sweeney

Scotland: G H Metcalfe; R C Kerr, A Craig, B J Laney, S C J Danielli; G P J Townsend, G Beveridge; G Kerr, G C Bulloch, B A F Douglas, S Murray (*captain*), S B Grimes, M D Leslie, J M Petrie, A L Mower *Substitutions:* N J Hines for Murray (30 mins); G R McIlwham for Douglas (40 mins); A K Dall for Leslie (61 mins); C D Paterson for Laney (71 mins); D W H Hall for Bulloch (74 mins)

Scorer *Penalty Goals:* Laney (3)

Referee C White (England)

30 August, Thomond Park, Limerick
Ireland 61 (6G 3PG 2T) Italy 6 (2PG)

Ireland: G T Dempsey; J P Kelly, B G O'Driscoll (*captain*), R A J Henderson, D A Hickie; D G Humphreys, G Easterby; M J Horan, J S Byrne, R Corrigan, G W Longwell, L F M Cullen, S H Easterby, V C P Costello, E R P Miller *Substitutions:* K Dawson for Costello (30 mins); J M Fitzpatrick for Corrigan (53 mins); J C Bell for O'Driscoll (67 mins); G E A Murphy for Hickie (72 mins); B T O'Meara for G Easterby (72 mins); P M Shields for Byrne (72 mins); D O'Callaghan for Miller (72 mins)

Scorers *Tries:* Hickie (4), Byrne, Kelly, Dempsey, Humphreys *Conversions:* Humphreys (6) *Penalty Goals:* Humphreys (3)

Italy: G Peens; N Mazzucato, C Stoica, M Barbini, D Saccá; F Mazzariol, A Troncon (*captain*); A Lo Cicero, F Ongaro, M-L Castrogiovanni, C Bezzi, M Giacheri, A de Rossi, S Parisse, Mauro Bergamasco *Substitutions:* A Masi for Sacca (24 mins); A R Persico for Masi (53 mins); C Festuccia for Ongaro (60 mins); M Phillips for Giacheri (60 mins)

Scorer *Penalty Goals:* Peens (2)

Referee S J Lander (England)

30 August, Stade Vélodrome, Marseilles
France 17 (3PG 1DG 1T) **England 16** (1G 3PG)

France: N Brusque; A Rougerie, Y Jauzion, D Traille, C Dominici; F Michalak, F Galthié (*captain*); J-J Crenca, Y Bru, S Marconnet, F Pelous, J Thion, S Betsen, I Harinordoquy, O Magne *Substitutions:* B Liebenberg for Traille (54 mins); R Ibañez for Bru (54 mins); D Auradou for Thion (65 mins); P Tabacco for Betsen (65 mins); O Milloud for Crenca (temp 5 to 9 mins, 38 to 41 mins and 66 mins); S Chabal for Magne (75 mins)

Scorers *Try:* Brusque *Penalty Goals:* Michalak (3) *Dropped Goal:* Michalak

England: I R Balshaw; O J Lewsey, O J Smith, M J Tindall, B C Cohen; P J Grayson, A S Healey; G C Rowntree, D E West (*captain*), J M White, S W Borthwick, D J Grewcock, M E Corry, A Sanderson, L W Moody *Substitutions:* S Thompson for West (50 mins); J Noon for Cohen (temp 10 to 16 mins) and for Balshaw (54 mins); J Leonard for White (temp 6 to 8 mins) and for Rowntree (61 mins); S D Shaw for Borthwick (61 mins); A C T Gomarsall for Tindall (76 mins)

Scorers *Try:* Tindall *Conversion:* Grayson *Penalty Goals:* Grayson (3)

Referee S M Lawrence (South Africa)

6 September, Murrayfield
Scotland 10 (1G 1PG) **Ireland 29** (3G 1PG 1T)

Scotland: G H Metcalfe; C D Paterson, A Craig,, A R Henderson, K M Logan; G Ross, M R L Blair; A F Jacobsen, G C Bulloch (*captain*), G R McIlwham, S B Grimes, N J Hines, R S Beattie, S M Taylor, A L Mower *Substitutions:* S Webster for Metcalfe (40 mins); J M Petrie for Beattie (62 mins); M C Proudfoot for McIlwham (62 mins); J G McLaren for Henderson (62 mins); R R Russell for Bulloch (67 mins); I A Fullarton for Grimes (temp 53 to 65 mins)

Scorers *Try:* Webster *Conversion:* Paterson *Penalty Goal:* Paterson

Ireland: G E A Murphy; A P Horgan, B G O'Driscoll, K M Maggs, D A Hickie; R J R O'Gara, P A Stringer; M J Horan, K G M Wood (*captain*), R Corrigan, M E O'Kelly, P J O'Connell, D P Wallace, V C P Costello, E R P Miller *Substitutions:* G T Dempsey for Murphy (21 mins); K Dawson for Miller (69 mins); S H Easterby for Costello (temp 51 to 55 mins) and for O'Connell (75 mins);

G Easterby for Stringer (75 mins); D G Humphreys for O'Driscoll (75 mins); S J Best for Corrigan (75 mins); J S Byrne for Wood (77 mins)

Scorers *Tries:* Maggs, Hickie, Horgan, Wallace *Conversions:* O'Gara (3) *Penalty Goal:* O'Gara

Referee N Whitehouse (Wales)

6 September, Stadio Communale Censin Bosia, Asti
Italy 31 (1G 3PG 3T) Georgia 22 (1G 4PG 1DG)

Italy: G Canale; Mirco Bergamasco, C Stoica, G Raineri, N Mazzucato; R Pez, A Troncon (*captain*); A Lo Cicero, F Ongaro, M-L Castrogiovanni, S Dellape, M Bortolami, A De Rossi, S Parisse, A R Persico *Substitutions:* G Peens for Canale; J-M Queirolo for Troncon; Mauro Bergamasco for De Rossi; C Checchinato for Dellape; S Perugini for Castrogiovanni; C Festuccia for Ongaro

Scorers *Tries:* Castrogiovanni, Lo Cicero, Troncon, Checchinato *Conversion:* Pez *Penalty Goals:* Pez (3)

Georgia: B Khamashuridze; M Urjukashvili, T Zibzibadze, I Guiorgadze, I Machkhaneli; P Jimsheladze, I Abusseridze; A Kopaliani, A Guiorgadze, A Margvelashvili, Z Mtchedlishvili, V Didebulidze, G Chkhaidze, I Zedguinidze (*captain*), G Yachvili *Substitutions:* G Khonelidze for Machkhaneli; D Dadunashvili for Kopaliani; G Shvelidze for Margvelashvili; V Nadiradze for Didebulidze; G Labadze for Zedguinidze

Scorers *Try:* Urjukashvili *Conversion:* Jimsheladze *Penalty Goals:* Jimsheladze (4) *Dropped Goal:* Urjukashvili

Referee D I Ramage (Scotland)

6 September, Twickenham
England 45 (4G 4PG 1T) France 14 (2PG 1DG 1T)

England: J Robinson; I R Balshaw, W J H Greenwood, S Abbott, B C Cohen; J P Wilkinson, K P P Bracken; T J Woodman, S Thompson, J M White, M O Johnson (*captain*), B J Kay, R A Hill, M E Corry, N A Back *Substitutions:* M J S Dawson for Bracken (34 mins); P J Grayson for Wilkinson (43 mins); S D Shaw for Johnson (43 mins); L W Moody for Corry (57 mins); O J Lewsey for Cohen (temp 47 to 53 mins) and for Abbott (60 mins); J Leonard for White (63 mins); D E West for Moody (temp 68 to 72 mins) and for Thompson (73 mins)

Scorers *Tries:* Cohen (2), Robinson, Balshaw, Lewsey *Conversions:* Wilkinson (3), Grayson *Penalty Goals:* Wilkinson (4)

France: C Poitrenaud; X Garbajosa, Y Jauzion, B Liebenberg, C Dominici; G Merceron, D Yachvili; O Milloud, R Ibañez (*captain*), J-B Poux, D Auradou, O Brouzet, P Tabacco, C Labit, S Chabal *Substitutions:* A Rougerie for Dominici (40 mins); O Magne for Chabal (50 mins); F Pelous for Brouzet (58 mins); Y Bru for Ibañez (70 mins); I Harinordoquy for Tabacco (73 mins); S Marconnet for Milloud (temp 62 to 73 mins) and for Poux (73 mins)

Scorers *Try:* Rougerie *Penalty Goals:* Merceron (2) *Dropped Goal:* Jauzion

Referee N Williams (Wales)

IRB WORLD RANKINGS

In September 2003, a month before the Rugby World Cup kick-off, the International Rugby Board announced the launch of their official IRB World Rankings for the fifteen-a-side international men's game.

The rankings will be the official indicator of the development of Unions. The system was chosen for its reliability, transparency and flexibility and has been tested on an extensive database of nearly 4,500 international matches dating back to 1871.

The state of the nations at the start of the World Cup is:

RANK	*NATION*	*SCORE*	*RANK*	*NATION*	*SCORE*
1	England	89.95	38	Switzerland	49.08
2	New Zealand	89.8	39	Cote d'Ivoire	48.87
3	Ireland	83.92	40	Netherlands	48.38
4	Australia	83.81	41	Madagascar	48.27
5	France	82.85	42	Kazakhstan	48.17
6	South Africa	80.92	43	Sweden	47.41
7	Argentina	80	44	Arabian Gulf	47.25
8	Samoa	74.67	45	Zimbabwe	47.22
9	Scotland	74.42	46	Latvia	47.17
10	Wales	74.24	47	China	47.05
11	Fiji	72.45	48	Peru	47.04
12	Tonga	70.08	49	Slovenia	46.98
13	Italy	69.98	50	Trinidad & Tobago	46.36
14	United States	68.42	51	Kenya	46.3
15	Romania	67.73	52	Bermuda	46.3
16	Canada	66.21	53	Belgium	46.18
17	Georgia	63.8	54	Thailand	45.65
18	Japan	62.68	55	Venezuela	45.52
19	Uruguay	62.65	56	Cook Islands	45.11
20	Portugal	62.03	57	Singapore	44.9
21	Morocco	60.8	58	Moldova	44.58
22	Korea	60.78	59	Yugoslavia	44.06
23	Russia	60.2	60	Papua N Guinea	43.52
24	Chile	59.65	61	Lithuania	43.39
25	Namibia	58.76	62	Zambia	42.9
26	Czech Republic	57.61	63	Sri Lanka	42.8
27	Ukraine	56.97	64	Andorra	42.6
28	Germany	54.96	65	Hungary	42.43
29	Hong Kong	54.67	66	Cayman Islands	42.03
30	Spain	54.28	67	Uganda	42.02
31	Tunisia	54.09	68	Malta	41.46
32	Chinese Taipei	53.09	69	Solomon Islands	40.27
33	Poland	52.82	70	Nigeria	40
34	Croatia	52.8	71	Guam	40
35	Brazil	51.87	72	Senegal	40
36	Paraguay	51.25	73	St Lucia	40
37	Denmark	49.75	74	Malaysia	39.44

RANK	*NATION*	*SCORE*
75	Niue Island	39.31
76	Cameroon	38.97
77	Guyana	38.95
78	Monaco	38.81
79	Tahiti	38.62
80	Colombia	38.5
81	Barbados	38.48
82	Jamaica	38.14
83	Swaziland	37.92
84	Bulgaria	36.99
85	Luxembourg	36.91

RANK	*NATION*	*SCORE*
86	Austria	36.76
87	Israel	35.95
88	Botswana	35.82
89	India	35.49
90	Vanuatu	35.16
91	Bahamas	34.2
92	Bosnia	33.94
93	Norway	33.62
94	Finland	33.06

SIX NATIONS 2003

England Slam the Door on Demons of Doubt

Mick Cleary

England laid to rest all those ghosts that had swirled around them for the last four years, taunting them over their repeated failure to land the Grand Slam. A combination of fate, arrogance, chance and rank bad tactics had cost them dear in years past. This time England made no attempt to hide from the significance of the challenge. Lawrence Dallaglio stated at the season's start that England deserved shooting if they failed again. There was never a moment throughout the championship when rifles were in danger of being loaded and triggers cocked.

England deserved their first Grand Slam in eight years, their 12th in all. In passing it should be recorded that they also notched their 25th outright championship title and 23rd Triple Crown. They were the highest points scorers in the championship, although their haul of 173 points was some way short of their own record mark of 229 points set in 2001. That was the year that the cruel Gods above intervened, the ravages of foot-and-mouth causing Ireland's match with England to be one of three games to be held over until the autumn.

Clive Woodward has taken it upon himself to cover most eventualities in his meticulous preparation but not even he could find a religious specialist to have an influential word with the Man above. In this championship Woodward used his natural resources shrewdly. He was not afraid to take some calculated risks, such as the selection of Sale fly-half, Charlie Hodgson, at centre for the first time in his career. He was thrown in for the opening match against France. Welcome to the big time Charlie.

Woodward's side ended on a thrilling note and gave one of the most vivid displays of the tournament in dispatching Ireland 42-6 on the final day of the championship. It was the game we had all been hoping for. That is, a contest that was full-blooded, relentless and compelling; a match that satisfied both heart and head, one that withstood scrutiny as both a good game of rugby as well as a grand occasion.

There were not that many other high-spots across the seven weeks. We can all admire the effort and work-ethic of these teams. We can admire sound defence. And applaud the big hits. But, please, where is the poetry to go with the heavy-duty prose? There were only sporadic glimpses in this championship.

The final table told its own story. Each of the sides beat the teams beneath them. The symmetry was appropriate. England had more depth to their game than anyone else, be it the unerring accuracy of Jonny Wilkinson's kicking – he was the top scorer with 77 points, four points ahead of Ireland fly-half, David Humphreys – or the ball-carrying thrusts of hooker Steve Thompson. Centre Mike Tindall came through strongly to lend a focal point to the England attack while the belated appearance of Josh Lewsey mid-way through the championship brought shape and direction.

Ireland have still to prove that they can go the extra mile. They were decent value as possible Grand Slam champions, looking to achieve the elusive status for the first time in 55 years. France never recovered their composure after their opening-day defeat by England. They lacked a quality goal-kicker and Gérald Merceron paid the price. France missed the absent Tony Marsh who had a cancer scare and prop Pieter de Villiers who failed a drugs test. The intermittent absence of captain Fabien Galthié also hindered them.

Italy were the delight of the championship, recording only their second-ever win when beating Wales. They responded well to the Kiwi-Italian promptings of new coach, John Kirwan. Their back-row of Andrea de Rossi, Matthew Phillips and Aaron Persico was particularly impressive. Italy twice went walkabout, against England and then France, only to recover their ground. If they can cure those mental lapses then they will be even more effective.

Scotland finished with a couple of victories but did little to suggest that they are close to emulating their Celtic cousins, Ireland. They struggled to get a settled midfield, a failing reflected in their poor points return of 81 points in five games.

Wales were whitewashed for the first time since 1995. Even though they battled bravely against England, and were only beaten in dramatic circumstances by Ireland, it was hard to mount much of a case in their defence. They got what they deserved from the championship. So too did England.

Six Nations 2003: Final Table

	P	*W*	*D*	*L*	*F*	*A*	*Pts*
England	5	5	0	0	173	46	10
Ireland	5	4	0	1	119	97	8
France	5	3	0	2	153	75	6
Scotland	5	2	0	3	81	161	4
Italy	5	1	0	4	100	185	2
Wales	5	0	0	5	82	144	0

Points: win 2; draw 1; defeat 0.

There were 708 points scored at an average of 47.2 a match. The Championship record (803 points at an average of 53.5 a match) was set in 2000. Jonny Wilkinson was the leading individual points scorer with 77, a dozen shy of the Championship record he set in 2001. Damien Traille scored most tries (four – four short of the all time record).

The England team celebrate winning the Six Nations Grand Slam after beating Ireland 42-6 at Lansdowne Road, Dublin in March.

15 February, Stadio Flaminio, Rome
Italy 30 (3G 1PG 2DG) **Wales 22** (2G 1PG 1T)

As one commentator noted, there are quite enough crumbling ruins in the Eternal City without the Welsh team making their own contribution. They disintegrated quite emphatically in the face of a raw-edged, robust Italian challenge, worthy virtues but hardly unique in international rugby. It was a lively, exciting but terribly fractured game: high in drama, low in genuine quality. The Welsh defence was pitiful.

Victory was no more than Italy deserved and was built on the foundations of a solid performance from a back-row of Andrea de Rossi, Matthew Phillips and Aaron Persico. It was only Italy's second win in the championship and should serve as an antidote to those who routinely question their right to be part of the Six Nations.

New coach John Kirwan fashioned a side that played with great heart and no little skill. The former All Black wing, not known for recklessness in his playing days, took a huge gamble by moving star flanker Mauro Bergamasco to the wing. Kirwan compared Bergamasco to Jonah Lomu, stating that he was out there to 'frighten opponents.' Bergamasco was probably pretty anxious himself in such unfamiliar territory.

Wales made six changes from the side that had lost to New Zealand. In the absence of Stephen Jones and Neil Jenkins, coach Steve Hansen was forced to pick Iestyn Harris at fly-half.

There was a pell-mell feel to the first half as both sides scored tries in slapdash circumstances. Giampiero de Carli opened the scoring in the fourth minute, ambling through for the try. Tom Shanklin's pass sent Steve Williams to the line three minutes later before Shanklin himself touched down in the 14th minute. The procession of scoring continued with a try by hooker Carlo Festuccia seven minutes later.

Diego Dominguez and Harris exchanged penalties before the Italian fly-half landed the first of his two drop goals just before half-time. The game swung Italy's way with Phillips's try in the 62nd minute, the Italian No 8 profiting from good pilfering work by Alessandro Troncon at the base of the Welsh scrum. Dwayne Peel's 80th minute try was no consolation whatsoever for Wales. Dominguez, whose Test career began with 27 points for his native Argentina, passed 1,000 points in international rugby.

Italy: P Vaccari; Mauro Bergamasco, C Stoica, G Raineri, D Dallan; D Dominguez, A Troncon (*captain*); G P De Carli, C Festuccia, R Martinez-Frugoni, C Bezzi, M Bortolami, A De Rossi, M Phillips, A R Persico
Substitutions: Mirco Bergamasco for Raineri (27 mins); S Perugini for Martinez-Frugoni (temp 58 mins to 60 mins)

Scorers *Tries:* De Carli, Festuccia, Phillips *Conversions:* Dominguez (3)
Penalty Goal: Dominguez *Drop Goals*: Dominguez (2)

Wales: G R Williams; G Thomas, T Shanklin, L B Davies, M A Jones; I R Harris, D Peel; I D Thomas, Mefin Davies, B R Evans, R Sidoli, S M Williams, M Owen, C L Charvis (*captain*), M E Williams
Substitutions: G J Williams for Mefin Davies (50 mins); D R Jones for S Williams

(50 mins); M J Watkins for L Davies (56 mins); Gavin Thomas for Charvis (68 mins); C Sweeney for M Jones (76 mins)

Scorers *Tries:* Shanklin, S Williams, Peel *Conversions:* Harris (2) *Penalty Goal:* Harris

Referee J Jutge (France)

15 February, Twickenham
England 25 (1G 5PG 1DG) **France 17** (1G 2T)

The mood was flat even if the game itself had its uplifting moments. The sudden death 24 hours earlier of 21-year-old Harlequins scrum-half, Nick Duncombe, cast a pall over proceedings. But for injury, Duncombe would have been on the England bench. His 'Quins teammate, wing Dan Luger, was close to pulling out. There were mixed feelings therefore for another 'Quins colleague, Jason Leonard as he led the side down the Twickenham tunnel to mark his 100th cap for England. The prop's enjoyment of the day was cut further short when he left the field with a hamstring injury after barely half an hour.

England were very self-critical in victory. Their downbeat air was only partly due to the tragic news. Even though they had comfortably accounted for supposedly their closest rivals for the Grand Slam, England lost their focus and their sharpness after an impressive opening hour. At that stage they led 25-7 and looked set to play merry with the previous year's champions. Instead it was France who bounced back off the ropes, scoring two well-crafted tries through Clément Poitrenaud in the 66th minute and Damien Traille in injury time. France, though, for all the finery of their late flourish could not match England's power.

They had no-one either to match the marksmanship of Jonny Wilkinson who was faultless in amassing 20 points from five penalties, a drop goal and the conversion of Jason Robinson's try. In contrast, France missed four simple kicks at goal.

England had been bold in selection, choosing Charlie Hodgson at centre, the first time in his career the Sale fly-half had played there. All Hodgson's previous five caps had been at No 10. It was a scratchy midfield debut. It was a charge-down of Hodgson's attempted clearance kick that led to France's opening try by Oliver Magne in the 17th minute. Hodgson and England regrouped. They began the second half at a rare old lick, momentum that led to a try for Jason Robinson, the full-back coming on to a deft pass from Will Greenwood to round off a sequence that had begun ten phases earlier.

France were stymied in the scrum by harsh interventions from referee Paul Honiss. England accounted for all their other troubles.

England: J Robinson; D D Luger, W J H Greenwood, C Hodgson, B C Cohen; J P Wilkinson, A C T Gomarsall; J Leonard, S Thompson, J M White, M O Johnson (*captain*), B J Kay, L W Moody, R A Hill, N A Back

Substitutions: G C Rowntree for Leonard (33 mins); L B N Dallaglio for Moody (44 mins); D J Grewcock for Kay (84 mins); M P Regan for Rowntree (temp 47 mins to 56 mins)

Scorers *Try:* Robinson *Conversion:* Wilkinson *Penalty Goals:* Wilkinson (5) *Dropped Goal:* Wilkinson

France: C Poitrenaud; A Rougerie, X Garbajosa, D Traille, V Clerc; G Merceron, F Galthié (*captain*); J-J Crenca, R Ibañez, C Califano, F Pelous, O Brouzet, S Betsen, I Harinordoquy, O Magne *Substitutions:* S Marconnet for Califano (62 mins); S Chabal for Betsen (62 mins); T Castaignède for Rougerie (64 mins); J-B Rué for Ibañez (74 mins)

Scorers *Tries:* Magne, Poitrenaud, Traille *Conversion:* Merceron

Referee P G Honiss (New Zealand)

16 February, Murrayfield
Scotland 6 (2PG) Ireland 36 (3G 5PG)

The Sabbath offered no rest or respite for a hapless Scotland. This was their first home defeat to Ireland since 1985, and also their heaviest ever loss to them at Murrayfield. For Ireland, the tale of the statistical tape was altogether more encouraging as they notched a record seventh successive Test win, overtaking the sequence established by Tom Kiernan's sides of 1968 and 1969. The omens of a promising autumn were bearing fruit.

Ireland had too much conviction and cohesion up front, and too much sheer brilliance behind to be much troubled by a limited challenge from Scotland. Victor Costello was the pick of the Irish forwards, centre and captain Brian O'Driscoll the king-pin of the back line.

It was O'Driscoll's brawny physique and delicate imagination that took the game out of Scotland's reach in the second quarter. The Leinster centre had already been rocked by a couple of dangerously high charges from Brendan Laney. Other players might have drawn breath: O'Driscoll hit back. A trademark knifing break faltered only when O'Driscoll slipped. The Irish pack were quick in support and from the ruck, wing Denis Hickie went over. Moments later only a super cover tackle by Andy Craig halted O'Driscoll at the end of a 50-metre run.

Scotland had their best spell after the interval but sustained pressure only brought two penalty goals for Gordon Ross. That was as good as it got for Scotland. Geordan Murphy, a 26th-minute replacement for Shane Horgan, stole away with a poorly-defended ball from the back of a Scottish ruck in the Ireland 22. A chip, chase and dribble saw Murphy score. David Humphreys, back in the No 10 jersey after Ronan O'Gara was ruled out through injury, rounded off the try-scoring and completed a fine match with a 26-point haul.

Scotland: G H Metcalfe; K M Logan, A Craig, B J Laney, C D Paterson; G Ross, B W Redpath (*captain*); T J Smith, G C Bulloch, B A F Douglas, S Murray, S B Grimes, M D Leslie, S M Taylor, A L Mower *Substitutions:* G Kerr for Douglas (62 mins); G P J Townsend for Ross (66 mins)

Scorer *Penalty Goals:* Ross (2)

Ireland: G T Dempsey; S P Horgan, B G O'Driscoll (*captain*), K M Maggs, D A Hickie; D G Humphreys, P A Stringer; R Corrigan, J S Byrne, J J Hayes, G W Longwell, M E O'Kelly, V C P Costello, A G Foley, K D Gleeson *Substitutions:* G E A Murphy for Horgan (25 mins); L F M Cullen for Longwell (66 mins); A Quinlan for Costello (69 mins); M J Horan for Corrigan (73 mins);

G Easterby for Stringer (76 mins); F J Sheahan for Byrne (76 mins); P A Burke for O'Driscoll (78 mins)

Scorers *Tries:* Humphreys, Hickie, Murphy *Conversions:* Humphreys (3) *Penalty Goals:* Humphreys (5)

Referee A Cole (Australia)

22 February, Stadio Flaminio, Rome
Italy 13 (1G 2PG) **Ireland 37** (3G 2PG 2T)

Ireland were in no mood to pose as Celtic whipping-boys. There was never the remotest hint of a reprise showing of the Italian victory over Wales seven days earlier. Ireland lived up to their billing as championship contenders with an assured five-try dismantling of their opponents.

Once again their line-out was firm and their scrum stable. With that sort of platform, the half-back pairing of Peter Stringer and David Humphreys needed no second bidding. Mind you, Humphreys, so measured a week earlier, had a ragged opening spell as the Italians targeted him. The Ireland fly-half fumbled and fretted, putting the men around him under acute pressure. Both he and the team came through that bumpy quarter-of-an-hour. From there, the traffic was one way and orderly, an uncommon event in Rome.

Peter Stringer scored the first Ireland try in the 19th minute, benefiting from thumping build-up work by Victor Costello. It was another back-row forward, Keith Gleeson, who did the significant work for Ireland's second try, the flanker popping the ball out of the tackle to help put John Kelly in at the corner.

Four minutes after the half-time break Gleeson was again actively involved when he leapt well to gather Humphreys's Garryowen. From there, a swift flurry of hands saw Denis Hickie go over.

Italy had their moments, notably just before half-time when only sterling defence by Anthony Foley and Kevin Maggs kept Italy's No 8 Matthew Phillips at bay. Italy had some return in the 56th minute when they somehow recycled the ball from beneath a pile of bodies to enable Denis Dallan to squeeze over.

Ireland came back strongly. Brian O'Driscoll gave cause for some historical rewriting when he touched down for his 18th international try, so breaking the record of Brendan Mullin.

The Ireland centre was also involved in Ireland's fifth try scored by Geordan Murphy.

Italy: P Vaccari; Mauro Bergamasco, C Stoica, G Raineri, D Dallan; D Dominguez, A Troncon (*captain*); G P De Carli, C Festuccia, R Martinez-Frugoni, C Bezzi, M Bortolami, A De Rossi, M Phillips, A R Persico *Substitutions:* R Pez for Dominguez (47 mins); L Castrogiovanni for Martinez-Frugoni (60 mins); S Palmer for Phillips (71 mins); Mirco Bergamasco for Dallan (74 mins)

Scorers *Try:* Dallan *Conversion:* Pez *Penalty Goals:* Dominguez, Pez

Ireland: G E A Murphy; J P Kelly, B G O'Driscoll (*captain*), K M Maggs, D A Hickie; D G Humphreys, P A Stringer; R Corrigan, J S Byrne, J J Hayes,

G W Longwell, M E O'Kelly, V C P Costello, A G Foley, K D Gleeson
Substitutions: M J Horan for Corrigan (41 mins); F J Sheahan for Byrne (63 mins); L F M Cullen for Longwell (63 mins); A Quinlan for Costello (71 mins); G Easterby for Stringer (78 mins); R A J Henderson for Kelly (78 mins)

Scorers *Tries:* Stringer, Kelly, Humphreys, O'Driscoll, Murphy
Conversions: Humphreys (3) *Penalty Goals:* Humphreys (2)

Referee A J Spreadbury (England)

22 February, Millennium Stadium, Cardiff Arms Park
Wales 9 (3PG) England 26 (2G 2PG 2DG)

Normal service was disrupted on the rail network by petty officialdom who objected to the 17.30 evening kick-off. The smooth delivery of England towards their final Grand Slam destination was also subjected to severe local interference, but progress along their historic route they eventually did.

Wales, who had feared the worst after their Roman nightmare, expressed as much in their team selection when they were forced into a desperate roll of the dice with the recall of former captain, 33-year-old hooker Jonathan Humphreys. The former Cardiff forward, who had moved to Bath the previous summer, had not played international rugby for four years. He took on the job with customary pride and defiance. 'This is not long-term,' said Humphreys. 'I see it as helping-out.' Previous captain, Colin Charvis, was dropped to the bench. There were five other changes in the Welsh line-up with a first start for Pontypridd fly-half Ceri Sweeney.

The Humphreys factor proved a relative success, if home defeat can ever be truly seen in those terms. Wales took the game to England and made them fight hard for their spoils. The scoreboard, if not the story, might have taken on a different hue if one gilt-edged chance just before half-time had not been wasted, centre Mark Taylor hanging on to the ball after a fine break when he had men outside him. England led by just 9-6 at half-time and a try at that juncture might have, at least, delayed the inevitable.

As it was England clicked into something like their smoothest form in the third quarter. They scored two tries in that period, the first in the 47th minute coming from Will Greenwood when they were down to 14 men. Phil Christophers was sent to the sin-bin for obstruction on Gareth Thomas barely a minute after coming on as a replacement. England's second try owed much to Lawrence Dallaglio who had a fine all-round game. His initial drive was taken on by Kyran Bracken who was checked. Joe Worsley was on hand to finish off.

Bracken had surprisingly been chosen ahead of Andy Gomarsall in the continuing absence of Matt Dawson, who had a calf injury. England also had injury problems at prop and were forced to turn to 21-year-old Northampton prop Robbie Morris after Julian White withdrew.

Wales: K A Morgan; G Thomas, M Taylor, T Shanklin, G R Williams; C Sweeney, G J Cooper; I D Thomas, J M Humphreys (*captain*), B R Evans, R Sidoli, S M Williams, D R Jones, Gavin Thomas, M E Williams *Substitutions:* G J Williams for Humphreys (57 mins); C L Charvis for Gavin Thomas (57 mins); G Jenkins for

Evans (57 mins); M J Watkins for Shanklin (65 mins); I R Harris for G R Williams (66 mins); G O Llewellyn for S Williams (73 mins)

Scorer *Penalty Goals:* Sweeney (3)

England: J Robinson; D D Luger, W J H Greenwood, C Hodgson, B C Cohen; J P Wilkinson, K P P Bracken; G C Rowntree, S Thompson, R Morris, M O Johnson (*captain*), B J Kay, R A Hill, L B N Dallaglio, N A Back
Substitutions: P Christophers for Robinson (39 mins); J P R Worsley for Back (56 mins); D J Grewcock for Kay (63 mins); J Simpson-Daniel for Hill (temp 40 mins to 50 mins) and for Wilkinson (77 mins); A C T Gomarsall for Luger (77 mins)

Scorers *Tries:* Greenwood, Worsley *Conversions:* Wilkinson (2)
Penalty Goals: Wilkinson (2) *Dropped Goals:* Wilkinson (2)

Referee S R Walsh (New Zealand)

23 February, Stade de France, Paris
France 38 (3G 4PG 1T) Scotland 3 (1PG)

First impressions did not lie. Those who had branded Scotland as championship also-rans after their opening day rout by Ireland had their views confirmed at the Stade de France. In a poor, disjointed game, Scotland never really troubled the scorers and returned home with a pitiful tally of just nine points on the ledger after two matches.

They had a few upbeat moments but these really were sporadic interludes. The experiment of moving Brendan Laney to fly-half, the fourth different position he had occupied since moving from Otago 18 months earlier to take up with Scotland, was not a success. The former Highlander was too jittery in his play and was substituted after an hour's play, Gregor Townsend moving infield to No 10.

France scored four tries but did not convince. 'Anyone would think we have lost and not won by 35 points,' said manager Jo Maso as he fended off critical inquiries afterwards.

France did score a memorable try on the hour when Damien Traille executed a perfectly-timed leap and catch to take the deft chip kick of François Gelez. Scotland tried a similar ploy later in the game only for debutant Borders centre, Kevin Utterson, to knock on Townsend's kick. It was that sort of afternoon for Scotland; minimal expectation bringing due return.

In a scruffy first half, France's only try was scored by lock Fabien Pelous, who was on the end of a hard-driving maul from a line-out. Laney's unhappy outing ended shortly after he had been caught in possession, the turnover enabling France to counter-attack, a move that ended with a try for Clément Poitrenaud.

France's fourth and final try heaped more ignominy on Scotland with Kenny Logan beaten by the cross-kick of Dimitri Yachvili that enabled Aurélien Rougerie to touch down.

France: C Poitrenaud; A Rougerie, X Garbajosa, D Traille, V Clerc; F Gelez, F Galthié (*captain*); J-J Crenca, R Ibañez, S Marconnet, F Pelous, O Brouzet, S Betsen, I Harinordoquy, O Magne *Substitutions:* C Califano for Marconnet (66 mins); D Auradou for Brouzet (66 mins); T Castaignède for Clerc (67 mins); S Chabal for Harinordoquy (73 mins); D Yachvili for Galthié (73 mins); J-B Rué for Ibañez (79 mins)

Scorers *Tries:* Pelous, Poitrenaud, Traille, Rougerie *Conversions:* Gelez (3) *Penalty Goals:* Gelez (4)

Scotland: G H Metcalfe; C D Paterson, G P J Townsend, K N Utterson, K M Logan; B J Laney, B W Redpath (*captain*); T J Smith, G C Bulloch, B A F Douglas, S Murray, S B Grimes, M D Leslie, S M Taylor, A L Mower *Substitutions:* J P R White for Murray (54 mins); A Craig for Laney (61 mins); J M Petrie for Mower (temp 39 mins to 40 mins and 69 mins); M R L Blair for Redpath (temp 25 mins to 37 mins and 76 mins); G Kerr for Douglas (62 mins); B A F Douglas for Kerr (69 mins)

Scorer *Penalty Goal:* Paterson

Referee P Marshall (Australia)

8 March, Lansdowne Road, Dublin
Ireland 15 (4PG 1DG) France 12 (4PG)

Even those emerald-clad diehards who streamed out into a filthy Dublin evening dreaming of, and drinking to, an Irish Grand Slam would concede that they had just witnessed a game of depressingly low quality. Blame the conditions, blame the tension, but also blame the players. Ireland were stifled by a lack of ambition; France by the absence of their comfort blanket, scrum-half and captain, Fabien Galthié. They really will have to learn to do without him if they are to be serious contenders for World Cup honours.

The Irish strategy worked in that they recorded the victory that kept them on course for a showdown with England. Their kicking game, however, depended for its ultimate success on France squandering several gilt-edged chances. Hooker Raphaël Ibañez alone knocked on twice with the line at his mercy. In other instances of fecklessness, Dimitri Yachvili kicked ahead with wing Aurélien Rougerie free while a late chip and chase by Vincent Clerc was foiled by Ireland's offside tactics.

The wet and blustery backdrop did signal the need for a tighter, more controlled approach, but it was galling to see the glittering talent of Brian O'Driscoll so deployed. At least his forward pack did not let him down. Fears that the scrum might come under pressure without the injured Reggie Corrigan proved groundless as Marcus Horan came of age at loose-head. Once again the pin-point throwing of hooker Shane Byrne was a precious asset for Ireland.

Ireland made clear their intention to snatch every little opening when Geordan Murphy let fly with a snap 40-metre drop goal in the second minute. That score set the tone. David Humphreys, winning his 50th cap, was again reliable with his kicking, his four penalty goals always keeping his side just ahead of France. François Gelez, again preferred to Gérald Merceron, with four goals ensured that Ireland felt the hot French breath on their necks right to the final whistle.

Ireland: G E A Murphy; J P Kelly, B G O'Driscoll (*captain*), K M Maggs, D A Hickie; D G Humphreys, P A Stringer; M J Horan, J S Byrne, J J Hayes, G W Longwell, M E O'Kelly, V C P Costello, A G Foley, K D Gleeson
Substitutions: L F M Cullen for Longwell (35 mins); A Quinlan for Costello (66 mins)

Scorers *Penalty Goals:* Humphreys (4) *Dropped Goal:* Murphy

France: C Poitrenaud; A Rougerie, X Garbajosa, D Traille, V Clerc; F Gelez, D Yachvili; J-J Crenca, R Ibañez, S Marconnet, F Pelous (*captain*), O Brouzet, S Betsen, I Harinordoquy, O Magne *Substitutions:* C Califano for Marconnet (50 mins); S Chabal for Betsen (73 mins)

Scorer *Penalty Goals:* Gelez (4)

Referee A J Watson (South Africa)

8 March, Murrayfield
Scotland 30 (3G 3PG) Wales 22 (2G 1PG 1T)

The depressing thump of the wooden spoon was enough to galvanise Scotland to some sort of productive performance while its sombre beat echoed in the thoughts of the many thousands of Welsh fans who had made the biennial pilgrimage north. They may well have deserved some status on the scoreboard for all their effort and endeavour, but even their most partisan backers cannot hide from the fact that two of their three tries came in stoppage time when the game was well and truly run.

There was at least more shape as well as substance to Scotland. Gregor Townsend was back in his favoured position at fly-half, the third choice in as many games by coach Ian McGeechan, and with Jason White adding his considerable power on the blind-side, Scotland were able to fashion a more sustained and structured approach.

It was a combination of Townsend's guile and White's ball-carrying drive that saw Scotland to an early 17-3 lead. In the 14th minute Townsend put Scotland in position. Stuart Grimes secured line-out ball from where prop Bruce Douglas blasted over. Seven minutes later a floated Townsend pass somehow found Simon Taylor on the wide outside. The No 8 then managed to weave through a flaky Welsh defence to score.

Wales, who had been forced into choosing flanker Martyn Williams as their third captain in as many games after Jonathan Humphreys withdrew with a shoulder injury, had a brief rally towards the end of the first half when Gareth Cooper wriggled over after a long sequence of play.

Chris Paterson, who had a fine game, completed the Scotland scoring with a try in the 80th minute. The Scotland wing landed all his six kicks at goal. Then came the consolation flurry for Wales with tries from Mark Taylor and Rhys Williams.

Scotland: G H Metcalfe; C D Paterson, J G McLaren, K N Utterson, K M Logan; G P J Townsend, B W Redpath (*captain*); T J Smith, G C Bulloch, B A F Douglas, S Murray, S B Grimes, J P R White, S M Taylor, A L Mower
Substitutions: A Craig for Utterson (51 mins); G Kerr for Douglas (60 mins); M R L Blair for Redpath (72 mins); N J Hines for Grimes (74 mins); R R Russell

for Bulloch (76 mins); J M Petrie for White (83 mins); G Ross for Townsend (83 mins)

Scorers *Tries:* Douglas, Taylor, Paterson *Conversions:* Paterson (3) *Penalty Goals:* Paterson (3)

Wales: K A Morgan; G Thomas, M Taylor, T Shanklin, G R Williams; S M Jones, G J Cooper; I D Thomas, G J Williams, B R Evans, R Sidoli, S M Williams, D R Jones, Gavin Thomas, M E Williams (*captain*)
Substitutions: G Jenkins for Evans (44 mins); G O Llewellyn for S Williams (58 mins); C L Charvis for Gavin Thomas (58 mins); M J Watkins for Morgan (62 mins); D Peel for Cooper (71 mins); I R Harris for Shanklin (71 mins); Mefin Davies for G J Williams (71 mins)

Scorers *Tries:* Cooper, Taylor, R Williams *Conversions:* S Jones (2) *Penalty Goals:* S Jones

Referee P C Deluca (Argentina) replaced by A J Spreadbury (England) (HT)

9 March, Twickenham
England 40 (5G 1T) **Italy 5** (1T)

The palate was teased but not sated. England served up a wonderfully appetising first course only to dump down cold suet for the main dish. It left a strange feeling.

England led 33-0 just after the first quarter, their five tries leaving the Italian defence so much at sea you expected to see distress flares tracing across the sky over Twickenham. But just as we reached for the record books to chart England's progress through the various milestones, the game took on an altogether different hue. It was not that England went hopelessly off the boil – although there was an element of that as their pack lost concentration – but more that Italy roused themselves and discovered some much-needed pride and conviction. The fact that the top five tacklers in the match were all Englishmen tells you all you need to know about the Italian revival. They scored a fine try through full-back Mirco Bergamasco in the 59th minute while the likes of centre Giovanni Raineri and open-side Aaron Persico caught the eye.

England were hampered by injury. They lost both fly-halves, Charlie Hodgson limping off after catching his studs in the turf only a few minutes after replacing Jonny Wilkinson in the 48th minute. Wilkinson's shoulder injury was not serious, but Hodgson's cruciate problem was to put his World Cup in jeopardy.

England, with Wilkinson as captain for the first time in place of the injured Martin Johnson, were quickly into their stride. Josh Lewsey, called up for the ailing Jason Robinson, had a fine return to the international scene, scoring two tries on his Twickenham debut. The first was a simple touchdown while the second (England's fourth) was a 65-metre solo sizzler. Hooker Steve Thompson blasted through for England's second while a fumble by Persico allowed James Simpson-Daniel to profit. Mike Tindall's try in the 22nd minute came from a crisp blind-side move.

All 14 substitutes were used which did little to improve the smooth flow of the game. There was a first cap for 20-year-old Leicester centre Ollie Smith, who came on for Hodgson. Italy ensured that there was to be no stroll to the final whistle for Smith.

England: O J Lewsey; J Simpson-Daniel, W J H Greenwood, M J Tindall, D D Luger; J P Wilkinson (*captain*), M J S Dawson; G C Rowntree, S Thompson, R Morris, D J Grewcock, B J Kay, J P R Worsley, L B N Dallaglio, R A Hill *Substitutions:* C Hodgson for Wilkinson (47 mins); O J Smith for Hodgson (53 mins); S D Shaw for Kay (57 mins); M A Worsley for Morris (59 mins); M P Regan for Thompson (65 mins); A Sanderson for Dallaglio (temp 19 mins to 26 mins) and for Hill (65 mins); K P P Bracken for Lewsey (71 mins)

Scorers *Tries:* Lewsey (2), Thompson, Simpson-Daniel, Tindall, Luger *Conversion:* Wilkinson (4), Dawson

Italy: Mirco Bergamasco; N Mazzucato, P Vaccari, G Raineri, D Dallan; R Pez, A Troncon (*captain*); G P De Carli, C Festuccia, R Martinez-Frugoni, C Bezzi, M Giacheri, A De Rossi, M Phillips, A R Persico *Substitutions:* A Masi for Dallan (16 mins); M Bortolami for Giacheri (temp 6 mins to 11 mins; and 47 mins); L Castrogiovanni for De Carli (49 mins); G Peens for Vaccari (65 mins); M Mazzantini for Troncon (68 mins); S Palmer for Phillips (71 mins); F Ongaro for Festuccia (74 mins)

Scorers *Try:* Mirco Bergamasco

Referee A C Rolland (Ireland)

22 March, Millennium Stadium, Cardiff Arms Park
Wales 24 (3G 1DG) Ireland 25 (4PG 1DG 2T)

The championship had been waiting for a nerve-shredder. The game itself may not have been of the highest sustained quality, but there was no doubting that its climax provided drama that will feature in fireside talk for many years to come.

Wales had played the more considered football throughout yet trailed at the interval and were still behind, 22-21, as the match headed into injury time. Ireland, whose pack were blowing hard, were clinging on.

Fortune finally favoured Wales, however, when Stephen Jones landed a 40-metre drop goal in the 82nd minute. It seemed as if the home side would clinch their first win of the championship. Ireland had other ideas. The restart was somehow deflected back by Malcolm O'Kelly, a notable contribution on the Leinster lock's 50th cap. From there the ball was fed back to Ronan O'Gara who had come on in the 71st minute. The fly-half took a swing and even he admitted that the pot at goal was not the most stylish thing he had ever hit, but it had probably the sweetest return as the ball wobbled through the posts.

There was still more to come. Jones had another drop that went wide. Then, with the stadium at bedlam-pitch, Wales attacked again. Ireland wing Justin Bishop came steaming up into the Welsh line to block a pass. It looked like a deliberate knock-on. Referee Steve Lander signalled an infringement but played advantage. Wales kept playing, not knowing if it would be a penalty or scrum. The ball again came to Jones, whose drop goal attempt was palmed down by Denis Hickie. Lander didn't go back to the original offence but blew for full-time. He later stated that it would have been a scrum for an accidental knock-on. Not many agreed with him.

And so Ireland completed a record run of ten successive victories by the narrowest of margins.

They had put themselves into position for their Grand Slam shoot-out thanks to two tries either side of half-time from Keith Gleeson. Wales had opened the try-scoring through Jones but still trailed 14-7 at the break. Gleeson's second took Ireland clear. Wales hit back, though, with tries in the final quarter from Martyn Williams and Gareth Thomas.

The stage was set. And the drama was played to its conclusion.

Wales: G R Williams; G Thomas, M Taylor, T Shanklin, M A Jones; S M Jones, G J Cooper; I D Thomas, J M Humphreys (*captain*), G Jenkins, R Sidoli, G O Llewellyn, C L Charvis, D R Jones, M E Williams *Substitutions:* M J Watkins for M Jones (11 mins); Mefin Davies for Humphreys (42 mins); D Peel for Cooper (50 mins); I R Harris for Taylor (62 mins); M Madden for Jenkins (76 mins)

Scorers *Tries:* S Jones, M Williams, G Thomas *Conversions:* S Jones (3) *Dropped Goal:* S Jones

Ireland: G E A Murphy; J P Bishop, B G O'Driscoll (*captain*), K M Maggs, D A Hickie; D G Humphreys, P A Stringer; M J Horan, J S Byrne, J J Hayes, L F M Cullen, M E O'Kelly, A Quinlan, A G Foley, K D Gleeson *Substitutions:* D O'Callaghan for Cullen (70 mins); R J R O'Gara for Humphreys (70 mins); J M Fitzpatrick for Horan (75 mins); E R P Miller for Foley (temp 31 mins to 39 mins) and for Quinlan (76 mins)

Scorers *Tries:* Gleeson (2) *Penalty Goals:* Humphreys (4) *Dropped Goal:* O'Gara

Referee S J Lander (England)

22 March, Twickenham
England 40 (4G 4PG) Scotland 9 (3PG)

England made their intentions clear in their selection. All their fit-again front-line players were recalled – Martin Johnson, Neil Back, Jason Leonard, Jason Robinson and Ben Cohen. Josh Lewsey was retained at full-back which meant that Robinson would line up on the wing for the first time in 18 months.

Scotland, too, were keen to lay down a few markers. There was a call-up for burly lock, Nathan Hines, whose claim to fame lay in the fact that he had become the first ever Scotland player to be sent off in a Test match when dismissed against the United States the previous summer. 'Nathan will give us some devil,' said Scotland forwards coach, Jim Telfer.

And so he did. Despite the lop-sided nature of the scoreline, Scotland did make England fight for every opening and every last inch of turf. As such, then, this was England's most impressive performance of the championship. They were more direct and orthodox in their approach work, using the hefty charges of Steve Thompson in the pack and Mike Tindall behind to set the targets. Lewsey's presence also gave their attack a more classical direction.

And in Robinson England possessed a sharp-heeled finisher. Appearing at centre after the 56th-minute departure of Mike Tindall, he lived up to his billing with two lovely scores in the second-half, both of which owed much to the opportunist instincts of Matt Dawson.

The scrum-half's tap penalty in the 64th minute breached the initial defence, a break that was tracked by Robinson who came on to the ball at pace and glided through for the try. Three minutes from time, it was Dawson's one-handed pass out of the tackle that teed-up Robinson's short sprint to the line.

Dawson was also involved in England's second try shortly after half-time, the scrum-half clipping the heels of his opposite number Bryan Redpath, allowing Ben Cohen to latch on to the loose ball and tumble over. England's first try in the 21st minute involved smart transference of the ball with Lewsey completing matters.

Paul Grayson came on as substitute and kicked the final conversion in his first England outing for four years.

England: O J Lewsey; J Robinson, W J H Greenwood, M J Tindall, B C Cohen; J P Wilkinson, M J S Dawson; G C Rowntree, S Thompson, J Leonard, M O Johnson (*captain*), B J Kay, R A Hill, L B N Dallaglio, N A Back
Substitutions: D D Luger for Tindall (56 mins); D J Grewcock for Kay (62 mins); P J Grayson for Wilkinson (66 mins); T J Woodman for Rowntree (66 mins); J P R Worsley for Dallaglio (74 mins)

Scorers *Tries:* Robinson (2), Lewsey, Cohen *Conversions:* Wilkinson (3), Grayson *Penalty Goals:* Wilkinson (4)

Scotland: G H Metcalfe; C D Paterson, J G McLaren, A Craig, K M Logan; G P J Townsend, B W Redpath (*captain*); T J Smith, G C Bulloch, B A F Douglas, S Murray, N J Hines, J P R White, S M Taylor, A L Mower *Substitutions:* S B Grimes for Murray (51 mins); K N Utterson for McLaren (56 mins); R S Beattie for Mower (67 mins); G Kerr for Douglas (72 mins)

Scorer *Penalty Goals:* Paterson (3)

Referee A Lewis (Ireland)

23 March, Stadio Flaminio, Rome
Italy 27 (2G 1PG 2T) France 53 (6G 2PG 1T)

A horrible sense of *déjà vu* must have swept over Italy coach, John Kirwan, as he watched the opening quarter unfold. It was a repeat of the Twickenham experience as his side waved Frenchman blithely on their way to the try-line in much the manner that they had done against England a fortnight earlier. France led 31-3 after just 22 minutes. Kirwan called his players 'mentally immature' which is a polite way of describing their generosity.

It was not just that Italy missed tackles in that disastrous spell. Their line-out was a shambles and they repeatedly failed to clear their lines. France took full advantage. Italy, as they had done at Twickenham, did regroup and finished strongly scoring three second-half tries through Mirco Bergamasco, Aaron Persico and Matthew Phillips. By then, of course, the game was well and truly up.

Serge Betsen was first on the try-scoring sheet, capitalising on a failed clearance from Ramiro Pez. In the 14th minute a poor line out throw from Italy cost them dear, Damien Traille rounding off matters. The French centre blasted to the line a few minutes later after another sliced Italian kick put them into trouble. Wing Aurélien Rougerie was on hand to score shortly afterwards.

The second quarter was not quite as damning for Italy. Frédéric Michalak did swoop to score after Paolo Vaccari had a kick charged down but at least Italy did get on the scoreboard themselves when Pez scrambled over just before half-time.

The other French tries were scored by Thomas Castaignède and Rougerie with Dimitri Yachvili weighing in with 18 points from six conversions and two penalties.

Italy: Mirco Bergamasco; N Mazzucato, P Vaccari, G Raineri, D Dallan; R Pez, A Troncon (*captain*); A Lo Cicero, C Festuccia, R Martinez-Frugoni, C Bezzi, M Giacheri, A De Rossi, M Phillips, A R Persico *Substitutions:* A Masi for Mazzucato (23 mins); S Palmer for De Rossi (54 mins); L Castrogiovanni for Martinez-Frugoni (54 mins); S Dellape for Giacheri (60 mins); G Peens for Vaccari (76 mins); M Mazzantini for Troncon (78 mins); F Ongaro for Festuccia (78 mins)

Scorers *Tries:* Pez, Mirco Bergamasco, Persico, Phillips *Conversions:* Pez (2) *Penalty Goal:* Pez

France: C Poitrenaud; A Rougerie, T Castaignède, D Traille, X Garbajosa; F Michalak, D Yachvili; J-J Crenca, R Ibañez, S Marconnet, F Pelous (*captain*), O Brouzet, S Betsen, I Harinordoquy, O Magne *Substitutions:* P Tabacco for Harinordoquy (68 mins); D Auradou for Brouzet (68 mins); O Milloud for Crenca (73 mins); J-B Rué for Ibañez (78 mins); G Merceron for Michalak (78 mins); J-B Elissalde for Yachvili (78 mins); V Clerc for Garbajosa (78 mins)

Scorers *Tries:* Traille (2), Rougerie (2), Betsen, Michalak, Castaignède *Conversions:* Yachvili (6) *Penalty Goals:* Yachvili (2)

Referee N Williams (Wales)

29 March, Stade de France, Paris
France 33 (3G 4PG) Wales 5 (1T)

No end-of-term fireworks on show at the Stade de France, just the dampest of damp squibs. The defending Grand Slam champions did not fall on their sword in any sort of style. They were lacklustre and disjointed for long stretches, as if sub-consciously tuned-in to the comments the previous day of their coach Bernard Laporte, who had dubbed this game as little more than a 'friendly.'

Tell that to the 80,000 who had bought tickets in good faith. There was a stifling lack of ambition as well as accuracy in so much of France's approach work. That they ran out convincing winners tells you much about the chronic limitations of Welsh rugby.

Wales did actually play with a decent amount of gusto, particularly in the early stages. They scored a try in the fourth minute through Gareth Thomas and were only denied – quite correctly – by the video referee when Craig Morgan lost control just in the act of trying to touch down. That was as good as it got for Wales, however, as their customary failings again afflicted them. They simply did not have the ball-carrying power to trouble France, or enough speed and thrust in the middle of the field to unlock defences. There was a lot of industry on show, particularly from the likes of Martyn Williams and Robert Sidoli, but precious little true class.

France had the personnel but not the attitude. Going through the motions proved enough to see off the championship wooden spoonists. Thomas Castaignède opened their try-scoring on the half-hour after a well-worked scissors with Damien Traille.

The second-half belonged to France. A neat pass from Clément Poitrenaud helped Vincent Clerc on his way to the line. Then, in the 67th minute, the sharp-eyed Olivier Magne filched a ball from a maul and sent Frédéric Michalak clear. Dimitri Yachvili had a good day with the boot to amass 18 points.

France: C Poitrenaud; A Rougerie, T Castaignède, D Traille, X Garbajosa; F Michalak, D Yachvili; J-J Crenca, R Ibañez, S Marconnet, F Pelous (*captain*), O Brouzet, S Betsen, I Harinordoquy, O Magne *Substitutions:* V Clerc for Rougerie (20 mins); P Tabacco for Harinordoquy (59 mins); D Auradou for Brouzet (59 mins); O Milloud for Marconnet (67 mins); J-B Rué for Ibañez (76 mins); G Merceron for Michalak (76 mins); J-B Elissalde for Yachvili (76 mins)

Scorers *Tries:* Castaignède, Clerc, Michalak *Conversions:* Yachvili (3) *Penalty Goals:* Yachvili (4)

Wales: G R Williams; G Thomas, M Taylor, I R Harris, C S Morgan; S M Jones, D Peel; I D Thomas, Mefin Davies, G Jenkins, R Sidoli, G O Llewellyn, C L Charvis, D R Jones, M E Williams (*captain*) *Substitutions:* G J Cooper for Peel (52 mins); M Madden for Jenkins (54 mins); G J Williams for Mefin Davies (68 mins); T Shanklin for Gareth Thomas (temp 62 mins to 52 mins) and for Harris (74 mins); S M Williams for Llewellyn (74 mins); Gavin Thomas for D R Jones (82 mins)

Scorer *Try:* Gareth Thomas

Referee P O'Brien (New Zealand)

29 March, Murrayfield
Scotland 33 (2G 3PG 2T) Italy 25 (2G 2PG 1T)

Be thankful for small mercies. Scotland had failed to trouble the scorers for much of this championship so it doesn't do to begrudge them the four tries they managed against Italy. Their overall game, however, was still flawed; edgy and uncertain in many aspects and put under pressure by a spirited Italian riposte.

There were encouraging signs for coach Ian McGeechan, especially in the form of the back three – Kenny Logan, Chris Paterson and Glenn Metcalfe. Logan, in his last ever Six Nations game, was named

Man-of-the-Match. It was a fitting time to score only his second ever championship try, the Wasps wing touching down after a jinking run by Metcalfe.

Scotland did manage to create openings but lacked sharpness in their finishing. They also faded after the break, having stirred themselves after Italy took the lead in the third minute, full-back Mirco Bergamasco scoring his third try of the tournament after Italy won quick ball from a ruck.

Scotland's reply was swift and decisive. A tap penalty from Andrew Mower sent Jason White crashing over. A lively run from Logan then created the position from where Gregor Townsend's floated pass found centre James McLaren, who completed the formalities.

A good run late in the first half by Italian wing Denis Dallan almost brought its own rewards. Dallan was hauled down but Ramiro Pez was on hand to finish.

The second-half was notable for Scotland's fourth try, a splendid chip and gather by Paterson. Italy were not finished themselves and managed to work Scott Palmer over the line.

Scotland: G H Metcalfe; C D Paterson, J G McLaren, A Craig, K M Logan; G P J Townsend, B W Redpath (*captain*); T J Smith, G C Bulloch, B A F Douglas, S Murray, N J Hines, J P R White, S M Taylor, A L Mower *Substitutions:* R S Beattie for White (42 mins); S B Grimes for Murray (59 mins); R R Russell for Bulloch (76 mins)

Scorers *Tries:* White, McLaren, Logan, Paterson *Conversions:* Paterson (2) *Penalty Goals:* Paterson (3)

Italy: Mirco Bergamasco; P Vaccari, A Masi, G Raineri, D Dallan; R Pez, A Troncon (*captain*); A Lo Cicero, C Festuccia, R Martinez-Frugoni, C Bezzi, M Giacheri, A De Rossi, M Phillips, A R Persico *Substitutions:* G Peens for Vaccari (40 mins); L Castrogiovanni for Martinez-Frugoni (53 mins); S Palmer for Phillips (temp 57 mins to 70 mins) and for De Rossi (70 mins); S Dellape for Giacheri (76 mins)

Scorers *Tries:* Mirco Bergamasco, Pez, Palmer *Conversions:* Pez (2) *Penalty Goals:* Pez (2)

Referee D T M McHugh (Ireland)

30 March, Lansdowne Road, Dublin
Ireland 6 (1PG 1DG) England 42 (4G 1PG 2DG 1T)

The finale did not disappoint. So often these showdowns are plagued by the jitters. So often players go into their shells as the stakes get higher. Not this time. The day, the crowd, the occasion and the match itself all matched and even exceeded expectation.

And lording over them all by the day's end were England, Grand Slam champions for the first time in eight years and deservedly so.

It was not as if Ireland were puff-pastry opposition. They gave as good as they got for the best part of an hour. It made for an absorbing contest. Ireland came back at England after Lawrence Dallaglio had opened the

Ireland's Malcolm O'Kelly tries to evade Richard Hill during the match between Ireland and England in March. England won the match 42 – 6 to take the Grand Slam for the first time since 1995.

try-scoring in the eighth minute, the rejuvenated back-row forward tracking Matt Dawson after the scrum-half had spoiled Peter Stringer's ball (and afternoon) at the base of a scrum with a helping hand from Richard Hill.

Ireland had actually gone into an early lead with a neat 40-metre drop goal from David Humphreys. But for all their effort and sparkle, their only other contribution to the scoreboard was to be a long-range Humphreys penalty goal towards the end of the first half. And that despite some nimble footwork from Geordan Murphy and some typical gung-ho charges from Kevin Maggs, who was winning his 50th cap. England held firm, and then, in a rare breakout worked Jonny Wilkinson into position for a drop goal. That hurt.

The real turning point came around the hour mark when Mike Tindall cut a clever and penetrating angle off Will Greenwood to blast past Brian O'Driscoll and steam all the way to the try-line. It was a powerful expression of England's intent. Ireland were on the back foot. The game was up.

England still had to work for their final scores but by now there was an air of inevitability about the outcome. It was exhibition stuff, the parade of champions. Will Greenwood scored two tries, the first courtesy of the white wedge of players that drove him relentlessly over the line just when he appeared to have been checked. The second was a piece of opportunism as he intercepted Murphy as Ireland tried to run from deep. There was still time for England to round off in style, Dan Luger getting the final touch to a move that had begun way back down the field.

Ireland: G E A Murphy; J P Bishop, B G O'Driscoll (*captain*), K M Maggs, D A Hickie; D G Humphreys, P A Stringer; M J Horan, J S Byrne, J J Hayes, G W Longwell, M E O'Kelly, V C P Costello, A G Foley, K D Gleeson
Substitutions: P J O'Connell for Longwell (57 mins); R J R O'Gara for Humphreys (63 mins); A Quinlan for Costello (68 mins); J M Fitzpatrick for Horan (75 mins); G T Dempsey for O'Driscoll (81 mins)

Scorer *Penalty Goal:* Humphreys *Dropped Goal:* Humphreys

England: O J Lewsey; J Robinson, W J H Greenwood, M J Tindall, B C Cohen; J P Wilkinson, M J S Dawson; G C Rowntree, S Thompson, J Leonard, M O Johnson (*captain*), B J Kay, R A Hill, L B N Dallaglio, N A Back
Substitutions: J P R Worsley for Hill (temp 22 mins to 29 mins); K P P Bracken for Dawson (temp 25 mins to 34 mins and 68 mins to 71 mins); T J Woodman for Rowntree (temp 37 mins to 40 mins and 45 mins); D J Grewcock for Kay (temp 45 mins to 51 mins); P J Grayson for Wilkinson (temp 54 mins to 60 mins); D D Luger for Tindall (68 mins)

Scorers *Tries:* Greenwood (2), Dallaglio, Tindall, Luger *Conversions:* Wilkinson (3), Grayson *Penalty Goal:* Wilkinson *Dropped Goals:* Wilkinson (2)

Referee J I Kaplan (South Africa)

INTERNATIONAL CHAMPIONSHIP RECORDS 1883-2003

Previous winners:

1883 England; 1884 England; 1885 Not completed; 1886 England & Scotland; 1887 Scotland; 1888 Not completed; 1889 Not completed; 1890 England & Scotland; 1891 Scotland; 1892 England; 1893 Wales; 1894 Ireland; 1895 Scotland; 1896 Ireland; 1897 Not completed; 1898 Not completed; 1899 Ireland; 1900 Wales; 1901 Scotland; 1902 Wales; 1903 Scotland; 1904 Scotland; 1905 Wales; 1906 Ireland & Wales; 1907 Scotland; 1908 Wales; 1909 Wales; 1910 England; 1911 Wales; 1912 England & Ireland; 1913 England; 1914 England; 1920 England & Scotland & Wales; 1921 England; 1922 Wales; 1923 England; 1924 England; 1925 Scotland; 1926 Scotland & Ireland; 1927 Scotland & Ireland; 1928 England; 1929 Scotland; 1930 England; 1931 Wales; 1932 England & Ireland & Wales; 1933 Scotland; 1934 England; 1935 Ireland; 1936 Wales; 1937 England; 1938 Scotland; 1939 England & Ireland & Wales; 1947 England & Wales; 1948 Ireland; 1949 Ireland; 1950 Wales; 1951 Ireland; 1952 Wales; 1953 England; 1954 England & Wales & France; 1955 Wales & France; 1956 Wales; 1957 England; 1958 England; 1959 France; 1960 England & France; 1961 France; 1962 France; 1963 England; 1964 Scotland & Wales; 1965 Wales; 1966 Wales; 1967 France; 1968 France; 1969 Wales; 1970 Wales & France; 1971 Wales; 1972 Not completed; 1973 Five Nations tie; 1974 Ireland; 1975 Wales; 1976 Wales; 1977 France; 1978 Wales; 1979 Wales; 1980 England; 1981 France; 1982 Ireland; 1983 Ireland & France; 1984 Scotland; 1985 Ireland; 1986 Scotland & France; 1987 France; 1988 Wales & France; 1989 France; 1990 Scotland; 1991 England; 1992 England; 1993 France; 1994 Wales; 1995 England; 1996 England; 1997 France; 1998 France; 1999 Scotland; 2000 England; 2001 England; 2002 France; 2003 England.

England have won the title outright 25 times; Wales 22; Scotland 14; France 13; Ireland 10; Italy 0.

Triple Crown winners:

England (23 times) 1883, 1884, 1892, 1913, 1914, 1921, 1923, 1924, 1928, 1934, 1937, 1954, 1957, 1960, 1980, 1991, 1992, 1995, 1996, 1997, 1998, 2002, 2003.

Wales (17 times) 1893, 1900, 1902, 1905, 1908, 1909, 1911, 1950, 1952, 1965, 1969, 1971, 1976, 1977, 1978, 1979, 1988.

Scotland (10 times) 1891, 1895, 1901, 1903, 1907, 1925, 1933, 1938, 1984, 1990.

Ireland (Six times) 1894, 1899, 1948, 1949, 1982, 1985.

Grand Slam winners:

England (12 times) 1913, 1914, 1921, 1923, 1924, 1928, 1957, 1980, 1991, 1992, 1995, 2003.

Wales (Eight times) 1908, 1909, 1911, 1950, 1952, 1971, 1976, 1978.

France (Seven times) 1968, 1977, 1981, 1987, 1997, 1998, 2002

Scotland (Three times) 1925, 1984, 1990.

Ireland (Once) 1948.

Chief Records:

Record	*Detail*		*Set*
Most team points in season	229 by England	in five matches	2001
Most team tries in season	29 by England	in five matches	2001
Highest team score	80 by England	80-23 v Italy	2001
Biggest team win	57 by England	80-23 v Italy	2001
Most team tries in match	12 by Scotland	v Wales	1887
Most appearances	56 for Ireland	C M H Gibson	1964 – 1979
Most points in matches	406 for Wales	N R Jenkins	1991 – 2001
Most points in season	89 for England	J P Wilkinson	2001
Most points in match	35 for England	J P Wilkinson	v Italy, 2001
Most tries in matches	24 for Scotland	I S Smith	1924 – 1933
Most tries in season	8 for England	C N Lowe	1914
	8 for Scotland	I S Smith	1925
Most tries in match	5 for Scotland	G C Lindsay	v Wales, 1887
Most cons in matches	74 for England	J P Wilkinson	1998 – 2003
Most cons in season	24 for England	J P Wilkinson	2001
Most cons in match	9 for England	J P Wilkinson	v Italy, 2001
Most pens in matches	93 for Wales	N R Jenkins	1991 – 2001
Most pens in season	18 for England	S D Hodgkinson	1991
	18 for England	J P Wilkinson	2000
	18 for France	G Merceron	2002
Most pens in match	7 for England	S D Hodgkinson	v Wales, 1991
	7 for England	C R Andrew	v Scotland, 1995
	7 for England	J P Wilkinson	v France, 1999
	7 for Wales	N R Jenkins	v Italy, 2000
	7 for France	G Merceron	v Italy, 2002
Most drops in matches	9 for France	J-P Lescarboura	1982 – 1988
	9 for England	C R Andrew	1985 – 1997
Most drops in season	5 for France	G Camberabero	1967
	5 for Italy	D Dominguez	2000
	5 for Wales	N R Jenkins	2001
	5 for England	J P Wilkinson	2003
Most drops in match	3 for France	P Albaladejo	v Ireland, 1960
	3 for France	J-P Lescarboura	v England, 1985
	3 for Italy	D Dominguez	v Scotland 2000
	3 for Wales	N R Jenkins	v Scotland 2001

THE SIX NATIONS CHAMPIONSHIP 2000-2003: COMPOSITE FOUR-SEASON TABLE

	P	*W*	*D*	*L*	*Pts*
England	20	17	0	3	34
Ireland	20	14	0	6	28
France	20	13	0	7	26
Scotland	20	7	1	12	15
Wales	20	6	1	13	13
Italy	20	2	0	18	4

TRI NATIONS 2003

The All Blacks Race to Triumph

Paul Dobson

The 2003 Tri Nations had a slightly unrealistic air about it as people looked ahead to the World Cup. Then the magnificent All Blacks, who played in the first two matches, came to the rescue to give it validity and vitality. They carried on where the Blues had left off in the Super 12, running rings in the most joyous ways around first the Springboks in Pretoria and then the Wallabies in Sydney. After just two matches the glorious All Blacks had scored 102 points with 14 tries. They were brilliant.

They were better on dry fields away from home than they were on their own rain-affected fields. In their two home matches they scored three tries, the same number Joe Rokocoko scored in Sydney where he became the first player to bag a hat-trick of tries in a Tri Nations match. The All Blacks finished with 17 tries for the series, just one fewer than South Africa scored in 1997. They became the fourth side to enjoy a clean sweep of the Tri Nations and the first since the Springboks in 1998. But really the numbers did not count as much as the style shown, especially on those dry days in Pretoria and Sydney.

If the All Blacks were the glory of the Tri Nations, the cantankerous Brisbane Test was the nadir. The incidents of the last ten minutes which led to the suspensions of Bakkies Botha and Robbie Kempson were unedifying. The six referees it should be added were excellent.

The Tri Nations brought its usual crop of new stars to light. The brightest of them was young Joe Rokocoko. The Fijian speedster who became an All Black without ever playing an NPC match scored six tries in his four matches. Other New Zealanders who shone were powerful Jerry Collins, a wonderful mixture of strength, speed and skill, and his Samoan-born team-mate Mils Muliaina, a centre-cum-wing who made a smooth transfer to full-back which gave rein to his sense of adventure. Two new forwards stood out – tall, athletic Ali Williams and action-man Keven Mealamu.

South Africa's new men were recent under-21 graduates Juan Smith at No 8 and darting, dancing Ashwin Willemse on the wing. Richard Bands, a 28-year-old converted flanker, also made an impression, most notably with his try in Dunedin but also for his mobility and tackling. For Australia Wendell Sailor and Lote Tuqiri, not new players but new to rugby union, had a decided and exciting impact.

Of the established players, George Smith made a valued contribution to the Wallabies and was sorely missed when injury struck. Toutai Kefu was always dependable and Stephen Larkham grew with the series as he

The All Blacks celebrate with the Bledisloe Cup and Tri Nations Trophy after beating the Wallabies at Eden Park, Auckland.

returned from injury. For the All Blacks there was the Laughing Cavalier, Doug Howlett, relentless Richie McCaw, calm and creative Aaron Mauger at inside-centre, versatile Chris Jack and the maestro, Carlos Spencer at fly-half. Victor Matfield for South Africa stood out as a star in his ever-changing side.

From the Tri Nations the players tumble on to the World Cup, but there will also be SANZAR talks and thoughts. One strong proposal is that the competition be expanded to include Argentina and a Pacific Islands team, either in a single round or spread over two years.

Tri Nations 2003 : Final Table

	P	*W*	*D*	*L*	*F*	*A*	*Bonus Points*	*Pts*
New Zealand	4	4	0	0	142	65	2	18
Australia	4	1	0	3	89	106	2	6
South Africa	4	1	0	3	62	122	0	4

Points: win 4; draw 2; four or more tries, or defeat by seven or fewer points 1

12 July, Newlands, Cape Town
South Africa 26 (2G 4PG) **Australia 22** (2G 1DG 1T)

The Springboks played with purpose and concentrated cohesion and although favourites Australia scored three tries to two, they were well beaten.

The start of the match suggested that Australia would win. From a line-out the Wallabies attacked with their usual routine of phases. Then George Gregan slung a pass back to Burke who kicked a wobbly drop. The Wallabies led 3-0 after two minutes. Clearly they expected more as they could afford to be prodigal in a situation that offered the possibility of a try.

At this stage Springbok full-back Jaco van der Westhuyzen left the field with a knee injury and was replaced by Brent Russell. It was a replacement made in heaven. The Springboks attacked through phases, going left and right, eschewing an easy penalty for a tap-and-go. Suddenly Louis Koen created a good position for Russell, who scuttled round Joe Roff for a try. After five minutes the Springboks led 7-3.

The Wallabies were next to score. It was their turn to opt for a try rather than a simple penalty kick. They won the post-penalty line-out and Mat Rogers flicked the ball inside to Wendell Sailor who scored the kind of try one expects from the Wallabies in such circumstances.

Koen landed a couple of penalties and the Springboks led 13-10 before they scored a try that will pass into rugby legend. Wendell Sailor ran down the right wing and near half-way cross-kicked. Russell, just outside his 22, caught the ball and started moving towards his right with rapid little steps that took him past would-be tacklers. He executed a long pass to his right to De Wet Barry, who made ground and passed back to Russell who was scurrying towards the 22 but close to touch. He bowled a high pass infield where Terblanche leapt, caught and sprinted. He in turn passed infield to lock Victor Matfield who pounded over for the try.

The scoring in the second half belonged to Australia. They scored two tries – one from a tap-penalty at the line and the other a sweeping movement as Burke burst past a falling Bakkies Botha to send Joe Roff on a sprint for the corner.

South Africa: J N B van der Westhuyzen; C S Terblanche, M C Joubert, D Barry, G M Delport; L J Koen, J H van der Westhuizen; L D Sephaka, D Coetzee, R E Bands, J P Botha, V Matfield, C P J Krigé (*captain*), J H Smith, J L van Heerden *Substitutions:* R B Russell for Van der Westhuyzen (2 mins); G Bobo for Joubert (40 mins); R B Kempson for Bands (48 mins); D Santon for Coetzee (68 mins); C S Boome for Botha (76 mins); P J Wannenburg for Krigé (temp 44 to 48 mins) and for Smith (70 mins)

Scorers *Tries*: Russell, Matfield *Conversions*: Koen (2) *Penalty Goals*: Koen (4)

Australia: M C Burke; W J Sailor, M S Rogers, S Kefu, J W Roff; E J Flatley, G M Gregan (*captain*); W K Young, B J Cannon, E P Noriega, D T Giffin, D J Vickerman, D J Lyons, R S T Kefu, P R Waugh *Substitutions:* N C Sharpe for Vickerman (50 mins); B J Darwin for Noriega (60 mins); S J Larkham for S Kefu (60 mins); L Tuqiri for Roff (62 mins); O D A Finegan for Waugh (temp 54 to 61 mins)and for Lyons (63 mins); A L Freier for Cannon (72 mins)

Scorers *Tries*: Sailor, Waugh, Roff *Conversions*: Burke (2) *Drop Goal*: Burke

Referee S R Walsh (New Zealand)

19 July, Securicor Loftus Versfeld, Pretoria
South Africa 16 (1G 2PG 1DG) **New Zealand 52** (4G 3PG 3T)

The Springboks started well enough and could have had a try when Brent Russell knocked on with the goal-line at his mercy. Within nine minutes of the start, the hero of Newlands had knocked on twice and missed the tackle on Chris Jack that gave Carlos Spencer the chance to skip over for the try which made the score 5-3 to New Zealand.

It was 8-6 when the Springboks were attacking and Stefan Terblanche toed the ball ahead deep into New Zealand territory. The result was a line-out to New Zealand some 10 metres from the Springbok line, so quickly did the All Blacks seize any opportunity to attack. From the line-out Aaron Mauger flicked a delicate pass inside to Doug Howlett who raced through for a try. And after Russell had mistakenly passed to Joe Rokocoko for the first of the New Zealand speedster's two tries, the match as a contest was over. At half-time the score was 22-9.

South Africa lost a golden chance to score early in the second half when De Wet Barry slashed through in the centre and Terblanche lost the ball in the act of scoring a try. That was their last chance. With 25 minutes to go it seemed that both sides had decided that the result was settled and began to make many substitutions.

In the last 20 minutes the All Blacks took the score from 28 to 52 while the Springboks got a try from their sole performer of note, young Ashwin Willemse on the left-wing who managed to skip and dance to good effect no matter how confined. Willemse's try came while Kees Meeuws was in the sin bin for using a petulant elbow on Robbie Kempson after scoring a try from a five-metre line-out. For the second week in a row Kempson's aggressor received a yellow card.

The All Blacks did not like having a try scored against them and hit back straightway as Howlett skated through for his second. From the very kick-off, Howlett was sweeping down the field again and this time Mauger raced a long way to score.

The All Blacks recorded their record victory over the Springboks. It was one of the great displays from one of the great rugby teams.

South Africa: R B Russell; C S Terblanche, A H Snyman, D Barry, A K Willemse; L J Koen, J H van der Westhuizen; L D Sephaka, D Coetzee, R E Bands, J P Botha, V Matfield, C P J Krigé (*captain*), J H Smith, J L van Heerden *Substitutions:* R B Kempson for Bands (53 mins); A S Pretorius for Russell (56 mins); D Santon for Coetzee (60 mins); C D Davidson for Van der Westhuizen (64 mins); P J Wannenburg for Van Heerden (65 mins); C S Boome for Botha (71 mins)

Scorers *Try*: Willemse *Conversion*: Koen *Penalty Goals*: Koen (2) *Dropped Goal:* Koen

New Zealand: M Muliaina; D C Howlett, J F Umaga, A J D Mauger, J T Rokococo; C J Spencer, S J Devine; D N Hewett, K F Mealamu, G M Somerville, C R Jack, A J Williams, R D Thorne (*captain*), J Collins, R H McCaw *Substitutions:* B C Thorn for Williams (51 mins); K J Meeuws for Hewett (54 mins); M G Hammett for Mealamu (60 mins); J W Marshall for Devine (63 mins); R So'oialo for McCaw (78 mins); D N Hewett for Collins (temp 70 to 76 mins)

Referee A C Rolland (Ireland)

Scorers *Tries*: Howlett (2), Rokococo (2), Spencer, Meeuws, Mauger *Conversions*: Spencer (4) *Penalty Goals*: Spencer (3)

26 July, Telstra Stadium Australia, Sydney
Australia 21 (2PG 3T) New Zealand 50 (3G 3PG 4T)

You could watch only in awe at this performance of the joyous All Blacks. It was all about speed, confidence and a spirit of fun, and at the end of it all the winner of the Tri Nations looked a foregone conclusion. It took New Zealand 21 minutes to get into the lead. Then they shared it and after 32 minutes went ahead again. That was it. For the next 50 minutes they just kept making the lead bigger as the world watched mouth agape.

Matthew Burke scored the Wallabies' first try after Phil Waugh had won one of the game's rare turnovers. New Zealand's first try came when Joe Rokococo ran past Wendell Sailor to score in the corner. Not long afterwards Sailor blotted his copybook with a reckless tackle for which he received a yellow card.

When he went to the sin bin, the score was 8-5 to New Zealand. When he emerged expiated, the All Blacks led 20-8. While he was away, Aaron Mauger waltzed past Patricio Noriega and gave Doug Howlett a sweet pass for the wing to sweep past George Gregan to score. Then from the kick off the All Blacks ran from their own quarter and Muliaina slipped Rokocoko a pass to send the pacy wing speeding for the corner.

Early in the second half Chris Jack deftly left-footed a long low kick into touch near the Wallabies' corner-flag. From the line-out Latham booted far down field, Rokocoko fielded the ball near his left touch-line and slung a long pass to Spencer who slung a long pass to Muliaina who made a half break and, with a quick inside pass, sent Tana Umaga surging for a try which took the score to 33-11. At this stage Spencer went off to be replaced by Daniel Carter, who was the next to score when Chris Latham lost the ball and the All Blacks made hay.

The Wallabies came back with two tries, the first by Wendell Sailor who ran half the length of the field from a line-out, and the second by Rogers from a long run for the corner. But by then Rokocoko had become the first player to score a try hat-trick in a Tri Nations Test and the fastest man in history to reach ten tries in major internationals. Before the final whistle the All Blacks got their seventh try when Mauger touched down beside the post.

Australia: M C Burke; W J Sailor, M S Rogers, E J Flatley, L Tuqiri; S J Larkham, G M Gregan (*captain*); W K Young, B J Cannon, E P Noriega, D T Giffin, D J Vickerman, G B Smith, R S T Kefu, P R Waugh *Substitutions:* B J Darwin for Noriega (45 mins); C E Latham for Burke (51 mins); N C Sharpe for Vickerman (54 mins); A L Freier for Cannon (temp 67 to 75 mins); O D A Finegan for Smith (67 mins); S Kefu for Flatley (69 mins)

Scorers *Tries*: Burke, Sailor, Rogers *Penalty Goals*: Burke (2)

New Zealand: M Muliaina; D C Howlett, J F Umaga, A J D Mauger, J T Rokocoko; C J Spencer, J W Marshall; D N Hewett, K F Mealamu, G M Somerville, C R Jack, A J Williams, R D Thorne (*captain*), J Collins, R H McCaw *Substitutions:* D W Carter for Spencer (53 mins); K J Meeuws for Somerville (61 mins); B C Thorn for Williams (63 mins); M R Holah for McCaw (71 mins); C S Ralph for Muliaina (71 mins); M G Hammett for Mealamu (71 mins); S J Devine for Howlett (78 mins)

Scorers *Tries*: Rokocoko (3), Howlett, Umaga, Carter, Mauger *Conversions*: Spencer (2), Carter *Penalty Goals*: Spencer (3)

Referee A J Spreadbury (England)

2 August, Suncorp Stadium, Brisbane
Australia 29 (2G 5PG) South Africa 9 (3PG)

Two players were cited and received hefty suspensions, yet apart from a lack of courtesies during the match there was nothing blatantly unpleasant. Where the Springboks had been much the better side at Newlands, so the Wallabies were much the better side in Brisbane as the teams clashed to avoid the wooden spoon.

The Springbok defence proved a tough nut to crack and at half-time the scores were 6-all. The Wallabies were given a gift try early in the second half when a loose pass by Louis Koen was snapped up by Mat Rogers who sped off half the length of the field to score. Their only other try was in the last movement of the match.

In between it was the Springboks' brittle discipline which cracked. Danie Coetzee and Robbie Kempson went to the sin bin for unintentional infringements in attacking positions and as South Africa conceded numerous penalties Elton Flatley's unerring boot accumulated the points.

Afterwards the match commissioner cited Bakkie Botha for attacking an opponent's face and Robbie Kempson for a dangerous tackle. Ten minutes from time Brendan Cannon tackled Botha and in the wrestling that followed Botha gave every impression of trying to bite Cannon on his right shoulder. When they rolled over he gave every impression of using his right thumb to attack Cannon's left eye.

In the last movement of the match the Wallabies attacked down their left through Lote Tuqiri and then spread to the right where they were certainly going to score. After Toutai Kefu passed to Phil Waugh, who did indeed score, Kempson tackled Kefu with a swinging right arm that hit him at about shoulder height and then went up higher. Kempson was suspended for four weeks and Botha for eight.

The result of the match meant that New Zealand had won the Tri Nations with Australia runners-up and South Africa, for the fifth season running, holders of the wooden spoon.

Australia: C E Latham; W J Sailor, M S Rogers, E J Flatley, L Tuqiri; S J Larkham, G M Gregan (*captain*); W K Young, B J Cannon, E P Noriega, D T Giffin, D J Vickerman, G B Smith, R S T Kefu, P R Waugh *Substitutions:* N C Sharpe for Vickerman (64 mins); G M Panoho for Noriega (65 mins); O D A Finegan for Smith (68 mins); J A Paul for Cannon (temp 36 to 40 mins and 75 mins); C J Whitaker for Gregan (77 mins); M C Burke for Rogers (78 mins); M J Giteau for Kefu (79 mins)

Scorers *Tries*: Rogers, Waugh *Conversions:* Flatley (2) *Penalty Goals*: Flatley (5)

South Africa: A S Pretorius; C S Terblanche, G P Müller, D Barry, A K Willemse; L J Koen, C D Davidson; R B Kempson, D Coetzee, R E Bands, C S Boome, V Matfield, C P J Krigé (*captain*), J H Smith, J C van Niekerk *Substitutions:* J C van der Westhuizen for Davidson (53 mins); J P Botha for Boome (55 mins); R B Russell for Terblanche (68 mins); L D Sephaka for Krigé (temp 72 to 77 mins) and for Bands (77 mins); J L van Heerden for Krigé (temp 34 to 38 mins); D Santon for Krigé (temp 38 to 40 mins) and for Smith (40 to 48 mins)

Scorer *Penalty Goals*: Koen (3)

Referee P D O'Brien (New Zealand)

9 August, Carisbrook, Dunedin
New Zealand 19 (1G 4PG) South Africa 11 (2PG 1T)

There can be honour in defeat. The Springboks proved that on a cold, cold night at Carisbrook. They came off a thrashing in Pretoria and the horror of Brisbane to show yet again that they are at their best when the chips are down.

It seemed set to be a repeat of Pretoria when in the sixth minute Aaron Mauger threaded through a grubber and Joe Rokocoko sped after it, scooped and scored. But that was the end of the All Black try-scoring. The

Springboks had the better of the first half with their aggressive defence and their close-quarter pick-and-drive. Safe, sound and unadventurous maybe, but there was one gem in it all and it was of breath-taking beauty.

Some 48 metres from the All Black line South Africa won a ruck and Joost van der Westhuizen popped a pass to tight-head prop Richard Bands. Off Bands went, short legs pumping for metre after metre. Carlos Spencer arrived in defence but the prop shrugged him aside. Aaron Mauger and Jerry Collins arrived but too late as Bands plunged for a try. It would have been a great try in anybody's book, but it was stupendous for a prop, possibly the greatest prop's try in the history of the game. There were no more tries for the next 64 minutes' playing time. Koen missed a penalty chance to put the Springboks 14-13 ahead at half-time.

In the second half the All Blacks, always more creative, were the better side. The Springboks conceded many penalties and in the end the difference was the kicking of Spencer. He didn't miss a kick at goal while Koen fluffed a conversion, two penalties and three drops. To be fair Spencer had the easier job because his were closer.

The end of the match was friendly as players smiled and swapped jerseys. The two old rivals were back to traditionally tough encounters – with respect for each other.

New Zealand: M Muliaina; D C Howlett, J F Umaga, A J D Mauger, J T Rokocoko; C J Spencer, J W Marshall; D N Hewett, M G Hammett, K J Meeuws, B C Thorn, A J Williams, R D Thorne (*captain*), J Collins, M R Holah *Substitutions:* C R Jack for Thorn (55 mins); G M Somerville for Meeuws (59 mins); K F Mealamu for Hammett (71 mins)

Scorers *Try*: Rokocoko *Conversion*: Spencer *Penalty Goals*: Spencer (4)

South Africa: G M Delport; C S Terblanche, G P Müller, G Bobo, A K Willemse; L J Koen, J H van der Westhuizen; L D Sephaka, D Coetzee, R E Bands, G Cronjé, V Matfield, C P J Krigé (*captain*), J H Smith, J C van Niekerk *Substitutions:* C J Bezuidenhout for Sephaka (40 mins); L van Biljon for Coetzee (60 mins); C S Boome for Cronjé (66 mins)

Scorers *Try:* Bands *Penalty Goals*: Koen (2)

Referee P Marshall (Australia)

16 August, Eden Park, Auckland
New Zealand 21 (1G 3PG 1T) **Australia 17** (4PG 1T)

New Zealand wanted to wrest the Bledisloe Cup from Australia's tenacious grasp. It was bad for the New Zealand psyche that the big cup had become settled on the other side of the Tasman Sea. It was also the 100th Bledisloe Cup match and a 100 years and a day since the inaugural Australia-New Zealand Test.

The rain pelted down and the match was very different from the Sydney fiesta. It was hard and relentless. This time the All Blacks' most potent weapon was not primarily the speed of their outside backs but the unrelenting, driving tackling of their defence as each inch was defended as if it were the goal-line.

In the end it was smiling Doug Howlett's speed which beat the Wallabies in two wonderful bursts. The first came when Mils Muliaina collected a deep but poor kick by Stephen Larkham. He started the counterattack and Richie McCaw carried it on. Then energetic hooker Keven Mealamu seized a half gap before letting his flying wing have the ball. Howlett scored, Carlos Spencer converted and the All Blacks led by seven points to an Elton Flatley penalty.

Two more Flatley penalties made it 9-7 to Australia. Then came the moment of the match. The Wallabies were about to win the ball at a crumbled tackle when Jerry Collins stepped forward, snatched the ball up from under George Gregan's nose and passed to his left. Spencer chipped and Howlett comfortably outpaced Flatley to the touch-down. Spencer gathered three points from a penalty and the All Blacks led by 15-9 at the break. It could well have been more as the All Blacks had had most of the half.

The second half was much better for the Wallabies as more and more they shut down the All Blacks. They also created better scoring opportunities. Twice the TMO, Roy Maybank of England, had to adjudicate and on both occasions he decided that there was insufficient evidence that the Wallabies had scored.

They did get a try five minutes from time. Australia won a turnover off Spencer, attacked at speed and George Smith surged over in Leon MacDonald's tackle. The Wallabies still had a chance to win when Flatley broke, but a pass went astray. Soon after, the whistle sounded victory for the All Blacks and heralded much expression of joy.

New Zealand: M Muliaina; D C Howlett, J F Umaga, A J D Mauger, J T Rokocoko; C J Spencer, J W Marshall; D N Hewett, K F Mealamu, G M Somerville, C R Jack, A J Williams, R D Thorne (*captain*), J Collins, R H McCaw *Substitution:* L R MacDonald for Muliaina (46 mins)

Scorers *Tries*: Howlett (2) *Conversion*: Spencer *Penalty Goals*: Spencer (3)

Australia: C E Latham; W J Sailor, M S Rogers, E J Flatley, L Tuqiri; S J Larkham, G M Gregan (*captain*); W K Young, B J Cannon, G M Panoho, D T Giffin, D J Vickerman, G B Smith, R S T Kefu, P R Waugh *Substitutions:* A K E Baxter for Panoho (38 mins); M C Burke for Sailor (40 mins); N C Sharpe for Vickerman (47 mins); O D A Finegan for Kefu (50 mins); J A Paul for Cannon (63 mins); M J Giteau for Larkham (66 mins)

Scorers *Try*: Smith *Penalty Goals*: Flatley (4)

Referee J I Kaplan (South Africa)

TRI NATIONS RECORDS 1996-2003

Previous winners: 1996 New Zealand; 1997 New Zealand; 1998 South Africa; 1999 New Zealand; 2000 Australia; 2001 Australia; 2002 New Zealand; 2003 New Zealand
Grand Slam winners: New Zealand (Three times) 1996, 1997, 2003; South Africa (Once) 1998

Team Record	*Detail*		*Set*
Most team points in season	159 by N Zealand	in four matches	1997
Most team tries in season	18 by S Africa	in four matches	1997
Highest team score	61 by S Africa	61-22 v Australia (h)	1997
Biggest team win	39 by S Africa	61-22 v Australia (h)	1997
Most team tries in match	8 by S Africa	v Australia	1997

Individual Record	*Detail*		*Set*
Most appearances	31 for N Zealand	J W Marshall	1996 to 2003
	31 for Australia	G M Gregan	1996 to 2003
Most points in matches	309 for N Zealand	A P Mehrtens	1996 to 2002
Most points in season	84 for N Zealand	C J Spencer	1997
Most points in match	29 for N Zealand	A P Mehrtens	v Australia (h) 1999
Most tries in matches	16 for N Zealand	C M Cullen	1996 to 2002
Most tries in season	7 for N Zealand	C M Cullen	2000
Most tries in match	3 for N Zealand	J T Rokocoko	v Australia (a) 2003
Most cons in matches	32 for N Zealand	A P Mehrtens	1996 to 2002
Most cons in season	13 for N Zealand	C J Spencer	1997
Most cons in match	6 for S Africa	J H de Beer	v Australia (h),1997
Most pens in matches	77 for N Zealand	A P Mehrtens	1996 to 2002
Most pens in season	19 for N Zealand	A P Mehrtens	1996
	19 for N Zealand	A P Mehrtens	1999
Most pens in match	9 for N Zealand	A P Mehrtens	v Australia (h) 1999

CHURCHILL CUP 2003

Young Squad Demonstrates England's Strength in Depth

John Griffiths

The seeds of this new competition were sown in November 2001 when the RFU's chief executive Francis Baron fleshed out radical proposals for a buddy system to help raise the game's international profile. His core proposal was that each of the eight senior members of the IRB 'adopt' two middle-ranking nations. The leading edge nations would offer continuous support with coaching and the development of the emerging players, and arrange regular representative matches at various levels.

The principle was warmly received by the IRB's member unions and the green light was given for England to feature in the inaugural competition of this kind, staged in British Columbia in June 2003. While the senior England players toured New Zealand and Australia, a developmental squad in the garb of England A took on the full might of Canada and the United States in a round-robin tournament that led to a grand final for the Churchill Cup. The women's game enjoyed a parallel competition.

For the England A players the tournament offered a welcome chance to define their reputations ahead of the World Cup. The trip was of considerable significance to England's World Cup plans with Clive Woodward releasing nine of his senior squad in New Zealand for the later stages of the tournament and the ensuing two-match visit to Japan. The United States and Canada also enjoyed their time in the limelight and benefited from the early-season opportunity of running the rule over their prospective World Cup squads.

Jim Mallinder and Steve Diamond shared the England A coaching duties and must have been quietly satisfied by the achievements of their squad. In the opening match in Vancouver their team set the tone with a convincing 43-7 defeat of Canada, leading from the first minute through a Dave Walder penalty.

The Canadians were disappointed with their error-strewn performance, but not half as dispirited as in midweek when they fell to arch-rivals the United States. Petty indiscipline was costly for the Canucks after full-back Quentin Fyffe had notched an early try to give them the lead. They conceded a string of penalties, and three Canadian players spent time in the sin bin as the Eagles defended tightly and took their chances to win 16-11. 'You can't win Test matches with actions like that,' said the disappointed Canadian coach Dave Clark. It was the United States' first win against Canada in four matches and only their ninth of the 34-match series.

The Eagles' victory meant that there was little at stake in their final match of the round-robin stage against England, both sides having already qualified for the final. Even so, the United States constructed several promising attacks and scored two sparkling tries despite a defeat by 36-10. Skipper Dave Hodges made one of his trademark charges for one try and centre Cayo Nicolau showed quick wits to exploit the advantage law for the other. 'We did very well. We're excited about reaching the Churchill Cup final,' said Eagles coach Tom Billups.

England, who scored three tries in each half, were forced to work hard for their success. Iain Balshaw ran confidently on the right-wing while full-back Michael Horak revelled in the firm conditions and scored four tries.

The English men stepped up a couple of gears to win the final a week later while their women's team beat the Canadians with a last-minute pushover try. The tournament was judged an unqualified success by players, supporters and administrators who enjoyed the varied attractions of Vancouver so much that the British Columbian venue has been given hosting rights for the next two years.

Churchill Cup 2003: Final Table

	P	*W*	*D*	*L*	*F*	*A*	*Pts*
England A	2	2	0	0	79	17	4
United States	2	1	0	1	26	47	2
Canada	2	0	0	2	18	59	0

Results

14 June, Thunderbird Stadium, Vancouver
Canada 7 (1G) England A 43 (2G 3PG 4T)

Canada: Q Fyffe; D Moonlight, N Witkowski, J Cannon, W U Stanley; R P Ross, M Williams; K Tkachuk, M Lawson, G Cooke, R Johnston, E Knaggs, J Cudmore, R Banks (*captain*), A van Staveren *Substitutions:* L Carlson for Knaggs (54 mins); P Riordan for Lawson (63 mins); K Wirachowski for Cooke (63 mins); E Fairhurst for Williams (65 mins); R Smith for Ross (65 mins); C Yukes for Cudmore (70 mins); C Plater for Tkachuk (75 mins)

Scorers *Try:* Williams *Conversion:* Ross

England A: D Scarbrough; M Cueto, F H H Waters, H Paul, P Christophers; D J H Walder, M B Wood; A Sheridan, A Titterell, W R Green, A Brown, A Codling, P Anglesea, H Vyvyan (*captain*), D Hyde *Substitutions:* M Cairns for Titterell (57 mins); D L Flatman for Sheridan (57 mins); N Hatley for Green (62 mins); C Jones for Anglesea (65 mins); M J Horak for Scarbrough (65 mins); O Barkley for Walder (70 mins); N P J Walshe for Wood (70 mins)

Scorers *Tries:* Scarbrough, Titterell, Wood, Waters, Cueto, Cairns *Conversions:* Walder, Flatman *Penalty Goals:* Walder (3)

Referee A Klemp (United States)

18 June, Thunderbird Stadium, Vancouver
Canada 11 (2PG 1T) **United States 16** (1G 3PG)

Canada: Q Fyffe; S Fauth, N Witkowski, M di Girolamo, W U Stanley; R P Ross, M Williams; K Tkachuk, M Lawson, G Cooke, J Cudmore, C Yukes, R Banks (*captain*), P Murphy, A van Staveren *Substitutions:* K Wirachowski for Van Staveren (temp 23 to 33 mins); P Riordan for Lawson (42 mins); J Cannon for Fyffe (70 mins)

Scorers *Try:* Fyffe *Penalty Goals:* Ross (2)

United States: L Wilfley; D Fee, P Eloff, K Cross, R van Zyl; C Nicolau, K Dalzell; M MacDonald, K Khasigian, D Dorsey, A Parker, D Hodges (*captain*), K Schubert, D Lyle, C Hodgson *Substitutions:* J Keyter for Nicolau (60 mins); J Tarpoff for Dorsey (73 mins); L Gross for Lyle (80 mins)

Scorers *Try:* Eloff *Conversion:* Wilfley *Penalty Goals:* Wilfley (3)

Referee R Maybank (England)

21 June, Thunderbird Stadium, Vancouver
United States 10 (2T) **England A 36** (3G 3T)

United States: L Wilfley; M Timoteo, J Keyter, C Nicolau, P Emerick; K Cross, K Kjar; J Tarpoff, M Griffin, J Waasdorp, A Parker, L Gross, J Gouws, D Hodges (*captain*), O Fifita *Substitutions:* J Buchholz for Wilfley (37 mins); K Schubert for Hodges (37 mins); B Surgener for Parker (57 mins)

Scorers *Tries:* Hodges, Nicolau

England A: M J Horak; I R Balshaw, F H H Waters, B Johnston, J Simpson-Daniel; O Barkley, N P J Walshe; M A Worsley, P B T Greening, D L Flatman, T Palmer, C Jones, P Volley, H Vyvyan (*captain*), A Hazell *Substitutions:* M Cairns for Palmer (31 mins); P Anglesea for Hazell (31 mins); H Paul for Waters (56 mins); W R Green for Worsley (63 mins); N Hatley for Flatman (63 mins); D Scarbrough for Horak (71 mins); M B Wood for Barkley (75 mins);

Scorers *Tries:* Horak (4), Balshaw, Anglesea *Conversions:* Barkley (3)

Referee I Hyde-Lay (Canada)

Churchill Cup Final 2003

28 June, Thunderbird Stadium, Vancouver
United States 6 (2PG) **England A 43** (5G 1PG 1T)

The feel-good factor running through English rugby after back-to-back victories over New Zealand and Australia was extended by their A side's success in the inaugural Churchill Cup final. The backs lifted their performance considerably from the standard shown in the earlier pool stages and ruthlessly capitalised on their opponents' mistakes.

Hugh Vyvyan inspired England by scoring a try just before half-time after the United States had defended efficiently in the early stages. The skipper's try, scored while Eagles full-back Link Wilfley was receiving attention for an injury, gave England a useful 17-6 interval advantage.

England cut loose in the second half to add four more cracking tries, including a beauty from centre Henry Paul who ran 40 metres to stretch England's lead to 31-6. After the match he spoke for the players when he paid tribute to the management. 'It's all about playing well as a squad,' he said. 'It's good that England has a pool of around 60 players to choose from rather than just 20 or so. The coaching staff have really fired us.'

So England completed their American duties and set off for Japan with the unbeaten record coach Jim Mallinder had wanted. If Winston Churchill had been the England manager for the tournament that bears his name, he might have said of his team, as he did in June 1940 in rather more serious circumstances: 'This was their finest hour.'

United States: L Wilfley; D Fee, P Eloff, K Cross, R van Zyl; M Sherman, K Kjar; M MacDonald, K Khasigian, D Dorsey, B Surgener, L Gross, K Schubert, D Lyle (*captain*), C Hodgson *Substitutions:* M Timoteo for Wilfley (40 mins); K Dalzell for Kjar (40 mins); J Keyter for Cross (58 mins); O Fifita for Lyle (63 mins); J Gouws for Surgener (64 mins); J Tarpoff for Dorsey (68 mins); M Griffin for Hodgson (73 mins)

Scorer *Penalty Goals:* Wilfley (2)

England A: I R Balshaw; M Cueto, B Johnston, H Paul, J Simpson-Daniel; D J H Walder, M B Wood; A Sheridan, A Titterell, W R Green, A Brown, A Codling, P Anglesea, H Vyvyan (*captain*), D Hyde *Substitutions:* M A Worsley for Sheridan (62 mins); P B T Greening for Titterell (62 mins); P Christophers for Paul (65 mins); C Jones for Vyvyan (66 mins); O Barkley for Walder (72 mins); P Volley for Hyde (72 mins)

Scorers *Tries:* Balshaw, Johnston, Paul, Anglesea, Vyvyan, Greening *Conversions:* Walder (4), Barkley *Penalty Goal:* Walder

Referee P C Deluca (Argentina)

Previous Churchill Cup winners: 2003 England

Churchill Cup winners' tour to Japan 2003

Tour party

Full-backs: I R Balshaw (Bath), M J Horak (London Irish)

Threequarters: M Cueto (Sale Sharks), D Scarbrough (Leeds Tykes), F H H Waters (London Wasps), B Johnston (Saracens), H Paul (Gloucester), J Simpson-Daniel (Gloucester), P Christophers (Leeds Tykes)

Half-backs: D J H Walder (Newcastle Falcons), O Barkley (Bath), M B Wood (Bath), N P J Walshe (Sale Sharks)

Forwards: A Titterell (Sale Sharks), P B T Greening (London Wasps), M A Worsley (NEC Harlequins), N Hatley (London Irish), W R Green (London Wasps), M Cairns (Sale Sharks), D L Flatman (Bath), A Sheridan (Sale Sharks), A Codling (Saracens), T Palmer (Leeds Tykes), C Jones (Sale Sharks), A Brown (Gloucester), P Anglesea (Sale Sharks), P Volley (London Wasps), A Hazell (Gloucester), D Hyde (Leeds Tykes), H Vyvyan (Newcastle Falcons) (*captain*)

Coach: J Mallinder **Assistant Coach:** S Diamond

Tour record P 2 W 2 For 92 Against 30
3 JulyWon 37-10 v JAPAN (Tokyo)
6 July Won 55-20 v JAPAN (Tokyo)

Tour details

First International 3 July, Ajinomoto Stadium, Tokyo
Japan 10 (1G 1PG) England A 37 (3G 2PG 2T)

Japan: M Tsutomu; D Ohata, H Namba, Y Motoki, T Kurihara; K Hirose, Y Sonoda; S Hasegawa, M Amino, M Toyoyama, H Kiso, A Parker, T Ito, Y Saito, T Miuchi (*captain*)

Scorers *Try:* Ohata *Conversion:* Hirose *Penalty Goal:* Kurihara

England A: M J Horak; D Scarbrough, F H H Waters, B Johnston, P Christophers; O Barkley, N P J Walshe; N Hatley, M Cairns, D L Flatman, A Brown, C Jones, P Volley, P Anglesea (*captain*), A Hazell *Substitutions:* H Vyvyan for Brown (40 mins); H Paul for Johnston (55 mins); D Hyde for Anglesea (57 mins); W R Green for Flatman (55 mins); A Sheridan for Hatley (67 mins); A Titterell for Cairns (67 mins); M B Wood for Walshe (72 mins)

Scorers *Tries:* Barkley (2), Anglesea, Christophers, Scarbrough *Conversions:* Barkley (3) *Penalty Goals:* Barkley (2)

Referee S Young (Australia)

Second International 6 July, National Stadium, Tokyo
Japan 20 (2G 2PG) England A 55 (5G 4T)

Japan: T Kurihara; D Ohata, H Namba, Y Motoki, H Onozawa; K Hirose, Y Sonoda; S Hasegawa, M Amino, M Toyoyama, H Kiso, A Parker, T Ito, Y Saito, T Miuchi (*captain*) *Substitutions:* T Yoshida for Kurihara; R Parkinson for Motoki; S Tsukida for Sonoda; H Tanuma for Parker; H Matsuo for Amino; M Yamamoto for Hasegawa

Scorers *Tries:* Namba, Yoshida *Conversions:* Hirose (2) *Penalty Goals:* Hirose (2)

England A: I R Balshaw; M Cueto, B Johnston, H Paul, J Simpson-Daniel; D J H Walder, M B Wood; M A Worsley, P B T Greening, W R Green, A Codling, C Jones, P Anglesea, H Vyvyan (*captain*), A Hazell *Substitutions:* P Volley for Codling (27 mins); N Hatley for Worsley (58 mins); A Sheridan for Jones (58 mins); D Hyde for Hazell (60 mins); A Titterell for Greening (65 mins); D Scarbrough for Cueto (67 mins); O Barkley for Walder (73 mins)

Scorers *Tries:* Balshaw (2), Wood (2), Green, Hatley, Johnston, Simpson-Daniel, Worsley *Conversions:* Walder (5)

Referee K M Deaker (New Zealand)

MAJOR TEST TOURS 2002-03

Romania to Ireland 2002

Tour party

Full-backs: G Brezoianu (Bègles-Bordeaux, Fra)

Threequarters: M Picoiu (Lavelanet, Fra), R Gontineac (Aurillac, Fra) (*captain*), V Maftei (Valence, Fra), M Vioreanu (DLSP, Ire), C Sauan (Rovigo, Ita), R Vusec (US Tours, Fra)

Half-backs: I Tofan (Racing Club de France), L Sirbu (Racing Club de France), C Podea (Universitatea Cluj)

Forwards: R Mavrodin (Tarbes, Fra), M Tincu (Pau, Fra), D Tudosa (Racing Club de France), P Toderasc (Farul Constanta), M Dumitru (Aurillac, Fra), M Dragomir (Dijon, Fra), C Petre (Racing Club de France), A Petrichei (Bourgoin, Fra), F Corodeanu (Grenoble, Fra), G Chiriac (Farul Constanta), A Manta (Bègles-Bordeaux, Fra), A Petrache (Toulon, Fra)

Manager: E Stoica **Coach:** B Charreyre

Tour record P 1 L 1 For 8 Against 39

7 September Lost 8-39 v IRELAND (Limerick)

Tour details

Test Match 7 September, Thomond Park, Limerick
Ireland 39 (4G 2PG 1T) **Romania 8** (1PG 1T)

Ireland: G T Dempsey; J P Kelly, B G O'Driscoll, K M Maggs, D A Hickie; R J R O'Gara, P A Stringer; R Corrigan, J S Byrne, J J Hayes, G W Longwell, M E O'Kelly, S H Easterby, A G Foley (*captain*), K D Gleeson *Substitutions:* R A J Henderson for O'Driscoll (40 mins); V C P Costello for S Easterby (65 mins); G Easterby for Stringer (70 mins); D G Humphreys for O'Gara (temp 23 to 34 mins and 75 mins); L F M Cullen for Foley (80 mins)

Scorers *Tries:* Hayes, Gleeson, penalty try, O'Driscoll, Henderson *Conversions:* O'Gara (3), Humphreys *Penalty Goals:* O'Gara (2)

Romania: G Brezoianu; C Sauan, V Maftei, R Gontineac (*captain*), M Vioreanu; I Tofan, L Sirbu; M Dumitru, R Mavrodin, M Tincu, M Dragomir, C Petre, G Chiriac, A Petrache, A Manta *Substitutions:* P Toderasc for Dumitru (41 mins); A Petrichei for Dragomir (41 mins); M Picoiu for Gontineac (56 mins); D Tudosa for Tincu (62 mins); R Vusec for Tofan (67 mins)

Scorers *Try:* Maftei *Penalty Goal:* Tofan

Referee G de Santis (Italy)

Romania to Wales and Scotland 2002

Tour party

Full-backs: G Brezoianu (Bègles-Bordeaux, Fra), *D Dumbrava (Steaua Bucaresti)

Threequarters: * I Teodorescu (Universitatea Cluj), M Picoiu (Lavelanet, Fra), R Gontineac (Aurillac, Fra) (*captain*), V Maftei (Valence, Fra), V Ghioc (Dinamo

Bucaresti), *M Coltineac (Universitatea Cluj)

Half-backs: I Tofan (Racing Club de France), R Lungu (Perigueux, Fra), P Mitu (Grenoble, Fra), L Sirbu (Racing Club de France), C Podea (Universitatea Cluj)

Forwards: R Mavrodin (Tarbes, Fra), M Tincu (Pau, Fra), M Constantin (CS Petrosani), M Socaciu (Rovigo, Ita), P Balan (Grenoble, Fra), P Toderasc (Farul Constanta), S Florea (Cannes-Mandelieu, Fra), D Dima (Stade Toulousain, Fra), C Mersiou (Steaua Bucaresti), M Socaciu (Rovigo, Ita), O Tonita (Biarritz Olympique, Fra), C Petre (Racing Club de France), A Petrichei (Bourgoin, Fra), S Socol (Brive, Fra), F Corodeanu (Grenoble, Fra), G Chiriac (Farul Constanta), A Manta (Bègles-Bordeaux, Fra), M Coltineac (Universitatea Cluj), * S Dragnea (Valence, Fra), A Petrache (Toulon, Fra)

Manager: E Stoica **Coach:** B Charreyre **Assistant Coaches:** R Tryancsev, H Dumitras

* Replacements during tour

Tour record P 3 L 3 For 31 Against 98

1 November Lost 3-40 v WALES (Wrexham)

5 November Lost 18-21 v Scotland A (Aberdeen)

9 November Lost 10-37 v SCOTLAND (Murrayfield)

Tour details

Test Match 1 November, The Racecourse Ground, Wrexham
Wales 40 (4G 4PG) Romania 3 (1PG)

Wales: G R Williams; M A Jones, T Shanklin, S Parker, Gareth Thomas; N R Jenkins, D Peel; G Jenkins, M Davies, M Madden, R Sidoli, S M Williams, M Owen, L S Quinnell, C L Charvis (*captain*) *Substitutions:* C S Morgan for G R Williams (43 mins); B R Evans for Madden (50 mins); Gavin Thomas & A L P Lewis for Quinnell & M Davies (66 mins); S M Jones for Shanklin (74 mins); G O Llewellyn for S M Williams (76 mins)

Scorers *Tries:* Quinnell, M A Jones, Gareth Thomas, penalty try *Conversions:* N R Jenkins (4) *Penalty Goals:* N R Jenkins (4)

Romania: D Dumbrava; V Ghioc, G Brezoianu, R Gontineac (*captain*), M Picoiu; I Tofan, P Mitu; P Toderasc, R Mavrodin, S Florea, S Socol, C Petre, F Corodeanu, O Tonita, A Petrache *Substitutions:* G Chiriac for Tonita (15 mins); D Dima & M Cultineac for Florea & Ghioc (40 mins); M Constantin for Mavrodin (48 mins); C Podea & M Socaciu for Mitu & Toderasc (69 mins); R Lungu for Picoiu (79 mins)

Scorer *Penalty Goal:* Tofan

Referee J Jutge (France)

5 November, Rubislaw, Aberdeen
Scotland A 21 (1G 3PG 1T) Romania XV 18 (1G 2PG 1T)

Scotland A scorers *Tries:* Howarth, R Kerr *Conversion:* Howarth *Penalty Goals:* Howarth (3)

Romania XV scorers *Tries:* Petrache, Tofan *Conversion:* Tofan *Penalty Goals:* Lungu (2)

Test Match 9 November, Murrayfield, Edinburgh
Scotland 37 (3G 2PG 2T) **Romania 10** (1G 1PG)

Scotland: J S D Moffat; N Walker, A Craig, B J Laney, C D Paterson; G Ross, B W Redpath (*captain*); T J Smith, G C Bulloch, B A F Douglas, S Murray, S B Grimes, M D Leslie, S M Taylor, A C Pountney *Substitutions:* M J Stewart for Smith (63 mins); N J Hines for Murray (64 mins); J M Petrie & G P J Townsend for Taylor & Ross (72 mins); B G Hinshelwood for Craig (74 mins); T J Smith for Stewart (77 mins); S Scott for Leslie (79 mins)

Scorers *Tries:* Grimes, Paterson, Leslie, Pountney, Moffat *Conversions:* Laney (3) *Penalty Goals:* Laney (2)

Romania: G Brezoianu; I Teodorescu, V Maftei, R Gontineac (*captain*), V Ghioc; I Tofan, P Mitu; P Balan, M Tincu, D Dima, A Petrichei, C Petre, F Corodeanu, A Petrache, G Chiriac *Substitutions:* P Toderasc & S Dragnea for Petrichei & Dima (40 mins); L Sirbu for Mitu (52 mins); C Mersoiu for Petrache (60 mins); M Socaciu for Balan (63 mins)

Scorer *Try:* Tofan *Conversion:* Tofan *Penalty Goal:* Tofan

Referee A D Turner (South Africa)

Australia to Argentina and Europe 2002

Tour party

Full-backs: M C Burke (Eastwood & NSW), M S Rogers (Randwick & NSW)

Threequarters: W J Sailor (Gold Coast & Queensland), S N G Staniforth (Eastwood & NSW), S A Mortlock (Gordon & ACT), B N Tune (GPS & Queensland), D J Herbert (GPS & Queensland), * M A Bartholomeusz (Canberra & ACT), E J Flatley (Brothers & Queensland)

Half-backs: S J Larkham (Wests & ACT), G M Gregan (*captain*), C J Whitaker (Randwick & NSW), M J Giteau (Canberra & ACT)

Forwards: J A Paul (Canberra & ACT), A L Freier (Randwick & NSW), * B J Cannon (Sydney University & NSW), E P Noriega (Eastern Suburbs & NSW), B J Darwin (Northern Suburbs & ACT), N B Stiles (University & Queensland), W K Young (Eastwood & ACT), O D A Finegan (Randwick & ACT), D T Giffin (Canberra & ACT), J B Harrison (Canberra & ACT), D J Vickerman (University & ACT), M J Cockbain (GPS & Queensland), G B Smith (Manly & ACT), D N Croft (Brothers & Queensland), D J Lyons (Sydney University & NSW), R S T Kefu (Souths & Queensland)

Manager: P Thomson **Coach:** E Jones **Coaching co-ordinator:** E J A McKenzie **Assistant Coach:** G Ella

* Replacement on tour

Tour record P 4 W 2 L 2 For 91 Against 59

2 November Won 17-6 v ARGENTINA (Buenos Aires)

9 November Lost 9-18 v IRELAND (Dublin)

16 November Lost 31-32 v ENGLAND (Twickenham)

23 November Won 34-3 v ITALY (Genoa)

Tour details

Test Match 2 November, River Plate Stadium, Buenos Aires
Argentina 6 (2PG) **Australia 17** (4PG 1T)

Argentina: I Corleto; J M Nuñez Piossek, J Orengo, L Arbizu (*captain*), D Albanese; F Contepomi, A Pichot; M Reggiardo, F E Mendez, O J Hasan-Jalil, C I Fernandez Lobbe, R Alvarez, S Phelan, G Longo, R A Martin *Substitutions:* M Durand for Martin (temp 37 to 39 mins) and for Phelan (68 mins); R D Grau for Reggiardo (52 mins); M E Ledesma for Mendez (58 mins)

Scorer *Penalty Goals:* F Contepomi (2)

Australia: M S Rogers; B N Tune, M C Burke, D J Herbert, S A Mortlock; S J Larkham, G M Gregan (*captain*); W K Young, J A Paul, E P Noriega, D J Vickerman, J B Harrison, M J Cockbain, R S T Kefu, G B Smith *Substitutions:* W J Sailor for Tune (14 mins); D N Croft for Cockbain (54 to 66 & 80 mins); A L Freier & D T Giffin for Paul & Vickerman (66 mins); E J Flatley for Burke (77 mins); B J Darwin for Noriega (80 mins); C J Whitaker for Rogers (80 mins)

Scorers *Try:* Mortlock *Penalty Goals:* Burke (3), Flatley

Referee K M Deaker (New Zealand)

Test Match 9 November, Lansdowne Road, Dublin
Ireland 18 (6PG) **Australia 9** (3PG)

Ireland: G T Dempsey; S P Horgan, B G O'Driscoll (*captain*), K M Maggs, D A Hickie; R J R O'Gara, P A Stringer; R Corrigan, J S Byrne, J J Hayes, G W Longwell, M E O'Kelly, V C P Costello, A G Foley, K D Gleeson *Substitutions:* F J Sheahan for Byrne (temp 27 to 37 mins and 80 mins); J P Kelly for Hickie (40 mins); L F M Cullen for Longwell (72 mins); A Quinlan for Costello (72 mins)

Scorer: *Penalty Goals:* O'Gara (6)

Australia: M C Burke; W J Sailor, S A Mortlock, D J Herbert, S N G Staniforth; S J Larkham, G M Gregan (*captain*); N B Stiles, A L Freier, E P Noriega, O D A Finegan, D T Giffin, M J Cockbain, R S T Kefu, G B Smith *Substitutions:* J B Harrison for Finegan (17 mins); B J Darwin for Stiles (60 mins); D N Croft for Smith (74 mins); E J Flatley for Larkham (74 mins); B J Cannon for Freier (temp 76 to 79 mins)

Scorer *Penalty Goals:* Burke (3)

Referee S R Walsh (New Zealand)

Test Match 16 November, Twickenham
England 32 (2G 6PG) **Australia 31** (2G 4PG 1T)

England: J Robinson; J Simpson-Daniel, W J H Greenwood, M J Tindall, B C Cohen; J P Wilkinson, M J S Dawson; J Leonard, S Thompson, P J Vickery, M O Johnson (*captain*), B J Kay, L W Moody, RA Hill, N A Back *Substitutions:* L B N Dallaglio for Hill (temp 41 to 51 mins); A S Healey for Tindall (80 mins)

Scorers *Tries:* Cohen (2) *Conversions:* Wilkinson (2) *Penalty Goals:* Wilkinson (6)

Australia: S J Larkham; W J Sailor, M C Burke, D J Herbert, S A Mortlock; E J Flatley, G M Gregan (*captain*); W K Young, J A Paul, E P Noriega,

D J Vickerman, J B Harrison, M J Cockbain, R S T Kefu, G B Smith *Substitutions:* D T Giffin for Vickerman (55 mins); A L Freier for Paul (69 mins); D N Croft for Harrison (temp 70 to 80 mins) and for Smith (80 mins); M J Giteau for Herbert (73 mins); B J Darwin for Noriega (77 mins)

Scorers *Tries:* Flatley (2), Sailor *Conversions:* Burke (2) *Penalty Goals:* Burke (4)

Referee P G Honiss (New Zealand)

Test Match 23 November, Stadio Luigi Ferraris, Genoa
Italy 3 (1PG) **Australia 34** (3G 1PG 2T)

Italy: Mirco Bergamasco; P Vaccari, C Stoica, M Barbini, N Mazzucato; R Pez, J-M Queirolo; A lo Cicero, F Ongaro, M-L Castrogiovanni, M Bortolami (*captain*), E Pavanello, A R Persico, S Parisse, Mauro Bergamasco *Substitutions:* S Palmer for Persico (temp 7 to 8 mins) and for Mauro Bergamasco (60 mins); G Peens for Mazzucato (57 mins); A Moretti & G Faliva for Ongaro & Lo Cicero (62 mins); M Giacheri for Pavanello (64 mins); C Zanoletti for Stoica (77 mins); A Troncon for Queirolo (80 mins)

Scorer *Penalty Goal:* Pez

Australia: S A Mortlock; W J Sailor, M C Burke, D J Herbert, S N G Staniforth; E J Flatley, G M Gregan (*captain*); W K Young, A L Freier, E P Noriega, D J Vickerman, J B Harrison, M J Cockbain, R S T Kefu, G B Smith *Substitutions:* D T Giffin for Harrison (53 mins); B J Darwin for Noriega (60 mins); D N Croft for Cockbain (65 mins); C J Whitaker for Gregan (69 mins); B J Cannon for Freier (74 mins); M J Giteau for Herbert (79 mins); M A Bartholomeusz for Mortlock (80 mins)

Scorers *Tries:* Staniforth (2), Harrison, Kefu, Mortlock *Conversions:* Burke (3) *Penalty Goal:* Burke

Referee P C Deluca (Argentina)

New Zealand to Europe 2002

Tour party

Full-backs: B A Blair (Canterbury), C M Cullen (Wellington)

Threequarters: D C Howlett (Auckland), J T Lomu (Wellington), J F Umaga (Wellington), R M King (Waikato), K R Lowen (Waikato), M P Robinson (Canterbury). * P C Steinmetz (Wellington)

Half-backs: A P Mehrtens (Canterbury), C J Spencer (Auckland), S J Devine (Auckland), D D Lee (Otago)

Forwards: A K Hore (Taranaki), K F Mealamu (Auckland), K J Meeuws (Auckland), J M McDonnell (Otago), C J Hayman (Otago), T D Woodcock (North Harbour), B M Mika (Auckland), K J Robinson (Waikato) A J Williams (Auckland),T C Randell (Otago) (*captain*), D J Braid (Auckland), M R Holah (Waikato), R So'oialo (Wellington) S R Broomhall (Canterbury)

Operations Manager: T Thorpe **Head Coach:** J E P Mitchell **Coaching co-ordinator:** R M Deans

* Replacement on tour

Tour record P 3 W 1 D 1 L 1 For 91 Against 68
9 November Lost 28-31 v ENGLAND (Twickenham)
16 November Drawn 20-20 v FRANCE (Paris)
23 November Won 43-17 v WALES (Cardiff)

Tour details

Test Match 9 November, Twickenham
England 31 (2G 3PG 1DG 1T) New Zealand 28 (4G)

England: J Robinson; J Simpson-Daniel, W J H Greenwood, M J Tindall, B C Cohen; J P Wilkinson, M J S Dawson; T J Woodman, S Thompson, P J Vickery, M O Johnson (*captain*), D J Grewcock, L W Moody, L B N Dallaglio, R A Hill *Substitutions:* B Johnston for Greenwood (40 mins); N A Back for Hill (temp 49 to 62 mins) and for Dallaglio (70 mins); B J Kay for Grewcock (61 mins); A S Healey for Simpson-Daniel (77 mins)

Scorers *Tries:* Moody, Wilkinson, Cohen *Conversions:* Wilkinson (2) *Penalty Goals:* Wilkinson (3) *Dropped Goal:* Wilkinson

New Zealand: B A Blair; D C Howlett, J F Umaga, K R Lowen, J T Lomu; C J Spencer, S J Devine; J M McDonnell, A K Hore, K J Meeuws, A J Williams, K J Robinson, T C Randell (*captain*), S R Broomhall, M R Holah *Substitutions:* D D Lee for Devine (30 mins); A P Mehrtens for Spencer (40 mins); M P Robinson for Umaga (temp 37 to 40 mins) and for Lowen (47 mins); B M Mika for K Robinson (62 mins)

Scorers *Tries:* Lomu (2), Howlett, Lee *Conversions:* Blair (2), Mehrtens (2)

Referee J I Kaplan (South Africa)

Test Match 16 November, Stade de France, Paris
France 20 (2G 2PG) New Zealand 20 (2G 2PG)

France: N Brusque; V Clerc, T Castaignède, D Traille, C Heymans; F Gelez, F Galthié (*captain*); J-J Crenca, R Ibañez, P de Villiers, F Pelous, O Brouzet, S Betsen, I Harinordoquy, O Magne *Substitution:* S Chabal for Magne (temp 11 to 17 mins)

Scorers *Tries:* Magne, Brusque *Conversions:* Gelez (2) *Penalty Goals:* Gelez (2)

New Zealand: C M Cullen; D C Howlett, J F Umaga, M P Robinson, J T Lomu; A P Mehrtens, D D Lee; J M McDonnell, A K Hore, K J Meeuws, A J Williams, B M Mika, T C Randell (*captain*), S R Broomhall, M R Holah *Substitutions:* K J Robinson for Mika (63 mins); C J Hayman for Broomhall (temp 17 to 20 mins)

Scorers *Tries:* Meeuws, Umaga *Conversions:* Mehrtens (2) *Penalty Goals:* Mehrtens (2)

Referee S M Young (Australia)

Test Match 23 November, Millennium Stadium, Cardiff
Wales 17 (2G 1PG) **New Zealand 43** (4G 5PG)

Wales: G R Williams; Gareth Thomas, J P Robinson, S Parker, M A Jones; S M Jones, D Peel; I D Thomas, R C McBryde, B R Evans, R Sidoli, G O Llewellyn, D R Jones, C L Charvis (*captain*), M E Williams *Substitutions:* I R Harris, G Jenkins & M Owen for S Jones, I Thomas & Llewellyn (64 mins); D R James for M Jones (72 mins)

Scorers *Tries:* Robinson, penalty try *Conversions:* S Jones, Harris *Penalty Goal:* S Jones

New Zealand: B A Blair; D C Howlett, R M King, J F Umaga, J T Lomu; A P Mehrtens, S J Devine; T D Woodcock, K F Mealamu, C J Hayman, K J Robinson, A J Williams, T C Randell (*captain*), R So'oialo, D J Braid *Substitutions:* M R Holah for Randell (49 mins); M P Robinson for Blair (56 mins); K J Meeuws for Hayman (60 mins); P C Steinmetz for M Robinson (78 mins); B M Mika for Williams (78 mins)

Scorers *Tries:* Howlett (2), Meeuws, King *Conversions:* Mehrtens (4) *Penalty Goals:* Mehrtens (5)

Referee W T S Henning (South Africa)

Fiji to Britain and Ireland 2002

Tour party

Full-backs: A Nariva (Namosi), N Ligairi (Southland, NZ), J Narruhn (Hino, Jap)

Threequarters: F Lasagavibau (Northland, NZ), I Mow (Suva), S Rabeni (Otago, NZ), V Satala (NEC Harlequins, Eng), E Ruivadra (Dravo), W Hughes (Suva), S Bai (Southland, NZ)

Half-backs: W Serevi (Mont-de-Marsan, Fra), N Little (Saracens, Eng), J Rauluni (Rotherham, Eng), S Rabaka (Mosi)

Forwards: G Smith (Waikato, NZ) (*captain*), I Rasila (Nadroga), V Gadolo (Suva), P Biu (Nadroga), V B Cavubati (Wellington, NZ), R Nyholt (Queensland University, Aus), J Soqoiwasa (West Subiaco, Perth, Aus), S Naivaluwaqa (Suva), E Katalau (Narberth, Wal), S Raiwalui (Newport, Wal), I Rawaqa (Lautoka), S Leawere (East Coast, NZ), A Naevo (Kaneka, Jap), K Salawa (Nadi), A Mocelutu (Neath, Wal), S Koyamaibole (Toyota, Jap), A Doviverata (Yamaha, Jap), S Tawake (Suva)

Manager: J Browne **Assistant Manager:** M Nailumu **Coach:** M McCallion
Trainer: G Fairhurst

Tour record P 5 W 1 L 4 For 156 Against 219

4 November Won 74-16 v Pontypool (Pontypool)

9 November Lost 14-58 v WALES (Cardiff)

17 November Lost 17-64 v IRELAND (Dublin)

20 November Lost 29-45 v Scotland A (Stirling)

24 November Lost 22-36 v SCOTLAND (Murrayfield)

Tour details

4 November, Pontypool Park
Pontypool 16 (1G 3PG) **Fiji XV 74** (7G 5T)

Pontypool scorers *Try:* Bowles *Conversion:* J Williams *Penalty Goals:*: J Williams (3)

Fiji XV scorers *Tries:* Lasagavibau (3), Naevo (2), Nariva, Mocelutu, Ruivadra, Rauluni, Ligairi, Cavubati, Narruhn *Conversions:* Little (3), Narruhn (2), Serevi (2)

Test Match 9 November, Millenium Stadium, Cardiff
Wales 58 (4G 5PG 3T) **Fiji 14** (2G)

Wales: G R Williams; Gareth Thomas, T Shanklin, S Parker, M A Jones; S M Jones, D Peel; I D Thomas, M Davies, B R Evans, R Sidoli, G O Llewellyn, D R Jones, C L Charvis (*captain*), M E Williams *Substitutions:* J P Robinson for Shanklin (10 mins); S M Williams for Llewellyn (41 mins); R Parks for M Williams (60 mins); M Madden for Evans (69 mins); I R Harris for S Jones (70 mins)

Scorers *Tries:* M A Jones (2), G R Williams, Parker, Charvis, Gareth Thomas, I Thomas a penalty try *Conversions:* S Jones (3), Harris *Penalty Goals:* S Jones (5)

Fiji: J Narruhn; F Lasagavibau, S Rabeni, S Bai, N Ligairi; N Little, J Rauluni; R Nyholt, G Smith (*captain*), V Cavubati, A Naevo, S Raiwalui, S Tawake, A Mocelutu, A Doviverata *Substitutions:* W Serevi for Narruhn (40 mins); E Ruivadra for Rabeni (47 mins); S Koyamaibole for Tawake (53 mins); S Rabaka for Rauluni (69 mins)

Scorers *Tries:* Lasagavibau, Serevi *Conversions:* Little, Serevi

Referee S J Dickinson (Australia)

Test Match 17 November, Lansdowne Road, Dublin
Ireland 64 (5G 3PG 4T) **Fiji 17** (2G 1PG)

Ireland: G E A Murphy; S P Horgan, B G O'Driscoll (*captain*), K M Maggs, J P Bishop; D G Humphreys, G Easterby; M J Horan, F J Sheahan, J J Hayes, L F M Cullen, M E O'Kelly, A Quinlan, A G Foley, K Dawson *Substitutions:* G M D'Arcy for O'Driscoll (55 mins); M R O'Driscoll, R Corrigan & E R P Miller for O'Kelly, Hayes & Foley (57 mins)

Scorers *Tries:* Maggs (3), Murphy (2), O'Driscoll, Bishop, Dawson, Foley *Conversions:* Humphreys (5) *Penalty Goals:* Humphreys (3)

Fiji: W Serevi; F Lasagavibau, V Satala, S Bai, N Ligairi; N Little, J Rauluni; R Nyholt, G Smith (*captain*), V B Cavubati, A Naevo, S Raiwalui, A Mocelutu, S Koyamaibole, A Doviverata *Substitutions:* S Tawake for Doviverata (47 mins); J Narruhn for Little (51 mins); I Rawaqa for Naevo (59 mins); S Rabaka for Rauluni (75 mins)

Scorers *Tries:* Doviverata, Narruhn *Conversions:* Little, Serevi *Penalty Goal:* Little

Referee A J Spreadbury (England)

20 November, Bridgehaugh, Stirling
Scotland A 45 (3G 3PG 3T) **Fiji XV 29** (1G 4PG 2T)

Scotland A scorers *Tries:* Rennick, Mower, Utterson, Howarth, Steel, Simpson *Conversions:* Howarth (2), Hodge *Penalty Goals:* Howarth (2), Hodge

Fiji XV scorers *Tries:* Tawake, Koyamaibole, Nariva *Conversion:* Narruhn *Penalty Goals:* Narruhn (4)

Test Match 24 November, Murrayfield, Edinburgh
Scotland 36 (1G 3PG 4T) **Fiji 22** (4PG 2T)

Scotland: B G Hinshelwood; N Walker, A Craig, B J Laney, C D Paterson; G P J Townsend, B W Redpath (*captain*); T J Smith, G C Bulloch, B A F Douglas, J P R White, S B Grimes, S M Taylor, J M Petrie, A C Pountney *Substitutions:* N J Hines for White (25 mins); J S D Moffat for Paterson (41 mins); M D Leslie for Petrie (55 mins); S Scott for Bulloch (68 mins); G Ross for Townsend (69 mins); G Beveridge for Redpath (76 mins)

Scorers *Tries:* Craig (3), Laney, Grimes *Conversion:* Laney *Penalty Goals:* Laney (3)

Fiji: A Nariva; F Lasagavibau, E Ruivadra, S Bai, N Ligairi; J Narruhn, J Rauluni; I Rasila, G Smith (*captain*), V B Cavubati, A Naevo, S Raiwalui, S Koyamaibole, S Tawake, A Mocelutu *Substitutions:* V Satala for Bai (49 mins); S Leawere for Naevo (54 mins); E Katalau for Tawake (69 mins); W Serevi for Rauluni (70 mins); V Gadolo for Mocelutu (temp 73 to 79 mins)

Scorers *Tries:* Naevo, Ligairi *Penalty Goals:* Narruhn (4)

Referee S M Lawrence (South Africa)

South Africa to Europe 2002

Tour party

Full-backs: W W Greeff (Western Province)

Threequarters: B J Paulse (Western Province), F Lombard (Free State Cheetahs), R B Russell (Pumas), J de Villiers (Western Province), R F Fleck (Western Province), A A Jacobs (Falcons), M C Joubert (Western Province)

Half-backs: A S Pretorius (Lions), A D James (Natal Sharks), J H Conradie (Western Province), N A de Kock (Wetsern Province), * N Jordaan (Western Province)

Forwards: J Dalton (Falcons), L van Biljon (Natal Sharks), W Meyer (Lions), W G Roux (Blue Bulls), L D Sephaka (Lions), P D Carstens (Natal Sharks), *C J van der Linde (Free State Cheetahs), J J Labuschagne (Lions), P J Wannenburg (Blue Bulls), M van Z Wentzel (Pumas), J P Botha (Blue Bulls), A J Venter (Natal Sharks), C P J Krigé (Western Province) (*captain*), P J Uys (Pumas), J C van Niekerk (Lions)

Manager: G Sam **Operations Manager:** M Hendricks **Coach:** R A W Straeuli
Assistant Coach: T A Lane

Tour record P 3 L 3 For 19 Against 104

9 November Lost 10-30 v FRANCE (Marseilles)

16 November Lost 6-21 v SCOTLAND (Murrayfield)

23 November Lost 3-53 v ENGLAND (Twickenham)

Tour details

Test Match 9 November, Stade Vélodrome, Marseilles
France 30 (1G 5PG 1DG 1T) South Africa 10 (1G 1PG)

France: N Brusque; V Clerc, T Castaignède, D Traille, C Heymans; F Gelez, F Galthié (*captain*); J-J Crenca, R Ibañez, P de Villiers, F Pelous, O Brouzet, S Betsen, I Harinordoquy, O Magne *Substitutions:* S Marconnet for De Villiers (67 mins); X Garbajosa for Castaignède (71 mins); S Chabal & J-B Rué for Harinordoquy & Ibañez (79 mins); T Privat for Brouzet (80 mins)

Scorers *Tries:* Heymans, Clerc *Conversion:* Gelez *Penalty Goals:* Gelez (5) *Dropped Goal:* Castaignède

South Africa: W W Greeff; B J Paulse, J de Villiers, A A Jacobs, R B Russell; A S Pretorius, N A de Kock; L D Sephaka, J Dalton, W Meyer, J P Botha, J J Labuschagne, C P J Krigé (*captain*), J C van Niekerk, A J Venter *Substitutions:* M C Joubert for J de Villiers (7 mins); W G Roux for Meyer (40 mins); L van Biljon for Sephaka (50 mins); P J Wannenburg for Botha (55 mins); M van Z Wentzel for Venter (67 mins); A D James for Greeff (80 mins)

Scorers *Try:* Van Niekerk *Conversion:* Pretorius *Penalty Goal:* Pretorius

Referee A C Rolland (Ireland)

Test Match 16 November, Murrayfield, Edinburgh
Scotland 21 (1G 3PG 1T) South Africa 6 (2PG)

Scotland: J S D Moffat; N Walker, A Craig, B J Laney, C D Paterson; G Ross, B W Redpath (*captain*); T J Smith, G C Bulloch, B A F Douglas, S Murray, S B Grimes, M D Leslie, S M Taylor, A C Pountney *Substitutions:* G P J Townsend for Ross (62 mins); J P R White for Grimes (72 mins); B G Hinshelwood for Walker (77 mins); D I W Hilton for Smith (78 mins); N J Hines for Murray (80 mins)

Scorers *Tries:* Pountney, Walker *Conversion:* Laney *Penalty Goals:* Laney (3)

South Africa: W W Greeff; B J Paulse, A A Jacobs, R F Fleck, F Lombard; A D James, J H Conradie; W G Roux, L van Biljon, P D Carstens, J J Labuschagne, M van Z Wentzel, C P J Krigé (*captain*), J C van Niekerk, P J Uys *Substitutions:* A S Pretorius for Jacobs (56 mins); A J Venter for Wentzel (66 mins); C J van der Linde for Carstens (77 mins)

Scorer *Penalty Goals:* James (2)

Referee N Williams (Wales)

Test Match 23 November, Twickenham
England 53 (6G 2PG 1T) South Africa 3 (1PG)

England: J Robinson; B C Cohen, W J H Greenwood, M J Tindall, P Christophers; J P Wilkinson, M J S Dawson; J Leonard, S Thompson, P J Vickery, M O Johnson (*captain*), B J Kay, L W Moody, R A Hill, N A Back *Substitutions:* L B N Dallaglio for Moody (15 mins); A S Healey for Wilkinson (44 mins); A C T Gomarsall for Dawson (57 mins); D J Grewcock for Kay (71 mins); T R G Stimpson for Greenwood (72 mins)

Scotland celebrate beating South Africa at Murrayfield in November. It was their first win against the Springboks for 33 years.

Scorers *Tries:* Greenwood (2), Cohen, Back, Hill, Dallaglio, Christophers a penalty try *Conversions:* Gomarsall (2), Stimpson (2), Wilkinson, Dawson *Penalty Goals:* Wilkinson (2)

South Africa: W W Greeff; B J Paulse, R F Fleck, A D James, F Lombard; A S Pretorius, J H Conradie; W G Roux, J Dalton, P D Carstens, J J Labuschagne, A J Venter, C P J Krigé (*captain*), J C van Niekerk, P J Wannenburg *Substitutions:* N Jordaan for Conradie (11 mins); R B Russell for Paulse (47 mins); A A Jacobs & L van Biljon for Pretorius & Dalton (55 mins); C J van der Linde for Carstens (62 mins)

Scorer *Penalty Goal:* Pretorius

Referee P D O'Brien (New Zealand)

Canada to Wales & France 2002

Tour party

Full-backs: W U Stanley (James Bay AA)

Threequarters: S Fauth (Castaway-Wanderers), F C Asselin (James Bay AA), N Witkowski (James Bay AA), J Cannon (Castaway-Wanderers & Rotherham, Eng), M di Girolamo (James Bay AA)

Half-backs: J Barker (James Bay AA & RC Arras, Fra), R P Ross (James Bay AA), M Williams (Saracens, Eng), E Fairhurst (University of Victoria)

Forwards: P Dunkley (James Bay AA), M Lawson (University of Victoria), J Thiel (Bridgend, Wal), K Tkachuk (Oxford University, Eng), R G A Snow (Newport, Wal), L Carlson (Ex-Brits RFC), J Cudmore (Capilano & Llanelli, Wal), M B James (Stade Français, Fra), R Banks (Burnaby Lake), J Tait (Cardiff, Wal), A van Staveren (Bayside), P Murphy (Perpignan, Fra), A J Charron (Ottawa Irish) (*captain*)

Manager: D Whidden **Coach:** D Clark **Assistant Coach:** G Johnston

Tour record P 2 L 2 For 24 Against 67

16 November Lost 21-32 v WALES (Cardiff)

23 November Lost 3-35 v FRANCE (Paris)

Tour details

Test Match 16 November, Millennium Stadium, Cardiff
Wales 32 (2G 6PG) Canada 21 (6PG 1DG)

Wales: G R Williams; Gareth Thomas, J P Robinson, S Parker, M A Jones; S M Jones, D Peel; I D Thomas, R C McBryde, B R Evans, V Cooper, G O Llewellyn, D R Jones, C L Charvis (*captain*), M E Williams *Substitutions:* M Owen for Cooper (52 mins); L S Quinnell for D Jones (55 mins); I R Harris for S Jones (72 mins); R D Powell for Peel (72 mins)

Scorers *Tries:* McBryde, Robinson *Conversions:* S Jones (2) *Penalty Goals:* S Jones (6)

Canada: W U Stanley; S Fauth, N Witkowski, J Cannon, F C Asselin; J Barker, M Williams; R G A Snow, P Dunkley (*captain*), J Thiel, J Tait, M B James, R Banks, P Murphy, A van Staveren *Substitutions:* J Cudmore for Murphy (63 mins); L Carlson for Tait (70 mins); M di Girolamo for Cannon (71 mins); E Fairhurst for Williams (74 mins); K Tkachuk for Van Staveren (temp 28 to 35 mins)

Scorers *Penalty Goals:* Barker (6) *Dropped Goal:* Williams

Referee G de Santis (Italy)

Test Match 23 November, Stade de France, Paris
France 35 (3G 3PG 1T) Canada 3 (1PG)

France: N Brusque; V Clerc, T Castaignède, D Traille, D Bory; G Merceron, F Galthié (*captain*); J-J Crenca, R Ibañez, P de Villiers, F Pelous, O Brouzet, S Betsen, I Harinordoquy, O Magne *Substitutions:* S Marconnet for Crenca (65 mins); S Chabal & J-B Rué for Magne & Ibañez (69 mins); D Yachvili for Galthié (74 mins); X Garbajosa for Castaignède (72 mins); D Auradou & F Gelez for Chabal & Merceron (76 mins)

Scorers *Tries:* Clerc (2), Bory, Traille *Conversions:* Merceron (2), Traille *Penalty Goals:* Merceron (3)

Canada: W U Stanley; S Fauth, N Witkowski, J Cannon, F C Asselin; R P Ross, M Williams; R G A Snow, P Dunkley, J Thiel, J Tait, M B James, A J Charron (*captain*), P Murphy, R Banks *Substitutions:* A van Staveren for Banks (46 mins); M di Girolamo for Cannon (51 mins); J Cudmore for Murphy (65 mins); M Lawson for Dunkley (72 mins); K Tkachuk for Snow (76 mins); E Fairhurst for Williams (76 mins)

Scorer *Penalty Goal:* Ross
Referee D T M McHugh (Ireland)

Argentina to Europe 2002

Tour party

Full-backs: I Corleto (Stade Français, Fra), B M Stortoni (Narbonne, Fra)

Threequarters: D Albanese (Leeds Tykes, Eng), G F Camardon (Roma, Ita), J-M Nuñez-Piossek (Huirapuca), L Arbizu (Bègles-Bordaux, Fra) (*captain*), J Orengo (Grenoble, Fra), H Senillosa (Hindu), M Gaitan (Biarritz Olympique, Fra), J-M Hernandez (Deportiva Francesa)

Half-backs: F Contepomi (Bristol Shoguns, Eng), M Contepomi (Newman), J de la C Fernandez Miranda (Hindu), N Fernandez Miranda (Natal Sharks, SA), A Pichot (Bristol Shoguns, Eng)

Forwards: M E Ledesma (RC Narbonne, Fra), J J Villar (CU Buenos Aires), M Reggiardo (Castres Olympique, Fra), S Gonzalez Bonorino (AS Béziers, Fra), R D Grau (Liceo), O J Hasan-Jalil (SU Agen, Fra), M Scelzo (Narbonne, Fra), C I Fernandez Lobbe (Castres Olympique, Fra), P L Sporleder (Curupayti), R Alvarez (USA Perpignan, Fra), P Bouza (Duendes), P Albacete (Belgrano), M Durand (Champagnat), R A Martin (San Isidro Club), G Longo (RC Narbonne, Fra), S Phelan (CA San Isidro), M Schusterman (San Isidro Club)

Manager: E Perasso **Head Coach:** M Loffreda **Assistant Coach:** D Baetti

Tour record P 4 W 3 L 1 For 112 Against 43

12 November Won 45-9 v Italy A (Coleferro)

16 November Won 36-6 v ITALY (Rome)

20 November Won 24-12 v Irish Development XV (Donnybrook)

23 November Lost 7-16 v IRELAND (Dublin)

Tour details

12 November, Stadio Maurizio Natali, Coleferro
Italy A 9 (3PG) **Argentina XV 45** (3G 3PG 3T)

Italy A scorer *Penalty Goals:* Eigner (3)

Argentina XV scorers *Tries:* Nuñez-Piossek (2), Gaitan, Albacete, Schusterman, Hernandez *Conversions:* J C Fernandez Miranda (3) *Penalty Goals:* J C Fernandez Miranda (3)

Test Match 16 November, Stadio Flaminio, Rome
Italy 6 (2PG) **Argentina 36** (4G 1PG 1T)

Italy: Mirco Bergamasco; P Vaccari, C Stoica, M Barbini, N Mazzucato; D Dominguez, A Troncon (*captain*); G Faliva, A Moretti, F Pucciariello, M Bortolami, S Dellape, S Garozzo, S Palmer, A R Persico *Substitutions:* G Peens for Dominguez (41 mins); E Pavanello for Dellape (56 mins); M-L Castrogiovanni for Pucciariello (56 mins); S Parisse for Garozzo (62 mins); C Zanoletti for Stoica (67 mins); F Ongaro for Moretti (78 mins)

Scorer *Penalty Goals:* Dominguez (2)

Argentina: I Corleto; G F Camardon, J Orengo, L Arbizu (*captain*), D Albanese; F Contepomi, A Pichot; R D Grau, M E Ledesma, O J Hasan-Jalil, C I Fernandez Lobbe, R Alvarez, S Phelan, G Longo, R A Martin *Substitutions:* M Reggiardo for Grau (47 mins); P L Sporleder for Alvarez (56 mins); J C Fernandez Miranda for F Contepomi (63 mins); M Durand for Longo (65 mins); N Fernandez Miranda for Pichot (78 mins)

Scorers *Tries:* Orengo, Corleto, Martin, Albanese, Durand *Conversions:* F Contepomi (2), J C Fernandez Miranda (2) *Penalty Goal:* F Contepomi

Referee A J Cole (Australia)

20 November, Donnybrook, Dublin
Irish Development XV 12 (4PG) Argentina XV 24 (2G 2T)

Irish Development XV scorer *Penalty Goals:* McHugh (4)

Argentina XV scorers *Tries:* penalty try, Senillosa, Gaitan, Reggiardo *Conversions:* J Fernandez Miranda (2)

Test Match 23 November, Lansdowne Road, Dublin
Ireland 16 (1G 3PG) Argentina 7 (1G)

Ireland: G T Dempsey; S P Horgan, B G O'Driscoll (*captain*), K M Maggs, J P Bishop; R J R O'Gara, P A Stringer; R Corrigan, J S Byrne, J J Hayes, G W Longwell, M E O'Kelly, V C P Costello, A G Foley, K D Gleeson *Substitutions:* L F M Cullen for Longwell (29 mins); A Quinlan for Costello (70 mins); M J Horan for Corrigan (75 mins)

Scorers *Try:* Dempsey *Conversion:* O'Gara *Penalty Goals:* O'Gara (3)

Argentina: I Corleto; G F Camardon, J Orengo, L Arbizu (*captain*), D Albanese; F Contepomi, A Pichot; M Reggiardo, M E Ledesma, O J Hasan-Jalil, C I Fernandez Lobbe, R Alvarez, S Phelan, G Longo, R A Martin *Substitutions:* P L Sporleder for Alvarez (64 mins); J de la C Fernandez Miranda for Arbizu (70 mins); M Durand for Phelan (77 mins)

Scorers *Try:* Martin *Conversion:* F Contepomi

Referee C White (England)

Scotland to South Africa 2003

Tour party

Full-back: G H Metcalfe (Glasgow Rugby)

Threequarters: C D Paterson (Edinburgh Rugby), S Webster (Edinburgh), K M Logan (London Wasps), A R Henderson (Glasgow Rugby), A Craig (Orrell), B J Laney (Edinburgh Rugby), J G McLaren (Bègles-Bordeaux, Fra)

Half-backs: G P J Townsend (The Borders), G Ross (Leeds Tykes), B W Redpath (Sale Sharks) (*captain*), M R L Blair (Edinburgh)

Forwards: G C Bulloch (Glasgow Rugby), R R Russell (Saracens), G R McIlwham (Bègles-Bordeaux, Fra), B A F Douglas (The Borders), G Kerr (Leeds Tykes), I A Fullarton (Sale Sharks), N J Hines (Edinburgh Rugby), S Murray (Edinburgh Rugby), A L Mower (Newcastle Falcons), M D Leslie

(Edinburgh Rugby), J M Petrie (Glasgow), J P R White (Sale Sharks), S M Taylor (Edinburgh Rugby), A Dall (Edinburgh Rugby)

Manager: D Morgan **Coach:** I R McGeechan **Assistant Coach:** H Campbell

Tour record P 2 L 2 For 44 Against 57

7 June Lost 25-29 v SOUTH AFRICA (Durban)

14 June Lost 19-28 v SOUTH AFRICA (Johannesburg)

Tour details

First Test Match 7 June, ABSA Stadium, King's Park, Durban
South Africa 29 (2G 5PG) Scotland 25 (2G 2PG 1T)

South Africa: R I P Loubscher; C S Terblanche, A H Snyman, T M Halstead, A K Willemse; L J Koen, J H van der Westhuizen (*captain*); L D Sephaka, D Coetzee, R E Bands, J P Botha, V Matfield, H J Gerber, P J Wannenburg, J L van Heerden *Substitutions:* C S Boome for Botha (68 mins); J H Smith for Wannenburg (69 mins); R B Kempson for Sephaka (71 mins); I J Visagie for Bands (75 mins); J N B van der Westhuyzen for Loubscher (78 mins)

Scorers *Tries:* Terblanche, Halstead *Conversions:* Koen (2) *Penalty Goals:* Koen (5)

Scotland: G H Metcalfe; C D Paterson, A Craig, A R Henderson, K M Logan; G P J Townsend, B W Redpath (*captain*); G Kerr, G C Bulloch, B A F Douglas, S Murray, N J Hines, J P R White, S M Taylor, A L Mower *Substitutions:* M D Leslie for White (62 mins); J M Petrie & R R Russell for Mower & Bulloch (72 mins); J G McLaren for Henderson (76 mins)

Scorers *Tries:* White, Craig, Paterson *Conversions:* Paterson (2) *Penalty Goals:* Paterson (2)

Referee J Jutge (France)

Second Test Match 14 June, Ellis Park, Johannesburg
South Africa 28 (1G 6PG 1DG) Scotland 19 (1G 4PG)

South Africa: J N B van der Westhuyzen; C S Terblanche, M C Joubert, T M Halstead, A K Willemse; L J Koen, J H van der Westhuizen (*captain*); L D Sephaka, D Coetzee, R E Bands, J P Botha, V Matfield, H J Gerber, P J Wannenburg, J L van Heerden *Substitutions:* R B Kempson & I J Visagie for Sephaka & Bands (50 mins); G Bobo for Halstead (57 mins); J H Smith for Gerber (63 mins); C S Boome for Botha (73 mins)

Scorers *Try:* Terblanche *Conversion:* Koen *Penalty Goals:* Koen (6) *Dropped Goal:* Koen

Scotland: G H Metcalfe; C D Paterson, A Craig, A R Henderson, K M Logan; G P J Townsend, B W Redpath (*captain*); G Kerr, G C Bulloch, B A F Douglas, S Murray, N J Hines, J P R White, S M Taylor, A L Mower *Substitutions:* M D Leslie for Hines (45 mins); R R Russell & G R McIlwham for Bulloch & Kerr (59 mins); G Ross for Townsend (61 mins); J M Petrie for Mower (64 mins); M R L Blair for Redpath (68 mins); B J Laney for Henderson (74 mins)

Scorers *Try:* Craig *Conversion:* Paterson *Penalty Goals:* Paterson (4)

Referee S Young (Australia)

Ireland to Southern Hemisphere 2003

Tour party

Full-backs: G T Dempsey (Terenure College & Leinster), M McHugh (St Mary's College & Connacht)

Threequarters: A P Horgan (Cork Constitution & Munster), J P Kelly (Cork Constitution & Munster), T G Howe (Dungannon & Ulster), J A Topping (Ballymena & Ulster), K M Maggs (Bath), J C Bell (Dungannon & Ulster), G E A Murphy (Leicester Tigers), M J Mullins (Old Crescent & Munster), G M D'Arcy (Lansdowne & Leinster)

Half-backs: P A Burke (NEC Harlequins), D G Humphreys (Dungannon & Ulster), R J R O'Gara (Cork Constitution & Munster), G Easterby (Llanelli), P A Stringer (Shannon & Munster), B T O'Meara (Cork Constitution & Leinster)

Forwards: J S Byrne (Blackrock College & Leinster), P M Shields (Ballymena & Ulster) S J Best (Belfast Harlequins & Ulster), M J Horan (Shannon & Munster), E Byrne (St Mary's College & Leinster), R Corrigan (Greystones & Leinster), J J Fitzpatrick (Dungannon & Ulster), G W Longwell (Ballymena & Ulster), D O'Callaghan (Cork Constitution & Munster), P J O'Connell (Young Munster & Munster), M E O'Kelly (St Mary's College & Leinster), L F M Cullen (Blackrock College & Leinster), A Quinlan (Shannon & Munster), K Dawson (London Irish), S H Easterby (Llanelli), K D Gleeson (St Mary's College & Leinster), A McCullen (Lansdowne & Leinster), D P Wallace (Garryowen & Munster) V C P Costello (St Mary's College & Leinster), E R P Miller (Terenure College & Leinster)

Manager: B A P O'Brien **Coach:** E O'Sullivan

Tour record P 3 W 2 L 1 For 96 Against 78

7 June Lost 16-45 v AUSTRALIA (Perth)

14 June Won 40-19 v TONGA (Nuku'alofa)

20 June Won 40-14 v SAMOA (Apia)

Tour details

Test Match 7 June, Subiaco Oval, Perth
Australia 45 (6G 1PG) **Ireland 16** (1G 3PG)

Australia: C E Latham; W J Sailor, M Turinui, S Kefu, J W Roff; E J Flatley, G M Gregan (*captain*); W K Young, J A Paul, E P Noriega, N C Sharpe, D T Giffin, D J Lyons, R S T Kefu, G B Smith *Substitutions:* B J Darwin for Noriega (54 mins); D J Vickerman for Sharpe (56 mins); L Tuqiri for Sailor (60 mins); B J Cannon for Paul (69 mins); P R Waugh & C J Whitaker for Smith & Gregan (70 mins); N P Grey for S Kefu (73 mins)

Scorers *Tries:* Gregan (2), Flatley (2 including a penalty try), S Kefu, Latham, *Conversions:* Flatley (6) *Penalty Goal:* Flatley

Ireland: G T Dempsey; J A Topping, G E A Murphy, K M Maggs, J P Kelly; D G Humphreys (*captain*), P A Stringer; M J Horan, J S Byrne, R Corrigan, G W Longwell, M E O'Kelly, A Quinlan, V C P Costello, K D Gleeson *Substitutions:* R J R O'Gara for Humphreys (temp 15 to 19 mins & 40 mins); P J O'Connell & E Byrne for Longwell & Corrigan (50 mins); R Corrigan for Horan (69 mins)

Scorers *Try:* Kelly *Conversion:* Humphreys *Penalty Goals:* Humphreys (2), O'Gara
Referee N Williams (Wales)

Test Match 14 June, Teufaiva Stadium, Nuku'alofa
Tonga 19 (3PG 2T) Ireland 40 (2G 2PG 4T)

Tonga: G Leger; P Hola, J Ngauamo, J Payne, S Mafileo; T Alatini, D Palu; T Lea'aetoa, V Ma'asi, H Lavaka, M Ngauamo, I Afeaki (*captain*), N Naufahu, S Latu, S Afeaki *Substitutions:* T Tulia for J Ngaumo (temp 30 to 40 mins); K Pulu for Lavaka (59 mins)

Scorer *Tries:* Hola (2) *Penalty Goals:* Hola (3)

Ireland: M McHugh; J P Kelly, M J Mullins, J C Bell, T G Howe; R J R O'Gara, G Easterby; J J Fitzpatrick, J S Byrne, R Corrigan (*captain*), L F M Cullen, P J O'Connell, S H Easterby, E R P Miller, K Dawson *Subsitutions:* D P Wallace for Miller (59 mins); S J Best for Fitzpatrick (63 mins); G M D'Arcy & D O'Callaghan for McHugh & Dawson (80 mins)

Scorers *Tries:* Kelly (2), G Easterby (2), Bell, McHugh *Conversions:* O'Gara (2) *Penalty Goals:* O'Gara (2)

Referee S R Walsh (New Zealand)

Test Match 20 June, Apia Park, Apia
Samoa 14 (2G) Ireland 40 (2G 6PG 1DG 1T)

Samoa: F Fili; L Fa'atau, D Rasmussen, B P Lima, R Fanuatanu; E Va'a, D Tyrell; K Lealamanua, T Leota, J Tomuli, O Palepoi, L Lafaiali'i, K Viliamu, S Sititi (*captain*), M Fa'asavalu *Substitutions:* T Leupola for Tomuli (44 mins); S So'oialo for Tyrell (50 mins); J Meredith for Leota (65 mins); D Tuiavi'i for Viliamu (70 mins); G Elisara for Rasmusen (73 mins)

Scorers *Tries:* Fanuatanu, Va'a *Conversions:* Va'a (2)

Ireland: G T Dempsey; J P Kelly, M J Mullins, J C Bell, A P Horgan; R J R O'Gara, G Easterby; M J Horan, J S Byrne, R Corrigan (*captain*), L F M Cullen, P J O'Connell, S H Easterby, E R P Miller, A McCullen *Substitutions:* D O'Callaghan for Cullen (18 mins); G M D'Arcy for Horgan (52 mins); P M Shields & E Byrne for J S Byrne & Corrigan (70 mins); B T O'Meara & P A Burke for G Easterby & O'Gara (76 mins); D P Wallace for Bell (79 mins)

Scorers *Tries:* O'Gara (2), Miller *Conversions:* O'Gara (2) *Penalty Goals:* O'Gara (5), Burke *Dropped Goal:* O'Gara

Referee P G Honiss (New Zealand)

England to Southern Hemisphere 2003

Tour party

Full-backs: O J Lewsey (London Wasps), I R Balshaw (Bath)

Threequarters: J Robinson (Sale Sharks), D D Luger (NEC Harelquins), J Simpson-Daniel (Gloucester), B C Cohen (Northampton Saints), W J H Greenwood (NEC Harlequins), M J Tindall (Bath), S Abbott (London Wasps), B Johnston (Saracens), J Noon (Newcastle Falcons)

Half-backs: J P Wilkinson (Newcastle Falcons), P J Grayson (Northampton Saints), A D King (London Wasps), M J S Dawson (Northampton Saints), K P P Bracken (Saracens), A C T Gomarsall (Gloucester)

Forwards: S Thompson (Northampton Saints), M P Regan (Leeds Tykes), D E West (Leicester Tigers), J Leonard (NEC Harlequins), M A Worsley (London Irish), T J Woodman (Gloucester), G C Rowntree (Leicester Tigers), P J Vickery (Gloucester), M O Johnson (Leicester Tigers) (*captain*), B J Kay (Leicester Tigers), T Palmer (Leeds Tykes), S W Borthwick (Bath), S D Shaw (London Wasps), R A Hill (Saracens), J P R Worsley (London Wasps), N A Back (Leicester Tigers), A R Hazell (Gloucester), P Volley (London Wasps), M E Corry (Leicester Tigers), L B N Dallaglio (London Wasps)

Manager/Head Coach: C R Woodward **Assistant Coaches** R A Robinson, P Larder, D Aldred

Tour record P 3 W 3 For 63 Against 36

9 June Won 23-9 v New Zealand Maori (New Plymouth)

14 June Won 15-13 v NEW ZEALAND (Wellington)

21 June Won 25-14 v AUSTRALIA (Melbourne)

Tour details

9 June, Yarrow Stadium, New Plymouth
New Zealand Maori 9 (3PG) England XV 23 (2G 3PG)

New Zealand Maori scorer *Penalty Goals:* Jackson (3)

England XV scorers *Tries:* Shaw, Gomarsall *Conversions:* Grayson (2) *Penalty Goals:* Grayson (3)

Test Match 14 June, WestpacTrust Stadium, Wellington
New Zealand 13 (1G 2PG) England 15 (4PG 1DG)

New Zealand: D C Howlett; J T Rokocoko, M Nonu, J F Umaga, C S Ralph; C J Spencer, J W Marshall; D N Hewett, A D Oliver, G M Somerville, C R Jack, A J Williams, R D Thorne (*captain*), R So'oialo, R H McCaw *Substitutions:* S J Devine for Marshall (48 mins); K F Mealamu for Oliver (56 mins); M Muliaina for Rokokoko (72 mins); J Collins for So'oialo (73 mins)

Scorers *Try:* Howlett *Conversion:* Spencer *Penalty Goals:* Spencer (2)

England: O J Lewsey; J Robinson, W J H Greenwood, M J Tindall, B C Cohen; J P Wilkinson, K P P Bracken; G C Rowntree, S Thompson, J Leonard, M O Johnson (*captain*), B J Kay, R A Hill, L B N Dallaglio, N A Back *Substitutions:* P J Vickery for Leonard (40 mins); J P R Worsley for Hill (72 mins); D D Luger for Lewsey (77 mins)

Scorer *Penalty Goals:* Wilkinson (4) *Dropped Goal:* Wilkinson

Referee S J Dickinson (Australia)

Test Match 21 June, Telstra Dome, Colonial Stadium, Melbourne
Australia 14 (3PG 1T) England 25 (2G 2PG 1T)

Australia: C E Latham; W J Sailor, M Turinui, S Kefu, J W Roff; N P Grey, G M Gregan (*captain*); W K Young, J A Paul, E P Noriega, D T Giffin, N C Sharpe, D J Lyons, R S T Kefu, P R Waugh *Substitutions:* D J Vickerman for Sharpe (44 mins); B J Cannon for Paul (53 mins); M S Rogers for Turinui (58 mins); B J Darwin for Noriega (65 mins); L Tuqiri for Grey (65 mins)

Scorers *Try:* Sailor *Penalty Goals:* Roff (3)

England: J Robinson; O J Lewsey, W J H Greenwood, M J Tindall, B C Cohen; J P Wilkinson, K P P Bracken; T J Woodman, S Thompson, P J Vickery, M O Johnson (*captain*), B J Kay, R A Hill, L B N Dallaglio, N A Back *Substitutions:* J P R Worsley & M J S Dawson for Hill & Bracken (53 mins); S W Borthwick for Kay (temp 62 to 67 mins)

Scorers *Tries:* Greenwood, Tindall, Cohen *Conversions:* Wilkinson (2) *Penalty Goals:* Wilkinson (2)

Referee D T M McHugh (Ireland)

Wales to Australia & New Zealand 2003

Tour party

Full-backs: G Evans (Llanelli), G R Williams (Cardiff)
Threequarters: M A Jones (Llanelli), J P Robinson (Cardiff), S Parker (Pontypridd), M Taylor (Swansea), T Shanklin (Saracens)

Half-backs: G L Henson (Swansea), C Sweeney (Pontypridd), S M Jones (Llanelli), D Peel (Llanelli), G J Cooper (Bath), M Phillips (Llanelli)

Forwards: R C McBryde (Neath), M Davies (Pontypridd), G Williams (Bridgend), I D Thomas (Llanelli), G Jenkins (Pontypridd), B R Evans (Cardiff), A Jones (Neath), R Sidoli (Pontypridd), G O Llewellyn (Neath), C P Wyatt (Llanelli), V Cooper (Llanelli), D R Jones (Llanelli), M E Williams (Cardiff)(*captain*), C L Charvis (Swansea), J Thomas (Swansea), A Popham (Leeds Tykes)

Manager: A J Phillips **Head Coach:** S Hansen **Assistant Coach:** C R Griffiths

Tour record P 2 L 2 For 13 Against 85

14 June Lost 10-30 v AUSTRALIA (Sydney)

21 June Lost 3-55 v NEW ZEALAND (Hamilton)

Test Match 14 June, Telstra Stadium Australia, Sydney
Australia 30 (1G 1PG 4T) Wales 10 (1G 1PG)

Australia: C E Latham; W J Sailor, M Turinui, S Kefu, J W Roff; E J Flatley, G M Gregan (*captain*); W K Young, J A Paul, E P Noriega, N C Sharpe, D T Giffin, D J Lyons, R S T Kefu, P R Waugh *Substitutions:* B J Darwin for Noriega (temp 38 to 40 mins and 53 mins); D J Vickerman for Giffin (61 mins); N P Grey for S Kefu (64 mins); B J Cannon for Paul (64 mins); D P Heenan for Lyons (66 mins); L Tuqiri for Roff (71 mins); C J Whitaker for Gregan (72 mins)

Scorers *Tries:* Sailor (2), Latham, Paul, Grey *Conversion:* Roff *Penalty Goal:* Flatley

Wales: G R Williams; T Shanklin, J P Robinson, M Taylor, M A Jones; S M Jones, G J Cooper; I D Thomas, R C McBryde, G Jenkins, R Sidoli,

G O Llewellyn, J Thomas, C L Charvis, M E Williams (*captain*) *Substitutions:* C P Wyatt for Llewellyn (66 mins); M Davies for McBryde (69 mins); A Popham for J Thomas (73 mins)

Scorers *Try:* Robinson *Conversion:* S Jones *Penalty Goal:* S Jones

Referee S M Lawrence (South Africa)

Test Match 21 June, Waikato Stadium, Rugby Park, Hamilton
New Zealand 55 (6G 1PG 2T) Wales 3 (1PG)

New Zealand: M Muliaina; D C Howlett, J F Umaga, D W Carter, J T Rokocoko; C J Spencer, S J Devine; C H Hoeft, K F Mealamu, K J Meeuws, C R Jack, A J Williams, R D Thorne (*captain*), J Collins, R H McCaw *Substitution:* B C Thorn for Williams (47 mins)

Scorers *Tries:* Rokokoko (2), Howlett, Spencer, Carter, Meeuws, Mealamu, Umaga *Conversions:* Carter (6) *Penalty Goal:* Carter

Wales: G R Williams; T Shanklin, J P Robinson, M Taylor, M A Jones; S M Jones, G J Cooper; I D Thomas, R C McBryde, G Jenkins, R Sidoli, G O Llewellyn, R D Jones, C L Charvis, M E Williams (*captain*) *Substitutions:* J Thomas for Charvis (23 mins); C P Wyatt for M Williams (temp 28 to 40 mins) and for Llewellyn (57 mins); M Davies for McBryde (51 mins); C Sweeney for Robinson (68 mins); G L Henson & D Peel for Shanklin & Cooper (75 mins)

Scorer *Penalty Goal:* S Jones

Referee A Lewis (Ireland)

All Black hooker Keven Mealamu is tackled by Mark Jones during New Zealand's record 55-3 win against Wales in Hamilton in June.

France to Argentina & New Zealand 2003

Tour party

Full-backs: C Poitrenaud (Stade Toulousain), P Elhorga (SU Agen)

Threequarters: V Clerc (Stade Toulousain), C Dominici (Stade Français), A Rougerie (AS Montferrand), Y Jauzion (Stade Toulousain), T Castaignède (Saracens, Eng), D Traille (Section Pau)

Half-backs: Y Delaigue (Stade Toulousain), G Merceron (AS Montferrand)*, F Michalak (Stade Toulousain), F Galthié (Stade Français) (*captain*)

Forwards: J-B Rué (SU Agen), Y Bru (Stade Toulousain), S Marconnet (Stade Français), P de Villiers (Stade Français), O Milloud (Bourgoin-Jallieu), N Mas (USA Perpignan), D Auradou (Stade Français), L Nallet (Bourgoin-Jallieu), J Thion (USA Perpignan), I Harinordoquy (Section Pau), S Chabal (Bourgoin-Jallieu), J Bouilhou (Stade Toulousain), E Vermeulen (AS Montferrand), P Tabacco (Stade Français), C Labit (Stade Toulousain)

Manager: J Maso **Coach:** B Laporte

* Replacement on tour

Tour record P 3 L 3 For 61 Against 74

14 June Lost 6-10 v ARGENTINA (Buenos Aires)

20 June Lost 32-33 v ARGENTINA (Buenos Aires)

28 June Lost 23-31 v NEW ZEALAND (Christchurch)

Tour details

First Test Match 14 June, Vélez Sarsfield Stadium, Buenos Aires
Argentina 10 (1G 1PG) **France 6** (2PG)

Argentina: I Corleto; J-M Nuñez-Piossek, M Contepomi, L Arbizu (*captain*), D Albanese; F Contepomi, N Fernandez Miranda; M Reggiardo, M E Ledesma, M Scelzo, C I Fernandez Lobbe, P Albacete, S Phelan, G Longo, L Ostiglia *Substitutions:* P L Sporleder for Fernandez Lobbe (54 mins); J-M Hernandez for Corleto (57 mins); S Gonzalez Bonarino for Scelzo (61 mins); F E Mendez for Ledesma (80 mins)

Scorers *Try:* Nuñez-Piossek *Conversion:* F Contepomi *Penalty Goal:* F Contepomi

France: C Poitrenaud; A Rougerie, T Castaignède, D Traille, C Dominici; Y Delaigue, F Galthié (*captain*); O Milloud, J-B Rué, P de Villiers, D Auradou, J Thion, J Bouilhou, C Labit, P Tabacco *Substitutions:* S Marconnet for Milloud (temp 31-33 mins & 71 mins); I Harinordoquy for Bouilhou (70 mins)

Scorers *Penalty Goals:* Traille, Delaigue

Referee S J Lander (England)

Second Test Match 20 June, Vélez Sarsfield Stadium, Buenos Aires
Argentina 33 (1G 5PG 2DG 1T) **France 32** (2G 6PG)

Argentina: J M Hernandez; H Senillosa, J Orengo, L Arbizu (*captain*), D Albanese; G Quesada, N Fernandez Miranda; R D Grau, F E Mendez, M Scelzo, C I Fernandez Lobbe, R Alvarez, S Phelan, L Ostiglia, R A Martin

Substitutions: B M Stortoni for Hernandez (51 mins); F Contepomi for Arbizu (55 mins)

Scorers *Tries:* Hernandez, Orengo *Conversion:* Quesada *Penalty Goals:* Quesada (5) *Dropped Goals:* Arbizu, Quesada

France: P Elhorga; A Rougerie, Y Jauzion, D Traille, V Clerc; Y Delaigue, F Galthié (*captain*); S Marconnet, Y Bru, P de Villiers, D Auradou, J Thion, I Harinordoquy, C Labit, S Chabal *Substitutions:* F Michalak for Delaigue (28 mins); J-B Rué for Bru (79 mins)

Scorers *Tries:* Jauzion, Elhorga *Conversions:* Michalak (2) *Penalty Goals:* Michalak (3), Delaigue (2), Traille

Referee A Cole (Australia)

Test Match 28 June, Jade Stadium, Lancaster Park, Christchurch
New Zealand 31 (2G 4PG 1T) France 23 (2G 2PG 1DG)

New Zealand: M Muliaina; D C Howlett, J F Umaga, D W Carter, J T Rokocoko; C J Spencer, S J Devine; D N Hewett, A D Oliver, G M Somerville, C R Jack, A J Williams, R D Thorne (*captain*), J Collins, R H McCaw *Substitutions:* K F Mealamu for Oliver (53 mins); B C Thorn for Williams (55 mins); B T Kelleher for Devine (60 mins); K J Meeuws for Hewett (64 mins); M R Holah for Collins (77 mins)

Scorers *Tries:* Rokocoko (3) *Conversions:* Carter (2) *Penalty Goals:* Carter (4)

France: C Poitrenaud; A Rougerie, Y Jauzion, D Traille, V Clerc; F Michalak, F Galthié (*captain*); S Marconnet, Y Bru, N Mas, L Nallet, J Thion, I Harinordoquy, E Vermeulen, P Tabacco *Substitutions:* P de Villiers for Mas (10 mins); S Chabal for Harinordoquy (39 mins); D Auradou for Nallet (49 mins); C Labit for Vermeulen (52 mins); G Merceron for Michalak (temp 49 to 52 mins and 64 mins); P Elhorga for Clerc (80 mins)

Scorers *Tries:* Marconnet, Jauzion *Conversions:* Michalak, Merceron *Penalty Goals:* Michalak, Traille *Dropped Goal:* Michalak

Referee A J Watson (South Africa)

Argentina to South Africa 2003

Tour party

Full-backs: B M Stortoni (RC Narbonne, Fra), J-M Hernandez (Deportivo Francesa)

Threequarters: D Albanese (Leeds Tykes, Eng), O Bartolucci (Atletico del Rosario), J-M Nuñez-Piossek (Huirapuca), M Contepomi (Newman), M Gaitan (Biarritz Olympique, Fra), J Orengo (Grenoble, Fra), H Senillosa (Hindu)

Half-backs: G Quesada (AS Beziers, Fra), F Contepomi (Bristol Shoguns, Eng), J Fernandez Miranda (Hindu), N Fernandez Miranda (Hindu), M Albina (Los Tilos)

Forwards: F E Mendez (Mendoza RC), M E Ledesma (RC Narbonne, Fra), S Gonzalez Bonarino (AS Béziers, Fra), R D Grau (Liceo), M Reggiardo (Castres Olympique, Fra), R Roncero (Gloucester, Eng), M Scelzo (RC Narbonne, Fra), P Albacete (Manuel Belrano), R Alvarez (USA Perpignan, Fra), C I Fernandez Lobbe (Castres Olympique, Fra), P L Sporleder (Curupayti), P Bouza (Duendes),

G Longo (RC Narbonne, Fra), R A Martin (SIC), L Ostiglia (Hindu), S Phelan (CASI), S Sanz (CASI)

Manager: A Coscia **Coaches:** M Loffreda, D Baetti

Tour record P 2 D 1 L 1 For 55 Against 56

25 June Drew 30-30 v South Africa A (Wellington)

28 June Lost 25-26 v SOUTH AFRICA (Port Elizabeth)

Tour details

25 June, Boland Stadium, Wellington
South Africa A 30 (3G 3PG) **Argentine XV 30** (3G 2PG 1DG)

South Africa A scorers *Tries:* Snyman (2), Sowerby *Conversions:* Delport (2), James *Penalty Goals:* Delport (3)

Argentine XV scorers *Tries:* Gaitan (2), Nuñez-Piossek *Conversions:* J Fernandez Miranda (3) *Penalty Goals:* J Fernandez Miranda (2) *Dropped Goal:* J Fernandez Miranda

Test Match 28 June, EPRFU Stadium, Port Elizabeth
South Africa 26 (2G 4PG) **Argentina 25** (2G 2PG 1T)

South Africa: J N B van der Westhuyzen; C S Terblanche, M C Joubert, G Bobo, P W G Rossouw; L J Koen, C D Davidson; R B Kempson, D Coetzee, I J Visagie, Q Davids, V Matfield, C P J Krigé (*captain*), P J Wannenburg, A J Venter *Substitutions:* R E Bands for Visagie (52 mins); C S Boome for Davids (57 mins); R B Skinstad for A J Venter (69 mins); R B Russell for Rossouw (72 mins)

Scorers *Tries:* Coetzee, Russell *Conversions:* Koen (2) *Penalty Goals:* Koen (4)

Argentina: J-M Hernandez; J-M Nuñez-Piossek, J Orengo, F Contepomi, D Albanese; G Quesada, N Fernandez Miranda; R D Grau, M E Ledesma, M Reggiardo, C I Fernandez Lobbe, R Alvarez, L Ostiglia, G Longo (*captain*), R A Martin *Substitutions:* S Gonzalez Bonorino for Reggiardo (41 mins); P Albacete for Fernandez Lobbe (48 mins); F E Mendez & S Phelan for Ledesma & Ostiglia (72 mins); H Senillosa for Nuñez-Piossek (78 mins); M Reggiardo for Ledesma (79 mins)

Scorers *Tries:* Hernandez, Nuñez-Piossek, F Contepomi *Conversions:* Quesada (2) *Penalty Goals:* Quesada (2)

Referee N Williams (Wales)

Fiji to New Zealand & South America 2003

Tour party

Full backs: A Uluinayau (Suntory, Jap), N Ligairi (Southland, NZ)

Threequarters: S Leawere (Navosa), M Vunibaka (Canterbury, NZ), V Delasau (Yamaha, Jap), S Rokini (Stade Montois, Fra), E Ruivadra (Tailevu), S Rabeni (Otago, NZ), A Tuilevu (Otago, NZ), R Caucau (Auckland, NZ), I Mow (Suva)

Half-backs: M Rauluni (Easts, Brisbane, Aus), S Rabaka (Nadi), N Little (Saracens, Eng), W Serevi (Stade Montois, Fra)

Forwards: G Smith (Waikato, NZ), V Gadolo (Suva), I Rasila (Nadroga) R Nyholt (Queensland University, Aus), J Veitayaki (Northland, NZ), P Biu (Nadroga), N Seru (Suva), E Katalau (Narberth, Wal), A Naevo (Northland, NZ), K Leawere (East Coast, NZ), I Rawaqa (Lautoka), S Koyamaibole (Nadroga), K Salawa (Nadi), A Doviverata (Yamaha, Jap) (*captain*), K Sewabu (Yamaha, Jap), A Mocelutu (Neath, Wal), S Tawake (Hino, Jap), V Maimuri (Auckland, NZ)

Tour record P 7 W 6 L 1 For 300 Against 147

3 August Won 46-17 v Canterbury Development XV (Christchurch)

6 August Won 41-38 v Canterbury (Christchurch)

9 August Won 75-12 v Marlborough (Blenheim)

13 August Won 24-3 v Uruguay XV (Montevideo)

18 August Lost 30-49 v ARGENTINA (Cordoba)

22 August Won 43-12 v Salta Selection (Salta)

24 August Won 41-16 v CHILE (Santiago)

Tour details

3 August, Rugby Park, Christchurch
Canterbury Development XV 17 (2G 1PG) Fiji XV 46 (5G 2PG 1T)

Canterbury Development XV scorers *Tries:* Luamanuvae, Roberts *Conversions:* Roberts (2) *Penalty Goal:* Roberts

Fiji XV scorers *Tries:* Ruivadra (2), Veitayaki, Rabaka, S Leawere, Sewabu *Conversions:* Little (3), Serevi (2) *Penalty Goals:* Little, Serevi

6 August, Jade Stadium, Christchurch
Canterbury 38 (1G 7PG 2T) Fiji XV 41 (5G 1PG 1DG)

Canterbury scorers *Tries:* Johnstone, Pupuailei, Blair *Conversion:* Mehrtens *Penalty Goals:* Mehrtens (7)

Fiji XV scorers *Tries:* Rabeni (3), Delasau, Vunibaka *Conversions:* Little (5) *Penalty Goal:* Little *Dropped Goal:* Little

9 August, Lansdowne Park, Blenheim
Marlborough 12 (1G 1T) Fiji XV 75 (10G 1T)

Marlborough scorers *Tries:* Campbell, Stewart *Conversion:* Dixon

Fiji XV scorers *Tries:* K Leawere (3), Vunibaka, Ruivadra, Rawaqa, Mocelutu, Rasila, Koyamaibole, Delasau, S Leawere *Conversions:* Serevi (10)

13 August, Luis Franzini Stadium, Montevideo
Uruguay XV 3 (1PG) Fiji XV 24 (3G 1PG)

Uruguay XV scorer *Penalty Goal:* Menchaca

Fiji XV scorers *Tries:* Ruivadra, Sewabu, Vunibaka *Conversions:* Little (3) *Penalty Goal:* Little

18 August, Cordoba Stadium, Cordoba
Argentina 49 (4G 2PG 3T) Fiji 30 (3G 3PG)

Argentina: B M Stortoni; H Senillosa, M Contepomi, M Gaitan, I Corleto; J Fernandez Miranda, M Albina; R Roncero, F Mendez, M Scelzo, M Sambucetti, R Alvarez, S Phelan, G Longo (*captain*), M Schusterman *Substitutions:* M Reggiardo for Scelzo (57 mins); P L Sporleder for Alvarez (63 mins); M Durand & M Ledesma for Phelan & Roncero (68 mins)

Scorers *Tries:* Scelzo (2), Roncero (2), Stortoni, J Fernandez Miranda, Durand *Conversions:* J Fernandez Miranda (4) *Penalty Goals:* J Fernandez Miranda (2)

Fiji: N Ligairi; S Leawere, A Tuilevu, S Rabeni, R Caucau; N Little, M Rauluni; R Nyholt, V Gadolo, J Veitayaki, E Katalau (*captain*), K Leawere, S Koyamaibole, A Mocelutu, K Salawa *Substitutions:* I Rawaqa for Katalau (40 mins); V Maimuri for Mocelutu (52 mins); I Rasila for Gadolo (55 mins); K Sewabu for Salawa (65 mins); N Seru for Maimuri (73 mins); W Serevi for Little (75 mins)

Scorers *Tries:* Koyamaibole, Tuilevu, Caucau *Conversions:* Little (2), Serevi *Penalty Goals:* Little (3)

Referee C White (England)

22 August, Salta
Salta Selection 12 (1G 1T) Fiji XV 43 (4G 3T)

Salta Selection scorers *Tries:* Fleming, Caro *Conversion:* R Moreno

Fiji XV scorers *Tries:* Caucau (4), Sewabu, Little, Rawaqa *Conversions:* Serevi (4)

24 August, Prince of Wales Club, Santiago
Chile 16 (1G 3PG) Fiji 41 (3G 4T)

Chile: R Infante; P Llorens, S Pizarro, B Echeverria, C Berti; C Gonzalez (*captain*), J Pizarro; C Iga, S Bossans, E Jouannet, S Valdes, N Leonicio, A Palacios, E Olfos, C Westerneck *Substitutions:* J Seron for Infante; T Platowsky for Echeverria; P Marsalli for Leonicio; J-P Gonzalez for Palacios; R Laccasie for Bossans; Gajardo for Iga

Scorers *Try:* S Pizarro *Conversion:* C Gonzalez *Penalty Goals:* C Gonzalez (3)

Fiji: N Ligairi; S Leawere, S Rokini, S Rabeni, R Caucau; N Little, M Rauluni; R Nyholt, V Gadolo, J Veitayaki, I Rawaqa, K Leawere, S Koyamaibole, A Mocelutu (*captain*), K Salawa *Substitutions:* W Serevi for Ligairi; S Tawake for Mocelutu; P Biu for Tawake; N Seru for Veityaki; I Rasila for Gadolo

Scorers *Tries:* Caucau (4), Rabeni, S Leawere, penalty try *Conversions:* Serevi (2), Little

Referee S Slinger (Uruguay)

Samoa to New Zealand, Australia & Southern Africa 2003

Tour Party

Full-backs: F Fili, R Robertson, T Vili

Three quarters: L Fa'atau, T Fanolua, R Fanuatanu, D Feaunati, B P Lima, D A Rasmussen, E Seveali'i, S Tagicakibau, F Tuilagi

Five-eighths: G Elisara, V Tuigamala, E Va'a

Half-backs: S So'oialo, D Tyrell

Forwards: M Fa'asavalu, J Paramore, P Petaia, P Segi, S Sititi (*captain*), P Tapelu, D Tuiavi'i, K Viliamu, N George, S F Lafaiali'i, O Palepoi, M von Dincklage, K Lealamanua, T Leupolu, M Luafalealo, F Pala'amo, J Tomuli, T Leota, J Meredith, M Schwalger

Manager: K Tu'uau **Coach:** J W Boe **Assistant Coach:** M N Jones

Tour record P 9 W 5 L 4 For 311 Against 280

31 May Won 30-27 v NZ Divisional XV (Pukekohe)

12 June Won 48-41 v New South Wales (Sydney)

15 June Lost 42-43 v Queensland (Brisbane)

2 July Lost 45-51 v Cheetahs (Bloemfontein)

5 July Won 34-32 v Golden Lions (Johannesburg)

8 July Lost 29-35 v Pumas (Secunda)

12 July Won 40-13 v NAMIBIA (Windhoek)

2 August Won 27-17 v Northland (Whangarei)

8 August Lost 16-21 v Auckland (Auckland)

Tour details

31 May, Pukekohe
NZ Divisional XV 27 (1G 5PG 1T) Samoa XV 30 (2G 2PG 2T)

NZ Divisional XV scorers *Tries:* Trigg, Ngarimu *Conversion:* Manawatu *Penalty Goals:* Manawatu (5)

Samoa XV scorers *Tries:* Rasmussen, Viliamu, Fa'asavalu, Vili *Conversions:* Va'a (2) *Penalty Goals:* Va'a (2)

12 June, Sydney
New South Wales 41 (4G 1PG 2T) Samoa XV 48 (5G 1DG 2T)

New South Wales scorers *Tries:* Berne (3), Freier, Sheedy, Tapuai *Conversions:* Berne (4) *Penalty Goal:* Berne

Samoa XV scorers *Tries:* Va'a, Fanuatanu, Lima, Fa'atau, Meredith, Vili, Leota *Conversions:* Fili (3), Vili, Va'a *Dropped Goal:* Fili

15 June, Brisbane
Queensland 43 (2G 3PG 4T) Samoa XV 42 (3G 2PG 3T)

Queensland scorers *Tries:* McIsaac, McVerry, Panoho, Cockbain, Hoo, Huxley *Conversions:* J Huxley (2) *Penalty Goals:* J Huxley (3)

Samoa XV scorers *Tries:* Fa'asavalu (2), Viliamu (2), Lima, Fa'atau *Conversions:* Fili (3) *Penalty Goals:* Fili (2)

2 July, Bloemfontein
Cheetahs 51 (5G 2PG 2T) **Samoa XV 45** (5G 2T)

Cheetahs scorers *Tries:* Du Plooy (2), Hendriks, Tsimba, Steenkamp, Lombard, Britz *Conversions:* Tsimba (5) *Penalty Goals:* Tsimba (2)

Samoa XV scorers *Tries:* Fanuatanu (2), Feaunati (2), Viliamu, Rasmussen, Meredith

Conversions: Va'a (5)

5 July, Johannesburg
Golden Lions 32 (3G 2PG 1T) **Samoa XV 34** (3G 1PG 2T)

Golden Lions scorers *Tries:* Van Niekerk, Fourie, Daniels, penalty try

Conversions: Fourie (2), Van Rensburg *Penalty Goals:* Fourie, Van Rensburg

Samoa XV scorers *Tries:* Fanolua (2), Sititi, Lima, Palepoi *Conversions:* Va'a (3)

Penalty Goal: Tyrell.

8 July, Witbank
Pumas 35 (3G 2PG 1DG 1T) **Samoa XV 29** (3G 1PG 1T)

Pumas scorers *Tries:* Schoeman (2), Saayman, Van Zyl

Conversions: Goosen (3) *Penalty Goals:* Goosen, Steyn *Dropped Goal:* Bartle

Samoa XV scorers *Tries:* Tagicakibau (2), Sititi, Lima *Conversions:* Va'a (3) *Penalty Goal:* Va'a

12 July, National Rugby Stadium, Windhoek
Namibia 18 (1G 2PG 1T) **Samoa 40** (3G 3PG 2T)

Samoa: F Fili; S Tagicakibau, T Fanolua, B P Lima, D Feaunati; E Va'a, S So'oialo; K Lealamanua, J Meredith, J Tomuli, O Palepoi, S F Lafaiali'i, D Tuiavai'i, S Sititi (*captain*), M Fa'asavalu *Substitutions:* D Tyrell for So'oialo; M Schwalger for Meredith; T Leupolu for Tomuli; P Petia for Tuiavai'i; D Rasmussen for Lima

Scorers *Tries:* Feaunati (3), Lima, Tagicakibau *Conversions:* Va'a (3) *Penalty Goals:* Va'a (3)

2 August, Whangarei
Northland 17 (1G 2T) **Samoa XV 27** (3G 2PG)

Northland scorers *Tries:* Naufahu, Storey, Lasagavibau *Conversion:* Peina

Samoa XV scorers *Tries:* Fanuatanu, Meredith, So'oialo *Conversions:* Va'a (3)

Penalty Goals: Va'a (2)

8 August, Auckland
Auckland 21 (1G 3PG 1T) **Samoa XV 16** (2PG 2T)

Auckland scorers *Tries:* Tanivula, Koonwaiyou *Conversion:* Ward *Penalty Goals:* Ward (3)

Samoa XV *Tries:* Lima, Tomuli *Penalty Goals:* Va'a, Vili

THE EUROPEAN NATIONS TOURNAMENT 2002-03

Portugal to the Fore

Chris Thau

As predicted in these pages, the Portuguese 'Lobos' have continued to grow into one of Continental Europe's powerhouses, defying the comparatively low status of the game in the country and its small constituency. At the end of the 2003 season, plucky Portugal were leading the table of the European Nations Cup (ENC), commonly referred to as Six Nations B, with an enviable played five, won five record – a clear statement about their talent, passion and, of course, expertise.

The only low note of this rather spectacular ascent is the fact that the team ably coached by Tomas Morais could not be crowned as Champions of Continental Europe, because the FIRA-AER regulations state that the ENC is held home and away over two years, with the Cup being awarded every other year. While this may be understandable from a sporting point of view, it does nothing to help the promotion of an event which unfortunately doesn't enjoy the status and exposure it deserves.

However, this unexpected and thoroughly welcome Portuguese winning sequence has enlivened a competition dominated in the past two years by the two Eastern European heavyweights Romania and Georgia. And as an old observer of the Continental scene pointed out, the quality and consistency of the Portuguese performance were probably as significant as the collection of scalps in itself.

In a season disrupted by severe weather, it was Portugal's first win over Georgia, who fielded most of its French professionals, and a rare success against the 'Oaks' of Romania that confirmed the steady progress of the 'Lobos' into a forceful outfit. It will be interesting to see whether the Portuguese maintain the momentum next season, when they will play most of their matches away from home.

It is true that the Romanians, who should have hosted the match in the Black Sea city of Constanta, agreed to play the match in Portugal, owing to the freezing weather conditions back home. But this had no real impact on the outcome of the match – a well-deserved Portuguese win, described by an inspired local pundit as David beating Goliath. The significantly bigger Romanian pack could find no answer to Portugal's bewildering brand of hit-and-run tactics.

To their credit the Romanians, unable to vary their game when confronted with the Portuguese array of commando tactics, did not seek excuses for their defeat and gave coach Morais and his admirable team credit for their gallant challenge. Portugal played intelligent, modern rugby and several of their players showed that they could hold their own in any company, something which may have come to the attention of the talent scouts of the professional clubs in search of new and cheaper talent.

Russia, still sore after their exclusion from the RWC for fielding several ineligible South African players, tried to prove a point by demolishing Spain 52-19 in the first match of their ENC campaign. But the 'winter Russian offensive' soon fizzled out. While some of their officials kept making bewildering statements about the seemingly sinister reasons behind Russia's expulsion from the RWC, the Bears were soundly beaten at home, first by arch-opponents Georgia then by Portugal, whose fly-half Goncalo Malheiro was in top form and inflicted most of the damage. Two further defeats away, at the hands of Romania in Bucharest and in Prague against the Czech Republic, who made great progress in their first year in the ENC, left Russia just one place above Spain at the bottom of the table.

Portugal's emphatic 43-10 win over the Czech Republic in round three was the first match for the Czechs after the postponement of their fixtures against Romania and Russia owing to freezing conditions in Prague. The Czechs recovered their composure after a drubbing at the hands of the Georgians in Prague and managed a spectacular and satisfying 40-38 win over Spain in Madrid, followed by an equally satisfying 27-13 win in Prague over the Russians, who were without their French professionals Sergei Sergeev, Vladimir Grachev and Konstantin Ratchkov. The Czechs were prepared by their veteran coach Jiri Stasny, helped by Frenchman Michel Bernardin and Jan Machacek, who was still playing at No 8.

Georgia, after their success in reaching the finals of the RWC for the first time, had a mixed year by their standards, but their win over Russia in Krasnodar compensated for the indignity of losing in Lisbon. The Romanians, under their new French coach Bernard Charreyre, seemed to have sorted out their priorities after the Portuguese accident and finished the season in style with wins over Russia, Georgia and by a record 42-5 score against the Czechs in Prague.

Results and scorers 2003

16 February in Palma

Spain 19 (*Try:* penalty try *Conversion:* M Cascara *Penalty Goals:* M Cascara 4) **Russia 52** (*Tries:* A Sergeev, S Sergeev, V Grachev, A Kouzin, V Fedchenko *Conversions:* K Rachkov 3 *Penalty Goals:* K Rachkov 6 *Dropped Goal:* K Rachkov) **Referee** D Pruvot (France)

16 February in Lisbon

Portugal 34 (*Tries:* Diogo Mateus, David Mateus, P Gonçalves *Conversions:* G Malheiro 2 *Penalty Goals:* G Malheiro 5) **Georgia 30** (*Tries:* V Katsadze 2, I Abusseridze, I Zedguinidze *Converions:* P Jimsheladze 2 *Penalty Goal:* P Jimsheladze *Dropped Goal:* P Jimsheladze) **Referee** N Owens (Wales)

22 February in Tbilisi

Georgia 34 (*Tries:* B Khekhelashvili, M Urjukashvili, G Yachvili, S Nikolaenko, I Gundishvili *Conversions:* P Jimsheladze 3 *Penalty Goal:* P Jimsheladze) **Spain 3** (*Penalty Goal:* M Cascara) **Referee** G Doyle (Ireland)

22 February in Lisbon

Portugal 16 (*Try:* N Garvão *Conversion:* G Malheiro *Penalty Goals:* G Malheiro 2 *Dropped Goal:* M Tomé) **Romania 15** (*Tries:* M Tincu, A Manta *Conversion:* I Tofan *Penalty Goal:* I Tofan) **Referee** B Gabbei (Germany)

8 March in Krasnodar

Russia 17 (*Try:* S Sergeev *Penalty Goals:* K Rachkov 2 *Dropped Goals:* K Rachkov 2) **Georgia 23** (*Try:* P Jimsheladze *Penalty Goals:* P Jimsheladze 6) **Referee** G Morandin (Italy)

8 March in Lisbon

Portugal 43 (*Tries:* G Malheiro 2, Diogo Mateus, David Mateus, M Frederico Nunes *Conversions:* M Tomé 2, G Malheiro *Penalty Goals:* G Malheiro 4) **Czech Republic 10** (*Try:* Z Žák *Conversion:* T Krejèí *Penalty Goal:* T Krejèí) **Referee** S Mallon (The Netherlands)

9 March in Madrid

Spain 6 (*Penalty Goal:* F Díez *Dropped Goal:* F Velazco) **Romania 31** (*Tries:* A Petrichei, I Tofan, S Socol *Conversions:* I Tofan 2 *Penalty Goals:* I Tofan 4) **Referee** A Lombardi (Italy)

22 March in Bucharest

Romania 23 (*Tries:* M Vioreanu, A Petrache, penalty try *Conversion:* I Tofan *Penalty Goals:* I Tofan 2) **Russia 12** (*Penalty Goals:* K Rachkov 4) **Referee** D Dartigeas (France)

22 March in Prague

Czech Republic 15 (*Penalty Goals:* M Kafka 4 *Dropped Goal:* M Kafka) **Georgia 30** (*Tries:* I Zedguinidze, G Schvelidze, B Khamashuridze, G Labadze, T Zibzibadze, *Conversion:* P Jimsheladze *Penalty Goal:* P Jimsheladze) **Referee** C Damasco (Italy)

23 March in Coimbra

Portugal 35 (*Tries:* F Sousa, A Cunha *Conversions:* G Malheiro 2 *Penalty Goals:* G Malheiro 5 *Dropped Goals:* G Malheiro 2) **Spain 16** (*Try:* S Tuineau *Conversion:* M Cascara *Penalty Goals:* M Cascara 2 *Dropped Goal:* A Kovalenco) **Referee** J-L Rebollal (France)

29 March in Krasnodar

Russia 14 (*Try:* I Dymchenko *Penalty Goals:* D Akulov 3) **Portugal 25** (*Try:* A Cunha *Conversion:* G Malheiro *Penalty Goals:* G Malheiro 5 *Dropped Goal:* G Malheiro) **Referee** M Parachivescu (Romania)

30 March in Tbilisi

Georgia 6 (*Penalty Goals:* P Jimsheladze 2) **Romania 19** (*Tries:* V Maftei, G Brezoianu, R Gontineac *Conversions:* I Tofan 2) **Referee** D Gillet (France)

30 March in Madrid

Spain 38 (*Tries:* S Loubsens, A Beltrán, M Cascara, D Zarzosa, D Monreal *Conversions:* M Cascara 2 *Penalty Goals:* M Cascara 3) **Czech Republic 40** (*Tries:* P Štastný, P Syrový, J Rohlík, R Šuster *Conversions:* M Kafka 4 *Penalty Goals:* M Kafka 4) **Referee** J Shauder (Israel)

14 June in Prague

Czech Republic 27 (*Tries:* P Èamrda, M Pekárek, J Rohlík *Conversions:* M Kafka 3 *Penalty Goals:* M Kafka 2) **Russia 13** (*Try:* A Lubkov *Conversion:* K Rachkov *Penalty Goals:* K Rachkov 2) **Referee** M Dordolo (Italy)

22 June in Prague

Czech Republic 5 (*Try:* P Štastný) **Romania 42** (*Tries:* C Sauan, G Brezoianu, I Tofan, C Popescu, V Ghioc *Conversions:* D Dumbrava 4 *Penalty Goals:* D Dumbrava 3) **Referee** D Pearson (England)

Final Division 1 European Nations Cup Table For 2003

	P	*W*	*D*	*L*	*For*	*Against*	*Pts*
Portugal	5	5	0	0	153	85	15
Romania	5	4	0	1	130	45	13
Georgia	5	3	0	2	123	88	11
Czech Republic	5	2	0	3	97	166	9
Russia	5	1	0	4	108	117	7
Spain	5	0	0	5	82	192	5

Three points for a win, two for a draw and one for a defeat

Previous European Nations Cup Winners: 1999-2000 Romania; 2000-01 Georgia (leaders at half-way stage); 2001-02 Romania (winners over the home-and-away two-year tournament); 2002-03 Portugal (leaders at half-way stage)

In the A section of the second division, the so-called European Nations Plate (ENP), the competition was equally exciting with Ukraine and Germany in contention for the elusive promotion slot before the second leg of matches take place next year. Poland and the Netherlands stayed in contention, but the East Europeans, who host Germany and the Netherlands next year, emerged as favourites for promotion.

In the B section of the division, Switzerland headed the table, but Croatia and Denmark were just one point behind and must view with optimism their chances for promotion next year. Paradoxically Belgium, despite a very poor season, might become the pool's powerbroker. Although without a win after four matches, the Belgians have both the ability and the resources to upset matters, hosting both Croatia and Switzerland in Brussels in 2003-04.

Further down the pyramid in Division 3, Latvia led the table in pool A with Moldova and Hungary in pursuit, while in pool B, unbeaten Malta led the table. The matches in Pool C of Division 3 involving Israel, Finland, Bulgaria and Norway were played in Palma de Majorca with the four teams playing two matches each. Bulgaria beat Israel 25-23 in the final.

Division 2 Pool A Results 2002-03

Sweden 7, Poland 14 (Lund); Ukraine 20, Poland 11 (Kiev); Germany 26, Ukraine 26 (Heidelberg); Germany 15, The Netherlands 3 (Hanover); Poland 15, Germany 37 (Gdynia); The Netherlands 18, Ukraine 24 (Amsterdam); Sweden 16, Germany 24 (Trelleborg); The Netherlands 39, Sweden 26 (Amsterdam); Poland 13, The Netherlands 13 (Gdynia); Ukraine 37, Sweden 0 (Kiev)

Final Division 2 Pool A Table For 2002-03

	P	*W*	*D*	*L*	*For*	*Against*	*Pts*
Ukraine	4	3	1	0	107	55	11
Germany	4	3	1	0	102	60	11
The Netherlands	4	1	1	2	73	78	7
Poland	4	1	1	2	53	77	7
Sweden	4	0	0	4	49	114	4

Three points for a win, two for a draw and one for a defeat

Division 2 Pool B Results 2002-03

Croatia 13, Slovenia 0 (Zagreb); Denmark 13, Switzerland 13 (Copenhagen); Slovenia 10, Denmark 13 (Ljubljana); Croatia 33, Belgium 12 (Sisak); Switzerland 24, Croatia 15 (Geneva); Switzerland 9, Belgium 6 (Basle); Belgium 24, Slovenia 32 (Liege); Belgium 6, Denmark 6 (Brussels); Denmark 8, Croatia 8 (Copenhagen); Slovenia 23, Switzerland 23 (Ljubljana)

Final Division 2 Pool B Table For 2002-03

	P	*W*	*D*	*L*	*For*	*Against*	*Pts*
Switzerland	4	2	2	0	69	57	10
Croatia	4	2	1	1	69	44	9
Denmark	4	1	3	0	40	37	9
Slovenia	4	1	1	2	65	73	7
Belgium	4	0	1	3	48	80	5

Three points for a win, two for a draw and one for a defeat

Division 3 Pool A Results 2002-03

Latvia 26, Hungary 5; Hungary 47, Serbia Montenegro 23; Latvia 43, Moldavia 0; Serbia Montenegro 18, Latvia 29; Moldavia 47, Hungary 11; Moldavia 17, Serbia Montenegro 17

Final Division 3 Pool A Table For 2002-03

	P	*W*	*D*	*L*	*For*	*Against*	*Pts*
Latvia	3	3	0	0	98	23	9
Moldavia	3	1	1	1	64	71	6
Hungary	3	1	0	2	63	96	5
Serbia Montenegro	3	0	1	2	58	93	4

Three points for a win, two for a draw and one for a defeat

Division 3 Pool B Results 2002-03

Lithuania 32, Austria 10; Luxembourg 21, Bosnia 5; Malta 22, Lithuania 18; Austria 16, Malta 25; Malta 34, Luxembourg 6; Bosnia 14, Malta 20; Luxembourg 25, Austria 14; Lithuania 60, Luxembourg 6; Bosnia 15, Lithuania 37; Austria 25, Bosnia 6

Final Division 3 Pool B Table For 2002-03

	P	*W*	*D*	*L*	*For*	*Against*	*Pts*
Malta	4	4	0	0	101	54	12
Lithuania	4	3	0	1	147	53	10
Luxembourg	4	2	0	2	58	113	8
Austria	4	1	0	3	65	88	6
Bosnia	4	0	0	4	40	103	4

Three points for a win, two for a draw and one for a defeat

Division 3 Pool C Results 2002-03

Semi-finals: Bulgaria 42, Finland 3; Israel 30, Norway 13;

Third/fourth place play-off: Norway 55, Finland 20

FINAL: Bulgaria 25, Israel 23

PAN AMERICAN TOURNAMENT 2003

Argentina Maintain their Impressive 100% Record

Frankie Deges & John Griffiths

The Pan American Rugby Association (PARA) tournament, conceived in 1994 and launched in 1995, has been staged regularly to advance the international game in the Americas. Canada, Uruguay, the United States and Argentina take part in a round-robin that lasts a week, one of the participating Unions hosting the event. To date the competition has been the exclusive domain of Argentina, who retained their 100% winning record in the fifth series that was staged in Buenos Aires in late August 2003.

In a tournament that doubled up conveniently as a World Cup warm-up stage for the four American nations, Los Pumas again swept aside the best that the United States, Uruguay or Canada could offer and won each of their three matches in the round-robin competition by handsome margins. The US Eagles, a team that had significantly improved since winning the final Repechage spot for the RWC finals, were defeated 42-8, while Uruguay took a 57-0 beating and Canada, in Los Pumas' best performance of the season, were trounced 62–22 on the final weekend, Argentina scoring nine tries in the process.

The Eagles' mid-week victory over Canada – their second of 2003 against the Canucks – put them in contention for the runners-up position. The 31-17 win against Uruguay on the final day of the competition consolidated that place after outside-half Mike Hercus gave a polished display of goal kicking. His match-winning haul of 16 points comprised a drop goal, two conversions and three penalty goals.

Results

23 August: Uruguay 11, Canada 21; Argentina 42, United States 8; **27 August** Argentina 57, Uruguay 0; United States 35, Canada 20; **30 August** Argentina 62, Canada 22; United States 31, Uruguay 17

Pan American Tournament 2003: Final Table

	P	*W*	*D*	*L*	*F*	*A*	*Pts*
Argentina	3	3	0	0	161	30	9
United States	3	2	0	1	74	79	6
Canada	3	1	0	2	63	108	3
Uruguay	3	0	0	3	28	109	0

Points: win 3; draw 1; defeat 0

Previous winners: 1995 Argentina; 1996 Argentina; 1998 Argentina; 2001 Argentina; 2003 Argentina

SUPERPOWERS CUP 2003

Russians Win Race to Superpowers Title

John Griffiths

If Rugby Union is to become a credible global sport like soccer then its profile in the relatively untapped markets of North America and Asia urgently needs to be raised. It is a development that ranks high on the IRB's list of priorities, and the launch of the Superpowers Cup in May 2003 was seen as an important step on the Board's gospel-spreading road.

One of the late Vernon Pugh's last missions was the encouragement of the expansion of the game in the People's Republic of China. The institution of the Four Nations Superpowers Cup was intended to assist the development of Chinese rugby through regular contact with the United States, Russia and Japan.

For this inaugural tournament, however, the SARS epidemic that hit South-Eastern Asia caused the Chinese to withdraw, leaving the three remaining superpowers to fit three Test matches into their already busy schedules.

The tournament kicked off in San Francisco when old rivals Japan and the United States met. The rugby rivalry between them dates from 1985 and this was their 15th meeting. On this occasion the Eagles were dominant, breaking a 17-all interval deadlock to run in eight second-half tries on their way to a landslide victory.

A week later at home in the Prince Chichibu Stadium the Japanese suffered their second defeat when the Russian forwards dominated the tight and the loose to lay the foundations for a convincing win. Toru Kurihara gave the home side an early lead with a 10th-minute penalty and the scores were level at 13-all until right-wing Iaroslav Retchnev crossed on the stroke of half-time to give the Russians an 18-13 lead.

The Japanese caved in during the second half, conceding early tries to Viktor Motorin and Alexei Sarychev and 15 points to full-back Konstantin Rachkov, who finished the day with 23 altogether. The consolation of two unconverted tries in the last five minutes lent some respectability to the Japanese score.

The result effectively set up the eagerly awaited Russia-United States match as the grand final for the Cup. For the Russians, there was a point to prove. Their earlier disqualification from the Rugby World Cup for fielding ineligible players in their repechage match with Spain had deprived them of a play-off against the Eagles for a place in Pool B in Australia.

Controversy followed with the announcement by Tom Billups, the United States' head coach, that he would select only his A side for the match. Some felt the selection was a slight to the tournament's profile, but the United States rugby media relations office took pains to point out: 'With player welfare a prominent concern in a long, World Cup season, most members of the US Test team were unavailable for July fixtures'.

In a move to judge the depth of talent in a squad preparing for the Pan American Championships and Rugby World Cup, Billups selected several players who were new to international rugby. The side prepared for the match in Northampton before flying out to Krasnoyarsk from London, though the coach made it perfectly clear that he was fully aware of the challenge ahead. 'We are pleased with our preparations, but that does not change the magnitude of the challenge we face,' he said.

The Russians in fact had played five matches in the European Nations Tournament as well as against the Japanese and were determined to repeat the 31-16 defeat inflicted by the then Soviet Union on the Eagles in an ill-tempered match in Moscow in 1988 when the superpowers first met.

The young untried American side defended well in the first half. Centre Salesi Sika crossed for a try after 20 minutes to put the Eagles ahead while the experienced Russians had to rely on the boot of full-back Rachkov, who landed four penalty goals, to keep them in touch.

The Eagles went into the break 13-12 in front before the Russians drew down an iron curtain on their front. Their back-row stifled American attempts to run the ball and Rachkov regained the lead. He landed a penalty, scored a try which he converted himself and then kicked his sixth penalty to put his side in the saddle at 25-13. Kouzin added a late try before Sika scored his second as the match moved into added time.

Superpowers Cup 2003: Final Table

	P	*W*	*D*	*L*	*F*	*A*	*Bonus*	*Pts*
Russia	2	2	0	0	73	55	1	9
United States	2	1	0	1	90	57	2	6
Japan	2	0	0	2	61	112	2	2

Points: win 4; draw 2; four or more tries, or defeat by seven or fewer points 1

Results

17 May, Boxer Stadium, Balbao, San Francisco
United States 69 (7G 4T) **Japan 27** (2G 1PG 2T)

United States: L Wilfley; D Fee, P Eloff, K Cross, R van Zyl; M Hercus, K Dalzell; M MacDonald, K Khasigian, D Dorsey, D Hodges (*captain*), L Gross, K Schubert, D Lyle, C Hodgson *Substitutions:* J Waasdorp for Dorsey (61 mins); S Paga for Schubert (66 mins); F Mo'unga for Hodgson (temp 49 to 61 mins) and for Paga (70 mins); M Timoteo for Fee (72 mins); C Nicolau for Eloff (74 mins); M Griffin for Khasigian (75 mins)

Scorers *Tries:* Cross (3), Wilfley (2), Van Zyl (2), Fee, Nicolau, Mo'unga, Timoteo *Conversions:* Hercus (7)

Japan: T Matsuda; D Ohata, H Namba, G Konia, Y Shinomiya; S Fuchigami, W Murata; S Hasegawa, M Sakata, M Toyoyama, K Kubo, A Parker, N Okubo, T Ito, T Miuchi (*captain*) *Substitutions:* Y Sonoda for Murata (54 mins); L T Vatuvei for Parker (67 mins); T Kurihara for Shinomiya (72 mins)

Scorers *Tries:* Ohata, Fuchigami, Shinomiya, Konia *Conversions:* Fuchigami (2) *Penalty Goal:* Fuchigami

Referee B Kuklinski (Canada)

25 May, Prince Chichibu Stadium, Tokyo
Japan 34 (3G 1PG 2T) Russia 43 (3G 4PG 2T)

Japan: T Kurihara; D Ohata, H Namba, R Parkinson, H Onozawa; S Fuchigami, Y Sonoda; Y Hisadomi, M Sakata, M Toyoyama, K Kubo, A Parker, T Okubo, T Ito, T Miuchi (*captain*) *Substitutes:* T Matsuda, G Konia

Scorers *Tries:* Kurihara (2), Ohata, Fuchigami, Ito *Conversions:* Kurihara (3) *Penalty Goal:* Kurihara

Russia: K Rachkov; I Retchnev, D Akulov, Z Veer, I Klyuchnikov; A Korobeinikov, V Motorin; A Travkin, I Nikolaichuk, O Shukailov, S Segeev (*captain*), V Fedchenko, A Sarychev, V Gratchev, V Zykov *Substitutions:* R Bikbov for Travkin; V Simonov for Klyuchnikov

Scorers *Tries:* Rachkov, Retchnev, Motorin, Shukailov, Sarychev *Conversions:* Rachkov (3) *Penalty Goals:* Rachkov (4)

Referee A Klemp (United States)

20 July, Central Stadium, Krasnoyarsk
Russia 30 (1G 6PG 1T) United States A 21 (1G 3PG 1T)

Russia: K Rachkov; A Kouzin, D Akulov, Z Veer, I Klyuchnikov; A Korobeinikov, V Motorin; A Travkin, R Romak, O Shukailov, S Segeev (*captain*), V Fedchenko, D Diatlov, V Gratchev, V Zykov *Substitutions:* I Prischipenko for Travkin; I Nikolaichuk for Romak; A Khrokin for Shukailov; M Uambaev for Diatlov; A Sarychev for Zykov; A Yanyushkin for Zeer; A Kazantsev for Yanyushkin

Scorers *Tries:* Rachkov, Kouzin *Conversion:* Rachkov *Penalty Goals:* Rachkov (6)

United States A: J Buchholz; P Emerick, A Tuipulotu, S Sika, M Timotei (*captain*); M Sherman, D Rowe; R Liddington, J Tarpoff, J Waasdorp, E Anderson, G Klerck, J Gouws, A Satchwell, C Long *Substitutions:* J Naqica for Rowe (50 mins); M Wyatt for Gouws (temp 6 to 16 mins) and for Tarpoff (60 mins); C Osentowski for Waasdorp (60 mins); R Hamilton for Tuipulotu (62 mins); S Lawrence for Gouws (65 mins); F Viljoen for Sherman (72 mins); A McGarry for Liddington (72 mins);

Scorers *Tries:* Sika (2) *Conversion:* Sherman *Penalty Goals:* Sherman (3)

Referee C Berdos (France)

Previous Superpowers Cup winners: 2003 Russia

IRB SEVENS 2002-03

England's Stern Challenge to New Zealand's Sevens Supremacy

Nick Jordan

Even though New Zealand retained the IRB Sevens title, the silver fern was not the dominant force of previous years. The Kiwis had enough points in reserve to hold on for their fourth championship, yet saw their margin reduce from the record 62 of 2002 to just four points in 2003.

Instead, the rose of England started to reach full bloom, winning three tournaments to New Zealand's two. 'It's been neck and neck right the way through,' said Kiwi coach Gordon Tietjens after the finale. 'I don't think people appreciate how close this series really is.'

England recorded historic successes at Brisbane, Hong Kong and Twickenham placing themselves among illustrious company: only New Zealand and Fiji have previously won back-to-back at Hong Kong, while, until this year, even the men in black had never collected a title at home.

Coach Joe Lydon, in his second season, quietly secured the support of the clubs and meticulously wove sevens into the master plan of chief coach Clive Woodward. Lydon and England made the rugby public sit up and take notice of a circuit that, although condensed from eleven tournaments to seven in unfortunate circumstances last year, is clearly growing in popularity and confirming itself both as a vehicle for developing rugby and a thrilling competition in its own right.

Where else in rugby could Samoa defeat New Zealand, Kenya topple Australia, the Cook Islands draw with and then defeat Wales, or the Welsh later claim the scalps of England and France on one day?

Among the 40 countries participating in the circuit Kenya, Tonga, France, Georgia, Wales and Italy all managed at least one finish in the last eight, while Canada, Namibia and Scotland were among the nations who won silverware in the subsidiary competitions.

The seven Cup finals featured five different combinations and no team won two tournaments in succession. Oddly, Argentina were runners-up one week and ended up in the Shield (bottom four) a week later.

This increased competitiveness in the circuit came amidst a year of misfortune. The SARS virus forced the cancellation of events in Beijing and Singapore whilst two tournaments – in Chile and Malaysia – were pulled for commercial and logistical reasons.

On the other hand, tickets for Wellington sold out in 90 minutes, Dubai returned to the circuit with a record attendance, the South African leg moved to the picturesque coastal town of George with resounding success and Brisbane and Twickenham met with more support.

The highlight of the year was the final between New Zealand and England at Wellington. Peter Jackson, of *Lord of the Rings*, could have directed the sevens epic in his hometown – and the sequels that followed in Hong Kong and Cardiff.

The evergreen Eric Rush, 38 a week after the tournament, led his side to a 38-26 triumph. 'We've won Wellington which is the one I came back for, the big carrot. It was four years coming but it was worth the wait,' he said.

The lead changed four times in a pulsating second spell in front of 35,000 revellers. Tafai Ioasa, the hero against Fiji with a last-ditch try in the semi, powered his way to three tries with impressive newcomer Roy Kinikinilau scoring two.

The Hong Kong final a month later was just as exciting. Richard Haughton, the exceptional Saracens athlete, scored two tries coming off the bench to clinch a 22-17 victory. For England, however, triumph was tinged with sadness. Nick Duncombe, one of the talents of the previous sevens season when he was a member of the England Commonwealth Games squad, died from blood poisoning in February. For the successful Hong Kong leg his name was embroidered beneath the rose emblem on the England players' shirts.

Tragedy also struck when former Fijian coach Ratu Kitione Vesikula Tuibua – 'Tukiti' – died aged 49 and Dave Tyler, a leading administrator at Twickenham, passed away aged 53.

Fiji, minus Serevi and other prodigies of Tukiti, were at their brilliant best at George in round two, winning the final over New Zealand, and finished third overall. Their latest sensation, 21-year old Nasoni Roko, topped both the point scoring (325) and try scoring (39) tallies and looks to follow a growing list of former stars of the circuit to higher honours.

Last year's leading scorer Brent Russell graduated to the full Springbok side between seasons while in June 2003 Joe Rokocoko and Mils Muliaina made the All Blacks.

South Africa's new talent, who twice lost to New Zealand by less than a try, eventually triumphed in Cardiff and finished the series in fourth place. Chester Williams's young Springboks defeated Fiji, England and Argentina at the Arms Park with Fabian Juries, the lightning-quick winger, touching down twice in the final.

In the end, though, the series hinged on another classic England v New Zealand tie. Simon Amor's team had to eliminate New Zealand early at Cardiff and Twickenham and go on to win both tournaments.

Inspired by their captain, returning from club final duty with Gloucester, and down to six men after the talented Ben Gollings was sent off, England managed the first part, holding out the Kiwis 14-10 in a nail-biting Cardiff quarter-final. A week later they took the Emirates Airline London Sevens, but South Africa's Cardiff success had virtually assured New Zealand of the title.

Hayden Reid of New Zealand faces Neori Buli of Fiji in Cardiff in June. New Zealand won 35-0 on their way to retaining the IRB Sevens title.

Yet England, powered by the strength of Pat Sanderson and Tony Roques, and with playmakers Amor, Gollings and Henry Paul beautifully orchestrating the pace of Haughton and Ugo Monye, still had almost the complete team by the season's end.

A young New Zealand, who have set the standards for four years but are likely to lose the services of both Tietjens and Rush, now face the prospect of someone else taking the mantle of world champion. It may not happen, but you can sense the possibility hanging in the air.

IRB Sevens Results from 2002-03 Tournaments

Team	*1*	*2*	*3*	*4*	*5*	*6*	*7*	*Points*
New Zealand	20	16	12	20	24	8	12	112
England	6	4	20	16	30	12	20	108
Fiji	8	20	16	12	18	4	16	94
South Africa	12	12	4	4	18	20	12	82
Australia	12	12	8	12	8	6	8	66
Samoa	16	6	6	8	8	12	2	58
Argentina	4	8	4	4	0	16	0	36
France	2	0	12	6	0	0	0	20
Wales	4	0	0	0	0	4	6	14
Kenya	0	4	0	0	8	0	0	12
Tonga	0	0	2	0	8	0	0	10
Canada	0	0	0	2	4	0	0	6
Scotland	0	0	0	0	3	2	0	5
Georgia	0	0	0	0	0	0	4	4
Italy	0	0	0	0	0	0	4	4
Namibia	0	2	0	0	0	0	0	2
Korea	0	0	0	0	2	0	0	2
Cook Islands	0	0	0	0	2	0	0	2
United States	0	0	0	0	1	0	0	1

Key to the tournaments and results in the final: 1 (Dubai) New Zealand 36 Samoa 0; 2 (George) Fiji 24 New Zealand 14; 3 (Brisbane) England 28 Fiji 14; 4 (Wellington) New Zealand 38 England 26; 5 (Hong Kong) England 22 New Zealand 17; 6 (Cardiff) South Africa 35 Argentina 17; 7 (London) England 31 Fiji 24

Previous IRB-World Sevens Series Winners: 1999-2000 New Zealand; 2000-01 New Zealand; 2001-02 New Zealand; 2002-03 New Zealand

IRB/FIRA-AER WORLD JUNIOR CHAMPIONSHIP 2003

South Africa Take Last Title of the FIRA Era

Chris Thau

The 35th IRB/FIRA-AER World U19 Championship, a mouthful of a name reflecting the ambiguous nature of the ownership of the event shared until this year between the IRB and the European Federation FIRA-AER, has brought to an end a romantic era that commenced in Spain in 1969. The European Federation, the founders of the U19 Tournament known for more than 30 years as FIRA U19, will no longer plan, administer and manage the world's leading developmental rugby competition. The IRB will take over the running of it from next year, when the 24-nation competition will be held in South Africa.

Since its launch in 1969, the U19 Championship has welcomed players from all corners of Europe then, as FIRA was looking to expand into other regions, from all over the World. Through its own momentum the tournament grew in stature and size into a formidable competition, due not only to the enormous value of the U19 age group to development in the participating countries but also to the diligent work of many FIRA officials and, during the last eight years, thanks to the IRB's financial support and guidance.

During these years, FIRA-AER have administered the competition with increased efficiency and confidence, but the anachronism of having a regional organisation in charge of a World Cup competition and the need to globalise the event has brought the 34-year long association between the U19 Tournament and the European governing body to an end.

Naturally, the 35th tournament, held in the Ile de France (Paris) region, was an emotional occasion for the many FIRA-AER veterans whose entire mature rugby career had been spent developing, strengthening and fine-tuning the U19 tournament.

However, the sense of frustration felt by the FIRA-AER administrators to what one described as 'the loss of a beloved child' must be put into perspective by the plan to launch a European U18 Championship, very much on the model of the old FIRA U19 Tournament. The FIRA-AER Senior Vice-President and IRB representative Jose-Maria Epalza has contacted most youth rugby organisations in Europe to sound out the level of interest for an U18 tournament. And according to FIRA-AER insiders, the proposal for an U18 FIRA-AER Championship is likely to be ratified at the annual meeting of the FIRA-AER Executive in Paris in December.

That means that while the U19 age group remains firmly in the hands of the IRB Tournaments Department, the base of the developmental pyramid is further enlarged by the U18 age-group, which acquires both meaning and status through the planned move. Several teams from the lower division have argued that this restructuring may adversely affect the growth of the game in the smaller nations, but the IRB hope that by introducing regional qualification series the new tournament will gather momentum and eventually become the genuine engine of the development process.

For the moment, the jury is still out regarding the future format of the U19 World Championships. There is strong support for a 16-team format now that the restrictive blueprint of the old U19 knockout competition is a thing of the past, while there are many who feel that the 24-team format might be just right. Arguably, the most significant thing that needs to be sorted out is the link between the U19 Tournament and the previous year's U18 competition. Ultimately a combination of cost and value for money will decide the optimum format, while the sister competition, the U21s, is equally busy trying to sort out its format, number of qualifiers and the mechanism to identify them. While there is a virtual consensus that the U19s should remain an annual event, the IRB planners are still debating whether the U21s should become a biennial competition.

On the field the 35th championship will be remembered for a truly outstanding U19 competition, with a beautifully balanced and resourceful South Africa snatching the World U19 crown from New Zealand in a memorable final. With their U21s 2002 world champions, South Africa could genuinely claim last April that its development programmes were an outstanding success.

In the third/fourth place play-off match, France had too much firepower against an Argentina side that still looked to be suffering the effects of their closely fought semi-final with New Zealand. The French ran out winners 45-24, but will be disappointed not to have reached the final in front of their home crowd.

Ireland finished top of the Home Unions after beating England to fifth place after a penalty shoot-out. The teams were tied at 22-apiece when the final whistle went, but Ireland held their nerve to win the shoot-out 4-3. For the second year running, Wales flattered to deceive and finished in seventh place despite high hopes leading in to the competition. They were cruelly exposed by France in the quarter-finals where they lost 43-26.

The second division (Group B) final between Uruguay and Chile ended 19-19 and also required a penalty-shoot-out. Uruguay won and earned the right to play among the top senior division teams at the 2004 U19 World Cup. Elsewhere in the group, performances from teams such as Tunisia and Portugal were shining examples of how important this tournament is for developing talent; ditto for the likes of Belgium, Spain and Germany for whom the U19 championship has been historically the conveyor belt of their development programmes. The infectious joy of the Lithuanian boys after their narrow win over the United States, and the skill of the Russians and Koreans in a match of such energy and commitment that made the onlooker feel exhausted augured well for the future of the game in these countries. The clash between the Italians and newly promoted Namibia had an intensity about it that has rarely been seen at this level before. The selection is better, the coaching is more comprehensive and intensive, the boys are bigger and stronger, and the skill levels are higher.

Among the new members of old rugby clans who experienced baptisms of fire were fly-half Yuri Kushnarev, the son of Victor the famous Russian flank forward of the 1980s, and Sebastian Cunha, another member of the Portuguese rugby dynasty.

Budding skippers grasped the opportunity to master the art of leadership, control and man-management. The calm composure of the incredibly young German scrum-half Franck Moutsiga from Berlin spoke volumes for the quality of the German U19 programme, while the athleticism of the Lithuanian captain Vilius Kucinas and the maturity of the United States' skipper Mike Petri, a symbol of the good things to come in US rugby, added to the wonder of this magnificent tournament.

Group B Results (9th/19th April 2003)

Round One: Uruguay 47, Hong Kong 0; Ukraine 5, Germany 13; Tunisia 32, Lithuania 19; United States 3, Belgium 16; Chile 54, Czech Republic 0; Paraguay 17, Morocco 6; Spain 72, Côte d'Ivoire 0; Portugal 34, Poland 15

Round Two: Uruguay 47, Germany 3; Tunisia 8, Belgium 3; Chile 46, Paraguay 13; Spain 3, Portugal 21; Hong Kong 0, Ukraine 54; Lithuania 15, United States 11; Czech Republic 5, Morocco 36; Côte d'Ivoire 18, Poland 41

Semi-final round: Uruguay 14, Tunisia 6; Chile 22, Portugal 14; Germany 7, Belgium 22; Paraguay 12, Spain 15; Ukraine 11, Lithuania 7; Morocco 37, Poland 17; Hong Kong 10, United States 25; Czech Republic 33, Côte d'Ivoire 3

Play-offs for Group B lower rankings: Tunisia 15, Portugal 15 (Portugal won 4-3 on penalties); Belgium 3, Spain 33; Germany 17, Paraguay 24; Ukraine 10, Morocco 24; Lithuania 10, Poland 25; United States 33, Czech Republic 15; Hong Kong won over Côte d'Ivoire

Group B Final: Uruguay 19, Chile 19 (Uruguay won 4-3 on penalties)

Group B Final Rankings: 1st Uruguay; 2nd Chile; 3rd Portugal; 4th Tunisia; 5th Spain; 6th Belgium; 7th Paraguay; 8th Germany; 9th Morocco; 10th Ukraine; 11th Poland; 12th Lithuania; 13th United States; 14th Czech Republic; 15th Hong Kong; 16th Côte d'Ivoire

Group A Results (10th/20th April 2003)

Round One: New Zealand 57, Namibia 11; Italy 7, Ireland 33; Scotland 38, Romania 8; Argentina 25, Japan 3; France 41, Canada 7; Wales 24, Georgia 7; South Africa 50, Korea 0; England 30, Russia 7

Round Two: New Zealand 43, Ireland 8; Scotland 17, Argentina 22; France 43, Wales 26; South Africa 19, England 3; Namibia 18, Italy 23; Romania 22, Japan 38; Georgia 31, Canada 7; Korea 25, Russia 26

Semi-final round: New Zealand 27, Argentina 24; France 15, South Africa 20; Ireland 28, Scotland 22; Wales 11, England 15; Italy 10, Japan 29; Georgia 16, Russia 8; Namibia 16, Romania 11; Canada 10, Korea 15

Play-offs for Group A lower rankings: Argentina 24, France 45; Ireland 22, England 22 (Ireland won 4-3 on penalties); Scotland 6, Wales 10; Japan 28, Georgia 20; Italy 6, Russia 3; Namibia 5, Korea 21; Romania 13, Canada 3

Final 20 April, Stade Bobin, Bondoufle, Paris
South Africa 22 (1G 4PG 1DG) New Zealand 18 (1G 2PG 1T)

The final was an epic occasion, with the two teams playing a brand of rugby unheard of and unseen at this age group a few years ago. The pace, skill, vision and overall ability of the two teams had to be seen to be believed.

New Zealand's Mia Nikora landed a penalty for an early lead, but South Africa bounced back with a try signed off by their outstanding scrum-half Paul Delport who went over at a scrum near the New Zealand line. Influential Earl Rose, who showed remarkable promise at centre, added the conversion. New Zealand hit back with tries by powerful North Harbour wing Hosea Gear and Waikato's dynamic blind-side flanker Steven Setephano, Nikora converting one of the two touchdowns. Just before half time Rose landed a penalty to keep South Africa in contention at 10-15.

Two more penalties after the break took South Africa into a precarious one-point lead, but New Zealand edged ahead through Nikora when South Africa were penalised for a high tackle. Another penalty by Rose and a late drop goal by fly-half Isam-eel-Dollie ended an epic battle which found New Zealand battering the heroically defended South African line to the bitter end.

South Africa: H Daniller; E Alexander, E Rose, P Grant, M Delport; I-E Dollie, P Delport (captain); S Ferreira, B du Plessis, N de Villiers, S Sykes, W de Jager, W Arlow, P Louw, G Kuün *Substitutions:* R Pienaar for P Delport; L Karemaker for Arlow; M Sangoni for Ferreira; D Murray for Dollie

Scorers *Try:* Delport *Conversion:* Rose *Penalty Goals:* Rose (4) *Dropped Goal:* Dollie

New Zealand: P Te Whare; M Rowe, R Wulf, B Williams-Stanley, H Gear; M Nikora, M France; J Mackintosh (captain), C Moke, B Franks, K Haiu, I Ross, S Setephano, L Messam, T Boys *Substitutions:* S Giddens for Rowe

Scorers *Tries:* Gear, Setephano *Conversion:* Nikora *Penalty Goals:* Nikora (2)

Referee H Watkins (Wales)

Group A Final Rankings: 1st South Africa; 2nd New Zealand; 3rd France; 4th Argentina; 5th Ireland; 6th England; 7th Wales; 8th Scotland; 9th Japan; 10th Georgia; 11th Italy; 12th Russia; 13th Korea; 14th Namibia; 15th Romania; 16 Canada

Previous IRB-FIRA World Junior Championship Winners: 1969 France (Barcelona); 1970 France (Vichy), 1971 France (Casablanca); 1972 Romania (Rome); 1973 Romania (Bucharest); 1974 France (Heidelberg); 1975 France (Madrid); 1976 France (Albi); 1977 France (Hilversum); 1978 France (Parma); 1979 France (Lisbon); 1980 France (Tunis); 1981 France (Madrid); 1982 France (Geneva); 1983 France (Casablanca); 1984 Italy (Warsaw); 1985 France (Brussels); 1986 France (Bucharest); 1987 Argentina (Berlin); 1988 France (Makarska); 1989 Argentina (Lisbon); 1990 Argentina (Brescia); 1991 France (Toulouse); 1992 France (Madrid); 1993 Argentina (Lille); 1994 South Africa (Lyon); 1995 France (Bucharest); 1996 Argentina (Brescia); 1997 Argentina (Buenos Aires); 1998 Ireland (Toulouse); 1999 New Zealand (Llanelli); 2000 France (Burgundy); 2001 New Zealand (Santiago de Chile); 2002 New Zealand (Treviso); 2003 South Africa (Paris)

IRB UNDER 21 WORLD CUP 2003

Southern Hemisphere Dominance Continues

John Griffiths

The RFU became the first northern hemisphere Union to host the Under-21 World Cup when Oxford, Henley and Newbury staged the ninth event of this competition in June. The tournament, originally launched as the SANZAR/UAR U21 World Cup in Argentina in 1995, has been organised by the IRB since 2002.

The competition, which has been dominated by the Tri Nations, continues to be an important proving ground for the upcoming generation of senior international players. Of the participants in the 2002 final, for instance, Ashwin Willemse, Juan Smith and Pedrie Wannenburg from the winning South African side went on to become fully-fledged Springboks in 2002-03 while Matt Giteau, Morgan Turinui and Daniel Heenan won their senior caps for Australia. Many among the class of 2003 in England will no doubt be added to the list of nearly 200 players who have appeared at these finals and progressed to full Test honours.

The developmental aspect of the competition is reflected in its structure. A dozen teams are seeded into four pools of three depending on their finishing positions in the previous year's competition and other Under-21 tournaments. Nations do not play within their own pool. Instead the pools are graded from A to D with the sides in Pool A meeting each of the three nations in Pool D. Pools B and C play off similarly in an opening round of three matches. Then the filtering process begins in a fourth round of matches that is used to decide the playing order for the final round. As a result, every nation's interest is maintained through five matches, each side playing in its own 'final' to determine the rankings for the next tournament.

Once again it was the precocious talent of the southern hemisphere that dominated the tournament, though South Africa, the reigning champions, struggled to dispose of Ireland in their opening match at Iffley Road. They lost No 8 Jacques Cronjé and their captain Schalk Burger to the sin bin before coming through 36-27 thanks to three tries from their wings Bronwyn Buys and Alaun Bock. Australia flattened England by 52-22 in the first round. Admittedly England were under strength with several of their promising youngsters on Churchill Cup duty in North America with the A side. But the gold rush served as a stark reminder of the healthy state of the Australian game. Mark Gerrard, the Brumbies' Super Twelve wing, contributed 20 points as the Junior Wallabies gave clear notice of their potential.

Wales, the reigning Under-21 Grand Slam winners in Europe, disposed of the Scots in the Home Unions' sole victory of the first round.

The second-round matches provided two exciting contests. Wales, spearheaded by Cardiff's Nicky Robinson, beat a typically physical Argentine side by 24-18 and France, making up for their disappointing performances of 2002, gave New Zealand a run for their money before losing by 23-26.The third round brought the top-seeded sides together. Wales managed a brave display before losing to holders South Africa while New Zealand and Australia shared a 37-all draw after the Junior Blacks had raced into a 24-0 lead. Lachlan MacKay, the Aussies' play-maker, lifted his men with two tries in an inspiring comeback that ended in a draw when Gerrard landed a penalty from half-way with the last kick of the match.

After the pool stages the seedings were re-set for the final play-offs. New Zealand were matched with South Africa and Australia were to play Argentina in the main tournament semi-finals. Ben Atiga, who had contributed 22 points to the draw with Australia, was the star attraction in the Baby Blacks' 38-16 win over the holders. South Africa had eliminated New Zealand at the corresponding stage in 2002 and at 16-9 ahead at the interval looked set to repeat the feat. But they had not reckoned with the skilful full-back's attacking potential. After landing the three penalties that had kept New Zealand in touch in the first half, Atiga's ability to launch counter-attacks was an important factor in his side's adventurous approach to a second half that yielded four tries without reply.

Australia went three tries better in their 48-25 defeat of Argentina, but the contest was far closer than the score suggested. The Pumitas had two tries disallowed and totally out-scrummaged their opponents before conceding a string of technical penalties that undermined their confidence.

Argentina beat the Junior Springboks to third place in a curtain raiser to the final at Oxford's Kassam Stadium before New Zealand went on to win the title with a convincing defeat of Australia. Wales were beaten 24-20 by France in the fifth/sixth place play-off but were elevated to fifth position after launching a successful appeal against France's failure to comply with the IRB's ruling on front-row replacements. During the match the referee had had to award uncontested scrums after France had been unable to field the requisite number of specialist front-row substitutes. In the seventh/eighth place play-off England opened a comfortable lead in the first half-hour before Nikki Walker and Graham Morton's points helped Scotland to a satisfying 33-22 victory.

Conditions throughout the tournament were ideal for open rugby and the modest crowds who attended enjoyed their first glances of the stars whose names will light up the game's future.

Results (13th/29th June 2003)

First round: South Africa 36, Ireland 27; Argentina 62, Canada 13; Scotland 19, Wales 37; Australia 52, England 22; France 34, Italy 7; Japan 14, New Zealand 61

Second round: South Africa 102, Canada 10; Argentina 18, Wales 24; Scotland 15, Ireland 21; Australia 24, Italy 5; France 23, New Zealand 26; Japan 3, England 69

Third round: South Africa 50, Wales 21; Argentina 30, Ireland 19; Scotland 34, Canada 19; Australia 37, New Zealand 37; France 21, England 16; Japan 34, Italy 47

Fourth round: Canada 21, Italy 27; Ireland 52, Japan 13; Scotland 12, France 48; Wales 44, England 27; Argentina 25, Australia 48; South Africa 16, New Zealand 38

Play-off finals: Japan 48, Canada 27; Ireland 24, Italy 19; England 22, Scotland 33; Wales 20, France 24; South Africa 30, Argentina 34

Final 29 June, Kassam Stadium, Oxford
New Zealand 21 (1G 3PG 1T) Australia 10 (1G 1PG)

The quick-witted Junior All Blacks were too slick for their Pacific neighbours in the final. They led from the 13th minute, when lock Ross Kennedy used his muscle and a neat piece of footwork to dodge past the Australian defence ten metres from the line, and never relaxed their iron grasp on the match.

Ben Atiga, New Zealand's prolific points scorer, had missed with shots at goal before fly-half Stephen Donald stepped up to kick penalties that took the score to 11-0 at the interval. His first, after 25 minutes, was awarded when Australian scrum-half Josh Valentine was sent to the sin bin for killing the ball. Australia, however, continued to stretch the laws and shortly after Valentine's return his half-back partner Lachlan MacKay was binned for failing to stay on his feet at the breakdown. Donald again added the penalty points.

Australia briefly staged a fight-back early in the second half when Mark Gerrard kicked a penalty, but New Zealand absorbed the pressure and remained firmly in control. Any hopes the Wallabies might have held of mounting a revival to match the epic comeback of their pool match were finally dispelled when Donald restored the 11-point advantage with his third penalty on the hour mark.

Five minutes from time Hayden Pedersen, who had earlier gone near to scoring in a thrilling kick and chase, carved out a neat passage to power through two tackles for a try wide out. Donald converted before Elia Tuqiri, cousin of Lote the new Wallaby wing, made a late dash for the best try of the afternoon. Gerrard converted, reducing the deficit to 11 points, but that was a margin that flattered Australia.

'We've worked hard for this, and I'm delighted for the boys,' said New Zealand's coach Bryce Woodward. Lachlan MacKay, Australia's captain, was generous in his praise of the winners. 'They outplayed us on the day,' he said.

New Zealand: B Atiga; H Pedersen, L Mafi, S Tuitupou (*captain*), P Te Whare; S Donald, J Cowan; J Afoa, J Pareanga, T Fairbrother, K Thompson, R Kennedy, J Kaino, T Waldrom, T Harding *Substitutions:* A Thomson for Kaino (69 mins);

S Tonga'uiha for Afoa (70 mins); A Koonwaiyou for Te Whare (73 mins); T Pisi for Tuitupou (77 mins)

Scorers *Tries:* Kennedy, Pedersen *Conversion:* Donald *Penalty Goals:* Donald (3)

Australia: M Gerrard; E Tuqiri, C Siale, G Fairbanks, P Hynes; L MacKay (*captain*), J Valentine; P Waring, S Moore, G Shepherdson, M Wilson, W Caldwell, R Elsom, J Tawake, L Tomiki *Substitutions:* L Doherty for Elsom (temp 31 to 40 mins) and for Tomiki (40 mins); D Mitchell for Siale (59 mins); M Cecere for Waring (70 mins); C Shepherd for Hynes (72 mins); N Churven for Moore (73 mins); N Haydon for Valentine (79 mins);

Referee R Debney (England)

Final Rankings: 1st New Zealand; 2nd Australia; 3rd Argentina; 4th South Africa; 5th Wales; 6th France; 7th Scotland; 8th England; 9th Ireland; 10th Italy; 11th Japan; 12th Canada

Previous SANZAR/UAR Under-21 World Cup Winners: 1995 New Zealand (Buenos Aires); 1996 Australia (Takapuna); 1997 Australia (Sydney); 1998 Australia (Cape Town); 1999 South Africa (Buenos Aires); 2000 New Zealand (Auckland); 2001 New Zealand (Sydney)

Previous IRB Under-21 World Cup Finals: 2002 South Africa 24, Australia 21 (Johannesburg); 2003 New Zealand 21, Australia 10 (Oxford)

ENGLAND'S TEST SEASON REVIEW 2002-2003

A Perfect Ten for England Impresses Judges Far and Wide

Mick Cleary

You might think that the sight of Neil Back sitting in a wheelie-bin full of ice on the third floor of one of Wellington's finest hotels had little bearing on England's most successful season in 46 years according to the stats and their most successful ever for those of us that judge these things by more subjective criteria. But it did. Back, as many of his team-mates also did during the build-up to the summer Test against the All Blacks, would regularly immerse his body for half-an-hour in a makeshift giant ice-bucket. The big chill, apparently, speeds up recovery.

It was this attention to detail, this constant search for the little edge, which characterised England's year. They were never satisfied. They never reached for the laurels and parked their backsides there. There was always a desire to seek out new horizons and then set about finding the quickest way to get there.

Such professionalism, such enthusiasm and dedication, had their fitting reward. England won all ten games in the season, their first invincible return since 1956-57. That side of long ago only had to win four matches. England chalked up their perfect ten the hard way. They book-ended their *annus mirabilis* with victories over the leading southern hemisphere lights, New Zealand and Australia.

For the first time ever England beat the Wallabies on Australian soil. For the first time ever they won back-to-back away victories over the Tri Nations sides. The Springboks were also in the mix, seen off 53-3 in the autumn on a dark day for South African rugby. Lock Jannes Labuschange was sent off for a late charge on Jonny Wilkinson and he was lucky that a couple of his pals didn't follow him down the tunnel for an early bath. The Springbok attitude was a disgrace as they set about roughing up England. It was cheap and mean-spirited. One of several high, reckless tackles by Butch James eventually found its target, forcing Wilkinson to leave the field.

But England survived that. And all that any opponent could throw at them. They won their first Grand Slam under Clive Woodward by beating Ireland 42-6 in a winner-takes-all showdown at Lansdowne Road. It was a monkey off the Woodward back, for much as he professed to say that the three previous failures to close out the Slam did not unduly bug him, it clearly did. That mental fault line needed to be rectified. And it was in quite some style.

Woodward deliberately stepped up the pressure on his team throughout the season, realising that if they were to win a World Cup, then they needed to be able to deal with the nerve-shredding burden of expectation. He set targets for his side, willing them to meet the challenge. 'I couldn't contemplate going back over the Severn Bridge not having won the game,' said Woodward prior to the game at the Millennium Stadium.

Woodward was able to make the return journey. Even though the Six Nations was wrapped up with considerable conviction in Dublin, there were still some doubters, those that felt that even though England were a mighty force at Twickenham, where they were unbeaten in capped games since the 1999 World Cup (the Barbarians did see off an England XV, 36-49, in the end-of-season shindig), they still did not have enough in the locker to win the big games on the road. The trip to the southern hemisphere knocked that theory into a cocked hat.

The All Blacks, in typically testing Wellington conditions, were beaten 15-13 while the 23-9 defeat of the Maori in New Plymouth five days earlier suggested that England's second string were no mugs either. That viewpoint was confirmed by the showing of the Jim Mallinder and Steve Diamond-coached side in the Churchill Cup where England A comfortably saw off the United States (twice) and Canada. Victories away from home across the globe and in different circumstances. Ah, but could England play rugby? They had beaten New Zealand without putting the ball through the hands. Yes – and they had done so because conditions dictated that they keep it tight. It was smart rugby, not dull rugby.

The following week in Melbourne England showed that they could mix it with the best. They showed the full deck in beating Australia 25-14, scoring three tries, all of them crackers in their own way. They also shunted the Wallaby pack 45 metres downfield in a trundling maul that will pass into rugby folklore. As will the Goal Line Stand by the six England forwards who held out against the All Blacks seven days earlier after Neil Back and Lawrence Dallaglio had been sin-binned.

England only conceded two tries in the two summer Tests, a relief to defence coach Phil Larder after he had seen seven tries run past his side during the autumn series. The win against New Zealand was the side's 12th consecutive Test victory, a new England record, and in Australia their 13th win broke the record for an unbeaten English Test run set by Temple Gurdon's sides back in the 1880s.

England improved on all fronts throughout a season in which the captaincy of Martin Johnson became an ever-more crucial factor. Johnson had one of his finest ever games in an England shirt – and there have been a few contenders – in the Wellington Test. Johnson would be the first to acknowledge that he has been well served by those around him. Jonny Wilkinson stepped into the breach against Italy to lead his country for the first time when Johnson had an Achilles problem. Lawrence Dallaglio came through strongly, too, after being dropped for the first time ever by England after the November Test against New Zealand.

'It's important that the message hits home,' said Woodward. 'We expect a very high work-rate from the back-row and Lawrence is not quite at the standard at which we know he can play. You have to be brutally honest in these situations and pick on what you see and not on reputation. No-one can afford to have a weak Test match because his place is under threat.'

The competition for places was intense through the year, particularly in the back-row where Neil Back found himself out of favour for that opening autumn Test in favour of Leicester colleague, Lewis Moody. The young flanker had matured over the previous 18 months into a fine international player. His season was to be cut short with a shoulder injury during the Six Nations.

Another to suffer cruelly was Charlie Hodgson. The Sale fly-half missed the autumn series with a knee injury and was then chosen at centre for the opening two Six Nations games against France and Wales, the first time in his career he had worn the No 12 shirt. Disaster struck in the game against Italy when Hodgson, who had only been on the field for six minutes after replacing Wilkinson, caught his studs in the turf and ruptured his cruciate ligament. Paul Grayson was recalled for the first time in four years to cover the No 10 shortfall.

England had front-row problems through the year, largely caused by injury, although the dismissal of Bristol's Julian White for butting Graham Rowntree in a club game in early October did not help their cause. White was banned for ten weeks. The Gloucester props Trevor Woodman and Phil Vickery, chosen against New Zealand in November, were not reunited until the last Test of the season against Australia. Northampton's Robbie Morris became the youngest prop to play for England when picked against Wales.

England had other disciplinary concerns when Bath lock Danny Grewcock was left out of the summer tour after being sent off in the Parker Pen final for punching Wasps captain, Lawrence Dallaglio.

By the time that tour came round England had a very settled line-up. Josh Lewsey made the most of an unexpected opening when called up against Italy in the absence of the injured Jason Robinson. Lewsey, with his more orthodox approach, scored two tries and kept his place.

Jason Leonard won his 100th cap for England against France, an occasion over-shadowed by the tragic news of Nick Duncombe's death the day before. Leonard had another notable landmark that day, pulling a hamstring for the first time in his career.

The England Sevens side, with victories in Hong Kong, Brisbane and London, were only narrowly pipped to the Grand Prix title by New Zealand. It was a good season for England on every front. It began with Woodward securing a deal with the Zurich Premiership clubs for 20 release dates for training. 'Other sports will look at this scheme, this union between club and country, and think Wow,' said Woodward. 'I'm as positive as a result of this agreement as I've ever been.'

Nine months later, with 10 victories under his belt, Woodward got his own reward when the RFU extended his contract through to the end of the

2007 Rugby World Cup. That tournament is to be held in France. England were the only other bidders. It was their only reverse in a quite splendid year.

England's Test Record in 2002-03: Played 13, won 12, lost 1

Opponents	*Date*	*Venue*	*Result*
France	6th September 2003	H	Won 45-14
France	30th August 2003	A	Lost 16-17
Wales	23rd August 2003	A	Won 43-9
Australia	21st June 2003	A	Won 25-14
New Zealand	14th June 2003	A	Won 15-13
Ireland	30th March 2003	A	Won 42-6
Scotland	22nd March 2003	H	Won 40-9
Italy	9th March 2003	H	Won 40-5
Wales	22nd February 2003	A	Won 26-9
France	15th February 2003	H	Won 25-17
South Africa	23rd November 2002	H	Won 53-3
Australia	16th November 2002	H	Won 32-31
New Zealand	9th November 2002	H	Won 31-28

ENGLAND INTERNATIONAL STATISTICS

(to 30 September 2003)

Match Records

MOST CONSECUTIVE TEST WINS

14 2002 *W, It, Arg, NZ, A, SA*, 2003 *F 1, W 1, It, S, I, NZ, A, W2*
11 2000 *SA 2, A, Arg, SA 3*, 2001 *W, It, S, F, C 1,2, US*
10 1882 *W*, 1883 *I, S*, 1884 *W, I, S*, 1885 *W, I*, 1886 *W, I*
10 1994 *R, C*, 1995 *I, F, W, S, Arg, It, WS, A*

MOST CONSECUTIVE TESTS WITHOUT DEFEAT

Matches	*Wins*	*Draws*	*Period*
14	14	0	2002 to 2003
12	10	2	1882 to 1887
11	10	1	1922 to 1924
11	11	0	2000 to 2001

MOST POINTS IN A MATCH

by the team

Pts	*Opponents*	*Venue*	*Year*
134	Romania	Twickenham	2001
110	Netherlands	Huddersfield	1998
106	United States	Twickenham	1999
101	Tonga	Twickenham	1999
80	Italy	Twickenham	2001
67	Italy	Twickenham	1999
60	Japan	Sydney	1987
60	Canada	Twickenham	1994
60	Wales	Twickenham	1998

by a player

Pts	*Player*	*Opponents*	*Venue*	*Year*
44	C Hodgson	Romania	Twickenham	2001
36	P J Grayson	Tonga	Twickenham	1999
35	J P Wilkinson	Italy	Twickenham	2001
32	J P Wilkinson	Italy	Twickenham	1999
30	C R Andrew	Canada	Twickenham	1994
30	P J Grayson	Netherlands	Huddersfield	1998
30	J P Wilkinson	Wales	Twickenham	2002
29	D J H Walder	Canada	Burnaby	2001
27	C R Andrew	South Africa	Pretoria	1994
27	J P Wilkinson	South Africa	Bloemfontein	2000
26	J P Wilkinson	United States	Twickenham	1999

MOST TRIES IN A MATCH

by the team

Tries	*Opponents*	*Venue*	*Year*
20	Romania	Twickenham	2001
16	Netherlands	Huddersfield	1998
16	United States	Twickenham	1999
13	Wales	Blackheath	1881
13	Tonga	Twickenham	1999
10	Japan	Sydney	1987
10	Fiji	Twickenham	1989
10	Italy	Twickenham	2001
9	France	Paris	1906
9	France	Richmond	1907
9	France	Paris	1914
9	Romania	Bucharest	1989

by a player

Tries	*Player*	*Opponents*	*Venue*	*Year*
5	D Lambert	France	Richmond	1907
5	R Underwood	Fiji	Twickenham	1989
4	G W Burton	Wales	Blackheath	1881
4	A Hudson	France	Paris	1906
4	R W Poulton	France	Paris	1914
4	C Oti	Romania	Bucharest	1989
4	J C Guscott	Netherlands	Huddersfield	1998
4	N A Back	Netherlands	Huddersfield	1998
4	J C Guscott	United States	Twickenham	1999
4	J Robinson	Romania	Twickenham	2001

MOST CONVERSIONS IN A MATCH

by the team

Cons	*Opponents*	*Venue*	*Year*
15	Netherlands	Huddersfield	1998
14	Romania	Twickenham	2001
13	United States	Twickenham	1999
12	Tonga	Twickenham	1999
9	Italy	Twickenham	2001
8	Romania	Bucharest	1989
7	Wales	Blackheath	1881
7	Japan	Sydney	1987
7	Argentina	Twickenham	1990
7	Wales	Twickenham	1998

by a player

Cons	Player	Opponents	Venue	Year
15	P J Grayson	Netherlands	Huddersfield	1998
14	C Hodgson	Romania	Twickenham	2001
13	J P Wilkinson	United States	Twickenham	1999
12	P J Grayson	Tonga	Twickenham	1999
9	J P Wilkinson	Italy	Twickenham	2001
8	S D Hodgkinson	Romania	Bucharest	1989
7	J M Webb	Japan	Sydney	1987
7	S D Hodgkinson	Argentina	Twickenham	1990
7	P J Grayson	Wales	Twickenham	1998

MOST PENALTIES IN A MATCH

by the team

Penalties	Opponents	Venue	Year
8	South Africa	Bloemfontein	2000
7	Wales	Cardiff	1991
7	Scotland	Twickenham	1995
7	France	Twickenham	1999
7	Fiji	Twickenham	1999
7	South Africa	Paris	1999
7	South Africa	Twickenham	2001
6	Wales	Twickenham	1986
6	Canada	Twickenham	1994
6	Argentina	Durban	1995
6	Scotland	Murrayfield	1996
6	Ireland	Twickenham	1996
6	South Africa	Twickenham	2000
6	Australia	Twickenham	2002

by a player

Penalties	Player	Opponents	Venue	Year
8	J P Wilkinson	South Africa	Bloemfontein	2000
7	S D Hodgkinson	Wales	Cardiff	1991
7	C R Andrew	Scotland	Twickenham	1995
7	J P Wilkinson	France	Twickenham	1999
7	J P Wilkinson	Fiji	Twickenham	1999
7	J P Wilkinson	South Africa	Twickenham	2001
6	C R Andrew	Wales	Twickenham	1986
6	C R Andrew	Canada	Twickenham	1994
6	C R Andrew	Argentina	Durban	1995
6	P J Grayson	Scotland	Murrayfield	1996
6	P J Grayson	Ireland	Twickenham	1996
6	P J Grayson	South Africa	Paris	1999
6	J P Wilkinson	South Africa	Twickenham	2000
6	J P Wilkinson	Australia	Twickenham	2002

MOST DROPPED GOALS IN A MATCH

by the team

Drops	Opponents	Venue	Year
2	Ireland	Twickenham	1970
2	France	Paris	1978
2	France	Paris	1980
2	Romania	Twickenham	1985
2	Fiji	Suva	1991
2	Argentina	Durban	1995
2	France	Paris	1996
2	Australia	Twickenham	2001
2	Wales	Cardiff	2003
2	Ireland	Dublin	2003

by a player

Drops	Player	Opponents	Venue	Year
2	R Hiller	Ireland	Twickenham	1970
2	A G B Old	France	Paris	1978
2	J P Horton	France	Paris	1980
2	C R Andrew	Romania	Twickenham	1985
2	C R Andrew	Fiji	Suva	1991
2	C R Andrew	Argentina	Durban	1995
2	P J Grayson	France	Paris	1996
2	J P Wilkinson	Australia	Twickenham	2001
2	J P Wilkinson	Wales	Cardiff	2003
2	J P Wilkinson	Ireland	Dublin	2003

Career Records

MOST CAPPED PLAYERS

Caps	Player	Career Span
106	J Leonard	1990 to 2003
85	R Underwood	1984 to 1996
77	M O Johnson	1993 to 2003
72	W D C Carling	1988 to 1997
71	C R Andrew	1985 to 1997
65	J C Guscott	1989 to 1999
64	B C Moore	1987 to 1995
60	N A Back	1994 to 2003
60	R A Hill	1997 to 2003
58	P J Winterbottom	1982 to 1993
58	L B N Dallaglio	1995 to 2003
56	M J Catt	1994 to 2001
55	W A Dooley	1985 to 1993
52	M J S Dawson	1995 to 2003
51	A S Healey	1997 to 2003
48	D Richards	1986 to 1996

MOST CONSECUTIVE TESTS

Tests	Player	Span
44	W D C Carling	1989 to 1995
40	J Leonard	1990 to 1995
36	J V Pullin	1968 to 1975
33	W B Beaumont	1975 to 1982
30	R Underwood	1992 to 1996

MOST TESTS AS CAPTAIN

Tests	Captain	Span
59	W D C Carling	1988 to 1996
33	M O Johnson	1998 to 2003
21	W B Beaumont	1978 to 1982
14	L B N Dallaglio	1997 to 1999
13	W W Wakefield	1924 to 1926
13	N M Hall	1949 to 1955
13	R E G Jeeps	1960 to 1962
13	J V Pullin	1972 to 1975

MOST TESTS IN INDIVIDUAL POSITIONS

Position	Player	Tests	Span
Full-back	M B Perry	35	1997 to 2001
Wing	R Underwood	85	1984 to 1996
Centre	W D C Carling	72	1988 to 1997
Fly-half	C R Andrew	70	1985 to 1997
Scrum-half	M J S Dawson	52	1995 to 2003
Prop	J Leonard	106	1990 to 2003
Hooker	B C Moore	64	1987 to 1995
Lock	M O Johnson	77	1993 to 2003
Flanker	N A Back	60	1994 to 2003
No 8	D Richards	48	1986 to 1996

Andrew and Perry were capped elsewhere

MOST POINTS IN TESTS

Points	Player	Tests	Career
704	J P Wilkinson	46	1998 to 2003
396	C R Andrew	71	1985 to 1997
327	P J Grayson	27	1995 to 2003
296	J M Webb	33	1987 to 1993
240	W H Hare	25	1974 to 1984
210	R Underwood	85	1984 to 1996

MOST TRIES IN TESTS

Tries	Player	Tests	Career
49	R Underwood	85	1984 to 1996
30	J C Guscott	65	1989 to 1999
25	W J H Greenwood	41	1997 to 2003
23	B C Cohen	29	2000 to 2003
22	D D Luger	34	1998 to 2003
18	C N Lowe	25	1913 to 1923
15	A S Healey	51	1997 to 2003
14	N A Back	60	1994 to 2003
13	T Underwood	27	1992 to 1998
13	M J S Dawson	52	1995 to 2003
13	L B N Dallaglio	58	1995 to 2003

MOST CONVERSIONS IN TESTS

Cons	Player	Tests	Career
113	J P Wilkinson	46	1998 to 2003
56	P J Grayson	27	1995 to 2003
41	J M Webb	33	1987 to 1993
35	S D Hodgkinson	14	1989 to 1991
33	C R Andrew	71	1985 to 1997
17	L Stokes	12	1875 to 1881
17	C Hodgson	8	2001 to 2003

MOST PENALTY GOALS IN TESTS

Penalties	Player	Tests	Career
138	J P Wilkinson	46	1998 to 2003
86	C R Andrew	71	1985 to 1997
67	W H Hare	25	1974 to 1984
66	J M Webb	33	1987 to 1993
64	P J Grayson	27	1995 to 2003
43	S D Hodgkinson	14	1989 to 1991

MOST DROPPED GOALS IN TESTS

Drops	Player	Tests	Career
21	C R Andrew	71	1985 to 1997
13	J P Wilkinson	46	1998 to 2003
6	P J Grayson	27	1995 to 2003
4	J P Horton	13	1978 to 1984

International Championship Records

Record	Detail		Set
Most points in season	229	in five matches	2001
Most tries in season	29	in five matches	2001
Highest Score	80	80-23 v Italy	2001
Biggest win	57	80-23 v Italy	2001
Highest score conceded	37	12-37 v France	1972

Biggest defeat	27	6-33 v Scotland	1986
Most appearances	53	J Leonard	1991 – 2003
Most points in matches	379	J P Wilkinson	1998-2003
Most points in season	89	J P Wilkinson	2001
Most points in match	35	J P Wilkinson	v Italy, 2001
Most tries in matches	18	C N Lowe	1913 – 1923
	18	R Underwood	1984 – 1996
Most tries in season	8	C N Lowe	1914
Most tries in match	4	R W Poulton	v France, 1914
Most cons in matches	74	J P Wilkinson	1998 – 2003
Most cons in season	24	J P Wilkinson	2001
Most cons in match	9	J P Wilkinson	v Italy, 2001
Most pens in matches	66	J P Wilkinson	1998 – 2003
Most pens in season	18	S D Hodgkinson	1991
	18	J P Wilkinson	2000
Most pens in match	7	S D Hodgkinson	v Wales, 1991
	7	C R Andrew	v Scotland, 1995
	7	J P Wilkinson	v France, 1999
Most drops in matches	9	C R Andrew	1985 – 1997
Most drops in season	5	J P Wilkinson	2003
Most drops in match	2	R Hiller	v Ireland, 1970
	2	A G B Old	v France, 1978
	2	J P Horton	v France, 1980
	2	P J Grayson	v France, 1996
	2	J P Wilkinson	v Wales, 2003
	2	J P Wilkinson	v Ireland, 2003

Miscellaneous Records

Record	*Holder*	*Detail*
Longest Test Career	G S Pearce	14 seasons, 1978-79 to 1991-92
	J Leonard	14 seasons, 1990 to 2003
Youngest Test Cap	H C C Laird	18 yrs 134 days in 1927
Oldest Test Cap	F Gilbert	38 yrs in 1923

Career Records of England International Players
(up to 30 September 2003)

PLAYER	*Debut*	*Caps*	*T*	*C*	*P*	*D*	*Pts*
Backs:							
S Abbott	2003 v W	2	1	0	0	0	5
I R Balshaw	2000 v I	16	6	0	0	0	30
K P P Bracken	1993 v NZ	47	3	0	0	0	15
M J Catt	1994 v W	56	5	14	22	3	128
P D Christophers	2002 v Arg	3	2*	0	0	0	10
B C Cohen	2000 v I	29	23	0	0	0	115
M J S Dawson	1995 v WS	52	13	6	3	0	86
P J Grayson	1995 v WS	27	1	56	64	6	327
A C T Gomarsall	1996 v It	13	4	2	0	0	24
W J H Greenwood	1997 v A	41	25	0	0	0	125
A S Healey	1997 v I	51	15	0	0	0	75
C Hodgson	2001 v R	8	2	17	5	0	59
B Johnston	2002 v Arg	2	0	0	0	0	0
A D King	1997 v Arg	5	1	3	3	1	23

O J Lewsey	1998 v NZ	13	8	0	0	0	40
D D Luger	1998 v H	34	22	0	0	0	110
J Noon	2001 v C	5	1	0	0	0	5
M B Perry	1997 v A	36	10	0	0	0	50
D L Rees	1997 v A	11	3	0	0	0	15
J Robinson	2001 v It	21	12	0	0	0	60
D Scarbrough	2003 v W	1	0	0	0	0	0
J Simpson-Daniel	2002 v NZ	5	1	0	0	0	5
O J Smith	2003 v It	3	0	0	0	0	0
T R G Stimpson	1996 v It	19	2	5	5	0	35
M J Tindall	2000 v I	27	8	0	0	0	40
D J H Walder	2001 v C	4	2	11	3	0	41
F H H Waters	2001 v US	1	0	0	0	0	0
J P Wilkinson	1998 v I	46	5	113	138	13	704
M B Wood	2001 v C	2	1	0	0	0	5
Forwards:							
G S Archer	1996 v S	21	0	0	0	0	0
N A Back	1994 v S	60	14	0	0	1	73
S W Borthwick	2001 v F	8	0	0	0	0	0
M E Corry	1997 v Arg	28	2	0	0	0	10
L B N Dallaglio	1995 v SA	58	13	0	0	0	65
D L Flatman	2000 v SA	8	0	0	0	0	0
D J Garforth	1997 v W	25	0	0	0	0	0
W R Green	1997 v A	4	0	0	0	0	0
P B T Greening	1996 v It	24	6	0	0	0	30
D J Grewcock	1997 v Arg	42	1	0	0	0	5
R A Hill	1997 v S	60	11	0	0	0	55
M O Johnson	1993 v F	77	2	0	0	0	10
B J Kay	2001 v C	22	2	0	0	0	10
J Leonard	1990 v Arg	106	1	0	0	0	5
L W Moody	2001 v C	17	5	0	0	0	25
R Morris	2003 v W	2	0	0	0	0	0
M P Regan	1995 v SA	26	2	0	0	0	10
G C Rowntree	1995 v S	45	0	0	0	0	0
A Sanderson	2001 v R	5	1	0	0	0	5
P H Sanderson	1998 v NZ	6	1	0	0	0	5
S D Shaw	1996 v It	23	2	0	0	0	10
S Thompson	2002 v S	18	1	0	0	0	5
P J Vickery	1998 v W	31	0	0	0	0	0
D E West	1998 v F	19	3	0	0	0	15
J M White	2000 v SA	17	0	0	0	0	0
T J Woodman	1999 v US	10	0	0	0	0	0
J P R Worsley	1999 v Tg	27	7	0	0	0	35
M A Worsley	2003 v It	1	0	0	0	0	0

* Christophers's figures include a penalty try awarded against South Africa in 2002.

ENGLISH INTERNATIONAL PLAYERS

(up to 30 September 2003)

Note: Years given for International Championship matches are for second half of season; eg 1972 means season 1971-72. Years for all other matches refer to the actual year of the match. When a series has taken place, figures have been used to denote the particular matches in which players have featured. Thus 1984 *SA* 2 indicates that a player appeared in the second Test of the series.

Aarvold, C D (Cambridge U, W Hartlepool, Headingley, Blackheath) 1928 *A, W, I, F, S*, 1929 *W, I, F*, 1931 *W, S, F*, 1932 *SA, W, I, S*, 1933 *W*
Abbott, S (Wasps) 2003 *W* 2, *F* 3
Ackford, P J (Harlequins) 1988 *A*, 1989 *S, I, F, W, R, Fj*, 1990 *I, F, W, S, Arg* 3, 1991 *W, S, I, F, A*, [*NZ, It, F, S, A*]
Adams, A A (London Hospital) 1910 *F*
Adams, F R (Richmond) 1875 *I, S*, 1876 *S*, 1877 *I*, 1878 *S*, 1879 *S, I*
Adebayo, A A (Bath) 1996, *It*, 1997 *Arg* 1,2, *A* 2, *NZ* 1, 1998 *S*
Adey, G J (Leicester) 1976 *I, F*
Adkins, S J (Coventry) 1950 *I, F, S*, 1953 *W, I, F, S*
Agar, A E (Harlequins) 1952 *SA, W, S, I, F*, 1953 *W, I*
Alcock, A (Guy's Hospital) 1906 *SA*
Alderson, F H R (Hartlepool R) 1891 *W, I, S*, 1892 *W, S*, 1893 *W*
Alexander, H (Richmond) 1900 *I, S*, 1901 *W, I, S*, 1902 *W, I*
Alexander, W (Northern) 1927 *F*
Allison, D F (Coventry) 1956 *W, I, S, F*, 1957 *W*, 1958 *W, S*
Allport, A (Blackheath) 1892 *W*, 1893 *I*, 1894 *W, I, S*
Anderson, S (Rockcliff) 1899 *I*
Anderson, W F (Orrell) 1973 *NZ* 1
Anderton, C (Manchester FW) 1889 *M*
Andrew, C R (Cambridge U, Nottingham, Wasps, Toulouse, Newcastle) 1985 *R, F, S, I, W*, 1986 *W, S, I, F*, 1987 *I, F, W*, [*J* (R), *US*], 1988 *S, I* 1,2, *A* 1,2, *Fj, A*, 1989 *S, I, F, W, R, Fj*, 1990 *I, F, W, S, Arg* 3, 1991 *W, S, I, F, Fj, A*, [*NZ, It, US, F, S, A*], 1992 *S, I, F, W, C, SA*, 1993 *F, W, NZ*, 1994 *S, I, F, W, SA* 1,2, *R, C*, 1995 *I, F, W, S*, [*Arg, It, A, NZ, F*], 1997 *W* (R)
Appleford, G (London Irish) 2002 *Arg*
Archer, G S (Bristol, Army, Newcastle) 1996 *S, I*, 1997 *A* 2, *NZ* 1, *SA, NZ* 2, 1998 *F, W, S, I, A* 1, *NZ* 1, *H, It*, 1999 *Tg, Fj*, 2000 *I, F, W, It, S*
Archer, H (Bridgwater A) 1909 *W, F, I*
Armstrong, R (Northern) 1925 *W*
Arthur, T G (Wasps) 1966 *W, I*
Ashby, R C (Wasps) 1966 *I, F*, 1967 *A*
Ashcroft, A (Waterloo) 1956 *W, I, S, F*, 1957 *W, I, F, S*, 1958 *W, A, I, F, S*, 1959 *I, F, S*
Ashcroft, A H (Birkenhead Park) 1909 *A*
Ashford, W (Richmond) 1897 *W, I*, 1898 *S, W*
Ashworth, A (Oldham) 1892 *I*
Askew, J G (Cambridge U) 1930 *W, I, F*
Aslett, A R (Richmond) 1926 *W, I, F, S*, 1929 *S, F*
Assinder, E W (O Edwardians) 1909 *A, W*
Aston, R L (Blackheath) 1890 *S, I*
Auty, J R (Headingley) 1935 *S*

Back, N A (Leicester) 1994 *S, I*, 1995 [*Arg* (t), *It, WS*], 1997 *NZ* 1(R), *SA, NZ* 2, 1998 *F, W, S, I, H, It, A* 2, *SA* 2, 1999 *S, I, F, W, A, US, C*, [*It, NZ, Fj, SA*], 2000 *I, F, W, It, S, SA* 1,2, *A, Arg, SA* 3, 2001 *W, It, S, F, I, A, R, SA*, 2002 *S, I, F, W, It, NZ* (t+R), *A, SA*, 2003 *F* 1, *W* 1, *S, I, NZ, A, F* 3
Bailey, M D (Cambridge U, Wasps) 1984 *SA* 1,2, 1987 [*US*], 1989 *Fj*, 1990 *I, F, S* (R)
Bainbridge, S (Gosforth, Fylde) 1982 *F, W*, 1983 *F, W, S, I, NZ*, 1984 *S, I, F, W*, 1985 *NZ* 1,2, 1987 *F, W, S*, [*J, US*]
Baker, D G S (OMTs) 1955 *W, I, F, S*
Baker, E M (Moseley) 1895 *W, I, S*, 1896 *W, I, S*, 1897 *W*
Baker, H C (Clifton) 1887 *W*
Balshaw, I R (Bath) 2000 *I* (R), *F* (R), *It* (R), *S* (R), *A* (R), *Arg, SA* 3(R), 2001 *W, It, S, F, I*, 2002 *S* (R), *I* (R), 2003 *F* 2,3
Bance, J F (Bedford) 1954 *S*
Barkley, O (Bath) 2001 *US* (R)
Barley, B (Wakefield) 1984 *I, F, W, A*, 1988 *A* 1,2, *Fj*
Barnes, S (Bristol, Bath) 1984 *A*, 1985 *R* (R), *NZ* 1,2, 1986 *S* (R), *F* (R), 1987 *I* (R), 1988 *Fj*, 1993 *S, I*
Barr, R J (Leicester) 1932 *SA, W, I*
Barrett, E I M (Lennox) 1903 *S*
Barrington, T J M (Bristol) 1931 *W, I*
Barrington-Ward, L E (Edinburgh U) 1910 *W, I, F, S*
Barron, J H (Bingley) 1896 *S*, 1897 *W, I*
Bartlett, J T (Waterloo) 1951 *W*
Bartlett, R M (Harlequins) 1957 *W, I, F, S*, 1958 *I, F, S*
Barton, J (Coventry) 1967 *I, F, W*, 1972 *F*
Batchelor, T B (Oxford U) 1907 *F*
Bates, S M (Wasps) 1989 *R*
Bateson, A H (Otley) 1930 *W, I, F, S*
Bateson, H D (Liverpool) 1879 *I*
Batson, T (Blackheath) 1872 *S*, 1874 *S*, 1875 *I*
Batten, J M (Cambridge U) 1874 *S*
Baume, J L (Northern) 1950 *S*
Baxendell, J J N (Sale) 1998 *NZ* 2, *SA* 1
Baxter, J (Birkenhead Park) 1900 *W, I, S*
Bayfield, M C (Northampton) 1991 *Fj, A*, 1992 *S, I, F, W, C, SA*, 1993 *F, W, S, I*, 1994 *S, I, SA* 1,2, *R, C*, 1995 *I, F, W, S*, [*Arg, It, A, NZ, F*], *SA, WS*, 1996 *F, W*
Bazley, R C (Waterloo) 1952 *I, F*, 1953 *W, I, F, S*, 1955 *W, I, F, S*
Beal, N D (Northampton) 1996 *Arg*, 1997 *A* 1, 1998 *NZ* 1,2, *SA* 1, *H* (R), *SA* 2, 1999 *S, F* (R), *A* (t), *C* (R), [*It* (R), *Tg* (R), *Fj, SA*]
Beaumont, W B (Fylde) 1975 I, *A* 1(R),2, 1976 *A, W, S, I, F*, 1977 *S, I, F, W*, 1978 *F, W, S, I, NZ*, 1979 *S, I, F, W, NZ*, 1980 *I, F, W, S*, 1981 *W, S, I, F, Arg* 1,2, 1982 *A, S*
Bedford, H (Morley) 1889 *M*, 1890 *S, I*
Bedford, L L (Headingley) 1931 *W, I*
Beer, I D S (Harlequins) 1955 *F, S*
Beese, M C (Liverpool) 1972 *W, I, F*
Beim, T D (Sale) 1998 *NZ* 1(R),2
Bell, F J (Northern) 1900 *W*
Bell, H (New Brighton) 1884 *I*
Bell, J L (Darlington) 1878 *I*
Bell, P J (Blackheath) 1968 *W, I, F, S*
Bell, R W (Northern) 1900 *W, I, S*
Bendon, G J (Wasps) 1959 *W, I, F, S*
Bennett, N O (St Mary's Hospital, Waterloo) 1947 *W, S, F*, 1948 *A, W, I, S*
Bennett, W N (Bedford, London Welsh) 1975 *S, A*1, 1976 *S* (R), 1979 *S, I, F, W*
Bennetts, B B (Penzance) 1909 *A, W*
Bentley, J (Sale, Newcastle) 1988 *I* 2, *A* 1, 1997 *A* 1, *SA*
Bentley, J E (Gipsies) 1871 *S*, 1872 *S*
Benton, S (Gloucester) 1998 *A* 1
Berridge, M J (Northampton) 1949 *W, I*
Berry, H (Gloucester) 1910 *W, I, F, S*
Berry, J (Tyldesley) 1891 *W, I, S*
Berry, J T W (Leicester) 1939 *W, I, S*
Beswick, E (Swinton) 1882 *I, S*
Biggs, J M (UCH) 1878 *S*, 1879 *I*
Birkett, J G G (Harlequins) 1906 *S, F, SA*, 1907 *F, W, S*, 1908 *F, W,I , S*, 1910 *W, I, S*, 1911 *W, F, I , S*, 1912 *W, I , S, F*
Birkett L (Clapham R) 1875 *S*, 1877 *I, S*
Birkett, R H (Clapham R) 1871 *S*, 1875 *S*, 1876 *S*, 1877 *I*
Bishop, C C (Blackheath) 1927 *F*
Black, B H (Blackheath) 1930 *W, I, F, S*, 1931 *W, I, S, F*, 1932 *S*, 1933 *W*
Blacklock, J H (Aspatria) 1898 *I*, 1899 *I*
Blakeway, P J (Gloucester) 1980 *I, F, W, S*, 1981 *W, S, I, F*, 1982 *I, F, W*, 1984 *I, F, W, SA* 1, 1985 *R, F, S, I*
Blakiston, A F (Northampton) 1920 *S*, 1921 *W, I, S, F*, 1922 *W*, 1923 *S, F*, 1924 *W, I, F, S*, 1925 *NZ, W, I, S, F*
Blatherwick, T (Manchester) 1878 *I*
Body, J A (Gipsies) 1872 *S*, 1873 *S*
Bolton, C A (United Services) 1909 *F*
Bolton, R (Harlequins) 1933 *W*, 1936 *S*, 1937 *S*, 1938 *W, I*
Bolton, W N (Blackheath) 1882 *I, S*, 1883 *W, I, S*, 1884 *W, I, S*, 1885 *I*, 1887 *I, S*
Bonaventura, M S (Blackheath) 1931 *W*
Bond, A M (Sale) 1978 *NZ*, 1979 *S, I, NZ*, 1980 *I*, 1982 *I*
Bonham-Carter, E (Oxford U) 1891 *S*

Bonsor, F (Bradford) 1886 *W, I, S*, 1887 *W, S*, 1889 *M*
Boobbyer, B (Rosslyn Park) 1950 *W, I, F, S*, 1951 *W, F*, 1952 *S, I, F*
Booth, L A (Headingley) 1933 *W, I, S*, 1934 *S*, 1935 *W, I, S*
Borthwick, S W (Bath) 2001 *F, C* 1,2(R), *US, R*, 2003 *A* (t), *W* 2(t), *F* 2
Botting, I J (Oxford U) 1950 *W, I*
Boughton, H J (Gloucester) 1935 *W, I, S*
Boyle, C W (Oxford U) 1873 *S*
Boyle, S B (Gloucester) 1983 *W, S, I*
Boylen, F (Hartlepool R) 1908 *F, W, I, S*
Bracken, K P P (Bristol, Saracens) 1993 *NZ*, 1994 *S, I, C*, 1995 *I, F, W, S*, [*It, WS* (t)], *SA*, 1996 *It* (R), 1997 *Arg* 1,2, *A* 2, *NZ* 1,2, 1998 *F, W*, 1999 *S*(R), *I, F, A*, 2000 *SA* 1,2, *A*, 2001 *It* (R), *S* (R), *F* (R), *C* 1,2, *US, I* (R), *A, R* (R), *SA*, 2002 *S, I, F, W, It*, 2003 *W* 1, *It* (R), *I* (t), *NZ, A, F* 3
Bradby, M S (United Services) 1922 *I, F*
Bradley, R (W Hartlepool) 1903 *W*
Bradshaw, H (Bramley) 1892 *S*, 1893 *W, I, S*, 1894 *W, I, S*
Brain, S E (Coventry) 1984 *SA* 2, *A* (R), 1985 *R, F, S, I, W, NZ* 1,2, 1986 *W, S, I, F*
Braithwaite, J (Leicester) 1905 *NZ*
Braithwaite-Exley, B (Headingley) 1949 *W*
Brettargh, A T (Liverpool OB) 1900 *W*, 1903 *I, S*, 1904 *W, I, S*, 1905 *I, S*
Brewer, J (Gipsies) 1876 *I*
Briggs, A (Bradford) 1892 *W, I, S*
Brinn, A (Gloucester) 1972 *W, I, S*
Broadley, T (Bingley) 1893 *W, S*, 1894 *W, I, S*, 1896 *S*
Bromet, W E (Richmond) 1891 *W, I*, 1892 *W, I, S*, 1893 *W, I, S*, 1895 *W, I, S*, 1896 *I*
Brook, P W P (Harlequins) 1930 *S*, 1931 *F*, 1936 *S*
Brooke, T J (Richmond) 1968 *F, S*
Brooks, F G (Bedford) 1906 *SA*
Brooks, M J (Oxford U) 1874 *S*
Brophy, T J (Liverpool) 1964 *I, F, S*, 1965 *W, I*, 1966 *W, I, F*
Brough, J W (Silloth) 1925 *NZ, W*
Brougham, H (Harlequins) 1912 *W, I, S, F*
Brown, A A (Exeter) 1938 *S*
Brown, L G (Oxford U, Blackheath) 1911 *W, F, I, S*, 1913 *SA, W, F, I, S*, 1914 *W, I, S, F*, 1921 *W, I, S, F*, 1922 *W*
Brown S P (Richmond) 1998 *A* 1, *SA* 1
Brown, T W (Bristol) 1928 *S*, 1929 *W, I, S, F*, 1932 *S*, 1933 *W, I, S*
Brunton, J (N Durham) 1914 *W, I, S*
Brutton, E B (Cambridge U) 1886 *S*
Bryden, C C (Clapham R) 1876 *I*, 1877 *S*
Bryden, H A (Clapham R) 1874 *S*
Buckingham, R A (Leicester) 1927 *F*
Bucknall, A L (Richmond) 1969 *SA*, 1970 *I, W, S, F*, 1971 *W, I, F, S* (2[1C])
Buckton, J R D (Saracens) 1988 *A* (R), 1990 *Arg* 1,2
Budd, A (Blackheath) 1878 *I*, 1879 *S, I*, 1881 *W, S*
Budworth, R T D (Blackheath) 1890 *W*, 1891 *W, S*
Bull, A G (Northampton) 1914 *W*
Bullough, E (Wigan) 1892 *W, I, S*
Bulpitt, M P (Blackheath) 1970 *S*
Bulteel, A J (Manchester) 1876 *I*
Bunting, W L (Moseley) 1897 *I, S*, 1898 *I, S, W*, 1899 *S*, 1900 *S*, 1901 *I, S*
Burland, D W (Bristol) 1931 *W, I, F*, 1932 *I, S*, 1933 *W, I, S*
Burns, B H (Blackheath) 1871 *S*
Burton, G W (Blackheath) 1879 *S, I*, 1880 *S*, 1881 *I, W, S*
Burton, H C (Richmond) 1926 *W*
Burton, M A (Gloucester) 1972 *W, I, F, S, SA*, 1974 *F, W*, 1975 *S*, A 1,2, 1976 *A, W, S, I, F*, 1978 *F, W*
Bush, J A (Clifton) 1872 *S*, 1873 *S*, 1875 *S*, 1876 *I, S*
Butcher, C J S (Harlequins) 1984 *SA* 1,2, *A*
Butcher, W V (Streatham) 1903 *S*, 1904 *W, I, S*, 1905 *W, I, S*
Butler, A G (Harlequins) 1937 *W, I*
Butler, P E (Gloucester) 1975 *A* 1, 1976 *F*
Butterfield, J (Northampton) 1953 *F, S*, 1954 *W, NZ, I, S, F*, 1955 *W, I, F, S*, 1956 *W, I, S, F*, 1957 *W, I, F, S*, 1958 *W, A, I, F, S*, 1959 *W, I, F, S*
Byrne, F A (Moseley) 1897 *W*
Byrne, J F (Moseley) 1894 *W, I, S*, 1895 *I, S*, 1896 *I*, 1897 *W, I, S*, 1898 *I, S, W*, 1899 *I*

Cain, J J (Waterloo) 1950 *W*
Callard, J E B (Bath) 1993 *NZ*, 1994 *S, I*, 1995 [*WS*], *SA*
Campbell, D A (Cambridge U) 1937 *W, I*
Candler, P L (St Bart's Hospital) 1935 *W*, 1936 *NZ, W, I, S*, 1937 *W, I, S*, 1938 *W, S*
Cannell, L B (Oxford U, St Mary's Hospital) 1948 *F*, 1949 *W, I, F, S*, 1950 *W, I, F, S*, 1952 *SA, W*, 1953 *W, I, F*, 1956 *I, S, F*, 1957 *W, I*
Caplan, D W N (Headingley) 1978 *S, I*
Cardus, R M (Roundhay) 1979 *F, W*
Carey, G M (Blackheath) 1895 *W, I, S*, 1896 *W, I*
Carleton, J (Orrell) 1979 *NZ*, 1980 *I, F, W, S*, 1981 *W, S, I, F, Arg* 1,2, 1982 *A, S, I, F, W*, 1983 *F, W, S, I, NZ*, 1984 *S, I, F, W, A*
Carling, W D C (Durham U, Harlequins) 1988 *F, W, S, I* 1,2, *A2, Fj*, A, 1989 *S, I, F, W, Fj*, 1990 *I, F, W, S, Arg* 1,2,3, 1991 *W, S, I, F, Fj, A*, [*NZ, It, US, F, S, A*], 1992 *S, I, F, W, C, SA*, 1993 *F, W, S, I, NZ*, 1994 *S, I, F, W, SA* 1,2, *R, C*, 1995 *I, F, W, S*, [*Arg, WS, A, NZ, F*], *SA, WS*, 1996 *F, W, S, I, It, Arg*, 1997 *S, I, F, W*
Carpenter, A D (Gloucester) 1932 *SA*
Carr, R S L (Manchester) 1939 *W, I, S*
Cartwright, V H (Nottingham) 1903 *W, I, S*, 1904 *W, S*, 1905 *W, I, S, NZ*, 1906 *W, I, S, F, SA*
Catcheside, H C (Percy Park) 1924 *W, I, F, S*, 1926 *W, I*, 1927 *I, S*
Catt, M J (Bath) 1994 *W* (R), *C* (R), 1995 *I, F, W, S*, [*Arg, It, WS, A, NZ, F*], *SA, WS*, 1996 *F, W, S, I, It, Arg*, 1997 *W, Arg* 1, *A* 1,2, *NZ* 1, *SA*, 1998 *F, W* (R), *I, A* 2(R), *SA* 2, 1999 *S, F, W, A, C* (R), [*Tg* (R), *Fj, SA* (R)], 2000 *I, F, W, It, S, SA* 1,2, *A, Arg*, 2001 *W, It, S, F, I, A, R* (R), *SA*
Cattell, R H B (Blackheath) 1895 *W, I, S*, 1896 *W, I, S*, 1900 *W*
Cave, J W (Richmond) 1889 *M*
Cave, W T C (Blackheath) 1905 *W*
Challis, R (Bristol) 1957 *I, F, S*
Chambers, E L (Bedford) 1908 *F*, 1910 *W, I*
Chantrill, B S (Bristol) 1924 *W, I, F, S*
Chapman, C E (Cambridge U) 1884 *W*
Chapman D E (Richmond) 1998 *A* 1(R)
Chapman, F E (Hartlepool) 1910 *W, I, F, S*, 1912 *W*, 1914 *W, I*
Cheesman, W I (OMTs) 1913 *SA, W, F, I*
Cheston, E C (Richmond) 1873 *S*, 1874 *S*, 1875 *I, S*, 1876 *S*
Chilcott, G J (Bath) 1984 *A*, 1986 *I, F*, 1987 *F* (R), *W*, [*J, US, W* (R)], 1988 *I* 2(R), *Fj*, 1989 *I* (R), *F, W, R*
Christophers, P (Bristol) 2002 *Arg, SA*, 2003 *W* 1(R)
Christopherson, P (Blackheath) 1891 *W, S*
Clark, C W H (Liverpool) 1876 *I*
Clarke, A J (Coventry) 1935 *W, I, S*, 1936 *NZ, W, I*
Clarke, B B (Bath, Richmond) 1992 *SA*, 1993 *F, W, S, I, NZ*, 1994 *S, F, W, SA* 1,2, *R, C*, 1995 *I, F, W, S*, [*Arg, It, A, NZ, F*], *SA, WS*, 1996 *F, W, S, I, Arg* (R), 1997 *W, Arg* 1,2, *A* 1(R), 1998 *A* 1(t),*NZ* 1,2, *SA* 1, *H, It*, 1999 *A* (R)
Clarke, S J S (Cambridge U, Blackheath) 1963 *W, I, F, S, NZ* 1,2, *A*, 1964 *NZ, W, I*, 1965 *I, F, S*
Clayton, J H (Liverpool) 1871 *S*
Clements, J W (O Cranleighans) 1959 *I, F, S*
Cleveland, C R (Blackheath) 1887 *W, S*
Clibborn, W G (Richmond) 1886 *W, I, S*, 1887 *W, I, S*
Clough, F J (Cambridge U, Orrell) 1986 *I, F*, 1987 [*J* (R), *US*]
Coates, C H (Yorkshire W) 1880 *S*, 1881 *S*, 1882 *S*
Coates, V H M (Bath) 1913 *SA, W, F, I, S*
Cobby, W (Hull) 1900 *W*
Cockerham, A (Bradford Olicana) 1900 *W*
Cockerill, R (Leicester) 1997 *Arg* 1(R),2, *A* 2(t+R), *NZ* 1, *SA, NZ* 2, 1998 *W, S, I, A* 1, *NZ* 1,2, *SA* 1, *H, It, A* 2, *SA* 2, 1999 *S, I, F, W, A, C* (R), [*It, NZ, Tg* (R), *Fj* (R)]
Codling, A (Harlequins) 2002 *Arg*
Cohen, B C (Northampton) 2000 *I, F, W, It, S, SA* 2, *Arg, SA* 3, 2001 *W, It, S, F, R*, 2002 *S, I, F, W, It, NZ, A, SA*, 2003 *F* 1, *W* 1, *S, I, NZ, A, F* 2,3
Colclough, M J (Angoulême, Wasps, Swansea) 1978 *S, I*, 1979 *NZ*, 1980 *F, W, S*, 1981 *W, S, I, F*, 1982 *A, S, I, F, W*, 1983 *F, NZ*, 1984 *S, I, F, W*, 1986 *W, S, I, F*
Coley, E (Northampton) 1929 *F*, 1932 *W*
Collins, P J (Camborne) 1952 *S, I, F*
Collins, W E (O Cheltonians) 1874 *S*, 1875 *I, S*, 1876 *I, S*
Considine, S G U (Bath) 1925 *F*
Conway, G S (Cambridge U, Rugby, Manchester) 1920 *F, I, S*, 1921 *F*, 1922 *W, I, F, S*, 1923 *W, I, S, F*, 1924 *W, I, F, S*, 1925 *NZ*, 1927 *W*
Cook, J G (Bedford) 1937 *S*
Cook, P W (Richmond) 1965 *I, F*
Cooke, D A (Harlequins) 1976 *W, S, I, F*
Cooke, D H (Harlequins) 1981 *W, S, I, F*, 1984 *I*, 1985 *R, F, S, I, W, NZ* 1,2

Cooke, P (Richmond) 1939 *W, I*
Coop, T (Leigh) 1892 *S*
Cooper, J G (Moseley) 1909 *A, W*
Cooper, M J (Moseley) 1973 *F, S, NZ* 2(R), 1975 *F, W*, 1976 *A, W*, 1977 *S, I, F, W*
Coopper, S F (Blackheath) 1900 *W*, 1902 *W, I*, 1905 *W, I, S*, 1907 *W*
Corbett, L J (Bristol) 1921 *F*, 1923 *W, I*, 1924 *W, I, F, S*, 1925 *NZ, W, I, S, F*, 1927 *W, I, S, F*
Corless, B J (Coventry, Moseley) 1976 *A, I* (R), 1977 *S, I, F, W*, 1978 *F, W, S, I*
Corry, M E (Bristol, Leicester) 1997 *Arg* 1,2, 1998 *H, It, SA* 2(t), 1999 *F*(R), *A, C* (t), [*It* (R), *NZ* (t+R), *SA* (R)], 2000 *I* (R), *F* (R), *W* (R), *It* (R), *S (R), Arg* (R), *SA* 3(t), 2001 *W* (R), *It* (R), *F* (t), *C* 1, *I*, 2002 *F* (t+R), *W* (t), 2003 *W* 2, *F* 2,3
Cotton, F E (Loughborough Colls, Coventry, Sale) 1971 *S* (2[1C]), *P*, 1973 *W, I, F, S, NZ* 2, *A*, 1974 *S, I*, 1975 *I, F, W*, 1976 *A, W, S, I, F*, 1977 *S, I, F, W*, 1978 *S, I*, 1979 *NZ*, 1980 *I, F, W, S*, 1981 *W*
Coulman, M J (Moseley) 1967 *A, I, F, S, W*, 1968 *W, I, F, S*
Coulson, T J (Coventry) 1927 *W*, 1928 *A, W*
Court, E D (Blackheath) 1885 *W*
Coverdale, H (Blackheath) 1910 *F*, 1912 *I, F*, 1920 *W*
Cove-Smith, R (OMTs) 1921 *S, F*, 1922 *I, F, S*, 1923 *W, I, S, F*, 1924 *W, I, S, F*, 1925 *NZ, W, I, S, F*, 1927 *W, I, S, F*, 1928 *A, W, I, F, S*, 1929 *W, I*
Cowling, R J (Leicester) 1977 *S, I, F, W*, 1978 *F, NZ*, 1979 *S, I*
Cowman, A R (Loughborough Colls, Coventry) 1971 *S* (2[1C]), *P*, 1973 *W, I*
Cox, N S (Sunderland) 1901 *S*
Cranmer, P (Richmond, Moseley) 1934 *W, I, S*, 1935 *W, I, S*, 1936 *NZ, W, I, S*, 1937 *W, I, S*, 1938 *W, I, S*
Creed, R N (Coventry) 1971 *P*
Cridlan, A G (Blackheath) 1935 *W, I, S*
Crompton, C A (Blackheath) 1871 *S*
Crosse, C W (Oxford U) 1874 *S*, 1875 *I*
Cumberlege, B S (Blackheath) 1920 *W, I, S*, 1921 *W, I, S, F*, 1922 *W*
Cumming, D C (Blackheath) 1925 *S, F*
Cunliffe, F L (RMA) 1874 *S*
Currey, F I (Marlborough N) 1872 *S*
Currie, J D (Oxford U, Harlequins, Bristol) 1956 *W, I, S, F*, 1957 *W, I, F, S*, 1958 *W, A, I, F, S*, 1959 *W, I, F, S*, 1960 *W, I, F, S*, 1961 *SA*, 1962 *W, I, F*
Cusani, D A (Orrell) 1987 *I*
Cusworth, L (Leicester) 1979 *NZ*, 1982 *F, W*, 1983 *F, W, NZ*, 1984 *S, I, F, W*, 1988 *F, W*

D'Aguilar, F B G (Royal Engineers) 1872 *S*
Dallaglio, L B N (Wasps) 1995 *SA* (R), *WS*, 1996 *F, W, S, I, It, Arg*, 1997 *S, I, F*, 1997 *A* 1,2, *NZ* 1, *SA, NZ* 2, 1998 *F, W, S, I, A* 2, *SA* 2, 1999 *S, I, F, W, US, C*, [*It, NZ, Tg, Fj, SA*], 2000 *I, F, W, It, S, SA* 1,2, *A, Arg, SA* 3, 2001 *W, It, S, F*, 2002 *It* (R), *NZ, A* (t), *SA* (R), 2003 *F* 1(R), *W* 1, *It, S, I, NZ, A*
Dalton, T J (Coventry) 1969 *S*(R)
Danby, T (Harlequins) 1949 *W*
Daniell, J (Richmond) 1899 *W*, 1900 *I, S*, 1902 *I, S*, 1904 *I, S*
Darby, A J L (Birkenhead Park) 1899 *I*
Davenport, A (Ravenscourt Park) 1871 *S*
Davey, J (Redruth) 1908 *S*, 1909 *W*
Davey, R F (Teignmouth) 1931 *W*
Davidson, Jas (Aspatria) 1897 *S*, 1898 *S, W*, 1899 *I, S*
Davidson, Jos (Aspatria) 1899 *W, S*
Davies, G H (Cambridge U, Coventry, Wasps) 1981 *S, I, F, Arg* 1,2, 1982 *A, S, I*, 1983 *F, W, S*, 1984 *S, SA* 1,2, 1985 *R* (R), *NZ* 1,2, 1986 *W, S, I, F*
Davies, P H (Sale) 1927 *I*
Davies, V G (Harlequins) 1922 *W*, 1925 *NZ*
Davies, W J A (United Services, RN) 1913 *SA, W, F, I, S*, 1914 *I, S, F*, 1920 *F, I, S*, 1921 *W, I, S, F*, 1922 *I, F, S*, 1923 *W, I, S, F*
Davies, W P C (Harlequins) 1953 *S*, 1954 *NZ, I*, 1955 *W, I, F, S*, 1956 *W*, 1957 *F, S*, 1958 *W*
Davis, A M (Torquay Ath, Harlequins) 1963 *W, I, S, NZ* 1,2, 1964 *NZ, W, I, F, S*, 1966 *W*, 1967 *A*, 1969 *SA*, 1970 *I, W, S*
Dawe, R G R (Bath) 1987 *I, F, W*, [*US*], 1995 [*WS*]
Dawson, E F (RIEC) 1878 *I*
Dawson, M J S (Northampton) 1995 *WS*, 1996 *F, W, S, I*, 1997 *A* 1, *SA, NZ* 2(R), 1998 *W* (R), *S, I, NZ* 1,2, *SA* 1, *H, It, A* 2, *SA* 2, 1999 *S, F*(R), *W, A*(R), *US, C*, [*It, NZ, Tg, Fj* (R), *SA*], 2000 *I, F, W, It, S, A* (R), *Arg, SA* 3, 2001 *W, It, S, F, I*, 2002 *W* (R), *It* (R), *NZ, A, SA*, 2003 *It, S, I, A* (R), *F* 3(R)

Day, H L V (Leicester) 1920 *W*, 1922 *W, F*, 1926 *S*
Dean, G J (Harlequins) 1931 *I*
Dee, J M (Hartlepool R) 1962 *S*, 1963 *NZ* 1
Devitt, Sir T G (Blackheath) 1926 *I, F*, 1928 *A, W*
Dewhurst, J H (Richmond) 1887 *W, I, S*, 1890 *W*
De Glanville, P R (Bath) 1992 *SA* (R), 1993 *W* (R), *NZ*, 1994 *S, I, F, W, SA* 1,2, *C* (R), 1995 [*Arg* (R), *It, WS*], *SA* (R), 1996 *W* (R), *I* (R), *It*, 1997 *S, I, F, W, Arg* 1,2, *A* 1,2, *NZ* 1,2, 1998 *W* (R), *S* (R), *I* (R), *A* 2, *SA* 2, 1999 *A* (R), *US*, [*It, NZ, Fj* (R), *SA*]
De Winton, R F C (Marlborough N) 1893 *W*
Dibble, R (Bridgwater A) 1906 *S, F, SA*, 1908 *F, W, I, S*, 1909 *A, W, F, I, S*, 1910 *S*, 1911 *W, F, S*, 1912 *W, I, S*
Dicks, J (Northampton) 1934 *W, I, S*, 1935 *W, I, S*, 1936 *S*, 1937 *I*
Dillon, E W (Blackheath) 1904 *W, I, S*, 1905 *W*
Dingle, A J (Hartlepool R) 1913 *I*, 1914 *S, F*
Diprose, A J (Saracens) 1997 *Arg* 1,2, *A* 2, *NZ* 1, 1998 *W* (R), *S* (R), *I, A* 1, *NZ* 2, *SA* 1
Dixon, P J (Harlequins, Gosforth) 1971 *P*, 1972 *W, I, F, S*, 1973 *I, F, S*, 1974 *S, I, F, W*, 1975 *I*, 1976 *F*, 1977 *S, I, F, W*, 1978 *F, S, I, NZ*
Dobbs, G E B (Devonport A) 1906 *W, I*
Doble, S A (Moseley) 1972 *SA*, 1973 *NZ* 1, *W*
Dobson, D D (Newton Abbot) 1902 *W, I, S*, 1903 *W, I, S*
Dobson, T H (Bradford) 1895 *S*
Dodge, P W (Leicester) 1978 *W, S, I, NZ*, 1979 *S, I, F, W*, 1980 *W, S*, 1981 *W, S, I, F, Arg* 1,2, 1982 *A, S, F, W*, 1983 *F, W, S, I, NZ*, 1985 *R, F, S, I, W, NZ* 1,2
Donnelly, M P (Oxford U) 1947 *I*
Dooley, W A (Preston Grasshoppers, Fylde) 1985 *R, F, S, I, W, NZ* 2(R), 1986 *W, S, I, F*, 1987 *F, W*, [*A, US, W*], 1988 *F, W, S, I* 1,2, *A* 1,2, *Fj*, A, 1989 *S, I, F, W, R, Fj*, 1990 *I, F, W, S, Arg* 1,2,3, 1991 *W, S, I, F*, [*NZ, US, F, S, A*], 1992 *S, I, F, W, C, SA*, 1993 *W, S, I*
Dovey, B A (Rosslyn Park) 1963 *W, I*
Down, P J (Bristol) 1909 *A*
Dowson, A O (Moseley) 1899 *S*
Drake-Lee, N J (Cambridge U, Leicester) 1963 *W, I, F, S*, 1964 *NZ, W, I*, 1965 *W*
Duckett, H (Bradford) 1893 *I, S*
Duckham, D J (Coventry) 1969 *I, F, S, W, SA*, 1970 *I, W, S, F*, 1971 *W, I, F, S* (2[1C]), *P*, 1972 *W, I, F, S*, 1973 *NZ* 1, *W, I, F, S, NZ* 2, *A*, 1974 *S, I, F, W*, 1975 *I, F, W*, 1976 *A, W, S*
Dudgeon, H W (Richmond) 1897 *S*, 1898 *I, S, W*, 1899 *W, I, S*
Dugdale, J M (Ravenscourt Park) 1871 *S*
Dun, A F (Wasps) 1984 *W*
Duncan, R F H (Guy's Hospital) 1922 *I, F, S*
Duncombe, N (Harlequins) 2002 *S* (R), *I* (R)
Dunkley, P E (Harlequins) 1931 *I, S*, 1936 *NZ, W, I, S*
Duthie, J (W Hartlepool) 1903 *W*
Dyson, J W (Huddersfield) 1890 *S*, 1892 *S*, 1893 *I, S*

Ebdon, P J (Wellington) 1897 *W, I*
Eddison, J H (Headingley) 1912 *W, I, S, F*
Edgar, C S (Birkenhead Park) 1901 *S*
Edwards, R (Newport) 1921 *W, I, S, F*, 1922 *W, F*, 1923 *W*, 1924 *W, F, S*, 1925 *NZ*
Egerton, D W (Bath) 1988 *I* 2, *A* 1, *Fj* (R), *A*, 1989 *Fj*, 1990 *I, Arg* 2(R)
Elliot, C H (Sunderland) 1886 *W*
Elliot, E W (Sunderland) 1901 *W, I, S*, 1904 *W*
Elliot, W (United Services, RN) 1932 *I, S*, 1933 *W, I, S*, 1934 *W, I*
Elliott, A E (St Thomas's Hospital) 1894 *S*
Ellis, J (Wakefield) 1939 *S*
Ellis, S S (Queen's House) 1880 *I*
Emmott, C (Bradford) 1892 *W*
Enthoven, H J (Richmond) 1878 *I*
Estcourt, N S D (Blackheath) 1955 *S*
Evans, B J (Leicester) 1988 *A* 2, *Fj*
Evans, E (Sale) 1948 *A*, 1950 *W*, 1951 *I, F, S*, 1952 *SA, W, S, I, F*, 1953 *I, F, S*, 1954 *W, NZ, I, F*, 1956 *W, I, S, F*, 1957 *W, I, F, S*, 1958 *W, A, I, F, S*
Evans, G W (Coventry) 1972 *S*, 1973 *W (R), F, S, NZ* 2, 1974 *S, I, F, W*
Evans, N L (RNEC) 1932 *W, I, S*, 1933 *W, I*
Evanson, A M (Richmond) 1883 *W, I, S*, 1884 *S*
Evanson, W A D (Richmond) 1875 *S*, 1877 *S*, 1878 *S*, 1879 *S, I*
Evershed, F (Blackheath) 1889 *M*, 1890 *W, S, I*, 1892 *W, I, S*, 1893 *W, I, S*

Eyres, W C T (Richmond) 1927 *I*

Fagan, A R St L (Richmond) 1887 *I*
Fairbrother, K E (Coventry) 1969 *I, F, S, W, SA*, 1970 *I, W, S, F*, 1971 *W, I, F*
Faithfull, C K T (Harlequins) 1924 *I*, 1926 *F, S*
Fallas, H (Wakefield T) 1884 *I*
Fegan, J H C (Blackheath) 1895 *W, I, S*
Fernandes, C W L (Leeds) 1881 *I, W, S*
Fidler, J H (Gloucester) 1981 *Arg* 1,2, 1984 *SA* 1,2
Fidler, R J (Gloucester) 1998 *NZ* 2, *SA* 1
Field, E (Middlesex W) 1893 *W, I*
Fielding, K J (Moseley, Loughborough Colls) 1969 *I, F, S, SA*, 1970 *I, F*, 1972 *W, I, F, S*
Finch, R T (Cambridge U) 1880 *S*
Finlan, J F (Moseley) 1967 *I, F, S, W, NZ*, 1968 *W, I*, 1969 *I, F, S, W*, 1970 *F*, 1973 *NZ* 1
Finlinson, H W (Blackheath) 1895 *W, I, S*
Finney, S (RIE Coll) 1872 *S*, 1873 *S*
Firth, F (Halifax) 1894 *W, I, S*
Flatman, D L (Saracens) 2000 *SA* 1(t),2(t+R), *A* (t), *Arg* (t+R), 2001 *F* (t), *C* 2(t+R), *US* (t+R), 2002 *Arg*
Fletcher, N C (OMTs) 1901 *W, I, S*, 1903 *S*
Fletcher, T (Seaton) 1897 *W*
Fletcher, W R B (Marlborough N) 1873 *S*, 1875 *S*
Fookes, E F (Sowerby Bridge) 1896 *W, I, S*, 1897 *W, I, S*, 1898 *I, W*, 1899 *I, S*
Ford, P J (Gloucester) 1964 *W, I, F, S*
Forrest, J W (United Services, RN) 1930 *W, I, F, S*, 1931 *W, I, S, F*, 1934 *I, S*
Forrest, R (Wellington) 1899 *W*, 1900 *S*, 1902 *I, S*, 1903 *I, S*
Foulds, R T (Waterloo) 1929 *W, I*
Fowler, F D (Manchester) 1878 *S*, 1879 *S*
Fowler, H (Oxford U) 1878 *S*, 1881 *W, S*
Fowler, R H (Leeds) 1877 *I*
Fox, F H (Wellington) 1890 *W, S*
Francis, T E S (Cambridge U) 1926 *W, I, F, S*
Frankcom, G P (Cambridge U, Bedford) 1965 *W, I, F, S*
Fraser, E C (Blackheath) 1875 *I*
Fraser, G (Richmond) 1902 *W, I, S*, 1903 *W, I*
Freakes, H D (Oxford U) 1938 *W*, 1939 *W, I*
Freeman, H (Marlborough N) 1872 *S*, 1873 *S*, 1874 *S*
French, R J (St Helens) 1961 *W, I, F, S*
Fry, H A (Liverpool) 1934 *W, I, S*
Fry, T W (Queen's House) 1880 *I, S*, 1881 *W*
Fuller, H G (Cambridge U) 1882 *I, S*, 1883 *W, I, S*, 1884 *W*

Gadney, B C (Leicester, Headingley) 1932 *I, S*, 1933 *I, S*, 1934 *W, I, S*, 1935 *S*, 1936 *NZ, W, I, S*, 1937 *S*, 1938 *W*
Gamlin, H T (Blackheath) 1899 *W, S*, 1900 *W, I, S*, 1901 *S*, 1902 *W, I, S*, 1903 *W, I, S*, 1904 *W, I, S*
Gardner, E R (Devonport Services) 1921 *W, I, S*, 1922 *W, I, F*, 1923 *W, I, S, F*
Gardner, H P (Richmond) 1878 *I*
Garforth, D J (Leicester) 1997 *W* (R), *Arg* 1,2, *A* 1, *NZ* 1, *SA, NZ* 2, 1998 *F, W* (R), *S, I, H, It, A* 2, *SA* 2, 1999 *S, I, F, W, A, C* (R), [*It* (R), *NZ* (R), *Fj*], 2000 *It*
Garnett, H W T (Bradford) 1877 *S*
Gavins, M N (Leicester) 1961 *W*
Gay, D J (Bath) 1968 *W, I, F, S*
Gent, D R (Gloucester) 1905 *NZ*, 1906 *W, I*, 1910 *W, I*
Genth, J S M (Manchester) 1874 *S*, 1875 *S*
George, J T (Falmouth) 1947 *S, F*, 1949 *I*
Gerrard, R A (Bath) 1932 *SA, W, I, S*, 1933 *W, I, S*, 1934 *W, I, S*, 1936 *NZ, W, I, S*
Gibbs, G A (Bristol) 1947 *F*, 1948 *I*
Gibbs, J C (Harlequins) 1925 *NZ, W*, 1926 *F*, 1927 *W, I, S, F*
Gibbs, N (Harlequins) 1954 *S, F*
Giblin, L F (Blackheath) 1896 *W, I*, 1897 *S*
Gibson, A S (Manchester) 1871 *S*
Gibson, C O P (Northern) 1901 *W*
Gibson, G R (Northern) 1899 *W*, 1901 *S*
Gibson, T A (Northern) 1905 *W, S*
Gilbert, F G (Devonport Services) 1923 *W, I*
Gilbert, R (Devonport A) 1908 *W, I, S*
Giles, J L (Coventry) 1935 *W, I*, 1937 *W, I*, 1938 *I, S*
Gittings, W J (Coventry) 1967 *NZ*
Glover, P B (Bath) 1967 *A*, 1971 *F, P*
Godfray, R E (Richmond) 1905 *NZ*
Godwin, H O (Coventry) 1959 *F, S*, 1963 *S, NZ* 1,2, *A*, 1964 *NZ, I, F, S*, 1967 *NZ*
Gomarsall, A C T (Wasps, Bedford, Gloucester) 1996 *It, Arg*, 1997 *S, I, F, Arg* 2(R) 2000 *It* (R), 2002 *Arg, SA* (R), 2003 *F* 1, *W* 1(R),2, *F* 2(R)
Gordon-Smith, G W (Blackheath) 1900 *W, I, S*
Gotley, A L H (Oxford U) 1910 *F, S*, 1911 *W, F, I, S*
Graham, D (Aspatria) 1901 *W*
Graham, H J (Wimbledon H) 1875 *I, S*, 1876 *I, S*
Graham, J D G (Wimbledon H) 1876 *I*
Gray, A (Otley) 1947 *W, I, S*
Grayson, P J (Northampton) 1995 *WS*, 1996 *F, W, S, I*, 1997 *S, I, F, A* 2(t), *SA* (R), *NZ* 2, 1998 *F, W, S, I, H, It, A* 2, 1999 *I*, [*NZ* (R), *Tg, Fj* (R), *SA*], 2003 *S* (R), *I* (t), *F* 2,3(R)
Green, J (Skipton) 1905 *I*, 1906 *S, F, SA*, 1907 *F, W, I, S*
Green, J F (West Kent) 1871 *S*
Green, W R (Wasps) 1997 *A* 2, 1998 *NZ* 1(t+R), 1999 *US* (R), 2003 *W* 2(R)
Greening, P B T (Gloucester, Wasps) 1996 *It* (R), 1997 *W* (R), *Arg* 1 1998 *NZ* 1(R),2(R), 1999 *A* (R), *US, C*, [*It* (R), *NZ* (R), *Tg, Fj, SA*], 2000 *I, F, W, It, S, SA* 1,2, *A, SA* 3, 2001 *F, I*
Greenstock, N J J (Wasps) 1997 *Arg* 1,2, *A* 1, *SA*
Greenwell, J H (Rockcliff) 1893 *W, I*
Greenwood, J E (Cambridge U, Leicester) 1912 *F*, 1913 *SA, W, F, I, S*, 1914 *W, S, F*, 1920 *W, F, I, S*
Greenwood, J R H (Waterloo) 1966 *I, F, S*, 1967 *A*, 1969 *I*
Greenwood, W J H (Leicester, Harlequins) 1997 *A* 2, *NZ* 1, *SA, NZ* 2, 1998 *F, W, S, I, H, It*, 1999 *C*, [*It, Tg, Fj, SA*], 2000 *Arg* (R), *SA* 3, 2001 *W, It, S, F, I, A, R, SA*, 2002 *S, I, F, W, It, NZ, A, SA*, 2003 *F* 1, *W* 1, *It, S, I, NZ, A, F* 3
Greg, W (Manchester) 1876 *I, S*
Gregory, G G (Bristol) 1931 *I, S, F*, 1932 *SA, W, I, S*, 1933 *W, I, S*, 1934 *W, I, S*
Gregory, J A (Blackheath) 1949 *W*
Grewcock, D J (Coventry, Saracens, Bath) 1997 *Arg* 2, *SA*, 1998 *W* (R), *S* (R), *I* (R), *A* 1, *NZ* 1, *SA* 2(R), 1999 *S* (R), *A* (R), *US, C*, [*It, NZ, Tg* (R), *SA*], 2000 *SA* 1,2, *A, Arg, SA* 3, 2001 *W, It, S, I, A, R* (R), *SA*, 2002 *S* (R), *I* (R), *F* (R), *W, It, NZ, SA* (R), 2003 *F* 1(R), *W* 1(R), *It, S* (R), *I* (t), *W* 2, *F* 2
Grylls, W M (Redruth) 1905 *I*
Guest, R H (Waterloo) 1939 *W, I, S*, 1947 *W, I, S, F*, 1948 *A, W, I, S*, 1949 *F, S*
Guillemard, A G (West Kent) 1871 *S*, 1872 *S*
Gummer, C H A (Plymouth A) 1929 *F*
Gunner, C R (Marlborough N) 1876 *I*
Gurdon, C (Richmond) 1880 *I, S*, 1881 *I, W, S*, 1882 *I, S*, 1883 *S*, 1884 *W, S*, 1885 *I*, 1886 *W, I, S*
Gurdon, E T (Richmond) 1878 *S*, 1879 *I*, 1880 *S*, 1881 *I, W, S*, 1882 S, 1883 *W, I, S*, 1884 *W, I, S*, 1885 *W, I*, 1886 *S*
Guscott, J C (Bath) 1989 *R, Fj*, 1990 *I, F, W, S, Arg* 3, 1991 *W, S, I, F, Fj, A*, [*NZ, It, F, S, A*], 1992 *S, I, F, W, C, SA*, 1993 *F, W, S, I*, 1994 *R, C*, 1995 *I, F, W, S*, [*Arg, It, A, NZ, F*], *SA, WS*, 1996 *F, W, S, I, Arg*, 1997 *I* (R), *W* (R), 1998 *F, W, S, I, H, It, A* 2, *SA* 2, 1999 *S, I, F, A, US, C*, [*It* (R), *NZ, Tg*]

Haag, M (Bath) 1997 *Arg* 1,2
Haigh, L (Manchester) 1910 *W, I, S*, 1911 *W, F, I, S*
Hale, P M (Moseley) 1969 *SA*, 1970 *I, W*
Hall, C (Gloucester) 1901 *I, S*
Hall, J (N Durham) 1894 *W, I, S*
Hall, J P (Bath) 1984 *S* (R), *I, F, SA* 1,2, *A*, 1985 *R, F, S, I, W, NZ* 1,2, 1986 *W, S*, 1987 *I, F, W, S*, 1990 *Arg* 3, 1994 *S*
Hall, N M (Richmond) 1947 *W, I, S, F*, 1949 *W, I*, 1952 *SA, W, S, I, F*, 1953 *W, I, F, S*, 1955 *W, I*
Halliday, S J (Bath, Harlequins) 1986 *W, S*, 1987 *S*, 1988 *S, I* 1,2, *A* 1, *A*, 1989 *S, I, F, W, R, Fj* (R), 1990 *W, S*, 1991 [*US, S, A*], 1992 *S, I, F, W*
Hamersley, A St G (Marlborough N) 1871 *S*, 1872 *S*, 1873 *S*, 1874 *S*
Hamilton-Hill, E A (Harlequins) 1936 *NZ, W, I*
Hamilton-Wickes, R H (Cambridge U) 1924 *I*, 1925 *NZ, W, I, S, F*, 1926 *W, I, S*, 1927 *W*
Hammett, E D G (Newport) 1920 *W, F, S*, 1921 *W, I, S, F*, 1922 *W*
Hammond, C E L (Harlequins) 1905 *S, NZ*, 1906 *W, I, S, F*, 1908 *W, I*
Hancock, A W (Northampton) 1965 *F, S*, 1966 *F*
Hancock, G E (Birkenhead Park) 1939 *W, I, S*
Hancock, J H (Newport) 1955 *W, I*
Hancock, P F (Blackheath) 1886 *W, I*, 1890 *W*
Hancock, P S (Richmond) 1904 *W, I, S*
Handford, F G (Manchester) 1909 *W, F, I, S*
Hands, R H M (Blackheath) 1910 *F, S*
Hanley, J (Plymouth A) 1927 *W, S, F*, 1928 *W, I, F, S*
Hanley, S M (Sale) 1999 *W*

Hannaford, R C (Bristol) 1971 *W, I, F*
Hanvey, R J (Aspatria) 1926 *W, I, F, S*
Harding, E H (Devonport Services) 1931 *I*
Harding, R M (Bristol) 1985 *R, F, S*, 1987 *S, [A, J, W]*, 1988 *I* 1(R),2, *A* 1,2, *Fj*
Harding, V S J (Saracens) 1961 *F, S*, 1962 *W, I, F, S*
Hardwick, P F (Percy Park) 1902 *I, S*, 1903 *W, I, S*, 1904 *W, I, S*
Hardwick, R J K (Coventry) 1996 *It* (R)
Hardy, E M P (Blackheath) 1951 *I, F, S*
Hare, W H (Nottingham, Leicester) 1974 *W*, 1978 *F, NZ*, 1979 *NZ*, 1980 *I, F, W, S*, 1981 *W, S, Arg* 1,2, 1982 *F, W*, 1983 *F, W, S, I, NZ*, 1984 *S, I, F, W, SA* 1,2
Harper, C H (Exeter) 1899 *W*
Harriman, A T (Harlequins) 1988 *A*
Harris, S W (Blackheath) 1920 *I, S*
Harris, T W (Northampton) 1929 *S*, 1932 *I*
Harrison, A C (Hartlepool R) 1931 *I, S*
Harrison, A L (United Services, RN) 1914 *I, F*
Harrison, G (Hull) 1877 *I, S*, 1879 *S, I*, 1880 *S*, 1885 *W, I*
Harrison, H C (United Services, RN) 1909 *S*, 1914 *I, S, F*
Harrison, M E (Wakefield) 1985 *NZ* 1,2, 1986 *S, I, F*, 1987 *I, F, W, S, [A, J, US, W]*, 1988 *F, W*
Hartley, B C (Blackheath) 1901 *S*, 1902 *S*
Haslett, L W (Birkenhead Park) 1926 *I, F*
Hastings, G W D (Gloucester) 1955 *W, I, F, S*, 1957 *W, I, F, S*, 1958 *W, A, I, F, S*
Havelock, H (Hartlepool R) 1908 *F, W, I*
Hawcridge, J J (Bradford) 1885 *W, I*
Hayward, L W (Cheltenham) 1910 *I*
Hazell, D St G (Leicester) 1955 *W, I, F, S*
Healey, A S (Leicester) 1997 *I* (R), *W, A* 1(R),2(R), *NZ* 1(R), *SA* (R), *NZ* 2, 1998 *F, W, S, I, A* 1, *NZ* 1,2, *H, It, A* 2, *SA* 2(R), 1999 *US, C, [It, NZ, Tg, Fj, SA* (R)], 2000 *I, F, W, It, S, SA* 1,2, *A, SA* 3(R), 2001 *W* (R), *It, S, F, I* (R), *A, R, SA*, 2002 *S, I, F, W, It* (R), *NZ* (R), *A* (R), *SA* (R), 2003 *F* 2
Hearn, R D (Bedford) 1966 *F, S*, 1967 *I, F, S, W*
Heath, A H (Oxford U) 1876 *S*
Heaton, J (Waterloo) 1935 *W, I, S*, 1939 *W, I, S*, 1947 *I, S, F*
Henderson, A P (Edinburgh Wands) 1947 *W, I, S, F*, 1948 *I, S, F*, 1949 *W, I*
Henderson, R S F (Blackheath) 1883 *W, S*, 1884 *W, S*, 1885 *W*
Heppell, W G (Devonport A) 1903 *I*
Herbert, A J (Wasps) 1958 *F, S*, 1959 *W, I, F, S*
Hesford, R (Bristol) 1981 *S* (R), 1982 *A, S, F* (R), 1983 *F* (R), 1985 *R, F, S, I, W*
Heslop, N J (Orrell) 1990 *Arg* 1,2,3, 1991 *W, S, I, F, [US, F]*, 1992 *W* (R)
Hetherington, J G G (Northampton) 1958 *A, I*, 1959 *W, I, F, S*
Hewitt, E N (Coventry) 1951 *W, I, F*
Hewitt, W W (Queen's House) 1881 *I, W, S*, 1882 *I*
Hickson, J L (Bradford) 1887 *W, I, S*, 1890 *W, S, I*
Higgins, R (Liverpool) 1954 *W, NZ, I, S*, 1955 *W, I, F, S*, 1957 *W, I, F, S*, 1959 *W*
Hignell, A J (Cambridge U, Bristol) 1975 *A* 2, 1976 *A, W, S, I*, 1977 *S, I, F, W*, 1978 *W*, 1979 *S, I, F, W*
Hill, B A (Blackheath) 1903 *I, S*, 1904 *W, I*, 1905 *W, NZ*, 1906 *SA*, 1907 *F, W*
Hill, R A (Saracens) 1997 *S, I, F, W, A* 1,2, *NZ* 1, *SA, NZ* 2, 1998 *F, W, H* (R), *It* (R), *A* 2, *SA* 2, 1999 *S, I, F, W, A, US, C, [It, NZ, Tg, Fj* (R), *SA]*, 2000 *I, F, W, It, S, SA* 1,2, *A, Arg, SA* 3, 2001 *W, It, S, F, I, A, SA*, 2002 *S, I, F, W, It, NZ, A, SA*, 2003 *F* 1, *W* 1, *It, S, I, NZ, A, F* 3
Hill, R J (Bath) 1984 *SA* 1,2, 1985 *I* (R), *NZ* 2(R), 1986 *F* (R), 1987 *I, F, W, [US]*, 1989 *Fj*, 1990 *I, F, W, S, Arg* 1,2,3, 1991 *W, S, I, F, Fj, A, [NZ, It, US, F, S, A]*
Hillard, R J (Oxford U) 1925 *NZ*
Hiller, R (Harlequins) 1968 *W, I, F, S*, 1969 *I, F, S, W, SA*, 1970 *I, W, S*, 1971 *I, F, S* (2[1C]), *P*, 1972 *W, I*
Hind, A E (Leicester) 1905 *NZ*, 1906 *W*
Hind, G R (Blackheath) 1910 *S*, 1911 *I*
Hobbs, R F A (Blackheath) 1899 *S*, 1903 *W*
Hobbs, R G S (Richmond) 1932 *SA, W, I, S*
Hodges, H A (Nottingham) 1906 *W, I*
Hodgkinson, S D (Nottingham) 1989 *R, Fj*, 1990 *I, F, W, S, Arg* 1,2,3, 1991 *W, S, I, F, [US]*
Hodgson, C (Sale) 2001 *R*, 2002 *S* (R), *I* (R), *It* (R), *Arg*, 2003 *F* 1, *W* 1, *It* (R)
Hodgson, J McD (Northern) 1932 *SA, W, I, S*, 1934 *W, I*, 1936 *I*
Hodgson, S A M (Durham City) 1960 *W, I, F, S*, 1961 *SA, W*, 1962 *W, I, F, S*, 1964 *W*
Hofmeyr, M B (Oxford U) 1950 *W, F, S*
Hogarth, T B (Hartlepool R) 1906 *F*
Holford, G (Gloucester) 1920 *W, F*
Holland, D (Devonport A) 1912 *W, I, S*
Holliday, T E (Aspatria) 1923 *S, F*, 1925 *I, S, F*, 1926 *F, S*
Holmes, C B (Manchester) 1947 *S*, 1948 *I, F*
Holmes, E (Manningham) 1890 *S, I*
Holmes, W A (Nuneaton) 1950 *W, I, F, S*, 1951 *W, I, F, S*, 1952 *SA, S, I, F*, 1953 *W, I, F, S*
Holmes, W B (Cambridge U) 1949 *W, I, F, S*
Hook, W G (Gloucester) 1951 *S*, 1952 *SA, W*
Hooper, C A (Middlesex W) 1894 *W, I, S*
Hopley, D P (Wasps) 1995 *[WS* (R)], *SA, WS*
Hopley, F J V (Blackheath) 1907 *F, W*, 1908 *I*
Horak, M J (London Irish) 2002 *Arg*
Hordern, P C (Gloucester) 1931 *I, S, F*, 1934 *W*
Horley, C H (Swinton) 1885 *I*
Hornby, A N (Manchester) 1877 *I, S*, 1878 *S, I*, 1880 *I*, 1881 *I, S*, 1882 *I, S*
Horrocks-Taylor, J P (Cambridge U, Leicester, Middlesbrough) 1958 *W, A*, 1961 *S*, 1962 *S*, 1963 *NZ* 1,2, *A*, 1964 *NZ, W*
Horsfall, E L (Harlequins) 1949 *W*
Horton, A L (Blackheath) 1965 *W, I, F, S*, 1966 *F, S*, 1967 *NZ*
Horton, J P (Bath) 1978 *W, S, I, NZ*, 1980 *I, F, W, S*, 1981 *W*, 1983 *S, I*, 1984 *SA* 1,2
Horton, N E (Moseley, Toulouse) 1969 *I, F, S, W*, 1971 *I, F, S*, 1974 *S*, 1975 *W*, 1977 *S, I, F, W*, 1978 *F, W*, 1979 *S, I, F, W*, 1980 *I*
Hosen, R W (Bristol, Northampton) 1963 *NZ* 1,2, *A*, 1964 *F, S*, 1967 *A, I, F, S, W*
Hosking, G R d'A (Devonport Services) 1949 *W, I, F, S*, 1950 *W*
Houghton, S (Runcorn) 1892 *I*, 1896 *W*
Howard, P D (O Millhillians) 1930 *W, I, F, S*, 1931 *W, I, S, F*
Hubbard, G C (Blackheath) 1892 *W, I*
Hubbard, J C (Harlequins) 1930 *S*
Hudson, A (Gloucester) 1906 *W, I, F*, 1908 *F, W, I, S*, 1910 *F*
Hughes, G E (Barrow) 1896 *S*
Hull, P A (Bristol, RAF) 1994 *SA* 1,2, *R, C*
Hulme, F C (Birkenhead Park) 1903 *W, I*, 1905 *W, I*
Hunt, J T (Manchester) 1882 *I, S*, 1884 *W*
Hunt, R (Manchester) 1880 *I*, 1881 *W, S*, 1882 *I*
Hunt, W H (Manchester) 1876 *S*, 1877 *I, S*, 1878 *I*
Hunter, I (Northampton) 1992 *C*, 1993 *F, W*, 1994 *F, W*, 1995 *[WS, F]*
Huntsman, R P (Headingley) 1985 *NZ* 1,2
Hurst, A C B (Wasps) 1962 *S*
Huskisson, T F (OMTs) 1937 *W, I, S*, 1938 *W, I*, 1939 *W, I, S*
Hutchinson, F (Headingley) 1909 *F, I, S*
Hutchinson, J E (Durham City) 1906 *I*
Hutchinson, W C (RIE Coll) 1876 *S*, 1877 *I*
Hutchinson, W H H (Hull) 1875 *I*, 1876 *I*
Huth, H (Huddersfield) 1879 *S*
Hyde, J P (Northampton) 1950 *F, S*
Hynes, W B (United Services, RN) 1912 *F*

Ibbitson, E D (Headingley) 1909 *W, F, I, S*
Imrie, H M (Durham City) 1906 *NZ*, 1907 *I*
Inglis, R E (Blackheath) 1886 *W, I, S*
Irvin, S H (Devonport A) 1905 *W*
Isherwood, F W (Ravenscourt Park) 1872 *S*

Jackett, E J (Leicester, Falmouth) 1905 *NZ*, 1906 *W, I, S, F, SA*, 1907 *W, I, S*, 1909 *W, F, I, S*
Jackson, A H (Blackheath) 1878 *I*, 1880 *I*
Jackson, B S (Broughton Park) 1970 *S* (R), *F*
Jackson, P B (Coventry) 1956 *W, I, F*, 1957 *W, I, F, S*, 1958 *W, A, F, S*, 1959 *W, I, F, S*, 1961 *S*, 1963 *W, I, F, S*
Jackson, W J (Halifax) 1894 *S*
Jacob, F (Cambridge U) 1897 *W, I, S*, 1898 *I, S, W*, 1899 *W, I*
Jacob, H P (Blackheath) 1924 *W, I, F, S*, 1930 *F*
Jacob, P G (Blackheath) 1898 *I*
Jacobs, C R (Northampton) 1956 *W, I, S, F*, 1957 *W, I, F, S*, 1958 *W, A, I, F, S*, 1960 *W, I, F, S*, 1961 *SA, W, I, F, S*, 1963 *NZ* 1,2, *A*, 1964 *W, I, F, S*
Jago, R A (Devonport A) 1906 *W, I, SA*, 1907 *W, I*
Janion, J P A G (Bedford) 1971 *W, I, F, S* (2[1C]), *P*, 1972 *W, S, SA*, 1973 *A*, 1975 *A* 1,2
Jarman, J W (Bristol) 1900 *W*

Jeavons, N C (Moseley) 1981 *S, I, F, Arg* 1,2, 1982 *A, S, I, F, W*, 1983 *F, W, S, I*
Jeeps, R E G (Northampton) 1956 *W*, 1957 *W, I, F, S*, 1958 *W, A, I, F, S*, 1959 *I*, 1960 *W, I, F, S*, 1961 *SA, W, I, F, S*, 1962 *W, I, F, S*
Jeffery, G L (Blackheath) 1886 *W, I, S*, 1887 *W, I, S*
Jennins, C R (Waterloo) 1967 *A, I, F*
Jewitt, J (Hartlepool R) 1902 *W*
Johns, W A (Gloucester) 1909 *W, F, I, S*, 1910 *W, I, F*
Johnson, M O (Leicester) 1993 *F, NZ*, 1994 *S, I, F, W, R, C*, 1995 *I, F, W, S*, [*Arg, It, WS, A, NZ, F*], *SA, WS*, 1996 *F, W, S, I, It, Arg*, 1997 *S, I, F, W, A* 2, *NZ* 1,2, 1998 *F, W, S, I, H, It, A* 2, *SA* 2, 1999 *S, I, F, W, A, US, C*, [*It, NZ, Tg, Fj, SA*], 2000 *SA* 1,2, *A, Arg, SA* 3, 2001 *W, It, S, F, SA*, 2002 *S, I, F, It* (t+R), *NZ, A, SA*, 2003 *F* 1, *W* 1, *S, I, NZ, A, F* 3
Johnston, B (Saracens) 2002 *Arg, NZ* (R)
Johnston, W R (Bristol) 1910 *W, I, S*, 1912 *W, I, S, F*, 1913 *SA, W, F, I, S*, 1914 *W, I, S, F*
Jones, F P (New Brighton) 1893 *S*
Jones, H A (Barnstaple) 1950 *W, I, F*
Jorden, A M (Cambridge U, Blackheath, Bedford) 1970 *F*, 1973 *I, F, S*, 1974 *F*, 1975 *W, S*
Jowett, D (Heckmondwike) 1889 *M*, 1890 *S, I*, 1891 *W, I, S*
Judd, P E (Coventry) 1962 *W, I, F, S*, 1963 *S, NZ* 1,2, *A*, 1964 *NZ*, 1965 *I, F, S*, 1966 *W, I, F, S*, 1967 *A, I, F, S, W, NZ*

Kay, B J (Leicester) 2001 *C* 1,2, *A, R, SA* (t+R), 2002 *S, I, F, W, It, Arg, NZ* (R), *A, SA*, 2003 *F* 1, *W* 1, *It, S, I, NZ, A, F* 3
Kayll, H E (Sunderland) 1878 *S*
Keeling, J H (Guy's Hospital) 1948 *A, W*
Keen, B W (Newcastle U) 1968 *W, I, F, S*
Keeton, G H (Leicester) 1904 *W, I, S*
Kelly, G A (Bedford) 1947 *W, I, S*, 1948 *W*
Kelly, T S (London Devonians) 1906 *W, I, S, F, SA*, 1907 *F, W, I, S*, 1908 *F, I, S*
Kemble, A T (Liverpool) 1885 *W, I*, 1887 *I*
Kemp, D T (Blackheath) 1935 *W*
Kemp, T A (Richmond) 1937 *W, I*, 1939 *S*, 1948 *A, W*
Kendall, P D (Birkenhead Park) 1901 *S*, 1902 *W*, 1903 *S*
Kendall-Carpenter, J MacG K (Oxford U, Bath) 1949 *I, F, S*, 1950 *W, I, F, S*, 1951 *I, F, S*, 1952 *SA, W, S, I, F*, 1953 *W, I, F, S*, 1954 *W, NZ, I, F*
Kendrew, D A (Leicester) 1930 *W, I*, 1933 *I, S*, 1934 *S*, 1935 *W, I*, 1936 *NZ, W, I*
Kennedy, R D (Camborne S of M) 1949 *I, F, S*
Kent, C P (Rosslyn Park) 1977 *S, I, F, W*, 1978 *F* (R)
Kent, T (Salford) 1891 *W, I, S*, 1892 *W, I, S*
Kershaw, C A (United Services, RN) 1920 *W, F, I, S*, 1921 *W, I, S, F*, 1922 *W, I, F, S*, 1923 *W, I, S, F*
Kewley, E (Liverpool) 1874 *S*, 1875 *S*, 1876 *I, S*, 1877 *I, S*, 1878 *S*
Kewney, A L (Leicester) 1906 *W, I, S, F*, 1909 *A, W, F, I, S*, 1911 *W, F, I, S*, 1912 *I, S*, 1913 *SA*
Key, A (O Cranleighans) 1930 *I*, 1933 *W*
Keyworth, M (Swansea) 1976 *A, W, S, I*
Kilner, B (Wakefield T) 1880 *I*
Kindersley, R S (Exeter) 1883 *W*, 1884 *S*, 1885 *W*
King, A D (Wasps) 1997 *Arg* 2(R), 1998 *SA* 2(R), 2000 *It* (R), 2001 *C* 2(R), 2003 *W* 2
King, I (Harrogate) 1954 *W, NZ, I*
King, J A (Headingley) 1911 *W, F, I, S*, 1912 *W, I, S*, 1913 *SA, W, F, I, S*
King, Q E M A (Army) 1921 *S*
Kingston, P (Gloucester) 1975 *A* 1,2, 1979 *I, F, W*
Kitching, A E (Blackheath) 1913 *I*
Kittermaster, H J (Harlequins) 1925 *NZ, W, I*, 1926 *W, I, F, S*
Knight, F (Plymouth) 1909 *A*
Knight, P M (Bristol) 1972 *F, S, SA*
Knowles, E (Millom) 1896 *S*, 1897 *S*
Knowles, T C (Birkenhead Park) 1931 *S*
Krige, J A (Guy's Hospital) 1920 *W*

Labuschagne, N A (Harlequins, Guy's Hospital) 1953 *W*, 1955 *W, I, F, S*
Lagden, R O (Richmond) 1911 *S*
Laird, H C C (Harlequins) 1927 *W, I, S*, 1928 *A, W, I, F, S*, 1929 *W, I*
Lambert, D (Harlequins) 1907 *F*, 1908 *F, W, S*, 1911 *W, F, I*
Lampkowski, M S (Headingley) 1976 *A, W, S, I*
Lapage, W N (United Services, RN) 1908 *F, W, I, S*
Larter, P J (Northampton, RAF) 1967 *A, NZ*, 1968 *W, I, F, S*, 1969 *I, F, S, W, SA*, 1970 *I, W, F, S*, 1971 *W, I, F, S* (2[1C]), *P*, 1972 *SA*, 1973 *NZ* 1, *W*
Law, A F (Richmond) 1877 *S*
Law, D E (Birkenhead Park) 1927 *I*
Lawrence, Hon H A (Richmond) 1873 *S*, 1874 *S*, 1875 *I, S*
Lawrie, P W (Leicester) 1910 *S*, 1911 *S*
Lawson, R G (Workington) 1925 *I*
Lawson, T M (Workington) 1928 *A, W*
Leadbetter, M M (Broughton Park) 1970 *F*
Leadbetter, V H (Edinburgh Wands) 1954 *S, F*
Leake, W R M (Harlequins) 1891 *W, I, S*
Leather, G (Liverpool) 1907 *I*
Lee, F H (Marlborough N) 1876 *S*, 1877 *I*
Lee, H (Blackheath) 1907 *F*
Le Fleming, J (Blackheath) 1887 *W*
Leonard, J (Saracens, Harlequins) 1990 *Arg* 1,2,3, 1991 *W, S, I, F, Fj, A*, [*NZ, It, US, F, S, A*], 1992 *S, I, F, W, C, SA*, 1993 *F, W, S, I, NZ*, 1994 *S, I, F, W, SA* 1,2, *R, C*, 1995 *I, F, W, S*, [*Arg, It, A, NZ, F*], *SA, WS*, 1996 *F, W, S, I, It, Arg*, 1997 *S, I, F, W, A* 2, *NZ* 1, *SA, NZ* 2, 1998 *F, W, S, I, H, It, A* 2 *SA* 2, 1999 *S, I, F, W, A, C* (R), [*It, NZ, Fj, SA*], 2000 *I, F, W, It, S, SA* 1,2, *A, Arg, SA* 3, 2001 *W, It, S, F, I, R*, 2002 *S* (R), *I* (R), *F* (R), *It* (R), *A, SA*, 2003 *F* 1, *S, I, NZ, W* 2, *F* 2(t+R),3(R)
Leslie-Jones, F A (Richmond) 1895 *W, I*
Lewis, A O (Bath) 1952 *SA, W, S, I, F*, 1953 *W, I, F, S*, 1954 *F*
Lewsey, O J (Wasps) 1998 *NZ* 1,2, *SA* 1, 2001 *C* 1,2, *US*, 2003 *It, S, I, NZ, A, F* 2,3(t+R)
Leyland, R (Waterloo) 1935 *W, I, S*
Linnett, M S (Moseley) 1989 *Fj*
Livesay, R O'H (Blackheath) 1898 *W*, 1899 *W*
Lloyd, L D (Leicester) 2000 *SA* 1(R),2(R), 2001 *C* 1,2, *US*
Lloyd, R H (Harlequins) 1967 *NZ*, 1968 *W, I, F, S*
Locke, H M (Birkenhead Park) 1923 *S, F*, 1924 *W, F, S*, 1925 *W, I, S, F*, 1927 *W, I, S*
Lockwood, R E (Heckmondwike) 1887 *W, I, S*, 1889 *M*, 1891 *W, I, S*, 1892 *W, I, S*, 1893 *W, I*, 1894 *W, I*
Login, S H M (RN Coll) 1876 *I*
Lohden, F C (Blackheath) 1893 *W*
Long, A E (Bath) 1997 *A* 2, 2001 *US* (R)
Longland, R J (Northampton) 1932 *S*, 1933 *W, S*, 1934 *W, I, S*, 1935 *W, I, S*, 1936 *NZ, W, I, S*, 1937 *W, I, S*, 1938 *W, I, S*
Lowe, C N (Cambridge U, Blackheath) 1913 *SA, W, F, I, S*, 1914 *W, I, S, F*, 1920 *W, F, I, S*, 1921 *W, I, S, F*, 1922 *W, I, F, S*, 1923 *W, I, S, F*
Lowrie, F (Wakefield T) 1889 *M*, 1890 *W*
Lowry, W M (Birkenhead Park) 1920 *F*
Lozowski, R A P (Wasps) 1984 *A*
Luddington, W G E (Devonport Services) 1923 *W, I, S, F*, 1924 *W, I, F, S*, 1925 *W, I, S, F*, 1926 *W*
Luger, D D (Harlequins, Saracens) 1998 *H, It, SA* 2, 1999 *S, I, F, W, A, US, C*, [*It, NZ, Tg, Fj, SA*], 2000 *SA* 1, *A, Arg, SA* 3, 2001 *W, I, A, R, SA*, 2002 *F* (R), *W, It*, 2003 *F* 1, *W* 1, *It, S* (R), *I* (R), *NZ* (R), *W* 2
Luscombe, F (Gipsies) 1872 *S*, 1873 *S*, 1875 *I, S*, 1876 *I, S*
Luscombe, J H (Gipsies) 1871 *S*
Luxmoore, A F C C (Richmond) 1900 *S*, 1901 *W*
Luya, H F (Waterloo, Headingley) 1948 *W, I, S, F*, 1949 *W*
Lyon, A (Liverpool) 1871 *S*
Lyon, G H d'O (United Services, RN) 1908 *S*, 1909 *A*

McCanlis, M A (Gloucester) 1931 *W, I*
McCarthy, N (Gloucester) 1999 *I* (t), *US* (R), 2000 *It* (R)
McFadyean, C W (Moseley) 1966 *I, F, S*, 1967 *A, I, F, S, W, NZ*, 1968 *W, I*
MacIlwaine, A H (United Services, Hull & E Riding) 1912 *W, I, S, F*, 1920 *I*
Mackie, O G (Wakefield T, Cambridge U) 1897 *S*, 1898 *I*
Mackinlay, J E H (St George's Hospital) 1872 *S*, 1873 *S*, 1875 *I*
MacLaren, W (Manchester) 1871 *S*
MacLennan, R R F (OMTs) 1925 *I, S, F*
McLeod, N F (RIE Coll) 1879 *S, I*
Madge, R J P (Exeter) 1948 *A, W, I, S*
Malir, F W S (Otley) 1930 *W, I, S*
Mallett, J A (Bath) 1995 [*WS* (R)]
Mallinder, J (Sale) 1997 *Arg* 1,2
Mangles, R H (Richmond) 1897 *W, I*
Manley, D C (Exeter) 1963 *W, I, F, S*
Mann, W E (United Services, Army) 1911 *W, F, I*
Mantell, N D (Rosslyn Park) 1975 *A* 1
Mapletoft, M S (Gloucester) 1997 *Arg* 2
Markendale, E T (Manchester R) 1880 *I*
Marques, R W D (Cambridge U, Harlequins) 1956 *W, I, S, F*, 1957 *W, I, F, S*, 1958 *W, A, I, F, S*, 1959 *W, I, F, S*, 1960 *W, I, F, S*, 1961 *SA, W*

Marquis, J C (Birkenhead Park) 1900 *I, S*
Marriott, C J B (Blackheath) 1884 *W, I, S*, 1886 *W, I, S*, 1887 *I*
Marriott, E E (Manchester) 1876 *I*
Marriott, V R (Harlequins) 1963 *NZ* 1,2, *A*, 1964 *NZ*
Marsden, G H (Morley) 1900 *W, I, S*
Marsh, H (RIE Coll) 1873 *S*
Marsh, J (Swinton) 1892 *I*
Marshall, H (Blackheath) 1893 *W*
Marshall, M W (Blackheath) 1873 *S*, 1874 *S*, 1875 *I, S*, 1876 *I, S*, 1877 *I, S*, 1878 *S, I*
Marshall, R M (Oxford U) 1938 *I, S*, 1939 *W, I, S*
Martin, C R (Bath) 1985 *F, S, I, W*
Martin, N O (Harlequins) 1972 *F* (R)
Martindale, S A (Kendal) 1929 *F*
Massey, E J (Leicester) 1925 *W, I, S*
Mather, B-J (Sale) 1999 *W*
Mathias, J L (Bristol) 1905 *W, I, S, NZ*
Matters, J C (RNE Coll) 1899 *S*
Matthews, J R C (Harlequins) 1949 *F, S*, 1950 *I, F, S*, 1952 *SA, W, S, I, F*
Maud, P (Blackheath) 1893 *W, I*
Maxwell, A W (New Brighton, Headingley) 1975 *A* 1, 1976 *A, W, S, I, F*, 1978 *F*
Maxwell-Hyslop, J E (Oxford U) 1922 *I, F, S*
Maynard, A F (Cambridge U) 1914 *W, I, S*
Meikle, G W C (Waterloo) 1934 *W, I, S*
Meikle, S S C (Waterloo) 1929 *S*
Mellish, F W (Blackheath) 1920 *W, F, I, S*, 1921 *W, I*
Melville, N D (Wasps) 1984 *A*, 1985 *I, W, NZ* 1,2, 1986 *W, S, I, F*, 1988 *F, W, S, I* 1
Merriam, L P B (Blackheath) 1920 *W, F*
Michell, A T (Oxford U) 1875 *I, S*, 1876 *I*
Middleton, B B (Birkenhead Park) 1882 *I*, 1883 *I*
Middleton, J A (Richmond) 1922 *S*
Miles, J H (Leicester) 1903 *W*
Millett, H (Richmond) 1920 *F*
Mills, F W (Marlborough N) 1872 *S*, 1873 *S*
Mills, S G F (Gloucester) 1981 *Arg* 1,2, 1983 *W*, 1984 *SA* 1, *A*
Mills, W A (Devonport A) 1906 *W, I, S, F, SA*, 1907 *F, W, I, S*, 1908 *F, W*
Milman, D L K (Bedford) 1937 *W*, 1938 *W, I, S*
Milton, C H (Camborne S of M) 1906 *I*
Milton, J G (Camborne S of M) 1904 *W, I, S*, 1905 *S*, 1907 *I*
Milton, W H (Marlborough N) 1874 *S*, 1875 *I*
Mitchell, F (Blackheath) 1895 *W, I, S*, 1896 *W, I, S*
Mitchell, W G (Richmond) 1890 *W, S, I*, 1891 *W, I, S*, 1893 *S*
Mobbs, E R (Northampton) 1909 *A, W, F, I, S*, 1910 *I, F*
Moberley, W O (Ravenscourt Park) 1872 *S*
Moody, L W (Leicester) 2001 *C* 1,2, *US, I* (R), *R, SA* (R), 2002 *I* (R), *W, It, Arg, NZ, A, SA*, 2003 *F* 1, *W* 2, *F* 2,3(R)
Moore, B C (Nottingham, Harlequins) 1987 *S*, [*A, J, W*], 1988 *F, W, S, I* 1,2, *A* 1, 2, *Fj, A*, 1989 *S, I, F, W, R, Fj*, 1990 *I, F, W, S, Arg* 1,2, 1991 *W, S, I, F, Fj, A*, [*NZ, It, F, S, A*], 1992 *S, I, F, W, SA*, 1993 *F, W, S, I, NZ*, 1994 *S, I, F, W, SA* 1,2, *R, C*, 1995 *I, F, W, S*, [*Arg, It, WS* (R), *A, NZ, F*]
Moore, E J (Blackheath) 1883 *I, S*
Moore, N J N H (Bristol) 1904 *W, I, S*
Moore, P B C (Blackheath) 1951 *W*
Moore, W K T (Leicester) 1947 *W, I*, 1949 *F, S*, 1950 *I, F, S*
Mordell, R J (Rosslyn Park) 1978 *W*
Morfitt, S (W Hartlepool) 1894 *W, I, S*, 1896 *W, I, S*
Morgan, J R (Hawick) 1920 *W*
Morgan, W G D (Medicals, Newcastle) 1960 *W, I, F, S*, 1961 *SA, W, I, F, S*
Morley, A J (Bristol) 1972 *SA*, 1973 *NZ* 1, *W, I*, 1975 *S, A* 1,2
Morris, A D W (United Services, RN) 1909 *A, W, F*
Morris, C D (Liverpool St Helens, Orrell) 1988 *A*, 1989 *S, I, F, W*, 1992 *S, I, F, W, C, SA*, 1993 *F, W, S, I*, 1994 *F, W, SA* 1,2, *R*, 1995 *S* (t), [*Arg, WS, A, NZ, F*]
Morris, R (Northampton) 2003 *W* 1, *It*
Morrison, P H (Cambridge U) 1890 *W, S, I*, 1891 *I*
Morse, S (Marlborough N) 1873 *S*, 1874 *S*, 1875 *S*
Mortimer, W (Marlborough N) 1899 *W*
Morton, H J S (Blackheath) 1909 *I, S*, 1910 *W, I*
Moss, F (Broughton) 1885 *W, I*, 1886 *W*
Mullins, A R (Harlequins) 1989 *Fj*
Mycock, J (Sale) 1947 *W, I, S, F*, 1948 *A*
Myers, E (Bradford) 1920 *I, S*, 1921 *W, I*, 1922 *W, I, F, S*, 1923 *W, I, S, F*, 1924 *W, I, F, S*, 1925 *S, F*
Myers, H (Keighley) 1898 *I*

Nanson, W M B (Carlisle) 1907 *F, W*
Nash, E H (Richmond) 1875 *I*
Neale, B A (Rosslyn Park) 1951 *I, F, S*
Neale, M E (Blackheath) 1912 *F*
Neame, S (O Cheltonians) 1879 *S, I*, 1880 *I, S*
Neary, A (Broughton Park) 1971 *W, I, F, S* (2[1C]), *P*, 1972 *W, I, F, S, SA*, 1973 *NZ* 1, *W, I, F, S, NZ* 2, *A*, 1974 *S, I, F, W*, 1975 *I, F, W, S, A* 1, 1976 *A, W, S, I, F*, 1977 *I*, 1978 *F* (R), 1979 *S, I, F, W, NZ*, 1980 *I, F, W, S*
Nelmes, B G (Cardiff) 1975 *A* 1,2, 1978 *W, S, I, NZ*
Newbold, C J (Blackheath) 1904 *W, I, S*, 1905 *W, I, S*
Newman, S C (Oxford U) 1947 *F*, 1948 *A, W*
Newton, A W (Blackheath) 1907 *S*
Newton, P A (Blackheath) 1882 *S*
Newton-Thompson, J O (Oxford U) 1947 *S, F*
Nichol, W (Brighouse R) 1892 *W, S*
Nicholas, P L (Exeter) 1902 *W*
Nicholson, B E (Harlequins) 1938 *W, I*
Nicholson, E S (Leicester) 1935 *W, I, S*, 1936 *NZ, W*
Nicholson, E T (Birkenhead Park) 1900 *W, I*
Nicholson, T (Rockcliff) 1893 *I*
Ninnes, B F (Coventry) 1971 *W*
Noon, J (Newcastle) 2001 *C* 1,2, *US*, 2003 *W* 2, *F* 2(t+R)
Norman, D J (Leicester) 1932 *SA, W*
North, E H G (Blackheath) 1891 *W, I, S*
Northmore, S (Millom) 1897 *I*
Novak, M J (Harlequins) 1970 *W, S, F*
Novis, A L (Blackheath) 1929 *S, F*, 1930 *W, I, F*, 1933 *I, S*

Oakeley, F E (United Services, RN) 1913 *S*, 1914 *I, S, F*
Oakes, R F (Hartlepool R) 1897 *W, I, S*, 1898 *I, S, W*, 1899 *W, S*
Oakley, L F L (Bedford) 1951 *W*
Obolensky, A (Oxford U) 1936 *NZ, W, I, S*
Ojomoh, S O (Bath, Gloucester) 1994 *I, F, SA* 1(R),2, *R*, 1995 *S* (R), [*Arg, WS, A* (t), *F*], 1996 *F*, 1998 *NZ* 1
Old, A G B (Middlesbrough, Leicester, Sheffield) 1972 *W, I, F, S, SA*, 1973 *NZ* 2, *A*, 1974 *S, I, F, W*, 1975 *I, A* 2, 1976 *S, I*, 1978 *F*
Oldham, W L (Coventry) 1908 *S*, 1909 *A*
Olver, C J (Northampton) 1990 *Arg* 3, 1991 [*US*], 1992 *C*
O'Neill, A (Teignmouth, Torquay A) 1901 *W, I, S*
Openshaw, W E (Manchester) 1879 *I*
Orwin, J (Gloucester, RAF, Bedford) 1985 *R, F, S, I, W, NZ* 1,2, 1988 *F, W, S, I* 1,2, *A* 1,2
Osborne, R R (Manchester) 1871 *S*
Osborne, S H (Oxford U) 1905 *S*
Oti, C (Cambridge U, Nottingham, Wasps) 1988 *S, I* 1, 1989 *S, I, F, W, R*, 1990 *Arg* 1,2, 1991 *Fj, A*, [*NZ, It*]
Oughtred, B (Hartlepool R) 1901 *S*, 1902 *W, I, S*, 1903 *W, I*
Owen, J E (Coventry) 1963 *W, I, F, S, A*, 1964 *NZ*, 1965 *W, I, F, S*, 1966 *I, F, S*, 1967 *NZ*
Owen-Smith, H G O (St Mary's Hospital) 1934 *W, I, S*, 1936 *NZ, W, I, S*, 1937 *W, I, S*

Page, J J (Bedford, Northampton) 1971 *W, I, F, S*, 1975 *S*
Pallant, J N (Notts) 1967 *I, F, S*
Palmer, A C (London Hospital) 1909 *I, S*
Palmer, F H (Richmond) 1905 *W*
Palmer, G V (Richmond) 1928 *I, F, S*
Palmer, J A (Bath) 1984 *SA* 1,2, 1986 *I* (R)
Palmer, T (Leeds) 2001 *US* (R)
Pargetter, T A (Coventry) 1962 *S*, 1963 *F, NZ* 1
Parker, G W (Gloucester) 1938 *I, S*
Parker, Hon S (Liverpool) 1874 *S*, 1875 *S*
Parsons, E I (RAF) 1939 *S*
Parsons, M J (Northampton) 1968 *W, I, F, S*
Patterson, W M (Sale) 1961 *SA, S*
Pattisson, R M (Blackheath) 1883 *I, S*
Paul, H (Gloucester) 2002 *F* (R)
Paul, J E (RIE Coll) 1875 *S*
Payne, A T (Bristol) 1935 *I, S*
Payne, C M (Harlequins) 1964 *I, F, S*, 1965 *I, F, S*, 1966 *W, I, F, S*
Payne, J H (Broughton) 1882 *S*, 1883 *W, I, S*, 1884 *I*, 1885 *W, I*
Pearce, G S (Northampton) 1979 *S, I, F, W*, 1981 *Arg* 1,2, 1982 *A*, S, 1983 *F, W, S, I, NZ*, 1984 *S, SA* 2, *A*, 1985 *R, F, S, I, W, NZ* 1,2, 1986 *W, S, I, F*, 1987 *I, F, W, S*, [*A, US, W*], 1988 *Fj*, 1991 [*US*]
Pears, D (Harlequins) 1990 *Arg* 1,2, 1992 *F* (R), 1994 *F*
Pearson, A W (Blackheath) 1875 *I, S*, 1876 *I, S*, 1877 *S*, 1878 *S, I*

Peart, T G A H (Hartlepool R) 1964 *F, S*
Pease, F E (Hartlepool R) 1887 *I*
Penny, S H (Leicester) 1909 *A*
Penny, W J (United Hospitals) 1878 *I*, 1879 *S, I*
Percival, L J (Rugby) 1891 *I*, 1892 *I*, 1893 *S*
Periton, H G (Waterloo) 1925 *W*, 1926 *W, I, F, S*, 1927 *W, I, S, F*, 1928 *A, I, F, S*, 1929 *W, I, S, F*, 1930 *W, I, F, S*
Perrott, E S (O Cheltonians) 1875 *I*
Perry, D G (Bedford) 1963 *F, S, NZ* 1,2, *A* 1964 *NZ, W, I*, 1965 *W, I, F, S*, 1966 *W, I, F*
Perry, M B (Bath) 1997 *A* 2, *NZ* 1, *SA, NZ* 2, 1998 *W, S, I, A* 1, *NZ* 1,2, *SA* 1, *H, It, A* 2, 1999 *I, F, W, A US, C*, [*It, NZ, Tg, Fj, SA*], 2000 *I, F, W, It, S, SA* 1,2, *A, SA* 3, 2001 *W* (R), *F* (R)
Perry, S V (Cambridge U, Waterloo) 1947 *W, I*, 1948 *A, W, I, S, F*
Peters, J (Plymouth) 1906 *S, F*, 1907 *I, S*, 1908 *W*
Phillips, C (Birkenhead Park) 1880 *S*, 1881 *I, S*
Phillips, M S (Fylde) 1958 *A, I, F, S*, 1959 *W, I, F, S*, 1960 *W, I, F, S*, 1961 *W*, 1963 *W, I, F, S, NZ* 1,2, *A*, 1964 *NZ, W, I, F, S*
Pickering, A S (Harrogate) 1907 *I*
Pickering, R D A (Bradford) 1967 *I, F, S, W*, 1968 *F, S*
Pickles, R C W (Bristol) 1922 *I, F*
Pierce, R (Liverpool) 1898 *I*, 1903 *S*
Pilkington, W N (Cambridge U) 1898 *S*
Pillman, C H (Blackheath) 1910 *W, I, F, S*, 1911 *W, F, I, S*, 1912 *W, F*, 1913 *SA, W, F, I, S*, 1914 *W, I, S*
Pillman, R L (Blackheath) 1914 *F*
Pinch, J (Lancaster) 1896 *W, I*, 1897 *S*
Pinching, W W (Guy's Hospital) 1872 *S*
Pitman, I J (Oxford U) 1922 *S*
Plummer, K C (Bristol) 1969 *W*, 1976 *S, I, F*
Pool-Jones, R J (Stade Francais) 1998 *A* 1
Poole, F O (Oxford U) 1895 *W, I, S*
Poole, R W (Hartlepool R) 1896 *S*
Pope, E B (Blackheath) 1931 *W, S, F*
Portus, G V (Blackheath) 1908 *F, I*
Potter, S (Leicester) 1998 *A* 1(t)
Poulton, R W (later Poulton Palmer) (Oxford U, Harlequins, Liverpool) 1909 *F, I, S*, 1910 *W*, 1911 *S*, 1912 *W, I, S*, 1913 *SA, W, F, I, S*, 1914 *W, I, S, F*
Powell, D L (Northampton) 1966 *W, I*, 1969 *I, F, S, W*, 1971 *W, I, F, S* (2[1C])
Pratten, W E (Blackheath) 1927 *S, F*
Preece, I (Coventry) 1948 *I, S, F*, 1949 *F, S*, 1950 *W, I, F, S*, 1951 *W, I, F*
Preece, P S (Coventry) 1972 *SA*, 1973 *NZ* 1, *W, I, F, S, NZ* 2, 1975 *I, F, W, A* 2, 1976 *W* (R)
Preedy, M (Gloucester) 1984 *SA* 1
Prentice, F D (Leicester) 1928 *I, F, S*
Prescott, R E (Harlequins) 1937 *W, I*, 1938 *I*, 1939 *W, I, S*
Preston, N J (Richmond) 1979 *NZ*, 1980 *I, F*
Price, H L (Harlequins) 1922 *I, S*, 1923 *W, I*
Price, J (Coventry) 1961 *I*
Price, P L A (RIE Coll) 1877 *I, S*, 1878 *S*
Price, T W (Cheltenham) 1948 *S, F*, 1949 *W, I, F, S*
Probyn, J A (Wasps, Askeans) 1988 *F, W, S, I* 1,2, *A* 1, 2, *A*, 1989 *S, I, R* (R), 1990 *I, F, W, S, Arg* 1,2,3, 1991 *W, S, I, F, Fj, A*, [*NZ, It, F, S, A*], 1992 *S, I, F, W*, 1993 *F, W, S, I*
Prout, D H (Northampton) 1968 *W, I*
Pullin, J V (Bristol) 1966 *W*, 1968 *W, I, F, S*, 1969 *I, F, S, W, SA*, 1970 *I, W, S, F*, 1971 *W, I, F, S* (2[1C]), *P*, 1972 *W, I, F, S, SA*, 1973 *NZ* 1, *W, I, F, S, NZ* 2, *A*, 1974 *S, I, F, W*, 1975 *I, W* (R), *S, A* 1,2, 1976 *F*
Purdy, S J (Rugby) 1962 *S*
Pyke, J (St Helens Recreation) 1892 *W*
Pym, J A (Blackheath) 1912 *W, I, S, F*

Quinn, J P (New Brighton) 1954 *W, NZ, I, S, F*

Rafter, M (Bristol) 1977 *S, F, W*, 1978 *F, W, S, I, NZ*, 1979 *S, I, F, W, NZ*, 1980 *W*(R), 1981 *W, Arg* 1,2
Ralston, C W (Richmond) 1971 *S* (C), *P*, 1972 *W, I, F, S, SA*, 1973 *NZ* 1, *W, I, F, S, NZ* 2, *A*, 1974 *S, I, F, W*, 1975 *I, F, W, S*
Ramsden, H E (Bingley) 1898 *W, S*
Ranson, J M (Rosslyn Park) 1963 *NZ* 1,2, *A*, 1964 *W, I, F, S*
Raphael, J E (OMTs) 1902 *W, I, S*, 1905 *W, S, NZ*, 1906 *W, S, F*
Ravenscroft, J (Birkenhead Park) 1881 *I*
Ravenscroft, S C W (Saracens) 1998 *A* 1, *NZ* 2(R)
Rawlinson, W C W (Blackheath) 1876 *S*
Redfern, S (Leicester) 1984 *I* (R)
Redman, N C (Bath) 1984 *A*, 1986 *S* (R), 1987 *I, S*, [*A, J, W*], 1988 *Fj*, 1990 *Arg* 1,2, 1991 *Fj*, [*It, US*], 1993 *NZ*, 1994 *F, W, SA* 1,2, 1997 *Arg* 1, *A* 1
Redmond, G F (Cambridge U) 1970 *F*
Redwood, B W (Bristol) 1968 *W, I*
Rees, D L (Sale) 1997 *A* 2, *NZ* 1, *SA, NZ* 2, 1998 *F, W, SA* 2(R), 1999 *S, I, F, A*
Rees, G W (Nottingham) 1984 *SA* 2(R), *A*, 1986 *I, F*, 1987 *F, W, S*, [*A, J, US, W*], 1988 *S* (R), *I* 1,2, *A* 1,2, *Fj*, 1989 *W* (R), *R* (R), *Fj* (R), 1990 *Arg* 3(R), 1991 *Fj*, [*US*]
Reeve, J S R (Harlequins) 1929 *F*, 1930 *W, I, F, S*, 1931 *W, I, S*
Regan, M (Liverpool) 1953 *W, I, F, S*, 1954 *W, NZ, I, S, F*, 1956 *I, S, F*
Regan, M P (Bristol, Bath, Leeds) 1995 *SA, WS*, 1996 *F, W, S, I, It, Arg*, 1997 *S, I, F, W, A* 1, *NZ* 2(R), 1998 *F*, 2000 SA 1(t), *A* (R), *Arg, SA* 3(t), 2001 *It* (R), *S* (R), *C* 2(R), *R*, 2003 *F* 1 (t), *It* (R), *W* 2
Rendall, P A G (Wasps, Askeans) 1984 *W, SA* 2, 1986 *W, S*, 1987 *I, F, S*, [*A, J, W*], 1988 *F, W, S, I* 1,2, *A* 1,2, *A*, 1989 *S, I, F, W, R*, 1990 *I, F, W, S*, 1991 [*It* (R)]
Rew, H (Blackheath) 1929 *S, F*, 1930 *F, S*, 1931 *W, S, F*, 1934 *W, I, S*
Reynolds, F J (O Cranleighans) 1937 *S*, 1938 *I, S*
Reynolds, S (Richmond) 1900 *W, I, S*, 1901 *I*
Rhodes, J (Castleford) 1896 *W, I, S*
Richards, D (Leicester) 1986 *I, F*, 1987 *S*, [*A, J, US, W*], 1988 *F, W, S, I* 1, *A* 1,2, *Fj, A*, 1989 *S, I, F, W, R*, 1990 *Arg* 3, 1991 *W, S, I, F, Fj, A*, [*NZ, It, US*], 1992 *S* (R), *F, W, C*, 1993 *NZ*, 1994 *W, SA* 1, *C*, 1995 *I, F, W, S*, [*WS, A, NZ*], 1996 *F* (t), *S, I*
Richards, E E (Plymouth A) 1929 *S, F*
Richards, J (Bradford) 1891 *W, I, S*
Richards, S B (Richmond) 1965 *W, I, F, S*, 1967 *A, I, F, S, W*
Richardson, J V (Birkenhead Park) 1928 *A, W, I, F, S*
Richardson, W R (Manchester) 1881 *I*
Rickards, C H (Gipsies) 1873 *S*
Rimmer, G (Waterloo) 1949 *W, I*, 1950 *W*, 1951 *W, I, F*, 1952 *SA, W*, 1954 *W, NZ, I, S*
Rimmer, L I (Bath) 1961 *SA, W, I, F, S*
Ripley, A G (Rosslyn Park) 1972 *W, I, F, S, SA*, 1973 *NZ* 1, *W, I, F, S, NZ* 2, *A*, 1974 *S, I, F, W*, 1975 *I, F, S, A* 1,2, 1976 *A, W, S*
Risman, A B W (Loughborough Coll) 1959 *W, I, F, S*, 1961 *SA, W, I, F*
Ritson, J A S (Northern) 1910 *F, S*, 1912 *F*, 1913 *SA, W, F, I, S*
Rittson-Thomas, G C (Oxford U) 1951 *W, I, F*
Robbins, G L (Coventry) 1986 *W, S*
Robbins, P G D (Oxford U, Moseley, Coventry) 1956 *W, I, S, F*, 1957 *W, I, F, S*, 1958 *W, A, I, S*, 1960 *W, I, F, S*, 1961 *SA, W*, 1962 *S*
Roberts, A D (Northern) 1911 *W, F, I, S*, 1912 *I, S, F*, 1914 *I*
Roberts, E W (RNE Coll) 1901 *W, I*, 1905 *NZ*, 1906 *W, I*, 1907 *S*
Roberts, G D (Harlequins) 1907 *S*, 1908 *F, W*
Roberts, J (Sale) 1960 *W, I, F, S*, 1961 *SA, W, I, F, S*, 1962 *W, I, F, S*, 1963 *W, I, F, S*, 1964 *NZ*
Roberts, R S (Coventry) 1932 *I*
Roberts, S (Swinton) 1887 *W, I*
Roberts, V G (Penryn, Harlequins) 1947 *F*, 1949 *W, I, F, S*, 1950 *I, F, S*, 1951 *W, I, F, S*, 1956 *W, I, S, F*
Robertshaw, A R (Bradford) 1886 *W, I, S*, 1887 *W, S*
Robinson, A (Blackheath) 1889 *M*, 1890 *W, S, I*
Robinson, E T (Coventry) 1954 *S*, 1961 *I, F, S*
Robinson, G C (Percy Park) 1897 *I, S*, 1898 *I*, 1899 *W*, 1900 *I, S*, 1901 *I, S*
Robinson, J (Sale) 2001 *It* (R), *S* (R), *F* (R), *I, A, R, SA*, 2002 *S, I, F, It, NZ, A, SA*, 2003 *F* 1, *W* 1, *S, I, NZ, A, F* 3
Robinson, J J (Headingley) 1893 *S*, 1902 *W, I, S*
Robinson, R A (Bath) 1988 *A* 2, *Fj, A*, 1989 *S, I, F, W*, 1995 *SA*
Robson, A (Northern) 1924 *W, I, F, S*, 1926 *W*
Robson, M (Oxford U) 1930 *W, I, F, S*
Rodber, T A K (Army, Northampton) 1992 *S, I*, 1993 *NZ*, 1994 *I, F, W, SA* 1,2, *R, C*, 1995 *I, F, W, S*, [*Arg, It, WS* (R), *A, NZ, F*], *SA, WS*, 1996 *W, S* (R), *I* (t), *It, Arg*, 1997 *S, I, F, W, A* 1, 1998 *H* (R), *It* (R), *A* 2, *SA* 2, 1999 *S, I, F, W, A, US* (R), [*NZ* (R), *Fj* (R)]
Rogers, D P (Bedford) 1961 *I, F, S*, 1962 *W, I, F*, 1963 *W, I, F, S, NZ* 1,2, *A*, 1964 *NZ, W, I, F, S*, 1965 *W, I, F, S*, 1966 *W, I, F, S*, 1967 *A, S, W, NZ*, 1969 *I, F, S, W*
Rogers, J H (Moseley) 1890 *W, S, I*, 1891 *S*
Rogers, W L Y (Blackheath) 1905 *W, I*

Rollitt, D M (Bristol) 1967 *I, F, S, W,* 1969 *I, F, S, W,* 1975 *S, A* 1,2
Roncoroni, A D S (West Herts, Richmond) 1933 *W, I, S*
Rose, W M H (Cambridge U, Coventry, Harlequins) 1981 *I, F,* 1982 *A, S, I,* 1987 *I, F, W, S,* [*A*]
Rossborough, P A (Coventry) 1971 *W,* 1973 *NZ* 2, *A,* 1974 *S, I,* 1975 *I, F*
Rosser, D W A (Wasps) 1965 *W, I, F, S,* 1966 *W*
Rotherham, Alan (Richmond) 1883 *W, S,* 1884 *W, S,* 1885 *W, I,* 1886 *W, I, S,* 1887 *W, I, S*
Rotherham, Arthur (Richmond) 1898 *S, W,* 1899 *W, I, S*
Roughley, D (Liverpool) 1973 *A,* 1974 *S, I*
Rowell, R E (Leicester) 1964 *W,* 1965 *W*
Rowley, A J (Coventry) 1932 *SA*
Rowley, H C (Manchester) 1879 *S, I,* 1880 *I, S,* 1881 *I, W, S,* 1882 *I, S*
Rowntree, G C (Leicester) 1995 *S* (t), [*It, WS*], *WS,* 1996 *F, W, S, I, It, Arg,* 1997 *S, I, F, W, A* 1, 1998 *A* 1, *NZ* 1, 2, *SA* 1, *H* (R), *It* (R), 1999 *US, C,* [*It* (R), *Tg, Fj* (R)], 2001 *C* 1,2, *US, I* (R), *A, R, SA,* 2002 *S, I, F, W, It,* 2003 *F* 1 (R), *W* 1, *It, S, I, NZ, F* 2
Royds, P M R (Blackheath) 1898 *S, W,* 1899 *W*
Royle, A V (Broughton R) 1889 *M*
Rudd, E L (Liverpool) 1965 *W, I, S,* 1966 *W, I, S*
Russell, R F (Leicester) 1905 *NZ*
Rutherford, D (Percy Park, Gloucester) 1960 *W, I, F, S,* 1961 *SA,* 1965 *W, I, F, S,* 1966 *W, I, F, S,* 1967 *NZ*
Ryalls, H J (New Brighton) 1885 *W, I*
Ryan, D (Wasps, Newcastle) 1990 *Arg* 1,2, 1992 *C,* 1998 *S*
Ryan, P H (Richmond) 1955 *W, I*

Sadler, E H (Army) 1933 *I, S*
Sagar, J W (Cambridge U) 1901 *W, I*
Salmon, J L B (Harlequins) 1985 *NZ* 1,2, 1986 *W, S,* 1987 *I, F, W, S,* [*A, J, US, W*]
Sample, C H (Cambridge U) 1884 *I,* 1885 *I,* 1886 *S*
Sampson, P C (Wasps) 1998 *SA* 1, 2001 *C* 1,2
Sanders, D L (Harlequins) 1954 *W, NZ, I, S, F,* 1956 *W, I, S, F*
Sanders, F W (Plymouth A) 1923 *I, S, F*
Sanderson, A (Sale) 2001 *R* (R), 2002 *Arg,* 2003 *It* (t+R), *W* 2(R), *F* 2
Sanderson, P H (Sale, Harlequins) 1998 *NZ* 1,2, *SA* 1, 2001 *C* 1(R),2(R), *US* (t+R)
Sandford, J R P (Marlborough N) 1906 *I*
Sangwin, R D (Hull and E Riding) 1964 *NZ, W*
Sargent, G A F (Gloucester) 1981 *I* (R)
Savage, K F (Northampton) 1966 *W, I, F, S,* 1967 *A, I, F, S, W, NZ,* 1968 *W, F, S*
Sawyer, C M (Broughton) 1880 *S,* 1881 *I*
Saxby, L E (Gloucester) 1932 *SA, W*
Scarbrough, D (Leeds) 2003 *W* 2
Schofield, J W (Manchester) 1880 *I*
Scholfield, J A (Preston Grasshoppers) 1911 *W*
Schwarz, R O (Richmond) 1899 *S,* 1901 *W, I*
Scorfield, E S (Percy Park) 1910 *F*
Scott, C T (Blackheath) 1900 *W, I,* 1901 *W, I*
Scott, E K (St Mary's Hospital, Redruth) 1947 *W,* 1948 *A, W, I, S*
Scott, F S (Bristol) 1907 *W*
Scott, H (Manchester) 1955 *F*
Scott, J P (Rosslyn Park, Cardiff) 1978 *F, W, S, I, NZ,* 1979 *S* (R), *I, F, W, NZ,* 1980 *I, F, W, S,* 1981 *W, S, I, F, Arg* 1,2, 1982 *I, F, W,* 1983 *F, W, S, I, NZ,* 1984 *S, I, F, W, SA* 1,2
Scott, J S M (Oxford U) 1958 *F*
Scott, M T (Cambridge U) 1887 *I,* 1890 *S, I*
Scott, W M (Cambridge U) 1889 *M*
Seddon, R L (Broughton R) 1887 *W, I, S*
Sellar, K A (United Services, RN) 1927 *W, I, S,* 1928 *A, W, I, F*
Sever, H S (Sale) 1936 *NZ, W, I, S,* 1937 *W, I, S,* 1938 *W, I, S*
Shackleton, I R (Cambridge U) 1969 *SA,* 1970 *I, W, S*
Sharp, R A W (Oxford U, Wasps, Redruth) 1960 *W, I, F, S,* 1961 *I, F,* 1962 *W, I, F,* 1963 *W, I, F, S,* 1967 *A*
Shaw, C H (Moseley) 1906 *S, SA,* 1907 *F, W, I, S*
Shaw, F (Cleckheaton) 1898 *I*
Shaw, J F (RNE Coll) 1898 *S, W*
Shaw, S D (Bristol, Wasps) 1996 *It, Arg,* 1997 *S, I, F, W, A* 1, *SA* (R), 2000 *I, F, W, It, S, SA* 1(R),2(R), 2001 *C* 1(R), 2, *US, I,* 2003 *It* (R), *W* 2, *F* 2(R),3(R)
Sheasby, C M A (Wasps) 1996 *It, Arg,* 1997 *W* (R), *Arg* 1(R),2(R), *SA* (R), *NZ* 2(t)
Sheppard, A (Bristol) 1981 *W* (R), 1985 *W*
Sherrard, C W (Blackheath) 1871 *S,* 1872 *S*
Sherriff, G A (Saracens) 1966 *S,* 1967 *A, NZ*
Shewring, H E (Bristol) 1905 *I, NZ,* 1906 *W, S, F, SA,* 1907 *F, W, I, S*
Shooter, J H (Morley) 1899 *I, S,* 1900 *I, S*
Shuttleworth, D W (Headingley) 1951 *S,* 1953 *S*
Sibree, H J H (Harlequins) 1908 *F,* 1909 *I, S*
Silk, N (Harlequins) 1965 *W, I, F, S*
Simms, K G (Cambridge U, Liverpool, Wasps) 1985 *R, F, S, I, W,* 1986 *I, F,* 1987 *I, F, W,* [*A, J, W*], 1988 *F, W*
Simpson, C P (Harlequins) 1965 *W*
Simpson, P D (Bath) 1983 *NZ,* 1984 *S,* 1987 *I*
Simpson, T (Rockcliff) 1902 *S,* 1903 *W, I, S,* 1904 *I, S,* 1905 *I, S,* 1906 *S, SA,* 1909 *F*
Simpson-Daniel, J (Gloucester) 2002 *NZ, A,* 2003 *W* 1 (t+R), *It, W* 2
Sims, D (Gloucester) 1998 *NZ* 1(R),2, *SA* 1
Skinner, M G (Harlequins) 1988 *F, W, S, I* 1,2, 1989 *Fj,* 1990 *I, F, W, S, Arg* 1,2, 1991 *Fj* (R), [*US, F, S, A*], 1992 *S, I, F, W*
Sladen, G M (United Services, RN) 1929 *W, I, S*
Sleightholme, J M (Bath) 1996 *F, W, S, I, It, Arg,* 1997 *S, I, F, W, Arg* 1,2
Slemen, M A C (Liverpool) 1976 *I, F,* 1977 *S, I, F, W,* 1978 *F, W, S, I, NZ,* 1979 *S, I, F, W, NZ,* 1980 *I, F, W, S,* 1981 *W, S, I, F,* 1982 *A, S, I, F, W,* 1983 *NZ,* 1984 *S*
Slocock, L A N (Liverpool) 1907 *F, W, I, S,* 1908 *F, W, I, S*
Slow, C F (Leicester) 1934 *S*
Small, H D (Oxford U) 1950 *W, I, F, S*
Smallwood, A M (Leicester) 1920 *F, I,* 1921 *W, I, S, F,* 1922 *I, S,* 1923 *W, I, S, F,* 1925 *I, S*
Smart, C E (Newport) 1979 *F, W, NZ,* 1981 *S, I, F, Arg* 1,2, 1982 *A, S, I, F, W,* 1983 *F, W, S, I*
Smart, S E J (Gloucester) 1913 *SA, W, F, I, S,* 1914 *W, I, S, F,* 1920 *W, I, S*
Smeddle, R W (Cambridge U) 1929 *W, I, S,* 1931 *F*
Smith, C C (Gloucester) 1901 *W*
Smith, D F (Richmond) 1910 *W, I*
Smith, J V (Cambridge U, Rosslyn Park) 1950 *W, I, F, S*
Smith, K (Roundhay) 1974 *F, W,* 1975 *W, S*
Smith, M J K (Oxford U) 1956 *W*
Smith, O J (Leicester) 2003 *It* (R), *W* 2(R), *F* 2
Smith, S J (Sale) 1973 *I, F, S, A,* 1974 *I, F,* 1975 *W* (R), 1976 *F,* 1977 *F* (R), 1979 *NZ,* 1980 *I, F, W, S,* 1981 *W, S, I, F, Arg* 1,2, 1982 *A, S, I, F, W,* 1983 *F, W, S*
Smith, S R (Richmond) 1959 *W, F, S,* 1964 *F, S*
Smith, S T (Wasps) 1985 *R, F, S, I, W, NZ* 1,2, 1986 *W, S*
Smith, T H (Northampton) 1951 *W*
Soane, F (Bath) 1893 *S,* 1894 *W, I, S*
Sobey, W H (O Millhillians) 1930 *W, F, S,* 1932 *SA, W*
Solomon, B (Redruth) 1910 *W*
Sparks, R H W (Plymouth A) 1928 *I, F, S,* 1929 *W, I, S,* 1931 *I, S, F*
Speed, H (Castleford) 1894 *W, I, S,* 1896 *S*
Spence, F W (Birkenhead Park) 1890 *I*
Spencer, J (Harlequins) 1966 *W*
Spencer, J S (Cambridge U, Headingley) 1969 *I, F, S, W, SA,* 1970 *I, W, S, F,* 1971 *W, I, S* (2[1C]), *P*
Spong, R S (O Millhillians) 1929 *F,* 1930 *W, I, F, S,* 1931 *F,* 1932 *SA, W*
Spooner, R H (Liverpool) 1903 *W*
Springman, H H (Liverpool) 1879 *S,* 1887 *S*
Spurling, A (Blackheath) 1882 *I*
Spurling, N (Blackheath) 1886 *I, S,* 1887 *W*
Squires, P J (Harrogate) 1973 *F, S, NZ* 2, *A,* 1974 *S, I, F, W,* 1975 *I, F, W, S, A* 1,2, 1976 *A, W,* 1977 *S, I, F, W,* 1978 *F, W, S, I, NZ,* 1979 *S, I, F, W*
Stafford R C (Bedford) 1912 *W, I, S, F*
Stafford, W F H (RE) 1874 *S*
Stanbury, E (Plymouth A) 1926 *W, I, S,* 1927 *W, I, S, F,* 1928 *A, W, I, F, S,* 1929 *W, I, S, F*
Standing, G (Blackheath) 1883 *W, I*
Stanger-Leathes, C F (Northern) 1905 *I*
Stark, K J (O Alleynians) 1927 *W, I, S, F,* 1928 *A, W, I, F, S*
Starks, A (Castleford) 1896 *W, I*
Starmer-Smith, N C (Harlequins) 1969 *SA,* 1970 *I, W, S, F,* 1971 *S* (C), *P*
Start, S P (United Services, RN) 1907 *S*
Steeds, J H (Saracens) 1949 *F, S,* 1950 *I, F, S*
Steele-Bodger, M R (Cambridge U) 1947 *W, I, S, F,* 1948 *A, W, I, S, F*
Steinthal, F E (Ilkley) 1913 *W, F*
Stephenson, M (Newcastle) 2001 *C* 1,2, *US*

Stevens, C B (Penzance-Newlyn, Harlequins) 1969 *SA*, 1970 *I, W, S*, 1971 *P*, 1972 *W, I, F, S, SA*, 1973 *NZ* 1, *W, I, F, S, NZ* 2, *A*, 1974 *S, I, F, W*, 1975 *I, F, W, S*
Still, E R (Oxford U, Ravenscourt P) 1873 *S*
Stimpson, T R G (Newcastle, Leicester) 1996 *It*, 1997 *S, I, F, W, A* 1, *NZ* 2(t+R), 1998 *A* 1, *NZ* 1,2(R), *SA* 1(R), 1999 *US* (R), *C* (R), 2000 *SA* 1, 2001 *C* 1(t),2(R), 2002 *W* (R), *Arg, SA* (R)
Stirling, R V (Leicester, RAF, Wasps) 1951 *W, I, F, S*, 1952 *SA, W, S, I, F*, 1953 *W, I, F, S*, 1954 *W, NZ, I, S, F*
Stoddart, A E (Blackheath) 1885 *W, I*, 1886 *W, I, S*, 1889 *M*, 1890 *W, I*, 1893 *W, S*
Stoddart, W B (Liverpool) 1897 *W, I, S*
Stokes, F (Blackheath) 1871 *S*, 1872 *S*, 1873 *S*
Stokes, L (Blackheath) 1875 *I*, 1876 *S*, 1877 *I, S*, 1878 *S*, 1879 *S, I*, 1880 *I, S*, 1881 *I, W, S*
Stone, F le S (Blackheath) 1914 *F*
Stoop, A D (Harlequins) 1905 *S*, 1906 *S, F, SA*, 1907 *F, W*, 1910 *W, I, S*, 1911 *W, F, I, S*, 1912 *W, S*
Stoop, F M (Harlequins) 1910 *S*, 1911 *F, I*, 1913 *SA*
Stout, F M (Richmond) 1897 *W, I*, 1898 *I, S, W*, 1899 *I, S*, 1903 *S*, 1904 *W, I, S*, 1905 *W, I, S*
Stout, P W (Richmond) 1898 *S, W*, 1899 *W, I, S*
Stringer, N C (Wasps) 1982 *A* (R), 1983 *NZ* (R), 1984 *SA* 1(R), *A*, 1985 *R*
Strong, E L (Oxford U) 1884 *W, I, S*
Sturnham B (Saracens) 1998 *A* 1, *NZ* 1(t),2(t)
Summerscales, G E (Durham City) 1905 *NZ*
Sutcliffe, J W (Heckmondwike) 1889 *M*
Swarbrick, D W (Oxford U) 1947 *W, I, F*, 1948 *A, W*, 1949 *I*
Swayne, D H (Oxford U) 1931 *W*
Swayne, J W R (Bridgwater) 1929 *W*
Swift, A H (Swansea) 1981 *Arg* 1,2, 1983 *F, W, S*, 1984 *SA* 2
Syddall, J P (Waterloo) 1982 *I*, 1984 *A*
Sykes, A R V (Blackheath) 1914 *F*
Sykes, F D (Northampton) 1955 *F, S*, 1963 *NZ* 2, *A*
Sykes, P W (Wasps) 1948 *F*, 1952 *S, I, F*, 1953 *W, I, F*
Syrett, R E (Wasps) 1958 *W, A, I, F*, 1960 *W, I, F, S*, 1962 *W, I, F*

Tallent, J A (Cambridge U, Blackheath) 1931 *S, F*, 1932 *SA, W*, 1935 *I*
Tanner, C C (Cambridge U, Gloucester) 1930 *S*, 1932 *SA, W, I, S*
Tarr, F N (Leicester) 1909 *A, W, F*, 1913 *S*
Tatham, W M (Oxford U) 1882 *S*, 1883 *W, I, S*, 1884 *W, I, S*
Taylor, A S (Blackheath) 1883 *W, I*, 1886 *W, I*
Taylor, E W (Rockcliff) 1892 *I*, 1893 *I*, 1894 *W, I, S*, 1895 *W, I, S*, 1896 *W, I*, 1897 *W, I, S*, 1899 *I*
Taylor, F (Leicester) 1920 *F, I*
Taylor, F M (Leicester) 1914 *W*
Taylor, H H (Blackheath) 1879 *S*, 1880 *S*, 1881 *I, W*, 1882 *S*
Taylor, J T (W Hartlepool) 1897 *I*, 1899 *I*, 1900 *I*, 1901 *W, I*, 1902 *W, I, S*, 1903 *W, I*, 1905 *S*
Taylor, P J (Northampton) 1955 *W, I*, 1962 *W, I, F, S*
Taylor, R B (Northampton) 1966 *W*, 1967 *I, F, S, W, NZ*, 1969 *F, S, W, SA*, 1970 *I, W, S, F*, 1971 *S* (2[1C])
Taylor, W J (Blackheath) 1928 *A, W, I, F, S*
Teague, M C (Gloucester, Moseley) 1985 *F* (R), *NZ* 1, 2, 1989 *S, I, F, W, R*, 1990 *F, W, S*, 1991 *W, S, I, F, Fj, A*, [*NZ, It, F, S, A*], 1992 *SA*, 1993 *F, W, S, I*
Teden, D E (Richmond) 1939 *W, I, S*
Teggin, A (Broughton R) 1884 *I*, 1885 *W*, 1886 *I, S*, 1887 *I, S*
Tetley, T S (Bradford) 1876 *S*
Thomas, C (Barnstaple) 1895 *W, I, S*, 1899 *I*
Thompson, P H (Headingley, Waterloo) 1956 *W, I, S, F*, 1957 *W, I, F, S*, 1958 *W, A, I, F, S*, 1959 *W, I, F, S*
Thompson, S (Northampton) 2002 *S, I, F, W, It, Arg, NZ, A, SA*, 2003 *F* 1, *W* 1, *It, S, I, NZ, A, F* 2(R),3
Thomson, G T (Halifax) 1878 *S*, 1882 *I, S*, 1883 *W, I, S*, 1884 *I, S*, 1885 *I*
Thomson, W B (Blackheath) 1892 *W*, 1895 *W, I, S*
Thorne, J D (Bristol) 1963 *W, I, F*
Tindall, M J (Bath) 2000 *I, F, W, It, S, SA* 1,2, *A Arg, SA* 3, 2001 *W* (R), *R, SA* (R), 2002 *S, I, F, W, It, NZ, A, SA*, 2003 *It, S, I, NZ, A, F* 2
Tindall, V R (Liverpool U) 1951 *W, I, F, S*
Tobin, F (Liverpool) 1871 *S*
Todd, A F (Blackheath) 1900 *I, S*
Todd, R (Manchester) 1877 *S*
Toft, H B (Waterloo) 1936 *S*, 1937 *W, I, S*, 1938 *W, I, S*, 1939 *W, I, S*
Toothill, J T (Bradford) 1890 *S, I*, 1891 *W, I*, 1892 *W, I, S*, 1893 *W, I, S*, 1894 *W, I*
Tosswill, L R (Exeter) 1902 *W, I, S*
Touzel, C J C (Liverpool) 1877 *I, S*
Towell, A C (Bedford) 1948 *F*, 1951 *S*
Travers, B H (Harlequins) 1947 *W, I*, 1948 *A, W*, 1949 *F, S*
Treadwell, W T (Wasps) 1966 *I, F, S*
Trick, D M (Bath) 1983 *I*, 1984 *SA* 1
Tristram, H B (Oxford U) 1883 *S*, 1884 *W, S*, 1885 *W*, 1887 *S*
Troop, C L (Aldershot S) 1933 *I, S*
Tucker, J S (Bristol) 1922 *W*, 1925 *NZ, W, I, S, F*, 1926 *W, I, F, S*, 1927 *W, I, S, F*, 1928 *A, W, I, F, S*, 1929 *W, I, F*, 1930 *W, I, F, S*, 1931 *W*
Tucker, W E (Blackheath) 1894 *W, I*, 1895 *W, I, S*
Tucker, W E (Blackheath) 1926 *I*, 1930 *W, I*
Turner, D P (Richmond) 1871 *S*, 1872 *S*, 1873 *S*, 1874 *S*, 1875 *I, S*
Turner, E B (St George's Hospital) 1876 *I*, 1877 *I*, 1878 *I*
Turner, G R (St George's Hospital) 1876 *S*
Turner, H J C (Manchester) 1871 *S*
Turner, M F (Blackheath) 1948 *S, F*
Turquand-Young, D (Richmond) 1928 *A, W*, 1929 *I, S, F*
Twynam, H T (Richmond) 1879 *I*, 1880 *I*, 1881 *W*, 1882 *I*, 1883 *I*, 1884 *W, I, S*

Ubogu, V E (Bath) 1992 *C, SA*, 1993 *NZ*, 1994 *S, I, F, W, SA* 1,2, *R, C*, 1995 *I, F, W, S*, [*Arg, WS, A, NZ, F*], *SA*, 1999 *F* (R), *W* (R), *A* (R)
Underwood, A M (Exeter) 1962 *W, I, F, S*, 1964 *I*
Underwood, R (Leicester, RAF) 1984 *I, F, W, A*, 1985 *R, F, S, I, W*, 1986 *W, I, F*, 1987 *I, F, W, S*, [*A, J, W*], 1988 *F, W, S, I* 1,2, *A* 1,2, *Fj, A*, 1989 *S, I, F, W, R, Fj*, 1990 *I, F, W, S, Arg* 3, 1991 *W, S, I, F, Fj, A*, [*NZ, It, US, F, S, A*], 1992 *S, I, F, W, SA*, 1993 *F, W, S, I, NZ*, 1994 *S, I, F, W, SA* 1,2, *R, C*, 1995 *I, F, W, S*, [*Arg, It, WS, A, NZ, F*], *SA, WS*, 1996 *F, W, S, I*
Underwood, T (Leicester, Newcastle) 1992 *C, SA*, 1993 *S, I, NZ*, 1994 *S, I, W, SA* 1,2, *R, C*, 1995 *I, F, W, S*, [*Arg, It, A, NZ*], 1996 *Arg*, 1997 *S, I, F, W*, 1998 *A* 2, *SA* 2
Unwin, E J (Rosslyn Park, Army) 1937 *S*, 1938 *W, I, S*
Unwin, G T (Blackheath) 1898 *S*
Uren, R (Waterloo) 1948 *I, S, F*, 1950 *I*
Uttley, R M (Gosforth) 1973 *I, F, S, NZ* 2, *A*, 1974 *I, F, W*, 1975 *F, W, S, A* 1,2, 1977 *S, I, F, W*, 1978 *NZ* 1979 *S*, 1980 *I, F, W, S*

Valentine J (Swinton) 1890 *W*, 1896 *W, I, S*
Vanderspar, C H R (Richmond) 1873 *S*
Van Ryneveld, C B (Oxford U) 1949 *W, I, F, S*
Varley, H (Liversedge) 1892 *S*
Vassall, H (Blackheath) 1881 *W, S*, 1882 *I, S*, 1883 *W*
Vassall, H H (Blackheath) 1908 *I*
Vaughan, D B (Headingley) 1948 *A, W, I, S*, 1949 *I, F, S*, 1950 *W*
Vaughan-Jones, A (Army) 1932 *I, S*, 1933 *W*
Verelst, C L (Liverpool) 1876 I, 1878 *I*
Vernon, G F (Blackheath) 1878 *S, I*, 1880 *I, S*, 1881 *I*
Vickery, G (Aberavon) 1905 *I*
Vickery, P J (Gloucester) 1998 *W, A* 1, *NZ* 1,2, *SA* 1, 1999 *US, C*, [*It, NZ, Tg, SA*], 2000 *I, F, W, S, A, Arg* (R), *SA* 3(R), 2001 *W, It, S, A, SA*, 2002 *I, F, Arg, NZ, A, SA*, 2003 *NZ* (R), *A*
Vivyan, E J (Devonport A) 1901 *W*, 1904 *W, I, S*
Voyce, A T (Gloucester) 1920 *I, S*, 1921 *W, I, S, F*, 1922 *W, I, F, S*, 1923 *W, I, S, F*, 1924 *W, I, F, S*, 1925 *NZ, W, I, S, F*, 1926 *W, I, F, S*
Voyce, T (Bath) 2001 *US* (R)

Wackett, J A S (Rosslyn Park) 1959 *W, I*
Wade, C G (Richmond) 1883 *W, I, S*, 1884 *W, S*, 1885 *W*, 1886 *W, I*
Wade, M R (Cambridge U) 1962 *W, I, F*
Wakefield, W W (Harlequins) 1920 *W, F, I, S*, 1921 *W, I, S, F*, 1922 *W, I, F, S*, 1923 *W, I, S, F*, 1924 *W, I, F, S*, 1925 *NZ, W, I, S, F*, 1926 *W, I, F, S*, 1927 *S, F*
Walder, D J H (Newcastle) 2001 *C* 1,2, *US*, 2003 *W* 2(R)
Walker, G A (Blackheath) 1939 *W, I*
Walker, H W (Coventry) 1947 *W, I, S, F*, 1948 *A, W, I, S, F*
Walker, R (Manchester) 1874 *S*, 1875 *I*, 1876 *S*, 1879 *S*, 1880 *S*
Wallens, J N S (Waterloo) 1927 *F*
Walton, E J (Castleford) 1901 *W, I*, 1902 *I, S*
Walton, W (Castleford) 1894 *S*

Ward, G (Leicester) 1913 *W, F, S*, 1914 *W, I, S*
Ward, H (Bradford) 1895 *W*
Ward, J I (Richmond) 1881 *I*, 1882 *I*
Ward, J W (Castleford) 1896 *W, I, S*
Wardlow, C S (Northampton) 1969 *SA* (R), 1971 *W, I, F, S* (2[1C])
Warfield, P J (Rosslyn Park, Durham U) 1973 *NZ* 1, *W, I*, 1975 *I, F, S*
Warr, A L (Oxford U) 1934 *W, I*
Waters, F H H (Wasps) 2001 *US*
Watkins, J A (Gloucester) 1972 *SA*, 1973 *NZ* 1, *W, NZ* 2, *A*, 1975 *F, W*
Watkins, J K (United Services, RN) 1939 *W, I, S*
Watson, F B (United Services, RN) 1908 *S*, 1909 *S*
Watson, J H D (Blackheath) 1914 *W, S, F*
Watt, D E J (Bristol) 1967 *I, F, S, W*
Webb, C S H (Devonport Services, RN) 1932 *SA, W, I, S*, 1933 *W, I, S*, 1935 *S*, 1936 *NZ, W, I, S*
Webb, J M (Bristol, Bath) 1987 [*A* (R), *J, US, W*], 1988 *F, W, S, I* 1,2, *A* 1,2, *A*, 1989 *S, I, F, W*, 1991 *Fj, A*, [*NZ, It, F, S, A*], 1992 *S, I, F, W, C, SA*, 1993 *F, W, S, I*
Webb, J W G (Northampton) 1926 *F, S*, 1929 *S*
Webb, R E (Coventry) 1967 *S, W, NZ*, 1968 *I, F, S*, 1969 *I, F, S, W*, 1972 *I, F*
Webb, St L H (Bedford) 1959 *W, I, F, S*
Webster, J G (Moseley) 1972 *W, I, SA*, 1973 *NZ* 1, *W, NZ* 2, 1974 *S, W*, 1975 *I, F, W*
Wedge, T G (St Ives) 1907 *F*, 1909 *W*
Weighill, R H G (RAF, Harlequins) 1947 *S, F*, 1948 *S, F*
Wells, C M (Cambridge U, Harlequins) 1893 *S*, 1894 *W, S*, 1896 *S*, 1897 *W, S*
West, B R (Loughborough Colls, Northampton) 1968 *W, I, F, S*, 1969 *SA*, 1970 *I, W, S*
West, D E (Leicester) 1998 *F* (R), *S* (R), 2000 *Arg* (R), 2001 *W, It, S, F* (t), *C* 1,2, *US, I* (R), *A, SA*, 2002 *F* (R), *W* (R), *It* (R), 2003 *W* 2(R), *F* 2,3(t+R)
West, R (Gloucester) 1995 [*WS*]
Weston, H T F (Northampton) 1901 *S*
Weston, L E (W of Scotland) 1972 *F, S*
Weston, M P (Richmond, Durham City) 1960 *W, I, F, S*, 1961 *SA, W, I, F, S*, 1962 *W, I, F*, 1963 *W, I, F, S, NZ* 1,2, *A*, 1964 *NZ, W, I, F, S*, 1965 *F, S*, 1966 *S*, 1968 *F, S*
Weston, W H (Northampton) 1933 *I, S*, 1934 *I, S*, 1935 *W, I, S*, 1936 *NZ, W, S*, 1937 *W, I, S*, 1938 *W, I, S*
Wheatley, A A (Coventry) 1937 *W, I, S*, 1938 *W, S*
Wheatley, H F (Coventry) 1936 *I*, 1937 *S*, 1938 *W, S*, 1939 *W, I, S*
Wheeler, P J (Leicester) 1975 *F, W*, 1976 *A, W, S, I*, 1977 *S, I, F, W*, 1978 *F, W, S, I, NZ*, 1979 *S, I, F, W, NZ*, 1980 *I, F, W, S*, 1981 *W, S, I, F*, 1982 *A, S, I, F, W*, 1983 *F, S, I, NZ*, 1984 *S, I, F, W*
White, C (Gosforth) 1983 *NZ*, 1984 *S, I, F*
White, D F (Northampton) 1947 *W, I, S*, 1948 *I, F*, 1951 *S*, 1952 *SA, W, S, I, F*, 1953 *W, I, S*
White, J (Saracens, Bristol, Leicester) 2000 *SA* 1,2, *Arg, SA* 3, 2001 *F, C* 1,2, *US, I, R* (R), 2002 *S, W, It*, 2003 *F* 1, *W* 2, *F* 2,3
White-Cooper, S (Harlequins) 2001 *C* 2, *US*
Whiteley, E C P (O Alleynians) 1931 *S, F*
Whiteley, W (Bramley) 1896 *W*
Whitely, H (Northern) 1929 *W*
Wightman, B J (Moseley, Coventry) 1959 *W*, 1963 *W, I, NZ* 2, *A*
Wigglesworth, H J (Thornes) 1884 *I*
Wilkins, D T (United Services, RN, Roundhay) 1951 *W, I, F, S*, 1952 *SA, W, S, I, F*, 1953 *W, I, F, S*
Wilkinson, E (Bradford) 1886 *W, I, S*, 1887 *W, S*
Wilkinson, H (Halifax) 1929 *W, I, S*, 1930 *F*
Wilkinson, H J (Halifax) 1889 *M*
Wilkinson, J P (Newcastle) 1998 *I* (R), *A* 1, *NZ* 1, 1999 *S, I, F, W, A, US, C*, [*It, NZ, Fj, SA* (R)], 2000 *I, F, W, It, S, SA* 2, *A, Arg, SA* 3, 2001 *W, It, S, F, I, A, SA*, 2002 *S, I, F, W, It, NZ, A, SA*, 2003 *F* 1, *W* 1, *It, S, I, NZ, A, F* 3
Wilkinson, P (Law Club) 1872 *S*
Wilkinson, R M (Bedford) 1975 *A* 2, 1976 *A, W, S, I, F*
Willcocks, T J (Plymouth) 1902 *W*
Willcox, J G (Oxford U, Harlequins) 1961 *I, F, S*, 1962 *W, I, F, S*, 1963 *W, I, F, S*, 1964 *NZ, W, I, F, S*
William-Powlett, P B R W (United Services, RN) 1922 *S*
Williams, C G (Gloucester, RAF) 1976 *F*
Williams, C S (Manchester) 1910 *F*
Williams, J E (O Millhillians, Sale) 1954 *F*, 1955 *W, I, F, S*, 1956 *I, S, F*, 1965 *W*
Williams, J M (Penzance-Newlyn) 1951 *I, S*
Williams, P N (Orrell) 1987 *S*, [*A, J, W*]
Williams, S G (Devonport A) 1902 *W, I, S*, 1903 *I, S*, 1907 *I, S*
Williams, S H (Newport) 1911 *W, F, I, S*
Williamson, R H (Oxford U) 1908 *W, I, S*, 1909 *A, F*
Wilson, A J (Camborne S of M) 1909 *I*
Wilson, C E (Blackheath) 1898 *I*
Wilson, C P (Cambridge U, Marlborough N) 1881 *W*
Wilson, D S (Met Police, Harlequins) 1953 *F*, 1954 *W, NZ, I, S, F*, 1955 *F, S*
Wilson, G S (Tyldesley) 1929 *W, I*
Wilson, K J (Gloucester) 1963 *F*
Wilson, R P (Liverpool OB) 1891 *W, I, S*
Wilson, W C (Richmond) 1907 *I, S*
Winn, C E (Rosslyn Park) 1952 *SA, W, S, I, F*, 1954 *W, S, F*
Winterbottom, P J (Headingley, Harlequins) 1982 *A, S, I, F, W*, 1983 *F, W, S, I, NZ*, 1984 *S, F, W, SA* 1,2, 1986 *W, S, I, F*, 1987 *I, F, W*, [*A, J, US, W*], 1988 *F, W, S*, 1989 *R, Fj*, 1990 *I, F, W, S, Arg* 1,2,3, 1991 *W, S, I, F, A*, [*NZ, It, F, S, A*], 1992 *S, I, F, W, C, SA*, 1993 *F, W, S, I*
Wintle, T C (Northampton) 1966 *S*, 1969 *I, F, S, W*
Wodehouse, N A (United Services, RN) 1910 *F*, 1911 *W, F, I, S*, 1912 *W, I, S, F*, 1913 *SA, W, F, I, S*
Wood, A (Halifax) 1884 *I*
Wood, A E (Gloucester, Cheltenham) 1908 *F, W, I*
Wood, G W (Leicester) 1914 *W*
Wood, M B, (Wasps) 2000 *C* 2(R), *US* (R)
Wood, R (Liversedge) 1894 *I*
Wood, R D (Liverpool OB) 1901 *I*, 1903 *W, I*
Woodgate, E E (Paignton) 1952 *W*
Woodhead, E (Huddersfield) 1880 *I*
Woodman, T J, (Gloucester) 1999 *US* (R), 2000 *I* (R), *It* (R), 2001 *W* (R), *It* (R), 2002 *NZ*, 2003 *S* (R), *I* (t+R), *A, F* 3
Woodruff, C G (Harlequins) 1951 *W, I, F, S*
Woods, S M J (Cambridge U, Wellington) 1890 *W, S, I*, 1891 *W, I, S*, 1892 *I, S*, 1893 *W, I*, 1895 *W, I, S*
Woods, T (Bridgwater) 1908 *S*
Woods, T (United Services, RN) 1920 *S*, 1921 *W, I, S, F*
Woodward, C R (Leicester) 1980 *I* (R), *F, W, S*, 1981 *W, S, I, F, Arg* 1,2, 1982 *A, S, I, F, W*, 1983 *I, NZ*, 1984 *S, I, F, W*
Woodward, J E (Wasps) 1952 *SA, W, S*, 1953 *W, I, F, S*, 1954 *W, NZ, I, S, F*, 1955 *W, I*, 1956 *S*
Wooldridge, C S (Oxford U, Blackheath) 1883 *W, I, S*, 1884 *W, I, S*, 1885 *I*
Wordsworth, A J (Cambridge U) 1975 *A* 1(R)
Worsley, J P R (Wasps) 1999 [*Tg, Fj*], 2000 *It* (R), *S* (R), *SA* 1(R),2(R), 2001 *It* (R), *S* (R), *F* (R), *C* 1,2, *US, A, R, SA*, 2002 *S, I, F, W* (t+R), *Arg*, 2003 *W* 1(R), *It, S* (R), *I* (t), *NZ* (R), *A* (R), *W* 2
Worsley, M A (London Irish) 2003 *It* (R)
Worton, J R B (Harlequins, Army) 1926 *W*, 1927 *W*
Wrench, D F B (Harlequins) 1964 *F, S*
Wright, C C G (Cambridge U, Blackheath) 1909 *I, S*
Wright, F T (Edinburgh Acady, Manchester) 1881 *S*
Wright, I D (Northampton) 1971 *W, I, F, S* (R)
Wright. J C (Met Police) 1934 *W*
Wright, J F (Bradford) 1890 *W*
Wright, T P (Blackheath) 1960 *W, I, F, S*, 1961 *SA, W, I, F, S*, 1962 *W, I, F, S*
Wright, W H G (Plymouth) 1920 *W, F*
Wyatt, D M (Bedford) 1976 *S* (R)

Yarranton, P G (RAF, Wasps) 1954 *W, NZ, I*, 1955 *F, S*
Yates, K P (Bath) 1997 *Arg* 1,2
Yiend, W (Hartlepool R, Gloucester) 1889 *M*, 1892 *W, I, S*, 1893 *I, S*
Young, A T (Cambridge U, Blackheath, Army) 1924 *W, I, F, S*, 1925 *NZ, F*, 1926 *I, F, S*, 1927 *I, S, F*, 1928 *A, W, I, F, S*, 1929 *I*
Young, J R C (Oxford U, Harlequins) 1958 *I*, 1960 *W, I, F, S*, 1961 *SA, W, I, F*
Young, M (Gosforth) 1977 *S, I, F, W*, 1978 *F, W, S, I, NZ*, 1979 *S*
Young, P D (Dublin Wands) 1954 *W, NZ, I, S, F*, 1955 *W, I, F, S*
Youngs, N G (Leicester) 1983 *I, NZ*, 1984 *S, I, F, W*

SCOTLAND'S TEST SEASON REVIEW 2002-2003

First Win for 33 Years Against South Africa the Highlight

Bill McMurtrie

For the second successive season Scotland's on-field profit and loss account in the Six Nations Championship comprised wins against Wales and Italy and defeats by Ireland, France, and England. The difference this time was that the wins were at home instead of in Cardiff and Rome. The Murrayfield support could thus enjoy two championship wins in a season for the first time since the 1999 victories against Ireland and Wales contributed to the securing of the trophy in the last Five Nations tournament.

Scotland's record in the 2003 RBS Six Nations Championship fell short of what might have been expected after the clean sweep in the 2002 Scottish Mutual Autumn Internationals, when wins against Romania (37-10) and Fiji (36-22) bracketed Scotland's first victory over South Africa since 1969. The 21-6 margin was wider than any of the Scots' three previous wins against the Springboks.

Seven months later South Africa had their revenge at home in a two-match Test series in June. The Springboks won by 29-25 in Durban and 28-19 in Johannesburg. For Scotland, though, those two results were in inverse proportion to their efforts, especially in the first Test.

Scotland's Six Nations Championship campaign opened with a disappointing defeat by Ireland. The margin was emphatic, 36-6, Ireland's widest in any game against Scotland.

Yet the Scots had enough of the game in the first half-hour on which to have based a far better result. However, Denis Hickie went in for the first of three Irish tries after 30 minutes, and David Humphreys not only converted but also added a second penalty goal for 13-0 at half-time. Thereafter the game slid steadily away from the home team despite two penalty goals by Gordon Ross.

Scotland's visit to Paris was even more disappointing, yet another record loss, this one by 38-3. The 35-point margin equalled the heaviest defeat Scotland have suffered at French hands.

Chris Paterson, promoted to front-line goal-kicker, scored Scotland's only points in that Paris match. However, the Edinburgh wing's penalty goal there was to launch him to a half-century of points in the championship, with 20 against Wales, 9 against England, and 18 against Italy. His two double-figure hauls each included a try, and his tally of points against Wales was the best by a Scot in that particular inter-country series.

Scotland led Wales by 20-10 at half-time after tries by Bruce Douglas and Simon Taylor. However, it was a nervous second half, and victory was ensured only with Paterson's try as the clock ran up to 80 minutes. It was a score made out of almost nothing as the wing followed up a kick through by Tom Smith. Paterson added the conversion, though two injury-time Welsh tries cut the winning scoreline to 30-22.

Stuart Moffat of Scotland breaks through to score a try on his Test debut during the match against Romania at Murrayfield in November. Scotland won 37-10.

Scotland, visiting Twickenham, found England on top of their game, especially in the second half. At the interval the home team led by only the margin of a major score (16-9), and Scotland's goal-line had survived even the eight minutes they were down to 13 men, with both Andrew Mower and Taylor in the sin-bin. In the second half, however, England pulled steadily away to win 40-9.

A win against Italy was needed for Scotland to avoid the wooden spoon, but the alarm bells were clanging loudly as Mirco Bergamasco ran in an early try for the visitors. Tries by Jason White and James McLaren helped to edge Scotland into the lead after quarter of an hour, and they kept ahead for the remainder of the game despite Italian persistence. Kenny Logan's try ensured an interval lead at 23-15, and Italy's territorial dominance of the second half was thwarted by Paterson's kick-and-chase try, his conversion, and his clinching penalty goal from close to halfway for a 33-25 victory.

In the first Test of the South African tour Scotland turned on a sterling performance, at least for the first hour. Tries by Jason White and Andy Craig gave the Scots the upper hand in the first half, and their command was extended when Kenny Logan sliced through around halfway to ignite a sparkling phase that Chris Paterson completed with the tourists' third try. Paterson's conversion took the Scots to 19-9. After 57 minutes they were even further ahead at 25-12, but a late surge by the Springboks, including tries by Stefan Terblanche and Trevor Halstead, overturned the lead, though the Scots mounted a late siege in which, off the last move of the game, Nathan Hines knocked on as he was driven over the line.

In the second Test the Scots again held the early initiative after Craig's interception close to his own line and a run the length of the pitch to score. However, Louis Koen's goal-kicking kept the Springboks in contention, and the contest turned on Terblanche's try soon after the interval.

Scotland's Test Record in 2002-2003: Played 13, won 6, lost 7

Opponents	*Date*	*Venue*	*Result*
Ireland	6th September 2003	H	Lost 10-29
Wales	30th August 2003	A	Lost 9-23
Italy	23rd August 2003	H	Won 47-15
South Africa	14th June 2003	A	Lost 19-28
South Africa	7th June 2003	A	Lost 25-29
Italy	29th March 2003	H	Won 33-25
England	22nd March 2003	A	Lost 9-40
Wales	8th March 2003	H	Won 30-22
France	23rd February 2003	A	Lost 3-38
Ireland	16th February 2003	H	Lost 6-36
Fiji	24th November 2002	H	Won 36-12
South Africa	16th November 2002	H	Won 21-6
Romania	9th November 2002	H	Won 37-10

SCOTLAND INTERNATIONAL STATISTICS

(to 30 September 2003)

Match Records

MOST CONSECUTIVE TEST WINS

6 1925 *F, W, I, E,* 1926 *F, W*
6 1989 *Fj, R,* 1990 *I, F, W, E*

MOST CONSECUTIVE TESTS WITHOUT DEFEAT

Matches	*Wins*	*Draws*	*Period*
9	6*	3	1885 to 1887
6	6	0	1925 to 1926
6	6	0	1989 to 1990
6	4	2	1877 to 1880
6	5	1	1983 to 1984

* includes an abandoned match

MOST POINTS IN A MATCH

by the team

Pts	*Opponents*	*Venue*	*Year*
89	Ivory Coast	Rustenburg	1995
65	United States	San Francisco	2002
60	Zimbabwe	Wellington	1987
60	Romania	Hampden Park	1999
55	Romania	Dunedin	1987
53	United States	Murrayfield	2000
51	Zimbabwe	Murrayfield	1991
49	Argentina	Murrayfield	1990
49	Romania	Murrayfield	1995

by a player

Pts	*Player*	*Opponents*	*Venue*	*Year*
44	A G Hastings	Ivory Coast	Rustenburg	1995
33	G P J Townsend	United States	Murrayfield	2000
31	A G Hastings	Tonga	Pretoria	1995
27	A G Hastings	Romania	Dunedin	1987
26	K M Logan	Romania	Hampden Park	1999
24	B J Laney	Italy	Rome	2002
23	G Ross	Tonga	Murrayfield	2001
21	A G Hastings	England	Murrayfield	1986
21	A G Hastings	Romania	Bucharest	1986

MOST TRIES IN A MATCH

by the team

Tries	*Opponents*	*Venue*	*Year*
13	Ivory Coast	Rustenburg	1995
12	Wales	Raeburn Place	1887
11	Zimbabwe	Wellington	1987
10	United States	San Francisco	2002
9	Romania	Dunedin	1987
9	Argentina	Murrayfield	1990

by a player

Tries	*Player*	*Opponents*	*Venue*	*Year*
5	G C Lindsay	Wales	Raeburn Place	1887
4	W A Stewart	Ireland	Inverleith	1913
4	I S Smith	France	Inverleith	1925
4	I S Smith	Wales	Swansea	1925
4	A G Hastings	Ivory Coast	Rustenburg	1995

MOST CONVERSIONS IN A MATCH

by the team

Cons	*Opponents*	*Venue*	*Year*
9	Ivory Coast	Rustenburg	1995
8	Zimbabwe	Wellington	1987
8	Romania	Dunedin	1987

by a player

Cons	*Player*	*Opponents*	*Venue*	*Year*
9	A G Hastings	Ivory Coast	Rustenburg	1995
8	A G Hastings	Zimbabwe	Wellington	1987
8	A G Hastings	Romania	Dunedin	1987

MOST PENALTIES IN A MATCH

by the team

Penalties	*Opponents*	*Venue*	*Year*
8	Tonga	Pretoria	1995
6	France	Murrayfield	1986

by a player

Penalties	*Player*	*Opponents*	*Venue*	*Year*
8	A G Hastings	Tonga	Pretoria	1995
6	A G Hastings	France	Murrayfield	1986

MOST DROPPED GOALS IN A MATCH

by the team

Drops	*Opponents*	*Venue*	*Year*
3	Ireland	Murrayfield	1973
2	on several	occasions	

by a player

Drops	Player	Opponents	Venue	Year
2	R C MacKenzie	Ireland	Belfast	1877
2	N J Finlay	Ireland	Glasgow	1880
2	B M Simmers	Wales	Murrayfield	1965
2	D W Morgan	Ireland	Murrayfield	1973
2	B M Gossman	France	Parc des Princes	1983
2	J Y Rutherford	New Zealand	Murrayfield	1983
2	J Y Rutherford	Wales	Murrayfield	1985
2	J Y Rutherford	Ireland	Murrayfield	1987
2	C M Chalmers	England	Twickenham	1995

Career Records

MOST CAPPED PLAYERS

Caps	Player	Career Span
77	G P J Townsend	1993 to 2003
65	S Hastings	1986 to 1997
65	K M Logan	1992 to 2003
61	A G Hastings	1986 to 1995
61	G W Weir	1990 to 2000
60	C M Chalmers	1989 to 1999
55	B W Redpath	1993 to 2003
54	G C Bulloch	1997 to 2003
52	J M Renwick	1972 to 1984
52	C T Deans	1978 to 1987
52	A G Stanger	1989 to 1998
52	A P Burnell	1989 to 1999
51	A R Irvine	1972 to 1982
51	G Armstrong	1988 to 1999
51	S Murray	1997 to 2003
51	S B Grimes	1997 to 2003

MOST CONSECUTIVE TESTS

Tests	Player	Span
49	A B Carmichael	1967 to 1978
40	H F McLeod	1954 to 1962
37	J M Bannerman	1921 to 1929
35	A G Stanger	1989 to 1994

MOST TESTS AS CAPTAIN

Tests	Captain	Span
25	D M B Sole	1989 to 1992
20	A G Hastings	1993 to 1995
19	J McLauchlan	1973 to 1979
17	B W Redpath	1998 to 2003
16	R I Wainwright	1995 to 1998
15	M C Morrison	1899 to 1904
15	A R Smith	1957 to 1962
15	A R Irvine	1980 to 1982

MOST TESTS IN INDIVIDUAL POSITIONS

Position	Player	Tests	Span
Full-back	A G Hastings	61	1986 to 1995
Wing	K M Logan	63	1992 to 2003
Centre	S Hastings	63	1986 to 1997
Fly-half	G P J Townsend	56	1993 to 2003
Scrum-half	B W Redpath	55	1993 to 2003
Prop	A P Burnell	52	1989 to 1999
Hooker	G C Bulloch	54	1997 to 2003
Lock	S Murray	51	1997 to 2003
	S B Grimes	51	1997 to 2003
Flanker	J Jeffrey	40	1984 to 1991
No 8	D B White	29	1982 to 1992
	E W Peters	29	1995 to 1999

Townsend and Logan have been capped elsewhere in the back division

MOST POINTS IN TESTS

Points	Player	Tests	Career
667	A G Hastings	61	1986 to 1995
273	A R Irvine	51	1972 to 1982
220	K M Logan	65	1992 to 2003
210	P W Dods	23	1983 to 1991
166	C M Chalmers	60	1989 to 1999
157	G P J Townsend	77	1993 to 2003
147	C D Paterson	35	1999 to 2003
141	B J Laney	16	2001 to 2003
123	D W Hodge	26	1997 to 2002
106	A G Stanger	52	1989 to 1998

MOST TRIES IN TESTS

Tries	Player	Tests	Career
24	I S Smith	32	1924 to 1933
24	A G Stanger	52	1989 to 1998
17	A G Hastings	61	1986 to 1995
17	A V Tait	27	1987 to 1999
16	G P J Townsend	77	1993 to 2003
15	I Tukalo	37	1985 to 1992
13	K M Logan	65	1992 to 2003
12	A R Smith	33	1955 to 1962

MOST CONVERSIONS IN TESTS

Cons	Player	Tests	Career
86	A G Hastings	61	1986 to 1995
34	K M Logan	65	1992 to 2003
26	P W Dods	23	1983 to 1991
25	A R Irvine	51	1972 to 1982
19	D Drysdale	26	1923 to 1929
17	B J Laney	16	2001 to 2003
15	D W Hodge	26	1997 to 2002
14	F H Turner	15	1911 to 1914

14	R J S Shepherd	20	1995 to 1998
14	C D Paterson	35	1999 to 2003

23	C D Paterson	35	1999 to 2003
21	M Dods	8	1994 to 1996
21	R J S Shepherd	20	1995 to 1998

MOST PENALTY GOALS IN TESTS

Penalties	*Player*	*Tests*	*Career*
140	A G Hastings	61	1986 to 1995
61	A R Irvine	51	1972 to 1982
50	P W Dods	23	1983 to 1991
32	C M Chalmers	60	1989 to 1999
29	K M Logan	65	1992 to 2003
29	B J Laney	16	2001 to 2003

MOST DROPPED GOALS IN TESTS

Drops	*Player*	*Tests*	*Career*
12	J Y Rutherford	42	1979 to 1987
9	C M Chalmers	60	1989 to 1999
7	I R McGeechan	32	1972 to 1979
7	G P J Townsend	77	1993 to 2003
6	D W Morgan	21	1973 to 1978
5	H Waddell	15	1924 to 1930

International Championship Records

Record	*Detail*	*Holder*	*Set*
Most points in season	120	in four matches	1999
Most tries in season	17	in four matches	1925
Highest Score	38	38-10 v Ireland	1997
Biggest win	28	31-3 v France	1912
	28	38-10 v Ireland	1997
Highest score conceded	51	16-51 v France	1998
Biggest defeat	40	3-43 v England	2001
Most appearances	43	G P J Townsend	1993 – 2003
Most points in matches	288	A G Hastings	1986 – 1995
Most points in season	60	B J Laney	2002
Most points in match	24	B J Laney	v Italy, 2002
Most tries in matches	24	I S Smith	1924 – 1933
Most tries in season	8	I S Smith	1925
Most tries in match	5	G C Lindsay	v Wales, 1887
Most cons in matches	20	A G Hastings	1986 – 1995
Most cons in season	11	K M Logan	1999
Most cons in match	5	F H Turner	v France, 1912
	5	J W Allan	v England, 1931
	5	R J S Shepherd	v Ireland, 1997
Most pens in matches	77	A G Hastings	1986 – 1995
Most pens in season	15	B J Laney	2002
Most pens in match	6	A G Hastings	v France, 1986
Most drops in matches	8	J Y Rutherford	1979 – 1987
	8	C M Chalmers	1989 – 1998
Most drops in season	3	J Y Rutherford	1987
Most drops in match	2	on several	occasions

Miscellaneous Records

Record	*Holder*	*Detail*
Longest Test Career	W C W Murdoch	14 seasons, 1934-35 to 1947-48
Youngest Test Cap	N J Finlay	17 yrs 36 days in 1875*
Oldest Test Cap	J McLauchlan	37 yrs 210 days in 1979

* C Reid, also 17 yrs 36 days on debut in 1881, was a day *older* than Finlay, having lived through an extra leap-year day.

Career Records of Scotland International Players
(up to 30 September 2003)

PLAYER	*Debut*	*Caps*	*T*	*C*	*P*	*D*	*Pts*
Backs:							
G Beveridge	2000 v NZ	5	0	0	0	0	0
M R L Blair	2002 v C	7	2	0	0	0	10
A J Bulloch	2000 v US	5	1	0	0	0	5
G G Burns	1999 v It	4	0	0	0	0	0
A Craig	2002 v C	14	6	0	0	0	30
J M Craig	1997 v A	4	0	0	0	0	0
S C J Danielli	2003 v It	2	1	0	0	0	5
M P di Rollo	2002 v US	1	0	0	0	0	0
I T Fairley	1999 v It	3	0	0	0	0	0
A R Henderson	2001 v I	10	2	0	0	0	10
B G Hinshelwood	2002 v C	5	0	0	0	0	0
D W Hodge	1997 v F	26	6	15	20	1	123
R C Kerr	2002 v C	3	1	0	0	0	5
B J Laney	2001 v NZ	16	4	17	29	0	141
D J Lee	1998 v I	9	1	4	7	0	34
J A Leslie	1998 v SA	23	4	0	0	0	20
K M Logan	1992 v A	65	13	34	29	0	220
S L Longstaff	1998 v F	15	2	0	0	0	10
J G McLaren	1999 v Arg	26	6	0	0	0	30
M J M Mayer	1998 v SA	8	0	0	0	0	0
G H Metcalfe	1998 v A	36	4	0	0	0	20
J S D Moffat	2002 v R	3	1	0	0	0	5
C C Moir	2000 v W	3	0	0	0	0	0
C A Murray	1998 v E	26	7	0	0	0	35
C D Paterson	1999 v Sp	35	10	14	23	0	147
B W Redpath	1993 v NZ	55	1	0	0	0	5
R E Reid	2001 v Tg	2	1	0	0	0	5
G Ross	2001 v Tg	9	1	6	10	0	47
J F Steel	2000 v US	5	0	0	0	0	0
G P J Townsend	1993 v E	77	16	7	14	7	157
K N Utterson	2003 v F	3	0	0	0	0	0
N Walker	2002 v R	3	1	0	0	0	5
S Webster	2003 v I	1	1	0	0	0	5
Forwards:							
R S Beattie	2000 v NZ	6	0	0	0	0	0
S J Brotherstone	1999 v I	8	0	0	0	0	0
G C Bulloch	1997 v SA	54	4	0	0	0	20
S J Campbell	1995 v C	17	0	0	0	0	0
A K Dall	2003 v W	1	0	0	0	0	0
B A F Douglas	2002 v R	12	1	0	0	0	5
I A Fullarton	2000 v NZ	5	0	0	0	0	0
G Graham	1997 v A	25	1	0	0	0	5
S B Grimes	1997 v A	51	4	0	0	0	20
A J A Hall	2002 v US	1	0	0	0	0	0
D W H Hall	2003 v W	1	0	0	0	0	0
D I W Hilton	1995 v C	42	1	0	0	0	5
N J Hines	2000 v NZ	14	1	0	0	0	5
A F Jacobsen	2002 v C	3	0	0	0	0	0
G Kerr	2003 v I	7	0	0	0	0	0

M D Leslie	1998 v SA	35	10	0	0	0	50
D J H Macfadyen	2002 v C	2	0	0	0	0	0
G R McIlwham	1998 v Fj	15	0	0	0	0	0
K D McKenzie	1994 v Arg	14	1	0	0	0	5
C G Mather	1999 v R	4	2	0	0	0	10
R Metcalfe	2000 v E	9	1	0	0	0	5
A L Mower	2001 v Tg	13	0	0	0	0	0
S Murray	1997 v A	51	2	0	0	0	10
J M Petrie	2000 v NZ	22	1	0	0	0	5
A C Pountney	1998 v SA	31	5	0	0	0	25
M C Proudfoot	1998 v Fj	4	0	0	0	0	0
S J Reid	1995 v WS	8	0	0	0	0	0
A J Roxburgh	1997 v A	8	0	0	0	0	0
R R Russell	1999 v R	15	1	0	0	0	5
S Scott	2000 v NZ	9	0	0	0	0	0
G L Simpson	1998 v A	15	3	0	0	0	15
C J Smith	2002 v C	2	0	0	0	0	0
T J Smith	1997 v E	46	5	0	0	0	25
B D Stewart	1996 v NZ	4	0	0	0	0	0
M J Stewart	1996 v It	34	0	0	0	0	0
S M Taylor	2000 v US	25	2	0	0	0	10
G W Weir	1990 v Arg	61	4	0	0	0	19
J P R White	2000 v E	27	4	0	0	0	20

SCOTTISH INTERNATIONAL PLAYERS

(up to 30 September 2003)

Note: Years given for International Championship matches are for second half of season; eg 1972 means season 1971-72. Years for all other matches refer to the actual year of the match. When a series has taken place, figures have been used to denote the particular matches in which players have featured. Thus 1981 *NZ* 1,2 indicates that a player appeared in the first and second Tests of the series.

Abercrombie, C H (United Services) 1910 *I, E,* 1911 *F, W,* 1913 *F, W*
Abercrombie, J G (Edinburgh U) 1949 *F, W, I,* 1950 *F, W, I, E*
Agnew, W C C (Stewart's Coll FP) 1930 *W, I*
Ainslie, R (Edinburgh Inst FP) 1879 *I, E,* 1880 *I, E,* 1881 *E,* 1882 *I, E*
Ainslie, T (Edinburgh Inst FP) 1881 *E,* 1882 *I, E,* 1883 *W, I, E,* 1884 *W, I, E,* 1885 *W, I* 1,2
Aitchison, G R (Edinburgh Wands) 1883 *I*
Aitchison, T G (Gala) 1929 *W, I, E*
Aitken, A I (Edinburgh Inst FP) 1889 *I*
Aitken, G G (Oxford U) 1924 *W, I, E,* 1925 *F, W, I, E,* 1929 *F*
Aitken, J (Gala) 1977 *E, I, F,* 1981 *F, W, E, I, NZ* 1,2, *R, A,* 1982 *E, I, F, W,* 1983 *F, W, E, NZ,* 1984 *W, E, I, F, R*
Aitken, R (London Scottish) 1947 *W*
Allan, B (Glasgow Acads) 1881 *I*
Allan, J (Edinburgh Acads) 1990 *NZ* 1, 1991, *W, I, R, [J, I, WS, E, NZ]*
Allan, J L (Melrose) 1952 *F, W, I,* 1953 *W*
Allan, J L F (Cambridge U) 1957 *I, E*
Allan, J W (Melrose) 1927 *F,* 1928 *I,* 1929 *F, W, I, E,* 1930 *F, E,* 1931 *F, W, I, E,* 1932 *SA, W, I,* 1934 *I, E*
Allan, R C (Hutchesons' GSFP) 1969 *I*
Allardice, W D (Aberdeen GSFP) 1947 *A,* 1948 *F, W, I,* 1949 *F, W, I, E*
Allen, H W (Glasgow Acads) 1873 *E*
Anderson, A H (Glasgow Acads) 1894 *I*
Anderson, D G (London Scottish) 1889 *I,* 1890 *W, I, E,* 1891 *W, E,* 1892 *W, E*
Anderson, E (Stewart's Coll FP) 1947 *I, E*
Anderson, J W (W of Scotland) 1872 *E*
Anderson, T (Merchiston) 1882 *I*
Angus, A W (Watsonians) 1909 *W,* 1910 *F, W, E,* 1911 *W, I,* 1912 *F, W, I, E, SA,* 1913 *F, W,* 1914 *E,* 1920 *F, W, I, E*
Anton, P A (St Andrew's U) 1873 *E*
Armstrong, G (Jedforest, Newcastle) 1988 *A,* 1989 *W, E, I, F, Fj, R,* 1990 *I, F, W, E, NZ* 1,2, *Arg,* 1991 *F, W, E, I, R, [J, I, WS, E, NZ],* 1993 *I, F, W, E,* 1994 *E, I,* 1996 *NZ,* 1,2, *A,* 1997 *W, SA* (R), 1998 *It, I, F, W, E, SA* (R), 1999 *W, E, I, F, Arg, R, [SA, U, Sm, NZ]*
Arneil, R J (Edinburgh Acads, Leicester and Northampton) 1968 *I, E, A,* 1969 *F, W, I, E, SA,* 1970 *F, W, I, E, A,* 1971 *F, W, I, E* (2[1C]), 1972 *F, W, E, NZ*
Arthur, A (Glasgow Acads) 1875 *E,* 1876 *E*
Arthur, J W (Glasgow Acads) 1871 *E,* 1872 *E*
Asher, A G G (Oxford U) 1882 *I,* 1884 *W, I, E,* 1885 *W,* 1886 *I, E*
Auld, W (W of Scotland) 1889 *W,* 1890 *W*
Auldjo, L J (Abertay) 1878 *E*

Bain, D McL (Oxford U) 1911 *E,* 1912 *F, W, E, SA,* 1913 *F, W, I, E,* 1914 *W, I*
Baird, G R T (Kelso) 1981 *A,* 1982 *E, I, F, W, A* 1,2, 1983 *I, F, W, E, NZ,* 1984 *W, E, I, F, A,* 1985 *I, W, E,* 1986 *F, W, E, I, R,* 1987 *E,* 1988 *I*
Balfour, A (Watsonians) 1896 *W, I, E,* 1897 *E*
Balfour, L M (Edinburgh Acads) 1872 *E*
Bannerman, E M (Edinburgh Acads) 1872 *E,* 1873 *E*
Bannerman, J M (Glasgow HSFP) 1921 *F, W, I, E,* 1922 *F, W, I, E,* 1923 *F, W, I, E,* 1924 *F, W, I, E,* 1925 *F, W, I, E,* 1926 *F, W, I, E,* 1927 *F, W, I, E, A,* 1928 *F, W, I, E,* 1929 *F, W, I, E*
Barnes, I A (Hawick) 1972 *W,* 1974 *F* (R), 1975 *E* (R), *NZ,* 1977 *I, F, W*
Barrie, R W (Hawick) 1936 *E*
Bearne, K R F (Cambridge U, London Scottish) 1960 *F, W*
Beattie, J A (Hawick) 1929 *F, W,* 1930 *W,* 1931 *F, W, I, E,* 1932 *SA, W, I, E,* 1933 *W, E, I,* 1934 *I, E,* 1935 *W, I, E, NZ,* 1936 *W, I, E*
Beattie, J R (Glasgow Acads) 1980 *I, F, W, E,* 1981 *F, W, E, I,* 1983 *F, W, E, NZ,* 1984 *E* (R), *R, A,* 1985 *I,* 1986 *F, W, E, I, R,* 1987 *I, F, W, E*
Beattie, R S (Newcastle, Bristol) 2000 *NZ* 1,2(R), *Sm* (R), 2003 *E* (R), *It* 1(R), *I* 2
Bedell-Sivright, D R (Cambridge U, Edinburgh U) 1900 *W,* 1901 *W, I, E,* 1902 *W, I, E,* 1903 *W, I,* 1904 *W, I, E,* 1905 *NZ,* 1906 *W, I, E, SA,* 1907 *W, I, E,* 1908 *W, I*
Bedell-Sivright, J V (Cambridge U) 1902 *W*
Begbie, T A (Edinburgh Wands) 1881 *I, E*
Bell, D L (Watsonians) 1975 *I, F, W, E*
Bell, J A (Clydesdale) 1901 *W, I, E,* 1902 *W, I, E*
Bell, L H I (Edinburgh Acads) 1900 *E,* 1904 *W, I*
Berkeley, W V (Oxford U) 1926 *F,* 1929 *F, W, I*
Berry, C W (Fettesian-Lorettonians) 1884 *I, E,* 1885 *W, I* 1, 1887 *I, W, E,* 1888 *W, I*
Bertram, D M (Watsonians) 1922 *F, W, I, E,* 1923 *F, W, I, E,* 1924 *W, I, E*
Beveridge, G (Glasgow) 2000 *NZ* 2(R), *US* (R), *Sm* (R), 2002 *Fj* (R), 2003 *W* 2
Biggar, A G (London Scottish) 1969 *SA,* 1970 *F, I, E, A,* 1971 *F, W, I, E* (2[1C]), 1972 *F, W*
Biggar, M A (London Scottish) 1975 *I, F, W, E,* 1976 *W, E, I,* 1977 *I, F, W,* 1978 *I, F, W, E, NZ,* 1979 *W, E, I, F, NZ,* 1980 *I, F, W, E*
Birkett, G A (Harlequins, London Scottish) 1975 *NZ*
Bishop, J M (Glasgow Acads) 1893 *I*
Bisset, A A (RIE Coll) 1904 *W*
Black, A W (Edinburgh U) 1947 *F, W,* 1948 *E,* 1950 *W, I, E*
Black, W P (Glasgow HSFP) 1948 *F, W, I, E,* 1951 *E*
Blackadder, W F (W of Scotland) 1938 *E*
Blaikie, C F (Heriot's FP) 1963 *I, E,* 1966 *E,* 1968 *A,* 1969 *F, W, I, E*
Blair, M R L (Edinburgh) 2002 *C, US,* 2003 *F* (t+R), *W* 1(R), *SA* 2(R), *It* 2, *I* 2
Blair, P C B (Cambridge U) 1912 *SA,* 1913 *F, W, I, E*
Bolton, W H (W of Scotland) 1876 *E*
Borthwick, J B (Stewart's Coll FP) 1938 *W, I*
Bos, F H ten (Oxford U, London Scottish) 1959 *E,* 1960 *F, W, SA,* 1961 *F, SA, W, I, E,* 1962 *F, W, I, E,* 1963 *F, W, I, E*
Boswell, J D (W of Scotland) 1889 *W, I,* 1890 *W, I, E,* 1891 *W, I, E,* 1892 *W, I, E,* 1893 *I, E,* 1894 *I, E*
Bowie, T C (Watsonians) 1913 *I, E,* 1914 *I, E*
Boyd, G M (Glasgow HSFP) 1926 *E*
Boyd, J L (United Services) 1912 *E, SA*
Boyle, A C W (London Scottish) 1963 *F, W, I*
Boyle, A H W (St Thomas's Hospital, London Scottish) 1966 *A,* 1967 *F, NZ,* 1968 *F, W, I*
Brash, J C (Cambridge U) 1961 *E*
Breakey, R W (Gosforth) 1978 *E*
Brewis, N T (Edinburgh Inst FP) 1876 *E,* 1878 *E,* 1879 *I, E,* 1880 *I, E*
Brewster, A K (Stewart's-Melville FP) 1977 *E,* 1980 *I, F,* 1986 *E, I, R*
Brotherstone, S J (Melrose, Brive, Newcastle) 1999 *I* (R), 2000 *F, W, E, US, A, Sm,* 2002 *C* (R)
Brown, A H (Heriot's FP) 1928 *E,* 1929 *F, W*
Brown, A R (Gala) 1971 *E* (2[1C]), 1972 *F, W, E*
Brown, C H C (Dunfermline) 1929 *E*
Brown, D I (Cambridge U) 1933 *W, E, I*
Brown, G L (W of Scotland) 1969 *SA,* 1970 *F, W* (R), *I, E, A,* 1971 *F, W, I, E* (2[1C]), 1972 *F, W, E, NZ,* 1973 *E* (R), *P,* 1974 *W, E, I, F,* 1975 *I, F, W, E, A,* 1976 *F, W, E, I*
Brown, J A (Glasgow Acads) 1908 *W, I*
Brown, J B (Glasgow Acads) 1879 *I, E,* 1880 *I, E,* 1881 *I, E,* 1882 *I, E,* 1883 *W, I, E,* 1884 *W, I, E,* 1885 *I* 1,2, 1886 *W, I, E*
Brown, P C (W of Scotland, Gala) 1964 *F, NZ, W, I, E,* 1965 *I, E, SA,* 1966 *A,* 1969 *I, E,* 1970 *W, E,* 1971 *F, W, I, E* (2[1C]), 1972 *F, W, E, NZ,* 1973 *F, W, I, E, P*
Brown, T G (Heriot's FP) 1929 *W*

Brown, W D (Glasgow Acads) 1871 *E*, 1872 *E*, 1873 *E*, 1874 *E*, 1875 *E*
Brown, W S (Edinburgh Inst FP) 1880 *I*, *E*, 1882 *I*, *E*, 1883 *W*, *E*
Browning, A (Glasgow HSFP) 1920 *I*, 1922 *F*, *W*, *I*, 1923 *W*, *I*, *E*
Bruce, C R (Glasgow Acads) 1947 *F*, *W*, *I*, *E*, 1949 *F*, *W*, *I*, *E*
Bruce, N S (Blackheath, Army and London Scottish) 1958 *F*, *A*, *I*, *E*, 1959 *F*, *W*, *I*, *E*, 1960 *F*, *W*, *I*, *E*, *SA*, 1961 *F*, *SA*, *W*, *I*, *E*, 1962 *F*, *W*, *I*, *E*, 1963 *F*, *W*, *I*, *E*, 1964 *F*, *NZ*, *W*, *I*, *E*
Bruce, R M (Gordonians) 1947 *A*, 1948 *F*, *W*, *I*
Bruce-Lockhart, J H (London Scottish) 1913 *W*, 1920 *E*
Bruce-Lockhart, L (London Scottish) 1948 *E*, 1950 *F*, *W*, 1953 *I*, *E*
Bruce-Lockhart, R B (Cambridge U and London Scottish) 1937 *I*, 1939 *I*, *E*
Bryce, C C (Glasgow Acads) 1873 *E*, 1874 *E*
Bryce, R D H (W of Scotland) 1973 *I* (R)
Bryce, W E (Selkirk) 1922 *W*, *I*, *E*, 1923 *F*, *W*, *I*, *E*, 1924 *F*, *W*, *I*, *E*
Brydon, W R C (Heriot's FP) 1939 *W*
Buchanan, A (Royal HSFP) 1871 *E*
Buchanan, F G (Kelvinside Acads and Oxford U) 1910 *F*, 1911 *F*, *W*
Buchanan, J C R (Stewart's Coll FP) 1921 *W*, *I*, *E*, 1922 *W*, *I*, *E*, 1923 *F*, *W*, *I*, *E*, 1924 *F*, *W*, *I*, *E*, 1925 *F*, *I*
Buchanan-Smith, G A E (London Scottish, Heriot's FP) 1989 *Fj* (R), 1990 *Arg*
Bucher, A M (Edinburgh Acads) 1897 *E*
Budge, G M (Edinburgh Wands) 1950 *F*, *W*, *I*, *E*
Bullmore, H H (Edinburgh U) 1902 *I*
Bulloch, A J (Glasgow) 2000 *US*, *A*, *Sm*, 2001 *F* (t+R), *E*
Bulloch, G C (West of Scotland, Glasgow) 1997 *SA*, 1998 *It*, *I*, *F*, *W*, *E*, *Fj*, *A* 1, *SA*, 1999 *W*, *E*, *It*, *I*, *F*, *Arg*, [*SA*, *U*, *Sm*, *NZ*], 2000 *It*, *I*, *W* (R), *NZ* 1,2, *A* (R), *Sm* (R), 2001 *F*, *W*, *E*, *It*, *I*, *Tg*, *Arg*, *NZ*, 2002 *E*, *It*, *I*, *F*, *W*, *C*, *US*, *R*, *SA*, *Fj*, 2003 *I* 1, *F*, *W* 1, *E*, *It* 1, *SA* 1,2, *It* 2(R), *W* 2, *I* 2
Burnell, A P (London Scottish, Montferrand) 1989 *E*, *I*, *F*, *Fj*, *R*, 1990 *I*, *F*, *W*, *E*, *Arg*, 1991 *F*, *W*, *E*, *I*, *R*, [*J*, *Z*, *I*, *WS*, *E*, *NZ*], 1992 *E*, *I*, *F*, *W*, 1993 *I*, *F*, *W*, *E*, *NZ*, 1994 *W*, *E*, *I*, *F*, *Arg* 1,2, *SA*, 1995 [*Iv*, *Tg* (R), *F* (R)], *WS*, 1998 *E*, *SA*, 1999 *W*, *E*, *It*, *I*, *F*, *Arg*, [*Sp*, *Sm* (R), *NZ*]
Burnet, P J (London Scottish and Edinburgh Acads) 1960 *SA*
Burnet, W (Hawick) 1912 *E*
Burnet, W A (W of Scotland) 1934 *W*, 1935 *W*, *I*, *E*, *NZ*, 1936 *W*, *I*, *E*
Burnett, J N (Heriot's FP) 1980 *I*, *F*, *W*, *E*
Burns, G G (Watsonians, Edinburgh) 1999 *It* (R), 2001 *Tg* (R), *NZ* (R), 2002 *US* (R)
Burrell, G (Gala) 1950 *F*, *W*, *I*, 1951 *SA*

Cairns, A G (Watsonians) 1903 *W*, *I*, *E*, 1904 *W*, *I*, *E*, 1905 *W*, *I*, *E*, 1906 *W*, *I*, *E*
Calder, F (Stewart's-Melville FP) 1986 *F*, *W*, *E*, *I*, *R*, 1987 *I*, *F*, *W*, *E*, [*F*, *Z*, *R*, *NZ*], 1988 *I*, *F*, *W*, *E*, 1989 *W*, *E*, *I*, *F*, *R*, 1990 *I*, *F*, *W*, *E*, *NZ* 1,2, 1991 *R*, [*J*, *I*, *WS*, *E*, *NZ*]
Calder, J H (Stewart's-Melville FP) 1981 *F*, *W*, *E*, *I*, *NZ* 1,2, *R*, *A*, 1982 *E*, *I*, *F*, *W*, *A* 1,2, 1983 *I*, *F*, *W*, *E*, *NZ*, 1984 *W*, *E*, *I*, *F*, *A*, 1985 *I*, *F*, *W*
Callander, G J (Kelso) 1984 *R*, 1988 *I*, *F*, *W*, *E*, *A*
Cameron, A (Glasgow HSFP) 1948 *W*, 1950 *I*, *E*, 1951 *F*, *W*, *I*, *E*, *SA*, 1953 *I*, *E*, 1955 *F*, *W*, *I*, *E*, 1956 *F*, *W*, *I*
Cameron, A D (Hillhead HSFP) 1951 *F*, 1954 *F*, *W*
Cameron, A W (Watsonians) 1887 *W*, 1893 *W*, 1894 *I*
Cameron, D (Glasgow HSFP) 1953 *I*, *E*, 1954 *F*, *NZ*, *I*, *E*
Cameron, N W (Glasgow U) 1952 *E*, 1953 *F*, *W*
Campbell, A J (Hawick) 1984 *I*, *F*, *R*, 1985 *I*, *F*, *W*, *E*, 1986 *F*, *W*, *E*, *I*, *R*, 1988 *F*, *W*, *A*
Campbell, G T (London Scottish) 1892 *W*, *I*, *E*, 1893 *I*, *E*, 1894 *W*, *I*, *E*, 1895 *W*, *I*, *E*, 1896 *W*, *I*, *E*, 1897 *I*, 1899 *I*, 1900 *E*
Campbell, H H (Cambridge U, London Scottish) 1947 *I*, *E*, 1948 *I*, *E*
Campbell, J A (W of Scotland) 1878 *E*, 1879 *I*, *E*, 1881 *I*, *E*
Campbell, J A (Cambridge U) 1900 *I*
Campbell, N M (London Scottish) 1956 *F*, *W*
Campbell, S J (Dundee HSFP) 1995 *C*, *I*, *F*, *W*, *E*, *R*, [*Iv*, *NZ* (R)], *WS* (t), 1996 *I*, *F*, *W*, *E*, 1997 *A*, *SA*, 1998 *Fj* (R), *A* 2(R)
Campbell-Lamerton, J R E (London Scottish) 1986 *F*, 1987 [*Z*, *R*(R)]
Campbell-Lamerton, M J (Halifax, Army, London Scottish) 1961 *F*, *SA*, *W*, *I*, 1962 *F*, *W*, *I*, *E*, 1963 *F*, *W*, *I*, *E*, 1964 *I*, *E*, 1965 *F*, *W*, *I*, *E*, *SA*, 1966 *F*, *W*, *I*, *E*
Carmichael, A B (W of Scotland) 1967 *I*, *NZ*, 1968 *F*, *W*, *I*, *E*, *A*, 1969 *F*, *W*, *I*, *E*, *SA*, 1970 *F*, *W*, *I*, *E*, *A*, 1971 *F*, *W*, *I*, *E* (2[1C]), 1972 *F*, *W*, *E*, *NZ*, 1973 *F*, *W*, *I*, *E*, *P*, 1974 *W*, *E*, *I*, *F*, 1975 *I*, *F*, *W*, *E*, *NZ*, *A*, 1976 *F*, *W*, *E*, *I*, 1977 *E*, *I* (R), *F*, *W*, 1978 *I*
Carmichael, J H (Watsonians) 1921 *F*, *W*, *I*
Carrick, J S (Glasgow Acads) 1876 *E*, 1877 *E*
Cassels, D Y (W of Scotland) 1880 *E*, 1881 *I*, 1882 *I*, *E*, 1883 *W*, *I*, *E*
Cathcart, C W (Edinburgh U) 1872 *E*, 1873 *E*, 1876 *E*
Cawkwell, G L (Oxford U) 1947 *F*
Chalmers, C M (Melrose) 1989 *W*, *E*, *I*, *F*, *Fj*, 1990 *I*, *F*, *W*, *E*, *NZ* 1,2, *Arg*, 1991 *F*, *W*, *E*, *I*, *R*, [*J*, *Z* (R), *I*, *WS*, *E*, *NZ*], 1992 *E*, *I*, *F*, *W*, *A* 1,2, 1993 *I*, *F*, *W*, *E*, *NZ*, 1994 *W*, *SA*, 1995 *C*, *I*, *F*, *W*, *E*, *R*, [*Iv*, *Tg*, *F*, *NZ*], *WS*, 1996 *A*, *It*, 1997 *W*, *I*, *F*, *A* (R), *SA*, 1998 *It*, *I*, *F*, *W*, *E*, 1999 *Arg* (R)
Chalmers, T (Glasgow Acads) 1871 *E*, 1872 *E*, 1873 *E*, 1874 *E*, 1875 *E*, 1876 *E*
Chambers, H F T (Edinburgh U) 1888 *W*, *I*, 1889 *W*, *I*
Charters, R G (Hawick) 1955 *W*, *I*, *E*
Chisholm, D H (Melrose) 1964 *I*, *E*, 1965 *E*, *SA*, 1966 *F*, *I*, *E*, *A*, 1967 *F*, *W*, *NZ*, 1968 *F*, *W*, *I*
Chisholm, R W T (Melrose) 1955 *I*, *E*, 1956 *F*, *W*, *I*, *E*, 1958 *F*, *W*, *A*, *I*, 1960 *SA*
Church, W C (Glasgow Acads) 1906 *W*
Clark, R L (Edinburgh Wands, Royal Navy) 1972 *F*, *W*, *E*, *NZ*, 1973 *F*, *W*, *I*, *E*, *P*
Clauss, P R A (Oxford U) 1891 *W*, *I*, *E*, 1892 *W*, *E*, 1895 *I*
Clay, A T (Edinburgh Acads) 1886 *W*, *I*, *E*, 1887 *I*, *W*, *E*, 1888 *W*
Clunies-Ross, A (St Andrew's U) 1871 *E*
Coltman, S (Hawick) 1948 *I*, 1949 *F*, *W*, *I*, *E*
Colville, A G (Merchistonians, Blackheath) 1871 *E*, 1872 *E*
Connell, G C (Trinity Acads and London Scottish) 1968 *E*, *A*, 1969 *F*, *E*, 1970 *F*
Cooper, M McG (Oxford U) 1936 *W*, *I*
Corcoran, I (Gala) 1992 *A* 1(R)
Cordial, I F (Edinburgh Wands) 1952 *F*, *W*, *I*, *E*
Cotter, J L (Hillhead HSFP) 1934 *I*, *E*
Cottington, G S (Kelso) 1934 *I*, *E*, 1935 *W*, *I*, 1936 *E*
Coughtrie, S (Edinburgh Acads) 1959 *F*, *W*, *I*, *E*, 1962 *W*, *I*, *E*, 1963 *F*, *W*, *I*, *E*
Couper, J H (W of Scotland) 1896 *W*, *I*, 1899 *I*
Coutts, F H (Melrose, Army) 1947 *W*, *I*, *E*
Coutts, I D F (Old Alleynians) 1951 *F*, 1952 *E*
Cowan, R C (Selkirk) 1961 *F*, 1962 *F*, *W*, *I*, *E*
Cowie, W L K (Edinburgh Wands) 1953 *E*
Cownie, W B (Watsonians) 1893 *W*, *I*, *E*, 1894 *W*, *I*, *E*, 1895 *W*, *I*, *E*
Crabbie, G E (Edinburgh Acads) 1904 *W*
Crabbie, J E (Edinburgh Acads, Oxford U) 1900 *W*, 1902 *I*, 1903 *W*, *I*, 1904 *E*, 1905 *W*
Craig, A (Orrell) 2002 *C*, *US*, *R*, *SA*, *Fj*, 2003 *I* 1, *F* (R), *W* 1(R), *E*, *It* 1, *SA* 1,2, *W* 2, *I* 2
Craig, J B (Heriot's FP) 1939 *W*
Craig, J M (West of Scotland, Glasgow) 1997 *A*, 2001 *W* (R), *E* (R), *It*
Cramb, R I (Harlequins) 1987 [*R*(R)], 1988 *I*, *F*, *A*
Cranston, A G (Hawick) 1976 *W*, *E*, *I*, 1977 *E*, *W*, 1978 *F* (R), *W*, *E*, *NZ*, 1981 *NZ* 1,2
Crawford, J A (Army, London Scottish) 1934 *I*
Crawford, W H (United Services, RN) 1938 *W*, *I*, *E*, 1939 *W*, *E*
Crichton-Miller, D (Gloucester) 1931 *W*, *I*, *E*
Crole, G B (Oxford U) 1920 *F*, *W*, *I*, *E*
Cronin, D F (Bath, London Scottish, Bourges, Wasps) 1988 *I*, *F*, *W*, *E*, *A*, 1989 *W*, *E*, *I*, *F*, *Fj*, *R*, 1990 *I*, *F*, *W*, *E*, *NZ* 1,2, 1991 *F*, *W*, *E*, *I*, *R*, [*Z*], 1992 *A* 2, 1993 *I*, *F*, *W*, *E*, *NZ*, 1995 *C*, *I*, *F*, [*Tg*, *F*, *NZ*], *WS*, 1996 *NZ* 1,2, *A*, *It*, 1997 *F* (R), 1998 *I*, *F*, *W*, *E*
Cross, M (Merchistonians) 1875 *E*, 1876 *E*, 1877 *I*, *E*, 1878 *E*, 1879 *I*, *E*, 1880 *I*, *E*
Cross, W (Merchistonians) 1871 *E*, 1872 *E*
Cumming, R S (Aberdeen U) 1921 *F*, *W*
Cunningham, G (Oxford U) 1908 *W*, *I*, 1909 *W*, *E*, 1910 *F*, *I*, *E*, 1911 *E*
Cunningham, R F (Gala) 1978 *NZ*, 1979 *W*, *E*
Currie, L R (Dunfermline) 1947 *A*, 1948 *F*, *W*, *I*, 1949 *F*, *W*, *I*, *E*

Cuthbertson, W (Kilmarnock, Harlequins) 1980 *I*, 1981 *W, E, I, NZ* 1,2, *R, A*, 1982 *E, I, F, W, A* 1,2, 1983 *I, F, W, NZ*, 1984 *W, E, A*

Dalgleish, A (Gala) 1890 *W, E*, 1891 *W, I*, 1892 *W*, 1893 *W*, 1894 *W, I*
Dalgleish, K J (Edinburgh Wands, Cambridge U) 1951 *I, E*, 1953 *F, W*
Dall, A K (Edinburgh) 2003 *W* 2(R)
Dallas, J D (Watsonians) 1903 *E*
Danielli, S C J (Bath) 2003 *It* 2, *W* 2
Davidson, J A (London Scottish, Edinburgh Wands) 1959 *E*, 1960 *I, E*
Davidson, J N G (Edinburgh U) 1952 *F, W, I, E*, 1953 *F, W*, 1954 *F*
Davidson, J P (RIE Coll) 1873 *E*, 1874 *E*
Davidson, R S (Royal HSFP) 1893 *E*
Davies, D S (Hawick) 1922 *F, W, I, E*, 1923 *F, W, I, E*, 1924 *F, E*, 1925 *W, I, E*, 1926 *F, W, I, E*, 1927 *F, W, I*
Dawson, J C (Glasgow Acads) 1947 *A*, 1948 *F, W*, 1949 *F, W, I*, 1950 *F, W, I, E*, 1951 *F, W, I, E, SA*, 1952 *F, W, I, E*, 1953 *E*
Deans, C T (Hawick) 1978 *F, W, E, NZ*, 1979 *W, E, I, F, NZ*, 1980 *I, F*, 1981 *F, W, E, I, NZ* 1,2, *R, A*, 1982 *E, I, F, W, A* 1,2, 1983 *I, F, W, E, NZ*, 1984 *W, E, I, F, A*, 1985 *I, F, W, E*, 1986 *F, W, E, I, R*, 1987 *I, F, W, E*, [*F, Z, R, NZ*]
Deans, D T (Hawick) 1968 *E*
Deas, D W (Heriot's FP) 1947 *F, W*
Dick, L G (Loughborough Colls, Jordanhill, Swansea) 1972 *W* (R), *E*, 1974 *W, E, I, F*, 1975 *I, F, W, E, NZ, A*, 1976 *F*, 1977 *E*
Dick, R C S (Cambridge U, Guy's Hospital) 1934 *W, I, E*, 1935 *W, I, E, NZ*, 1936 *W, I, E*, 1937 *W*, 1938 *W, I, E*
Dickson, G (Gala) 1978 *NZ*, 1979 *W, E, I, F, NZ*, 1980 *W*, 1981 *F*, 1982 *W* (R)
Dickson, M R (Edinburgh U) 1905 *I*
Dickson, W M (Blackheath, Oxford U) 1912 *F, W, E, SA*, 1913 *F, W, I*
Di Rollo, M P (Edinburgh) 2002 *US* (R)
Dobson, J (Glasgow Acads) 1911 *E*, 1912 *F, W, I, E, SA*
Dobson, J D (Glasgow Acads) 1910 *I*
Dobson, W G (Heriot's FP) 1922 *W, I, E*
Docherty, J T (Glasgow HSFP) 1955 *F, W*, 1956 *E*, 1958 *F, W, A, I, E*
Dods, F P (Edinburgh Acads) 1901 *I*
Dods, J H (Edinburgh Acads) 1895 *W, I, E*, 1896 *W, I, E*, 1897 *I, E*
Dods, M (Gala, Northampton) 1994 *I* (t), *Arg* 1,2, 1995 *WS*, 1996 *I, F, W, E*
Dods, P W (Gala) 1983 *I, F, W, E, NZ*, 1984 *W, E, I, F, R, A*, 1985 *I, F, W, E*, 1989 *W, E, I, F*, 1991 *I* (R), *R*, [*Z, NZ* (R)]
Donald, D G (Oxford U) 1914 *W, I*
Donald, R L H (Glasgow HSFP) 1921 *W, I, E*
Donaldson, W P (Oxford U, W of Scotland) 1893 *I*, 1894 *I*, 1895 *E*, 1896 *I, E*, 1899 *I*
Don-Wauchope, A R (Fettesian-Lorettonians) 1881 *E*, 1882 *E*, 1883 *W*, 1884 *W, I, E*, 1885 *W, I* 1,2, 1886 *W, I, E*, 1888 *I*
Don-Wauchope, P H (Fettesian-Lorettonians) 1885 *I* 1,2, 1886 *W*, 1887 *I, W, E*
Dorward, A F (Cambridge U, Gala) 1950 *F*, 1951 *SA*, 1952 *W, I, E*, 1953 *F, W, E*, 1955 *F*, 1956 *I, E*, 1957 *F, W, I, E*
Dorward, T F (Gala) 1938 *W, I, E*, 1939 *I, E*
Douglas, B A F (Borders) 2002 *R, SA, Fj*, 2003 *I* 1, *F, W* 1, *E, It* 1, *SA* 1,2, *It* 2, *W* 2
Douglas, G (Jedforest) 1921 *W*
Douglas, J (Stewart's Coll FP) 1961 *F, SA, W, I, E*, 1962 *F, W, I, E*, 1963 *F, W, I*
Douty, P S (London Scottish) 1927 *A*, 1928 *F, W*
Drew, D (Glasgow Acads) 1871 *E*, 1876 *E*
Druitt, W A H (London Scottish) 1936 *W, I, E*
Drummond, A H (Kelvinside Acads) 1938 *W, I*
Drummond, C W (Melrose) 1947 *F, W, I, E*, 1948 *F, I, E*, 1950 *F, W, I, E*
Drybrough, A S (Edinburgh Wands, Merchistonians) 1902 *I*, 1903 *I*
Dryden, R H (Watsonians) 1937 *E*
Drysdale, D (Heriot's FP) 1923 *F, W, I, E*, 1924 *F, W, I, E*, 1925 *F, W, I, E*, 1926 *F, W, I, E*, 1927 *F, W, I, E, A*, 1928 *F, W, I, E*, 1929 *F*
Duff, P L (Glasgow Acads) 1936 *W, I*, 1938 *W, I, E*, 1939 *W*
Duffy, H (Jedforest) 1955 *F*
Duke, A (Royal HSFP) 1888 *W, I*, 1889 *W, I*, 1890 *W, I*
Duncan, A W (Edinburgh U) 1901 *W, I, E*, 1902 *W, I, E*
Duncan, D D (Oxford U) 1920 *F, W, I, E*
Duncan, M D F (W of Scotland) 1986 *F, W, E, R*, 1987 *I, F, W, E*, [*F, Z, R, NZ*], 1988 *I, F, W, E, A*, 1989 *W*
Duncan, M M (Fettesian-Lorettonians) 1888 *W*
Dunlop, J W (W of Scotland) 1875 *E*
Dunlop, Q (W of Scotland) 1971 *E* (2[1C])
Dykes, A S (Glasgow Acads) 1932 *E*
Dykes, J C (Glasgow Acads) 1922 *F, E*, 1924 *I*, 1925 *F, W, I*, 1926 *F, W, I, E*, 1927 *F, W, I, E, A*, 1928 *F, I*, 1929 *F, W, I*
Dykes, J M (Clydesdale, Glasgow HSFP) 1898 *I, E*, 1899 *W, E*, 1900 *W, I*, 1901 *W, I, E*, 1902 *E*

Edwards, D B (Heriot's FP) 1960 *I, E, SA*
Edwards, N G B (Harlequins, Northampton) 1992 *E, I, F, W, A* 1, 1994 *W*
Elgie, M K (London Scottish) 1954 *NZ, I, E, W*, 1955 *F, W, I, E*
Elliot, C (Langholm) 1958 *E*, 1959 *F*, 1960 *F*, 1963 *E*, 1964 *F, NZ, W, I, E*, 1965 *F, W, I*
Elliot, M (Hawick) 1895 *W*, 1896 *E*, 1897 *I, E*, 1898 *I, E*
Elliot, T (Gala) 1905 *E*
Elliot, T (Gala) 1955 *W, I, E*, 1956 *F, W, I, E*, 1957 *F, W, I, E*, 1958 *W, A, I*
Elliot, T G (Langholm) 1968 *W, A*, 1969 *F, W*, 1970 *E*
Elliot, W I D (Edinburgh Acads) 1947 *F, W, E, A*, 1948 *F, W, I, E*, 1949 *F, W, I, E*, 1950 *F, W, I, E*, 1951 *F, W, I, E, SA*, 1952 *F, W, I, E*, 1954 *NZ, I, E, W*
Ellis, D G (Currie) 1997 *W, E, I, F*
Emslie, W D (Royal HSFP) 1930 *F*, 1932 *I*
Eriksson, B R S (London Scottish) 1996 *NZ* 1, A, 1997 *E*
Evans, H L (Edinburgh U) 1885 *I* 1,2
Ewart, E N (Glasgow Acads) 1879 *E*, 1880 *I, E*

Fahmy, Dr E C (Abertillery) 1920 *F, W, I, E*
Fairley, I T (Kelso, Edinburgh) 1999 *It, I* (R), [*Sp* (R)]
Fasson, F H (London Scottish, Edinburgh Wands) 1900 *W*, 1901 *W, I*, 1902 *W, E*
Fell, A N (Edinburgh U) 1901 *W, I, E*, 1902 *W, E*, 1903 *W, E*
Ferguson, J H (Gala) 1928 *W*
Ferguson, W G (Royal HSFP) 1927 *A*, 1928 *F, W, I, E*
Fergusson, E A J (Oxford U) 1954 *F, NZ, I, E, W*
Finlay, A B (Edinburgh Acads) 1875 *E*
Finlay, J F (Edinburgh Acads) 1871 *E*, 1872 *E*, 1874 *E*, 1875 *E*
Finlay, N J (Edinburgh Acads) 1875 *E*, 1876 *E*, 1878 *E*, 1879 *I, E*, 1880 *I, E*, 1881 *I, E*
Finlay, R (Watsonians) 1948 *E*
Fisher, A T (Waterloo, Watsonians) 1947 *I, E*
Fisher, C D (Waterloo) 1975 *NZ, A*, 1976 *W, E, I*
Fisher, D (W of Scotland) 1893 *I*
Fisher, J P (Royal HSFP, London Scottish) 1963 *E*, 1964 *F, NZ, W, I, E*, 1965 *F, W, I, E, SA*, 1966 *F, W, I, E, A*, 1967 *F, W, I, E, NZ*, 1968 *F, W, I, E*
Fleming, C J N (Edinburgh Wands) 1896 *I, E*, 1897 *I*
Fleming, G R (Glasgow Acads) 1875 *E*, 1876 *E*
Fletcher, H N (Edinburgh U) 1904 *E*, 1905 *W*
Flett, A B (Edinburgh U) 1901 *W, I, E*, 1902 *W, I*
Forbes, J L (Watsonians) 1905 *W*, 1906 *I, E*
Ford, D St C (United Services, RN) 1930 *I, E*, 1931 *E*, 1932 *W, I*
Ford, J R (Gala) 1893 *I*
Forrest, J E (Glasgow Acads) 1932 *SA*, 1935 *E, NZ*
Forrest, J G S (Cambridge U) 1938 *W, I, E*
Forrest, W T (Hawick) 1903 *W, I, E*, 1904 *W, I, E*, 1905 *W, I*
Forsayth, H H (Oxford U) 1921 *F, W, I, E*, 1922 *W, I, E*
Forsyth, I W (Stewart's Coll FP) 1972 *NZ*, 1973 *F, W, I, E, P*
Forsyth, J (Edinburgh U) 1871 *E*
Foster, R A (Hawick) 1930 *W*, 1932 *SA, I, E*
Fox, J (Gala) 1952 *F, W, I, E*
Frame, J N M (Edinburgh U, Gala) 1967 *NZ*, 1968 *F, W, I, E*, 1969 *W, I, E, SA*, 1970 *F, W, I, E, A*, 1971 *F, W, I, E* (2[1C]), 1972 *F, W, E*, 1973 *P* (R)
France, C (Kelvinside Acads) 1903 *I*
Fraser, C F P (Glasgow U) 1888 *W*, 1889 *W*
Fraser, J W (Edinburgh Inst FP) 1881 *E*
Fraser, R (Cambridge U) 1911 *F, W, I, E*
French, J (Glasgow Acads) 1886 *W*, 1887 *I, W, E*
Frew, A (Edinburgh U) 1901 *W, I, E*
Frew, G M (Glasgow HSFP) 1906 *SA*, 1907 *W, I, E*, 1908 *W, I, E*, 1909 *W, I, E*, 1910 *F, W, I*, 1911 *I, E*
Friebe, J P (Glasgow HSFP) 1952 *E*
Fullarton, I A (Edinburgh) 2000 *NZ* 1(R),2, 2001 *NZ* (R), 2003 *It* 2(R), *I* 2(t)

Fulton, A K (Edinburgh U, Dollar Acads) 1952 *F*, 1954 *F*
Fyfe, K C (Cambridge U, Sale, London Scottish) 1933 *W*, *E*, 1934 *E*, 1935 *W*, *I*, *E*, *NZ*, 1936 *W*, *E*, 1939 *I*

Gallie, G H (Edinburgh Acads) 1939 *W*
Gallie, R A (Glasgow Acads) 1920 *F*, *W*, *I*, *E*, 1921 *F*, *W*, *I*, *E*
Gammell, W B B (Edinburgh Wands) 1977 *I*, *F*, *W*, 1978 *W*, *E*
Geddes, I C (London Scottish) 1906 *SA*, 1907 *W*, *I*, *E*, 1908 *W*, *E*
Geddes, K I (London Scottish) 1947 *F*, *W*, *I*, *E*
Gedge, H T S (Oxford U, London Scottish, Edinburgh Wands) 1894 *W*, *I*, *E*, 1896 *E*, 1899 *W*, *E*
Gedge, P M S (Edinburgh Wands) 1933 *I*
Gemmill, R (Glasgow HSFP) 1950 *F*, *W*, *I*, *E*, 1951 *F*, *W*, *I*
Gibson, W R (Royal HSFP) 1891 *I*, *E*, 1892 *W*, *I*, *E*, 1893 *W*, *I*, *E*, 1894 *W*, *I*, *E*, 1895 *W*, *I*, *E*
Gilbert-Smith, D S (London Scottish) 1952 *E*
Gilchrist, J (Glasgow Acads) 1925 *F*
Gill, A D (Gala) 1973 *P*, 1974 *W*, *E*, *I*, *F*
Gillespie, J I (Edinburgh Acads) 1899 *E*, 1900 *W*, *E*, 1901 *W*, *I*, *E*, 1902 *W*, *I*, 1904 *I*, *E*
Gillies, A C (Watsonians) 1924 *W*, *I*, *E*, 1925 *F*, *W*, *E*, 1926 *F*, *W*, 1927 *F*, *W*, *I*, *E*
Gilmour, H R (Heriot's FP) 1998 *Fj*
Gilray, C M (Oxford U, London Scottish) 1908 *E*, 1909 *W*, *E*, 1912 *I*
Glasgow, I C (Heriot's FP) 1997 *F* (R)
Glasgow, R J C (Dunfermline) 1962 *F*, *W*, *I*, *E*, 1963 *I*, *E*, 1964 *I*, *E*, 1965 *W*, *I*
Glen, W S (Edinburgh Wands) 1955 *W*
Gloag, L G (Cambridge U) 1949 *F*, *W*, *I*, *E*
Goodfellow, J (Langholm) 1928 *W*, *I*, *E*
Goodhue, F W J (London Scottish) 1890 *W*, *I*, *E*, 1891 *W*, *I*, *E*, 1892 *W*, *I*, *E*
Gordon, R (Edinburgh Wands) 1951 *W*, 1952 *F*, *W*, *I*, *E*, 1953 *W*
Gordon, R E (Royal Artillery) 1913 *F*, *W*, *I*
Gordon, R J (London Scottish) 1982 *A* 1,2
Gore, A C (London Scottish) 1882 *I*
Gossman, B M (W of Scotland) 1980 *W*, 1983 *F*, *W*
Gossman, J S (W of Scotland) 1980 *E* (R)
Gowans, J J (Cambridge U, London Scottish) 1893 *W*, 1894 *W*, *E*, 1895 *W*, *I*, *E*, 1896 *I*, *E*
Gowland, G C (London Scottish) 1908 *W*, 1909 *W*, *E*, 1910 *F*, *W*, *I*, *E*
Gracie, A L (Harlequins) 1921 *F*, *W*, *I*, *E*, 1922 *F*, *W*, *I*, *E*, 1923 *F*, *W*, *I*, *E*, 1924 *F*
Graham, G (Newcastle) 1997 *A* (R), *SA* (R), 1998 *I*, *F* (R), *W* (R), 1999 *F* (R), *Arg* (R), *R*, [*SA*, *U*, *Sm*, *NZ* (R)], 2000 *I* (R), *US*, *A*, *Sm*, 2001 *I* (R), *Tg* (R), *Arg* (R), *NZ* (R), 2002 *E* (R), *It* (R), *I* (R), *F* (R), *W* (R)
Graham, I N (Edinburgh Acads) 1939 *I*, *E*
Graham, J (Kelso) 1926 *I*, *E*, 1927 *F*, *W*, *I*, *E*, *A*, 1928 *F*, *W*, *I*, *E*, 1930 *I*, *E*, 1932 *SA*, *W*
Graham, J H S (Edinburgh Acads) 1876 *E*, 1877 *I*, *E*, 1878 *E*, 1879 *I*, *E*, 1880 *I*, *E*, 1881 *I*, *E*
Grant, D (Hawick) 1965 *F*, *E*, *SA*, 1966 *F*, *W*, *I*, *E*, *A*, 1967 *F*, *W*, *I*, *E*, *NZ*, 1968 *F*
Grant, D M (East Midlands) 1911 *W*, *I*
Grant, M L (Harlequins) 1955 *F*, 1956 *F*, *W*, 1957 *F*
Grant, T O (Hawick) 1960 *I*, *E*, *SA*, 1964 *F*, *NZ*, *W*
Grant, W St C (Craigmount) 1873 *E*, 1874 *E*
Gray, C A (Nottingham) 1989 *W*, *E*, *I*, *F*, *Fj*, *R*, 1990 *I*, *F*, *W*, *E*, *NZ* 1,2, *Arg*, 1991 *F*, *W*, *E*, *I*, [*J*, *I*, *WS*, *E*, *NZ*]
Gray, D (W of Scotland) 1978 *E*, 1979 *I*, *F*, *NZ*, 1980 *I*, *F*, *W*, *E*, 1981 *F*
Gray, G L (Gala) 1935 *NZ*, 1937 *W*, *I*, *E*
Gray, T (Northampton, Heriot's FP) 1950 *E*, 1951 *F*, *E*
Greenlees, H D (Leicester) 1927 *A*, 1928 *F*, *W*, 1929 *I*, *E*, 1930 *E*
Greenlees, J R C (Cambridge U, Kelvinside Acads) 1900 *I*, 1902 *W*, *I*, *E*, 1903 *W*, *I*, *E*
Greenwood, J T (Dunfermline and Perthshire Acads) 1952 *F*, 1955 *F*, *W*, *I*, *E*, 1956 *F*, *W*, *I*, *E*, 1957 *F*, *W*, *E*, 1958 *F*, *W*, *A*, *I*, *E*, 1959 *F*, *W*, *I*
Greig, A (Glasgow HSFP) 1911 *I*
Greig, L L (Glasgow Acads, United Services) 1905 *NZ*, 1906 *SA*, 1907 *W*, 1908 *W*, *I*
Greig, R C (Glasgow Acads) 1893 *W*, 1897 *I*
Grieve, C F (Oxford U) 1935 *W*, 1936 *E*
Grieve, R M (Kelso) 1935 *W*, *I*, *E*, *NZ*, 1936 *W*, *I*, *E*
Grimes, S B (Watsonians, Newcastle) 1997 *A* (t+R), 1998 *I* (R), *F* (R), *W* (R), *E* (R), *Fj*, *A* 1, 2, 1999 *W* (R), *E*, *It*, *I*, *F*, *Arg*, *R*, [*SA*, *U*, *Sm* (R), *NZ* (R)], 2000 *It*, *I*, *F* (R), *W*, *US*, *A*, *Sm* (R), 2001 *F* (R), *W* (R), *E* (R), *It*, *I* (R), *Tg*, *Arg*, *NZ*, 2002 *E*, *It*, *I*, *F* (R), *W* (R), *C*, *US*, *R*, *SA*, *Fj*, 2003 *I* 1, *F*, *W* 1, *E* (R), *It* 1(R), *W* 2, *I* 2
Gunn, A W (Royal HSFP) 1912 *F*, *W*, *I*, *SA*, 1913 *F*

Hall, A J A (Glasgow) 2002 *US* (R)
Hall, D W H (Edinburgh) 2003 *W* 2(R)
Hamilton, A S (Headingley) 1914 *W*, 1920 *F*
Hamilton, H M (W of Scotland) 1874 *E*, 1875 *E*
Hannah, R S M (W of Scotland) 1971 *I*
Harrower, P R (London Scottish) 1885 *W*
Hart, J G M (London Scottish) 1951 *SA*
Hart, T M (Glasgow U) 1930 *W*, *I*
Hart, W (Melrose) 1960 *SA*
Harvey, L (Greenock Wands) 1899 *I*
Hastie, A J (Melrose) 1961 *W*, *I*, *E*, 1964 *I*, *E*, 1965 *E*, *SA*, 1966 *F*, *W*, *I*, *E*, *A*, 1967 *F*, *W*, *I*, *NZ*, 1968 *F*, *W*
Hastie, I R (Kelso) 1955 *F*, 1958 *F*, *E*, 1959 *F*, *W*, *I*
Hastie, J D H (Melrose) 1938 *W*, *I*, *E*
Hastings, A G (Cambridge U, Watsonians, London Scottish) 1986 *F*, *W*, *E*, *I*, *R*, 1987 *I*, *F*, *W*, *E*, [*F*, *Z*, *R*, *NZ*], 1988 *I*, *F*, *W*, *E*, *A*, 1989 *Fj*, *R*, 1990 *I*, *F*, *W*, *E*, *NZ* 1,2, *Arg*, 1991 *F*, *W*, *E*, *I*, [*J*, *I*, *WS*, *E*, *NZ*], 1992 *E*, *I*, *F*, *W*, *A* 1, 1993 *I*, *F*, *W*, *E*, *NZ*, 1994 *W*, *E*, *I*, *F*, *SA*, 1995 *C*, *I*, *F*, *W*, *E*, *R*, [*Iv*, *Tg*, *F*, *NZ*]
Hastings, S (Watsonians) 1986 *F*, *W*, *E*, *I*, *R*, 1987 *I*, *F*, *W*, [*R*], 1988 *I*, *F*, *W*, *A*, 1989 *W*, *E*, *I*, *F*, *Fj*, *R*, 1990 *I*, *F*, *W*, *E*, *NZ* 1,2, *Arg*, 1991 *F*, *W*, *E*, *I*, [*J*, *Z*, *I*, *WS*, *E*, *NZ*], 1992 *E*, *I*, *F*, *W*, *A* 1,2, 1993 *I*, *F*, *W*, *E*, *NZ*, 1994 *E*, *I*, *F*, *SA*, 1995 *W*, *E*, *R* (R), [*Tg*, *F*, *NZ*], 1996 *I*, *F*, *W*, *E*, *NZ* 2, *It*, 1997 *W*, *E* (R)
Hay, B H (Boroughmuir) 1975 *NZ*, *A*, 1976 *F*, 1978 *I*, *F*, *W*, *E*, *NZ*, 1979 *W*, *E*, *I*, *F*, *NZ*, 1980 *I*, *F*, *W*, *E*, 1981 *F*, *W*, *E*, *I*, *NZ* 1,2
Hay, J A (Hawick) 1995 *WS*
Hay-Gordon, J R (Edinburgh Acads) 1875 *E*, 1877 *I*, *E*
Hegarty, C B (Hawick) 1978 *I*, *F*, *W*, *E*
Hegarty, J J (Hawick) 1951 *F*, 1953 *F*, *W*, *I*, *E*, 1955 *F*
Henderson, A R (Glasgow) 2001 *I* (R), *Tg* (R), *NZ* (R), 2002 *It*, *I*, *US* (R), 2003 *SA* 1,2, *It* 2, *I* 2
Henderson, B C (Edinburgh Wands) 1963 *E*, 1964 *F*, *I*, *E*, 1965 *F*, *W*, *I*, *E*, 1966 *F*, *W*, *I*, *E*
Henderson, F W (London Scottish) 1900 *W*, *I*
Henderson, I C (Edinburgh Acads) 1939 *I*, *E*, 1947 *F*, *W*, *E*, *A*, 1948 *I*, *E*
Henderson, J H (Oxford U, Richmond) 1953 *F*, *W*, *I*, *E*, 1954 *F*, *NZ*, *I*, *E*, *W*
Henderson, J M (Edinburgh Acads) 1933 *W*, *E*, *I*
Henderson, J Y M (Watsonians) 1911 *E*
Henderson, M M (Dunfermline) 1937 *W*, *I*, *E*
Henderson, N F (London Scottish) 1892 *I*
Henderson, R G (Newcastle Northern) 1924 *I*, *E*
Hendrie, K G P (Heriot's FP) 1924 *F*, *W*, *I*
Hendry, T L (Clydesdale) 1893 *W*, *I*, *E*, 1895 *I*
Henriksen, E H (Royal HSFP) 1953 *I*
Hepburn, D P (Woodford) 1947 *A*, 1948 *F*, *W*, *I*, *E*, 1949 *F*, *W*, *I*, *E*
Heron, G (Glasgow Acads) 1874 *E*, 1875 *E*
Hill, C C P (St Andrew's U) 1912 *F*, *I*
Hilton, D I W (Bath, Glasgow) 1995 *C*, *I*, *F*, *W*, *E*, *R*, [*Tg*, *F*, *NZ*], *WS*, 1996 *I*, *F*, *W*, *E*, *NZ* 1,2, *A*, *It*, 1997 *W*, *A*, *SA*, 1998 *It*, *I* (R), *F*, *W*, *E*, *A* 1,2, *SA* (R), 1999 *W* (R), *E* (R), *It* (R), *I* (R), *F*, *R* (R), [*SA* (R), *U* (R), *Sp*], 2000 *It* (R), *F* (R), *W* (R), 2002 *SA* (R)
Hines, N J (Edinburgh, Glasgow) 2000 *NZ* 2(R), 2002 *C*, *US*, *R* (R), *SA* (R), *Fj* (R), 2003 *W* 1(R), *E*, *It* 1, *SA* 1,2, *It* 2, *W* 2(R), *I* 2
Hinshelwood, A J W (London Scottish) 1966 *F*, *W*, *I*, *E*, *A*, 1967 *F*, *W*, *I*, *E*, *NZ*, 1968 *F*, *W*, *I*, *E*, *A*, 1969 *F*, *W*, *I*, *SA*, 1970 *F*, *W*
Hinshelwood, B G (Worcester) 2002 *C* (R), *R* (R), *SA* (R), *Fj*, 2003 *It* 2
Hodge D W (Watsonians, Edinburgh) 1997 *F* (R), *A*, *SA* (t+R), 1998 *A* 2(R), *SA*, 1999 *W*, *Arg*, *R*, [*Sp*, *Sm* (R)], 2000 *F* (R), *W*, *E*, *NZ* 1,2, *US* (R), *Sm* (R), 2001 *F* (R), *W*, *E*, *It*, *I* (R), 2002 *E*, *W* (R), *C*, *US*
Hodgson, C G (London Scottish) 1968 *I*, *E*
Hogg, C D (Melrose) 1992 *A* 1,2, 1993 *NZ* (R), 1994 *Arg* 1,2
Hogg, C G (Boroughmuir) 1978 *F* (R), *W* (R)
Holmes, S D (London Scottish) 1998 *It*, *I*, *F*
Holms, W F (RIE Coll) 1886 *W*, *E*, 1887 *I*, *E*, 1889 *W*, *I*

Horsburgh, G B (London Scottish) 1937 *W, I, E*, 1938 *W, I, E*, 1939 *W, I, E*
Howie, D D (Kirkcaldy) 1912 *F, W, I, E, SA*, 1913 *F, W*
Howie, R A (Kirkcaldy) 1924 *F, W, I, E*, 1925 *W, I, E*
Hoyer-Millar, G C (Oxford U) 1953 *I*
Huggan, J L (London Scottish) 1914 *E*
Hume, J (Royal HSFP) 1912 *F*, 1920 *F*, 1921 *F, W, I, E*, 1922 *F*
Hume, J W G (Oxford U, Edinburgh Wands) 1928 *I*, 1930 *F*
Hunter, F (Edinburgh U) 1882 *I*
Hunter, I G (Selkirk) 1984 *I* (R), 1985 *F* (R), *W, E*
Hunter, J M (Cambridge U) 1947 *F*
Hunter, M D (Glasgow High) 1974 *F*
Hunter, W J (Hawick) 1964 *F, NZ, W*, 1967 *F, W, I, E*
Hutchison, W R (Glasgow HSFP) 1911 *E*
Hutton, A H M (Dunfermline) 1932 *I*
Hutton, J E (Harlequins) 1930 *E*, 1931 *F*

Inglis, H M (Edinburgh Acads) 1951 *F, W, I, E, SA*, 1952 *W, I*
Inglis, J M (Selkirk) 1952 *E*
Inglis, W M (Cambridge U, Royal Engineers) 1937 *W, I, E*, 1938 *W, I, E*
Innes, J R S (Aberdeen GSFP) 1939 *W, I, E*, 1947 *A*, 1948 *F, W, I, E*
Ireland, J C H (Glasgow HSFP) 1925 *W, I, E*, 1926 *F, W, I, E*, 1927 *F, W, I, E*
Irvine, A R (Heriot's FP) 1972 *NZ*, 1973 *F, W, I, E, P*, 1974 *W, E, I, F*, 1975 *I, F, W, E, NZ, A*, 1976 *F, W, E, I*, 1977 *E, I, F, W*, 1978 *I, F, E, NZ*, 1979 *W, E, I, F, NZ*, 1980 *I, F, W, E*, 1981 *F, W, E, I, NZ* 1,2, *R, A*, 1982 *E, I, F, W, A* 1,2
Irvine, D R (Edinburgh Acads) 1878 *E*, 1879 *I, E*
Irvine, R W (Edinburgh Acads) 1871 *E*, 1872 *E*, 1873 *E*, 1874 *E*, 1875 *E*, 1876 *E*, 1877 *I, E*, 1878 *E*, 1879 *I, E*, 1880 *I, E*
Irvine T W (Edinburgh Acads) 1885 *I* 1,2, 1886 *W, I, E*, 1887 *I, W, E*, 1888 *W, I*, 1889 *I*

Jackson, K L T (Oxford U) 1933 *W, E, I*, 1934 *W*
Jackson, T G H (Army) 1947 *F, W, E, A*, 1948 *F, W, I, E*, 1949 *F, W, I, E*
Jackson, W D (Hawick) 1964 *I*, 1965 *E, SA*, 1968 *A*, 1969 *F, W, I, E*
Jacobsen, A F (Edinburgh) 2002 *C* (R), *US*, 2003 *I* 2
Jamieson, J (W of Scotland) 1883 *W, I, E*, 1884 *W, I, E*, 1885 *W, I* 1,2
Jardine, I C (Stirling County) 1993 *NZ*, 1994 *W, E* (R), *Arg* 1,2, 1995 *C, I, F*, [*Tg, F* (t & R), *NZ* (R)], 1996 *I, F, W, E, NZ* 1,2, 1998 *Fj*
Jeffrey, J (Kelso) 1984 *A*, 1985 *I, E*, 1986 *F, W, E, I, R*, 1987 *I, F, W, E*, [*F, Z, R*], 1988 *I, W, A*, 1989 *W, E, I, F, Fj, R*, 1990 *I, F, W, E, NZ* 1,2, *Arg*, 1991 *F, W, E, I*, [*J, I, WS, E, NZ*]
Johnston, D I (Watsonians) 1979 *NZ*, 1980 *I, F, W, E*, 1981 *R, A*, 1982 *E, I, F, W, A* 1,2, 1983 *I, F, W, NZ*, 1984 *W, E, I, F, R*, 1986 *F, W, E, I, R*
Johnston, H H (Edinburgh Collegian FP) 1877 *I, E*
Johnston, J (Melrose) 1951 *SA*, 1952 *F, W, I, E*
Johnston, W C (Glasgow HSFP) 1922 *F*
Johnston, W G S (Cambridge U) 1935 *W, I*, 1937 *W, I, E*
Joiner, C A (Melrose, Leicester) 1994 *Arg* 1,2, 1995 *C, I, F, W, E, R*, [*Iv, Tg, F, NZ*], 1996 *I, F, W, E, NZ* 1, 1997 *SA*, 1998 *It, I, A* 2(R), 1999 *R* (R), 2000 *NZ* 1(R),2, *US* (R)
Jones, P M (Gloucester) 1992 *W* (R)
Junor, J E (Glasgow Acads) 1876 *E*, 1877 *I, E*, 1878 *E*, 1879 *E*, 1881 *I*

Keddie, R R (Watsonians) 1967 *NZ*
Keith, G J (Wasps) 1968 *F, W*
Keller, D H (London Scottish) 1949 *F, W, I, E*, 1950 *F, W, I*
Kelly, R F (Watsonians) 1927 *A*, 1928 *F, W, E*
Kemp, J W Y (Glasgow HSFP) 1954 *W*, 1955 *F, W, I, E*, 1956 *F, W, I, E*, 1957 *F, W, I, E*, 1958 *F, W, A, I, E*, 1959 *F, W, I, E*, 1960 *F, W, I, E, SA*
Kennedy, A E (Watsonians) 1983 *NZ*, 1984 *W, E, A*
Kennedy, F (Stewart's Coll FP) 1920 *F, W, I, E*, 1921 *E*
Kennedy, N (W of Scotland) 1903 *W, I, E*
Ker, A B M (Kelso) 1988 *W, E*
Ker, H T (Glasgow Acads) 1887 *I, W, E*, 1888 *I*, 1889 *W*, 1890 *I, E*
Kerr, D S (Heriot's FP) 1923 *F, W*, 1924 *F*, 1926 *I, E*, 1927 *W, I, E*, 1928 *I, E*
Kerr, G (Leeds) 2003 *I* 1, *F* (R), *W* 1(R), *E* (R), *SA* 1,2, *W* 2
Kerr, G C (Old Dunelmians, Edinburgh Wands) 1898 *I, E*, 1899 *I, W, E*, 1900 *W, I, E*
Kerr, J M (Heriot's FP) 1935 *NZ*, 1936 *I, E*, 1937 *W, I*
Kerr, R C (Glasgow) 2002 *C, US*, 2003 *W* 2
Kerr, W (London Scottish) 1953 *E*
Kidston, D W (Glasgow Acads) 1883 *W, E*
Kidston, W H (W of Scotland) 1874 *E*
Kilgour, I J (RMC Sandhurst) 1921 *F*
King, J H F (Selkirk) 1953 *F, W, E*, 1954 *E*
Kininmonth, P W (Oxford U, Richmond) 1949 *F, W, I, E*, 1950 *F, W, I, E*, 1951 *F, W, I, E, SA*, 1952 *F, W, I*, 1954 *F, NZ, I, E, W*
Kinnear, R M (Heriot's FP) 1926 *F, W, I*
Knox, J (Kelvinside Acads) 1903 *W, I, E*
Kyle, W E (Hawick) 1902 *W, I, E*, 1903 *W, I, E*, 1904 *W, I, E*, 1905 *W, I, E, NZ*, 1906 *W, I, E*, 1908 *E*, 1909 *W, I, E*, 1910 *W*

Laidlaw, A S (Hawick) 1897 *I*
Laidlaw, F A L (Melrose) 1965 *F, W, I, E, SA*, 1966 *F, W, I, E, A*, 1967 *F, W, I, E, NZ*, 1968 *F, W, I, A*, 1969 *F, W, I, E, SA*, 1970 *F, W, I, E, A*, 1971 *F, W, I*
Laidlaw, R J (Jedforest) 1980 *I, F, W, E*, 1981 *F, W, E, I, NZ* 1,2, *R, A*, 1982 *E, I, F, W, A* 1,2, 1983 *I, F, W, E, NZ*, 1984 *W, E, I, F, R, A*, 1985 *I, F*, 1986 *F, W, E, I, R*, 1987 *I, F, W, E*, [*F, R, NZ*], 1988 *I, F, W, E*
Laing, A D (Royal HSFP) 1914 *W, I, E*, 1920 *F, W, I*, 1921 *F*
Lambie, I K (Watsonians) 1978 *NZ* (R), 1979 *W, E, NZ*
Lambie, L B (Glasgow HSFP) 1934 *W, I, E*, 1935 *W, I, E, NZ*
Lamond, G A W (Kelvinside Acads) 1899 *W, E*, 1905 *E*
Laney, B J (Edinburgh) 2001 *NZ*, 2002 *E, It, I, F, W, C, US, R, SA, Fj*, 2003 *I* 1, *F, SA* 2(R), *It* 2(R), *W* 2
Lang, D (Paisley) 1876 *E*, 1877 *I*
Langrish, R W (London Scottish) 1930 *F*, 1931 *F, W, I*
Lauder, W (Neath) 1969 *I, E, SA*, 1970 *F, W, I, A*, 1973 *F*, 1974 *W, E, I, F*, 1975 *I, F, NZ, A*, 1976 *F*, 1977 *E*
Laughland, I H P (London Scottish) 1959 *F*, 1960 *F, W, I, E*, 1961 *SA, W, I, E*, 1962 *F, W, I, E*, 1963 *F, W, I*, 1964 *F, NZ, W, I, E*, 1965 *F, W, I, E, SA*, 1966 *F, W, I, E*, 1967 *E*
Lawrie, J R (Melrose) 1922 *F, W, I, E*, 1923 *F, W, I, E*, 1924 *W, I, E*
Lawrie, K G (Gala) 1980 *F* (R), *W, E*
Lawson, A J M (Edinburgh Wands, London Scottish) 1972 *F* (R), *E*, 1973 *F*, 1974 *W, E*, 1976 *E, I*, 1977 *E*, 1978 *NZ*, 1979 *W, E, I, F, NZ*, 1980 *W* (R)
Lawther, T H B (Old Millhillians) 1932 *SA, W*
Ledingham, G A (Aberdeen GSFP) 1913 *F*
Lee, D J (London Scottish, Edinburgh) 1998 *I* (R), *F, W, E, Fj, A* 1,2, *SA*, 2001 *Arg*
Lees, J B (Gala) 1947 *I, A*, 1948 *F, W, E*
Leggatt, H T O (Watsonians) 1891 *W, I, E*, 1892 *W, I*, 1893 *W, E*, 1894 *I, E*
Lely, W G (Cambridge U, London Scottish) 1909 *I*
Leslie, D G (Dundee HSFP, W of Scotland, Gala) 1975 *I, F, W, E, NZ, A*, 1976 *F, W, E, I*, 1978 *NZ*, 1980 *E*, 1981 *W, E, I, NZ* 1,2, *R, A*, 1982 *E*, 1983 *I, F, W, E*, 1984 *W, E, I, F, R*, 1985 *F, W, E*
Leslie, J A (Glasgow, Northampton) 1998 *SA*, 1999 *W, E, It, I, F*, [*SA*], 2000 *It, F, W, US, A, Sm*, 2001 *F, W, E, It, I, Tg, Arg, NZ*, 2002 *F, W*
Leslie, M D (Glasgow, Edinburgh) 1998 *SA* (R), 1999 *W, E, It, I, F, R*, [*SA, U, Sm, NZ*], 2000 *It, I, F, W, E, NZ* 1,2, 2001 *F, W, E, It*, 2002 *It* (R), *I* (R), *F, W, R, SA, Fj* (R), 2003 *I* 1, *F, SA* 1(R),2(R), *It* 2(R), *W* 2
Liddell, E H (Edinburgh U) 1922 *F, W, I*, 1923 *F, W, I, E*
Lind, H (Dunfermline) 1928 *I*, 1931 *F, W, I, E*, 1932 *SA, W, E*, 1933 *W, E, I*, 1934 *W, I, E*, 1935 *I*, 1936 *E*
Lindsay, A B (London Hospital) 1910 *I*, 1911 *I*
Lindsay, G C (London Scottish) 1884 *W*, 1885 *I* 1, 1887 *W, E*
Lindsay-Watson, R H (Hawick) 1909 *I*
Lineen, S R P (Boroughmuir) 1989 *W, E, I, F, Fj, R*, 1990 *I, F, W, E, NZ* 1,2, *Arg*, 1991 *F, W, E, I, R*, [*J, Z, I, E, NZ*], 1992 *E, I, F, W, A* 1,2
Little, A W (Hawick) 1905 *W*
Logan, K M (Stirling County, Wasps) 1992 *A* 2, 1993 *E* (R), *NZ* (t), 1994 *W, E, I, F, Arg* 1,2, *SA*, 1995 *C, I, F, W, E, R*, [*Iv, Tg, F, NZ*], *WS*, 1996 *W* (R), NZ 1,2, *A, It*, 1997 *W, E, I, F, A*, 1998 *I, F, SA* (R), 1999 *W, E, It, I, F, Arg, R*, [*SA, U, Sm, NZ*], 2000 *It, I, F, Sm*, 2001 *F, W, E, It*, 2002 *I* (R), *F* (R), *W*, 2003 *I* 1, *F, W* 1, *E, It* 1, *SA* 1,2, *It* 2, *I* 2
Logan, W R (Edinburgh U, Edinburgh Wands) 1931 *E*, 1932 *SA, W, I*, 1933 *W, E, I*, 1934 *W, I, E*, 1935 *W, I, E, NZ*, 1936 *W, I, E*, 1937 *W, I, E*

Longstaff, S L (Dundee HSFP, Glasgow) 1998 *F* (R), *W, E, Fj, A* 1,2 1999 *It* (R), *I* (R), *Arg* (R), *R*, [*U* (R), *Sp*], 2000 *It, I, NZ* 1
Lorraine, H D B (Oxford U) 1933 *W, E, I*
Loudoun-Shand, E G (Oxford U) 1913 *E*
Lowe, J D (Heriot's FP) 1934 *W*
Lumsden, I J M (Bath, Watsonians) 1947 *F, W, A*, 1949 *F, W, I, E*
Lyall, G G (Gala) 1947 *A*, 1948 *F, W, I, E*
Lyall, W J C (Edinburgh Acads) 1871 *E*

Mabon, J T (Jedforest) 1898 *I, E*, 1899 *I*, 1900 *I*
Macarthur, J P (Waterloo) 1932 *E*
MacCallum, J C (Watsonians) 1905 *E, NZ*, 1906 *W, I, E, SA*, 1907 *W, I, E*, 1908 *W, I, E*, 1909 *W, I, E*, 1910 *F, W, I, E*, 1911 *F, I, E*, 1912 *F, W, I, E*
McClung, T (Edinburgh Acads) 1956 *I, E*, 1957 *W, I, E*, 1959 *F, W, I*, 1960 *W*
McClure, G B (W of Scotland) 1873 *E*
McClure, J H (W of Scotland) 1872 *E*
McCowan, D (W of Scotland) 1880 *I, E*, 1881 *I, E*, 1882 *I, E*, 1883 *I, E*, 1884 *I, E*
McCowat, R H (Glasgow Acads) 1905 *I*
McCrae, I G (Gordonians) 1967 *E*, 1968 *I*, 1969 *F* (R), *W*, 1972 *F, NZ*
McCrow, J W S (Edinburgh Acads) 1921 *I*
Macdonald, A E D (Heriot's FP) 1993 *NZ*
McDonald, C (Jedforest) 1947 *A*
Macdonald, D C (Edinburgh U) 1953 *F, W*, 1958 *I, E*
Macdonald, D S M (Oxford U, London Scottish, W of Scotland) 1977 *E, I, F, W*, 1978 *I, W, E*
Macdonald, J D (London Scottish, Army) 1966 *F, W, I, E*, 1967 *F, W, I, E*
Macdonald, J M (Edinburgh Wands) 1911 *W*
Macdonald, J S (Edinburgh U) 1903 *E*, 1904 *W, I, E*, 1905 *W*
Macdonald, K R (Stewart's Coll FP) 1956 *F, W, I*, 1957 *W, I, E*
Macdonald, R (Edinburgh U) 1950 *F, W, I, E*
McDonald, W A (Glasgow U) 1889 *W*, 1892 *I, E*
Macdonald, W G (London Scottish) 1969 *I* (R)
Macdougall, J B (Greenock Wands, Wakefield) 1913 *F*, 1914 *I*, 1921 *F, I, E*
McEwan, M C (Edinburgh Acads) 1886 *E*, 1887 *I, W, E*, 1888 *W, I*, 1889 *W, I*, 1890 *W, I, E*, 1891 *W, I, E*, 1892 *E*
MacEwan, N A (Gala, Highland) 1971 *F, W, I, E* (2[1C]), 1972 *F, W, E, NZ*, 1973 *F, W, I, E, P*, 1974 *W, E, I, F*, 1975 *W, E*
McEwan, W M C (Edinburgh Acads) 1894 *W, E*, 1895 *W, E*, 1896 *W, I, E*, 1897 *I, E*, 1898 *I, E*, 1899 *I, W, E*, 1900 *W, E*
MacEwen, R K G (Cambridge U, London Scottish) 1954 *F, NZ, I, W*, 1956 *F, W, I, E*, 1957 *F, W, I, E*, 1958 *W*
Macfadyen, D J H (Glasgow) 2002 *C* (R), *US*
Macfarlan, D J (London Scottish) 1883 *W*, 1884 *W, I, E*, 1886 *W, I*, 1887 *I*, 1888 *I*
McFarlane, J L H (Edinburgh U) 1871 *E*, 1872 *E*, 1873 *E*
McGaughey, S K (Hawick) 1984 *R*
McGeechan, I R (Headingley) 1972 *NZ*, 1973 *F, W, I, E, P*, 1974 *W, E, I, F*, 1975 *I, F, W, E, NZ, A*, 1976 *F, W, E, I*, 1977 *E, I, F, W*, 1978 *I, F, W, NZ*, 1979 *W, E, I, F*
McGlashan, T P L (Royal HSFP) 1947 *F, I, E*, 1954 *F, NZ, I, E, W*
MacGregor, D G (Watsonians, Pontypridd) 1907 *W, I, E*
MacGregor, G (Cambridge U) 1890 *W, I, E*, 1891 *W, I, E*, 1893 *W, I, E*, 1894 *W, I, E*, 1896 *E*
MacGregor, I A A (Hillhead HSFP, Llanelli) 1955 *I, E*, 1956 *F, W, I, E*, 1957 *F, W, I*
MacGregor, J R (Edinburgh U) 1909 *I*
McGuinness, G M (W of Scotland) 1982 *A* 1,2, 1983 *I*, 1985 *I, F, W, E*
McHarg, A F (W of Scotland, London Scottish) 1968 *I, E, A*, 1969 *F, W, I, E*, 1971 *F, W, I, E* (2[1C]), 1972 *F, E, NZ*, 1973 *F, W, I, E, P*, 1974 *W, E, I, F*, 1975 *I, F, W, E, NZ, A*, 1976 *F, W, E, I*, 1977 *E, I, F, W*, 1978 *I, F, W, NZ*, 1979 *W, E*
McIlwham, G R (Glasgow Hawks, Glasgow, Bordeaux-Bègles) 1998 *Fj, A* 2(R), 2000 *E* (R), *NZ* 2(R), *US* (R), *A* (R), *Sm* (R), 2001 *F* (R), *W* (R), *E* (R), *It* (R), 2003 *SA* 2(R), *It* 2(R), *W* 2(R), *I* 2
McIndoe, F (Glasgow Acads) 1886 *W, I*
MacIntyre, I (Edinburgh Wands) 1890 *W, I, E*, 1891 *W, I, E*
McIvor, D J (Edinburgh Acads) 1992 *E, I, F, W*, 1993 *NZ*, 1994 *SA*
Mackay, E B (Glasgow Acads) 1920 *W*, 1922 *E*
McKeating, E (Heriot's FP) 1957 *F, W*, 1961 *SA, W, I, E*
McKelvey, G (Watsonians) 1997 *A*
McKendrick, J G (W of Scotland) 1889 *I*
Mackenzie, A D G (Selkirk) 1984 *A*
Mackenzie, C J G (United Services) 1921 *E*
Mackenzie, D D (Edinburgh U) 1947 *W, I, E*, 1948 *F, W, I*
Mackenzie, D K A (Edinburgh Wands) 1939 *I, E*
Mackenzie, J M (Edinburgh U) 1905 *NZ*, 1909 *W, I, E*, 1910 *W, I, E*, 1911 *W, I*
McKenzie, K D (Stirling County) 1994 *Arg* 1,2, 1995 *R*, [*Iv*], 1996 *I, F, W, E, NZ* 1,2, *A, It*, 1998 *A* 1(R), 2
Mackenzie, R C (Glasgow Acads) 1877 *I, E*, 1881 *I, E*
Mackie, G Y (Highland) 1975 *A*, 1976 *F, W*, 1978 *F*
MacKinnon, A (London Scottish) 1898 *I, E*, 1899 *I, W, E*, 1900 *E*
Mackintosh, C E W C (London Scottish) 1924 *F*
Mackintosh, H S (Glasgow U, W of Scotland) 1929 *F, W, I, E*, 1930 *F, W, I, E*, 1931 *F, W, I, E*, 1932 *SA, W, I, E*
MacLachlan, L P (Oxford U, London Scottish) 1954 *NZ, I, E, W*
Maclagan, W E (Edinburgh Acads) 1878 *E*, 1879 *I, E*, 1880 *I, E*, 1881 *I, E*, 1882 *I, E*, 1883 *W, I, E*, 1884 *W, I, E*, 1885 *W, I* 1,2, 1887 *I, W, E*, 1888 *W, I*, 1890 *W, I, E*
McLaren, A (Durham County) 1931 *F*
McLaren, E (London Scottish, Royal HSFP) 1923 *F, W, I, E*, 1924 *F*
McLaren, J G (Bourgoin, Glasgow, Bordeaux-Bègles) 1999 *Arg, R*, [*Sp, Sm*], 2000 *It* (R), *F, E, NZ* 1, 2001 *F, W, E* (R), *I, Tg, Arg, NZ*, 2002 *E, It, I, F, W*, 2003 *W* 1, *E, It* 1, *SA* 1(R), *It* 2, *I* 2(R)
McLauchlan, J (Jordanhill) 1969 *E, SA*, 1970 *F, W*, 1971 *F, W, I, E* (2[1C]), 1972 *F, W, E, NZ*, 1973 *F, W, I, E, P*, 1974 *W, E, I, F*, 1975 *I, F, W, E, NZ, A*, 1976 *F, W, E, I*, 1977 *W*, 1978 *I, F, W, E, NZ*, 1979 *W, E, I, F, NZ*
McLean, D I (Royal HSFP) 1947 *I, E*
Maclennan, W D (Watsonians) 1947 *F, I*
MacLeod, D A (Glasgow U) 1886 *I, E*
MacLeod, G (Edinburgh Acads) 1878 *E*, 1882 *I*
McLeod, H F (Hawick) 1954 *F, NZ, I, E, W*, 1955 *F, W, I, E*, 1956 *F, W, I, E*, 1957 *F, W, I, E*, 1958 *F, W, A, I, E*, 1959 *F, W, I, E*, 1960 *F, W, I, E, SA*, 1961 *F, SA, W, I, E*, 1962 *F, W, I, E*
MacLeod, K G (Cambridge U) 1905 *NZ*, 1906 *W, I, E, SA*,1907 *W, I, E*, 1908 *I, E*
MacLeod, L M (Cambridge U) 1904 *W, I, E*, 1905 *W, I, NZ*
Macleod, W M (Fettesian-Lorettonians, Edinburgh Wands) 1886 *W, I*
McMillan, K H D (Sale) 1953 *F, W, I, E*
MacMillan, R G (London Scottish) 1887 *W, I, E*, 1890 *W, I, E*, 1891 *W, E*, 1892 *W, I, E*, 1893 *W, E*, 1894 *W, I, E*, 1895 *W, I, E*, 1897 *I, E*
MacMyn, D J (Cambridge U, London Scottish) 1925 *F, W, I, E*, 1926 *F, W, I, E*, 1927 *E, A*, 1928 *F*
McNeil, A S B (Watsonians) 1935 *I*
McPartlin, J J (Harlequins, Oxford U) 1960 *F, W*, 1962 *F, W, I, E*
Macphail, J A R (Edinburgh Acads) 1949 *E*, 1951 *SA*
Macpherson, D G (London Hospital) 1910 *I, E*
Macpherson, G P S (Oxford U, Edinburgh Acads) 1922 *F, W, I, E*, 1924 *W, E*, 1925 *F, W, E*, 1927 *F, W, I, E*, 1928 *F, W, E*, 1929 *I, E*, 1930 *F, W, I, E*, 1931 *W, E*, 1932 *SA, E*
Macpherson, N C (Newport) 1920 *W, I, E*, 1921 *F, E*, 1923 *I, E*
McQueen, S B (Waterloo) 1923 *F, W, I, E*
Macrae, D J (St Andrew's U) 1937 *W, I, E*, 1938 *W, I, E*, 1939 *W, I, E*
Madsen, D F (Gosforth) 1974 *W, E, I, F*, 1975 *I, F, W, E*, 1976 *F*, 1977 *E, I, F, W*, 1978 *I*
Mair, N G R (Edinburgh U) 1951 *F, W, I, E*
Maitland, G (Edinburgh Inst FP) 1885 *W, I* 2
Maitland, R (Edinburgh Inst FP) 1881 *E*, 1882 *I, E*, 1884 *W*, 1885 *W*
Maitland, R P (Royal Artillery) 1872 *E*
Malcolm, A G (Glasgow U) 1888 *I*
Manson, J J (Dundee HSFP) 1995 *E* (R)
Marsh, J (Edinburgh Inst FP) 1889 *W, I*
Marshall, A (Edinburgh Acads) 1875 *E*
Marshall, G R (Selkirk) 1988 *A* (R), 1989 *Fj*, 1990 *Arg*, 1991 [*Z*]
Marshall, J C (London Scottish) 1954 *F, NZ, I, E, W*
Marshall, K W (Edinburgh Acads) 1934 *W, I, E*, 1935 *W, I, E*, 1936 *W*, 1937 *E*
Marshall, T R (Edinburgh Acads) 1871 *E*, 1872 *E*, 1873 *E*, 1874 *E*
Marshall, W (Edinburgh Acads) 1872 *E*

Martin, H (Edinburgh Acads, Oxford U) 1908 *W, I, E*, 1909 *W, E*
Masters, W H (Edinburgh Inst FP) 1879 *I*, 1880 *I, E*
Mather, C G (Edinburgh) 1999 *R* (R), [*Sp, Sm* (R)], 2000 *F* (t)
Maxwell, F T (Royal Engineers) 1872 *E*
Maxwell, G H H P (Edinburgh Acads, RAF, London Scottish) 1913 *I, E*, 1914 *W, I, E*, 1920 *W, E*, 1921 *F, W, I, E*, 1922 *F, E*
Maxwell, J M (Langholm) 1957 *I*
Mayer, M J M (Watsonians, Edinburgh) 1998 *SA*, 1999 [*SA* (R), *U, Sp, Sm, NZ*], 2000 *It, I*
Mein, J (Edinburgh Acads) 1871 *E*, 1872 *E*, 1873 *E*, 1874 *E*, 1875 *E*
Melville, C L (Army) 1937 *W, I, E*
Menzies, H F (W of Scotland) 1893 *W, I*, 1894 *W, E*
Metcalfe, G H (Glasgow Hawks, Glasgow) 1998 *A* 1,2, 1999 *W, E, It, I, F, Arg, R*, [*SA, U, Sm, NZ*], 2000 *It, I, F, W, E*, 2001 *I, Tg*, 2002 *E, It, I, F, W* (R), *C, US*, 2003 *I* 1, *F, W* 1, *E, It* 1, *SA* 1,2, *W* 2, *I* 2
Metcalfe, R (Northampton, Edinburgh) 2000 *E, NZ* 1,2, *US* (R), *A* (R), *Sm*, 2001 *F, W, E*
Methuen, A (London Scottish) 1889 *W, I*
Michie, E J S (Aberdeen U, Aberdeen GSFP) 1954 *F, NZ, I, E*, 1955 *W, I, E*, 1956 *F, W, I, E*, 1957 *F, W, I, E*
Millar, J N (W of Scotland) 1892 *W, I, E*, 1893 *W*, 1895 *I, E*
Millar, R K (London Scottish) 1924 *I*
Millican, J G (Edinburgh U) 1973 *W, I, E*
Milne, C J B (Fettesian-Lorettonians, W of Scotland) 1886 *W, I, E*
Milne, D F (Heriot's FP) 1991 [*J*(R)]
Milne, I G (Heriot's FP, Harlequins) 1979 *I, F, NZ*, 1980 *I, F*, 1981 *NZ* 1,2, *R, A*, 1982 *E, I, F, W, A* 1,2, 1983 *I, F, W, E, NZ*, 1984 *W, E, I, F, A*, 1985 *F, W, E*, 1986 *F, W, E, I, R*, 1987 *I, F, W, E*, [*F, Z, NZ*], 1988 *A*, 1989 *W*, 1990 *NZ* 1,2
Milne, K S (Heriot's FP) 1989 *W, E, I, F, Fj, R*, 1990 *I, F, W, E, NZ* 2, *Arg*, 1991 *F, W* (R), *E*, [*Z*], 1992 *E, I, F, W, A* 1, 1993 *I, F, W, E, NZ*, 1994 *W, E, I, F, SA*, 1995 *C, I, F, W, E*, [*Tg, F, NZ*]
Milne, W M (Glasgow Acads) 1904 *I, E*, 1905 *W, I*
Milroy, E (Watsonians) 1910 *W*, 1911 *E*, 1912 *W, I, E, SA*, 1913 *F, W, I, E*, 1914 *I, E*
Mitchell, G W E (Edinburgh Wands) 1967 *NZ*, 1968 *F, W*
Mitchell, J G (W of Scotland) 1885 *W, I* 1,2
Moffat, J S D (Edinburgh) 2002 *R, SA, Fj* (R)
Moir, C C (Northampton) 2000 *W, E, NZ* 1
Moncreiff, F J (Edinburgh Acads) 1871 *E*, 1872 *E*, 1873 *E*
Monteith, H G (Cambridge U, London Scottish) 1905 *E*, 1906 *W, I, E, SA*, 1907 *W, I*, 1908 *E*
Monypenny, D B (London Scottish) 1899 *I, W, E*
Moodie, A R (St Andrew's U) 1909 *E*, 1910 *F*, 1911 *F*
Moore, A (Edinburgh Acads) 1990 *NZ* 2, *Arg*, 1991 *F, W, E*
Morgan, D W (Stewart's-Melville FP) 1973 *W, I, E, P*, 1974 *I, F*, 1975 *I, F, W, E, NZ, A*, 1976 *F, W*, 1977 *I, F, W*, 1978 *I, F, W, E*
Morrison, I R (London Scottish) 1993 *I, F, W, E*, 1994 *W, SA*, 1995 *C, I, F, W, E, R*, [*Tg, F, NZ*]
Morrison, M C (Royal HSFP) 1896 *W, I, E*, 1897 *I, E*, 1898 *I, E*, 1899 *I, W, E*, 1900 *W, E*, 1901 *W, I, E*, 1902 *W, I, E*, 1903 *W, I*, 1904 *W, I, E*
Morrison, R H (Edinburgh U) 1886 *W, I, E*
Morrison, W H (Edinburgh Acads) 1900 *W*
Morton, D S (W of Scotland) 1887 *I, W, E*, 1888 *W, I*, 1889 *W, I*, 1890 *I, E*
Mowat, J G (Glasgow Acads) 1883 *W, E*
Mower, A L (Newcastle) 2001 *Tg, Arg, NZ*, 2002 *It*, 2003 *I* 1, *F, W* 1, *E, It* 1, *SA* 1,2, *W* 2, *I* 2
Muir, D E (Heriot's FP) 1950 *F, W, I, E*, 1952 *W, I, E*
Munnoch, N M (Watsonians) 1952 *F, W, I*
Munro, D S (Glasgow High Kelvinside) 1994 *W, E, I, F, Arg* 1,2, 1997 *W* (R)
Munro, P (Oxford U, London Scottish) 1905 *W, I, E, NZ*, 1906 *W, I, E, SA*, 1907 *I, E*, 1911 *F, W, I*
Munro, R (St Andrew's U) 1871 *E*
Munro, S (Ayr, W of Scotland) 1980 *I, F*, 1981 *F, W, E, I, NZ* 1,2, *R*, 1984 *W*
Munro, W H (Glasgow HSFP) 1947 *I, E*
Murdoch, W C W (Hillhead HSFP) 1935 *E, NZ*, 1936 *W, I*, 1939 *E*, 1948 *F, W, I, E*
Murray, C A (Hawick, Edinburgh) 1998 *E* (R), *Fj, A* 1,2, *SA*, 1999 *W, E, It, I, F, Arg*, [*SA, U, Sp, Sm, NZ*], 2000 *NZ* 2, *US, A, Sm*, 2001 *F, W, E, It* (R), *Tg, Arg*
Murray, G M (Glasgow Acads) 1921 *I*, 1926 *W*
Murray, H M (Glasgow U) 1936 *W, I*
Murray, K T (Hawick) 1985 *I, F, W*
Murray, R O (Cambridge U) 1935 *W, E*
Murray, S (Bedford, Saracens, Edinburgh) 1997 *A, SA*, 1998 *It, Fj, A* 1,2, *SA*, 1999 *W, E, It, I, F, Arg, R*, [*SA, U, Sm, NZ*], 2000 *It, I, F, W, E, NZ* 1, *US, A, Sm*, 2001 *F, W, E, It, I, Tg, Arg, NZ*, 2002 *E, It, I, F, W, R, SA*, 2003 *I* 1, *F, W* 1, *E, It* 1, *SA* 1,2, *It* 2, *W* 2
Murray, W A K (London Scottish) 1920 *F, I*, 1921 *F*

Napier, H M (W of Scotland) 1877 *I, E*, 1878 *E*, 1879 *I, E*
Neill, J B (Edinburgh Acads) 1963 *E*, 1964 *F, NZ, W, I, E*, 1965 *F*
Neill, R M (Edinburgh Acads) 1901 *E*, 1902 *I*
Neilson, G T (W of Scotland) 1891 *W, I, E*, 1892 *W, E*, 1893 *W*, 1894 *W, I*, 1895 *W, I, E*, 1896 *W, I, E*
Neilson, J A (Glasgow Acads) 1878 *E*, 1879 *E*
Neilson, R T (W of Scotland) 1898 *I, E*, 1899 *I, W*, 1900 *I, E*
Neilson, T (W of Scotland) 1874 *E*
Neilson, W (Merchiston, Cambridge U, London Scottish) 1891 *W, E*, 1892 *W, I, E*, 1893 *I, E*, 1894 *E*, 1895 *W, I, E*, 1896 *I*, 1897 *I, E*
Neilson, W G (Merchistonians) 1894 *E*
Nelson, J B (Glasgow Acads) 1925 *F, W, I, E*, 1926 *F, W, I, E*, 1927 *F, W, I, E*, 1928 *I, E*, 1929 *F, W, I, E*, 1930 *F, W, I, E*, 1931 *F, W, I*
Nelson, T A (Oxford U) 1898 *E*
Nichol, J A (Royal HSFP) 1955 *W, I, E*
Nichol, S A (Selkirk) 1994 *Arg* 2(R)
Nicol, A D (Dundee HSFP, Bath, Glasgow) 1992 *E, I, F, W, A* 1,2, 1993 *NZ*, 1994 *W*, 1997 *A, SA*, 2000 *I* (R), *F, W, E, NZ* 1,2, 2001 *F, W, E, I* (R), *Tg, Arg, NZ*
Nimmo, C S (Watsonians) 1920 *E*

Ogilvy, C (Hawick) 1911 *I, E*, 1912 *I*
Oliver, G H (Hawick) 1987 [*Z*], 1990 *NZ* 2(R), 1991 [*Z*]
Oliver, G K (Gala) 1970 *A*
Orr, C E (W of Scotland) 1887 *I, E, W*, 1888 *W, I*, 1889 *W, I*, 1890 *W, I, E*, 1891 *W, I, E*, 1892 *W, I, E*
Orr, H J (London Scottish) 1903 *W, I, E*, 1904 *W, I*
Orr, J E (W of Scotland) 1889 *I*, 1890 *W, I, E*, 1891 *W, I, E*, 1892 *W, I, E*, 1893 *I, E*
Orr, J H (Edinburgh City Police) 1947 *F, W*
Osler, F L (Edinburgh U) 1911 *F, W*

Park, J (Royal HSFP) 1934 *W*
Paterson, C D (Edinburgh) 1999 [*Sp*], 2000 *F, W, E, NZ* 1,2, *US, A, Sm*, 2001 *F, W, E, It, I, NZ*, 2002 *E, It, I, F, W, C, US, R, SA, Fj*, 2003 *I* 1, *F, W* 1, *E, It* 1, *SA* 1,2, *It* 2(R), *W* 2(R), *I* 2
Paterson, D S (Gala) 1969 *SA*, 1970 *I, E, A*, 1971 *F, W, I, E* (2[1C]), 1972 *W*
Paterson, G Q (Edinburgh Acads) 1876 *E*
Paterson, J R (Birkenhead Park) 1925 *F, W, I, E*, 1926 *F, W, I, E*, 1927 *F, W, I, E, A*, 1928 *F, W, I, E*, 1929 *F, W, I, E*
Patterson, D (Hawick) 1896 *W*
Patterson, D W (West Hartlepool) 1994 *SA*, 1995 [*Tg*]
Pattullo, G L (Panmure) 1920 *F, W, I, E*
Paxton, I A M (Selkirk) 1981 *NZ* 1,2, *R, A*, 1982 *E, I, F, W, A* 1,2, 1983 *I, E, NZ*, 1984 *W, E, I, F*, 1985 *I* (R), *F, W, E*, 1986 *W, E, I, R*, 1987 *I, F, W, E*, [*F, Z, R, NZ*], 1988 *I, E, A*
Paxton, R E (Kelso) 1982 *I, A* 2(R)
Pearson, J (Watsonians) 1909 *I, E*, 1910 *F, W, I, E*, 1911 *F*, 1912 *F, W, SA*, 1913 *I, E*
Pender, I M (London Scottish) 1914 *E*
Pender, N E K (Hawick) 1977 *I*, 1978 *F, W, E*
Penman, W M (RAF) 1939 *I*
Peterkin, W A (Edinburgh U) 1881 *E*, 1883 *I*, 1884 *W, I, E*, 1885 *W, I* 1,2
Peters, E W (Bath) 1995 *C, I, F, W, E, R*, [*Tg, F, NZ*], 1996 *I, F, W, E, NZ* 1,2, *A, It*, 1997 *A, SA*, 1998 *W, E, Fj, A* 1,2, *SA*, 1999 *W, E, It, I*
Petrie, A G (Royal HSFP) 1873 *E*, 1874 *E*, 1875 *E*, 1876 *E*, 1877 *I, E*, 1878 *E*, 1879 *I, E*, 1880 *I, E*
Petrie, J M (Glasgow) 2000 *NZ* 2, *US, A, Sm*, 2001 *F, W, It* (R), *I* (R), *Tg, Arg*, 2002 *F* (t), *W* (R), *C, R* (R), *Fj*, 2003 *F* (t+R), *W* 1(R), *SA* 1(R),2(R), *It* 2, *W* 2, *I* 2(R)
Philp, A (Edinburgh Inst FP) 1882 *E*
Pocock, E I (Edinburgh Wands) 1877 *I, E*
Pollock, J A (Gosforth) 1982 *W*, 1983 *E, NZ*, 1984 *E* (R), *I, F, R*, 1985 *F*
Polson, A H (Gala) 1930 *E*

Pountney, A C (Northampton) 1998 *SA*, 1999 *W* (t+R), *E* (R), *It* (t+R), *I* (R), *F*, *Arg*, [*SA*, *U*, *Sm*, *NZ*], 2000 *It*, *I*, *F*, *W*, *E*, *US*, *A*, *Sm*, 2001 *F*, *W*, *E*, *It*, *I*, 2002 *E*, *I*, *F*, *W*, *R*, *SA*, *Fj*
Proudfoot, M C (Melrose, Glasgow) 1998 *Fj*, *A* 1,2, 2003 *I* 2(R)
Purdie, W (Jedforest) 1939 *W*, *I*, *E*
Purves, A B H L (London Scottish) 1906 *W*, *I*, *E*, *SA*, 1907 *W*, *I*, *E*, 1908 *W*, *I*, *E*
Purves, W D C L (London Scottish) 1912 *F*, *W*, *I*, *SA*, 1913 *I*, *E*

Rea, C W W (W of Scotland, Headingley) 1968 *A*, 1969 *F*, *W*, *I*, *SA*, 1970 *F*, *W*, *I*, *A*, 1971 *F*, *W*, *E* (2[1C])
Redpath, B W (Melrose, Narbonne, Sale) 1993 *NZ* (t), 1994 *E* (t), *F*, *Arg* 1,2, 1995 *C*, *I*, *F*, *W*, *E*, *R*, [*Iv*, *F*, *NZ*], *WS*, 1996 *I*, *F*, *W*, *E*. *A* (R), *It*, 1997 *E*, *I*, *F*, 1998 *Fj*, *A* 1,2, *SA*, 1999 *R* (R), [*U* (R), *Sp*], 2000 *It*, *I*, *US*, *A*, *Sm*, 2001 *F* (R), *E* (R), *It*, *I*, 2002 *E*, *It*, *I*, *F*, *W*, *R*, *SA*, *Fj*, 2003 *I* 1, *F*, *W* 1, *E*, *It* 1, *SA* 1,2
Reed, A I (Bath, Wasps) 1993 *I*, *F*, *W*, *E*, 1994 *E*, *I*, *F*, *Arg* 1,2, *SA*, 1996 *It*, 1997 *W*, *E*, *I*, *F*, 1999 *It* (R), *F* (R), [*Sp*]
Reid, C (Edinburgh Acads) 1881 *I*, *E*, 1882 *I*, *E*, 1883 *W*, *I*, *E*, 1884 *W*, *I*, *E*, 1885 *W*, *I* 1,2, 1886 *W*, *I*, *E*, 1887 *I*, *W*, *E*, 1888 *W*, *I*
Reid, J (Edinburgh Wands) 1874 *E*, 1875 *E*, 1876 *E*, 1877 *I*, *E*
Reid, J M (Edinburgh Acads) 1898 *I*, *E*, 1899 *I*
Reid, M F (Loretto) 1883 *I*, *E*
Reid, R E (Glasgow) 2001 *Tg* (R), *Arg*
Reid, S J (Boroughmuir, Leeds, Narbonne) 1995 *WS*, 1999 *F*, *Arg*, [*Sp*], 2000 *It* (t), *F*, *W*, *E* (t)
Reid-Kerr, J (Greenock Wand) 1909 *E*
Relph, W K L (Stewart's Coll FP) 1955 *F*, *W*, *I*, *E*
Renny-Tailyour, H W (Royal Engineers) 1872 *E*
Renwick, J M (Hawick) 1972 *F*, *W*, *E*, *NZ*, 1973 *F*, 1974 *W*, *E*, *I*, *F*, 1975 *I*, *F*, *W*, *E*, *NZ*, *A*, 1976 *F*, *W*, *E* (R), 1977 *I*, *F*, *W*, 1978 *I*, *F*, *W*, *E*, *NZ*, 1979 *W*, *E*, *I*, *F*, *NZ*, 1980 *I*, *F*, *W*, *E*, 1981 *F*, *W*, *E*, *I*, *NZ* 1,2, *R*, *A*, 1982 *E*, *I*, *F*, *W*, 1983 *I*, *F*, *W*, *E*, 1984 *R*
Renwick, W L (London Scottish) 1989 *R*
Renwick, W N (London Scottish, Edinburgh Wands) 1938 *E*, 1939 *W*
Richardson, J F (Edinburgh Acads) 1994 *SA*
Ritchie, G (Merchistonians) 1871 *E*
Ritchie, G F (Dundee HSFP) 1932 *E*
Ritchie, J M (Watsonians) 1933 *W*, *E*, *I*, 1934 *W*, *I*, *E*
Ritchie, W T (Cambridge U) 1905 *I*, *E*
Robb, G H (Glasgow U) 1881 *I*, 1885 *W*
Roberts, G (Watsonians) 1938 *W*, *I*, *E*, 1939 *W*, *E*
Robertson, A H (W of Scotland) 1871 *E*
Robertson, A W (Edinburgh Acads) 1897 *E*
Robertson, D (Edinburgh Acads) 1875 *E*
Robertson, D D (Cambridge U) 1893 *W*
Robertson, I (London Scottish, Watsonians) 1968 *E*, 1969 *E*, *SA*, 1970 *F*, *W*, *I*, *E*, *A*
Robertson, I P M (Watsonians) 1910 *F*
Robertson, J (Clydesdale) 1908 *E*
Robertson, K W (Melrose) 1978 *NZ*, 1979 *W*, *E*, *I*, *F*, *NZ*, 1980 *W*, *E*, 1981 *F*, *W*, *E*, *I*, *R*, *A*, 1982 *E*, *I*, *F*, *A* 1,2, 1983 *I*, *F*, *W*, *E*, 1984 *E*, *I*, *F*, *R*, *A*, 1985 *I*, *F*, *W*, *E*, 1986 *I*, 1987 *F* (R), *W*, *E*, [*F*, *Z*, *NZ*], 1988 *E*, *A*, 1989 *E*, *I*, *F*
Robertson, L (London Scottish United Services) 1908 *E*, 1911 *W*, 1912 *W*, *I*, *E*, *SA*, 1913 *W*, *I*, *E*
Robertson, M A (Gala) 1958 *F*
Robertson, R D (London Scottish) 1912 *F*
Robson, A (Hawick) 1954 *F*, 1955 *F*, *W*, *I*, *E*, 1956 *F*, *W*, *I*, *E*, 1957 *F*, *W*, *I*, *E*, 1958 *W*, *A*, *I*, *E*, 1959 *F*, *W*, *I*, *E*, 1960 *F*
Rodd, J A T (United Services, RN, London Scottish) 1958 *F*, *W*, *A*, *I*, *E*, 1960 *F*, *W*, 1962 *F*, 1964 *F*, *NZ*, *W*, 1965 *F*, *W*, *I*
Rogerson, J (Kelvinside Acads) 1894 *W*
Roland, E T (Edinburgh Acads) 1884 *I*, *E*
Rollo, D M D (Howe of Fife) 1959 *E*, 1960 *F*, *W*, *I*, *E*, *SA*, 1961 *F*, *SA*, *W*, *I*, *E*, 1962 *F*, *W*, *E*, 1963 *F*, *W*, *I*, *E*, 1964 *F*, *NZ*, *W*, *I*, *E*, 1965 *F*, *W*, *I*, *E*, *SA*, 1966 *F*, *W*, *I*, *E*, *A*, 1967 *F*, *W*, *E*, *NZ*, 1968 *F*, *W*, *I*
Rose, D M (Jedforest) 1951 *F*, *W*, *I*, *E*, *SA*, 1953 *F*, *W*
Ross, A (Kilmarnock) 1924 *F*, *W*
Ross, A (Royal HSFP) 1905 *W*, *I*, *E*, 1909 *W*, *I*
Ross, A R (Edinburgh U) 1911 *W*, 1914 *W*, *I*, *E*
Ross, E J (London Scottish) 1904 *W*
Ross, G (Edinburgh, Leeds) 2001 *Tg*, 2002 *R*, *SA*, *Fj* (R), 2003 *I* 1, *W* 1(R), *SA* 2(R), *It* 2, *I* 2
Ross, G T (Watsonians) 1954 *NZ*, *I*, *E*, *W*
Ross, I A (Hillhead HSFP) 1951 *F*, *W*, *I*, *E*
Ross, J (London Scottish) 1901 *W*, *I*, *E*, 1902 *W*, 1903 *E*
Ross, K I (Boroughmuir FP) 1961 *SA*, *W*, *I*, *E*, 1962 *F*, *W*, *I*, *E*, 1963 *F*, *W*, *E*
Ross, W A (Hillhead HSFP) 1937 *W*, *E*
Rottenburg, H (Cambridge U, London Scottish) 1899 *W*, *E*, 1900 *W*, *I*, *E*
Roughead, W N (Edinburgh Acads, London Scottish) 1927 *A*, 1928 *F*, *W*, *I*, *E*, 1930 *I*, *E*, 1931 *F*, *W*, *I*, *E*, 1932 *W*
Rowan, N A (Boroughmuir) 1980 *W*, *E*, 1981 *F*, *W*, *E*, *I*, 1984 *R*, 1985 *I*, 1987 [*R*], 1988 *I*, *F*, *W*, *E*
Rowand, R (Glasgow HSFP) 1930 *F*, *W*, 1932 *E*, 1933 *W*, *E*, *I*, 1934 *W*
Roxburgh, A J (Kelso) 1997 *A*, 1998 *It*, *F* (R), *W*, *E*, *Fj*, *A* 1(R),2(R)
Roy, A (Waterloo) 1938 *W*, *I*, *E*, 1939 *W*, *I*, *E*
Russell, R R (Saracens) 1999 *R*, [*U* (R), *Sp*, *Sm* (R), *NZ* (R)], 2000 *I* (R), 2001 *F* (R), 2002 *F* (R), *W* (R), 2003 *W* 1(R), *It* 1(R), *SA* 1(R),2(R), *It* 2, *I* 2(R)
Russell, W L (Glasgow Acads) 1905 *NZ*, 1906 *W*, *I*, *E*
Rutherford, J Y (Selkirk) 1979 *W*, *E*, *I*, *F*, *NZ*, 1980 *I*, *F*, *E*, 1981 *F*, *W*, *E*, *I*, *NZ* 1,2, *A*, 1982 *E*, *I*, *F*, *W*, *A* 1,2, 1983 *E*, *NZ*, 1984 *W*, *E*, *I*, *F*, *R*, 1985 *I*, *F*, *W*, *E*, 1986 *F*, *W*, *E*, *I*, *R*, 1987 *I*, *F*, *W*, *E*, [*F*]

Sampson, R W F (London Scottish) 1939 *W*, 1947 *W*
Sanderson, G A (Royal HSFP) 1907 *W*, *I*, *E*, 1908 *I*
Sanderson, J L P (Edinburgh Acads) 1873 *E*
Schulze, D G (London Scottish) 1905 *E*, 1907 *I*, *E*, 1908 *W*, *I*, *E*, 1909 *W*, *I*, *E*, 1910 *W*, *I*, *E*, 1911 *W*
Scobie, R M (Royal Military Coll) 1914 *W*, *I*, *E*
Scotland, K J F (Heriot's FP, Cambridge U, Leicester) 1957 *F*, *W*, *I*, *E*, 1958 *E*, 1959 *F*, *W*, *I*, *E*, 1960 *F*, *W*, *I*, *E*, 1961 *F*, *SA*, *W*, *I*, *E*, 1962 *F*, *W*, *I*, *E*, 1963 *F*, *W*, *I*, *E*, 1965 *F*
Scott, D M (Langholm, Watsonians) 1950 *I*, *E*, 1951 *W*, *I*, *E*, *SA*, 1952 *F*, *W*, *I*, 1953 *F*
Scott, J M B (Edinburgh Acads) 1907 *E*, 1908 *W*, *I*, *E*, 1909 *W*, *I*, *E*, 1910 *F*, *W*, *I*, *E*, 1911 *F*, *W*, *I*, 1912 *W*, *I*, *E*, *SA*, 1913 *W*, *I*, *E*
Scott, J S (St Andrew's U) 1950 *E*
Scott, J W (Stewart's Coll FP) 1925 *F*, *W*, *I*, *E*, 1926 *F*, *W*, *I*, *E*, 1927 *F*, *W*, *I*, *E*, *A*, 1928 *F*, *W*, *E*, 1929 *E*, 1930 *F*
Scott, M (Dunfermline) 1992 *A* 2
Scott, R (Hawick) 1898 *I*, 1900 *I*, *E*
Scott, S (Edinburgh, Borders) 2000 *NZ* 2 (R), *US* (t+R), 2001 *It* (R), *I* (R), *Tg* (R), *NZ* (R), 2002 *US* (R), *R* (R), *Fj* (R)
Scott, T (Langholm, Hawick) 1896 *W*, 1897 *I*, *E*, 1898 *I*, *E*, 1899 *I*, *W*, *E*, 1900 *W*, *I*, *E*
Scott, T M (Hawick) 1893 *E*, 1895 *W*, *I*, *E*, 1896 *W*, *E*, 1897 *I*, *E*, 1898 *I*, *E*, 1900 *W*, *I*
Scott, W P (W of Scotland) 1900 *I*, *E*, 1902 *I*, *E*, 1903 *W*, *I*, *E*, 1904 *W*, *I*, *E*, 1905 *W*, *I*, *E*, *NZ*, 1906 *W*, *I*, *E*, *SA*, 1907 *W*, *I*, *E*
Scoular, J G (Cambridge U) 1905 *NZ*, 1906 *W*, *I*, *E*, *SA*
Selby, J A R (Watsonians) 1920 *W*, *I*
Shackleton, J A P (London Scottish) 1959 *E*, 1963 *F*, *W*, 1964 *NZ*, *W*, 1965 *I*, *SA*
Sharp, A V (Bristol) 1994 *E*, *I*, *F*, *Arg* 1,2 *SA*
Sharp, G (Stewart's FP, Army) 1960 *F*, 1964 *F*, *NZ*, *W*
Shaw, G D (Sale) 1935 *NZ*, 1936 *W*, 1937 *W*, *I*, *E*, 1939 *I*
Shaw, I (Glasgow HSFP) 1937 *I*
Shaw, J N (Edinburgh Acads) 1921 *W*, *I*
Shaw, R W (Glasgow HSFP) 1934 *W*, *I*, *E*, 1935 *W*, *I*, *E*, *NZ*, 1936 *W*, *I*, *E*, 1937 *W*, *I*, *E*, 1938 *W*, *I*, *E*, 1939 *W*, *I*, *E*
Shedden, D (W of Scotland) 1972 *NZ*, 1973 *F*, *W*, *I*, *E*, *P*, 1976 *W*, *E*, *I*, 1977 *I*, *F*, *W*, 1978 *I*, *F*, *W*
Shepherd, R J S (Melrose) 1995 *WS*, 1996 *I*, *F*, *W*, *E*, *NZ* 1,2, *A*, *It*, 1997 *W*, *E*, *I*, *F*, *SA*, 1998 *It*, *I*, *W* (R), *Fj* (t), *A* 1,2
Shiel, A G (Melrose, Edinburgh) 1991 [*I* (R), *WS*], 1993 *I*, *F*, *W*, *E*, *NZ*, 1994 *Arg* 1,2, *SA*, 1995 *R*, [*Iv*, *F*, *NZ*], *WS*, 2000 *I*, *NZ* 1(R),2
Shillinglaw, R B (Gala, Army) 1960 *I*, *E*, *SA*, 1961 *F*, *SA*
Simmers, B M (Glasgow Acads) 1965 *F*, *W*, 1966 *A*, 1967 *F*, *W*, *I*, 1971 *F* (R)
Simmers, W M (Glasgow Acads) 1926 *W*, *I*, *E*, 1927 *F*, *W*, *I*, *E*, *A*, 1928 *F*, *W*, *I*, *E*, 1929 *F*, *W*, *I*, *E*, 1930 *F*, *W*, *I*, *E*, 1931 *F*, *W*, *I*, *E*, 1932 *SA*, *W*, *I*, *E*
Simpson, G L (Kirkcaldy, Glasgow) 1998 *A* 1,2, 1999 *Arg* (R), *R*, [*SA*, *U*, *Sm*, *NZ*], 2000 *It*, *I*, *NZ* 1(R), 2001 *I*, *Tg* (R), *Arg* (R), *NZ*
Simpson, J W (Royal HSFP) 1893 *I*, *E*, 1894 *W*, *I*, *E*, 1895 *W*, *I*, *E*, 1896 *W*, *I*, 1897 *E*, 1899 *W*, *E*
Simpson, R S (Glasgow Acads) 1923 *I*

Simson, E D (Edinburgh U, London Scottish) 1902 *E*, 1903 *W, I, E*, 1904 *W, I, E*, 1905 *W, I, E, NZ*, 1906 *W, I, E*, 1907 *W, I, E*
Simson, J T (Watsonians) 1905 *NZ*, 1909 *W, I, E*, 1910 *F, W*, 1911 *I*
Simson, R F (London Scottish) 1911 *E*
Sloan, A T (Edinburgh Acads) 1914 *W*, 1920 *F, W, I, E*, 1921 *F, W, I, E*
Sloan, D A (Edinburgh Acads, London Scottish) 1950 *F, W, E*, 1951 *W, I, E*, 1953 *F*
Sloan, T (Glasgow Acads, Oxford U) 1905 *NZ*, 1906 *W, SA*, 1907 *W, E*, 1908 *W*, 1909 *I*
Smeaton, P W (Edinburgh Acads) 1881 *I*, 1883 *I, E*
Smith, A R (Oxford U) 1895 *W, I, E*, 1896 *W, I*, 1897 *I, E*, 1898 *I, E*, 1900 *I, E*
Smith, A R (Cambridge U, Gosforth, Ebbw Vale, Edinburgh Wands) 1955 *W, I, E*, 1956 *F, W, I, E*, 1957 *F, W, I, E*, 1958 *F, W, A, I*, 1959 *F, W, I, E*, 1960 *F, W, I, E, SA*, 1961 *F, SA, W, I, E*, 1962 *F, W, I, E*
Smith, C J (Edinburgh) 2002 *C, US* (R)
Smith, D W C (London Scottish) 1949 *F, W, I, E*, 1950 *F, W, I*, 1953 *I*
Smith, E R (Edinburgh Acads) 1879 *I*
Smith, G K (Kelso) 1957 *I, E*, 1958 *F, W, A*, 1959 *F, W, I, E*, 1960 *F, W, I, E*, 1961 *F, SA, W, I, E*
Smith, H O (Watsonians) 1895 *W*, 1896 *W, I, E*, 1898 *I, E*, 1899 *W, I, E*, 1900 *E*, 1902 *E*
Smith, I R (Gloucester, Moseley) 1992 *E, I, W, A* 1,2, 1994 *E* (R), *I, F, Arg* 1,2, 1995 [*Iv*], *WS*, 1996 *I, F, W, E, NZ* 1,2, *A, It*, 1997 *E, I, F, A, SA*
Smith, I S (Oxford U, Edinburgh U) 1924 *W, I, E*, 1925 *F, W, I, E*, 1926 *F, W, I, E*, 1927 *F, I, E*, 1929 *F, W, I, E*, 1930 *F, W, I*, 1931 *F, W, I, E*, 1932 *SA, W, I, E*, 1933 *W, E, I*
Smith I S G (London Scottish) 1969 *SA*, 1970 *F, W, I, E*, 1971 *F, W, I*
Smith, M A (London Scottish) 1970 *W, I, E, A*
Smith, R T (Kelso) 1929 *F, W, I, E*, 1930 *F, W, I*
Smith, S H (Glasgow Acads) 1877 *I*, 1878 *E*
Smith, T J (Gala) 1983 *E, NZ*, 1985 *I, F*
Smith T J (Watsonians, Dundee HSFP, Glasgow, Brive, Northampton) 1997 *E, I, F*, 1998 *SA*, 1999 *W, E, It, I, Arg, R*, [*SA, U, Sm, NZ*], 2000 *It, I, F, W, E, NZ* 1,2, *US, A, Sm*, 2001 *F, W, E, It, I, Tg, Arg, NZ*, 2002 *E, It, I, F, W, R, SA, Fj*, 2003 *I* 1, *F, W* 1, *E, It* 1,2
Sole, D M B (Bath, Edinburgh Acads) 1986 *F, W*, 1987 *I, F, W, E*, [*F, Z, R, NZ*], 1988 *I, F, W, E, A*, 1989 *W, E, I, F, Fj, R*, 1990 *I, F, W, E, NZ* 1,2, *Arg*, 1991 *F, W, E, I, R*, [*J, I, WS, E, NZ*], 1992 *E, I, F, W, A* 1,2
Somerville, D (Edinburgh Inst FP) 1879 *I*, 1882 *I*, 1883 *W, I, E*, 1884 *W*
Speirs, L M (Watsonians) 1906 *SA*, 1907 *W, I, E*, 1908 *W, I, E*, 1910 *F, W, E*
Spence, K M (Oxford U) 1953 *I*
Spencer, E (Clydesdale) 1898 *I*
Stagg, P K (Sale) 1965 *F, W, E, SA*, 1966 *F, W, I, E, A*, 1967 *F, W, I, E, NZ*, 1968 *F, W, I, E, A*, 1969 *F, W, I* (R), *SA*, 1970 *F, W, I, E, A*
Stanger, A G (Hawick) 1989 *Fj, R*, 1990 *I, F, W, E, NZ* 1,2, *Arg*, 1991 *F, W, E, I, R*, [*J, Z, I, WS, E, NZ*], 1992 *E, I, F, W, A* 1,2, 1993 *I, F, W, E, NZ*, 1994 *W, E, I, F, SA*, 1995 *R*, [*Iv*], 1996 *NZ* 2, *A, It*, 1997 *W, E, I, F, A, SA*, 1998 *It, I* (R), *F, W, E*
Stark, D A (Boroughmuir, Melrose, Glasgow Hawks) 1993 *I, F, W, E*, 1996 *NZ* 2(R), *It* (R), 1997 *W* (R), *E, SA*
Steel, J F (Glasgow) 2000 *US, A*, 2001 *I, Tg, NZ*
Steele, W C C (Langholm, Bedford, RAF, London Scottish) 1969 *E*, 1971 *F, W, I, E* (2[1C]), 1972 *F, W, E, NZ*, 1973 *F, W, I, E*, 1975 *I, F, W, E, NZ* (R), 1976 *W, E, I*, 1977 *E*
Stephen, A E (W of Scotland) 1885 *W*, 1886 *I*
Steven, P D (Heriot's FP) 1984 *A*, 1985 *F, W, E*
Steven, R (Edinburgh Wands) 1962 *I*
Stevenson, A K (Glasgow Acads) 1922 *F*, 1923 *F, W, E*
Stevenson, A M (Glasgow U) 1911 *F*
Stevenson, G D (Hawick) 1956 *E*, 1957 *F*, 1958 *F, W, A, I, E*, 1959 *W, I, E*, 1960 *W, I, E, SA*, 1961 *F, SA, W, I, E*, 1963 *F, W, I*, 1964 *E*, 1965 *F*
Stevenson, H J (Edinburgh Acads) 1888 *W, I*, 1889 *W, I*, 1890 *W, I, E*, 1891 *W, I, E*, 1892 *W, I, E*, 1893 *I, E*
Stevenson, L E (Edinburgh U) 1888 *W*
Stevenson, R C (London Scottish) 1897 *I, E*, 1898 *E*, 1899 *I, W, E*
Stevenson, R C (St Andrew's U) 1910 *F, I, E*, 1911 *F, W, I*
Stevenson, W H (Glasgow Acads) 1925 *F*
Stewart, A K (Edinburgh U) 1874 *E*, 1876 *E*
Stewart, A M (Edinburgh Acads) 1914 *W*
Stewart, B D (Edinburgh Acads, Edinburgh) 1996 *NZ* 2, *A*, 2000 *NZ* 1,2
Stewart, C A R (W of Scotland) 1880 *I, E*
Stewart, C E B (Kelso) 1960 *W*, 1961 *F*
Stewart, J (Glasgow HSFP) 1930 *F*
Stewart, J L (Edinburgh Acads) 1921 *I*
Stewart M J (Northampton) 1996 *It*, 1997 *W, E, I, F, A, SA*, 1998 *It, I, F, W, Fj* (R), 2000 *It, I, F, W, E, NZ* 1(R), 2001 *F, W, E, It, I, Tg, Arg, NZ*, 2002 *E, It, I, F, W, C, US, R* (R)
Stewart, M S (Stewart's Coll FP) 1932 *SA, W, I*, 1933 *W, E, I*, 1934 *W, I, E*
Stewart, W A (London Hospital) 1913 *F, W, I*, 1914 *W*
Steyn, S S L (Oxford U) 1911 *E*, 1912 *I*
Strachan, G M (Jordanhill) 1971 *E* (C) (R), 1973 *W, I, E, P*
Stronach, R S (Glasgow Acads) 1901 *W, E*, 1905 *W, I, E*
Stuart, C D (W of Scotland) 1909 *I*, 1910 *F, W, I, E*, 1911 *I, E*
Stuart, L M (Glasgow HSFP) 1923 *F, W, I, E*, 1924 *F*, 1928 *E*, 1930 *I, E*
Suddon, N (Hawick) 1965 *W, I, E, SA*, 1966 *A*, 1968 *E, A*, 1969 *F, W, I*, 1970 *I, E, A*
Sutherland, W R (Hawick) 1910 *W, E*, 1911 *F, E*, 1912 *F, W, E, SA*, 1913 *F, W, I, E*, 1914 *W*
Swan, J S (Army, London Scottish, Leicester) 1953 *E*, 1954 *F, NZ, I, E, W*, 1955 *F, W, I, E*, 1956 *F, W, I, E*, 1957 *F, W*, 1958 *F*
Swan, M W (Oxford U, London Scottish) 1958 *F, W, A, I, E*, 1959 *F, W, I*
Sweet, J B (Glasgow HSFP) 1913 *E*, 1914 *I*
Symington, A W (Cambridge U) 1914 *W, E*

Tait, A V (Kelso, Newcastle, Edinburgh) 1987 [*F*(R), *Z, R, NZ*], 1988 *I, F, W, E*, 1997 *I, F, A*, 1998 *It, I, F, W, E, SA*, 1999 *W* (R), *E, It, I, F, Arg, R*, [*SA, U, NZ*]
Tait, J G (Edinburgh Acads) 1880 *I*, 1885 *I* 2
Tait, P W (Royal HSFP) 1935 *E*
Taylor, E G (Oxford U) 1927 *W, A*
Taylor, R C (Kelvinside-West) 1951 *W, I, E, SA*
Taylor, S M (Edinburgh) 2000 *US, A*, 2001 *E, It, I, NZ* (R), 2002 *E, It, I, F, W, C, US, R, SA, Fj*, 2003 *I* 1, *F, W* 1, *E, It* 1, *SA* 1,2, *It* 2, *I* 2
Telfer, C M (Hawick) 1968 *A*, 1969 *F, W, I, E*, 1972 *F, W, E*, 1973 *W, I, E, P*, 1974 *W, E, I*, 1975 *A*, 1976 *F*
Telfer, J W (Melrose) 1964 *F, NZ, W, I, E*, 1965 *F, W, I*, 1966 *F, W, I, E*, 1967 *W, I, E*, 1968 *E, A*, 1969 *F, W, I, E, SA*, 1970 *F, W, I*
Tennent, J M (W of Scotland) 1909 *W, I, E*, 1910 *F, W, E*
Thom, D A (London Scottish) 1934 *W*, 1935 *W, I, E, NZ*
Thom, G (Kirkcaldy) 1920 *F, W, I, E*
Thom, J R (Watsonians) 1933 *W, E, I*
Thomson, A E (United Services) 1921 *F, W, E*
Thomson, A M (St Andrew's U) 1949 *I*
Thomson, B E (Oxford U) 1953 *F, W, I*
Thomson, I H M (Heriot's FP, Army) 1951 *W, I*, 1952 *F, W, I*, 1953 *I, E*
Thomson, J S (Glasgow Acads) 1871 *E*
Thomson, R H (London Scottish, PUC) 1960 *I, E, SA*, 1961 *F, SA, W, I, E*, 1963 *F, W, I, E*, 1964 *F, NZ, W*
Thomson, W H (W of Scotland) 1906 *SA*
Thomson, W J (W of Scotland) 1899 *W, E*, 1900 *W*
Timms, A B (Edinburgh U, Edinburgh Wands) 1896 *W*, 1900 *W, I*, 1901 *W, I, E*, 1902 *W, E*, 1903 *W, E*, 1904 *I, E*, 1905 *I, E*
Tod, H B (Gala) 1911 *F*
Tod, J (Watsonians) 1884 *W, I, E*, 1885 *W, I* 1,2, 1886 *W, I, E*
Todd, J K (Glasgow Acads) 1874 *E*, 1875 *E*
Tolmie, J M (Glasgow HSFP) 1922 *E*
Tomes, A J (Hawick) 1976 *E, I*, 1977 *E*, 1978 *I, F, W, E, NZ*, 1979 *W, E, I, F, NZ*, 1980 *F, W, E*, 1981 *F, W, E, I, NZ* 1,2, *R, A*, 1982 *E, I, F, W, A* 1,2, 1983 *I, F, W*, 1984 *W, E, I, F, R, A*, 1985 *W, E*, 1987 *I, F, E* (R), [*F, Z, R, NZ*]
Torrie, T J (Edinburgh Acads) 1877 *E*
Townsend, G P J (Gala, Northampton, Brive, Castres, Borders) 1993 *E* (R), 1994 *W, E, I, F, Arg* 1,2, 1995 *C, I, F, W, E, WS*, 1996 *I, F, W, E, NZ* 1,2, *A, It*, 1997 *W, E, I, F, A, SA*, 1998 *It, I, F, W, E, Fj, A* 1,2, *SA* (R), 1999 *W, E, It, I, F*, [*SA, U, Sp* (R), *Sm, NZ*], 2000 *It, I, F, W, E, NZ* 1,2, *US, A, Sm*, 2001 *F, It, I, Arg, NZ*, 2002 *E, It, I, F, W, R* (R), *SA* (R), *Fj*, 2003 *I* 1, *F, W* 1, *E, It* 1, *SA* 1,2, *W* 2
Tukalo, I (Selkirk) 1985 *I*, 1987 *I, F, W, E*, [*F, Z, R, NZ*], 1988 *F, W, E, A*, 1989 *W, E, I, F, Fj*, 1990 *I, F, W, E, NZ* 1, 1991 *I, R*, [*J, Z, I, WS, E, NZ*], 1992 *E, I, F, W, A* 1,2

Turk, A S (Langholm) 1971 *E* (R)
Turnbull, D J (Hawick) 1987 [*NZ*], 1988 *F, E*, 1990 *E* (R), 1991 *F, W, E, I, R*, [*Z*], 1993 *I, F, W, E*, 1994 *W*
Turnbull, F O (Kelso) 1951 *F, SA*
Turnbull, G O (W of Scotland) 1896 *I, E*, 1897 *I, E*, 1904 *W*
Turnbull, P (Edinburgh Acads) 1901 *W, I, E*, 1902 *W, I, E*
Turner, F H (Oxford U, Liverpool) 1911 *F, W, I, E*, 1912 *F, W, I, E, SA*, 1913 *F, W, I, E*, 1914 *I, E*
Turner, J W C (Gala) 1966 *W, A*, 1967 *F, W, I, E, NZ*, 1968 *F, W, I, E, A*, 1969 *F*, 1970 *E, A*, 1971 *F, W, I, E* (2[1C])

Usher, C M (United Services, Edinburgh Wands) 1912 *E*, 1913 *F, W, I, E*, 1914 *E*, 1920 *F, W, I, E*, 1921 *W, E*, 1922 *F, W, I, E*
Utterson, K N (Borders) 2003 *F, W* 1, *E* (R)

Valentine, A R (RNAS, Anthorn) 1953 *F, W, I*
Valentine, D D (Hawick) 1947 *I, E*
Veitch, J P (Royal HSFP) 1882 *E*, 1883 *I*, 1884 *W, I, E*, 1885 *I* 1,2, 1886 *E*
Villar, C (Edinburgh Wands) 1876 *E*, 1877 *I, E*

Waddell, G H (London Scottish, Cambridge U) 1957 *E*, 1958 *F, W, A, I, E*, 1959 *F, W, I, E*, 1960 *I, E, SA*, 1961 *F*, 1962 *F, W, I, E*
Waddell, H (Glasgow Acads) 1924 *F, W, I, E*, 1925 *I, E*, 1926 *F, W, I, E*, 1927 *F, W, I, E*, 1930 *W*
Wade, A L (London Scottish) 1908 *E*
Wainwright, R I (Edinburgh Acads, West Hartlepool, Watsonians, Army, Dundee HSFP) 1992 *I* (R), *F, A* 1,2, 1993 *NZ*, 1994 *W, E*, 1995 *C, I, F, W, E, R*, [*Iv, Tg, F, NZ*], *WS*, 1996 *I, F, W, E, NZ* 1,2, 1997 *W, E, I, F, SA*, 1998 *It, I, F, W, E, Fj, A* 1,2
Walker, A (W of Scotland) 1881 *I*, 1882 *E*, 1883 *W, I, E*
Walker, A W (Cambridge U, Birkenhead Park) 1931 *F, W, I, E*, 1932 *I*
Walker, J G (W of Scotland) 1882 *E*, 1883 *W*
Walker, M (Oxford U) 1952 *F*
Walker, N (Borders) 2002 *R, SA, Fj*
Wallace, A C (Oxford U) 1923 *F*, 1924 *F, W, E*, 1925 *F, W, I, E*, 1926 *F*
Wallace, W M (Cambridge U) 1913 *E*, 1914 *W, I, E*
Wallace, M I (Glasgow High Kelvinside) 1996 *A, It*, 1997 *W*
Walls, W A (Glasgow Acads) 1882 *E*, 1883 *W, I, E*, 1884 *W, I, E*, 1886 *W, I, E*
Walter, M W (London Scottish) 1906 *I, E, SA*, 1907 *W, I*, 1908 *W, I*, 1910 *I*
Walton, P (Northampton, Newcastle) 1994 *E, I, F, Arg* 1,2, 1995 [*Iv*], 1997 *W, E, I, F, SA* (R), 1998 *I, F, SA*, 1999 *W, E, It, I, F* (R), *Arg, R*, [*SA* (R), *U* (R), *Sp*]
Warren, J R (Glasgow Acads) 1914 *I*
Warren, R C (Glasgow Acads) 1922 *W, I*, 1930 *W, I, E*
Waters, F H (Cambridge U, London Scottish) 1930 *F, W, I, E*, 1932 *SA, W, I*
Waters, J A (Selkirk) 1933 *W, E, I*, 1934 *W, I, E*, 1935 *W, I, E, NZ*, 1936 *W, I, E*, 1937 *W, I, E*
Waters, J B (Cambridge U) 1904 *I, E*
Watherston, J G (Edinburgh Wands) 1934 *I, E*
Watherston, W R A (London Scottish) 1963 *F, W, I*
Watson, D H (Glasgow Acads) 1876 *E*, 1877 *I, E*
Watson, W S (Boroughmuir) 1974 *W, E, I, F*, 1975 *NZ*, 1977 *I, F, W*, 1979 *I, F*
Watt, A G J (Glasgow High Kelvinside) 1991 [*Z*], 1993 *I, NZ*, 1994 *Arg* 2(t & R)
Watt, A G M (Edinburgh Acads) 1947 *F, W, I, A*, 1948 *F, W*
Weatherstone, T G (Stewart's Coll FP) 1952 *E*, 1953 *I, E*, 1954 *F, NZ, I, E, W*, 1955 *F*, 1958 *W, A, I, E*, 1959 *W, I, E*
Webster, S (Edinburgh) 2003 *I* 2(R)
Weir, G W (Melrose, Newcastle) 1990 *Arg*, 1991 *R*, [*J, Z, I, WS, E, NZ*], 1992 *E, I, F, W, A* 1,2, 1993 *I, F, W, E, NZ*, 1994 *W* (R), *E, I, F, SA*, 1995 *F* (R), *W, E, R*, [*Iv, Tg, F, NZ*], *WS*, 1996 *I, F, W, E, NZ* 1,2, *A, It* (R), 1997 *W, E, I, F*, 1998 *It, I, F, W, E, SA*, 1999 *W, Arg* (R), *R* (R), [*SA* (R), *Sp, Sm, NZ*], 2000 *It* (R), *I* (R), *F*
Welsh, R (Watsonians) 1895 *W, I, E*, 1896 *W*
Welsh, R B (Hawick) 1967 *I, E*
Welsh, W B (Hawick) 1927 *A*, 1928 *F, W, I*, 1929 *I, E*, 1930 *F, W, I, E*, 1931 *F, W, I, E*, 1932 *SA, W, I, E*, 1933 *W, E, I*
Welsh, W H (Edinburgh U) 1900 *I, E*, 1901 *W, I, E*, 1902 *W, I, E*
Wemyss, A (Gala, Edinburgh Wands) 1914 *W, I*, 1920 *F, E*, 1922 *F, W, I*
West, L (Edinburgh U, West Hartlepool) 1903 *W, I, E*, 1905 *I, E, NZ*, 1906 *W, I, E*
Weston, V G (Kelvinside Acads) 1936 *I, E*
White, D B (Gala, London Scottish) 1982 *F, W, A* 1,2, 1987 *W, E*, [*F, R, NZ*], 1988 *I, F, W, E, A*, 1989 *W, E, I, F, Fj, R*, 1990 *I, F, W, E, NZ* 1,2, 1991 *F, W, E, I, R*, [*J, Z, I, WS, E, NZ*], 1992 *E, I, F, W*
White, D M (Kelvinside Acads) 1963 *F, W, I, E*
White, J P R (Glasgow) 2000 *E, NZ* 1,2, *US* (R), *A* (R), *Sm*, 2001 *F* (R), *I, Tg, Arg, NZ*, 2002 *E, It, I, F, W, C, US, SA* (R), *Fj*, 2003 *F* (R), *W* 1, *E, It* 1, *SA* 1,2, *It* 2
White, T B (Edinburgh Acads) 1888 *W, I*, 1889 *W*
Whittington, T P (Merchistonians) 1873 *E*
Whitworth, R J E (London Scottish) 1936 *I*
Whyte, D J (Edinburgh Wands) 1965 *W, I, E, SA*, 1966 *F, W, I, E, A*, 1967 *F, W, I, E*
Will, J G (Cambridge U) 1912 *F, W, I, E*, 1914 *W, I, E*
Wilson, A W (Dunfermline) 1931 *F, I, E*
Wilson, G A (Oxford U) 1949 *F, W, E*
Wilson, G R (Royal HSFP) 1886 *E*, 1890 *W, I, E*, 1891 *I*
Wilson, J H (Watsonians) 1953 *I*
Wilson, J S (St Andrew's U) 1931 *F, W, I, E*, 1932 *E*
Wilson, J S (United Services, London Scottish) 1908 *I*, 1909 *W*
Wilson, R (London Scottish) 1976 *E, I*, 1977 *E, I, F*, 1978 *I, F*, 1981 *R*, 1983 *I*
Wilson, R L (Gala) 1951 *F, W, I, E, SA*, 1953 *F, W, E*
Wilson, R W (W of Scotland) 1873 *E*, 1874 *E*
Wilson, S (Oxford U, London Scottish) 1964 *F, NZ, W, I, E*, 1965 *W, I, E, SA*, 1966 *F, W, I, A*, 1967 *F, W, I, E, NZ*, 1968 *F, W, I, E*
Wood, A (Royal HSFP) 1873 *E*, 1874 *E*, 1875 *E*
Wood, G (Gala) 1931 *W, I*, 1932 *W, I, E*
Woodburn, J C (Kelvinside Acads) 1892 *I*
Woodrow, A N (Glasgow Acads) 1887 *I, W, E*
Wotherspoon, W (W of Scotland) 1891 *I*, 1892 *I*, 1893 *W, E*, 1894 *W, I, E*
Wright, F A (Edinburgh Acads) 1932 *E*
Wright, H B (Watsonians) 1894 *W*
Wright, K M (London Scottish) 1929 *F, W, I, E*
Wright, P H (Boroughmuir) 1992 *A* 1,2, 1993 *F, W, E*, 1994 *W*, 1995 *C, I, F, W, E, R*, [*Iv, Tg, F, NZ*], 1996 *W, E, NZ* 1
Wright, R W J (Edinburgh Wands) 1973 *F*
Wright, S T H (Stewart's Coll FP) 1949 *E*
Wright, T (Hawick) 1947 *A*
Wyllie, D S (Stewart's-Melville FP) 1984 *A*, 1985 *W* (R), *E*, 1987 *I, F*, [*F, Z, R, NZ*], 1989 *R*, 1991 *R*, [*J* (R), *Z*], 1993 *NZ* (R), 1994 *W* (R), *E, I, F*

Young, A H (Edinburgh Acads) 1874 *E*
Young, E T (Glasgow Acads) 1914 *E*
Young, R G (Watsonians) 1970 *W*
Young, T E B (Durham) 1911 *F*
Young, W B (Cambridge U, London Scottish) 1937 *W, I, E*, 1938 *W, I, E*, 1939 *W, I, E*, 1948 *E*

IRELAND TEST SEASON REVIEW 2002-03

The Busiest Test Season to Date

Peter O'Reilly

It was entirely appropriate that Ireland's season should end with players dropping from exhaustion and dehydration in the searing 95°F heat of Apia. For this season was a test of endurance as much as anything else – 14 Test matches in the space of 10 months is by some distance the busiest international schedule in Ireland's history.

In terms of wins and losses, it was also one of the most profitable. A highly impressive success rate of 85% was a significant improvement on the previous term, when Ireland lost more often than they won. At one stage, Ireland had won a record 10 games in succession and Brian O'Driscoll, a surprise choice as skipper when Keith Wood got injured, was being hailed as Captain Fantastic. There was a truly heroic triumph over the world champion Wallabies and another victory against France – that's three wins from the last four games against *Les Tricolores*. Ireland also came within one victory of their first Grand Slam in over half a century.

Yet somehow, at the end of it all, there was still a sense of deflation among supporters. It's the price of success, of course – failure hits that much harder. And when failure comes as spectacularly as it did in games 11 and 12 on the programme, it's inevitable that there will be some disillusionment.

The end-of-season defeats to England and Australia served as a timely reminder of Ireland's real position in the world order. Eddie O'Sullivan's men can justifiably claim to have opened up some daylight between themselves and their Celtic cousins; they also have the organisation and the fire-power to cause problems for any of their superiors. Yet that doesn't put them in the same league as the superpowers of the game.

Against England, they played some of their best attacking rugby of the year yet still ended up on the end of a 42-6 hammering. Then came the re-match against the Australians in Perth, where injuries forced both teams into radical re-structuring. The Wallabies coped much better, walloping the tourists 45-16. The only conclusion to be drawn was that Ireland would still need quite a lot going for them if they are to realise their ambition of a first-ever World Cup semi-final slot. They'd need all their best players available, all playing at peak form. They'd probably need a bit of luck too.

One of the main reasons the calendar was so cluttered was Ireland's wretched performance at the previous World Cup – failure to emerge from their pool in 1999 meant they had to negotiate the qualifying route this time around. So it was that the players found themselves in the odd position of playing Test rugby in September.

They played like it was silly season, too. There was very little impressive in their victories over Russia and Georgia, or in their warm-up game against Romania in Thomond Park – Limerick's first Ireland Test match in over a century. To make matters worse, there was a major casualty of the long and punishing trip to the Siberian city of Krasnoyarsk, where Ireland played Russia. Keith Wood hurt his neck during the game at the Centralny Stadium and then aggravated the injury on the cramped flight home.

It was to be Wood's last full game for the season – having sorted his neck out, he then picked up a serious shoulder injury while playing for Harlequins. In previous years, this would have been a disaster. Not only did O'Sullivan come up with a solution for the November Tests against Australia and Argentina (both World Cup pool opponents), he found one that gave the team an added dimension.

In Wood's absence, the ball-carrying role went to Victor Costello, the 31-year-old from Leinster who had barely featured for Ireland in four seasons. When it transpired that both games would be played in a downpour on a Lansdowne Road pitch with serious drainage problems, Costello's role became even more significant. Not only did he deliver on the yardage front, he also defended well out of position at blind-side flanker and provided a target for Shane Byrne at the line-out.

Byrne was the other Leinster player to benefit from Wood's absence. In fact, there were as many as six Leinster forwards on the field at one stage in the game against the Pumas – appropriate enough given Leinster would be the form team in Europe.

Yet none of the forwards' grunt would have counted for much were it not for the phenomenal place-kicking of Ronan O'Gara. The Munster out-half ignored the appalling conditions to kick a perfect ten out of ten place kicks in the games against Australia and Argentina. Having established himself as Ireland's first-choice out-half, he was horribly unfortunate to be the victim of a cynical ankle-stamp by Neath flanker Brett Sinkinson during the Celtic League final, only a fortnight before the beginning of the Six Nations championship.

In this instance, the beneficiary was David Humphreys. The Ulster pivot scored 26 points as Ireland ended an 18-year drought in Murrayfield against a wretchedly weak Scottish side. Then, six days later in Rome, he overcame a second consecutive nervy start to score 17 more against Italy. Even if O'Gara was now fit again, he wasn't going to dislodge his rival.

Ireland's primary concern coming into the game against France was the scrum – Reggie Corrigan had fractured his wrist in Rome and there were fears that his replacement Marcus Horan would be exposed by the French scrum. They proved unfounded. What's more, Ireland produced another stirring defensive effort in poor conditions at Lansdowne Road to squeeze home 15-12 – so far they had conceded the grand total of one try in three championship games.

Three down, two to go. Already, O'Sullivan was banning any mention of the words 'grand' and 'slam'. Wales in Cardiff should have been a formality

Ireland's Kevin Maggs is tackled by Seremaia Bai of Fiji during the match at Lansdowne Road on November 17, 2002. Ireland won 64-17, Maggs scoring a hat trick of tries.

– after all, weren't Ireland unbeaten there since 1983? As it turned out they conceded three tries to two and had to rely on a late, late drop-goal by substitute O'Gara to win by a point.

It was all set up for a splendid Grand Slam Sunday at the end of March, which transpired to be a massive anti-climax. It wasn't that Ireland played particularly badly, just that England were in a different league. Mike Ford's defence system, which had been one of the real success stories of the season, crumbled under the weight of English pressure to yield five tries, four of them in the final quarter.

After this sobering experience, and with the players needing rest before the World Cup, the last thing O'Sullivan needed was a summer tour. Senior players like O'Driscoll, Denis Hickie and John Hayes cried off injured and those who made it to Perth for the one-off Test against Australia played like they were already in holiday mode. Once again, the defence system failed as six tries were leaked.

O'Sullivan can look back and take comfort from an exceptional win-loss ratio and several other things. There was the brilliance of Geordan Murphy, who vied with Malcolm O'Kelly for player of the season. There was the re-emergence of Costello and Corrigan as international forces, and the first appearance in an Irish shirt of Donncha O'Callaghan, a startling talent.

As he took a well-earned rest, there was plenty for the coach to ponder, not least the fact that the next season would be almost as busy as the last – if that were possible.

Ireland's Test Record in 2002-2003: Played 17, won 15, lost 2

Opponents	*Date*	*Venue*	*Result*
Scotland	6th September 2003	A	Won 29-10
Italy	30th August 2003	H	Won 61-6
Wales	16th August 2003	H	Won 35-12
Samoa	20th June 2003	A	Won 40-14
Tonga	14th June 2003	A	Won 40-19
Australia	7th June 2003	A	Lost 16-45
England	30th March 2003	H	Lost 6-42
Wales	22nd March 2003	A	Won 25-24
France	8th March 2003	H	Won 15-12
Italy	22nd February 2003	A	Won 37-13
Scotland	16th February 2003	A	Won 36-6
Argentina	23rd November 2002	H	Won 16-7
Fiji	17th November 2002	H	Won 64-17
Australia	9th November 2002	H	Won 18-9
Georgia	28th September 2002	H	Won 63-14
Russia	21st September 2002	A	Won 35-3
Romania	7th September 2002	H	Won 39-8

IRELAND INTERNATIONAL STATISTICS

(up to 30 September 2003)

Match Records

MOST CONSECUTIVE TEST WINS

10 2002 *R, Ru, Gg, A, Fj, Arg,* 2003 *S* 1, *It* 1, *F, W* 1

6 1968 *S, W, A,* 1969 *F, E, S*

MOST CONSECUTIVE TESTS WITHOUT DEFEAT

Matches	*Wins*	*Draws*	*Period*
10	10	0	2002 to 2003
7	6	1	1968 to 1969
5	4	1	1972 to 1973

MOST POINTS IN A MATCH

by the team

Pts	*Opponents*	*Venue*	*Year*
83	United States	Manchester (NH)	2000
78	Japan	Dublin	2000
70	Georgia	Dublin	1998
64	Fiji	Dublin	2002
63	Georgia	Dublin	2002
61	Italy	Limerick	2003
60	Romania	Dublin	1986
60	Italy	Dublin	2000
55	Zimbabwe	Dublin	1991
54	Wales	Dublin	2002
53	Romania	Dublin	1998
53	United States	Dublin	1999
50	Japan	Bloemfontein	1995

by a player

Pts	*Player*	*Opponents*	*Venue*	*Year*
32	R J R O'Gara	Samoa	Apia	2003
30	R J R O'Gara	Italy	Dublin	2000
26	D G Humphreys	Scotland	Murrayfield	2003
26	D G Humphreys	Italy	Limerick	2003
24	P A Burke	Italy	Dublin	1997
24	D G Humphreys	Argentina	Lens	1999
23	R P Keyes	Zimbabwe	Dublin	1991
23	R J R O'Gara	Japan	Dublin	2000
22	D G Humphreys	Wales	Dublin	2002
21	S O Campbell	Scotland	Dublin	1982
21	S O Campbell	England	Dublin	1983
21	R J R O'Gara	Italy	Rome	2001
20	M J Kiernan	Romania	Dublin	1986
20	E P Elwood	Romania	Dublin	1993
20	S J P Mason	Samoa	Dublin	1996
20	E P Elwood	Georgia	Dublin	1998
20	K G M Wood	United States	Dublin	1999
20	D A Hickie	Italy	Limerick	2003

MOST TRIES IN A MATCH

by the team

Tries	*Opponents*	*Venue*	*Year*
13	United States	Manchester (NH)	2000
11	Japan	Dublin	2000
10	Romania	Dublin	1986
10	Georgia	Dublin	1998
9	Fiji	Dublin	2003
8	Western Samoa	Dublin	1988
8	Zimbabwe	Dublin	1991
8	Georgia	Dublin	2002
8	Italy	Limerick	2003
7	Japan	Bloemfontein	1995
7	Romania	Dublin	1998
7	United States	Dublin	1999

by a player

Tries	*Player*	*Opponents*	*Venue*	*Year*
4	B F Robinson	Zimbabwe	Dublin	1991
4	K G M Wood	United States	Dublin	1999
4	D A Hickie	Italy	Limerick	2003
3	R Montgomery	Wales	Birkenhead	1887
3	J P Quinn	France	Cork	1913
3	E O'D Davy	Scotland	Murrayfield	1930
3	S J Byrne	Scotland	Murrayfield	1953
3	K D Crossan	Romania	Dublin	1986
3	B J Mullin	Tonga	Brisbane	1987
3	M R Mostyn	Argentina	Dublin	1999
3	B G O'Driscoll	France	Paris	2000
3	M J Mullins	United States	Manchester (NH)	2000
3	D A Hickie	Japan	Dublin	2000
3	R A J Henderson	Italy	Rome	2001
3	B G O'Driscoll	Scotland	Dublin	2002
3	K M Maggs	Fiji	Dublin	2002

MOST CONVERSIONS IN A MATCH

by the team

Cons	*Opponents*	*Venue*	*Year*
10	Georgia	Dublin	1998
10	Japan	Dublin	2000
9	United States	Manchester (NH)	2000
7	Romania	Dublin	1986
7	Georgia	Dublin	2002
6	Japan	Bloemfontein	1995

6	Romania	Dublin	1998
6	United States	Dublin	1999
6	Italy	Dublin	2000
6	Italy	Limerick	2003

by a player

Cons	Player	Opponents	Venue	Year
10	E P Elwood	Georgia	Dublin	1998
10	R J R O'Gara	Japan	Dublin	2000
8	R J R O'Gara	United States	Manchester (NH)	2000
7	M J Kiernan	Romania	Dublin	1986
6	P A Burke	Japan	Bloemfontein	1995
6	R J R O'Gara	Italy	Dublin	2000
6	D G Humphreys	Italy	Limerick	2003
5	M J Kiernan	Canada	Dunedin	1987
5	E P Elwood	Romania	Dublin	1999
5	R J R O'Gara	Georgia	Dublin	2002
5	D G Humphreys	Fiji	Dublin	2002

MOST PENALTIES IN A MATCH

by the team

Penalties	Opponents	Venue	Year
8	Italy	Dublin	1997
7	Argentina	Lens	1999
6	Scotland	Dublin	1982
6	Romania	Dublin	1993
6	United States	Atlanta	1996
6	Western Samoa	Dublin	1996
6	Italy	Dublin	2000
6	Wales	Dublin	2002
6	Australia	Dublin	2002
6	Samoa	Apia	2003

by a player

Penalties	Player	Opponents	Venue	Year
8	P A Burke	Italy	Dublin	1997
7	D G Humphreys	Argentina	Lens	1999
6	S O Campbell	Scotland	Dublin	1982
6	E P Elwood	Romania	Dublin	1993
6	S J P Mason	Western Samoa	Dublin	1996
6	R J R O'Gara	Italy	Dublin	2000
6	D G Humphreys	Wales	Dublin	2002
6	R J R O'Gara	Australia	Dublin	2002

MOST DROPPED GOALS IN A MATCH

by the team

Drops	Opponents	Venue	Year
2	Australia	Dublin	1967
2	France	Dublin	1975
2	Australia	Sydney	1979
2	England	Dublin	1981
2	Canada	Dunedin	1987
2	England	Dublin	1993
2	Wales	Wembley	1999
2	New Zealand	Dublin	2001

by a player

Drops	Player	Opponents	Venue	Year
2	C M H Gibson	Australia	Dublin	1967
2	W M McCombe	France	Dublin	1975
2	S O Campbell	Australia	Sydney	1979
2	E P Elwood	England	Dublin	1993
2	D G Humphreys	Wales	Wembley	1999
2	D G Humphreys	New Zealand	Dublin	2001

Career Records

MOST CAPPED PLAYERS

Caps	Player	Career Span
69	C M H Gibson	1964 to 1979
63	W J McBride	1962 to 1975
61	J F Slattery	1970 to 1984
59	P S Johns	1990 to 2000
58	P A Orr	1976 to 1987
56	D G Humphreys	1996 to 2003
55	B J Mullin	1984 to 1995
54	T J Kiernan	1960 to 1973
54	P M Clohessy	1993 to 2002
53	K M Maggs	1997 to 2003
53	K G M Wood	1994 to 2003
52	D G Lenihan	1981 to 1992
52	M E O'Kelly	1997 to 2003
51	M I Keane	1974 to 1984
48	N J Popplewell	1989 to 1998

MOST CONSECUTIVE TESTS

Tests	Player	Span
52	W J McBride	1964 to 1975
49	P A Orr	1976 to 1986
43	D G Lenihan	1981 to 1989
39	M I Keane	1974 to 1981
37	G V Stephenson	1920 to 1929

MOST TESTS AS CAPTAIN

Tests	Captain	Span
31	K G M Wood	1996 to 2003
24	T J Kiernan	1963 to 1973
19	C F Fitzgerald	1982 to 1986
17	J F Slattery	1979 to 1981
17	D G Lenihan	1986 to 1990

MOST TESTS IN INDIVIDUAL POSITIONS

Position	Player	Tests	Span
Full-back	T J Kiernan	54	1960 to 1973
Wing	K D Crossan	41	1982 to 1992
Centre	B J Mullin	55	1984 to 1995
Fly-half	D G Humphreys	52	1996 to 2003
Scrum-half	M T Bradley	40	1984 to 1995
Prop	P A Orr	58	1976 to 1987
Hooker	K G M Wood	52	1994 to 2003
Lock	W J McBride	63	1962 to 1975
Flanker	J F Slattery	61	1970 to 1984
No 8	A G Foley	41	1995 to 2003

Humphreys, Foley and Wood have also been capped elsewhere in the team

MOST POINTS IN TESTS

Points	Player	Tests	Career
465*	D G Humphreys	56	1996 to 2003
323	R J R O'Gara	32	2000 to 2003
308	M J Kiernan	43	1982 to 1991
296	E P Elwood	35	1993 to 1999
217	S O Campbell	22	1976 to 1984
158	T J Kiernan	54	1960 to 1973
113	A J P Ward	19	1978 to 1987

** Humphreys's total includes a penalty try against Scotland in 1999*

MOST TRIES IN TESTS

Tries	Player	Tests	Career
20	D A Hickie	40	1997 to 2003
18	B G O'Driscoll	41	1999 to 2003
17	B J Mullin	55	1984 to 1995
14	G V Stephenson	42	1920 to 1930
14	K G M Wood	53	1994 to 2003
13	K M Maggs	53	1997 to 2003
12	K D Crossan	41	1982 to 1992
11	A T A Duggan	25	1963 to 1972
11	S P Geoghegan	37	1991 to 1996

MOST CONVERSIONS IN TESTS

Cons	Player	Tests	Career
59	R J R O'Gara	33	2000 to 2003
57	D G Humphreys	56	1996 to 2003
43	E P Elwood	35	1993 to 1999
40	M J Kiernan	43	1982 to 1991
26	T J Kiernan	54	1960 to 1973
16	R A Lloyd	19	1910 to 1920
15	S O Campbell	22	1976 to 1984

MOST PENALTY GOALS IN TESTS

Penalties	Player	Tests	Career
99	D G Humphreys	56	1996 to 2003
68	E P Elwood	35	1993 to 1999
62	M J Kiernan	43	1982 to 1991
61	R J R O'Gara	33	2000 to 2003
54	S O Campbell	22	1976 to 1984
31	T J Kiernan	54	1960 to 1973
29	A J P Ward	19	1978 to 1987

MOST DROPPED GOALS IN TESTS

Drops	Player	Tests	Career
8	D G Humphreys	56	1996 to 2003
7	R A Lloyd	19	1910 to 1920
7	S O Campbell	22	1976 to 1984
6	C M H Gibson	69	1964 to 1979
6	B J McGann	25	1969 to 1976
6	M J Kiernan	43	1982 to 1991

International Championship Records

Record	Detail		Set
Most points in season	168	in five matches	2000
Most tries in season	17	in five matches	2000
Highest Score	60	60-13 v Italy	2000
Biggest win	47	60-13 v Italy	2000
Highest score conceded	50	18-50 v England	2000
Biggest defeat	40	6-46 v England	1997
Most appearances	56	C M H Gibson	1964 – 1979
Most points in matches	269	D G Humphreys	1996 – 2003
Most points in season	73	D G Humphreys	2003
Most points in match	30	R J R O'Gara	v Italy, 2000
Most tries in matches	14	G V Stephenson	1920 – 1930
Most tries in season	5	J E Arigho	1928

	5	B G O'Driscoll	2000
Most tries in match	3	R Montgomery	v Wales, 1887
	3	J P Quinn	v France, 1913
	3	E O'D Davy	v Scotland, 1930
	3	S J Byrne	v Scotland, 1953
	3	B G O'Driscoll	v France, 2000
	3	R A J Henderson	v Italy, 2001
	3	B G O'Driscoll	v Scotland, 2002
Most cons in matches	24	D G Humphreys	1996 – 2003
Most cons in season	11	R J R O'Gara	2000
Most cons in match	6	R J R O'Gara	v Italy, 2000
Most pens in matches	62	D G Humphreys	1996 – 2003
Most pens in season	16	D G Humphreys	2002
	16	D G Humphreys	2003
Most pens in match	6	S O Campbell	v Scotland, 1982
	6	R J R O'Gara	v Italy, 2000
	6	D G Humphreys	v Wales, 2002
Most drops in matches	7	R A Lloyd	1910 – 1920
Most drops in season	2	on several	Occasions
Most drops in match	2	W M McCombe	v France, 1975
	2	E P Elwood	v England, 1993
	2	D G Humphreys	v Wales, 1999

Miscellaneous Records

Record	*Holder*	*Detail*
Longest Test Career	A J F O'Reilly	16 seasons, 1954-55 to 1969-70
	C M H Gibson	16 seasons, 1963-64 to 1979
Youngest Test Cap	F S Hewitt	17 yrs 157 days in 1924
Oldest Test Cap	C M H Gibson	36 yrs 195 days in 1979

Career Records of Ireland International Players
(up to 30 September 2003)

PLAYER	*Debut*	*Caps*	*T*	*C*	*P*	*D*	*Pts*
Backs:							
J C Bell	1994 v A	36	8	0	0	0	40
J P Bishop	1998 v SA	25	8	0	0	0	40
P A Burke	1995 v E	13	0	12	27	1	108
D J Crotty	1996 v A	5	0	0	0	0	0
G M D'Arcy	1999 v R	5	0	0	0	0	0
G T Dempsey	1998 v Gg	38	10	0	0	0	50
G Easterby	2000 v US	19	5	0	0	0	25
R A J Henderson	1996 v WS	29	6	0	0	0	30
D A Hickie	1997 v W	40	20	0	0	0	100
A P Horgan	2003 v Sm	3	1	0	0	0	5
S P Horgan	2000 v S	19	8	0	0	0	40
T G Howe	2000 v US	10	4	0	0	0	20
D G Humphreys	1996 v F	56	6*	57	99	8	465
J P Kelly	2002 v It	13	7	0	0	0	35
M McHugh	2003 v Tg	1	1	0	0	0	5
K M Maggs	1997 v NZ	53	13	0	0	0	65
S J P Mason	1996 v W	3	0	3	12	0	42
M R Mostyn	1999 v A	6	3	0	0	0	15

M J Mullins	1999 v Arg	16	3	0	0	0	15
G E A Murphy	2000 v US	20	10	1	0	1	55
B G O'Driscoll	1999 v A	41	18	0	0	3	99
R J R O'Gara	2000 v S	33	5	59	61	2	332
B T O'Meara	1997 v E	9	0	0	0	0	0
J W Staunton	2001 v Sm	1	1	0	0	0	5
P A Stringer	2000 v S	36	2	0	0	0	10
T A Tierney	1999 v A	8	1	0	0	0	5
J A Topping	1996 v WS	8	1	0	0	0	5
Forwards:							
S J Best	2003 v Tg	3	0	0	0	0	0
T Brennan	1998 v SA	12	0	0	0	0	0
E Byrne	2001 v It	9	0	0	0	0	0
J S Byrne	2001 v R	22	1	0	0	0	5
R E Casey	1999 v A	5	0	0	0	0	0
R Corrigan	1997 v C	26	0	0	0	0	0
V C P Costello	1996 v US	32	3	0	0	0	15
L F M Cullen	2002 v NZ	14	0	0	0	0	0
J W Davidson	1995 v Fj	32	0	0	0	0	0
K Dawson	1997 v NZ	21	2	0	0	0	10
S H Easterby	2000 v S	23	4	0	0	0	20
J M Fitzpatrick	1998 v SA	26	0	0	0	0	0
A G Foley	1995 v E	45	3	0	0	0	15
M J Galwey	1991 v F	41	3	0	0	0	15
K D Gleeson	2002 v W	16	4	0	0	0	20
J J Hayes	2000 v S	34	1	0	0	0	5
M J Horan	2000 v US	12	0	0	0	0	0
G W Longwell	2000 v J	25	1	0	0	0	5
A McCullen	2003 v Sm	1	0	0	0	0	0
E R P Miller	1997 v It	35	3	0	0	0	15
P J O'Connell	2002 v W	10	3	0	0	0	15
D O'Callaghan	2003 v W	5	0	0	0	0	0
M R O'Driscoll	2001 v R	2	0	0	0	0	0
M E O'Kelly	1997 v NZ	54	5	0	0	0	25
A Quinlan	1999 v R	16	2	0	0	0	10
F J Sheahan	2000 v US	13	1	0	0	0	5
P M Shields	2003 v Sm	2	0	0	0	0	0
D P Wallace	2000 v Arg	18	2	0	0	0	10
P S Wallace	1995 v J	45	5	0	0	0	25
A J Ward	1998 v F	28	3	0	0	0	15
K G M Wood	1994 v A	53	14	0	0	0	70

* Humphreys's figures include a penalty try awarded against Scotland in 1999

IRISH INTERNATIONAL PLAYERS

(up to 30 September 2003)

Note: Years given for International Championship matches are for second half of season; eg 1972 means season 1971-72. Years for all other matches refer to the actual year of the match. When a series has taken place, figures have been used to denote the particular matches in which players have featured. Thus 1981 *SA* 2 indicates that a player appeared in the second Test of the series.

Abraham, M (Bective Rangers) 1912 *E, S, W, SA*, 1914 *W*
Adams, C (Old Wesley), 1908 *E*, 1909 *E, F*, 1910 *F*, 1911 *E, S, W, F*, 1912 *S, W, SA*, 1913 *W, F*, 1914 *F, E, S*
Agar, R D (Malone) 1947 *F, E, S, W*, 1948 *F*, 1949 *S, W*, 1950 *F, E, W*
Agnew, P J (CIYMS) 1974 *F* (R), 1976 *A*
Ahearne, T (Queen's Coll, Cork) 1899 *E*
Aherne, L F P (Dolphin, Lansdowne) 1988 *E* 2, *WS, It*, 1989 *F, W, E, S, NZ*, 1990 *E, S, F, W* (R), 1992 *E, S, F, A*
Alexander, R (NIFC, Police Union) 1936 *E, S, W*, 1937 *E, S, W*, 1938 *E, S*, 1939 *E, S, W*
Allen, C E (Derry, Liverpool) 1900 *E, S, W*, 1901 *E, S, W*, 1903 *S, W*, 1904 *E, S, W*, 1905 *E, S, W, NZ*, 1906 *E, S, W, SA*, 1907 *S, W*
Allen, G G (Derry, Liverpool) 1896 *E, S, W*, 1897 *E, S*, 1898 *E, S*, 1899 *E, W*
Allen, T C (NIFC) 1885 *E, S* 1
Allen, W S (Wanderers) 1875 *E*
Allison, J B (Edinburgh U) 1899 *E, S*, 1900 *E, S, W*, 1901 *E, S, W*, 1902 *E, S, W*, 1903 *S*
Anderson, F E (Queen's U, Belfast, NIFC) 1953 *F, E, S, W*, 1954 *NZ, F, E, S, W*, 1955 *F, E, S, W*
Anderson, H J (Old Wesley) 1903 *E, S*, 1906 *E, S*
Anderson, W A (Dungannon) 1984 *A*, 1985 *S, F, W, E*, 1986 *F, S, R*, 1987 *E, S, F, W*, [*W, C, Tg, A*], 1988 *S, F, W, E* 1,2, 1989 *F, W, E, NZ*, 1990 *E, S*
Andrews, G (NIFC) 1875 *E*, 1876 *E*
Andrews, H W (NIFC) 1888 *M*, 1889 *S, W*
Archer, A M (Dublin U, NIFC) 1879 *S*
Arigho, J E (Lansdowne) 1928 *F, E, W*, 1929 *F, E, S, W*, 1930 *F, E, S, W*, 1931 *F, E, S, W, SA*
Armstrong, W K (NIFC) 1960 *SA*, 1961 *E*
Arnott, D T (Lansdowne) 1876 *E*
Ash, W H (NIFC) 1875 *E*, 1876 *E*, 1877 *S*
Aston, H R (Dublin U) 1908 *E, W*
Atkins, A P (Bective Rangers) 1924 *F*
Atkinson, J M (NIFC) 1927 *F, A*
Atkinson, J R (Dublin U) 1882 *W, S*

Bagot, J C (Dublin U, Lansdowne) 1879 *S, E*, 1880 *E, S*, 1881 *S*
Bailey, A H (UC Dublin, Lansdowne) 1934 *W*, 1935 *E, S, W, NZ*, 1936 *E, S, W*, 1937 *E, S, W*, 1938 *E, S*
Bailey, N (Northampton) 1952 *E*
Bardon, M E (Bohemians) 1934 *E*
Barlow, M (Wanderers) 1875 *E*
Barnes, R J (Dublin U, Armagh) 1933 *W*
Barr, A (Methodist Coll, Belfast) 1898 *W*, 1899 *S*, 1901 *E, S*
Barry, N J (Garryowen) 1991 *Nm* 2(R)
Beamish, C E St J (RAF, Leicester) 1933 *W, S*, 1934 *S, W*, 1935 *E, S, W, NZ*, 1936 *E, S, W*, 1938 *W*
Beamish, G R (RAF, Leicester) 1925 *E, S, W*, 1928 *F, E, S, W*, 1929 *F, E, S, W*, 1930 *F, S, W*, 1931 *F, E, S, W, SA*, 1932 *E, S, W*, 1933 *E, W, S*
Beatty, W J (NIFC, Richmond) 1910 *F*, 1912 *F, W*
Becker, V A (Lansdowne) 1974 *F, W*
Beckett, G G P (Dublin U) 1908 *E, S, W*
Bell, J C (Ballymena, Northampton, Dungannon) 1994 *A* 1,2, *US*, 1995 *S, It*, [*NZ, W, F*], *Fj*, 1996 *US, S, F, W, E, WS, A*, 1997 *It* 1, *F, W, E, S*, 1998 *Gg, R, SA* 3, 1999 *F, W, S It* (R), *A* 2, [*US* (R), *A* 3(R), *R*], 2001 *R* (R), 2003 *Tg, Sm, It* 2(R)
Bell, R J (NIFC) 1875 *E*, 1876 *E*
Bell, W E (Belfast Collegians) 1953 *F, E, S, W*
Bennett, F (Belfast Collegians) 1913 *S*
Bent, G C (Dublin U) 1882 *W, E*
Berkery, P J (Lansdowne) 1954 *W*, 1955 *W*, 1956 *S, W*, 1957 *F, E, S, W*, 1958 *A, E, S*
Bermingham, J J C (Blackrock Coll) 1921 *E, S, W, F*
Best, S J (Belfast Harlequins) 2003 *Tg* (R), *W* 2, *S* 2(R)
Bishop, J P (London Irish) 1998 *SA*, 1,2, *Gg, R, SA* 3, 1999 *F, W, E, S, It, A* 1,2, *Arg* 1, [*US, A* 3, *Arg* 2], 2000 *E, Arg, C*, 2002 *NZ* 1,2, *Fj, Arg*, 2003 *W* 1, *E*
Blackham, J C (Queen's Coll, Cork) 1909 *S, W, F*, 1910 *E, S, W*
Blake-Knox, S E F (NIFC) 1976 *E, S*, 1977 *F* (R)
Blayney, J J (Wanderers) 1950 *S*
Bond, A T W (Derry) 1894 *S, W*
Bornemann, W W (Wanderers) 1960 *E, S, W, SA*
Bowen, D St J (Cork Const) 1977 *W, E, S*
Boyd, C A (Dublin U) 1900 *S*, 1901 *S, W*
Boyle, C V (Dublin U) 1935 *NZ*, 1936 *E, S, W*, 1937 *E, S, W*, 1938 *W*, 1939 *W*
Brabazon, H M (Dublin U) 1884 *E*, 1885 *S* 1, 1886 *E*
Bradley, M J (Dolphin) 1920 *W, F*, 1922 *E, S, W, F*, 1923 *E, S, W, F*, 1925 *F, S, W*, 1926 *F, E, S, W*, 1927 *F, W*
Bradley, M T (Cork Constitution) 1984 *A*, 1985 *S, F, W, E*, 1986 *F, W, E, S, R*, 1987 *E, S, F, W*, [*W, C, Tg, A*], 1988 *S, F, W, E* 1, 1990 *W*, 1992 *NZ* 1,2, 1993 *S, F, W, E, R*, 1994 *F, W, E, S, A* 1,2, *US*, 1995 *S, F*, [*NZ*]
Bradshaw, G (Belfast Collegians) 1903 *W*
Bradshaw, R M (Wanderers) 1885 *E, S* 1,2
Brady, A M (UC Dublin, Malone) 1966 *S*, 1968 *E, S, W*
Brady, J A (Wanderers) 1976 *E, S*
Brady, J R (CIYMS) 1951 *S, W*, 1953 *F, E, S, W*, 1954 *W*, 1956 *W*, 1957 *F, E, S, W*
Bramwell, T (NIFC) 1928 *F*
Brand, T N (NIFC) 1924 *NZ*
Brennan, J I (CIYMS) 1957 *S, W*
Brennan, T (St Mary's Coll, Barnhall) 1998 *SA* 1(R),2(R), 1999 *F* (R), *S* (R), *It, A* 2, *Arg* 1, [*US, A* 3], 2000 *E* (R), 2001 *W* (R), *E* (R), *Sm* (R)
Bresnihan, F P K (UC Dublin, Lansdowne, London Irish) 1966 *E, W*, 1967 *A* 1, *E, S, W, F*, 1968 *F, E, S, W, A*, 1969 *F, E, S, W*, 1970 *SA, F, E, S, W*, 1971 *F, E, S, W*
Brett, J T (Monkstown) 1914 *W*
Bristow, J R (NIFC) 1879 *E*
Brophy, N H (Blackrock Coll, UC Dublin, London Irish) 1957 *F, E*, 1959 *E, S, W, F*, 1960 *F, SA*, 1961 *S, W*, 1962 *E, S, W*, 1963 *E, W*, 1967 *E, S, W, F, A* 2
Brown, E L (Instonians) 1958 *F*
Brown, G S (Monkstown, United Services) 1912 *S, W, SA*
Brown, H (Windsor) 1877 *E*
Brown, T (Windsor) 1877 *E, S*
Brown, W H (Dublin U) 1899 *E*
Brown, W J (Malone) 1970 *SA, F, S, W*
Brown, W S (Dublin U) 1893 *S, W*, 1894 *E, S, W*
Browne, A W (Dublin U) 1951 *SA*
Browne, D (Blackrock Coll) 1920 *F*
Browne, H C (United Services and RN) 1929 *E, S, W*
Browne, W F (United Services and Army) 1925 *E, S, W*, 1926 *S, W*, 1927 *F, E, S, W, A*, 1928 *E, S*
Browning, D R (Wanderers) 1881 *E, S*
Bruce, S A M (NIFC) 1883 *E, S*, 1884 *E*
Brunker, A A (Lansdowne) 1895 *E, W*
Bryant, C H (Cardiff) 1920 *E, S*
Buchanan, A McM (Dublin U) 1926 *E, S, W*, 1927 *S, W, A*
Buchanan, J W B (Dublin U) 1882 *S*, 1884 *E, S*
Buckley, J H (Sunday's Well) 1973 *E, S*
Bulger, L Q (Lansdowne) 1896 *E, S, W*, 1897 *E, S*, 1898 *E, S, W*
Bulger, M J (Dublin U) 1888 *M*
Burges, J H (Rosslyn Park) 1950 *F, E*
Burgess, R B (Dublin U) 1912 *SA*
Burke, P A (Cork Constitution, Bristol, Harlequins) 1995 *E, S, W* (R), *It*, [*J*], *Fj*, 1996 *US* (R), *A*, 1997 *It* 1, *S* (R), 2001 *R* (R), 2003 *S* 1(R), *Sm* (R)
Burkitt, J C S (Queen's Coll, Cork) 1881 *E*
Burns, I J (Wanderers) 1980 *E* (R)
Butler, L G (Blackrock Coll) 1960 *W*
Butler, N (Bective Rangers) 1920 *E*

Byers, R M (NIFC) 1928 *S, W*, 1929 *E, S, W*
Byrne, E (St Mary's Coll) 2001 *It* (R), *F* (R), *S* (R), *W* (R), *E* (R), *Sm, NZ* (R), 2003 *A* (R), *Sm* (R)
Byrne, E M J (Blackrock Coll) 1977 *S, F*, 1978 *F, W, E, NZ*
Byrne, J S (Blackrock Coll) 2001 *R* (R), 2002 *W* (R), *E* (R), *S* (R), *It, NZ* 2(R), *R, Ru* (R), *Gg, A, Arg*, 2003 *S* 1, *It* 1, *F, W* 1, *E, A, Tg, Sm, W* 2(R), *It* 2, *S* 2(R)
Byrne, N F (UC Dublin) 1962 *F*
Byrne, S J (UC Dublin, Lansdowne) 1953 *S, W*, 1955 *F*
Byron, W G (NIFC) 1896 *E, S, W*, 1897 *E, S*, 1898 *E, S, W*, 1899 *E, S, W*

Caddell, E D (Dublin U, Wanderers) 1904 *S*, 1905 *E, S, W, NZ*, 1906 *E, S, W, SA*, 1907 *E, S*, 1908 *S, W*
Cagney, S J (London Irish) 1925 *W*, 1926 *F, E, S, W*, 1927 *F*, 1928 *E, S, W*, 1929 *F, E, S, W*
Callan, C P (Lansdowne) 1947 *F, E, S, W*, 1948 *F, E, S, W*, 1949 *F, E*
Cameron, E D (Bective Rangers) 1891 *S, W*
Campbell, C E (Old Wesley) 1970 *SA*
Campbell, E F (Monkstown) 1899 *S, W*, 1900 *E, W*
Campbell, S B B (Derry) 1911 *E, S, W, F*, 1912 *F, E, S, W, SA*, 1913 *E, S, F*
Campbell, S O (Old Belvedere) 1976 *A*, 1979 *A* 1,2, 1980 *E, S, F, W*, 1981 *F, W, E, S, SA* 1, 1982 *W, E, S, F*, 1983 *S, F, W, E*, 1984 *F, W*
Canniffe, D M (Lansdowne) 1976 *W, E*
Cantrell, J L (UC Dublin, Blackrock Coll) 1976 *A, F, W, E, S*, 1981 *S, SA* 1,2, *A*
Carey, R W (Dungannon) 1992 *NZ* 1,2
Carpendale, M J (Monkstown) 1886 *S*, 1887 *W*, 1888 *W, S*
Carr, N J (Ards) 1985 *S, F, W, E*, 1986 *W, E, S, R*, 1987 *E, S, W*
Carroll, C (Bective Rangers) 1930 *F*
Carroll, R (Lansdowne) 1947 *F*, 1950 *S, W*
Casement, B N (Dublin U) 1875 *E*, 1876 *E*, 1879 *E*
Casement, F (Dublin U) 1906 *E, S, W*
Casey, J C (Young Munster) 1930 *S*, 1932 *E*
Casey, P J (UC Dublin, Lansdowne) 1963 *F, E, S, W, NZ*, 1964 *E, S, W, F*, 1965 *F, E, S*
Casey, R E (Blackrock Coll) 1999 [*A* 3(t), *Arg* 2(R)], 2000 *E, US* (R), *C* (R)
Chambers, J (Dublin U) 1886 *E, S*, 1887 *E, S, W*
Chambers, R R (Instonians) 1951 *F, E, S, W*, 1952 *F, W*
Clancy, T P J (Lansdowne) 1988 *W, E* 1,2, *WS, It*, 1989 *F, W, E, S*
Clarke, A T H (Northampton, Dungannon) 1995 *Fj* (R), 1996 *W, E, WS*, 1997 *F* (R), *It* 2(R), 1998 *Gg* (R), *R*
Clarke, C P (Terenure Coll) 1993 *F, W, E*, 1998 *W, E*
Clarke, D J (Dolphin) 1991 *W, Nm* 1,2, [*J, A*], 1992 *NZ* 2(R)
Clarke, J A B (Bective Rangers) 1922 *S, W, F*, 1923 *F*, 1924 *E, S, W*
Clegg, R J (Bangor) 1973 *F*, 1975 *E, S, F, W*
Clifford, J T (Young Munster) 1949 *F, E, S, W*, 1950 *F, E, S, W*, 1951 *F, E, SA*, 1952 *F, S, W*
Clinch, A D (Dublin U, Wanderers) 1892 *S*, 1893 *W*, 1895 *E, S, W*, 1896 *E, S, W*, 1897 *E, S*
Clinch, J D (Wanderers, Dublin U) 1923 *W*, 1924 *F, E, S, W, NZ*, 1925 *F, E, S*, 1926 *E, S, W*, 1927 *F*, 1928 *F, E, S, W*, 1929 *F, E, S, W*, 1930 *F, E, S, W*, 1931 *F, E, S, W, SA*
Clohessy, P M (Young Munster) 1993 *F, W, E*, 1994 *F, W, E, S, A* 1,2, *US*, 1995 *E, S, F, W*, 1996 *S, F*, 1997 *It* 2, 1998 *F* (R), *W* (R), *SA* 2(R), *Gg, R, SA* 3, 1999 *F, W, E, S, It, A* 1,2 *Arg* 1, [*US, A* 3(R)], 2000 *E, S, It, F, W, Arg, J, SA*, 2001 *It, F, R, S, W, E, Sm* (R), *NZ*, 2002 *W, E, S, It, F*
Clune, J J (Blackrock Coll) 1912 *SA*, 1913 *W, F*, 1914 *F, E, W*
Coffey, J J (Lansdowne) 1900 *E*, 1901 *W*, 1902 *E, S, W*, 1903 *E, S, W*, 1905 *E, S, W, NZ*, 1906 *E, S, W, SA*, 1907 *E*, 1908 *W*, 1910 *F*
Cogan, W St J (Queen's Coll, Cork) 1907 *E, S*
Collier, S R (Queen's Coll, Belfast) 1883 *S*
Collins, P C (Lansdowne, London Irish) 1987 [*C*], 1990 *S* (R)
Collis, W R F (KCH, Harlequins) 1924 *F, W, NZ*, 1925 *F, E, S*, 1926 *F*
Collis, W S (Wanderers) 1884 *W*
Collopy, G (Bective Rangers) 1891 *S*, 1892 *S*
Collopy, R (Bective Rangers) 1923 *E, S, W, F*, 1924 *F, E, S, W, NZ*, 1925 *F, E, S, W*
Collopy, W P (Bective Rangers) 1914 *F, E, S, W*, 1921 *E, S, W, F*, 1922 *E, S, W, F*, 1923 *S, W, F*, 1924 *F, E, S, W*
Combe, A (NIFC) 1875 *E*
Condon, H C (London Irish) 1984 *S* (R)
Cook, H G (Lansdowne) 1884 *W*
Coote, P B (RAF, Leicester) 1933 *S*
Corcoran, J C (London Irish) 1947 *A*, 1948 *F*
Corken, T S (Belfast Collegians) 1937 *E, S, W*
Corkery, D S (Cork Constitution, Bristol) 1994 *A* 1,2, *US*, 1995 *E*, [*NZ, J, W, F*], *Fj*, 1996 *US, S, F, W, E, WS, A*, 1997 *It* 1, *F, W, E, S*, 1998 *S, F, W, E*, 1999 *A* 1(R),2(R)
Corley, H H (Dublin U, Wanderers) 1902 *E, S, W*, 1903 *E, S, W*, 1904 *E, S*
Cormac, H S T (Clontarf) 1921 *E, S, W*
Corrigan, R (Greystones, Lansdowne) 1997 *C* (R), *It* 2, 1998 *S, F, W, E, SA* 3(R), 1999 *A* 1(R),2(R), [*Arg* 2], 2002 *NZ* 1,2, *R, Ru, Gg, A, Fj* (R), *Arg*, 2003 *S* 1, *It* 1, *A, Tg, Sm, W* 2, *It* 2, *S* 2
Costello, P (Bective Rangers) 1960 *F*
Costello, R A (Garryowen) 1993 *S*
Costello, V C P (St Mary's Coll, London Irish) 1996 *US, F, W, E. WS* (R), 1997 *C, It* 2(R), 1998 *S* (R), *F, W, E, SA* 1,2, *Gg, R, SA* 3, 1999 *F, W* (R), *E, S* (R), *It, A* 1, 2002 *R* (R), *A, Arg*, 2003 *S* 1, *It* 1, *F, E, A, It* 2, *S* 2
Cotton, J (Wanderers) 1889 *W*
Coulter, H H (Queen's U, Belfast) 1920 *E, S, W*
Courtney, A W (UC Dublin) 1920 *S, W, F*, 1921 *E, S, W, F*
Cox, H L (Dublin U) 1875 *E*, 1876 *E*, 1877 *E, S*
Craig, R G (Queen's U, Belfast) 1938 *S, W*
Crawford, E C (Dublin U) 1885 *E, S* 1
Crawford, W E (Lansdowne) 1920 *E, S, W, F*, 1921 *E, S, W, F*, 1922 *E, S*, 1923 *E, S, W, F*, 1924 *F, E, W, NZ*, 1925 *F, E, S, W*, 1926 *F, E, S, W*, 1927 *F, E, S, W*
Crean, T J (Wanderers) 1894 *E, S, W*, 1895 *E, S, W*, 1896 *E, S, W*
Crichton, R Y (Dublin U) 1920 *E, S, W, F*, 1921 *F*, 1922 *E*, 1923 *W, F*, 1924 *F, E, S, W, NZ*, 1925 *E, S*
Croker, E W D (Limerick) 1878 *E*
Cromey, G E (Queen's U, Belfast) 1937 *E, S, W*, 1938 *E, S, W*, 1939 *E, S, W*
Cronin, B M (Garryowen) 1995 *S*, 1997 *S*
Cronyn, A P (Dublin U, Lansdowne) 1875 *E*, 1876 *E*, 1880 *S*
Crossan, K D (Instonians) 1982 *S*, 1984 *F, W, E, S*, 1985 *S, F, W, E*, 1986 *E, S, R*, 1987 *E, S, F, W*, [*W, C, Tg, A*], 1988 *S, F, W, E* 1, *WS, It*, 1989 *W, S, NZ*, 1990 *E, S, F, W, Arg*, 1991 *E, S, Nm* 2 [*Z, J, S*], 1992 *W*
Crotty, D J (Garryowen) 1996 *A*, 1997 *It* 1, *F, W*, 2000 *C*
Crowe, J F (UC Dublin) 1974 *NZ*
Crowe, L (Old Belvedere) 1950 *E, S, W*
Crowe, M P (Lansdowne) 1929 *W*, 1930 *E, S, W*, 1931 *F, S, W, SA*, 1932 *S, W*, 1933 *W, S*, 1934 *E*
Crowe, P M (Blackrock Coll) 1935 *E*, 1938 *E*
Cullen, L F M (Blackrock Coll) 2002 *NZ* 2(R), *R* (R), *Ru* (R), *Gg* (R), *A* (R), *Fj, Arg* (R), 2003 *S* 1(R), *It* 1(R), *F* (R), *W* 1, *Tg, Sm, It* 2
Cullen, T J (UC Dublin) 1949 *F*
Cullen, W J (Monkstown and Manchester) 1920 *E*
Culliton, M G (Wanderers) 1959 *E, S, W, F*, 1960 *E, S, W, F, SA*, 1961 *E, S, W, F*, 1962 *S, F*, 1964 *E, S, W, F*
Cummins, W E A (Queen's Coll, Cork) 1879 *S*, 1881 *E*, 1882 *E*
Cunningham, D McC (NIFC) 1923 *E, S, W*, 1925 *F, E, W*
Cunningham, M J (UC Cork) 1955 *F, E, S, W*, 1956 *F, S, W*
Cunningham, V J G (St Mary's Coll) 1988 *E* 2, *It*, 1990 *Arg* (R), 1991 *Nm* 1,2, [*Z, J*(R)], 1992 *NZ* 1,2, *A*, 1993 *S, F, W, E, R*, 1994 *F*
Cunningham, W A (Lansdowne) 1920 *W*, 1921 *E, S, W, F*, 1922 *E*, 1923 *S, W*
Cuppaidge, J L (Dublin U) 1879 *E*, 1880 *E, S*
Currell, J (NIFC) 1877 *S*
Curtis, A B (Oxford U) 1950 *F, E, S*
Curtis, D M (London Irish) 1991 *W, E, S, Nm* 1,2, [*Z, J, S, A*], 1992 *W, E, S* (R), *F*
Cuscaden, W A (Dublin U, Bray) 1876 *E*
Cussen, D J (Dublin U) 1921 *E, S, W, F*, 1922 *E*, 1923 *E, S, W, F*, 1926 *F, E, S, W*, 1927 *F, E*

Daly, J C (London Irish) 1947 *F, E, S, W*, 1948 *E, S, W*
Daly, M J (Harlequins) 1938 *E*
Danaher, P P A (Lansdowne, Garryowen) 1988 *S, F, W, WS, It*, 1989 *F, NZ* (R), 1990 *F*, 1992 *S, F, NZ* 1, *A*, 1993 *S, F, W, E, R*, 1994 *F, W, E, S, A* 1,2, *US*, 1995 *E, S, F, W*
D'Arcy, G M (Lansdowne) 1999 [*R* (R)], 2002 *Fj* (R), 2003 *Tg* (R), *Sm* (R), *W* 2(R)
Dargan, M J (Old Belvedere) 1952 *S, W*
Davidson, C T (NIFC) 1921 *F*

Davidson, I G (NIFC) 1899 *E*, 1900 *S, W*, 1901 *E, S, W*, 1902 *E, S, W*
Davidson, J C (Dungannon) 1969 *F, E, S, W*, 1973 *NZ*, 1976 *NZ*
Davidson, J W (Dungannon, London Irish, Castres) 1995 *Fj*, 1996 *S, F, W, E, WS, A*, 1997 *It* 1, *F, W, E, S*, 1998 *Gg* (R), *R* (R), *SA* 3(R), 1999 *F, W, E, S, It, A* 1,2(R), *Arg* 1, [*US,R* (R), *Arg* 2], 2000 *S* (R), *W (R), US, C*, 2001 *It* (R), *S*
Davies, F E (Lansdowne) 1892 *S, W*, 1893 *E, S, W*
Davis, J L (Monkstown) 1898 *E, S*
Davis, W J N (Edinburgh U, Bessbrook) 1890 *S, W, E*, 1891 *E, S, W*, 1892 *E, S*, 1895 *S*
Davison, W (Belfast Academy) 1887 *W*
Davy, E O'D (UC Dublin, Lansdowne) 1925 *W*, 1926 *F, E, S, W*, 1927 *F, E, S, W, A*, 1928 *F, E, S, W*, 1929 *F, E, S, W*, 1930 *F, E, S, W*, 1931 *F, E, S, W, SA*, 1932 *E, S, W*, 1933 *E, W, S*, 1934 *E*
Dawson, A R (Wanderers) 1958 *A, E, S, W, F*, 1959 *E, S, W, F*, 1960 *F, SA*, 1961 *E, S, W, F, SA*, 1962 *S, F, W*, 1963 *F, E, S, W, NZ*, 1964 *E, S, F*
Dawson, K (London Irish) 1997 *NZ, C*, 1998 *S*, 1999 [*R, Arg* 2], 2000 *E, S, It, F, W, J, SA*, 2001 *R, S, W* (R), *E* (R), *Sm*, 2002 *Fj*, 2003 *Tg, It* 2(R), *S* 2(R)
Dean, P M (St Mary's Coll) 1981 *SA* 1,2, *A*, 1982 *W, E, S, F*, 1984 *A*, 1985 *S, F, W, E*, 1986 *F, W, R*, 1987 *E, S, F, W*, [*W, A*], 1988 *S, F, W, E* 1,2, *WS, It*, 1989 *F, W, E, S*
Deane, E C (Monkstown) 1909 *E*
Deering, M J (Bective Rangers) 1929 *W*
Deering, S J (Bective Rangers) 1935 *E, S, W, NZ*, 1936 *E, S, W*, 1937 *E, S*
Deering, S M (Garryowen, St Mary's Coll) 1974 *W*, 1976 *F, W, E, S*, 1977 *W, E*, 1978 *NZ*
de Lacy, H (Harlequins) 1948 *E, S*
Delany, M G (Bective Rangers) 1895 *W*
Dempsey, G T (Terenure Coll) 1998 *Gg* (R). *SA* 3, 1999 *F, E, S, It, A* 2, 2000 *E* (R), *S, It, F, W, SA*, 2001 *It, F, S, W, E, NZ*, 2002 *W, E, S, It, F, NZ* 1,2, *R, Ru, Gg, A, Arg*, 2003 *S* 1, *E* (R), *A, Sm, W* 2(R), *It* 2, *S* 2(R)
Dennison, S P (Garryowen) 1973 *F*, 1975 *E, S*
Dick, C J (Ballymena) 1961 *W, F, SA*, 1962 *W*, 1963 *F, E, S, W*
Dick, J S (Queen's U, Belfast) 1962 *E*
Dick, J S (Queen's U, Cork) 1887 *E, S, W*
Dickson, J A N (Dublin U) 1920 *E, W, F*
Doherty, A E (Old Wesley) 1974 *P* (R)
Doherty, W D (Guy's Hospital) 1920 *E, S, W*, 1921 *E, S, W, F*
Donaldson, J A (Belfast Collegians) 1958 *A, E, S, W*
Donovan, T M (Queen's Coll, Cork) 1889 *S*
Dooley, J F (Galwegians) 1959 *E, S, W*
Doran, B R W (Lansdowne) 1900 *S, W*, 1901 *E, S, W*, 1902 *E, S, W*
Doran, E F (Lansdowne) 1890 *S, W*
Doran, G P (Lansdowne) 1899 *S, W*, 1900 *E, S*, 1902 *S, W*, 1903 *W*, 1904 *E*
Douglas, A C (Instonians) 1923 *F*, 1924 *E, S*, 1927 *A*, 1928 *S*
Downing, A J (Dublin U) 1882 *W*
Dowse, J C A (Monkstown) 1914 *F, S, W*
Doyle, J A P (Greystones) 1984 *E, S*
Doyle, J T (Bective Rangers) 1935 *W*
Doyle, M G (Blackrock Coll, UC Dublin, Cambridge U, Edinburgh Wands) 1965 *F, E, S, W, SA*, 1966 *F, E, S, W*, 1967 *A* 1, *E, S, W, F, A* 2, 1968 *F, E, S, W, A*
Doyle, T J (Wanderers) 1968 *E, S, W*
Duggan, A T A (Lansdowne) 1963 *NZ*, 1964 *F*, 1966 *W*, 1967 *A* 1, *S, W, A* 2, 1968 *F, E, S, W*, 1969 *F, E, S, W*, 1970 *SA, F, E, S, W*, 1971 *F, E, S, W*, 1972 *F* 2
Duggan, W (UC Cork) 1920 *S, W*
Duggan, W P (Blackrock Coll) 1975 *E, S, F, W*, 1976 *A, F, W, S, NZ*, 1977 *W, E, S, F*, 1978 *S, F, W, E, NZ*, 1979 *E, S, A* 1,2, 1980 *E*, 1981 *F, W, E, S, SA* 1,2, *A*, 1982 *W, E, S*, 1983 *S, F, W, E*, 1984 *F, W, E, S*
Duignan, P (Galwegians) 1998 *Gg, R*
Duncan, W R (Malone) 1984 *W, E*
Dunlea, F J (Lansdowne) 1989 *W, E, S*
Dunlop, R (Dublin U) 1889 *W*, 1890 *S, W, E*, 1891 *E, S, W*, 1892 *E, S*, 1893 *W*, 1894 *W*
Dunn, P E F (Bective Rangers) 1923 *S*
Dunn, T B (NIFC) 1935 *NZ*
Dunne, M J (Lansdowne) 1929 *F, E, S*, 1930 *F, E, S, W*, 1932 *E, S, W*, 1933 *E, W, S*, 1934 *E, S, W*
Dwyer, P J (UC Dublin) 1962 *W*, 1963 *F, NZ*, 1964 *S, W*

Easterby, G (Ebbw Vale, Ballynahinch, Llanelli) 2000 *US, C* (R), 2001 *R* (R), *S, W* (R), *Sm* (R), 2002 *W* (R), *S* (R), *R* (R), *Ru* (R), *Gg* (R), *Fj*, 2003 *S* 1(R), *It* 1(R), *Tg, Sm, W* 2(R), *It* 2, *S* 2(R)
Easterby, S H (Llanelli) 2000 *S, It, F, W, Arg, US, C*, 2001 *S, Sm* (R), 2002 *W, E* (R), *S* (R), *It, F, NZ* 1,2, *R, Ru, Gg*, 2003 *Tg, Sm, It* 2, *S* 2(t+R)
Edwards, H G (Dublin U) 1877 *E*, 1878 *E*
Edwards, R W (Malone) 1904 *W*
Edwards, T (Lansdowne) 1888 *M*, 1890 *S, W, E*, 1892 *W*, 1893 *E*
Edwards, W V (Malone) 1912 *F, E*
Egan, J D (Bective Rangers) 1922 *S*
Egan, J T (Cork Constitution) 1931 *F, E, SA*
Egan, M S (Garryowen) 1893 *E*, 1895 *S*
Ekin, W (Queen's Coll, Belfast) 1888 *W, S*
Elliott, W R J (Bangor) 1979 *S*
Elwood, E P (Lansdowne, Galwegians) 1993 *W, E, R*, 1994 *F, W, E, S, A* 1,2, 1995 *F, W*, [*NZ, W, F*], 1996 *US, S*, 1997 *F, W, E, NZ, C, It* 2(R), 1998 *F, W, E, SA* 1,2, *Gg, R, SA* 3, 1999 *It, Arg* 1(R), [*US* (R), *A* 3(R), *R*]
English, M A F (Lansdowne, Limerick Bohemians) 1958 *W, F*, 1959 *E, S, F*, 1960 *E, S*, 1961 *S, W, F*, 1962 *F, W*, 1963 *E, S, W, NZ*
Ennis, F N G (Wanderers) 1979 *A* 1(R)
Ensor, A H (Wanderers) 1973 *W, F*, 1974 *F, W, E, S, P, NZ*, 1975 *E, S, F, W*, 1976 *A, F, W, E, NZ*, 1977 *E*, 1978 *S, F, W, E*
Entrican, J C (Queen's U, Belfast) 1931 *S*
Erskine, D J (Sale) 1997 *NZ* (R), *C, It* 2

Fagan, G L (Kingstown School) 1878 *E*
Fagan, W B C (Wanderers) 1956 *F, E, S*
Farrell, J L (Bective Rangers) 1926 *F, E, S, W*, 1927 *F, E, S, W, A*, 1928 *F, E, S, W*, 1929 *F, E, S, W*, 1930 *F, E, S, W*, 1931 *F, E, S, W, SA*, 1932 *E, S, W*
Feddis, N (Lansdowne) 1956 *E*
Feighery, C F P (Lansdowne) 1972 *F* 1, *E, F* 2
Feighery, T A O (St Mary's Coll) 1977 *W, E*
Ferris, H H (Queen's Coll, Belfast) 1901 *W*
Ferris, J H (Queen's Coll, Belfast) 1900 *E, S, W*
Field, M J (Malone) 1994 *E, S, A* 1(R), 1995 *F* (R), *W* (t), *It* (R), [*NZ*(t + R), *J*], *Fj*, 1996 *F* (R), *W, E, A* (R), 1997 *F, W, E, S*
Finlay, J E (Queen's Coll, Belfast) 1913 *E, S, W*, 1920 *E, S, W*
Finlay, W (NIFC) 1876 *E*, 1877 *E, S*, 1878 *E*, 1879 *S, E*, 1880 *S*, 1882 *S*
Finn, M C (UC Cork, Cork Constitution) 1979 *E*, 1982 *W, E, S, F*, 1983 *S, F, W, E*, 1984 *E, S, A*, 1986 *F, W*
Finn, R G A (UC Dublin) 1977 *F*
Fitzgerald, C C (Glasgow U, Dungannon) 1902 *E*, 1903 *E, S*
Fitzgerald, C F (St Mary's Coll) 1979 *A* 1,2, 1980 *E, S, F, W*, 1982 *W, E, S, F*, 1983 *S, F, W, E*, 1984 *F, W, A*, 1985 *S, F, W, E*, 1986 *F, W, E, S*
Fitzgerald, D C (Lansdowne, De La Salle Palmerston) 1984 *E, S*, 1986 *W, E, S, R*, 1987 *E, S, F, W*, [*W, C, A*], 1988 *S, F, W, E* 1, 1989 *NZ* (R), 1990 *E, S, F, W, Arg*, 1991 *F, W, E, S, Nm* 1,2, [*Z, S, A*], 1992 *W, S* (R)
Fitzgerald, J (Wanderers) 1884 *W*
Fitzgerald, J J (Young Munster) 1988 *S, F*, 1990 *S, F, W*, 1991 *F, W, E, S*, [*J*], 1994 *A* 1,2
Fitzgibbon, M J J (Shannon) 1992 *W, E, S, F, NZ* 1,2
Fitzpatrick, J M (Dungannon) 1998 *SA* 1,2 *Gg* (R), *R* (R), *SA* 3, 1999 *F* (R), *W* (R), *E* (R), *It, Arg* 1(R), [*US* (R), *A* 3, *R, Arg* 2(t&R)], 2000 *S* (R), *It* (R), *Arg* (R), *US, C, SA* (t&R), 2001 *R* (R), 2003 *W* 1(R), *E* (R), *Tg, W* 2(R), *It* 2(R)
Fitzpatrick, M P (Wanderers) 1978 *S*, 1980 *S, F, W*, 1981 *F, W, E, S, A*, 1985 *F* (R)
Flavin, P (Blackrock Coll) 1997 *F* (R), *S*
Fletcher, W W (Kingstown) 1882 *W, S*, 1883 *E*
Flood, R S (Dublin U) 1925 *W*
Flynn, M K (Wanderers) 1959 *F*, 1960 *F*, 1962 *E, S, F, W*, 1964 *E, S, W, F*, 1965 *F, E, S, W, SA*, 1966 *F, E, S*, 1972 *F* 1, *E, F* 2, 1973 *NZ*
Fogarty, T (Garryowen) 1891 *W*
Foley, A G (Shannon) 1995 *E, S, F, W, It*, [*J*(t + R)], 1996 *A*, 1997 *It* 1, *E* (R), 2000 *E, S, It, F, W, Arg, C, J, SA*, 2001 *It, F, R, S, W, E, Sm, NZ*, 2002 *W, E, S, It, F, NZ* 1,2, *R, Ru, Gg, A, Fj, Arg*, 2003 *S* 1, *It* 1, *F, W* 1, *E, W* 2
Foley, B O (Shannon) 1976 *F, E*, 1977 *W* (R), 1980 *F, W*, 1981 *F, E, S, SA* 1,2, *A*
Forbes, R E (Malone) 1907 *E*

Forrest, A J (Wanderers) 1880 *E*, *S*, 1881 *E*, *S*, 1882 *W*, *E*, 1883 *E*, 1885 *S* 2
Forrest, E G (Wanderers) 1888 *M*, 1889 *S*, *W*, 1890 *S*, *E*, 1891 *E*, 1893 *S*, 1894 *E*, *S*, *W*, 1895 *W*, 1897 *E*, *S*
Forrest, H (Wanderers) 1893 *S*, *W*
Fortune, J J (Clontarf) 1963 *NZ*, 1964 *E*
Foster, A R (Derry) 1910 *E*, *S*, *F*, 1911 *E*, *S*, *W*, *F*, 1912 *F*, *E*, *S*, *W*, 1914 *E*, *S*, *W*, 1921 *E*, *S*, *W*
Francis, N P J (Blackrock Coll, London Irish, Old Belvedere) 1987 [*Tg*, *A*], 1988 *WS*, *It*, 1989 *S*, 1990 *E*, *F*, *W*, 1991 *E*, *S*, *Nm* 1,2, [*Z*, *J*, *S*, *A*], 1992 *W*, *E*, *S*, 1993 *F*, *R*, 1994 *F*, *W*, *E*, *S*, *A* 1,2, *US*, 1995 *E*, [*NZ*, *J*, *W*, *F*], *Fj*, 1996 *US*, *S*
Franks, J G (Dublin U) 1898 *E*, *S*, *W*
Frazer, E F (Bective Rangers) 1891 *S*, 1892 *S*
Freer, A E (Lansdowne) 1901 *E*, *S*, *W*
Fulcher, G M (Cork Constitution, London Irish) 1994 *A* 2, *US*, 1995 *E* (R), *S*, *F*, *W*, *It*, [*NZ*, *W*, *F*], *Fj*, 1996 *US*, *S*, *F*, *W*, *E*, *A*, 1997 *It* 1, *W* (R), 1998 *SA* 1(R)
Fulton, J (NIFC) 1895 *S*, *W*, 1896 *E*, 1897 *E*, 1898 *W*, 1899 *E*, 1900 *W*, 1901 *E*, 1902 *E*, *S*, *W*, 1903 *E*, *S*, *W*, 1904 *E*, *S*
Furlong, J N (UC Galway) 1992 *NZ* 1,2

Gaffikin, W (Windsor) 1875 *E*
Gage, J H (Queen's U, Belfast) 1926 *S*, *W*, 1927 *S*, *W*
Galbraith, E (Dublin U) 1875 *E*
Galbraith, H T (Belfast Acad) 1890 *W*
Galbraith, R (Dublin U) 1875 *E*, 1876 *E*, 1877 *E*
Galwey, M J (Shannon) 1991 *F*, *W*, *Nm* 2(R), [*J*], 1992 *E*, *S*, *F*, *NZ* 1,2, *A*, 1993 *F*, *W*, *E*, *R*, 1994 *F*, *W*, *E*, *S*, *A* 1, *US* (R), 1995 *E*, 1996 *WS*, 1998 *F* (R), 1999 *W* (R), 2000 *E* (R), *S*, *It*, *F*, *W*, *Arg*, *C*, 2001 *It*, *F*, *R*, *W*, *E*, *Sm*, *NZ*, 2002 *W*, *E*, *S*
Ganly, J B (Monkstown) 1927 *F*, *E*, *S*, *W*, *A*, 1928 *F*, *E*, *S*, *W*, 1929 *F*, *S*, 1930 *F*
Gardiner, F (NIFC) 1900 *E*, *S*, 1901 *E*, *W*, 1902 *E*, *S*, *W*, 1903 *E*, *W*, 1904 *E*, *S*, *W*, 1906 *E*, *S*, *W*, 1907 *S*, *W*, 1908 *S*, *W*, 1909 *E*, *S*, *F*
Gardiner, J B (NIFC) 1923 *E*, *S*, *W*, *F*, 1924 *F*, *E*, *S*, *W*, *NZ*, 1925 *F*, *E*, *S*, *W*
Gardiner, S (Belfast Albion) 1893 *E*, *S*
Gardiner, W (NIFC) 1892 *E*, *S*, 1893 *E*, *S*, *W*, 1894 *E*, *S*, *W*, 1895 *E*, *S*, *W*, 1896 *E*, *S*, *W*, 1897 *E*, *S*, 1898 *W*
Garry, M G (Bective Rangers) 1909 *E*, *S*, *W*, *F*, 1911 *E*, *S*, *W*
Gaston, J T (Dublin U) 1954 *NZ*, *F*, *E*, *S*, *W*, 1955 *W* 1956 *F*, *E*
Gavin, T J (Moseley, London Irish) 1949 *F*, *E*
Geoghegan, S P (London Irish, Bath) 1991 *F*, *W*, *E*, *S*, *Nm* 1, [*Z*, *S*, *A*], 1992 *E*, *S*, *F*, *A*, 1993 *S*, *F*, *W*, *E*, *R*, 1994 *F*, *W*, *E*, *S*, *A* 1,2, *US*, 1995 *E*, *S*, *F*, *W*, [*NZ*, *J*, *W*, *F*], *Fj*, 1996 *US*, *S*, *W*, *E*
Gibson, C M H (Cambridge U, NIFC) 1964 *E*, *S*, *W*, *F*, 1965 *F*, *E*, *S*, *W*, *SA*, 1966 *F*, *E*, *S*, *W*, 1967 *A* 1, *E*, *S*, *W*, *F*, *A* 2, 1968 *E*, *S*, *W*, *A*, 1969 *E*, *S*, *W*, 1970 *SA*, *F*, *E*, *S*, *W*, 1971 *F*, *E*, *S*, *W*, 1972 *F* 1, *E*, *F* 2, 1973 *NZ*, *E*, *S*, *W*, *F*, 1974 *F*, *W*, *E*, *S*, *P*, 1975 *E*, *S*, *F*, *W*, 1976 *A*, *F*, *W*, *E*, *S*, *NZ*, 1977 *W*, *E*, *S*, *F*, 1978 *F*, *W*, *E*, *NZ*, 1979 *S*, *A* 1,2
Gibson, M E (Lansdowne, London Irish) 1979 *F*, *W*, *E*, *S*, 1981 *W* (R), 1986 *R*, 1988 *S*, *F*, *W*, *E* 2
Gifford, H P (Wanderers) 1890 *S*
Gillespie, J C (Dublin U) 1922 *W*, *F*
Gilpin, F G (Queen's U, Belfast) 1962 *E*, *S*, *F*
Glass, D C (Belfast Collegians) 1958 *F*, 1960 *W*, 1961 *W*, *SA*
Gleeson, K D (St Mary's Coll) 2002 *W* (R), *F* (R), *NZ* 1,2, *R*, *Ru*, *Gg*, *A*, *Arg*, 2003 *S* 1, *It* 1, *F*, *W* 1, *E*, *A*, *W* 2
Glennon, B T (Lansdowne) 1993 *F* (R)
Glennon, J J (Skerries) 1980 *E*, *S*, 1987 *E*, *S*, *F*, [*W* (R)]
Godfrey, R P (UC Dublin) 1954 *S*, *W*
Goodall, K G (City of Derry, Newcastle U) 1967 *A* 1, *E*, *S*, *W*, *F*, *A* 2, 1968 *F*, *E*, *S*, *W*, *A*, 1969 *F*, *E*, *S*, 1970 *SA*, *F*, *E*, *S*, *W*
Gordon, A (Dublin U) 1884 *S*
Gordon, T G (NIFC) 1877 *E*, *S*, 1878 *E*
Gotto, R P C (NIFC) 1906 *SA*
Goulding, W J (Cork) 1879 *S*
Grace, T O (UC Dublin, St Mary's Coll) 1972 *F* 1, *E*, 1973 *NZ*, *E*, *S*, *W*, 1974 *E*, *S*, *P*, *NZ*, 1975 *E*, *S*, *F*, *W*, 1976 *A*, *F*, *W*, *E*, *S*, *NZ*, 1977 *W*, *E*, *S*, *F*, 1978 *S*
Graham, R I (Dublin U) 1911 *F*
Grant, E L (CIYMS) 1971 *F*, *E*, *S*, *W*
Grant, P J (Bective Rangers) 1894 *S*, *W*
Graves, C R A (Wanderers) 1934 *E*, *S*, *W*, 1935 *E*, *S*, *W*, *NZ*, 1936 *E*, *S*, *W*, 1937 *E*, *S*, 1938 *E*, *S*, *W*
Gray, R D (Old Wesley) 1923 *E*, *S*, 1925 *F*, 1926 *F*
Greene, E H (Dublin U, Kingstown) 1882 *W*, 1884 *W*, 1885 *E*, *S* 2, 1886 *E*
Greer, R (Kingstown) 1876 *E*
Greeves, T J (NIFC) 1907 *E*, *S*, *W*, 1909 *W*, *F*
Gregg, R J (Queen's U, Belfast) 1953 *F*, *E*, *S*, *W*, 1954 *F*, *E*, *S*
Griffin, C S (London Irish) 1951 *F*, *E*
Griffin, J L (Wanderers) 1949 *S*, *W*
Griffiths, W (Limerick) 1878 *E*
Grimshaw, C (Queen's U, Belfast) 1969 *E* (R)
Guerin, B N (Galwegians) 1956 *S*
Gwynn, A P (Dublin U) 1895 *W*
Gwynn, L H (Dublin U) 1893 *S*, 1894 *E*, *S*, *W*, 1897 *S*, 1898 *E*, *S*

Hakin, R F (CIYMS) 1976 *W*, *S*, *NZ*, 1977 *W*, *E*, *F*
Hall, R O N (Dublin U) 1884 *W*
Hall, W H (Instonians) 1923 *E*, *S*, *W*, *F*, 1924 *F*, *S*
Hallaran, C F G T (Royal Navy) 1921 *E*, *S*, *W*, 1922 *E*, *S*, *W*, 1923 *E*, *F*, 1924 *F*, *E*, *S*, *W*, 1925 *F*, 1926 *F*, *E*
Halpin, G F (Wanderers, London Irish) 1990 *E*, 1991 [*J*], 1992 *E*, *S*, *F*, 1993 *R*, 1994 *F* (R), 1995 *It*, [*NZ*, *W*, *F*]
Halpin, T (Garryowen) 1909 *S*, *W*, *F*, 1910 *E*, *S*, *W*, 1911 *E*, *S*, *W*, *F*, 1912 *F*, *E*, *S*
Halvey, E O (Shannon) 1995 *F*, *W*, *It*, [*J*, *W* (t), *F* (R)], 1997 *NZ*, *C* (R)
Hamilton, A J (Lansdowne) 1884 *W*
Hamilton, G F (NIFC) 1991 *F*, *W*, *E*, *S*, *Nm* 2, [*Z*, *J*, *S*, *A*], 1992 *A*
Hamilton, R L (NIFC) 1926 *F*
Hamilton, R W (Wanderers) 1893 *W*
Hamilton, W J (Dublin U) 1877 *E*
Hamlet, G T (Old Wesley) 1902 *E*, *S*, *W*, 1903 *E*, *S*, *W*, 1904 *S*, *W*, 1905 *E*, *S*, *W*, *NZ*, 1906 *SA*, 1907 *E*, *S*, *W*, 1908 *E*, *S*, *W*, 1909 *E*, *S*, *W*, *F*, 1910 *E*, *S*, *F*, 1911 *E*, *S*, *W*, *F*
Hanrahan, C J (Dolphin) 1926 *S*, *W*, 1927 *E*, *S*, *W*, *A*, 1928 *F*, *E*, *S*, 1929 *F*, *E*, *S*, *W*, 1930 *F*, *E*, *S*, *W*, 1931 *F*, 1932 *S*, *W*
Harbison, H T (Bective Rangers) 1984 *W* (R), *E*, *S*, 1986 *R*, 1987 *E*, *S*, *F*, *W*
Hardy, G G (Bective Rangers) 1962 *S*
Harman, G R A (Dublin U) 1899 *E*, *W*
Harper, J (Instonians) 1947 *F*, *E*, *S*
Harpur, T G (Dublin U) 1908 *E*, *S*, *W*
Harrison, T (Cork) 1879 *S*, 1880 *S*, 1881 *E*
Harvey, F M W (Wanderers) 1907 *W*, 1911 *F*
Harvey, G A D (Wanderers) 1903 *E*, *S*, 1904 *W*, 1905 *E*, *S*
Harvey, T A (Dublin U) 1900 *W*, 1901 *S*, *W*, 1902 *E*, *S*, *W*, 1903 *E*, *W*
Haycock, P P (Terenure Coll) 1989 *E*
Hayes, J J (Shannon) 2000 *S*, *It*, *F*, *W*, *Arg*, *C*, *J*, *SA*, 2001 *It*, *F*, *R*, *S*, *W*, *E*, *Sm*, *NZ*, 2002 *W*, *E*, *S*, *It*, *F*, *NZ* 1,2, *R*, *Ru*, *Gg*, *A*, *Fj*, *Arg*, 2003 *S* 1, *It* 1, *F*, *W* 1, *E*
Headon, T A (UC Dublin) 1939 *S*, *W*
Healey, P (Limerick) 1901 *E*, *S*, *W*, 1902 *E*, *S*, *W*, 1903 *E*, *S*, *W*, 1904 *S*
Heffernan, M R (Cork Constitution) 1911 *E*, *S*, *W*, *F*
Hemphill, R (Dublin U) 1912 *F*, *E*, *S*, *W*
Henderson, N J (Queen's U, Belfast, NIFC) 1949 *S*, *W*, 1950 *F*, 1951 *F*, *E*, *S*, *W*, *SA*, 1952 *F*, *S*, *W*, *E*, 1953 *F*, *E*, *S*, *W*, 1954 *NZ*, *F*, *E*, *S*, *W*, 1955 *F*, *E*, *S*, *W*, 1956 *S*, *W*, 1957 *F*, *E*, *S*, *W*, 1958 *A*, *E*, *S*, *W*, *F*, 1959 *E*, *S*, *W*, *F*
Henderson R A J (London Irish, Wasps, Young Munster) 1996 *WS*, 1997 *NZ*, *C*, 1998 *F*, *W*, *SA* 1(R),2(R), 1999 *F* (R), *E*, *S* (R), *It*, 2000 *S* (R), *It* (R), *F*, *W*, *Arg*, *US*, *J* (R), *SA*, 2001 *It*, *F*, 2002 *W* (R), *E* (R), *F*, *R* (R), *Ru* (t), *Gg* (R), 2003 *It* 1(R),2
Henebrey, G J (Garryowen) 1906 *E*, *S*, *W*, *SA*, 1909 *W*, *F*
Heron, A G (Queen's Coll, Belfast) 1901 *E*
Heron, J (NIFC) 1877 *S*, 1879 *E*
Heron, W T (NIFC) 1880 *E*, *S*
Herrick, R W (Dublin U) 1886 *S*
Heuston, F S (Kingstown) 1882 *W*, 1883 *E*, *S*
Hewitt, D (Queen's U, Belfast, Instonians) 1958 *A*, *E*, *S*, *F*, 1959 *S*, *W*, *F*, 1960 *E*, *S*, *W*, *F*, 1961 *E*, *S*, *W*, *F*, 1962 *S*, *F*, 1965 *W*
Hewitt, F S (Instonians) 1924 *W*, *NZ*, 1925 *F*, *E*, *S*, 1926 *E*, 1927 *E*, *S*, *W*
Hewitt, J A (NIFC) 1981 *SA* 1(R),2(R)
Hewitt, T R (Queen's U, Belfast) 1924 *W*, *NZ*, 1925 *F*, *E*, *S*, 1926 *F*, *E*, *S*, *W*
Hewitt, V A (Instonians) 1935 *S*, *W*, *NZ*, 1936 *E*, *S*, *W*
Hewitt, W J (Instonians) 1954 *E*, 1956 *S*, 1959 *W*, 1961 *SA*
Hewson, F T (Wanderers) 1875 *E*
Hickie, D A (St Mary's Coll) 1997 *W*, *E*, *S*, *NZ*, *C*, *It* 2, 1998 *S*, *F*, *W*, *E*, *SA* 1,2, 2000 *S*, *It*, *F*, *W*, *J*, *SA*, 2001 *F*, *R*, *S*, *W*, *E*, *NZ*, 2002 *W*, *E*, *S*, *It*, *F*, *R*, *Ru*, *Gg*, *A*, 2003 *S* 1, *It* 1, *F*, *W* 1, *E*, *It* 2, *S* 2

Hickie, D J (St Mary's Coll) 1971 *F, E, S, W*, 1972 *F* 1, *E*
Higgins, J A D (Civil Service) 1947 *S, W, A*, 1948 *F, S, W*
Higgins, W W (NIFC) 1884 *E, S*
Hillary, M F (UC Dublin) 1952 *E*
Hingerty, D J (UC Dublin) 1947 *F, E, S, W*
Hinton, W P (Old Wesley) 1907 *W*, 1908 *E, S, W*, 1909 *E, S*, 1910 *E, S, W, F*, 1911 *E, S, W*, 1912 *F, E, W*
Hipwell, M L (Terenure Coll) 1962 *E, S*, 1968 *F, A*, 1969 *F* (R), *S* (R), *W*, 1971 *F, E, S, W*, 1972 *F* 2
Hobbs, T H M (Dublin U) 1884 *S*, 1885 *E*
Hobson, E W (Dublin U) 1876 *E*
Hogan, N A (Terenure Coll, London Irish) 1995 *E, W*, [*J, W, F*], 1996 *F, W, E, WS*, 1997 *F, W, E, It* 2
Hogan, P (Garryowen) 1992 *F*
Hogg, W (Dublin U) 1885 *S* 2
Holland, J J (Wanderers) 1981 *SA* 1,2, 1986 *W*
Holmes, G W (Dublin U) 1912 *SA*, 1913 *E, S*
Holmes, L J (Lisburn) 1889 *S, W*
Hooks, K J (Queen's U, Belfast, Ards, Bangor) 1981 *S*, 1989 *NZ*, 1990 *F, W, Arg*, 1991 *F*
Horan, A K (Blackheath) 1920 *E, W*
Horan, M (Shannon) 2000 *US* (R), 2002 *Fj, Arg* (R), 2003 *S* 1(R), *It* 1(R), *F, W* 1, *E, A, Sm, It* 2, *S* 2
Horgan, A P (Cork Const) 2003 *Sm, W* 2, *S* 2
Horgan, S P (Lansdowne) 2000 *S, It, W, Arg, C, J, SA* (R), 2001 *It, S, W, E, NZ*, 2002 *S, It, F, A, Fj, Arg*, 2003 *S* 1
Houston, K J (Oxford U, London Irish) 1961 *SA*, 1964 *S, W*, 1965 *F, E, SA*
Howe, T G (Dungannon, Ballymena) 2000 *US, J, SA*, 2001 *It, F, R, Sm*, 2002 *It* (R), 2003 *Tg, W* 2
Hughes, R W (NIFC) 1878 *E*, 1880 *E, S*, 1881 *S*, 1882 *E, S*, 1883 *E, S*, 1884 *E, S*, 1885 *E*, 1886 *E*
Humphreys, D G (London Irish, Dungannon) 1996 *F, W, E, WS*, 1997 *E* (R), *S, It* 2, 1998 *S, E* (R), *SA* 2(t + R), *R* (R), 1999 *F, W, E, S, A* 1,2, *Arg* 1, [*US, A* 3, *Arg* 2], 2000 *E, S* (R), *F* (t&R), *W* (R), *Arg, US* (R), *C, J* (R), *SA* (R), 2001 *It* (R), *R, S* (R), *W, E, NZ*, 2002 *W, E, S, It, F, NZ* 1(R),2(R), *R* (t+R), *Ru* (R), *Gg* (R), *Fj*, 2003 *S* 1, *It* 1, *F, W* 1, *E, A, W* 2, *It* 2, *S* 2(R)
Hunt, E W F de Vere (Army, Rosslyn Park) 1930 *F*, 1932 *E, S, W*, 1933 *E*
Hunter, D V (Dublin U) 1885 *S* 2
Hunter, L (Civil Service) 1968 *W, A*
Hunter, W R (CIYMS) 1962 *E, S, W, F*, 1963 *F, E, S*, 1966 *F, E, S*
Hurley, H D (Old Wesley, Moseley) 1995 *Fj* (t), 1996 *WS*
Hutton, S A (Malone) 1967 *S, W, F, A* 2

Ireland J (Windsor) 1876 *E*, 1877 *E*
Irvine, H A S (Collegians) 1901 *S*
Irwin, D G (Queen's U, Belfast, Instonians) 1980 *F, W*, 1981 *F, W, E, S, SA* 1,2, *A*, 1982 *W*, 1983 *S, F, W, E*, 1984 *F, W*, 1987 [*Tg, A* (R)], 1989 *F, W, E, S, NZ*, 1990 *E, S*
Irwin, J W S (NIFC) 1938 *E, S*, 1939 *E, S, W*
Irwin, S T (Queen's Coll, Belfast) 1900 *E, S, W*, 1901 *E, W*, 1902 *E, S, W*, 1903 *S*

Jack, H W (UC Cork) 1914 *S, W*, 1921 *W*
Jackson, A R V (Wanderers) 1911 *E, S, W, F*, 1913 *W, F*, 1914 *F, E, S, W*
Jackson, F (NIFC) 1923 *E*
Jackson, H W (Dublin U) 1877 *E*
Jameson, J S (Lansdowne) 1888 *M*, 1889 *S, W*, 1891 *W*, 1892 *E, W*, 1893 *S*
Jeffares, E W (Wanderers) 1913 *E, S*
Johns, P S (Dublin U, Dungannon, Saracens) 1990 *Arg*, 1992 *NZ* 1,2, *A*, 1993 *S, F, W, E, R*, 1994 *F, W, E, S, A* 1,2, *US*, 1995 *E, S, W, It*, [*NZ, J, W, F*], *Fj*, 1996 *US, S, F, WS*, 1997 *It* 1(R), *F, W, E, S, NZ, C, It* 2, 1998 *S, F, W, E, SA* 1,2, *Gg, R, SA* 3, 1999 *F, W, E, S, It, A* 1,2, *Arg* 1, [*US, A* 3, *R*], 2000 *F* (R), *J*
Johnston, J (Belfast Acad) 1881 *S*, 1882 *S*, 1884 *S*, 1885 *S* 1,2, 1886 *E*, 1887 *E, S, W*
Johnston, M (Dublin U) 1880 *E, S*, 1881 *E, S*, 1882 *E*, 1884 *E, S*, 1886 *E*
Johnston, R (Wanderers) 1893 *E, W*
Johnston, R W (Dublin U) 1890 *S, W, E*
Johnston, T J (Queen's Coll, Belfast) 1892 *E, S, W*, 1893 *E, S*, 1895 *E*
Johnstone, W E (Dublin U) 1884 *W*
Johnstone-Smyth, T R (Lansdowne) 1882 *E*

Kavanagh, J R (UC Dublin, Wanderers) 1953 *F, E, S, W*, 1954 *NZ, S, W*, 1955 *F, E*, 1956 *E, S, W*, 1957 *F, E, S, W*, 1958 *A, E, S, W*, 1959 *E, S, W, F*, 1960 *E, S, W, F, SA*, 1961 *E, S, W, F, SA*, 1962 *F*
Kavanagh, P J (UC Dublin, Wanderers) 1952 *E*, 1955 *W*
Keane, K P (Garryowen) 1998 *E* (R)
Keane, M I (Lansdowne) 1974 *F, W, E, S, P, NZ*, 1975 *E, S, F, W*, 1976 *A, F, W, E, S, NZ*, 1977 *W, E, S, F*, 1978 *S, F, W, E, NZ*, 1979 *F, W, E, S, A* 1,2, 1980 *E, S, F, W*, 1981 *F, W, E, S*, 1982 *W, E, S, F*, 1983 *S, F, W, E*, 1984 *F, W, E, S*
Kearney, R K (Wanderers) 1982 *F*, 1984 *A*, 1986 *F, W*
Keeffe, E (Sunday's Well) 1947 *F, E, S, W, A*, 1948 *F*
Kelly, H C (NIFC) 1877 *E, S*, 1878 *E*, 1879 *S*, 1880 *E, S*
Kelly, J C (UC Dublin) 1962 *F, W*, 1963 *F, E, S, W, NZ*, 1964 *E, S, W, F*
Kelly, J P (Cork Constitution) 2002 *It, NZ* 1,2, *R, Ru, Gg, A* (R), 2003 *It* 1, *F, A, Tg, Sm, It* 2
Kelly, S (Lansdowne) 1954 *S, W*, 1955 *S*, 1960 *W, F*
Kelly, W (Wanderers) 1884 *S*
Kennedy, A G (Belfast Collegians) 1956 *F*
Kennedy, A P (London Irish) 1986 *W, E*
Kennedy, F (Wanderers) 1880 *E*, 1881 *E*, 1882 *W*
Kennedy, F A (Wanderers) 1904 *E, W*
Kennedy, H (Bradford) 1938 *S, W*
Kennedy, J M (Wanderers) 1882 *W*, 1884 *W*
Kennedy, K W (Queen's U, Belfast, London Irish) 1965 *F, E, S, W, SA*, 1966 *F, E, W*, 1967 *A* 1, *E, S, W, F, A* 2, 1968 *F, A*, 1969 *F, E, S, W*, 1970 *SA, F, E, S, W*, 1971 *F, E, S, W*, 1972 *F* 1, *E, F* 2, 1973 *NZ, E, S, W, F*, 1974 *F, W, E, S, P, NZ*, 1975 *F, W*
Kennedy, T J (St Mary's Coll) 1978 *NZ*, 1979 *F, W, E* (R), *A* 1,2, 1980 *E, S, F, W*, 1981 *SA* 1,2, *A*
Kenny, P (Wanderers) 1992 *NZ* 2(R)
Keogh, F S (Bective Rangers) 1964 *W, F*
Keon, J J (Limerick) 1879 *E*
Keyes, R P (Cork Constitution) 1986 *E*, 1991 [*Z, J, S, A*], 1992 *W, E, S*
Kidd, F W (Dublin U, Lansdowne) 1877 *E, S*, 1878 *E*
Kiely, M D (Lansdowne) 1962 *W*, 1963 *F, E, S, W*
Kiernan, M J (Dolphin, Lansdowne) 1982 *W* (R), *E, S, F*, 1983 *S, F, W, E*, 1984 *E, S, A*, 1985 *S, F, W, E*, 1986 *F, W, E, S, R*, 1987 *E, S, F, W*, [*W, C, A*], 1988 *S, F, W, E* 1,2, *WS*, 1989 *F, W, E, S*, 1990 *E, S, F, W, Arg*, 1991 *F*
Kiernan, T J (UC Cork, Cork Const) 1960 *E, S, W, F, SA*, 1961 *E, S, W, F, SA*, 1962 *E, W*, 1963 *F, S, W, NZ*, 1964 *E, S*, 1965 *F, E, S, W, SA*, 1966 *F, E, S, W*, 1967 *A* 1, *E, S, W, F, A* 2, 1968 *F, E, S, W, A*, 1969 *F, E, S, W*, 1970 *SA, F, E, S, W*, 1971 *F*, 1972 *F* 1, *E, F* 2, 1973 *NZ, E, S*
Killeen, G V (Garryowen) 1912 *E, S, W*, 1913 *E, S, W, F*, 1914 *E, S, W*
King, H (Dublin U) 1883 *E, S*
Kingston, T J (Dolphin) 1987 [*W, Tg, A*], 1988 *S, F, W, E* 1, 1990 *F, W*, 1991 [*J*], 1993 *F, W, E, R*, 1994 *F, W, E, S*, 1995 *F, W, It*, [*NZ, J* (R), *W, F*], *Fj*, 1996 *US, S, F*
Knox, J H (Dublin U, Lansdowne) 1904 *W*, 1905 *E, S, W, NZ*, 1906 *E, S, W*, 1907 *W*, 1908 *S*
Kyle, J W (Queen's U, Belfast, NIFC) 1947 *F, E, S, W, A*, 1948 *F, E, S, W*, 1949 *F, E, S, W*, 1950 *F, E, S, W*, 1951 *F, E, S, W, SA*, 1952 *F, S, W, E*, 1953 *F, E, S, W*, 1954 *NZ, F*, 1955 *F, E, W*, 1956 *F, E, S, W*, 1957 *F, E, S, W*, 1958 *A, E, S*

Lambert, N H (Lansdowne) 1934 *S, W*
Lamont, R A (Instonians) 1965 *F, E, SA*, 1966 *F, E, S, W*, 1970 *SA, F, E, S, W*
Landers, M F (Cork Const) 1904 *W*, 1905 *E, S, W, NZ*
Lane, D (UC Cork) 1934 *S, W*, 1935 *E, S*
Lane, M F (UC Cork) 1947 *W*, 1949 *F, E, S, W*, 1950 *F, E, S, W*, 1951 *F, S, W, SA*, 1952 *F, S*, 1953 *F, E*
Lane, P (Old Crescent) 1964 *W*
Langan, D J (Clontarf) 1934 *W*
Langbroek, J A (Blackrock Coll) 1987 [*Tg*]
Lavery, P (London Irish) 1974 *W*, 1976 *W*
Lawlor, P J (Clontarf) 1951 *S, SA*, 1952 *F, S, W, E*, 1953 *F*, 1954 *NZ, E, S*, 1956 *F, E*
Lawlor, P J (Bective Rangers) 1935 *E, S, W*, 1937 *E, S, W*
Lawlor, P J (Bective Rangers) 1990 *Arg*, 1992 *A*, 1993 *S*
Leahy, K T (Wanderers) 1992 *NZ* 1
Leahy, M W (UC Cork) 1964 *W*
Lee, S (NIFC) 1891 *E, S, W*, 1892 *E, S, W*, 1893 *E, S, W*, 1894 *E, S, W*, 1895 *E, W*, 1896 *E, S, W*, 1897 *E*, 1898 *E*
Le Fanu, V C (Cambridge U, Lansdowne) 1886 *E, S*, 1887 *E, W*, 1888 *S*, 1889 *W*, 1890 *E*, 1891 *E*, 1892 *E, S, W*

Lenihan, D G (UC Cork, Cork Const) 1981 *A*, 1982 *W, E, S, F*, 1983 *S, F, W, E*, 1984 *F, W, E, S, A*, 1985 *S, F, W, E*, 1986 *F, W, E, S, R*, 1987 *E, S, F, W*, [*W, C, Tg, A*], 1988 *S, F, W, E* 1,2, *WS, It*, 1989 *F, W, E, S, NZ*, 1990 *S, F, W, Arg*, 1991 *Nm* 2, [*Z, S, A*], 1992 *W*
L'Estrange, L P F (Dublin U) 1962 *E*
Levis, F H (Wanderers) 1884 *E*
Lightfoot, E J (Lansdowne) 1931 *F, E, S, W, SA*, 1932 *E, S, W*, 1933 *E, W, S*
Lindsay, H (Dublin U, Armagh) 1893 *E, S, W*, 1894 *E, S, W*, 1895 *E*, 1896 *E, S, W*, 1898 *E, S, W*
Little, T J (Bective Rangers) 1898 *W*, 1899 *S, W*, 1900 *S, W*, 1901 *E, S*
Lloyd, R A (Dublin U, Liverpool) 1910 *E, S*, 1911 *E, S, W, F*, 1912 *F, E, S, W, SA*, 1913 *E, S, W, F*, 1914 *F, E*, 1920 *E, F*
Longwell, G W (Ballymena) 2000 *J* (R), *SA*, 2001 *F* (R), *R, S* (R), *Sm, NZ* (R), 2002 *W* (R), *E* (R), *S* (R), *It, F, NZ* 1,2, *R, Ru, Gg, A, Arg*, 2003 *S* 1, *It* 1, *F, E, A, It* 2
Lydon, C T J (Galwegians) 1956 *S*
Lyle, R K (Dublin U) 1910 *W, F*
Lyle, T R (Dublin U) 1885 *E, S* 1,2, 1886 *E*, 1887 *E, S*
Lynch, J F (St Mary's Coll) 1971 *F, E, S, W*, 1972 *F* 1, *E, F* 2, 1973 *NZ, E, S, W*, 1974 *F, W, E, S, P, NZ*
Lynch, L (Lansdowne) 1956 *S*
Lytle, J H (NIFC) 1894 *E, S, W*, 1895 *W*, 1896 *E, S, W*, 1897 *E, S*, 1898 *E, S*, 1899 *S*
Lytle, J N (NIFC) 1888 *M*, 1889 *W*, 1890 *E*, 1891 *E, S*, 1894 *E, S, W*
Lyttle, V J (Collegians, Bedford) 1938 *E*, 1939 *E, S*

McAleese, D R (Ballymena) 1992 *F*
McAllan, G H (Dungannon) 1896 *S, W*
Macauley, J (Limerick) 1887 *E, S*
McBride, W D (Malone) 1988 *W, E* 1, *WS, It*, 1989 *S*, 1990 *F, W, Arg*, 1993 *S, F, W, E, R*, 1994 *W, E, S, A* 1(R), 1995 *S, F*, [*NZ, W, F*], *Fj* (R), 1996 *W, E, WS, A*, 1997 *It* 1(R), *F, W, E, S*
McBride, W J (Ballymena) 1962 *E, S, F, W*, 1963 *F, E, S, W, NZ*, 1964 *E, S, F*, 1965 *F, E, S, W, SA*, 1966 *F, E, S, W*, 1967 *A* 1, *E, S, W, F, A* 2, 1968 *F, E, S, W, A*, 1969 *F, E, S, W*, 1970 *SA, F, E, S, W*, 1971 *F, E, S, W*, 1972 *F* 1, *E, F* 2, 1973 *NZ, E, S, W, F*, 1974 *F, W, E, S, P, NZ*, 1975 *E, S, F, W*
McCahill, S A (Sunday's Well) 1995 *Fj* (t)
McCall, B W (London Irish) 1985 *F* (R), 1986 *E, S*
McCall, M C (Bangor, Dungannon, London Irish) 1992 *NZ* 1(R),2, 1994 *W*, 1996 *E* (R), *A*, 1997 *It* 1, *NZ, C, It* 2, 1998 *S, E, SA* 1,2
McCallan, B (Ballymena) 1960 *E, S*
McCarten, R J (London Irish) 1961 *E, W, F*
McCarthy, E A (Kingstown) 1882 *W*
McCarthy, J S (Dolphin) 1948 *F, E, S, W*, 1949 *F, E, S, W*, 1950 *W*, 1951 *F, E, S, W, SA*, 1952 *F, S, W, E*, 1953 *F, E, S*, 1954 *NZ, F, E, S, W*, 1955 *F, E*
McCarthy, P D (Cork Const) 1992 *NZ* 1,2, *A*, 1993 *S, R* (R)
MacCarthy, St G (Dublin U) 1882 *W*
McCarthy, T (Cork) 1898 *W*
McClelland, T A (Queen's U, Belfast) 1921 *E, S, W, F*, 1922 *E, W, F*, 1923 *E, S, W, F*, 1924 *F, E, S, W, NZ*
McClenahan, R O (Instonians) 1923 *E, S, W*
McClinton, A N (NIFC) 1910 *W, F*
McCombe, W McM (Dublin U, Bangor) 1968 *F*, 1975 *E, S, F, W*
McConnell, A A (Collegians) 1947 *A*, 1948 *F, E, S, W*, 1949 *F, E*
McConnell, G (Derry, Edinburgh U) 1912 *F, E*, 1913 *W, F*
McConnell, J W (Lansdowne) 1913 *S*
McCormac, F M (Wanderers) 1909 *W*, 1910 *W, F*
McCormick, W J (Wanderers) 1930 *E*
McCoull, H C (Belfast Albion) 1895 *E, S, W*, 1899 *E*
McCourt, D (Queen's U, Belfast) 1947 *A*
McCoy, J J (Dungannon, Bangor, Ballymena) 1984 *W, A*, 1985 *S, F, W, E*, 1986 *F*, 1987 [*Tg*], 1988 *E* 2, *WS, It*, 1989 *F, W, E, S, NZ*
McCracken, H (NIFC) 1954 *W*
McCullen, A (Lansdowne) 2003 *Sm*
McDermott, S J (London Irish) 1955 *S, W*
Macdonald, J A (Methodist Coll, Belfast) 1875 *E*, 1876 *E*, 1877 *S*, 1878 *E*, 1879 *S*, 1880 *E*, 1881 *S*, 1882 *E, S*, 1883 *E, S*, 1884 *E, S*
McDonald, J P (Malone) 1987 [*C*], 1990 *E* (R), *S, Arg*
McDonnell, A C (Dublin U) 1889 *W*, 1890 *S, W*, 1891 *E*
McDowell, J C (Instonians) 1924 *F, NZ*
McFarland, B A T (Derry) 1920 *S, W, F*, 1922 *W*
McGann, B J (Lansdowne) 1969 *F, E, S, W*, 1970 *SA, F, E, S, W*, 1971 *F, E, S, W*, 1972 *F* 1, *E, F* 2, 1973 *NZ, E, S, W*, 1976 *F, W, E, S, NZ*
McGowan, A N (Blackrock Coll) 1994 *US*
McGown, T M W (NIFC) 1899 *E, S*, 1901 *S*
McGrath, D G (UC Dublin, Cork Const) 1984 *S*, 1987 [*W, C, Tg, A*]
McGrath, N F (Oxford U, London Irish) 1934 *W*
McGrath, P J (UC Cork) 1965 *E, S, W, SA*, 1966 *F, E, S, W*, 1967 *A* 1, *A* 2
McGrath, R J M (Wanderers) 1977 *W, E, F* (R), 1981 *SA* 1,2, *A*, 1982 *W, E, S, F*, 1983 *S, F, W, E*, 1984 *F, W*
McGrath, T (Garryowen) 1956 *W*, 1958 *F*, 1960 *E, S, W, F*, 1961 *SA*
McGuinness, C D (St Mary's Coll) 1997 *NZ, C*, 1998 *F, W, E, SA* 1,2, *Gg, R* (R), *SA* 3, 1999 *F, W, E, S*
McGuire, E P (UC Galway) 1963 *E, S, W, NZ*, 1964 *E, S, W, F*
MacHale, S (Lansdowne) 1965 *F, E, S, W, SA*, 1966 *F, E, S, W*, 1967 *S, W, F*
McHugh, M (St Mary's Coll) 2003 *Tg*
McIldowie, G (Malone) 1906 *SA*, 1910 *E, S, W*
McIlrath, J A (Ballymena) 1976 *A, F, NZ*, 1977 *W, E*
McIlwaine, E H (NIFC) 1895 *S, W*
McIlwaine, E N (NIFC) 1875 *E*, 1876 *E*
McIlwaine, J E (NIFC) 1897 *E, S*, 1898 *E, S, W*, 1899 *E, W*
McIntosh, L M (Dublin U) 1884 *S*
MacIvor, C V (Dublin U) 1912 *F, E, S, W*, 1913 *E, S, F*
McIvor, S C (Garryowen) 1996 *A*, 1997 *It* 1, *S* (R)
McKay, J W (Queen's U, Belfast) 1947 *F, E, S, W, A*, 1948 *F, E, S, W*, 1949 *F, E, S, W*, 1950 *F, E, S, W*, 1951 *F, E, S, W, SA*, 1952 *F*
McKee, W D (NIFC) 1947 *A*, 1948 *F, E, S, W*, 1949 *F, E, S, W*, 1950 *F, E*, 1951 *SA*
McKeen, A J W (Lansdowne) 1999 [*R* (R)]
McKelvey, J M (Queen's U, Belfast) 1956 *F, E*
McKenna, P (St Mary's Coll) 2000 *Arg*
McKibbin, A R (Instonians, London Irish) 1977 *W, E, S*, 1978 *S, F, W, E, NZ*, 1979 *F, W, E, S*, 1980 *E, S*
McKibbin, C H (Instonians) 1976 *S* (R)
McKibbin, D (Instonians) 1950 *F, E, S, W*, 1951 *F, E, S, W*
McKibbin, H R (Queen's U, Belfast) 1938 *W*, 1939 *E, S, W*
McKinney, S A (Dungannon) 1972 *F* 1, *E, F* 2, 1973 *W, F*, 1974 *F, E, S, P, NZ*, 1975 *E, S*, 1976 *A, F, W, E, S, NZ*, 1977 *W, E, S*, 1978 *S* (R), *F, W, E*
McLaughlin, J H (Derry) 1887 *E, S*, 1888 *W, S*
McLean, R E (Dublin U) 1881 *S*, 1882 *W, E, S*, 1883 *E, S*, 1884 *E, S*, 1885 *E, S* 1
Maclear, B (Cork County, Monkstown) 1905 *E, S, W, NZ*, 1906 *E, S, W, SA*, 1907 *E, S, W*
McLennan, A C (Wanderers) 1977 *F*, 1978 *S, F, W, E, NZ*, 1979 *F, W, E, S*, 1980 *E, F*, 1981 *F, W, E, S, SA* 1,2
McLoughlin, F M (Northern) 1976 *A*
McLoughlin, G A J (Shannon) 1979 *F, W, E, S, A* 1,2, 1980 *E*, 1981 *SA* 1,2, 1982 *W, E, S, F*, 1983 *S, F, W, E*, 1984 *F*
McLoughlin, R J (UC Dublin, Blackrock Coll, Gosforth) 1962 *E, S, F*, 1963 *E, S, W, NZ*, 1964 *E, S*, 1965 *F, E, S, W, SA*, 1966 *F, E, S, W*, 1971 *F, E, S, W*, 1972 *F* 1, *E, F* 2, 1973 *NZ, E, S, W, F*, 1974 *F, W, E, S, P, NZ*, 1975 *E, S, F, W*
McMahon, L B (Blackrock Coll, UC Dublin) 1931 *E, SA*, 1933 *E*, 1934 *E*, 1936 *E, S, W*, 1937 *E, S, W*, 1938 *E, S*
McMaster, A W (Ballymena) 1972 *F* 1, *E, F* 2, 1973 *NZ, E, S, W, F*, 1974 *F, E, S, P*, 1975 *F, W*, 1976 *A, F, W, NZ*
McMordie, J (Queen's Coll, Belfast) 1886 *S*
McMorrow, A (Garryowen) 1951 *W*
McMullen, A R (Cork) 1881 *E, S*
McNamara, V (UC Cork) 1914 *E, S, W*
McNaughton, P P (Greystones) 1978 *S, F, W, E*, 1979 *F, W, E, S, A* 1,2, 1980 *E, S, F, W*, 1981 *F*
MacNeill, H P (Dublin U, Oxford U, Blackrock Coll, London Irish) 1981 *F, W, E, S, A*, 1982 *W, E, S, F*, 1983 *S, F, W, E*, 1984 *F, W, E, A*, 1985 *S, F, W, E*, 1986 *F, W, E, S, R*, 1987 *E, S, F, W*, [*W, C, Tg, A*], 1988 *S* (R), *E* 1,2
McQuilkin, K P (Bective Rangers, Lansdowne) 1996 *US, S, F*, 1997 *F* (t & R), *S*
MacSweeney, D A (Blackrock Coll) 1955 *S*
McVicker, H (Army, Richmond) 1927 *E, S, W, A*, 1928 *F*
McVicker, J (Collegians) 1924 *F, E, S, W, NZ*, 1925 *F, E, S, W*, 1926 *F, E, S, W*, 1927 *F, E, S, W, A*, 1928 *W*, 1930 *F*
McVicker, S (Queen's U, Belfast) 1922 *E, S, W, F*
McWeeney, J P J (St Mary's Coll) 1997 *NZ*
Madden, M N (Sunday's Well) 1955 *E, S, W*
Magee, J T (Bective Rangers) 1895 *E, S*

Magee, A M (Louis) (Bective Rangers, London Irish) 1895 *E, S, W*, 1896 *E, S, W*, 1897 *E, S*, 1898 *E, S, W*, 1899 *E, S, W*, 1900 *E, S, W*, 1901 *E, S, W*, 1902 *E, S, W*, 1903 *E, S, W*, 1904 *W*
Maggs, K M (Bristol, Bath) 1997 *NZ* (R), *C, It* 2, 1998 *S, F, W, E, SA* 1,2, *Gg, R* (R), *SA* 3, 1999 *F, W, E, S, It, A* 1,2, *Arg* 1, [*US, A* 3, *Arg* 2], 2000 *E, F, Arg, US* (R), *C*, 2001 *It* (R), *F* (R), *R, S* (R), *W, E, Sm, NZ*, 2002 *W, E, S, R, Ru, Gg, A, Fj, Arg*, 2003 *S* 1, *It* 1, *F, W* 1, *E, A, W* 2, *S* 2
Maginiss, R M (Dublin U) 1875 *E*, 1876 *E*
Magrath, R M (Cork Constitution) 1909 *S*
Maguire, J F (Cork) 1884 *S*
Mahoney, J (Dolphin) 1923 *E*
Malcolmson, G L (RAF, NIFC) 1935 *NZ*, 1936 *E, S, W*, 1937 *E, S, W*
Malone, N G (Oxford U, Leicester) 1993 *S, F*, 1994 *US* (R)
Mannion, N P (Corinthians, Lansdowne, Wanderers) 1988 *WS, It*, 1989 *F, W, E, S, NZ*, 1990 *E, S, F, W, Arg*, 1991 *Nm* 1(R),2, [*J*], 1993 *S*
Marshall, B D E (Queen's U, Belfast) 1963 *E*
Mason, S J P (Orrell, Richmond) 1996 *W, E, WS*
Massey-Westropp, R H (Limerick, Monkstown) 1886 *E*
Matier, R N (NIFC) 1878 *E*, 1879 *S*
Matthews, P M (Ards, Wanderers) 1984 *A*, 1985 *S, F, W, E*, 1986 *R*, 1987 *E, S, F, W*, [*W, Tg, A*], 1988 *S, F, W, E* 1,2, *WS, It*, 1989 *F, W, E, S, NZ*, 1990 *E, S*, 1991 *F, W, E, S, Nm* 1 [*Z, S, A*], 1992 *W, E, S*
Mattsson, J (Wanderers) 1948 *E*
Mayne, R B (Queen's U, Belfast) 1937 *W*, 1938 *E, W*, 1939 *E, S, W*
Mayne, R H (Belfast Academy) 1888 *W, S*
Mayne, T (NIFC) 1921 *E, S, F*
Mays, K M A (UC Dublin) 1973 *NZ, E, S, W*
Meares, A W D (Dublin U) 1899 *S, W*, 1900 *E, W*
Megaw, J (Richmond, Instonians) 1934 *W*, 1938 *E*
Millar, A (Kingstown) 1880 *E, S*, 1883 *E*
Millar, H J (Monkstown) 1904 *W*, 1905 *E, S, W*
Millar, S (Ballymena) 1958 *F*, 1959 *E, S, W, F*, 1960 *E, S, W, F, SA*, 1961 *E, S, W, F, SA*, 1962 *E, S, F*, 1963 *F, E, S, W*, 1964 *F*, 1968 *F, E, S, W, A*, 1969 *F, E, S, W*, 1970 *SA, F, E, S, W*
Millar, W H J (Queen's U, Belfast) 1951 *E, S, W*, 1952 *S, W*
Miller, E R P (Leicester, Terenure Coll) 1997 *It* 1, *F, W, E, NZ, It* 2, 1998 *S, W* (R), *Gg, R*, 1999 *F, W, E* (R), *S, Arg* 1(R), [*US* (R), *A* 3(t&R), *Arg* 2(R)], 2000 *US, C* (R), *SA*, 2001 *R, W, E, Sm, NZ*, 2002 *E, S, It* (R), *Fj* (R), 2003 *E* (t+R), *Tg, Sm, It* 2, *S* 2
Miller, F H (Wanderers) 1886 *S*
Milliken, R A (Bangor) 1973 *E, S, W, F*, 1974 *F, W, E, S, P, NZ*, 1975 *E, S, F, W*
Millin, T J (Dublin U) 1925 *W*
Minch, J B (Bective Rangers) 1912 *SA*, 1913 *E, S*, 1914 *E, S*
Moffat, J (Belfast Academy) 1888 *W, S, M*, 1889 *S*, 1890 *S, W*, 1891 *S*
Moffatt, J E (Old Wesley) 1904 *S*, 1905 *E, S, W*
Moffett, J W (Ballymena) 1961 *E, S*
Molloy, M G (UC Galway, London Irish) 1966 *F, E*, 1967 *A* 1, *E, S, W, F, A* 2, 1968 *F, E, S, W, A*, 1969 *F, E, S, W*, 1970 *F, E, S, W*, 1971 *F, E, S, W*, 1973 *F*, 1976 *A*
Moloney, J J (St Mary's Coll) 1972 *F* 1, *E, F* 2, 1973 *NZ, E, S, W, F*, 1974 *F, W, E, S, P, NZ*, 1975 *E, S, F, W*, 1976 *S*, 1978 *S, F, W, E*, 1979 *A* 1,2, 1980 *S, W*
Moloney, L A (Garryowen) 1976 *W* (R), *S*, 1978 *S* (R), *NZ*
Molony, J U (UC Dublin) 1950 *S*
Monteith, J D E (Queen's U, Belfast) 1947 *E, S, W*
Montgomery, A (NIFC) 1895 *S*
Montgomery, F P (Queen's U, Belfast) 1914 *E, S, W*
Montgomery, R (Cambridge U) 1887 *E, S, W*, 1891 *E*, 1892 *W*
Moore, C M (Dublin U) 1887 *S*, 1888 *W, S*
Moore, D F (Wanderers) 1883 *E, S*, 1884 *E, W*
Moore, F W (Wanderers) 1884 *W*, 1885 *E, S* 2, 1886 *S*
Moore, H (Windsor) 1876 *E*, 1877 *S*
Moore, H (Queen's U, Belfast) 1910 *S*, 1911 *W, F*, 1912 *F, E, S, W, SA*
Moore, T A P (Highfield) 1967 *A* 2, 1973 *NZ, E, S, W, F*, 1974 *F, W, E, S, P, NZ*
Moore, W D (Queen's Coll, Belfast) 1878 *E*
Moran, F G (Clontarf) 1936 *E*, 1937 *E, S, W*, 1938 *S, W*, 1939 *E, S, W*
Morell, H B (Dublin U) 1881 *E, S*, 1882 *W, E*
Morgan, G J (Clontarf) 1934 *E, S, W*, 1935 *E, S, W, NZ*, 1936 *E, S, W*, 1937 *E, S, W*, 1938 *E, S, W*, 1939 *E, S, W*
Moriarty, C C H (Monkstown) 1899 *W*
Moroney, J C M (Garryowen) 1968 *W, A*, 1969 *F, E, S, W*
Moroney, R J M (Lansdowne) 1984 *F, W*, 1985 *F*
Moroney, T A (UC Dublin) 1964 *W*, 1967 *A* 1, *E*
Morphy, E McG (Dublin U) 1908 *E*
Morris, D P (Bective Rangers) 1931 *W*, 1932 *E*, 1935 *E, S, W, NZ*
Morrow, J W R (Queen's Coll, Belfast) 1882 *S*, 1883 *E, S*, 1884 *E, W*, 1885 *S* 1,2, 1886 *E, S*, 1888 *S*
Morrow, R D (Bangor) 1986 *F, E, S*
Mortell, M (Bective Rangers, Dolphin) 1953 *F, E, S, W*, 1954 *NZ, F, E, S, W*
Morton, W A (Dublin U) 1888 *S*
Mostyn, M R (Galwegians) 1999 *A* 1, *Arg* 1, [*US, A* 3, *R, Arg* 2]
Moyers, L W (Dublin U) 1884 *W*
Moylett, M M F (Shannon) 1988 *E* 1
Mulcahy, W A (UC Dublin, Bective Rangers, Bohemians) 1958 *A, E, S, W, F*, 1959 *E, S, W, F*, 1960 *E, S, W, SA*, 1961 *E, S, W, SA*, 1962 *E, S, F, W*, 1963 *F, E, S, W, NZ*, 1964 *E, S, W, F*, 1965 *F, E, S, W, SA*
Mullan, B (Clontarf) 1947 *F, E, S, W*, 1948 *F, E, S, W*
Mullane, J P (Limerick Bohemians) 1928 *W*, 1929 *F*
Mullen, K D (Old Belvedere) 1947 *F, E, S, W, A*, 1948 *F, E, S, W*, 1949 *F, E, S, W*, 1950 *F, E, S, W*, 1951 *F, E, S, W, SA*, 1952 *F, S, W*
Mulligan, A A (Wanderers) 1956 *F, E*, 1957 *F, E, S, W*, 1958 *A, E, S, F*, 1959 *E, S, W, F*, 1960 *E, S, W, F, SA*, 1961 *W, F, SA*
Mullin, B J (Dublin U, Oxford U, Blackrock Coll, London Irish) 1984 *A*, 1985 *S, W, E*, 1986 *F, W, E, S, R*, 1987 *E, S, F, W*, [*W, C, Tg, A*], 1988 *S, F, W, E* 1,2, *WS, It*, 1989 *F, W, E, S, NZ*, 1990 *E, S, W, Arg*, 1991 *F, W, E, S, Nm* 1,2, [*J, S, A*], 1992 *W, E, S*, 1994 *US*, 1995 *E, S, F, W, It*, [*NZ, J, W, F*]
Mullins, M J (Young Munster, Old Crescent) 1999 *Arg* 1(R), [*R*], 2000 *E, S, It, Arg* (t&R), *US, C*, 2001 *It, R, W* (R), *E* (R), *Sm* (R), *NZ* (R), 2003 *Tg, Sm*
Murphy, C J (Lansdowne) 1939 *E, S, W*, 1947 *F, E*
Murphy, G E A (Leicester) 2000 *US, C* (R), *J*, 2001 *R, S, Sm*, 2002 *W, E, NZ* 1,2, *Fj*, 2003 *S* 1(R), *It* 1, *F, W* 1, *E, A, W* 2, *It* 2(R), *S* 2
Murphy, J G M W (London Irish) 1951 *SA*, 1952 *S, W, E*, 1954 *NZ*, 1958 *W*
Murphy, J J (Greystones) 1981 *SA* 1, 1982 *W* (R), 1984 *S*
Murphy, J N (Greystones) 1992 *A*
Murphy, K J (Cork Constitution) 1990 *E, S, F, W, Arg*, 1991 *F, W* (R), *S* (R), 1992 *S, F, NZ* 2(R)
Murphy, N A A (Cork Constitution) 1958 *A, E, S, W, F*, 1959 *E, S, W, F*, 1960 *E, S, W, F, SA*, 1961 *E, S, W*, 1962 *E*, 1963 *NZ*, 1964 *E, S, W, F*, 1965 *F, E, S, W, SA*, 1966 *F, E, S, W*, 1967 *A* 1, *E, S, W, F*, 1969 *F, E, S, W*
Murphy, N F (Cork Constitution) 1930 *E, W*, 1931 *F, E, S, W, SA*, 1932 *E, S, W*, 1933 *E*
Murphy-O'Connor, J (Bective Rangers) 1954 *E*
Murray, H W (Dublin U) 1877 *S*, 1878 *E*, 1879 *E*
Murray, J B (UC Dublin) 1963 *F*
Murray, P F (Wanderers) 1927 *F*, 1929 *F, E, S*, 1930 *F, E, S, W*, 1931 *F, E, S, W, SA*, 1932 *E, S, W*, 1933 *E, W, S*
Murtagh, C W (Portadown) 1977 *S*
Myles, J (Dublin U) 1875 *E*

Nash, L C (Queen's Coll, Cork) 1889 *S*, 1890 *W, E*, 1891 *E, S, W*
Neely, M R (Collegians) 1947 *F, E, S, W*
Neill, H J (NIFC) 1885 *E, S* 1,2, 1886 *S*, 1887 *E, S, W*, 1888 *W, S*
Neill, J McF (Instonians) 1926 *F*
Nelson, J E (Malone) 1947 *A*, 1948 *E, S, W*, 1949 *F, E, S, W*, 1950 *F, E, S, W*, 1951 *F, E, W*, 1954 *F*
Nelson, R (Queen's Coll, Belfast) 1882 *E, S*, 1883 *S*, 1886 *S*
Nesdale, R P (Newcastle) 1997 *W, E, S, NZ* (R), *C*, 1998 *F* (R), *W* (R), *Gg, SA* 3(R), 1999 *It, A* 2(R), [*US* (R), *R*]
Nesdale, T J (Garryowen) 1961 *F*
Neville, W C (Dublin U) 1879 *S, E*
Nicholson, P C (Dublin U) 1900 *E, S, W*
Norton, G W (Bective Rangers) 1949 *F, E, S, W*, 1950 *F, E, S, W*, 1951 *F, E, S*
Notley, J R (Wanderers) 1952 *F, S*
Nowlan, K W (St Mary's Coll) 1997 *NZ, C, It* 2

O'Brien, B (Derry) 1893 *S, W*
O'Brien, B A P (Shannon) 1968 *F, E, S*
O'Brien, D J (London Irish, Cardiff, Old Belvedere) 1948 *E, S, W*, 1949 *F, E, S, W*, 1950 *F, E, S, W*, 1951 *F, E, S, W, SA*, 1952 *F, S, W, E*

O'Brien, K A (Broughton Park) 1980 *E*, 1981 *SA* 1(R),2
O'Brien-Butler, P E (Monkstown) 1897 *S*, 1898 *E, S*, 1899 *S, W*, 1900 *E*
O'Callaghan, C T (Carlow) 1910 *W, F*, 1911 *E, S, W, F*, 1912 *F*
O'Callaghan, D (Cork Const) 2003 *W* 1(R), *Tg* (R), *Sm* (R), *W* 2(R), *It* 2(R)
O'Callaghan, M P (Sunday's Well) 1962 *W*, 1964 *E, F*
O'Callaghan, P (Dolphin) 1967 *A* 1, *E, A* 2, 1968 *F, E, S, W*, 1969 *F, E, S, W*, 1970 *SA, F, E, S, W*, 1976 *F, W, E, S, NZ*
O'Connell, K D (Sunday's Well) 1994 *F, E* (t)
O'Connell, P (Bective Rangers) 1913 *W, F*, 1914 *F, E, S, W*
O'Connell, P J (Young Munster) 2002 *W, It* (R), *F* (R), *NZ* 1, 2003 *E* (R), *A* (R), *Tg, Sm, W* 2, *S* 2
O'Connell, W J (Lansdowne) 1955 *F*
O'Connor, H S (Dublin U) 1957 *F, E, S, W*
O'Connor, J (Garryowen) 1895 *S*
O'Connor, J H (Bective Rangers) 1888 *M*, 1890 *S, W, E*, 1891 *E, S*, 1892 *E, W*, 1893 *E, S*, 1894 *E, S, W*, 1895 *E*, 1896 *E, S, W*
O'Connor, J J (Garryowen) 1909 *F*
O'Connor, J J (UC Cork) 1933 *S*, 1934 *E, S, W*, 1935 *E, S, W, NZ*, 1936 *S, W*, 1938 *S*
O'Connor, P J (Lansdowne) 1887 *W*
O'Cuinneagain, D (Sale, Ballymena) 1998 *SA* 1,2, *Gg* (R), *R* (R), *SA* 3, 1999 *F, W, E, S, It, A* 1,2, *Arg* 1, [*US, A* 3, *R, Arg* 2], 2000 *E, It* (R)
Odbert, R V M (RAF) 1928 *F*
O'Donnell, R C (St Mary's Coll) 1979 *A* 1,2, 1980 *S, F, W*
O'Donoghue, P J (Bective Rangers) 1955 *F, E, S, W*, 1956 *W*, 1957 *F, E*, 1958 *A, E, S, W*
O'Driscoll, B G (Blackrock Coll) 1999 *A* 1,2, *Arg* 1, [*US, A* 3, *R* (R), *Arg* 2], 2000 *E, S, It, F, W, J, SA*, 2001 *F, S, W, E, Sm, NZ*, 2002 *W, E, S, It, F, NZ* 1,2, *R, Ru, Gg, A, Fj, Arg*, 2003 *S* 1, *It* 1, *F, W* 1, *E, W* 2, *It* 2, *S* 2
O'Driscoll, B J (Manchester) 1971 *F* (R), *E, S, W*
O'Driscoll, J B (London Irish, Manchester) 1978 *S*, 1979 *A* 1,2, 1980 *E, S, F, W*, 1981 *F, W, E, S, SA* 1,2, *A*, 1982 *W, E, S, F*, 1983 *S, F, W, E*, 1984 *F, W, E, S*
O'Driscoll, M (Cork Const) 2001 *R* (R), 2002 *Fj* (R)
O'Flanagan, K P (London Irish) 1947 *A*
O'Flanagan, M (Lansdowne) 1948 *S*
O'Gara, R J R (Cork Const) 2000 *S, It, F, W, Arg* (R), *US, C* (R), *J, SA*, 2001 *It, F, S, W* (R), *E* (R), *Sm*, 2002 *W* (R), *E* (R), *S* (R), *It* (t), *F* (R), *NZ* 1,2, *R, Ru, Gg, A, Arg*, 2003 *W* 1(R), *E* (R), *A* (t+R), *Tg, Sm, S* 2
O'Grady, D (Sale) 1997 *It* 2
O'Hanlon, B (Dolphin) 1947 *E, S, W*, 1948 *F, E, S, W*, 1949 *F, E, S, W*, 1950 *F*
O'Hara, P T J (Sunday's Well, Cork Const) 1988 *WS* (R), 1989 *F, W, E, NZ*, 1990 *E, S, F, W*, 1991 *Nm* 1, [*J*], 1993 *F, W, E*, 1994 *US*
O'Kelly, M E (London Irish, St Mary's Coll) 1997 *NZ, C, It* 2, 1998 *S, F, W, E, SA* 1,2, *Gg, R, SA* 3, 1999 *A* 1(R),2, *Arg* 1(R), [*US* (R), *A* 3, *R, Arg* 2], 2000 *E, S, It, F, W, Arg, US, J, SA*, 2001 *It, F, S, W, E, NZ*, 2002 *E, S, It, F, NZ* 1(R),2, *R, Ru, Gg, A, Fj, Arg*, 2003 *S* 1, *It* 1, *F, W* 1, *E, A, W* 2, *S* 2
O'Leary, A (Cork Constitution) 1952 *S, W, E*
O'Loughlin, D B (UC Cork) 1938 *E, S, W*, 1939 *E, S, W*
O'Mahony, D W (UC Dublin, Moseley, Bedford) 1995 *It*, [*F*], 1997 *It* 2, 1998 *R*
O'Mahony, David (Cork Constitution) 1995 *It*
O'Meara, B T (Cork Constitution) 1997 *E* (R), *S, NZ* (R), 1998 *S*, 1999 [*US* (R), *R* (R)], 2001 *It* (R), 2003 *Sm* (R), *It* 2(R)
O'Meara, J A (UC Cork, Dolphin) 1951 *F, E, S, W, SA*, 1952 *F, S, W, E*, 1953 *F, E, S, W*, 1954 *NZ, F, E, S*, 1955 *F, E*, 1956 *S, W*, 1958 *W*
O'Neill, H O'H (Queen's U, Belfast, UC Cork) 1930 *E, S, W*, 1933 *E, S, W*
O'Neill, J B (Queen's U, Belfast) 1920 *S*
O'Neill, W A (UC Dublin, Wanderers) 1952 *E*, 1953 *F, E, S, W*, 1954 *NZ*
O'Reilly, A J F (Old Belvedere, Leicester) 1955 *F, E, S, W*, 1956 *F, E, S, W*, 1957 *F, E, S, W*, 1958 *A, E, S, W, F*, 1959 *E, S, W, F*, 1960 *E*, 1961 *E, F, SA*, 1963 *F, S, W*, 1970 *E*
Orr, P A (Old Wesley) 1976 *F, W, E, S, NZ*, 1977 *W, E, S, F*, 1978 *S, F, W, E, NZ*, 1979 *F, W, E, S, A* 1,2, 1980 *E, S, F, W*, 1981 *F, W, E, S, SA* 1,2, *A*, 1982 *W, E, S, F*, 1983 *S, F, W, E*, 1984 *F, W, E, S, A*, 1985 *S, F, W, E*, 1986 *F, S, R*, 1987 *E, S, F, W*, [*W, C, A*]
O'Shea, C M P (Lansdowne, London Irish) 1993 *R*, 1994 *F, W, E, S, A* 1,2, *US*, 1995 *E, S*, [*J, W, F*], 1997 *It* 1, *F, S* (R), 1998 *S, F, SA* 1,2, *Gg, R, SA* 3, 1999 *F, W, E, S, It, A* 1, *Arg* 1, [*US, A* 3, *R, Arg* 2], 2000 *E*
O'Sullivan, A C (Dublin U) 1882 *S*
O'Sullivan, J M (Limerick) 1884 *S*, 1887 *S*
O'Sullivan, P J A (Galwegians) 1957 *F, E, S, W*, 1959 *E, S, W, F*, 1960 *SA*, 1961 *E, S*, 1962 *F, W*, 1963 *F, NZ*
O'Sullivan, W (Queen's Coll, Cork) 1895 *S*
Owens, R H (Dublin U) 1922 *E, S*

Parfrey, P (UC Cork) 1974 *NZ*
Parke, J C (Monkstown) 1903 *W*, 1904 *E, S, W*, 1905 *W, NZ*, 1906 *E, S, W, SA*, 1907 *E, S, W*, 1908 *E, S, W*, 1909 *E, S, W, F*
Parr, J S (Wanderers) 1914 *F, E, S, W*
Patterson, C S (Instonians) 1978 *NZ*, 1979 *F, W, E, S, A* 1,2, 1980 *E, S, F, W*
Patterson, R d'A (Wanderers) 1912 *F, S, W, SA*, 1913 *E, S, W, F*
Payne, C T (NIFC) 1926 *E*, 1927 *F, E, S, A*, 1928 *F, E, S, W*, 1929 *F, E, W*, 1930 *F, E, S, W*
Pedlow, A C (CIYMS) 1953 *W*, 1954 *NZ, F, E*, 1955 *F, E, S, W*, 1956 *F, E, S, W*, 1957 *F, E, S, W*, 1958 *A, E, S, W, F*, 1959 *E*, 1960 *E, S, W, F, SA*, 1961 *S*, 1962 *W*, 1963 *F*
Pedlow, J (Bessbrook) 1882 *S*, 1884 *W*
Pedlow, R (Bessbrook) 1891 *W*
Pedlow, T B (Queen's Coll, Belfast) 1889 *S, W*
Peel, T (Limerick) 1892 *E, S, W*
Peirce, W (Cork) 1881 *E*
Phipps, G C (Army) 1950 *E, W*, 1952 *F, W, E*
Pike, T O (Lansdowne) 1927 *E, S, W, A*, 1928 *F, E, S, W*
Pike, V J (Lansdowne) 1931 *E, S, W, SA*, 1932 *E, S, W*, 1933 *E, W, S*, 1934 *E, S, W*
Pike, W W (Kingstown) 1879 *E*, 1881 *E, S*, 1882 *E*, 1883 *S*
Pinion, G (Belfast Collegians) 1909 *E, S, W, F*
Piper, O J S (Cork Constitution) 1909 *E, S, W, F*, 1910 *E, S, W, F*
Polden, S E (Clontarf) 1913 *W, F*, 1914 *F*, 1920 *F*
Popham, I (Cork Constitution) 1922 *S, W, F*, 1923 *F*
Popplewell, N J (Greystones, Wasps, Newcastle) 1989 *NZ*, 1990 *Arg*, 1991 *Nm* 1,2, [*Z, S, A*], 1992 *W, E, S, F, NZ* 1,2, *A*, 1993 *S, F, W, E, R*, 1994 *F, W, E, S, US*, 1995 *E, S, F, W, It*, [*NZ, J, W, F*], *Fj*, 1996 *US, S, F, W, E, A*, 1997 *It* 1, *F, W, E, NZ, C*, 1998 *S* (t), *F* (R)
Potterton, H N (Wanderers) 1920 *W*
Pratt, R H (Dublin U) 1933 *E, W, S*, 1934 *E, S*
Price, A H (Dublin U) 1920 *S, F*
Pringle, J C (NIFC) 1902 *S, W*
Purcell, N M (Lansdowne) 1921 *E, S, W, F*
Purdon, H (NIFC) 1879 *S, E*, 1880 *E*, 1881 *E, S*
Purdon, W B (Queen's Coll, Belfast) 1906 *E, S, W*
Purser, F C (Dublin U) 1898 *E, S, W*

Quinlan, A (Shannon) 1999 [*R* (R)], 2001 *It, F*, 2002 *NZ* 2(R), *Ru* (R), *Gg* (R), *A* (R), *Fj, Arg* (R), 2003 *S* 1(R), *It* 1(R), *F* (R), *W* 1, *E* (R), *A, W* 2
Quinlan, S V J (Blackrock Coll) 1956 *F, E, W*, 1958 *W*
Quinn, B T (Old Belvedere) 1947 *F*
Quinn, F P (Old Belvedere) 1981 *F, W, E*
Quinn, J P (Dublin U) 1910 *E, S*, 1911 *E, S, W, F*, 1912 *E, S, W*, 1913 *E, W, F*, 1914 *F, E, S*
Quinn, K (Old Belvedere) 1947 *F, A*, 1953 *F, E, S*
Quinn, M A M (Lansdowne) 1973 *F*, 1974 *F, W, E, S, P, NZ*, 1977 *S, F*, 1981 *SA* 2
Quirke, J M T (Blackrock Coll) 1962 *E, S*, 1968 *S*

Rainey, P I (Ballymena) 1989 *NZ*
Rambaut, D F (Dublin U) 1887 *E, S, W*, 1888 *W*
Rea, H H (Edinburgh U) 1967 *A* 1, 1969 *F*
Read, H M (Dublin U) 1910 *E, S*, 1911 *E, S, W, F*, 1912 *F, E, S, W, SA*, 1913 *E, S*
Reardon, J V (Cork Constitution) 1934 *E, S*
Reid, C (NIFC) 1899 *S, W*, 1900 *E*, 1903 *W*
Reid, J L (Richmond) 1934 *S, W*
Reid, P J (Garryowen) 1947 *A*, 1948 *F, E, W*
Reid, T E (Garryowen) 1953 *E, S, W*, 1954 *NZ, F*, 1955 *E, S*, 1956 *F, E*, 1957 *F, E, S, W*
Reidy, C J (London Irish) 1937 *W*
Reidy, G F (Dolphin, Lansdowne) 1953 *W*, 1954 *F, E, S, W*
Richey, H A (Dublin U) 1889 *W*, 1890 *S*
Ridgeway, E C (Wanderers) 1932 *S, W*, 1935 *E, S, W*
Rigney, B J (Greystones) 1991 *F, W, E, S, Nm* 1, 1992 *F, NZ* 1(R),2

Ringland, T M (Queen's U, Belfast, Ballymena) 1981 *A*, 1982 *W, E, F*, 1983 *S, F, W, E*, 1984 *F, W, E, S, A*, 1985 *S, F, W, E*, 1986 *F, W, E, S, R*, 1987 *E, S, F, W*, [*W, C, Tg, A*], 1988 *S, F, W, E* 1
Riordan, W F (Cork Constitution) 1910 *E*
Ritchie, J S (London Irish) 1956 *F, E*
Robb, C G (Queen's Coll, Belfast) 1904 *E, S, W*, 1905 *NZ*, 1906 *S*
Robbie, J C (Dublin U, Greystones) 1976 *A, F, NZ*, 1977 *S, F*, 1981 *F, W, E, S*
Robinson, B F (Ballymena, London Irish) 1991 *F, W, E, S, Nm* 1,2, [*Z, S, A*], 1992 *W, E, S, F, NZ* 1,2, *A*, 1993 *W, E, R*, 1994 *F, W, E, S, A* 1,2
Robinson, T T H (Wanderers) 1904 *E, S*, 1905 *E, S, W, NZ*, 1906 *SA*, 1907 *E, S, W*
Roche, J (Wanderers) 1890 *S, W, E*, 1891 *E, S, W*, 1892 *W*
Roche, R E (UC Galway) 1955 *E, S*, 1957 *S, W*
Roche, W J (UC Cork) 1920 *E, S, F*
Roddy, P J (Bective Rangers) 1920 *S, F*
Roe, R (Lansdowne) 1952 *E*, 1953 *F, E, S, W*, 1954 *F, E, S, W*, 1955 *F, E, S, W*, 1956 *F, E, S, W*, 1957 *F, E, S, W*
Rolland, A C (Blackrock Coll) 1990 *Arg*, 1994 *US* (R), 1995 *It* (R)
Rooke, C V (Dublin U) 1891 *E, W*, 1892 *E, S, W*, 1893 *E, S, W*, 1894 *E, S, W*, 1895 *E, S, W*, 1896 *E, S, W*, 1897 *E, S*
Ross, D J (Belfast Academy) 1884 *E*, 1885 *S* 1,2, 1886 *E, S*
Ross, G R P (CIYMS) 1955 *W*
Ross, J F (NIFC) 1886 *S*
Ross, J P (Lansdowne) 1885 *E, S* 1,2, 1886 *E, S*
Ross, N G (Malone) 1927 *F, E*
Ross, W McC (Queen's U, Belfast) 1932 *E, S, W*, 1933 *E, W, S*, 1934 *E, S*, 1935 *NZ*
Russell, J (UC Cork) 1931 *F, E, S, W, SA*, 1933 *E, W, S*, 1934 *E, S, W*, 1935 *E, S, W*, 1936 *E, S, W*, 1937 *E, S*
Russell, P (Instonians) 1990 *E*, 1992 *NZ* 1,2, *A*
Rutherford, W G (Tipperary) 1884 *E, S*, 1885 *E, S* 1, 1886 *E*, 1888 *W*
Ryan, E (Dolphin) 1937 *W*, 1938 *E, S*
Ryan, J (Rockwell Coll) 1897 *E*, 1898 *E, S, W*, 1899 *E, S, W*, 1900 *S, W*, 1901 *E, S, W*, 1902 *E*, 1904 *E*
Ryan, J G (UC Dublin) 1939 *E, S, W*
Ryan, M (Rockwell Coll) 1897 *E, S*, 1898 *E, S, W*, 1899 *E, S, W*, 1900 *E, S, W*, 1901 *E, S, W*, 1903 *E*, 1904 *E, S*

Saunders, R (London Irish) 1991 *F, W, E, S, Nm* 1,2, [*Z, J, S, A*], 1992 *W*, 1994 *F* (t)
Saverimutto, C (Sale) 1995 *Fj*, 1996 *US, S*
Sayers, H J M (Lansdowne) 1935 *E, S, W*, 1936 *E, S, W*, 1938 *W*, 1939 *E, S, W*
Scally, C J (U C Dublin) 1998 *Gg* (R), *R*, 1999 *S* (R), *It*
Schute, F (Wanderers) 1878 *E*, 1879 *E*
Schute, F G (Dublin U) 1912 *SA*, 1913 *E, S*
Scott, D (Malone) 1961 *F, SA*, 1962 *S*
Scott, R D (Queen's U, Belfast) 1967 *E, F*, 1968 *F, E, S*
Scovell, R H (Kingstown) 1883 *E*, 1884 *E*
Scriven, G (Dublin U) 1879 *S, E*, 1880 *E, S*, 1881 *E*, 1882 *S*, 1883 *E, S*
Sealy, J (Dublin U) 1896 *E, S, W*, 1897 *S*, 1899 *E, S, W*, 1900 *E, S*
Sexton, J F (Dublin U, Lansdowne) 1988 *E* 2, *WS, It*, 1989 *F*
Sexton, W J (Garryowen) 1984 *A*, 1988 *S, E* 2
Shanahan, T (Lansdowne) 1885 *E, S* 1,2, 1886 *E*, 1888 *S, W*
Shaw, G M (Windsor) 1877 *S*
Sheahan, F J (Cork Const) 2000 *US* (R), 2001 *It* (R), *R, W* (R), *Sm*, 2002 *W, E, S, Gg* (R), *A* (t+R), *Fj*, 2003 *S* 1(R), *It* 1(R)
Sheehan, M D (London Irish) 1932 *E*
Sherry, B F (Terenure Coll) 1967 *A* 1, *E, S, A* 2, 1968 *F, E*
Sherry, M J A (Lansdowne) 1975 *F, W*
Shields, P M (Ballymena) 2003 *Sm* (R), *It* 2(R)
Siggins, J A E (Belfast Collegians) 1931 *F, E, S, W, SA*, 1932 *E, S, W*, 1933 *E, W, S*, 1934 *E, S, W*, 1935 *E, S, W, NZ*, 1936 *E, S, W*, 1937 *E, S, W*
Slattery, J F (UC Dublin, Blackrock Coll) 1970 *SA, F, E, S, W*, 1971 *F, E, S, W*, 1972 *F* 1, *E, F* 2, 1973 *NZ, E, S, W, F*, 1974 *F, W, E, S, P, NZ*, 1975 *E, S, F, W*, 1976 *A*, 1977 *S, F*, 1978 *S, F, W, E, NZ*, 1979 *F, W, E, S, A* 1,2, 1980 *E, S, F, W*, 1981 *F, W, E, S, SA* 1,2, *A*, 1982 *W, E, S, F*, 1983 *S, F, W, E*, 1984 *F*
Smartt, F N B (Dublin U) 1908 *E, S*, 1909 *E*
Smith, B A (Oxford U, Leicester) 1989 *NZ*, 1990 *S, F, W, Arg*, 1991 *F, W, E, S*
Smith, J H (London Irish) 1951 *F, E, S, W, SA*, 1952 *F, S, W, E*, 1954 *NZ, W, F*
Smith, R E (Lansdowne) 1892 *E*
Smith, S J (Ballymena) 1988 *E* 2, *WS, It*, 1989 *F, W, E, S, NZ*, 1990 *E*, 1991 *F, W, E, S, Nm* 1,2, [*Z, S, A*], 1992 *W, E, S, F, NZ* 1,2, 1993 *S*
Smithwick, F F S (Monkstown) 1898 *S, W*
Smyth, J T (Queen's U, Belfast) 1920 *F*
Smyth, P J (Belfast Collegians) 1911 *E, S, F*
Smyth, R S (Dublin U) 1903 *E, S*, 1904 *E*
Smyth, T (Malone, Newport) 1908 *E, S, W*, 1909 *E, S, W*, 1910 *E, S, W, F*, 1911 *E, S, W*, 1912 *E*
Smyth, W S (Belfast Collegians) 1910 *W, F*, 1920 *E*
Solomons, B A H (Dublin U) 1908 *E, S, W*, 1909 *E, S, W, F*, 1910 *E, S, W*
Spain, A W (UC Dublin) 1924 *NZ*
Sparrow, W (Dublin U) 1893 *W*, 1894 *E*
Spillane, B J (Bohemians) 1985 *S, F, W, E*, 1986 *F, W, E*, 1987 *F, W*, [*W, C, A* (R)], 1989 *E* (R)
Spring, D E (Dublin U) 1978 *S, NZ*, 1979 *S*, 1980 *S, F, W*, 1981 *W*
Spring, R M (Lansdowne) 1979 *F, W, E*
Spunner, H F (Wanderers) 1881 *E, S*, 1884 *W*
Stack, C R R (Dublin U) 1889 *S*
Stack, G H (Dublin U) 1875 *E*
Staples, J E (London Irish, Harlequins) 1991 *W, E, S, Nm* 1,2, [*Z, J, S, A*], 1992 *W, E, NZ* 1,2, *A*, 1995 *F, W, It*, [*NZ*], *Fj*, 1996 *US, S, F, A*, 1997 *W, E, S*
Staunton, J W (Garryowen) 2001 *Sm*
Steele, H W (Ballymena) 1976 *E*, 1977 *F*, 1978 *F, W, E*, 1979 *F, W, E, A* 1,2
Stephenson, G V (Queen's U, Belfast, London Hosp) 1920 *F*, 1921 *E, S, W, F*, 1922 *E, S, W, F*, 1923 *E, S, W, F*, 1924 *F, E, S, W, NZ*, 1925 *F, E, S, W*, 1926 *F, E, S, W*, 1927 *F, E, S, W, A*, 1928 *F, E, S, W*, 1929 *F, E, W*, 1930 *F, E, S, W*
Stephenson, H W V (United Services) 1922 *S, W, F*, 1924 *F, E, S, W, NZ*, 1925 *F, E, S, W*, 1927 *A*, 1928 *E*
Stevenson, J (Dungannon) 1888 *M*, 1889 *S*
Stevenson, J B (Instonians) 1958 *A, E, S, W, F*
Stevenson, R (Dungannon) 1887 *E, S, W*, 1888 *M*, 1889 *S, W*, 1890 *S, W, E*, 1891 *W*, 1892 *W*, 1893 *E, S, W*
Stevenson, T H (Belfast Acad) 1895 *E, W*, 1896 *E, S, W*, 1897 *E, S*
Stewart, A L (NIFC) 1913 *W, F*, 1914 *F*
Stewart, W J (Queen's U, Belfast, NIFC) 1922 *F*, 1924 *S*, 1928 *F, E, S, W*, 1929 *F, E, S, W*
Stoker, E W (Wanderers) 1888 *W, S*
Stoker, F O (Wanderers) 1886 *S*, 1888 *W, M*, 1889 *S*, 1891 *W*
Stokes, O S (Cork Bankers) 1882 *E*, 1884 *E*
Stokes, P (Garryowen) 1913 *E, S*, 1914 *F*, 1920 *E, S, W, F*, 1921 *E, S, F*, 1922 *W, F*
Stokes, R D (Queen's Coll, Cork) 1891 *S, W*
Strathdee, E (Queen's U, Belfast) 1947 *E, S, W, A*, 1948 *W, F*, 1949 *E, S, W*
Stringer, P A (Shannon) 2000 *S, It, F, W, Arg, C, J, SA*, 2001 *It, F, R, S* (R), *W, E, Sm, NZ*, 2002 *W, E, S, It, F, NZ* 1,2, *R, Ru, Gg, A, Arg*, 2003 *S* 1, *It* 1, *F, W* 1, *E, A, W* 2, *S* 2
Stuart, C P (Clontarf) 1912 *SA*
Stuart, I M B (Dublin U) 1924 *E, S*
Sugars, H S (Dublin U) 1905 *NZ*, 1906 *SA*, 1907 *S*
Sugden, M (Wanderers) 1925 *F, E, S, W*, 1926 *F, E, S, W*, 1927 *E, S, W, A*, 1928 *F, E, S, W*, 1929 *F, E, S, W*, 1930 *F, E, S, W*, 1931 *F, E, S, W*
Sullivan, D B (UC Dublin) 1922 *E, S, W, F*
Sweeney, J A (Blackrock Coll) 1907 *E, S, W*
Symes, G R (Monkstown) 1895 *E*
Synge, J S (Lansdowne) 1929 *S*

Taggart, T (Dublin U) 1887 *W*
Taylor, A S (Queen's Coll, Belfast) 1910 *E, S, W*, 1912 *F*
Taylor, D R (Queen's Coll, Belfast) 1903 *E*
Taylor, J (Belfast Collegians) 1914 *E, S, W*
Taylor, J W (NIFC) 1879 *S*, 1880 *E, S*, 1881 *S*, 1882 *E, S*, 1883 *E, S*
Tector, W R (Wanderers) 1955 *F, E, S*
Tedford, A (Malone) 1902 *E, S, W*, 1903 *E, S, W*, 1904 *E, S, W*, 1905 *E, S, W, NZ*, 1906 *E, S, W, SA*, 1907 *E, S, W*, 1908 *E, S, W*
Teehan, C (UC Cork) 1939 *E, S, W*
Thompson, C (Belfast Collegians) 1907 *E, S*, 1908 *E, S, W*, 1909 *E, S, W, F*, 1910 *E, S, W, F*
Thompson, J A (Queen's Coll, Belfast) 1885 *S* 1,2

Thompson, J K S (Dublin U) 1921 *W*, 1922 *E, S, F*, 1923 *E, S, W, F*
Thompson, R G (Lansdowne) 1882 *W*
Thompson, R H (Instonians) 1951 *SA*, 1952 *F*, 1954 *NZ, F, E, S, W*, 1955 *F, S, W*, 1956 *W*
Thornhill, T (Wanderers) 1892 *E, S, W*, 1893 *E*
Thrift, H (Dublin U) 1904 *W*, 1905 *E, S, W, NZ*, 1906 *E, W, SA*, 1907 *E, S, W*, 1908 *E, S, W*, 1909 *E, S, W, F*
Tierney, D (UC Cork) 1938 *S, W*, 1939 *E*
Tierney, T A (Garryowen) 1999 *A* 1,2, *Arg* 1, [*US, A* 3, *R, Arg* 2], 2000 *E*
Tillie, C R (Dublin U) 1887 *E, S*, 1888 *W, S*
Todd, A W P (Dublin U) 1913 *W, F*, 1914 *F*
Topping, J A (Ballymena) 1996 *WS, A*, 1997 *It* 1, *F, E*, 1999 [*R*], 2000 *US*, 2003 *A*
Torrens, J D (Bohemians) 1938 *W*, 1939 *E, S, W*
Tucker, C C (Shannon) 1979 *F, W*, 1980 *F* (R)
Tuke, B B (Bective Rangers) 1890 *E*, 1891 *E, S*, 1892 *E*, 1894 *E, S, W*, 1895 *E, S*
Turley, N (Blackrock Coll) 1962 *E*
Tweed, D A (Ballymena) 1995 *F, W, It*, [*J*]
Tydings, J J (Young Munster) 1968 *A*
Tyrrell, W (Queen's U, Belfast) 1910 *F*, 1913 *E, S, W, F*, 1914 *F, E, S, W*

Uprichard, R J H (Harlequins, RAF) 1950 *S, W*

Waide, S L (Oxford U, NIFC) 1932 *E, S, W*, 1933 *E, W*
Waites, J (Bective Rangers) 1886 *S*, 1888 *M*, 1889 *W*, 1890 *S, W, E*, 1891 *E*
Waldron, O C (Oxford U, London Irish) 1966 *S, W*, 1968 *A*
Walker, S (Instonians) 1934 *E, S*, 1935 *E, S, W, NZ*, 1936 *E, S, W*, 1937 *E, S, W*, 1938 *E, S, W*
Walkington, D B (NIFC) 1887 *E, W*, 1888 *W*, 1890 *W, E*, 1891 *E, S, W*
Walkington, R B (NIFC) 1875 *E*, 1876 *E*, 1877 *E, S*, 1878 *E*, 1879 *S*, 1880 *E, S*, 1882 *E, S*
Wall, H (Dolphin) 1965 *S, W*
Wallace, D P (Garryowen) 2000 *Arg, US*, 2001 *It, F, R* (R), *S* (R), *W, E, NZ*, 2002 *W, E, S, It, F*, 2003 *Tg* (R), *Sm* (R), *W* 2(t+R), *S* 2
Wallace, Jas (Wanderers) 1904 *E, S*
Wallace, Jos (Wanderers) 1903 *S, W*, 1904 *E, S, W*, 1905 *E, S, W, NZ*, 1906 *W*
Wallace, P S (Blackrock Coll, Saracens) 1995 [*J*], *Fj*, 1996 *US, W, E, WS, A*, 1997 *It* 1, *F, W, E, S, NZ, C*, 1998 *S, F, W, E, SA* 1,2, *Gg, R*, 1999 *F, W, E, S, It* (R), 1999 *A* 1,2, *Arg* 1, [*US, A* 3, *R, Arg* 2], 2000 *E, US, C* (R), 2002 *W* (R), *E* (R), *S* (R), *It* (R), *F* (R), *NZ* 2(R), *Ru* (R), *Gg* (R)
Wallace, R M (Garryowen, Saracens) 1991 *Nm* 1(R), 1992 *W, E, S, F, A*, 1993 *S, F, W, E, R*, 1994 *F, W, E, S*, 1995 *W, It*, [*NZ, J, W*], *Fj*, 1996 *US, S, F, WS*, 1998 *S, F, W, E*
Wallace, T H (Cardiff) 1920 *E, S, W*
Wallis, A K (Wanderers) 1892 *E, S, W*, 1893 *E, W*
Wallis, C O'N (Old Cranleighans, Wanderers) 1935 *NZ*
Wallis, T G (Wanderers) 1921 *F*, 1922 *E, S, W, F*
Wallis, W A (Wanderers) 1880 *S*, 1881 *E, S*, 1882 *W*, 1883 *S*
Walmsley, G (Bective Rangers) 1894 *E*
Walpole, A (Dublin U) 1888 *S, M*
Walsh, E J (Lansdowne) 1887 *E, S, W*, 1892 *E, S, W*, 1893 *E*
Walsh, H D (Dublin U) 1875 *E*, 1876 *E*
Walsh, J C (UC Cork, Sunday's Well) 1960 *S, SA*, 1961 *E, S, F, SA*, 1963 *E, S, W, NZ*, 1964 *E, S, W, F*, 1965 *F, S, W, SA*, 1966 *F, S, W*, 1967 *E, S, W, F, A* 2
Ward, A J (Ballynahinch) 1998 *F, W, E, SA* 1,2, *Gg, R, SA* 3, 1999 *W, E, S, It* (R), *A* 1,2, *Arg* 1, [*US, A* 3, *R, Arg* 2], 2000 *F* (R), *W* (t&R), *Arg* (R), *US* (R), *C, J, SA* (R), 2001 *It* (R), *F* (R)
Ward, A J P (Garryowen, St Mary's Coll, Greystones) 1978 *S, F, W, E, NZ*, 1979 *F, W, E, S*, 1981 *W, E, S, A*, 1983 *E* (R), 1984 *E, S*, 1986 *S*, 1987 [*C, Tg*]
Warren, J P (Kingstown) 1883 *E*
Warren, R G (Lansdowne) 1884 *W*, 1885 *E, S* 1,2, 1886 *E*, 1887 *E, S, W*, 1888 *W, S, M*, 1889 *S, W*, 1890 *S, W, E*
Watson, R (Wanderers) 1912 *SA*
Wells, H G (Bective Rangers) 1891 *S, W*, 1894 *E, S*
Westby, A J (Dublin U) 1876 *E*
Wheeler, G H (Queen's Coll, Belfast) 1884 *S*, 1885 *E*
Wheeler, J R (Queen's U, Belfast) 1922 *E, S, W, F*, 1924 *E*
Whelan, P C (Garryowen) 1975 *E, S*, 1976 *NZ*, 1977 *W, E, S, F*, 1978 *S, F, W, E, NZ*, 1979 *F, W, E, S*, 1981 *F, W, E*
White, M (Queen's Coll, Cork) 1906 *E, S, W, SA*, 1907 *E, W*
Whitestone, A M (Dublin U) 1877 *E*, 1879 *S, E*, 1880 *E*, 1883 *S*
Whittle, D (Bangor) 1988 *F*
Wilkinson, C R (Malone) 1993 *S*
Wilkinson, R W (Wanderers) 1947 *A*
Williamson, F W (Dolphin) 1930 *E, S, W*
Willis, W J (Lansdowne) 1879 *E*
Wilson, F (CIYMS) 1977 *W, E, S*
Wilson, H G (Glasgow U, Malone) 1905 *E, S, W, NZ*, 1906 *E, S, W, SA*, 1907 *E, S, W*, 1908 *E, S, W*, 1909 *E, S, W*, 1910 *W*
Wilson, W H (Bray) 1877 *E, S*
Withers, H H C (Army, Blackheath) 1931 *F, E, S, W, SA*
Wolfe, E J (Armagh) 1882 *E*
Wood, G H (Dublin U) 1913 *W*, 1914 *F*
Wood, B G M (Garryowen) 1954 *E, S*, 1956 *F, E, S, W*, 1957 *F, E, S, W*, 1958 *A, E, S, W, F*, 1959 *E, S, W, F*, 1960 *E, S, W, F, SA*, 1961 *E, S, W, F, SA*
Wood, K G M (Garryowen, Harlequins) 1994 *A* 1,2, *US*, 1995 *E, S*, [*J*], 1996 *A*, 1997 *It* 1, *F*, 1997 *NZ, It* 2, 1998 *S, F, W, E, SA* 1,2, *R* (R), *SA* 3, 1999 *F, W, E, S, It* (R), *A* 1,2, *Arg* 1, [*US, A* 3, *R* (R), *Arg* 2], 2000 *E, S, It, F, W, Arg, US, C, J, SA*, 2001 *It, F, S, W, E, NZ*, 2002 *F, NZ* 1,2, *Ru*, 2003 *W* 2, *S* 2
Woods, D C (Bessbrook) 1888 *M*, 1889 *S*
Woods, N K P J (Blackrock Coll, London Irish) 1994 *A* 1,2, 1995 *E, F*, 1996 *F, W, E*, 1999 *W*
Wright, R A (Monkstown) 1912 *S*

Yeates, R A (Dublin U) 1889 *S, W*
Young, G (UC Cork) 1913 *E*
Young, R M (Collegians) 1965 *F, E, S, W, SA*, 1966 *F, E, S, W*, 1967 *W, F*, 1968 *W, A*, 1969 *F, E, S, W*, 1970 *SA, F, E, S, W*, 1971 *F, E, S, W*

WALES TEST SEASON REVIEW 2002-2003

Will Regional Way Improve Playing Standards?

John Billot

A whitewash in the Six Nations together with defeats in Australia and New Zealand, the latter by a record margin, gave further credence to the reformation of the club game at the top level to a regional structure. David Moffett, the new WRU group chief executive, arrived in October 2002 to drag Welsh rugby kicking and shrieking into the new era he envisaged. 'I am here to see change and I'll make it happen,' he promised. With an impressive record as a sports administrator in New Zealand and Australia, he was selected from more than 100 applicants. But his head-to-head with the major clubs proved a pretty rough affair with threats of legal action and eventually he had to compromise over the regional plan imposed on the Premier Division.

This was all designed to benefit playing standards for the national team and make the regions more competitive in the European competitions and an expanded Celtic League. He urged a four-team regional concept, including a North Wales-based side. That enraged the clubs. They saw the newcomer as determined to cull them after, at a WRU emergency special meeting, the small clubs had imposed their will on the professional clubs. They ruled regional teams to be the way forward.

Cardiff and Llanelli declined to amalgamate with other clubs. They insisted on stand-alone status within a five-team system. Mr Moffett compromised. He dismissed accusations that he had failed to deliver four regions. 'I don't regard it as failure to be close to improving Welsh rugby,' he asserted. 'We don't always get what we want in life. You win some, you lose some.'

So the five-team line-up was implemented for the start of the 2003-04 season. Cardiff and Llanelli retained their identity while mergers involved Bridgend/Pontypridd, Neath/Swansea and Ebbw Vale/Newport. Few of them were pleased with the situation. There would be a 16-club second tier of semi-pro clubs incorporating all the famous names, but funding was far less than required. 'The WRU is in a parlous financial state and everybody is having to take some pain, perhaps more than we envisaged,' explained Moffett. 'The bottom line is we can't afford the money we have been paying, whether that be to players, clubs or backroom staff.'

Players were unsympathetic. It all became melodramatic. Almost a Mexican stand-off when they held an impromptu protest meeting in a motorway service station car park en route to Heathrow for the journey

Down Under to face Australia and New Zealand. It was Moffett who had to rush to the centre of events to quell the rebellion over the pay structure.

'There was straight talking in strong terms,' admitted Wales team manager Alan Phillips after it was disclosed that the players were ordered on to the bus or face the sack. They went, but two hours late and missed their flight. They had to pay their own overnight hotel expenses and the rugby world wondered what the game was coming to when players caused their country so many embarrassing problems.

Steve Lewis, the WRU general manager, pointed out, 'Our intelligence tells us that it was due to four or five senior internationals while the rest of the players are thoroughly embarrassed.' He explained that the WRU had spent £5.6M on the Wales squad with senior players receiving between £147,000 and £217,000 during the last four seasons. The playing record of the national team during that period was dismal. Just six victories in the Six Nations and three of those against Italy. Yet the players, subjected to considerable pay cuts, nursed a grievance over reductions and it was an unhappy way to leave for a short-haul tour. The WRU were in hock to the bank. Skint! It had to be faced. Professionalism certainly brought its problems.

Perhaps this was the signal for the WRU chairman Glanmor Griffiths to depart the scene after nearly 20 years with the union. A few days after the car park contretemps, he decided to stand down. He had become honorary treasurer in 1987 and 10 years later succeeded the late Vernon Pugh as WRU chairman. Griffiths continued in financial governance and then added a third role as chairman of Millennium Stadium plc. Glanmor 'Three Jobs' certainly left his mark with his energy in achieving the completion of the Stadium in time for the 1999 World Cup at a cost some £126M. However, he was bitterly disappointed that the WRU were left with debt in excess of £66M, annual interest repayments of £4M and a refusal from the National Assembly to help with a cash grant. He could have left with far happier memories. Moffett shouldered all the burdens.

Not that there were any cheery moments worth recall for the Welsh team in the Six Nations. There was no recovery after the shock defeat in Rome. Scott Quinnell had quit the international arena during the autumn programme of matches, playing his 52nd and final match as a replacement against Canada. He said he wanted to spend more time with his family. So Wales had no high-profile pathfinder to carry the ball.

Coach Steve Hansen, in desperation, called Jonathan Humphreys back from his twilight years at Bath to take over the captaincy duties from Colin Charvis, who had failed to fire his team in Rome. Humphreys was tasked with infusing spirit and steel in his pack. He certainly did that against England, who were made to look less than impressive, though they were winners by 26-9 in Cardiff. There were no Welsh tries; just three Ceri Sweeney penalty goals and the Pontypridd outside-half, a precocious talent, showed he was never out of his depth as deputy for the injured Stephen Jones.

Debate still exercised thoughts whether Iestyn Harris was better suited to inside-centre than outside-half. He had little opportunity to float through like a zephyr and the jury is still out. Gareth Thomas's consistent aggression brought him Welsh Player of the Year recognition while Llanelli scrum-half Michael Phillips, third in the pecking order for his club, was voted the most promising player and Wales took him with them Down Under in June.

As if they had not suffered enough, Wales trooped off to Australia and New Zealand on the 'suicide tour' and accepted the inevitable. Had the Wallabies kicked their goals it would have given them victory in Sydney far more conclusively than by 30-10. The All Blacks made no mistakes with their goal kicks and Daniel Carter marked his debut with 15 goal points plus a try in his 20 points. So his side won by their biggest tally against Wales by 55-3. Eight tries to nil. Say no more.

Hansen occasionally revealed irritability with the media. Any coach with his wretched record probably is entitled to feel edgy. The match against Ireland, the most charismatic of Six Nations sides, could have saved the season and victory appeared for Wales's taking in Cardiff at 24-22 after Stephen Jones dropped a breathtaking 40-metre goal in the second minute of stoppage time. Alas, Ronan O'Gara emulated the feat just one minute later, the ball crawling over the bar for Irish success by 25-24. If ever the bell tolled for Wales's season it was then.

If O'Gara had missed, perhaps Glanmor would have stayed a while longer, Hansen may have smiled at least once, and Moffett might have found a little extra cash in the corner of an empty bag to mollify the players. If only . . .

Wales's Test Record in 2002-2003: Played 15, won 5, lost 10

Opponents	*Date*	*Venue*	*Result*
Scotland	30th August 2003	H	Won 23-9
Romania	27th August 2003	H	Won 54-8
England	23rd August 2003	H	Lost 9-43
Ireland	16th August 2003	A	Lost 12-35
New Zealand	21st June 2003	A	Lost 3-55
Australia	14th June 2003	A	Lost 10-30
France	29th March 2003	A	Lost 5-33
Ireland	22nd March 2003	H	Lost 24-25
Scotland	8th March 2003	A	Lost 22-30
England	22nd February 2003	H	Lost 9-26
Italy	15th February 2003	A	Lost 22-30
New Zealand	23rd November 2002	H	Lost 17-43
Canada	16th November 2002	H	Won 32-21
Fiji	9th November 2002	H	Won 58-14
Romania	1st November 2002	H	Won 40-3

WALES INTERNATIONAL STATISTICS

(up to 30 September 2003)

Match Records

MOST CONSECUTIVE TEST WINS

11 1907 *I*, 1908 *E, S, F, I, A*, 1909 *E, S, F, 0 I*, 1910 *F*
10 1999 *F 1, It, E, Arg 1,2, SA, C, F 2, Arg 3, J*
8 1970 *F*, 1971 *E, S, I, F*, 1972 *E, S, F*

MOST CONSECUTIVE TESTS WITHOUT DEFEAT

Matches	*Wins*	*Draws*	*Period*
11	11	0	1907 to 1910
10	10	0	1999 to 1999
8	8	0	1970 to 1972

MOST POINTS IN A MATCH

by the team

Pts	*Opponents*	*Venue*	*Year*
102	Portugal	Lisbon	1994
81	Romania	Cardiff	2001
70	Romania	Wrexham	1997
64	Japan	Cardiff	1999
64	Japan	Osaka	2001
60	Italy	Treviso	1999
58	Fiji	Cardiff	2002
57	Japan	Bloemfontein	1995
55	Japan	Cardiff	1993

by a player

Pts	*Player*	*Opponents*	*Venue*	*Year*
30	N R Jenkins	Italy	Treviso	1999
29	N R Jenkins	France	Cardiff	1999
28	N R Jenkins	Canada	Cardiff	1999
28	N R Jenkins	France	Paris	2001
27	N R Jenkins	Italy	Cardiff	2000
26	S M Jones	Romania	Cardiff	2001
24	N R Jenkins	Canada	Cardiff	1993
24	N R Jenkins	Italy	Cardiff	1994
24	G L Henson	Romania	Wrexham	2003
23	A C Thomas	Romania	Wrexham	1997
23	N R Jenkins	Argentina	Llanelli	1998
23	N R Jenkins	Scotland	Murrayfield	2001
22	N R Jenkins	Portugal	Lisbon	1994
22	N R Jenkins	Japan	Bloemfontein	1995
22	N R Jenkins	England	Wembley	1999
22	S M Jones	Canada	Cardiff	2002

MOST TRIES IN A MATCH

by the team

Tries	*Opponents*	*Venue*	*Year*
16	Portugal	Lisbon	1994
11	France	Paris	1909
11	Romania	Wrexham	1997
11	Romania	Cardiff	2001
10	France	Swansea	1910
10	Japan	Osaka	2001
9	France	Cardiff	1908
9	Japan	Cardiff	1993
9	Japan	Cardiff	1999
9	Japan	Tokyo	2001

by a player

Tries	*Player*	*Opponents*	*Venue*	*Year*
4	W Llewellyn	England	Swansea	1899
4	R A Gibbs	France	Cardiff	1908
4	M C R Richards	England	Cardiff	1969
4	I C Evans	Canada	Invercargill	1987
4	N Walker	Portugal	Lisbon	1994
4	G Thomas	Italy	Treviso	1999
4	S M Williams	Japan	Osaka	2001

MOST CONVERSIONS IN A MATCH

by the team

Cons	*Opponents*	*Venue*	*Year*
11	Portugal	Lisbon	1994
10	Romania	Cardiff	2001
8	France	Swansea	1910
8	Japan	Cardiff	1999
7	France	Paris	1909
7	Japan	Osaka	2001

by a player

Cons	*Player*	*Opponents*	*Venue*	*Year*
11	N R Jenkins	Portugal	Lisbon	1994
10	S M Jones	Romania	Cardiff	2001
8	J Bancroft	France	Swansea	1910
8	N R Jenkins	Japan	Cardiff	1999
7	S M Jones	Japan	Osaka	2001
6	J Bancroft	France	Paris	1909
6	G L Henson	Romania	Wrexham	2003

MOST PENALTIES IN A MATCH

by the team

Penalties	Opponents	Venue	Year
9	France	Cardiff	1999
8	Canada	Cardiff	1993
7	Italy	Cardiff	1994
7	Canada	Cardiff	1999
7	Italy	Cardiff	2000
6	France	Cardiff	1982
6	Tonga	Nuku'alofa	1994
6	England	Wembley	1999
6	Canada	Cardiff	2002

by a player

Penalties	Player	Opponents	Venue	Year
9	N R Jenkins	France	Cardiff	1999
8	N R Jenkins	Canada	Cardiff	1993
7	N R Jenkins	Italy	Cardiff	1994
7	N R Jenkins	Canada	Cardiff	1999
7	N R Jenkins	Italy	Cardiff	2000
6	G Evans	France	Cardiff	1982
6	N R Jenkins	Tonga	Nuku'alofa	1994
6	N R Jenkins	England	Wembley	1999
6	S M Jones	Canada	Cardiff	2002

MOST DROPPED GOALS IN A MATCH

by the team

Drops	Opponents	Venue	Year
3	Scotland	Murrayfield	2001
2	Scotland	Swansea	1912
2	Scotland	Cardiff	1914
2	England	Swansea	1920
2	Scotland	Swansea	1921
2	France	Paris	1930
2	England	Cardiff	1971
2	France	Cardiff	1978
2	England	Twickenham	1984
2	Ireland	Wellington	1987
2	Scotland	Cardiff	1988
2	France	Paris	2001

by a player

Drops	Player	Opponents	Venue	Year
3	N R Jenkins	Scotland	Murrayfield	2001
2	J Shea	England	Swansea	1920
2	A Jenkins	Scotland	Swansea	1921
2	B John	England	Cardiff	1971
2	M Dacey	England	Twickenham	1984
2	J Davies	Ireland	Wellington	1987
2	J Davies	Scotland	Cardiff	1988
2	N R Jenkins	France	Paris	2001

Career Records

MOST CAPPED PLAYERS

Caps	Player	Career Span
87	N R Jenkins	1991 to 2002
79	G O Llewellyn	1989 to 2003
72	I C Evans	1987 to 1998
68	Gareth Thomas	1995 to 2003
59	R Howley	1996 to 2002
59	C L Charvis	1996 to 2003
58	G R Jenkins	1991 to 2000
55	J P R Williams	1969 to 1981
54	R N Jones	1986 to 1995
53	G O Edwards	1967 to 1978
53	I S Gibbs	1991 to 2001
52	L S Quinnell	1993 to 2002
51	D Young	1987 to 2001
46	T G R Davies	1966 to 1978
46	P T Davies	1985 to 1995
44	K J Jones	1947 to 1957
42	M R Hall	1988 to 1995

MOST CONSECUTIVE TESTS

Tests	Player	Span
53	G O Edwards	1967 to 1978
43	K J Jones	1947 to 1956
39	G Price	1975 to 1983
38	T M Davies	1969 to 1976
33	W J Bancroft	1890 to 1901

MOST TESTS AS CAPTAIN

Tests	Captain	Span
28	I C Evans	1991 to 1995
22	R Howley	1998 to 1999
19	J M Humphreys	1995 to 2003
18	A J Gould	1889 to 1897
14	D C T Rowlands	1963 to 1965
14	W J Trew	1907 to 1913

MOST TESTS IN INDIVIDUAL POSITIONS

Position	Player	Tests	Span
Full-back	J P R Williams	54	1969 to 1981
Wing	I C Evans	72	1987 to 1998
Centre	I S Gibbs	53	1991 to 2001
Fly-half	N R Jenkins	70	1991 to 2002
Scrum-half	R Howley	59	1996 to 2002
Prop	D Young	51	1987 to 2002
Hooker	G R Jenkins	57	1991 to 2000
Lock	G O Llewellyn	78	1989 to 2003
Flanker	C L Charvis	46	1996 to 2003
No 8	L S Quinnell	51	1993 to 2002

JPR Williams started one match as a flanker, Jenkins was also capped elsewhere in the back division. Llewellyn, Charvis and Quinnell were capped elsewhere in the pack

MOST POINTS IN TESTS

Points	Player	Tests	Career
1049	N R Jenkins	87	1991 to 2002
304	P H Thorburn	37	1985 to 1991
244	S M Jones	31	1998 to 2003
211	A C Thomas	23	1996 to 2000
166	P Bennett	29	1969 to 1978
157	I C Evans	72	1987 to 1998

MOST TRIES IN TESTS

Tries	Player	Tests	Career
33	I C Evans	72	1987 to 1998
31	Gareth Thomas	68	1995 to 2003
20	G O Edwards	53	1967 to 1978
20	T G R Davies	46	1966 to 1978
17	R A Gibbs	16	1906 to 1911
17	J L Williams	17	1906 to 1911
17	K J Jones	44	1947 to 1957

MOST CONVERSIONS IN TESTS

Cons	Player	Tests	Career
130	N R Jenkins	87	1991 to 2002
47	S M Jones	31	1998 to 2003
43	P H Thorburn	37	1985 to 1991
38	J Bancroft	18	1909 to 1914
30	A C Thomas	23	1996 to 2000
20	W J Bancroft	33	1890 to 1901

MOST PENALTY GOALS IN TESTS

Penalties	Player	Tests	Career
235	N R Jenkins	87	1991 to 2002
70	P H Thorburn	37	1985 to 1991
43	S M Jones	31	1998 to 2003
36	P Bennett	29	1969 to 1978
35	S P Fenwick	30	1975 to 1981
32	A C Thomas	23	1996 to 2000
22	G Evans	10	1981 to 1983

MOST DROPPED GOALS IN TESTS

Drops	Player	Tests	Career
13	J Davies	32	1985 to 1997
10	N R Jenkins	87	1991 to 2002
8	B John	25	1966 to 1972
7	W G Davies	21	1978 to 1985

International Championship Records

Record	Detail		Set
Most points in season	125	in five matches	2001
Most tries in season	21	in four matches	1910
Highest Score	49	49-14 v France	1910
Biggest win	35	49-14 v France	1910
Highest score conceded	60	26-60 v England	1998
Biggest defeat	51	0-51 v France	1998
Most appearances	45	G O Edwards	1967 – 1978
Most points in matches	406	N R Jenkins	1991 – 2001
Most points in season	74	N R Jenkins	2001
Most points in match	28	N R Jenkins	v France, 2001
Most tries in matches	18	G O Edwards	1967 – 1978
Most tries in season	6	M C R Richards	1969
Most tries in match	4	W Llewellyn	v England, 1899
	4	M C R Richards	v England, 1969
Most cons in matches	41	N R Jenkins	1991 – 2001
Most cons in season	10	S M Jones	2002
Most cons in match	8	J Bancroft	v France, 1910
Most pens in matches	93	N R Jenkins	1991 – 2001
Most pens in season	16	P H Thorburn	1986
	16	N R Jenkins	1999
Most pens in match	7	N R Jenkins	v Italy, 2000

Most drops in matches	8	J Davies	1985 – 1997
Most drops in season	5	N R Jenkins	2001
Most drops in match	3	N R Jenkins	v Scotland, 2001

Miscellaneous Records

Record	*Holder*	*Detail*
Longest Test Career	D Young	15 seasons, 1987 to 2001
	G O Llewellyn	15 seasons, 1989 to 2003
Youngest Test Cap	N Biggs	18 yrs 49 days in 1888
Oldest Test Cap	T H Vile	38 yrs 152 days in 1921

Career Records of Wales International Players *(up to 30 September 2003)*

PLAYER	*Debut*	*Caps*	*T*	*C*	*P*	*D*	*Pts*
Backs:							
N Brew	2003 v R	1	1	0	0	0	5
J Bryant	2003 v R	1	0	0	0	0	0
G J Cooper	2001 v F	10	2	0	0	0	10
L B Davies	1996 v It	21	4	0	0	0	20
A P R Durston	2001 v J	2	1	0	0	0	5
G R Evans	1998 v SA	3	1	0	0	0	5
I R Harris	2001 v Arg	17	1	11	17	0	78
B I Hayward	1998 v Z	2	3	0	0	0	15
G L Henson	2001 v J	4	0	6	4	0	24
R Howley	1996 v E	59	10	0	0	0	50
D R James	1996 v A	41	13	0	0	0	65
L Jarvis	1997 v R	1	0	1	0	0	2
N R Jenkins	1991 v E	87	11	130	235	10	1049
Paul John	1994 v Tg	10	1	0	0	0	5
M A Jones	2001 v E	12	4	0	0	0	20
S M Jones	1998 v SA	31	3	47	43	2	244
H Luscombe	2003 v S	1	0	0	0	0	0
A W N Marinos	2002 v I	8	1	0	0	0	5
C S Morgan	2002 v I	9	2	0	0	0	10
K A Morgan	1997 v US	24	5	0	0	0	25
S Parker	2002 v R	5	1	0	0	0	5
D Peel	2001 v J	20	1	0	0	0	5
M Phillips	2003 v R	1	1	0	0	0	5
R D Powell	2002 v SA	3	0	0	0	0	0
J P Robinson	2001 v J	13	5	0	0	0	25
N J Robinson	2003 v I	2	0	0	0	0	0
T Shanklin	2001 v J	15	3	0	0	0	15
C Sweeney	2003 v It	5	0	0	3	1	12
M Taylor	1994 v SA	40	9	0	0	0	45
Gareth Thomas	1995 v J	68	31	0	0	0	155
M J Watkins	2003 v It	6	0	0	0	0	0
A Williams	2003 v R	1	0	0	0	0	0
G R Williams	2000 v I	30	7	0	0	0	35
S M Williams	2000 v F	11	12	0	0	0	60
G Wyatt	1997 v Tg	2	1	0	0	0	5

Forwards:

C T Anthony	1997 v US	17	1	0	0	0	5
J Bater	2003 v R	1	0	0	0	0	0
H Bennett	2003 v I	2	0	0	0	0	0
C L Charvis	1996 v A	59	9	0	0	0	45
B Cockbain	2003 v R	1	0	0	0	0	0
V Cooper	2002 v C	3	0	0	0	0	0
Mefin Davies	2002 v SA	11	0	0	0	0	0
B R Evans	1998 v SA	24	0	0	0	0	0
I M Gough	1998 v SA	21	1	0	0	0	5
J Griffiths	2000 v Sm	1	0	0	0	0	0
J M Humphreys	1995 v NZ	35	2	0	0	0	10
P James	2003 v R	1	0	0	0	0	0
Gethin Jenkins	2002 v R	10	0	0	0	0	0
Adam Jones	2003 v E	2	0	0	0	0	0
D L Jones	2000 v Sm	2	0	0	0	0	0
D R Jones	2002 v Fj	10	0	0	0	0	0
Duncan Jones	2001 v A	5	0	0	0	0	0
Steve Jones	2001 v J	1	0	0	0	0	0
A L P Lewis	1996 v It	28	0	0	0	0	0
G Lewis	1998 v SA	16	0	0	0	0	0
G O Llewellyn	1989 v NZ	79	5	0	0	0	24
A Lloyd	2001 v J	1	1	0	0	0	5
R C McBryde	1994 v Fj	26	1	0	0	0	5
M Madden	2002 v SA	5	0	0	0	0	0
D R Morris	1998 v Z	15	1	0	0	0	5
R Oakley	2003 v I	2	0	0	0	0	0
M Owen	2002 v SA	8	1	0	0	0	5
R Parks	2002 v SA	4	0	0	0	0	0
A Popham	2003 v A	4	1	0	0	0	5
L S Quinnell	1993 v C	52	11	0	0	0	55
J Ringer	2001 v J	2	0	0	0	0	0
R Sidoli	2002 v SA	13	0	0	0	0	0
Gavin Thomas	2001 v J	16	4	0	0	0	20
I D Thomas	2000 v Sm	25	1*	0	0	0	5
J Thomas	2003 v A	4	0	0	0	0	0
G J Williams	2003 v It	5	0	0	0	0	0
M E Williams	1996 v Bb	36	1	0	0	0	5
S M Williams	1994 v Tg	28	2	0	0	0	10
C P Wyatt	1998 v Z	36	2	0	0	0	10
P Young	2003 v R	1	0	0	0	0	0

* Iestyn Thomas's figures include a penalty try awarded against Fiji in 2002.

WELSH INTERNATIONAL PLAYERS

(up to 30 September 2003)

Note: Years given for International Championship matches are for second half of season; eg 1972 means season 1971-72. Years for all other matches refer to the actual year of the match. When a series has taken place, figures have been used to denote the particular matches in which players have featured. Thus 1969 *NZ* 2 indicates that a player appeared in the second Test of the series.

Ackerman, R A (Newport, London Welsh) 1980 *NZ*, 1981 *E, S, A*, 1982 *I, F, E, S*, 1983 *S, I, F, R*, 1984 *S, I, F, E, A*, 1985 *S, I, F, E, Fj*
Alexander, E P (Llandovery Coll, Cambridge U) 1885 *S*, 1886 *E, S*, 1887 *E, I*
Alexander, W H (Llwynypia) 1898 *I, E*, 1899 *E, S, I*, 1901 *S, I*
Allen, A G (Newbridge) 1990 *F, E, I*
Allen, C P (Oxford U, Beaumaris) 1884 *E, S*
Andrews, F (Pontypool) 1912 *SA*, 1913 *E, S, I*
Andrews, F G (Swansea) 1884 *E, S*
Andrews, G E (Newport) 1926 *E, S*, 1927 *E, F, I*
Anthony, C T (Swansea, Newport) 1997 *US* 1(R),2(R), *C* (R), *Tg* (R), 1998 *SA* 2, *Arg*, 1999 *S, I* (R), 2001 *J* 1,2, *I* (R), 2002 *I, F, It, E, S*, 2003 *R* (R)
Anthony, L (Neath) 1948 *E, S, F*
Appleyard, R C (Swansea) 1997 *C, R, Tg, NZ*, 1998 *It, E* (R), *S, I, F*
Arnold, P (Swansea) 1990 *Nm* 1, 2, *Bb*, 1991 *E, S, I, F* 1, *A*, [*Arg, A*], 1993 *F* (R), *Z* 2, 1994 *Sp, Fj*, 1995 *SA*, 1996 *Bb* (R)
Arnold, W R (Swansea) 1903 *S*
Arthur, C S (Cardiff) 1888 *I, M*, 1891 *E*
Arthur, T (Neath) 1927 *S, F, I*, 1929 *E, S, F, I*, 1930 *E, S, I, F*, 1931 *E, S, F, I, SA*, 1933 *E, S*
Ashton, C (Aberavon) 1959 *E, S, I*, 1960 *E, S, I*, 1962 *I*
Attewell, S L (Newport) 1921 *E, S, F*

Back, M J (Bridgend) 1995 *F* (R), *E* (R), *S, I*
Badger, O (Llanelli) 1895 *E, S, I*, 1896 *E*
Baker, A (Neath) 1921 *I*, 1923 *E, S, F, I*
Baker, A M (Newport) 1909 *S, F*, 1910 *S*
Bancroft, J (Swansea) 1909 *E, S, F, I*, 1910 *F, E, S, I*, 1911 *E, F, I*, 1912 *E, S, I*, 1913 *I*, 1914 *E, S, F*
Bancroft, W J (Swansea) 1890 *S, E, I*, 1891 *E, S, I*, 1892 *E, S, I*, 1893 *E, S, I*, 1894 *E, S, I*, 1895 *E, S, I*, 1896 *E, S, I*, 1897 *E*, 1898 *I, E*, 1899 *E, S, I*, 1900 *E, S, I*, 1901 *E, S, I*
Barlow, T M (Cardiff) 1884 *I*
Barrell, R J (Cardiff) 1929 *S, F, I*, 1933 *I*
Bartlett, J D (Llanelli) 1927 *S*, 1928 *E, S*
Bassett, A (Cardiff) 1934 *I*, 1935 *E, S, I*, 1938 *E, S*
Bassett, J A (Penarth) 1929 *E, S, F, I*, 1930 *E, S, I*, 1931 *E, S, F, I, SA*, 1932 *E, S, I*
Bateman, A G (Neath, Richmond, Northampton) 1990 *S, I, Nm* 1,2, 1996 *SA*, 1997 *US, S, F, E, R, NZ*, 1998 *It, E, S, I*, 1999 *S, Arg* 1,2, *SA, C*, [*J, A* (R)], 2000 *It, E, S, I, Sm, US, SA*, 2001 *E* (R), *It* (t), *R, I, Art* (R), *Tg*
Bater, J (Neath/Swansea) 2003 *R* (R)
Bayliss, G (Pontypool) 1933 *S*
Bebb, D I E (Carmarthen TC, Swansea) 1959 *E, S, I, F*, 1960 *E, S, I, F, SA*, 1961 *E, S, I, F*, 1962 *E, S, F, I*, 1963 *E, F, NZ*, 1964 *E, S, F, SA*, 1965 *E, S, I, F*, 1966 *F, A*, 1967 *S, I, F, E*
Beckingham, G (Cardiff) 1953 *E, S*, 1958 *F*
Bennett, A M (Cardiff) 1995 [*NZ*] *SA, Fj*
Bennett, H (Neath/ Swansea) 2003 *I* 2(R), *S* 2(R)
Bennett, I (Aberavon) 1937 *I*
Bennett, P (Cardiff Harlequins) 1891 *E, S*, 1892 *S, I*
Bennett, P (Llanelli) 1969 *F* (R), 1970 *SA, S, F*, 1972 *S* (R), *NZ*, 1973 *E, S, I, F, A*, 1974 *S, I, F, E*, 1975 *S* (R), *I*, 1976 *E, S, I, F*, 1977 *I, F, E, S*, 1978 *E, S, I, F*
Bergiers, R T E (Cardiff Coll of Ed, Llanelli) 1972 *E, S, F, NZ*, 1973 *E, S, I, F, A*, 1974 *E*, 1975 *I*
Bevan, G W (Llanelli) 1947 *E*
Bevan, J A (Cambridge U) 1881 *E*
Bevan, J C (Cardiff, Cardiff Coll of Ed) 1971 *E, S, I, F*, 1972 *E, S, F, NZ*, 1973 *E, S*
Bevan, J D (Aberavon) 1975 *F, E, S, A*
Bevan, S (Swansea) 1904 *I*
Beynon, B (Swansea) 1920 *E, S*
Beynon, G E (Swansea) 1925 *F, I*
Bidgood, R A (Newport) 1992 *S*, 1993 *Z* 1,2, *Nm, J* (R)
Biggs, N W (Cardiff) 1888 *M*, 1889 *I*, 1892 *I*, 1893 *E, S, I*, 1894 *E, I*
Biggs, S H (Cardiff) 1895 *E, S*, 1896 *S*, 1897 *E*, 1898 *I, E*, 1899 *S, I*, 1900 *I*
Birch, J (Neath) 1911 *S, F*
Birt, F W (Newport) 1911 *E, S*, 1912 *E, S, I, SA*, 1913 *E*
Bishop, D J (Pontypool) 1984 *A*
Bishop, E H (Swansea) 1889 *S*
Blackmore, J H (Abertillery) 1909 *E*
Blackmore, S W (Cardiff) 1987 *I*, [*Tg* (R), *C, A*]
Blake, J (Cardiff) 1899 *E, S, I*, 1900 *E, S, I*, 1901 *E, S, I*
Blakemore, R E (Newport) 1947 *E*
Bland, A F (Cardiff) 1887 *E, S, I*, 1888 *S, I, M*, 1890 *S, E, I*
Blyth, L (Swansea) 1951 *SA*, 1952 *E, S*
Blyth, W R (Swansea) 1974 *E*, 1975 *S* (R), 1980 *F, E, S, I*
Boobyer, N (Llanelli) 1993 *Z* 1(R),2, *Nm*, 1994 *Fj, Tg*, 1998 *F*, 1999 *It* (R)
Boon, R W (Cardiff) 1930 *S, F*, 1931 *E, S, F, I, SA*, 1932 *E, S, I*, 1933 *E, I*
Booth, J (Pontymister) 1898 *I*
Boots, J G (Newport) 1898 *I, E*, 1899 *I*, 1900 *E, S, I*, 1901 *E, S, I*, 1902 *E, S, I*, 1903 *E, S, I*, 1904 *E*
Boucher, A W (Newport) 1892 *E, S, I*, 1893 *E, S, I*, 1894 *E*, 1895 *E, S, I*, 1896 *E, I*, 1897 *E*
Bowcott, H M (Cardiff, Cambridge U) 1929 *S, F, I*, 1930 *E*, 1931 *E, S*, 1933 *E, I*
Bowdler, F A (Cross Keys) 1927 *A*, 1928 *E, S, I, F*, 1929 *E, S, F, I*, 1930 *E*, 1931 *SA*, 1932 *E, S, I*, 1933 *I*
Bowen, B (S Wales Police, Swansea) 1983 *R*, 1984 *S, I, F, E*, 1985 *Fj*, 1986 *E, S, I, F, Fj, Tg, WS*, 1987 [*C, E, NZ*], *US*, 1988 *E, S, I, F, WS*, 1989 *S, I*
Bowen, C A (Llanelli) 1896 *E, S, I*, 1897 *E*
Bowen, D H (Llanelli) 1883 *E*, 1886 *E, S*, 1887 *E*
Bowen, G E (Swansea) 1887 *S, I*, 1888 *S, I*
Bowen, W (Swansea) 1921 *S, F*, 1922 *E, S, I, F*
Bowen, Wm A (Swansea) 1886 *E, S*, 1887 *E, S, I*, 1888 *M*, 1889 *S, I*, 1890 *S, E, I*, 1891 *E, S*
Brace, D O (Llanelli, Oxford U) 1956 *E, S, I, F*, 1957 *E*, 1960 *S, I, F*, 1961 *I*
Braddock, K J (Newbridge) 1966 *A*, 1967 *S, I*
Bradshaw, K (Bridgend) 1964 *E, S, I, F, SA*, 1966 *E, S, I, F*
Brew, N (Gwent Dragons) 2003 *R*
Brewer, T J (Newport) 1950 *E*, 1955 *E, S*
Brice, A B (Aberavon) 1899 *E, S, I*, 1900 *E, S, I*, 1901 *E, S, I*, 1902 *E, S, I*, 1903 *E, S, I*, 1904 *E, S, I*
Bridges, C J (Neath) 1990 *Nm* 1,2, *Bb*, 1991 *E* (R), *I, F* 1, *A*
Bridie, R H (Newport) 1882 *I*
Britton, G R (Newport) 1961 *S*
Broughton, A S (Treorchy) 1927 *A*, 1929 *S*
Brown, A (Newport) 1921 *I*
Brown, J (Cardiff) 1925 *I*
Brown, J A (Cardiff) 1907 *E, S, I*, 1908 *E, S, F*, 1909 *E*
Brown, M (Pontypool) 1983 *R*, 1986 *E, S, Fj* (R), *Tg, WS*
Bryant, D J (Bridgend) 1988 *NZ* 1,2, *WS, R*, 1989 *S, I, F, E*
Bryant, J (Celtic Warriors) 2003 *R* (R)
Buchanan, A (Llanelli) 1987 [*Tg, E, NZ, A*], 1988 *I*
Buckett, I M (Swansea) 1994 *Tg*, 1997 *US* 2, *C*
Budgett, N J (Ebbw Vale, Bridgend) 2000 *S, I, Sm* (R), *US, SA*, 2001 *J* 1(R),2, 2002 *I, F, It, E, S*
Burcher, D H (Newport) 1977 *I, F, E, S*
Burgess, R C (Ebbw Vale) 1977 *I, F, E, S*, 1981 *I, F*, 1982 *F, E, S*
Burnett, R (Newport) 1953 *E*
Burns, J (Cardiff) 1927 *F, I*
Bush, P F (Cardiff) 1905 *NZ*, 1906 *E, SA*, 1907 *I*, 1908 *E, S*, 1910 *S, I*
Butler, E T (Pontypool) 1980 *F, E, S, I, NZ* (R), 1982 *S*, 1983 *E, S, I, F, R*, 1984 *S, I, F, E, A*

Cale, W R (Newbridge, Pontypool) 1949 *E, S, I*, 1950 *E, S, I, F*
Cardey, M D (Llanelli) 2000 *S*
Carter, A J (Newport) 1991 *E, S*
Cattell, A (Llanelli) 1883 *E, S*
Challinor, C (Neath) 1939 *E*
Charvis, C L (Swansea) 1996 *A* 3(R), *SA*, 1997 *US, S, I, F*, 1998 *It* (R), *E, S, I, F, Z* (R), *SA* 1,2, *Arg*, 1999 *S, I, F* 1, *It, E, Arg* 1, *SA, F* 2, [*Arg* 3, *A*], 2000 *F, It* (R), *E, S, I, Sm, US, SA*, 2001 *E, S, F, It, R, I, Arg, Tg, A*, 2002 *E* (R), *S, SA* 1,2, *R, Fj, C, NZ*, 2003 *It, E* 1(R), *S* 1(R), *I* 1, *F, A, NZ, E* 2, *S* 2
Clapp, T J S (Newport) 1882 *I*, 1883 *E, S*, 1884 *E, S, I*, 1885 *E, S*, 1886 *S*, 1887 *E, S, I*, 1888 *S, I*
Clare, J (Cardiff) 1883 *E*
Clark, S S (Neath) 1882 *I*, 1887 *I*
Cleaver, W B (Cardiff) 1947 *E, S, F, I, A*, 1948 *E, S, F, I*, 1949 *I*, 1950 *E, S, I, F*
Clegg, B G (Swansea) 1979 *F*
Clement, A (Swansea) 1987 *US* (R), 1988 *E, NZ* 1, *WS* (R), *R*, 1989 *NZ*, 1990 *S* (R), *I* (R), *Nm* 1,2, 1991 *S* (R), *A* (R), *F* 2, [*WS, A*], 1992 *I, F, E, S*, 1993 *I* (R), *F, J, C*, 1994 *S, I, F, Sp, C* (R), *Tg, WS, It, SA*, 1995 *F, E*, [*J, NZ, I*]
Clement, W H (Llanelli) 1937 *E, S, I*, 1938 *E, S, I*
Cobner, T J (Pontypool) 1974 *S, I, F, E*, 1975 *F, E, S, I, A*, 1976 *E, S*, 1977 *F, E, S*, 1978 *E, S, I, F, A* 1
Cockbain, B (Celtic Warriors) 2003 *R*
Coldrick, A P (Newport) 1911 *E, S, I*, 1912 *E, S, F*
Coleman, E (Newport) 1949 *E, S, I*
Coles, F C (Pontypool) 1960 *S, I, F*
Collins, J (Aberavon) 1958 *A, E, S, F*, 1959 *E, S, I, F*, 1960 *E*, 1961 *F*
Collins, R G (S Wales Police, Cardiff, Pontypridd) 1987 *E* (R), *I*, [*I, E, NZ*], *US*, 1988 *E, S, I, F, R*, 1990 *E, S, I*, 1991 *A, F* 2, [*WS*], 1994 *C, Fj, Tg, WS, R, It, SA*, 1995 *F, E, S, I*
Collins, T (Mountain Ash) 1923 *I*
Conway-Rees, J (Llanelli) 1892 *S*, 1893 *E*, 1894 *E*
Cook, T (Cardiff) 1949 *S, I*
Cooper, G J (Bath, Celtic Warriors) 2001 *F, J* 1,2, 2003 E 1, *S* 1, *I* 1, *F* (R), *A, NZ, E* 2
Cooper, V (Llanelli) 2002 *C*, 2003 *I* 2(R), *S* 2
Cope, W (Cardiff, Blackheath) 1896 *S*
Copsey, A H (Llanelli) 1992 *I, F, E, S, A*, 1993 *E, S, I, J, C*, 1994 *E* (R), *Pt, Sp* (R), *Fj, Tg, WS* (R)
Cornish, F H (Cardiff) 1897 *E*, 1898 *I, E*, 1899 *I*
Cornish, R A (Cardiff) 1923 *E, S*, 1924 *E*, 1925 *E, S, F*, 1926 *E, S, I, F*
Coslett, K (Aberavon) 1962 *E, S, F*
Cowey, B T V (Welch Regt, Newport) 1934 *E, S, I*, 1935 *E*
Cresswell, B (Newport) 1960 *E, S, I, F*
Cummins, W (Treorchy) 1922 *E, S, I, F*
Cunningham, L J (Aberavon) 1960 *E, S, I, F*, 1962 *E, S, F, I*, 1963 *NZ*, 1964 *E, S, I, F, SA*

Dacey, M (Swansea) 1983 *E, S, I, F, R*, 1984 *S, I, F, E, A*, 1986 *Fj, Tg, WS*, 1987 *F* (R), [*Tg*]
Daniel, D J (Llanelli) 1891 *S*, 1894 *E, S, I*, 1898 *I, E*, 1899 *E, I*
Daniel, L T D (Newport) 1970 *S*
Daniels, P C T (Cardiff) 1981 *A*, 1982 *I*
Darbishire, G (Bangor) 1881 *E*
Dauncey, F H (Newport) 1896 *E, S, I*
Davey, C (Swansea) 1930 *F*, 1931 *E, S, F, I, SA*, 1932 *E, S, I*, 1933 *E, S*, 1934 *E, S, I*, 1935 *E, S, I, NZ*, 1936 *S*, 1937 *E, I*, 1938 *E, I*
David, R J (Cardiff) 1907 *I*
David, T P (Llanelli, Pontypridd) 1973 *F, A*, 1976 *I, F*
Davidge, G D (Newport) 1959 *F*, 1960 *S, I, F, SA*, 1961 *E, S, I*, 1962 *F*
Davies, A (Cambridge U, Neath, Cardiff) 1990 *Bb* (R), 1991 *A*, 1993 *Z* 1,2, *J, C*, 1994 *Fj*, 1995 [*J, I*]
Davies, A C (London Welsh) 1889 *I*
Davies, A E (Llanelli) 1984 *A*
Davies, B (Llanelli) 1895 *E*, 1896 *E*
Davies, C (Cardiff) 1947 *S, F, I, A*, 1948 *E, S, F, I*, 1949 *F*, 1950 *E, S, I, F*, 1951 *E, S, I*
Davies, C (Llanelli) 1988 *WS*, 1989 *S, I* (R), *F*
Davies, C H A (Llanelli, Cardiff) 1957 *I*, 1958 *A, E, S, I*, 1960 *SA*, 1961 *E*
Davies, C L (Cardiff) 1956 *E, S, I*
Davies, C R (Bedford, RAF) 1934 *E*
Davies, D (Bridgend) 1921 *I*, 1925 *I*
Davies, D B (Llanelli) 1907 *E*
Davies, D B (Llanelli) 1962 *I*, 1963 *E, S*
Davies, D G (Cardiff) 1923 *E, S*
Davies, D H (Neath) 1904 *S*
Davies, D H (Aberavon) 1924 *E*
Davies, D I (Swansea) 1939 *E*
Davies, D J (Neath) 1962 *I*
Davies, D M (Somerset Police) 1950 *E, S, I, F*, 1951 *E, S, I, F, SA*, 1952 *E, S, I, F*, 1953 *I, F, NZ*, 1954 *E*
Davies, E (Aberavon) 1947 *A*, 1948 *I*
Davies, E (Maesteg) 1919 *NZA*
Davies, E G (Cardiff) 1912 *E, F*
Davies, E G (Cardiff) 1928 *F*, 1929 *E*, 1930 *S*
Davies, G (Swansea) 1900 *E, S, I*, 1901 *E, S, I*, 1905 *E, S, I*
Davies, G (Cambridge U, Pontypridd) 1947 *S, A*, 1948 *E, S, F, I*, 1949 *E, S, F*, 1951 *E, S*
Davies, G (Llanelli) 1921 *F, I*, 1925 *F*
Davies, H (Swansea) 1898 *I, E*, 1901 *S, I*
Davies, H (Swansea, Llanelli) 1939 *S, I*, 1947 *E, S, F, I*
Davies, H (Neath) 1912 *E, S*
Davies, H (Bridgend) 1984 *S, I, F, E*
Davies, H J (Cambridge U, Aberavon) 1959 *E, S*
Davies, H J (Newport) 1924 *S*
Davies, I T (Llanelli) 1914 *S, F, I*
Davies, J (Neath, Llanelli, Cardiff) 1985 *E, Fj*, 1986 *E, S, I, F, Fj, Tg, WS*, 1987 *F, E, S, I*, [*I, Tg* (R), *C, E, NZ, A*], 1988 *E, S, I, F, NZ* 1,2, *WS, R*, 1996 *A* 3, 1997 *US* (t), *S* (R), *F* (R), *E*
Davies, Rev J A (Swansea) 1913 *S, F, I*, 1914 *E, S, F, I*
Davies, J D (Neath, Richmond) 1991 *I, F* 1, 1993 *F* (R), *Z* 2, *J, C*, 1994 *S, I, F, E, Pt, Sp, C, WS, R, It, SA*, 1995 *F, E*, [*J, NZ, I*] *SA*, 1996 *It, E, S, I, F* 1, *A* 1, *Bb, F* 2, *It*, 1998 *Z, SA* 1
Davies, J H (Aberavon) 1923 *I*
Davies, L (Swansea) 1939 *S, I*
Davies, L (Bridgend) 1966 *E, S, I*
Davies, L B (Neath, Cardiff, Llanelli) 1996 *It, E, S, I, F* 1, *A* 1, *Bb, F* 2, *It* (R), 1997 *US* 1,2, *C, R, Tg, NZ* (R), 1998 *E* (R), *I, F*, 1999 *C*, 2001 *I*, 2003 *It*
Davies, L M (Llanelli) 1954 *F, S*, 1955 *I*
Davies, M (Swansea) 1981 *A*, 1982 *I*, 1985 *Fj*
Davies, Mefin (Pontypridd, Celtic Warriors) 2002 *SA* 2(R), *R, Fj*, 2003 *It, S* 1(R), *I* 1(R), *F, A* (R), *NZ* (R), *I* 2, *R*
Davies, M J (Blackheath) 1939 *S, I*
Davies, N G (London Welsh) 1955 *E*
Davies, N G (Llanelli) 1988 *NZ* 2, *WS*, 1989 *S, I*, 1993 *F*, 1994 *S, I, E, Pt, Sp, C, Fj, Tg* (R), *WS, R, It*, 1995 *E, S, I, Fj*, 1996 *E, S, I, F* 1, *A* 1,2, *Bb, F* 2, 1997 *E*
Davies, P T (Llanelli) 1985 *E, Fj*, 1986 *E, S, I, F, Fj, Tg, WS*, 1987 *F, E, I*, [*Tg, C, NZ*], 1988 *WS, R*, 1989 *S, I, F, E, NZ*, 1990 *F, E, S*, 1991 *I, F* 1, *A, F* 2, [*WS, Arg, A*], 1993 *F, Z* 1, *Nm*, 1994 *S, I, F, E, C, Fj* (R), *WS, R, It*, 1995 *F, I*
Davies, R H (Oxford U, London Welsh) 1957 *S, I, F*, 1958 *A*, 1962 *E, S*
Davies, S (Treherbert) 1923 *I*
Davies, S (Swansea) 1992 *I, F, E, S, A*, 1993 *E, S, I, Z* 1(R),2, *Nm, J*, 1995 *F*, [*J, I*], 1998 *I* (R), *F*
Davies, T G R (Cardiff, London Welsh) 1966 *A*, 1967 *S, I, F, E*, 1968 *E, S*, 1969 *S, I, F, NZ* 1,2, *A*, 1971 *E, S, I, F*, 1972 *E, S, F, NZ*, 1973 *E, S, I, F, A*, 1974 *S, F, E*, 1975 *F, E, S, I*, 1976 *E, S, I, F*, 1977 *I, F, E, S*, 1978 *E, S, I, A* 1,2
Davies, T J (Devonport Services, Swansea, Llanelli) 1953 *E, S, I, F*, 1957 *E, S, I, F*, 1958 *A, E, S, F*, 1959 *E, S, I, F*, 1960 *E, SA*, 1961 *E, S, F*
Davies, T M (London Welsh, Swansea) 1969 *S, I, F, E, NZ* 1,2, *A*, 1970 *SA, S, E, I, F*, 1971 *E, S, I, F*, 1972 *E, S, F, NZ*, 1973 *E, S, I, F, A*, 1974 *S, I, F, E*, 1975 *F, E, S, I, A*, 1976 *E, S, I, F*
Davies, W (Cardiff) 1896 *S*
Davies, W (Swansea) 1931 *SA*, 1932 *E, S, I*
Davies, W A (Aberavon) 1912 *S, I*
Davies, W G (Cardiff) 1978 *A* 1,2, *NZ*, 1979 *S, I, F, E*, 1980 *F, E, S, NZ*, 1981 *E, S, A*, 1982 *I, F, E, S*, 1985 *S, I, F*
Davies, W T H (Swansea) 1936 *I*, 1937 *E, I*, 1939 *E, S, I*
Davis, C E (Newbridge) 1978 *A* 2, 1981 *E, S*
Davis, M (Newport) 1991 *A*
Davis, W E N (Cardiff) 1939 *E, S, I*
Dawes, S J (London Welsh) 1964 *I, F, SA*, 1965 *E, S, I, F*, 1966 *A*, 1968 *I, F*, 1969 *E, NZ* 2, *A*, 1970 *SA, S, E, I, F*, 1971 *E, S, I, F*
Day, H C (Newport) 1930 *S, I, F*, 1931 *E, S*
Day, H T (Newport) 1892 *I*, 1893 *E, S*, 1894 *S, I*
Day, T B (Swansea) 1931 *E, S, F, I, SA*, 1932 *E, S, I*, 1934 *S, I*, 1935 *E, S, I*
Deacon, J T (Swansea) 1891 *I*, 1892 *E, S, I*
Delahay, W J (Bridgend) 1922 *E, S, I, F*, 1923 *E, S, F, I*, 1924 *NZ*, 1925 *E, S, F, I*, 1926 *E, S, I, F*, 1927 *S*

Delaney, L (Llanelli) 1989 *I, F, E*, 1990 *E*, 1991 *F* 2, [*WS, Arg, A*], 1992 *I, F, E*
Devereux, D (Neath) 1958 *A, E, S*
Devereux, J A (S Glamorgan Inst, Bridgend) 1986 *E, S, I, F, Fj, Tg, WS*, 1987 *F, E, S, I*, [*I, C, E, NZ, A*], 1988 *NZ* 1,2, *R*, 1989 *S, I*
Diplock, R (Bridgend) 1988 *R*
Dobson, G (Cardiff) 1900 *S*
Dobson, T (Cardiff) 1898 *I, E*, 1899 *E, S*
Donovan, A J (Swansea) 1978 *A* 2, 1981 *I* (R), *A*, 1982 *E, S*
Donovan, R (S Wales Police) 1983 *F* (R)
Douglas, M H J (Llanelli) 1984 *S, I, F*
Douglas, W M (Cardiff) 1886 *E, S*, 1887 *E, S*
Dowell, W H (Newport) 1907 *E, S, I*, 1908 *E, S, F, I*
Durston, A (Bridgend) 2001 *J* 1,2
Dyke, J C M (Penarth) 1906 *SA*
Dyke, L M (Penarth, Cardiff) 1910 *I*, 1911 *S, F, I*

Edmunds, D A (Neath) 1990 *I* (R), *Bb*
Edwards, A B (London Welsh, Army) 1955 *E, S*
Edwards, B O (Newport) 1951 *I*
Edwards, D (Glynneath) 1921 *E*
Edwards, G O (Cardiff, Cardiff Coll of Ed) 1967 *F, E, NZ*, 1968 *E, S, I, F*, 1969 *S, I, F, E, NZ* 1,2, *A*, 1970 *SA, S, E, I, F*, 1971 *E, S, I, F*, 1972 *E, S, F, NZ*, 1973 *E, S, I, F, A*, 1974 *S, I, F, E*, 1975 *F, E, S, I, A*, 1976 *E, S, I, F*, 1977 *I, F, E, S*, 1978 *E, S, I, F*
Eidman, I H (Cardiff) 1983 *S, R*, 1984 *I, F, E, A*, 1985 *S, I, Fj*, 1986 *E, S, I, F*
Elliott, J E (Cardiff) 1894 *I*, 1898 *I, E*
Elsey, W J (Cardiff) 1895 *E*
Emyr, Arthur (Swansea) 1989 *E, NZ*, 1990 *F, E, S, I, Nm* 1,2, 1991 *F* 1,2, [*WS, Arg, A*]
Evans, A (Pontypool) 1924 *E, I, F*
Evans, B (Swansea) 1933 *S*
Evans, B (Llanelli) 1933 *E, S*, 1936 *E, S, I*, 1937 *E*
Evans, B R (Swansea, Cardiff) 1998 *SA* 2(R), 1999 *F* 1, *It, E, Arg* 1,2, *C*, [*J* (R), *Sm* (R), *A* (R)], 2000 *Sm, US*, 2001 *J* 1(R), 2002 *SA* 1,2, *R* (R), *Fj, C, NZ*, 2003 *It, E* 1, *S* 1, *I* 2, *R*
Evans, B S (Llanelli) 1920 *E*, 1922 *E, S, I, F*
Evans, C (Pontypool) 1960 *E*
Evans, D (Penygraig) 1896 *S, I*, 1897 *E*, 1898 *E*
Evans, D B (Swansea) 1926 *E*
Evans, D D (Cheshire, Cardiff U) 1934 *E*
Evans, D P (Llanelli) 1960 *SA*
Evans, D W (Cardiff) 1889 *S, I*, 1890 *E, I*, 1891 *E*
Evans, D W (Oxford U, Cardiff, Treorchy) 1989 *F, E, NZ*, 1990 *F, E, S, I, Bb*, 1991 *A* (R), *F* 2(R), [*A* (R)], 1995 [*J* (R)]
Evans, E (Llanelli) 1937 *E*, 1939 *S, I*
Evans, F (Llanelli) 1921 *S*
Evans, G (Cardiff) 1947 *E, S, F, I, A*, 1948 *E, S, F, I*, 1949 *E, S, I*
Evans, G (Maesteg) 1981 *S* (R), *I, F, A*, 1982 *I, F, E, S*, 1983 *F, R*
Evans, G L (Newport) 1977 *F* (R), 1978 *F, A* 2(R)
Evans, G R (Llanelli) 1998 *SA* 1, 2003 *I* 2, *S* 2
Evans, I (London Welsh) 1934 *S, I*
Evans, I (Swansea) 1922 *E, S, I, F*
Evans, I C (Llanelli, Bath) 1987 *F, E, S, I*, [*I, C, E, NZ, A*], 1988 *E, S, I, F, NZ* 1,2, 1989 *I, F, E*, 1991 *E, S, I, F* 1, *A, F* 2, [*WS, Arg, A*], 1992 *I, F, E, S, A*, 1993 *E, S, I, F, J, C*, 1994 *S, I, E, Pt, Sp, C, Fj, Tg, WS, R*, 1995 *E, S, I*, [*J, NZ, I*], *SA, Fj*, 1996 *It, E, S, I, F* 1, *A* 1,2, *Bb, F* 2, *A* 3, *SA*, 1997 *US, S, I, F*, 1998 *It*
Evans, I L (Llanelli) 1991 *F* 2(R)
Evans, J (Llanelli) 1896 *S, I*, 1897 *E*
Evans, J (Blaina) 1904 *E*
Evans, J (Pontypool) 1907 *E, S, I*
Evans, J D (Cardiff) 1958 *I, F*
Evans, J E (Llanelli) 1924 *S*
Evans, J R (Newport) 1934 *E*
Evans, O J (Cardiff) 1887 *E, S*, 1888 *S, I*
Evans, P D (Llanelli) 1951 *E, F*
Evans, R (Cardiff) 1889 *S*
Evans, R (Bridgend) 1963 *S, I, F*
Evans, R L (Llanelli) 1993 *E, S, I, F*, 1994 *S, I, F, E, Pt, Sp, C, Fj, WS, R, It, SA*, 1995 *F*, [*NZ, I* (R)]
Evans, R T (Newport) 1947 *F, I*, 1950 *E, S, I, F*, 1951 *E, S, I, F*
Evans, S (Swansea, Neath) 1985 *F, E*, 1986 *Fj, Tg, WS*, 1987 *F, E*, [*I, Tg*]
Evans, T (Swansea) 1924 *I*
Evans, T G (London Welsh) 1970 *SA, S, E, I*, 1972 *E, S, F*
Evans, T H (Llanelli) 1906 *I*, 1907 *E, S, I*, 1908 *I, A*, 1909 *E, S, F, I*, 1910 *F, E, S, I*, 1911 *E, S, F, I*
Evans, T P (Swansea) 1975 *F, E, S, I, A*, 1976 *E, S, I, F*, 1977 *I*
Evans, V (Neath) 1954 *I, F, S*
Evans, W (Llanelli) 1958 *A*
Evans, W F (Rhymney) 1882 *I*, 1883 *S*
Evans, W G (Brynmawr) 1911 *I*
Evans, W H (Llwynypia) 1914 *E, S, F, I*
Evans, W J (Pontypool) 1947 *S*
Evans, W R (Bridgend) 1958 *A, E, S, I, F*, 1960 *SA*, 1961 *E, S, I, F*, 1962 *E, S, I*
Everson, W A (Newport) 1926 *S*

Faulkner, A G (Pontypool) 1975 *F, E, S, I, A*, 1976 *E, S, I, F*, 1978 *E, S, I, F, A* 1,2, *NZ*, 1979 *S, I, F*
Faull, J (Swansea) 1957 *I, F*, 1958 *A, E, S, I, F*, 1959 *E, S, I*, 1960 *E, F*
Fauvel, T J (Aberavon) 1988 *NZ* 1(R)
Fear, A G (Newport) 1934 *S, I*, 1935 *S, I*
Fender, N H (Cardiff) 1930 *I, F*, 1931 *E, S, F, I*
Fenwick, S P (Bridgend) 1975 *F, E, S, A*, 1976 *E, S, I, F*, 1977 *I, F, E, S*, 1978 *E, S, I, F, A* 1,2, *NZ*, 1979 *S, I, F, E*, 1980 *F, E, S, I, NZ*, 1981 *E, S*
Finch, E (Llanelli) 1924 *F, NZ*, 1925 *F, I*, 1926 *F*, 1927 *A*, 1928 *I*
Finlayson, A A J (Cardiff) 1974 *I, F, E*
Fitzgerald, D (Cardiff) 1894 *S, I*
Ford, F J V (Welch Regt, Newport) 1939 *E*
Ford, I (Newport) 1959 *E, S*
Ford, S P (Cardiff) 1990 *I, Nm* 1,2, *Bb*, 1991 *E, S, I, A*
Forward, A (Pontypool, Mon Police) 1951 *S, SA*, 1952 *E, S, I, F*
Fowler, I J (Llanelli) 1919 *NZA*
Francis, D G (Llanelli) 1919 *NZA*, 1924 *S*
Francis, P (Maesteg) 1987 *S*
Funnell, J S (Ebbw Vale) 1998 *Z* (R), *SA* 1

Gabe, R T (Cardiff, Llanelli) 1901 *I*, 1902 *E, S, I*, 1903 *E, S, I*, 1904 *E, S, I*, 1905 *E, S, I, NZ*, 1906 *E, I, SA*, 1907 *E, S, I*, 1908 *E, S, F, I*
Gale, N R (Swansea, Llanelli) 1960 *I*, 1963 *E, S, I, NZ*, 1964 *E, S, I, F, SA*, 1965 *E, S, I, F*, 1966 *E, S, I, F, A*, 1967 *E, NZ*, 1968 *E*, 1969 *NZ* 1(R),2, *A*
Gallacher, I S (Llanelli) 1970 *F*
Garrett, R M (Penarth) 1888 *M*, 1889 *S*, 1890 *S, E, I*, 1891 *S, I*, 1892 *E*
Geen, W P (Oxford U, Newport) 1912 *SA*, 1913 *E, I*
George, E E (Pontypridd, Cardiff) 1895 *S, I*, 1896 *E*
George, G M (Newport) 1991 *E, S*
Gething, G I (Neath) 1913 *F*
Gibbs, A (Newbridge) 1995 *I, SA*, 1996 *A* 2, 1997 *US* 1,2, *C*
Gibbs, I S (Neath, Swansea) 1991 *E, S, I, F* 1, *A, F* 2, [*WS, Arg, A*], 1992 *I, F, E, S, A*, 1993 *E, S, I, F, J, C*, 1996 *It, A* 3, *SA*, 1997 *US, S, I, F, Tg, NZ*, 1998 *It, E, S, SA* 2, *Arg*, 1999 *S, I, F* 1, *It, E, C, F* 2, [*Arg* 3, *J, Sm, A*], 2000 *I, Sm, US, SA*, 2001 *E, S, F, It*
Gibbs, R A (Cardiff) 1906 *S, I*, 1907 *E, S*, 1908 *E, S, F, I*, 1910 *F, E, S, I*, 1911 *E, S, F, I*
Giles, R (Aberavon) 1983 *R*, 1985 *Fj* (R), 1987 [*C*]
Girling, B E (Cardiff) 1881 *E*
Goldsworthy, S J (Swansea) 1884 *I*, 1885 *E, S*
Gore, J H (Blaina) 1924 *I, F, NZ*, 1925 *E*
Gore, W (Newbridge) 1947 *S, F, I*
Gough, I M (Newport, Pontypridd) 1998 *SA* 1, 1999 *S*, 2000 *F, It* (R), *E* (R), *S, I, Sm, US, SA*, 2001 *E, S, F, It, Tg, A*, 2002 *I* (R), *F* (R), *It, S*, 2003 *R*
Gould, A J (Newport) 1885 *E, S*, 1886 *E, S*, 1887 *E, S, I*, 1888 *S*, 1889 *I*, 1890 *S, E, I*, 1892 *E, S, I*, 1893 *E, S, I*, 1894 *E, S*, 1895 *E, S, I*, 1896 *E, S, I*, 1897 *E*
Gould, G H (Newport) 1892 *I*, 1893 *S, I*
Gould, R (Newport) 1882 *I*, 1883 *E, S*, 1884 *E, S, I*, 1885 *E, S*, 1886 *E*, 1887 *E, S*
Graham, T C (Newport) 1890 *I*, 1891 *S, I*, 1892 *E, S*, 1893 *E, S, I*, 1894 *E, S*, 1895 *E, S*
Gravell, R W R (Llanelli) 1975 *F, E, S, I, A*, 1976 *E, S, I, F*, 1978 *E, S, I, F, A* 1,2, *NZ*, 1979 *S, I*, 1981 *I, F*, 1982 *F, E, S*
Gray, A J (London Welsh) 1968 *E, S*
Greenslade, D (Newport) 1962 *S*
Greville, H G (Llanelli) 1947 *A*
Griffin, Dr J (Edinburgh U) 1883 *S*
Griffiths, C (Llanelli) 1979 *E* (R)
Griffiths, D (Llanelli) 1888 *M*, 1889 *I*

Griffiths, G (Llanelli) 1889 *I*
Griffiths, G M (Cardiff) 1953 *E, S, I, F, NZ*, 1954 *I, F, S*, 1955 *I, F*, 1957 *E, S*
Griffiths, J (Swansea) 2000 *Sm* (R)
Griffiths, J L (Llanelli) 1988 *NZ* 2, 1989 *S*
Griffiths, M (Bridgend, Cardiff, Pontypridd) 1988 *WS, R*, 1989 *S, I, F, E, NZ*, 1990 *F, E, Nm* 1,2, *Bb*, 1991 *I, F* 1,2, [*WS, Arg, A*], 1992 *I, F, E, S, A*, 1993 *Z* 1,2, *Nm, J, C*, 1995 *F* (R), *E, S, I*, [*J, I*], 1998 *SA* 1
Griffiths, V M (Newport) 1924 *S, I, F*
Gronow, B (Bridgend) 1910 *F, E, S, I*
Gwilliam, J A (Cambridge U, Newport) 1947 *A*, 1948 *I*, 1949 *E, S, I, F*, 1950 *E, S, I, F*, 1951 *E, S, I, SA*, 1952 *E, S, I, F*, 1953 *E, I, F, NZ*, 1954 *E*
Gwynn, D (Swansea) 1883 *E*, 1887 *S*, 1890 *E, I*, 1891 *E, S*
Gwynn, W H (Swansea) 1884 *E, S, I*, 1885 *E, S*

Hadley, A M (Cardiff) 1983 *R*, 1984 *S, I, F, E*, 1985 *F, E, Fj*, 1986 *E, S, I, F, Fj, Tg*, 1987 *S* (R), *I*, [*I, Tg, C, E, NZ, A*], *US*, 1988 *E, S, I, F*
Hall, I (Aberavon) 1967 *NZ*, 1970 *SA, S, E*, 1971 *S*, 1974 *S, I, F*
Hall, M R (Cambridge U, Bridgend, Cardiff) 1988 *NZ* 1(R),2, *WS, R*, 1989 *S, I, F, E, NZ*, 1990 *F, E, S*, 1991 *A, F* 2, [*WS, Arg, A*], 1992 *I, F, E, S, A*, 1993 *E, S, I*, 1994 *S, I, F, E, Pt, Sp, C, Tg, R, It, SA*, 1995 *F, S, I*, [*J, NZ, I*]
Hall, W H (Bridgend) 1988 *WS*
Hancock, F E (Cardiff) 1884 *I*, 1885 *E, S*, 1886 *S*
Hannan, J (Newport) 1888 *M*, 1889 *S, I*, 1890 *S, E, I*, 1891 *E*, 1892 *E, S, I*, 1893 *E, S, I*, 1894 *E, S, I*, 1895 *E, S, I*
Harding, A F (London Welsh) 1902 *E, S, I*, 1903 *E, S, I*, 1904 *E, S, I*, 1905 *E, S, I, NZ*, 1906 *E, S, I, SA*, 1907 *I*, 1908 *E, S*
Harding, G F (Newport) 1881 *E*, 1882 *I*, 1883 *E, S*
Harding, R (Swansea, Cambridge U) 1923 *E, S, F, I*, 1924 *I, F, NZ*, 1925 *F, I*, 1926 *E, I, F*, 1927 *E, S, F, I*, 1928 *E*
Harding, T (Newport) 1888 *M*, 1889 *S, I*
Harris, D J E (Pontypridd, Cardiff) 1959 *I, F*, 1960 *S, I, F, SA*, 1961 *E, S*
Harris, I R (Cardiff) 2001 *Arg, Tg, A*, 2002 *I, It* (R), *E, S* (R), *Fj* (R), *C* (R), *NZ* (R), 2003 *It, E* 1(R), *S* 1(R), *I* 1(R), *F, I* 2, *S* 2
Harris, T (Aberavon) 1927 *A*
Hathway, G F (Newport) 1924 *I, F*
Havard, Rev W T (Llanelli) 1919 *NZA*
Hawkins, F (Pontypridd) 1912 *I, F*
Hayward, B I (Ebbw Vale) 1998 *Z* (R), *SA* 1
Hayward, D (Newbridge) 1949 *E, F*, 1950 *E, S, I, F*, 1951 *E, S, I, F, SA*, 1952 *E, S, I, F*
Hayward, D J (Cardiff) 1963 *E, NZ*, 1964 *S, I, F, SA*
Hayward, G (Swansea) 1908 *S, F, I, A*, 1909 *E*
Hellings, R (Llwynypia) 1897 *E*, 1898 *I, E*, 1899 *S, I*, 1900 *E, I*, 1901 *E, S*
Henson, G L (Swansea) 2001 *J* 1(R), *R*, 2003 *NZ* (R), *R*
Herrerá, R C (Cross Keys) 1925 *S, F, I*, 1926 *E, S, I, F*, 1927 *E*
Hiams, H (Swansea) 1912 *I, F*
Hickman, A (Neath) 1930 *E*, 1933 *S*
Hiddlestone, D D (Neath) 1922 *E, S, I, F*, 1924 *NZ*
Hill, A F (Cardiff) 1885 *S*, 1886 *E, S*, 1888 *S, I, M*, 1889 *S*, 1890 *S, I*, 1893 *E, S, I*, 1894 *E, S, I*
Hill, S D (Cardiff) 1993 *Z* 1,2, *Nm*, 1994 *I* (R), *F, SA*, 1995 *F, SA*, 1996 *A* 2, *F* 2(R), *It*, 1997 *E*
Hinam, S (Cardiff) 1925 *I*, 1926 *E, S, I, F*
Hinton, J T (Cardiff) 1884 *I*
Hirst, G L (Newport) 1912 *S*, 1913 *S*, 1914 *E, S, F, I*
Hodder, W (Pontypool) 1921 *E, S, F*
Hodges, J J (Newport) 1899 *E, S, I*, 1900 *E, S, I*, 1901 *E, S*, 1902 *E, S, I*, 1903 *E, S, I*, 1904 *E, S*, 1905 *E, S, I, NZ*, 1906 *E, S, I*
Hodgson, G T R (Neath) 1962 *I*, 1963 *E, S, I, F, NZ*, 1964 *E, S, I, F, SA*, 1966 *S, I, F*, 1967 *I*
Hollingdale, H (Swansea) 1912 *SA*, 1913 *E*
Hollingdale, T H (Neath) 1927 *A*, 1928 *E, S, I, F*, 1930 *E*
Holmes, T D (Cardiff) 1978 *A* 2, *NZ*, 1979 *S, I, F, E*, 1980 *F, E, S, I, NZ*, 1981 *A*, 1982 *I, F, E*, 1983 *E, S, I, F*, 1984 *E*, 1985 *S, I, F, E, Fj*
Hopkin, W H (Newport) 1937 *S*
Hopkins, K (Cardiff, Swansea) 1985 *E*, 1987 *F, E, S*, [*Tg, C* (R)], *US*
Hopkins, P L (Swansea) 1908 *A*, 1909 *E, I*, 1910 *E*
Hopkins, R (Maesteg) 1970 *E* (R)
Hopkins, T (Swansea) 1926 *E, S, I, F*
Hopkins, W J (Aberavon) 1925 *E, S*
Howarth, S P (Sale, Newport) 1998 *SA* 2, *Arg*, 1999 *S, I, F* 1, *It, E, Arg* 1,2, *SA, C, F* 2, [*Arg* 3, *J, Sm, A*], 2000 *F, It, E*
Howells, B (Llanelli) 1934 *E*
Howells, W G (Llanelli) 1957 *E, S, I, F*
Howells, W H (Swansea) 1888 *S, I*
Howley, R (Bridgend, Cardiff) 1996 *E, S, I, F* 1, *A* 1,2, *Bb, F* 2, *It, A* 3, *SA*, 1997 *US, S, I, F, E, Tg* (R), *NZ*, 1998 *It, E, S, I, F, Z, SA* 2, *Arg*, 1999 *S, I, F* 1, *It, E, Arg* 1,2, *SA, C, F* 2, [*Arg* 3, *J, Sm, A*], 2000 *F, It, E, Sm, US, SA*, 2001 *E, S, F, R, I, Arg, Tg, A*, 2002 *I, F, It, E, S*
Hughes, D (Newbridge) 1967 *NZ*, 1969 *NZ* 2, 1970 *SA, S, E, I*
Hughes, G (Penarth) 1934 *E, S, I*
Hughes, H (Cardiff) 1887 *S*, 1889 *S*
Hughes, K (Cambridge U, London Welsh) 1970 *I*, 1973 *A*, 1974 *S*
Hullin, W (Cardiff) 1967 *S*
Humphreys, J M (Cardiff, Bath) 1995 [*NZ, I*], *SA, Fj*, 1996 *It, E, S, I, F* 1, *A* 1,2, *Bb, It, A* 3, *SA*, 1997 *S, I, F, E, Tg* (R), *NZ* (R), 1998 *It* (R), *E* (R), *S* (R), *I* (R), *F* (R), *SA* 2, *Arg*, 1999 *S, Arg* 2(R), *SA* (R), *C*, [*J* (R)], 2003 *E* 1, *I*
Hurrell, J (Newport) 1959 *F*
Hutchinson, F (Neath) 1894 *I*, 1896 *S, I*
Huxtable, R (Swansea) 1920 *F, I*
Huzzey, H V P (Cardiff) 1898 *I, E*, 1899 *E, S, I*
Hybart, A J (Cardiff) 1887 *E*

Ingledew, H M (Cardiff) 1890 *I*, 1891 *E, S*
Isaacs, I (Cardiff) 1933 *E, S*

Jackson, T H (Swansea) 1895 *E*
James, B (Bridgend) 1968 *E*
James, C R (Llanelli) 1958 *A, F*
James, D (Swansea) 1891 *I*, 1892 *S, I*, 1899 *E*
James, D R (Treorchy) 1931 *F, I*
James, D R (Bridgend, Pontypridd, Llanelli) 1996 *A* 2(R), *It, A* 3, *SA*, 1997 *I, Tg* (R), 1998 *F* (R), *Z, SA* 1,2, *Arg*, 1999 *S, I, F* 1, *It, E, Arg* 1,2, *SA, F* 2, [*Arg* 3, *Sm, A*], 2000 *F, It* (R), *I* (R), *Sm* (R), *US, SA*, 2001 *E, S, F, It, R, I*, 2002 *I, F, It, E, S* (R), *NZ* (R)
James, E (Swansea) 1890 *S*, 1891 *I*, 1892 *S, I*, 1899 *E*
James, M (Cardiff) 1947 *A*, 1948 *E, S, F, I*
James, P (Neath/ Swansea) 2003 *R*
James, T O (Aberavon) 1935 *I*, 1937 *S*
James, W J (Aberavon) 1983 *E, S, I, F, R*, 1984 *S*, 1985 *S, I, F, E, Fj*, 1986 *E, S, I, F, Fj, Tg, WS*, 1987 *E, S, I*
James, W P (Aberavon) 1925 *E, S*
Jarman, H (Newport) 1910 *E, S, I*, 1911 *E*
Jarrett, K S (Newport) 1967 *E*, 1968 *E, S*, 1969 *S, I, F, E, NZ* 1,2, *A*
Jarvis, L (Cardiff) 1997 *R* (R)
Jeffery, J J (Cardiff Coll of Ed, Newport) 1967 *NZ*
Jenkin, A M (Swansea) 1895 *I*, 1896 *E*
Jenkins, A (Llanelli) 1920 *E, S, F, I*, 1921 *S, F*, 1922 *F*, 1923 *E, S, F, I*, 1924 *NZ*, 1928 *S, I*
Jenkins, D M (Treorchy) 1926 *E, S, I, F*
Jenkins, D R (Swansea) 1927 *A*, 1929 *E*
Jenkins, E (Newport) 1910 *S, I*
Jenkins, E M (Aberavon) 1927 *S, F, I, A*, 1928 *E, S, I, F*, 1929 *F*, 1930 *E, S, I, F*, 1931 *E, S, F, I, SA*, 1932 *E, S, I*
Jenkins, G (Pontypridd, Celtic Warriors) 2002 *R, NZ* (R), 2003 *E* 1(R), *S* 1(R), *I* 1, *F, A, NZ, I* 2(R), *E* 2
Jenkins, G R (Pontypool, Swansea) 1991 *F* 2, [*WS* (R), *Arg, A*], 1992 *I, F, E, S, A*, 1993 *C*, 1994 *S, I, F, E, Pt, Sp, C, Tg, WS, R, It, SA*, 1995 *F, E, S, I*, [*J*], *SA* (R), *Fj* (t), 1996 *E* (R), 1997 *US, US* 1, *C*, 1998 *S, I, F, Z, SA* 1(R), 1999 *I* (R), *F* 1, *It, E, Arg* 1,2, *SA, F* 2, [*Arg* 3, *J, Sm, A*], 2000 *F, It, E, S, I, Sm, US, SA*
Jenkins, J C (London Welsh) 1906 *SA*
Jenkins, J L (Aberavon) 1923 *S, F*
Jenkins, L H (Mon TC, Newport) 1954 *I*, 1956 *E, S, I, F*
Jenkins, N R (Pontypridd, Cardiff) 1991 *E, S, I, F* 1, 1992 *I, F, E, S*, 1993 *E, S, I, F, Z* 1,2, *Nm, J, C*, 1994 *S, I, F, E, Pt, Sp, C, Tg, WS, R, It, SA*, 1995 *F, E, S, I*, [*J, NZ, I*], *SA, Fj*, 1996 *F* 1, *A* 1,2, *Bb, F* 2, *It, A* 3(R), *SA*, 1997 *S, I, F, E, Tg, NZ*, 1998 *It, E, S, I, F, SA* 2, *Arg*, 1999 *S, I, F* 1, *It, E, Arg* 1,2, *SA, C, F* 2, [*Arg* 3, *J, Sm, A*], 2000 *F, It, E, I* (R), *Sm* (R), *US* (R), *SA*, 2001 *E, S, F, It*, 2002 *SA* 1(R),2(R), *R*
Jenkins, V G J (Oxford U, Bridgend, London Welsh) 1933 *E, I*, 1934 *S, I*, 1935 *E, S, NZ*, 1936 *E, S, I*, 1937 *E*, 1938 *E, S*, 1939 *E*
Jenkins, W (Cardiff) 1912 *I, F*, 1913 *S, I*

John, B (Llanelli, Cardiff) 1966 *A*, 1967 *S, NZ*, 1968 *E, S, I, F*, 1969 *S, I, F, E, NZ* 1,2, *A*, 1970 *SA, S, E, I*, 1971 *E, S, I, F*, 1972 *E, S, F*
John, D A (Llanelli) 1925 *I*, 1928 *E, S, I*
John, D E (Llanelli) 1923 *F, I*, 1928 *E, S, I*
John, E R (Neath) 1950 *E, S, I, F*, 1951 *E, S, I, F, SA*, 1952 *E, S, I, F*, 1953 *E, S, I, F, NZ*, 1954 *E*
John G (St Luke's Coll, Exeter) 1954 *E, F*
John, J H (Swansea) 1926 *E, S, I, F*, 1927 *E, S, F, I*
John, P (Pontypridd) 1994 *Tg*, 1996 *Bb* (t), 1997 *US* (R), *US* 1,2, *C, R, Tg*, 1998 *Z* (R), *SA* 1
John, S C (Llanelli, Cardiff) 1995 *S, I*, 1997 *E* (R), *Tg, NZ* (R), 2000 *F* (R), *It* (R), *E* (R), *Sm* (R), *SA* (R), 2001 *E* (R), *S* (R), *Tg* (R), *A*, 2002 *I, F, It* (R), *S* (R)
Johnson, T A (Cardiff) 1921 *E, F, I*, 1923 *E, S, F*, 1924 *E, S, NZ*, 1925 *E, S, F*
Johnson, W D (Swansea) 1953 *E*
Jones, Adam (Neath/ Swansea) 2003 *E* 2(R), *S* 2
Jones, A H (Cardiff) 1933 *E, S*
Jones, B (Abertillery) 1914 *E, S, F, I*
Jones, Bert (Llanelli) 1934 *S, I*
Jones, Bob (Llwynypia) 1901 *I*
Jones, B J (Newport) 1960 *I, F*
Jones, B Lewis (Devonport Services, Llanelli) 1950 *E, S, I, F*, 1951 *E, S, SA*, 1952 *E, I, F*
Jones, C W (Cambridge U, Cardiff) 1934 *E, S, I*, 1935 *E, S, I, NZ*, 1936 *E, S, I*, 1938 *E, S, I*
Jones, C W (Bridgend) 1920 *E, S, F*
Jones, D (Neath) 1927 *A*
Jones, D (Aberavon) 1897 *E*
Jones, D (Swansea) 1947 *E, F, I*, 1949 *E, S, I, F*
Jones, D (Treherbert) 1902 *E, S, I*, 1903 *E, S, I*, 1905 *E, S, I, NZ*, 1906 *E, S, SA*
Jones, D (Newport) 1926 *E, S, I, F*, 1927 *E*
Jones, D (Llanelli) 1948 *E*
Jones, D (Cardiff) 1994 *SA*, 1995 *F, E, S*, [*J, NZ, I*], *SA, Fj*, 1996 *It, E, S, I, F* 1, *A* 1,2, *Bb, It, A* 3
Jones, Duncan (Neath) 2001 *A* (R), 2002 *I* (R), *F* (R), 2003 *I* 2, *S* 2
Jones, D K (Llanelli, Cardiff) 1962 *E, S, F, I*, 1963 *E, F, NZ*, 1964 *E, S, SA*, 1966 *E, S, I, F*
Jones, D L (Ebbw Vale, Celtic Warriors) 2000 *Sm*, 2003 *R* (R)
Jones, D P (Pontypool) 1907 *I*
Jones, D R (Llanelli) 2002 *Fj, C, NZ*, 2003 *It* (R), *E* 1, *S* 1, *I* 1, *F, NZ, E* 2
Jones, E H (Neath) 1929 *E, S*
Jones, E L (Llanelli) 1930 *F*, 1933 *E, S, I*, 1935 *E*
Jones, Elvet L (Llanelli) 1939 *S*
Jones, G (Ebbw Vale) 1963 *S, I, F*
Jones, G (Llanelli) 1988 *NZ* 2, 1989 *F, E, NZ*, 1990 *F*
Jones, G G (Cardiff) 1930 *S*, 1933 *I*
Jones, G H (Bridgend) 1995 *SA*
Jones, H (Penygraig) 1902 *S, I*
Jones, H (Neath) 1904 *I*
Jones, H (Swansea) 1930 *I, F*
Jones, Iorwerth (Llanelli) 1927 *A*, 1928 *E, S, I, F*
Jones, I C (London Welsh) 1968 *I*
Jones, Ivor E (Llanelli) 1924 *E, S*, 1927 *S, F, I, A*, 1928 *E, S, I, F*, 1929 *E, S, F, I*, 1930 *E, S*
Jones, J (Aberavon) 1901 *E*
Jones, J (Swansea) 1924 *F*
Jones, Jim (Aberavon) 1919 *NZA*, 1920 *E, S*, 1921 *S, F, I*
Jones, J A (Cardiff) 1883 *S*
Jones, J P (Tuan) (Pontypool) 1913 *S*
Jones, J P (Pontypool) 1908 *A*, 1909 *E, S, F, I*, 1910 *F, E*, 1912 *E, F*, 1913 *F, I*, 1920 *F, I*, 1921 *E*
Jones, K D (Cardiff) 1960 *SA*, 1961 *E, S, I*, 1962 *E, F*, 1963 *E, S, I, NZ*
Jones, K J (Newport) 1947 *E, S, F, I, A*, 1948 *E, S, F, I*, 1949 *E, S, I, F*, 1950 *E, S, I, F*, 1951 *E, S, I, F, SA*, 1952 *E, S, I, F*, 1953 *E, S, I, F, NZ*, 1954 *E, I, F, S*, 1955 *E, S, I, F*, 1956 *E, S, I, F*, 1957 *S*
Jones, K P (Ebbw Vale) 1996 *Bb, F* 2, *It, A* 3, 1997 *I* (R), *E*, 1998 *S, I, F* (R), *SA* 1
Jones, K W J (Oxford U, London Welsh) 1934 *E*
Jones, M A (Neath, Ebbw Vale) 1987 *S*, 1988 *NZ* 2(R), 1989 *S, I, F, E, NZ*, 1990 *F, E, S, I, Nm* 1,2, *Bb*, 1998 *Z*
Jones, M A (Llanelli) 2001 *E* (R), *S, J* 1, 2002 *R, Fj, C, NZ*, 2003 *It, I* 1, *A, NZ, E* 2
Jones, P (Newport) 1912 *SA*, 1913 *E, S, F*, 1914 *E, S, F, I*
Jones, P B (Newport) 1921 *S*
Jones, R (Swansea) 1901 *I*, 1902 *E*, 1904 *E, S, I*, 1905 *E*, 1908 *F, I, A*, 1909 *E, S, F, I*, 1910 *F, E*
Jones, R (London Welsh) 1929 *E*
Jones, R (Northampton) 1926 *E, S, F*
Jones, R (Swansea) 1927 *A*, 1928 *F*
Jones, R B (Cambridge U) 1933 *E, S*
Jones, R E (Coventry) 1967 *F, E*, 1968 *S, I, F*
Jones, R G (Llanelli, Cardiff) 1996 *It, E, S, I, F* 1, *A* 1, 1997 *US* (R), *S* (R), *US* 1,2, *R, Tg, NZ*
Jones, R L (Llanelli) 1993 *Z* 1,2, *Nm, J, C*
Jones, R N (Swansea) 1986 *E, S, I, F, Fj, Tg, WS*, 1987 *F, E, S, I*, [*I, Tg, E, NZ, A*], *US*, 1988 *E, S, I, F, NZ* 1, *WS, R*, 1989 *I, F, E, NZ*, 1990 *F, E, S, I*, 1991 *E, S, F* 2, [*WS, Arg, A*], 1992 *I, F, E, S, A*, 1993 *E, S, I*, 1994 *I* (R), *Pt*, 1995 *F, E, S, I*, [*NZ, I*]
Jones, S (Neath) 2001 *J* 1(R)
Jones, S M (Llanelli) 1998 *SA* 1(R), 1999 *C* (R), [*J* (R)], 2000 *It* (R), *S, I*, 2001 *E, F* (R), *J* 1,2, *R, I, Arg, Tg, A*, 2002 *I, F, It, S, SA* 1,2, *R* (R), *Fj, C, NZ*, 2003 *S* 1, *I* 1, *F, A, NZ, E* 2
Jones, S T (Pontypool) 1983 *S, I, F, R*, 1984 *S*, 1988 *E, S, F, NZ* 1,2
Jones, Tom (Newport) 1922 *E, S, I, F*, 1924 *E, S*
Jones, T B (Newport) 1882 *I*, 1883 *E, S*, 1884 *S*, 1885 *E, S*
Jones, W (Cardiff) 1898 *I, E*
Jones, W (Mountain Ash) 1905 *I*
Jones, W I (Llanelli, Cambridge U) 1925 *E, S, F, I*
Jones, W J (Llanelli) 1924 *I*
Jones, W K (Cardiff) 1967 *NZ*, 1968 *E, S, I, F*
Jones-Davies, T E (London Welsh) 1930 *E, I*, 1931 *E, S*
Jones-Hughes, J (Newport) 1999 [*Arg* 3(R), *J*], 2000 *F*
Jordan, H M (Newport) 1885 *E, S*, 1889 *S*
Joseph, W (Swansea) 1902 *E, S, I*, 1903 *E, S, I*, 1904 *E, S*, 1905 *E, S, I, NZ*, 1906 *E, S, I, SA*
Jowett, W F (Swansea) 1903 *E*
Judd, S (Cardiff) 1953 *E, S, I, F, NZ*, 1954 *E, F, S*, 1955 *E, S*
Judson, J H (Llanelli) 1883 *E, S*

Kedzlie, Q D (Cardiff) 1888 *S, I*
Keen, L (Aberavon) 1980 *F, E, S, I*
Knight, P (Pontypridd) 1990 *Nm* 1,2, *Bb* (R), 1991 *E, S*
Knill, F M D (Cardiff) 1976 *F* (R)

Lamerton, A E H (Llanelli) 1993 *F, Z* 1,2, *Nm, J*
Lane, S M (Cardiff) 1978 *A* 1(R),2, 1979 *I* (R), 1980 *S, I*
Lang, J (Llanelli) 1931 *F, I*, 1934 *S, I*, 1935 *E, S, I, NZ*, 1936 *E, S, I*, 1937 *E*
Lawrence, S (Bridgend) 1925 *S, I*, 1926 *S, I, F*, 1927 *E*
Law, V J (Newport) 1939 *I*
Legge, W S G (Newport) 1937 *I*, 1938 *I*
Leleu, J (London Welsh, Swansea) 1959 *E, S*, 1960 *F, SA*
Lemon, A (Neath) 1929 *I*, 1930 *S, I, F*, 1931 *E, S, F, I, SA*, 1932 *E, S, I*, 1933 *I*
Lewis, A J L (Ebbw Vale) 1970 *F*, 1971 *E, I, F*, 1972 *E, S, F*, 1973 *E, S, I, F*
Lewis, A L P (Cardiff) 1996 *It, E, S, I, A* 2(t), 1998 *It, E, S, I, F, SA* 2, *Arg*, 1999 *F* 1(R), *E* (R), *Arg* 1(R),2(R), *SA* (R), *C* (R), [*J* (R), *Sm* (R), *A* (R)], 2000 *Sm* (R), *US* (R), SA (R), 2001 *F* (R), *J* 1,2, 2002 *R* (R)
Lewis, A R (Abertillery) 1966 *E, S, I, F, A*, 1967 *I*
Lewis, B R (Swansea, Cambridge U) 1912 *I*, 1913 *I*
Lewis, C P (Llandovery Coll) 1882 *I*, 1883 *E, S*, 1884 *E, S*
Lewis, D H (Cardiff) 1886 *E, S*
Lewis, E J (Llandovery) 1881 *E*
Lewis, E W (Llanelli, Cardiff) 1991 *I, F* 1, *A, F* 2, [*WS, Arg, A*], 1992 *I, F, S, A*, 1993 *E, S, I, F, Z* 1,2, *Nm, J, C*, 1994 *S, I, F, E, Pt, Sp, Fj, WS, R, It, SA*, 1995 *E, S, I*, [*J, I*], 1996 *It, E, S, I, F* 1
Lewis, G (Pontypridd, Swansea) 1998 *SA* 1(R), 1999 *It* (R), *Arg* 2, *C*, [*J*], 2000 *F* (R), *It, S, I, Sm, US* (t+R), 2001 *F* (R), *J* 1,2, *R, I*
Lewis, G W (Richmond) 1960 *E, S*
Lewis, H (Swansea) 1913 *S, F, I*, 1914 *E*
Lewis, J G (Llanelli) 1887 *I*
Lewis, J M C (Cardiff, Cambridge U) 1912 *E*, 1913 *S, F, I*, 1914 *E, S, F, I*, 1921 *I*, 1923 *E, S*
Lewis, J R (S Glam Inst, Cardiff) 1981 *E, S, I, F*, 1982 *F, E, S*
Lewis, M (Treorchy) 1913 *F*
Lewis, P I (Llanelli) 1984 *A*, 1985 *S, I, F, E*, 1986 *E, S, I*
Lewis, T W (Cardiff) 1926 *E*, 1927 *E, S*
Lewis, W (Llanelli) 1925 *F*
Lewis, W H (London Welsh, Cambridge U) 1926 *I*, 1927 *E, F, I, A*, 1928 *F*
Llewelyn, D B (Newport, Llanelli) 1970 *SA, S, E, I, F*, 1971 *E, S, I, F*, 1972 *E, S, F, NZ*

Llewellyn, D S (Ebbw Vale, Newport) 1998 *SA* 1(R), 1999 *F* 1(R), *It* (R), [*J* (R)]
Llewellyn, G D (Neath) 1990 *Nm* 1,2, *Bb*, 1991 *E, S, I, F* 1, *A, F* 2
Llewellyn, G O (Neath, Harlequins) 1989 *NZ*, 1990 *E, S, I*, 1991 *E, S, A* (R), 1992 *I, F, E, S, A*, 1993 *E, S, I, F, Z* 1,2, *Nm, J, C*, 1994 *S, I, F, E, Pt, Sp, C, Tg, WS, R, It, SA*, 1995 *F, E, S, I*, [*J, NZ, I*], 1996 *It, E, S, I, F* 1, *A* 1,2, *Bb, F* 2, *It, A* 3, *SA*, 1997 *US, S, I, F, E, US* 1,2, *NZ*, 1998 *It, E*, 1999 *C* (R), [*Sm*], 2002 *E* (R), *SA* 1,2, *R* (R), *Fj, C, NZ*, 2003 *E* 1(R), *S* 1(R), *I* 1, *F, A, NZ, I* 2, *S* 2(R)
Llewellyn, P D (Swansea) 1973 *I, F, A*, 1974 *S, E*
Llewellyn, W (Llwynypia) 1899 *E, S, I*, 1900 *E, S, I*, 1901 *E, S, I*, 1902 *E, S, I*, 1903 *I*, 1904 *E, S, I*, 1905 *E, S, I, NZ*
Lloyd, A (Bath) 2001 *J* 1
Lloyd, D J (Bridgend) 1966 *E, S, I, F, A*, 1967 *S, I, F, E*, 1968 *S, I, F*, 1969 *S, I, F, E, NZ* 1, *A*, 1970 *F*, 1972 *E, S, F*, 1973 *E, S*
Lloyd, E (Llanelli) 1895 *S*
Lloyd, G L (Newport) 1896 *I*, 1899 *S, I*, 1900 *E, S*, 1901 *E, S*, 1902 *S, I*, 1903 *E, S, I*
Lloyd, P (Llanelli) 1890 *S, E*, 1891 *E, I*
Lloyd, R A (Pontypool) 1913 *S, F, I*, 1914 *E, S, F, I*
Lloyd, T (Maesteg) 1953 *I, F*
Lloyd, T C (Neath) 1909 *F*, 1913 *F, I*, 1914 *E, S, F, I*
Loader, C D (Swansea) 1995 *SA, Fj*, 1996 *F* 1, *A* 1,2, *Bb, F* 2, *It, A* 3, *SA*, 1997 *US, S, I, F, E, US* 1, *R, Tg, NZ*
Lockwood, T W (Newport) 1887 *E, S, I*
Long, E C (Swansea) 1936 *E, S, I*, 1937 *E, S*, 1939 *S, I*
Luscombe, H (Gwent Dragons) 2003 *S* 2(R)
Lyne, H S (Newport) 1883 *S*, 1884 *E, S, I*, 1885 *E*

McBryde, R C (Swansea, Llanelli, Neath) 1994 *Fj, SA* (t), 1997 *US* 2, 2000 *I* (R), 2001 *E, S, F, It, R, I, Arg, Tg, A*, 2002 *I, F, It, E, S* (R), *SA* 1,2, *C, NZ*, 2003 *A, NZ, E* 2, *S* 2
McCall, B E W (Welch Regt, Newport) 1936 *E, S, I*
McCarley, A (Neath) 1938 *E, S, I*
McCutcheon, W M (Swansea) 1891 *S*, 1892 *E, S*, 1893 *E, S, I*, 1894 *E*
McIntosh, D L M (Pontypridd) 1996 *SA*, 1997 *E* (R)
Madden, M (Llanelli) 2002 *SA* 1(R), *R, Fj* (R), 2003 *I* 1(R), *F* (R)
Maddock, H T (London Welsh) 1906 *E, S, I*, 1907 *E, S*, 1910 *F*
Maddocks, K (Neath) 1957 *E*
Main, D R (London Welsh) 1959 *E, S, I, F*
Mainwaring, H J (Swansea) 1961 *F*
Mainwaring, W T (Aberavon) 1967 *S, I, F, E, NZ*, 1968 *E*
Major, W C (Maesteg) 1949 *F*, 1950 *S*
Male, B O (Cardiff) 1921 *F*, 1923 *S*, 1924 *S, I*, 1927 *E, S, F, I*, 1928 *S, I, F*
Manfield, L (Mountain Ash, Cardiff) 1939 *S, I*, 1947 *A*, 1948 *E, S, F, I*
Mann, B B (Cardiff) 1881 *E*
Mantle, J T (Loughborough Colls, Newport) 1964 *E, SA*
Margrave, F L (Llanelli) 1884 *E, S*
Marinos, A W N (Newport, Gwent Dragons) 2002 *I* (R), *F, It, E, S, SA* 1,2, 2003 *R*
Marsden-Jones, D (Cardiff) 1921 *E*, 1924 *NZ*
Martin, A J (Aberavon) 1973 *A*, 1974 *S, I*, 1975 *F, E, S, I, A*, 1976 *E, S, I, F*, 1977 *I, F, E, S*, 1978 *E, S, I, F, A* 1,2, *NZ*, 1979 *S, I, F, E*, 1980 *F, E, S, I, NZ*, 1981 *I, F*
Martin, W J (Newport) 1912 *I, F*, 1919 *NZA*
Mason, J (Pontypridd) 1988 *NZ* 2(R)
Mathews, Rev A A (Lampeter) 1886 *S*
Mathias, R (Llanelli) 1970 *F*
Matthews, C (Bridgend) 1939 *I*
Matthews, J (Cardiff), 1947 *E, A*, 1948 *E, S, F*, 1949 *E, S, I, F*, 1950 *E, S, I, F*, 1951 *E, S, I, F*
May, P S (Llanelli) 1988 *E, S, I, F, NZ* 1,2, 1991 [*WS*]
Meek, N N (Pontypool) 1993 *E, S, I*
Meredith, A (Devonport Services) 1949 *E, S, I*
Meredith, B V (St Luke's Coll, London Welsh, Newport) 1954 *I, F, S*, 1955 *E, S, I, F*, 1956 *E, S, I, F*, 1957 *E, S, I, F*, 1958 *A, E, S, I*, 1959 *E, S, I, F*, 1960 *E, S, F, SA*, 1961 *E, S, I*, 1962 *E, S, F, I*
Meredith, C C (Neath) 1953 *S, NZ*, 1954 *E, I, F, S*, 1955 *E, S, I, F*, 1956 *E, I*, 1957 *E, S*
Meredith, J (Swansea) 1888 *S, I*, 1890 *S, E*
Merry, A E (Pill Harriers) 1912 *I, F*
Michael, G (Swansea) 1923 *E, S, F*
Michaelson, R C B (Aberavon, Cambridge U) 1963 *E*
Miller, F (Mountain Ash) 1896 *I*, 1900 *E, S, I*, 1901 *E, S, I*
Mills, F M (Swansea, Cardiff) 1892 *E, S, I*, 1893 *E, S, I*, 1894 *E, S, I*, 1895 *E, S, I*, 1896 *E*
Moon, R H StJ B (Llanelli) 1993 *F, Z* 1,2, *Nm, J, C*, 1994 *S, I, F, E, Sp, C, Fj, WS, R, It, SA*, 1995 *E* (R), 2000 *S, I, Sm* (R), *US* (R), 2001 *E* (R), *S* (R)
Moore, A P (Cardiff) 1995 [*J*], *SA, Fj*, 1996 *It*
Moore, A P (Swansea) 1995 *SA* (R), *Fj*, 1998 *S, I, F, Z, SA* 1, 1999 *C*, 2000 *S, I, US* (R), 2001 *E* (R), *S, F, It, J* 1,2, *R, I, Arg, Tg, A*, 2002 *F, It, E, S*
Moore, S J (Swansea, Moseley) 1997 *C, R, Tg*
Moore, W J (Bridgend) 1933 *I*
Morgan, C H (Llanelli) 1957 *I, F*
Morgan, C I (Cardiff) 1951 *I, F, SA*, 1952 *E, S, I*, 1953 *S, I, F, NZ*, 1954 *E, I, S*, 1955 *E, S, I, F*, 1956 *E, S, I, F*, 1957 *E, S, I, F*, 1958 *E, S, I, F*
Morgan, C S (Cardiff) 2002 *I, F, It, E, S, SA* 1,2, *R* (R), 2003 *F*
Morgan, D (Swansea) 1885 *S*, 1886 *E, S*, 1887 *E, S, I*, 1889 *I*
Morgan, D (Llanelli) 1895 *I*, 1896 *E*
Morgan, D R R (Llanelli) 1962 *E, S, F, I*, 1963 *E, S, I, F, NZ*
Morgan, E (Llanelli) 1920 *I*, 1921 *E, S, F*
Morgan, Edgar (Swansea) 1914 *E, S, F, I*
Morgan, E T (London Welsh) 1902 *E, S, I*, 1903 *I*, 1904 *E, S, I*, 1905 *E, S, I, NZ*, 1906 *E, S, I, SA*, 1908 *F*
Morgan, F L (Llanelli) 1938 *E, S, I*, 1939 *E*
Morgan, H J (Abertillery) 1958 *E, S, I, F*, 1959 *I, F*, 1960 *E*, 1961 *E, S, I, F*, 1962 *E, S, F, I*, 1963 *S, I, F*, 1965 *E, S, I, F*, 1966 *E, S, I, F, A*
Morgan, H P (Newport) 1956 *E, S, I, F*
Morgan, I (Swansea) 1908 *A*, 1909 *E, S, F, I*, 1910 *F, E, S, I*, 1911 *E, F, I*, 1912 *S*
Morgan, J L (Llanelli) 1912 *SA*, 1913 *E*
Morgan, K A (Pontypridd, Swansea) 1997 *US* 1,2, *C, R, NZ*, 1998 *S, I, F*, 2001 *J* 1,2, *R, I, Arg, Tg, A*, 2002 *I, F, It, E, S, SA* 1,2, 2003 *E* 1, *S* 1
Morgan, M E (Swansea) 1938 *E, S, I*, 1939 *E*
Morgan, N (Newport) 1960 *S, I, F*
Morgan, P E J (Aberavon) 1961 *E, S, F*
Morgan, P J (Llanelli) 1980 *S* (R), *I, NZ* (R), 1981 *I*
Morgan, R (Newport) 1984 *S*
Morgan, T (Llanelli) 1889 *I*
Morgan, W G (Cambridge U) 1927 *F, I*, 1929 *E, S, F, I*, 1930 *I, F*
Morgan, W L (Cardiff) 1910 *S*
Moriarty, R D (Swansea) 1981 *A*, 1982 *I, F, E, S*, 1983 *E*, 1984 *S, I, F, E*, 1985 *S, I, F*, 1986 *Fj, Tg, WS*, 1987 [*I, Tg, C* (R), *E, NZ, A*]
Moriarty, W P (Swansea) 1986 *I, F, Fj, Tg, WS*, 1987 *F, E, S, I*, [*I, Tg, C, E, NZ, A*], *US*, 1988 *E, S, I, F, NZ* 1
Morley, J C (Newport) 1929 *E, S, F, I*, 1930 *E, I*, 1931 *E, S, F, I, SA*, 1932 *E, S, I*
Morris, D R (Neath, Swansea) 1998 *Z, SA* 1(R),2(R), 1999 *S, I, It* (R), 2000 *US, SA*, 2001 *E, S, F, It, Arg, Tg, A*
Morris, G L (Swansea) 1882 *I*, 1883 *E, S*, 1884 *E, S*
Morris, H T (Cardiff) 1951 *F*, 1955 *I, F*
Morris, J I T (Swansea) 1924 *E, S*
Morris, M S (S Wales Police, Neath) 1985 *S, I, F*, 1990 *I, Nm* 1,2, *Bb*, 1991 *I, F* 1, [*WS* (R)], 1992 *E*
Morris, R R (Swansea, Bristol) 1933 *S*, 1937 *S*
Morris, S (Cross Keys) 1920 *E, S, F, I*, 1922 *E, S, I, F*, 1923 *E, S, F, I*, 1924 *E, S, F, NZ*, 1925 *E, S, F*
Morris, W (Abertillery) 1919 *NZA*, 1920 *F*, 1921 *I*
Morris, W (Llanelli) 1896 *S, I*, 1897 *E*
Morris, W D (Neath) 1967 *F, E*, 1968 *E, S, I, F*, 1969 *S, I, F, E, NZ* 1,2, *A*, 1970 *SA, S, E, I, F*, 1971 *E, S, I, F*, 1972 *E, S, F, NZ*, 1973 *E, S, I, A*, 1974 *S, I, F, E*
Morris, W J (Newport) 1965 *S*, 1966 *F*
Morris, W J (Pontypool) 1963 *S, I*
Moseley, K (Pontypool, Newport) 1988 *NZ* 2, *R*, 1989 *S, I*, 1990 *F*, 1991 *F* 2, [*WS, Arg, A*]
Murphy, C D (Cross Keys) 1935 *E, S, I*
Mustoe, L (Cardiff) 1995 *Fj*, 1996 *A* 1(R),2, 1997 *US* 1,2, *C, R* (R), 1998 *E* (R), *I* (R), *F* (R)

Nash, D (Ebbw Vale) 1960 *SA*, 1961 *E, S, I, F*, 1962 *F*
Newman, C H (Newport) 1881 *E*, 1882 *I*, 1883 *E, S*, 1884 *E, S*, 1885 *E, S*, 1886 *E*, 1887 *E*
Nicholas, D L (Llanelli) 1981 *E, S, I, F*
Nicholas, T J (Cardiff) 1919 *NZA*
Nicholl, C B (Cambridge U, Llanelli) 1891 *I*, 1892 *E, S, I*, 1893 *E, S, I*, 1894 *E, S*, 1895 *E, S, I*, 1896 *E, S, I*
Nicholl, D W (Llanelli) 1894 *I*

Nicholls, E G (Cardiff) 1896 *S, I*, 1897 *E*, 1898 *I, E*, 1899 *E, S, I*, 1900 *S, I*, 1901 *E, S, I*, 1902 *E, S, I*, 1903 *I*, 1904 *E*, 1905 *I, NZ*, 1906 *E, S, I, SA*
Nicholls, F E (Cardiff Harlequins) 1892 *I*
Nicholls, H (Cardiff) 1958 *I*
Nicholls, S H (Cardiff) 1888 *M*, 1889 *S, I*, 1891 *S*
Norris, C H (Cardiff) 1963 *F*, 1966 *F*
Norster, R L (Cardiff) 1982 *S*, 1983 *E, S, I, F*, 1984 *S, I, F, E, A*, 1985 *S, I, F, E, Fj*, 1986 *Fj, Tg, WS*, 1987 *F, E, S, I*, [*I, C, E*], *US*, 1988 *E, S, I, F, NZ* 1, *WS*, 1989 *F, E*
Norton, W B (Cardiff) 1882 *I*, 1883 *E, S*, 1884 *E, S, I*

Oakley, R (Gwnet Dragons) 2003 *I* 2, *S* 2(R)
O'Connor, A (Aberavon) 1960 *SA*, 1961 *E, S*, 1962 *F, I*
O'Connor, R (Aberavon) 1957 *E*
O'Neill, W (Cardiff) 1904 *S, I*, 1905 *E, S, I*, 1907 *E, I*, 1908 *E, S, F, I*
O'Shea, J P (Cardiff) 1967 *S, I*, 1968 *S, I, F*
Oliver, G (Pontypool) 1920 *E, S, F, I*
Osborne, W T (Mountain Ash) 1902 *E, S, I*, 1903 *E, S, I*
Ould, W J (Cardiff) 1924 *E, S*
Owen, A (Swansea) 1924 *E*
Owen, G D (Newport) 1955 *I, F*, 1956 *E, S, I, F*
Owen, M (Pontypridd, Gwent Dragons) 2002 *SA* 1,2, *R, C* (R), *NZ* (R), 2003 *It, I* 2, *S* 2
Owen, R M (Swansea) 1901 *I*, 1902 *E, S, I*, 1903 *E, S, I*, 1904 *E, S, I*, 1905 *E, S, I, NZ*, 1906 *E, S, I, SA*, 1907 *E, S*, 1908 *F, I, A*, 1909 *E, S, F, I*, 1910 *F, E*, 1911 *E, S, F, I*, 1912 *E, S*

Packer, H (Newport) 1891 *E*, 1895 *S, I*, 1896 *E, S, I*, 1897 *E*
Palmer, F (Swansea) 1922 *E, S, I*
Parfitt, F C (Newport) 1893 *E, S, I*, 1894 *E, S, I*, 1895 *S*, 1896 *S, I*
Parfitt, S A (Swansea) 1990 *Nm* 1(R), *Bb*
Parker, D S (Swansea) 1924 *I, F, NZ*, 1925 *E, S, F, I*, 1929 *F, I*, 1930 *E*
Parker, S (Pontypridd, Celtic Warriors) 2002 *R, Fj, C, NZ*, 2003 *E* 2
Parker, T (Swansea) 1919 *NZA*, 1920 *E, S, I*, 1921 *E, S, F, I*, 1922 *E, S, I, F*, 1923 *E, S, F*
Parker, W (Swansea) 1899 *E, S*
Parks, R (Pontypridd, Celtic Warriors) 2002 *SA* 1(R), *Fj* (R), 2003 *I* 2, *S* 2
Parsons, G W (Newport) 1947 *E*
Pascoe, D (Bridgend) 1923 *F, I*
Pask, A E I (Abertillery) 1961 *F*, 1962 *E, S, F, I*, 1963 *E, S, I, F, NZ*, 1964 *E, S, I, F, SA*, 1965 *E, S, I, F*, 1966 *E, S, I, F, A*, 1967 *S, I*
Payne, G W (Army, Pontypridd) 1960 *E, S, I*
Payne, H (Swansea) 1935 *NZ*
Peacock, H (Newport) 1929 *S, F, I*, 1930 *S, I, F*
Peake, E (Chepstow) 1881 *E*
Pearce, G P (Bridgend) 1981 *I, F*, 1982 *I* (R)
Pearson, T W (Cardiff, Newport) 1891 *E, I*, 1892 *E, S*, 1894 *S, I*, 1895 *E, S, I*, 1897 *E*, 1898 *I, E*, 1903 *E*
Peel, D (Llanelli) 2001 *J* 2(R), *R* (R), *Tg* (R), 2002 *I* (R), *It* (R), *E* (R), *S* (R), *SA* 1,2, *R, Fj, C, NZ*, 2003 *It, S* 1(R), *I* 1(R), *F, NZ* (R), *I* 2, *S* 2
Pegge, E V (Neath) 1891 *E*
Perego, M A (Llanelli) 1990 *S*, 1993 *F, Z* 1, *Nm* (R), 1994 *S, I, F, E, Sp*
Perkins, S J (Pontypool) 1983 *S, I, F, R*, 1984 *S, I, F, E, A*, 1985 *S, I, F, E, Fj*, 1986 *E, S, I, F*
Perrett, F L (Neath) 1912 *SA*, 1913 *E, S, F, I*
Perrins, V C (Newport) 1970 *SA, S*
Perry, W (Neath) 1911 *E*
Phillips, A J (Cardiff) 1979 *E*, 1980 *F, E, S, I, NZ*, 1981 *E, S, I, F, A*, 1982 *I, F, E, S*, 1987 [*C, E, A*]
Phillips, B (Aberavon) 1925 *E, S, F, I*, 1926 *E*
Phillips, D H (Swansea) 1952 *F*
Phillips, H P (Newport) 1892 *E*, 1893 *E, S, I*, 1894 *E, S*
Phillips, H T (Newport) 1927 *E, S, F, I, A*, 1928 *E, S, I, F*
Phillips, K H (Neath) 1987 *F*, [*I, Tg, NZ*], *US*, 1988 *E, NZ* 1, 1989 *NZ*, 1990 *F, E, S, I, Nm* 1,2, *Bb*, 1991 *E, S, I, F* 1, *A*
Phillips, L A (Newport) 1900 *E, S, I*, 1901 *S*
Phillips, M (Llanelli) 2003 *R*
Phillips, R (Neath) 1987 *US*, 1988 *E, S, I, F, NZ* 1,2, *WS*, 1989 *S, I*
Phillips, W D (Cardiff) 1881 *E*, 1882 *I*, 1884 *E, S, I*
Pickering, D F (Llanelli) 1983 *E, S, I, F, R*, 1984 *S, I, F, E, A*, 1985 *S, I, F, E, Fj*, 1986 *E, S, I, F, Fj*, 1987 *F, E, S*
Plummer, R C S (Newport) 1912 *S, I, F, SA*, 1913 *E*
Pook, T (Newport) 1895 *S*
Popham, A (Leeds) 2003 *A* (R), *I* 2, *R, S* 2
Powell, G (Ebbw Vale) 1957 *I, F*
Powell, J (Cardiff) 1906 *I*
Powell, J (Cardiff) 1923 *I*
Powell, R D (Cardiff) 2002 *SA* 1(R),2(R), *C* (R)
Powell, R W (Newport) 1888 *S, I*
Powell, W C (London Welsh) 1926 *S, I, F*, 1927 *E, F, I*, 1928 *S, I, F*, 1929 *E, S, F, I*, 1930 *S, I, F*, 1931 *E, S, F, I, SA*, 1932 *E, S, I*, 1935 *E, S, I*
Powell, W J (Cardiff) 1920 *E, S, F, I*
Price, B (Newport) 1961 *I, F*, 1962 *E, S*, 1963 *E, S, F, NZ*, 1964 *E, S, I, F, SA*, 1965 *E, S, I, F*, 1966 *E, S, I, F, A*, 1967 *S, I, F, E*, 1969 *S, I, F, NZ* 1,2, *A*
Price, G (Pontypool) 1975 *F, E, S, I, A*, 1976 *E, S, I, F*, 1977 *I, F, E, S*, 1978 *E, S, I, F, A* 1,2, *NZ*, 1979 *S, I, F, E*, 1980 *F, E, S, I, NZ*, 1981 *E, S, I, F, A*, 1982 *I, F, E, S*, 1983 *E, I, F*
Price, M J (Pontypool, RAF) 1959 *E, S, I, F*, 1960 *E, S, I, F*, 1962 *E*
Price, R E (Weston-s-Mare) 1939 *S, I*
Price, T G (Llanelli) 1965 *E, S, I, F*, 1966 *E, A*, 1967 *S, F*
Priday, A J (Cardiff) 1958 *I*, 1961 *I*
Pritchard, C (Pontypool) 1928 *E, S, I, F*, 1929 *E, S, F, I*
Pritchard, C C (Newport, Pontypool) 1904 *S, I*, 1905 *NZ*, 1906 *E, S*
Pritchard, C M (Newport) 1904 *I*, 1905 *E, S, NZ*, 1906 *E, S, I, SA*, 1907 *E, S, I*, 1908 *E*, 1910 *F, E, A* 1,2, *Bb, F* 2, *It, A* 3, 1997 *E* (R)
Proctor, W T (Llanelli) 1992 *A*, 1993 *E, S, Z* 1,2, *Nm, C*, 1994 *I, C, Fj, WS, R, It, SA*, 1995 *S, I*, [*NZ*], *Fj*, 1996 *It, E, S, I, A* 1,2, *Bb, F* 2, *It, A* 3, 1997 E(R), *US* 1,2, *C, R*, 1998 *E* (R), *S, I, F, Z*, 2001 *A*
Prosser, D R (Neath) 1934 *S, I*
Prosser, G (Neath) 1934 *E, S, I*, 1935 *NZ*
Prosser, G (Pontypridd) 1995 [*NZ*]
Prosser, J (Cardiff) 1921 *I*
Prosser, T R (Pontypool) 1956 *S, F*, 1957 *E, S, I, F*, 1958 *A, E, S, I, F*, 1959 *E, S, I, F*, 1960 *E, S, I, F, SA*, 1961 *I, F*
Prothero, G J (Bridgend) 1964 *S, I, F*, 1965 *E, S, I, F*, 1966 *E, S, I, F*
Pryce-Jenkins, T J (London Welsh) 1888 *S, I*
Pugh, C (Maesteg) 1924 *E, S, I, F, NZ*, 1925 *E, S*
Pugh, J D (Neath) 1987 *US*, 1988 *S* (R), 1990 *S*
Pugh, P (Neath) 1989 *NZ*
Pugsley, J (Cardiff) 1910 *E, S, I*, 1911 *E, S, F, I*
Pullman, J J (Neath) 1910 *F*
Purdon, F T (Newport) 1881 *E*, 1882 *I*, 1883 *E, S*

Quinnell, D L (Llanelli) 1972 *F* (R), *NZ*, 1973 *E, S, A*, 1974 *S, F*, 1975 *E* (R), 1977 *I* (R), *F, E, S*, 1978 *E, S, I, F, A* 1, *NZ*, 1979 *S, I, F, E*, 1980 *NZ*
Quinnell, J C (Llanelli, Richmond, Cardiff) 1995 *Fj*, 1996 *A* 3(R), 1997 *US* (R), *S* (R), *I* (R), *E* (R), 1998 *SA* 2, *Arg*, 1999 *I, F* 1, *It, E, Arg* 1,2, *SA, C, F* 2, [*Arg* 3, *J, A*], 2000 *It, E*, 2001 *S* (R), *F* (R), *It* (R), *J* 1,2, *R* (R), *I* (R), *Arg*, 2002 *I, F*
Quinnell, L S (Llanelli, Richmond) 1993 *C*, 1994 *S, I, F, E, Pt, Sp, C, WS*, 1997 *US, S, I, F, E*, 1998 *It, E, S* (R), *Z, SA* 2, *Arg*, 1999 *S, I, F* 1, *It, E, Arg* 1,2, *SA, C, F* 2, [*Arg* 3, *Sm, A*], 2000 *F, It, E, Sm, US, SA*, 2001 *E, S, F, It, Arg, Tg, A*, 2002 *I, F, It, E, R, C* (R)

Radford, W J (Newport) 1923 *I*
Ralph, A R (Newport) 1931 *F, I, SA*, 1932 *E, S, I*
Ramsey, S H (Treorchy) 1896 *E*, 1904 *E*
Randell, R (Aberavon) 1924 *I, F*
Raybould, W H (London Welsh, Cambridge U, Newport) 1967 *S, I, F, E, NZ*, 1968 *I, F*, 1970 *SA, E, I, F* (R)
Rayer, M A (Cardiff) 1991 [*WS* (R), *Arg, A* (R)], 1992 *E* (R), *A*, 1993 *E, S, I, Z* 1, *Nm, J* (R), 1994 *S* (R), *I* (R), *F, E, Pt, C, Fj, WS, R, It*
Rees, Aaron (Maesteg) 1919 *NZA*
Rees, Alan (Maesteg) 1962 *E, S, F*
Rees, A M (London Welsh) 1934 *E*, 1935 *E, S, I, NZ*, 1936 *E, S, I*, 1937 *E, S, I*, 1938 *E, S*
Rees, B I (London Welsh) 1967 *S, I, F*
Rees, C F W (London Welsh) 1974 *I*, 1975 *A*, 1978 *NZ*, 1981 *F, A*, 1982 *I, F, E, S*, 1983 *E, S, I, F*
Rees, D (Swansea) 1968 *S, I, F*
Rees, Dan (Swansea) 1900 *E*, 1903 *E, S*, 1905 *E, S*
Rees, E B (Swansea) 1919 *NZA*
Rees, H (Cardiff) 1937 *S, I*, 1938 *E, S, I*
Rees, H E (Neath) 1979 *S, I, F, E*, 1980 *F, E, S, I, NZ*, 1983 *E, S, I, F*

Rees, J (Swansea) 1920 *E, S, F, I*, 1921 *E, S, I*, 1922 *E*, 1923 *E, F, I*, 1924 *E*
Rees, J I (Swansea) 1934 *E, S, I*, 1935 *S, NZ*, 1936 *E, S, I*, 1937 *E, S, I*, 1938 *E, S, I*
Rees, L M (Cardiff) 1933 *I*
Rees, P (Llanelli) 1947 *F, I*
Rees, P M (Newport) 1961 *E, S, I*, 1964 *I*
Rees, R (Swansea) 1998 *Z*
Rees, T (Newport) 1935 *S, I, NZ*, 1936 *E, S, I*, 1937 *E, S*
Rees, T A (Llandovery) 1881 *E*
Rees, T E (London Welsh) 1926 *I, F*, 1927 *A*, 1928 *E*
Rees-Jones, G R (Oxford U, London Welsh) 1934 *E, S*, 1935 *I, NZ*, 1936 *E*
Reeves, F (Cross Keys) 1920 *F, I*, 1921 *E*
Reynolds, A (Swansea) 1990 *Nm* 1,2(R), 1992 *A* (R)
Rhapps, J (Penygraig) 1897 *E*
Rice-Evans, W (Swansea) 1890 *S*, 1891 *E, S*
Richards, B (Swansea)1960 *F*
Richards, C (Pontypool) 1922 *E, S, I, F*, 1924 *I*
Richards, D S (Swansea) 1979 *F, E*, 1980 *F, E, S, I, NZ*, 1981 *E, S, I, F*, 1982 *I, F*, 1983 *E, S, I, R* (R)
Richards, E G (Cardiff) 1927 *S*
Richards, E S (Swansea) 1885 *E*, 1887 *S*
Richards, H D (Neath) 1986 *Tg* (R), 1987 [*Tg, E* (R), *NZ*]
Richards, I (Cardiff) 1925 *E, S, F*
Richards, K H L (Bridgend) 1960 *SA*, 1961 *E, S, I, F*
Richards, M C R (Cardiff) 1968 *I, F*, 1969 *S, I, F, E, NZ* 1,2, *A*
Richards, R (Aberavon) 1913 *S, F, I*
Richards, R (Cross Keys) 1956 *F*
Richards, T L (Maesteg) 1923 *I*
Richardson, S J (Aberavon) 1978 *A* 2(R), 1979 *E*
Rickards, A R (Cardiff) 1924 *F*
Ring, J (Aberavon) 1921 *E*
Ring, M G (Cardiff, Pontypool) 1983 *E*, 1984 *A*, 1985 *S, I, F*, 1987 *I*, [*I, Tg, A*], *US*, 1988 *E, S, I, F, NZ* 1,2, 1989 *NZ*, 1990 *F, E, S, I, Nm* 1,2, *Bb*, 1991 *E, S, I, F* 1,2, [*WS, Arg, A*]
Ringer, J (Bridgend) 2001 *J* 1(R),2(R)
Ringer, P (Ebbw Vale, Llanelli) 1978 *NZ*, 1979 *S, I, F, E*, 1980 *F, E, NZ*
Roberts, C (Neath) 1958 *I, F*
Roberts, D E A (London Welsh) 1930 *E*
Roberts, E (Llanelli) 1886 *E*, 1887 *I*
Roberts, E J (Llanelli) 1888 *S, I*, 1889 *I*
Roberts, G J (Cardiff) 1985 *F* (R), *E*, 1987 [*I, Tg, C, E, A*]
Roberts, H M (Cardiff) 1960 *SA*, 1961 *E, S, I, F*, 1962 *S, F*, 1963 *I*
Roberts, J (Cardiff) 1927 *E, S, F, I, A*, 1928 *E, S, I, F*, 1929 *E, S, F, I*
Roberts, M G (London Welsh) 1971 *E, S, I, F*, 1973 *I, F*, 1975 *S*, 1979 *E*
Roberts, T (Newport, Risca) 1921 *S, F, I*, 1922 *E, S, I, F*, 1923 *E, S*
Roberts, W (Cardiff) 1929 *E*
Robins, J D (Birkenhead Park) 1950 *E, S, I, F*, 1951 *E, S, I, F*, 1953 *E, I, F*
Robins, R J (Pontypridd) 1953 *S*, 1954 *F, S*, 1955 *E, S, I, F*, 1956 *E, F*, 1957 *E, S, I, F*
Robinson, I R (Cardiff) 1974 *F, E*
Robinson, J P (Cardiff) 2001 *J* 1(R),2(R), *Arg* (R), *Tg* (R), *A*, 2002 *I, Fj* (R), *C, NZ*, 2003 *A, NZ, I* 2, *S* 2
Robinson, M F D (Swansea) 1999 *S, I, F* 1, *Arg* 1
Robinson, N J (Cardiff) 2003 *I* 2, *R*
Rocyn-Jones, D N (Cambridge U) 1925 *I*
Roderick, W B (Llanelli) 1884 *I*
Rogers, P J D (London Irish, Newport, Cardiff) 1999 *F* 1, *It, E, Arg* 1,2, *SA, C, F* 2, [*Arg* 3, *J, Sm, A*], 2000 *F, It, E, S, I, SA*
Rosser, M A (Penarth) 1924 *S, F*
Rowland, E M (Lampeter) 1885 *E*
Rowlands, C F (Aberavon) 1926 *I*
Rowlands, D C T (Pontypool) 1963 *E, S, I, F, NZ*, 1964 *E, S, I, F, SA*, 1965 *E, S, I, F*
Rowlands, G (RAF, Cardiff) 1953 *NZ*, 1954 *E, F*, 1956 *F*
Rowlands, K A (Cardiff) 1962 *F, I*, 1963 *I*, 1965 *I, F*
Rowles, G R (Penarth) 1892 *E*
Rowley, M (Pontypridd) 1996 *SA*, 1997 *US, S, I, F, R*
Roy, W S (Cardiff) 1995 [*J* (R)]
Russell, S (London Welsh) 1987 *US*

Samuel, D (Swansea) 1891 *I*, 1893 *I*
Samuel, F (Mountain Ash) 1922 *S, I, F*
Samuel, J (Swansea) 1891 *I*
Scourfield, T (Torquay) 1930 *F*
Scrine, G F (Swansea) 1899 *E, S*, 1901 *I*
Shanklin, J L (London Welsh) 1970 *F*, 1972 *NZ*, 1973 *I, F*
Shanklin, T (Saracens, Cardiff) 2001 *J* 2, 2002 *F, It, SA* 1(R),2(R), *R, Fj*, 2003 *It, E* 1, *S* 1, *I* 1, *F* (t+R), *A, NZ, S* 2
Shaw, G (Neath) 1972 *NZ*, 1973 *E, S, I, F, A*, 1974 *S, I, F, E*, 1977 *I, F*
Shaw, T W (Newbridge) 1983 *R*
Shea, J (Newport) 1919 *NZA*, 1920 *E, S*, 1921 *E*
Shell, R C (Aberavon) 1973 *A* (R)
Sidoli, R (Pontypridd, Celtic Warriors) 2002 *SA* 1(R),2(R), *R, Fj, NZ*, 2003 *It, E* 1, *S* 1, *I* 1, *F, A, NZ, E* 2
Simpson, H J (Cardiff) 1884 *E, S, I*
Sinkinson, B D (Neath) 1999 *F* 1, *It, E, Arg* 1,2, *SA, F* 2, [*Arg* 3, *J, Sm, A*], 2000 *F, It, E*, 2001 *R* (R), *I, Arg* (R), *Tg, A*, 2002 *It* (R)
Skrimshire, R T (Newport) 1899 *E, S, I*
Skym, A (Llanelli) 1928 *E, S, I, F*, 1930 *E, S, I, F*, 1931 *E, S, F, I, SA*, 1932 *E, S, I*, 1933 *E, S, I*, 1935 *E*
Smith, J S (Cardiff) 1884 *E, I*, 1885 *E*
Smith, R (Ebbw Vale) 2000 *F* (R)
Sparks, B (Neath) 1954 *I*, 1955 *E, F*, 1956 *E, S, I*, 1957 *S*
Spiller, W J (Cardiff) 1910 *S, I*, 1911 *E, S, F, I*, 1912 *E, F, SA*, 1913 *E*
Squire, J (Newport, Pontypool) 1977 *I, F*, 1978 *E, S, I, F, A* 1, *NZ*, 1979 *S, I, F, E*, 1980 *F, E, S, I, NZ*, 1981 *E, S, I, F, A*, 1982 *I, F, E*, 1983 *E, S, I, F*
Stadden, W J W (Cardiff) 1884 *I*, 1886 *E, S*, 1887 *I*, 1888 *S, M*, 1890 *S, E*
Stephens, C (Bridgend) 1998 *E* (R), 2001 *J* 2(R)
Stephens, C J (Llanelli) 1992 *I, F, E, A*
Stephens, G (Neath) 1912 *E, S, I, F, SA*, 1913 *E, S, F, I*, 1919 *NZA*
Stephens, I (Bridgend) 1981 *E, S, I, F, A*, 1982 *I, F, E, S*, 1984 *I, F, E, A*
Stephens, Rev J G (Llanelli) 1922 *E, S, I, F*
Stephens, J R G (Neath) 1947 *E, S, F, I*, 1948 *I*, 1949 *S, I, F*, 1951 *F, SA*, 1952 *E, S, I, F*, 1953 *E, S, I, F, NZ*, 1954 *E, I*, 1955 *E, S, I, F*, 1956 *S, I, F*, 1957 *E, S, I, F*
Stock, A (Newport) 1924 *F, NZ*, 1926 *E, S*
Stone, P (Llanelli) 1949 *F*
Strand-Jones, J (Llanelli) 1902 *E, S, I*, 1903 *E, S*
Sullivan, A C (Cardiff) 2001 *Arg, Tg*
Summers, R H B (Haverfordwest) 1881 *E*
Sutton, S (Pontypool, S Wales Police) 1982 *F, E*, 1987 *F, E, S, I*, [*C, NZ* (R), *A*]
Sweeney, C (Pontypridd, Celtic Warriors) 2003 *It* (R), *E, NZ* (R), *I* 2, *S* 2
Sweet-Escott, R B (Cardiff) 1891 *S*, 1894 *I*, 1895 *I*

Tamplin, W E (Cardiff) 1947 *S, F, I, A*, 1948 *E, S, F*
Tanner, H (Swansea, Cardiff) 1935 *NZ*, 1936 *E, S, I*, 1937 *E, S, I*, 1938 *E, S, I*, 1939 *E, S, I*, 1947 *E, S, F, I*, 1948 *E, S, F, I*, 1949 *E, S, I, F*
Tarr, D J (Swansea, Royal Navy) 1935 *NZ*
Taylor, A R (Cross Keys) 1937 *I*, 1938 *I*, 1939 *E*
Taylor, C G (Ruabon) 1884 *E, S, I*, 1885 *E, S*, 1886 *E, S*, 1887 *E, I*
Taylor, H T (Cardiff) 1994 *Pt, C, Fj, Tg, WS* (R), *R, It, SA*, 1995 *E, S*, [*J, NZ, I*], *SA, Fj*, 1996 *It, E, S, I, F* 1, *A* 1,2, *It, A* 3
Taylor, J (London Welsh) 1967 *S, I, F, E, NZ*, 1968 *I, F*, 1969 *S, I, F, E, NZ* 1, *A*, 1970 *F*, 1971 *E, S, I, F*, 1972 *E, S, F, NZ*, 1973 *E, S, I, F*
Taylor, M (Pontypool, Swansea) 1994 *SA*, 1995 *F, E, SA* (R), 1998 *Z, SA* 1,2, *Arg*, 1999 *I, F* 1, *It, E, Arg* 1,2, *SA, F* 2, [*Arg* 3, *J, Sm, A*], 2000 *F, It, E, S, Sm, US*, 2001 *E, S, F, It*, 2002 *S, SA* 1,2, 2003 *E* 1, *S* 1, *I* 1, *F, A, NZ, E* 2
Thomas, A (Newport) 1963 *NZ*, 1964 *E*
Thomas, A C (Bristol, Swansea) 1996 *It, E, S, I, F* 2(R), *SA*, 1997 *US, S, I, F, US* 1,2, *C, R, NZ* (t), 1998 *It, E, S* (R), *Z, SA* 1, 2000 *Sm, US, SA* (R)
Thomas, A G (Swansea, Cardiff) 1952 *E, S, I, F*, 1953 *S, I, F*, 1954 *E, I, F*, 1955 *S, I, F*
Thomas, Bob (Swansea) 1900 *E, S, I*, 1901 *E*
Thomas, Brian (Neath, Cambridge U) 1963 *E, S, I, F, NZ*, 1964 *E, S, I, F, SA*, 1965 *E*, 1966 *E, S, I*, 1967 *NZ*, 1969 *S, I, F, E, NZ* 1,2
Thomas, C (Bridgend) 1925 *E, S*
Thomas, C J (Newport) 1888 *I, M*, 1889 *S, I*, 1890 *S, E, I*, 1891 *E, I*
Thomas, D (Aberavon) 1961 *I*
Thomas, D (Llanelli) 1954 *I*
Thomas, Dick (Mountain Ash) 1906 *SA*, 1908 *F, I*, 1909 *S*

Thomas, D J (Swansea) 1904 *E*, 1908 *A*, 1910 *E, S, I*, 1911 *E, S, F, I*, 1912 *E*
Thomas, D J (Swansea) 1930 *S, I*, 1932 *E, S, I*, 1933 *E, S*, 1934 *E*, 1935 *E, S, I*
Thomas, D L (Neath) 1937 *E*
Thomas, E (Newport) 1904 *S, I*, 1909 *S, F, I*, 1910 *F*
Thomas, G (Llanelli) 1923 *E, S, F, I*
Thomas, G (Newport) 1888 *M*, 1890 *I*, 1891 *S*
Thomas, G (Bridgend, Cardiff, Celtic Warriors) 1995 [*J, NZ, I*], *SA, Fj*, 1996 *F* 1, *A* 1,2, *Bb, F* 2, *It, A* 3, 1997 *US, S, I, F, E, US* 1,2, *C, R, Tg, NZ*, 1998 *It, E, S, I, F, SA* 2, *Arg*, 1999 *F* 1(R), *It, E, Arg* 2, *SA, F* 2, [*Arg* 3, *J* (R), *Sm, A*], 2000 *F, It, E, S, I, US* (R), *SA*, 2001 *E, F, It, J* 1,2, *R, Arg, Tg, A*, 2002 *E, R, Fj, C, NZ*, 2003 *It, E* 1, S 1, *I* 1, *F, I* 2, *E* 2
Thomas, G (Bath, Neath/Swansea) 2001 *J* 1,2, *R, I* (R), *Arg, Tg* (R), *A* (R), 2002 *S* (R), *SA* 2(R), *R* (R), 2003 *It* (R), *E* 1, *S* 1, *F* (R), *E* 2(R), *R*
Thomas, H (Llanelli) 1912 *F*
Thomas, H (Neath) 1936 *E, S, I*, 1937 *E, S, I*
Thomas, H W (Swansea) 1912 *SA*, 1913 *E*
Thomas, I (Bryncethin) 1924 *E*
Thomas, I D (Ebbw Vale, Llanelli) 2000 *Sm, US* (R), *SA* (R), 2001 *J* 1,2, *R, I, Arg* (R), *Tg*, 2002 *It, E, S, SA* 1,2, *Fj, C, NZ*, 2003 *It, E* 1, *S* 1, *I* 1, *F, A, NZ, E* 2
Thomas, J (Swansea) 2003 *A, NZ* (R), *E* 2(R), *R*
Thomas, L C (Cardiff) 1885 *E, S*
Thomas, M C (Newport, Devonport Services) 1949 *F*, 1950 *E, S, I, F*, 1951 *E, S, I, F, SA*, 1952 *E, S, I, F*, 1953 *E*, 1956 *E, S, I, F*, 1957 *E, S*, 1958 *E, S, I, F*, 1959 *I, F*
Thomas, M G (St Bart's Hospital) 1919 *NZA*, 1921 *S, F, I*, 1923 *F*, 1924 *E*
Thomas, N (Bath) 1996 *SA* (R), 1997 *US* 1(R),2, *C* (R), *R, Tg, NZ*, 1998 *Z, SA* 1
Thomas, R (Pontypool) 1909 *F, I*, 1911 *S, F*, 1912 *E, S, SA*, 1913 *E*
Thomas, R C C (Swansea) 1949 *F*, 1952 *I, F*, 1953 *S, I, F, NZ*, 1954 *E, I, F, S*, 1955 *S, I*, 1956 *E, S, I*, 1957 *E*, 1958 *A, E, S, I, F*, 1959 *E, S, I, F*
Thomas, R L (London Welsh) 1889 *S, I*, 1890 *I*, 1891 *E, S, I*, 1892 *E*
Thomas, S (Llanelli) 1890 *S, E*, 1891 *I*
Thomas, W D (Llanelli) 1966 *A*, 1968 *S, I, F*, 1969 *E, NZ* 2, *A*, 1970 *SA, S, E, I, F*, 1971 *E, S, I, F*, 1972 *E, S, F, NZ*, 1973 *E, S, I, F*, 1974 *E*
Thomas, W G (Llanelli, Waterloo, Swansea) 1927 *E, S, F, I*, 1929 *E*, 1931 *E, S, SA*, 1932 *E, S, I*, 1933 *E, S, I*
Thomas, W H (Llandovery Coll, Cambridge U) 1885 *S*, 1886 *E, S*, 1887 *E, S*, 1888 *S, I*, 1890 *E, I*, 1891 *S, I*
Thomas, W J (Cardiff) 1961 *F*, 1963 *F*
Thomas, W J L (Llanelli, Cardiff) 1995 *SA, Fj*, 1996 *It, E, S, I, F* 1, 1996 *Bb* (R), 1997 *US*
Thomas, W L (Newport) 1894 *S*, 1895 *E, I*
Thomas, W T (Abertillery) 1930 *E*
Thompson, J F (Cross Keys) 1923 *E*
Thorburn, P H (Neath) 1985 *F, E, Fj*, 1986 *E, S, I, F*, 1987 *F*, [*I, Tg, C, E, NZ, A*], *US*, 1988 *S, I, F, WS, R* (R), 1989 *S, I, F, E, NZ*, 1990 *F, E, S, I, Nm* 1,2, *Bb*, 1991 *E, S, I, F* 1, *A*
Titley, M H (Bridgend, Swansea) 1983 *R*, 1984 *S, I, F, E, A*, 1985 *S, I, Fj*, 1986 *F, Fj, Tg, WS*, 1990 *F, E*
Towers, W H (Swansea) 1887 *I*, 1888 *M*
Travers, G (Pill Harriers) 1903 *E, S, I*, 1905 *E, S, I, NZ*, 1906 *E, S, I, SA*, 1907 *E, S, I*, 1908 *E, S, F, I, A*, 1909 *E, S, I*, 1911 *S, F, I*
Travers, W H (Newport) 1937 *S, I*, 1938 *E, S, I*, 1939 *E, S, I*, 1949 *E, S, I, F*
Treharne, E (Pontypridd) 1881 *E*, 1883 *E*
Trew, W J (Swansea) 1900 *E, S, I*, 1901 *E, S*, 1903 *S*, 1905 *S*, 1906 *S*, 1907 *E, S*, 1908 *E, S, F, I, A*, 1909 *E, S, F, I*, 1910 *F, E, S*, 1911 *E, S, F, I*, 1912 *S*, 1913 *S, F*
Trott, R F (Cardiff) 1948 *E, S, F, I*, 1949 *E, S, I, F*
Truman, W H (Llanelli) 1934 *E*, 1935 *E*
Trump, L C (Newport) 1912 *E, S, I, F*
Turnbull, B R (Cardiff) 1925 *I*, 1927 *E, S*, 1928 *E, F*, 1930 *S*
Turnbull, M J L (Cardiff) 1933 *E, I*
Turner, P (Newbridge) 1989 *I* (R), *F, E*

Uzzell, H (Newport) 1912 *E, S, I, F*, 1913 *S, F, I*, 1914 *E, S, F, I*, 1920 *E, S, F, I*
Uzzell, J R (Newport) 1963 *NZ*, 1965 *E, S, I, F*

Vickery, W E (Aberavon) 1938 *E, S, I*, 1939 *E*
Vile, T H (Newport) 1908 *E, S*, 1910 *I*, 1912 *I, F, SA*, 1913 *E*, 1921 *S*
Vincent, H C (Bangor) 1882 *I*
Voyle, M J (Newport, Llanelli, Cardiff) 1996 *A* 1(t), *F* 2, 1997 *E, US* 1,2, *C, Tg, NZ*, 1998 *It, E, S, I, F, Arg* (R), 1999 *S* (R), *I* (t), *It* (R), *SA* (R), *F* 2(R), [*J, A* (R)], 2000 *F* (R)

Wakeford, J D M (S Wales Police) 1988 *WS, R*
Waldron, R (Neath) 1965 *E, S, I, F*
Walker, N (Cardiff) 1993 *I, F, J*, 1994 *S, F, E, Pt, Sp*, 1995 *F, E*, 1997 *US* 1,2, *C, R* (R), *Tg, NZ*, 1998 *E*
Waller, P D (Newport) 1908 *A*, 1909 *E, S, F, I*, 1910 *F*
Walne, N J (Richmond, Cardiff) 1999 *It* (R), *E* (R), *C*
Walters, N (Llanelli) 1902 *E*
Wanbon, R (Aberavon) 1968 *E*
Ward, W S (Cross Keys) 1934 *S, I*
Warlow, J (Llanelli) 1962 *I*
Waters, D R (Newport) 1986 *E, S, I, F*
Waters, K (Newbridge) 1991 [*WS*]
Watkins, D (Newport) 1963 *E, S, I, F, NZ*, 1964 *E, S, I, F, SA*, 1965 *E, S, I, F*, 1966 *E, S, I, F*, 1967 *I, F, E*
Watkins, E (Neath) 1924 *E, S, I, F*
Watkins, E (Blaina) 1926 *S, I, F*
Watkins, E (Cardiff) 1935 *NZ*, 1937 *S, I*, 1938 *E, S, I*, 1939 *E, S*
Watkins, H (Llanelli) 1904 *S, I*, 1905 *E, S, I*, 1906 *E*
Watkins, I J (Ebbw Vale) 1988 *E* (R), *S, I, F, NZ* 2, *R*, 1989 *S, I, F, E*
Watkins, L (Oxford U, Llandaff) 1881 *E*
Watkins, M J (Newport) 1984 *I, F, E, A*
Watkins, M J (Llanelli) 2003 *It* (R), *E* 1(R), *S* 1(R), *I* 1(R), *R*, *S* 2
Watkins, S J (Newport, Cardiff) 1964 *S, I, F*, 1965 *E, S, I, F*, 1966 *E, S, I, F, A*, 1967 *S, I, F, E, NZ*, 1968 *E, S*, 1969 *S, I, F, E, NZ* 1, 1970 *E, I*
Watkins, W R (Newport) 1959 *F*
Watts, D (Maesteg) 1914 *E, S, F, I*
Watts, J (Llanelli) 1907 *E, S, I*, 1908 *E, S, F, I, A*, 1909 *S, F, I*
Watts, W (Llanelli) 1914 *E*
Watts, W H (Newport) 1892 *E, S, I*, 1893 *E, S, I*, 1894 *E, S, I*, 1895 *E, I*, 1896 *E*
Weatherley, D J (Swansea) 1998 *Z*
Weaver, D (Swansea) 1964 *E*
Webb, J (Abertillery) 1907 *S*, 1908 *E, S, F, I, A*, 1909 *E, S, F, I*, 1910 *F, E, S, I*, 1911 *E, S, F, I*, 1912 *E, S*
Webb, J E (Newport) 1888 *M*, 1889 *S*
Webbe, G M C (Bridgend) 1986 *Tg* (R), *WS*, 1987 *F, E, S*, [*Tg*], *US*, 1988 *F* (R), *NZ* 1, *R*
Webster, R E (Swansea) 1987 [*A*], 1990 *Bb*, 1991 [*Arg, A*], 1992 *I, F, E, S, A*, 1993 *E, S, I, F*
Wells, G T (Cardiff) 1955 *E, S*, 1957 *I, F*, 1958 *A, E, S*
Westacott, D (Cardiff) 1906 *I*
Wetter, H (Newport) 1912 *SA*, 1913 *E*
Wetter, J J (Newport) 1914 *S, F, I*, 1920 *E, S, F, I*, 1921 *E*, 1924 *I, NZ*
Wheel, G A D (Swansea) 1974 *I, E* (R), 1975 *F, E, I, A*, 1976 *E, S, I, F*, 1977 *I, E, S*, 1978 *E, S, I, F, A* 1,2, *NZ*, 1979 *S, I*, 1980 *F, E, S, I*, 1981 *E, S, I, F, A*, 1982 *I*
Wheeler, P J (Aberavon) 1967 *NZ*, 1968 *E*
Whitefoot, J (Cardiff) 1984 *A* (R), 1985 *S, I, F, E, Fj*, 1986 *E, S, I, F, Fj, Tg, WS*, 1987 *F, E, S, I*, [*I, C*]
Whitfield, J (Newport) 1919 *NZA*, 1920 *E, S, F, I*, 1921 *E*, 1922 *E, S, I, F*, 1924 *S, I*
Whitson, G K (Newport) 1956 *F*, 1960 *S, I*
Wilkins, G (Bridgend) 1994 *Tg*
Williams, A (Neath/ Swansea) 2003 *R* (R)
Williams, A (Bridgend, Swansea) 1990 *Nm* 2(R), 1995 *Fj* (R)
Williams, B (Llanelli) 1920 *S, F, I*
Williams, B H (Neath, Richmond, Bristol) 1996 *F* 2, 1997 *R, Tg, NZ*, 1998 *It, E, Z* (R), *SA* 1, *Arg* (R), 1999 *S* (R), *I, It* (R), 2000 *F* (R), *It* (R), *E* (t+R), 2001 *R* (R), *I* (R), *Tg* (R), *A* (R), 2002 *I* (R), *F* (R), *It* (R), *E* (R), *S*
Williams, B L (Cardiff) 1947 *E, S, F, I, A*, 1948 *E, S, F, I*, 1949 *E, S, I*, 1951 *I, SA*, 1952 *S*, 1953 *E, S, I, F, NZ*, 1954 *S*, 1955 *E*
Williams, B R (Neath) 1990 *S, I, Bb*, 1991 *E, S*
Williams, C (Llanelli) 1924 *NZ*, 1925 *E*
Williams, C (Aberavon, Swansea) 1977 *E, S*, 1980 *F, E, S, I, NZ*, 1983 *E*
Williams, C D (Cardiff, Neath) 1955 *F*, 1956 *F*
Williams, D (Llanelli) 1998 *SA* 1(R)
Williams, D (Ebbw Vale) 1963 *E, S, I, F*, 1964 *E, S, I, F, SA*, 1965 *E, S, I, F*, 1966 *E, S, I, A*, 1967 *F, E, NZ*, 1968 *E*, 1969 *S, I, F, E, NZ* 1,2, *A*, 1970 *SA, S, E, I*, 1971 *E, S, I, F*
Williams, D B (Newport, Swansea) 1978 *A* 1, 1981 *E, S*

Williams, E (Neath) 1924 *NZ*, 1925 *F*
Williams, E (Aberavon) 1925 *E, S*
Williams, F L (Cardiff) 1929 *S, F, I*, 1930 *E, S, I, F*, 1931 *F, I, SA*, 1932 *E, S, I*, 1933 *I*
Williams, G (Aberavon) 1936 *E, S, I*
Williams, G (London Welsh) 1950 *I, F*, 1951 *E, S, I, F, SA*, 1952 *E, S, I, F*, 1953 *NZ*, 1954 *E*
Williams, G (Bridgend) 1981 *I, F*, 1982 *E* (R), *S*
Williams, G J (Bridgend, Cardiff) 2003 *It* (R), *E* 1(R), *S* 1, *F* (R), *E* 2(R)
Williams, G P (Bridgend) 1980 *NZ*, 1981 *E, S, A*, 1982 *I*
Williams, G R (Cardiff) 2000 *I, Sm, US, SA*, 2001 *S, F, It, R* (R), *I* (R), *Arg, Tg* (R), *A* (R), 2002 *F* (R), *It* (R), *E* (R), *S, SA* 1,2, *R, Fj, C, NZ*, 2003 *It, E* 1, *S* 1, *I* 1, *F, A, NZ, E* 2
Williams, J (Blaina) 1920 *E, S, F, I*, 1921 *S, F, I*
Williams, J F (London Welsh) 1905 *I, NZ*, 1906 *S, SA*
Williams, J J (Llanelli) 1973 *F* (R), *A*, 1974 *S, I, F, E*, 1975 *F, E, S, I, A*, 1976 *E, S, I, F*, 1977 *I, F, E, S*, 1978 *E, S, I, F, A* 1,2, *NZ*, 1979 *S, I, F, E*
Williams, J L (Cardiff) 1906 *SA*, 1907 *E, S, I*, 1908 *E, S, I, A*, 1909 *E, S, F, I*, 1910 *I*, 1911 *E, S, F, I*
Williams, J P R (London Welsh, Bridgend) 1969 *S, I, F, E, NZ* 1,2, *A*, 1970 *SA, S, E, I, F*, 1971 *E, S, I, F*, 1972 *E, S, F, NZ*, 1973 *E, S, I, F, A*, 1974 *S, I, F*, 1975 *F, E, S, I, A*, 1976 *E, S, I, F*, 1977 *I, F, E, S*, 1978 *E, S, I, F, A* 1,2, *NZ*, 1979 *S, I, F, E*, 1980 *NZ*, 1981 *E, S*
Williams, L (Llanelli, Cardiff) 1947 *E, S, F, I, A*, 1948 *I*, 1949 *E*
Williams, L H (Cardiff) 1957 *S, I, F*, 1958 *E, S, I, F*, 1959 *E, S, I*, 1961 *F*, 1962 *E, S*
Williams, M (Newport) 1923 *F*
Williams, M E (Pontypridd, Cardiff) 1996 *Bb, F* 2, *It* (t), 1998 *It, E, Z, SA* 2, *Arg*, 1999 *S, I, C, J*, [*Sm*], 2000 *E* (R), 2001 *E, S, F, It*, 2002 *I, F, It, E, S, SA* 1,2, *Fj, C, NZ*, 2003 *It, E* 1, *S* 1, *I* 1, *F, A, NZ, E* 2
Williams, O (Bridgend) 1990 *Nm* 2
Williams, O (Llanelli) 1947 *E, S, A*, 1948 *E, S, F, I*
Williams, R (Llanelli) 1954 *S*, 1957 *F*, 1958 *A*
Williams, R D G (Newport) 1881 *E*
Williams, R F (Cardiff) 1912 *SA*, 1913 *E, S*, 1914 *I*
Williams, R H (Llanelli) 1954 *I, F, S*, 1955 *S, I, F*, 1956 *E, S, I*, 1957 *E, S, I, F*, 1958 *A, E, S, I, F*, 1959 *E, S, I, F*, 1960 *E*
Williams, S (Llanelli) 1947 *E, S, F, I*, 1948 *S, F*
Williams, S A (Aberavon) 1939 *E, S, I*
Williams, S M (Neath, Cardiff, Northampton) 1994 *Tg*, 1996 *E* (t), *A* 1,2, *Bb, F* 2, *It, A* 3, *SA*, 1997 *US, S, I, F, E, US* 1,2(R), *C, R* (R), *Tg* (R), *NZ* (t+R), 2002 *SA* 1,2, *R, Fj* (R), 2003 *It, E* 1, *S* 1, *F* (R), *R*
Williams, S M (Neath) 2000 *F* (R), *It, E, S, I, Sm, SA* (R), 2001 *J* 1,2, *I*
Williams, T (Pontypridd) 1882 *I*
Williams, T (Swansea) 1888 *S, I*
Williams, T (Swansea) 1912 *I*, 1913 *F*, 1914 *E, S, F, I*
Williams, Tudor (Swansea) 1921 *F*
Williams, T G (Cross Keys) 1935 *S, I, NZ*, 1936 *E, S, I*, 1937 *S, I*
Williams, W A (Crumlin) 1927 *E, S, F, I*
Williams, W A (Newport) 1952 *I, F*, 1953 *E*
Williams, W E O (Cardiff) 1887 *S, I*, 1889 *S*, 1890 *S, E*
Williams, W H (Pontymister) 1900 *E, S, I*, 1901 *E*
Williams, W O G (Swansea, Devonport Services) 1951 *F, SA*, 1952 *E, S, I, F*, 1953 *E, S, I, F, NZ*, 1954 *E, I, F, S*, 1955 *E, S, I, F*, 1956 *E, S, I*
Williams, W P J (Neath) 1974 *I, F*
Williams-Jones, H (S Wales Police, Llanelli) 1989 *S* (R), 1990 *F* (R), *I*, 1991 *A*, 1992 *S, A*, 1993 *E, S, I, F, Z* 1, *Nm*, 1994 *Fj, Tg, WS* (R), *It* (t), 1995 *E* (R)
Willis, W R (Cardiff) 1950 *E, S, I, F*, 1951 *E, S, I, F, SA*, 1952 *E, S*, 1953 *S, NZ*, 1954 *E, I, F, S*, 1955 *E, S, I, F*
Wiltshire, M L (Aberavon) 1967 *NZ*, 1968 *E, S, F*
Windsor, R W (Pontypool) 1973 *A*, 1974 *S, I, F, E*, 1975 *F, E, S, I, A*, 1976 *E, S, I, F*, 1977 *I, F, E, S*, 1978 *E, S, I, F, A* 1,2, *NZ*, 1979 *S, I, F*
Winfield, H B (Cardiff) 1903 *I*, 1904 *E, S, I*, 1905 *NZ*, 1906 *E, S, I*, 1907 *S, I*, 1908 *E, S, F, I, A*
Winmill, S (Cross Keys) 1921 *E, S, F, I*
Wintle, M E (Llanelli) 1996 *It*
Wintle, R V (London Welsh) 1988 *WS* (R)
Wooller, W (Sale, Cambridge U, Cardiff) 1933 *E, S, I*, 1935 *E, S, I, NZ*, 1936 *E, S, I*, 1937 *E, S, I*, 1938 *S, I*, 1939 *E, S, I*
Wyatt, C P (Llanelli) 1998 *Z* (R), *SA* 1(R),2, *Arg*, 1999 *S, I, F* 1, *It, E, Arg* 1,2, *SA, C* (R), *F* 2, [*Arg* 3, *J* (R), *Sm, A*], 2000 *F, It, E, US, SA*, 2001 *E, R, I, Arg* (R), *Tg* (R), *A* (R), 2002 *I, It* (R), *E, S* (R), 2003 *A* (R), *NZ* (t+R), *E* 2
Wyatt, G (Pontypridd, Celtic Warriors) 1997 *Tg*, 2003 *R* (R)
Wyatt, M A (Swansea) 1983 *E, S, I, F*, 1984 *A*, 1985 *S, I*, 1987 *E, S, I*

Young, D (Swansea, Cardiff) 1987 [*E, NZ*], *US*, 1988 *E, S, I, F, NZ* 1,2, *WS, R*, 1989 *S, NZ*, 1990 *F*, 1996 *A* 3, *SA*, 1997 *US, S, I, F, E, R, NZ*, 1998 *It, E, S, I, F*, 1999 *I, E* (R), *Arg* 1(R),2(R), *SA, C* (R), *F* 2, [*Arg* 3, *J, Sm, A*], 2000 *F, It, E, S, I*, 2001 *E, S, F, It, R, I, Arg*
Young, G A (Cardiff) 1886 *E, S*
Young, J (Harrogate, RAF, London Welsh) 1968 *S, I, F*, 1969 *S, I, F, E, NZ* 1, 1970 *E, I, F*, 1971 *E, S, I, F*, 1972 *E, S, F, NZ*, 1973 *E, S, I, F*
Young, P (Gwent Dragons) 2003 *R* (R)

FRANCE TEST SEASON REVIEW 2002-03

Roller-coaster ride for the French

Ian Borthwick

This was a season of mixed fortunes for the French, who despite failing to capitalise on the success of the previous year, still managed to finish their international campaign on a positive note. After winning the Grand Slam in 2002 and after walking off with all the major awards at the IRB ceremonies (team of the year and player of the year for Fabien Galthié), this ought to have been a year of consolidation for Bernard Laporte and his men. But it was instead a year of doubt, in which *Les Bleus* not only lost as many games as they won, but the charismatic coach was also forced to change his strategy and adopt a completely different game plan from the one that had been so successful a year earlier.

The international season seemed to start rather well with an apparently convincing (30-10) victory over the Springboks in Marseilles, although the Springboks' subsequent defeat at Murrayfield and the 53-3 thrashing at Twickenham rapidly put this result into perspective. Signs that all was not well, however, surfaced the following week at Stade de France when, against an experimental All Black side twice reduced to 14 men after referee Scott Young brandished the yellow cards, they only managed a 20-20 draw, the first draw ever between the two countries. Fly-half François Gelez, whose goal-kicking had been so successful the week before, choked on two vital occasions in the dying minutes of the game, letting the New Zealanders off the hook. The Agen fly-half's woes were to be symptomatic of the French season as they searched desperately for a world-class goal-kicker to see them through the World Cup, and before the end of the season Laporte would try four different candidates in the No 10 jersey – Gelez, Gérald Merceron, Frédéric Michalak and Yann Delaigue – before settling on Merceron and Michalak for the World Cup.

From the French point of view, the Six Nations got off to the worst possible start with a 25-17 loss to favourites England at Twickenham. Once again Laporte had fought a losing battle with the vested interests of the clubs as he tried to bring his players together as often as possible, and the *Tricolores* went into the game with only four days' preparation. Despite the absence of tight-head prop Pieter de Villiers, suspended by the FFR after testing positive for cocaine and Ecstasy, France definitely had the measure of England, scoring three tries to one. But Merceron's failure with the boot robbed the French of what they considered to be a victory well within their reach.

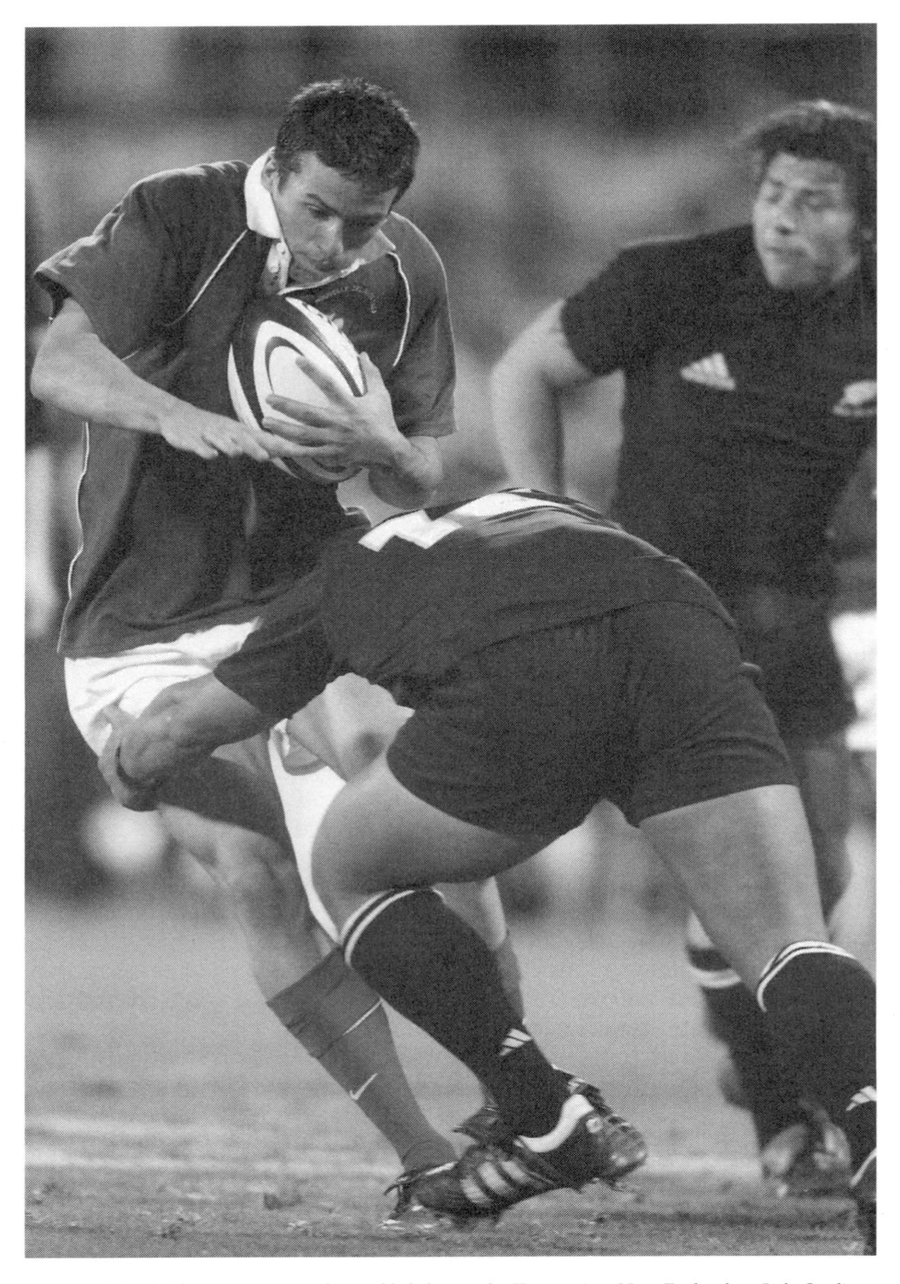

French full-back Clement Poitrenaud is tackled during the Test against New Zealand at Jade Stadium, Christchurch, in June. New Zealand won a close match 31-23.

The turning point came in fact early in the game when loose-head prop Jean-Jacques Crenca was penalised for the third time in the scrum and threatened with a yellow card. From the very first scrum, Crenca had totally dominated the English tight-head Julian White who repeatedly pulled up to relieve the pressure. Instead of rewarding the French for their superior strength and technique, however, referee Paul Honiss penalised them and, after only twelve minutes of play the French were forced to de-power their scrum to avoid the risk of a yellow card.

Against Scotland a week later, France bounced back with style, winning 38-3 and running in four tries to none, but the loss to Ireland in Dublin on 8 March was undoubtedly the low point of the season. While having claimed almost a moral victory against England, Laporte was forced to admit that against Ireland his team had gone back to its bad old ways in terms of discipline and that the 15-12 loss represented 'une regression monumentale'.

'We will never be World Champions with a team like the one which played in Dublin,' blurted the outspoken coach in an interview with *L'Equipe*, accusing his players of being 'liars and cheats' and of having lost the essential team spirit which one season before had made them 'une grande équipe.'

After this widely-published outburst, the air was cleared, the *Tricolores* regrouped, and the subsequent games against Italy (53-27) and Wales (33-5) enabled them to finish off the Championship in style, with no fewer than nine tries (six and three) from the two encounters.

Three months later, with French clubs dominating the final phases of the European Cup, and with Stade Français and Stade Toulousain playing in the club final, Laporte opted to rest a number of his key players for the perilous summer tour to Argentina and New Zealand. Fabien Pelous, Olivier Brouzet, Olivier Magne, Serge Betsen, Jean-Jacques Crenca, Raphaël Ibañez and Xavier Garbajosa were all given the summer off to recuperate and, very much like John Mitchell's experimental All Black side which toured Europe in November 2002, the French headed off to the Southern Hemisphere with a largely untried group, aimed purely at identifying the remaining eight or nine World Cup spots still up for grabs.

There were surprises in store, however, as the French roller-coaster once again plumbed the depths of mediocrity, losing both Tests to the Pumas in Buenos Aires, and this despite dominating Argentina in terms of both territory and possession. After the second Test, played on a Friday evening to give *Les Bleus* a better chance of recovering from the jet-lag and travel fatigue before playing the All Blacks, Laporte once again let rip, accusing his players of being 'idiots' and of only losing to Argentina because 'we were more stupid than they were.'

Once again his tongue-lashing, aided by some skilful cajoling from the captain Fabien Galthié, had the desired effect and, for the final game of the tour, the French once again looked like a team which could go all the way in the 2003 World Cup.

After the debacle in Argentina, many observers were predicting a 40-point defeat at the hands of a rampant All Black side which had just beaten Wales 55-3. But with a makeshift side featuring at best only four first-choice players, Galthié and his men pushed the All Blacks to the limit in Christchurch. Although eventually losing by 31-23, they not only recovered from an early 19-3 deficit, but also played with the very qualities of courage and commitment that Laporte had been looking for all season. To such an extent that, despite the season's balance sheet looking distinctly dodgy, with five wins, five losses and a draw, Laporte headed back to France with a smile on his face. And while the knives were out in New Zealand for local coach, the taciturn John Mitchell, the ebullient Frenchman remained secure in his job, and secure in the knowledge that, despite the hiccups, France were once again back on track.

France's Test record in 2002-03: Played 14, won 7, drew 1, lost 6

Opponents	*Date*	*Venue*	*Result*
England	6th September 2003	A	Lost 14-45
England	30th August 2003	H	Won 17-16
Romania	22nd August 2003	H	Won 56-8
New Zealand	28th June 2003	A	Lost 23-31
Argentina	20th June 2003	A	Lost 32-33
Argentina	14th June 2003	A	Lost 6-10
Wales	29th March 2003	H	Won 33-5
Italy	23rd March 2003	A	Won 53-27
Ireland	8th March 2003	A	Lost 12-15
Scotland	23rd February 2003	H	Won 38-3
England	15th February 2003	A	Lost 17-25
Canada	23rd November 2002	H	Won 35-3
New Zealand	16th November 2002	H	Drew 20-20
South Africa	9th November 2002	H	Won 30-10

FRANCE INTERNATIONAL STATISTICS

(to 30 September 2003)

Match Records

MOST CONSECUTIVE TEST WINS

10 1931 *E, G,* 1932 *G,* 1933 *G,* 1934 *G,* 1935 *G,* 1936 *G 1,2,* 1937 *G,It*
8 1998 *E, S, I, W, Arg 1,2, Fj, Arg 3*
8 2001 *SA 3 A, Fj* 2002 *It, W, E, S, I*

MOST CONSECUTIVE TESTS WITHOUT DEFEAT

Matches	*Wins*	*Draws*	*Period*
10	10	0	1931 to 1938
10	8	2	1958 to 1959
10	9	1	1986 to 1987

MOST POINTS IN A MATCH

by the team

Pts	*Opponents*	*Venue*	*Year*
77	Fiji	Saint Etienne	2001
70	Zimbabwe	Auckland	1987
67	Romania	Bucharest	2000
64	Romania	Aurillac	1996
62	Romania	Castres	1999
60	Italy	Toulon	1967
59	Romania	Paris	1924
56	Romania	Lens	2003

by a player

Pts	*Player*	*Opponents*	*Venue*	*Year*
30	D Camberabero	Zimbabwe	Auckland	1987
28	C Lamaison	New Zealand	Twickenham	1999
27	G Camberabero	Italy	Toulon	1967
27	C Lamaison	New Zealand	Marseilles	2000
27	G Merceron	South Africa	Johannesburg	2001
26	T Lacroix	Ireland	Durban	1995
25	J-P Romeu	United States	Chicago	1976
25	P Berot	Romania	Agen	1987
25	T Lacroix	Tonga	Pretoria	1995

MOST TRIES IN A MATCH

by the team

Tries	*Opponents*	*Venue*	*Year*
13	Romania	Paris	1924
13	Zimbabwe	Auckland	1987
12	Fiji	Saint Etienne	2001
11	Italy	Toulon	1967
10	Romania	Aurillac	1996
10	Romania	Bucharest	2000

by a player

Tries	*Player*	*Opponents*	*Venue*	*Year*
4	A Jauréguy	Romania	Paris	1924
4	M Celhay	Italy	Paris	1937

MOST CONVERSIONS IN A MATCH

by the team

Cons	*Opponents*	*Venue*	*Year*
9	Italy	Toulon	1967
9	Zimbabwe	Auckland	1987
8	Romania	Wellington	1987
8	Romania	Lens	2003

by a player

Cons	*Player*	*Opponents*	*Venue*	*Year*
9	G Camberabero	Italy	Toulon	1967
9	D Camberabero	Zimbabwe	Auckland	1987
8	G Laporte	Romania	Wellington	1987

MOST PENALTIES IN A MATCH

by the team

Penalties	*Opponents*	*Venue*	*Year*
8	Ireland	Durban	1995
7	Wales	Paris	2001
7	Italy	Paris	2002
6	Argentina	Buenos Aires	1977
6	Scotland	Paris	1997
6	Italy	Auch	1997
6	Ireland	Paris	2000
6	South Africa	Johannesburg	2001
6	Argentina	Buenos Aires	2003

by a player

Penalties	*Player*	*Opponents*	*Venue*	*Year*
8	T Lacroix	Ireland	Durban	1995
7	G Merceron	Italy	Paris	2002
6	J-M Aguirre	Argentina	Buenos Aires	1977
6	C Lamaison	Scotland	Paris	1997
6	C Lamaison	Italy	Auch	1997
6	G Merceron	Ireland	Paris	2000
6	G Merceron	South Africa	Johannesburg	2001

MOST DROPPED GOALS IN A MATCH

by the team

Drops	Opponents	Venue	Year
3	Ireland	Paris	1960
3	England	Twickenham	1985
3	New Zealand	Christchurch	1986
3	Australia	Sydney	1990
3	Scotland	Paris	1991
3	New Zealand	Christchurch	1994

by a player

Drops	Player	Opponents	Venue	Year
3	P Albaladejo	Ireland	Paris	1960
3	J-P Lescarboura	England	Twickenham	1985
3	J-P Lescarboura	New Zealand	Christchurch	1986
3	D Camberabero	Australia	Sydney	1990

Career Records

MOST CAPPED PLAYERS

Caps	Player	Career Span
111	P Sella	1982 to 1995
93	S Blanco	1980 to 1991
80	F Pelous	1995 to 2003
78	A Benazzi	1990 to 2001
71	J-L Sadourny	1991 to 2001
69	R Bertranne	1971 to 1981
69	P Saint-André	1990 to 1997
69	C Califano	1994 to 2003
66	O Brouzet	1994 to 2003
66	R Ibañez	1996 to 2003
66	O Magne	1997 to 2003
63	M Crauste	1957 to 1966
63	B Dauga	1964 to 1972

MOST CONSECUTIVE TESTS

Tests	Player	Span
46	R Bertranne	1973 to 1979
45	P Sella	1982 to 1987
44	M Crauste	1960 to 1966
35	B Dauga	1964 to 1968

MOST TESTS AS CAPTAIN

Tests	Captain	Span
34	J-P Rives	1978 to 1984
34	P Saint-André	1994 to 1997
27	R Ibanez	1998 to 2003
25	D Dubroca	1986 to 1988
24	G Basquet	1948 to 1952
22	M Crauste	1961 to 1966

MOST TESTS IN INDIVIDUAL POSITIONS

Position	Player	Tests	Span
Full-back	S Blanco	81	1980 to 1991
Wing	P Saint-André	67	1990 to 1997
Centre	P Sella	104	1982 to 1995
Fly-half	J-P Romeu	33	1972 to 1977
Scrum-half	F Galthié	59	1991 to 2003
Prop	C Califano	69	1994 to 2003
Hooker	R Ibañez	64	1997 to 2003
Lock	F Pelous	68	1995 to 2003
Flanker	O Magne	66	1997 to 2003
No 8	G Basquet	33	1945 to 1952

Ibañez and Pelous have also been capped in the back-row

MOST POINTS IN TESTS

Points	Player	Tests	Career
380	C Lamaison	37	1996 to 2001
367	T Lacroix	43	1989 to 1997
354	D Camberabero	36	1982 to 1993
265	J-P Romeu	34	1972 to 1977
252	G Merceron	26	1999 to 2003
235	T Castaignède	43	1995 to 2003
233	S Blanco	93	1980 to 1991
200	J-P Lescarboura	28	1982 to 1990

MOST TRIES IN TESTS

Tries	Player	Tests	Career
38	S Blanco	93	1980 to 1991
33	P Saint-André	69	1990 to 1997
30	P Sella	111	1982 to 1995
26	E Ntamack	46	1994 to 2000
26	P Bernat Salles	41	1992 to 2001
23	C Darrouy	40	1957 to 1967

MOST CONVERSIONS IN TESTS

Cons	Player	Tests	Career
59	C Lamaison	37	1996 to 2001
48	D Camberabero	36	1982 to 1993
45	M Vannier	43	1953 to 1961
41	T Castaignède	43	1995 to 2003
36	R Dourthe	31	1995 to 2001
33	G Merceron	26	1999 to 2003
32	T Lacroix	43	1989 to 1997
29	P Villepreux	34	1967 to 1972

MOST PENALTY GOALS IN TESTS

Penalties	Player	Tests	Career
89	T Lacroix	43	1989 to 1997
78	C Lamaison	37	1996 to 2001
59	D Camberabero	36	1982 to 1993
56	J-P Romeu	34	1972 to 1977
54	G Merceron	26	1999 to 2003
33	P Villepreux	34	1967 to 1972
33	P Bérot	19	1986 to 1989

MOST DROPPED GOALS IN TESTS

Drops	Player	Tests	Career
15	J-P Lescarboura	28	1982 to 1990
12	P Albaladejo	30	1954 to 1964
11	G Camberabero	14	1961 to 1968
11	D Camberabero	36	1982 to 1993
9	J-P Romeu	34	1972 to 1977

International Championship Records

Record	Detail		Set
Most points in season	156	in five matches	2002
Most tries in season	18	in four matches	1998
Highest Score	53	53-27 v Italy	2003
Biggest win	51	51 – 0 v Wales	1998
Highest score conceded	49	14-49 v Wales	1910
Biggest defeat	37	0-37 v England	1911
Most appearances	50	P Sella	1983 – 1995
Most points in matches	144	C Lamaison	1997 – 2001
Most points in season	80	G Merceron	2002
Most points in match	24	S Viars	v Ireland, 1992
	24	C Lamaison	v Scotland, 1997
Most tries in matches	14	S Blanco	1981 – 1991
	14	P Sella	1983 – 1995
Most tries in season	5	P Estève	1983
	5	E Bonneval	1987
	5	E Ntamack	1999
	5	P Bernat Salles	2001
Most tries in match	3	M Crauste	v England, 1962
	3	C Darrouy	v Ireland, 1963
	3	E Bonneval	v Scotland, 1987
	3	D Venditti	v Ireland, 1997
	3	E Ntamack	v Wales, 1999
Most cons in matches	23	C Lamaison	1997 – 2001
Most cons in season	9	C Lamaison	1998
	9	G Merceron	2002
	9	D Yachvili	2003
Most cons in match	6	D Yachvili	v Italy, 2003
Most pens in matches	34	G Merceron	2000 – 2003
Most pens in season	18	G Merceron	2002
Most pens in match	7	G Merceron	v Italy, 2002
Most drops in matches	9	J-P Lescarboura	1982 – 1988
Most drops in season	5	G Camberabero	1967
Most drops in match	3	P Albaladejo	v Ireland, 1960
	3	J-P Lescarboura	v England, 1985

Miscellaneous Records

Record	Holder	Detail
Longest Test Career	F Haget	14 seasons, 1974 to 1987
Youngest Test Cap	C Dourthe	18 yrs 7 days in 1966
Oldest Test Cap	A Roques	37 yrs 329 days in 1963

Career Records of France International Players
(up to 30 September 2003)

PLAYER	*Debut*	*Caps*	*T*	*C*	*P*	*D*	*Pts*
Backs:							
P Bondouy	1997 v S	5	2	0	0	0	10
S Bonetti	2001 v It	3	2	0	0	0	10
D Bory	2000 v I	16	2	0	0	0	10
N Brusque	1997 v R	11	5	0	0	0	25
T Castaignède	1995 v R	43	15	41	21	5	235
F Cermeno	2000 v R	1	0	0	0	0	0
J-C Cistacq	2000 v R	1	0	0	0	0	0
V Clerc	2002 SA	10	4	0	0	0	20
Y Delaigue	1994 v S	12	2	0	3	2	25
C Desbrosse	1999 v Nm	2	0	0	0	0	0
C Dominici	1998 v E	30	12	0	0	0	60
P Elhorga	2001 v NZ	6	1	0	0	0	5
J-B Elissalde	2000 v S	4	1	0	0	0	5
F Galthié	1991 v R	59	9	0	0	0	44
X Garbajosa	1998 v I	32	7	0	0	0	35
F Gelez	2001 v SA	8	0	6	23	0	81
C Heymans	2000 v It	5	1	0	0	0	5
Y Jauzion	2001 v SA	10	3	0	0	1	18
N Jeanjean	2001 v SA	9	2	0	0	0	10
C Laussucq	1999 v S	4	1	0	0	0	5
B Liebenberg	2003 v R	3	1	0	0	0	5
T Lombard	1998 v Arg	12	1	0	0	0	5
J Marlu	1998 v Fj	3	0	0	0	0	0
T Marsh	2001 v SA	11	6	0	0	0	30
G Merceron	1999 v R	26	3	33	54	3	252
F Michalak	2001 v SA	12	2	10	8	2	60
P Mignoni	1997 v R	13	3	0	0	0	15
U Mola	1997 v S	12	6	0	0	0	30
C Poitrenaud	2001 v SA	11	3	0	0	0	15
A Rougerie	2001 v SA	22	11	0	0	0	55
D Skrela	2001 v NZ	1	0	0	4	0	12
J-M Souverbie	2000 v R	1	1	0	0	0	5
D Traille	2001 v SA	24	7	1	8	0	61
D Yachvili	2002 v C	7	0	9	6	0	36
Forwards:							
J-L Aqua	1999 v R	3	0	0	0	0	0
A Audebert	2000 v R	2	0	0	0	0	0
D Auradou	1999 v E	34	0	0	0	0	0
O Azam	1995 v R	10	0	0	0	0	0
F Belot	2000 v I	1	0	0	0	0	0
S Betsen	1997 v It	31	7	0	0	0	35
J Bouilhou	2001 v NZ	2	0	0	0	0	0
O Brouzet	1994 v S	66	2	0	0	0	10
Y Bru	2001 v A	8	0	0	0	0	0
S Bruno	2002 v W	1	0	0	0	0	0
C Califano	1994 v NZ	69	6	0	0	0	30
S Chabal	2000 v S	17	0	0	0	0	0
J-J Crenca	1996 v SA	28	2	0	0	0	10

P de Villiers	1999 v W	32	0	0	0	0	0
A Galasso	2000 v R	2	0	0	0	0	0
S Hall	2002 v It	2	0	0	0	0	0
I Harinordoquy	2002 v W	20	2	0	0	0	10
R Ibañez	1996 v W	66	5	0	0	0	25
C Labit	1999 v S	12	0	0	0	0	0
O Magne	1997 v W	66	11	0	0	0	55
L Mallier	1999 v R	5	1	0	0	0	5
S Marconnet	1998 v Arg	33	2	0	0	0	10
R Martin	2002 v E	3	0	0	0	0	0
A Martinez	2002 v A	1	0	0	0	0	0
N Mas	2003 v NZ	1	0	0	0	0	0
O Milloud	2000 v R	10	0	0	0	0	0
C Moni	1996 v R	8	1	0	0	0	5
L Nallet	2000 v R	9	1	0	0	0	5
F Ntamack	2001 v SA	1	0	0	0	0	0
F Pelous	1995 v R	80	6	0	0	0	30
C Porcu	2002 v Arg	3	0	0	0	0	0
J-B Poux	2001 v Fj	7	2	0	0	0	10
T Privat	2001 v SA	7	0	0	0	0	0
J-B Rué	2002 v SA	8	0	0	0	0	0
C Soulette	1997 v R	13	2	0	0	0	10
P Tabacco	2001 v SA	12	0	0	0	0	0
J Thion	2003 v Arg	5	0	0	0	0	0
E Vermeulen	2001 v SA	3	0	0	0	0	0

FRENCH INTERNATIONAL PLAYERS

(up to 30 September 2003)

Note: Years given for International Championship matches are for second half of season, eg 1972 refers to season 1971-72. Years for all other matches refer to the actual year of the match. When a series has taken place, or more than one match has been played against a country in the same year, figures have been used to denote the particular matches in which players have featured. Thus 1967 *SA* 2,4 indicates that a player appeared in the second and fourth Tests of the 1967 series against South Africa. This list includes only those players who have appeared in FFR International Matches *'donnant droit au titre d'international'*.

Abadie, A (Pau) 1964 *I*
Abadie, A (Graulhet) 1965 *R*, 1967 *SA* 1,3,4, *NZ*, 1968 *S*, *I*
Abadie, L (Tarbes) 1963 *R*
Accoceberry, G (Bègles) 1994 *NZ* 1,2, *C* 2, 1995 *W*, *E*, *S*, *I*, *R* 1, [*Iv*, *S*], *It*, 1996 *I*, *W* 1, *R*, *Arg* 1, *W* 2(R), *SA* 2, 1997 *S*, *It* 1
Aguerre, R (Biarritz O) 1979 *S*
Aguilar, D (Pau) 1937 *G*
Aguirre, J-M (Bagnères) 1971 *A* 2, 1972 *S*, 1973 *W*, *I*, *J*, *R*, 1974 *I*, *W*, *Arg* 2, *R*, *SA* 1, 1976 *W* (R), *E*, *US*, *A* 2, *R*, 1977 *W*, *E*, *S*, *I*, *Arg* 1,2, *NZ* 1,2, *R*, 1978 *E*, *S*, *I*, *W*, *R*, 1979 *I*, *W*, *E*, *S*, *NZ* 1,2, *R*, 1980 *W*, *I*
Ainciart, E (Bayonne) 1933 *G*, 1934 *G*, 1935 *G*, 1937 *G*, *It*, 1938 *G* 1
Albaladejo, P (Dax) 1954 *E*, *It*, 1960 *W*, *I*, *It*, *R*, 1961 *S*, *SA*, *E*, *W*, *I*, *NZ* 1,2, *A*, 1962 *S*, *E*, *W*, *I*, 1963 *S*, *I*, *E*, *W*, *It*, 1964 *S*, *NZ*, *W*, *It*, *I*, *SA*, *Fj*
Albouy, A (Castres) 2002 *It* (R)
Alvarez, A-J (Tyrosse) 1945 *B*2, 1946 *B*, *I*, *K*, *W*, 1947 *S*, *I*, *W*, *E*, 1948 *I*, *A*, *S*, *W*, *E*, 1949 *I*, *E*, *W*, 1951 *S*, *E*, *W*
Amand, H (SF) 1906 *NZ*
Ambert, A (Toulouse) 1930 *S*, *I*, *E*, *G*, *W*
Amestoy, J-B (Mont-de-Marsan) 1964 *NZ*, *E*
André, G (RCF) 1913 *SA*, *E*, *W*, *I*, 1914 *I*, *W*, *E*
Andrieu, M (Nîmes) 1986 *Arg* 2, *NZ* 1, *R* 2, *NZ* 2, 1987 [*R*, *Z*], *R*, 1988 *E*, *S*, *I*, *W*, *Arg* 1,2,3,4, *R*, 1989 *I*, *W*, *E*, *S*, *NZ* 2, *B*, *A* 2, 1990 *W*, *E*, *I* (R)
Anduran, J (SCUF) 1910 *W*
Aqua, J-L (Toulon) 1999 *R*, *Tg*, *NZ* 1(R)
Araou, R (Narbonne) 1924 *R*
Arcalis, R (Brive) 1950 *S*, *I*, 1951 *I*, *E*, *W*
Arino, M (Agen) 1962 *R*
Aristouy, P (Pau) 1948 *S*, 1949 *Arg* 2, 1950 *S*, *I*, *E*, *W*
Arlettaz, P (Perpignan) 1995 *R* 2
Armary, L (Lourdes) 1987 [*R*], *R*, 1988 *S*, *I*, *W*, *Arg* 3,4, *R*, 1989 *W*, *S*, *A* 1,2, 1990 *W*, *E*, *S*, *I*, *A* 1,2,3, *NZ* 1, 1991 *W* 2, 1992 *S*, *I*, *R*, *Arg* 1,2, *SA* 1,2, *Arg*, 1993 *E*, *S*, *I*, *W*, *SA* 1,2, *R* 2, *A* 1,2, 1994 *I*, *W*, *NZ* 1(t),2(t), 1995 *I*, *R* 1 [*Tg*, *I*, *SA*]
Arnal, J-M (RCF) 1914 *I*, *W*
Arnaudet, M (Lourdes) 1964 *I*, 1967 *It*, *W*
Arotca, R (Bayonne) 1938 *R*
Arrieta, J (SF) 1953 *E*, *W*
Arthapignet, P (see Harislur-Arthapignet)
Artiguste, E (Castres) 1999 *WS*
Astre, R (Béziers) 1971 *R*, 1972 *I* 1, 1973 *E* (R), 1975 *E*, *S*, *I*, *SA* 1,2, *Arg* 2, 1976 *A* 2, *R*
Aucagne, D (Pau) 1997 *W* (R), *S*, *It* 1, *R* 1(R), *A* 1, *R* 2(R), *SA* 2(R), 1998 *S* (R), *W* (R), *Arg* 2(R), *Fj* (R), *Arg* 3, *A*, 1999 *W* 1(R), *S* (R)
Audebert, A (Montferrand) 2000 *R*, 2002 *W* (R)
Aué, J-M (Castres) 1998 *W* (R)
Augé, J (Dax) 1929 *S*, *W*
Augras-Fabre, L (Agen) 1931 *I*, *S*, *W*
Auradou, D (SF) 1999 *E* (R), *S* (R), *WS* (R), *Tg*, *NZ* 1, *W* 2(R), [*Arg* (R)], 2000 *A* (R), *NZ* 1,2, 2001 *S*, *I*, *It*, *W*, *E* (R), *SA* 1,2, *NZ* (R), *SA* 3, *A*, *Fj*, 2002 *It*, *E*, *I* (R), *C* (R), 2003 *S* (R), *It* (R), *W* (R), *Arg*, 1,2, *NZ* (R), *R* (R), *E* 2(R),3
Averous, J-L (La Voulte) 1975 *S*, *I*, *SA* 1,2, 1976 *I*, *W*, *E*, *US*, *A* 1,2, *R*, 1977 *W*, *E*, *S*, *I*, *Arg* 1, *R*, 1978 *E*, *S*, *I*, 1979 *NZ* 1,2, 1980 *E*, *S*, 1981 *A* 2
Azam, O (Montferrand, Gloucester) 1995 *R* 2, *Arg* (R), 2000 *A* (R), *NZ* 2(R), 2001 *SA* 2(R), *NZ*, 2002 *E* (R), *I* (R), *Arg* (R), *A* 1
Azarete, J-L (Dax, St Jean-de-Luz) 1969 *W*, *R*, 1970 *S*, *I*, *W*, *R*, 1971 *S*, *I*, *E*, *SA* 1,2, *A* 1, 1972 *E*, *W*, *I* 2, *A* 1, *R*, 1973 *NZ*, *W*, *I*, *R*, 1974 *I*, *R*, *SA* 1,2, 1975 *W*

Bacqué, N (Pau) 1997 *R* 2
Bader, E (Primevères) 1926 *M*, 1927 *I*, *S*
Badin, C (Chalon) 1973 *W*, *I*, 1975 *Arg* 1
Baillette, M (Perpignan) 1925 *I*, *NZ*, *S*, 1926 *W*, *M*, 1927 *I*, *W*, *G* 2, 1929 *G*, 1930 *S*, *I*, *E*, *G*, 1931 *I*, *S*, *E*, 1932 *G*
Baladie, G (Agen) 1945 *B* 1,2, *W*, 1946 *B*, *I*, *K*
Ballarin, J (Tarbes) 1924 *E*, 1925 *NZ*, *S*
Baquey, J (Toulouse) 1921 *I*
Barbazanges, A (Roanne) 1932 *G*, 1933 *G*
Barrau, M (Beaumont, Toulouse) 1971 *S*, *E*, *W*, 1972 *E*, *W*, *A* 1,2, 1973 *S*, *NZ*, *E*, *I*, *J*, *R*, 1974 *I*, *S*
Barrère, P (Toulon) 1929 *G*, 1931 *W*
Barrière, R (Béziers) 1960 *R*
Barthe, E (SBUC) 1925 *W*, *E*
Barthe, J (Lourdes) 1954 *Arg* 1,2, 1955 *S*, 1956 *I*, *W*, *It*, *E*, *Cz*, 1957 *S*, *I*, *E*, *W*, *R* 1,2, 1958 *S*, *E*, *A*, *W*, *It*, *I*, *SA* 1,2, 1959 *S*, *E*, *It*, *W*
Basauri, R (Albi) 1954 *Arg* 1
Bascou, P (Bayonne) 1914 *E*
Basquet, G (Agen) 1945 *W*, 1946 *B*, *I*, *K*, *W*, 1947 *S*, *I*, *W*, *E*, 1948 *I*, *A*, *S*, *W*, *E*, 1949 *S*, *I*, *E*, *W*, *Arg* 1, 1950 *S*, *I*, *E*, *W*, 1951 *S*, *I*, *E*, *W*, 1952 *S*, *I*, *SA*, *W*, *E*, *It*
Bastiat, J-P (Dax) 1969 *R*, 1970 *S*, *I*, *W*, 1971 *S*, *I*, *SA* 2, 1972 *S*, *A* 1, 1973 *E*, 1974 *Arg* 1,2, *SA* 2, 1975 *W*, *Arg* 1,2, *R*, 1976 *S*, *I*, *W*, *E*, *A* 1,2, *R*, 1977 *W*, *E*, *S*, *I*, 1978 *E*, *S*, *I*, *W*
Baudry, N (Montferrand) 1949 *S*, *I*, *W*, *Arg* 1,2
Baulon, R (Vienne, Bayonne) 1954 *S*, *NZ*, *W*, *E*, *It*, 1955 *I*, *E*, *W*, *It*, 1956 *S*, *I*, *W*, *It*, *E*, *Cz*, 1957 *S*, *I*, *It*
Baux, J-P (Lannemezan) 1968 *NZ* 1,2, *SA* 1,2
Bavozet, J (Lyon) 1911 *S*, *E*, *W*
Bayard, J (Toulouse) 1923 *S*, *W*, *E*, 1924 *W*, *R*, *US*
Bayardon, J (Chalon) 1964 *S*, *NZ*, *E*
Beaurin-Gressier, C (SF) 1907 *E*, 1908 *E*
Bégu, J (Dax) 1982 *Arg* 2(R), 1984 *E*, *S*
Béguerie, C (Agen) 1979 *NZ* 1
Beguet, L (RCF) 1922 *I*, 1923 *S*, *W*, *E*, *I*, 1924 *S*, *I*, *E*, *R*, *US*
Behoteguy, A (Bayonne, Cognac) 1923 *E*, 1924 *S*, *I*, *E*, *W*, *R*, *US*, 1926 *E*, 1927 *E*, *G* 1,2, 1928 *A*, *I*, *E*, *G*, *W*, 1929 *S*, *W*, *E*
Behoteguy, H (RCF, Cognac) 1923 *W*, 1928 *A*, *I*, *E*, *G*, *W*
Belascain, C (Bayonne) 1977 *R*, 1978 *E*, *S*, *I*, *W*, *R*, 1979 *I*, *W*, *E*, *S*, 1982 *W*, *E*, *S*, *I*, 1983 *E*, *S*, *I*, *W*
Belletante, G (Nantes) 1951 *I*, *E*, *W*
Belot, F (Toulouse) 2000 *I* (R)
Benazzi, A (Agen) 1990 *A* 1,2,3, *NZ* 1,2, 1991 *E*, *US* 1(R),2, [*R*, *Fj*, *C*], 1992 *SA* 1(R),2, *Arg*, 1993 *E*, *S*, *I*, *W*, *A* 1,2, 1994 *I*, *W*, *E*, *S*, *C* 1, *NZ* 1,2, *C* 2, 1995 *W*, *E*, *S*, *I*, [*Tg*, *Iv*, *S*, *I*, *SA*, *E*], *NZ* 1,2, 1996 *E*, *S*, *I*, *W* 1, *Arg* 1,2, *W* 2, *SA* 1,2, 1997 *I*, *W*, *E*, *S*, *R* 1, *A* 1,2, *It* 2, *R* 2(R), *Arg*, *SA* 1,2, 1999 *R*, *WS*, *W* 2, [*C*, *Nm* (R), *Fj*, *Arg*, *NZ* 2, *A*], 2000 *W*, *E*, *I*, *It* (R), *R*, 2001 *S* (R), *I* (t&R), *E*
Bénésis, R (Narbonne) 1969 *W*, *R*, 1970 *S*, *I*, *W*, *E*, *R*, 1971 *S*, *I*, *E*, *W*, *A* 2, *R*, 1972 *S*, *I* 1, *E*, *W*, *I* 2, *A* 1, *R*, 1973 *NZ*, *E*, *W*, *I*, *J*, *R*, 1974 *I*, *W*, *E*, *S*
Benetière, J (Roanne) 1954 *It*, *Arg* 1
Benetton, P (Agen) 1989 *B*, 1990 *NZ* 2, 1991 *US* 2, 1992 *Arg* 1,2(R), *SA* 1(R),2, *Arg*, 1993 *E*, *S*, *I*, *W*, *SA* 1,2, *R* 2, *A* 1,2, 1994 *I*, *W*, *E*, *S*, *C* 1, *NZ* 1,2, *C* 2, 1995 *W*, *E*, *S*, *I*, [*Tg*, *Iv* (R), *S*], *It*, *R* 2(R), *Arg*, *NZ* 1,2, 1996 *Arg* 1,2, *W* 2, *SA* 1,2, 1997 *I*, *It* 1,2(R), *R* 2, *Arg*, *SA* 1,2 1998 *E*, *S* (R), *I* (R), *W* (R), *Arg* 1(R),2(R), *Fj* (R), 1999 *I*, *W* 1, *S* (R)
Benezech, L (RCF) 1994 *E*, *S*, *C* 1, *NZ* 1,2, *C* 2, 1995 *W*, *E*, [*Iv*, *S*, *E*], *R* 2, *Arg*, *NZ* 1,2
Berbizier, P (Lourdes, Agen) 1981 *S*, *I*, *W*, *E*, *NZ* 1,2, 1982 *I*, *R*, 1983 *S*, *I*, 1984 *S* (R), *NZ* 1,2, 1985 *Arg* 1,2, 1986 *S*, *I*, *W*, *E*, *R* 1, *Arg* 1, *A*, *NZ* 1, *R* 2, *NZ* 2,3, 1987 *W*, *E*, *S*, *I*, [*S*, *R*, *Fj*, *A*, *NZ*], *R*, 1988 *E*, *S*, *I*, *W*, *Arg* 1,2, 1989 *I*, *W*, *E*, *S*, *NZ* 1,2, *B*, *A* 1, 1990 *W*, *E*, 1991 *S*, *I*, *W* 1, *E*
Berejnoi, J-C (Tulle) 1963 *R*, 1964 *S*, *W*, *It*, *I*, *SA*, *Fj*, *R*, 1965 *S*, *I*, *E*, *W*, *It*, *R*, 1966 *S*, *I*, *E*, *W*, *It*, *R*, 1967 *S*, *A*, *E*, *It*, *W*, *I*, *R*
Berges, B (Toulouse) 1926 *I*
Berges-Cau, R (Lourdes) 1976 *E* (R)
Bergese, F (Bayonne) 1936 *G* 2, 1937 *G*, *It*, 1938 *G* 1, *R*, *G* 2

Bergougnan, Y (Toulouse) 1945 *B* 1, *W*, 1946 *B, I, K, W*, 1947 *S, I, W, E*, 1948 *S, W, E*, 1949 *S, E, Arg* 1,2
Bernard, R (Bergerac) 1951 *S, I, E, W*
Bernat-Salles, P (Pau, Bègles-Bordeaux, Biarritz) 1992 *Arg*, 1993 *R* 1, *SA* 1,2, *R* 2, *A* 1,2, 1994 *I*, 1995 *E, S*, 1996 *E* (R), 1997 *R* 1, *A* 1,2, 1998 *E, S, I, W, Arg* 1,2, *Fj, Arg* 3(R), *A* 1999 *I, W* 1, *R, Tg*, [*Nm, Fj, Arg, NZ* 2, *A*], 2000 *I, It, NZ* 1(R),2, 2001 *S, I, It, W, E*
Bernon, J (Lourdes) 1922 *I*, 1923 *S*
Bérot, J-L (Toulouse) 1968 *NZ* 3, *A*, 1969 *S, I*, 1970 *E, R*, 1971 *S, I, E, W, SA* 1,2, *A* 1,2, *R*, 1972 *S, I* 1, *E, W, A* 1, 1974 *I*
Bérot, P (Agen) 1986 *R* 2, *NZ* 2,3, 1987 *W, E, S, I, R*, 1988 *E, S, I, Arg* 1,2,3,4, *R*, 1989 *S, NZ* 1,2
Bertrand, P (Bourg) 1951 *I, E, W*, 1953 *S, I, E, W, It*
Bertranne, R (Bagnères) 1971 *E, W, SA* 2, *A* 1,2, 1972 *S, I* 1, 1973 *NZ, E, J, R*, 1974 *I, W, E, S, Arg* 1,2, *R, SA* 1,2, 1975 *W, E, S, I, SA* 1,2, *Arg* 1,2, *R*, 1976 *S, I, W, E, US, A* 1,2, *R*, 1977 *W, E, S, I, Arg* 1,2, *NZ* 1,2, *R*, 1978 *E, S, I, W, R*, 1979 *I, W, E, S, R*, 1980 *W, E, S, I, SA, R*, 1981 *S, I, W, E, R, NZ* 1,2
Berty, D (Toulouse) 1990 *NZ* 2, 1992 *R* (R), 1993 *R* 2, 1995 *NZ* 1(R), 1996 *W* 2(R), *SA* 1
Besset, E (Grenoble) 1924 *S*
Besset, L (SCUF) 1914 *W, E*
Besson, M (CASG) 1924 *I*, 1925 *I, E*, 1926 *S, W*, 1927 *I*
Besson, P (Brive) 1963 *S, I, E*, 1965 *R*, 1968 *SA* 1
Betsen, S (Biarritz) 1997 *It* 1(R), 2000 *W* (R), *E* (R), *A* (R), *NZ* 1(R),2(R), 2001 *S* (R), *I* (R), *It* (R), *W* (R), *SA* 3(R), *A, Fj*, 2002 *It, W, E, S, I, Arg, A* 1,2, *SA, NZ, C*, 2003 *E* 1, *S, I, It, W, R, E* 2
Bianchi, J (Toulon) 1986 *Arg* 1
Bichindaritz, J (Biarritz O) 1954 *It, Arg* 1,2
Bidart, L (La Rochelle) 1953 *W*
Biemouret, P (Agen) 1969 *E, W*, 1970 *I, W, E*, 1971 *W, SA* 1,2, *A* 1, 1972 *E, W, I* 2, *A* 2, *R*, 1973 *S, NZ, E, W, I*
Biénès, R (Cognac) 1950 *S, I, E, W*, 1951 *S, I, E, W*, 1952 *S, I, SA, W, E, It*, 1953 *S, I, E*, 1954 *S, I, NZ, W, E, Arg* 1,2, 1956 *S, I, W, It, E*
Bigot, C (Quillan) 1930 *S, E*, 1931 *I, S*
Bilbao, L (St Jean-de-Luz) 1978 *I*, 1979 *I*
Billac, E (Bayonne) 1920 *S, E, W, I, US*, 1921 *S, W*, 1922 *W*, 1923 *E*
Billière, M (Toulouse) 1968 *NZ* 3
Bioussa, A (Toulouse) 1924 *W, US*, 1925 *I, NZ, S, E*, 1926 *S, I, E*, 1928 *E, G, W*, 1929 *I, S, W, E*, 1930 *S, I, E, G, W*
Bioussa, C (Toulouse) 1913 *W, I*, 1914 *I*
Biraben, M (Dax) 1920 *W, I, US*, 1921 *S, W, E, I*, 1922 *S, E, I*
Blain, A (Carcassonne) 1934 *G*
Blanco, S (Biarritz O) 1980 *SA, R*, 1981 *S, W, E, A* 1,2, *R, NZ* 1,2, 1982 *W, E, S, I, R, Arg* 1,2, 1983 *E, S, I, W*, 1984 *I, W, E, S, NZ* 1,2, *R*, 1985 *E, S, I, W, Arg* 1,2, 1986 *S, I, W, E, R* 1, *Arg* 2, *A, NZ* 1, *R* 2, *NZ* 2,3, 1987 *W, E, S, I*, [*S, R, Fj, A, NZ*], *R*, 1988 *E, S, I, W, Arg* 1,2,3,4, *R*, 1989 *I, W, E, S, NZ* 1,2, *B, A* 1, 1990 *E, S, I, R, A* 1,2,3, *NZ* 1,2, 1991 *S, I, W* 1, *E, R, US* 1,2, *W* 2, [*R, Fj, C, E*]
Blond, J (SF) 1935 *G*, 1936 *G* 2, 1937 *G*, 1938 *G* 1, *R, G* 2
Blond, X (RCF) 1990 *A* 3, 1991 *S, I, W* 1, *E*, 1994 *NZ* 2(R)
Boffelli, V (Aurillac) 1971 *A* 2, *R*, 1972 *S, I* 1, 1973 *J, R*, 1974 *I, W, E, S, Arg* 1,2, *R, SA* 1,2, 1975 *W, S, I*
Bonal, J-M (Toulouse) 1968 *E, W, Cz, NZ* 2,3, *SA* 1,2, *R*, 1969 *S, I, E, R*, 1970 *W, E*
Bonamy, R (SB) 1928 *A, I*
Bondouy, P (Narbonne, Toulouse) 1997 *S* (R), *It* 1, *A* 2(R), *R* 2, 2000 *R* (R)
Bonetti, S (Biarritz) 2001 *It, W, NZ* (R)
Boniface, A (Mont-de-Marsan) 1954 *I, NZ, W, E, It, Arg* 1,2, 1955 *S, I*, 1956 *S, I, W, It, Cz*, 1957 *S, I, W, R* 2, 1958 *S, E*, 1959 *E*, 1961 *NZ* 1,3, *A, R*, 1962 *E, W, I, It, R*, 1963 *S, I, E, W, It, R*, 1964 *S, NZ, E, W, It*, 1965 *W, It, R*, 1966 *S, I, E, W*
Boniface, G (Mont-de-Marsan) 1960 *W, I, It, R, Arg* 1,2,3, 1961 *S, SA, E, W, It, I, NZ* 1,2,3, *R*, 1962 *R*, 1963 *S, I, E, W, It, R*, 1964 *S*, 1965 *S, I, E, W, It, R*, 1966 *S, I, E, W*
Bonnes, E (Narbonne) 1924 *W, R, US*
Bonneval, E (Toulouse) 1984 *NZ* 2(R), 1985 *W, Arg* 1, 1986 *W, E, R* 1, *Arg* 1,2, *A, R* 2, *NZ* 2,3, 1987 *W, E, S, I*, [*Z*], 1988 *E*
Bonnus, F (Toulon) 1950 *S, I, E, W*
Bonnus, M (Toulon) 1937 *It*, 1938 *G* 1, *R, G* 2, 1940 *B*
Bontemps, D (La Rochelle) 1968 *SA* 2
Borchard, G (RCF) 1908 *E*, 1909 *E, W, I*, 1911 *I*
Borde, F (RCF) 1920 *I, US*, 1921 *S, W, E*, 1922 *S, W*, 1923 *S, I*, 1924 *E*, 1925 *I*, 1926 *E*
Bordenave, L (Toulon) 1948 *A, S, W, E*, 1949 *S*
Bory, D (Montferrand) 2000 *I, It, A, NZ* 1, 2001 *S, I, SA* 1,2,3, *A, Fj*, 2002 *It, E, S, I, C*
Boubée, J (Tarbes) 1921 *S, E, I*, 1922 *E, W*, 1923 *E, I*, 1925 *NZ, S*
Boudreaux, R (SCUF) 1910 *W, S*
Bouet, D (Dax) 1989 *NZ* 1,2, *B, A* 2, 1990 *A* 3
Bouguyon, G (Grenoble) 1961 *SA, E, W, It, I, NZ* 1,2,3, *A*
Bouic, G (Agen) 1996 *SA* 1
Bouilhou, J (Toulouse) 2001 *NZ*, 2003 *Arg* 1
Boujet, C (Grenoble) 1968 *NZ* 2, *A* (R), *SA* 1
Bouquet, J (Bourgoin, Vienne) 1954 *S*, 1955 *E*, 1956 *S, I, W, It, E, Cz*, 1957 *S, E, W, R* 2, 1958 *S, E*, 1959 *S, It, W, I*, 1960 *S, E, W, I, R*, 1961 *S, SA, E, W, It, I, R*, 1962 *S, E, W, I*
Bourdeu, J R (Lourdes) 1952 *S, I, SA, W, E, It*, 1953 *S, I, E*
Bourgarel, R (Toulouse) 1969 *R*, 1970 *S, I, E, R*, 1971 *W, SA* 1,2, 1973 *S*
Bourguignon, G (Narbonne) 1988 *Arg* 3, 1989 *I, E, B, A* 1, 1990 *R*
Bousquet, A (Béziers) 1921 *E, I*, 1924 *R*
Bousquet, R (Albi) 1926 *M*, 1927 *I, S, W, E, G* 1, 1929 *W, E*, 1930 *W*
Boyau, M (SBUC) 1912 *I, S, W, E*, 1913 *W, I*
Boyer, P (Toulon) 1935 *G*
Branca, G (SF) 1928 *S*, 1929 *I, S*
Branlat, A (RCF) 1906 *NZ, E*, 1908 *W*
Brejassou, R (Tarbes) 1952 *S, I, SA, W, E*, 1953 *W, E*, 1954 *S, I, NZ*, 1955 *S, I, E, W, It*
Brethes, R (St Sever) 1960 *Arg* 2
Bringeon, A (Biarritz O) 1925 *W*
Brouzet, O (Grenoble, Bègles, Northampton, Montferrand) 1994 *S, NZ* 2(R), 1995 *E, S, I, R* 1, [*Tg, Iv, E* (t)], *It, Arg* (R), 1996 *W* 1(R), 1997 *R* 1, *A* 1,2, *It* 2, *Arg, SA* 1,2, 1998 *E, S, I, W, Arg* 1,2, *Fj, Arg* 3, *A*, 1999 *I, W* 1, *E, S, R*, [*C* (R), *Nm, Fj* (R), *Arg, NZ* 2(R), *A* (R)], 2000 *W, E, S, I, It, A, NZ* 1(R),2(R), 2001 *SA* 1,2, *NZ*, 2002 *W, E, S, I, Arg, A* 1(R),2, *SA, NZ, C*, 2003 *E* 1, *S, I, It, W, E* 3
Bru, Y (Toulouse) 2001 *A* (R), *Fj* (R), 2002 *It*, 2003 *Arg* 2, *NZ, R, E* 2,3(R)
Brun, G (Vienne) 1950 *E, W*, 1951 *S, E, W*, 1952 *S, I, SA, W, E, It*, 1953 *E, W, It*
Bruneau, M (SBUC) 1910 *W, E*, 1913 *SA, E*
Brunet, Y (Perpignan) 1975 *SA* 1, 1977 *Arg* 1
Bruno, S (Béziers) 2002 *W* (R)
Brusque, N (Pau, Biarritz) 1997 *R* 2(R), 2002 *W, E, S, I, Arg, A* 2, *SA, NZ, C*, 2003 *E* 2
Buchet, E (Nice) 1980 *R*, 1982 *E, R* (R), *Arg* 1,2
Buisson, H (see Empereur-Buisson)
Buonomo, Y (Béziers) 1971 *A* 2, *R*, 1972 *I* 1
Burgun, M (RCF) 1909 *I*, 1910 *W, S, I*, 1911 *S, E*, 1912 *I, S*, 1913 *S, E*, 1914 *E*
Bustaffa, D (Carcassonne) 1977 *Arg* 1,2, *NZ* 1,2, 1978 *W, R*, 1980 *W, E, S, SA, R*
Buzy, C-E (Lourdes) 1946 *K, W*, 1947 *S, I, W, E*, 1948 *I, A, S, W, E*, 1949 *S, I, E, W, Arg* 1,2

Cabanier, J-M (Montauban) 1963 *R*, 1964 *S, Fj*, 1965 *S, I, W, It, R*, 1966 *S, I, E, W, It, R*, 1967 *S, A, E, It, W, I, SA* 1,3, *NZ, R*, 1968 *S, I*
Cabannes, L (RCF, Harlequins) 1990 *NZ* 2(R), 1991 *S, I, W* 1, *E, US* 2, *W* 2, [*R, Fj, C, E*], 1992 *W, E, S, I, R, Arg* 2, *SA* 1,2, 1993 *E, S, I, W, R* 1, *SA* 1,2, 1994 *E, S, C* 1, *NZ* 1,2, 1995 *W, E, S, R* 1, [*Tg* (R), *Iv, S, I, SA, E*], 1996 *E, S, I, W* 1, 1997 *It* 2, *Arg, SA* 1,2
Cabrol, H (Béziers) 1972 *A* 1(R),2, 1973 *J*, 1974 *SA* 2
Cadenat, J (SCUF) 1910 *S, E*, 1911 *W, I*, 1912 *W, E*, 1913 *I*
Cadieu, J-M (Toulouse) 1991 *R, US* 1, [*R, Fj, C, E*], 1992 *W, I, R, Arg* 1,2, *SA* 1
Cahuc, F (St Girons) 1922 *S*
Califano, C (Toulouse, Saracens) 1994 *NZ* 1,2, *C* 2, 1995 *W, E, S, I*, [*Iv, S, I, SA, E*], *It, Arg, NZ* 1,2, 1996 *E, S, I, W* 1, *R, Arg* 1,2, *SA* 1,2, 1997 *I, W, E, A* 1,2, *It* 2, *R* 2(R), *Arg, SA* 1,2, 1998 *E, S, I, W*, 1999 *I, W* 1, *E* (R), *S, WS, Tg* (R), *NZ* 1, *W* 2, [*C, Nm, Fj*], 2000 *W, E, S, I, It, R, A, NZ* 1,2(R), 2001 *S* (R), *I* (R), *It, W, SA* 1(R),2(R), *NZ*, 2003 *E* 1, *S* (R), *I* (R)
Cals, R (RCF) 1938 *G* 1
Calvo, G (Lourdes) 1961 *NZ* 1,3
Camberabero, D (La Voulte, Béziers) 1982 *R, Arg* 1,2, 1983 *E, W*, 1987 [*R* (R), *Z, Fj* (R), *A, NZ*], 1988 *I*, 1989 *B, A* 1, 1990 *W, S, I, R, A* 1,2,3, *NZ* 1,2, 1991 *S, I, W* 1, *E, R, US* 1,2, *W* 2, [*R, Fj, C*], 1993 *E, S, I*
Camberabero, G (La Voulte) 1961 *NZ* 3, 1962 *R*, 1964 *R*, 1967 *A, E, It, W, I, SA* 1,3,4, 1968 *S, E, W*

Camberabero, L (La Voulte) 1964 *R*, 1965 *S*, *I*, 1966 *E*, *W*, 1967 *A*, *E*, *It*, *W*, *I*, 1968 *S*, *E*, *W*
Cambré, T (Oloron) 1920 *E*, *W*, *I*, *US*
Camel, A (Toulouse) 1928 *S*, *A*, *I*, *E*, *G*, *W*, 1929 *W*, *E*, *G*, 1930 *S*, *I*, *E*, *G*, *W*, 1935 *G*
Camel, M (Toulouse) 1929 *S*, *W*, *E*
Camicas, F (Tarbes) 1927 *G* 2, 1928 *S*, *I*, *E*, *G*, *W*, 1929 *I*, *S*, *W*, *E*
Camo, E (Villeneuve) 1931 *I*, *S*, *W*, *E*, *G*, 1932 *G*
Campaes, A (Lourdes) 1965 *W*, 1967 *NZ*, 1968 *S*, *I*, *E*, *W*, *Cz*, *NZ* 1,2, *A*, 1969 *S*, *W*, 1972 *R*, 1973 *NZ*
Campan, O (Agen) 1993 *SA* 1(R),2(R), *R* 2(R), 1996 *I*, *W* 1, *R*
Cantoni, J (Béziers) 1970 *W*, *R*, 1971 *S*, *I*, *E*, *W*, *SA* 1,2, *R*, 1972 *S*, *I* 1, 1973 *S*, *NZ*, *W*, *I*, 1975 *W* (R)
Capdouze, J (Pau) 1964 *SA*, *Fj*, *R*, 1965 *S*, *I*, *E*
Capendeguy, J-M (Bègles) 1967 *NZ*, *R*
Capitani, P (Toulon) 1954 *Arg* 1,2
Capmau, J-L (Toulouse) 1914 *E*
Carabignac, G (Agen) 1951 *S*, *I*, 1952 *SA*, *W*, *E*, 1953 *S*, *I*
Carbonne, J (Perpignan) 1927 *W*
Carbonneau, P (Toulouse, Brive, Pau) 1995 *R* 2, *Arg*, *NZ* 1,2, 1996 *E*, *S*, *R* (R), *Arg* 2, *W* 2, *SA* 1, 1997 *I* (R), *W*, *E*, *S* (R), *R* 1(R), *A* 1,2, 1998 *E*, *S*, *I*, *W*, *Arg* 1,2, *Fj*, *Arg* 3, *A*, 1999 *I*, *W* 1, *E*, *S*, 2000 *NZ* 2(R), 2001 *I*
Carminati, A (Béziers, Brive) 1986 *R* 2, *NZ* 2, 1987 [*R*, *Z*], 1988 *I*, *W*, *Arg* 1,2, 1989 *I*, *W*, *S*, *NZ* 1(R),2, *A* 2, 1990 *S*, 1995 *It*, *R* 2, *Arg*, *NZ* 1,2
Caron, L (Lyon O, Castres) 1947 *E*, 1948 *I*, *A*, *W*, *E*, 1949 *S*, *I*, *E*, *W*, *Arg* 1
Carpentier, M (Lourdes) 1980 *E*, *SA*, *R*, 1981 *S*, *I*, *A* 1, 1982 *E*, *S*
Carrère, C (Toulon) 1966 *R*, 1967 *S*, *A*, *E*, *W*, *I*, *SA* 1,3,4, *NZ*, *R*, 1968 *S*, *I*, *E*, *W*, *Cz*, *NZ* 3, *A*, *R*, 1969 *S*, *I*, 1970 *S*, *I*, *W*, *E*, 1971 *E*, *W*
Carrère, J (Vichy, Toulon) 1956 *S*, 1957 *E*, *W*, *R* 2, 1958 *S*, *SA* 1,2, 1959 *I*
Carrère, R (Mont-de-Marsan) 1953 *E*, *It*
Casadei, D (Brive) 1997 *S*, *R* 1, *SA* 2(R)
Casaux, L (Tarbes) 1959 *I*, *It*, 1962 *S*
Cassagne, P (Pau) 1957 *It*
Cassayet-Armagnac, A (Tarbes, Narbonne) 1920 *S*, *E*, *W*, *US*, 1921 *W*, *E*, *I*, 1922 *S*, *E*, *W*, 1923 *S*, *W*, *E*, *I*, 1924 *S*, *E*, *W*, *R*, *US*, 1925 *I*, *NZ*, *S*, *W*, 1926 *S*, *I*, *E*, *W*, *M*, 1927 *I*, *S*, *W*
Cassiède, M (Dax) 1961 *NZ* 3, *A*, *R*
Castaignède, S (Mont-de-Marsan) 1999 *W* 2, [*C* (R), *Nm* (R), *Fj*, *Arg* (R), *NZ* 2(R), *A* (R)]
Castaignède, T (Toulouse, Castres, Saracens) 1995 *R* 2, *Arg*, *NZ* 1,2, 1996 *E*, *S*, *I*, *W* 1, *Arg* 1,2, 1997 *I*, *A* 1,2, *It* 2, 1998 *E*, *S*, *I*, *W*, *Arg* 1,2, *Fj*, 1999 *I*, *W* 1, *E*, *S*, *R*, *WS*, *Tg* (R), *NZ* 1, *W* 2, [*C*], 2000 *W*, *E*, *S*, *It*, 2002 *SA*, *NZ*, *C*, 2003 *E* 1(R), *S* (R), *It*, *W*, *Arg* 1
Castel, R (Toulouse, Béziers) 1996 *I*, *W* 1, *W* 2, *SA* 1(R),2, 1997 *I* (R), *W*, *E* (R), *S* (R), *A* 1(R), 1998 *Arg* 3(R), *A* (R), 1999 *W* 1(R), *E*, *S*
Castets, J (Toulon) 1923 *W*, *E*, *I*
Caujolle, J (Tarbes) 1909 *E*, 1913 *SA*, *E*, 1914 *W*, *E*
Caunègre, R (SB) 1938 *R*, *G* 2
Caussade, A (Lourdes) 1978 *R*, 1979 *I*, *W*, *E*, *NZ* 1,2, *R*, 1980 *W*, *E*, *S*, 1981 *S* (R), *I*
Caussarieu, G (Pau) 1929 *I*
Cayrefourcq, E (Tarbes) 1921 *E*
Cazalbou, J (Toulouse) 1997 *It* 2(R), *R* 2, *Arg*, *SA* 2(R)
Cazals, P (Mont-de-Marsan) 1961 *NZ* 1, *A*, *R*
Cazenave, A (Pau) 1927 *E*, *G* 1, 1928 *S*, *A*, *G*
Cazenave, F (RCF) 1950 *E*, 1952 *S*, 1954 *I*, *NZ*, *W*, *E*
Cecillon, M (Bourgoin) 1988 *I*, *W*, *Arg* 2,3,4, *R*, 1989 *I*, *E*, *NZ* 1,2, *A* 1, 1991 *S*, *I*, *E* (R), *R*, *US* 1, *W* 2, [*E*], 1992 *W*, *E*, *S*, *I*, *R*, *Arg* 1,2, *SA* 1,2, 1993 *E*, *S*, *I*, *W*, *R* 1, *SA* 1,2, *R* 2, *A* 1,2, 1994 *I*, *W*, *NZ* 1(R), 1995 *I*, *R* 1, [*Tg*, *S* (R), *I*, *SA*]
Celaya, M (Biarritz O, SBUC) 1953 *E*, *W*, *It*, 1954 *I*, *E*, *It*, *Arg* 1,2, 1955 *S*, *I*, *E*, *W*, *It*, 1956 *S*, *I*, *W*, *It*, *E*, *Cz* 1957 *S*, *I*, *E*, *W*, *R* 2, 1958 *S*, *E*, *A*, *W*, *It*, 1959 *S*, *E*, 1960 *S*, *E*, *W*, *I*, *R*, *Arg* 1,2,3, 1961 *S*, *SA*, *E*, *W*, *It*, *I*, *NZ* 1,2,3, *A*, *R*
Celhay, M (Bayonne) 1935 *G*, 1936 *G* 1, 1937 *G*, *It*, 1938 *G* 1, 1940 *B*
Cermeno, F (Perpignan) 2000 *R*
Cessieux, N (Lyon) 1906 *NZ*
Cester, E (TOEC, Valence) 1966 *S*, *I*, *E*, 1967 *W*, 1968 *S*, *I*, *E*, *W*, *Cz*, *NZ* 1,3, *A*, *SA* 1,2, *R*, 1969 *S*, *I*, *E*, *W*, 1970 *S*, *I*, *W*, *E*, 1971 *A* 1, 1972 *R*, 1973 *S*, *NZ*, *W*, *I*, *J*, *R*, 1974 *I*, *W*, *E*, *S*
Chabal, S (Bourgoin) 2000 *S*, 2001 *SA* 1,2, *NZ* (R), *Fj* (R), 2002 *Arg* (R), *A* 2, *SA* (R), *NZ* (t), *C* (R), 2003 *E* 1(R), *S* (R), *I* (R), *Arg* 2, *NZ* (R), *E* 2(R),3
Chaban-Delmas, J (CASG) 1945 *B* 2
Chabowski, H (Nice, Bourgoin) 1985 *Arg* 2, 1986 *R* 2, *NZ* 2, 1989 *B* (R)
Chadebech, P (Brive) 1982 *R*, *Arg* 1,2, 1986 *S*, *I*
Champ, E (Toulon) 1985 *Arg* 1,2, 1986 *I*, *W*, *E*, *R* 1, *Arg* 1,2, *A*, *NZ* 1, *R* 2, *NZ* 2,3, 1987 *W*, *E*, *S*, *I*, [*S*, *R*, *Fj*, *A*, *NZ*], *R*, 1988 *E*, *S*, *Arg* 1,3,4, *R*, 1989 *W*, *S*, *A* 1,2, 1990 *W*, *E*, *NZ* 1, 1991 *R*, *US* 1, [*R*, *Fj*, *C*, *E*]
Chapuy, L (SF) 1926 *S*
Charpentier, G (SF) 1911 *E*, 1912 *W*, *E*
Charton, P (Montferrand) 1940 *B*
Charvet, D (Toulouse) 1986 *W*, *E*, *R* 1, *Arg* 1, *A*, *NZ* 1,3, 1987 *W*, *E*, *S*, *I*, [*S*, *R*, *Z*, *Fj*, *A*, *NZ*], *R*, 1989 *E* (R), 1990 *W*, *E*, 1991 *S*, *I*
Chassagne, J (Montferrand) 1938 *G* 1
Chatau, A (Bayonne) 1913 *SA*
Chaud, E (Toulon) 1932 *G*, 1934 *G*, 1935 *G*
Chazalet, A (Bourgoin) 1999 *Tg*
Chenevay, C (Grenoble) 1968 *SA* 1
Chevallier, B (Montferrand) 1952 *S*, *I*, *SA*, *W*, *E*, *It*, 1953 *E*, *W*, *It*, 1954 *S*, *I*, *NZ*, *W*, *Arg* 1, 1955 *S*, *I*, *E*, *W*, *It*, 1956 *S*, *I*, *W*, *It*, *E*, *Cz*, 1957 *S*
Chiberry, J (Chambéry) 1955 *It*
Chilo, A (RCF) 1920 *S*, *W*, 1925 *I*, *NZ*
Cholley, G (Castres) 1975 *E*, *S*, *I*, *SA* 1,2, *Arg* 1,2, *R*, 1976 *S*, *I*, *W*, *E*, *A* 1,2, *R*, 1977 *W*, *E*, *S*, *I*, *Arg* 1,2, *NZ* 1,2, *R*, 1978 *E*, *S*, *I*, *W*, *R*, 1979 *I*, *S*
Choy J (Narbonne) 1930 *S*, *I*, *E*, *G*, *W*, 1931 *I*, 1933 *G*, 1934 *G*, 1935 *G*, 1936 *G* 2
Cigagna, A (Toulouse) 1995 [*E*]
Cimarosti, J (Castres) 1976 *US* (R)
Cistacq, J-C (Agen) 2000 *R* (R)
Clady, A (Lezignan) 1929 *G*, 1931 *I*, *S*, *E*, *G*
Clarac, H (St Girons) 1938 *G* 1
Claudel, R (Lyon) 1932 *G*, 1934 *G*
Clauzel, F (Béziers) 1924 *E*, *W*, 1925 *W*
Clavé, J (Agen) 1936 *G* 2, 1938 *R*, *G* 2
Claverie, H (Lourdes) 1954 *NZ*, *W*
Cléda, T (Pau) 1998 *E* (R), *S* (R), *I* (R), *W* (R), *Arg* 1(R), *Fj* (R), *Arg* 3(R), 1999 *I* (R), *S*
Clément, G (RCF) 1931 *W*
Clément, J (RCF) 1921 *S*, *W*, *E*, 1922 *S*, *E*, *W*, *I*, 1923 *S*, *W*, *I*
Clemente, M (Oloron) 1978 *R*, 1980 *S*, *I*
Clerc, V (Toulouse) 2002 *SA*, *NZ*, *C*, 2003 *E* 1, *S*, *I*, *It* (R), *W* (R), *Arg* 2, *NZ*
Cluchague, L (Biarritz O) 1924 *S*, 1925 *E*
Coderc, J (Chalon) 1932 *G*, 1933 *G*, 1934 *G*, 1935 *G*, 1936 *G* 1
Codorniou, D (Narbonne) 1979 *NZ* 1,2, *R*, 1980 *W*, *E*, *S*, *I*, 1981 *S*, *W*, *E*, *A* 2, 1983 *E*, *S*, *I*, *W*, *A* 1,2, *R*, 1984 *I*, *W*, *E*, *S*, *NZ* 1,2, *R*, 1985 *E*, *S*, *I*, *W*, *Arg* 1,2
Coeurveille, C (Agen) 1992 *Arg* 1(R),2
Cognet, L (Montferrand) 1932 *G*, 1936 *G* 1,2, 1937 *G*, *It*
Collazo, P (Bègles) 2000 *R*
Colombier, J (St Junien) 1952 *SA*, *W*, *E*
Colomine, G (Narbonne) 1979 *NZ* 1
Comba, F (SF) 1998 *Arg* 1,2, *Fj*, *Arg* 3, 1999 *I*, *W* 1, *E*, *S*, 2000 *A*, *NZ* 1,2, 2001 *S*, *I*
Combe, J (SF) 1910 *S*, *E*, *I*, 1911 *S*
Combes, G (Fumel) 1945 *B* 2
Communeau, M (SF) 1906 *NZ*, *E*, 1907 *E*, 1908 *E*, *W*, 1909 *E*, *W*, *I*, 1910 *S*, *E*, *I*, 1911 *S*, *E*, *I*, 1912 *I*, *S*, *W*, *E*, 1913 *SA*, *E*, *W*
Condom, J (Boucau, Biarritz O) 1982 *R*, 1983 *E*, *S*, *I*, *W*, *A* 1,2, *R*, 1984 *I*, *W*, *E*, *S*, *NZ* 1,2, *R*, 1985 *E*, *S*, *I*, *W*, *Arg* 1,2, 1986 *S*, *I*, *W*, *E*, *R* 1, *Arg* 1,2, *NZ* 1, *R* 2, *NZ* 2,3, 1987 *W*, *E*, *S*, *I*, [*S*, *R*, *Z*, *A*, *NZ*], *R*, 1988 *E*, *S*, *W*, *Arg* 1,2,3,4, *R*, 1989 *I*, *W*, *E*, *S*, *NZ* 1,2, *A* 1, 1990 *I*, *R*, *A* 2,3(R)
Conilh de Beyssac, J-J (SBUC) 1912 *I*, *S*, 1914 *I*, *W*, *E*
Constant, G (Perpignan) 1920 *W*
Coscolla, G (Béziers) 1921 *S*, *W*
Costantino, J (Montferrand) 1973 *R*
Costes, A (Montferrand) 1994 *C* 2, 1995 *R* 1, [*Iv*], 1997 *It* 1, 1999 *WS*, *Tg* (R), *NZ* 1, [*Nm* (R), *Fj* (R), *Arg* (R), *NZ* 2(R), *A* (t&R)], 2000 *S* (R), *I*
Costes, F (Montferrand) 1979 *E*, *S*, *NZ* 1,2, *R*, 1980 *W*, *I*
Couffignal, H (Colomiers) 1993 *R* 1
Coulon, E (Grenoble) 1928 *S*
Courtiols, M (Bègles) 1991 *R*, *US* 1, *W* 2

Crabos, R (RCF) 1920 *S, E, W, I, US*, 1921 *S, W, E, I*, 1922 *S, E, W, I*, 1923 *S, I*, 1924 *S, I*
Crampagne, J (Bègles) 1967 *SA* 4
Crancee, R (Lourdes) 1960 *Arg* 3, 1961 *S*
Crauste, M (RCF, Lourdes) 1957 *R* 1,2, 1958 *S, E, A, W, It, I*, 1959 *E, It, W, I*, 1960 *S, E, W, I, It, R, Arg* 1,3, 1961 *S, SA, E, W, It, I, NZ* 1,2,3, *A, R*, 1962 *S, E, W, I, It, R*, 1963 *S, I, E, W, It, R*, 1964 *S, NZ, E, W, It, I, SA, Fj, R*, 1965 *S, I, E, W, It, R*, 1966 *S, I, E, W, It*
Cremaschi, M (Lourdes) 1980 *R*, 1981 *R, NZ* 1,2, 1982 *W, S*, 1983 *A* 1,2, *R*, 1984 *I, W*
Crenca, J-J (Agen) 1996 *SA* 2(R), 1999 *R, Tg, WS* (R), *NZ* 1(R), 2001 *SA* 1,2, *NZ* (R), *SA* 3, *A, Fj*, 2002 *It, W, E, S, I, Arg, A* 2, *SA, NZ, C*, 2003 *E* 1, *S, I, It, W, R, E* 2
Crichton, W H (Le Havre) 1906 *NZ, E*
Cristina, J (Montferrand) 1979 *R*
Cussac, P (Biarritz O) 1934 *G*
Cutzach, A (Quillan) 1929 *G*

Daguerre, F (Biarritz O) 1936 *G* 1
Daguerre, J (CASG) 1933 *G*
Dal Maso, M (Mont-de-Marsan, Agen, Colomiers) 1988 *R* (R), 1990 *NZ* 2, 1996 *SA* 1(R),2, 1997 *I, W, E, S, It* 1, *R* 1(R), *A* 1,2, *It* 2, *Arg, SA* 1,2, 1998 *W* (R), *Arg* 1(t), *Fj* (R), 1999 *R* (R), *WS* (R), *Tg, NZ* 1(R), *W* 2(R), [*Nm* (R), *Fj* (R), *Arg* (R), *A* (R)], 2000 *W, E, S, I, It*
Danion, J (Toulon) 1924 *I*
Danos, P (Toulon, Béziers) 1954 *Arg* 1,2, 1957 *R* 2, 1958 *S, E, W, It, I, SA* 1,2, 1959 *S, E, It, W, I*, 1960 *S, E*
Dantiacq, D (Pau) 1997 *R* 1
Darbos, P (Dax) 1969 *R*
Darracq, R (Dax) 1957 *It*
Darrieussecq, A (Biarritz O) 1973 *E*
Darrieussecq, J (Mont-de-Marsan) 1953 *It*
Darrouy, C (Mont-de-Marsan) 1957 *I, E, W, It, R* 1, 1959 *E*, 1961 *R*, 1963 *S, I, E, W, It*, 1964 *NZ, E, W, It, I, SA, Fj, R*, 1965 *S, I, E, It, R*, 1966 *S, I, E, W, It, R*, 1967 *S, A, E, It, W, I, SA* 1,2,4
Daudé, J (Bourgoin) 2000 *S*
Daudignon, G (SF) 1928 *S*
Dauga, B (Mont-de-Marsan) 1964 *S, NZ, E, W, It, I, SA, Fj, R*, 1965 *S, I, E, W, It, R*, 1966 *S, I, E, W, It, R*, 1967 *S, A, E, It, W, I, SA* 1,2,3,4, *NZ, R*, 1968 *S, I, NZ* 1,2,3, *A, SA* 1,2, *R*, 1969 *S, I, E, R*, 1970 *S, I, W, E, R*, 1971 *S, I, E, W, SA* 1,2, *A* 1,2, *R*, 1972 *S, I* 1, *W*
Dauger, J (Bayonne) 1945 *B* 1,2, 1953 *S*
Daulouede, P (Tyrosse) 1937 *G, It*, 1938 *G* 1, 1940 *B*
De Besombes, S (Perpignan) 1998 *Arg* 1(R), *Fj* (R)
Decamps, P (RCF) 1911 *S*
Dedet, J (SF) 1910 *S, E, I*, 1911 *W, I*, 1912 *S*, 1913 *E, I*
Dedeyn, P (RCF) 1906 *NZ*
Dedieu, P (Béziers) 1963 *E, It*, 1964 *W, It, I, SA, Fj, R*, 1965 *S, I, E, W*
De Gregorio, J (Grenoble) 1960 *S, E, W, I, It, R, Arg* 1,2, 1961 *S, SA, E, W, It, I*, 1962 *S, E, W*, 1963 *S, W, It*, 1964 *NZ, E*
Dehez, J-L (Agen) 1967 *SA* 2, 1969 *R*
De Jouvencel, E (SF) 1909 *W, I*
De Laborderie, M (RCF) 1921 *I*, 1922 *I*, 1925 *W, E*
Delage, C (Agen) 1983 *S, I*
De Malherbe, H (CASG) 1932 *G*, 1933 *G*
De Malmann, R (RCF) 1908 *E, W*, 1909 *E, W, I*, 1910 *E, I*
De Muizon, J J (SF) 1910 *I*
Delaigue, G (Toulon) 1973 *J, R*
Delaigue, Y (Toulon, Toulouse) 1994 *S, NZ* 2(R), *C* 2, 1995 *I, R* 1, [*Tg, Iv*], *It, R* 2(R), 1997 *It* 1, 2003 *Arg* 1,2
Delmotte, G (Toulon) 1999 *R, Tg*
Delque, A (Toulouse) 1937 *It*, 1938 *G* 1, *R, G* 2
De Rougemont, M (Toulon) 1995 *E* (t), *R* 1(t), [*Iv*], *NZ* 1,2, 1996 *I* (R), *Arg* 1,2, *W* 2, *SA* 1, 1997 *E* (R), *S* (R), *It* 1
Desbrosse, C (Toulouse) 1999 [*Nm* (R)], 2000 *I*
Descamps, P (SB) 1927 *G* 2
Desclaux, F (RCF) 1949 *Arg* 1,2, 1953 *It*
Desclaux, J (Perpignan) 1934 *G*, 1935 *G*, 1936 *G* 1,2, 1937 *G, It*, 1938 *G* 1, *R, G* 2, 1945 *B* 1
Deslandes, C (RCF) 1990 *A* 1, *NZ* 2, 1991 *W* 1, 1992 *R, Arg* 1,2
Desnoyer, L (Brive) 1974 *R*
Destarac, L (Tarbes) 1926 *S, I, E, W, M*, 1927 *W, E, G* 1,2
Desvouges, R (SF) 1914 *W*
Detrez, P-E (Nîmes) 1983 *A* 2(R), 1986 *Arg* 1(R),2, *A* (R), *NZ*1
Devergie, T (Nîmes) 1988 *R*, 1989 *NZ* 1,2, *B, A* 2, 1990 *W, E, S, I, R, A* 1,2,3, 1991 *US* 2, *W* 2, 1992 *R* (R), *Arg* 2(R)
De Villiers, P (SF) 1999 *W* 2, [*Arg* (R), *NZ* 2(R), *A* (R)], 2000 *W* (R), *E* (R), *S* (R), *I* (R), *It* (R), *NZ* 1(R),2, 2001 *S, I, It, W, E, SA* 1,2, *NZ* (R), *SA* 3, *A, Fj*, 2002 *It, W, E, I, SA, NZ, C*, 2003 *Arg* 1,2, *NZ* (R)
Deygas, M (Vienne) 1937 *It*
Deylaud, C (Toulouse) 1992 *R, Arg* 1,2, *SA* 1, 1994 *C* 1, *NZ* 1,2, 1995 *W, E, S*, [*Iv* (R), *S, I, SA*], *It, Arg*
Dintrans, P (Tarbes) 1979 *NZ* 1,2, *R*, 1980 *E, S, I, SA, R*, 1981 *S, I, W, E, A* 1,2, *R, NZ* 1,2, 1982 *W, E, S, I, R, Arg* 1,2, 1983 *E, W, A* 1,2, *R*, 1984 *I, W, E, S, NZ* 1,2, *R*, 1985 *E, S, I, W, Arg* 1,2, 1987 [*R*], 1988 *Arg* 1,2,3, 1989 *W, E, S*, 1990 *R*
Dispagne, S (Toulouse) 1996 *I* (R), *W* 1
Dizabo, P (Tyrosse) 1948 *A, S, E*, 1949 *S, I, E, W, Arg* 2, 1950 *S, I*, 1960 *Arg* 1,2,3
Domec, A (Carcassonne) 1929 *W*
Domec, H (Lourdes) 1953 *W, It*, 1954 *S, I, NZ, W, E, It*, 1955 *S, I, E, W*, 1956 *I, W, It*, 1958 *E, A, W, It, I*
Domenech, A (Vichy, Brive) 1954 *W, E, It*, 1955 *S, I, E, W*, 1956 *S, I, W, It, E, Cz*, 1957 *S, I, E, W, It, R* 1,2, 1958 *S, E, It*, 1959 *It*, 1960 *S, E, W, I, It, R, Arg* 1,2,3, 1961 *S, SA, E, W, It, I, NZ* 1,2,3, *A, R*, 1962 *S, E, W, I, It, R*, 1963 *W, It*
Domercq, J (Bayonne) 1912 *I, S*
Dominici, C (SF) 1998 *E, S, Arg* 1,2, 1999 *E, S, WS, NZ* 1, *W* 2, [*C, Fj, Arg, NZ* 2, *A*], 2000 *W, E, S, R*, 2001 *I* (R), *It, W, E, SA* 1,2, *NZ, Fj*, 2003 *Arg* 1, *R, E* 2,3
Dorot, J (RCF) 1935 *G*
Dospital, P (Bayonne) 1977 *R*, 1980 *I*, 1981 *S, I, W, E*, 1982 *I, R, Arg* 1,2, 1983 *E, S, I, W*, 1984 *E, S, NZ* 1,2, *R*, 1985 *E, S, I, W, Arg* 1
Dourthe, C (Dax) 1966 *R*, 1967 *S, A, E, W, I, SA* 1,2,3, *NZ*, 1968 *W, NZ* 3, *SA* 1,2, 1969 *W*, 1971 *SA* 2(R), *R*, 1972 *I* 1,2, *A* 1,2, *R*, 1973 *S, NZ, E*, 1974 *I, Arg* 1,2, *SA* 1,2, 1975 *W, E, S*
Dourthe, M (Dax) 2000 *NZ* 2(t)
Dourthe, R (Dax, SF, Béziers) 1995 *R* 2, *Arg, NZ* 1,2, 1996 *E, R*, 1996 *Arg* 1,2, *W* 2, *SA* 1,2, 1997 *W, A* 1, 1999 *I, W* 1,2, [*C, Nm, Fj, Arg, NZ* 2, *A*], 2000 *W, E, It, R, A, NZ* 1,2, 2001 *S, I*
Doussau, E (Angoulême) 1938 *R*
Droitecourt, M (Montferrand) 1972 *R*, 1973 *NZ* (R), *E*, 1974 *E, S, Arg* 1, *SA* 2, 1975 *SA* 1,2, *Arg* 1,2, *R*, 1976 *S, I, W, A* 1, 1977 *Arg* 2
Dubertrand, A (Montferrand) 1971 *A* 1,2, *R*, 1972 *I* 2, 1974 *I, W, E, SA* 2, 1975 *Arg* 1,2, *R*, 1976 *S, US*
Dubois, D (Bègles) 1971 *S*
Dubroca, D (Agen) 1979 *NZ* 2, 1981 *NZ* 2(R), 1982 *E, S*, 1984 *W, E, S*, 1985 *Arg* 2, 1986 *S, I, W, E, R* 1, *Arg* 2, *A, NZ* 1, *R* 2, *NZ* 2,3, 1987 *W, E, S, I*, [*S, Z, Fj, A, NZ*], *R*, 1988 *E, S, I, W*
Duché, A (Limoges) 1929 *G*
Duclos, A (Lourdes) 1931 *S*
Ducousso, J (Tarbes) 1925 *S, W, E*
Dufau, G (RCF) 1948 *I, A*, 1949 *I, W*, 1950 *S, E, W*, 1951 *S, I, E, W*, 1952 *SA, W*, 1953 *S, I, E, W*, 1954 *S, I, NZ, W, E, It*, 1955 *S, I, E, W, It*, 1956 *S, I, W, It*, 1957 *S, I, E, W, It, R* 1
Dufau, J (Biarritz) 1912 *I, S, W, E*
Duffaut, Y (Agen) 1954 *Arg* 1,2
Duffour, R (Tarbes) 1911 *W*
Dufourcq, J (SBUC) 1906 *NZ, E*, 1907 *E*, 1908 *W*
Duhard, Y (Bagnères) 1980 *E*
Duhau, J (SF) 1928 *I*,1930 *I, G*, 1931 *I, S, W*, 1933 *G*
Dulaurens, C (Toulouse) 1926 *I*, 1928 *S*, 1929 *W*
Duluc, A (Béziers) 1934 *G*
Du Manoir, Y le P (RCF) 1925 *I, NZ, S, W, E*, 1926 *S*, 1927 *I, S*
Dupont, C (Lourdes) 1923 *S, W, I*, 1924 *S, I, W, R, US*, 1925 *S*, 1927 *E, G* 1,2, 1928 *A, G, W*, 1929 *I*
Dupont, J-L (Agen) 1983 *S*
Dupont, L (RCF) 1934 *G*, 1935 *G*, 1936 *G* 1,2, 1938 *R, G* 2
Dupouy, A (SB) 1924 *W, R*
Duprat, B (Bayonne) 1966 *E, W, It, R*, 1967 *S, A, E, SA* 2,3, 1968 *S, I*, 1972 *E, W, I* 2, *A* 1
Dupré, P (RCF) 1909 *W*
Dupuy, J (Tarbes) 1956 *S, I, W, It, E, Cz*, 1957 *S, I, E, W, It, R* 2, 1958 *S, E, SA* 1,2, 1959 *S, E, It, W, I*, 1960 *W, I, It, Arg* 1,3, 1961 *S, SA, E, NZ* 2, *R*, 1962 *S, E, W, I, It*, 1963 *W, It, R*, 1964 *S*
Du Souich, C J (see Judas du Souich)
Dutin, B (Mont-de-Marsan) 1968 *NZ* 2, *A, SA* 2, *R*
Dutour, F X (Toulouse) 1911 *E, I*, 1912 *S, W, E*, 1913 *S*
Dutrain, H (Toulouse) 1945 *W*, 1946 *B, I*, 1947 *E*, 1949 *I, E, W, Arg* 1
Dutrey, J (Lourdes) 1940 *B*

Duval, R (SF) 1908 *E, W*, 1909 *E*, 1911 *E, W, I*

Echavé, L (Agen) 1961 *S*
Elhorga, P (Agen) 2001 *NZ*, 2002 *A* 1,2, 2003 *Arg* 2, *NZ* (R), *R*
Elissalde, E (Bayonne) 1936 *G* 2, 1940 *B*
Elissalde, J-B (La Rochelle, Toulouse) 2000 *S* (R), *R* (R), 2003 *It* (R), *W* (R)
Elissalde, J-P (La Rochelle) 1980 *SA, R*, 1981 *A* 1,2, *R*
Empereur-Buisson, H (Béziers) 1931 *E, G*
Erbani, D (Agen) 1981 *A* 1,2, *NZ* 1,2, 1982 *Arg* 1,2, 1983 *S* (R), *I, W, A* 1,2, *R*, 1984 *W, E, R*, 1985 *E, W* (R), *Arg* 2, 1986 *S, I, W, E, R* 1, *Arg* 2, *NZ* 1,2(R),3, 1987 *W, E, S, I*, [*S, R, Fj, A, NZ*], 1988 *E, S*, 1989 *I* (R), *W, E, S, NZ* 1, *A* 2, 1990 *W, E*
Escaffre, P (Narbonne) 1933 *G*, 1934 *G*
Escommier, M (Montelimar) 1955 *It*
Esponda, J-M (RCF) 1967 *SA* 1,2, *R*, 1968 *NZ* 1,2, *SA* 2, *R*, 1969 *S, I* (R), *E*
Estève, A (Béziers) 1971 *SA* 1, 1972 *I* 1, *E, W, I* 2, *A* 2, *R*, 1973 *S, NZ, E, I*, 1974 *I, W, E, S, R, SA* 1,2, 1975 *W, E*
Estève, P (Narbonne, Lavelanet) 1982 *R, Arg* 1,2, 1983 *E, S, I, W, A* 1,2, *R*, 1984 *I, W, E, S, NZ* 1,2, *R*, 1985 *E, S, I, W*, 1986 *S, I*, 1987 [*S, Z*]
Etcheberry, J (Rochefort, Cognac) 1923 *W, I*, 1924 *S, I, E, W, R, US*, 1926 *S, I, E, M*, 1927 *I, S, W, G* 2
Etchenique, J-M (Biarritz O) 1974 *R, SA* 1, 1975 *E, Arg* 2
Etchepare, A (Bayonne) 1922 *I*
Etcheverry, M (Pau) 1971 *S, I*
Eutrope, A (SCUF) 1913 *I*

Fabre, E (Toulouse) 1937 *It*, 1938 *G* 1,2
Fabre, J (Toulouse) 1963 *S, I, E, W, It*, 1964 *S, NZ, E*
Fabre, L (Lezignan) 1930 *G*
Fabre, M (Béziers) 1981 *A* 1, *R, NZ* 1,2, 1982 *I, R*
Failliot, P (RCF) 1911 *S, W, I*, 1912 *I, S, E*, 1913 *E, W*
Fargues, G (Dax) 1923 *I*
Fauré, F (Tarbes) 1914 *I, W, E*
Fauvel, J-P (Tulle) 1980 *R*
Favre, M (Lyon) 1913 *E, W*
Ferrand, L (Chalon) 1940 *B*
Ferrien, R (Tarbes) 1950 *S, I, E, W*
Finat, R (CASG) 1932 *G*, 1933 *G*
Fite, R (Brive) 1963 *W, It*
Forestier, J (SCUF) 1912 *W*
Forgues, F (Bayonne) 1911 *S, E, W*, 1912 *I, W, E*, 1913 *S, SA, W*, 1914 *I, E*
Fort, J (Agen) 1967 *It, W, I, SA* 1,2,3,4
Fourcade, G (BEC) 1909 *E, W*
Foures, H (Toulouse) 1951 *S, I, E, W*
Fournet, F (Montferrand) 1950 *W*
Fouroux, J (La Voulte) 1972 *I* 2, *R*, 1974 *W, E, Arg* 1,2, *R, SA* 1,2, 1975 *W, Arg* 1, *R*, 1976 *S, I, W, E, US, A* 1, 1977 *W, E, S, I, Arg* 1,2, *NZ* 1,2, *R*
Francquenelle, A (Vaugirard) 1911 *S*, 1913 *W, I*
Furcade, R (Perpignan) 1952 *S*

Gabernet, S (Toulouse) 1980 *E, S*, 1981 *S, I, W, E, A* 1,2, *R, NZ* 1,2, 1982 *I*, 1983 *A* 2, *R*
Gachassin, J (Lourdes) 1961 *S, I*, 1963 *R*, 1964 *S, NZ, E, W, It, I, SA, Fj, R*, 1965 *S, I, E, W, It, R*, 1966 *S, I, E, W*, 1967 *S, A, It, W, I, NZ*, 1968 *I, E*, 1969 *S, I*
Galasso, A (Toulon, Montferrand) 2000 *R* (R), 2001 *E* (R)
Galau, H (Toulouse) 1924 *S, I, E, W, US*
Galia, J (Quillan) 1927 *E, G* 1,2, 1928 *S, A, I, E, W*, 1929 *I, E, G*, 1930 *S, I, E, G, W*, 1931 *S, W, E, G*
Gallart, P (Béziers) 1990 *R, A* 1,2(R),3, 1992 *S, I, R, Arg* 1,2, *SA* 1,2, *Arg*, 1994 *I, W, E*, 1995 *I* (t), *R* 1, [*Tg*]
Gallion, J (Toulon) 1978 *E, S, I, W*, 1979 *I, W, E, S, NZ* 2, *R*, 1980 *W, E, S, I*, 1983 *A* 1,2, *R*, 1984 *I, W, E, S, R*, 1985 *E, S, I, W*, 1986 *Arg* 2
Galthié, F (Colomiers, SF) 1991 *R, US* 1, [*R, Fj, C, E*], 1992 *W, E, S, R, Arg*, 1994 *I, W, E*, 1995 [*SA, E*], 1996 *W* 1(R), 1997 *I, It* 2, *SA* 1,2, 1998 *W* (R), *Fj* (R), 1999 *R, WS* (R), *Tg, NZ* 1(R), [*Fj* (R), *Arg, NZ* 2, *A*], 2000 *W, E, A, NZ* 1,2, 2001 *S, It, W, E, SA* 1,2, *NZ, SA* 3, *A, Fj*, 2002 *E, S, I, SA, NZ, C*, 2003 *E* 1, *S, Arg* 1,2, *NZ, R, E* 2
Galy, J (Perpignan) 1953 *W*
Garbajosa, X (Toulouse) 1998 *I, W, Arg* 2(R), *Fj*, 1999 *W* 1(R), *E, S, WS, NZ* 1, *W* 2, [*C, Nm* (R), *Fj* (R), *Arg, NZ* 2, *A*], 2000 *A, NZ* 1,2, 2001 *S, I, E*, 2002 *It* (R), *W, SA* (R), *C* (R), 2003 *E* 1, *S, I, It, W, E* 3
Garuet-Lempirou, J-P (Lourdes) 1983 *A* 1,2, *R*, 1984 *I, NZ* 1,2, *R*, 1985 *E, S, I, W, Arg* 1, 1986 *S, I, W, E, R* 1, *Arg* 1, *NZ* 1, *R* 2, *NZ* 2,3, 1987 *W, E, S, I*, [*S, R, Fj, A, NZ*], 1988 *E, S, Arg* 1,2, *R*, 1989 *E* (R), *S, NZ* 1,2, 1990 *W, E*
Gasc, J (Graulhet) 1977 *NZ* 2
Gasparotto, G (Montferrand) 1976 *A* 2, *R*
Gauby, G (Perpignan) 1956 *Cz*
Gaudermen, P (RCF) 1906 *E*
Gayraud, W (Toulouse) 1920 *I*
Gelez, F (Agen) 2001 *SA* 3, 2002 *I* (R), *A* 1, *SA, NZ, C* (R), 2003 *S, I*
Geneste, R (BEC) 1945 *B* 1, 1949 *Arg* 2
Genet, J-P (RCF) 1992 *S, I, R*
Gensane, R (Béziers) 1962 *S, E, W, I, It, R*, 1963 *S*
Gerald, G (RCF) 1927 *E, G* 2, 1928 *S*, 1929 *I, S, W, E, G*, 1930 *S, I, E, G, W*, 1931 *I, S, E, G*
Gérard, D (Bègles) 1999 *Tg*
Gerintes, G (CASG) 1924 *R*, 1925 *I*, 1926 *W*
Geschwind, P (RCF) 1936 *G* 1,2
Giacardy, M (SBUC) 1907 *E*
Gimbert, P (Bègles) 1991 *R, US* 1, 1992 *W, E*
Giordani, P (Dax) 1999 *E, S*
Glas, S (Bourgoin) 1996 *S* (t), *I* (R), *W* 1, *R, Arg* 2(R), *W* 2, *SA* 1,2, 1997 *I, W, E, S, It* 2(R), *R* 2, *Arg, SA* 1,2, 1998 *E, S, I, W, Arg* 1,2, *Fj, Arg* 3, *A*, 1999 *W* 2, [*C, Nm, Arg* (R), *NZ* 2(R), *A* (t&R)], 2000 *I*, 2001 *E, SA* 1,2, *NZ*
Gomès, A (SF) 1998 *Arg* 1,2, *Fj, Arg* 3, *A*, 1999 *I* (R)
Gommes, J (RCF) 1909 *I*
Gonnet, C-A (Albi) 1921 *E, I*, 1922 *E, W*, 1924 *S, E*, 1926 *S, I, E, W, M*, 1927 *I, S, W, E, G* 1
Gonzalez, J-M (Bayonne) 1992 *Arg* 1,2, *SA* 1,2, *Arg*, 1993 *R* 1, *SA* 1,2, *R* 2, *A* 1,2, 1994 *I, W, E, S, C* 1, *NZ* 1,2, *C* 2, 1995 *W, E, S, I, R* 1, [*Tg, S, I, SA, E*], *It, Arg*, 1996 *E, S, I, W* 1
Got, R (Perpignan) 1920 *I, US*, 1921 *S, W*, 1922 *S, E, W, I*, 1924 *I, E, W, R, US*
Gourdon, J-F (RCF, Bagnères) 1974 *S, Arg* 1,2, *R, SA* 1,2, 1975 *W, E, S, I, R*, 1976 *S, I, W, E*, 1978 *E, S*, 1979 *W, E, S, R*, 1980 *I*
Gourragne, J-F (Béziers) 1990 *NZ* 2, 1991 *W* 1
Goyard, A (Lyon U) 1936 *G* 1,2, 1937 *G, It*, 1938 *G* 1, *R, G* 2
Graciet, R (SBUC) 1926 *I, W*, 1927 *S, G* 1, 1929 *E*, 1930 *W*
Graou, S (Auch, Colomiers) 1992 *Arg* (R), 1993 *SA* 1,2, *R* 2, *A* 2(R), 1995 *R* 2, *Arg* (t), *NZ* 2(R)
Gratton, J (Agen) 1984 *NZ* 2, *R*, 1985 *E, S, I, W, Arg* 1,2, 1986 *S, NZ* 1
Graule, V (Arl Perpignan) 1926 *I, E, W*, 1927 *S, W*, 1931 *G*
Greffe, M (Grenoble) 1968 *W, Cz, NZ* 1,2, *SA* 1
Griffard, J (Lyon U) 1932 *G*, 1933 *G*, 1934 *G*
Gruarin, A (Toulon) 1964 *W, It, I, SA, Fj, R*, 1965 *S, I, E, W, It*, 1966 *S, I, E, W, It, R*, 1967 *S, A, E, It, W, I, NZ*, 1968 *S, I*
Guelorget, P (RCF) 1931 *E, G*
Guichemerre, A (Dax) 1920 *E*, 1921 *E, I*, 1923 *S*
Guilbert, A (Toulon) 1975 *E, S, I, SA* 1,2, 1976 *A* 1, 1977 *Arg* 1,2, *NZ* 1,2, *R*, 1979 *I, W, E*
Guillemin, P (RCF) 1908 *E, W*, 1909 *E, I*, 1910 *W, S, E, I*, 1911 *S, E, W*
Guilleux, P (Agen) 1952 *SA, It*
Guiral, M (Agen) 1931 *G*, 1932 *G*, 1933 *G*
Guiraud, H (Nîmes) 1996 *R*

Haget, A (PUC) 1953 *E*, 1954 *I, NZ, E, Arg* 2, 1955 *E, W, It*, 1957 *I, E, It, R* 1, 1958 *It, SA* 2
Haget, F (Agen, Biarritz O) 1974 *Arg* 1,2, 1975 *SA* 2, *Arg* 1,2, *R*, 1976 *S*, 1978 *S, I, W, R*, 1979 *I, W, E, S, NZ* 1,2, *R*, 1980 *W, S, I*, 1984 *S, NZ* 1,2, *R*, 1985 *E, S, I*, 1986 *S, I, W, E, R* 1, *Arg* 1, *A, NZ* 1, 1987 *S, I*, [*R, Fj*]
Haget, H (CASG) 1928 *S*, 1930 *G*
Halet, R (Strasbourg) 1925 *NZ, S, W*
Hall, S (Béziers) 2002 *It, W*
Harinordoquy, I (Pau) 2002 *W, E, S, I, A* 1,2, *SA, NZ, C*, 2003 *E* 1, *S, I, It, W, Arg* 1(R),2, *NZ, R, E* 2,3(R)
Harislur-Arthapignet, P (Tarbes) 1988 *Arg* 4(R)
Harize, D (Cahors, Toulouse) 1975 *SA* 1,2, 1976 *A* 1,2, *R*, 1977 *W, E, S, I*
Hauc, J (Toulon) 1928 *E, G*, 1929 *I, S, G*
Hauser, M (Lourdes) 1969 *E*
Hedembaigt, M (Bayonne) 1913 *S, SA*, 1914 *W*
Hericé, D (Bègles) 1950 *I*
Herrero, A (Toulon) 1963 *R*, 1964 *NZ, E, W, It, I, SA, Fj, R*, 1965 *S, I, E, W*, 1966 *W, It, R*, 1967 *S, A, E, It, I, R*
Herrero, B (Nice) 1983 *I*, 1986 *Arg* 1
Heyer, F (Montferrand) 1990 *A* 2
Heymans, C (Agen, Toulouse) 2000 *It* (R) *R*, 2002 *A* 2(R), *SA, NZ*
Hiquet, J-C (Agen) 1964 *E*

Hoche, M (PUC) 1957 I, E, W, It, R 1

Hondagné-Monge, M (Tarbes) 1988 Arg 2(R)

Hontas, P (Biarritz) 1990 S, I, R, 1991 R, 1992 Arg, 1993 E, S, I, W

Hortoland, J-P (Béziers) 1971 A 2

Houblain, H (SCUF) 1909 E, 1910 W

Houdet, R (SF) 1927 S, W, G 1, 1928 G, W, 1929 I, S, E, 1930 S, E

Hourdebaigt, A (SBUC) 1909 I, 1910 W, S, E, I

Hubert, A (ASF) 1906 E, 1907 E, 1908 E, W, 1909 E, W, I

Hueber, A (Lourdes, Toulon) 1990 A 3, NZ 1, 1991 US 2, 1992 I, Arg 1,2, SA 1,2, 1993 E, S, I, W, R 1, SA 1,2, R 2, A 1,2, 1995 [Tg, S (R), I], 2000 It, R

Hutin, R (CASG) 1927 I, S, W

Hyardet, A (Castres) 1995 It, Arg (R)

Ibanez, R (Dax, Perpignan, Castres) 1996 W 1(R), 1997 It 1(R), R 1, It 2(R), R 2, SA 2(R), 1998 E, S, I, W, Arg 1,2, Fj, Arg 3, A, 1999 I, W 1, E, S, R, WS, Tg (R), NZ 1, W 2, [C, Nm, Fj, Arg, NZ 2, A], 2000 W (R), E (R), S (R), I (R), It (R), R, 2001 S, I, It, W, E, SA 1,2, NZ (R), SA 3, A, Fj, 2002 It (R), W, E, S, I, Arg, A 1(R),2, SA, NZ, C, 2003 E 1, S, I, It, W, R (R), E 2(R),3

Icard, J (SF) 1909 E, W

Iguiniz, E (Bayonne) 1914 E

Ihingoué, D (BEC) 1912 I, S

Imbernon, J-F (Perpignan) 1976 I, W, E, US, A 1, 1977 W, E, S, I, Arg 1,2, NZ 1,2, 1978 E, R, 1979 I, 1981 S, I, W, E, 1982 I, 1983 I, W

Iraçabal, J (Bayonne) 1968 NZ 1,2, SA 1, 1969 S, I, W, R, 1970 S, I, W, E, R, 1971 W, SA 1,2, A 1, 1972 E, W, I 2, A 2, R, 1973 S, NZ, E, W, I, J, 1974 I, W, E, S, Arg 1,2, SA 2(R)

Isaac, H (RCF) 1907 E, 1908 E

Ithurra, E (Biarritz O) 1936 G 1,2, 1937 G

Janeczek, T (Tarbes) 1982 Arg 1,2, 1990 R

Janik, K (Toulouse) 1987 R

Jarasse, A (Brive) 1945 B 1

Jardel, J (SB) 1928 I, E

Jauréguy, A (RCF, Toulouse, SF) 1920 S, E, W, I, US, 1922 S, W, 1923 S, W, E, I, 1924 S, W, R, US, 1925 I, NZ, 1926 S, E, W, M, 1927 I, E, 1928 S, A, E, G, W, 1929 I, S, E

Jauréguy, P (Toulouse) 1913 S, SA, W, I

Jauzion, Y (Colomiers, Toulouse) 2001 SA 1,2, NZ, 2002 A 1(R),2(R), 2003 Arg 2, NZ, R, E 2,3

Jeangrand, M-H (Tarbes) 1921 I

Jeanjean, N (Toulouse) 2001 SA 1,2, NZ, SA 3(R), A (R), Fj (R), 2002 It, Arg, A 1

Jeanjean, P (Toulon) 1948 I

Jérôme, G (SF) 1906 NZ, E

Joinel, J-L (Brive) 1977 NZ 1, 1978 R, 1979 I, W, E, S, NZ 1,2, R, 1980 W, E, S, I, SA, 1981 S, I, W, E, R, NZ 1,2, 1982 E, S, I, R, 1983 E, S, I, W, A 1,2, R, 1984 I, W, E, S, NZ 1,2, 1985 S, I, W, Arg 1, 1986 S, I, W, E, R 1, Arg 1,2, A, 1987 [Z]

Jol, M (Biarritz O) 1947 S, I, W, E, 1949 S, I, E, W, Arg 1,2

Jordana, J-L (Pau, Toulouse) 1996 R (R), Arg 1(t),2, W 2, 1997 I (t), W, S (R)

Judas du Souich, C (SCUF) 1911 W, I

Juillet, C (Montferrand, SF) 1995 R 2, Arg, 1999 E, S, WS, NZ 1, [C, Fj, Arg, NZ 2, A], 2000 A, NZ 1,2, 2001 S, I, It, W

Junquas, L (Tyrosse) 1945 B 1,2, W, 1946 B, I, K, W, 1947 S, I, W, E, 1948 S, W

Kaczorowski, D (Le Creusot) 1974 I (R)

Kaempf, A (St Jean-de-Luz) 1946 B

Labadie, P (Bayonne) 1952 S, I, SA, W, E, It, 1953 S, I, It, 1954 S, I, NZ, W, E, Arg 2, 1955 S, I, E, W, 1956 I, 1957 I

Labarthete, R (Pau) 1952 S

Labazuy, A (Lourdes) 1952 I, 1954 S, W, 1956 E, 1958 A, W, I, 1959 S, E, It, W

Labit, C (Toulouse) 1999 S, R (R), WS (R), Tg, 2000 R (R), 2002 Arg, A 1(R), 2003 Arg 1,2, NZ (R), R (R), E 3

Laborde, C (RCF) 1962 It, R, 1963 R, 1964 SA, 1965 E

Labrousse, T (Brive) 1996 R, SA 1

Lacans, P (Béziers) 1980 SA, 1981 W, E, A 2, R, 1982 W

Lacassagne, H (SBUC) 1906 NZ, 1907 E

Lacaussade, R (Bègles) 1948 A, S

Lacaze, C (Lourdes, Angoulême) 1961 NZ 2,3, A, R, 1962 E, W, I, It, 1963 W, R, 1964 S, NZ, E, 1965 It, R, 1966 S, I, E, W, It, R, 1967 S, E, SA 1,3,4, R, 1968 S, E, W, Cz, NZ 1, 1969 E

Lacaze, H (Périgueux) 1928 I, G, W, 1929 I, W

Lacaze, P (Lourdes) 1958 SA 1,2, 1959 S, E, It, W, I

Lacazedieu, C (Dax) 1923 W, I, 1928 A, I, 1929 S

Lacombe, B (Agen) 1989 B, 1990 A 2

Lacome, M (Pau) 1960 Arg 2

Lacoste, R (Tarbes) 1914 I, W, E

Lacrampe, F (Béziers) 1949 Arg 2

Lacroix, P (Mont-de-Marsan, Agen) 1958 A, 1960 W, I, It, R, Arg 1,2,3, 1961 S, SA, E, W, I, NZ 1,2,3, A, R, 1962 S, E, W, I, R, 1963 S, I, E, W

Lacroix, T (Dax, Harlequins) 1989 A 1(R),2, 1991 W 1(R),2(R), [R, C (R), E], 1992 SA 2, 1993 E, S, I, W, SA 1,2, R 2, A 1,2, 1994 I, W, E, S, C 1, NZ 1,2, C 2, 1995 W, E, S, R 1, [Tg, Iv, S, I, SA, E], 1996 E, S, I, 1997 It 2, R 2, Arg, SA 1,2

Lafarge, Y (Montferrand) 1978 R, 1979 NZ 1, 1981 I (R)

Laffitte, R (SCUF) 1910 W, S

Laffont, H (Narbonne) 1926 W

Lafond, A (Bayonne) 1922 E

Lafond, J-B (RCF) 1983 A 1, 1985 Arg 1,2 1986 S, I, W, E, R 1, 1987 I (R), 1988 W, 1989 I, W, E, 1990 W, A 3(R), NZ 2, 1991 S, I, W 1, E, R, US 1, W 2, [R (R), Fj, C, E], 1992 W, E, S, I (R), SA 2, 1993 E, S, I, W

Lagisquet, P (Bayonne) 1983 A 1,2, R, 1984 I, W, NZ 1,2, 1986 R 1(R), Arg 1,2, A, NZ 1, 1987 [S, R, Fj, A, NZ], R, 1988 S, I, W, Arg 1,2,3,4, R, 1989 I, W, E, S, NZ 1,2, B, A 1,2, 1990 W, E, S, I, A 1,2,3, 1991 S, I, US 2, [R]

Lagrange, J-C (RCF) 1966 It

Lalande, M (RCF) 1923 S, W, I

Lalanne, F (Mont-de-Marsan) 2000 R

Lamaison, C (Brive, Agen) 1996 SA 1(R),2, 1997 W, E, S, R 1, A 2, It 2, R 2, Arg, SA 1,2, 1998 E, S, I, W, Arg 3(R), A, 1999 R, WS (R), Tg, NZ 1(R), W 2(R), [C (R), Nm, Fj, Arg, NZ 2, A], 2000 W, A, NZ 1,2, 2001 S, I, It, W (R)

Landreau, F (SF) 2000 A, NZ 1,2, 2001 E (R)

Lane, G (RCF) 1906 NZ, E, 1907 E, 1908 E, W, 1909 E, W, I, 1910 W, E, 1911 S, W, 1912 I, W, E, 1913 S

Langlade, J-C (Hyères) 1990 R, A 1, NZ 1

Laperne, D (Dax) 1997 R 1(R)

Laporte, G (Graulhet) 1981 I, W, E, R, NZ 1,2, 1986 S, I, W, E, R 1, Arg 1, A (R), 1987 [R, Z (R), Fj]

Larreguy, P (Bayonne) 1954 It

Larribau, J (Périgueux) 1912 I, S, W, E, 1913 S, 1914 I, E

Larrieu, J (Tarbes) 1920 I, US, 1921 W, 1923 S, W, E, I

Larrieux, M (SBUC) 1927 G 2

Larrue, H (Carmaux) 1960 W, I, It, R, Arg 1,2,3

Lasaosa, P (Dax) 1950 I, 1952 S, I, E, It, 1955 It

Lascubé, G (Agen) 1991 S, I, W 1, E, US 2, W 2, [R, Fj, C, E], 1992 W, E

Lassegue, J-B (Toulouse) 1946 W, 1947 S, I, W, 1948 W, 1949 I, E, W, Arg 1

Lasserre, F (René) (Bayonne, Cognac, Grenoble) 1914 I, 1920 S, 1921 S, W, I, 1922 S, E, W, I, 1923 W, E, 1924 S, I, R, US

Lasserre, J-C (Dax) 1963 It, 1964 S, NZ, E, W, It, I, Fj, 1965 W, It, R, 1966 R, 1967 S

Lasserre, M (Agen) 1967 SA 2,3, 1968 E, W, Cz, NZ 3, A, SA 1,2, 1969 S, I, E, 1970 E, 1971 E, W

Laterrade, G (Tarbes) 1910 E, I, 1911 S, E, I

Laudouar, J (Soustons, SBUC) 1961 NZ 1,2, R, 1962 I, R

Lauga, P (Vichy) 1950 S, I, E, W

Laurent, A (Biarritz O) 1925 NZ, S, W, E, 1926 W

Laurent, J (Bayonne) 1920 S, E, W

Laurent, M (Auch) 1932 G, 1933 G, 1934 G, 1935 G, 1936 G 1

Laussucq, C (SF) 1999 S (R), 2000 W (R), S, I

Lavail, G (Perpignan) 1937 G, 1940 B

Lavaud, R (Carcassonne) 1914 I, W

Lavergne, P (Limoges) 1950 S

Lavigne, B (Agen) 1984 R, 1985 E

Lavigne, J (Dax) 1920 E, W

Lazies, H (Auch) 1954 Arg 2, 1955 It, 1956 E, 1957 S

Le Bourhis, R (La Rochelle) 1961 R

Lecointre, M (Nantes) 1952 It

Le Droff, J (Auch) 1963 It, R, 1964 S, NZ, E, 1970 E, R, 1971 S, I

Lefevre, R (Brive) 1961 NZ 2

Leflamand, L (Bourgoin) 1996 SA 2, 1997 W, E, S, It 2, Arg, SA 1,2(R)

Lefort, J-B (Biarritz O) 1938 G 1

Le Goff, R (Métro) 1938 R, G 2

Legrain, M (SF) 1909 I, 1910 I, 1911 S, E, W, I, 1913 S, SA, E, I, 1914 I, W

Lemeur, Y (RCF) 1993 R 1

Lenient, J-J (Vichy) 1967 R

Lepatey, J (Mazamet) 1954 It, 1955 S, I, E, W

Lepatey, L (Mazamet) 1924 *S, I, E*
Lescarboura, J-P (Dax) 1982 *W, E, S, I*, 1983 *A* 1,2, *R*, 1984 *I, W, E, S, NZ* 1,2, *R*, 1985 *E, S, I, W, Arg* 1,2, 1986 *Arg* 2, *A, NZ* 1, *R* 2, *NZ* 2, 1988 *S, W*, 1990 *R*
Lesieur, E (SF) 1906 *E*, 1908 *E, W*, 1909 *E, W, I*, 1910 *S, E, I*, 1911 *E, I*, 1912 *W*
Leuvielle, M (SBUC) 1908 *W*, 1913 *S, SA, E, W*, 1914 *W, E*
Levasseur, R (SF) 1925 *W, E*
Levée, H (RCF) 1906 *NZ*
Lewis, E W (Le Havre) 1906 *E*
Lhermet, J-M (Montferrand) 1990 *S, I*, 1993 *R* 1
Libaros, G (Tarbes) 1936 *G* 1, 1940 *B*
Liebenberg, B (SF) 2003 *R* (R), *E* 2(R),3
Lievremont, M (Perpignan, SF) 1995 *It, R* 2, *Arg* (R), *NZ* 2(R), 1996 *R, Arg* 1(R), *SA* 2(R), 1997 *R* 1, *A* 2(R), 1998 *E* (R), *S, I, W, Arg* 1,2, *Fj, Arg* 3, *A*, 1999 *W* 2, [*C, Nm, Fj, Arg, NZ* 2, *A*]
Lievremont, T (Perpignan, SF, Biarritz) 1996 *W* 2(R), 1998 *E, S, I, W, Arg* 1,2, *Fj, Arg* 3, *A*, 1999 *I, W* 1, *E, W* 2, [*Nm*], 2000 *W* (R), *E* (R), *S* (R), *I, It*, 2001 *E* (R)
Lira, M (La Voulte) 1962 *R*, 1963 *I, E, W, It, R*, 1964 *W, It, I, SA*, 1965 *S, I, R*
Llari, R (Carcassonne) 1926 *S*
Lobies, J (RCF) 1921 *S, W, E*
Lombard, F (Narbonne) 1934 *G*, 1937 *It*
Lombard, T (SF) 1998 *Arg* 3, *A*, 1999 *I, W* 1, *S* (R), 2000 *W, E, S, A, NZ* 1, 2001 *It, W*
Lombarteix, R (Montferrand) 1938 *R, G* 2
Londios, J (Montauban) 1967 *SA* 3
Loppy, L (Toulon) 1993 *R* 2
Lorieux, A (Grenoble, Aix) 1981 *A* 1, *R, NZ* 1,2, 1982 *W*, 1983 *A* 2, *R*, 1984 *I, W, E*, 1985 *Arg* 1,2(R), 1986 *R* 2, *NZ* 2,3, 1987 *W, E*, [*S, Z, Fj, A, NZ*], 1988 *S, I, W, Arg* 1,2,4, 1989 *W, A* 2
Loury, A (RCF) 1927 *E, G* 1,2, 1928 *S, A, I*
Loustau, M (Dax) 1923 *E*
Lubin-Lebrère, M-F (Toulouse) 1914 *I, W, E*, 1920 *S, E, W, I, US*, 1921 *S*, 1922 *S, E, W*, 1924 *W, US*, 1925 *I*
Lubrano, A (Béziers) 1972 *A* 2, 1973 *S*
Lux, J-P (Tyrosse, Dax) 1967 *E, It, W, I, SA* 1,2,4, *R*, 1968 *I, E, Cz, NZ* 3, *A, SA* 1,2, 1969 *S, I, E*, 1970 *S, I, W, E, R*, 1971 *S, I, E, W, A* 1,2, 1972 *S, I* 1, *E, W, I* 2, *A* 1,2, *R*, 1973 *S, NZ, E*, 1974 *I, W, E, S, Arg* 1,2, 1975 *W*

Macabiau, A (Perpignan) 1994 *S, C* 1
Maclos, P (SF) 1906 *E*, 1907 *E*
Magne, O (Dax, Brive, Montferrand) 1997 *W* (R), *E, S, R* 1(R), *A* 1,2, *It* 2(R), *R* 2, *Arg* (R), 1998 *E, S, I, W, Arg* 1,2, *Fj, Arg* 3, *A*, 1999 *I, R, WS, NZ* 1, *W* 2, [*C, Nm, Fj, Arg, NZ* 2, *A*], 2000 *W, E, S, It, R, A, NZ* 1,2, 2001 *S, I, It, W, E, SA* 1,2, *NZ, SA* 3, *A, Fj*, 2002 *It, E, S, I, Arg, A* 1,2(R), *SA, NZ, C*, 2003 *E* 1, *S, I, It, W, R, E* 2,3(R)
Magnanou, C (RCF) 1923 *E*, 1925 *W, E*, 1926 *S*, 1929 *S, W*, 1930 *S, I, E, W*
Magnol, L (Toulouse) 1928 *S*, 1929 *S, W, E*
Magois, H (La Rochelle) 1968 *SA* 1,2, *R*
Majerus, R (SF) 1928 *W*, 1929 *I, S*, 1930 *S, I, E, G, W*
Malbet, J-C (Agen) 1967 *SA* 2,4
Maleig, A (Oloron) 1979 *W, E, NZ* 2, 1980 *W, E, SA, R*
Mallier, L (Brive) 1999 *R, W* 2(R), [*C* (R)], 2000 *I* (R), *It*
Malquier, Y (Narbonne) 1979 *S*
Manterola, T (Lourdes) 1955 *It*, 1957 *R* 1
Mantoulan, C (Pau) 1959 *I*
Marcet, J (Albi) 1925 *I, NZ, S, W, E*, 1926 *I, E*
Marchal, J-F (Lourdes) 1979 *S, R*, 1980 *W, S, I*
Marconnet, S (SF) 1998 *Arg* 3, A, 1999 *I* (R), *W* 1(R), *E, S* (R), *R, Tg*, 2000 *A, NZ* 1,2, 2001 *S, I, It* (R), *W* (R), *E*, 2002 *S* (R), *Arg* (R), *A* 1,2, *SA* (R), *C* (R), 2003 *E* 1(R), *S, I, It, W, Arg* 1(t+R),2, *NZ, R, E* 2,3(t+R)
Marchand, R (Poitiers) 1920 *S, W*
Marfaing, M (Toulouse) 1992 *R, Arg* 1
Marlu, J (Montferrand) 1998 *Fj* (R), 2002 *S* (R), *I* (R)
Marocco, P (Montferrand) 1968 *S, I, W, E, R* 1, *Arg* 1,2, *A*, 1988 *Arg* 4, 1989 *I*, 1990 *E* (R), *NZ* 1(R), 1991 *S, I, W* 1, *E, US* 2, [*R, Fj, C, E*]
Marot, A (Brive) 1969 *R*, 1970 *S, I, W*, 1971 *SA* 1, 1972 *I* 2, 1976 *A* 1
Marquesuzaa, A (RCF) 1958 *It, SA* 1,2, 1959 *S, E, It, W*, 1960 *S, E, Arg* 1
Marracq, H (Pau) 1961 *R*
Marsh, T (Montferrand) 2001 *SA* 3, *A, Fj*, 2002 *It, W, E, S, I, Arg, A* 1,2
Martin, C (Lyon) 1909 *I*, 1910 *W, S*
Martin, H (SBUC) 1907 *E*, 1908 *W*
Martin, J-L (Béziers) 1971 *A* 2, *R*, 1972 *S, I* 1
Martin, L (Pau) 1948 *I, A, S, W, E*, 1950 *S*
Martin, R (SF) 2002 *E* (t+R), *S* (R), *I* (R)
Martine, R (Lourdes) 1952 *S, I, It*, 1953 *It*, 1954 *S, I, NZ, W, E, It, Arg* 2, 1955 *S, I, W*, 1958 *A, W, It, I, SA* 1,2, 1960 *S, E, Arg* 3, 1961 *S, It*
Martinez, A (Narbonne) 2002 *A* 1
Martinez, G (Toulouse) 1982 *W, E, S, Arg* 1,2, 1983 *E, W*
Mas, F (Béziers) 1962 *R*, 1963 *S, I, E, W*
Mas, N (Perpignan) 2003 *NZ*
Maso, J (Perpignan, Narbonne) 1966 *It, R*, 1967 *S, R*, 1968 *S, W, Cz, NZ* 1,2,3, *A, R*, 1969 *S, I, W*, 1971 *SA* 1,2, *R*, 1972 *E, W, A* 2, 1973 *W, I, J, R*
Massare, J (PUC) 1945 *B* 1,2, *W*, 1946 *B, I, W*
Massé, A (SBUC) 1908 *W*, 1909 *E, W*, 1910 *W, S, E, I*
Masse, H (Grenoble) 1937 *G*
Matheu-Cambas, J (Agen) 1945 *W*, 1946 *B, I, K, W*, 1947 *S, I, W, E*, 1948 *I, A, S, W, E*, 1949 *S, I, E, W, Arg* 1,2, 1950 *E, W*, 1951 *S, I*
Matiu, L (Biarritz) 2000 *W, E*
Mauduy, G (Périgueux) 1957 *It, R* 1,2, 1958 *S, E*, 1961 *W, It*
Mauran, J (Castres) 1952 *SA, W, E, It*, 1953 *I, E*
Mauriat, P (Lyon) 1907 *E*, 1908 *E, W*, 1909 *W, I*, 1910 *W, S, E, I*, 1911 *S, E, W, I*, 1912 *I, S*, 1913 *S, SA, W, I*
Maurin, G (ASF) 1906 *E*
Maury, A (Toulouse) 1925 *I, NZ, S, W, E*, 1926 *S, I, E*
Mayssonnié, A (Toulouse) 1908 *E, W*, 1910 *W*
Mazas, L (Colomiers, Biarritz) 1992 *Arg*, 1996 *SA* 1
Melville, E (Toulon) 1990 *I* (R), *A* 1,2,3, *NZ* 1, 1991 *US* 2
Menrath, R (SCUF) 1910 *W*
Menthiller, Y (Romans) 1964 *W, It, SA, R*, 1965 *E*
Merceron, G (Montferrand) 1999 *R* (R), *Tg*, 2000 *S, I, R*, 2001 *S* (R), *W, E, SA* 1,2, *NZ* (R), *Fj*, 2002 *It, W, E, S, I, Arg, A* 2, *C*, 2003 *E* 1, *It* (R), *W* (R), *NZ* (t+R), *R* (R), *E* 3
Meret, F (Tarbes) 1940 *B*
Mericq, S (Agen) 1959 *I*, 1960 *S, E, W*, 1961 *I*
Merle, O (Grenoble, Montferrand) 1993 *SA* 1,2, *R* 2, *A* 1,2, 1994 *I, W, E, S, C* 1, *NZ* 1,2, *C* 2, 1995 *W, I, R* 1, [*Tg, S, I, SA, E*], *It, R* 2, *Arg, NZ* 1,2, 1996 *E, S, R, Arg* 1,2, *W* 2, *SA* 2, 1997 *I, W, E, S, It* 1, *R* 1, *A* 1,2, *It* 2, *R* 2, *SA* 1(R),2
Merquey, J (Toulon)1950 *S, I, E, W*
Mesnel, F (RCF) 1986 *NZ* 2(R),3, 1987 *W, E, S, I*, [*S, Z, Fj, A, NZ*], *R*, 1988 *E, Arg* 1,2,3,4, *R*, 1989 *I, W, E, S, NZ* 1, *A* 1,2, 1990 *E, S, I, A* 2,3, *NZ* 1,2, 1991 *S, I, W* 1, *E, R, US* 1,2, *W* 2, [*R, Fj, C, E*], 1992 *W, E, S, I, SA* 1,2, 1993 *E* (R), *W*, 1995 *I, R* 1, [*Iv, E*]
Mesny, P (RCF, Grenoble) 1979 *NZ* 1,2, 1980 *SA, R*, 1981 *I, W* (R), *A* 1,2, *R, NZ* 1,2, 1982 *I, Arg* 1,2
Meyer, G-S (Périgueux) 1960 *S, E, It, R, Arg* 2
Meynard, J (Cognac) 1954 *Arg* 1, 1956 *Cz*
Mias, L (Mazamet) 1951 *S, I, E, W*, 1952 *I, SA, W, E, It*, 1953 *S, I, W, It*, 1954 *S, I, NZ, W*, 1957 *R* 2, 1958 *S, E, A, W, I, SA* 1,2, 1959 *S, It, W, I*
Michalak, F (Toulouse) 2001 *SA* 3(R), *A, Fj* (R), 2002 *It, A* 1,2, 2003 *It, W, Arg* 2(R), *NZ, R, E* 2
Mignoni, P (Béziers) 1997 *R* 2(R), *Arg* (t), 1999 *R* (R), *WS, NZ* 1, *W* 2(R), [*C, Nm*], 2002 *W, E* (R), *I* (R), *Arg, A* 2(R)
Milhères, C (Biarritz) 2001 *E*
Milliand, P (Grenoble) 1936 *G* 2, 1937 *G, It*
Milloud, O (Bourgoin) 2000 *R* (R), 2001 *NZ*, 2002 *W* (R), *E* (R), 2003 *It* (R), *W* (R), *Arg* 1, *R* (R), *E* 2(t+R),3
Minjat, R (Lyon) 1945 *B* 1
Miorin, H (Toulouse) 1996 *R, SA* 1, 1997 *I, W, E, S, It* 1, 2000 *It* (R), *R* (R)
Mir, J-H (Lourdes) 1967 *R*, 1968 *I*
Mir, J-P (Lourdes) 1967 *A*
Modin, R (Brive) 1987 [*Z*]
Moga, A-M-A (Bègles) 1945 *B* 1,2, *W*, 1946 *B, I, K, W*, 1947 *S, I, W, E*, 1948 *I, A, S, W, E*, 1949 *S, I, E, W, Arg* 1,2
Mola, U (Dax, Castres) 1997 *S* (R), 1999 *R* (R), *WS, Tg* (R), *NZ* 1, *W* 2, [*C, Nm, Fj, Arg* (R), *NZ* 2(R), *A* (R)]
Mommejat, B (Cahors, Albi) 1958 *It, I, SA* 1,2, 1959 *S, E, It, W, I*, 1960 *S, E, I, R*, 1962 *S, E, W, I, It, R*, 1963 *S, I, W*
Moncla, F (RCF, Pau) 1956 *Cz*, 1957 *I, E, W, It, R* 1, 1958 *SA* 1,2, 1959 *S, E, It, W, I*, 1960 *S, E, W, I, It, R, Arg* 1,2,3, 1961 *S, SA, E, W, It, I, NZ* 1,2,3
Moni, C (Nice, SF) 1996 *R*, 2000 *A, NZ* 1,2, 2001 *S, I, It, W*
Monié, R (Perpignan) 1956 *Cz*, 1957 *E*
Monier, R (SBUC) 1911 *I*, 1912 *S*
Monniot, M (RCF) 1912 *W, E*
Montade, A (Perpignan) 1925 *I, NZ, S, W*, 1926 *W*
Montlaur, P (Agen) 1992 *E* (R), 1994 *S* (R)

Moraitis, B (Toulon) 1969 *E, W*
Morel, A (Grenoble) 1954 *Arg* 2
Morere, J (Toulouse) 1927 *E, G* 1, 1928 *S, A*
Moscato, V (Bègles) 1991 *R, US* 1, 1992 *W, E*
Mougeot, C (Bègles) 1992 *W, E, Arg*
Mouniq, P (Toulouse) 1911 *S, E, W, I*,1912 *I, E*, 1913 *S, SA, E*
Moure, H (SCUF) 1908 *E*
Moureu, P (Béziers) 1920 *I, US*, 1921 *W, E, I*, 1922 *S, W, I*, 1923 *S, W, E, I*, 1924 *S, I, E, W*, 1925 *E*
Mournet, A (Bagnères) 1981 *A* 1(R)
Mouronval, F (SF) 1909 *I*
Muhr, A H (RCF) 1906 *NZ, E*, 1907 *E*
Murillo, G (Dijon) 1954 *It, Arg* 1

Nallet, L (Bourgoin) 2000 *R*, 2001 *E, SA* 1(R),2(R), *NZ, SA* 3(R), *A* (R), *Fj* (R), 2003 *NZ*
Namur, R (Toulon) 1931 *E, G*
Noble, J-C (La Voulte) 1968 *E, W, Cz, NZ* 3, *A, R*
Normand, A (Toulouse) 1957 *R* 1
Novès, G (Toulouse) 1977 *NZ* 1,2, *R*, 1978 *W, R*, 1979 *I, W*
Ntamack, E (Toulouse) 1994 *W, C* 1, *NZ* 1,2, *C* 2, 1995 *W, I, R* 1, [*Tg, S, I, SA, E*], *It, R* 2, *Arg, NZ* 1,2, 1996 *E, S, I, W* 1, *R* (R), *Arg* 1,2, *W* 2, 1997 *I*, 1998 *Arg* 3, 1999 *I, W* 1, *E, S, WS, NZ* 1, *W* 2(R), [*C* (R), *Nm, Fj, Arg, NZ* 2, *A*], 2000 *W, E, S, I, It*
Ntamack F (Colomiers) 2001 *SA* 3

Olive, D (Montferrand) 1951 *I*, 1952 *I*
Ondarts, P (Biarritz O) 1986 *NZ* 3, 1987 *W, E, S, I*, [*S, Z, Fj, A, NZ*], *R*, 1988 *E, I, W, Arg* 1,2,3,4, *R*, 1989 *I, W, E, NZ* 1,2, *A* 2, 1990 *W, E, S, I, R* (R), *NZ* 1,2, 1991 *S, I, W* 1, *E, US* 2, *W* 2, [*R, Fj, C, E*]
Orso, J-C (Nice, Toulon) 1982 *Arg* 1,2, 1983 *E, S, A* 1, 1984 *E* (R), *S, NZ* 1, 1985 *I* (R), *W*, 1988 *I*
Othats, J (Dax) 1960 *Arg* 2,3
Ougier, S (Toulouse) 1992 *R, Arg* 1, 1993 *E* (R), 1997 *It* 1

Paco, A (Béziers) 1974 *Arg* 1,2, *R, SA* 1,2, 1975 *W, E, Arg* 1,2, *R*, 1976 *S, I, W, E, US, A* 1,2, *R*, 1977 *W, E, S, I, NZ* 1,2, *R*, 1978 *E, S, I, W, R*, 1979 *I, W, E, S*, 1980 *W*
Palat, J (Perpignan) 1938 *G* 2
Palmié, M (Béziers) 1975 *SA* 1,2, *Arg* 1,2, *R*, 1976 *S, I, W, E, US*, 1977 *W, E, S, I, Arg* 1,2, *NZ* 1,2, *R*, 1978 *E, S, I, W*
Paoli, R (see Simonpaoli)
Paparemborde, R (Pau) 1975 *SA* 1,2, *Arg* 1,2, *R*, 1976 *S, I, W, E, US, A* 1,2, *R*, 1977 *W, E, S, I, Arg* 1, *NZ* 1,2, 1978 *E, S, I, W, R*, 1979 *I, W, E, S, NZ* 1,2, *R*, 1980 *W, E, S, SA, R*, 1981 *S, I, W, E, A* 1,2, *R, NZ* 1,2, 1982 *W, I, R, Arg* 1,2 1983 *E, S, I, W*
Pardo, L (Hendaye) 1924 *I, E*
Pardo, L (Bayonne) 1980 *SA, R*, 1981 *S, I, W, E, A* 1, 1982 *W, E, S*, 1983 *A* 1(R), 1985 *S, I, Arg* 2
Pargade, J-H (Lyon U) 1953 *It*
Paries, L (Biarritz O) 1968 *SA* 2, *R*, 1970 *S, I, W*, 1975 *E, S, I*
Pascalin, P (Mont-de-Marsan) 1950 *I, E, W*, 1951 *S, I, E, W*
Pascarel, J-R (TOEC) 1912 *W, E*, 1913 *S, SA, E, I*
Pascot, J (Perpignan) 1922 *S, E, I*, 1923 *S*, 1926 *I*, 1927 *G* 2
Paul, R (Montferrand) 1940 *B*
Pauthe, G (Graulhet) 1956 *E*
Pebeyre, E-J (Fumel, Brive) 1945 *W*, 1946 *I, K, W*, 1947 *S, I, W, E*
Pebeyre, M (Vichy, Montferrand) 1970 *E, R*, 1971 *I, SA* 1,2, *A* 1, 1973 *W*
Pecune, J (Tarbes) 1974 *W, E, S*, 1975 *Arg* 1,2, *R*, 1976 *I, W, E, US*
Pedeutour, P (Begles) 1980 *I*
Pellissier, L (RCF) 1928 *A, I, E, G, W*
Pelous, F (Dax, Toulouse) 1995 *R* 2, *Arg, NZ* 1,2, 1996 *E, S, I, R* (R), *Arg* 1,2, *W* 2, *SA* 1,2, 1997 *I, W, E, S, It* 1, *R* 1, *A* 1,2, *It* 2, *R* 2, *Arg, SA* 1,2(R), 1998 *E, S, I, W, Arg* 1,2, *Fj, Arg* 3, *A*, 1999 *I, W* 1, *E, R* (R), *WS, Tg* (R), *NZ* 1, *W* 2, [*C, Nm, Fj, NZ* 2, *A*], 2000 *W, E, S, I, It, A, NZ* 1,2, 2001 *S, I, It, W, E*, 2002 *It* (R), *W* (R), *E* (R), *S, I, Arg, A* 1,2, *SA, NZ, C*, 2003 *E* 1, *S, I, It, W, R, E* 2,3(R)
Penaud, A (Brive, Toulouse) 1992 *W, E, S, I, R, Arg* 1,2, *SA* 1,2, *Arg*, 1993 *R* 1, *SA* 1,2, *R* 2, *A* 1,2, 1994 *I, W, E*, 1995 *NZ* 1,2, 1996 *S, R, Arg* 1,2, *W* 2, 1997 *I, E, R* 1, *A* 2, 2000 *W* (R), *It*
Périé, M (Toulon) 1996 *E, S, I* (R)
Peron, P (RCF) 1975 *SA* 1,2
Perrier, P (Bayonne) 1982 *W, E, S, I* (R)
Pesteil, J-P (Béziers) 1975 *SA* 1, 1976 *A* 2, *R*
Petit, C (Lorrain) 1931 *W*
Peyrelade, H (Tarbes) 1940 *B*
Peyroutou, G (Périgueux) 1911 *S, E*
Phliponeau, J-F (Montferrand) 1973 *W, I*
Piazza, A (Montauban) 1968 *NZ* 1, *A*
Picard, T (Montferrand) 1985 *Arg* 2, 1986 *R* 1(R), *Arg* 2
Pierrot, G (Pau) 1914 *I, W, E*
Pilon, J (Périgueux) 1949 *E*, 1950 *E*
Piqué, J (Pau) 1961 *NZ* 2,3, *A*, 1962 *S, It*, 1964 *NZ, E, W, It, I, SA, Fj, R*, 1965 *S, I, E, W, It*
Piquemal, M (Tarbes) 1927 *I, S*, 1929 *I, G*, 1930 *S, I, E, G, W*
Piquiral, E (RCF) 1924 *S, I, E, W, R, US*, 1925 *E*, 1926 *S, I, E, W, M*, 1927 *I, S, W, E, G* 1,2, 1928 *E*
Piteu, R (Pau) 1921 *S, W, E, I*, 1922 *S, E, W, I*, 1923 *E*, 1924 *E*, 1925 *I, NZ, W, E*, 1926 *E*
Plantefol, A (RCF) 1967 *SA* 2,3,4, *NZ, R*, 1968 *E, W, Cz, NZ* 2, 1969 *E, W*
Plantey, S (RCF) 1961 *A*, 1962 *It*
Podevin, G (SF) 1913 *W, I*
Poeydebasque, F (Bayonne) 1914 *I, W*
Poirier, A (SCUF) 1907 *E*
Poitrenaud, C (Toulouse) 2001 *SA* 3, *A, Fj*, 2003 *E* 1, *S, I, It, W, Arg* 1, *NZ, E* 3
Pomathios, M (Agen, Lyon U, Bourg) 1948 *I, A, S, W, E*, 1949 *S, I, E, W, Arg* 1,2, 1950 *S, I, W*, 1951 *S, I, E, W*, 1952 *W, E*, 1953 *S, I, W*, 1954 *S*
Pons, P (Toulouse) 1920 *S, E, W*, 1921 *S, W*, 1922 *S*
Porcu, C (Agen) 2002 *Arg* (R), *A* 1,2(R)
Porra, M (Lyon) 1931 *I*
Porthault, A (RCF) 1951 *S, E, W*, 1952 *I*, 1953 *S, I, It*
Portolan, C (Toulouse) 1986 *A*, 1989 *I, E*
Potel, A (Begles) 1932 *G*
Poux, J-B (Narbonne) 2001 *Fj* (R), 2002 *S, I* (R), *Arg, A* 1(R),2(R), 2003 *E* 3
Prat, J (Lourdes) 1945 *B* 1,2, *W*, 1946 *B, I, K, W*, 1947 *S, I, W, E*, 1948 *I, A, S, W, E*, 1949 *S, I, E, W, Arg* 1,2, 1950 *S, I, E, W*, 1951 *S, E, W*, 1952 *S, I, SA, W, E, It*, 1953 *S, I, E, W, It*, 1954 *S, I, NZ, W, E, It*, 1955 *S, I, E, W, It*
Prat, M (Lourdes) 1951 *I*, 1952 *S, I, SA, W, E*, 1953 *S, I, E*, 1954 *I, NZ, W, E, It*, 1955 *S, I, E, W, It*, 1956 *I, W, It, Cz*, 1957 *S, I, W, It, R* 1, 1958 *A, W, I*
Prevost, A (Albi) 1926 *M*, 1927 *I, S, W*
Prin-Clary, J (Cavaillon, Brive) 1945 *B* 1,2, *W*, 1946 *B, I, K, W*, 1947 *S, I, W*
Privat, T (Béziers) 2001 *SA* 3, *A, Fj*, 2002 *It, W, S* (R), *SA* (R)
Puech, L (Toulouse) 1920 *S, E, I*, 1921 *E, I*
Puget, M (Toulouse) 1961 *It*, 1966 *S, I, It*, 1967 *SA* 1,3,4, *NZ*, 1968 *Cz, NZ* 1,2, *SA* 1,2, *R*, 1969 *E, R*, 1970 *W*
Puig, A (Perpignan) 1926 *S, E*
Pujol, A (SOE Toulouse) 1906 *NZ*
Pujolle, M (Nice) 1989 *B, A* 1, 1990 *S, I, R, A* 1,2, *NZ* 2

Quaglio, A (Mazamet) 1957 *R* 2, 1958 *S, E, A, W, I, SA* 1,2, 1959 *S, E, It, W, I*
Quilis, A (Narbonne) 1967 *SA* 1,4, *NZ*, 1970 *R*, 1971 *I*

Ramis, R (Perpignan) 1922 *E, I*, 1923 *W*
Rancoule, H (Lourdes, Toulon, Tarbes) 1955 *E, W, It*, 1958 *A, W, It, I, SA* 1, 1959 *S, It, W*, 1960 *I, It, R, Arg* 1,2, 1961 *SA, E, W, It, NZ* 1,2, 1962 *S, E, W, I, It*
Rapin, A (SBUC) 1938 *R*
Raymond, F (Toulouse) 1925 *S*, 1927 *W*, 1928 *I*
Raynal, F (Perpignan) 1935 *G*, 1936 *G* 1,2, 1937 *G, It*
Raynaud, F (Carcassonne) 1933 *G*
Raynaud, M (Narbonne) 1999 *W* 1, *E* (R)
Razat, J-P (Agen) 1962 *R*, 1963 *S, I, R*
Rebujent, R (RCF) 1963 *E*
Revailler, D (Graulhet) 1981 *S, I, W, E, A* 1,2, *R, NZ* 1,2, 1982 *W, S, I, R, Arg* 1
Revillon, J (RCF) 1926 *I, E*, 1927 *S*
Ribère, E (Perpignan, Quillan) 1924 *I*, 1925, *I, NZ, S*, 1926 *S, I, W, M*, 1927 *I, S, W, E, G* 1,2, 1928 *S, A, I, E, G, W*, 1929 *I, E, G*, 1930 *S, I, E, W*, 1931 *I, S, W, E, G*, 1932 *G*, 1933 *G*
Rives, J-P (Toulouse, RCF) 1975 *E, S, I, Arg* 1,2, *R*, 1976 *S, I, W, E, US, A* 1,2, *R*, 1977 *W, E, S, I, Arg* 1,2, *R*, 1978 *E, S, I, W, R*, 1979 *I, W, E, S, NZ* 1,2, *R*, 1980 *W, E, S, I, SA*, 1981 *S, I, W, E, A* 2, 1982 *W, E, S, I, R*, 1983 *E, S, I, W, A* 1,2, *R*, 1984 *I, W, E, S*
Rochon, A (Montferrand) 1936 *G* 1
Rodrigo, M (Mauléon) 1931 *I, W*
Rodriguez, L (Mont-de-Marsan, Montferrand, Dax) 1981 *A* 1,2, *R, NZ* 1,2, 1982 *W, E, S, I, R*, 1983 *E, S*, 1984 *I, NZ* 1,2,

R, 1985 *E, S, I, W*, 1986 *Arg* 1, *A, R* 2, *NZ* 2,3, 1987 *W, E, S, I*, [*S, Z, Fj, A, NZ*], *R*, 1988 *E, S, I, W, Arg* 1,2,3,4, *R*, 1989 *I, E, S, NZ* 1,2, *B, A* 1, 1990 *W, E, S, I, NZ* 1
Rogé, L (Béziers) 1952 *It*, 1953 *E, W, It*, 1954 *S, Arg* 1,2, 1955 *S, I*, 1956 *W, It, E*, 1957 *S*, 1960 *S, E*
Rollet, J (Bayonne) 1960 *Arg* 3, 1961 *NZ* 3, *A*, 1962 *It*, 1963 *I*
Romero, H (Montauban) 1962 *S, E, W, I, It, R*, 1963 *E*
Romeu, J-P (Montferrand) 1972 *R*, 1973 *S, NZ, E, W, I, R*, 1974 *W, E, S, Arg* 1,2, *R, SA* 1,2(R), 1975 *W, SA* 2, *Arg* 1,2, *R*, 1976 *S, I, W, E, US*, 1977 *W, E, S, I, Arg* 1,2, *NZ* 1,2, *R*
Roques, A (Cahors) 1958 *A, W, It, I, SA* 1,2, 1959 *S, E, W, I*, 1960 *S, E, W, I, It, Arg* 1,2,3, 1961 *S, SA, E, W, It, I*, 1962 *S, E, W, I, It*, 1963 *S*
Roques, J-C (Brive) 1966 *S, I, It, R*
Rossignol, J-C (Brive) 1972 *A* 2
Rouan, J (Narbonne) 1953 *S, I*
Roucaries, G (Perpignan) 1956 *S*
Rouffia, L (Narbonne) 1945 *B* 2, *W*, 1946 *W*, 1948 *I*
Rougerie, A (Montferrand) 2001 *SA* 3, *A, Fj* (R), 2002 *It, W, E, S, I, Arg, A* 1,2, 2003 *E* 1, *S, I, It, W, Arg* 1,2, *NZ, R, E* 2,3(R)
Rougerie, J (Montferrand) 1973 *J*
Rougé-Thomas, P (Toulouse) 1989 *NZ* 1,2
Roujas, F (Tarbes) 1910 *I*
Roumat, O (Dax) 1989 *NZ* 2(R), *B*, 1990 *W, E, S, I, R, A* 1,2,3, *NZ* 1,2, 1991 *S, I, W* 1, *E, R, US* 1, *W* 2, [*R, Fj, C, E*], 1992 *W* (R), *E* (R), *S, I, SA* 1,2, *Arg*, 1993 *E, S, I, W, R* 1, *SA* 1,2, *R* 2, *A* 1,2, 1994 *I, W, E, C* 1, *NZ* 1,2, *C* 2, 1995 *W, E, S*, [*Iv, S, I, SA, E*], 1996 *E, S, I, W* 1, *Arg* 1,2
Rousie, M (Villeneuve) 1931 *S, G*, 1932 *G*, 1933 *G*
Rousset, G (Béziers) 1975 *SA* 1, 1976 *US*
Rué, J-B (Agen) 2002 *SA* (R), *C* (R), 2003 *E* 1(R), *S* (R), *It* (R), *W* (R), *Arg* 1,2(R)
Ruiz, A (Tarbes) 1968 *SA* 2, *R*
Rupert, J-J (Tyrosse) 1963 *R*, 1964 *S, Fj*, 1965 *E, W, It*, 1966 *S, I, E, W, It*, 1967 *It, R*, 1968 *S*

Sadourny, J-L (Colomiers) 1991 *W* 2(R), [*C* (R)], 1992 *E* (R), *S, I, Arg* 1(R),2, *SA* 1,2, 1993 *R* 1, *SA* 1,2, *R* 2, *A* 1,2, 1994 *I, W, E, S, C* 1, *NZ* 1,2, *C* 2, 1995 *W, E, S, I, R* 1, [*Tg, S, I, SA, E*], *It, R* 2, *Arg, NZ* 1,2, 1996 *E, S, I, W* 1, *Arg* 1,2, *W* 2, *SA* 1,2, 1997 *I, W, E, S, It* 1, *R* 1, *A* 1,2, *It* 2, *R* 2, *Arg, SA* 1,2, 1998 *E, S, I, W*, 1999 *R, Tg, NZ* 1(R), 2000 *NZ* 2, 2001 *It, W, E*
Sagot, P (SF) 1906 *NZ*, 1908 *E*, 1909 *W*
Sahuc, A (Métro) 1945 *B* 1,2
Sahuc, F (Toulouse) 1936 *G* 2
Saint-André, P (Montferrand, Gloucester) 1990 *R, A* 3, *NZ* 1,2, 1991 *I* (R), *W* 1, *E, US* 1,2, *W* 2, [*R, Fj, C, E*], 1992 *W, E, S, I, R, Arg* 1,2, *SA* 1,2, 1993 *E, S, I, W, SA* 1,2, *A* 1,2, 1994 *I, W, E, S, C* 1, *NZ* 1,2, *C* 2, 1995 *W, E, S, I, R* 1, [*Tg, Iv, S, I, SA, E*], *It, R* 2, *Arg, NZ* 1,2, 1996 *E, S, I, W* 1, *R, Arg* 1,2, *W* 2, 1997 *It* 1,2, *R* 2, *Arg, SA* 1,2
Saisset, O (Béziers) 1971 *R*, 1972 *S, I* 1, *A* 1,2, 1973 *S, NZ, E, W, I, J, R*, 1974 *I, Arg* 2, *SA* 1,2, 1975 *W*
Salas, P (Narbonne) 1979 *NZ* 1,2, *R*, 1980 *W, E*, 1981 *A* 1, 1982 *Arg* 2
Salinié, R (Perpignan) 1923 *E*
Sallefranque, M (Dax) 1981 *A* 2, 1982 *W, E, S*
Salut, J (TOEC) 1966 *R*, 1967 *S*, 1968 *I, E, Cz, NZ* 1, 1969 *I*
Samatan, R (Agen) 1930 *S, I, E, G, W*, 1931 *I, S, W, E, G*
Sanac, A (Perpignan) 1952 *It*, 1953 *S, I*, 1954 *E*, 1956 *Cz*, 1957 *S, I, E, W, It*
Sangalli, F (Narbonne) 1975 *I, SA* 1,2, 1976 *S, A* 1,2, *R*, 1977 *W, E, S, I, Arg* 1,2, *NZ* 1,2
Sanz, H (Narbonne) 1988 *Arg* 3,4, *R*, 1989 *A* 2, 1990 *S, I, R, A* 1,2, *NZ* 2, 1991 *W* 2
Sappa, M (Nice) 1973 *J, R*, 1977 *R*
Sarrade, R (Pau) 1929 *I*
Sarraméa, O (Castres) 1999 *R, WS* (R), *Tg, NZ* 1
Saux, J-P (Pau) 1960 *W, It, Arg* 1,2, 1961 *SA, E, W, It, I, NZ* 1,2,3, *A*, 1962 *S, E, W, I, It*, 1963 *S, I, E, It*
Savitsky, M (La Voulte) 1969 *R*
Savy, M (Montferrand) 1931 *I, S, W, E*, 1936 *G* 1
Sayrou, J (Perpignan) 1926 *W, M*, 1928 *E, G, W*, 1929 *S, W, E, G*
Scohy, R (BEC) 1931 *S, W, E, G*
Sébedio, J (Tarbes) 1913 *S, E*, 1914 *I*, 1920 *S, I, US*, 1922 *S, E*, 1923 *S*
Seguier, N (Béziers) 1973 *J, R*
Seigne, L (Agen, Merignac) 1989 *B, A* 1, 1990 *NZ* 1, 1993 *E, S, I, W, R* 1, *A* 1,2, 1994 *S, C* 1, 1995 *E* (R), *S*
Sella, P (Agen) 1982 *R, Arg* 1,2, 1983 *E, S, I, W, A* 1,2, *R*, 1984 *I, W, E, S, NZ* 1,2, *R*, 1985 *E, S, I, W, Arg* 1,2, 1986 *S, I, W, E, R* 1, *Arg* 1,2, *A, NZ* 1, *R* 2, *NZ* 2,3, 1987 *W, E, S, I*, [*S, R, Z* (R), *Fj, A, NZ*], 1988 *E, S, I, W, Arg* 1,2,3,4, *R*, 1989 *I, W, E, S, NZ* 1,2, *B, A* 1,2, 1990 *W, E, S, I, A* 1,2,3, 1991 *W* 1, *E, R, US* 1,2, *W* 2, [*Fj, C, E*], 1992 *W, E, S, I, Arg*, 1993 *E, S, I, W, R* 1, *SA* 1,2, *R* 2, *A* 1,2, 1994 *I, W, E, S, C* 1, *NZ* 1,2, *C* 2, 1995 *W, E, S, I*, [*Tg, S, I, SA, E*]
Semmartin, J (SCUF) 1913 *W, I*
Senal, G (Béziers) 1974 *Arg* 1,2, *R, SA* 1,2, 1975 *W*
Sentilles, J (Tarbes) 1912 *W, E*, 1913 *S, SA*
Serin, L (Béziers) 1928 *E*, 1929 *W, E, G*, 1930 *S, I, E, G, W*, 1931 *I, W, E*
Serre, P (Perpignan) 1920 *S, E*
Serrière, P (RCF) 1986 *A*, 1987 *R*, 1988 *E*
Servole, L (Toulon) 1931 *I, S, W, E, G*, 1934 *G*, 1935 *G*
Sicart, N (Perpignan) 1922 *I*
Sillières, J (Tarbes) 1968 *R*, 1970 *S, I*, 1971 *S, I, E*, 1972 *E, W*
Siman, M (Montferrand) 1948 *E*, 1949 *S*, 1950 *S, I, E, W*
Simon, S (Bègles) 1991 *R, US* 1
Simonpaoli, R (SF) 1911 *I*, 1912 *I, S*
Sitjar, M (Agen) 1964 *W, It, I, R*, 1965 *It, R*, 1967 *A, E, It, W, I, SA* 1,2
Skrela, D (Colomiers) 2001 *NZ*
Skrela, J-C (Toulouse) 1971 *SA* 2, *A* 1,2, 1972 *I* 1(R), *E, W, I* 2, *A* 1, 1973 *W, J, R*, 1974 *W, E, S, Arg* 1, *R*, 1975 *W* (R), *E, S, I, SA* 1,2, *Arg* 1,2, *R*, 1976 *S, I, W, E, US, A* 1,2, *R*, 1977 *W, E, S, I, Arg* 1,2, *NZ* 1,2, *R*, 1978 *E, S, I, W*
Soler, M (Quillan) 1929 *G*
Soro, R (Lourdes, Romans) 1945 *B* 1,2, *W*, 1946 *B, I, K*, 1947 *S, I, W, E*, 1948 *I, A, S, W, E*, 1949 *S, I, E, W, Arg* 1,2
Sorondo, L-M (Montauban) 1946 *K*, 1947 *S, I, W, E*, 1948 *I*
Soulette, C (Béziers, Toulouse) 1997 *R* 2, 1998 *S* (R), *I* (R), *W* (R), *Arg* 1,2, *Fj*, 1999 *W* 2(R), [*C* (R), *Nm* (R), *Arg, NZ* 2, *A*]
Soulié, E (CASG) 1920 *E, I, US*, 1921 *S, E, I*, 1922 *E, W, I*
Sourgens, J (Bègles) 1926 *M*
Souverbie, J-M (Bègles) 2000 *R*
Spanghero, C (Narbonne) 1971 *E, W, SA* 1,2, *A* 1,2, *R*, 1972 *S, E, W, I* 2, *A* 1,2, 1974 *I, W, E, S, R, SA* 1, 1975 *E, S, I*
Spanghero, W (Narbonne) 1964 *SA, Fj, R*, 1965 *S, I, E, W, It, R*, 1966 *S, I, E, W, It, R*, 1967 *S, A, E, SA* 1,2,3,4, *NZ*, 1968 *S, I, E, W, NZ* 1,2,3, *A, SA* 1,2, *R*, 1969 *S, I, W*, 1970 *R*, 1971 *E, W, SA* 1, 1972 *E, I* 2, *A* 1,2, *R*, 1973 *S, NZ, E, W, I*
Stener, G (PUC) 1956 *S, I, E*, 1958 *SA* 1,2
Struxiano, P (Toulouse) 1913 *W, I*, 1920 *S, E, W, I, US*
Sutra, G (Narbonne) 1967 *SA* 2, 1969 *W*, 1970 *S, I*
Swierczinski, C (Bègles) 1969 *E*, 1977 *Arg* 2

Tabacco, P (SF) 2001 *SA* 1,2, *NZ, SA* 3, *A, Fj*, 2003 *It* (R), *W* (R), *Arg* 1, *NZ, E* 2(R),3
Tachdjian, M (RCF) 1991 *S, I, E*
Taffary, M (RCF) 1975 *W, E, S, I*
Taillantou, J (Pau) 1930 *I, G, W*
Tarricq, P (Lourdes) 1958 *A, W, It, I*
Tavernier, H (Toulouse) 1913 *I*
Techoueyres, W (SBUC) 1994 *E, S*, 1995 [*Iv*]
Terreau, M-M (Bourg) 1945 *W*, 1946 *B, I, K, W*, 1947 *S, I, W, E*, 1948 *I, A, W, E*, 1949 *S, Arg* 1,2, 1951 *S*
Theuriet, A (SCUF) 1909 *E, W*, 1910 *S*, 1911 *W*, 1913 *E*
Thevenot, M (SCUF) 1910 *W, E, I*
Thierry, R (RCF) 1920 *S, E, W, US*
Thiers, P (Montferrand) 1936 *G* 1,2, 1937 *G, It*, 1938 *G* 1,2, 1940 *B*, 1945 *B*, 1,2
Thion, J (Perpignan) 2003 *Arg* 1,2, *NZ, R, E* 2
Tignol, P (Toulouse) 1953 *S, I*
Tilh, H (Nantes) 1912 *W, E*, 1913 *S, SA, E, W*
Tolot, J-L (Agen) 1987 [*Z*]
Tordo, J-F (Nice) 1991 *US* 1(R), 1992 *W, E, S, I, R, Arg* 1,2, *SA* 1, *Arg*, 1993 *E, S, I, W, R* 1
Torossian, F (Pau) 1997 *R* 1
Torreilles, S (Perpignan) 1956 *S*
Tournaire, F (Narbonne, Toulouse) 1995 *It*, 1996 *I, W* 1, *R, Arg* 1,2(R), *W* 2, *SA* 1,2, 1997 *I, E, S, It* 1, *R* 1, *A* 1,2, *It* 2, *R* 2, *Arg, SA* 1,2, 1998 *E, S, I, W, Arg* 1,2, *Fj, Arg* 3, *A*, 1999 *I, W* 1, *E, S, R* (R), *WS, NZ* 1, [*C, Nm, Fj, Arg, NZ* 2, *A*], 2000 *W, E, S, I, It, A* (R)
Tourte, R (St Girons) 1940 *B*
Traille, D (Pau) 2001 *SA* 3, *A, Fj*, 2002 *It, W, E, S, I, Arg, A* 1,2, *SA, NZ, C*, 2003 *E* 1, *S, I, It, W, Arg*, 1,2, *NZ, R, E* 2
Trillo, J (Bègles) 1967 *SA* 3,4, *NZ, R*, 1968 *S, I, NZ* 1,2,3, *A*, 1969 *I, E, W, R*, 1970 *E, R*, 1971 *S, I, SA* 1,2, *A* 1,2, 1972 *S, A* 1,2, *R*, 1973 *S, E*

Triviaux, R (Cognac) 1931 *E, G*
Tucco-Chala, M (PUC) 1940 *B*

Ugartemendia, J-L (St Jean-de-Luz) 1975 *S, I*

Vaills, G (Perpignan) 1928 *A*, 1929 *G*
Vallot, C (SCUF) 1912 *S*
Van Heerden, A (Tarbes) 1992 *E, S*
Vannier, M (RCF, Chalon) 1953 *W*, 1954 *S, I, Arg* 1,2, 1955 *S, I, E, W, It*, 1956 *S, I, W, It, E*, 1957 *S, I, E, W, It, R* 1,2, 1958 *S, E, A, W, It, I*, 1960 *S, E, W, I, It, R, Arg* 1,3, 1961 *SA, E, W, It, I, NZ* 1, *A*
Vaquer, F (Perpignan) 1921 *S, W*, 1922 *W*
Vaquerin, A (Béziers) 1971 *R*, 1972 *S, I* 1, *A* 1, 1973 *S*, 1974 *W, E, S, Arg* 1,2, *R, SA* 1,2, 1975 *W, E, S, I*, 1976 *US, A* 1(R),2, *R*, 1977 *Arg* 2, 1979 *W, E*, 1980 *S, I*
Vareilles, C (SF) 1907 *E*, 1908 *E, W*, 1910 *S, E*
Varenne, F (RCF) 1952 *S*
Varvier, T (RCF) 1906 *E*, 1909 *E, W*, 1911 *E, W*, 1912 *I*
Vassal, G (Carcassonne) 1938 *R, G* 2
Vaysse, J (Albi) 1924 *US*, 1926 *M*
Vellat, E (Grenoble) 1927 *I, E, G* 1,2, 1928 *A*
Venditti, D (Bourgoin, Brive) 1996 *R, SA* 1(R),2, 1997 *I, W, E, S, R* 1, *A* 1, *SA* 2, 2000 *W* (R), *E, S, It* (R)
Vergé, L (Bègles) 1993 *R* 1(R)
Verger, A (SF) 1927 *W, E, G* 1, 1928 *I, E, G, W*
Verges, S-A (SF) 1906 *NZ, E*, 1907 *E*
Vermeulen, E (Brive, Montferrand) 2001 *SA* 1(R),2(R), 2003 *NZ*
Viard, G (Narbonne) 1969 *W*, 1970 *S, R*, 1971 *S, I*
Viars, S (Brive) 1992 *W, E, I, R, Arg* 1,2, *SA* 1,2(R), *Arg*, 1993 *R* 1, 1994 *C* 1(R), *NZ* 1(t), 1995 *E* (R), [*Iv*], 1997 *R* 1(R), *A* 1(R),2
Vigerie, M (Agen) 1931 *W*
Vigier, R (Montferrand) 1956 *S, W, It, E, Cz*, 1957 *S, E, W, It, R* 1,2, 1958 *S, E, A, W, It, I, SA* 1,2, 1959 *S, E, It, W, I*
Vigneau, A (Bayonne) 1935 *G*
Vignes, C (RCF) 1957 *R* 1,2, 1958 *S, E*
Vila, E (Tarbes) 1926 *M*
Vilagra, J (Vienne) 1945 *B* 2
Villepreux, P (Toulouse) 1967 *It, I, SA* 2, *NZ*, 1968 *I, Cz, NZ* 1,2,3, *A*, 1969 *S, I, E, W, R*, 1970 *S, I, W, E, R*, 1971 *S, I, E, W, A* 1,2, *R*, 1972 *S, I* 1, *E, W, I* 2, *A* 1,2
Viviès, B (Agen) 1978 *E, S, I, W*, 1980 *SA, R*, 1981 *S, A* 1, 1983 *A* 1(R)
Volot, M (SF) 1945 *W*, 1946 *B, I, K, W*

Weller, S (Grenoble) 1989 *A* 1,2, 1990 *A* 1, *NZ* 1
Wolf, J-P (Béziers) 1980 *SA, R*, 1981 *A* 2, 1982 *E*

Yachvili, D (Biarritz) 2002 *C* (R), 2003 *S* (R), *I, It, W, R* (R), *E* 3
Yachvili, M (Tulle, Brive) 1968 *E, W, Cz, NZ* 3, *A, R*, 1969 *S, I, R*, 1971 *E, SA* 1,2 *A* 1, 1972 *R*, 1975 *SA* 2

Zago, F (Montauban) 1963 *I, E*

ITALY TEST SEASON REVIEW 2002-03

Best Ever Finish in the Six Nations Championship

Paolo Pacitti

Italian rugby is still in search of a new identity. There have been some peaks, such as the success in the Six Nations opening game against Wales, but the same problems remain. There are many directions to follow, many ways to reach the international standards that their coach John Kirwan has in mind. But on the field itself, the final result is still proving elusive.

The international season started in Valladolid where Italy hammered Spain in the first Rugby World Cup qualifying game. This was a good chance for Kirwan to find new faces in some crucial positions. Diego Dominguez wasn't in Spain. At the end of the day it was a useful opportunity to check out some options in the midfield position switching between Treviso fly-half Francesco Mazzariol and Rovigo outside-half Andrea Scanavacca.

Kirwan used Spain and Romania to test the future. But if against Spain Italy offered a sparkling performance in the attacking patterns, when they played in Parma against Romania they offered a poor defensive game. Italy actually took the risk of losing the game against a Romanian side that changed dramatically their own attacking game plan.

In the autumn Tests against Argentina in Rome and Australia in Genoa, Italy gave a poor performance not only in the attacking strategy but also in the defensive patterns. The Pumas shocked Italy with a 36-6 victory at the Flaminio Stadium. The South Americans led 15-6 at half-time thanks to first-half tries from centre José Orengo and wing Ignacio Corleto, and one conversion and one penalty by Felipe Contepomi. Italy scored two early penalties from Diego Dominguez. In the second half, flanker Rolando Martín, Leeds winger Diego Albanese and replacement loose forward Martin Durand put the final Puma flourish on the match.

Seven days later, in Genoa and without Diego Dominguez, Italy lost 34-3 to the Wallabies as they rounded off their troubled European tour.

Tries from Toutai Kefu, Stirling Mortlock and Justin Harrison, with a couple from Scott Staniforth, helped give Australia a comfortable margin of victory. Former Rotherham fly-half Ramiro Pez contributed only three points despite the high consideration in which he was held by Kirwan, who saw him as a genuine alternative to Diego Dominguez. But at the end of the day, the autumn Test ended with no tries for Italy. It was not a great return just a couple of months before the beginning of the Six Nations Championship.

Moreover, it was clear that without Dominguez there would be a different Italy. And Pez himself gave confidence to the team only in the attacking patterns. In the defence structure, his presence in the midfield forced Aaron Persico to play behind him to cover the space in the not rare eventuality of a missed tackle. This caused problems that could only be solved with either a different tactical strategy or, better, with Diego wearing the No 10 jersey from the beginning.

And then it was Six Nations time. One week before the opening game against Wales in Rome, Italy managed a practice game in Treviso against the All Stars. The opposition were a good team, very attacking oriented, coached by Craig Green (another 1987 All Black Rugby World Cup winner), with lots of talent that put the Azzurri under pressure. In the end Italy won, scoring five tries but conceding another five. What could you say seven days before the start of the competition? Some of the executive board members were not happy about John Kirwan's role. And so the Wales game became crucial to Italy's future.

Against the Dragons, Italy played a great game. Despite an injury, Dominguez recovered in time for the match. Steve Hansen was disappointed about that. And you can say the same for Welsh outside-half Stephen Jones, who left the No 10 jersey to Iestyn Harris. This gave Dominguez an easy job to control the source of Wales's attacking pattern. There were three tries each (De Carli, Phillips and first cap Festuccia for Italy) plus 15 points scored by Dominguez. It was a poor game for Wales who failed to force the Italian defence, leaving space for the Azzurri's creativity. For the Italians it was extremely easy to control the development of the Welsh attack. At the end, it was 30-22 for Italy and the flavour was the same after the glorious day when Italy won against Scotland in the very debut of the Six Nations tournament.

Against the Dragons, Italy collected the victory everyone expected in the previous two years when they earned a couple of wooden spoons. Kirwan saved his position and started to push the federation in order to confirm his contract for another season. But first it was another Six Nations match with Ireland in opposition. A different job. Much stronger than the Welsh, Eddie O'Sullivan's team hammered Italy with five tries and it was a great day for David Humphreys. Overcoming a nervous start, he kicked five out of seven attempts at goal (two penalties and three conversions), and also scored a fine try that put the Italians on their knees. He made the same impression as Gregor Townsend did on the Italian crowd the year before when Scotland were at the Flaminio Stadium.

And then England. Or better, David against Goliath. A team searching for the Grand Slam against fifteen men with nothing to lose. Despite a first half which England controlled with 33 points in 40 minutes, John Kirwan's team put the whites under pressure earning a wonderful try by Mirco Bergamasco in the second half. That game confirmed the difference between hell and heaven, but in the same way showed the ability of the Italian players to face any opponent if they had the right attitude.

The Twickenham game gave the Azzurri the strength to build with more confidence towards the next match, at home against France. Bernard Laporte landed in Rome with some injury problems. On the eve of the match Fabien Galthié pulled out, a withdrawal that strengthened Italian hopes. But on the ground the music sounded just the same. Like at Twickenham, the impressive start of the French put a stone on the match. 41-10 at halftime; 53-27 at the final whistle. A late first-half try from Ramiro Pez opened the Italian scoring, and the Azzurri had the honour to win the second half 17-12 after a further three tries from full-back Mirco Bergamasco, open-side Aaron Persico and No 8 Matthew Phillips. This was a real step ahead considering the way Italy had left the Stadio Flaminio in the previous two years.

The final game was at Murrayfield. Maybe this would be the occasion to record an historic double after the opening victory earned against Wales. The match was well played by both sides. A clear lesson in open rugby that Scotland and Italy helped with a light presence in defence and with many handling mistakes. It was a sort of an answer to the critics who want Italy out of the Championship because of the quality of their rugby. That is a harsh and unfair judgement. At the least, Italy have reached the level of other countries. And the road is still long. In McGeechan's last championship game, Scotland won 33-25. The three tries scored by Scott Palmer, Mirco Bergamasco and Ramiro Pez impressed for the quality of the attack. But Italy failed to be aggressive in defence, conceding four tries. Chris Paterson's quality kicking made up the rest of the total. The wooden spoon passed to Wales. It was handed over with great relief. The Azzurri had completed their best ever Six Nations.

The last part of the season was dedicated to New Zealand. The scheduled matches in Canada and United States were cancelled, so the federation took the opportunity of travelling to New Zealand for a two-week tour facing only provincial teams. Some players asked for a rest after the domestic season and stayed at home. John Kirwan was confirmed for another year as head coach, and Italy collected three defeats against Southland, Bay of Plenty and Waikato. They won against Taranaki and Manukau Steelers, but as in the wake of any defeat rumours about the ability of the group started to grow louder. At the end of the day the balance of the Italian season is to be considered positive. Despite the results in black and white, Kirwan gave the Azzurri new spirit. He introduced to the squad players like strong centre Andrea Masi and hooker Carlo Festuccia, who impressed in the Championship opening game against Wales. He also gave confidence to Ramiro Pez, who needs only to be more conspicuous in defence.

Italy's Test Record in 2002-2003: Played 12, won 4, lost 8

Opponents	*Date*	*Venue*	*Result*
Georgia	6th September 2003	H	Won 31-22
Ireland	30th August 2003	A	Lost 6-61
Scotland	23rd August 2003	A	Lost 15-47
Scotland	29th March 2003	A	Lost 25-33
France	23rd March 2003	H	Lost 27-53
England	9th March 2003	A	Lost 5-40
Ireland	22nd February 2003	H	Lost 13-37
Wales	15th February 2003	H	Won 30-22
Australia	23rd November 2002	H	Lost 3-34
Argentina	16th November 2002	H	Lost 6-36
Romania	28th September 2002	H	Won 25-17
Spain	21st September 2002	A	Won 50-3

ITALY INTERNATIONAL STATISTICS

(to 30 September 2003)

Match Records

MOST CONSECUTIVE TEST WINS

6 1968 Pt, G, Y, 1969 Bu, Sp, Be

MOST CONSECUTIVE TESTS WITHOUT DEFEAT

Matches	Wins	Draws	Period
6	6	0	1968-69
5	4	1	1982-83

MOST POINTS IN A MATCH

by the team

Pts	Opponents	Venue	Year
104	Czech Republic	Viadana	1994
78	Croatia	Perpignan	1993
70	Morocco	Carcassonne	1993
67	Netherlands	Huddersfield	1998
66	Fiji	Treviso	2001
64	Portugal	Lisbon	1996

by a player

Pts	Player	Opponents	Venue	Year
29	S Bettarello	Canada	Toronto	1983
29	D Dominguez	Scotland	Rome	2000
29	D Dominguez	Fiji	Treviso	2001
28	D Dominguez	Netherlands	Calvisano	1994
27	D Dominguez	Ireland	Bologna	1997
25	D Dominguez	Romania	Tarbes	1997
24	L Troiani	Spain	Parma	1994

MOST TRIES IN A MATCH

by the team

Tries	Opponents	Venue	Year
16	Czech Republic	Viadana	1994
11	Croatia	Perpignan	1993
11	Netherlands	Huddersfield	1998
10	Belgium	Paris	1937
10	Morocco	Carcassonne	1993
10	Portugal	Lisbon	1996

by a player

Tries	Player	Opponents	Venue	Year
4	R Cova	Belgium	Paris	1937
4	I Francescato	Morocco	Carcassonne	1993

MOST CONVERSIONS IN A MATCH

by the team

Cons	Opponents	Venue	Year
12	Czech Republic	Viadana	1994
10	Croatia	Perpignan	1993
10	Morocco	Carcassonne	1993
8	Spain	Parma	1994

by a player

Cons	Player	Opponents	Venue	Year
12	L Troiani	Czech Reuplic	Viadana	1994
10	L Troiani	Croazia	Perpignan	1993
10	G Filizzola	Morocco	Carcassonne	1993
8	L Troiani	Spain	Parma	1994

MOST PENALTIES IN A MATCH

by the team

Penalties	Opponents	Venue	Year
8	Romania	Catania	1994
7	Fiji	Treviso	2001
6	Scotland	Rovigo	1993
6	Argentina	Lourdes	1997
6	Ireland	Bologna	1997
6	Scotland	Treviso	1998
6	Tonga	Leicester	1999
6	Scotland	Rome	2000
6	Romania	Parma	2002

by a player

Penalties	Player	Opponents	Venue	Year
8	D Dominguez	Romania	Catania	1994
7	D Dominguez	Fiji	Treviso	2001
6	D Dominguez	Scotland	Rovigo	1993
6	D Dominguez	Argentina	Lourdes	1997
6	D Dominguez	Ireland	Bologna	1997
6	D Dominguez	Scotland	Treviso	1998
6	D Dominguez	Tonga	Leicester	1999
6	D Dominguez	Scotland	Rome	2000
6	G Peens	Romania	Parma	2002

MOST DROPPED GOALS IN A MATCH

by the team

Drops	Opponents	Venue	Year
3	Transvaal	Johannesburg	1973

3	Scotland	Rome	2000

by a player

Drops	Player	Opponents	Venue	Year
3	R Caligiuri	Tranvaal	Johannesburg	1973
3	D Dominguez	Scotland	Rome	2000

Career Records

MOST CAPPED PLAYERS

Caps	Player	Career Span
79	A Troncon	1994-2003
76	C Checchinato	1990-2003
74	D Dominguez	1991-2003
69	Massimo Cuttitta	1990-2000
64	P Vaccari	1991-2003
60	S Ghizzoni	1977-87
60	M Giovanelli	1989-2000
55	S Bettarello	1979-88
54	M Mascioletti	1977-90
54	Marcello Cuttitta	1987-99
54	F Properzi-Curti	1990-2001
53	G Pivetta	1979-93

MOST CONSECUTIVE TESTS

Tests	Player	Span
31	A Moscardi	1999-2002
29	M Bollesan	1968-72
27	Massimo Cuttitta	1991-94
25	C Orlandi	1995-98
25	A R Persico	2001-03
24	D Dominguez	1995-99
23	A Sgorlon	1995-98
23	C Stoica	1999-2001

MOST TESTS AS CAPTAIN

Tests	Captain	Span
37	M Giovanelli	1992-99
34	M Bollesan	1969-75
22	Massimo Cuttitta	1993-99
20	M Innocenti	1985-88

MOST TESTS IN INDIVIDUAL POSITIONS

Position	Player	Tests	Span
Full-back	L Troiani	41	1985-95
Wing	Marcello Cuttitta	54	1987-99
Centre	C Stoica	41	1997-2003
Fly-half	D Dominguez	68	1991-2003
Scrum-half	A Troncon	79	1994-2003
Prop	M Cuttitta	69	1990-2000
Hooker	A Moscardi	44	1993-2002
Lock	M Giacheri	47	1992-2003
Flanker	M Giovanelli	60	1989-2000
No 8	C Checchinato	42	1991-2002

Checchinato and Stoica have also been capped elsewhere

MOST POINTS IN TESTS

Points	Player	Tests	Career
983	D Dominguez	74	1991-2003
483	S Bettarello	55	1979-88
296	L Troiani	47	1985-95
133	E Ponzi	20	1973-77
110	Marc Cuttitta	54	1987-99

MOST TRIES IN TESTS

Tries	Player	Tests	Career
25	Marc Cuttitta	54	1987-99
22	P Vaccari	64	1991-2003
21	M Marchetto	43	1972-81
20	C Checchinato	75	1990-2002
17	S Ghizzoni	60	1977-87
17	M Mascioletti	54	1977-90

MOST CONVERSIONS IN TESTS

Cons	Player	Tests	Career
127	D Dominguez	74	1991-2003
58	L Troiani	47	1985-95
46	S Bettarello	55	1979-88
17	E Ponzi	20	1973-77
16	G Filizzola	12	1993-95

MOST PENALTY GOALS IN TESTS

Penalties	Player	Tests	Career
209	D Dominguez	74	1991-2003
104	S Bettarello	55	1979-88
57	L Troiani	47	1985-95
31	E Ponzi	20	1973-77

MOST DROPPED GOALS IN TESTS

Drops	Player	Tests	Career
19	D Dominguez	74	1991-2003
17	S Bettarello	55	1979-88
5	M Bonomi	34	1988-96
5	O Collodo	15	1977-87

International Championship Records

Record	*Detail*		*Set*
Most points in season	106	in five matches	2000
	106	in five matches	2001
Most tries in season	12	in five matches	2003
Highest Score	34	34-20 v Scotland	2000
Biggest win	14	34-20 v Scotland	2000
Highest score conceded	80	23-80 v England	2001
Biggest defeat	57	23-80 v England	2001
Most appearances	18	D Dallan	2000 – 2003
Most points in matches	161	D Dominguez	2000 – 2003
Most points in season	61	D Dominguez	2000
Most points in match	29	D Dominguez	v Scotland, 2000
Most tries in matches	4	C Checchinato	2000 – 2002
Most tries in season	3	C Checchinato	2001
	3	Mirco Bergamasco	2003
Most tries in match	2	A Troncon	v France, 2000
Most cons in matches	16	D Dominguez	2000 – 2003
Most cons in season	8	D Dominguez	2000
Most cons in match	4	D Dominguez	v France, 2000
Most pens in matches	35	D Dominguez	2000 – 2003
Most pens in season	13	D Dominguez	2001
Most pens in match	6	D Dominguez	v Scotland, 2000
Most drops in matches	8	D Dominguez	2000 – 2003
Most drops in season	5	D Dominguez	2000
Most drops in match	3	D Dominguez	v Scotland, 2000

Miscellaneous Records

Record	*Holder*	*Detail*
Longest Test Career	S Lanfranchi	16 seasons, 1949 to 1964

Career Records Of Italy International Players
(up to 30 September 2003)

PLAYER	*Debut*	*Caps*	*T*	*C*	*P*	*D*	*Pts*
Backs:							
J A Antoni	2001 v Nm	2	0	0	0	0	0
M Barbini	2002 v NZ	5	1	0	0	0	5
M Baroni	1999 v F	6	1	0	0	0	5
Mirco Bergamasco	2002 v F	12	3	0	0	0	15
G Canale	2003 v S	2	0	0	0	0	0
A Ceppolino	1999 v U	5	1	0	0	0	5
D Dallan	1999 v F	30	4	0	0	0	20
M Dallan	1997 v Arg	13	3	0	0	0	15
D Dominguez	1991 v F	74	9	127	209	19	983
J S Francesio	2000 v W	4	0	0	0	0	0
F Frati	2000 v C	4	0	0	0	0	0
E Galon	2001 v I	1	0	0	0	0	0
L Martin	1997 v F	38	9	0	0	0	45
A Masi	1999 v Sp	6	1	0	0	0	5
M Mazzantini	2000 v S	7	0	0	0	0	0
F Mazzariol	1995 v F	29	2	12	14	0	76

G Mazzi	1998 v H	5	1	0	0	0	5
N Mazzucato	1995 v SA	29	4	0	0	0	20
S Pace	2001 v SA	2	0	0	0	0	0
R Pedrazzi	2001 v Nm	5	0	0	0	0	0
G Peens	2002 v W	14	0	8	11	1	52
M Perziano	2000 v NZ	10	3	0	0	0	15
R Pez	2000 v Sm	16	3	13	16	1	92
C Pilat	1997 v I	7	2	0	1	0	13
W Pozzebon	2001 v I	14	3	0	0	0	15
G Preo	1999 v I	7	0	1	0	0	2
J-M Queirolo	2000 v Sm	9	0	0	0	0	0
G Raineri	1998 v H	22	2	0	1	0	13
M Ravazzolo	1993 v Cr	23	3	0	0	0	15
M Rivaro	2000 v S	4	0	0	0	0	0
F Roselli	1995 v F	16	5	0	0	0	25
D Saccá	2003 v I	1	0	0	0	0	0
A Scanavacca	1999 v U	4	0	3	3	0	15
C Stoica	1997 v I	52	10	0	0	0	50
A Troncon	1994 v Sp	79	15	0	0	0	75
P Vaccari	1991 v Nm	64	22	0	0	0	107
L Villagra	2000 v Sm	2	0	0	0	0	0
C Zanoletti	2001 v Sm	6	0	0	0	0	0
N Zisti	1999 v E	4	0	0	0	0	0
Forwards:							
A Benatti	2001 v Fj	4	1	0	0	0	5
Mauro Bergamasco	1998 v H	32	6	0	0	0	30
C Bezzi	2003 v W	6	0	0	0	0	0
M Birtig	1998 v H	2	0	0	0	0	0
M Bortolami	2001 v Nm	20	1	0	0	0	5
C Caione	1995 v R	25	3	0	0	0	15
A Castellani	1994 v Cz	20	1	0	0	0	5
M-L Castrogiovanni	2002 v NZ	11	1	0	0	0	5
C Checchinato	1990 v Sp	76	21	0	0	0	105
L Cornella	1999 v Sp	1	0	0	0	0	0
D Dal Maso	2000 v Sm	4	0	0	0	0	0
G P de Carli	1996 v W	32	5	0	0	0	25
A de Rossi	1999 v U	25	2	0	0	0	10
S Dellapè	2002 v F	11	0	0	0	0	0
G Faliva	1999 v SA	4	0	0	0	0	0
C Festuccia	2003 v W	8	1	0	0	0	5
S Garozzo	2001 v U	3	0	0	0	0	0
M Giacheri	1992 v R	48	0	0	0	0	0
A Gritti	1996 v Pt	15	0	0	0	0	0
G Lanzi	1998 v Arg	8	0	0	0	0	0
A Lo Cicero	2000 v E	26	4	0	0	0	20
R Martinez-Frugoni	2002 v NZ	9	0	0	0	0	0
L Mastrodomenico	2000 v Sm	5	0	0	0	0	0
A Moreno	1999 v Tg	4	0	0	0	0	0
A Moretti	1997 v R	12	0	0	0	0	0
A Moscardi	1993 v Pt	44	6	0	0	0	30
A Muraro	2000 v C	13	0	0	0	0	0
C Nieto	2002 v E	1	0	0	0	0	0
F Ongaro	2000 v C	12	0	0	0	0	0

S Palmer	2002 v Arg	7	2	0	0	0	10
C Paoletti	2000 v S	15	0	0	0	0	0
S Parisse	2002 v NZ	8	0	0	0	0	0
E Pavanello	2002 v R	3	0	0	0	0	0
A R Persico	2000 v S	33	2	0	0	0	10
S Perugini	2000 v I	15	0	0	0	0	0
M Phillips	2002 v F	12	2	0	0	0	10
R Piovan	1996 v Pt	4	0	0	0	0	0
F Pucciariello	1999 v Sp	8	1	0	0	0	5
R Rampazzo	1996 v W	2	0	0	0	0	0
S Saviozzi	1998 v Ru	14	2	0	0	0	10
D Sesenna	1992 v R	5	0	0	0	0	0
S Stocco	1998 v H	4	1	0	0	0	5
L Travini	1999 v SA	5	0	0	0	0	0
W Visser	1999 v I	22	1	0	0	0	5
M Zaffiri	2000 v Fj	5	0	0	0	0	0

SOUTH AFRICA TEST SEASON REVIEW 2002-2003

Springboks Struggle

Dan Retief

'With the final hooter already having sounded, full-back Werner Greeff cut in on the angle to score the try and conversion that gave the Springboks a 33-31 victory (over Australia) and, most South Africans believe, cast the die for a bright new passage in Springbok history.'

Well, how wrong can one be! The above extract is the final paragraph in the South African Test review that appeared in the 2002-2003 IRB Yearbook, but subsequent events in what for the Springboks turned out to be an *annus horriblis* render those sentiments almost laughable.

In fact, it is debatable whether in the time frame under review the Springboks might in fact not have come through the worst period in their history.

There was a particularly dismal spell in the mid-60s when South Africa lost seven Tests in a row, but a run of record defeats from November 2002 to July 2003 would certainly rival those dark days.

In 1964 the Springboks lost 8-6 to France in Springs and set in motion a disastrous run in which they dropped six more Tests in a row – to Ireland and Scotland on a hastily arranged tour in 1965 and then twice each to Australia and New Zealand when they toured down under before arresting the run with a famous 19-16 win in the mud of the old Lancaster Park in Christchurch.

But juxtapose that with what can best be described as coach Rudolf Straueli's nightmare in the year under review.

After yet again ending up as the bottom team in the 2002 Tri Nations – despite the aforementioned victory at Ellis Park – the Springboks set off on their habitual tour to the northern hemisphere to play France, Scotland and England.

With Straeuli deciding to allow some stalwarts to stay home to recover from injuries the squad was jam-packed with many new faces representing what was thought to be a bright new era for South African rugby.

The victory over the Wallabies was hailed as a watershed but the ambush that awaits touring sides in the Stade Vélodrome in Marseilles brought a thudding reality check as the Boks went down 30-10 – a record margin of victory for the French.

The coach responded by not only putting his charges through some punishing practice sessions but also by making wholesale changes for the next international against Scotland at Murrayfield.

But instead of the desired galvanizing effect Straeuli's ministrations begot the opposite outcome as the Springboks, inexperienced and struggling to come to terms with the cold and wet conditions, stumbled to a 21-6 defeat – the 15-point margin being another record as it exceeded Scotland's previous biggest win over South Africa; 6-0 in 1906!

After two matches and two record defeats the portents for the third and last match of the tour against England were not promising but not even the most pessimistic could have foreseen what turned out to be a horror story for the Springboks at Twickenham.

South Africa were already trailing 8-0 in the 23rd minute when New Zealand referee Paddy O'Brien made the crucial decision to send off (red card) Bok lock Jannes Labuschagne for a late and dangerous challenge on England's kingpin Jonny Wilkinson.

Although the official's ruling seemed harsh, O'Brien had just moments before issued a general warning to both teams to cut out the niggle and as Labuschagne trudged off it seemed he took his team's resolve and spirit with him.

England were a side challenging for the No 1 ranking and they proceeded to administer the worst beating a Springbok side has ever suffered – 53-3. The margin surpassed a 28-0 defeat by New Zealand in 1999 and represented the second time the Boks had conceded 50 points – the other being 55 against the All Blacks in Auckland in 1997.

England's seven tries equalled the record (set by the All Blacks when they scored 55 points) against South Africa and upped the ante for Rugby World Cup 2003 as the two teams are drawn in the same pool.

After the disastrous tour concerns for the standard of Springbok rugby heightened as South Africa's four teams struggled through the Super 12 tournament – the Bulls eventually finishing up as the country's best team in sixth place with the Sharks and the Cats occupying the bottom two rungs.

The problems were compounded by a ravaging run of injuries – including the coach's preferred captain Corné Krige – and Straeuli stepped in towards the end of the tournament to order rest and recuperation for players he had identified for the World Cup.

In keeping with most other countries much of the focus was on the World Cup but first the Boks had to negotiate two Tests against Scotland and one against Argentina before the Tri Nations.

Straeuli's first teams of the year predictably leant towards the Bulls but while the record defeat against Scotland was avenged with a 29-25 win in Durban and a 28-19 result in Johannesburg, the manner of the victories was everything but convincing with the Scots, who led 25-12 into the last quarter at King's Park, unlucky not to have won at least one of the Tests.

The Springbok hero was fly-half Louis Koen, replacing the injured André Pretorius and getting the nod ahead of Butch James because of the latter's questionable discipline. Koen contributed 19 out of the 29 points in Durban and 23 out of the 28 at Ellis Park.

Koen, who had done well for the Blue Bulls in the Super Twelve, would be an even bigger hero two weeks later when South Africa played Argentina in Port Elizabeth. The Springboks found themselves trailing 16-25 into the last 10 minutes before a try by Brent Russell, converted by Koen, pulled them to within two points.

It seemed the Pumas were set to score their first ever victory over the Springboks – although the South American Jaguars, Argentina in all but name and captained by Hugo Porta who scored all his side's points, had beaten South Africa 21-12 during the Apartheid years in Bloemfontein in 1982 – when a last-gasp break-out led to the Boks being awarded a penalty.

The time-keeper's hooter had gone and with literally the last kick of the match (five metres from touch on the right and 32 metres out) Koen raised the flags to give the Springboks a 26-25 victory most felt they did not deserve.

The Tri Nations was next on the agenda but with inopportune injuries continuing to militate against continuity in selection South Africa's prospects were grim as they headed for Newlands to face the Wallabies.

But, as has often been the case in South Africa, the world champions were out of sorts. The Springboks, with Sevens specialist Brent Russell (who had come on in the second minute to replace the injured full-back Jaco van der Westhuyzen) playing a starring role, eked out a 26-22 victory that was much closer than Straeuli and his fellow coaches seemed to realise.

The Wallabies scored three tries to two, but Straeuli took the opportunity to lambaste the Press for their pessimism and negativity and talk was of a new dawn for Springbok rugby.

But the euphoria lasted only a week before the Boks were literally cut to pieces by the All Blacks. The warm weather and firm, fast pitch played into the hands of the super-charged New Zealanders, fielding arguably the fastest back-line in world rugby, who ran up a record 52-16 victory that included seven tries.

Straeuli continued to ring the changes, sometimes inexplicably, but to no avail. The return Test against the Wallabies in Brisbane degenerated into a mean-spirited affair in which both Robbie Kempson (for a dangerous tackle) and Bakkies Botha (for attacking the face of a player) were cited and suspended for four and eight weeks respectively.

South Africa had never previously won at Carisbrook and, although Krigé and his men produced a performance of great spirit, that record remained intact, the All Blacks getting home 19-11.

The Springbok forwards performed admirably with Richard Bands scoring probably the greatest try by a tight-head prop in the annals of the game, but the stark reality was that they had finished bottom of the Tri Nations table for the fifth time in succession and there was no real conviction they had the material to get through a World Cup draw that required them to beat either England or New Zealand to go beyond the quarter-finals.

That the Springboks were no longer the force they once were was confirmed by their record in the period under review – two 50-pointers conceded, four record defeats against France, Scotland, England and New Zealand, and only four wins in 10 internationals. The question was: were the Boks fifth (on the world rankings) and sliding or fifth and climbing. Most believed the former.

South Africa's Test Record in 2002-2003: Played 10, won 4, lost 6

Opponents	*Date*	*Venue*	*Result*
New Zealand	9th August 2003	A	Lost 11-19
Australia	2nd August 2003	A	Lost 9-29
New Zealand	19th July 2003	H	Lost 16-52
Australia	12th July 2003	H	Won 26-22
Argentina	28th June 2003	H	Won 26-25
Scotland	14th June 2003	H	Won 28-19
Scotland	7th June 2003	H	Won 29-25
England	23rd November 2002	A	Lost 3-53
Scotland	16thNovember 2002	A	Lost 6-21
France	9th November 2002	A	Lost 10-30

SOUTH AFRICA INTERNATIONAL STATISTICS

(up to 30 September 2003)

Match Records

MOST CONSECUTIVE TEST WINS

17 1997 *A* 2, *It*, *F* 1,2, *E*, *S*, 1998 *I* 1,2, *W* 1, *E* 1, *A* 1, *NZ* 1,2, *A* 2, *W* 2, *S*, *I* 3
15 1994 *Arg* 1,2, *S*, *W* 1995 *WS*, *A*, *R*, *C*, *WS*, *F*, *NZ*, *W*, *It*, *E*, 1996 *Fj*

MOST CONSECUTIVE TESTS WITHOUT DEFEAT

Matches	Wins	Draws	Period
17	17	0	1997 to 1998
16	15	1	1994 to 1996
15	12	3	1960 to 1963

MOST POINTS IN A MATCH

by the team

Pts	Opponents	Venue	Year
101	Italy	Durban	1999
96	Wales	Pretoria	1998
74	Tonga	Cape Town	1997
74	Italy	Port Elizabeth	1999
68	Scotland	Murrayfield	1997
62	Italy	Bologna	1997
61	Australia	Pretoria	1997

by a player

Pts	Player	Opponents	Venue	Year
34	J H de Beer	England	Paris	1999
31	P C Montgomery	Wales	Pretoria	1998
29	G S du Toit	Italy	Port Elizabeth	1999
28	G K Johnson	W Samoa	Johannesburg	1995
26	J H de Beer	Australia	Pretoria	1997
26	P C Montgomery	Scotland	Murrayfield	1997
25	J T Stransky	Australia	Bloemfontein	1996
25	C S Terblanche	Italy	Durban	1999

MOST TRIES IN A MATCH

by the team

Tries	Opponents	Venue	Year
15	Wales	Pretoria	1998
15	Italy	Durban	1999
12	Tonga	Cape Town	1997
11	Italy	Port Elizabeth	1999
10	Ireland	Dublin	1912
10	Scotland	Murrayfield	1997

by a player

Tries	Player	Opponents	Venue	Year
5	C S Terblanche	Italy	Durban	1999
4	C M Williams	W Samoa	Johannesburg	1995
4	P W G Rossouw	France	Parc des Princes	1997
4	C S Terblanche	Ireland	Bloemfontein	1998

MOST CONVERSIONS IN A MATCH

by the team

Cons	Opponents	Venue	Year
13	Italy	Durban	1999
9	Scotland	Murrayfield	1997
9	Wales	Pretoria	1998
8	Italy	Port Elizabeth	1999
7	Scotland	Murrayfield	1951
7	Tonga	Cape Town	1997
7	Italy	Bologna	1997
7	France	Parc des Princes	1997
7	Italy	Genoa	2001
7	Samoa	Pretoria	2002

by a player

Cons	Player	Opponents	Venue	Year
9	P C Montgomery	Wales	Pretoria	1998
8	P C Montgomery	Scotland	Murrayfield	1997
8	G S du Toit	Italy	Port Elizabeth	1999
8	G S du Toit	Italy	Durban	1999
7	A O Geffin	Scotland	Murrayfield	1951
7	J M F Lubbe	Tonga	Cape Town	1997
7	H W Honiball	Italy	Bologna	1997
7	H W Honiball	France	Parc des Princes	1997
7	A S Pretorius	Samoa	Pretoria	2002

MOST PENALTIES IN A MATCH

by the team

Penalties	Opponents	Venue	Year
7	France	Pretoria	1975
6	Australia	Bloemfontein	1996
6	Australia	Twickenham	1999
6	England	Pretoria	2000
6	Australia	Durban	2000
6	France	Johannesburg	2001
6	Scotland	Johannesburg	2003

by a player

Penalties	Player	Opponents	Venue	Year
6	G R Bosch	France	Pretoria	1975
6	J T Stransky	Australia	Bloemfontein	1996
6	J H de Beer	Australia	Twickenham	1999
6	A J J van Straaten	England	Pretoria	2000
6	A J J van Straaten	Australia	Durban	2000
6	P C Montgomery	France	Johannesburg	2001
6	L J Koen	Scotland	Johannesburg	2003
5	A O Geffin	N Zealand	Cape Town	1949
5	R Blair	World XV	Pretoria	1977
5	H E Botha	N Zealand	Wellington	1981
5	J W Heunis	England	Port Elizabeth	1984
5	H E Botha	NZ Cavaliers	Johannesburg	1986
5	J T J van Rensburg	France	Durban	1993
5	A J Joubert	England	Pretoria	1994
5	P C Montgomery	Australia	Johannesburg	1998
5	J H de Beer	England	Paris	1999
5	A D James	France	Durban	2001
5	A J J van Straaten	Australia	Pretoria	2001
5	A J J van Straaten	New Zealand	Auckland	2001
5	L J Koen	Scotland	Durban	2003

MOST DROPPED GOALS IN A MATCH

by the team

Drops	Opponents	Venue	Year
5	England	Paris	1999
3	S America	Durban	1980
3	Ireland	Durban	1981

by a player

Drops	Player	Opponents	Venue	Year
5	J H de Beer	England	Paris	1999
3	H E Botha	S America	Durban	1980
3	H E Botha	Ireland	Durban	1981
2	B L Osler	N Zealand	Durban	1928
2	H E Botha	NZ Cavaliers	Cape Town	1986
2	J T Stransky	N Zealand	Johannesburg	1995
2	J H de Beer	N Zealand	Johannesburg	1997
2	P C Montgomery	N Zealand	Cardiff	1999

Career Records

MOST CAPPED PLAYERS

Caps	Player	Career Span
85	J H van der Westhuizen	1993 to 2003
77	M G Andrews	1994 to 2001
66	A G Venter	1996 to 2001
54	A-H le Roux	1994 to 2002
50	P C Montgomery	1997 to 2001
47	J T Small	1992 to 1997
43	J Dalton	1994 to 2002
43	P W G Rossouw	1997 to 2003
42	G H Teichmann	1995 to 1999
39	J P du Randt	1994 to 1999
39	B J Paulse	1999 to 2002
38	F C H du Preez	1961 to 1971
38	J H Ellis	1965 to 1976
38	K Otto	1995 to 2000

MOST CONSECUTIVE TESTS

Tests	Player	Span
39	G H Teichmann	1996 to 1999
26	A H Snyman	1996 to 1998
26	A N Vos	1999 to 2001
25	S H Nomis	1967 to 1972
25	A G Venter	1997 to 1999
25	A-H le Roux	1998 to 1999
24	P C Montgomery	1997 to 1999
24	P W G Rossouw	1997 to 1999

MOST TESTS AS CAPTAIN

Tests	Captain	Span
36	G H Teichmann	1996 to 1999
29	J F Pienaar	1993 to 1996
22	D J de Villiers	1965 to 1970
16	A N Vos	1999 to 2001
15	C P J Krigé	1999 to 2003
15	M du Plessis	1975 to 1980
11	J F K Marais	1971 to 1974

MOST TESTS IN INDIVIDUAL POSITIONS

Position	Player	Tests	Span
Full-back	P C Montgomery	36	1997 to 2001
Wing	J T Small	43*	1992 to 1997
	P W G Rossouw	43	1997 to 2003
Centre	J C Mulder	34	1994 to 2001
Fly-half	H E Botha	28	1980 to 1992
Scrum-half	J H van der Westhuizen	83	1993 to 2003
Prop	A-H Le Roux	52	1994 to 2002
Hooker	J Dalton	43	1994 to 2002
Lock	M G Andrews	75	1994 to 2001
Flanker	A G Venter	56	1996 to 2001
No 8	G H Teichmann	42	1995 to 1999

* *excludes an appearance as a temporary replacement*

Montgomery, Small, Van der Westhuizen, Le Roux, Andrews and Venter won caps in other positions

MOST POINTS IN TESTS

Points	Player	Tests	Career
312	H E Botha	28	1980 to 1992
261	P C Montgomery	50	1997 to 2001
240	J T Stransky	22	1993 to 1996
221	A J J van Straaten	21	1999 to 2001
181	J H de Beer	13	1997 to 1999
175	J H van der Westhuizen	85	1993 to 2003
156	H W Honiball	35	1993 to 1999
130	P J Visagie	25	1967 to 1971

MOST TRIES IN TESTS

Tries	Player	Tests	Career
35	J H van der Westhuizen	85	1993 to 2003
21	P W G Rossouw	43	1997 to 2003
20	J T Small	47	1992 to 1997
19	D M Gerber	24	1980 to 1992
19	C S Terblanche	36	1998 to 2003
17*	B J Paulse	39	1999 to 2002
15	P C Montgomery	50	1997 to 2001
14	C M Williams	27	1993 to 2000

* includes a penalty try

MOST CONVERSIONS IN TESTS

Cons	Player	Tests	Career
50	H E Botha	28	1980 to 1992
42	P C Montgomery	50	1997 to 2001
38	H W Honiball	35	1993 to 1999
33	J H de Beer	13	1997 to 1999
30	J T Stransky	22	1993 to 1996
23	A J J van Straaten	21	1999 to 2001
22	A S Pretorius	12	2002 to 2003
20	P J Visagie	25	1967 to 1971
20	G S du Toit	6	1998 to 1999

MOST PENALTY GOALS IN TESTS

Penalties	Player	Tests	Career
55	A J J van Straaten	21	1999 to 2001
50	H E Botha	28	1980 to 1992
47	J T Stransky	22	1993 to 1996
31	P C Montgomery	50	1997 to 2001
29	L J Koen	11	2000 to 2003
27	J H de Beer	13	1997 to 1999
25	H W Honiball	35	1993 to 1999
23	G R Bosch	9	1974 to 1976
19	P J Visagie	25	1967 to 1971

MOST DROPPED GOALS IN TESTS

Drops	Player	Tests	Career
18	H E Botha	28	1980 to 1992
8	J H de Beer	13	1997 to 1999
5	J D Brewis	10	1949 to 1953
5	P J Visagie	25	1967 to 1971
4	B L Osler	17	1924 to 1933

Tri Nations Records

Record	Detail		Set
Most points in season	148	in four matches	1997
Most tries in season	18	in four matches	1997
Highest Score	61	61-22 v Australia (h)	1997
Biggest win	39	61-22 v Australia (h)	1997
Highest score conceded	55	35-55 v N Zealand (a)	1997
Biggest defeat	36	16-52 v N Zealand (h)	2003
Most points in matches	94	A J J van Straaten	1999 to 2001
Most points in season	64	J H de Beer	1997
Most points in match	26	J H de Beer	v Australia (h),1997
Most tries in matches	4	J H vd Westhuizen	1996 to 2003
	4	R B Skinstad	1998 to 2002
Most tries in season	3	P C Montgomery	1997
	3	M C Joubert	2002
Most tries in match	2	P C Montgomery	v Australia (h),1997
	2	R F Fleck	v New Zealand (h) 2000
	2	W Swanepoel	v New Zealand (h) 2000
	2	M C Joubert	v Australia (a) 2002
	2	B J Paulse	v Australia (h) 2002
Most cons in matches	13	J H de Beer	1997 to 1999
Most cons in season	12	J H de Beer	1997

Most cons in match	6	J H de Beer	v Australia (h),1997
Most pens in matches	28	A J J van Straaten	1999 to 2001
Most pens in season	13	A J J van Straaten	2000
	13	A J J van Straaten	2001
Most pens in match	6	J T Stransky	v Australia (h),1996
	6	A J J van Straaten	v Australia (h),2000

Series Records

Record	*Holder*	*Detail*
Most tries	P W G Rossouw	8 in Europe, 1997
Most points	H E Botha	69 v NZ Cavaliers, 1986

Miscellaneous Records

Record	*Holder*	*Detail*
Longest Test Career	J M Powell/B H Heatlie/ D M Gerber/H E Botha	13 seasons, 1891-1903/1891-1903/ 1980-1992/1980-1992
Youngest Test Cap	A J Hartley	18 yrs 18 days in 1891
Oldest Test Cap	W H Morkel	36 yrs 258 days in 1921

Career Records Of South Africa International Players
(up to 30 September 2003)

PLAYER	*Debut*	*Caps*	*T*	*C*	*P*	*D*	*Pts*
Backs:							
D W Barry	2000 v C	19	3	0	0	0	15
G Bobo	2003 v S	4	0	0	0	0	0
J H Conradie	2002 v W	10	1	0	0	0	5
C D Davidson	2002 v W	5	2	0	0	0	10
N A de Kock	2001 v It	6	1	0	0	0	5
J de Villiers	2002 v F	1	0	0	0	0	0
G M Delport	2000 v C	14	2	0	0	0	10
R F Fleck	1999 v It	31	10	0	0	0	50
W W Greeff	2002 v Arg	9	3	4	0	1	26
T M Halstead	2001 v F	6	3	0	0	0	15
A A Jacobs	2001 v It	10	1	0	0	0	5
A D James	2001 v F	9	0	0	7	0	21
N Jordaan	2002 v E	1	0	0	0	0	0
M C Joubert	2001 v NZ	13	4	0	0	0	20
L J Koen	2000 v A	11	0	16	29	2	125
F Lombard	2002 v S	2	0	0	0	0	0
R I P Loubscher	2002 v W	2	0	0	0	0	0
G P Müller	2003 v A	2	0	0	0	0	0
B J Paulse	1999 v It	39	17*	0	0	0	85
A S Pretorius	2002 v W	12	2	22	15	1	102
P W G Rossouw	1997 v BI	43	21	0	0	0	105
R B Russell	2002 v W	12	5	0	0	0	25
A H Snyman	1996 v NZ	36	9	0	0	0	45
C S Terblanche	1998 v I	36	19	0	0	0	95
J H van der Westhuizen	1993 v Arg	85	35	0	0	0	175
J N B van der Westhuyzen	2000 v NZ	6	0	0	0	0	0
A K Willemse	2003 v S	5	1	0	0	0	5

Forwards:							
R E Bands	2003 v S	7	1	0	0	0	5
C J Bezuidenhout	2003 v NZ	1	0	0	0	0	0
C S Boome	1999 v It	17	2	0	0	0	10
J P Botha	2002 v F	6	0	0	0	0	0
P D Carstens	2002 v S	2	0	0	0	0	0
D Coetzee	2002 v Sm	8	1	0	0	0	5
G Cronjé	2003 v NZ	1	0	0	0	0	0
J Dalton	1994 v Arg	43	5	0	0	0	25
Q Davids	2002 v W	4	0	0	0	0	0
H J Gerber	2003 v S	2	0	0	0	0	0
R B Kempson	1998 v I	37	1	0	0	0	5
C P J Krige	1999 v It	36	2	0	0	0	10
J J Labuschagne	2000 v NZ	11	0	0	0	0	0
V Matfield	2001 v It	20	4	0	0	0	20
W Meyer	1997 v S	26	1	0	0	0	5
W G Roux	2002 v F	3	0	0	0	0	0
D Santon	2003 v A	3	0	0	0	0	0
L D Sephaka	2001 v US	13	0	0	0	0	0
R B Skinstad	1997 v E	34	10	0	0	0	50
J H Smith	2003 v S	6	0	0	0	0	0
P J Uys	2002 v S	1	0	0	0	0	0
L van Biljon	2001 v It	13	1	0	0	0	5
C J van der Linde	2002 v S	2	0	0	0	0	0
J L van Heerden	2003 v S	5	0	0	0	0	0
J C van Niekerk	2001 v NZ	19	3	0	0	0	15
A J Venter	2000 v W	16	0	0	0	0	0
I J Visagie	1999 v It	29	0	0	0	0	0
P J Wannenburg	2002 v F	7	0	0	0	0	0
M van Z Wentzel	2002 v F	2	0	0	0	0	0

* Paulse's figures include a penalty try awarded against Wales in 2002

SOUTH AFRICAN INTERNATIONAL PLAYERS

(up to 30 September 2003)

Ackermann, D S P (WP) 1955 *BI* 2,3,4, 1956 *A* 1,2, *NZ* 1,3, 1958 *F* 2
Ackermann, J N (NT, BB) 1996 *Fj, A* 1, *NZ* 1, *A* 2, 2001 *F* 2(R), *It* 1, *NZ* 1(R), *A* 1
Aitken, A D (WP) 1997 *F* 2(R), *E,* 1998 *I* 2(R), *W* 1(R), *NZ* 1,2(R), *A* 2(R)
Albertyn, P K (SWD) 1924 *BI* 1,2,3,4
Alexander, F A (GW) 1891 *BI* 1,2
Allan, J (N) 1993 *A* 1(R), *Arg* 1,2(R), 1994 *E* 1,2, *NZ* 1,2,3, 1996 *Fj, A* 1, *NZ* 1, *A* 2, *NZ* 2
Allen, P B (EP) 1960 *S*
Allport, P H (WP) 1910 *BI* 2,3
Anderson, J W (WP) 1903 *BI* 3
Anderson, J H (WP) 1896 *BI* 1,3,4
Andrew, J B (Tvl) 1896 *BI* 2
Andrews, K S (WP) 1992 *E,* 1993 *F* 1,2, *A* 1(R), 2,3, *Arg* 1(R), 2, 1994 *NZ* 3
Andrews, M G (N) 1994 *E* 2, *NZ* 1,2,3, *Arg* 1,2, *S, W,* 1995 *WS,* [*A, WS, F, NZ*], *W, It, E,* 1996 *Fj, A* 1, *NZ* 1, *A* 2, *NZ* 2,3,4,5, *Arg* 1,2, *F* 1,2, *W,* 1997 *Tg* (R), *BI* 1,2, *NZ* 1, *A* 1, *NZ* 2, *A* 2, *It, F* 1,2, *E, S,* 1998 *I* 1,2, *W* 1, *E* 1, *A* 1, *NZ* 1,2, *A* 2, *W* 2, *S, I* 3, *E* 2, 1999 *NZ* 1,2(R), *A* 2(R), [*S, U, E, A* 3, *NZ* 3], 2000 *A* 2, *NZ* 2, *A* 3, *Arg, I, W, E* 3, 2001 *F* 1,2, *It* 1, *NZ* 1, *A* 1,2, *NZ* 2, *F* 3, *E*
Antelme, M J G (Tvl) 1960 *NZ* 1,2,3,4, 1961 *F*
Apsey, J T (WP) 1933 *A* 4,5, 1938 *BI* 2
Ashley, S (WP) 1903 *BI* 2
Aston, F T D (Tvl) 1896 *BI* 1,2,3,4
Atherton, S (N) 1993 *Arg* 1,2, 1994 *E* 1,2, *NZ* 1,2,3, 1996 *NZ* 2
Aucamp, J (WT) 1924 *BI* 1,2

Baard, A P (WP) 1960 *I*
Babrow, L (WP) 1937 *A* 1,2, *NZ* 1,2,3
Badenhorst, C (OFS) 1994 *Arg* 2, 1995 *WS* (R)
Bands, R E (BB) 2003 *S* 1,2, *Arg* (R), *A* 1, *NZ* 1, *A* 2, *NZ* 2
Barnard, A S (EP) 1984 *S Am* 1,2, 1986 *Cv* 1,2
Barnard, J H (Tvl) 1965 *S, A* 1,2, *NZ* 3,4
Barnard, R W (Tvl) 1970 *NZ* 2(R)
Barnard, W H M (NT) 1949 *NZ* 4, 1951 *W*
Barry, D W (WP) 2000 *C, E* 1,2, *A* 1(R), *NZ* 1, *A* 2, 2001 *F* 1,2, *US* (R), 2002 *W* 2, *Arg, Sm, NZ* 1, *A* 1, *NZ* 2, *A* 2, 2003 *A* 1, *NZ* 1, *A* 2
Barry, J (WP) 1903 *BI* 1,2,3
Bartmann, W J (Tvl, N) 1986 *Cv* 1,2,3,4, 1992 *NZ, A, F,* 1,2
Bastard, W E (N) 1937 *A* 1, *NZ* 1,2,3, 1938 *BI* 1,3
Bates, A J (WT) 1969 *E,* 1970 *NZ* 1,2, 1972 *E*
Bayvel, P C R (Tvl) 1974 *BI* 2,4, *F* 1,2, 1975 *F* 1,2, 1976 *NZ* 1,2,3,4
Beck, J J (WP) 1981 *NZ* 2(R), 3(R), *US*
Bedford, T P (N) 1963 *A* 1,2,3,4, 1964 *W, F,* 1965 *I, A* 1,2, 1968 *BI* 1,2,3,4, *F* 1,2, 1969 *A* 1,2,3,4, *S, E,* 1970 *I, W,* 1971 *F* 1,2
Bekker, H J (WP) 1981 *NZ* 1,3
Bekker, H P J (NT) 1952 *E, F,* 1953 *A* 1,2,3,4, 1955 *BI* 2,3,4, 1956 *A* 1,2, *NZ* 1,2,3,4
Bekker, M J (NT) 1960 *S*
Bekker, R P (NT) 1953 *A* 3,4
Bekker, S (NT) 1997 *A* 2(t)
Bennett, R G (Border) 1997 *Tg* (R), *BI* 1(R), 3, *NZ* 1, *A* 1, *NZ* 2
Bergh, W F (SWD) 1931 *W, I,* 1932 *E, S,* 1933 *A* 1,2,3,4,5, 1937 *A* 1,2, *NZ* 1,2,3, 1938 *BI* 1,2,3
Bestbier, A (OFS) 1974 *F* 2(R)
Bester, J J N (WP) 1924 *BI* 2,4
Bester, J L A (WP) 1938 *BI* 2,3
Beswick, A M (Bor) 1896 *BI* 2,3,4
Bezuidenhout, C E (NT) 1962 *BI* 2,3,4
Bezuidenhout, C J (Pumas) 2003 *NZ* 2(R)
Bezuidenhout, N S E (NT) 1972 *E,* 1974 *BI* 2,3,4, *F* 1,2, 1975 *F* 1,2, 1977 *Wld*
Bierman, J N (Tvl) 1931 *I*
Bisset, W M (WP) 1891 *BI* 1,3
Blair, R (WP) 1977 *Wld*
Bobo, G (GL) 2003 *S* 2(R), *Arg, A* 1(R), *NZ* 2
Boome, C S (WP) 1999 *It* 1,2, *W, NZ* 1(R), *A* 1, *NZ* 2, *A* 2, 2000 *C, E* 1,2, 2003 *S* 1(R),2(R), *Arg* (R), *A* 1(R), *NZ* 1(R), *A* 2, *NZ* 2(R)
Bosch, G R (Tvl) 1974 *BI* 2, *F* 1,2, 1975 *F* 1,2, 1976 *NZ* 1,2,3,4
Bosman, N J S (Tvl) 1924 *BI* 2,3,4
Botha, D S (NT) 1981 *NZ* 1
Botha, H E (NT) 1980 *S Am* 1,2, *BI* 1,2,3,4, *S Am* 3,4, *F,* 1981 *I* 1,2, *NZ* 1,2,3, *US,* 1982 *S Am* 1,2, 1986 *Cv* 1,2,3,4, 1989 *Wld* 1,2, 1992 *NZ, A, F* 1,2, *E*
Botha, J A (Tvl) 1903 *BI* 3
Botha, J P (BB) 2002 *F,* 2003 *S* 1,2, *A* 1, *NZ* 1, *A* 2(R)
Botha, J P F (NT) 1962 *BI* 2,3,4
Botha, P H (Tvl) 1965 *A* 1,2
Boyes, H C (GW) 1891 *BI* 1,2
Brand, G H (WP) 1928 *NZ* 2,3, 1931 *W, I,* 1932 *E, S,* 1933 *A* 1,2,3,4,5, 1937 *A* 1,2, *NZ* 2,3, 1938 *BI* 1
Bredenkamp, M J (GW) 1896 *BI* 1,3
Breedt, J C (Tvl) 1986 *Cv* 1,2,3,4, 1989 *Wld* 1,2, 1992 *NZ, A*
Brewis, J D (NT) 1949 *NZ* 1,2,3,4, 1951 *S, I, W,* 1952 *E, F,* 1953 *A* 1
Briers, T P D (WP) 1955 *BI* 1,2,3,4, 1956 *NZ* 2,3,4
Brink D J (WP) 1906 *S, W, E*
Brink, R (WP) 1995 [*R, C*]
Britz, W K (N) 2002 *W* 1
Brooks, D (Bor) 1906 *S*
Brosnihan, W (GL, N) 1997 *A* 2, 2000 *NZ* 1(t+R), *A* 2(t+R), *NZ* 2(R), *A* 3(R), *E* 3(R)
Brown, C B (WP) 1903 *BI* 1,2,3
Brynard, G S (WP) 1965 *A* 1, *NZ* 1,2,3,4, 1968 *BI* 3,4
Buchler, J U (Tvl) 1951 *S, I, W,* 1952 *E, F,* 1953 *A* 1,2,3,4, 1956 *A* 2
Burdett, A F (WP) 1906 *S, I*
Burger, J M (WP) 1989 *Wld* 1,2
Burger, M B (NT) 1980 *BI* 2(R), *S Am* 3, 1981 *US* (R)
Burger, S W P (WP) 1984 *E* 1,2, 1986 *Cv* 1,2,3,4
Burger, W A G (Bor) 1906 *S, I, W,* 1910 *BI* 2

Carelse, G (EP) 1964 *W, F,* 1965 *I, S,* 1967 *F* 1,2,3, 1968 *F* 1,2, 1969 *A* 1,2,3,4, *S*
Carlson, R A (WP) 1972 *E*
Carolin, H W (WP) 1903 *BI* 3, 1906 *S, I*
Carstens, P D (N) 2002 *S, E*
Castens, H H (WP) 1891 *BI* 1
Chignell, T W (WP) 1891 *BI* 3
Cilliers, G D (OFS) 1963 *A* 1,3,4
Cilliers, N V (WP) 1996 *NZ* 3(t)
Claassen, J T (WT) 1955 *BI* 1,2,3,4, 1956 *A* 1,2, *NZ* 1,2,3,4, 1958 *F* 1,2, 1960 *S, NZ* 1,2,3, *W, I,* 1961 *E, S, F, I, A* 1,2, 1962 *BI* 1,2,3,4
Claassen, W (N) 1981 *I* 1,2, *NZ* 2,3, *US,* 1982 *S Am* 1,2
Clark, W H G (Tvl) 1933 *A* 3
Clarkson, W A (N) 1921 *NZ* 1,2, 1924 *BI* 1
Cloete, H A (WP) 1896 *BI* 4
Cockrell, C H (WP) 1969 *S,* 1970 *I, W*
Cockrell, R J (WP) 1974 *F* 1,2, 1975 *F* 1,2, 1976 *NZ* 1,2, 1977 *Wld,* 1981 *NZ* 1,2(R), 3, *US*
Coetzee, D (BB) 2002 *Sm,* 2003 *S* 1,2, *Arg, A* 1, *NZ* 1, *A* 2, *NZ* 2
Coetzee, J H H (WP) 1974 *BI* 1, 1975 *F* 2(R), 1976 *NZ* 1,2,3,4
Conradie, J H (WP) 2002 *W* 1,2, *Arg* (R), *Sm, NZ* 1, *A* 1, *NZ* 2(R), *A* 2(R), *S, E*
Cope, D K (Tvl) 1896 *BI* 2
Cotty, W (GW) 1896 *BI* 3
Crampton, G (GW) 1903 *BI* 2
Craven, D H (WP) 1931 *W, I,* 1932 *S,* 1933 *A* 1,2,3,4,5, 1937 *A* 1,2, *NZ* 1,2,3, 1938 *BI* 1,2,3,
Cronjé, G (BB) 2003 *NZ* 2
Cronje, P A (Tvl) 1971 *F* 1,2, *A* 1,2,3, 1974 *BI* 3,4
Crosby, J H (Tvl) 1896 *BI* 2
Crosby, N J (Tvl) 1910 *BI* 1,3
Currie, C (GW) 1903 *BI* 2

D'Alton, G (WP) 1933 *A* 1
Dalton, J (Tvl, GL, Falcons) 1994 *Arg* 1(R), 1995 [*A, C*], *W, It, E*, 1996 *NZ* 4(R),5, *Arg* 1,2, *F* 1,2, *W*, 1997 *Tg* (R), *BI* 3, *NZ* 2, *A* 2, *It, F* 1,2, *E, S*, 1998 *I* 1,2, *W* 1, *E* 1, *A* 1, *NZ* 1,2, *A* 2, *W* 2, *S, I* 3, *E* 2, 2002 *W* 1,2, *Arg, NZ* 1, *A* 1, *NZ* 2, *A* 2, *F, E*
Daneel, G M (WP) 1928 *NZ* 1,2,3,4, 1931 *W, I*, 1932 *E, S*
Daneel, H J (WP) 1906 *S, I, W, E*
Davidson, C D (N) 2002 *W* 2(R), *Arg*, 2003 *Arg, NZ* 1(R), *A* 2
Davids, Q (WP) 2002 *W* 2, *Arg* (R), *Sm* (R), 2003 *Arg*
Davison, P M (EP) 1910 *BI* 1
De Beer, J H (OFS) 1997 *BI* 3, *NZ* 1, *A* 1, *NZ* 2, *A* 2, *F* 2(R), *S*, 1999 *A* 2, [*S, Sp, U, E, A* 3]
De Bruyn, J (OFS) 1974 *BI* 3
De Jongh, H P K (WP) 1928 *NZ* 3
De Klerk, I J (Tvl) 1969 *E*, 1970 *I, W*
De Klerk, K B H (Tvl) 1974 *BI* 1,2,3(R), 1975 *F* 1,2, 1976 *NZ* 2(R), 3,4, 1980 *S Am* 1,2, *BI* 2, 1981 *I* 1,2
De Kock, A N (GW) 1891 *BI* 2
De Kock, D (Falcons) 2001 *It* 2(R), *US*
De Kock, J S (WP) 1921 *NZ* 3, 1924 *BI* 3
De Kock, N A (WP) 2001 *It* 1, 2002 *Sm* (R), *NZ* 1(R),2, *A* 2, *F*
Delport, G M (GL, Worcester) 2000 *C* (R), *E* 1(t+R), *A* 1, *NZ* 1, *A* 2, *NZ* 2, *A* 3, *Arg, I, W*, 2001 *F* 2, *It* 1, 2003 *A* 1, *NZ* 2
Delport, W H (EP) 1951 *S, I, W*, 1952 *E, F*, 1953 *A* 1,2,3,4
De Melker, S C (GW) 1903 *BI* 2, 1906 *E*
Devenish, C E (GW) 1896 *BI* 2
Devenish, G St L (Tvl) 1896 *BI* 2
Devenish, G E (Tvl) 1891 *BI* 1
De Villiers, D I (Tvl) 1910 *BI* 1,2,3
De Villiers, D J (WP, Bol) 1962 *BI* 2,3, 1965 *I, NZ* 1,3,4, 1967 *F* 1,2,3,4, 1968 *BI* 1,2,3,4, *F* 1,2, 1969 *A* 1,4, *E*, 1970 *I, W, NZ* 1,2,3,4
De Villiers, H A (WP) 1906 *S, W, E*
De Villiers, H O (WP) 1967 *F* 1,2,3,4, 1968 *F* 1,2, 1969 *A* 1,2,3,4, *S, E*, 1970 *I, W*
De Villiers, J (WP) 2002 *F*
De Villiers, P du P (WP) 1928 *NZ* 1,3,4, 1932 *E*, 1933 *A* 4, 1937 *A* 1,2, *NZ* 1
Devine, D (Tvl) 1924 *BI* 3, 1928 *NZ* 2
De Vos, D J J (WP) 1965 *S*, 1969 *A* 3, *S*
De Waal, A N (WP) 1967 *F* 1,2,3,4
De Waal, P J (WP) 1896 *BI* 4
De Wet, A E (WP) 1969 *A* 3,4, *E*
De Wet, P J (WP) 1938 *BI* 1,2,3
Dinkelmann, E E (NT) 1951 *S, I*, 1952 *E, F*, 1953 *A* 1,2
Dirksen, C W (NT) 1963 *A* 4, 1964 *W*, 1965 *I, S*, 1967 *F* 1,2,3,4, 1968 *BI* 1,2
Dobbin, F J (GW) 1903 *BI* 1,2, 1906 *S, W, E*, 1910 *BI* 1, 1912 *S, I, W*
Dobie, J A R (Tvl) 1928 *NZ* 2
Dormehl, P J (WP) 1896 *BI* 3,4
Douglass, F W (EP) 1896 *BI* 1
Drotské, A E (OFS) 1993 *Arg* 2, 1995 [*WS* (R)], 1996 *A* 1(R), 1997 *Tg, BI* 1,2,3(R), *NZ* 1, *A* 1, *NZ* 2(R), 1998 *I* 2(R), *W* 1(R), *I* 3(R), 1999 *It* 1,2, *W, NZ* 1, *A* 1, *NZ* 2, *A* 2, [*S, Sp* (R), *U, E, A* 3, *NZ* 3]
Dryburgh, R G (WP) 1955 *BI* 2,3,4, 1956 *A* 2, *NZ* 1,4, 1960 *NZ* 1,2
Duff, B R (WP) 1891 *BI* 1,2,3
Duffy, B A (Bor) 1928 *NZ* 1
Du Plessis, C J (WP) 1982 *S Am* 1,2, 1984 *E* 1,2, *S Am* 1,2, 1986 *Cv* 1,2,3,4, 1989 *Wld* 1,2
Du Plessis, D C (NT) 1977 *Wld*, 1980 *S Am* 2
Du Plessis, F (Tvl) 1949 *NZ* 1,2,3
Du Plessis, M (WP) 1971 *A* 1,2,3, 1974 *BI* 1,2, *F* 1,2, 1975 *F* 1,2, 1976 *NZ* 1,2,3,4, 1977 *Wld*, 1980 *S Am* 1,2, *BI* 1,2,3,4, *S Am* 4, *F*
Du Plessis, M J (WP) 1984 *S Am* 1,2, 1986 *Cv* 1,2,3,4, 1989 *Wld* 1,2
Du Plessis, N J (WT) 1921 *NZ* 2,3, 1924 *BI* 1,2,3
Du Plessis, P G (NT) 1972 *E*
Du Plessis, T D (NT) 1980 *S Am* 1,2
Du Plessis, W (WP) 1980 *S Am* 1,2, *BI* 1,2,3,4, *S Am* 3,4, *F*, 1981 *NZ* 1,2,3, 1982 *S Am* 1,2
Du Plooy, A J J (EP) 1955 *BI* 1
Du Preez, F C H (NT) 1961 *E, S, A* 1,2, 1962 *BI* 1,2,3,4, 1963 *A* 1, 1964 *W, F*, 1965 *A* 1,2, *NZ* 1,2,3,4, 1967 *F* 4, 1968 *BI* 1,2,3,4, *F* 1,2, 1969 *A* 1,2, *S*, 1970 *I, W, NZ* 1,2,3,4, 1971 *F* 1,2, *A* 1,2,3
Du Preez, G J D (GL) 2002 *Sm* (R), *A* 1(R)
Du Preez, J G H (WP) 1956 *NZ* 1
Du Preez, R J (N) 1992 *NZ, A*, 1993 *F* 1,2, *A* 1,2,3
Du Rand, J A (R, NT) 1949 *NZ* 2,3, 1951 *S, I, W*, 1952 *E, F*, 1953 *A* 1,2,3,4, 1955 *BI* 1,2,3,4, 1956 *A* 1,2, *NZ* 1,2,3,4
Du Randt, J P (OFS) 1994 *Arg* 1,2, *S, W*, 1995 *WS*, [*A, WS, F, NZ*], 1996 *Fj, A* 1, *NZ* 1, *A* 2, *NZ* 2,3,4, 1997 *Tg, BI* 1,2,3, *NZ* 1, *A* 1, *NZ* 2, *A* 2, *It, F* 1,2, *E, S*, 1999 *NZ* 1, *A* 1, *NZ* 2, *A* 2, [*S, Sp* (R), *U, E, A* 3, *NZ* 3]
Du Toit, A F (WP) 1928 *NZ* 3,4
Du Toit, B A (Tvl) 1938 *BI* 1,2,3
Du Toit, G S (GW) 1998 *I* 1, 1999 *It* 1,2, *W* (R), *NZ* 1,2
Du Toit, P A (NT) 1949 *NZ* 2,3,4, 1951 *S, I, W*, 1952 *E, F*
Du Toit, P G (WP) 1981 *NZ* 1, 1982 *S Am* 1,2, 1984 *E* 1,2
Du Toit, P S (WP) 1958 *F* 1,2, 1960 *NZ* 1,2,3,4, *W, I*, 1961 *E, S, F, I, A* 1,2
Duvenhage, F P (GW) 1949 *NZ* 1,3

Edwards, P (NT) 1980 *S Am* 1,2
Ellis, J H (SWA) 1965 *NZ* 1,2,3,4, 1967 *F* 1,2,3,4, 1968 *BI* 1,2,3,4, *F* 1,2, 1969 *A* 1,2,3,4, *S*, 1970 *I, W, NZ* 1,2,3,4, 1971 *F* 1,2, *A* 1,2,3, 1972 *E*, 1974 *BI* 1,2,3,4, *F* 1,2, 1976 *NZ* 1
Ellis, M C (Tvl) 1921 *NZ* 2,3, 1924 *BI* 1,2,3,4
Els, W W (OFS) 1997 *A* 2(R)
Engelbrecht, J P (WP) 1960 *S, W, I*, 1961 *E, S, F, A* 1,2, 1962 *BI* 2,3,4, 1963 *A* 2,3, 1964 *W, F*, 1965 *I, S, A* 1,2, *NZ* 1,2,3,4, 1967 *F* 1,2,3,4, 1968 *BI* 1,2, *F* 1,2, 1969 *A* 1,2
Erasmus, F S (NT, EP) 1986 *Cv* 3,4, 1989 *Wld* 2
Erasmus, J C (OFS, GL) 1997 *BI* 3, *A* 2, *It, F* 1,2, *S*, 1998 *I* 1,2, *W* 1, *E* 1, *A* 1, *NZ* 2, *A* 2, *S, W* 2, *I* 3, *E* 2, 1999 *It* 1,2, *W, A* 1, *NZ* 2, *A* 2, [*S, U, E, A* 3, *NZ* 3], 2000 *C, E* 1, *A* 1, *NZ* 1,2, *A* 3, 2001 *F* 1,2
Esterhuizen, G (GL) 2000 *NZ* 1(R),2, *A* 3, *Arg, I, W* (R), *E* 3(t)
Etlinger, T E (WP) 1896 *BI* 4

Ferreira, C (OFS) 1986 *Cv* 1,2
Ferreira, P S (WP) 1984 *S Am* 1,2
Ferris, H H (Tvl) 1903 *BI* 3
Fleck R F (WP) 1999 *It* 1,2, *NZ* 1(R), *A* 1, *NZ* 2(R), *A* 2, [*S, U, E, A* 3, *NZ* 3], 2000 *C, E* 1,2, *A* 1, *NZ* 1, *A* 2, *NZ* 2, *A* 3, *Arg, I, W, E* 3, 2001 *F* 1(R),2, *It* 1, *NZ* 1, *A* 1,2, 2002 *S, E*
Forbes, H H (Tvl) 1896 *BI* 2
Fourie, C (EP) 1974 *F* 1,2, 1975 *F* 1,2
Fourie, T T (SET) 1974 *BI* 3
Fourie, W L (SWA) 1958 *F* 1,2
Francis, J A J (Tvl) 1912 *S, I, W*, 1913 *E, F*
Frederickson, C A (Tvl) 1974 *BI* 2, 1980 *S Am* 1,2
Frew, A (Tvl) 1903 *BI* 1
Froneman, D C (OFS) 1977 *Wld*
Froneman, I L (Bor) 1933 *A* 1
Fuls, H T (Tvl, EP) 1992 *NZ* (R), 1993 *F* 1,2, *A* 1,2,3, *Arg* 1,2
Fry, S P (WP) 1951 *S, I, W*, 1952 *E, F*, 1953 *A* 1,2,3,4, 1955 *BI* 1,2,3,4
Fynn, E E (N) 2001 *F* 1, *It* 1(R)
Fyvie, W (N) 1996 *NZ* 4(t & R), 5(R), *Arg* 2(R)

Gage, J H (OFS) 1933 *A* 1
Gainsford, J L (WP) 1960 *S, NZ* 1,2,3,4, *W, I*, 1961 *E, S, F, A* 1,2, 1962 *BI* 1,2,3,4, 1963 *A* 1,2,3,4, 1964 *W, F*, 1965 *I, S, A* 1,2, *NZ* 1,2,3,4, 1967 *F* 1,2,3
Garvey, A C (N) 1996 *Arg* 1,2, *F* 1,2, *W*, 1997 *Tg, BI* 1,2,3(R), *A* 1(t), *It, F* 1,2, *E, S*, 1998 *I* 1,2, *W* 1, *E*1, *A* 1, *NZ* 1,2 *A* 2, *W* 2, *S, I* 3, *E* 2, 1999 [*Sp*]
Geel, P J (OFS) 1949 *NZ* 3
Geere, V (Tvl) 1933 *A* 1,2,3,4,5
Geffin, A O (Tvl) 1949 *NZ* 1,2,3,4, 1951 *S, I, W*
Geldenhuys, A (EP) 1992 *NZ, A, F* 1,2
Geldenhuys, S B (NT) 1981 *NZ* 2,3, *US*, 1982 *S Am* 1,2, 1989 *Wld* 1,2
Gentles, T A (WP) 1955 *BI* 1,2,4, 1956 *NZ* 2,3, 1958 *F* 2
Geraghty, E M (Bor) 1949 *NZ* 4
Gerber, D M (EP, WP) 1980 *S Am* 3,4, *F*, 1981 *I* 1,2, *NZ* 1,2,3, *US*, 1982 *S Am* 1,2, 1984 *E* 1,2, *S Am* 1,2, 1986 *Cv* 1,2,3,4, 1992 *NZ, A, F* 1,2, *E*
Gerber, H J (WP) 2003 *S* 1,2
Gerber, M C (EP) 1958 *F* 1,2, 1960 *S*
Gericke, F W (Tvl) 1960 *S*
Germishuys, J S (OFS, Tvl) 1974 *BI* 2, 1976 *NZ* 1,2,3,4, 1977 *Wld*, 1980 *S Am* 1,2, *BI* 1,2,3,4, *S Am* 3,4, *F*, 1981 *I* 1,2, *NZ* 2,3, *US*
Gibbs, B (GW) 1903 *BI* 2
Goosen, C P (OFS) 1965 *NZ* 2

Gorton, H C (Tvl) 1896 *BI* 1
Gould, R L (N) 1968 *BI* 1,2,3,4
Gray, B G (WP) 1931 *W*, 1932 *E*, *S*, 1933 *A* 5
Greeff, W W (WP) 2002 *Arg* (R), *Sm*, *NZ* 1, *A* 1, *NZ* 2, *A* 2, *F*, *S*, *E*
Greenwood, C M (WP) 1961 *I*
Greyling, P J F (OFS) 1967 *F* 1,2,3,4, 1968 *BI* 1, *F* 1,2, 1969 *A* 1,2,3,4, *S*, *E*, 1970 *I*, *W*, *NZ* 1,2,3,4, 1971 *F* 1,2, *A* 1,2,3, 1972 *E*
Grobler, C J (OFS) 1974 *BI* 4, 1975 *F* 1,2
Guthrie, F H (WP) 1891 *BI* 1,3, 1896 *BI* 1

Hahn, C H L (Tvl) 1910 *BI* 1,2,3
Hall, D B (GL) 2001 *F* 1,2, *NZ* 1, *A* 1,2, *NZ* 2, *It* 2, *E*, *US*, 2002 *Sm*, *NZ* 1,2, *A* 2
Halstead, T M (N) 2001 *F* 3, *It* 2, *E*, *US* (R), 2003 *S* 1,2
Hamilton, F (EP) 1891 *BI* 1
Harris, T A (Tvl) 1937 *NZ* 2,3, 1938 *BI* 1,2,3
Hartley, A J (WP) 1891 *BI* 3
Hattingh, H (NT) 1992 *A* (R), *F* 2(R), *E*, 1994 *Arg* 1,2
Hattingh, L B (OFS) 1933 *A* 2
Heatlie, B H (WP) 1891 *BI* 2,3, 1896 *BI* 1,4, 1903 *BI* 1,3
Hendricks, M (Bol) 1998 *I* 2(R), *W* 1(R)
Hendriks, P (Tvl) 1992 *NZ*, *A*, 1994 *S*, *W*, 1995 [*A*, *R*, *C*], 1996 *A* 1, *NZ* 1, *A* 2, *NZ* 2,3,4,5
Hepburn, T B (WP) 1896 *BI* 4
Heunis, J W (NT) 1981 *NZ* 3(R), *US*, 1982 *S Am* 1,2, 1984 *E* 1,2, *S Am* 1,2, 1986 *Cv* 1,2,3,4, 1989 *Wld* 1,2
Hill, R A (R) 1960 *W*, *I*, 1961 *I*, *A* 1,2, 1962 *BI* 4, 1963 *A* 3
Hills, W G (NT) 1992 *F* 1,2, *E*, 1993 *F* 1,2, *A* 1
Hirsch, J G (EP) 1906 *I*, 1910 *BI* 1
Hobson, T E C (WP) 1903 *BI* 3
Hoffman, R S (Bol) 1953 *A* 3
Holton, D N (EP) 1960 *S*
Honiball, H W (N) 1993 *A* 3(R), *Arg* 2, 1995 *WS* (R), 1996 *Fj*, *A* 1, *NZ* 5, *Arg* 1,2, *F* 1,2, *W*, 1997 *Tg*, *BI* 1,2,3(R), *NZ* 1(R), *A* 1(R), *NZ* 2, *A* 2, *It*, *F* 1,2, *E*, 1998 *W* 1(R), *E* 1, *A* 1, *NZ* 1,2, *A* 2, *W* 2, *S*, *I* 3, *E* 2, 1999 [*A* 3(R), *NZ* 3]
Hopwood, D J (WP) 1960 *S*, *NZ* 3,4, *W*, 1961 *E*, *S*, *F*, *I*, *A* 1,2, 1962 *BI* 1,2,3,4, 1963 *A* 1,2,4, 1964 *W*, *F*, 1965 *S*, *NZ* 3,4
Howe, B F (Bor) 1956 *NZ* 1,4
Howe-Browne, N R F G (WP) 1910 *BI* 1,2,3
Hugo, D P (WP) 1989 *Wld* 1,2
Human, D C F (WP) 2002 *W* 1,2, *Arg* (R), *Sm* (R)
Hurter, M H (NT) 1995 [*R*, *C*], *W*, 1996 *Fj*, *A* 1, *NZ* 1,2,3,4,5, 1997 *NZ* 1,2, *A* 2

Immelman, J H (WP) 1913 *F*

Jackson, D C (WP) 1906 *I*, *W*, *E*
Jackson, J S (WP) 1903 *BI* 2
Jacobs, A A (Falcons) 2001 *It* 2(R), *US*, 2002 *W* 1(R), *Arg*, *Sm* (R), *NZ* 1(t+R), *A* 1(R), *F*, *S*, *E* (R)
James, A D (N) 2001 *F* 1,2, *NZ* 1, *A* 1,2, *NZ* 2, 2002 *F* (R), *S*, *E*
Jansen, E (OFS) 1981 *NZ* 1
Jansen, J S (OFS) 1970 *NZ* 1,2,3,4, 1971 *F* 1,2, *A* 1,2,3, 1972 *E*
Jantjes, C A (GL) 2001 *It* 1, *A* 1,2, *NZ* 2, *F* 3, *It* 2, *E*, *US*
Jennings, C B (Bor) 1937 *NZ* 1
Johnson, G K (Tvl) 1993 *Arg* 2, 1994 *NZ* 3, *Arg* 1, 1995 *WS*, [*R*, *C*, *WS*]
Johnstone, P G A (WP) 1951 *S*, *I*, *W*, 1952 *E*, *F*, 1956 *A* 1, *NZ* 1,2,4
Jones, C H (Tvl) 1903 *BI* 1,2
Jones, P S T (WP) 1896 *BI* 1,3,4
Jordaan, N (BB) 2002 *E* (R)
Jordaan, R P (NT) 1949 *NZ* 1,2,3,4
Joubert, A J (OFS, N) 1989 *Wld* 1(R), 1993 *A* 3, *Arg* 1, 1994 *E* 1,2, *NZ* 1,2(R), 3, *Arg* 2, *S*, *W*, 1995 [*A*, *C*, *WS*, *F*, *NZ*], *W*, *It*, *E*, 1996 *Fj*, *A* 1, *NZ* 1,3,4,5, *Arg* 1,2, *F* 1,2, *W*, 1997 *Tg*, *BI* 1,2, *A* 2
Joubert, M C (Bol, WP) 2001 *NZ* 1, 2002 *W* 1,2, *Arg* (R), *Sm*, *NZ* 1, *A*1, *NZ* 2, *A* 2, *F* (R), 2003 *S* 2, *Arg*, *A* 1
Joubert, S J (WP) 1906 *I*, *W*, *E*
Julies, W (Bol) 1999 [*Sp*]

Kahts, W J H (NT) 1980 *BI* 1,2,3, *S Am* 3,4, *F*, 1981 *I* 1,2, *NZ* 2, 1982 *S Am* 1,2
Kaminer, J (Tvl) 1958 *F* 2
Kayser, D J (EP, N) 1999 *It* 2(R), *A* 1(R), *NZ* 2, *A* 2, [*S*, *Sp* (R), *U*, *E*, *A* 3], 2001 *It* 1(R), *NZ* 1(R), *A* 2(R), *NZ* 2(R)
Kebble, G R (N) 1993 *Arg* 1,2, 1994 *NZ* 1(R), 2
Kelly, E W (GW) 1896 *BI* 3
Kempson, R B (N, WP, Ulster) 1998 *I* 2(R), *W* 1, *E* 1, *A* 1, *NZ* 1,2 *A* 2, *W* 2, *S*, *I* 3, *E* 2, 1999 *It* 1,2, *W*, 2000 *C*, *E* 1,2, *A* 1, *NZ* 1, *A* 2,3, *Arg*, *I*, *W*, *E* 3, 2001 *F* 1,2(R), *NZ* 1, *A* 1,2, *NZ* 2, 2003 *S* 1(R),2(R), *Arg*, *A* 1(R), *NZ* 1(R), *A* 2
Kenyon, B J (Bor) 1949 *NZ* 4
Kipling, H G (GW) 1931 *W*, *I*, 1932 *E*, *S*, 1933 *A* 1,2,3,4,5
Kirkpatrick, A I (GW) 1953 *A* 2, 1956 *NZ* 2, 1958 *F* 1, 1960 *S*, *NZ* 1,2,3,4, *W*, *I*, 1961 *E*, *S*, *F*
Knight, A S (Tvl) 1912 *S*, *I*, *W*, 1913 *E*, *F*
Knoetze, F (WP) 1989 *Wld* 1,2
Koch, A C (Bol) 1949 *NZ* 2,3,4, 1951 *S*, *I*, *W*, 1952 *E*, *F*, 1953 *A* 1,2,4, 1955 *BI* 1,2,3,4, 1956 *A* 1, *NZ* 2,3, 1958 *F* 1,2, 1960 *NZ* 1,2
Koch, H V (WP) 1949 *NZ* 1,2,3,4
Koen, L J (GL, BB) 2000 *A* 1, 2001 *It* 2, *E*, *US*, 2003 *S* 1,2, *Arg*, *A* 1, *NZ* 1, *A* 2, *NZ* 2
Kotze, G J M (WP) 1967 *F* 1,2,3,4
Krantz, E F W (OFS) 1976 *NZ* 1, 1981 *I* 1,
Krige, C P J (WP) 1999 *It* 2, *W*, *NZ* 1, 2000 *C* (R), *E* 1(R),2, *A* 1(R), *NZ* 1, *A* 2, *NZ* 2, *A* 3, *Arg*, *I*, *W*, *E* 3, 2001 *F* 1,2, *It* 1(R), *A* 1(t+R), *It* 2(R), *E* (R), 2002 *W* 2, *Arg*, *Sm*, *NZ* 1, *A* 1, *NZ* 2, *A* 2, *F*, *S*, *E*, 2003 *Arg*, *A* 1, *NZ* 1, *A* 2, *NZ* 2
Krige, J D (WP) 1903 *BI* 1,3, 1906 *S*, *I*, *W*
Kritzinger, J L (Tvl) 1974 *BI* 3,4, *F* 1,2, 1975 *F* 1,2, 1976 *NZ* 4
Kroon, C M (EP) 1955 *BI* 1
Kruger, P E (Tvl) 1986 *Cv* 3,4
Kruger, R J (NT, BB) 1993 *Arg* 1,2, 1994 *S*, *W*, 1995 *WS*, [*A*, *R*, *WS*, *F*, *NZ*], *W*, *It*, *E*, 1996 *Fj*, *A* 1, *NZ* 1, *A* 2, *NZ* 2,3,4,5, *Arg* 1,2, *F* 1,2, *W*, 1997 *Tg*, *BI* 1,2, *NZ* 1, *A* 1, *NZ* 2, 1999 *NZ* 2, *A* 2(R), [*Sp*, *NZ* 3(R)]
Kruger, T L (Tvl) 1921 *NZ* 1,2, 1924 *BI* 1,2,3,4, 1928 *NZ* 1,2
Kuhn, S P (Tvl) 1960 *NZ* 3,4, *W*, *I*, 1961 *E*, *S*, *F*, *I*, *A* 1,2, 1962 *BI* 1,2,3,4, 1963 *A* 1,2,3, 1965 *I*, *S*

Labuschagne, J J (GL) 2000 *NZ* 1(R), 2002 *W* 1,2, *Arg*, *NZ* 1, *A* 1, *NZ* 2, *A*2, *F*, *S*, *E*
La Grange, J B (WP) 1924 *BI* 3,4
Larard, A (Tvl) 1896 *BI* 2,4
Lategan, M T (WP) 1949 *NZ* 1,2,3,4, 1951 *S*, *I*, *W*, 1952 *E*, *F*, 1953 *A* 1,2
Laubscher, T G (WP) 1994 *Arg* 1,2, *S*, *W*, 1995 *It*, *E*
Lawless, M J (WP) 1964 *F*, 1969 *E* (R), 1970 *I*, *W*
Ledger, S H (GW) 1912 *S*, *I*, 1913 *E*, *F*
Leonard, A (WP, SWD) 1999 *A* 1, [*Sp*]
Le Roux, A H (OFS, N) 1994 *E* 1, 1998 *I* 1,2, *W* 1(R), *E* 1(R), *A* 1(R), *NZ* 1(R),2(R), *A* 2(R), *W* 2(R), *S* (R), *I* 3(R), *E* 2(t+R), 1999 *It* 1(R),2(R), *W* (R), *NZ* 1(R), *A* 1(R), *NZ* 2(R), *A* 2(R), [*S*(R), *Sp*, *U* (R), *E* (R), *A* 3(R), *NZ* 3(R)], 2000 *E* 1(t+R),2(R), *A* 1(R),2(R), *NZ* 2, *A* 3(R), *Arg* (R), *I* (t), *W* (R), *E* 3(R), 2001 *F* 1(R),2, *It* 1, *NZ* 1(R), *A* 1(R),2(R), *NZ* 2(R), *F* 3, *It* 2, *E*, *US* (R), 2002 *W* 1(R),2(R), *Arg*, *NZ* 1(R), *A* 1(R), *NZ* 2(R), *A* 2(R)
Le Roux, H P (Tvl) 1993 *F* 1,2, 1994 *E* 1,2, *NZ* 1,2,3, *Arg* 2, *S*, *W*, 1995 *WS* [*A*, *R*, *C* (R), *WS*, *F*, *NZ*], *W*, *It*, *E*, 1996 *Fj*, *NZ* 2, *Arg* 1,2, *F* 1,2, *W*
Le Roux, J H S (Tvl) 1994 *E* 2, *NZ* 1,2
Le Roux, M (OFS) 1980 *BI* 1,2,3,4, *S Am* 3,4, *F*, 1981 *I* 1
Le Roux, P A (WP) 1906 *I*, *W*, *E*
Little, E M (GW) 1891 *BI* 1,3
Lochner, G P (WP) 1955 *BI* 3, 1956 *A* 1,2, *NZ* 1,2,3,4, 1958 *F* 1,2
Lochner, G P (EP) 1937 *NZ* 3, 1938 *BI* 1,2
Lockyear, R J (GW) 1960 *NZ* 1,2,3,4, 1960 *I*, 1961 *F*
Lombard, A C (EP) 1910 *BI* 2
Lombard, F (Cheetahs) 2002 *S*, *E*
Lötter, D (Tvl) 1993 *F* 2, *A* 1,2
Lotz, J W (Tvl) 1937 *A* 1,2, *NZ* 1,2,3, 1938 *BI* 1,2,3
Loubscher, R I P (Elephants) 2002 *W* 1, 2003 *S* 1
Loubser, J A (WP) 1903 *BI* 3, 1906 *S*, *I*, *W*, *E*, 1910 *BI* 1,3
Lourens, M J (NT) 1968 *BI* 2,3,4
Louw, F H (WP) 2002 *W* 2(R), *Arg*, *Sm*
Louw, J S (Tvl) 1891 *BI* 1,2,3
Louw, M J (Tvl) 1971 *A* 2,3
Louw, M M (WP) 1928 *NZ* 3,4, 1931 *W*, *I*, 1932 *E*, *S*, 1933 *A* 1,2,3,4,5, 1937 *A* 1,2, *NZ* 2,3, 1938 *BI* 1,2,3
Louw, R J (WP) 1980 *S Am* 1,2, *BI* 1,2,3,4 *S Am* 3,4, *F*, 1981 *I* 1,2, *NZ* 1,3, 1982 *S Am* 1,2, 1984 *E* 1,2, *S Am* 1,2
Louw, S C (WP) 1933 *A* 1,2,3,4,5, 1937 *A* 1, *NZ* 1,2,3, 1938 *BI* 1,2,3
Lubbe, E (GW) 1997 *Tg*, *BI* 1
Luyt, F P (WP) 1910 *BI* 1,2,3, 1912 *S*, *I*, *W*, 1913 *E*

Luyt, J D (EP) 1912 *S, W*, 1913 *E, F*
Luyt, R R (W P) 1910 *BI* 2,3, 1912 *S, I, W*, 1913 *E, F*
Lyons, D J (EP) 1896 *BI* 1
Lyster, P J (N) 1933 *A* 2,5, 1937 *NZ* 1

McCallum, I D (WP) 1970 *NZ* 1,2,3,4, 1971 *F* 1,2, *A* 1,2,3, 1974 *BI* 1,2
McCallum, R J (WP) 1974 *BI* 1
McCulloch, J D (GW) 1913 *E, F*
MacDonald, A W (R) 1965 *A* 1, *NZ* 1,2,3,4
Macdonald, D A (WP) 1974 *BI* 2
Macdonald, I (Tvl) 1992 *NZ, A*, 1993 *F* 1, *A* 3, 1994 *E* 2, 1995 *WS* (R)
McDonald, J A J (WP) 1931 *W, I*, 1932 *E, S*
McEwan, W M C (Tvl) 1903 *BI* 1,3
McHardy, E E (OFS) 1912 *S, I, W*, 1913 *E, F*
McKendrick, J A (WP) 1891 *BI* 3
Malan, A S (Tvl) 1960 *NZ* 1,2,3,4, *W, I*, 1961 *E, S, F*, 1962 *BI* 1, 1963 *A* 1,2,3, 1964 *W*, 1965 *I, S*
Malan, A W (NT) 1989 *Wld* 1,2, 1992 *NZ, A, F* 1,2, *E*
Malan, E (NT) 1980 *BI* 3(R), 4
Malan, G F (WP) 1958 *F* 2, 1960 *NZ* 1,3,4, 1961 *E, S, F*, 1962 *BI* 1,2,3, 1963 *A* 1,2,4, 1964 *W*, 1965 *A* 1,2, *NZ* 1,2
Malan, P (Tvl) 1949 *NZ* 4
Mallett, N V H (WP) 1984 *S Am* 1,2
Malotana K (Bor) 1999 [*Sp*]
Mans, W J (WP) 1965 *I, S*
Marais, C F (WP) 1999 *It* 1(R),2(R), 2000 *C, E* 1,2, *A* 1, *NZ* 1, *A* 2, *NZ* 2, *A* 3, *Arg* (R), *W* (R)
Marais, F P (Bol) 1949 *NZ* 1,2, 1951 *S*, 1953 *A* 1,2
Marais, J F K (WP) 1963 *A* 3, 1964 *W, F*, 1965 *I, S, A* 2, 1968 *BI*, 1,2,3,4, *F* 1,2, 1969 *A* 1,2,3,4, *S, E*, 1970 *I, W, NZ* 1,2,3,4, 1971 *F* 1,2, *A* 1,2,3, 1974 *BI* 1,2,3,4, *F* 1,2
Maré, D S (Tvl) 1906 *S*
Marsberg, A F W (GW) 1906 *S, W, E*
Marsberg, P A (GW) 1910 *BI* 1
Martheze, W C (GW) 1903 *BI* 2, 1906 *I, W*
Martin, H J (Tvl) 1937 *A* 2
Matfield, V (BB) 2001 *It* 1(R), *NZ* 1, *A* 2, *NZ* 2, *F* 3, *It* 2, *E, US*, 2002 *W* 1, *Sm, NZ* 1, *A* 1, *NZ* 2(R), 2003 *S* 1,2, *Arg, A* 1, *NZ* 1, *A* 2, *NZ* 2
Mellet, T B (GW) 1896 *BI* 2
Mellish, F W (WP) 1921 *NZ* 1,3, 1924 *BI* 1,2,3,4
Merry, J (EP) 1891 *BI* 1
Metcalf, H D (Bor) 1903 *BI* 2
Meyer, C du P (WP) 1921 *NZ* 1,2,3
Meyer, P J (GW) 1896 *BI* 1
Meyer, W (OFS, GL) 1997 *S* (R), 1999 *It* 2, *NZ* 1(R), *A* 1(R), 2000 *C* (R), *E* 1, *NZ* 1(R),2(R), *Arg, I, W, E* 3, 2001 *F* 1(R),2, *It* 1, *F* 3(R), *It* 2, *E, US* (t+R), 2002 *W* 1,2, *Arg, NZ* 1,2, *A* 2, *F*
Michau, J M (Tvl) 1921 *NZ* 1
Michau, J P (WP) 1921 *NZ* 1,2,3
Millar, W A (WP) 1906 *E*, 1910 *BI* 2,3, 1912 *I, W*, 1913 *F*
Mills, W J (WP) 1910 *BI* 2
Moll, T (Tvl) 1910 *BI* 2
Montini, P E (WP) 1956 *A* 1,2
Montgomery, P C (WP) 1997 *BI* 2,3, *NZ* 1, *A* 1, *NZ* 2, *A* 2, *F* 1,2, *E, S*, 1998 *I* 1,2, *W* 1, *E* 1, *A* 1, *NZ* 1,2, *A* 2, *W* 2, *S, I* 3, *E* 2, 1999 *It* 1,2, *W, NZ* 1, *A* 1, *NZ* 2, *A* 2, [*S, U, E, A* 3, *NZ* 3], 2000 *C, E* 1,2, *A* 1, *NZ* 1, *A* 2(R), *Arg, I, W, E* 3, 2001 *F* 1, 2(t), *It* 1, *NZ* 1, *F* 3(R), *It* 2(R)
Moolman, L C (NT) 1977 *Wld*, 1980 *S Am* 1,2, *BI* 1,2,3,4, *S Am* 3,4, *F*, 1981 *I* 1,2, *NZ* 1,2,3, *US*, 1982 *S Am* 1,2, 1984 *S Am* 1,2, 1986 *Cv* 1,2,3,4
Mordt, R H (Z-R, NT) 1980 *S Am* 1,2, *BI* 1,2,3,4, *S Am* 3,4, *F*, 1981 *I* 2, *NZ* 1,2,3, *US*, 1982 *S Am* 1,2, 1984 *S Am* 1,2
Morkel, D A (Tvl) 1903 *BI* 1
Morkel, D F T (Tvl) 1906 *I, E*, 1910 *BI* 1,3, 1912 *S, I, W*, 1913 *E, F*
Morkel, H J (WP) 1921 *NZ* 1
Morkel, H W (WP) 1921 *NZ* 1,2
Morkel, J A (WP) 1921 *NZ* 2,3
Morkel, J W H (WP) 1912 *S, I, W*, 1913 *E, F*
Morkel, P G (WP) 1912 *S, I, W*, 1913 *E, F*, 1921 *NZ* 1,2,3
Morkel, P K (WP) 1928 *NZ* 4
Morkel, W H (WP) 1910 *BI* 3, 1912 *S, I, W*, 1913 *E, F*, 1921 *NZ* 1,2,3
Morkel, W S (Tvl) 1906 *S, I, W, E*
Moss, C (N) 1949 *NZ* 1,2,3,4
Mostert, P J (WP) 1921 *NZ* 1,2,3, 1924 *BI* 1,2,4, 1928 *NZ* 1,2,3,4, 1931 *W, I*, 1932 *E, S*
Mulder, J C (Tvl, GL) 1994 *NZ* 2,3, *S, W*, 1995 *WS*, [*A, WS, F, NZ*], *W, It, E*, 1996 *Fj, A* 1, *NZ* 1, *A* 2, *NZ* 2,5, *Arg* 1,2, *F* 1,2, *W*, 1997 *Tg, BI* 1, 1999 *It* 1(R),2, *W, NZ* 1, 2000 *C*(R), *A* 1, *E* 3, 2001 *F* 1, *It* 1
Muller, G H (WP) 1969 *A* 3,4, *S*, 1970 *W, NZ* 1,2,3,4, 1971 *F* 1,2, 1972 *E*, 1974 *BI* 1,3,4
Muller, G P (GL) 2003 *A* 2, *NZ* 2
Muller, H L (OFS) 1986 *Cv* 4(R), 1989 *Wld* 1(R)
Muller, H S V (Tvl) 1949 *NZ* 1,2,3,4, 1951 *S, I, W*, 1952 *E, F*, 1953 *A* 1,2,3,4
Muller, L J J (N) 1992 *NZ, A*
Muller, P G (N) 1992 *NZ, A, F* 1,2, *E*, 1993 *F* 1,2, *A* 1,2,3, *Arg* 1,2, 1994 *E* 1,2, *NZ* 1, *S, W*, 1998 *I* 1,2, *W* 1, *E* 1, *A* 1, *NZ* 1,2, *A* 2, 1999 *It* 1, *W, NZ* 1, *A* 1, [*Sp, E, A* 3, *NZ* 3]
Muir, D J (WP) 1997 *It, F* 1,2, *E, S*
Myburgh, F R (EP) 1896 *BI* 1
Myburgh, J L (NT) 1962 *BI* 1, 1963 *A* 4, 1964 *W, F*, 1968 *BI* 1,2,3, *F* 1,2, 1969 *A* 1,2,3,4, *E*, 1970 *I, W, NZ* 3,4
Myburgh, W H (WT) 1924 *BI* 1

Naude, J P (WP) 1963 *A* 4, 1965 *A* 1,2, *NZ* 1,3,4, 1967 *F* 1,2,3,4, 1968 *BI* 1,2,3,4
Neethling, J B (WP) 1967 *F* 1,2,3,4, 1968 *BI* 4, 1969 *S*, 1970 *NZ* 1,2
Nel, J A (Tvl) 1960 *NZ* 1,2, 1963 *A* 1,2, 1965 *A* 2, *NZ* 1,2,3,4, 1970 *NZ* 3,4
Nel, J J (WP) 1956 *A* 1,2, *NZ* 1,2,3,4, 1958 *F* 1,2
Nel, P A R O (Tvl) 1903 *BI* 1,2,3
Nel, P J (N) 1928 *NZ* 1,2,3,4, 1931 *W, I*, 1932 *E, S*, 1933 *A* 1,3,4,5, 1937 *A* 1,2, *NZ* 2,3
Nimb, C F (WP) 1961 *I*
Nomis, S H (Tvl) 1967 *F* 4, 1968 *BI* 1,2,3,4, *F* 1,2, 1969 *A* 1,2,3,4, *S, E*, 1970 *I, W, NZ* 1,2,3,4, 1971 *F* 1,2, *A* 1,2,3, 1972 *E*
Nykamp, J L (Tvl) 1933 *A* 2

Ochse, J K (WP) 1951 *I, W*, 1952 *E, F*, 1953 *A* 1,2,4
Oelofse, J S A (Tvl) 1953 *A* 1,2,3,4
Oliver, J F (Tvl) 1928 *NZ* 3,4
Olivier, E (WP) 1967 *F* 1,2,3,4, 1968 *BI* 1,2,3,4, *F* 1,2, 1969 *A* 1,2,3,4, *S, E*
Olivier, J (NT) 1992 *F* 1,2, *E*, 1993 *F* 1,2 *A* 1,2,3, *Arg* 1, 1995 *W, It* (R), *E*, 1996 *Arg* 1,2, *F* 1,2, *W*
Olver, E (EP) 1896 *BI* 1
Oosthuizen, J J (WP) 1974 *BI* 1, *F* 1,2, 1975 *F* 1,2, 1976 *NZ* 1,2,3,4
Oosthuizen, O W (NT, Tvl) 1981 *I* 1(R), 2, *NZ* 2,3, *US*, 1982 *S Am* 1,2, 1984 *E* 1,2
Osler, B L (WP) 1924 *BI* 1,2,3,4, 1928 *NZ* 1,2,3,4, 1931 *W, I*, 1932 *E, S*, 1933 *A* 1,2,3,4,5
Osler, S G (WP) 1928 *NZ* 1
Otto, K (NT, BB) 1995 [*R, C* (R), *WS* (R)], 1997 *BI* 3, *A* 1, *NZ* 2, *A* 2, *It, F* 1,2, *E, S*, 1998 *I* 1,2, *W* 1, *E* 1, *A* 1, *NZ* 1,2, *A* 2, *W* 2, *S, I* 3, *E* 2, 1999 *It* 1, *W, NZ* 1, *A* 1, [*S* (R), *Sp, U, E, A* 3, *NZ* 3], 2000 *C, E* 1,2, *A* 1
Oxlee, K (N) 1960 *NZ* 1,2,3,4, *W, I*, 1961 *S, A* 1,2, 1962 *BI* 1,2,3,4, 1963 *A* 1,2,4, 1964 *W*, 1965 *NZ* 1,2

Pagel, G L (WP) 1995 [*A* (R), *R, C, NZ* (R)], 1996 *NZ* 5(R)
Parker, W H (EP) 1965 *A* 1,2
Partridge, J E C (Tvl) 1903 *BI* 1
Paulse, B J (WP) 1999 *It* 1,2, *NZ* 1, *A* 1,2(R), [*S* (R), *Sp, NZ* 3], 2000 *C, E* 1,2, *A* 1, *NZ* 1, *A* 2, *NZ* 2, *A* 3, *Arg, W, E* 3, 2001 *F* 1,2, *It* 1, *NZ* 1, *A* 1,2, *NZ* 2, *F* 3, *It* 2, *E*, 2002 *W* 1,2, *Arg, Sm* (R), *A* 1, *NZ* 2, *A* 2, *F, S, E*
Payn, C (N) 1924 *BI* 1,2
Pelser, H J M (Tvl) 1958 *F* 1, 1960 *NZ* 1,2,3,4, *W, I*, 1961 *F, I, A* 1,2
Pfaff, B D (WP) 1956 *A* 1
Pickard, J A J (WP) 1953 *A* 3,4, 1956 *NZ* 2, 1958 *F* 2
Pienaar, J F (Tvl) 1993 *F* 1,2, *A* 1,2,3, *Arg* 1,2, 1994 *E* 1,2, *NZ* 2,3, *Arg* 1,2, *S, W*, 1995 *WS*, [*A, C, WS, F, NZ*], *W, It, E*, 1996 *Fj, A* 1, *NZ* 1, *A* 2, *NZ* 2
Pienaar, Z M J (OFS) 1980 *S Am* 2(R), *BI* 1,2,3,4, *S Am* 3,4, *F*, 1981 *I* 1,2, *NZ* 1,2,3
Pitzer, G (NT) 1967 *F* 1,2,3,4, 1968 *BI* 1,2,3,4, *F* 1,2, 1969 *A* 3,4
Pope, C F (WP) 1974 *BI* 1,2,3,4, 1975 *F* 1,2, 1976 *NZ* 2,3,4
Potgieter, H J (OFS) 1928 *NZ* 1,2
Potgieter, H L (OFS) 1977 *Wld*
Powell, A W (GW) 1896 *BI* 3
Powell, J M (GW) 1891 *BI* 2, 1896 *BI* 3, 1903 *BI* 1,2
Prentis, R B (Tvl) 1980 *S Am* 1,2, *BI* 1,2,3,4, *S Am* 3,4, *F*, 1981 *I* 1,2

Pretorius, A S (GL) 2002 *W* 1,2, *Arg, Sm, NZ* 1, *A* 1, *NZ* 2, *F, S* (R), *E,* 2003 *NZ* 1(R), *A* 1
Pretorius, N F (Tvl) 1928 *NZ* 1,2,3,4
Prinsloo, J (Tvl) 1958 *F* 1,2
Prinsloo, J (NT) 1963 *A* 3
Prinsloo, J P (Tvl) 1928 *NZ* 1
Putter, D J (WT) 1963 *A* 1,2,4

Raaff, J W E (GW) 1903 *BI* 1,2, 1906 *S, W, E,* 1910 *BI* 1
Ras, W J de Wet (OFS) 1976 *NZ* 1(R), 1980 *S Am* 2(R)
Rautenbach, S J (WP) 2002 *W* 1(R),2(t+R), *Arg* (R), *Sm, NZ* 1(R), *A* 1, *NZ* 2(R), *A* 2(R)
Reece-Edwards, H (N) 1992 *F* 1,2, 1993 *A* 2
Reid, A (WP) 1903 *BI* 3
Reid, B C (Bor) 1933 *A* 4
Reinach, J (OFS) 1986 *Cv* 1,2,3,4
Rens, I J (Tvl) 1953 *A* 3,4
Retief, D F (NT) 1955 *BI* 1,2,4, 1956 *A* 1,2, *NZ* 1,2,3,4
Reyneke, H J (WP) 1910 *BI* 3
Richards, A R (WP) 1891 *BI* 1,2,3
Richter, A (NT) 1992 *F* 1,2, *E,* 1994 *E* 2, *NZ* 1,2,3, 1995 [*R, C, WS* (R)]
Riley, N M (ET) 1963 *A* 3
Riordan, C A (Tvl) 1910 *BI* 1,2
Robertson, I W (R) 1974 *F* 1,2, 1976 *NZ* 1,2,4
Rodgers, P H (NT, Tvl) 1989 *Wld* 1,2, 1992 *NZ, F* 1,2
Rogers, C D (Tvl) 1984 *E* 1,2, *S Am* 1,2
Roos, G D (WP) 1910 *BI* 2,3
Roos, P J (WP) 1903 *BI* 3, 1906 *I, W, E*
Rosenberg, W (Tvl) 1955 *BI* 2,3,4, 1956 *NZ* 3, 1958 *F* 1
Rossouw, C L C (Tvl, N) 1995 *WS,* [*R, WS, F, NZ*], 1999 *NZ* 2(R), *A* 2(t), [*Sp, NZ* 3(R)]
Rossouw, D H (WP) 1953 *A* 3, 4
Rossouw, P W G (WP) 1997 *BI* 2,3, *NZ* 1, *A* 1, *NZ* 2(R), *A* 2(R), *It, F* 1,2, *E, S,* 1998 *I* 1,2, *W* 1, *E* 1, *A* 1, *NZ* 1,2, *A* 2, *W* 2, *S, I* 3, *E* 2, 1999 *It* 1, *W, NZ* 1, *A* 1(R), *NZ* 2, *A* 2, [*S, U, E, A* 3], 2000 *C, E* 1,2, *A* 2, *Arg* (R), *I, W,* 2001 *F* 3, *US,* 2003 *Arg*
Rousseau, W P (WP) 1928 *NZ* 3,4
Roux, F du T (WP) 1960 *W,* 1961 *A* 1,2, 1962 *BI* 1,2,3,4, 1963 *A* 2, 1965 *A* 1,2, *NZ* 1,2,3,4, 1968 *BI* 3,4, *F* 1,2 1969 *A* 1,2,3,4, 1970 *I, NZ* 1,2,3,4
Roux, J P (Tvl) 1994 *E* 2, *NZ* 1,2,3, *Arg* 1, 1995 [*R, C, F* (R)], 1996 *A* 1(R), *NZ* 1, *A* 2, *NZ* 3
Roux, O A (NT) 1969 *S, E,* 1970 *I, W,* 1972 *E,* 1974 *BI* 3,4
Roux, W G (BB) 2002 *F* (R), *S, E*
Russell, R B (Pumas, Natal) 2002 *W* 1(R),2, *Arg, A* 1(R), *NZ* 2(R), *A* 2, *F, E* (R), 2003 *Arg* (R), *A* 1(R), *NZ* 1, *A* 2(R)

Samuels, T A (GW) 1896 *BI* 2,3,4
Santon, D (Bol) 2003 *A* 1(R), *NZ* 1(R), *A* 2(t)
Sauermann, J T (Tvl) 1971 *F* 1,2, *A* 1, 1972 *E,* 1974 *BI* 1
Schlebusch, J J J (OFS) 1974 *BI* 3,4, 1975 *F* 2
Schmidt, L U (NT) 1958 *F* 2, 1962 *BI* 2
Schmidt, U L (NT, Tvl) 1986 *Cv* 1,2,3,4, 1989 *Wld* 1,2, 1992 *NZ, A,* 1993 *F* 1,2, *A* 1,2,3, 1994 *Arg* 1,2, *S, W*
Schoeman, J (WP) 1963 *A* 3,4, 1965 *I, S, A* 1, *NZ* 1,2
Scholtz, C P (WP, Tvl) 1994 *Arg* 1, 1995 [*R, C, WS*]
Scholtz, H (FSC) 2002 *A* 1(R), *NZ* 2(R), *A* 2(R)
Scholtz, H H (WP) 1921 *NZ* 1,2
Schutte, P J W (Tvl) 1994 *S, W*
Scott, P A (Tvl) 1896 *BI* 1,2,3,4
Sendin, W D (GW) 1921 *NZ* 2
Sephaka, L D (GL) 2001 *US,* 2002 *Sm, NZ* 1, *A* 1, *NZ* 2, *A* 2, *F,* 2003 *S* 1,2, *A* 1, *NZ* 1, *A* 2(t+R), *NZ* 2
Serfontein, D J (WP) 1980 *BI* 1,2,3,4, *S Am* 3,4, *F,* 1981 *I* 1,2, *NZ* 1,2,3, *US,* 1982 *S Am* 1,2, 1984 *E* 1,2, *S Am* 1,2
Shand, R (GW) 1891 *BI* 2,3
Sheriff, A R (Tvl) 1938 *BI* 1,2,3
Shum, E H (Tvl) 1913 *E*
Sinclair, D J (Tvl) 1955 *BI* 1,2,3,4
Sinclair, J H (Tvl) 1903 *BI* 1
Skene, A L (WP) 1958 *F* 2
Skinstad, R B (WP, GL) 1997 *E* (t), 1998 *W* 1(R), *E* 1(t), *NZ* 1(R),2(R), *A* 2(R), *W* 2(R), *S, I* 3, *E* 2, 1999 [*S, Sp* (R), *U, E, A* 3], 2001 *F* 1(R),2(R), *It* 1, *NZ* 1, *A* 1,2, *NZ* 2, *F* 3, *It* 2, *E,* 2002 *W* 1,2, *Arg, Sm, NZ* 1, *A* 1, *NZ* 2, *A* 2, 2003 *Arg* (R)
Slater, J T (EP) 1924 *BI* 3,4, 1928 *NZ* 1
Smal, G P (WP) 1986 *Cv* 1,2,3,4, 1989 *Wld* 1,2
Small, J T (Tvl, N, WP) 1992 *NZ, A, F* 1,2, *E,* 1993 *F* 1,2, *A* 1,2,3, *Arg* 1,2, 1994 *E* 1,2, *NZ* 1,2,3(t), *Arg* 1, 1995 *WS,* [*A, R, F, NZ*], *W, It, E* (R), 1996 *Fj, A* 1, *NZ* 1, *A* 2, *NZ* 2, *Arg* 1,2, *F* 1,2, *W,* 1997 *Tg, BI* 1, *NZ* 1(R), *A* 1(R), *NZ* 2, *A* 2, *It, F* 1,2, *E, S*
Smit, F C (WP) 1992 *E*
Smit, W J (N) 2000 *C* (t), *A* 1(R), *NZ* 1(t+R), *A* 2(R), *NZ* 2(R), *A* 3(R), *Arg, I, W, E* 3, 2001 *F* 1,2, *It* 1, *NZ* 1(R), *A* 1(R),2(R), *NZ* 2(R), *F* 3(R), *It* 2, *E, US* (R)
Smith, C M (OFS) 1963 *A* 3,4, 1964 *W, F,* 1965 *A* 1,2, *NZ* 2
Smith, C W (GW) 1891 *BI* 2, 1896 *BI* 2,3
Smith, D (GW) 1891 *BI* 2
Smith D J (Z-R) 1980 *BI* 1,2,3,4
Smith, G A C (EP) 1938 *BI* 3
Smith, J H (Cheetahs) 2003 *S* 1(R),2(R), *A* 1, *NZ* 1, *A* 2, *NZ* 2
Smith, P F (GW) 1997 *S* (R), 1998 *I* 1(t),2, *W* 1, *NZ* 1(R),2(R), *A* 2(R), *W* 2, 1999 *NZ* 2
Smollan, F C (Tvl) 1933 *A* 3,4,5
Snedden, R C D (GW) 1891 *BI* 2
Snyman, A H (NT, BB, N) 1996 *NZ* 3,4, *Arg* 2(R), *W* (R), 1997 *Tg, BI* 1,2,3, *NZ* 1, *A* 1, *NZ* 2, *A* 2, *It, F* 1,2, *E, S,* 1998 *I* 1,2, *W* 1, *E* 1, *A* 1, *NZ* 1,2, *A* 2, *W* 2, *S, I* 3, *E* 2, 1999 *NZ* 2, 2001 *NZ* 2, *F* 3, *US,* 2002 *W* 1, 2003 *S* 1, *NZ* 1
Snyman, D S L (WP) 1972 *E,* 1974 *BI* 1,2(R), *F* 1,2, 1975 *F* 1,2, 1976 *NZ* 2,3, 1977 *Wld*
Snyman, J C P (OFS) 1974 *BI* 2,3,4
Sonnekus, G H H (OFS) 1974 *BI* 3, 1984 *E* 1,2
Sowerby, R S (N) 2002 *Sm* (R)
Spies, J J (NT) 1970 *NZ* 1,2,3,4
Stander, J C J (OFS) 1974 *BI* 4(R), 1976 *NZ* 1,2,3,4
Stapelberg, W P (NT) 1974 *F* 1,2
Starke, J J (WP) 1956 *NZ* 4
Starke, K T (WP) 1924 *BI* 1,2,3,4
Steenekamp, J G A (Tvl) 1958 *F* 1
Stegmann, A C (WP) 1906 *S, I*
Stegmann, J A (Tvl) 1912 *S, I, W,* 1913 *E, F*
Stewart, C (WP) 1998 *S, I* 3, *E* 2
Stewart, D A (WP) 1960 *S,* 1961 *E, S, F, I,* 1963 *A* 1,3,4, 1964 *W, F,* 1965 *I*
Stofberg, M T S (OFS, NT, WP) 1976 *NZ* 2,3, 1977 *Wld,* 1980 *S Am* 1,2, *BI* 1,2,3,4, *S Am* 3,4, *F,* 1981 *I* 1,2, *NZ* 1,2, *US,* 1982 *S Am* 1,2, 1984 *E* 1,2
Strachan, L C (Tvl) 1932 *E, S,* 1937 *A* 1,2, *NZ* 1,2,3, 1938 *BI* 1,2,3
Stransky, J (N, WP) 1993 *A* 1,2,3, *Arg* 1, 1994 *Arg* 1,2, 1995 *WS,* [*A, R* (t), *C, F, NZ*], *W, It, E,* 1996 *Fj* (R), *NZ* 1, *A* 2, *NZ* 2,3,4,5(R)
Straeuli, R A W (Tvl) 1994 *NZ* 1, *Arg* 1,2, *S, W,* 1995 *WS,* [*A, WS, NZ* (R)], *E* (R)
Strauss, C P (WP) 1992 *F* 1,2, *E,* 1993 *F* 1,2, *A* 1,2,3, *Arg* 1,2, 1994 *E* 1, *NZ* 1,2, *Arg* 1,2
Strauss, J A (WP) 1984 *S Am* 1,2
Strauss, J H P (Tvl) 1976 *NZ* 3,4, 1980 *S Am* 1
Strauss, S S F (GW) 1921 *NZ* 3
Strydom, C F (OFS) 1955 *BI* 3, 1956 *A* 1,2, *NZ* 1,4, 1958 *F* 1,
Strydom, J J (Tvl, GL) 1993 *F* 2, *A* 1,2,3, *Arg* 1,2, 1994 *E* 1, 1995 [*A, C, F, NZ*], 1996 *A* 2(R), *NZ* 2(R), 3,4, *W* (R), 1997 *Tg, BI* 1,2,3, *A* 2
Strydom, L J (NT) 1949 *NZ* 1,2
Styger, J J (OFS) 1992 *NZ* (R), *A, F* 1,2, *E,* 1993 *F* 2(R), *A* 3(R)
Suter, M R (N) 1965 *I, S*
Swanepoel, W (OFS, GL) 1997 *BI* 3(R), *A* 2(R), *F* 1(R), 2, *E, S,* 1998 *I* 2(R), *W* 1(R), *E* 2(R), 1999 *It* 1,2(R), *W, A* 1, [*Sp, NZ* 3(t)], 2000 *A* 1, *NZ* 1, *A* 2, *NZ* 2, *A* 3
Swart, J (WP) 1996 *Fj, NZ* 1(R), *A* 2, *NZ* 2,3,4,5, 1997 *BI* 3(R), *It, S* (R)
Swart, J J N (SWA) 1955 *BI* 1
Swart, I S (Tvl) 1993 *A* 1,2,3, *Arg* 1, 1994 *E* 1,2, *NZ* 1,3, *Arg* 2(R), 1995 *WS,* [*A, WS, F, NZ*], *W,* 1996 *A* 2

Taberer, W S (GW) 1896 *BI* 2
Taylor, O B (N) 1962 *BI* 1
Terblanche, C S (Bol, N) 1998 *I* 1,2, *W* 1, *E* 1, *A* 1, *NZ* 1,2, *A* 2, *W* 2, *S, I* 3, *E* 2, 1999 *It* 1(R),2, *W, A* 1, *NZ* 2(R), [*Sp, E* (R), *A* 3(R), *NZ* 3], 2000 *E* 3, 2002 *W* 1,2, *Arg, Sm, NZ* 1, *A* 1,2(R), 2003 *S* 1,2, *Arg, A* 1, *NZ* 1, *A* 2, *NZ* 2
Teichmann, G H (N) 1995 *W,* 1996 *Fj, A* 1, *NZ* 1, *A* 2, *NZ* 2,3,4,5, *Arg* 1,2, *F* 1,2, *W,* 1997 *Tg, BI* 1,2,3, *NZ* 1, *A* 1, *NZ* 2, *A* 2, *It, F* 1,2 *E, S,* 1998 *I* 1,2, *W* 1, *E* 1, *A* 1, *NZ* 1,2, *A* 2, *W* 2, *S, I* 3, *E* 2, 1999 *It* 1, *W, NZ* 1
Theron, D F (GW) 1996 *A* 2(R), *NZ* 2(R), 5, *Arg* 1,2, *F* 1,2, *W,* 1997 *BI* 2(R), 3, *NZ* 1(R), *A* 1, *NZ* 2(R)
Theunissen, D J (GW) 1896 *BI* 3
Thompson, G (WP) 1912 *S, I, W*
Tindall, J C (WP) 1924 *BI* 1, 1928 *NZ* 1,2,3,4
Tobias, E G (SARF, Bol) 1981 *I* 1,2, 1984 *E* 1,2, *S Am* 1,2
Tod, N S (N) 1928 *NZ* 2
Townsend, W H (N) 1921 *NZ* 1
Trenery, W E (GW) 1891 *BI* 2

Joost van der Westhuizen sets his backs moving in the Tri Nations match against Australia at Suncorp Stadium, Brisbane.

Tromp, H (NT) 1996 *NZ*3,4, *Arg* 2(R), *F* 1(R)
Truter, D R (WP) 1924 *BI* 2,4
Truter, J T (N) 1963 *A* 1, 1964 *F*, 1965 *A* 2
Turner, F G (EP) 1933 *A* 1,2,3, 1937 *A* 1,2, *NZ* 1,2,3, 1938 *BI* 1,2,3
Twigge, R J (NT) 1960 *S*

Ulyate, C A (Tvl) 1955 *BI* 1,2,3,4, 1956 *NZ* 1,2,3
Uys, P de W (NT) 1960 *W*, 1961 *E, S, I, A* 1,2, 1962 *BI* 1,4, 1963 *A* 1,2, 1969 *A* 1(R), 2
Uys, P J (Pumas) 2002 *S*

Van Aswegen, H J (WP) 1981 *NZ* 1, 1982 *S Am* 2(R)
Van Biljon, L (N) 2001 *It* 1(R), *NZ* 1, *A* 1,2, *NZ* 2, *F* 3, *It* 2(R), *E* (R), *US*, 2002 *F* (R), *S, E* (R), 2003 *NZ* 2(R)
Van Broekhuizen, H D (WP) 1896 *BI* 4
Van Buuren, M C (Tvl) 1891 *BI* 1
Van de Vyver, D F (WP) 1937 *A* 2
Van den Berg, D S (N) 1975 *F* 1,2, 1976 *NZ* 1,2
Van den Berg, M A (WP) 1937 *A* 1, *NZ* 1,2,3
Van den Berg, P A (WP, GW, N) 1999 *It* 1(R),2, *NZ* 2, *A* 2, [*S, U* (t+R), *E* (R), *A* 3(R), *NZ* 3(R)], 2000 *E* 1(R), *A* 1, *NZ* 1, *A* 2, *NZ* 2(R), *A* 3(t+R), *Arg, I, W, E* 3, 2001 *F* 1(R),2, *A* 2(R), *NZ* 2(R), *US*
Van den Bergh, E (EP) 1994 *Arg* 2(t & R)
Van der Linde, A (WP) 1995 *It, E*, 1996 *Arg* 1(R), 2(R), *F* 1(R), *W* (R), 2001 *F* 3(R)
Van der Linde, C J (Cheetahs) 2002 *S* (R), *E* (R)
Van der Merwe, A J (Bol) 1955 *BI* 2,3,4, 1956 *A* 1,2, *NZ* 1,2,3,4, 1958 *F* 1, 1960 *S, NZ* 2
Van der Merwe, A V (WP) 1931 *W*
Van der Merwe, B S (NT) 1949 *NZ* 1
Van der Merwe, H S (NT) 1960 *NZ* 4, 1963 *A* 2,3,4, 1964 *F*
Van der Merwe, J P (WP) 1970 *W*
Van der Merwe, P R (SWD, WT, GW) 1981 *NZ* 2,3, *US*, 1986 *Cv* 1,2, 1989 *Wld* 1
Vanderplank, B E (N) 1924 *BI* 3,4
Van der Schyff, J H (GW) 1949 *NZ* 1,2,3,4, 1955 *BI* 1
Van der Watt, A E (WP) 1969 *S* (R), *E*, 1970 *I*
Van der Westhuizen, J C (WP) 1928 *NZ* 2,3,4, 1931 *I*
Van der Westhuizen, J H (WP) 1931 *I*, 1932 *E, S*
Van der Westhuizen, J H (NT, BB) 1993 *Arg* 1,2, 1994 *E* 1,2(R), *Arg* 2, *S, W*, 1995 *WS*, [*A, C* (R), *WS, F, NZ*], *W, It, E*, 1996 *Fj, A* 1,2(R), *NZ* 2,3(R), 4,5, *Arg* 1,2, *F* 1,2, *W*, 1997 *Tg, BI* 1,2,3, *NZ* 1, *A* 1, *NZ* 2, *A* 2, *It, F* 1, 1998 *I* 1,2, *W* 1, *E* 1, *A* 1, *NZ* 1,2, *A* 2, *W* 2, *S, I* 3, *E* 2, 1999 *NZ* 2, *A* 2, [*S, Sp* (R), *U, E, A* 3, *NZ* 3], 2000 *C, E* 1,2, *A* 1(R), *NZ* 1(R), *A* 2(R), *Arg, I, W, E* 3, 2001 *F* 1,2, *It* 1(R), *NZ* 1, *A* 1,2, *NZ* 2, *F* 3, *It* 2, *E, US* (R), 2003 *S* 1,2, *A* 1, *NZ* 1, *A* 2(R), *NZ* 2
Van der Westhuyzen, J N B (Mp, BB) 2000 *NZ* 2(R), 2001 *It* 1(R), 2003 *S* 1(R),2, *Arg, A* 1
Van Druten, N J V (Tvl) 1924 *BI* 1,2,3,4, 1928 *NZ* 1,2,3,4
Van Heerden, A J (Tvl) 1921 *NZ* 1,3
Van Heerden, F J (WP) 1994 *E* 1,2(R), *NZ* 3, 1995 *It, E*, 1996 *NZ* 5(R), *Arg* 1(R),2(R), 1997 *Tg, BI* 2(t+R),3(R), *NZ* 1(R),2(R), 1999 [*Sp*]
Van Heerden, J L (NT, Tvl) 1974 *BI* 3,4, *F* 1,2, 1975 *F* 1,2, 1976 *NZ* 1,2,3,4, 1977 *Wld*, 1980 *BI* 1,3,4, *S Am* 3,4, *F*
Van Heerden, J L (BB) 2003 *S* 1,2, *A* 1, *NZ* 1, *A* 2(t)
Van Jaarsveld, C J (Tvl) 1949 *NZ* 1
Van Jaarsveldt, D C (R) 1960 *S*
Van Niekerk, J A (WP) 1928 *NZ* 4
Van Niekerk, J C (GL) 2001 *NZ* 1(R), *A* 1(R), *NZ* 2(t+R), *F* 3(R), *It*2, *US*, 2002 *W* 1(R),2(R), *Arg* (R), *Sm, NZ* 1, *A* 1, *NZ* 2, *A* 2, *F, S, E*, 2003 *A* 2, *NZ* 2
Van Reenen, G L (WP) 1937 *A* 2, *NZ* 1
Van Renen, C G (WP) 1891 *BI* 3, 1896 *BI* 1,4
Van Renen, W (WP) 1903 *BI* 1,3
Van Rensburg, J T J (Tvl) 1992 *NZ, A, E*, 1993 *F* 1,2, *A* 1, 1994 *NZ* 2
Van Rooyen, G W (Tvl) 1921 *NZ* 2,3
Van Ryneveld, R C B (WP) 1910 *BI* 2,3
Van Schalkwyk, D (NT) 1996 *Fj* (R), *NZ* 3,4,5, 1997 *BI* 2,3, *NZ* 1, *A* 1
Van Schoor, R A M (R) 1949 *NZ* 2,3,4, 1951 *S, I, W*, 1952 *E, F*, 1953 *A* 1,2,3,4
Van Straaten, A J J (WP) 1999 *It* 2(R), *W, NZ* 1(R), *A* 1, 2000 *C, E* 1,2, *NZ* 1, *A* 2, *NZ* 2, *A* 3, *Arg* (R), *I* (R), *W, E* 3, 2001 *A* 1,2, *NZ* 2, *F* 3, *It* 2, *E*
Van Vollenhoven, K T (NT) 1955 *BI* 1,2,3,4, 1956 *A* 1,2, *NZ* 3
Van Vuuren, T F (EP) 1912 *S, I, W*, 1913 *E, F*
Van Wyk, C J (Tvl) 1951 *S, I, W*, 1952 *E, F*, 1953 *A* 1,2,3,4, 1955 *BI* 1
Van Wyk, J F B (NT) 1970 *NZ* 1,2,3,4, 1971 *F* 1,2, *A* 1,2,3, 1972 *E*, 1974 *BI* 1,3,4, 1976 *NZ* 3,4
Van Wyk, S P (WP) 1928 *NZ* 1,2
Van Zyl, B P (WP) 1961 *I*
Van Zyl, C G P (OFS) 1965 *NZ* 1,2,3,4
Van Zyl, D J (WP) 2000 *E* 3(R)
Van Zyl, G H (WP) 1958 *F* 1, 1960 *S, NZ* 1,2,3,4, *W, I*, 1961 *E, S, F, I, A* 1,2, 1962 *BI* 1,3,4
Van Zyl, H J (Tvl) 1960 *NZ* 1,2,3,4, *I*, 1961 *E, S, I, A* 1,2
Van Zyl, P J (Bol) 1961 *I*
Veldsman, P E (WP) 1977 *Wld*
Venter, A G (OFS) 1996 *NZ* 3,4,5, *Arg* 1,2, *F* 1,2, *W*, 1997 *Tg, BI* 1,2,3, *NZ* 1, *A* 1, *NZ* 2, *It, F* 1,2, *E, S*, 1998 *I* 1,2, *W* 1, *E* 1, *A* 1, *NZ* 1,2, *A* 2, *W* 2, *S* (R), *I* 3(R), *E* 2(R), 1999 *It* 1,2(R), *W* (R), *NZ* 1, *A* 1, *NZ* 2, *A* 2, [*S, U, E, A* 3, *NZ* 3], 2000 *C, E* 1,2, *A* 1, *NZ* 1, *A* 2, *NZ* 2, *A* 3, *Arg, I, W, E* 3, 2001 *F* 1, *It* 1, *NZ* 1, *A* 1,2, *NZ* 2, *F* 3(R), *It* 2(R), *E* (t+R), *US* (R)
Venter, A J (N) 2000 *W* (R), *E* 3(R), 2001 *F* 3, *It* 2, *E, US*, 2002 *W* 1,2, *Arg, NZ* 1(R),2, *A* 2, *F, S* (R), *E*, 2003 *Arg*
Venter, B (OFS) 1994 *E* 1,2, *NZ* 1,2,3, *Arg* 1,2, 1995 [*R, C, WS* (R), *NZ* (R)], 1996 *A* 1, *NZ* 1, *A* 2, 1999 *A* 2, [*S, U*]
Venter, F D (Tvl) 1931 *W*, 1932 *S*, 1933 *A* 3
Versfeld, C (WP) 1891 *BI* 3
Versfeld, M (WP) 1891 *BI* 1,2,3
Vigne, J T (Tvl) 1891 *BI* 1,2,3
Viljoen, J F (GW) 1971 *F* 1,2, *A* 1,2,3, 1972 *E*
Viljoen, J T (N) 1971 *A* 1,2,3
Villet, J V (WP) 1984 *E* 1,2
Visagie, I J (WP) 1999 *It* 1, *W, NZ* 1, *A* 1, *NZ* 2, *A* 2, [*S, U, E, A* 3, *NZ* 3], 2000 *C, E* 2, *A* 1, *NZ* 1, *A* 2, *NZ* 2, *A* 3, 2001 *NZ* 1, *A* 1,2, *NZ* 2, *F* 3, *It* 2(R), *E* (t+R), *US*, 2003 *S* 1(R),2(R), *Arg*
Visagie, P J (GW) 1967 *F* 1,2,3,4, 1968 *BI* 1,2,3,4, *F* 1,2, 1969 *A* 1,2,3,4, *S, E*, 1970 *NZ* 1,2,3,4, 1971 *F* 1,2, *A* 1,2,3
Visagie, R G (OFS, N) 1984 *E* 1,2, *S Am* 1,2, 1993 *F* 1
Visser, J de V (WP) 1981 *NZ* 2, *US*
Visser, M (WP) 1995 *WS* (R)
Visser, P J (Tvl) 1933 *A* 2
Viviers, S S (OFS) 1956 *A* 1,2, *NZ* 2,3,4
Vogel, M L (OFS) 1974 *BI* 2(R)
Von Hoesslin, D J B (GW) 1999 *It* 1(R),2, *W* (R), *NZ* 1, *A* 1(R)
Vos, A N (GL) 1999 *It* 1(t+R),2, *NZ* 1(R),2(R), *A* 2, [*S* (R), *Sp, E* (R), *A* 3(R), *NZ* 3], 2000 *C, E* 1,2, *A* 1, *NZ* 1, *A* 2, *NZ* 2, *A* 3, *Arg, I, W, E* 3, 2001 *F* 1,2, *It* 1, *NZ* 1, *A* 1,2, *NZ* 2, *F* 3, *It* 2, *E, US*

Wagenaar, C (NT) 1977 *Wld*
Wahl, J J (WP) 1949 *NZ* 1
Walker, A P (N) 1921 *NZ* 1,3, 1924 *BI* 1,2,3,4
Walker, H N (OFS) 1953 *A* 3, 1956 *A* 2, *NZ* 1,4
Walker, H W (Tvl) 1910 *BI* 1,2,3
Walton, D C (N) 1964 *F*, 1965 *I, S, NZ* 3,4, 1969 *A* 1,2, *E*
Wannenburg, P J (BB) 2002 *F* (R), *E*, 2003 *S* 1,2, *Arg, A* 1(t+R), *NZ* 1(R)
Waring, F W (WP) 1931 *I*, 1932 *E*, 1933 *A* 1,2,3,4,5
Wegner, N (WP) 1993 *F* 2, *A* 1,2,3
Wentzel, M van Z (Pumas) 2002 *F* (R), *S*
Wessels, J J (WP) 1896 *BI* 1,2,3
Whipp, P J M (WP) 1974 *BI* 1,2, 1975 *F* 1, 1976 *NZ* 1,3,4, 1980 *S Am* 1,2
White, J (Bor) 1931 *W*, 1933 *A* 1,2,3,4,5, 1937 *A* 1,2, *NZ* 1,2
Wiese, J J (Tvl) 1993 *F* 1, 1995 *WS*, [*R, C, WS, F, NZ*], *W, It, E*, 1996 *NZ* 3(R), 4(R), 5, *Arg* 1,2, *F* 1,2, *W*
Willemse, A K (GL) 2003 *S* 1,2, *NZ* 1, *A* 2, *NZ* 2
Williams, A E (GW) 1910 *BI* 1
Williams, A P (WP) 1984 *E* 1,2
Williams, C M (WP, GL) 1993 *Arg* 2, 1994 *E* 1,2, *NZ* 1,2,3, *Arg* 1,2, *S, W*, 1995 *WS*, [*WS, F, NZ*], *It, E*, 1998 *A* 1(t), *NZ* 1(t), 2000 *C* (R), *E* 1(t),2(R), *A* 1(R), *NZ* 2, *A* 3, *Arg, I, W* (R)
Williams, D O (WP) 1937 *A* 1,2, *NZ* 1,2,3, 1938 *BI* 1,2,3
Williams, J G (NT) 1971 *F* 1,2, *A* 1,2,3, 1972 *E*, 1974 *BI* 1,2,4, *F* 1,2, 1976 *NZ* 1,2
Wilson, L G (WP) 1960 *NZ* 3,4, *W, I*, 1961 *E, F, I, A* 1,2, 1962 *BI* 1,2,3,4, 1963 *A* 1,2,3,4, 1964 *W, F*, 1965 *I, S, A* 1,2, *NZ* 1,2,3,4
Wolmarans, B J (OFS) 1977 *Wld*
Wright, G D (EP, Tvl) 1986 *Cv* 3,4, 1989 *Wld* 1,2, 1992 *F* 1,2, *E*
Wyness, M R K (WP) 1962 *BI* 1,2,3,4, 1963 *A* 2

Zeller, W C (N) 1921 *NZ* 2,3
Zimerman, M (WP) 1931 *W, I*, 1932 *E, S*

NEW ZEALAND TEST SEASON REVIEW 2002-2003

Fitting End to a Century of New Zealand Test Rugby

Don Cameron

In mid-August 2003, New Zealand rugby reached one of those remarkable peaks that come perhaps once in a generation. Suitable preparations had been made to celebrate, when the All Blacks finished their Tri Nations series with the Test against Australia at Eden Park on 16 August, the centenary of All Black Tests which had stretched back to the defeat of Australia in Dunedin on 15 August 1903.

A handsome book written by Ron Palenski, a formidable rugby journalist and historian (who made his own history when he succeeded in taking the place of the incumbent Colin Weatherall as chairman of the Otago union) started the parade. Then came victories in the first three games of the Tri Nations series, with half-century away wins against both South Africa and Australia, and by 19-11 against South Africa at home. Nearer to the climax was the last of a series of special dinners, followed by a dinner at which past All Blacks, and former captains of both Australia and New Zealand, were guests.

These glittering affairs were splendidly presented and publicised. So by the time the Wallabies and the All Blacks ran out onto Eden Park in damp weather the stage had been handsomely set. There was the glamour of the centenary, the honouring of the past greats, as well as the possibility of a clean-sweep of Tri Nations wins and the recovery of the Bledisloe Cup which Australia had held since 1998.

Twelve months before, the two countries had been at each other's throats over the co-hosting fiasco for the October/November 2003 Rugby World Cup. At that stage the Tasman Sea had never been so deep or stormy. Sensible compromise on both sides of the Tasman had repaired the damage – the old brotherhood was restored, perhaps stronger than ever.

For the match, Eden Park was filled to the brim, a rain shower or two not disturbing the vigour or the majesty of the occasion. At the end, with New Zealand winners by 21-17, the All Blacks broke their usual stoical stance and hugged each other with glee. In the stands dozens of great and old All Blacks and Wallabies greeted with joy a marvellous rugby occasion – the sometimes scrappy play disregarded – befitting the lustrous history of the trans-Tasman rivalry.

Within 24 hours the newspapers and radio stations were proclaiming that a broad, smooth road led to ultimate victory in the Rugby World Cup final nine or ten weeks away. The All Blacks, said the cheerleaders, were facing another moment of glory to compare with the Cup win of 1987, or the laying by the Incomparables in 1996 of the jinx which had foiled so many All Black attempts to win a Test series in South Africa.

Which just goes to show that even the keenest New Zealand rugby memories are very, very short. Two or three months beforehand, the same thousands who greeted the return of the Bledisloe Cup with such optimistic glee were saying the opposite – that the All Blacks were annoyingly erratic, the coach John Mitchell was some rather dense fellow who delivered only rugby-speak platitudes, and that Reuben Thorne's captaincy ability was so modest that his grading had been reduced from 'Captain Impossible' to 'Captain Invisible.'

Mitchell was blamed for this low state of New Zealand rugby morale from the time he took a 'development' All Black side on a three-Test expedition to Europe in November 2002. Nine top-ranked All Blacks – including Thorne and six other leading forwards – were left behind. Taine Randell was pressed into taking the captaincy when everyone knew he was not Mitchell's long-term favourite as a leader or player.

There were cries that Mitchell was cheapening the thread of the All Black jersey by promoting so many half-All Blacks. The clamour became louder as the All Blacks lost to England, drew with France and defeated Wales. It became louder still when crowd favourites such as Christian Cullen, Taine Randell and Andrew Mehrtens were later left beyond the sideline and Jonah Lomu was so stricken by his kidney problem that he was under dialysis treatment. And the conservative South almost rebelled when Carlos Spencer, regarded in southern parts as a flighty butterfly of a player, became Mitchell's tactical hinge at five-eighths – and Mehrtens faded further into the background.

There was some warmer commendation for the promotion of a full-back of all-round talent, Mils Muliaina, in place of Leon MacDonald who was a concussion risk; of a boisterous No 8 Jerry Collins; the former rugby league hard man Brad Thorn; a talented young mid-fielder Daniel Carter and a Fijian flier, Joe Rococoko, as wing partner for the flying Doug Howlett.

The All Blacks took a backward step when England out-muscled them 15-13 at Wellington, a curious game that showed the New Zealanders' lack of tactical nous, especially when they could not score a try against an England side temporarily reduced to 13 men. Wales were dismissed 55-3, but France were, for what they regarded as a below-strength side, disconcertingly dangerous even though the All Blacks squeezed out a 31-23 win.

The French had re-opened the wounds in the All Black line-out. The New Zealand back play was brittle while the defence was of thistledown substance as France ran in two simple forward tries. Public dissatisfaction deepened with the news that Cullen would be lost to Munster and Randell to Saracens – further blots, so it seemed, on the Mitchell escutcheon.

The public ill-humour poured down on the All Blacks, so much so that two or three senior players said they looked forward to the freedom they would have away from their home-folk as they played their first two Tri Nations matches at Pretoria and Sydney.

A fortnight later the mood had changed completely. There were seven spanking tries when the All Black backs destroyed South Africa 52-16 and, a week later, another seven-try haul in the 50-21 drubbing of a disjointed Wallaby side at Sydney. In those eight days Thorne, Mitchell and their players were apparently changed from the ugliest ducklings to serenely beautiful swans. Mitchell further proved his point by resting half his best pack, and with a superb defensive effort ground out an old-fashioned arm-wrestle of a win, 19-11, over South Africa at Dunedin.

So the scene was set for the stunning rugby occasion that was Eden Park, 16 August, 2003. The Tri Nations contest was taken 4-0 and the Bledisloe Cup was back in its original home. And, as a fitting footnote, the final All Black triumph owed much to Thorne's level-headed captaincy during the Test series, and a brilliant tour-de-force as he took complete control of the ball in the last twitchy ten minutes when the Wallabies went close to what would have been a miraculous win. 'Captain Invisible' had become 'Captain Invincible.' Thorne, his team and all New Zealand were now almost confident of bringing home the World Cup.

New Zealand's Test Record in 2002-2003: Played 10, won 7, drawn 1, lost 2

Opponents	*Date*	*Venue*	*Result*
Australia	16th August 2003	H	Won 21-17
South Africa	9th August 2003	H	Won 19-11
Australia	26th July 2003	A	Won 50-21
South Africa	19th July 2003	A	Won 52-16
France	28th June 2003	H	Won 31-23
Wales	21st June 2003	H	Won 55-3
England	14th June 2003	H	Lost 13-15
Wales	23rd November 2002	A	Won 43-17
France	16th November 2002	A	Drawn 20-20
England	9th November 2002	A	Lost 28-31

NEW ZEALAND INTERNATIONAL STATISTICS

(up to 30 September 2003)

Match Records

MOST CONSECUTIVE TEST WINS

17 1965 *SA* 4, 1966 *BI* 1,2,3,4, 1967 *A,E,W,F,S,* 1968 *A* 1,2, *F* 1,2,3, 1969 *W* 1,2
12 1988 *A* 3, 1989 *F* 1,2, *Arg* 1,2, *A,W,I,* 1990 *S* 1,2, *A* 1,2

MOST CONSECUTIVE TESTS WITHOUT DEFEAT

Matches	*Wins*	*Draws*	*Period*
23	22	1	1987 to 1990
17	15	2	1961 to 1964
17	17	0	1965 to 1969

MOST POINTS IN A MATCH

by the team

Pts	*Opponents*	*Venue*	*Year*
145	Japan	Bloemfontein	1995
102	Tonga	Albany	2000
101	Italy	Huddersfield	1999
93	Argentina	Wellington	1997
74	Fiji	Christchurch	1987
73	Canada	Auckland	1995
71	Fiji	Albany	1997
71	Samoa	Albany	1999

by a player

Pts	*Player*	*Opponents*	*Venue*	*Year*
45	S D Culhane	Japan	Bloemfontein	1995
36	T E Brown	Italy	Huddersfield	1999
33	C J Spencer	Argentina	Wellington	1997
33	A P Mehrtens	Ireland	Dublin	1997
32	T E Brown	Tonga	Albany	2000
30	M C G Ellis	Japan	Bloemfontein	1995
30	T E Brown	Samoa	Albany	2001
29	A P Mehrtens	Australia	Auckland	1999
29	A P Mehrtens	France	Paris	2000
28	A P Mehrtens	Canada	Auckland	1995

MOST TRIES IN A MATCH

by the team

Tries	*Opponents*	*Venue*	*Year*
21	Japan	Bloemfontein	1995
15	Tonga	Albany	2000
14	Argentina	Wellington	1997
14	Italy	Huddersfield	1999
13	U S A	Berkeley	1913
12	Italy	Auckland	1987
12	Fiji	Christchurch	1987

by a player

Tries	*Player*	*Opponents*	*Venue*	*Year*
6	M C G Ellis	Japan	Bloemfontein	1995
5	J W Wilson	Fiji	Albany	1997
4	D McGregor	England	Crystal Palace	1905
4	C I Green	Fiji	Christchurch	1987
4	J A Gallagher	Fiji	Christchurch	1987
4	J J Kirwan	Wales	Christchurch	1988
4	J T Lomu	England	Cape Town	1995
4	C M Cullen	Scotland	Dunedin	1996
4	J W Wilson	Samoa	Albany	1999

MOST CONVERSIONS IN A MATCH

by the team

Cons	*Opponents*	*Venue*	*Year*
20	Japan	Bloemfontein	1995
12	Tonga	Albany	2000
11	Italy	Huddersfield	1999
10	Fiji	Christchurch	1987
10	Argentina	Wellington	1997
8	Italy	Auckland	1987
8	Wales	Auckland	1988
8	Fiji	Albany	1997
8	Italy	Hamilton	2002

by a player

Cons	*Player*	*Opponents*	*Venue*	*Year*
20	S D Culhane	Japan	Bloemfontein	1995
12	T E Brown	Tonga	Albany	2000
11	T E Brown	Italy	Huddersfield	1999
10	G J Fox	Fiji	Christchurch	1987
10	C J Spencer	Argentina	Wellington	1997
8	G J Fox	Italy	Auckland	1987
8	G J Fox	Wales	Auckland	1988
8	A P Mehrtens	Italy	Hamilton	2002

MOST PENALTIES IN A MATCH

by the team

Penalties	*Opponents*	*Venue*	*Year*
9	Australia	Auckland	1999
9	France	Paris	2000
7	Western Samoa	Auckland	1993

7	South Africa	Pretoria	1999
6	British/Irish Lions	Dunedin	1959
6	England	Christchurch	1985
6	Argentina	Wellington	1987
6	Scotland	Christchurch	1987
6	France	Paris	1990
6	South Africa	Auckland	1994
6	Australia	Brisbane	1996
6	Ireland	Dublin	1997
6	South Africa	Cardiff	1999
6	Scotland	Murrayfield	2001

by a player

Penalties	Player	Opponents	Venue	Year
9	A P Mehrtens	Australia	Auckland	1999
9	A P Mehrtens	France	Paris	2000
7	G J Fox	Western Samoa	Auckland	1993
7	A P Mehrtens	South Africa	Pretoria	1999
6	D B Clarke	British/Irish Lions	Dunedin	1959
6	K J Crowley	England	Christchurch	1985
6	G J Fox	Argentina	Wellington	1987
6	G J Fox	Scotland	Christchurch	1987
6	G J Fox	France	Paris	1990
6	S P Howarth	South Africa	Auckland	1994
6	A P Mehrtens	Australia	Brisbane	1996
6	A P Mehrtens	Ireland	Dublin	1997
6	A P Mehrtens	South Africa	Cardiff	1999
6	A P Mehrtens	Scotland	Murrayfield	2001

MOST DROPPED GOALS IN A MATCH

by the team

Drops	Opponents	Venue	Year
3	France	Christchurch	1986

by a player

Drops	Player	Opponents	Venue	Year
2	O D Bruce	Ireland	Dublin	1978
2	F M Botica	France	Christchurch	1986
2	A P Mehrtens	Australia	Auckland	1995

Career Records

MOST CAPPED PLAYERS

Caps	Player	Career Span
92	S B T Fitzpatrick	1986 to 1997
79	I D Jones	1990 to 1999
66	A P Mehrtens	1995 to 2002
65	J W Marshall	1995 to 2003
63	J J Kirwan	1984 to 1994
63	J T Lomu	1994 to 2002
62	R M Brooke	1992 to 1999
60	C W Dowd	1993 to 2001
60	J W Wilson	1993 to 2001
58	G W Whetton	1981 to 1991
58	Z V Brooke	1987 to 1997
58	C M Cullen	1996 to 2002
56	O M Brown	1992 to 1998
55	C E Meads	1957 to 1971
55	F E Bunce	1992 to 1997
55	M N Jones	1987 to 1998
54	J A Kronfeld	1995 to 2000

MOST CONSECUTIVE TESTS

Tests	Player	Span
63	S B T Fitzpatrick	1986 to 1995
51	C M Cullen	1996 to 2000
49	R M Brooke	1995 to 1999
41	J W Wilson	1996 to 1999
40	G W Whetton	1986 to 1991

MOST TESTS AS CAPTAIN

Tests	Captain	Span
51	S B T Fitzpatrick	1992 to 1997
30	W J Whineray	1958 to 1965
22	T C Randell	1998 to 2002
19	G N K Mourie	1977 to 1982
18	B J Lochore	1966 to 1970
17	A G Dalton	1981 to 1985

MOST TESTS IN INDIVIDUAL POSITIONS

Position	Player	Tests	Span
Full-back	C M Cullen	45	1996 to 2002
Wing	J J Kirwan	63	1984 to 1994
	J T Lomu	63	1994 to 2002
Centre	F E Bunce	55	1992 to 1997
Fly-half	A P Mehrtens	66	1995 to 2002
Scrum-half	J W Marshall	64	1995 to 2003
Prop	C W Dowd	58	1993 to 2000
Hooker	S B T Fitzpatrick	92	1986 to 1997
Lock	I D Jones	79	1990 to 1999
Flanker	J A Kronfeld	54	1995 to 2000
No 8	Z V Brooke	52	1990 to 1997

Cullen and Marshall have been capped elsewhere in the back division

MOST POINTS IN TESTS

Points	Player	Tests	Career
932	A P Mehrtens	66	1995 to 2002
645	G J Fox	46	1985 to 1993
250	C J Spencer	22	1997 to 2003
236	C M Cullen	58	1996 to 2002

234	J W Wilson	60	1993 to 2001
207	D B Clarke	31	1956 to 1964
201	A R Hewson	19	1981 to 1984
185	J T Lomu	63	1994 to 2002

MOST TRIES IN TESTS

Tries	*Player*	*Tests*	*Career*
46	C M Cullen	58	1996 to 2002
44	J W Wilson	60	1993 to 2001
37	J T Lomu	63	1994 to 2002
35	J J Kirwan	63	1984 to 1994
27*	J F Umaga	52	1999 to 2003
24	D C Howlett	31	2000 to 2003
22	J W Marshall	65	1995 to 2003
20	F E Bunce	55	1992 to 1997
19	S S Wilson	34	1977 to 1983
19	T J Wright	30	1986 to 1991

** Umaga's haul includes a penalty try*

MOST CONVERSIONS IN TESTS

Cons	*Player*	*Tests*	*Career*
162	A P Mehrtens	66	1995 to 2002
118	G J Fox	46	1985 to 1993
48	C J Spencer	22	1997 to 2003
43	T E Brown	18	1999 to 2001
33	D B Clarke	31	1956 to 1964
32	S D Culhane	6	1995 to 1996

MOST PENALTY GOALS IN TESTS

Penalties	*Player*	*Tests*	*Career*
181	A P Mehrtens	66	1995 to 2003
128	G J Fox	46	1985 to 1993
43	A R Hewson	19	1981 to 1984
38	D B Clarke	31	1956 to 1964
38	C J Spencer	22	1997 to 2003
24	W F McCormick	16	1965 to 1971

MOST DROPPED GOALS IN TESTS

Drops	*Player*	*Tests*	*Career*
10	A P Mehrtens	66	1995 to 2002
7	G J Fox	46	1985 to 1993
5	D B Clarke	31	1956 to 1964
5	M A Herewini	10	1962 to 1967
5	O D Bruce	14	1976 to 1978

Tri Nations Records

Record	*Detail*	*Holder*	*Set*
Most points in season	159	in four matches	1997
Most tries in season	17	in four matches	1997
	17	in four matches	2003
Highest Score	55	55-35 v S Africa (h)	1997
Biggest win	37	43-6 v Australia (h)	1996
Highest score conceded	46	40-46 v S Africa (a)	2000
Biggest defeat	21	7-28 v Australia (a)	1999
Most points in matches	309	A P Mehrtens	1996 to 2002
Most points in season	84	C J Spencer	1997
Most points in match	29	A P Mehrtens	v Australia (h) 1999
Most tries in matches	16	C M Cullen	1996 to 2002
Most tries in season	7	C M Cullen	2000
Most tries in match	3	J T Rokocoko	v Australia (a) 2003
Most cons in matches	32	A P Mehrtens	1996 to 2002
Most cons in season	13	C J Spencer	1997
Most cons in match	4	C J Spencer	v S Africa (h) 1997
	4	A P Mehrtens	v Australia (a) 2000
	4	A P Mehrtens	v S Africa (a) 2000
	4	C J Spencer	v S Africa (a) 2003
Most pens in matches	77	A P Mehrtens	1996 to 2002
Most pens in season	19	A P Mehrtens	1996
	19	A P Mehrtens	1999
Most pens in match	9	A P Mehrtens	v Australia (h) 1999

Series Records

Record	Holder	Detail
Most tries	C M Cullen	7 v Tri Nations 2000
Most points	C J Spencer	84 v Tri Nations 1997

Miscellaneous Records

Record	Holder	Detail
Longest Test Career	E Hughes/ C E Meads	15 seasons, 1907-21/1957-71
Youngest Test Cap	J T Lomu	19 yrs 45 days in 1994
Oldest Test Cap	E Hughes	40 yrs 123 days in 1921

Career Records Of New Zealand International Players
(up to 30 September 2003)

	Debut	Caps	T	C	P	D	Pts
Backs:							
B A Blair	2001 v S	4	0	2	0	0	4
D W Carter	2003 v W	3	2	9	5	0	43
C M Cullen	1996 v WS	58	46	3	0	0	236
S J Devine	2002 v E	7	0	0	0	0	0
D C Howlett	2000 v Tg	31	24	0	0	0	120
B T Kelleher	1999 v WS	24	4	0	0	0	20
R M King	2002 v W	1	1	0	0	0	5
D D Lee	2002 v E	2	1	0	0	0	5
J T Lomu	1994 v F	63	37	0	0	0	185
K R Lowen	2002 v E	1	0	0	0	0	0
L R MacDonald	2000 v S	19	7*	0	0	0	35
J W Marshall	1995 v F	65	22	0	0	0	110
A J D Mauger	2001 v I	15	5	5	1	0	38
A P Mehrtens	1995 v C	66	7	162	181	10	932
M Muliaina	2003 v E	7	0	0	0	0	0
M Nonu	2003 v E	1	0	0	0	0	0
C S Ralph	1998 v E	10	4	0	0	0	20
M P Robinson	2000 v S	9	1	0	0	0	5
J T Rokocoko	2003 v E	7	11	0	0	0	55
C J Spencer	1997 v Arg	22	8	48	38	0	250
P C Steinmetz	2002 v W	1	0	0	0	0	0
J F Umaga	1997 v Fj	52	27*	0	0	0	135
Forwards:							
D J Braid	2002 v W	1	0	0	0	0	0
S R Broomhall	2002 v SA	4	0	0	0	0	0
J Collins	2001 v Arg	8	0	0	0	0	0
G E Feek	1999 v WS	10	0	0	0	0	0
M G Hammett	1999 v F	24	3	0	0	0	15
S Harding	2002 v Fj	1	0	0	0	0	0
C J Hayman	2001 v Sm	8	0	0	0	0	0
D N Hewett	2001 v I	16	2	0	0	0	10
C H Hoeft	1998 v E	28	0	0	0	0	0
M R Holah	2001 v Sm	17	2	0	0	0	10
A K Hore	2002 v E	2	0	0	0	0	0

C R Jack	2001 v Arg	20	2	0	0	0	10
R H McCaw	2001 v I	14	1	0	0	0	5
J M McDonnell	2002 v It	8	1	0	0	0	5
T S Maling	2002 v It	7	0	0	0	0	0
K F Mealamu	2002 v W	8	1	0	0	0	5
K J Meeuws	1998 v A	29	7	0	0	0	35
B M Mika	2002 v E	3	0	0	0	0	0
A D Oliver	1997 v Fj	41	2	0	0	0	10
T C Randell	1997 v Fj	51	12	0	0	0	60
S M Robertson	1998 v A	23	4	0	0	0	20
K J Robinson	2002 v E	3	0	0	0	0	0
R So'oialo	2002 v W	3	0	0	0	0	0
G M Somerville	2000 v Tg	28	0	0	0	0	0
B C Thorn	2003 v W	5	0	0	0	0	0
R D Thorne	1999 v SA	34	3	0	0	0	15
A J Williams	2002 v E	10	0	0	0	0	0
T E Willis	2002 v It	5	0	0	0	0	0
T D Woodcock	2002 v W	1	0	0	0	0	0

NB MacDonald's figures include a penalty try awarded against South Africa in 2001 and Umaga's a penalty try awarded against South Africa in 2002.

NEW ZEALAND INTERNATIONAL PLAYERS

(up to 30 September 2003)

Abbott, H L (Taranaki) 1906 *F*
Aitken, G G (Wellington) 1921 *SA* 1,2
Alatini, P F (Otago) 1999 *F* 1(R), [*It, SA* 3(R)], 2000 *Tg, S* 1, *A* 1, *SA* 1, *A* 2, *SA* 2, *It*, 2001 *Sm, Arg* 1, *F, SA* 1, *A* 1, *SA* 2, *A* 2
Allen, F R (Auckland) 1946 *A* 1,2, 1947 *A* 1,2, 1949 *SA* 1,2
Allen, M R (Taranaki, Manawatu) 1993 *WS* (t), 1996 *S* 2 (t), 1997 *Arg* 1(R),2(R), *SA* 2(R), *A* 3(R), *E* 2, *W* (R)
Allen, N H (Counties) 1980 *A* 3, *W*
Alley, G T (Canterbury) 1928 *SA* 1,2,3
Anderson, A (Canterbury) 1983 *S, E*, 1984 *A* 1,2,3, 1987 [*Fj*]
Anderson, B L (Wairarapa-Bush) 1986 *A* 1
Archer, W R (Otago, Southland) 1955 *A* 1,2, 1956 *SA* 1,3
Argus, W G (Canterbury) 1946 *A* 1,2, 1947 *A* 1,2
Arnold, D A (Canterbury) 1963 *I, W*, 1964 *E, F*
Arnold, K D (Waikato) 1947 *A* 1,2
Ashby, D L (Southland) 1958 *A* 2
Asher, A A (Auckland) 1903 *A*
Ashworth, B G (Auckland) 1978 *A* 1,2
Ashworth, J C (Canterbury, Hawke's Bay) 1978 *A* 1,2,3, 1980 *A* 1,2,3, 1981 *SA* 1,2,3, 1982 *A* 1,2, 1983 *BI* 1,2,3,4, *A*, 1984 *F* 1,2, *A* 1,2,3, 1985 *E* 1,2, *A*
Atkinson, H (West Coast) 1913 *A* 1
Avery, H E (Wellington) 1910 *A* 1,2,3

Bachop, G T M (Canterbury) 1989 *W, I*, 1990 *S* 1,2, *A* 1,2,3, *F* 1,2, 1991 *Arg* 1,2, *A* 1,2, [*E, US, C, A, S*], 1992 *Wld* 1, 1994 *SA* 1,2,3, *A*, 1995 *C*, [*I, W, S, E, SA*], *A* 1,2
Bachop, S J (Otago) 1994 *F* 2, *SA* 1,2,3, *A*
Badeley, C E O (Auckland) 1921 *SA* 1,2
Baird, J A S (Otago) 1913 *A* 2
Ball, N (Wellington) 1931 *A*, 1932 *A* 2,3, 1935 *W*, 1936 *E*
Barrett, J (Auckland) 1913 *A* 2,3
Barry, E F (Wellington) 1934 *A* 2
Barry, L J (North Harbour) 1995 *F* 2
Batty, G B (Wellington, Bay of Plenty) 1972 *W, S*, 1973 *E* 1, *I, F, E* 2, 1974 *A* 1,3, *I*, 1975 *S*, 1976 *SA* 1,2,3,4, 1977 *BI* 1
Batty, W (Auckland) 1930 *BI* 1,3,4, 1931 *A*
Beatty, G E (Taranaki) 1950 *BI* 1
Bell, R H (Otago) 1951 *A* 3, 1952 *A* 1,2
Bellis, E A (Wanganui) 1921 *SA* 1,2,3
Bennet, R (Otago) 1905 *A*
Berghan, T (Otago) 1938 *A* 1,2,3
Berry, M J (Wairarapa-Bush) 1986 *A* 3(R)
Berryman, N R (Northland) 1998 *SA* 2(R)
Bevan, V D (Wellington) 1949 *A* 1,2, 1950 *BI* 1,2,3,4
Birtwistle, W M (Canterbury) 1965 *SA* 1,2,3,4, 1967 *E, W, S*
Black, J E (Canterbury) 1977 *F* 1, 1979 *A*, 1980 *A* 3
Black, N W (Auckland) 1949 *SA* 3
Black, R S (Otago) 1914 *A* 1
Blackadder, T J (Canterbury) 1998 *E* 1(R),2, 2000 *Tg, S* 1,2, *A* 1, *SA* 1, *A* 2, *SA* 2, *F 1,2, It*
Blair, B A (Canterbury) 2001 *S* (R), *Arg* 2, 2002 *E, W*
Blake, A W (Wairarapa) 1949 *A* 1
Blowers, A F (Auckland) 1996 *SA* 2(R),4(R), 1997 *I, E* 1(R), *W* (R), 1999 *F* 1(R), *SA* 1, *A* 1(R), *SA* 2, *A* 2(R), [*It*]
Boggs, E G (Auckland) 1946 *A* 2, 1949 *SA* 1
Bond, J G (Canterbury) 1949 *A* 2
Booth, E E (Otago) 1906 *F*, 1907 *A* 1,3
Boroevich, K G (Wellington) 1986 *F* 1, *A* 1, *F* 3(R)
Botica, F M (North Harbour) 1986 *F* 1, *A* 1,2,3, *F* 2,3, 1989 *Arg* 1(R)
Bowden, N J G (Taranaki) 1952 *A* 2
Bowers, R G (Wellington) 1954 *I, F*
Bowman, A W (Hawke's Bay) 1938 *A* 1,2,3
Braid, D J (Auckland) 2002 *W*
Braid, G J (Bay of Plenty) 1983 *S, E*
Bremner, S G (Auckland, Canterbury) 1952 *A* 2, 1956 *SA* 2
Brewer, M R (Otago, Canterbury) 1986 *F* 1, *A* 1,2,3, *F* 2,3, 1988 *A* 1, 1989 *A, W, I*, 1990 *S* 1,2, *A* 1,2,3, *F* 1,2, 1992 *I* 2, *A* 1, 1994 *F* 1,2, *SA* 1,2,3, *A*, 1995 *C*, [*I, W, E, SA*], *A* 1,2
Briscoe, K C (Taranaki) 1959 *BI* 2, 1960 *SA* 1,2,3,4, 1963 *I, W*, 1964 *E, S*
Brooke, R M (Auckland) 1992 *I* 2, *A* 1,2,3, *SA*, 1993 *BI* 1,2,3, *A, WS*, 1994 *SA* 2,3, 1995 *C*, [*J, S, E, SA*], *A* 1,2, *It, F* 1,2, 1996 *WS, S* 1,2, *A* 1, *SA* 1, *A* 2, *SA* 2,3,4,5, 1997 *Fj, Arg* 1,2, *A* 1, *SA* 1, *A* 2, *SA* 2, *A* 3, *I, E* 1, *W, E* 2, 1998 *E* 1,2, *A* 1, *SA* 1, *A* 2, *SA* 2, *A* 3, 1999 *WS, F* 1, *SA* 1, *A* 1, *SA* 2, *A* 2, [*Tg, E, It* (R), *S, F* 2]
Brooke, Z V (Auckland) 1987 [*Arg*], 1989 *Arg* 2(R), 1990 *A* 1,2,3, *F* 1(R), 1991 *Arg* 2, *A* 1,2, [*E, It, C, A, S*], 1992 *A* 2,3, *SA*, 1993 *BI* 1,2,3(R), *WS* (R), *S, E*, 1994 *F* 2, *SA* 1,2,3, *A*, 1995 [*J, S, E, SA*], *A* 1,2, *It, F* 1,2, 1996 *WS, S* 1,2, *A* 1, *SA* 1, *A* 2, *SA* 2,3,4,5, 1997 *Arg* 1,2, *A* 1, *SA* 1, *A* 2, *SA* 2, *A* 3, *I, E* 1, *W, E* 2
Brooke-Cowden, M (Auckland) 1986 *F* 1, *A* 1, 1987 [*W*]
Broomhall, S R (Canterbury) 2002 *SA* 1(R),2(R), *E, F*
Brown, C (Taranaki) 1913 *A* 2,3
Brown, O M (Auckland) 1992 *I* 2, *A* 1,2,3, *SA*, 1993 *BI* 1,2,3, *A, S, E*, 1994 *F* 1,2, *SA* 1,2,3, *A*, 1995 *C*, [*I, W, S, E, SA*], *A* 1,2, *It, F* 1,2, 1996 *WS, S* 1,2, *A* 1, *SA* 1, *A* 2, *SA* 2,3,4,5, 1997 *Fj, Arg* 1,2, *A* 1, *SA* 1, *A* 2, *SA* 2, *A* 3, *I, E* 1, *W, E* 2, 1998 *E* 1,2, *A* 1, *SA* 1, *A* 2, *SA* 2
Brown, R H (Taranaki) 1955 *A* 3, 1956 *SA* 1,2,3,4, 1957 *A* 1,2, 1958 *A* 1,2,3, 1959 *BI* 1,3, 1961 *F* 1,2,3, 1962 *A* 1
Brown, T E (Otago) 1999 *WS, F* 1(R), *SA* 1(R), *A* 1(R),2(R), [*E* (R), *It, S* (R)], 2000 *Tg, S* 2(R), *A* 1(R), *SA* 1(R), *A* 2(R), 2001 *Sm, Arg* 1(R), *F, SA* 1, *A* 1
Brownlie, C J (Hawke's Bay) 1924 *W*, 1925 *E, F*
Brownlie, M J (Hawke's Bay) 1924 *I, W*, 1925 *E, F*, 1928 *SA* 1,2,3,4
Bruce, J A (Auckland) 1914 *A* 1,2
Bruce, O D (Canterbury) 1976 *SA* 1,2,4, 1977 *BI* 2,3,4, *F* 1,2, 1978 *A* 1,2, *I, W, E, S*
Bryers, R F (King Country) 1949 *A* 1
Budd, T A (Southland) 1946 *A* 2, 1949 *A* 2
Bullock-Douglas, G A H (Wanganui) 1932 *A* 1,2,3, 1934 *A* 1,2
Bunce, F E (North Harbour) 1992 *Wld* 1,2,3, *I* 1,2, *A* 1,2,3, *SA*, 1993 *BI* 1,2,3, *A, WS, S, E*, 1994 *F* 1,2, *SA* 1,2,3, *A*, 1995 *C*, [*I, W, S, E, SA*], *A* 1,2, *It, F* 1,2, 1996 *WS, S* 1,2, *A*1, *SA* 1, *A* 2, *SA* 2,3,4,5, 1997 *Fj, Arg* 1,2, *A* 1, *SA* 1, *A* 2, *SA* 2, *A* 3, *I, E* 1, *W, E* 2
Burgess, G A J (Auckland) 1981 *SA* 2
Burgess, G F (Southland) 1905 *A*
Burgess, R E (Manawatu) 1971 *BI* 1,2,3, 1972 *A* 3, *W*, 1973 *I, F*
Burke, P S (Taranaki) 1955 *A* 1, 1957 *A* 1,2
Burns, P J (Canterbury) 1908 *AW* 2, 1910 *A* 1,2,3, 1913 *A* 3
Bush, R G (Otago) 1931 *A*
Bush, W K (Canterbury) 1974 *A* 1,2, 1975 *S*, 1976 *I, SA*, 2,4, 1977 *BI* 2,3,4(R), 1978 *I, W*, 1979 *A*
Buxton, J B (Canterbury) 1955 *A* 3, 1956 *SA* 1

Cain, M J (Taranaki) 1913 *US*, 1914 *A* 1,2,3
Callesen, J A (Manawatu) 1974 *A* 1,2,3, 1975 *S*
Cameron, D (Taranaki) 1908 *AW* 1,2,3
Cameron, L M (Manawatu) 1980 *A* 3, 1981 *SA* 1(R),2,3, *R*
Carleton, S R (Canterbury) 1928 *SA* 1,2,3, 1929 *A* 1,2,3
Carrington, K R (Auckland) 1971 *BI* 1,3,4
Carter, D W (Canterbury) 2003 *W, F, A* 1(R)
Carter, M P (Auckland) 1991 *A* 2, [*It, A*], 1997 *Fj* (R), *A* 1(R), 1998 *E* 2(R), *A* 2
Casey, S T (Otago) 1905 *S, I, E, W*, 1907 *A* 1,2,3, 1908 *AW* 1
Cashmore, A R (Auckland) 1996 *S* 2(R), 1997 *A* 2(R)
Catley, E H (Waikato) 1946 *A* 1, 1947 *A* 1,2, 1949 *SA* 1,2,3,4
Caughey, T H C (Auckland) 1932 *A* 1,3, 1934 *A* 1,2, 1935 *S, I*, 1936 *E, A* 1, 1937 *SA* 3
Caulton, R W (Wellington) 1959 *BI* 2,3,4, 1960 *SA* 1,4, 1961 *F* 2, 1963 *E* 1,2, *I, W*, 1964 *E, S, F, A* 1,2,3
Cherrington, N P (North Auckland) 1950 *BI* 1
Christian, D L (Auckland) 1949 *SA* 4
Clamp, M (Wellington) 1984 *A* 2,3
Clark, D W (Otago) 1964 *A* 1,2
Clark, W H (Wellington) 1953 *W*, 1954 *I, E, S*, 1955 *A* 1,2, 1956 *SA* 2,3,4
Clarke, A H (Auckland) 1958 *A* 3, 1959 *BI* 4, 1960 *SA* 1
Clarke, D B (Waikato) 1956 *SA* 3,4, 1957 *A* 1,2, 1958 *A* 1,3, 1959 *BI* 1,2,3,4, 1960 *SA* 1,2,3,4, 1961 *F* 1,2,3, 1962 *A* 1,2,3,4,5, 1963 *E* 1,2, *I, W*, 1964 *E, S, F, A* 2,3
Clarke, E (Auckland) 1992 *Wld* 2,3, *I* 1,2, 1993 *BI* 1,2, *S* (R), *E*, 1998 *SA* 2, *A* 3

Clarke, I J (Waikato) 1953 *W*, 1955 *A* 1,2,3, 1956 *SA* 1,2,3,4, 1957 *A* 1,2, 1958 *A* 1,3, 1959 *BI* 1,2, 1960 *SA* 2,4, 1961 *F* 1,2,3, 1962 *A* 1,2,3, 1963 *E* 1,2
Clarke, R L (Taranaki) 1932 *A* 2,3
Cobden, D G (Canterbury) 1937 *SA* 1
Cockerill, M S (Taranaki) 1951 *A* 1,2,3
Cockroft, E A P (South Canterbury) 1913 *A* 3, 1914 *A* 2,3
Codlin, B W (Counties) 1980 *A* 1,2,3
Collins, A H (Taranaki) 1932 *A* 2,3, 1934 *A* 1
Collins, J (Wellington) 2001 *Arg* 1, 2003 *E* (R), *W, F, SA* 1, *A* 1, *SA* 2, *A* 2
Collins, J L (Poverty Bay) 1964 *A* 1, 1965 *SA* 1,4
Colman, J T H (Taranaki) 1907 *A* 1,2, 1908 *AW* 1,3
Connor, D M (Auckland) 1961 *F* 1,2,3, 1962 *A* 1,2,3,4,5, 1963 *E* 1,2, 1964 *A* 2,3
Conway, R J (Otago, Bay of Plenty) 1959 *BI* 2,3,4, 1960 *SA* 1,3,4, 1965 *SA* 1,2,3,4
Cooke, A E (Auckland, Wellington) 1924 *I, W*, 1925 *E, F*, 1930 *BI* 1,2,3,4
Cooke, R J (Canterbury) 1903 *A*
Cooksley, M S B (Counties, Waikato) 1992 *Wld* 1, 1993 *BI* 2,3(R), *A*, 1994 *F* 1,2, *SA* 1,2, *A*, 2001 *A* 1(R), *SA* 2(t&R)
Cooper, G J L (Auckland, Otago) 1986 *F* 1, *A* 1,2, 1992 *Wld* 1,2,3, *I* 1
Cooper, M J A (Waikato) 1992 *I* 2, *SA* (R), 1993 *BI* 1(R),3(t), *WS* (t), *S*, 1994 *F* 1,2
Corner, M M N (Auckland) 1930 *BI* 2,3,4, 1931 *A*, 1934 *A* 1, 1936 *E*
Cossey, R R (Counties) 1958 *A* 1
Cottrell, A I (Canterbury) 1929 *A* 1,2,3, 1930 *BI* 1,2,3,4, 1931 *A*, 1932 *A* 1,2,3
Cottrell, W D (Canterbury) 1968 *A* 1,2, *F* 2,3, 1970 *SA* 1, 1971 *BI* 1,2,3,4
Couch, M B R (Wairarapa) 1947 *A* 1, 1949 *A* 1,2
Coughlan, T D (South Canterbury) 1958 *A* 1
Creighton, J N (Canterbury) 1962 *A* 4
Cribb, R T (North Harbour) 2000 *S* 1,2, *A* 1, *SA* 1, *A* 2, *SA* 2, *F* 1,2, *It*, 2001 *Sm, F, SA* 1, *A* 1, *SA* 2, *A* 2
Crichton, S (Wellington) 1983 *S, E*
Cross, T (Canterbury) 1904 *BI*, 1905 *A*
Crowley, K J (Taranaki) 1985 *E* 1,2, *A, Arg* 1,2, 1986 *A* 3, *F* 2,3, 1987 [*Arg*], 1990 *S* 1,2, *A* 1,2,3, *F* 1,2, 1991 *Arg* 1,2, [*A*]
Crowley, P J B (Auckland) 1949 *SA* 3,4, 1950 *BI* 1,2,3,4
Culhane, S D (Southland) 1995 [*J*], *It, F* 1,2, 1996 *SA* 3,4
Cullen C M (Manawatu, Central Vikings, Wellington) 1996 *WS, S* 1,2, *A* 1, *SA* 1, *A* 2, *SA* 2,3,4,5, 1997 *Fj, Arg* 1,2, *A* 1, *SA* 1, *A* 2, *SA* 2, *A* 3, *I, E* 1, *W, E* 2, 1998 *E* 1,2, *A* 1, *SA* 1, *A* 2, *SA* 2, *A* 3, 1999 *WS, F* 1, *SA* 1, *A* 1, *SA* 2, *A* 2, [*Tg, E, It* (R), *S, F* 2, *SA* 3], 2000 *Tg, S* 1,2, *A* 1, *SA* 1, *A* 2, *SA* 2, *F* 1,2, *It*, 2001 *A* 2(R), 2002 *It, Fj, A* 1, *SA* 1, *A* 2, *F*
Cummings, W (Canterbury) 1913 *A* 2,3
Cundy, R T (Wairarapa) 1929 *A* 2(R)
Cunningham, G R (Auckland) 1979 *A, S, E*, 1980 *A* 1,2
Cunningham, W (Auckland) 1905 *S, I*, 1906 *F*, 1907 *A* 1,2,3, 1908 *AW* 1,2,3
Cupples, L F (Bay of Plenty) 1924 *I, W*
Currie, C J (Canterbury) 1978 *I, W*
Cuthill, J E (Otago) 1913 *A* 1, *US*

Dalley, W C (Canterbury) 1924 *I*, 1928 *SA* 1,2,3,4
Dalton, A G (Counties) 1977 *F* 2, 1978 *A* 1,2,3, *I, W, E, S*, 1979 *F* 1,2, *S*, 1981 *S* 1,2, *SA* 1,2,3, *R, F* 1,2, 1982 *A* 1,2,3, 1983 *BI* 1,2,3,4, *A*, 1984 *F* 1,2, *A* 1,2,3, 1985 *E* 1,2, *A*
Dalton, D (Hawke's Bay) 1935 *I, W*, 1936 *A* 1,2, 1937 *SA* 1,2,3, 1938 *A* 1,2
Dalton, R A (Wellington) 1947 *A* 1,2
Dalzell, G N (Canterbury) 1953 *W*, 1954 *I, E, S, F*
Davie, M G (Canterbury) 1983 *E* (R)
Davies, W A (Auckland, Otago) 1960 *SA* 4, 1962 *A* 4,5
Davis, K (Auckland) 1952 *A* 2, 1953 *W*, 1954 *I, E, S, F*, 1955 *A* 2, 1958 *A* 1,2,3
Davis, L J (Canterbury) 1976 *I*, 1977 *BI* 3,4
Davis, W L (Hawke's Bay) 1967 *A, E, W, F, S*, 1968 *A* 1,2, *F* 1, 1969 *W* 1,2, 1970 *SA* 2
Deans, I B (Canterbury) 1988 *W* 1,2, *A* 1,2,3, 1989 *F* 1,2, *Arg* 1,2, *A*
Deans, R G (Canterbury) 1905 *S, I, E, W*, 1908 *AW* 3
Deans, R M (Canterbury) 1983 *S, E*, 1984 *A* 1(R),2,3
Delamore, G W (Wellington) 1949 *SA* 4
Devine, S J (Auckland) 2002 *E, W* 2003 *E* (R), *W, F, SA* 1, *A* 1(R)
Dewar, H (Taranaki) 1913 *A* 1, *US*
Diack, E S (Otago) 1959 *BI* 2
Dick, J (Auckland) 1937 *SA* 1,2, 1938 *A* 3
Dick, M J (Auckland) 1963 *I, W*, 1964 *E, S, F*, 1965 *SA* 3, 1966 *BI* 4, 1967 *A, E, W, F*, 1969 *W* 1,2, 1970 *SA* 1,4
Dixon, M J (Canterbury) 1954 *I, E, S, F*, 1956 *SA* 1,2,3,4, 1957 *A* 1,2
Dobson, R L (Auckland) 1949 *A* 1
Dodd, E H (Wellington) 1905 *A*
Donald, A J (Wanganui) 1983 *S, E*, 1984 *F* 1,2, *A* 1,2,3
Donald, J G (Wairarapa) 1921 *SA* 1,2
Donald, Q (Wairarapa) 1924 *I, W*, 1925 *E, F*
Donaldson, M W (Manawatu) 1977 *F* 1,2, 1978 *A* 1,2,3, *I, E, S*, 1979 *F* 1,2, *A, S* (R), 1981 *SA* 3(R)
Dougan, J P (Wellington) 1972 *A* 1, 1973 *E* 2
Dowd, C W (Auckland) 1993 *BI* 1,2,3, *A, WS, S, E*, 1994 *SA* 1(R), 1995 *C*, [*I, W, J, E, SA*], *A* 1,2, *It, F* 1,2, 1996 *WS, S* 1,2, *A* 1, *SA* 1, *A* 2, *SA* 2,3,4,5, 1997 *Fj, Arg* 1,2, *A* 1, *SA* 1, *A* 2, *SA* 2, *A* 3, *I, E* 1, *W*, 1998 *E* 1,2, *A* 1, *SA* 1, *A* 2,3(R), 1999 *SA* 2(R), *A* 2(R), [*Tg* (R), *E, It, S, F* 2, *SA* 3], 2000 *Tg, S* 1(R),2(R), *A* 1(R), *SA* 1(R), *A* 2(R)
Dowd, G W (North Harbour) 1992 *I* 1(R)
Downing, A J (Auckland) 1913 *A* 1, *US*, 1914 *A* 1,2,3
Drake, J A (Auckland) 1986 *F* 2,3, 1987 [*Fj, Arg, S, W, F*], *A*
Duff, R H (Canterbury) 1951 *A* 1,2,3, 1952 *A* 1,2, 1955 *A* 2,3, 1956 *SA* 1,2,3,4
Duggan, R J L (Waikato) 1999 [*It* (R)]
Duncan, J (Otago) 1903 *A*
Duncan, M G (Hawke's Bay) 1971 *BI* 3(R),4
Duncan, W D (Otago) 1921 *SA* 1,2,3
Dunn, E J (North Auckland) 1979 *S*, 1981 *S* 1
Dunn, I T W (North Auckland) 1983 *BI* 1,4, *A*
Dunn, J M (Auckland) 1946 *A* 1

Earl, A T (Canterbury) 1986 *F* 1, *A* 1, *F* 3(R), 1987 [*Arg*], 1989 *W, I*, 1991 *Arg* 1(R),2, *A* 1, [*E* (R), *US, S*], 1992 *A* 2,3(R)
Eastgate, B P (Canterbury) 1952 *A* 1,2, 1954 *S*
Elliott, K G (Wellington) 1946 *A* 1,2
Ellis, M C G (Otago) 1993 *S, E*, 1995 *C*, [*I* (R), *W, J, S, SA* (R)]
Elsom, A E G (Canterbury) 1952 *A* 1,2, 1953 *W*, 1955 *A* 1,2,3
Elvidge, R R (Otago) 1946 *A* 1,2, 1949 *SA* 1,2,3,4, 1950 *BI* 1,2,3
Erceg, C P (Auckland) 1951 *A* 1,2,3, 1952 *A* 1
Evans, D A (Hawke's Bay) 1910 *A* 2
Eveleigh, K A (Manawatu) 1976 *SA* 2,4, 1977 *BI* 1,2

Fanning, A H N (Canterbury) 1913 *A* 3
Fanning, B J (Canterbury) 1903 *A*, 1904 *BI*
Farrell, C P (Auckland) 1977 *BI* 1,2
Fawcett, C L (Auckland) 1976 *SA* 2,3
Fea, W R (Otago) 1921 *SA* 3
Feek, G E (Canterbury) 1999 *WS* (R), *A* 1(R), *SA* 2, [*E* (t), *It*], 2000 *F* 1,2, *It*, 2001 *I, S*
Finlay, B E L (Manawatu) 1959 *BI* 1
Finlay, J (Manawatu) 1946 *A* 1
Finlayson, I (North Auckland) 1928 *SA* 1,2,3,4, 1930 *BI* 1,2
Fitzgerald, J T (Wellington) 1952 *A* 1
Fitzpatrick, B B J (Wellington) 1953 *W*, 1954 *I, F*
Fitzpatrick, S B T (Auckland) 1986 *F* 1, *A* 1, *F* 2,3, 1987 [*It, Fj, Arg, S, W, F*], *A*, 1988 *W* 1,2, *A* 1,2,3, 1989 *F* 1,2, *Arg* 1,2, *A, W, I*, 1990 *S* 1,2, *A* 1,2,3, *F* 1,2, 1991 *Arg* 1,2, *A* 1,2, [*E, US, It, C, A, S*], 1992 *Wld* 1,2,3, *I* 1,2, *A* 1,2,3, *SA*, 1993 *BI* 1,2,3, *A, WS, S, E*, 1994 *F* 1,2, *SA* 1,2,3, *A*, 1995 *C*, [*I, W, S, E, SA*], *A* 1,2, *It, F* 1,2, 1996 *WS, S* 1,2, *A* 1, *SA* 1, *A* 2, *SA* 2,3,4,5, 1997 *Fj, Arg* 1,2, *A* 1, *SA* 1, *A* 2, *SA* 2, *A* 3, *W* (R)
Flavell, T V (North Harbour) 2000 *Tg, S* 1(R), *A* 1(R), *SA* 1,2(t), *F* 1(R),2(R), *It*, 2001 *Sm, Arg* 1, *F, SA* 1, *A* 1, *SA* 2, *A* 2
Fleming, J K (Wellington) 1979 *S, E*, 1980 *A* 1,2,3
Fletcher, C J C (North Auckland) 1921 *SA* 3
Fogarty, R (Taranaki) 1921 *SA* 1,3
Ford, B R (Marlborough) 1977 *BI* 3,4, 1978 *I*, 1979 *E*
Forster, S T (Otago) 1993 *S, E*, 1994 *F* 1,2, 1995 *It, F* 1
Fox, G J (Auckland) 1985 *Arg* 1, 1987 [*It, Fj, Arg, S, W, F*], *A*, 1988 *W* 1,2, *A* 1,2,3, 1989 *F* 1,2, *Arg* 1,2, *A, W, I*, 1990 *S* 1,2, *A* 1,2,3, *F* 1,2, 1991 *Arg* 1,2, *A* 1,2, [*E, It, C, A*], 1992 *Wld* 1,2(R), *A* 1,2,3, *SA*, 1993 *BI* 1,2,3, *A, WS*
Francis, A R H (Auckland) 1905 *A*, 1907 *A* 1,2,3, 1908 *AW* 1,2,3, 1910 *A* 1,2,3
Francis, W C (Wellington) 1913 *A* 2,3, 1914 *A* 1,2,3
Fraser, B G (Wellington) 1979 *S, E*, 1980 *A* 3, *W*, 1981 *S* 1,2, *SA* 1,2,3, *R, F* 1,2, 1982 *A* 1,2,3, 1983 *BI* 1,2,3,4, *A, S, E*, 1984 *A* 1

Frazer, H F (Hawke's Bay) 1946 *A* 1,2, 1947 *A* 1,2, 1949 *SA* 2
Fryer, F C (Canterbury) 1907 *A* 1,2,3, 1908 *AW* 2
Fuller, W B (Canterbury) 1910 *A* 1,2
Furlong, B D M (Hawke's Bay) 1970 *SA* 4

Gallagher, J A (Wellington) 1987 [*It, Fj, S, W, F*], *A*, 1988 *W* 1,2, *A* 1,2,3, 1989 *F* 1,2, *Arg* 1,2, *A, W, I*
Gallaher, D (Auckland) 1903 *A*, 1904 *BI*, 1905 *S, E, W*, 1906 *F*
Gard, P C (North Otago) 1971 *BI* 4
Gardiner, A J (Taranaki) 1974 *A* 3
Geddes, J H (Southland) 1929 *A* 1
Geddes, W McK (Auckland) 1913 *A* 2
Gemmell, B McL (Auckland) 1974 *A* 1,2
George, V L (Southland) 1938 *A* 1,2,3
Gibson, D P E (Canterbury) 1999 *WS, F* 1, *SA* 1, *A* 1, *SA* 2, *A* 2, [*Tg* (R), *E* (R), *It, S* (R), *F* 2(R)], 2000 *F* 1,2, 2002 *It, I* 1(R),2(R), *Fj*, A 2(R), *SA* 2(R)
Gilbert, G D M (West Coast) 1935 *S, I, W*, 1936 *E*
Gillespie, C T (Wellington) 1913 *A* 2
Gillespie, W D (Otago) 1958 *A* 3
Gillett, G A (Canterbury, Auckland) 1905 *S, I, E, W*, 1907 *A* 2,3, 1908 *AW* 1,3
Gillies, C C (Otago) 1936 *A* 2
Gilray, C M (Otago) 1905 *A*
Glasgow, F T (Taranaki, Southland) 1905 *S, I, E, W*, 1906 *F*, 1908 *AW* 3
Glenn, W S (Taranaki) 1904 *BI*, 1906 *F*
Goddard, M P (South Canterbury) 1946 *A* 2, 1947 *A* 1,2, 1949 *SA* 3,4
Going, S M (North Auckland) 1967 *A, F*, 1968 *F* 3, 1969 *W* 1,2, 1970 *SA* 1(R),4, 1971 *BI* 1,2,3,4, 1972 *A* 1,2,3, *W, S*, 1973 *E* 1, *I, F, E* 2, 1974 *I*, 1975 *S*, 1976 *I* (R), *SA* 1,2,3,4, 1977 *BI* 1,2
Gordon, S B (Waikato) 1993 *S, E*
Graham, D J (Canterbury) 1958 *A* 1,2, 1960 *SA* 2,3, 1961 *F* 1,2,3, 1962 *A* 1,2,3,4,5, 1963 *E* 1,2, *I, W*, 1964 *E, S, F, A* 1,2,3
Graham, J B (Otago) 1913 *US*, 1914 *A* 1,3
Graham, W G (Otago) 1979 *F* 1(R)
Grant, L A (South Canterbury) 1947 *A* 1,2, 1949 *SA* 1,2
Gray, G D (Canterbury) 1908 *AW* 2, 1913 *A* 1, *US*
Gray, K F (Wellington) 1963 *I, W*, 1964 *E, S, F, A* 1,2,3, 1965 *SA* 1,2,3,4, 1966 *BI* 1,2,3,4, 1967 *W, F, S*, 1968 *A* 1, *F* 2,3, 1969 *W* 1,2
Gray, W N (Bay of Plenty) 1955 *A* 2,3, 1956 *SA* 1,2,3,4
Green, C I (Canterbury) 1983 *S* (R), *E*, 1984 *A* 1,2,3, 1985 *E* 1,2, *A, Arg* 1,2, 1986 *A* 2,3, *F* 2,3, 1987 [*It, Fj, S, W, F*], *A*
Grenside, B A (Hawke's Bay) 1928 *SA* 1,2,3,4, 1929 *A* 2,3
Griffiths, J L (Wellington) 1934 *A* 2, 1935 *S, I, W*, 1936 *A* 1,2, 1938 *A* 3
Guy, R A (North Auckland) 1971 *BI* 1,2,3,4

Haden, A M (Auckland) 1977 *BI* 1,2,3,4, *F* 1,2, 1978 *A* 1,2,3, *I, W, E, S*, 1979 *F* 1,2, *A, S, E*, 1980 *A* 1,2,3, *W*, 1981 *S* 2, *SA* 1,2,3, *R, F* 1,2, 1982 *A* 1,2,3, 1983 *BI* 1,2,3,4, *A*, 1984 *F* 1,2, 1985 *Arg* 1,2
Hadley, S (Auckland) 1928 *SA* 1,2,3,4
Hadley, W E (Auckland) 1934 *A* 1,2, 1935 *S, I, W*, 1936 *E, A* 1,2
Haig, J S (Otago) 1946 *A* 1,2
Haig, L S (Otago) 1950 *BI* 2,3,4, 1951 *A* 1,2,3, 1953 *W*, 1954 *E, S*
Hales, D A (Canterbury) 1972 *A* 1,2,3, *W*
Hamilton, D C (Southland) 1908 *AW* 2
Hammett, MG (Canterbury) 1999 *F* 1(R), *SA* 2(R), [*It, S* (R), *SA* 3], 2000 *Tg, S* 1(R),2(t&R), *A* 1(R), *SA* 1(R), *A* 2(R), *SA* 2(R), *F* 2(R), *It* (R), 2001 *Arg* 1(t), 2002 *It* (R), *I* 1,2, *A* 1, *SA* 1,2(R), 2003 *SA* 1(R), *A* 1(R), *SA* 2
Hammond, I A (Marlborough) 1952 *A* 2
Harper, E T (Canterbury) 1904 *BI*, 1906 *F*
Harding, S (Otago) 2002 *Fj*
Harris, P C (Manawatu) 1976 *SA* 3
Hart, A H (Taranaki) 1924 *I*
Hart, G F (Canterbury) 1930 *BI* 1,2,3,4, 1931 *A*, 1934 *A* 1, 1935 *S, I, W*, 1936 *A* 1,2
Harvey, B A (Wairarapa-Bush) 1986 *F* 1
Harvey, I H (Wairarapa) 1928 *SA* 4
Harvey, L R (Otago) 1949 *SA* 1,2,3,4, 1950 *BI* 1,2,3,4
Harvey, P (Canterbury) 1904 *BI*
Hasell, E W (Canterbury) 1913 *A* 2,3
Hayman, C J (Otago) 2001 *Sm* (R), *Arg* 1, *F* (R), *A* 1(R), *SA* 2(R), *A* 2(R), 2002 *F* (t), *W*
Hayward, H O (Auckland) 1908 *AW* 3
Hazlett, E J (Southland) 1966 *BI* 1,2,3,4, 1967 *A, E*
Hazlett, W E (Southland) 1928 *SA* 1,2,3,4, 1930 *BI* 1,2,3,4
Heeps, T R (Wellington) 1962 *A* 1,2,3,4,5
Heke, W R (North Auckland) 1929 *A* 1,2,3
Hemi, R C (Waikato) 1953 *W*, 1954 *I, E, S, F*, 1955 *A* 1,2,3, 1956 *SA* 1,3,4, 1957 *A* 1,2, 1959 *BI* 1,3,4
Henderson, P (Wanganui) 1949 *SA* 1,2,3,4, 1950 *BI* 2,3,4
Henderson, P W (Otago) 1991 *Arg* 1, [*C*], 1992 *Wld* 1,2,3, *I* 1, 1995 [*J*]
Herewini, M A (Auckland) 1962 *A* 5, 1963 *I*, 1964 *S, F*, 1965 *SA* 4, 1966 *BI* 1,2,3,4, 1967 *A*
Hewett, D N (Canterbury) 2001 *I* (R), *S* (R), *Arg* 2, 2002 *It* (R), *I* 1,2, *A* 1, *SA* 1, *A* 2, *SA* 2, 2003 *E, F, SA* 1, *A* 1, *SA* 2, *A* 2
Hewett, J A (Auckland) 1991 [*It*]
Hewitt, N J (Southland) 1995 [*I* (t), *J*], 1996 *A* 1(R), 1997 *SA* 1(R), *I, E* 1, *W, E* 2, 1998 *E* 2(t + R)
Hewson, A R (Wellington) 1981 *S* 1,2, *SA* 1,2,3, *R, F* 1,2, 1982 *A* 1,2,3, 1983 *BI* 1,2,3,4, *A*, 1984 *F* 1,2, *A* 1
Higginson, G (Canterbury, Hawke's Bay) 1980 *W*, 1981 *S* 1, *SA* 1, 1982 *A* 1,2, 1983 *A*
Hill, S F (Canterbury) 1955 *A* 3, 1956 *SA* 1,3,4, 1957 *A* 1,2, 1958 *A* 3, 1959 *BI* 1,2,3,4
Hines, G R (Waikato) 1980 *A* 3
Hobbs, M J B (Canterbury) 1983 *BI* 1,2,3,4, *A, S, E*, 1984 *F* 1,2, *A* 1,2,3, 1985 *E* 1,2, *A, Arg* 1,2, 1986 *A* 2,3, *F* 2,3
Hoeft, C H (Otago) 1998 *E* 2(t + R), *A* 2(R), *SA* 2, *A* 3, 1999 *WS, F* 1, *SA* 1, *A* 1,2, [*Tg,E, S, F* 2, *SA* 3(R)], 2000 *S* 1,2, *A* 1, *SA* 1, *A* 2, *SA* 2, 2001 *Sm, Arg* 1, *F, SA* 1, *A* 1, *SA* 2, *A* 2, 2003 *W*
Holah, M R (Waikato) 2001 *Sm, Arg* 1(t&R), *F* (R), *SA* 1(R), *A* 1(R), *SA* 2(R), *A* 2(R), 2002 *It, I* 2(R), *A* 2(t), *E, F, W* (R), 2003 *W, F* (R), *A* 1(R), *SA* 2
Holder, E C (Buller) 1934 *A* 2
Hook, L S (Auckland) 1929 *A* 1,2,3
Hooper, J A (Canterbury) 1937 *SA* 1,2,3
Hopkinson, A E (Canterbury) 1967 *S*, 1968 *A* 2, *F* 1,2,3, 1969 *W* 2, 1970 *SA* 1,2,3
Hore, A K (Taranaki) 2002 *E, F*
Hore, J (Otago) 1930 *BI* 2,3,4, 1932 *A* 1,2,3, 1934 *A* 1,2, 1935 *S*, 1936 *E*
Horsley, R H (Wellington) 1960 *SA* 2,3,4
Hotop, J (Canterbury) 1952 *A* 1,2, 1955 *A* 3
Howarth, S P (Auckland) 1994 *SA* 1,2,3, *A*
Howlett, D C (Auckland) 2000 *Tg* (R), *F* 1,2, *It*, 2001 *Sm, Arg* 1(R), *F* (R), *SA* 1, *A* 1,2, *I, S, Arg* 2, 2002 *It, I* 1,2(R), *Fj, A* 1, *SA* 1, *A* 2, *SA* 2, *E, F, W*, 2003 *E, W, F, SA* 1, *A* 1, *SA* 2, *A* 2
Hughes, A M (Auckland) 1949 *A* 1,2, 1950 *BI* 1,2,3,4
Hughes, E (Southland, Wellington) 1907 *A* 1,2,3, 1908 *AW* 1, 1921 *SA* 1,2
Hunter, B A (Otago) 1971 *BI* 1,2,3
Hunter, J (Taranaki) 1905 *S, I, E, W*, 1906 *F*, 1907 *A* 1,2,3, 1908 *AW* 1,2,3
Hurst, I A (Canterbury) 1973 *I, F, E* 2, 1974 *A* 1,2

Ieremia, A (Wellington) 1994 *SA* 1,2,3, 1995 [*J*], 1996 *SA* 2(R),5(R), 1997 *A* 1(R), *SA* 1(R), *A* 2, *SA* 2, *A* 3, *I, E* 1, 1999 *WS, F* 1, *SA* 1, *A* 1, *SA* 2, *A* 2, [*Tg, E, S, F* 2, *SA* 3], 2000 *Tg, S* 1,2, *A* 1,2, *SA* 2
Ifwersen, K D (Auckland) 1921 *SA* 3
Innes, C R (Auckland) 1989 *W, I*, 1990 *A* 1,2,3, *F* 1,2, 1991 *Arg* 1,2, *A* 1,2, [*E, US, It, C, A, S*]
Innes, G D (Canterbury) 1932 *A* 2
Irvine, I B (North Auckland) 1952 *A* 1
Irvine, J G (Otago) 1914 *A* 1,2,3
Irvine, W R (Hawke's Bay, Wairarapa) 1924 *I, W*, 1925 *E, F*, 1930 *BI* 1
Irwin, M W (Otago) 1955 *A* 1,2, 1956 *SA* 1, 1958 *A* 2, 1959 *BI* 3,4, 1960 *SA* 1

Jack, C R (Canterbury) 2001 *Arg* 1(R), *SA* 1(R),2, *A* 2, *I, S, Arg* 2, 2002 *I* 1,2, *A* 1, *SA* 1, *A* 2, *SA* 2, 2003 *E, W, F, SA* 1, *A* 1, *SA* 2(R), *A* 2
Jackson, E S (Hawke's Bay) 1936 *A* 1,2, 1937 *SA* 1,2,3, 1938 *A* 3
Jaffray, J L (Otago, South Canterbury) 1972 *A* 2, 1975 *S*, 1976 *I, SA* 1, 1977 *BI* 2, 1979 *F* 1,2
Jarden, R A (Wellington) 1951 *A* 1,2, 1952 *A* 1,2, 1953 *W*, 1954 *I, E, S, F*, 1955 *A* 1,2,3, 1956 *SA* 1,2,3,4
Jefferd, A C R (East Coast) 1981 *S* 1,2, *SA* 1
Jessep, E M (Wellington) 1931 *A*, 1932 *A* 1

Johnson, L M (Wellington) 1928 *SA* 1,2,3,4
Johnston, W (Otago) 1907 *A* 1,2,3
Johnstone, B R (Auckland) 1976 *SA* 2, 1977 *BI* 1,2, *F* 1,2, 1978 *I, W, E, S*, 1979 *F* 1,2, *S, E*
Johnstone, P (Otago) 1949 *SA* 2,4, 1950 *BI* 1,2,3,4, 1951 *A* 1,2,3
Jones, I D (North Auckland, North Harbour) 1990 *S* 1,2, *A* 1,2,3, *F* 1,2, 1991 *Arg* 1,2, *A* 1,2, [*E, US, It, C, A, S*], 1992 *Wld* 1,2,3, *I* 1,2, *A* 1,2,3, *SA*, 1993 *BI* 1,2(R),3, *WS, S, E*, 1994 *F* 1,2, *SA* 1,3, *A*, 1995 *C*, [*I, W, S, E, SA*], *A* 1,2, *It, F* 1,2, 1996 *WS, S* 1,2, *A* 1, *SA* 1, *A* 2, *SA* 2,3,4,5, 1997 *Fj, Arg* 1,2, *A* 1, *SA* 1, *A* 2, *SA* 2, *A* 3, *I, E* 1, *W, E* 2, 1998 *E* 1,2, *A* 1, *SA* 1, *A* 2,3(R), 1999 *F* 1(R), [*It, S* (R)]
Jones, M G (North Auckland) 1973 *E* 2
Jones, M N (Auckland) 1987 [*It, Fj, S, F*], *A*, 1988 *W* 1,2, *A* 2,3, 1989 *F* 1,2, *Arg* 1,2, 1990 *F* 1,2, 1991 *Arg* 1,2, *A* 1,2, [*E, US, S*], 1992 *Wld* 1,3, *I* 2, *A* 1,3, *SA*, 1993 *BI* 1,2,3, *A, WS*, 1994 *SA* 3(R), *A*, 1995 *A* 1(R),2, *It, F* 1,2, 1996 *WS, S* 1,2, *A* 1, *SA* 1, *A* 2, *SA* 2,3,4,5, 1997 *Fj*, 1998 *E* 1, *A* 1, *SA* 1, *A* 2
Jones, P F H (North Auckland) 1954 *E, S*, 1955 *A* 1,2, 1956 *SA* 3,4, 1958 *A* 1,2,3, 1959 *BI* 1, 1960 *SA* 1
Joseph, H T (Canterbury) 1971 *BI* 2,3
Joseph, J W (Otago) 1992 *Wld* 2,3(R), *I* 1, *A* 1(R),3, *SA*, 1993 *BI* 1,2,3, *A, WS, S, E*, 1994 *SA* 2(t), 1995 *C*, [*I, W, J* (R), *S, SA* (R)]

Karam, J F (Wellington, Horowhenua) 1972 *W, S*, 1973 *E* 1, *I, F*, 1974 *A* 1,2,3, *I*, 1975 *S*
Katene, T (Wellington) 1955 *A* 2
Kearney, J C (Otago) 1947 *A* 2, 1949 *SA* 1,2,3
Kelleher, B T (Otago) 1999 *WS* (R), *SA* 1(R), *A* 2(R), [*Tg* (R), *E* (R), *It, F* 2], 2000 *S* 1, *A* 1(R),2(R), *It* (R), 2001 *Sm, F* (R), *A* 1(R), *SA* 2, *A* 2, *I, S*, 2002 *It, I* 2(R), *Fj, SA* 1(R),2(R), 2003 *F* (R)
Kelly, J W (Auckland) 1949 *A* 1,2
Kember, G F (Wellington) 1970 *SA* 4
Ketels, R C (Counties) 1980 *W*, 1981 *S* 1,2, *R, F* 1
Kiernan, H A D (Auckland) 1903 *A*
Kilby, F D (Wellington) 1932 *A* 1,2,3, 1934 *A* 2
Killeen, B A (Auckland) 1936 *A* 1
King, R M (Waikato) 2002 *W*
King, R R (West Coast) 1934 *A* 2, 1935 *S, I, W*, 1936 *E, A* 1,2, 1937 *SA* 1,2,3, 1938 *A* 1,2,3
Kingstone, C N (Taranaki) 1921 *SA* 1,2,3
Kirk, D E (Auckland) 1985 *E* 1,2, *A, Arg* 1, 1986 *F* 1, *A* 1,2,3, *F* 2,3, 1987 [*It, Fj, Arg, S, W, F*], *A*
Kirkpatrick, I A (Canterbury, Poverty Bay) 1967 *F*, 1968 *A* 1(R),2, *F* 1,2,3, 1969 *W* 1,2, 1970 *SA* 1,2,3,4, 1971 *BI* 1,2,3,4, 1972 *A* 1,2,3, *W, S*, 1973 *E* 1, *I, F, E* 2, 1974 *A* 1,2,3, *I* 1975 *S*, 1976 *I, SA* 1,2,3,4, 1977 *BI* 1,2,3,4
Kirton, E W (Otago) 1967 *E, W, F, S*, 1968 *A* 1,2, *F* 1,2,3, 1969 *W* 1,2, 1970 *SA* 2,3
Kirwan, J J (Auckland) 1984 *F* 1,2, 1985 *E* 1,2, *A, Arg* 1,2, 1986 *F* 1, *A* 1,2,3, *F* 2,3, 1987 [*It, Fj, Arg, S, W, F*], *A*, 1988 *W* 1,2, *A* 1,2,3, 1989 *F* 1,2, *Arg* 1,2, *A*, 1990 *S* 1,2, *A* 1,2,3, *F* 1,2, 1991 *Arg* 2, *A* 1,2, [*E, It, C, A, S*], 1992 *Wld* 1,2(R),3, *I* 1,2, *A* 1,2,3, *SA*, 1993 *BI* 2,3, *A, WS*, 1994 *F* 1,2, *SA* 1,2,3
Kivell, A L (Taranaki) 1929 *A* 2,3
Knight, A (Auckland) 1934 *A* 1
Knight, G A (Manawatu) 1977 *F* 1,2, 1978 *A* 1,2,3, *E, S*, 1979 *F* 1,2, *A*, 1980 *A* 1,2,3, *W*, 1981 *S* 1,2, *SA* 1,3, 1982 *A* 1,2,3, 1983 *BI* 1,2,3,4, *A*, 1984 *F* 1,2, *A* 1,2,3, 1985 *E* 1,2, *A*, 1986 *A* 2,3
Knight, L G (Poverty Bay) 1977 *BI* 1,2,3,4, *F* 1,2
Koteka, T T (Waikato) 1981 *F* 2, 1982 *A* 3
Kreft, A J (Otago) 1968 *A* 2
Kronfeld, J A (Otago) 1995 *C*, [*I, W, S, E, SA*], *A* 1,2(R) 1996 *WS, S* 1,2, *A* 1, *SA* 1, *A* 2, *SA* 2,3,4,5, 1997 *Fj, Arg* 1,2, *A* 1, *SA* 1, *A* 2, *SA* 2, *A* 3, *I* (R), *E* 1, *W, E* 2, 1998 *E* 1,2, *A* 1, *SA* 1,2 *A* 3, 1999 *WS, F* 1, *SA* 1, *A* 1, *SA* 2, *A* 2, [*Tg, E, S, F* 2, *SA* 3], 2000 *Tg, S* 1(R),2, *A* 1(R), *SA* 1, *A* 2, *SA* 2

Laidlaw, C R (Otago, Canterbury) 1964 *F, A* 1, 1965 *SA* 1,2,3,4, 1966 *BI* 1,2,3,4, 1967 *E, W, S*, 1968 *A* 1,2, *F* 1,2, 1970 *SA* 1,2,3
Laidlaw, K F (Southland) 1960 *SA* 2,3,4
Lambert, K K (Manawatu) 1972 *S* (R), 1973 *E* 1, *I, F, E* 2, 1974 *I*, 1976 *SA* 1,3,4, 1977 *BI* 1,4
Lambourn, A (Wellington) 1934 *A* 1,2, 1935 *S, I, W*, 1936 *E*, 1937 *SA* 1,2,3, 1938 *A* 3
Larsen, B P (North Harbour) 1992 *Wld* 2,3, *I* 1, 1994 *F* 1,2, *SA* 1,2,3, *A* (t), 1995 [*I, W, J, E*(R)], *It, F* 1, 1996 *S* 2(t), *SA* 4(R)
Le Lievre, J M (Canterbury) 1962 *A* 4
Lee, D D (Otago) 2002 *E* (R), *F*
Lendrum, R N (Counties) 1973 *E* 2
Leslie, A R (Wellington) 1974 *A* 1,2,3, *I*, 1975 *S*, 1976 *I, SA* 1,2,3,4
Leys, E T (Wellington) 1929 *A* 3
Lilburne, H T (Canterbury, Wellington) 1928 *SA* 3,4, 1929 *A* 1,2,3, 1930 *BI* 1,4, 1931 *A*, 1932 *A* 1, 1934 *A* 2
Lindsay, D F (Otago) 1928 *SA* 1,2,3
Lineen, T R (Auckland) 1957 *A* 1,2, 1958 *A* 1,2,3, 1959 *BI* 1,2,3,4, 1960 *SA* 1,2,3
Lister, T N (South Canterbury) 1968 *A* 1,2, *F* 1, 1969 *W* 1,2, 1970 *SA* 1,4, 1971 *BI* 4
Little, P F (Auckland) 1961 *F* 2,3, 1962 *A* 2,3,5, 1963 *I, W*, 1964 *E, S, F*
Little, W K (North Harbour) 1990 *S* 1,2, *A* 1,2,3, *F* 1,2, 1991 *Arg* 1,2, *A* 1, [*It, S*], 1992 *Wld* 1,2,3, *I* 1,2, *A* 1,2,3, *SA*, 1993 *BI* 1, *WS* (R), 1994 *SA* 2(R), *A*, 1995 *C*, [*I, W, S, E, SA*], *A* 1,2, *It, F* 1,2, 1996 *S* 2, *A* 1, *SA* 1, *A* 2, *SA* 2,3,4,5, 1997 *W, E* 2, 1998 *E* 1, *A* 1, *SA* 1, *A* 2
Loader, C J (Wellington) 1954 *I, E, S, F*
Lochore, B J (Wairarapa) 1964 *E, S*, 1965 *SA* 1,2,3,4, 1966 *BI* 1,2,3,4, 1967 *A, E, W, F, S*, 1968 *A* 1, *F* 2,3, 1969 *W* 1,2, 1970 *SA* 1,2,3,4, 1971 *BI* 3
Loe, R W (Waikato, Canterbury) 1987 [*It, Arg*], 1988 *W* 1,2, *A* 1,2,3, 1989 *F* 1,2, *Arg* 1,2, *A, W, I*, 1990 *S* 1,2, *A* 1,2,3, *F* 1,2, 1991 *Arg* 1,2, *A* 1,2, [*E, It, C, A, S*], 1992 *Wld* 1,2,3, *I* 1, *A* 1,2,3, *SA*, 1994 *F* 1,2, *SA* 1,2,3, *A*, 1995 [*J, S, SA* (R)], *A* 2(t), *F* 2(R)
Lomu, J T (Counties Manukau, Wellington) 1994 *F* 1,2, 1995 [*I, W, S, E, SA*], *A* 1,2, *It, F* 1,2, 1996 *WS, S* 1, *A* 1, *SA* 1, *A* 2, 1997 *E* 1, *W, E* 2, 1998 *E* 1,2, *A* 1(R), *SA* 1, *A* 2, *SA* 2, *A* 3, 1999 *WS* (R), *SA* 1(R), *A* 1(R), *SA* 2(R), *A* 2(R), [*Tg, E, It, S, F* 2, *SA* 3], 2000 *Tg, S* 1,2, *A* 1, *SA* 1, *A* 2, *SA* 2, *F* 1, 2001 *Arg* 1, *F, SA* 1, *A* 1, *SA* 2, *A* 2, *I, S, Arg* 2, 2002 *It* (R), *I* 1(R),2, *Fj, SA* 1(R), *E, F, W*
Long, A J (Auckland) 1903 *A*
Loveridge, D S (Taranaki) 1978 *W*, 1979 *S, E*, 1980 *A* 1,2,3, *W*, 1981 *S* 1,2, *SA* 1,2,3, *R, F* 1,2, 1982 *A* 1,2,3, 1983 *BI* 1,2,3,4, *A*, 1985 *Arg* 2
Lowen, K R (Waikato) 2002 *E*
Lucas, F W (Auckland) 1924 *I*, 1925 *F*, 1928 *SA* 4, 1930 *BI* 1,2,3,4
Lunn, W A (Otago) 1949 *A* 1,2
Lynch, T W (South Canterbury) 1913 *A* 1, 1914 *A* 1,2,3
Lynch, T W (Canterbury) 1951 *A* 1,2,3

McAtamney, F S (Otago) 1956 *SA* 2
McCahill, B J (Auckland) 1987 [*Arg, S* (R), *W* (R)], 1989 *Arg* 1(R),2(R), 1991 *A* 2, [*E, US, C, A*]
McCaw, R H (Canterbury) 2001 *I, S, Arg* 2, 2002 *I* 1,2, *A* 1, *SA* 1, *A* 2, *SA* 2, 2003 *E, F, SA* 1, *A* 1,2
McCaw, W A (Southland) 1951 *A* 1,2,3, 1953 *W*, 1954 *F*
McCool, M J (Wairarapa-Bush) 1979 *A*
McCormick, W F (Canterbury) 1965 *SA* 4, 1967 *E, W, F, S*, 1968 *A* 1,2, *F* 1,2,3, 1969 *W* 1,2, 1970 *SA* 1,2,3, 1971 *BI* 1
McCullough, J F (Taranaki) 1959 *BI* 2,3,4
McDonald, A (Otago) 1905 *S, I, E, W*, 1907 *A* 1, 1908 *AW* 1, 1913 *A* 1, *US*
Macdonald, H H (Canterbury, North Auckland) 1972 *W, S*, 1973 *E* 1, *I, F, E* 2, 1974 *I*, 1975 *S*, 1976 *I, SA* 1,2,3
MacDonald, L R (Canterbury) 2000 *S* 1(R),2(R), *SA* 1(t),2(R), 2001 *Sm, Arg* 1, *F, SA* 1(R), *A* 1(R), *SA* 2, *A* 2, *I, S*, 2002 *I* 1,2, *Fj* (R), *A* 2(R), *SA* 2, 2003 *A* 2(R)
McDonnell, J M (Otago) 2002 *It, I* 1(R),2(R), *Fj, SA* 1(R), *A* 2(R), *E, F*
McDowell, S C (Auckland, Bay of Plenty) 1985 *Arg* 1,2, 1986 *A* 2,3, *F* 2,3, 1987 [*It, Fj, S, W, F*], *A*, 1988 *W* 1,2, *A* 1,2,3, 1989 *F* 1,2, *Arg* 1,2, *A, W, I*, 1990 *S* 1,2, *A* 1,2,3, *F* 1,2, 1991 *Arg* 1,2, *A* 1,2, [*E, US, It, C, A, S*], 1992 *Wld* 1,2,3, *I* 1,2
McEldowney, J T (Taranaki) 1977 *BI* 3,4
MacEwan, I N (Wellington) 1956 *SA* 2, 1957 *A* 1,2, 1958 *A* 1,2,3, 1959 *BI* 1,2,3, 1960 *SA* 1,2,3,4, 1961 *F* 1,2,3, 1962 *A* 1,2,3,4
McGrattan, B (Wellington) 1983 *S, E*, 1985 *Arg* 1,2, 1986 *F* 1, *A* 1
McGregor, A J (Auckland) 1913 *A* 1, *US*
McGregor, D (Canterbury, Southland) 1903 *A*, 1904 *BI*, 1905 *E, W*
McGregor, N P (Canterbury) 1924 *W*, 1925 *E*
McGregor, R W (Auckland) 1903 *A*, 1904 *BI*
McHugh, M J (Auckland) 1946 *A* 1,2, 1949 *SA* 3
McIntosh, D N (Wellington) 1956 *SA* 1,2, 1957 *A* 1,2

McKay, D W (Auckland) 1961 *F* 1,2,3, 1963 *E* 1,2
McKechnie, B J (Southland) 1977 *F* 1,2, 1978 *A* 2(R),3, *W* (R), *E, S*, 1979 *A*, 1981 *SA* 1(R), *F* 1
McKellar, G F (Wellington) 1910 *A* 1,2,3
McKenzie, R J (Wellington) 1913 *A* 1, *US*, 1914 *A* 2,3
McKenzie, R McC (Manawatu) 1934 *A* 1, 1935 *S*, 1936 *A* 1, 1937 *SA* 1,2,3, 1938 *A* 1,2,3
McLachlan, J S (Auckland) 1974 *A* 2
McLaren, H C (Waikato) 1952 *A* 1
McLean, A L (Bay of Plenty) 1921 *SA* 2,3
McLean, H F (Wellington, Auckland) 1930 *BI* 3,4, 1932 *A* 1,2,3, 1934 *A* 1, 1935 *I, W*, 1936 *E*
McLean, J K (King Country, Auckland) 1947 *A* 1, 1949 *A* 2
McLeod, B E (Counties) 1964 *A* 1,2,3, 1965 *SA* 1,2,3,4, 1966 *BI* 1,2,3,4, 1967 *E, W, F, S*, 1968 *A* 1,2, *F* 1,2,3, 1969 *W* 1,2, 1970 *SA* 1,2
McLeod, S J (Waikato) 1996 *WS, S* 1, 1997 *Fj* (R), *Arg* 2(t + R), *I* (R), *E* 1(R), *W* (t), *E* 2(R), 1998 *A* 1, *SA* 1(R)
McMinn, A F (Wairarapa, Manawatu) 1903 *A*, 1905 *A*
McMinn, F A (Manawatu) 1904 *BI*
McMullen, R F (Auckland) 1957 *A* 1,2, 1958 *A* 1,2,3, 1959 *BI* 1,2,3, 1960 *SA* 2,3,4
McNab, J R (Otago) 1949 *SA* 1,2,3, 1950 *BI* 1,2,3
McNaughton, A M (Bay of Plenty) 1971 *BI* 1,2,3
McNeece, J (Southland) 1913 *A* 2,3, 1914 *A* 1,2,3
McPhail, B E (Canterbury) 1959 *BI* 1,4
Macpherson, D G (Otago) 1905 *A*
MacPherson, G L (Otago) 1986 *F* 1
MacRae, I R (Hawke's Bay) 1966 *BI* 1,2,3,4, 1967 *A, E, W, F, S*, 1968 *F* 1,2, 1969 *W* 1,2, 1970 *SA* 1,2,3,4
McRae, J A (Southland) 1946 *A* 1(R),2
McWilliams, R G (Auckland) 1928 *SA* 2,3,4, 1929 *A* 1,2,3, 1930 *BI* 1,2,3,4
Mackrell, W H C (Auckland) 1906 *F*
Macky, J V (Auckland) 1913 *A* 2
Maguire, J R (Auckland) 1910 *A* 1,2,3
Mahoney, A (Bush) 1935 *S, I, W*, 1936 *E*
Mains, L W (Otago) 1971 *BI* 2,3,4, 1976 *I*
Major, J (Taranaki) 1967 *A*
Maka, I (Otago) 1998 *E* 2(R), *A* 1(R), *SA* 1(R),2
Maling, T S (Otago) 2002 *It, I* 2(R), *Fj, A* 1, *SA* 1, *A* 2, *SA* 2
Manchester, J E (Canterbury) 1932 *A* 1,2,3, 1934 *A* 1,2, 1935 *S, I, W*, 1936 *E*
Mannix, S J (Wellington) 1994 *F* 1
Marshall, J W (Southland, Canterbury) 1995 *F* 2, 1996 *WS, S* 1,2, *A* 1, *SA* 1, *A* 2, *SA* 2,3,4,5, 1997 *Fj, Arg* 1,2, *A* 1, *SA* 1, *A* 2, *SA* 2, *A* 3, *I, E* 1, *W, E* 2, 1998 *A* 1, *SA* 1, *A* 2, *SA* 2, *A* 3, 1999 *WS, F* 1, *SA* 1, *A* 1, *SA* 2, *A* 2, [*Tg, E, S, F* 2(R), *SA* 3], 2000 *Tg, S* 2, *A* 1, *SA* 1, *A* 2, *SA* 2, *F* 1,2, *It*, 2001 *Arg* 1, *F, SA* 1, *A* 1,2(R), 2002 *I* 1,2, *Fj* (R), *A* 1, *SA* 1, *A* 2, *SA* 2, 2003 *E, SA* 1(R), *A* 1, *SA* 2, *A* 2
Mason, D F (Wellington) 1947 *A* 2(R)
Masters, R R (Canterbury) 1924 *I, W*, 1925 *E, F*
Mataira, H K (Hawke's Bay) 1934 *A* 2
Matheson, J D (Otago) 1972 *A* 1,2,3, *W, S*
Mauger, A J D (Canterbury) 2001 *I, S, Arg* 2, 2002 *It* (R), *I* 1,2, *Fj, A* 1, *SA* 1, *A* 2, *SA* 2, 2003 *SA* 1, *A* 1, *SA* 2, *A* 2
Max, D S (Nelson) 1931 *A*, 1934 *A* 1,2
Maxwell, N M C (Canterbury) 1999 *WS, F* 1, *SA* 1, *A* 1, *SA* 2, *A* 2, [*Tg, E, S, F* 2, *SA* 3], 2000 *S* 1,2, *A* 1, *SA* 1(R), *A* 2, *SA* 2, *F* 1,2, *It* (R), 2001 *Sm, Arg* 1, *F, SA* 1, *A* 1, *SA* 2, A2, *I, S, Arg* 2, 2002 *It, I* 1,2, *Fj*
Mayerhofler, M A (Canterbury) 1998 *E* 1,2, *SA* 1, *A* 2, *SA* 2, *A* 3
Meads, C E (King Country) 1957 *A* 1,2, 1958 *A* 1,2,3, 1959 *BI* 2,3,4, 1960 *SA* 1,2,3,4, 1961 *F* 1,2,3, 1962 *A* 1,2,3,5, 1963 *E* 1,2, *I, W*, 1964 *E, S, F, A* 1,2,3, 1965 *SA* 1,2,3,4, 1966 *BI* 1,2,3,4, 1967 *A, E, W, F, S*, 1968 *A* 1,2, *F* 1,2,3, 1969 *W* 1,2, 1970 *SA* 3,4, 1971 *BI* 1,2,3,4
Meads, S T (King Country) 1961 *F* 1, 1962 *A* 4,5, 1963 *I*, 1964 *A* 1,2,3, 1965 *SA* 1,2,3,4, 1966 *BI* 1,2,3,4
Mealamu, K F (Auckland) 2002 *W*, 2003 *E* (R), *W, F* (R), *SA* 1, *A* 1, *SA* 2(R), *A* 2
Meates, K F (Canterbury) 1952 *A* 1,2
Meates, W A (Otago) 1949 *SA* 2,3,4, 1950 *BI* 1,2,3,4
Meeuws, K J (Otago, Auckland) 1998 *A* 3, 1999 *WS, F* 1, *SA* 1, *A* 1, *SA* 2, *A* 2, [*Tg, It* (R), *S* (R), *F* 2(R), *SA* 3], 2000 *Tg* (R), *S* 2, *A* 1, *SA* 1, *A* 2, *SA* 2, 2001 *Arg* 2, 2002 *It, Fj, E, F, W* (R), 2003 *W, F* (R), *SA* 1(R), *A* 1(R), *SA* 2
Mehrtens, A P (Canterbury) 1995 *C*, [*I, W, S, E, SA*], *A* 1,2, 1996 *WS, S* 1,2, *A* 1, *SA* 1, *A* 2, *SA* 2,5, 1997 *Fj, SA* 2(R), *I, E* 1, *W, E* 2, 1998 *E* 1,2, *A* 1, *SA* 1(R), *A* 2, *SA* 2, *A* 3, 1999 *F* 1, *SA* 1, *A* 1, *SA* 2, *A* 2, [*Tg, E, S, F* 2, *SA* 3], 2000 *S* 1,2, *A* 1, *SA* 1, *A* 2, *SA* 2, *F* 1,2, *It* (R), 2001 *Arg* 1, *A* 1(R), *SA* 2, *A* 2, *I, S, Arg* 2, 2002 *It, I* 1,2, *Fj* (R), *A* 1, *SA* 1, *A* 2, *SA* 2, *E* (R), *F, W*
Metcalfe, T C (Southland) 1931 *A*, 1932 *A* 1
Mexted, G G (Wellington) 1950 *BI* 4
Mexted, M G (Wellington) 1979 *S, E*, 1980 *A* 1,2,3, *W*, 1981 *S* 1,2, *SA* 1,2,3, *R, F* 1,2, 1982 *A* 1,2,3, 1983 *BI* 1,2,3,4, *A, S, E*, 1984 *F* 1,2, *A* 1,2,3, 1985 *E* 1,2, *A, Arg* 1,2
Mika, B M (Auckland) 2002 *E* (R), *F, W* (R)
Mika, D G (Auckland) 1999 *WS, F* 1, *SA* 1(R), *A* 1,2, [*It, SA* 3(R)]
Mill, J J (Hawke's Bay, Wairarapa) 1924 *W*, 1925 *E, F*, 1930 *BI* 1
Milliken, H M (Canterbury) 1938 *A* 1,2,3
Milner, H P (Wanganui) 1970 *SA* 3
Mitchell, N A (Southland, Otago) 1935 *S, I, W*, 1936 *E, A* 2, 1937 *SA* 3, 1938 *A* 1,2
Mitchell, T W (Canterbury) 1976 *SA* 4(R)
Mitchell, W J (Canterbury) 1910 *A* 2,3
Mitchinson, F E (Wellington) 1907 *A* 1,2,3, 1908 *AW* 1,2,3, 1910 *A* 1,2,3, 1913 *A* 1(R), *US*
Moffitt, J E (Wellington) 1921 *SA* 1,2,3
Moore, G J T (Otago) 1949 *A* 1
Moreton, R C (Canterbury) 1962 *A* 3,4, 1964 *A* 1,2,3, 1965 *SA* 2,3
Morgan, J E (North Auckland) 1974 *A* 3, *I*, 1976 *SA* 2,3,4
Morris, T J (Nelson Bays) 1972 *A* 1,2,3
Morrison, T C (South Canterbury) 1938 *A* 1,2,3
Morrison, T G (Otago) 1973 *E* 2(R)
Morrissey, P J (Canterbury) 1962 *A* 3,4,5
Mourie, G N K (Taranaki) 1977 *BI* 3,4, *F* 1,2, 1978 *I, W, E, S*, 1979 *F* 1,2, *A, S, E*, 1980 *W*, 1981 *S* 1,2, *F* 1,2, 1982 *A* 1,2,3
Muliaina, M (Auckland) 2003 *E* (R), *W, F, SA* 1, *A* 1, *SA* 2, *A* 2
Muller, B L (Taranaki) 1967 *A, E, W, F*, 1968 *A* 1, *F* 1, 1969 *W* 1, 1970 *SA* 1,2,4, 1971 *BI* 1,2,3,4
Mumm, W J (Buller) 1949 *A* 1
Murdoch, K (Otago) 1970 *SA* 4, 1972 *A* 3, *W*
Murdoch, P H (Auckland) 1964 *A* 2,3, 1965 *SA* 1,2,3
Murray, H V (Canterbury) 1913 *A* 1, *US*, 1914 *A* 2,3
Murray, P C (Wanganui) 1908 *AW* 2
Myers, R G (Waikato) 1978 *A* 3
Mynott, H J (Taranaki) 1905 *I, W*, 1906 *F*, 1907 *A* 1,2,3, 1910 *A* 1,3

Nathan, W J (Auckland) 1962 *A* 1,2,3,4,5, 1963 *E* 1,2, *W*, 1964 *F*, 1966 *BI* 1,2,3,4, 1967 *A*
Nelson, K A (Otago) 1962 *A* 4,5
Nepia, G (Hawke's Bay, East Coast) 1924 *I, W*, 1925 *E, F*, 1929 *A* 1, 1930 *BI* 1,2,3,4
Nesbit, S R (Auckland) 1960 *SA* 2,3
Newton, F (Canterbury) 1905 *E, W*, 1906 *F*
Nicholls, H E (Wellington) 1921 *SA* 1
Nicholls, M F (Wellington) 1921 *SA* 1,2,3, 1924 *I, W*, 1925 *E, F*, 1928 *SA* 4, 1930 *BI* 2,3
Nicholson, G W (Auckland) 1903 *A*, 1904 *BI*, 1907 *A* 2,3
Nonu, M (Wellington) 2003 *E*
Norton, R W (Canterbury) 1971 *BI* 1,2,3,4, 1972 *A* 1,2,3, *W, S*, 1973 *E* 1, *I, F, E* 2, 1974 *A* 1,2,3, *I*, 1975 *S*, 1976 *I, SA* 1,2,3,4, 1977 *BI* 1,2,3,4

O'Brien, J G (Auckland) 1914 *A* 1
O'Callaghan, M W (Manawatu) 1968 *F* 1,2,3
O'Callaghan, T R (Wellington) 1949 *A* 2
O'Donnell, D H (Wellington) 1949 *A* 2
O'Halloran, J D (Wellington) 2000 *It* (R)
Old, G H (Manawatu) 1981 *SA* 3, *R* (R), 1982 *A* 1(R)
O'Leary, M J (Auckland) 1910 *A* 1,3, 1913 *A* 2,3
Oliver, A D (Otago) 1997 *Fj* (t), 1998 *E* 1,2, *A* 1, *SA* 1, *A* 2, *SA* 2, *A* 3, 1999 *WS, F* 1, *SA* 1, *A* 1, *SA* 2, *A* 2, [*Tg, E, S, F* 2, *SA* 3(R)], 2000 *Tg* (R), *S* 1,2, *A* 1, *SA* 1, *A* 2, *SA* 2, *F* 1,2, *It*, 2001 *Sm, Arg* 1, *F, SA* 1, *A* 1, *SA* 2, *A* 2, *I, S, Arg* 2, 2003 *E, F*
Oliver, C J (Canterbury) 1929 *A* 1,2, 1934 *A* 1, 1935 *S, I, W*, 1936 *E*
Oliver, D J (Wellington) 1930 *BI* 1,2
Oliver, D O (Otago) 1954 *I, F*
Oliver, F J (Southland, Otago, Manawatu) 1976 *SA* 4, 1977 *BI* 1,2,3,4, *F* 1,2, 1978 *A* 1,2,3, *I, W, E, S*, 1979 *F* 1,2, 1981 *SA* 2
Orr, R W (Otago) 1949 *A* 1
Osborne, G M (North Harbour) 1995 *C*, [*I, W, J, E, SA*], *A* 1,2, *F* 1(R),2, 1996 *SA* 2,3,4,5, 1997 *Arg* 1(R), *A* 2,3, *I*, 1999 [*It*]

Osborne, W M (Wanganui) 1975 *S*, 1976 *SA* 2(R),4(R), 1977 *BI* 1,2,3,4, *F* 1(R),2, 1978 *I, W, E, S*, 1980 *W*, 1982 *A* 1,3
O'Sullivan, J M (Taranaki) 1905 *S, I, E, W*, 1907 *A* 3
O'Sullivan, T P A (Taranaki) 1960 *SA* 1, 1961 *F* 1, 1962 *A* 1,2

Page, J R (Wellington) 1931 *A*, 1932 *A* 1,2,3, 1934 *A* 1,2
Palmer, B P (Auckland) 1929 *A* 2, 1932 *A* 2,3
Parker, J H (Canterbury) 1924 *I, W*, 1925 *E*
Parkhill, A A (Otago) 1937 *SA* 1,2,3, 1938 *A* 1,2,3
Parkinson, R M (Poverty Bay) 1972 *A* 1,2,3, *W, S*, 1973 *E* 1,2
Paterson, A M (Otago) 1908 *AW* 2,3, 1910 *A* 1,2,3
Paton, H (Otago) 1910 *A* 1,3
Pene, A R B (Otago) 1992 *Wld* 1(R),2,3, *I* 1,2, *A* 1,2(R), 1993 *BI* 3, *A, WS, S, E*, 1994 *F* 1,2(R), *SA* 1(R)
Phillips, W J (King Country) 1937 *SA* 2, 1938 *A* 1,2
Philpott, S (Canterbury) 1991 [*It* (R), *S* (R)]
Pickering, E A R (Waikato) 1958 *A* 2, 1959 *BI* 1,4
Pierce, M J (Wellington) 1985 *E* 1,2, *A, Arg* 1, 1986 *A* 2,3, *F* 2,3, 1987 [*It, Arg, S, W, F*], *A*, 1988 *W* 1,2, *A* 1,2,3, 1989 *F* 1,2, *Arg* 1,2, *A, W, I*
Pokere, S T (Southland, Auckland) 1981 *SA* 3, 1982 *A* 1,2,3, 1983 *BI* 1,2,3,4, *A, S, E*, 1984 *F* 1,2, *A* 2,3, 1985 *E* 1,2, *A*
Pollock, H R (Wellington) 1932 *A* 1,2,3, 1936 *A* 1,2
Porter, C G (Wellington) 1925 *F*, 1929 *A* 2,3, 1930 *BI* 1,2,3,4
Preston, J P (Canterbury, Wellington) 1991 [*US, S*], 1992 *SA* (R), 1993 *BI* 2,3, *A, WS*, 1996 *SA* 4(R), 1997 *I* (R), *E* 1(R)
Procter, A C (Otago) 1932 *A* 1
Purdue, C A (Southland) 1905 *A*
Purdue, E (Southland) 1905 *A*
Purdue, G B (Southland) 1931 *A*, 1932 *A* 1,2,3
Purvis, G H (Waikato) 1991 [*US*], 1993 *WS*
Purvis, N A (Otago) 1976 *I*

Quaid, C E (Otago) 1938 *A* 1,2

Ralph, C S (Auckland, Canterbury) 1998 *E* 2, 2002 *It, I* 1,2, *A* 1, *SA* 1, *A* 2, *SA* 2, 2003 *E, A* 1(R)
Ranby, R M (Waikato) 2001 *Sm* (R)
Randell, T C (Otago) 1997 *Fj, Arg* 1,2, *A* 1, *SA* 1, *A* 2, *SA* 2, *A* 3, *I, E* 1, *W, E* 2, 1998 *E* 1,2, *A* 1, *SA* 1, *A* 2, *SA* 2, *A* 3, 1999 *WS, F* 1, *SA* 1, *A* 1, *SA* 2, *A* 2, [*Tg, E, It, S, F* 2, *SA* 3], 2000 *Tg, S* 1,2(R), *A* 1, *SA* 1, *A* 2, *SA* 2, *F* 2(R), *It* (R), 2001 *Arg* 1, *F, SA* 1, *A* 1, *SA* 2, *A* 2, 2002 *It, Fj, E, F, W*
Rangi, R E (Auckland) 1964 *A* 2,3, 1965 *SA* 1,2,3,4, 1966 *BI* 1,2,3,4
Rankin, J G (Canterbury) 1936 *A* 1,2, 1937 *SA* 2
Reedy, W J (Wellington) 1908 *AW* 2,3
Reid, A R (Waikato) 1952 *A* 1, 1956 *SA* 3,4, 1957 *A* 1,2
Reid, H R (Bay of Plenty) 1980 *A* 1,2, *W*, 1983 *S, E*, 1985 *Arg* 1,2, 1986 *A* 2,3
Reid, K H (Wairarapa) 1929 *A* 1,3
Reid, S T (Hawke's Bay) 1935 *S, I, W*, 1936 *E, A* 1,2, 1937 *SA* 1,2,3
Reihana, B T (Waikato) 2000 *F* 2, *It*
Reside, W B (Wairarapa) 1929 *A* 1
Rhind, P K (Canterbury) 1946 *A* 1,2
Richardson, J (Otago, Southland) 1921 *SA* 1,2,3, 1924 *I, W*, 1925 *E, F*
Rickit, H (Waikato) 1981 *S* 1,2
Riechelmann, C C (Auckland) 1997 *Fj* (R), *Arg* 1(R), *A* 1(R), *SA* 2(t), *I* (R), *E* 2(t)
Ridland, A J (Southland) 1910 *A* 1,2,3
Roberts, E J (Wellington) 1914 *A* 1,2,3, 1921 *SA* 2,3
Roberts, F (Wellington) 1905 *S, I, E, W*, 1907 *A* 1,2,3, 1908 *AW* 1,3, 1910 *A* 1,2,3
Roberts, R W (Taranaki) 1913 *A* 1, *US*, 1914 *A* 1,2,3
Robertson, B J (Counties) 1972 *A* 1,3, *S*, 1973 *E* 1, *I, F*, 1974 *A* 1,2,3, *I*, 1976 *I, SA* 1,2,3,4, 1977 *BI* 1,3,4, *F* 1,2, 1978 *A* 1,2,3, *W, E, S*, 1979 *F* 1,2, *A*, 1980 *A* 2,3, *W*, 1981 *S* 1,2
Robertson, D J (Otago) 1974 *A* 1,2,3, *I*, 1975 *S*, 1976 *I, SA* 1,3,4, 1977 *BI* 1
Robertson, S M (Canterbury) 1998 *A* 2(R), *SA* 2(R), *A* 3(R), 1999 [*It* (R)], 2000 *Tg* (R), *S* 1,2(R), *A* 1, *SA* 1(R),2(R), *F* 1,2, *It*, 2001 *I, S, Arg* 2, 2002 *I* 1,2, *Fj* (R), *A* 1, *SA* 1, *A* 2, *SA* 2
Robilliard, A C C (Canterbury) 1928 *SA* 1,2,3,4
Robinson, C E (Southland) 1951 *A* 1,2,3, 1952 *A* 1,2
Robinson, K J (Waikato) 2002 *E, F* (R), *W*
Robinson, M D (North Harbour) 1998 *E* 1(R), 2001 *S* (R), *Arg* 2
Robinson, M P (Canterbury) 2000 *S* 2, *SA* 1, 2002 *It, I* 2, *A* 1, *SA* 1, *E* (t&R), *F, W* (R)
Rokocoko, J T (Auckland) 2003 *E, W, F, SA* 1, *A* 1, *SA* 2, *A* 2
Rollerson, D L (Manawatu) 1980 *W*, 1981 *S* 2, *SA* 1,2,3, *R, F* 1(R),2
Roper, R A (Taranaki) 1949 *A* 2, 1950 *BI* 1,2,3,4
Rowley, H C B (Wanganui) 1949 *A* 2
Rush, E J (North Harbour) 1995 [*W* (R), *J*], *It, F* 1,2, 1996 *S* 1(R),2, *A* 1(t), *SA* 1(R)
Rush, X J (Auckland) 1998 *A* 3
Rutledge, L M (Southland) 1978 *A* 1,2,3, *I, W, E, S*, 1979 *F* 1,2, *A*, 1980 *A* 1,2,3
Ryan, J (Wellington) 1910 *A* 2, 1914 *A* 1,2,3

Sadler, B S (Wellington) 1935 *S, I, W*, 1936 *A* 1,2
Salmon, J L B (Wellington) 1981 *R, F* 1,2(R)
Savage, L T (Canterbury) 1949 *SA* 1,2,4
Saxton, C K (South Canterbury) 1938 *A* 1,2,3
Schuler, K J (Manawatu, North Harbour) 1990 *A* 2(R), 1992 *A* 2, 1995 [*I* (R), *J*]
Schuster, N J (Wellington) 1988 *A* 1,2,3, 1989 *F* 1,2, *Arg* 1,2, *A, W, I*
Scott, R W H (Auckland) 1946 *A* 1,2, 1947 *A* 1,2, 1949 *SA* 1,2,3,4, 1950 *BI* 1,2,3,4, 1953 *W*, 1954 *I, E, S, F*
Scown, A I (Taranaki) 1972 *A* 1,2,3, *W* (R), *S*
Scrimshaw, G (Canterbury) 1928 *SA* 1
Seear, G A (Otago) 1977 *F* 1,2, 1978 *A* 1,2,3, *I, W, E, S*, 1979 *F* 1,2, *A*
Seeling, C E (Auckland) 1904 *BI*, 1905 *S, I, E, W*, 1906 *F*, 1907 *A* 1,2, 1908 *AW* 1,2,3
Sellars, G M V (Auckland) 1913 *A* 1, *US*
Shaw, M W (Manawatu, Hawke's Bay) 1980 *A* 1,2,3(R), *W*, 1981 *S* 1,2, *SA* 1,2, *R, F* 1,2, 1982 *A* 1,2,3, 1983 *BI* 1,2,3,4, *A, S, E*, 1984 *F* 1,2, *A* 1, 1985 *E* 1,2, *A, Arg* 1,2, 1986 *A* 3
Shelford, F N K (Bay of Plenty) 1981 *SA* 3, *R*, 1984 *A* 2,3
Shelford, W T (North Harbour) 1986 *F* 2,3, 1987 [*It, Fj, S, W, F*], *A*, 1988 *W* 1,2, *A* 1,2,3, 1989 *F* 1,2, *Arg* 1,2, *A, W, I*, 1990 *S* 1,2
Siddells, S K (Wellington) 1921 *SA* 3
Simon, H J (Otago) 1937 *SA* 1,2,3
Simpson, J G (Auckland) 1947 *A* 1,2, 1949 *SA* 1,2,3,4, 1950 *BI* 1,2,3
Simpson, V L J (Canterbury) 1985 *Arg* 1,2
Sims, G S (Otago) 1972 *A* 2
Skeen, J R (Auckland) 1952 *A* 2
Skinner, K L (Otago, Counties) 1949 *SA* 1,2,3,4, 1950 *BI* 1,2,3,4, 1951 *A* 1,2,3, 1952 *A* 1,2, 1953 *W*, 1954 *I, E, S, F*, 1956 *SA* 3,4
Skudder, G R (Waikato) 1969 *W* 2
Slater, G L (Taranaki) 2000 *F* 1(R),2(R), *It* (R)
Sloane, P H (North Auckland) 1979 *E*
Smith, A E (Taranaki) 1969 *W* 1,2, 1970 *SA* 1
Smith, B W (Waikato) 1984 *F* 1,2, *A* 1
Smith, G W (Auckland) 1905 *S, I*
Smith, I S T (Otago, North Otago) 1964 *A* 1,2,3, 1965 *SA* 1,2,4, 1966 *BI* 1,2,3
Smith, J B (North Auckland) 1946 *A* 1, 1947 *A* 2, 1949 *A* 1,2
Smith, R M (Canterbury) 1955 *A* 1
Smith, W E (Nelson) 1905 *A*
Smith, W R (Canterbury) 1980 *A* 1, 1982 *A* 1,2,3, 1983 *BI* 2,3, *S, E*, 1984 *F* 1,2, *A* 1,2,3, 1985 *E* 1,2, *A, Arg* 2
Snow, E M (Nelson) 1929 *A* 1,2,3
Solomon, F (Auckland) 1931 *A*, 1932 *A* 2,3
Somerville, G M (Canterbury) 2000 *Tg, S* 1, *SA* 2(R), *F* 1,2, *It*, 2001 *Sm, Arg* 1(R), *F, SA* 1, *A* 1, *SA* 2, *A* 2, *I, S, Arg* 2(t+R), 2002 *I* 1,2, *A* 1, *SA* 1, *A* 2, *SA* 2, 2003 *E, F, SA* 1, *A* 1, *SA* 2(R), *A* 2
Sonntag, W T C (Otago) 1929 *A* 1,2,3
So'oialo, R (Wellington) 2002 *W*, 2003 *E, SA* 1(R)
Speight, M W (Waikato) 1986 *A* 1
Spencer, C J (Auckland) 1997 *Arg* 1,2, *A* 1, *SA* 1, *A* 2, *SA* 2, *A* 3, *E* 2(R), 1998 *E* 2(R), *A* 1(R), *SA* 1, *A* 3(R), 2000 *F* 1(t&R), *It*, 2002 *E*, 2003 *E, W, F, SA* 1, *A* 1, *SA* 2, *A* 2
Spencer, J C (Wellington) 1905 *A*, 1907 *A* 1(R)
Spiers, J E (Counties) 1979 *S, E*, 1981 *R, F* 1,2
Spillane, A P (South Canterbury) 1913 *A* 2,3
Stanley, J T (Auckland) 1986 *F* 1, *A* 1,2,3, *F* 2,3, 1987 [*It, Fj, Arg, S, W, F*], *A*, 1988 *W* 1,2, *A* 1,2,3, 1989 *F* 1,2, *Arg* 1,2, *A, W, I*, 1990 *S* 1,2
Stead, J W (Southland) 1904 *BI*, 1905 *S, I, E*, 1906 *F*, 1908 *AW* 1,3
Steel, A G (Canterbury) 1966 *BI* 1,2,3,4, 1967 *A, F, S*, 1968 *A* 1,2
Steel, J (West Coast) 1921 *SA* 1,2,3, 1924 *W*, 1925 *E, F*
Steele, L B (Wellington) 1951 *A* 1,2,3

Steere, E R G (Hawke's Bay) 1930 *BI* 1,2,3,4, 1931 *A*, 1932 *A* 1
Steinmetz, P C (Wellington) 2002 *W* (R)
Stensness, L (Auckland) 1993 *BI* 3, *A*, *WS*, 1997 *Fj*, *Arg* 1,2, *A* 1, *SA* 1
Stephens, O G (Wellington) 1968 *F* 3
Stevens, I N (Wellington) 1972 *S*, 1973 *E* 1, 1974 *A* 3
Stewart, A J (Canterbury, South Canterbury) 1963 *E* 1,2, *I*, *W*, 1964 *E*, *S*, *F*, *A* 3
Stewart, J D (Auckland) 1913 *A* 2,3
Stewart, K W (Southland) 1973 *E* 2, 1974 *A* 1,2,3, *I*, 1975 *S*, 1976 *I*, *SA* 1,3, 1979 *S*, *E*, 1981 *SA* 1,2
Stewart, R T (South Canterbury, Canterbury) 1928 *SA* 1,2,3,4, 1930 *BI* 2
Stohr, L B (Taranaki) 1910 *A* 1,2,3
Stone, A M (Waikato, Bay of Plenty) 1981 *F* 1,2, 1983 *BI* 3(R), 1984 *A* 3, 1986 *F* 1, *A* 1,3, *F* 2,3
Storey, P W (South Canterbury) 1921 *SA* 1,2
Strachan, A D (Auckland, North Harbour) 1992 *Wld* 2,3, *I* 1,2, *A* 1,2,3, *SA*, 1993 *BI* 1, 1995 [*J*, *SA* (t)]
Strahan, S C (Manawatu) 1967 *A*, *E*, *W*, *F*, *S*, 1968 *A* 1,2, *F* 1,2,3, 1970 *SA* 1,2,3, 1972 *A* 1,2,3, 1973 *E* 2
Strang, W A (South Canterbury) 1928 *SA* 1,2, 1930 *BI* 3,4, 1931 *A*
Stringfellow, J C (Wairarapa) 1929 *A* 1(R),3
Stuart, K C (Canterbury) 1955 *A* 1
Stuart, R C (Canterbury) 1949 *A* 1,2, 1953 *W*, 1954 *I*, *E*, *S*, *F*
Stuart, R L (Hawke's Bay) 1977 *F* 1(R)
Sullivan, J L (Taranaki) 1937 *SA* 1,2,3, 1938 *A* 1,2,3
Sutherland, A R (Marlborough) 1970 *SA* 2,4, 1971 *BI* 1, 1972 *A* 1,2,3, *W*, 1973 *E* 1, *I*, *F*
Svenson, K S (Wellington) 1924 *I*, *W*, 1925 *E*, *F*
Swain, J P (Hawke's Bay) 1928 *SA* 1,2,3,4

Tanner, J M (Auckland) 1950 *BI* 4, 1951 *A* 1,2,3, 1953 *W*
Tanner, K J (Canterbury) 1974 *A* 1,2,3, *I*, 1975 *S*, 1976 *I*, *SA* 1
Taylor, G L (Northland) 1996 *SA* 5(R)
Taylor, H M (Canterbury) 1913 *A* 1, *US*, 1914 *A* 1,2,3
Taylor, J M (Otago) 1937 *SA* 1,2,3, 1938 *A* 1,2,3
Taylor, M B (Waikato) 1979 *F* 1,2, *A*, *S*, *E*, 1980 *A* 1,2
Taylor, N M (Bay of Plenty, Hawke's Bay) 1977 *BI* 2,4(R), *F* 1,2, 1978 *A* 1,2,3, *I*, 1982 *A* 2
Taylor, R (Taranaki) 1913 *A* 2,3
Taylor, W T (Canterbury) 1983 *BI* 1,2,3,4, *A*, *S*, 1984 *F* 1,2, *A* 1,2, 1985 *E* 1,2, *A*, *Arg* 1,2, 1986 *A* 2, 1987 [*It*, *Fj*, *S*, *W*, *F*], *A*, 1988 *W* 1,2
Tetzlaff, P L (Auckland) 1947 *A* 1,2
Thimbleby, N W (Hawke's Bay) 1970 *SA* 3
Thomas, B T (Auckland, Wellington) 1962 *A* 5, 1964 *A* 1,2,3
Thomson, H D (Wellington) 1908 *AW* 1
Thorn, B C (Conterbury) 2003 *W* (R), *F* (R), *SA* 1(R), *A* 1(R), *SA* 2
Thorne, G S (Auckland) 1968 *A* 1,2, *F* 1,2,3, 1969 *W* 1, 1970 *SA* 1,2,3,4
Thorne, R D (Canterbury) 1999 *SA* 2(R), [*Tg*, *E*, *S*, *F* 2, *SA* 3], 2000 *Tg*, *S* 2, *A* 2(R), *F* 1,2, 2001 *Sm*, *Arg* 1, *F*, *SA* 1, *A* 1, *I*, *S*, *Arg* 2, 2002 *It*, *I* 1,2, *Fj*, *A* 1, SA 1, *A*2, *SA* 2, 2003 *E*, *W*, *F*, *SA* 1, *A* 1, *SA* 2, *A* 2
Thornton, N H (Auckland) 1947 *A* 1,2, 1949 *SA* 1
Tiatia, F I (Wellington) 2000 *Tg* (R), *It*
Tilyard, J T (Wellington) 1913 *A* 3
Timu, J K R (Otago) 1991 *Arg* 1, *A* 1,2, [*E*, *US*, *C*, *A*], 1992 *Wld* 2, *I* 2, *A* 1,2,3, *SA*, 1993 *BI* 1,2,3, *A*, *WS*, *S*, *E*, 1994 *F* 1,2, *SA* 1,2,3, *A*
Tindill, E W T (Wellington) 1936 *E*
Tonu'u, O F J (Auckland) 1997 *Fj* (R), *A* 3(R), 1998 *E* 1,2, *SA* 1(R)
Townsend, L J (Otago) 1955 *A* 1,3
Tremain, K R (Canterbury, Hawke's Bay) 1959 *BI* 2,3,4, 1960 *SA* 1,2,3,4, 1961 *F* 2,3 1962 *A* 1,2,3, 1963 *E* 1,2, *I*, *W*, 1964 *E*, *S*, *F*, *A* 1,2,3, 1965 *SA* 1,2,3,4, 1966 *BI* 1,2,3,4, 1967 *A*, *E*, *W*, *S*, 1968 *A* 1, *F* 1,2,3
Trevathan, D (Otago) 1937 *SA* 1,2,3
Tuck, J M (Waikato) 1929 *A* 1,2,3
Tuigamala, V L (Auckland) 1991 [*US*, *It*, *C*, *S*], 1992 *Wld* 1,2,3, *I* 1, *A* 1,2,3, *SA*, 1993 *BI* 1,2,3, *A*, *WS*, *S*, *E*
Turner, R S (North Harbour) 1992 *Wld* 1,2(R)
Turtill, H S (Canterbury) 1905 *A*
Twigden, T M (Auckland) 1980 *A* 2,3
Tyler, G A (Auckland) 1903 *A*, 1904 *BI*, 1905 *S*, *I*, *E*, *W*, 1906 *F*

Udy, D K (Wairarapa) 1903 *A*
Umaga, J F (Wellington) 1997 *Fj*, *Arg* 1,2, *A* 1, *SA* 1,2, 1999 *WS*, *F* 1, *SA* 1, *A* 1, *SA* 2, *A* 2, [*Tg*, *E*, *S*, *F* 2, *SA* 3], 2000 *Tg*, *S* 1,2, *A* 1, *SA* 1, *A* 2, *SA* 2, *F* 1,2, *It*, 2001 *Sm*, *Arg* 1, *F*, *SA* 1, *A* 1, *SA* 2, *A* 2, *I*, *S*, *Arg* 2, 2002 *I* 1, *Fj*, *SA* 1(R), *A* 2, *SA* 2, *E*, *F*, *W*, 2003 *E*, *W*, *F*, *SA* 1, *A* 1, *SA* 2, *A* 2
Urbahn, R J (Taranaki) 1959 *BI* 1,3,4
Urlich, R A (Auckland) 1970 *SA* 3,4
Uttley, I N (Wellington) 1963 *E* 1,2

Vidiri, J (Counties Manukau) 1998 *E* 2(R), *A* 1
Vincent, P B (Canterbury) 1956 *SA* 1,2
Vodanovich, I M H (Wellington) 1955 *A* 1,2,3

Wallace, W J (Wellington) 1903 *A*, 1904 *BI*, 1905 *S*, *I*, *E*, *W*, 1906 *F*, 1907 *A* 1,2,3, 1908 *AW* 2
Waller, D A G (Wellington) 2001 *Arg* 2(t)
Walsh, P T (Counties) 1955 *A* 1,2,3, 1956 *SA* 1,2,4, 1957 *A* 1,2, 1958 *A* 1,2,3, 1959 *BI* 1, 1963 *E* 2
Ward, R H (Southland) 1936 *A* 2, 1937 *SA* 1,3
Waterman, A C (North Auckland) 1929 *A* 1,2
Watkins, E L (Wellington) 1905 *A*
Watt, B A (Canterbury) 1962 *A* 1,4, 1963 *E* 1,2, *W*, 1964 *E*, *S*, *A* 1
Watt, J M (Otago) 1936 *A* 1,2
Watt, J R (Wellington) 1958 *A* 2, 1960 *SA* 1,2,3,4, 1961 *F* 1,3, 1962 *A* 1,2
Watts, M G (Taranaki) 1979 *F* 1,2, 1980 *A* 1,2,3(R)
Webb, D S (North Auckland) 1959 *BI* 2
Wells, J (Wellington) 1936 *A* 1,2
West, A H (Taranaki) 1921 *SA* 2,3
Whetton, A J (Auckland) 1984 *A* 1(R),3(R), 1985 *A* (R), *Arg* 1(R), 1986 *A* 2, 1987 [*It*, *Fj*, *Arg*, *S*, *W*, *F*], *A*, 1988 *W* 1,2, *A* 1,2,3, 1989 *F* 1,2, *Arg* 1,2, *A*, 1990 *S* 1,2, *A* 1,2,3, *F* 1,2, 1991 *Arg* 1, [*E*, *US*, *It*, *C*, *A*]
Whetton, G W (Auckland) 1981 *SA* 3, *R*, *F* 1,2, 1982 *A* 3, 1983 *BI* 1,2,3,4, 1984 *F* 1,2, *A* 1,2,3, 1985 *E* 1,2, *A*, *Arg* 2, 1986 *A* 2,3, *F* 2,3, 1987 [*It*, *Fj*, *Arg*, *S*, *W*, *F*], *A*, 1988 *W* 1,2, *A* 1,2,3, 1989 *F* 1,2, *Arg* 1,2, *A*, *W*, *I*, 1990 *S* 1,2, *A* 1,2,3, *F* 1,2, 1991 *Arg* 1,2, *A* 1,2, [*E*, *US*, *It*, *C*, *A*, *S*]
Whineray, W J (Canterbury, Waikato, Auckland) 1957 *A* 1,2, 1958 *A* 1,2,3, 1959 *BI* 1,2,3,4, 1960 *SA* 1,2,3,4, 1961 *F* 1,2,3, 1962 *A* 1,2,3,4,5, 1963 *E* 1,2, *I*, *W*, 1964 *E*, *S*, *F*, 1965 *SA* 1,2,3,4
White, A (Southland) 1921 *SA* 1, 1924 *I*, 1925 *E*, *F*
White, H L (Auckland) 1954 *I*, *E*, *F*, 1955 *A* 3
White, R A (Poverty Bay) 1949 *A* 1,2, 1950 *BI* 1,2,3,4, 1951 *A* 1,2,3, 1952 *A* 1,2, 1953 *W*, 1954 *I*, *E*, *S*, *F*, 1955 *A* 1,2,3, 1956 *SA* 1,2,3,4
White, R M (Wellington) 1946 *A* 1,2, 1947 *A* 1,2
Whiting, G J (King Country) 1972 *A* 1,2, *S*, 1973 *E* 1, *I*, *F*
Whiting, P J (Auckland) 1971 *BI* 1,2,4, 1972 *A* 1,2,3, *W*, *S*, 1973 *E* 1, *I*, *F*, 1974 *A* 1,2,3, *I*, 1976 *I*, *SA* 1,2,3,4
Williams, A J (Auckland) 2002 *E*, *F*, *W*, 2003 *E*, *W*, *F*, *SA* 1, *A* 1, *SA* 2, *A* 2
Williams, B G (Auckland) 1970 *SA* 1,2,3,4, 1971 *BI* 1,2,4, 1972 *A* 1,2,3, *W*, *S*, 1973 *E* 1, *I*, *F*, *E* 2, 1974 *A* 1,2,3, *I*, 1975 *S*, 1976 *I*, *SA* 1,2,3,4, 1977 *BI* 1,2,3,4, *F* 1, 1978 *A* 1,2,3, *I* (R), *W*, *E*, *S*
Williams, G C (Wellington) 1967 *E*, *W*, *F*, *S*, 1968 *A* 2
Williams, P (Otago) 1913 *A* 1
Williment, M (Wellington) 1964 *A* 1, 1965 *SA* 1,2,3, 1966 *BI* 1,2,3,4, 1967 *A*
Willis, R K (Waikato) 1998 *SA* 2, *A* 3, 1999 *SA* 1(R), *A* 1(R), *SA* 2(R), *A* 2(R), [*Tg* (R), *E* (R), *It*, *F* 2(R), *SA* 3], 2002 *SA* 1(R)
Willis, T E (Otago) 2002 *It*, *Fj*, *SA* 2(R), *A* 2, *SA* 2
Willocks, C (Otago) 1946 *A* 1,2, 1949 *SA* 1,3,4
Wilson, B W (Otago) 1977 *BI* 3,4, 1978 *A* 1,2,3, 1979 *F* 1,2, *A*
Wilson, D D (Canterbury) 1954 *E*, *S*
Wilson, H W (Otago) 1949 *A* 1, 1950 *BI* 4, 1951 *A* 1,2,3
Wilson, J W (Otago) 1993 *S*, *E*, 1994 *A*, 1995 *C*, [*I*, *J*, *S*, *E*, *SA*], *A* 1,2, *It*, *F* 1, 1996 *WS*, *S* 1,2, *A* 1, *SA* 1, *A* 2, *SA* 2,3,4,5, 1997 *Fj*, *Arg* 1,2, *A* 1, *SA* 1, *A* 2, *SA* 2, *A* 3, *I*, *E* 1, *W*, *E* 2, 1998 *E* 1,2, *A* 1, *SA* 1, *A* 2, *SA* 2, *A* 3, 1999 *WS*, *F* 1, *SA* 1, *A* 1, *SA* 2, *A* 2, [*Tg*, *E*, *It*, *S*, *F* 2, *SA* 3], 2001 *Sm*, *Arg* 1, *F*, *SA* 1, *A* 1, *SA* 2
Wilson, N A (Wellington) 1908 *AW* 1,2, 1910 *A* 1,2,3, 1913 *A* 2,3, 1914 *A* 1,2,3
Wilson, N L (Otago) 1951 *A* 1,2,3
Wilson, R G (Canterbury) 1979 *S*, *E*

Wilson, S S (Wellington) 1977 *F* 1,2, 1978 *A* 1,2,3, *I, W, E, S,* 1979 *F* 1,2, *A, S, E,* 1980 *A* 1, *W,* 1981 *S* 1,2, *SA* 1,2,3, *R, F* 1,2, 1982 *A* 1,2,3, 1983 *BI* 1,2,3,4, *A, S, E*

Wolfe, T N (Wellington, Taranaki) 1961 *F* 1,2,3, 1962 *A* 2,3, 1963 *E* 1

Wood, M E (Canterbury, Auckland) 1903 *A*, 1904 *BI*

Woodcock, T D (North Harbour) 2002 *W*

Woodman, F A (North Auckland) 1981 *SA* 1,2, *F* 2

Wrigley, E (Wairarapa) 1905 *A*

Wright, T J (Auckland) 1986 *F* 1, *A* 1, 1987 [*Arg*], 1988 *W* 1,2, *A* 1,2,3, 1989 *F* 1,2, *Arg* 1,2, *A, W, I,* 1990 *S* 1,2, *A* 1,2,3, *F* 1,2, 1991 *Arg* 1,2, *A* 1,2, [*E, US, It, S*]

Wylie, J T (Auckland) 1913 *A* 1, *US*

Wyllie, A J (Canterbury) 1970 *SA* 2,3, 1971 *BI* 2,3,4, 1972 *W, S,* 1973 *E* 1, *I, F, E* 2

Yates, V M (North Auckland) 1961 *F* 1,2,3

Young, D (Canterbury) 1956 *SA* 2, 1958 *A* 1,2,3, 1960 *SA* 1,2,3,4, 1961 *F* 1,2,3, 1962 *A* 1,2,3,5, 1963 *E* 1,2, *I, W,* 1964 *E, S, F*

AUSTRALIA TEST SEASON REVIEW 2002-03

And then there was One . . .

Peter Jenkins

The Australian trophy cabinet was further raided in the countdown to the game's 2003 global showpiece as the All Blacks, for the first time since 1997, lifted the Bledisloe Cup. New Zealand had stunned the Wallabies in Sydney to complete an awesome away start to the Tri Nations series. After piling on a half-century of points in thrashing the Springboks in Pretoria, the All Blacks arrived down under the following week to inflict the same humiliation. Capitalising on a dreadful Australian kicking game, the Kiwis unleashed a back three of unequalled pace and precision, and raced to a 50-21 victory. It was Australia's worst defeat on home soil and the most points they had ever conceded to the All Blacks. Only once, in a 61-22 loss to the Springboks six years earlier, had they leaked more points in a major Test.

Under the two-game format to decide the Bledisloe trophy, the Wallabies could still retain the big-bellied silverware with a win in the return match at Eden Park, Auckland, a few weeks later. But the glory deeds and miracle escape acts of previous seasons were beyond the Australians. Despite a late try to fan the flames of hope, they went down 21-17 and the Bledisloe Cup was gone. It went the same way as the Tri Nations trophy the previous year. The All Blacks now held both.

The Cook Cup had earlier been retained by England and suddenly, where once Australia had the most sought-after trophy collection in the game, they were left with a single golden memento, albeit the most important of all – the Webb Ellis Cup. The one they will defend on home soil in October/ November.

But the 11 Tests the Wallabies played between their tour to Argentina and Europe in November 2002, through to inbound matches against northern visitors in June 2003 and on to the Tri Nations series over the two months that followed suggested the World Cup trophy was also at severe risk of being removed from Australian Rugby Union headquarters in Sydney.

The Wallabies had won just five of the 11 internationals, losing the other six. It was not what national coach Eddie Jones had counted on at the start of a campaign that kicked off in Buenos Aires some 12 months before the same two sides were scheduled to meet in the 2003 World Cup opener at Stadium Australia on October 10.

Australia has a poor record in Argentina. They have yet to win a two-match series there. But, on this occasion, they managed to silence –

well, almost – a crowd of 70,000 at River Plate Stadium with a 17-6 victory. The Wallabies would later complain they were spat on by sections of the crowd.

The angst from the grandstands, however, was soon forgotten. A more lasting disappointment would be the injury toll exacted by the game. Full-back Mat Rogers, in his first starting Test in the position he filled for the NSW Waratahs, left the match early with damaged ribs and would not play again on tour. Nor would winger Ben Tune, who badly tore a hamstring. He would, the following Australian season, damage a knee and be ruled out of World Cup contention. He had not played another Test since his Buenos Aires mishap.

But if South America was his nightmare, his Wallabies team-mates found theirs the following week in Dublin. Ireland had not beaten Australia since 1979. But on a miserable afternoon at Lansdowne Road, with the Australian tactical kicking game again shown up as completely inadequate, the Irish triumphed 18-9. Irish fly-half Ronan O'Gara's kicking was faultless – out of hand and from the tee. His six penalty goals against the three by Wallabies full-back Matthew Burke settled the match. Ireland led 12-3 at halftime.

The Australians had been forced to make several changes after the injuries sustained in Argentina, but they still presented a Test side of experience and supposed quality. Not that their senior players shone on the day. Burke was disappointing at full-back, so too Larkham at fly-half. Owen Finegan, trialled as a lock, was replaced early on owing to a shoulder injury that would later require a full reconstruction. The day was one to forget for the Wallabies whose captain George Gregan, only minutes after the match, was rushed by taxi to the airport so he could fly home for the birth of his second child. Gregan would return within 72 hours to ensure he could start against England at Twickenham.

Coach Jones, in the lead-up to the Test, was criticised for not telling his skipper to take a week off, especially when the opportunity to give his perennial standby Chris Whitaker the chance to start a match had clearly presented itself. Jones decided not to experiment. Gregan went into the team and the Wallabies went down to England 32-31.

England led 16-6 late in the first half before fly-half Elton Flatley crossed for the Wallabies to reduce the deficit – with the ensuing conversion – to just three points. Flatley had been named at inside-centre but was shifted to the No 10 shirt before kick-off in a revamp which saw Larkham moved to full-back, Burke from full-back to outside-centre and Daniel Herbert from No 13 to No 12.

Flatley excelled in the pivot role, and grabbed an intercept try in the second half to complete a five-point double. It followed a try to winger Wendell Sailor and the Australians led 28-16. When England fly-half Jonny Wilkinson slotted three penalties to one from Burke, the score favoured

Australia 31-25. The killer blow for the Wallabies came 11 minutes before time when winger Ben Cohen powered over for his second try of the match and Wilkinson converted.

On to Genoa where Sailor, after struggling to make a genuine impact in his previous Test appearances, finally produced the power running for which he had been brought across from rugby league to showcase. Australia won 34-3 in a rain-affected affair where Stirling Mortlock became the Wallabies' fifth full-back in as many matches after Chris Latham, Rogers, Burke and Larkham.

The tour had shown Australia needed remedial work to several crucial areas. One was tactical kicking, forward mobility was another while the inability of a star-studded back-line to show the cohesion Jones was relying on flagged a need for better combinations. Injuries were considered a critical factor, but as the Tests of 2003 would show, they could not be used as camouflage for the fact that the Wallabies were struggling to find the winning habit of previous seasons.

The opening international in June against Ireland in Perth was predictable. The Irish had arrived without their two talismans, hooker Keith Wood and centre Brian O'Driscoll. While they harassed a new-look Australian back-line that featured Steve Kefu and the youngster Morgan Turinui in the centres, they were unable to spring an upset as they had seven months earlier and Australia won 45-16.

The Welsh were as expected. Enthusiastic but out-muscled and out-classed, and Australia won 30-10 with Sailor scoring a memorable try. After retrieving a loose ball in his in-goal area, he raced 105 metres and beat five defenders along the way to score one of the great solo tries in Test rugby. If it had been against the All Blacks, England or South Africa, it would have been replayed for weeks on end. That it was achieved against the struggling Welsh failed to win him the accolades the effort deserved. Even Welsh coach Steve Hansen, while praising Sailor later, offered the advice that the former league star would have to learn to kick if he wanted to reach the top in rugby.

There were doubts about the English when they arrived in Australia. They had beaten New Zealand but could they end their long-running drought on the other side of the Tasman? They had never won a Test on Australian shores. But as the Wallabies struggled to match the athleticism of England's Dad's Army pack, and the backs again lacked a sense of creativity, the watershed result finally arrived. England won 25-14. The highlight for the Wallabies was another solo effort from Sailor, this time cutting back on the angle and in behind forwards during a 30-metre dash to the right corner.

South Africa served up further problems for Jones when they beat the Wallabies 26-22 in Cape Town. A fast-advancing defence unsettled Kefu at inside-centre while Rogers, back in the starting side at outside-centre after injury, had little opportunity to display his running skills. The alarm bells were clanging. The Australians had lost two in a row and would, if they went down to the All Blacks, lose three in succession for the first time since 1995.

Lose they did, by a monstrous margin. The Kiwis ran amok and the Australian defence, with three former league players in the back-line in Sailor, Rogers and winger Lote Tuqiri, was all at sea. The kicking game of Larkham was again shown up and the Wallabies were, in some quarters, written off as World Cup pretenders.

A 29-9 victory over South Africa in Brisbane was a confidence boost. But it was a start, only a start, in their bid to turn around a year in danger of turning pear-shaped. New Zealand beat the Wallabies in Auckland, leaving them with just one win from their past five internationals and critics, this one included, calling for changes.

One of the few positives for Jones as he searched for solutions was the knowledge that key backs Joe Roff and Stirling Mortlock would be back in action for the World Cup. Roff missed the Tri Nations series with injury while Mortlock had not played a Test all year after major shoulder damage.

Australia's Test Record in 2002-2003: Played 11, won 5, lost 6

Opponents	*Date*	*Venue*	*Result*
New Zealand	16th August 2003	A	Lost 17-21
South Africa	2nd August 2003	H	Won 29-9
New Zealand	26th July 2003	H	Lost 21-50
South Africa	12th July 2003	A	Lost 22-26
England	21st June 2003	H	Lost 14-25
Wales	14th June 2003	H	Won 30-10
Ireland	7th June 2003	H	Won 45-16
Italy	23rd November 2002	A	Won 34-3
England	16th November 2002	A	Lost 31-32
Ireland	9th November 2002	A	Lost 9-18
Argentina	2nd November 2002	A	Won 17-6

AUSTRALIA INTERNATIONAL STATISTICS

(up to 30 September 2003)

Match Records

MOST CONSECUTIVE TEST WINS

10 1991 *Arg, WS, W, I, NZ, E,* 1992 *S* 1,2, *NZ* 1,2
10 1998 *NZ* 3, *Fj, Tg, Sm, F, E* 2, 1999 *I* 1,2, *E, SA* 1
10 1999 *NZ* 2, *R, I* 3, *US, W, SA* 3, *F,* 2000 *Arg* 1,2, *SA* 1

MOST CONSECUTIVE TESTS WITHOUT DEFEAT

Matches	*Wins*	*Draws*	*Period*
10	10	0	1991 to 1992
10	10	0	1998 to 1999
10	10	0	1999 to 2000

MOST POINTS IN A MATCH

by the team

Pts	*Opponents*	*Venue*	*Year*
92	Spain	Madrid	2001
76	England	Brisbane	1998
74	Canada	Brisbane	1996
74	Tonga	Canberra	1998
73	Western Samoa	Sydney	1994
67	United States	Brisbane	1990

by a player

Pts	*Player*	*Opponents*	*Venue*	*Year*
39	M C Burke	Canada	Brisbane	1996
29	S A Mortlock	South Africa	Melbourne	2000
28	M P Lynagh	Argentina	Brisbane	1995
25	M C Burke	Scotland	Sydney	1998
25	M C Burke	France	Cardiff	1999
25	M C Burke	British/Irish Lions	Melbourne	2001
25	E J Flatley*	Ireland	Perth	2003
24	M P Lynagh	United States	Brisbane	1990
24	M P Lynagh	France	Brisbane	1990
24	M C Burke	New Zealand	Melbourne	1998
24	M C Burke	South Africa	Twickenham	1999

** includes a penalty try*

MOST TRIES IN A MATCH

by the team

Tries	*Opponents*	*Venue*	*Year*
13	South Korea	Brisbane	1987
13	Spain	Madrid	2001
12	United States	Brisbane	1990
12	Wales	Brisbane	1991
12	Tonga	Canberra	1998
11	Western Samoa	Sydney	1994
11	England	Brisbane	1998

by a player

Tries	*Player*	*Opponents*	*Venue*	*Year*
4	G Cornelsen	New Zealand	Auckland	1978
4	D I Campese	United States	Sydney	1983
4	J S Little	Tonga	Canberra	1998
4	C E Latham	Argentina	Brisbane	2000
3	R L Raymond	NZ Maori	Sydney	1922
3	A D McLean	NZ Maori	Palmerston N	1936
3	J R Ryan	Japan	Brisbane	1975
3	M P Burke	Canada	Brisbane	1985
3	M P Burke	South Korea	Brisbane	1987
3	D I Campese	Italy	Rome	1988
3	A S Nuiqila	Italy	Rome	1988
3	D I Campese	Canada	Calgary	1993
3	M Burke	Canada	Brisbane	1996
3	S J Larkham	England	Brisbane	1998
3	B N Tune	England	Brisbane	1998
3	C P Strauss	Ireland	Brisbane	1999
3	R S T Kefu	Romania	Belfast	1999
3	C E Latham	Spain	Madrid	2001

MOST CONVERSIONS IN A MATCH

by the team

Cons	*Opponents*	*Venue*	*Year*
12	Spain	Madrid	2001
9	Canada	Brisbane	1996
9	Fiji	Parramatta	1998
8	Italy	Rome	1988
8	United States	Brisbane	1990
7	Canada	Sydney	1985
7	Tonga	Canberra	1998

by a player

Cons	*Player*	*Opponents*	*Venue*	*Year*
10	M C Burke	Spain	Madrid	2001
9	M C Burke	Canada	Brisbane	1996
9	J A Eales	Fiji	Parramatta	1998
8	M P Lynagh	Italy	Rome	1988
8	M P Lynagh	United States	Brisbane	1990
7	M P Lynagh	Canada	Sydney	1985

MOST PENALTIES IN A MATCH

by the team

Penalties	Opponents	Venue	Year
8	South Africa	Twickenham	1999
7	New Zealand	Sydney	1999
7	France	Cardiff	1999
7	Wales	Cardiff	2001
6	New Zealand	Sydney	1984
6	France	Sydney	1986
6	England	Brisbane	1988
6	Argentina	Buenos Aires	1997
6	Ireland	Perth	1999
6	France	Paris	2000
6	British/Irish Lions	Melbourne	2001

by a player

Penalties	Player	Opponents	Venue	Year
8	M C Burke	South Africa	Twickenham	1999
7	M C Burke	New Zealand	Sydney	1999
7	M C Burke	France	Cardiff	1999
7	M C Burke	Wales	Cardiff	2001
6	M P Lynagh	France	Sydney	1986
6	M P Lynagh	England	Brisbane	1988
6	D J Knox	Argentina	Buenos Aires	1997
6	M C Burke	France	Paris	2000
6	M C Burke	British/Irish Lions	Melbourne	2001

MOST DROPPED GOALS IN A MATCH

by the team

Drops	Opponents	Venue	Year
3	England	Twickenham	1967
3	Ireland	Dublin	1984
3	Fiji	Brisbane	1985

by a player

Drops	Player	Opponents	Venue	Year
3	P FHawthorne	England	Twickenham	1967
2	M G Ella	Ireland	Dublin	1984
2	D J Knox	Fiji	Brisbane	1985

Career Records

MOST CAPPED PLAYERS

Caps	Player	Career Span
101	D I Campese	1982 to 1996
89	G M Gregan	1994 to 2003
86	J A Eales	1991 to 2001
80	T J Horan	1989 to 2000
79	D J Wilson	1992 to 2000
76	J W C Roff	1995 to 2003
75	J S Little	1989 to 2000
72	M P Lynagh	1984 to 1995
72	M C Burke	1993 to 2003
67	P N Kearns	1989 to 1999
67	D J Herbert	1994 to 2002
63	N C Farr Jones	1984 to 1993
60	R S T Kefu	1997 to 2003
59	S P Poidevin	1980 to 1991
59	S J Larkham	1996 to 2003

MOST CONSECUTIVE TESTS

Tests	Player	Span
62	J W C Roff	1996 to 2001
46	P N Kearns	1989 to 1995
42	D I Campese	1990 to 1995
37	P G Johnson	1959 to 1968

MOST TESTS AS CAPTAIN

Tests	Captain	Span
55	J A Eales	1996 to 2001
36	N C Farr Jones	1988 to 1992
21	G M Gregan	2001 to 2003
19	A G Slack	1984 to 1987
16	J E Thornett	1962 to 1967
16	G V Davis	1969 to 1972

MOST TESTS IN INDIVIDUAL POSITIONS

Position	Player	Tests	Span
Full-back	M C Burke	53	1993 to 2003
Wing	D I Campese	85	1982 to 1996
Centre	T J Horan	69	1989 to 2000
Fly-half	M P Lynagh	64	1984 to 1995
Scrum-half	G M Gregan	89	1994 to 2003
Prop	E J A McKenzie	51	1990 to 1997
Hooker	P N Kearns	66	1989 to 1999
Lock	J A Eales	84	1991 to 2001
Flanker	D J Wilson	79	1992 to 2000
No 8	R S T Kefu	58	1998 to 2003

Burke, Campese, Horan, Lynagh, Eales and Kefu have been capped in other positions

MOST POINTS IN TESTS

Points	Player	Tests	Career
911	M P Lynagh	72	1984 to 1995
851	M C Burke	72	1993 to 2003
315	D I Campese	101	1982 to 1996
260	P E McLean	30	1974 to 1982
189	J W Roff	76	1995 to 2003
173	J A Eales	86	1991 to 2001

MOST TRIES IN TESTS

Tries	Player	Tests	Career
64	D I Campese	101	1982 to 1996
30	T J Horan	80	1989 to 2000
28	J W Roff	76	1995 to 2003
26	M C Burke	72	1993 to 2003
24	B N Tune	46	1996 to 2002
21	J S Little	75	1989 to 2000

MOST CONVERSIONS IN TESTS

Cons	Player	Tests	Career
140	M P Lynagh	72	1984 to 1995
101	M C Burke	72	1993 to 2003
31	J A Eales	86	1991 to 2001
27	P E McLean	30	1974 to 1982
19	D J Knox	13	1985 to 1997

MOST PENALTY GOALS IN TESTS

Penalties	Player	Tests	Career
177	M P Lynagh	72	1984 to 1995
172	M C Burke	72	1993 to 2003
62	P E McLean	30	1974 to 1982
34	J A Eales	86	1991 to 2001
25	S A Mortlock	20	2000 to 2002
23	M C Roebuck	23	1991 to 1993

MOST DROPPED GOALS IN TESTS

Drops	Player	Tests	Career
9	P F Hawthorne	21	1962 to 1967
9	M P Lynagh	72	1984 to 1995
8	M G Ella	25	1980 to 1984
4	P E McLean	30	1974 to 1982

Tri Nations Records

Record	Detail	Holder	Set
Most points in season	104	in four matches	2000
Most tries in season	13	in four matches	1997
Highest Score	38	38-27 v S Africa (h)	2002
Biggest win	26	32-6 v S Africa (h)	1999
Highest score conceded	61	22-61 v S Africa (a)	1997
Biggest defeat	39	22-61 v S Africa (a)	1997
Most points in matches	263	M C Burke	1996 to 2003
Most points in season	71	S A Mortlock	2000
Most points in match	24	M C Burke	v N Zealand (h) 1998
Most tries in matches	9	J W C Roff	1996 to 2003
Most tries in season	4	S A Mortlock	2000
Most tries in match	2	B N Tune	v S Africa (h) 1997
	2	M C Burke	v N Zealand (h) 1998
	2	J W C Roff	v S Africa (h) 1999
	2	S A Mortlock	v N Zealand (h) 2000
	2	C E Latham	v S Africa (h) 2002
Most cons in matches	18	M C Burke	1996 to 2003
Most cons in season	7	D J Knox	1997
Most cons in match	3	D J Knox	v S Africa (h) 1997
	3	M C Burke	v S Africa (h) 1999
	3	M C Burke	v S Africa (h) 2002
Most pens in matches	63	M C Burke	1996 to 2003
Most pens in season	14	M C Burke	2001
Most pens in match	7	M C Burke	v N Zealand (h) 1999

Series Records

Record	Holder	Detail
Most tries	D I Campese	6 in Europe 1988
Most points	M C Burke	74 in Europe 1996

Miscellaneous Records

Record	*Holder*	*Detail*
Longest Test Career	G M Cooke/A R Miller	16 seasons, 1932-1947-48/1952-67
Youngest Test Cap	B W Ford	18 yrs 90 days in 1957
Oldest Test Cap	A R Miller	38 yrs 113 days in 1967

Career Records of Australian International Players
(up to 30 September 2003)

PLAYER	*Debut*	*Caps*	*T*	*C*	*P*	*D*	*Pts*
Backs:							
M A Bartholomeusz	2002 v It	1	0	0	0	0	0
M C Burke	1993 v SA	72	26	101	172	1	851
E J Flatley	1997 v E	27	4*	12	12	0	80
M J Giteau	2002 v E	4	0	0	0	0	0
G M Gregan	1994 v It	89	13	0	0	2	71
N P Grey	1998 v S	33	6	0	0	0	30
D J Herbert	1994 v I	67	11	0	0	0	55
S Kefu	2001 v W	6	1	0	0	0	5
S J Larkham	1996 v W	59	15	2	0	1	82
C E Latham	1998 v F	38	19	0	0	0	95
S A Mortlock	2000 v Arg	20	12	10	25	0	155
J W Roff	1995 v C	76	28*	11	9	0	189
M S Rogers	2002 v F	12	4	0	0	0	20
W J Sailor	2002 v F	13	6	0	0	0	30
B N Tune	1996 v W	46	24	0	0	0	120
L Tuqiri	2003 v I	7	0	0	0	0	0
M Turinui	2003 v I	3	0	0	0	0	0
S N G Staniforth	1999 v US	3	4	0	0	0	20
C J Whitaker	1998 v SA	15	2	0	0	0	10
Forwards:							
A K E Baxter	2003 v NZ	1	0	0	0	0	0
B J Cannon	2001 v BI	18	1	0	0	0	5
M J Cockbain	1997 v F	56	1	0	0	0	5
D N Croft	2002 v Arg	4	0	0	0	0	0
B J Darwin	2001 v BI	22	0	0	0	0	0
O D A Finegan	1996 v W	55	6	0	0	0	30
A L Freier	2002 v Arg	6	0	0	0	0	0
D T Giffin	1996 v W	45	0	0	0	0	0
S P Hardman	2002 v F	1	0	0	0	0	0
J B Harrison	2001 v BI	17	1	0	0	0	5
D P Heenan	2003 v W	1	0	0	0	0	0
R S T Kefu	1997 v SA	60	10	0	0	0	50
D J Lyons	2000 v Arg	14	0	0	0	0	0
E P Noriega	1998 v F	24	0	0	0	0	0
G M Panoho	1998 v SA	21	0	0	0	0	0
J A Paul	1998 v S	37	6	0	0	0	30
N C Sharpe	2002 v F	13	1	0	0	0	5
G B Smith	2000 v F	28	2	0	0	0	10
N B Stiles	2001 v BI	12	1	0	0	0	5
D J Vickerman	2002 v F	11	0	0	0	0	0
P R Waugh	2000 v E	15	3	0	0	0	15
W K Young	2000 v F	19	0	0	0	0	0

* Roff's figures include a penalty try awarded against New Zealand in 2001 and Flatley's one awarded against Ireland in 2003

AUSTRALIAN INTERNATIONAL PLAYERS

(up to 30 September 2003)

Abrahams, A M F (NSW) 1967 *NZ*, 1968 *NZ* 1, 1969 *W*
Adams, N J (NSW) 1955 *NZ* 1
Adamson, R W (NSW) 1912 *US*
Allan, T (NSW) 1946 *NZ* 1, *M*, *NZ* 2, 1947 *NZ* 2, *S*, *I*, *W*, 1948 *E*, *F*, 1949 *M* 1,2,3, *NZ* 1,2
Anderson, R P (NSW) 1925 *NZ* 1
Anlezark, E A (NSW) 1905 *NZ*
Armstrong, A R (NSW) 1923 *NZ* 1,2
Austin, L R (NSW) 1963 *E*

Baker, R L (NSW) 1904 *BI* 1,2
Baker, W H (NSW) 1914 *NZ* 1,2,3
Ballesty, J P (NSW) 1968 *NZ* 1,2, *F*, *I*, *S*, 1969 *W*, *SA* 2,3,4,
Bannon, D P (NSW) 1946 *M*
Bardsley, E J (NSW) 1928 *NZ* 1,3, *M* (R)
Barker, H S (NSW) 1952 *Fj* 1,2, *NZ* 1,2, 1953 *SA* 4, 1954 *Fj* 1,2
Barnett, J T (NSW) 1907 *NZ* 1,2,3, 1908 *W*, 1909 *E*
Barry, M J (Q) 1971 *SA* 3
Bartholomeusz, M A (ACT) 2002 *It* (R)
Barton, R F D (NSW) 1899 *BI* 3
Batch, P G (Q) 1975 *S*, *W*, 1976 *E*, *Fj* 1,2,3, *F* 1,2, 1978 *W* 1,2, *NZ* 1,2,3, 1979 *Arg* 2
Batterham, R P (NSW) 1967 *NZ*, 1970 *S*
Battishall, B R (NSW) 1973 *E*
Baxter, A J (NSW) 1949 *M* 1,2,3, *NZ* 1,2, 1951 *NZ* 1,2, 1952 *NZ* 1,2
Baxter, A K E (NSW) 2003 *NZ* 2(R)
Baxter, T J (Q) 1958 *NZ* 3
Beith, B McN (NSW) 1914 *NZ* 3, 1920 *NZ* 1,2,3
Bell, K R (Q) 1968 *S*
Bell, M D NSW) 1996 *C*
Bennett, W G (Q) 1931 *M*, 1933 *SA* 1,2,3,
Bermingham, J V (Q) 1934 *NZ* 1,2, 1937 *SA* 1
Berne, J E (NSW) 1975 *S*
Besomo, K S (NSW) 1979 *I* 2
Betts, T N (Q) 1951 *NZ* 2,3, 1954 *Fj* 2
Biilmann, R R (NSW) 1933 *SA* 1,2,3,4
Birt, R (Q) 1914 *NZ* 2
Black, J W (NSW) 1985 *C* 1,2, *NZ*, *Fj* 1
Blackwood, J G (NSW) 1922 *M* 1, *NZ* 1,2,3, 1923 *M* 1, *NZ* 1,2,3, 1924 *NZ* 1,2,3, 1925 *NZ* 1,4, 1926 *NZ* 1,2,3, 1927 *I*, *W*, *S*, 1928 *E*, *F*
Blades, A T (NSW) 1996 *S*, *I*, *W* 3, 1997 *NZ* 1(R), *E* 1(R), *SA* 1(R), *NZ* 3, *SA* 2, *Arg* 1,2, *E* 2, *S*, 1998 *E* 1, *S* 1,2, *NZ* 1, *SA* 1, *NZ* 2, *SA* 2, *NZ* 3, *Fj*, *WS*, *F*, *E* 2, 1999 *I* 1(R), *SA* 2, *NZ* 2, [*R*, *I* 3, *W*, *SA* 3, *F*]
Blades, C D (NSW) 1997 *E* 1
Blair, M R (NSW) 1928 *F*, 1931 *M*, *NZ*
Bland, G V (NSW) 1928 *NZ* 3, *M*, 1932 *NZ* 1,2,3, 1933 *SA* 1,2,4,5
Blomley, J (NSW) 1949 *M* 1,2,3, *NZ* 1,2, 1950 *BI* 1,2
Boland, S B (Q) 1899 *BI* 3,4, 1903 *NZ*
Bond, G S G (ACT) 2001 *SA* 2(R), *Sp* (R), *E* (R), *F*, *W*
Bond, J H (NSW) 1920 *NZ* 1,2,3, 1921 *NZ*
Bondfield, C (NSW) 1925 *NZ* 2
Bonis, E T (Q) 1929 *NZ* 1,2,3, 1930 *BI*, 1931 *M*, *NZ*, 1932 *NZ* 1,2,3, 1933 *SA* 1,2,3,4,5, 1934 *NZ* 1,2, 1936 *NZ* 1,2, *M*, 1937 *SA* 1, 1938 *NZ* 1
Bonner, J E (NSW) 1922 *NZ* 1,2,3, 1923 *M* 1,2,3, 1924 *NZ* 1,2
Bosler, J M (NSW) 1953 *SA* 1
Bouffler, R G (NSW) 1899 *BI* 3
Bourke, T K (Q) 1947 *NZ* 2
Bowden, R (NSW) 1926 *NZ* 4
Bowen, S (NSW) 1993 *SA* 1,2,3, 1995 [*R*], *NZ* 1,2, 1996 *C*, *NZ* 1, *SA* 2
Bowers, A J A (NSW) 1923 *M* 2(R),3, *NZ*, 3, 1925 *NZ* 1,4, 1926 *NZ* 1, 1927 *I*
Bowman, T M (NSW) 1998 *E* 1, *S* 1,2, *NZ* 1, *SA* 1, *NZ* 2, *SA* 2, *NZ* 3, *Fj*, *WS*, *F*, *E* 2, 1999 *I* 1,2, *SA* 2, [*US*]
Boyce, E S (NSW) 1962 *NZ* 1,2, 1964 *NZ* 1,2,3, 1965 *SA* 1,2, 1966 *W*, *S*, 1967 *E*, *I* 1, *F*, *I* 2
Boyce, J S (NSW) 1962 *NZ* 3,4,5, 1963 *E*, *SA* 1,2,3,4, 1964 *NZ* 1,3, 1965 *SA* 1,2
Boyd, A (NSW) 1899 *BI* 3
Boyd, A F McC (Q) 1958 *M* 1
Brass, J E (NSW) 1966 *BI* 2, *W*, *S*, 1967 *E*, *I* 1, *F*, *I* 2, *NZ*, 1968 *NZ* 1, *F*, *I*, *S*
Breckenridge, J W (NSW) 1925 *NZ* 2(R),3, 1927 *I*, *W*, *S*, 1928 *E*, *F*, 1929 *NZ* 1,2,3, 1930 *BI*
Brial, M C (NSW) 1993 *F* 1(R), 2, 1996 *W* 1(R), 2, *C*, *NZ* 1, *SA* 1, *NZ* 2, *SA* 2, *It*, *I*, *W* 3, 1997 *NZ* 2
Bridle, O L (V) 1931 *M*, 1932 *NZ* 1,2,3, 1933 *SA* 3,4,5, 1934 *NZ* 1,2, 1936 *NZ* 1,2, *M*
Broad, E G (Q) 1949 *M* 1
Brockhoff, J D (NSW) 1949 *M* 2,3, *NZ* 1,2, 1950 *BI* 1,2, 1951 *NZ* 2,3
Brown, B R (Q) 1972 *NZ* 1,3
Brown, J V (NSW) 1956 *SA* 1,2, 1957 *NZ* 1,2, 1958 *W*, *I*, *E*, *S*, *F*
Brown, R C (NSW) 1975 *E* 1,2
Brown, S W (NSW) 1953 *SA* 2,3,4
Bryant, H (NSW) 1925 *NZ* 1,3,4
Buchan, A J (NSW) 1946 *NZ* 1,2, 1947 *NZ* 1,2, *S*, *I*, *W*, 1948 *E*, *F*, 1949 *M* 3
Buchanan, P N (NSW) 1923 *M* 2(R),3
Bull, D (NSW) 1928 *M*
Buntine, H (NSW) 1923 *NZ* 1(R), 1924 *NZ* 2
Burdon, A (NSW) 1903 *NZ*, 1904 *BI* 1,2, 1905 *NZ*
Burge, A B (NSW) 1907 *NZ* 3, 1908 *W*
Burge, P H (NSW) 1907 *NZ* 1,2,3
Burge, R (NSW) 1928 *NZ* 1,2,3(R), *M* (R)
Burke, B T (NSW) 1988 *S* (R)
Burke, C T (NSW) 1946 *NZ* 2, 1947 *NZ* 1,2, *S*, *I*, *W*, 1948 *E*, *F*, 1949 *M* 2,3, *NZ* 1,2, 1950 *BI* 1,2, 1951 *NZ* 1,2,3, 1953 *SA* 2,3,4, 1954 *Fj* 1, 1955 *NZ* 1,2,3, 1956 *SA* 1,2,
Burke, M C (NSW) 1993 *SA* 3(R), *F* 1, 1994 *I* 1,2, *It* 1,2, 1995 [*C*, *R*, *E*], *NZ* 1,2, 1996 *W* 1,2, *C*, *NZ* 1, *SA* 1, *NZ* 2, *SA* 2, *It*, *S*, *I*, *W* 3, 1997 *E* 1, *NZ* 2 , 1998 *E* 1, *S* 1,2, *NZ* 1, *SA* 1, *NZ* 2, *SA* 2, *NZ* 3, 1999 *I* 2(R), *E* (R), *SA* 1, *NZ* 1, *SA* 2, *NZ* 2, [*R*, *I* 3, *US*, *W*, *SA* 3, *F*], 2000 *F*, *S*, *E*, 2001 *BI* 1(R),2,3, *SA* 1, *NZ* 1, *SA* 2, *NZ* 2, *Sp*, *E*, *F*, *W*, 2002 *F* 1,2, *NZ* 1, *SA* 1, *NZ* 2, *SA* 2, *Arg*, *I*, *E*, *It*, 2003 *SA* 1, *NZ* 1, *SA* 2(R), *NZ* 2(R)
Burke, M P (NSW) 1984 *E* (R), *I*, 1985 *C* 1,2, *NZ*, *Fj* 1,2, 1986 *It* (R), *F*, *Arg* 1,2, *NZ* 1,2,3, 1987 *SK*, [*US*, *J*, *I*, *F*, *W*], *NZ*, *Arg* 1,2
Burnet, D R (NSW) 1972 *F* 1,2, *NZ* 1,2,3, *Fj*
Butler, O F (NSW) 1969 *SA* 1,2, 1970 *S*, 1971 *SA* 2,3, *F* 1,2

Calcraft, W J (NSW) 1985 *C* 1, 1986 *It*, *Arg* 2
Caldwell, B C (NSW) 1928 *NZ* 3
Cameron, A S (NSW) 1951 *NZ* 1,2,3, 1952 *Fj* 1,2, *NZ* 1,2, 1953 *SA* 1,2,3,4, 1954 *Fj* 1,2, 1955 *NZ* 1,2,3, 1956 *SA* 1,2, 1957 *NZ* 1, 1958 *I*
Campbell, J D (NSW) 1910 *NZ* 1,2,3
Campbell, W A (Q) 1984 *Fj*, 1986 *It*, *F*, *Arg* 1,2, *NZ* 1,2,3, 1987 *SK*, [*E*, *US*, *J* (R), *I*, *F*], *NZ*, 1988 *E*, 1989 *BI* 1,2,3, *NZ*, 1990 *NZ* 2,3
Campese, D I (ACT, NSW) 1982 *NZ* 1,2,3, 1983 *US*, *Arg* 1,2, *NZ*, *It*, *F* 1,2, 1984 *Fj*, *NZ* 1,2,3, *E*, *I*, *W*, *S*, 1985 *Fj* 1,2, 1986 *It*, *F*, *Arg* 1,2, *NZ* 1,2,3, 1987 [*E*, *US*, *J*, *I*, *F*, *W*], *NZ*, 1988 *E* 1,2, *NZ* 1,2,3, *E*, *S*, *It*, 1989 *BI* 1,2,3, *NZ*, *F* 1,2, 1990 *F* 2,3, *US*, *NZ* 1,2,3, 1991 *W*, *E*, *NZ* 1,2, [*Arg*, *WS*, *W*, *I*, *NZ*, *E*], 1992 *S* 1,2, *NZ* 1,2,3, *SA*, *I*, *W*, 1993 *Tg*, *NZ*, *SA* 1,2,3, *C*, *F* 1,2, 1994 *I* 1,2, *It* 1,2, *WS*, *NZ*, 1995 *Arg* 1,2, [*SA*, *C*, *E*], *NZ* 2(R), 1996 *W* 1,2, *C*, *NZ* 1, *SA* 1, *NZ* 2, *SA* 2, *It*, *W*3
Canniffe, W D (Q) 1907 *NZ* 2
Cannon, B J (NSW) 2001 *BI* 2(R), *NZ* 1(R), *Sp* (R), *F* (R), *W* (R), 2002 *F* 1(R),2, *SA* 1(t),2(R), *I* (t), *It* (R), 2003 *I* (R), *W* (R), *E* (R), *SA* 1, *NZ* 1, *SA* 2, *NZ* 2
Caputo, M E (ACT) 1996 *W* 1,2, 1997 *F* 1,2, *NZ* 1
Carberry, C M (NSW, Q) 1973 *Tg* 2, *E*, 1976 *I*, *US*, *Fj* 1,2,3, 1981 *F* 1,2, *I*, *W*, *S*, 1982 *E*
Cardy, A M (NSW) 1966 *BI* 1,2, *W*, *S*, 1967 *E*, *I* 1, *F*, 1968 *NZ* 1,2
Carew, P J (Q) 1899 *BI* 1,2,3,4
Carmichael, P (Q) 1904 *BI* 2, 1907 *NZ* 1, 1908 *W*, 1909 *E*
Carozza, P V (Q) 1990 *F* 1,2,3, *NZ* 2,3, 1992 *S* 1,2, *NZ* 1,2,3, *SA*, *I*, *W*, 1993 *Tg*, *NZ*
Carpenter, M G (V) 1938 *NZ* 1,2,
Carr, E T A (NSW) 1913 *NZ* 1,2,3, 1914 *NZ* 1,2,3

Carr, E W (NSW) 1921 *SA* 1,2,3, *NZ* (R)
Carroll, D B (NSW) 1908 *W*, 1912 *US*
Carroll, J C (NSW) 1953 *SA* 1
Carroll, J H (NSW) 1958 *M* 2,3, *NZ* 1,2,3, 1959 *BI* 1,2
Carson, J (NSW) 1899 *BI* 1
Carson, P J (NSW) 1979 *NZ*, 1980 *NZ* 3
Carter, D G (NSW) 1988 *E* 1,2, *NZ* 1, 1989 *F* 1,2
Casey, T V (NSW) 1963 *SA* 2,3,4, 1964 *NZ* 1,2,3
Catchpole, K W (NSW) 1961 *Fj* 1,2,3, *SA* 1,2, *F*, 1962 *NZ* 1,2,4, 1963 *SA* 2,3,4, 1964 *NZ* 1,2,3, 1965 *SA* 1,2, 1966 *BI* 1,2, *W*, *S*, 1967 *E*, *I* 1, *F*, *I* 2, *NZ*, 1968 *NZ* 1
Cawsey, R M (NSW) 1949 *M* 1, *NZ* 1,2
Cerutti, W H (NSW) 1928 *NZ* 1,2,3, *M*, 1929 *NZ* 1,2,3, 1930 *BI*, 1931 *M*, *NZ*, 1932 *NZ* 1,2,3, 1933 *SA* 1,2,3,4,5, 1936 *M*, 1937 *SA* 1,2
Challoner, R L (NSW) 1899 *BI* 2
Chambers, R (NSW) 1920 *NZ* 1,3
Chapman, G A (NSW) 1962 *NZ* 3,4,5
Clark, J G (Q) 1931 *M*, *NZ*, 1932 *NZ* 1,2, 1933 *SA* 1
Clarken, J C (NSW) 1905 *NZ*, 1910 *NZ* 1,2,3
Cleary, M A (NSW) 1961 *Fj* 1,2,3, *SA* 1,2, *F*
Clements, P (NSW) 1982 *NZ* 3
Clifford, M (NSW) 1938 *NZ* 3
Cobb, W G (NSW) 1899 *BI* 3,4
Cockbain, M J (Q) 1997 *F* 2(R), *NZ* 1, *SA* 1,2, 1998 *E* 1, *S* 1,2, *NZ* 1, *SA* 1, *NZ* 2, *SA* 2, *NZ* 3, *Fj*, *Tg* (R), *WS*, *F*, *E* 2, 1999 *I* 1,2, *E*, *SA* 1, *NZ* 1, *SA* 2, *NZ* 2, [*US* (t&R), *W*, *SA* 3, *F*], 2000 *Arg* 1,2, *SA* 2(t&R),3(t&R), *F*, *S*, *E* (R), 2001 *BI* 1(R),2(R),3(R), *SA* 1(R), *NZ* 1(R), *SA* 2(R), *NZ* 2(R), *Sp* (R), *E* (R), *F* (t+R), *W*, 2002 *F* 1(R),2(R), *NZ* 1(R), *SA* 1(R), *NZ* 2(R), *SA* 2(R), *Arg*, *I*, *E*, *It*
Cocks, M R (NSW, Q) 1972 *F* 1,2, *NZ* 2,3, *Fj*, 1973 *Tg* 1,2, *W*, *E*, 1975 *J* 1
Codey, D (NSW Country, Q) 1983 *Arg* 1, 1984 *E*, *W*, *S*, 1985 *C* 2, *NZ*, 1986 *F*, *Arg* 1, 1987 [*US*, *J*, *F* (R), *W*], *NZ*
Cody, E W (NSW) 1913 *NZ* 1,2,3
Coker, T (Q, ACT) 1987 [*E*, *US*, *F*, *W*], 1991 *NZ* 2, [*Arg*, *WS*, *NZ*, *E*], 1992 *NZ* 1,2,3, *W* (R), 1993 *Tg*, *NZ*, 1995 *Arg* 2, *NZ* 1(R), 1997 *F* 1(R), 2, *NZ* 1, *E* 1, *NZ* 2(R), *SA* 1(R), *NZ* 3, *SA* 2, *Arg* 1,2
Colbert, R (NSW) 1952 *Fj* 2, *NZ* 1,2, 1953 *SA* 2,3,4
Cole, J W (NSW) 1968 *NZ* 1,2, *F*, *I*, *S*, 1969 *W*, *SA* 1,2,3,4, 1970 *S*, 1971 *SA* 1,2,3, *F* 1,2, 1972 *NZ* 1,2,3, 1973 *Tg* 1,2, 1974 *NZ* 1,2,3
Collins, P K (NSW) 1937 *SA* 2, 1938 *NZ* 2,3
Colton, A J (Q) 1899 *BI* 1,3
Colton, T (Q) 1904 *BI* 1,2
Comrie-Thomson, I R (NSW) 1926 *NZ* 4, 1928 *NZ* 1,2,3 *M*
Connor, D M (Q) 1958 *W*, *I*, *E*, *S*, *F*, *M* 2,3, *NZ* 1,2,3, 1959 *BI* 1,2
Connors, M R (Q) 1999 *SA* 1(R), *NZ* 1(R), *SA* 2(R), *NZ* 2, [*R* (R), *I* 3, *US*, *W* (R), *SA* 3(R), *F*(R)], 2000 *Arg* 1(R),2(R), *SA* 1, *NZ* 1, *SA* 2, *NZ* 2(t&R), *SA* 3, *F* (R), *S* (R), *E* (R)
Constable, R (Q) 1994 *I* 2(t & R)
Cook, M T (Q) 1986 *F*, 1987 *SK*, [*J*], 1988 *E* 1,2, *NZ* 1,2,3, *E*, *S*, *It*
Cooke, B P (Q) 1979 *I* 1
Cooke, G M (Q) 1932 *NZ* 1,2,3, 1933 *SA* 1,2,3, 1946 *NZ* 2, 1947 *NZ* 2, *S*, *I*, *W*, 1948 *E*, *F*
Coolican, J E (NSW) 1982 *NZ* 1, 1983 *It*, *F* 1,2
Cooney, R C (NSW) 1922 *M* 2
Cordingley, S J (Q) 2000 *Arg* 1(R), *SA* 1(R), *F*, *S*, *E*
Corfe, A C (Q) 1899 *BI* 2
Cornelsen, G (NSW) 1974 *NZ* 2,3, 1975 *J* 2, *S*, *W*, 1976 *E*, *F* 1,2, 1978 *W* 1,2, *NZ* 1,2,3, 1979 *I* 1,2, *NZ*, *Arg* 1,2, 1980 *NZ* 1,2,3, 1981 *I*, *W*, *S*, 1982 *E*
Cornes, J R (Q) 1972 *Fj*
Cornforth, R G W (NSW) 1947 *NZ* 1, 1950 *BI* 2
Cornish, P (ACT) 1990 *F* 2,3, *NZ* 1
Costello, P P S (Q) 1950 *BI* 2
Cottrell, N V (Q) 1949 *M* 1,2,3, *NZ* 1,2, 1950 *BI* 1,2, 1951 *NZ* 1,2,3, 1952 *Fj* 1,2, *NZ* 1,2
Cowper, D L (V) 1931 *NZ*, 1932 *NZ* 1,2,3, 1933 *SA* 1,2,3,4,5
Cox, B P (NSW) 1952 *Fj* 1,2, *NZ* 1,2, 1954 *Fj* 2, 1955 *NZ* 1, 1956 *SA* 2, 1957 *NZ* 1,2
Cox, M H (NSW) 1981 *W*, *S*
Cox, P A (NSW) 1979 *Arg* 1,2, 1980 *Fj*, *NZ* 1,2, 1981 *W* (R), *S*, 1982 *S* 1,2, *NZ* 1,2,3, 1984 *Fj*, *NZ* 1,2,3
Craig, R R (NSW) 1908 *W*
Crakanthorp, J S (NSW) 1923 *NZ* 3
Cremin, J F (NSW) 1946 *NZ* 1,2, 1947 *NZ* 1
Crittle, C P (NSW) 1962 *NZ* 4,5, 1963 *SA* 2,3,4, 1964 *NZ* 1,2,3, 1965 *SA* 1,2, 1966 *BI* 1,2, *S*, 1967 *E*, *I*
Croft, B H D (NSW) 1928 *M*
Croft, D N (Q) 2002 *Arg* (t&R), *I* (R), *E* (t&R), *It* (R)
Cross, J R (NSW) 1955 *NZ* 1,2,3
Cross, K A (NSW) 1949 *M* 1, *NZ* 1,2, 1950 *BI* 1,2, 1951 *NZ* 2,3, 1952 *NZ* 1, 1953 *SA* 1,2,3,4, 1954 *Fj* 1,2, 1955 *NZ* 3, 1956 *SA* 1,2, 1957 *NZ* 1,2
Crossman, O C (NSW) 1923 *M* 1(R),2,3, 1924, *NZ* 1,2,3, 1925 *NZ* 1,3,4, 1926 *NZ* 1,2,3,4, 1929 *NZ* 2, 1930 *BI*
Crowe, P J (NSW) 1976 *F* 2, 1978 *W* 1,2, 1979 *I* 2, *NZ*, *Arg* 1
Crowley, D J (Q) 1989 *BI* 1,2,3, 1991 [*WS*], 1992 *I*, *W*, 1993 *C* (R), 1995 *Arg* 1,2, [*SA*, *E*], *NZ* 1, 1996 *W* 2(R), *C*, *NZ* 1, *SA* 1,2, *I*, *W* 3, 1998 *E* 1(R), *S* 1(R),2(R), *NZ* 1(R), *SA* 1, *NZ* 2, *SA* 2, *NZ* 3, *Tg*, *WS*, 1999 *I* 1,2(R), *E* (R), *SA* 1, *NZ* 1(R), [*R* (R), *I* 3(t&R), *US*, *F*(R)]
Curley, T G P (NSW) 1957 *NZ* 1,2, 1958 *W*, *I*, *E*, *S*, *F*, *M* 1, *NZ* 1,2,3
Curran, D J (NSW) 1980 *NZ* 3, 1981 *F* 1,2, *W*, 1983 *Arg* 1
Currie, E W (Q) 1899 *BI* 2
Cutler, S A G (NSW) 1982 *NZ* 2(R), 1984 *NZ* 1,2,3, *E*, *I*, *W*, *S*, 1985 *C* 1,2, *NZ*, *Fj* 1,2, 1986 *It*, *F*, *NZ* 1,2,3, 1987 *SK*, [*E*, *J*, *I*, *F*, *W*], *NZ*, *Arg* 1,2, 1988 *E* 1,2, *NZ* 1,2,3, *E*, *S*, *It*, 1989 *BI* 1,2,3, *NZ*, 1991 [*WS*]

Daly, A J (NSW) 1989 *NZ*, *F* 1,2, 1990 *F* 1,2,3, *US*, *NZ* 1,2,3, 1991 *W*, *E*, *NZ* 1,2, [*Arg*, *W*, *I*, *NZ*, *E*], 1992 *S* 1,2, *NZ* 1,2,3, *SA*, 1993 *Tg*, *NZ*, *SA* 1,2,3, *C*, *F* 1,2, 1994 *I* 1,2, *It* 1,2, *WS*, *NZ*, 1995 [*C*, *R*]
D'Arcy, A M (Q) 1980 *Fj*, *NZ* 3, 1981 *F* 1,2, *I*, *W*, *S*, 1982 *E*, *S* 1,2
Darveniza, P (NSW) 1969 *W*, *SA* 2,3,4
Darwin, B J (ACT) 2001 *BI* 1(R), *SA* 1(R), *NZ* 1(R), *SA* 2(R), *NZ* 2(t&R), *Sp*, *E*, *F*, *W*, 2002 *NZ* 1(R), *SA* 1(R), *NZ* 2(R), *SA* 2, *Arg* (R), *I* (R), *E* (R), *It* (R), 2003 *I* (R), *W* (t&R), *E* (R), *SA* 1(R), *NZ* 1(R)
Davidson, R A L (NSW) 1952 *Fj* 1,2, *NZ* 1,2, 1953 *SA* 1, 1957 *NZ* 1,2, 1958 *W*, *I*, *E*, *S*, *F*, *M* 1
Davis, C C (NSW) 1949 *NZ* 1, 1951 *NZ* 1,2,3
Davis, E H (V) 1947 *S*, *W*, 1949 *M* 1,2
Davis, G V (NSW) 1963 *E*, *SA* 1,2,3,4, 1964 *NZ* 1,2,3, 1965 *SA* 1, 1966 *BI* 1,2, *W*, *S*, 1967 *E*, *I* 1, *F*, *I* 2, *NZ*, 1968 *NZ* 1,2, *F*, *I*, *S*, 1969 *W*, *SA* 1,2,3,4, 1970 *S*, 1971 *SA* 1,2,3, *F* 1,2, 1972 *F* 1,2, *NZ* 1,2,3
Davis, G W G (NSW) 1955 *NZ* 2,3
Davis, R A (NSW) 1974 *NZ* 1,2,3
Davis, T S R (NSW) 1920 *NZ* 1,2,3, 1921 *SA* 1,2,3, *NZ*, 1922 *M* 1,2,3, *NZ* 1,2,3, 1923 *M* 3, *NZ* 1,2,3, 1924 *NZ* 1,2, 1925 *NZ* 1
Davis, W (NSW) 1899 *BI* 1,3,4
Dawson, W L (NSW) 1946 *NZ* 1,2
Diett, L J (NSW) 1959 *BI* 1,2
Dix, W (NSW) 1907 *NZ* 1,2,3, 1909 *E*
Dixon, E J (Q) 1904 *BI* 3
Donald, K J (Q) 1957 *NZ* 1, 1958 *W*, *I*, *E*, *S*, *M* 2,3, 1959 *BI* 1,2
Dore, E (Q) 1904 *BI* 1
Dore, M J (Q) 1905 *NZ*
Dorr, R W (V) 1936 *M*, 1937 *SA* 1
Douglas, J A (V) 1962 *NZ* 3,4,5
Douglas, W A (NSW) 1922 *NZ* 3(R)
Dowse, J H (NSW) 1961 *Fj* 1,2, *SA* 1,2
Dunbar, A R (NSW) 1910 *NZ* 1,2,3, 1912 *US*
Duncan, J L (NSW) 1926 *NZ* 4
Dunlop, E E (V) 1932 *NZ* 3, 1934 *NZ* 1
Dunn, P K (NSW) 1958 *NZ* 1,2,3, 1959 *BI* 1,2
Dunn, V A (NSW) 1920 *NZ* 1,2,3, 1921 *SA* 1,2,3, *NZ*
Dunworth, D A (Q) 1971 *F* 1,2, 1972 *F* 1,2, 1976 *Fj* 2
Dwyer, L J (NSW) 1910 *NZ* 1,2,3, 1912 *US*, 1913 *NZ* 3, 1914 *NZ* 1,2,3
Dyson, F J (Q) 2000 *Arg* 1,2, *SA* 1, *NZ* 1, *SA* 2, *NZ* 2, *SA* 3, *F*, *S*, *E*

Eales, J A (Q) 1991 *W*, *E*, *NZ* 1,2, [*Arg*, *WS*, *W*, *I*, *NZ*, *E*], 1992 *S* 1,2, *NZ* 1,2,3, *SA*, *I*, 1994 *I* 1,2, *It* 1,2, *WS*, *NZ*, 1995 *Arg* 1,2, [*SA*, *C*, *R*, *E*], *NZ* 1,2, 1996 *W* 1,2, *C*, *NZ* 1, *SA* 1, *NZ* 2, *SA* 2, *It*, *S*, *I*, 1997 *F* 1,2, *NZ* 1, *E* 1, *NZ* 2, *SA* 1, *Arg* 1,2, *E* 2, *S*, 1998 *E* 1, *S* 1,2, *NZ* 1, *SA* 1, *NZ* 2, *SA* 2, *NZ* 3, *Fj*, *Tg*, *WS*, *F*, *E* 2, 1999 [*R*, *I* 3, *W*, *SA* 3, *F*], 2000 *Arg* 1,2, *SA* 1, *NZ* 1, *SA* 2, *NZ* 2, *SA* 3, *F*, *S*, *E*, 2001 *BI* 1,2,3, *SA* 1, *NZ* 1, *SA* 2, *NZ* 2
Eastes, C C (NSW) 1946 *NZ* 1,2, 1947 *NZ* 1,2, 1949 *M* 1,2
Edmonds, M H M (NSW) 1998 *Tg*, 2001 *SA* 1(R)
Egerton, R H (NSW) 1991 *W*, *E*, *NZ* 1,2, [*Arg*, *W*, *I*, *NZ*, *E*]

Ella, G A (NSW) 1982 *NZ* 1,2, 1983 *F* 1,2, 1988 *E* 2, *NZ* 1
Ella, G J (NSW) 1982 *S* 1, 1983 *It*, 1985 *C* 2(R), *Fj* 2
Ella, M G (NSW) 1980 *NZ* 1,2,3, 1981 *F* 2, *S*, 1982 *E*, *S* 1, *NZ* 1,2,3, 1983 *US*, *Arg* 1,2, *NZ*, *It*, *F* 1,2, 1984 *Fj*, *NZ* 1,2,3, *E*, *I*, *W*, *S*
Ellem, M A (NSW) 1976 *Fj* 3(R)
Elliott, F M (NSW) 1957 *NZ* 1
Elliott, R E (NSW) 1920 *NZ* 1, 1921 *NZ*, 1922 *M* 1,2, *NZ* 1(R),2,3, 1923 *M* 1,2,3, *NZ* 1,2,3
Ellis, C S (NSW) 1899 *BI* 1,2,3,4
Ellis, K J (NSW) 1958 *NZ* 1,2,3, 1959 *BI* 1,2
Ellwood, B J (NSW) 1958 *NZ* 1,2,3, 1961 *Fj* 2,3, *SA* 1, *F*, 1962 *NZ* 1,2,3,4,5, 1963 *SA* 1,2,3,4, 1964 *NZ* 3, 1965 *SA* 1,2, 1966 *BI* 1
Emanuel, D M (NSW) 1957 *NZ* 2, 1958 *W*, *I*, *E*, *S*, *F*, *M* 1,2,3
Emery, N A (NSW) 1947 *NZ* 2, *S*, *I*, *W*, 1948 *E*, *F*, 1949 *M* 2,3, *NZ* 1,2
Erasmus, D J (NSW) 1923 *NZ* 1,2
Erby, A B (NSW) 1923 *M* 1,2, *NZ* 2,3, 1925 *NZ* 2
Evans, L J (Q) 1903 *NZ*, 1904 *BI* 1,3
Evans, W T (Q) 1899 *BI* 1,2

Fahey, E J (NSW) 1912 *US*, 1913 *NZ* 1,2, 1914 *NZ* 3
Fairfax, R L (NSW) 1971 *F* 1,2, 1972 *F* 1,2, *NZ* 1, *Fj*, 1973 *W*, *E*
Farmer, E H (Q) 1910 *NZ* 1
Farquhar, C R (NSW) 1920 *NZ* 2
Farr-Jones, N C (NSW) 1984 *E*, *I*, *W*, *S*, 1985 *C* 1,2, *NZ*, *Fj* 1,2, 1986 *It*, *F*, *Arg* 1,2, *NZ* 1,2,3, 1987 *SK*, [*E*, *I*, *F*, *W* (R)], *NZ*, *Arg* 2, 1988 *E* 1,2, *NZ* 1,2,3, *E*, *S*, *It*, 1989 *BI* 1,2,3, *NZ*, *F* 1,2, 1990 *F* 1,2,3, *US*, *NZ* 1,2,3, 1991 *W*, *E*, *NZ* 1,2, [*Arg*, *WS*, *I*, *NZ*, *E*], 1992 *S* 1,2, *NZ* 1,2,3, *SA*, 1993 *NZ*, *SA* 1,2,3
Fay, G (NSW) 1971 *SA* 2, 1972 *NZ* 1,2,3, 1973 *Tg* 1,2, *W*, *E*, 1974 *NZ* 1,2,3, 1975 *E* 1,2, *J* 1, *S*, *W*, 1976 *I*, *US*, 1978 *W* 1,2, *NZ* 1,2,3, 1979 *I* 1
Fenwicke, P T (NSW) 1957 *NZ* 1, 1958 *W*, *I*, *E*, 1959 *BI* 1,2
Ferguson, R T (NSW) 1922 *M* 3, *NZ* 1, 1923 *M* 3, *NZ* 3
Fihelly, J A (Q) 1907 *NZ* 2
Finau, S F (NSW) 1997 *NZ* 3
Finegan, O D A (ACT) 1996 *W* 1,2, *C*, *NZ* 1, *SA* 1(t), *S*, *W* 3, 1997 *SA* 1, *NZ* 3, *SA* 2, *Arg* 1,2, *E* 2, *S*, 1998 *E* 1(R), *S* 1(t + R),2(t + R), *NZ* 1(R), *SA* 1(t),2(R), *NZ* 3(R), *Fj* (R), *Tg*, *WS* (t + R), *F* (R), *E* 2(R), 1999 *NZ* 2(R), [*R*, *I* 3(R), *US*, *W* (R), *SA* 3(R), *F* (R)], 2001 *BI* 1,2,3, *SA* 1, *NZ* 1, *SA* 2, *NZ* 2, *Sp*, *E*, *F*, *W*, 2002 *F* 1,2, *NZ* 1, *SA* 1, *NZ* 2, *SA* 2, *I*, 2003 *SA* 1(t&R), *NZ* 1(R), *SA* 2(R), *NZ* 2(R)
Finlay, A N (NSW) 1926 *NZ* 1,2,3, 1927 *I*, *W*, *S*, 1928 *E*, *F*, 1929 *NZ* 1,2,3, 1930 *BI*
Finley, F G (NSW) 1904 *BI* 3
Finnane, S C (NSW) 1975 *E* 1, *J* 1,2, 1976 *E*, 1978 *W* 1,2
FitzSimons, P (NSW) 1989 *F* 1,2, 1990 *F* 1,2,3, *US*, *NZ* 1
Flanagan, P (Q) 1907 *NZ* 1,2
Flatley, E J (Q) 1997 *E* 2, *S*, 2000 *S* (R), 2001 *BI* 1(R),2(R),3, *SA* 1, *NZ* 1(R),2(R), *Sp* (R), *F* (R), *W*, 2002 *F* 1(R),2(R), *NZ* 1(t+R), *SA* 1(R), *NZ* 2(t), *Arg* (R), *I* (R), *E*, *It*, 2003 *I*, *W*, *SA* 1, *NZ* 1, *SA* 2, *NZ* 2
Flett, J A (NSW) 1990 *US*, *NZ* 2,3, 1991 [*WS*]
Flynn, J P (Q) 1914 *NZ* 1,2
Fogarty, J R (Q) 1949 *M* 2,3
Foley, M A (Q) 1995 [*C* (R), *R*], 1996 *W* 2(R), *NZ* 1, *SA* 1, *NZ* 2, *SA* 2, *It*, *S*, *I*, *W* 3, 1997 *NZ* 1(R), *E* 1, *NZ* 2, *SA* 1, *NZ* 3, *SA* 2, *Arg* 1,2, *E* 2, *S*, 1998 *Tg* (R), *F* (R), *E* 2(R), 1999 *NZ* 2(R), [*US*, *W*, *SA* 3, *F*], 2000 *Arg* 1,2, *SA* 1, *NZ* 1, *SA* 2, *NZ* 2, *SA* 3, *F*, *S*, *E*, 2001 *BI* 1(R),2,3, *SA* 1, *NZ* 1, *SA* 2, *NZ* 2, *Sp*, *E*, *F*, *W*
Foote, R H (NSW) 1924 *NZ* 2,3, 1926 *NZ* 2
Forbes, C F (Q) 1953 *SA* 2,3,4, 1954 *Fj* 1, 1956 *SA* 1,2
Ford, B (Q) 1957 *NZ* 2
Ford, E E (NSW) 1927 *I*, *W*, *S*, 1928 *E*, *F*, 1929 *NZ* 1,3
Ford, J A (NSW) 1925 *NZ* 4, 1926 *NZ* 1,2, 1927 *I*, *W*, *S*, 1928 *E*, 1929 *NZ* 1,2,3, 1930 *BI*
Forman, T R (NSW) 1968 *I*, *S*, 1969 *W*, *SA* 1,2,3,4
Fowles, D G (NSW) 1921 *SA* 1,2,3, 1922 *M* 2,3, 1923 *M* 2,3
Fox, C L (NSW) 1920 *NZ* 1,2,3, 1921 *SA* 1, *NZ*, 1922 *M* 1,2, *NZ* 1, 1924 *NZ* 1,2,3, 1925 *NZ* 1,2,3, 1926 *NZ* 1,3, 1928 *F*
Fox, O G (NSW) 1958 *F*
Francis, E (Q) 1914 *NZ* 1,2
Frawley, D (Q, NSW) 1986 *Arg* 2(R), 1987 *Arg* 1,2, 1988 *E* 1,2, *NZ* 1,2,3, *S*, *It*
Freedman, J E (NSW) 1962 *NZ* 3,4,5, 1963 *SA* 1
Freeman, E (NSW) 1946 *NZ* 1(R), *M*
Freier, A L (NSW) 2002 *Arg* (R), *I*, *E* (R), *It*, 2003 *SA* 1(R), *NZ* 1(t)
Freney, M E (Q) 1972 *NZ* 1,2,3, 1973 *Tg* 1, *W*, *E* (R)
Friend, W S (NSW) 1920 *NZ* 3, 1921 *SA* 1,2,3, 1922 *NZ* 1,2,3, 1923 *M* 1,2,3
Furness, D C (NSW) 1946 *M*
Futter, F C (NSW) 1904 *BI* 3

Gardner, J M (Q) 1987 *Arg* 2, 1988 *E* 1, *NZ* 1, *E*
Gardner, W C (NSW) 1950 *BI* 1
Garner, R L (NSW) 1949 *NZ* 1,2
Gavin, K A (NSW) 1909 *E*
Gavin, T B (NSW) 1988 *NZ* 2,3, *S*, *It* (R), 1989 *NZ* (R), *F* 1,2, 1990 *F* 1,2,3, *US*, *NZ* 1,2,3, 1991 *W*, *E*, *NZ* 1, 1992 *S* 1,2, *SA*, *I*, *W*, 1993 *Tg*, *NZ*, *SA* 1,2,3, *C*, *F* 1,2, 1994 *I* 1,2, *It* 1,2, *WS*, *NZ*, 1995 *Arg* 1,2, [*SA*, *C*, *R*, *E*], *NZ* 1,2, 1996 *NZ* 2(R), *SA* 2, *W* 3
Gelling, A M (NSW) 1972 *NZ* 1, *Fj*
George, H W (NSW) 1910 *NZ* 1,2,3, 1912 *US*, 1913 *NZ* 1,3, 1914 *NZ* 1,3
George, W G (NSW) 1923 *M* 1,3, *NZ* 1,2, 1924 *NZ* 3, 1925 *NZ* 2,3, 1926 *NZ* 4, 1928 *NZ* 1,2,3, *M*
Gibbons, E de C (NSW) 1936 *NZ* 1,2, *M*
Gibbs, P R (V) 1966 *S*
Giffin, D T (ACT) 1996 *W* 3, 1997 *F* 1,2, 1999 *I* 1,2, *E*, *SA* 1, *NZ* 1, *SA* 2, *NZ* 2, [*R*, *I* 3, *US* (R), *W*, *SA* 3, *F*], 2000 *Arg* 1,2, *SA* 1, *NZ* 1, *SA* 2, *NZ* 2, *SA* 3, *F*, *S*, *E*, 2001 *BI* 1,2, *SA* 1, *NZ* 2, *Sp*, *E*, *F*, *W*, 2002 *Arg* (R), *I*, *E* (R), *It* (R), 2003 *I*, *W*, *E*, *SA* 1, *NZ* 1, *SA* 2, *NZ* 2
Gilbert, H (NSW) 1910 *NZ* 1,2,3
Girvan, B (ACT) 1988 *E*
Giteau, M J (ACT) 2002 *E* (R), *It* (R), 2003 *SA* 2(R), *NZ* 2(R)
Gordon, G C (NSW) 1929 *NZ* 1
Gordon, K M (NSW) 1950 *BI* 1,2
Gould, R G (Q) 1980 *NZ* 1,2,3, 1981 *I*, *W*, *S*, 1982 *S* 2, *NZ* 1,2,3, 1983 *US*, *Arg* 1, *F* 1,2, 1984 *NZ* 1,2,3, *E*, *I*, *W*, *S*, 1985 *NZ*, 1986 *It*, 1987 *SK*, [*E*]
Gourley, S R (NSW) 1988 *S*, *It*, 1989 *BI* 1,2,3
Graham, C S (Q) 1899 *BI* 2
Graham, R (NSW) 1973 *Tg* 1,2, *W*, *E*, 1974 *NZ* 2,3, 1975 *E* 2, *J* 1,2, *S*, *W*, 1976 *I*, *US*, *Fj* 1,2,3, *F* 1,2
Gralton, A S I (Q) 1899 *BI* 1,4, 1903 *NZ*
Grant, J C (NSW) 1988 *E* 1, *NZ* 2,3, *E*
Graves, R H (NSW) 1907 *NZ* 1(R)
Greatorex, E N (NSW) 1923 *M* 3, *NZ* 3, 1924 *NZ* 1,2,3, 1925 *NZ* 1, 1928 *E*, *F*
Gregan, G M (ACT) 1994 *It* 1,2, *WS*, *NZ*, 1995 *Arg* 1,2, [*SA*, *C* (R), *R*, *E*], 1996 *W* 1, *C* (t), *SA* 1, *NZ* 2, *SA* 2, *It*, *I*, *W* 3, 1997 *F* 1,2, *NZ* 1, *E* 1, *NZ* 2, *SA* 1, *NZ* 3, *SA* 2, *Arg* 1,2, *E* 2, *S*, 1998 *E* 1, *S* 1,2, *NZ* 1, *SA* 1, *NZ* 2, *SA* 2, *NZ* 3, *Fj*, *WS*, *F*, *E* 2, 1999 *I* 1,2, *E*, *SA* 1, *NZ* 1, *SA* 2, *NZ* 2, [*R*, *I* 3, *W*, *SA* 3, *F*], 2000 *Arg* 1,2, *SA* 1, *NZ* 1, *SA* 2, *NZ* 2, *SA* 3, 2001 *BI* 1,2,3, *SA* 1, *NZ* 1, *SA* 2, *NZ* 2, *Sp*, *E*, *F*, *W*, 2002 *F* 1,2, *NZ* 1, *SA* 1, *NZ* 2, SA 2, *Arg*, *I*, *E*, *It*, 2003 *I*, *W*, *E*, *SA* 1, *NZ* 1, *SA* 2, *NZ* 2
Gregory, S C (Q) 1968 *NZ* 3, *F*, *I*, *S*, 1969 *SA* 1,3, 1971 *SA* 1,3, *F* 1,2, 1972 *F* 1,2, 1973 *Tg* 1,2, *W*, *E*
Grey, G O (NSW) 1972 *F* 2(R), *NZ* 1,2,3, *Fj* (R)
Grey, N P (NSW) 1998 *S* 2(R), *SA* 2(R), *Fj* (R), *Tg* (R), *F*, *E* 2, 1999 *I* 1(R),2(R), *E*, *SA* 1, *NZ* 1, *SA* 2, *NZ* 2(t&R), [*R* (R), *I* 3(R), *US*, *SA* 3(R), *F* (R)], 2000 *S* (R), *E* (R), 2001 *BI* 1,2,3, *SA* 1, *NZ* 1, *SA* 2, *NZ* 2, *Sp*, *E*, *F*, 2003 *I* (R), *W (R)*, *E*
Griffin, T S (NSW) 1907 *NZ* 1,3, 1908 *W*, 1910 *NZ* 1,2, 1912 *US*
Grigg, P C (Q) 1980 *NZ* 3, 1982 *S* 2, *NZ* 1,2,3, 1983 *Arg* 2, *NZ*, 1984 *Fj*, *W*, *S*, 1985 *C* 1,2, *NZ*, *Fj* 1,2, 1986 *Arg* 1,2, *NZ* 1,2, 1987 *SK*, [*E*, *J*, *I*, *F*, *W*]
Grimmond, D N (NSW) 1964 *NZ* 2
Gudsell, K E (NSW) 1951 *NZ* 1,2,3
Guerassimoff, J (Q) 1963 *SA* 2,3,4, 1964 *NZ* 1,2,3, 1965 *SA* 2, 1966 *BI* 1,2, 1967 *E*, *I*, *F*
Gunther, W J (NSW) 1957 *NZ* 2

Hall, D (Q) 1980 *Fj*, *NZ* 1,2,3, 1981 *F* 1,2, 1982 *S* 1,2, *NZ* 1,2, 1983 *US*, *Arg* 1,2, *NZ*, *It*
Hamalainen, H A (Q) 1929 *NZ* 1,2,3
Hamilton, B G (NSW) 1946 *M*
Hammand, C A (NSW) 1908 *W*, 1909 *E*
Hammon, J D C (V) 1937 *SA* 2
Handy, C B (Q) 1978 *NZ* 3, 1979 *NZ*, *Arg* 1,2, 1980 *NZ* 1,2
Hanley, R G (Q) 1983 *US* (R), *It* (R), 1985 *Fj* 2(R)
Hardcastle, P A (NSW) 1946 *NZ* 1, *M*, *NZ* 2, 1947 *NZ* 1, 1949 *M* 3
Hardcastle, W R (NSW) 1899 *BI* 4, 1903 *NZ*
Harding, M A (NSW) 1983 *It*

Hardman, S P (Q) 2002 *F* 2(R)
Hardy, M D (ACT) 1997 *F* 1(t), 2(R), *NZ* 1(R), 3(R), *Arg* 1(R), 2(R), 1998 *Tg*, *WS*
Harrison, J B (ACT) 2001 *BI* 3, *NZ* 1, *SA* 2, *Sp*, *E*, *F*, *W* (R), 2002 *F* 1,2, *NZ* 1, *SA* 1, *NZ* 2, *SA* 2, *Arg*, *I* (R), *E*, *It*
Harry, R L L (NSW) 1996 *W* 1,2, *NZ* 1, *SA* 1(t), *NZ* 2, *It*, *S*, 1997 *F* 1,2, *NZ* 1,2, *SA* 1, *NZ* 3, *SA* 2, *Arg* 1,2, *E* 2, *S*, 1998 *E* 1, *S* 1,2, *NZ* 1, *Fj*, 1999 *SA* 2, *NZ* 2, [*R*, *I* 3, *W*, *SA* 3, *F*], 2000 *Arg* 1,2, *SA* 1, *NZ* 1, *SA* 2, *NZ* 2, *SA* 3
Hartill, M N (NSW) 1986 *NZ* 1,2,3, 1987 *SK*, [*J*], *Arg* 1, 1988 *NZ* 1,2, *E*, *It*, 1989 *BI* 1(R), 2,3, *F* 1,2, 1995 *Arg* 1(R), 2(R), [*C*], *NZ* 1,2
Harvey, P B (Q) 1949 *M* 1,2
Harvey, R M (NSW) 1958 *F*, *M* 3
Hatherell, W I (Q) 1952 *Fj* 1,2
Hauser, R G (Q) 1975 *J* 1(R), 2, *W* (R), 1976 *E*, *I*, *US*, *Fj* 1,2,3, *F* 1,2, 1978 *W* 1,2, 1979 *I* 1,2
Hawker, M J (NSW) 1980 *Fj*, *NZ* 1,2,3, 1981 *F* 1,2, *I*, *W*, 1982 *E*, *S* 1,2, *NZ* 1,2,3, 1983 *US*, *Arg* 1,2, *NZ*, *It*, *F* 1,2, 1984 *NZ* 1,2,3, 1987 *NZ*
Hawthorne, P F (NSW) 1962 *NZ* 3,4,5, 1963 *E*, *SA* 1,2,3,4, 1964 *NZ* 1,2,3, 1965 *SA* 1,2, 1966 *BI* 1,2, *W*, 1967 *E*, *I* 1, *F*, *I* 2, *NZ*
Hayes, E S (Q) 1934 *NZ* 1,2, 1938 *NZ* 1,2,3
Heath, A (NSW) 1996 *C*, *SA* 1, *NZ* 2, *SA* 2, *It*, 1997 *NZ* 2, *SA* 1, *E* 2(R)
Heenan, D P (Q) 2003 *W*
Heinrich, E L (NSW) 1961 *Fj* 1,2,3, *SA* 2, *F*, 1962 *NZ* 1,2,3, 1963 *E*, *SA* 1
Heinrich, V W (NSW) 1954 *Fj* 1,2
Heming, R J (NSW) 1961 *Fj* 2,3, *SA* 1,2, *F*, 1962 *NZ* 2,3,4,5, 1963 *SA* 2,3,4, 1964 *NZ* 1,2,3, 1965 *SA* 1,2, 1966 *BI* 1,2, *W*, 1967 *F*
Hemingway, W H (NSW) 1928 *NZ* 2,3, 1931 *M*, *NZ*, 1932 *NZ* 3
Henry, A R (Q) 1899 *BI* 2
Herbert, A G (Q) 1987 *SK* (R), [*F* (R)], 1990 *F* 1(R), *US*, *NZ* 2,3, 1991 [*WS*], 1992 *NZ* 3(R), 1993 *NZ* (R), *SA* 2(R)
Herbert, D J (Q) 1994 *I* 2, *It* 1,2, *WS* (R), 1995 *Arg* 1,2, [*SA*, *R*], 1996 *C*, *SA* 2, *It*, *S*, *I*, 1997 *NZ* 1, 1998 *E* 1, *S* 1,2, *NZ* 1, *SA* 1, *NZ* 2, *SA* 2, *Fj*, *Tg*, *WS*, *F*, *E* 2, 1999 *I* 1,2, *E*, *SA* 1, *NZ* 1, *SA* 2, *NZ* 2, [*R*, *I* 3, *W*, *SA* 3, *F*], 2000 *Arg* 1,2, *SA* 1, *NZ* 1, *SA* 2, *NZ* 2, *SA* 3, *F*, *S*, *E*, 2001 *BI* 1,2,3, *SA* 1, *NZ* 1, *SA* 2, *NZ* 2, *Sp*, *E*, 2002 *F* 1,2, *NZ* 1, *SA* 1, *NZ* 2, *SA* 2, *Arg*, *I*, *E*, *It*
Herd, H V (NSW) 1931 *M*
Hickey, J (NSW) 1908 *W*, 1909 *E*
Hill, J (NSW) 1925 *NZ* 1
Hillhouse, D W (Q) 1975 *S*, 1976 *E*, *Fj* 1,2,3, *F* 1,2, 1978 *W* 1,2, 1983 *US*, *Arg* 1,2, *NZ*, *It*, *F* 1,2
Hills, E F (V) 1950 *BI* 1,2
Hindmarsh, J A (Q) 1904 *BI* 1
Hindmarsh, J C (NSW) 1975 *J* 2, *S*, *W*, 1976 *US*, *Fj* 1,2,3, *F* 1,2
Hipwell, J N B (NSW) 1968 *NZ* 1(R), 2, *F*, *I*, *S*, 1969 *W*, *SA* 1,2,3,4, 1970 *S*, 1971 *SA* 1,2, *F* 1,2, 1972 *F* 1,2, 1973 *Tg* 1, *W*, *E*, 1974 *NZ* 1,2,3, 1975 *E* 1,2, *J* 1, *S*, *W*, 1978 *NZ* 1,2,3, 1981 *F* 1,2, *I*, *W*, 1982 *E*
Hirschberg, W A (NSW) 1905 *NZ*
Hodgins, C H (NSW) 1910 *NZ* 1,2,3
Hodgson, A J (NSW) 1933 *SA* 2,3,4, 1934 *NZ* 1, 1936 *NZ* 1,2, *M*, 1937 *SA* 2, 1938 *NZ* 1,2,3
Holbeck, J C (ACT) 1997 *NZ* 1(R), *E* 1, *NZ* 2, *SA* 1, *NZ* 3, *SA* 2, 2001 *BI* 3(R)
Holdsworth, J W (NSW) 1921 *SA* 1,2,3, 1922 *M* 2,3, *NZ* 1(R)
Holt, N C (Q) 1984 *Fj*
Honan, B D (Q) 1968 *NZ* 1(R), 2, *F*, *I*, *S*, 1969 *SA* 1,2,3,4
Honan, R E (Q) 1964 *NZ* 1,2
Horan, T J (Q) 1989 *NZ*, *F* 1,2, 1990 *F* 1, *NZ* 1,2,3, 1991 *W*, *E*, *NZ* 1,2, [*Arg*, *WS*, *W*, *I*, *NZ*, *E*], 1992 *S* 1,2, *NZ* 1,2,3, *SA*, *I*, *W*, 1993 *Tg*, *NZ*, *SA* 1,2,3, *C*, *F* 1,2, 1995 [*C*, *R*, *E*], *NZ* 1,2, 1996 *W* 1,2, *C*, *NZ* 1, *SA* 1, *It*, *S*, *I*, *W* 3, 1997 *F* 1,2, *NZ* 1, *E* 1, *NZ* 2, *Arg* 1,2, *E* 2, *S*, 1998 *E* 1, *S* 1,2, *NZ* 1, *SA* 1, *NZ* 2, *SA* 2, *NZ* 3, *Fj*, *Tg*, *WS*, 1999 *I* 1,2, *E*, *SA* 1, *NZ* 1, *SA* 2, *NZ* 2, [*R*, *I* 3, *W*, *SA* 3, *F*], 2000 *Arg* 1
Horodam, D J (Q) 1913 *NZ* 2
Horsley, G R (Q) 1954 *Fj* 2
Horton, P A (NSW) 1974 *NZ* 1,2,3, 1975 *E* 1,2, *J* 1,2, *S*, *W*, 1976 *E*, *F* 1,2, 1978 *W* 1,2, *NZ* 1,2,3, 1979 *NZ*, *Arg* 1
Hoskins, J E (NSW) 1924 *NZ* 1,2,3
How, R A (NSW) 1967 *I* 2
Howard, J (Q) 1938 *NZ* 1,2
Howard, J L (NSW) 1970 *S*, 1971 *SA* 1, 1972 *F* 1(R), *NZ* 2, 1973 *Tg* 1,2, *W*
Howard, P W (Q, ACT) 1993 *NZ*, 1994 *WS*, *NZ*, 1995 *NZ* 1(R), 2(t), 1996 *W* 1,2, *SA* 1, *NZ* 2, *SA* 2, *It*, *S*, *W* 3, 1997 *F* 1,2, *NZ* 1, *Arg* 1,2, *E* 2, *S*
Howell, M L (NSW) 1946 *NZ* 1(R), 1947 *NZ* 1, *S*, *I*, *W*
Hughes, B D (NSW) 1913 *NZ* 2,3
Hughes, J C (NSW) 1907 *NZ* 1,3
Hughes, N McL (NSW) 1953 *SA* 1,2,3,4, 1955 *NZ* 1,2,3, 1956 *SA* 1,2, 1958 *W*, *I*, *E*, *S*, *F*
Humphreys, O W (NSW) 1920 *NZ* 3, 1921 *NZ*, 1922 *M* 1,2,3, 1925 *NZ* 1
Hutchinson, E E (NSW) 1937 *SA* 1,2
Hutchinson, F E (NSW) 1936 *NZ* 1,2, 1938 *NZ* 1,3

Ide, W P J (Q) 1938 *NZ* 2,3
Ives, W N (NSW) 1926 *NZ* 1,2,3,4, 1929 *NZ* 3

James, P M (Q) 1958 *M* 2,3
James, S L (NSW) 1987 *SK* (R), [*E* (R)], *NZ*, *Arg* 1,2, 1988 *NZ* 2(R)
Jamieson, A E (NSW) 1925 *NZ* 3(R)
Jaques, T (ACT) 2000 *SA* 1(R), *NZ* 1(R)
Jessep, E M (V) 1934 *NZ* 1,2
Johnson, A P (NSW) 1946 *NZ* 1, *M*
Johnson, B B (NSW) 1952 *Fj* 1,2, *NZ* 1,2, 1953 *SA* 2,3,4, 1955 *NZ* 1,2
Johnson, P G (NSW) 1959 *BI* 1,2, 1961 *Fj* 1,2,3, *SA* 1,2, *F*, 1962 *NZ* 1,2,3,4,5, 1963 *E*, *SA* 1,2,3,4, 1964 *NZ* 1,2,3, 1965 *SA* 1,2, 1966 *BI* 1,2, *W*, *S*, 1967 *E*, *I* 1, *F*, *I* 2, *NZ*, 1968 *NZ* 1,2, *F*, *I*, *S*, 1970 *S*, 1971 *SA* 1,2, *F* 1,2
Johnstone, B (Q) 1993 *Tg* (R)
Jones, G G (Q) 1952 *Fj* 1,2, 1953 *SA* 1,2,3,4, 1954 *Fj* 1,2, 1955 *NZ* 1,2,3, 1956 *SA* 1
Jones, H (NSW) 1913 *NZ* 1,2,3
Jones, P A (NSW) 1963 *E*, *SA* 1
Jorgensen, P (NSW) 1992 *S* 1(R), 2(R)
Joyce, J E (NSW) 1903 *NZ*
Judd, H A (NSW) 1903 *NZ*, 1904 *BI* 1,2,3, 1905 *NZ*
Judd, P B (NSW) 1925 *NZ* 4, 1926 *NZ* 1,2,3,4, 1927 *I*, *W*, *S*, 1928 *E*, 1931 *M*, *NZ*
Junee, D K (NSW) 1989 *F* 1(R), 2(R), 1994 *WS* (R), *NZ* (R)

Kafer, R B (ACT) 1999 *NZ* 2, [*R*, *US* (R)], 2000 *Arg* 1(R),2, *SA* 1, *NZ* 1(t&R), *SA* 2(R),3(R), *F*, *S*, *E*
Kahl, P R (Q) 1992 *W*
Kassulke, N (Q) 1985 *C* 1,2
Kay, A R (V) 1958 *NZ* 2, 1959 *BI* 2
Kay, P (NSW) 1988 *E* 2
Kearney, K H (NSW) 1947 *NZ* 1,2, *S*, *I*, *W*, 1948 *E*, *F*
Kearns, P N (NSW) 1989 *NZ*, *F* 1,2, 1990 *F* 1,2,3, *US*, *NZ* 1,2,3, 1991 *W*, *E*, *NZ* 1,2, [*Arg*, *WS*, *W*, *I*, *NZ*, *E*], 1992 *S* 1,2, *NZ* 1,2,3, *SA*, *I*, *W*, 1993 *Tg*, *NZ*, *SA* 1,2,3, *C*, *F* 1,2, 1994 *I* 1,2, *It* 1,2, *WS*, *NZ*, 1995 *Arg* 1,2, [*SA*, *C*, *E*], *NZ* 1,2, 1998 *E* 1, *S* 1,2, *NZ* 1, *SA* 1, *NZ* 2, *SA* 2, *NZ* 3, *Fj*, *WS*, *F*, *E* 2, 1999 *I* 2(R), *SA* 1(R),2, *NZ* 2, [*R*, *I* 3]
Kefu, R S T (Q) 1997 *SA* 2(R), 1998 *E* 1, *S* 1,2, *NZ* 1, *SA* 1, *NZ* 2, *SA* 2, *NZ* 3, *Fj* (R), *Tg*, *WS* (R), *F*, *E* 2, 1999 *I* 1,2, *E*, *SA* 1, *NZ* 1(R), *SA* 2, *NZ* 2, [*R*, *I* 3, *SA* 3, *F*], 2000 *SA* 1(t&R), *NZ* 1(R), *SA* 2(R), *NZ* 2, *SA* 3(R), *F*, *S*, *E*, 2001 *BI* 1,2,3, *SA* 1, *NZ* 1, *SA* 2, *NZ* 2, *Sp*, *E*, *F*, *W*, 2002 *F* 1, *NZ* 1, *SA* 1, *NZ* 2, *SA* 2, *Arg*, *I*, *E*, *It*, 2003 *I*, *W*, *E*, *SA* 1, *NZ* 1, *SA* 2, *NZ* 2
Kefu, S (Q) 2001 *W* (R), 2003 *I*, *W*, *E*, *SA* 1, *NZ* 1(R)
Kelaher, J D (NSW) 1933 *SA* 1,2,3,4,5, 1934 *NZ* 1,2, 1936 *NZ* 1,2, *M*, 1937 *SA* 1,2, 1938 *NZ* 3
Kelaher, T P (NSW) 1992 *NZ* 1, *I* (R), 1993 *NZ*
Kelleher, R J (Q) 1969 *SA* 2,3
Keller, D H (NSW) 1947 *NZ* 1, *S*, *I*, *W*, 1948 *E*, *F*
Kelly, A J (NSW) 1899 *BI* 1
Kelly, R L F (NSW) 1936 *NZ* 1,2, *M*, 1937 *SA* 1,2, 1938 *NZ* 1,2
Kent, A (Q) 1912 *US*
Kerr, F R (V) 1938 *NZ* 1
King, S C (NSW) 1926 *NZ* 1,2,3,4(R), 1927 *W*, *S*, 1928 *E*, *F*, 1929 *NZ* 1,2,3, 1930 *BI*, 1932 *NZ* 1,2
Knight, M (NSW) 1978 *W* 1,2, *NZ* 1
Knight, S O (NSW) 1969 *SA* 2,4, 1970 *S*, 1971 *SA* 1,2,3
Knox, D J (NSW, ACT) 1985 *Fj* 1,2, 1990 *US* (R), 1994 *WS*, *NZ*, 1996 *It*, *S*, *I*, 1997 *SA* 1, *NZ* 3, *SA* 2, *Arg* 1,2
Kraefft, D F (NSW) 1947 *NZ* 2, *S*, *I*, *W*, 1948 *E*, *F*
Kreutzer, S D (Q) 1914 *NZ* 2

Lamb, J S (NSW) 1928 *NZ* 1,2, *M*
Lambie, J K (NSW) 1974 *NZ* 1,2,3, 1975 *W*
Lane, R E (NSW) 1921 *SA* 1
Lane, T A (Q) 1985 *C* 1,2, *NZ*
Lang, C W P (V) 1938 *NZ* 2,3
Langford, J F (ACT) 1997 *NZ* 3, *SA* 2, *E* 2, *S*
Larkham, S J (ACT) 1996 *W* 2(R), 1997 *F* 1,2, *NZ* 1,2(R), *SA* 1, *NZ* 3, *SA* 2, *Arg* 1,2, *E* 2, *S*, 1998 *E* 1, *S* 1,2, *NZ* 1, *SA* 1, *NZ* 2, *SA* 2, *NZ* 3, *Fj*, *Tg* (t), *WS*, *F*, *E* 2, 1999 [*I* 3, *US*, *W*, *SA* 3, *F*], 2000 *Arg* 1,2, *SA* 1, *NZ* 1, *SA* 2, *NZ* 2, *SA* 3, 2001 *BI* 1,2, *NZ* 1, *SA* 2, *NZ* 2, *Sp*, *E*, *F*, *W*, 2002 *F* 1,2, *NZ* 1, *SA* 1, *NZ* 2, *SA* 2, *Arg*, *I*, *E*, 2003 *SA* 1(R), *NZ* 1, *SA* 2, *NZ* 2
Larkin, E R (NSW) 1903 *NZ*
Larkin, K K (Q) 1958 *M* 2,3
Latham, C E (Q) 1998 *F*, *E* 2, 1999 *I* 1,2, *E*, [*US*], 2000 *Arg* 1,2, *SA* 1, *NZ* 1, *SA* 2, *NZ* 2, *SA* 3, *F*, *S*, *E*, 2001 *BI* 1,2(R), *SA* 1(R), *NZ* 1(R), *SA* 2, *NZ* 2, *Sp*, *E*, *F*, *W* (R), 2002 *F* 1,2, *NZ* 1, *SA* 1, *NZ* 2, *SA* 2, 2003 *I*, *W*, *E*, *NZ* 1(R), *SA* 2, *NZ* 2
Latimer, N B (NSW) 1957 *NZ* 2
Lawton, R (Q) 1988 *E* 1, *NZ* 2(R), 3, *S*
Lawton, T (NSW, Q) 1920 *NZ* 1,2, 1925 *NZ* 4, 1927 *I*, *W*, *S*, 1928 *E*, *F*, 1929 *NZ* 1,2,3, 1930 *BI*, 1932 *NZ* 1,2
Lawton, T A (Q) 1983 *F* 1(R), 2, 1984 *Fj*, *NZ* 1,2,3, *E*, *I*, *W*, *S*, 1985 *C* 1,2, *NZ*, *Fj* 1, 1986 *It*, *F*, *Arg* 1,2, *NZ* 1,2,3, 1987 *SK*, [*E*, *US*, *I*, *F*, *W*], *NZ*, *Arg* 1,2, 1988 *E* 1,2, *NZ* 1,2,3, *E*, *S*, *It*, 1989 *BI* 1,2,3
Laycock, W M B (NSW) 1925 *NZ* 2,3,4, 1926 *NZ* 2
Leeds, A J (NSW) 1986 *NZ* 3, 1987 [*US*, *W*], *NZ*, *Arg* 1,2, 1988 *E* 1,2, *NZ* 1,2,3, *E*, *S*, *It*
Lenehan, J K (NSW) 1958 *W*, *E*, *S*, *F*, *M* 1,2,3, 1959 *BI* 1,2, 1961 *SA* 1,2, *F*, 1962 *NZ* 2,3,4,5, 1965 *SA* 1,2, 1966 *W*, *S*, 1967 *E*, *I* 1, *F*, *I* 2
L'Estrange, R D (Q) 1971 *F* 1,2, 1972 *NZ* 1,2,3, 1973 *Tg* 1,2, *W*, *E*, 1974 *NZ* 1,2,3, 1975 *S*, *W*, 1976 *I*, *US*
Lewis, L S (Q) 1934 *NZ* 1,2, 1936 *NZ* 2, 1938 *NZ* 1
Lidbury, S (NSW) 1987 *Arg* 1, 1988 *E* 2
Lillicrap, C P (Q) 1985 *Fj* 2, 1987 [*US*, *I*, *F*, *W*], 1989 *BI* 1, 1991 [*WS*]
Lindsay, R T G (Q) 1932 *NZ* 3
Lisle, R J (NSW) 1961 *Fj* 1,2,3, *SA* 1
Little, J S (Q, NSW) 1989 *F* 1,2, 1990 *F* 1,2,3, *US*, 1991 *W*, *E*, *NZ* 1,2, [*Arg*, *W*, *I*, *NZ*, *E*], 1992 *NZ* 1,2,3, *SA*, *I*, *W*, 1993 *Tg*, *NZ*, *SA* 1,2,3, *C*, *F* 1,2, 1994 *WS*, *NZ*, 1995 *Arg* 1,2, [*SA*, *C*, *E*], *NZ* 1,2, 1996 *It* (R), *I*, *W* 3, 1997 *F* 1,2, *E* 1, *NZ* 2, *SA* 1, *NZ* 3, *SA* 2, 1998 *E* 1(R), *S* 2(R), *NZ* 2, *SA* 2(R), *NZ* 3, *Fj*, *Tg*, *WS*, *F*, *E* 2, 1999 *I* 1(R),2, *SA* 2(R), *NZ* 2, [*R*, *I* 3(t&R), *US*, *W* (R), *SA* 3(t&R), *F* (R)], 2000 *Arg* 1(R),2(R), *SA* 1(R), *NZ* 1, *SA* 2, *NZ* 2, *SA* 3
Livermore, A E (Q) 1946 *NZ* 1, *M*
Loane, M E (Q) 1973 *Tg* 1,2, 1974 *NZ* 1, 1975 *E* 1,2, *J* 1, 1976 *E*, *I*, *Fj* 1,2,3, *F* 1,2, 1978 *W* 1,2, 1979 *I* 1,2, *NZ*, *Arg* 1,2, 1981 *F* 1,2, *I*, *W*, *S*, 1982 *E*, *S* 1,2
Logan, D L (NSW) 1958 *M* 1
Loudon, D B (NSW) 1921 *NZ*, 1922 *M* 1,2,3
Loudon, R B (NSW) 1923 *NZ* 1(R), 2,3, 1928 *NZ* 1,2,3, *M*, 1929 *NZ* 2, 1933 *SA* 2,3,4,5, 1934 *NZ* 2
Love, E W (NSW) 1932 *NZ* 1,2,3
Lowth, D R (NSW) 1958 *NZ* 1
Lucas, B C (Q) 1905 *NZ*
Lucas, P W (NSW) 1982 *NZ* 1,2,3
Lutge, D (NSW) 1903 *NZ*, 1904 *BI* 1,2,3
Lynagh, M P (Q) 1984 *Fj*, *E*, *I*, *W*, *S*, 1985 *C* 1,2, *NZ*, 1986 *It*, *F*, *Arg* 1,2, *NZ* 1,2,3, 1987 [*E*, *US*, *J*, *I*, *F*, *W*], *Arg* 1,2, 1988 *E* 1,2, *NZ* 1,3(R), *E*, *S*, *It*, 1989 *BI* 1,2,3, *NZ*, *F* 1,2, 1990 *F* 1,2,3, *US*, *NZ* 1,2,3, 1991 *W*, *E*, *NZ* 1,2, [*Arg*, *WS*, *W*, *I*, *NZ*, *E*], 1992 *S* 1,2, *NZ* 1,2,3, *SA*, *I*, 1993 *Tg*, *C*, *F* 1,2, 1994 *I* 1,2, *It* 1, 1995 *Arg* 1,2, [*SA*, *C*, *E*]
Lyons, D J (NSW) 2000 *Arg* 1(t&R),2(R), 2001 *BI* 1(R), *SA* 1(R), 2002 *F* 1(R),2, *NZ* 1(R), *SA* 1(R), *NZ* 2(R), *SA* 2(t+R), 2003 *I*, *W*, *E*, *SA* 1

McArthur, M (NSW) 1909 *E*
McBain, M I (Q) 1983 *It*, *F* 1, 1985 *Fj* 2, 1986 *It* (R), 1987 [*J*], 1988 *E* 2(R), 1989 *BI* 1(R)
MacBride, J W T (NSW) 1946 *NZ* 1, *M*, *NZ* 2, 1947 *NZ* 1,2, *S*, *I*, *W*, 1948 *E*, *F*
McCabe, A J M (NSW) 1909 *E*
McCall, R J (Q) 1989 *F* 1,2, 1990 *F* 1,2,3, *US*, *NZ* 1,2,3, 1991 *W*, *E*, *NZ* 1,2, [*Arg*, *W*, *I*, *NZ*, *E*], 1992 *S* 1,2, *NZ* 1,2,3, *SA*, *I*, *W*, 1993 *Tg*, *NZ*, *SA* 1,2,3, *C*, *F* 1,2, 1994 *It* 2, 1995 *Arg* 1,2, [*SA*, *R*, *E*]
McCarthy, F J C (Q) 1950 *BI* 1
McCowan, R H (Q) 1899 *BI* 1,2,4
McCue, P A (NSW) 1907 *NZ* 1,3, 1908 *W*, 1909 *E*
McDermott, L C (Q) 1962 *NZ* 1,2
McDonald, B S (NSW) 1969 *SA* 4, 1970 *S*
McDonald, J C (Q) 1938 *NZ* 2,3
Macdougall, D G (NSW) 1961 *Fj* 1, *SA* 1
Macdougall, S G (NSW, ACT) 1971 *SA* 3, 1973 *E*, 1974 *NZ* 1,2,3, 1975 *E* 1,2, 1976 *E*
McGhie, G H (Q) 1929 *NZ* 2,3, 1930 *BI*
McGill, A N (NSW) 1968 *NZ* 1,2, *F*, 1969 *W*, *SA* 1,2,3,4, 1970 *S*, 1971 *SA* 1,2,3, *F* 1,2, 1972 *F* 1,2, *NZ* 1,2,3, 1973 *Tg* 1,2
McIntyre, A J (Q) 1982 *NZ* 1,2,3, 1983 *F* 1,2, 1984 *Fj*, *NZ* 1,2,3, *E*, *I*, *W*, *S*, 1985 *C* 1,2, *NZ*, *Fj* 1,2, 1986 *It*, *F*, *Arg* 1,2, 1987 [*E*, *US*, *I*, *F*, *W*], *NZ*, *Arg* 2, 1988 *E* 1,2, *NZ* 1,2,3, *E*, *S*, *It*, 1989 *NZ*
McKay, G R (NSW) 1920 *NZ* 2, 1921 *SA* 2,3, 1922 *M* 1,2,3
McKenzie, E J A (NSW, ACT) 1990 *F* 1,2,3, *US*, *NZ* 1,2,3, 1991 *W*, *E*, *NZ* 1,2, [*Arg*, *W*, *I*, *NZ*, *E*], 1992 *S* 1,2, *NZ* 1,2,3, *SA*, *I*, *W*, 1993 *Tg*, *NZ*, *SA* 1,2,3, *C*, *F* 1,2, 1994 *I* 1,2, *It* 1,2, *WS*, *NZ*, 1995 *Arg* 1,2, [*SA*, *C* (R), *R*, *E*], *NZ* 2, 1996 *W* 1,2, 1997 *F* 1,2, *NZ* 1, *E* 1
McKid, W A (NSW) 1976 *E*, *Fj* 1, 1978 *NZ* 2,3, 1979 *I* 1,2
McKinnon, A (Q) 1904 *BI* 2
McKivat, C H (NSW) 1907 *NZ* 1,3, 1908 *W*, 1909 *E*
McLaren, S D (NSW) 1926 *NZ* 4
McLaughlin, R E M (NSW) 1936 *NZ* 1,2
McLean, A D (Q) 1933 *SA* 1,2,3,4,5, 1934 *NZ* 1,2, 1936 *NZ* 1,2, *M*
McLean, J D (Q) 1904 *BI* 2,3, 1905 *NZ*
McLean, J J (Q) 1971 *SA* 2,3, *F* 1,2, 1972 *F* 1,2, *NZ* 1,2,3, *Fj*, 1973 *W*, *E*, 1974 *NZ* 1
McLean, P E (Q) 1974 *NZ* 1,2,3, 1975 *J* 1,2, *S*, *W*, 1976 *E*, *I*, *Fj* 1,2,3, *F* 1,2, 1978 *W* 1,2, *NZ* 2, 1979 *I* 1,2, *NZ*, *Arg* 1,2, 1980 *Fj*, 1981 *F* 1,2, *I*, *W*, *S*, 1982 *E*, *S* 2
McLean, P W (Q) 1978 *NZ* 1,2,3, 1979 *I* 1,2, *NZ*, *Arg* 1,2, 1980 *Fj* (R), *NZ* 3, 1981 *I*, *W*, *S*, 1982 *E*, *S* 1,2
McLean, R A (NSW) 1971 *SA* 1,2,3, *F* 1,2
McLean, W M (Q) 1946 *NZ* 1, *M*, *NZ* 2, 1947 *NZ* 1,2
McMahon, M J (Q) 1913 *NZ* 1
McMaster, R E (Q) 1946 *NZ* 1, *M*, *NZ* 2, 1947 *NZ* 1,2, *I*, *W*
MacMillan, D I (Q) 1950 *BI* 1,2
McMullen, K V (NSW) 1962 *NZ* 3,5, 1963 *E*, *SA* 1
McShane, J M S (NSW) 1937 *SA* 1,2
Mackay, G (NSW) 1926 *NZ* 4
Mackney, W A R (NSW) 1933 *SA* 1,5, 1934 *NZ* 1,2
Magrath, E (NSW) 1961 *Fj* 1, *SA* 2, *F*
Maguire, D J (Q) 1989 *BI* 1,2,3
Malcolm, S J (NSW) 1927 *S*, 1928 *E*, *F*, *NZ* 1,2, *M*, 1929 *NZ* 1,2,3, 1930 *BI*, 1931 *NZ*, 1932 *NZ* 1,2,3, 1933 *SA* 4,5, 1934 *NZ* 1,2
Malone, J H (NSW) 1936 *NZ* 1,2, *M*, 1937 *SA* 2
Malouf, B P (NSW) 1982 *NZ* 1
Mandible, E F (NSW) 1907 *NZ* 2,3, 1908 *W*
Manning, J (NSW) 1904 *BI* 2
Manning, R C S (Q) 1967 *NZ*
Mansfield, B W (NSW) 1975 *J* 2
Manu, D T (NSW) 1995 [*R* (t)], *NZ* 1,2, 1996 *W* 1,2(R), *SA* 1, *NZ* 2, *It*, *S*, *I*, 1997 *F* 1, *NZ* 1(t), *E* 1, *NZ* 2, *SA* 1
Marks, H (NSW) 1899 *BI* 1,2
Marks, R J P (Q) 1962 *NZ* 4,5, 1963 *E*, *SA* 2,3,4, 1964 *NZ* 1,2,3, 1965 *SA* 1,2, 1966 *W*, *S*, 1967 *E*, *I* 1, *F*, *I* 2
Marrott, R (NSW) 1920 *NZ* 1,3
Marrott, W J (NSW) 1922 *NZ* 2,3, 1923 *M* 1,2,3, *NZ* 1,2
Marshall, J S (NSW) 1949 *M* 1
Martin, G J (Q) 1989 *BI* 1,2,3, *NZ*, *F* 1,2, 1990 *F* 1,3(R), *NZ* 1
Martin, M C (NSW) 1980 *Fj*, *NZ* 1,2, 1981 *F* 1,2, *W* (R)
Massey-Westropp, M (NSW) 1914 *NZ* 3
Mathers, M J (NSW) 1980 *Fj*, *NZ* 2(R)
Maund, J W (NSW) 1903 *NZ*
Mayne, A V (NSW) 1920 *NZ* 1,2,3, 1922 *M* 1
Meadows, J E C (V, Q) 1974 *NZ* 1, 1975 *S*, *W*, 1976 *I*, *US*, *Fj* 1,3, *F* 1,2, 1978 *NZ* 1,2,3, 1979 *I* 1,2, 1981 *I*, *S*, 1982 *E*, *NZ* 2,3, 1983 *US*, *Arg* 2, *NZ*
Meadows, R W (NSW) 1958 *M* 1,2,3, *NZ* 1,2,3
Meagher, F W (NSW) 1923 *NZ* 3, 1924 *NZ* 3, 1925 *NZ* 4, 1926 *NZ* 1,2,3, 1927 *I*, *W*
Meibusch, J H (Q) 1904 *BI* 3
Meibusch, L S (Q) 1912 *US*
Melrose, T C (NSW) 1978 *NZ* 3, 1979 *I* 1,2, *NZ*, *Arg* 1,2
Merrick, S (NSW) 1995 *NZ* 1,2
Messenger, H H (NSW) 1907 *NZ* 2,3
Middleton, S A (NSW) 1909 *E*, 1910 *NZ* 1,2,3

Miller, A R (NSW) 1952 *Fj* 1,2, *NZ* 1,2, 1953 *SA* 1,2,3,4, 1954 *Fj* 1,2, 1955 *NZ* 1,2,3, 1956 *SA* 1,2, 1957 *NZ* 1,2, 1958 *W, E, S, F, M* 1,2,3, 1959 *BI* 1,2, 1961 *Fj* 1,2,3, *SA* 2, *F*, 1962 *NZ* 1,2, 1966 *BI* 1,2, *W, S*, 1967 *I* 1, *F, I* 2, *NZ*
Miller, J M (NSW) 1962 *NZ* 1, 1963 *E, SA* 1, 1966 *W, S*, 1967 *E*
Miller, J S (Q) 1986 *NZ* 2,3, 1987 *SK*, [*US, I, F*], *NZ, Arg* 1,2, 1988 *E* 1,2, *NZ* 2,3, *E, S, It*, 1989 *BI* 1,2,3, *NZ*, 1990 *F* 1,3, 1991 *W*, [*WS, W, I*]
Miller, S W J (NSW) 1899 *BI* 3
Mingey, N (NSW) 1920 *NZ* 3, 1921 *SA* 1,2,3, 1923 *M* 1, *NZ* 1,2
Monaghan, L E (NSW) 1973 *E*, 1974 *NZ* 1,2,3, 1975 *E* 1,2, *S, W*, 1976 *E, I, US, F* 1, 1978 *W* 1,2, *NZ* 1, 1979 *I* 1,2
Monti, C I A (Q) 1938 *NZ* 2
Moon, B J (Q) 1978 *NZ* 2,3, 1979 *I* 1,2, *NZ, Arg* 1,2, 1980 *Fj, NZ* 1,2,3, 1981 *F* 1,2, *I, W, S*, 1982 *E, S* 1,2, 1983 *US, Arg* 1,2, *NZ, It, F* 1,2, 1984 *Fj, NZ* 1,2,3, *E*, 1986 *It, F, Arg* 1,2
Mooney, T P (Q) 1954 *Fj* 1,2
Moore, R C (ACT, NSW) 1999 [*US*], 2001 *BI* 2,3, *SA* 1, *NZ* 1, *SA* 2, *NZ* 2, *Sp* (R), *E* (R), *F* (R), *W* (R), 2002 *F* 1(R),2(R), *SA* 2(R)
Moran, H M (NSW) 1908 *W*
Morgan, G (Q) 1992 *NZ* 1(R), 3(R), *W*, 1993 *Tg, NZ, SA* 1,2,3, *C, F* 1,2, 1994 *I* 1,2, *It* 1, *WS, NZ*, 1996 *W* 1,2, *C, NZ* 1, *SA* 1, *NZ* 2, 1997 *E* 1, *NZ* 2
Morrissey, C V (NSW) 1925 *NZ* 2,3,4, 1926 *NZ* 2,3
Morrissey, W (Q) 1914 *NZ* 2
Mortlock, S A (ACT) 2000 *Arg* 1,2, *SA* 1, *NZ* 1, *SA* 2, *NZ* 2, *SA* 3, *F, S, E*, 2002 *F* 1,2, *NZ* 1, *SA* 1, *NZ* 2, *SA* 2, *Arg, I, E, It*
Morton, A R (NSW) 1957 *NZ* 1,2, 1958 *F, M* 1,2,3, *NZ* 1,2,3, 1959 *BI* 1,2
Mossop, R P (NSW) 1949 *NZ* 1,2, 1950 *BI* 1,2, 1951 *NZ* 1
Moutray, I E (NSW) 1963 *SA* 2
Mulligan, P J (NSW) 1925 *NZ* 1(R)
Munsie, A (NSW) 1928 *NZ* 2
Murdoch, A R (NSW) 1993 *F* 1, 1996 *W* 1
Murphy, P J (Q) 1910 *NZ* 1,2,3, 1913 *NZ* 1,2,3, 1914 *NZ* 1,2,3
Murphy, W (Q) 1912 *US*

Nasser, B P (Q) 1989 *F* 1,2, 1990 *F* 1,2,3, *US, NZ* 2, 1991 [*WS*]
Newman, E W (NSW) 1922 *NZ* 1
Nicholson, F C (Q) 1904 *BI* 3
Nicholson, F V (Q) 1903 *NZ*, 1904 *BI* 1
Niuqila, A S (NSW) 1988 *S, It*, 1989 *BI* 1
Noriega, E P (ACT, NSW) 1998 *F, E* 2, 1999 *I* 1,2, *E, SA* 1, *NZ* 1, *SA* 2(R), *NZ* 2(R), 2002 *F* 1,2, *NZ* 1, *SA* 1, *NZ* 2, *Arg, I, E, It*, 2003 *I, W, E, SA* 1, *NZ* 1, *SA* 2
Nothling, O E (NSW) 1921 *SA* 1,2,3, *NZ*, 1922 *M* 1,2,3, *NZ* 1,2,3, 1923 *M* 1,2,3, *NZ* 1,2,3, 1924 *NZ* 1,2,3
Nucifora, D V (Q) 1991 [*Arg* (R)], 1993 *C* (R)

O'Brien, F W H (NSW) 1937 *SA* 2, 1938 *NZ* 3
O'Connor, J A (NSW) 1928 *NZ* 1,2,3, *M*
O'Connor, M (ACT) 1994 *I* 1
O'Connor, M D (ACT, Q) 1979 *Arg* 1,2, 1980 *Fj, NZ* 1,2,3, 1981 *F* 1,2, *I*, 1982 *E, S* 1,2
O'Donnell, C (NSW) 1913 *NZ* 1,2
O'Donnell, I C (NSW) 1899 *BI* 3,4
O'Donnell, J B (NSW) 1928 *NZ* 1,3, *M*
O'Donnell, J M (NSW) 1899 *BI* 4
O'Gorman, J F (NSW) 1961 *Fj* 1, *SA* 1,2, *F*, 1962 *NZ* 2, 1963 *E, SA* 1,2,3,4, 1965 *SA* 1,2, 1966 *W, S*, 1967 *E, I* 1, *F, I* 2
O'Neill, D J (Q) 1964 *NZ* 1,2
O'Neill, J M (Q) 1952 *NZ* 1,2, 1956 *SA* 1,2
Ofahengaue, V (NSW) 1990 *NZ* 1,2,3, 1991 *W, E, NZ* 1,2, [*Arg, W, I, NZ, E*], 1992 *S* 1,2, *SA, I, W*, 1994 *WS, NZ*, 1995 *Arg* 1,2(R), [*SA, C, E*], *NZ* 1,2, 1997 *Arg* 1(t + R), 2(R), *E* 2, *S*, 1998 *E* 1(R), *S* 1(R),2(R), *NZ* 1(R), *SA* 1(R), *NZ* 2(R), *SA* 2(R), *NZ* 3(R), *Fj, WS, F* (R)
Ormiston, I W L (NSW) 1920 *NZ* 1,2,3
Osborne, D H (V) 1975 *E* 1,2, *J* 1
Outterside, R (NSW) 1959 *BI* 1,2
Oxenham, A McE (Q) 1904 *BI* 2, 1907 *NZ* 2
Oxlade, A M (Q) 1904 *BI* 2,3, 1905 *NZ*, 1907 *NZ* 2
Oxlade, B D (Q) 1938 *NZ* 1,2,3

Palfreyman, J R L (NSW) 1929 *NZ* 1, 1930 *BI*, 1931 *NZ*, 1932 *NZ* 3
Panoho, G M (Q) 1998 *SA* 2(R), *NZ* 3(R), *Fj* (R), *Tg, WS* (R), 1999 *I* 2, *E, SA* 1(R), *NZ* 1, 2000 *Arg* 1(R),2(R), *SA* 1(R), *NZ* 1(R), *SA* 2(R),3(R), *F* (R), *S* (R), *E* (R), 2001 *BI* 1, 2003 *SA* 2(R), *NZ* 2
Papworth, B (NSW) 1985 *Fj* 1,2, 1986 *It, Arg* 1,2, *NZ* 1,2,3, 1987 [*E, US, J* (R), *I, F*], *NZ, Arg* 1,2
Parker, A J (Q) 1983 *Arg* 1(R), 2, *NZ*
Parkinson, C E (Q) 1907 *NZ* 2
Paul, J A (ACT) 1998 *S* 1(R), *NZ* 1(R), *SA* 1(t), *Fj* (R), *Tg*, 1999 *I* 1,2, *E, SA* 1, *NZ* 1, [*R* (R), *I* 3(R), *W* (t), *F* (R)], 2000 *Arg* 1(R),2(R), *SA* 1(R), *NZ* 1(R), *SA* 2(R), *NZ* 2(R), *SA* 3(R), *F* (R), *S* (R), *E* (R), 2001 *BI* 1, 2002 *F* 1, *NZ* 1, *SA* 1, *NZ* 2, *SA* 2, *Arg, E*, 2003 *I, W, E, SA* 2(t&R), *NZ* 2(R)
Pashley, J J (NSW) 1954 *Fj* 1,2, 1958 *M* 1,2,3
Pauling, T P (NSW) 1936 *NZ* 1, 1937 *SA* 1
Payne, S J (NSW) 1996 *W* 2, *C, NZ* 1, *S*, 1997 *F* 1(t), *NZ* 2(R), *Arg* 2(t)
Pearse, G K (NSW) 1975 *W* (R), 1976 *I, US, Fj* 1,2,3, 1978 *NZ* 1,2,3
Penman, A P (NSW) 1905 *NZ*
Perrin, P D (Q) 1962 *NZ* 1
Perrin, T D (NSW) 1931 *M, NZ*
Phelps, R (NSW) 1955 *NZ* 2,3, 1956 *SA* 1,2, 1957 *NZ* 1,2, 1958 *W, I, E, S, F, M* 1, *NZ* 1,2,3, 1961 *Fj* 1,2,3, *SA* 1,2, *F*, 1962 *NZ* 1,2
Phipps, J A (NSW) 1953 *SA* 1,2,3,4, 1954 *Fj* 1,2, 1955 *NZ* 1,2,3, 1956 *SA* 1,2
Phipps, W J (NSW) 1928 *NZ* 2
Piggott, H R (NSW) 1922 *M* 3(R)
Pilecki, S J (Q) 1978 *W* 1,2, *NZ* 1,2, 1979 *I* 1,2, *NZ, Arg* 1,2, 1980 *Fj, NZ* 1,2, 1982 *S* 1,2, 1983 *US, Arg* 1,2, *NZ*
Pini, M (Q) 1994 *I* 1, *It* 2, *WS, NZ*, 1995 *Arg* 1,2, [*SA, R* (t)]
Piper, B J C (NSW) 1946 *NZ* 1, *M, NZ* 2, 1947 *NZ* 1, *S, I, W*, 1948 *E, F*, 1949 *M*, 1,2,3
Poidevin, S P (NSW) 1980 *Fj, NZ* 1,2,3, 1981 *F* 1,2, *I, W, S*, 1982 *E, NZ* 1,2,3, 1983 *US, Arg* 1,2, *NZ, It, F* 1,2, 1984 *Fj, NZ* 1,2,3, *E, I, W, S*, 1985 *C* 1,2, *NZ, Fj* 1,2, 1986 *It, F, Arg* 1,2, *NZ* 1,2,3, 1987 *SK*, [*E, J, I, F, W*], *Arg* 1, 1988 *NZ* 1,2,3, 1989 *NZ*, 1991 *E, NZ* 1,2, [*Arg, W, I, NZ, E*]
Pope, A M (Q) 1968 *NZ* 2(R)
Potter, R T (Q) 1961 *Fj* 2
Potts, J M (NSW) 1957 *NZ* 1,2, 1958 *W, I*, 1959 *BI* 1
Prentice, C W (NSW) 1914 *NZ* 3
Prentice, W S (NSW) 1908 *W*, 1909 *E*, 1910 *NZ* 1,2,3, 1912 *US*
Price, R A (NSW) 1974 *NZ* 1,2,3, 1975 *E* 1,2, *J* 1,2, 1976 *US*
Primmer, C J (Q) 1951 *NZ* 1,3
Proctor, I J (NSW)) 1967 *NZ*
Prosser, R B (NSW) 1967 *E, I* 1,2, *NZ*, 1968 *NZ* 1,2, *F, I, S*, 1969 *W, SA* 1,2,3,4, 1971 *SA* 1,2,3, *F* 1,2, 1972 *F* 1,2, *NZ* 1,2,3, *Fj*
Pugh, G H (NSW) 1912 *US*
Purcell, M P (Q) 1966 *W, S*, 1967 *I* 2
Purkis, E M (NSW) 1958 *S, M* 1
Pym, J E (NSW) 1923 *M* 1

Rainbow, A E (NSW) 1925 *NZ* 1
Ramalli, C (NSW) 1938 *NZ* 2,3
Ramsay, K M (NSW) 1936 *M*, 1937 *SA* 1, 1938 *NZ* 1,3
Rankin, R (NSW) 1936 *NZ* 1,2, *M*, 1937 *SA* 1,2, 1938 *NZ* 1,2
Rathie, D S (Q) 1972 *F* 1,2
Raymond, R L (NSW) 1920 *NZ* 1,2, 1921 *SA* 2,3, *NZ*, 1922 *M* 1,2,3, *NZ* 1,2,3, 1923 *M* 1,2
Redwood, C (Q) 1903 *NZ*, 1904 *BI* 1,2,3
Reid, E J (NSW) 1925 *NZ* 2,3,4
Reid, T W (NSW) 1961 *Fj* 1,2,3, *SA* 1, 1962 *NZ* 1
Reilly, N P (Q) 1968 *NZ* 1,2, *F, I, S*, 1969 *W, SA* 1,2,3,4
Reynolds, L J (NSW) 1910 *NZ* 2(R), 3
Reynolds, R J (NSW) 1984 *Fj, NZ* 1,2,3, 1985 *Fj* 1,2, 1986 *Arg* 1,2, *NZ* 1, 1987 [*J*]
Richards, E W (Q) 1904 *BI* 1,3, 1905 *NZ*, 1907 *NZ* 1(R), 2
Richards, G (NSW) 1978 *NZ* 2(R), 3, 1981 *F* 1
Richards, T J (Q) 1908 *W*, 1909 *E*, 1912 *US*
Richards, V S (NSW) 1936 *NZ* 1,2(R), *M*, 1937 *SA* 1, 1938 *NZ* 1
Richardson, G C (Q) 1971 *SA* 1,2,3, 1972 *NZ* 2,3, *Fj*, 1973 *Tg* 1,2, *W*
Rigney, W A (NSW) 1925 *NZ* 2,4, 1926 *NZ* 4
Riley, S A (NSW) 1903 *NZ*
Ritchie, E V (NSW) 1924 *NZ* 1,3, 1925 *NZ* 2,3

Roberts, B T (NSW) 1956 *SA* 2
Roberts, H F (Q) 1961 *Fj* 1,3, *SA* 2, *F*
Robertson, I J (NSW) 1975 *J* 1,2
Robinson, B J (ACT) 1996 *It* (R), *S* (R), *I* (R), 1997 *F* 1,2, *NZ* 1, *E* 1, *NZ* 2, *SA* 1(R), *NZ* 3(R), *SA* 2(R), *Arg* 1,2, *E* 2, *S*, 1998 *Tg*
Roche, C (Q) 1982 *S* 1,2, *NZ* 1,2,3, 1983 *US*, *Arg* 1,2, *NZ*, *It*, *F* 1,2, 1984 *Fj*, *NZ* 1,2,3, *I*
Rodriguez, E E (NSW) 1984 *Fj*, *NZ* 1,2,3, *E*, *I*, *W*, *S*, 1985 *C* 1,2, *NZ*, *Fj* 1, 1986 *It*, *F*, *Arg* 1,2, *NZ* 1,2,3, 1987 *SK*, [*E*, *J*, *W* (R)], *NZ*, *Arg* 1,2
Roebuck, M C (NSW) 1991 *W*, *E*, *NZ* 1,2, [*Arg*, *WS*, *W*, *I*, *NZ*, *E*], 1992 *S* 1,2, *NZ* 2,3, *SA*, *I*, *W*, 1993 *Tg*, *SA* 1,2,3, *C*, *F* 2
Roff, J W (ACT) 1995 [*C*, *R*], *NZ* 1,2, 1996 *W* 1,2, *NZ* 1, *SA* 1, *NZ* 2, *SA* 2(R), *S*, *I*, *W* 3, 1997 *F* 1,2, *NZ* 1, *E* 1, *NZ* 2, *SA* 1, *NZ* 3, *SA* 2, *Arg* 1,2, *E* 2, *S*, 1998 *E* 1, *S* 1,2, *NZ* 1 , *SA* 1, *NZ* 2, *SA* 2, *NZ* 3, *Fj*, *Tg*, *WS*, *F*, *E* 2, 1999 *I* 1,2, *E*, *SA* 1, *NZ* 1, *SA* 2, *NZ* 2(R), [*R* (R), *I* 3, *US* (R), *W*, *SA* 3, *F*], 2000 *Arg* 1,2, *SA* 1, *NZ* 1, *SA* 2, *NZ* 2, *SA* 3, *F*, *S*, *E*, 2001 *BI* 1,2,3, *SA* 1, *NZ* 1, *SA* 2, *NZ* 2, *Sp*, *E*, *F*, *W*, 2003 *I*, *W*, *E*, *SA* 1
Rogers, M S (NSW) 2002 *F* 1(R),2(R), *NZ* 1(R), *SA* 1(R), *NZ* 2(R), *SA* 2(t&R), *Arg*, 2003 *E* (R), *SA* 1, *NZ* 1, *SA* 2, *NZ* 2
Rose, H A (NSW), 1967 *I* 2, *NZ*, 1968 *NZ* 1,2, *F*, *I*, *S*, 1969 *W*, *SA* 1,2,3,4, 1970 *S*
Rosenblum, M E (NSW) 1928 *NZ* 1,2,3, *M*
Rosenblum, R G (NSW) 1969 *SA* 1,3, 1970 *S*
Rosewell, J S H (NSW) 1907 *NZ* 1,3
Ross, A W (NSW) 1925 *NZ* 1,2,3, 1926 *NZ* 1,2,3, 1927 *I*, *W*, *S*, 1928 *E*, *F*, 1929 *NZ* 1, 1930 *BI*, 1931 *M*, *NZ*, 1932 *NZ* 2,3, 1933 *SA* 5, 1934 *NZ* 1,2
Ross, W S (Q) 1979 *I* 1,2, *Arg* 2, 1980 *Fj*, *NZ* 1,2,3, 1982 *S* 1,2, 1983 *US*, *Arg* 1,2, *NZ*
Rothwell, P R (NSW) 1951 *NZ* 1,2,3, 1952 *Fj* 1
Row, F L (NSW) 1899 *BI* 1,3,4
Row, N E (NSW) 1907 *NZ* 1,3, 1909 *E*, 1910 *NZ* 1,2,3
Rowles, P G (NSW) 1972 *Fj*, 1973 *E*
Roxburgh, J R (NSW) 1968 *NZ* 1,2, *F*, 1969 *W*, *SA* 1,2,3,4, 1970 *S*
Ruebner, G (NSW) 1966 *BI* 1,2
Russell, C J (NSW) 1907 *NZ* 1,2,3, 1908 *W*, 1909 *E*
Ryan, J R (NSW) 1975 *J* 2, 1976 *I*, *US*, *Fj* 1,2,3
Ryan, K J (Q) 1958 *E*, *M* 1, *NZ* 1,2,3
Ryan, P F (NSW) 1963 *E*, *SA* 1, 1966 *BI* 1,2
Rylance, M H (NSW) 1926 *NZ* 4(R)

Sailor, W J (Q) 2002 *F* 1,2, *Arg* (R), *I*, *E*, *It*, 2003 *I*, *W*, *E*, *SA* 1, *NZ* 1, *SA* 2, *NZ* 2
Sampson, J H (NSW) 1899 *BI* 4
Sayle, J L (NSW) 1967 *NZ*
Schulte, B G (Q) 1946 *NZ* 1, *M*
Scott, P R I (NSW) 1962 *NZ* 1,2
Scott-Young, S J (Q) 1990 *F* 2,3(R), *US*, *NZ* 3, 1992 *NZ* 1,2,3
Shambrook, G G (Q) 1976 *Fj* 2,3
Sharpe, N C (Q) 2002 *F* 1,2, *NZ* 1, *SA* 1, *NZ* 2, *SA* 2, 2003 *I*, *W*, *E*, *SA* 1(R), *NZ* 1(R), *SA* 2(R), *NZ* 2(R)
Shaw, A A (Q) 1973 *W*, *E*, 1975 *E* 1,2, *J* 2, *S*, *W*, 1976 *E*, *I*, *US*, *Fj* 1,2,3, *F* 1,2, 1978 *W* 1,2, *NZ* 1,2,3, 1979 *I* 1,2, *NZ*, *Arg* 1,2, 1980 *Fj*, *NZ* 1,2,3, 1981 *F* 1,2, *I*, *W*, *S*, 1982 *S* 1,2
Shaw, C (NSW) 1925 *NZ* 2,3,4(R)
Shaw, G A (NSW) 1969 *W*, *SA* 1(R), 1970 *S*, 1971 *SA* 1,2,3, *F* 1,2, 1973 *W*, *E*, 1974 *NZ* 1,2,3, 1975 *E* 1,2, *J* 1,2, *W*, 1976 *E*, *I*, *US*, *Fj* 1,2,3, *F* 1,2, 1979 *NZ*
Sheehan, W B J (NSW) 1921 *SA* 1,2,3, 1922 *NZ* 1,2,3, 1923 *M* 1,2, *NZ* 1,2,3, 1924 *NZ* 1,2, 1926 *NZ* 1,2,3, 1927 *W*, *S*
Shehadie, N M (NSW) 1947 *NZ* 2, 1948 *E*, *F*, 1949 *M* 1,2,3, *NZ* 1,2, 1950 *BI* 1,2, 1951 *NZ* 1,2,3, 1952 *Fj* 1,2, *NZ* 2, 1953 *SA* 1,2,3,4, 1954 *Fj* 1,2, 1955 *NZ* 1,2,3, 1956 *SA* 1,2, 1957 *NZ* 2, 1958 *W*, *I*
Sheil, A G R (Q) 1956 *SA* 1
Shepherd, D J (V) 1964 *NZ* 3, 1965 *SA* 1,2, 1966 *BI* 1,2
Shute, J L (NSW) 1920 *NZ* 3, 1922 *M* 2,3
Simpson, R J (NSW) 1913 *NZ* 2
Skinner, A J (NSW) 1969 *W*, *SA* 4, 1970 *S*
Slack, A G (Q) 1978 *W* 1,2, *NZ* 1,2, 1979 *NZ*, *Arg* 1,2, 1980 *Fj*, 1981 *I*, *W*, *S*, 1982 *E*, *S* 1, *NZ* 3, 1983 *US*, *Arg* 1,2 *NZ*, *It*, 1984 *Fj*, *NZ* 1,2,3, *E*, *I*, *W*, *S*, 1986 *It*, *F*, *NZ* 1,2,3, 1987 *SK*, [*E*, *US*, *J*, *I*, *F*, *W*]
Slater, S H (NSW) 1910 *NZ* 3
Slattery, P J (Q) 1990 *US* (R), 1991 *W* (R), *E* (R), [*WS* (R), *W*, *I* (R)], 1992 *I*, *W*, 1993 *Tg*, *C*, *F* 1,2, 1994 *I* 1,2, *It* 1(R), 1995 [*C*, *R* (R)]
Smairl, A M (NSW) 1928 *NZ* 1,2,3
Smith, B A (Q) 1987 *SK*, [*US*, *J*, *I* (R), *W*], *Arg* 1
Smith, D P (Q) 1993 *SA* 1,2,3, *C*, *F* 2, 1994 *I* 1,2, *It* 1,2, *WS*, *NZ*, 1995 *Arg* 1,2, [*SA*, *R*, *E*], *NZ* 1,2, 1998 *SA* 1(R), *NZ* 3(R), *Fj*
Smith, F B (NSW) 1905 *NZ*, 1907 *NZ* 1,2,3
Smith, G B (ACT) 2000 *F*, *S*, *E*, 2001 *BI* 1,2,3, *SA* 1, *NZ* 1, *SA* 2, *NZ* 2, *Sp*, *E*, *F* (R), *W* (R), 2002 *F* 1,2, *NZ* 1, *SA* 1, *NZ* 2, *SA* 2, *Arg*, *I*, *E*, *It*, 2003 *I*, *NZ* 1, *SA* 2, *NZ* 2
Smith, L M (NSW) 1905 *NZ*
Smith, N C (NSW) 1922 *NZ* 2,3, 1923 *NZ* 1, 1924 *NZ* 1,3(R), 1925 *NZ* 2,3
Smith, P V (NSW) 1967 *NZ*, 1968 *NZ* 1,2, *F*, *I*, *S*, 1969 *W*, *SA* 1
Smith, R A (NSW) 1971 *SA* 1,2, 1972 *F* 1,2, *NZ* 1,2(R), 3, *Fj*, 1975 *E* 1,2, *J* 1,2, *S*, *W*, 1976 *E*, *I*, *US*, *Fj* 1,2,3, *F* 1,2
Smith, T S (NSW) 1921 *SA* 1,2,3, *NZ*, 1922 *M* 2,3, *NZ* 1,2,3, 1925 *NZ* 1,3,4
Snell, H W (NSW) 1925 *NZ* 2,3, 1928 *NZ* 3
Solomon, H J (NSW) 1949 *M* 3, *NZ* 2, 1950 *BI* 1,2, 1951 *NZ* 1,2, 1952 *Fj* 1,2, *NZ* 1,2, 1953 *SA* 1,2,3, 1955 *NZ* 1
Spooner, N R (Q) 1999 *I* 1,2
Spragg, S A (NSW) 1899 *BI* 1,2,3,4
Staniforth, S N G (NSW) 1999 [*US*], 2002 *I*, *It*
Stanley, R G (NSW) 1921 *NZ*, 1922 *M* 1,2,3, *NZ* 1,2,3, 1923 *M* 2,3, *NZ* 1,2,3, 1924 *NZ* 1,3
Stapleton, E T (NSW) 1951 *NZ* 1,2,3, 1952 *Fj* 1,2, *NZ* 1,2, 1953 *SA* 1,2,3,4, 1954 *Fj* 1, 1955 *NZ* 1,2,3, 1958 *NZ* 1
Steggall, J C (Q) 1931 *M*, *NZ*, 1932 *NZ* 1,2,3, 1933 *SA* 1,2,3,4,5
Stegman, T R (NSW) 1973 *Tg* 1,2
Stephens, O G (NSW) 1973 *Tg* 1,2, *W*, 1974 *NZ* 2,3
Stewart, A A (NSW) 1979 *NZ*, *Arg* 1,2
Stiles, N B (Q) 2001 *BI* 1,2,3, *SA* 1, *NZ* 1, *SA* 2, *NZ* 2, *Sp*, *E*, *F*, *W*, 2002 *I*
Stone, A H (NSW) 1937 *SA* 2, 1938 *NZ* 2,3
Stone, C G (NSW) 1938 *NZ* 1
Stone, J M (NSW) 1946 *M*, *NZ* 2
Storey, G P (NSW) 1926 *NZ* 4, 1927 *I*, *W*, *S*, 1928 *E*, *F*, 1929 *NZ* 3(R), 1930 *BI*
Storey, K P (NSW) 1936 *NZ* 2
Storey, N J D (NSW) 1962 *NZ* 1
Strachan, D J (NSW) 1955 *NZ* 2,3
Strauss, C P (NSW) 1999 *I* 1(R),2(R), *E* (R), *SA* 1(R), *NZ* 1, *SA* 2(R), *NZ* 2(R), [*R* (R), *I* 3(R), *US*, *W*]
Street, N O (NSW) 1899 *BI* 2
Streeter, S F (NSW) 1978 *NZ* 1
Stuart, R (NSW) 1910 *NZ* 2,3
Stumbles, B D (NSW) 1972 *NZ* 1(R), 2,3, *Fj*
Sturtridge, G S (V) 1929 *NZ* 2, 1932 *NZ* 1,2,3, 1933 *SA* 1,2,3,4,5
Sullivan, P D (NSW) 1971 *SA* 1,2,3, *F* 1,2, 1972 *F* 1,2, *NZ* 1,2, *Fj*, 1973 *Tg* 1,2, *W*
Summons, A J (NSW) 1958 *W*, *I*, *E*, *S*, *M* 2, *NZ* 1,2,3, 1959 *BI* 1,2
Suttor, D C (NSW) 1913 *NZ* 1,2,3
Swannell, B I (NSW) 1905 *NZ*
Sweeney, T L (Q) 1953 *SA* 1

Taafe, B S (NSW) 1969 *SA* 1, 1972 *F* 1,2
Tabua, I (Q) 1993 *SA* 2,3, *C*, *F* 1, 1994 *I* 1,2, *It* 1,2, 1995 [*C*, *R*]
Tancred, A J (NSW) 1927 *I*, *W*, *S*
Tancred, H E (NSW) 1923 *M* 1,2
Tancred, J L (NSW) 1926 *NZ* 3,4, 1928 *F*
Tanner, W H (Q) 1899 *BI* 1,2
Tarleton, K (NSW) 1925 *NZ* 2,3
Tasker, W G (NSW) 1913 *NZ* 1,2,3, 1914 *NZ* 1,2,3
Tate, M J (NSW) 1951 *NZ* 3, 1952 *Fj* 1,2, *NZ* 1,2, 1953 *SA* 1, 1954 *Fj* 1,2
Taylor, D A (Q) 1968 *NZ* 1,2, *F*, *I*, *S*
Taylor, H C (NSW) 1923 *NZ* 1,2,3, 1924 *NZ* 4
Taylor, J I (NSW) 1971 *SA* 1, 1972 *F* 1,2, *Fj*
Taylor, J M (NSW) 1922 *M* 1,2
Teitzel, R G (Q) 1966 *W*, *S*, 1967 *E*, *I* 1, *F*, *I* 2, *NZ*
Telford, D G (NSW) 1926 *NZ* 3(R)
Thompson, C E (NSW) 1922 *M* 1, 1923 M 1,2, *NZ* 1, 1924 *NZ* 2,3
Thompson, E G (Q) 1929 *NZ* 1,2,3, 1930 *BI*
Thompson, F (NSW) 1913 *NZ* 1,2,3, 1914 *NZ* 1,2,3
Thompson, J (Q) 1914 *NZ* 1
Thompson, P D (Q) 1950 *BI* 1
Thompson, R J (WA) 1971 *SA* 3, *F* 2(R), 1972 *Fj*
Thorn, A M (NSW) 1921 *SA* 1,2,3, *NZ*, 1922 *M* 1,3

Thorn, E J (NSW) 1922 *NZ* 1,2,3, 1923 *NZ* 1,2,3, 1924 *NZ* 1,2,3, 1925 *NZ* 1,2, 1926 *NZ* 1,2,3,4
Thornett, J E (NSW) 1955 *NZ* 1,2,3, 1956 *SA* 1,2, 1958 *W, I, S, F, M* 2,3, *NZ* 2,3, 1959 *BI* 1,2, 1961 *Fj* 2,3, *SA* 1,2, *F*, 1962 *NZ* 2,3,4,5, 1963 *E, SA* 1,2,3,4, 1964 *NZ* 1,2,3, 1965 *SA* 1,2, 1966 *BI* 1,2, 1967 *F*
Thornett, R N (NSW) 1961 *Fj* 1,2,3, *SA* 1,2, *F*, 1962 *NZ* 1,2,3,4,5
Thorpe, A C (NSW) 1929 *NZ* 1(R)
Timbury, F R V (Q) 1910 *NZ* 1,2,
Tindall, E N (NSW) 1973 *Tg* 2
Toby, A E (NSW) 1925 *NZ* 1,4
Tolhurst, H A (NSW) 1931 *M, NZ*
Tombs, R C (NSW) 1992 *S* 1,2, 1994 *I* 2, *It* 1, 1996 *NZ* 2
Tonkin, A E J (NSW) 1947 *S, I, W*, 1948 *E, F*, 1950 *BI* 2
Tooth, R M (NSW) 1951 *NZ* 1,2,3, 1954 *Fj* 1,2, 1955 *NZ* 1,2,3, 1957 *NZ* 1,2
Towers, C H T (NSW) 1926 *NZ* 1,3(R),4, 1927 *I*, 1928 *E, F, NZ* 1,2,3, *M*, 1929 *NZ* 1,3, 1930 *BI*, 1931 *M, NZ*, 1934 *NZ* 1,2, 1937 *SA* 1,2
Trivett, R K (Q) 1966 *BI* 1,2
Tune, B N (Q) 1996 *W* 2, *C, NZ* 1, *SA* 1, *NZ* 2, *SA* 2, 1997 *F* 1,2, *NZ* 1, *E* 1, *NZ* 2, *SA* 1, *NZ* 3, *SA* 2, *Arg*, 1,2, *E* 2, *S*, 1998 *E* 1, *S* 1,2, *NZ* 1, *SA* 1,2, *NZ* 3, 1999 *I* 1, *E, SA* 1, *NZ* 1, *SA* 2, *NZ* 2, [*R, I* 3, *W, SA* 3, *F*], 2000 *SA* 2(R), *NZ* 2(t&R), *SA* 3(R), 2001 *F* (R), *W*, 2002 *NZ* 1, *SA* 1, *NZ* 2, *SA* 2, *Arg*
Tuqiri, L (NSW) 2003 *I* (R), *W* (R), *E* (R), *SA* 1(R), *NZ* 1, *SA* 2, *NZ* 2
Turinui, M (NSW) 2003 *I, W, E*
Turnbull, A (V) 1961 *Fj* 3
Turnbull, R V (NSW) 1968 *I*
Tuynman, S N (NSW) 1983 *F* 1,2, 1984 *E, I, W, S*, 1985 *C* 1,2, *NZ, Fj* 1,2, 1986 *It, F, Arg* 1,2, *NZ* 1,2,3, 1987 *SK*, [*E, US, J, I, W*], *NZ, Arg* 1(R), 2, 1988 *E, It*, 1989 *BI* 1,2,3, *NZ*, 1990 *NZ* 1
Tweedale, E (NSW) 1946 *NZ* 1,2, 1947 *NZ* 2, *S, I*, 1948 *E, F*, 1949 *M* 1,2,3

Vaughan, D (NSW) 1983 *US, Arg* 1, *It, F* 1,2
Vaughan, G N (V) 1958 *E, S, F, M* 1,2,3
Verge, A (NSW) 1904 *BI* 1,2
Vickerman, D J (ACT) 2002 *F* 2(R), *Arg, E, It*, 2003 *I* (R), *W* (R), *E* (R), *SA* 1, *NZ* 1, *SA* 2, *NZ* 2

Walden, R J (NSW) 1934 *NZ* 2, 1936 *NZ* 1,2, *M*
Walker, A K (NSW) 1947 *NZ* 1, 1948 *E, F*, 1950 *BI* 1,2
Walker, A M (ACT) 2000 *NZ* 1(R), 2001 *BI* 1,2,3, *SA* 1, *NZ* 1,2(R)
Walker, A S B (NSW) 1912 *US*, 1920 *NZ* 1,2, 1921 *SA* 1,2,3, *NZ*, 1922 *M* 1,3, *NZ* 1,2,3, 1923 *M* 2,3, 1924 *NZ* 1,2
Walker, L F (NSW) 1988 *NZ* 2,3, *S, It*, 1989 *BI* 1,2,3, *NZ*
Walker, L R (NSW) 1982 *NZ* 2,3
Wallace, A C (NSW) 1921 *NZ*, 1926 *NZ* 3,4, 1927 *I, W, S*, 1928 *E, F*
Wallace, T M (NSW) 1994 *It* 1(R), 2
Wallach, C (NSW) 1913 *NZ* 1,3, 1914 *NZ* 1,2,3
Walsh, J J (NSW) 1953 *SA* 1,2,3,4
Walsh, P B (NSW) 1904 *BI* 1,2,3
Walsham, K P (NSW) 1962 *NZ* 3, 1963 *E*
Ward, P G (NSW) 1899 *BI* 1,2,3,4
Ward, T (Q) 1899 *BI* 2
Watson, G W (Q) 1907 *NZ* 1
Watson, W T (NSW) 1912 *US*, 1913 *NZ* 1,2,3, 1914 *NZ* 1, 1920 *NZ* 1,2,3
Waugh, P R (NSW) 2000 *E* (R), 2001 *NZ* 1(R), *SA* 2(R), *NZ* 2(R), *Sp* (R), *E* (R), *F, W*, 2003 *I* (R), *W, E, SA* 1, *NZ* 1, *SA* 2, *NZ*2
Waugh, W W (NSW, ACT) 1993 *SA* 1, 1995 [*C*], *NZ* 1,2, 1996 *S, I*, 1997 *Arg* 1,2
Weatherstone, L J (ACT) 1975 *E* 1,2, *J* 1,2, *S* (R), 1976 *E, I*
Webb, W (NSW) 1899 *BI* 3,4
Welborn J P (NSW) 1996 *SA* 2, *It*, 1998 *Tg*, 1999 *E, SA* 1, *NZ* 1
Wells, B G (NSW) 1958 *M* 1
Westfield, R E (NSW) 1928 *NZ* 1,2,3, *M*, 1929 *NZ* 2,3
Whitaker, C J (NSW) 1998 *SA* 2(R), *Fj* (R), *Tg*, 1999 *NZ* 2(R), [*R* (R), *US, F* (R)], 2000 *S* (R), 2001 *Sp* (R), *W* (R), 2002 *Arg* (R), *It* (R), 2003 *I* (R), *W* (R), *SA* 2(R)
White, C J B (NSW) 1899 *BI* 1, 1903 *NZ*, 1904 *BI* 1
White, J M (NSW) 1904 *BI* 3
White, J P L (NSW) 1958 *NZ* 1,2,3, 1961 *Fj* 1,2,3, *SA* 1,2, *F*, 1962 *NZ* 1,2,3,4,5, 1963 *E, SA* 1,2,3,4, 1964 *NZ* 1,2,3, 1965 *SA* 1,2
White, M C (Q) 1931 *M, NZ* 1932 *NZ* 1,2, 1933 *SA* 1,2,3,4,5
White, S W (NSW) 1956 *SA* 1,2, 1958 *I, E, S, M* 2,3
White, W G S (Q) 1933 *SA* 1,2,3,4,5, 1934 *NZ* 1,2, 1936 *NZ* 1,2, *M*
White, W J (NSW) 1928 *NZ* 1, *M*, 1932 *NZ* 1
Wickham, S M (NSW) 1903 *NZ*, 1904 *BI* 1,2,3, 1905 *NZ*
Williams, D (Q) 1913 *NZ* 3, 1914 *NZ* 1,2,3
Williams, I M (NSW) 1987 *Arg* 1,2, 1988 *E* 1,2, *NZ* 1,2,3, 1989 *BI* 2,3, *NZ, F* 1,2, 1990 *F* 1,2,3, *US, NZ* 1
Williams, J L (NSW) 1963 *SA* 1,3,4
Williams, R W (ACT) 1999 *I* 1(t&R),2(t&R), *E* (R), [*US*], 2000 *Arg* 1,2, *SA* 1, *NZ* 1, *SA* 2, *NZ* 2, *SA* 3, *F* (R), *S* (R), *E*
Williams, S A (NSW) 1980 *Fj, NZ* 1,2, 1981 *F* 1,2, 1982 *E, NZ* 1,2,3, 1983 *US, Arg* 1(R), 2, *NZ, It, F* 1,2, 1984 *NZ* 1,2,3, *E, I, W, S*, 1985 *C* 1,2, *NZ, Fj* 1,2
Wilson, B J (NSW) 1949 *NZ* 1,2
Wilson, C R (Q) 1957 *NZ* 1, 1958 *NZ* 1,2,3
Wilson, D J (Q) 1992 *S* 1,2, *NZ* 1,2,3, *SA, I, W*, 1993 *Tg, NZ, SA* 1,2,3, *C, F* 1,2, 1994 *I* 1,2, *It* 1,2, *WS, NZ*, 1995 *Arg* 1,2, [*SA, R, E*], 1996 *W* 1,2, *C, NZ* 1, *SA* 1, *NZ* 2, *SA* 2, *It, S, I, W* 3, 1997 *F* 1,2, *NZ* 1, *E* 1(t + R), *NZ* 2(R), *SA* 1, *NZ* 3, *SA* 2, *E* 2(R), *S* (R), 1998 *E* 1, *S* 1,2, *NZ* 1, *SA* 1, *NZ* 2, *SA* 2, *NZ* 3, *Fj, WS, F, E* 2, 1999 *I* 1,2, *E, SA* 1, *NZ* 1, *SA* 2, *NZ* 2, [*R, I* 3, *W, SA* 3, *F*], 2000 *Arg* 1,2, *SA* 1, *NZ* 1, *SA* 2, *NZ* 2, *SA* 3
Wilson, V W (Q) 1937 *SA* 1,2, 1938 *NZ* 1,2,3
Windon, C J (NSW) 1946 *NZ* 1,2, 1947 *NZ* 1, *S, I, W*, 1948 *E, F*, 1949 *M* 1,2,3, *NZ* 1,2, 1951 *NZ* 1,2,3, 1952 *Fj* 1,2, *NZ* 1,2
Windon, K S (NSW) 1937 *SA* 1,2, 1946 *M*
Windsor, J C (Q) 1947 *NZ* 2
Winning, K C (Q) 1951 *NZ* 1
Wogan, L W (NSW) 1913 *NZ* 1,2,3, 1914 *NZ* 1,2,3, 1920 *NZ* 1,2,3, 1921 *SA* 1,2,3, *NZ*, 1922 *M* 3, *NZ* 1,2,3, 1923 *M* 1,2, 1924 *NZ* 1,2,3
Wood, F (NSW) 1907 *NZ* 1,2,3, 1910 *NZ* 1,2,3, 1913 *NZ* 1,2,3, 1914 *NZ* 1,2,3
Wood, R N (Q) 1972 *Fj*
Woods, H F (NSW) 1925 *NZ* 4, 1926 *NZ* 1,2,3, 1927 *I, W, S*, 1928 *E*
Wright, K J (NSW) 1975 *E* 1,2, *J* 1, 1976 *US, F* 1,2, 1978 *NZ* 1,2,3
Wyld, G (NSW) 1920 *NZ* 2

Yanz, K (NSW) 1958 *F*
Young, W K (ACT) 2000 *F, S, E*, 2002 *F* 1,2, *NZ* 1, *SA* 1, *NZ* 2, *SA* 2, *Arg, E, It*, 2003 *I, W, E, SA* 1, *NZ* 1, *SA* 2, *NZ* 2

CANADA TEST SEASON REVIEW 2002-2003

Rugby World Cup Quarter-Final Place Canada's Goal

Peter McMullan

Give Canadian coach David Clark credit for taking a bold view of current adversities. With six games played and lost leading up to August's Pan-American Rugby Championship (PARA), in Buenos Aires, he bravely declared that a 2003 Rugby World Cup quarter-final place was definitely an achievable goal. Of the RWC squad he noted: 'It will be the best prepared, best organized and fittest ever to leave Canada.'

PARA saw Canada open with a 21-11 win over Uruguay before sustaining further losses to the United States (35-20), a major disappointment, and Argentina (62-22) in a game where Canada did well to score three tries, two after the Pumas had established a 48-10 advantage early in the second half.

To reach the last eight in the World Cup, Canada must win three of four pool games against Wales, New Zealand, Italy and Tonga in that order, an achievement that would give them their best ever RWC record.

The build-up to RWC 2003 was less than impressive, all the more so in the context of the P7 W6 L1 record achieved in 2001-02, albeit against lesser-ranked opposition excepting the touring Scots. Canada subsequently won all but the game in Uruguay in the RWC Americas qualifying series.

That was the end of the good times. November saw Canada away losers to Wales and France before 2003 brought home ground setbacks at the hands of England's second string, the United States and the truly formidable if internationally unranked New Zealand Maori. Who knows what would have happened in mid-August had not Georgia's financial problems led to the cancellation of the Test scheduled for Edmonton?

The 26-player PARA squad was led by Ryan Banks in the continuing absence of Al Charron, Canada's best known player whose 73-cap record, extending back to 1990 and encompassing three World Cups, speaks volumes for his physical commitment and absolute dedication to the game he has served so well.

Charron, comfortable at lock or in the back row, came home from France for the winter and then sustained a serious knee ligament injury in May. Surgery followed but he was still named to captain the World Cup squad in the hopes that he will be fully recovered by October.

All being well Charron, like Gareth Rees in 1999, will be attending his fourth RWC as will David Lougheed, back in harness as a robust wing or centre after a three-year retirement. Lougheed started in all six games in 1995 and 1999 but saw no action in 1991 when the wings were Pat Palmer, Steve Gray and Scott Stewart.

Two significant RWC 2003 absentees, in an era when so much hinges on the effectiveness of the forward effort, are flanker Dan Baugh (27 caps) and lock John Tait (37 caps), highly regarded and very experienced Canadians who will be appearing for Cardiff and Brive respectively in the months ahead. Baugh, whose last appearance was against Chile in August 2002, ruled himself out over an ongoing insurance issue while Tait has put family first as his young daughter has been unwell.

The demands of the professional game overseas continue to leave their mark on Canada and while the teams picked against Wales and France were not so far off full strength, the same could not be said for the mid-June hosting of the inaugural Churchill Cup, against England and the United States, and later for the two matches against the visiting Maori.

Props Rod Snow (Newport) and John Thiel (Sale), along with Tait, Baugh and Charron, were absentees following the November internationals while lock Mike James (Stade Français), another very influential French-based asset, only returned in time for the Maori and PARA series with Snow and Thiel back on board for the PARA trip.

Canada continues to earn credit for effort but no national team anywhere in the world can give of its best on a consistent basis while deprived of so many accomplished and experienced first choice players. More especially when they are forwards. Most certainly this has to relate to the fact that, in the nine-game period under review, Canada was outscored by 39 tries to 14 and by 329 points to 141.

All this gave Clark an opportunity to see how less experienced names performed under pressure with 34 players used as first-choice selections. Only Winston Stanley (Leeds) started in all nine matches, twice at full-back before reverting to his original role as a winger. Stanley leads all Canadian try scorers over the years with 24 while his 63 caps since 1994 are bettered only by Charron's 73 and Scott Stewart's 65.

New caps in 2003 included an intriguing Australian pair qualified through a parent or grandparent. James Pritchard, of Randwick and then Bedford, confirmed his qualities as a player and leading goal kicker with the Saskatchewan Prairie Fire in the Rugby Canada Super League before appearing at full-back against the Maori. Eastwood's Jeff Reid came on as a replacement No 8 in the tourists' first match but could not be considered a week later after injuring a hand in training before the visitors defeated the Rugby Canada All Stars 52-11, in Ottawa.

Pritchard held his place for the three PARA fixtures with Reid picked as a flanker against the United States and Argentina after team captain Ryan Banks suffered a knee ligament injury early in the opening game against Uruguay.

Other new caps included full-back Quentin Fyffe, wing David Moonlight (both against England) and No 8 Josh Jackson (against the United States).

Outside-half Ryan Smith was picked for the second game with the Maori after being used in a replacement role in the first match and against England, while flanker Jim Douglas earned his first cap as a replacement and then started a week later against the New Zealanders and in two PARA games.

Penalties dominated the scoring as Wales beat Canada 32-21, in Cardiff on 16 November. Each team landed six with outside-half Jared Barker the Canadian kicker while scrum-half Morgan Williams dropped a goal. Wales also scored two tries, both questioned by the losers. A run of injuries then held Barker back until the second game against the United States when he went over on an ankle and was replaced for the second half.

Charron missed the Wales game following the death of his father but was back a week later for the 35-3 wet weather loss to France. Canada's points came from a first half penalty by outside-half Bob Ross. France led 13-0 at half-time and finished with four tries.

The new and very well-received Churchill Cup tournament was staged in perfect conditions in Vancouver in July. England's big guns were busy in Australia but the quality of those left behind was such that Canada was overcome 43-7 conceding six tries while scoring one early on through Williams which Ross converted.

Hopes of a second chance finale against the English were dashed by a nightmarish 16-11 mid-week loss to the United States, a converted try and three penalties to a try, by Fyffe, and two Ross penalties.

The New Zealand Maori, strong and fast despite a number of late withdrawals, inevitably gave Canada hard games on successive August Saturdays, in Calgary and Toronto. They won the first one 65-27 and were then held to 30-9 by a far more spirited Canadian effort. Centre Nik Witkowski, Stanley, Ross and prop Kevin Tkachuk had tries first time around with Ross kicking a penalty and two conversions. In Toronto, the Maori added five tries to the nine scored in Calgary while limiting Canada to three Pritchard penalties.

Against Uruguay, wing Sean Fauth and Tkachuk were try scorers as replacements, along with Stanley while Ross had two penalties. For the second time the mid-week selection was then outplayed four tries to two by the United States. Hooker Mark Lawson and Williams, a replacement for the only time in the nine matches, claimed the tries while Pritchard kicked both conversions and two penalties with Canada 20-6 down at half-time.

Argentina led Canada 27-10 at the interval winning by nine tries, seven converted, and a penalty, to Canada's three, from Stanley, Tkachuk, again in a replacement role, and Pritchard leaving Ross to add a penalty and two conversions. As against Uruguay, Canada lost their captain in the opening minutes when James went down with a back problem.

Now for RWC 2003 and the definitive judgment on what has or has not been achieved in the four years since 1999.

Canada's Test Record in 2002-2003: Played 9, won 1, lost 8

Opponents	*Date*	*Venue*	*Result*
Argentina	30th August 2003	A	Lost 22-62
United States	27th August 2003	A	Lost 20-35
Uruguay	23rd August 2003	A	Won 21-11
NZ Maori	2nd August 2003	H	Lost 9-30
NZ Maori	26th July 2003	H	Lost 27-65
United States	18th June 2003	H	Lost 11-16
England A	14th June 2003	H	Lost 7-43
France	23rd November 2002	A	Lost 3-35
Wales	16th November 2002	A	Lost 21-32

CANADA INTERNATIONAL STATISTICS

(up to 30 September 2003)

Match Records

MOST CONSECUTIVE TEST WINS

6 1990 *Arg* 2, 1991 *J, S, US, F, R*
6 1998 *US* 1,2, *HK, J, U, US* 3

MOST CONSECUTIVE TESTS WITHOUT DEFEAT

Matches	*Wins*	*Draws*	*Period*
6	6	0	1990 to 1991
6	6	0	1998 to 1998

MOST POINTS IN A MATCH

by the team

Pts	*Opponents*	*Venue*	*Year*
72	Namibia	Toulouse	1999
62	Japan	Markham	2000
57	Hong Kong	Vancouver	1996
53	United States	Vancouver	1997
51	Japan	Vancouver	1996
51	Uruguay	Edmonton	2002

by a player

Pts	*Player*	*Opponents*	*Venue*	*Year*
27	G L Rees	Namibia	Toulouse	1999
26	R P Ross	Japan	Vancouver	1996
24	M A Wyatt	Scotland	Saint John	1991
23	G L Rees	Argentina	Buenos Aires	1998
22	R P Ross	Hong Kong	Vancouver	1996
22	G L Rees	Japan	Vancouver	1997
22	G L Rees	United States	Burlington	1998
22	J Barker	Japan	Markham	2000

MOST TRIES IN A MATCH

by the team

Tries	*Opponents*	*Venue*	*Year*
9	Namibia	Toulouse	1999
8	Tonga	Napier	1987
8	Japan	Vancouver	1991
8	Japan	Markham	2000
7	Hong Kong	Vancouver	1996
7	United States	Vancouver	1997

by a player

Tries	*Player*	*Opponents*	*Venue*	*Year*
4	K S Nichols	Japan	Markham	2000
3	S D Gray	United States	Vancouver	1987

MOST CONVERSIONS IN A MATCH

by the team

Cons	*Opponents*	*Venue*	*Year*
9	Namibia	Toulouse	1999
8	Japan	Markham	2000
7	Japan	Vancouver	1991
6	United States	Vancouver	1997
5	Hong Kong	Vancouver	1996

by a player

Cons	*Player*	*Opponents*	*Venue*	*Year*
9	G L Rees	Namibia	Toulouse	1999
8	J Barker	Japan	Markham	2000
7	M A Wyatt	Japan	Vancouver	1991
6	G L Rees	United States	Vancouver	1997
5	R P Ross	Hong Kong	Vancouver	1996

MOST PENALTIES IN A MATCH

by the team

Penalties	*Opponents*	*Venue*	*Year*
8	Scotland	Saint John	1991
7	Argentina	Buenos Aires	1998
6	United States	Vancouver	1985
6	Ireland	Victoria	1989
6	France	Nepean	1994
6	United States	Burlington	1998
6	Wales	Cardiff	2002

by a player

Penalties	*Player*	*Opponents*	*Venue*	*Year*
8	M A Wyatt	Scotland	Saint John	1991
7	G L Rees	Argentina	Buenos Aires	1998
6	M A Wyatt	United States	Vancouver	1985
6	M A Wyatt	Ireland	Victoria	1989
6	G L Rees	France	Nepean	1994
6	G L Rees	United States	Burlington	1998
6	J Barker	Wales	Cardiff	2002

MOST DROPPED GOALS IN A MATCH

by the team

Drops	Opponents	Venue	Year
2	United States	Saranac Lake (NY)	1980
2	United States	Tucson	1986
2	Hong Kong	Hong Kong	1997
2	Fiji	Tokyo	2001

by a player

Drops	Player	Opponents	Venue	Year
2	R P Ross	Hong Kong	Hong Kong	1997
2	R P Ross	Fiji	Tokyo	2001

Career Records

MOST CAPPED PLAYERS

Caps	Player	Career Span
73	A J Charron	1990 to 2002
64	D S Stewart	1989 to 2001
63	W U Stanley	1994 to 2003
55	G L Rees	1986 to 1999
55	R P Ross	1989 to 2003
54	J D Graf	1989 to 1999
50	J Hutchinson	1993 to 2000
50	R G A Snow	1995 to 2003
49	E A Evans	1986 to 1998
48	M B James	1994 to 2003
47	S D Gray	1984 to 1997

MOST CONSECUTIVE TESTS

Tests	Player	Span
40	J Hutchinson	1995 to 1999
25	J N Tait	1998 to 2001
21	W U Stanley	1998 to 2000
17	R P Ross	1996 to 1997
15	S D Gray	1991 to 1994

MOST TESTS AS CAPTAIN

Tests	Captain	Span
25	G L Rees	1994 to 1999
22	A J Charron	1996 to 2002
16	J D Graf	1995 to 1999
9	M A Wyatt	1990 to 1991
8	M Luke	1974 to 1981
8	H de Goede	1984 to 1987

MOST TESTS IN INDIVIDUAL POSITIONS

Position	Player	Tests	Span
Full-back	D S Stewart	46	1989 to 2001
Wing	W U Stanley	42	1994 to 2003
Centre	S D Gray	31	1984 to 1997
Fly-half	G L Rees	49	1986 to 1999
Scrum-half	J D Graf	39	1989 to 1999
Prop	R G A Snow	50	1995 to 2003
Hooker	P Dunkley	37	1998 to 2003
Lock	M B James	48	1994 to 2003
Flanker	J Hutchinson	46	1995 to 1999
No 8	C McKenzie	25	1992 to 1997

Stewart, Stanley, Rees, Graf, Hutchinson and Gray have been capped elsewhere.

MOST POINTS IN TESTS

Points	Player	Tests	Career
492	G L Rees	55	1986 to 1999
403	R P Ross	55	1989 to 2003
263	M A Wyatt	29	1982 to 1991
163	J Barker	12	2000 to 2003
123	W U Stanley	63	1994 to 2003
90	J D Graf	54	1989 to 1999

MOST TRIES IN TESTS

Tries	Player	Tests	Career
24	W U Stanley	63	1994 to 2003
10	K S Nichols	26	1996 to 2002
9	P Palmer	17	1983 to 1992
9	J D Graf	54	1989 to 1999
9	G L Rees	55	1986 to 1999
9	A J Charron	72	1990 to 2002

MOST CONVERSIONS IN TESTS

Cons	Player	Tests	Career
52	R P Ross	55	1989 to 2003
51	G L Rees	55	1986 to 1999
24	M A Wyatt	29	1982 to 1991
20	J Barker	12	2000 to 2003
9	D S Stewart	64	1989 to 2001

MOST PENALTY GOALS IN TESTS

Penalties	Player	Tests	Career
110	G L Rees	55	1986 to 1999
79	R P Ross	55	1989 to 2003
64	M A Wyatt	29	1982 to 1991
40	J Barker	12	2000 to 2003
14	D S Stewart	64	1989 to 2001
9	J D Graf	54	1989 to 1999
8	M D Schiefler	9	1980 to 1984

MOST DROPPED GOALS IN TESTS

Drops	Player	Tests	Career
9	G L Rees	55	1986 to 1999
9	R P Ross	49	1989 to 2002
5	M A Wyatt	29	1982 to 1991

Career Records of Canada International Players
(up to 30 September 2003)

PLAYER	Debut	Caps	T	C	P	D	Pts
Backs:							
F C Asselin	1999 v Fj	15	3	0	0	0	15
J Barker	2000 v Tg	12	0	20	40	1	163
J Cannon	2001 v US	21	0	0	0	0	0
M di Girolamo	2001 v U	12	3	0	0	0	15
E Fairhurst	2001 v Arg	11	1	0	0	0	5
S Fauth	2000 v Tg	27	6	0	0	0	30
Q Fyffe	2003 v E	2	1	0	0	0	5
M King	2002 v US	4	0	0	0	0	0
D Moonlight	2003 v E	1	0	0	0	0	0
J Pritchard	2003 v M	5	1	2	5	0	24
R P Ross	1989 v I	55	7	52	79	9	403
R Smith	2003 v E	6	0	0	0	0	0
W U Stanley	1994 v US	63	24	0	0	1	123
M Williams	1999 v Tg	31	6	0	0	0	30
N Witkowski	1998 v US	28	5	0	0	0	25
Forwards:							
R Banks	1999 v J	34	3	0	0	0	15
L Carlson	2002 v U	3	0	0	0	0	0
A J Charron	1990 v Arg	73	9	0	0	0	44
G G Cooke	2000 v Tg	11	0	0	0	0	0
J Cudmore	2002 v US	6	0	0	0	0	0
J Douglas	2003 v M	5	0	0	0	0	0
P Dunkley	1998 v J	37	3	0	0	0	15
J Jackson	2003 v U	3	0	0	0	0	0
M B James	1994 v US	48	3	0	0	0	15
R Johnstone	2001 v U	7	0	0	0	0	0
E R P Knaggs	2000 v Tg	17	0	0	0	0	0
M Lawson	2002 v US	13	1	0	0	0	5
P Murphy	2000 v Tg	19	5	0	0	0	25
C Plater	2003 v E	1	0	0	0	0	0
J Reid	2003 v M	3	0	0	0	0	0
P Riordan	2003 v E	2	0	0	0	0	0
R G A Snow	1995 v Arg	50	8	0	0	0	40
J N Tait	1997 v US	34	1	0	0	0	5
J Thiel	1998 v HK	32	3	0	0	0	15
K Tkachuk	2000 v Tg	20	3	0	0	0	15
A van Staveren	2000 v Tg	17	0	0	0	0	0
K M Wirachowski	1992 v E	19	3	0	0	0	15
C Yukes	2001 v U	13	0	0	0	0	0

ARGENTINA TEST SEASON REVIEW 2002-2003

First Series Win against France Highlight of World Cup Preparations

Frankie Deges

As below-par as Argentina were at the end of 2002, Los Pumas were at times right on their mettle come 2003, a good omen with the World Cup around the corner. Yet many of the problems chronicled in the last two editions of this Yearbook remain. Los Pumas still don't have a regular competition and will continue to suffer if no place is found for them in a major tournament. Moreover, with most of Argentina's star players performing in Europe, domestic rugby has suffered a deterioration of playing standards. The question remains, what will happen when the current Test players finally retire?

The answers could lie in the superb tournaments played by both the U19 and U21 teams. Los Pumitas (U19s) came within a minute of beating the Baby Blacks in Paris, losing by 24-27, before running out of steam in the third/fourth place play-off against the host nation. Returning home as the fourth best team in the world was a wonderful achievement for a side that had struggled with their games in the regional South American Championship. The U19s, once kings of the former FIRA championship with seven titles in little over a decade, had been losing touch with the bigger nations, unable to finish above seventh in 1999, 2000 or 2001. Now they are rated the fourth-best team in this age group after losing the play-off two seasons running.

The U21s, who were below their best at the inaugural U21 World Cup in 2002, managed the bronze medal in 2003. Many eyes were on a team that is expected to produce the next generation of Los Pumas, particularly as a large number of current Test players will retire after the World Cup. It was with flying honours that they returned from the Second World Cup in Oxfordshire, a number of players standing out to add a rosy hue to the future.

The international season divided into three distinct periods: the autumn Tests in November, followed by the home matches in the spring and late summer.

The first leg included the match at a packed River Plate Stadium against the Wallabies. In arguably Argentina's worst performance since the previous World Cup, many fingers were pointed at Bristol's Felipe Contepomi for his failed kicks. But it was generally a bad night for a team that was lucky not to lose by a larger score. They failed to create any attacking threat and the lacklustre Wallabies won by 17-6.

The coaches, hopeful of giving players beyond the Test squad their chances on a tour of Italy and Ireland, decided to retain the usual starting XV, missing a wonderful opportunity to blood players not always seen at this level. Italy were duly beaten 36-6 in Rome, and on a wet, cold day at Lansdowne Road the game that promised a foretaste of this year's World Cup opener in Australia disappointed. Ireland won 16-7 but Argentina were again below their best, the weather certainly being a distracting factor. If anything, the Argentine defence during these three Autumn Tests was superb – the try conceded against Australia came from a failed tackle and the one against Ireland from a high ball that descended with gallons of water attached to it. By the end of the tour the team seemed on the verge of self-destruction, too many factions within it complaining off the record. The break between seasons allowed tempers to cool down.

The Navy survival camp the team experienced in early April set the foundations for what was an extremely positive 2003. Players agreed to put the team and the World Cup as a priority and a real sense of unity resurfaced. A home-based XV again took control of the South American Championship with ease; defence was a standout as they scored wins against Paraguay 144-0, Chile 49-3 and Uruguay 32-0, with their line never crossed.

France arrived in the country desperate to claim vengeance from their loss a full calendar year before. It wasn't to be for Bernard Laporte's team. Scoring in the second minute, Argentina then withstood everything France threw at them to win a low-scoring game by 10-6. A week later, Los Pumas managed their first ever series win against the French since matches began in 1949. This time the game was very enjoyable and nerve-racking, a last-second drop-goal from fly-half Gonzalo Quesada (who had not played for almost a year) bringing a 33-32 win.

With spirits high, they travelled to South Africa for two games. A last-gasp penalty gave them a draw against South Africa A, although the luck would be on the Springboks' side in the Test. Los Pumas 'scored' four tries – one by the new find of Argentine rugby, 20-year-old Juan Martín Hernández – although only three were awarded. Felipe Contepomi had crossed for a great score only to be called back for an earlier infringement that, at least on television, was doubtful. Louis Koen's polished boot kicked a last-minute penalty for the Springboks to win 26-25. It would have been Argentina's first ever win against South Africa.

For the third part of the season – the final workout prior to the World Cup – professional players were obliged to take a month-and-a-half's rest – which they loved doing. A squad of 37 players (later trimmed to 30 for RWC requirements) appeared in the final four Tests, 'as we wanted to be fair and give every player that has been working with us in the last couple of years an opportunity to stake a claim on the World Cup squad,' said coach Marcelo Loffreda.

Even with fifteens that were clearly not first choice World Cup selections, four wins were secured. Fiji were met in the first ever Test staged in Córdoba. Although Argentina won 49-30 scoring seven tries, three were conceded. Los Pumas wrapped up their World Cup preparations with a clean sweep of the fifth Pan American Championship.

The World Cup will be the end of the road for many warriors who have made Argentine rugby proud in the last few years. Maybe the failure to capitalize on a strong team that could compete on equal terms against the best in the world when at its peak might bring problems for the future. A new generation will take time to find its feet in Test rugby, and much good could be undone. Without a regular meaningful international competition, tours will remain the bread and butter of Argentine rugby. That alone, however, will not be enough for a young team that will have to develop extra fast in a rugby economy that needs overseas assistance.

Argentina's Test Record in 2002-2003: Played 13, won 10, lost 3

Opponents	*Date*	*Venue*	*Result*
Canada	30th August 2003	H	Won 62-22
Uruguay	27th August 2003	H	Won 57-0
United States	23rd August 2003	H	Won 42-8
Fiji	19th August 2003	H	Won 49-30
South Africa	28th June 2003	A	Lost 25-26
France	20th June 2003	H	Won 33-32
France	14th June 2003	H	Won 10-6
Uruguay	3rd May 2003	A	Won 32-0
Chile	30th April 2003	A	Won 49-3
Paraguay	27th April 2003	A	Won 144-0
Ireland	23rd November 2002	A	Lost 7-16
Italy	16th November 2002	A	Won 36-6
Australia	2nd November 2002	H	Lost 6-17

ARGENTINA INTERNATIONAL STATISTICS

(up to 30 September 2003)

Match Records

MOST CONSECUTIVE TEST WINS

10 1992 *Sp 1,2, R, F,* 1993 *J 1,2, Br, Ch, P, U*
7 1972 *Gz 2,* 1973 *P, U, Br, Ch, R 1,2*

MOST CONSECUTIVE TESTS WITHOUT DEFEAT

Matches	Wins	Draws	Period
10	10	0	1992 to 1993
7	7	0	1972 to 1973

MOST POINTS IN A MATCH

by the team

Pts	Opponents	Venue	Year
152	Paraguay	Mendoza	2002
144	Paraguay	Montevidoe	2003
114	Brazil	Sao Paulo	1993
109	Brazil	Santiago	1979
103	Paraguay	Asuncion	1995
103	Brazil	Montevideo	1989
102	Paraguay	Asuncion	1985
98	Paraguay	San Pablo	1973
96	Brazil	San Pablo	1973

by a player

Pts	Player	Opponents	Venue	Year
50	E Morgan	Paraguay	San Pablo	1973
45	J M Nunez Piossek	Paraguay	Montevideo	2003
40	G M Jorge	Brazil	Sao Paulo	1993
32	M Sansot	Brazil	Tucuman	1977
32	J-L Cilley	Paraguay	Mendoza	2002
31	E Morgan	Uruguay	San Pablo	1973
31	E De Forteza	Paraguay	Asuncion	1975
31	J Luna	Romania	Buenos Aires	1995
30	J Capalbo	Uruguay	Tucuman	1977
29	P Guarrochena	Paraguay	Tucuman	1977
29	S E Meson	Canada	Buenos Aires	1995
29	G Quesada	Canada	Buenos Aires	1998
28	E Morgan	Chile	San Pablo	1973
27	G Quesada	Samoa	Llanelli	1999

MOST TRIES IN A MATCH

by the team

Tries	Opponents	Venue	Year
24	Paraguay	Mendoza	2002
24	Paraguay	Montevideo	2003
19	Brazil	Santiago	1979
19	Paraguay	Asuncion	1985
18	Paraguay	San Pablo	1973
18	Brazil	San Pablo	1973
18	Brazil	Sao Paulo	1993
17	Brazil	Buenos Aires	1991
16	Paraguay	Asuncion	1995
15	Paraguay	Asuncion	1975
14	Paraguay	Montevideo	1989
14	Brazil	Montevideo	1961

by a player

Tries	Player	Opponents	Venue	Year
9	J M Nunez Piossek	Paraguay	Montevideo	2003
8	G M Jorge	Brazil	Sao Paulo	1993
6	E Morgan	Paraguay	San Pablo	1973
6	G M Jorge	Brazil	Montevideo	1989
5	H Goti	Brazil	Montevideo	1961
5	M Rodriguez Jurado	Brazil	Montevideo	1971
5	P Grande	Paraguay	Asuncion	1998

MOST CONVERSIONS IN A MATCH

by the team

Cons	Opponents	Venue	Year
16	Paraguay	Mendoza	2002
15	Brazil	Santiago	1979
13	Paraguay	San Pablo	1973
13	Paraguay	Asuncion	1985
12	Paraguay	Asuncion	1975
12	Brazil	Buenos Aires	1993
12	Paraguay	Montevideo	2003
10	Paraguay	Tucuman	1977
10	Brazil	Montevideo	1989

by a player

Cons	Player	Opponents	Venue	Year
16	J-L Cilley	Paraguay	Mendoza	2002
13	E Morgan	Paraguay	San Pablo	1973
13	H Porta	Paraguay	Asuncion	1985
11	E De Forteza	Paraguay	Asuncion	1975
10	P Guarrochena	Paraguay	Tucuman	1977
10	S E Meson	Brazil	Montevideo	1989
10	S E Meson	Brazil	Sao Paulo	1993

MOST PENALTIES IN A MATCH

by the team

Penalties	Opponents	Venue	Year
8	Canada	Buenos Aires	1995
8	Samoa	Llanelli	1999
7	France	Buenos Aires	1974
7	France	Nantes	1992
7	Canada	Buenos Aires	1998
7	Japan	Cardiff	1999
7	Ireland	Lens	1999

by a player

Penalties	Player	Opponents	Venue	Year
8	S E Meson	Canada	Buenos Aires	1995
8	G Quesada	Samoa	Llanelli	1999
7	H Porta	France	Buenos Aires	1974
7	S E Meson	France	Nantes	1992
7	G Quesada	Canada	Buenos Aires	1998
7	G Quesada	Japan	Cardiff	1999
7	G Quesada	Ireland	Lens	1999

MOST DROPPED GOALS IN A MATCH

by the team

Drops	Opponents	Venue	Year
3	SA Gazelles	Pretoria	1971
3	Uruguay	Asuncion	1975
3	Australia	Buenos Aires	1979
3	New Zealand	Buenos Aires	1985
3	Canada	Markham	2001
2	SA Gazelles	Buenos Aires	1966
2	Scotland	Buenos Aires	1969
2	Uruguay	Montevideo	1971
2	Chile	Asuncion	1975
2	New Zealand	Dunedin	1979
2	Australia	Buenos Aires	1987
2	Chile	Santiago	1991
2	Australia	Llanelli	1991

by a player

Drops	Player	Opponents	Venue	Year
3	T Harris Smith	SA Gazelles	Pretoria	1971
3	H Porta	Australia	Buenos Aires	1979
3	H Porta	New Zealand	Buenos Aires	1985
3	J D Fernandez Miranda	Canada	Markham	2001
2	E Poggi	SA Gazelles	Buenos Aires	1966
2	T Harris Smith	Scotland	Buenos Aires	1969
2	H Porta	Uruguay	Montevideo	1971
2	E De Forteza	Chile	Asuncion	1975
2	H Porta	New Zealand	Dunedin	1979
2	H Porta	Australia	Buenos Aires	1987
2	L Arbizu	Chile	Santiago	1991
2	L Arbizu	Australia	Llanelli	1991

Career Records

MOST CAPPED PLAYERS

Caps	Player	Career Span
83	R Martin	1994 to 2003
82	L Arbizu	1990 to 2003
76	P L Sporleder	1990 to 2003
66	F E Mendez	1990 to 2003
63	D Cuesta Silva	1983 to 1995
58	H Porta	1971 to 1990
52	D Albanese	1995 to 2003
48	M Reggiardo	1996 to 2003
47	A Pichot	1995 to 2003
46	M Loffreda	1978 to 1994
45	R D Grau	1993 to 2003
43	G A Llanes	1990 to 2000
42	O J Hasan	1995 to 2003
41	G F Camardon	1990 to 2002
40	E Branca	1976 to 1990
40	S Phelan	1997 to 2003

MOST POINTS IN TESTS

Points	Player	Tests	Career
590	H Porta	58	1971 to 1990
451	G Quesada	34	1996 to 2003
364	S E Meson	34	1987 to 1997
240	F Contepomi	34	1998 to 2003
178	L Arbizu	82	1990 to 2003
138	J-L Cilley	13	1994 to 2002
134	J Fernandez Miranda	18	1997 to 2003
129	J Luna	8	1995 to 1997
127	E Morgan	12	1972 to 1975
125	D Cuesta Silva	63	1983 to 1995

MOST TRIES IN TESTS

Tries	Player	Tests	Career
28	D Cuesta Silva	63	1983 to 1995
24	J M Nunez Piossek	13	2001 to 2003
23	G M Jorge	22	1989 to 1994
19	R Martin	83	1994 to 2003
18	F Soler	26	1996 to 2002
15	L Arbizu	82	1990 to 2003
13	G Morgan	7	1977 to 1979
13	G Alvarez	9	1975 to 1977

MOST CONVERSIONS IN TESTS

Cons	Player	Tests	Career
84	H Porta	58	1971 to 1990
68	S E Meson	34	1987 to 1997
58	G Quesada	34	1996 to 2003

33	J Fernandez Miranda	18	1997 to 2003
32	F Contepomi	34	1998 to 2003
31	J-L Cilley	13	1994 to 2002
26	E Morgan	12	1972 to 1975
26	J Luna	8	1995 to 1997

MOST PENALTY GOALS IN TESTS

Penalties	Player	Tests	Career
101	H Porta	58	1971 to 1990
99	G Quesada	34	1996 to 2003
63	S E Meson	34	1987 to 1997

46	F Contepomi	34	1998 to 2003
22	J L Cilley	13	1994 to 2002
19	J Luna	8	1995 to 1997

MOST DROPPED GOALS IN TESTS

Drops	Player	Tests	Career
26	H Porta	58	1971 to 1990
11	L Arbizu	82	1990 to 2003
6	G Quesada	34	1996 to 2003
5	J Fernandez Miranda	18	1997 to 2003
5	T Harris Smith	5	1969 to 1972

Career Records of Argentina International Players
(up to 30 September 2003)

PLAYER	Debut	Caps	T	C	P	D	Pts
Backs:							
D Albanese	1995 v U	52	10	0	0	0	50
M Albina	2001 v US	4	2	0	0	0	10
L Arbizu	1990 v I	82	15	14	14	11	178
O Bartolucci	1996 v US	19	9	0	0	0	45
L Borges	2003 v Pg	3	3	0	0	0	15
G Bustos	2003 v Pg	2	0	9	0	0	18
G Camardon	1990 v E	41	9	0	0	0	45
F Contepomi	1998 v Ch	34	7	32	46	1	240
M Contepomi	1998 v US	14	2	0	0	0	10
I Corleto	1998 v J	20	9	0	0	0	45
J Fernandez Miranda	1997 v U	18	4	33	11	5	134
N Fernandez Miranda	1994 v US	31	4	0	0	0	20
J Freixas	2003 v Ch	2	1	0	0	0	5
M Gaitan	2002 v Pg	4	3	0	0	0	15
J M Hernandez	2003 v Pg	6	3	2	0	0	19
M Nannini	2002 v U	5	4	0	0	0	20
J M Nunez Piossek	2001 v U	13	24	0	0	0	120
J Orengo	1996 v U	32	8	0	0	0	40
A Pichot	1995 v A	47	12	0	0	0	60
G Quesada	1996 v US	34	4	58	99	6	451
S Sanz	2003 v US	1	0	0	0	0	0
H Senillosa	2002 v U	10	12	0	0	1	63
F Serra	2003 v Ch	1	0	0	0	0	0
B Stortoni	1998 v J	14	7	1	0	0	37
Forwards:							
P Albacete	2003 v Pg	6	0	0	0	0	0
R Alvarez	1998 v Pg	16	3	0	0	0	15
S G Bonorino	2001 v U	7	0	0	0	0	0
P Bouza	1996 v F	18	3	0	0	0	15
F Cortopasso	2003 v Ch	2	0	0	0	0	0
M Durand	1998 v Ch	25	6	0	0	0	30
R D Grau	1993 v J	45	2	0	0	0	10
E Guinazu	2003 v Pg	3	0	0	0	0	0

O Hasan	1995 v U	42	1	0	0	0	5
F Lecot	2003 v Pg	2	0	0	0	0	0
M Ledesma	1996 v U	39	0	0	0	0	0
C I Fernandez Lobbe	1996 v US	42	4	0	0	0	20
G Longo	1999 v W	30	2	0	0	0	10
R Martin	1994 v US	83	19	0	0	0	95
F E Mendez	1990 v I	66	12	0	0	0	60
L Ortiz	2003 v Pg	3	0	0	0	0	0
L Ostiglia	1999 v W	19	3	0	0	0	15
S Phelan	1997 v U	40	1	0	0	0	5
M Reggiardo	1996 v U	48	3	0	0	0	15
R Roncero	2002 v U	5	3	0	0	0	15
M Rospide	2003 v Pg	3	0	0	0	0	0
M Sambucetti	2001 v U	7	3	0	0	0	15
M Scelzo	1996 v US	17	7	0	0	0	35
M Schusterman	2003 v Pg	2	1	0	0	0	5
P L Sporleder	1990 v I	76	12	0	0	0	60

PACIFIC TEST SEASON REVIEW 2002-03

The Asian divide

Jeremy Duxbury

Despite regularly overwhelming their nearest Asian rivals, Japan often fail when confronted by the real world of rugby. In December 2002, the second-string Japan team overwhelmed Hong Kong and Chinese Taipei before suffering a shock defeat to neighbours Korea in the final. Few worried, however, as Japan had already qualified for the World Cup.

The Koreans thought this ideal preparation for their World Cup repechage matches against Tonga, who finished bottom of the Oceania qualifying pool. But the Asian divide reared its ugly head again in March as Tonga triumphed 75-0 and 119-0 without breaking sweat. In June, the Koreans were swept aside by 86-3 by the full Japanese side.

Japan, though, also wondered what they have to do to become competitive overseas. Despite talk of a bid to stage the 2011 World Cup, they spent so much on the national team's preparation with tours hither and zither that the Japanese Rugby Union reportedly accumulated a considerable debt.

And how much good did it do them? The Pool B results in October will yield the final answer, but conceding 80-plus points to Sydney and the ACT Brumbies B team in April before twice losing at home to Australia A tells a sorry tale.

Coach Shogo Mukai selected four New Zealanders in this year's squad, but they still fell to the United States and Russia in the Superpowers Cup. And to complete Japan's RWC preparations, England A went to Tokyo and twice conquered the Cherry Blossoms.

On the positive side, dashing wing Daisuke Ohata continues his try-scoring sprees unabated (he now has 38 tries from 36 Tests) while several experienced players from the 1999 tournament, centre Yukio Motoki, lock Hiroyuki Tanuma, flanker Takeomi Ito and prop Shin Hasagawa hold the side together.

Japan's Test Record in 2002-2003: Played 7, won 1, lost 6

Opponents	*Date*	*Venue*	*Result*
England A	6th July 2003	H	Lost 20-55
England A	3rd July 2003	H	Lost 10-37
Korea	15th June 2003	H	Won 86-3
Australia A	8th June 2003	H	Lost 15-66
Australia A	5th June 2003	H	Lost 5-63

Russia	25th May 2003	H	Lost 34-43
United States	17th May 2003	A	Lost 27-69

*The Superpowers Cup match against China scheduled for 28*th *May was cancelled owing to the SARS epidemic*

In the South Pacific, Fiji's improvement in the Boardroom over the past 18 months led to a vastly superior structure at Rugby House in Suva and the national side, having topped the RWC qualifiers from Oceania, headed for the United Kingdom in November 2002 in confident mood.

There was a setback, however, when Fiji were destroyed 58-14 by Wales in a match they had held high hopes of winning. Fiji struggled in the set pieces and lacked decent defensive patterns. An hour into the match, Fiji trailed 46-0. Two smart moves from replacement full-back Waisale Serevi then ended in converted tries to give Fiji some hope.

But in Dublin a week later, Fiji produced arguably their worst ever performance, losing 64-17 as the Irish backs ran amok to score seven of the team's nine tries. Fiji finally headed to Murrayfield to face a Scottish team that had just beaten the Springboks. Putting two passionless displays behind them, Fiji dug deep to play a respectable game that went a long way to restoring some credibility. Despite a 36-22 defeat by the Scots, the Fijians created two good tries.

Coach Mac McCallion believed that his side's biggest fault was a lack of preparation before the tour. So, in their build-up for the 2003 World Cup, the bulk of the Fiji squad spent four months together, in camp and on tour, as most of the FRU's hard-earned dollars went towards compensating players for loss of club contracts. The resulting wins over Tonga (at home) and Chile, but defeats to Tonga (away) and Argentina don't really reflect the considerable investment of this financially-challenged developing union.

McCallion's men began 2003 with a fortunate 34-31 win over Tonga at Prince Charles Park in Nadi but, one week later, Jim Love's Tonga went one better to pull off a 23-22 victory over Fiji and show that they too will be competitive in RWC Pool D in October.

In South America, the Pumas took their lead from Tonga and deployed a similar game plan in August, defeating Fiji in Cordoba. While Argentina had an easy time employing their line-out drives against a weakened Fijian pack, the game was significant for the Test debut of wing sensation Rupeni Caucau, who had been openly courted by the New Zealand Rugby Union all year.

Caucau had already starred in numerous sevens tournaments for Fiji, and he didn't disappoint at this level either. He dotted down one try and scored four more in the win against Chile six days later.

Fiji head for the World Cup with dazzling backline potential, the Highlanders' pair Seru Rabeni and Aisea Tuilevu in the centres working effectively with Caucau and Vilimoni Delasau outside them. This quartet carries the team's hopes for upsets over France and Scotland, but Fiji's Achilles' heel remains the questionable ball-winning ability of the forwards and the slowness to spin the ball wide.

Fiji's Test Record in 2002-2003: Played 7, won 2, lost 5

Opponents	*Date*	*Venue*	*Result*
Chile	24th August 2003	A	Won 41-16
Argentina	18th August 2003	A	Lost 30-49
Tonga	11th July 2003	A	Lost 22-23
Tonga	4th July 2003	H	Won 34-31
Scotland	24th November 2002	A	Lost 22-36
Ireland	17th November 2002	A	Lost 17-64
Wales	9th November 2002	A	Lost 14-58

Tonga's year was hardly marked with stunning victories over class opposition, but wily coach Jim Love trod a patient path that saw steady progress. Wales, Canada and Italy must be wary of the ŒIkale Tahi in Pool D. Tonga were forced to play no less than eight matches to qualify for this year's tournament: four Oceania qualifiers, then four in the repechage.

They began by annihilating Papua New Guinea and South Korea with an aggregate point advantage of 325-26 over the four repechage matches. The results included 17 converted tries in a national record win of 119-0 against the Koreans. Later, however, Tonga only managed a draw with a NZ Divisional XV, a narrow win over Queensland A and a defeat against a Wallaby-less ACT Brumbies.

In their four most recent Tests, they lost 47-12 against an All Black-laden NZ Maori team, went down bravely at home 40-19 to Ireland after leading until half-time, and shared the home-and-away series with Fiji.

Traditionally, the Tongans have had a strong set of hard-running loose forwards, and it's this quality that Love, who once coached the Maori to a 25-match unbeaten run against international opposition, has seized upon to teach them how to use the maul as an attacking weapon. Tonga have also worked hard on their set-piece play and dominated Fiji in both their July Tests.

Love has been with the team nearly two years and has put as much time into improving the off-field structure and management as he has coaching rugby. 'We have worked hard to restore some pride in the national game,' he says, looking ahead to the World Cup. 'We've set ourselves a realistic target. Our ambition is to make the quarter-finals.'

Tonga's Test Record in 2002-2003: Played 8, won 5, lost 3

Opponents	*Date*	*Venue*	*Result*
Fiji	11th July 2003	H	Won 23-22
Fiji	4th July 2003	A	Lost 31-34
Ireland	14th June 2003	H	Lost 19-40
NZ Maori	2nd June 2003	A	Lost 12-47
Korea	21st March 2003	H	Won 119-0
Korea	15th March 2003	A	Won 75-0
Papua New Guinea	7th December 2002	H	Won 84-12
Papua New Guinea	30th November 2002	A	Won 47-14

Producing shock results at the Rugby World Cup has become the hallmark of Manu Samoa, who enjoyed wins against Wales and Argentina at previous tournaments. But 2003 will bring Samoa's toughest challenge yet, as they must conquer either England or South Africa to reach the knock-out stages.

Their build-up has been fragmented because of problems of player availability and scheduling. Brief tours to Australia and Southern Africa brought an impressive tally of 36 tries in seven matches, the only drawback being that they conceded 31.

John Boe's team played only two Test matches in the last 12 months, losing at home to Ireland before defeating Namibia in Windhoek to win the first-ever Test match between the two nations. The match was a personal triumph for left-wing Dominic Feaunati who dotted down for a try either side of the interval before completing his hat-trick near the end.

Now in his fourth year with the Manu, Boe has built up a solid relationship with the players and with the country. He has often stuck up for the team to his own detriment, blaming missed job opportunities on his stance against New Zealand unions over player releases. 'I just cannot see why NPC and Super 12 players who are not going to be All Blacks can't play for their island teams,' he says. And when he points out how much Samoans have done for New Zealand rugby, it's hard not to sympathise with him: 'Six of the current All Blacks squad are Samoans, so I think Samoa has given plenty to New Zealand rugby. We're not getting a fair deal in return.'

As for the World Cup, Boe admits that South Africa's recent lapses in form have the Samoans talking of another quarter-final appearance with slightly more conviction. 'We'll have a crack at them. I do believe that on our day we can have a crack at anyone. We have that Polynesian flair and speed.'

Samoa's Test Record in 2002-2003: Played 2, won 1, lost 1

Opponents	*Date*	*Venue*	*Result*
Namibia	12th July 2003	A	Won 40-13
Ireland	20th June 2003	H	Lost 14-40

JAPAN INTERNATIONAL STATISTICS

(to 30 September 2003)

Match Records

MOST CONSECUTIVE TEST WINS

5 1980 *SK* 1981 *AU* 1982 *HK, C* 1,2

MOST CONSECUTIVE TESTS WITHOUT DEFEAT

Matches	*Wins*	*Draws*	*Period*
5	5	0	1980 to 1982

MOST POINTS IN A MATCH

by the team

Pts	*Opponents*	*Venue*	*Year*
155	Chinese Taipei	Tokyo	2002
134	Chinese Taipei	Singapore	1998
120	Chinese Taipei	Tainan	2002
90	South Korea	Tokyo	2002
86	South Korea	Tokyo	2003

by a player

Pts	*Player*	*Opponents*	*Venue*	*Year*
60	T Kurihara	Chinese Taipei	Tainan	2002
40	D Ohata	Chinese Taipei	Tokyo	2002
35	T Kurihara	South Korea	Tokyo	2002
34	K Hirose	Tonga	Tokyo	1999
29	T Kurihara	Russia	Tokyo	2002

MOST TRIES IN A MATCH

by the team

Tries	*Opponents*	*Venue*	*Year*
23	Chinese Taipei	Tokyo	2002
20	Chinese Taipei	Singapore	1998
18	Chinese Taipei	Tainan	2002
13	South Korea	Tokyo	2002
12	South Korea	Tokyo	2003
11	Chinese Taipei	Taiwan	2001

by a player

Tries	*Player*	*Opponents*	*Venue*	*Year*
8	D Ohata	Chinese Taipei	Tokyo	2002
6	T Kurihara	Chinese Taipei	Tainan	2002
5	T Masuho	Chinese Taipei	Singapore	1998
4	Y Sakata	NZ Juniors	Wellington	1968
4	T Hirao	Chinese Taipei	Taiwan	2001
4	D Ohata	South Korea	Tokyo	2002

MOST CONVERSIONS IN A MATCH

by the team

Cons	*Opponents*	*Venue*	*Year*
20	Chinese Taipei	Tokyo	2002
17	Chinese Taipei	Singapore	1998
15	Chinese Taipei	Tainan	2002
11	South Korea	Tokyo	2002

by a player

Cons	*Player*	*Opponents*	*Venue*	*Year*
15	T Kurihara	Chinese Taipei	Tainan	2002
12	A Miller	Chinese Taipei	Tokyo	2002
11	T Kurihara	South Korea	Tokyo	2002
10	K Hirose	Chinese Taipei	Singapore	1998
8	T Kurihara	Chinese Taipei	Tokyo	2002

MOST PENALTIES IN A MATCH

by the team

Penalties	*Opponents*	*Venue*	*Year*
9	Tonga	Tokyo	1999
6	Tonga	Tokyo	1990
5	Argentina (1st Test)	Buenos Aires	1993
5	Argentina (2nd Test)	Buenos Aires	1993
5	South Korea	Tokyo	2001

by a player

Penalties	*Player*	*Opponents*	*Venue*	*Year*
9	K Hirose	Tonga	Tokyo	1999
6	T Hosokawa	Tonga	Tokyo	1990
5	T Hosokawa	Argentina (1st Test)	Buenos Aires	1993
5	T Hosokawa	Argentina (2nd Test)	Buenos Aires	1993
5	T Kurihara	South Korea	Tokyo	2001

MOST DROPPED GOALS IN A MATCH

by the team

Drops	*Opponents*	*Venue*	*Year*
2	Argentina	Tokyo	1998

by a player

Drops	*Player*	*Opponents*	*Venue*	*Year*
2	K Iwabuchi	Argentina	Tokyo	1998

Career Records

MOST CAPPED PLAYERS

Caps	Player	Career Span
61	Y Motoki	1991 to 2003
49	T Ito	1996 to 2003
47	T Masuho	1991 to 2001
44	Y Sakuraba	1986 to 1999
43	M Kunda	1991 to 1999
40	T Matsuda	1992 to 2003
40	H Tanuma	1996 to 2003
38	T Hayashi	1980 to 1992
36	S Hasagawa	1997 to 2003
36	S Hirao	1983 to 1995
36	K Hirose	1994 to 2003
36	W Murata	1991 to 2003
36	D Ohata	1996 to 2003

MOST CONSECUTIVE TESTS

Tests	Player	Span
28	Y Motoki	1994 to 1998
26	Y Yoshida	1988 to 1995
18	S Mori	1974 to 1978
18	T Ishizuka	1978 to 1982
17	Y Konishi	1982 to 1986
17	B Ferguson	1993 to 1996

MOST TESTS AS CAPTAIN

Tests	Captain	Span
16	M Kunda	1993 to 1998
16	A McCormick	1998 to 1999
13	T Hayashi	1984 to 1987
13	S Hirao	1989 to 1991
13	Y Motoki	1996 to 1997
11	T Miuchi	2002 to 2003

MOST TESTS IN INDIVIDUAL POSITIONS

Position	Player	Tests	Span
Full-back	T Matsuda	35	1992 to 2003
Wing	T Masuho	47	1991 to 2001
Centre	Y Motoki	59	1991 to 2003
Fly-half	K Hirose	36	1994 to 2003
Scrum-half	W Murata	36	1991 to 2003
Prop	S Hasagawa	33	1997 to 2003
Hooker	M Kunda	43	1991 to 1999
Lock	Y Sakuraba	44	1986 to 1999
Flanker	H Kajihara	31	1989 to 1997
No 8	Sinali Latu	27	1996 to 2003

MOST POINTS IN TESTS

Points	Player	Tests	Career
353	K Hirose	36	1994 to 2003
307	T Kurihara	22	2000 to 2002
190	D Ohata	36	1996 to 2003
152	T Masuho	47	1991 to 2001
115	T Hosokawa	11	1990 to 1993

MOST TRIES IN TESTS

Tries	Player	Tests	Career
38	D Ohata	36	1996 to 2003
30	T Masuho	47	1991 to 2001
20	T Kurihara	22	2000 to 2003
19	T Itoh	19	1963 to 1974
18	Y Yoshida	26	1988 to 1995

MOST CONVERSIONS IN TESTS

Cons	Player	Tests	Career
66	T Kurihara	22	2000 to 2003
60	K Hirose	36	1994 to 2003
17	Y Yamaguchi	13	1967 to 1973
14	N Ueyama	21	1973 to 1980
14	T Hosokawa	11	1990 to 1993

MOST PENALTY GOALS IN TESTS

Penalties	Player	Tests	Career
70	K Hirose	36	1994 to 2003
25	T Kurihara	22	2000 to 2003
24	T Hosokawa	11	1990 to 1993
18	Y Yamaguchi	13	1967 to 1973
16	N Ueyama	21	1973 to 1980

MOST DROPPED GOALS IN TESTS

Drops	Player	Tests	Career
3	Y Matsuo	24	1974 to 1984
2	K Matsuo	24	1986 to 1995
2	K Iwabuchi	19	1997 to 2002

Career Records of Japan International Players
(up to 30 September 2003)

PLAYER	*Debut*	*Caps*	*T*	*C*	*P*	*D*	*Pts*
Backs:							
S Fuchigama	2000 v I	5	3	2	1	0	22
K Hirose	1994 v SK	36	4	60	70	1	353
T Kurihara	2000 v Fj	22	20	66	25	0	307
A Miller	2002 v Ru	6	5	16	0	0	57
T Matsuda	1992 v HK	40	11	0	0	0	55
Y Motoki	1991 v US	61	7	0	0	0	35
W Murata	1991 v US	36	5	13	11	0	84
H Nanba	2000 v Fj	23	6	0	0	0	30
G Konia	2003 v US	3	1	0	0	0	5
D Ohata	1996 v SK	36	38	0	0	0	190
H Onozawa	2001 v W	13	11	0	0	0	55
R Parkinson	2003 v Ru	3	0	0	0	0	0
Y Shinomiya	2003 v US	3	2	0	0	0	10
Y Sonoda	2000 v Fj	14	1	0	0	0	5
S Tsukida	2001 v SK	9	0	3	1	0	9
T Yoshida	2002 v Tg	4	3	0	0	0	15
Forwards:							
M Amino	2000 v SK	7	0	0	0	0	0
R Asano	2003 v A	2	0	0	0	0	0
S Hasagawa	1997 v HK	36	1	1	1	0	10
Y Hisadomi	2002 v Ru	5	0	0	0	0	0
T Ito	1996 v HK	49	6	0	0	0	30
H Kiso	2001 v CT	7	0	0	0	0	0
K Kubo	2000 v I	13	3	0	0	0	15
H Matsuo	2003 v A	5	0	0	0	0	0
T Miuchi	2002 v Ru	11	1	0	0	0	5
N T Okubo	1999 v Tg	16	0	0	0	0	0
A Parker	2002 v Ru	13	2	0	0	0	10
Y Saito	2001 v CT	12	4	0	0	0	20
M Sakata	1996 v C	30	4	0	0	0	20
H Tanuma	1996 v SK	40	2	0	0	0	10
M Toyoyama	2000 v Fj	21	3	0	0	0	15
L Vatuvai	2001 v SK	14	7	0	0	0	35
Y Watanabe	1996 v HK	20	4	0	0	0	20
M Yamamoto	2002 v Ru	10	0	0	0	0	0
R Yamamura	2001 v W	5	1	0	0	0	5

SAMOA INTERNATIONAL STATISTICS

(to 30 September 2003)

Match Records

MOST CONSECUTIVE TEST WINS

8 1990 SK, *Tg* 1, J, *Tg* 2, *Fj* 1991 *Tg*, *Fj*, *W*

MOST CONSECUTIVE TESTS WITHOUT DEFEAT

Matches	*Wins*	*Draws*	*Period*
8	8	0	1990 to 1991

MOST POINTS IN A MATCH

by the team

Pts	*Opponents*	*Venue*	*Year*
74	South Korea	Tokyo	1990
68	Japan	Apia	2000
62	Tonga	Apia	1997
55	West Germany	Bonn	1989
47	Japan	Tokyo	2001
43	Japan	Apia	1999
43	Italy	Apia	2000

by a player

Pts	*Player*	*Opponents*	*Venue*	*Year*
23	A Aiolupo	South Korea	Tokyo	1990
23	S Leaega	Japan	Apia	1999
23	T Samania	Italy	Apia	2000
22	D J Kellett	Tonga	Moamoa	1994
21	M Vaea	Fiji	Apia	1991
20	E Seveali'i	Japan	Apia	2000

MOST TRIES IN A MATCH

by the team

Tries	*Opponents*	*Venue*	*Year*
13	South Korea	Tokyo	1990
10	West Germany	Bonn	1989
10	Tonga	Apia	1997
10	Japan	Apia	2000
8	Tonga	Apia	1991
7	Japan	Tokyo	2001
7	Canada	Apia	2000

by a player

Tries	*Player*	*Opponents*	*Venue*	*Year*
4	T Fa'amasino	Tonga	Apia	1991
4	E Seveali'i	Japan	Apia	2000
3	T Fa'amasino	South Korea	Tokyo	1990
3	B P Lima	Fiji	Apia	1991
3	A So'oalo	Tonga	Apia	1997
3	D Feaunati	Namibia	Windhoek	2003

MOST CONVERSIONS IN A MATCH

by the team

Cons	*Opponents*	*Venue*	*Year*
8	South Korea	Tokyo	1990
6	West Germany	Bonn	1989
6	Tonga	Apia	1997
6	Japan	Apia	2000
6	Japan	Tokyo	2001
5	Belgium	Brussels	1989
5	Japan	Apia	1990
5	Wales	Cardiff	1999

by a player

Cons	*Player*	*Opponents*	*Venue*	*Year*
8	A Aiolupo	South Korea	Tokyo	1990
6	T Vili	Japan	Apia	2000
6	E Va'a	Japan	Tokyo	2001
5	A Aiolupo	Belgium	Brussels	1989
5	A Aiolupo	Japan	Apia	1990
5	S Leaega	Tonga	Apia	1997
5	S Leaega	Wales	Cardiff	1999

MOST PENALTIES IN A MATCH

by the team

Penalties	*Opponents*	*Venue*	*Year*
5	Tonga	Moamoa	1994
5	Wales	Moamoa	1994
5	Argentina	East London	1995
5	Japan	Osaka	1999
4	Tonga	Suva	1988
4	Fiji	Apia	1997
4	Japan	Apia	1999
4	Italy	Apia	2000
4	Tonga	Nuku'alofa	2002

by a player

Penalties	*Player*	*Opponents*	*Venue*	*Year*
5	D J Kellett	Tonga	Moamoa	1994
5	D J Kellett	Wales	Moamoa	1994
5	D J Kellett	Argentina	East London	1995
5	S Leaega	Japan	Osaka	1999
4	A Aiolupo	Tonga	Suva	1988

4	E Va'a	Fiji	Apia	1997
4	S Leaega	Japan	Apia	1999
4	S Leaega	Italy	Apia	2000
4	E Va'a	Tonga	Nuku'alofa	2002

MOST DROPPED GOALS IN A MATCH

by the team

Drops	*Opponents*	*Venue*	*Year*
1	Fiji	Nadi	1981
1	South Korea	Tokyo	1990
1	Fiji	Apia	1991
1	Scotland	Murrayfield	1991
1	Tonga	Moamoa	1994

by a player

Drops	*Player*	*Opponents*	*Venue*	*Year*
1	A Palamo	Fiji	Nadi	1981
1	J Ah Kuoi	South Korea	Tokyo	1990
1	S J Bachop	Fiji	Apia	1991
1	S J Bachop	Scotland	Murrayfield	1991
1	D J Kellett	Tonga	Moamoa	1994

Career Records

MOST CAPPED PLAYERS

Caps	*Player*	*Career Span*
60	T Vaega	1986 to 2001
50	B P Lima	1991 to 2003
37	A Aiolupo	1983 to 1994
35	P R Lam	1991 to 1999
34	P P Fatialofa	1988 to 1996
31	O Palepoi	1998 to 2003
29	T Leota	1997 to 2003
29	S To'omalatai	1985 to 1995
28	S Vaifale	1989 to 1997
27	T Salesa	1979 to 1989
26	P J Paramore	1991 to 2001
26	S Sititi	1999 to 2003

MOST POINTS IN TESTS

Points	*Player*	*Tests*	*Career*
180	A Aiolupo	37	1983 to 1994
160	S Leaega	17	1997 to 2002
157	D J Kellett	13	1993 to 1995
135	E Va'a	24	1996 to 2003
129	B P Lima	50	1991 to 2003
114	T Salesa	27	1979 to 1989
75	A So'oalo	19	1996 to 2001
73	T Vili	16	1999 to 2001
66	T Vaega	60	1986 to 2001
64	S J Bachop	18	1991 to 1999

MOST TRIES IN TESTS

Tries	*Player*	*Tests*	*Career*
27	B P Lima	50	1991 to 2003
15	T Vaega	60	1986 to 2001
15	A So'oalo	19	1996 to 2001
13	R Koko	22	1983 to 1994
11	T Fa'amasino	20	1988 to 1996
10	G E Leaupepe	25	1995 to 1999

MOST CONVERSIONS IN TESTS

Cons	*Player*	*Tests*	*Career*
35	A Aiolupo	37	1983 to 1994
26	S Leaega	17	1997 to 2002
23	E Va'a	24	1996 to 2003
18	D J Kellett	13	1993 to 1995
14	T Salesa	27	1979 to 1989
14	T Vili	16	1999 to 2001

MOST PENALTY GOALS IN TESTS

Penalties	*Player*	*Tests*	*Career*
35	D J Kellett	13	1993 to 1995
31	S Leaega	17	1997 to 2002
27	A Aiolupo	37	1983 to 1994
23	E Va'a	24	1996 to 2003
22	T Salesa	27	1979 to 1989

MOST DROPPED GOALS IN TESTS

Drops	*Player*	*Tests*	*Career*
2	S J Bachop	18	1991 to 1999
1	A Palamo	9	1979 to 1982
1	J Ah Kuoi	5	1987 to 1990
1	D J Kellett	13	1993 to 1995

Career Records Of Samoa International Players
(up to 30 September 2003)

PLAYER	*Debut*	*Caps*	*T*	*C*	*P*	*D*	*Pts*
Backs:							
L M Fa'atau	2000 v Fj	10	3	0	0	0	15
T Fanolua	1996 v NZ	21	6	0	0	0	30
R Fanuatanu	2003 v I	1	1	0	0	0	5
D S Feaunati	2003 v Nm	1	3	0	0	0	15
F Fili	2003 v I	2	0	0	0	0	0
S Leaega	1997 v Tg	17	3	26	31	0	160
B P Lima	1991 v Tg	50	27	0	0	0	129
C Manu	2002 v Fj	4	0	0	0	0	0
D A Rasmussen	2003 v I	2	0	0	0	0	0
E Seveali'i	2000 v Fj	14	9	0	0	0	45
S So'oialo	1998 v Tg	24	4	0	0	0	20
S Tagicakibau	2003 v Nm	1	1	0	0	0	5
A Tuilagi	2002 v Fj	3	0	0	0	0	0
F Tuilagi	1992 v Tg	16	2	0	0	0	10
D Tyrell	2000 v Fj	9	1	0	0	0	5
E Va'a	1996 v I	24	4	23	23	0	135
T Vili	1999 v C	16	3	14	10	0	73
Forwards:							
M Fa'asavalu	2002 v SA	3	0	0	0	0	0
S F Lafaiali'i	2001 v Tg	11	0	0	0	0	0
F Lalomilo	2001 v I	2	0	0	0	0	0
K Lealamanua	2000 v Fj	16	1	0	0	0	5
T Leota	1997 v Tg	29	1	0	0	0	5
T Leupolu	2001 v I	9	0	0	0	0	0
J Meredith	2001 v I	9	1	0	0	0	5
O Palepoi	1998 v Tg	31	1	0	0	0	5
P Petia	2003 v Nm	1	0	0	0	0	0
M M Schwalger	2000 v W	3	0	0	0	0	0
P Segi	2001 v Fj	9	1	0	0	0	5
S Sititi	1999 v J	26	6	0	0	0	30
G Stowers	2001 v I	1	0	0	0	0	0
P Tapelu	2002 v SA	1	0	0	0	0	0
J Tomuli	2001 v I	9	0	0	0	0	0
D Tuiavai'i	2003 v Nm	1	0	0	0	0	0
H Tuilagi	2002 v Fj	4	0	0	0	0	0
S Vaili	2002 v Fj	4	0	0	0	0	0
K Viliamu	2001 v I	5	1	0	0	0	5

FIJI INTERNATIONAL STATISTICS

(up to 30 September 2003)

Match Records

MOST CONSECUTIVE TEST WINS

6 1955 *WS 1*, *WS 2*, *WS 3*, 1957 *M 1*, *M 2*, 1958 *Tg*

MOST CONSECUTIVE TESTS WITHOUT DEFEAT

Matches	*Wins*	*Draws*	*Period*
6	6	0	1955 to 1958

MOST POINTS IN A MATCH

by the team

Pts	*Opponents*	*Venue*	*Year*
120	Niue	Apia	1983
113	Solomon Islands	Port Moresby	1969
88	Papua New Guinea	Port Moresby	1969
86	Solomons Islands	Apia	1983
86	Papua New Guinea	Suva	1979
79	Papua New Guinea	Port Moresby	1969
76	Belgium	Liege	1989

by a player

Pts	*Player*	*Opponents*	*Venue*	*Year*
36	S Koroduadua	Niue	Apia	1983
25	N Little	Italy	L'Aquila	1999
24	S Sikivou	Solomons	Port Moresby	1969
24	T Makutu	Papua New Guinea	Suva	1979
24	S Laulau	Solomons	Apia	1983
24	N Little	Hong Kong	Aberdeen	1996
23	N Little	Samoa	Tokyo	2001
23	N Little	Italy	Lautoka	2000

MOST TRIES IN A MATCH

by the team

Tries	*Opponents*	*Venue*	*Year*
25	Solomons Islands	Port Moresby	1969
21	Niue	Apia	1983
20	Papua New Guinea	Port Moresby	1969
19	Papua New Guinea	Port Moresby	1969
18	Papua New Guinea	Suva	1979
16	Solomons	Apia	1983
14	Belgium	Liege	1989

by a player

Tries	*Player*	*Opponents*	*Venue*	*Year*
6	T Makutu	Papua New Guinea	Suva	1979
6	S Laulau	Solomons	Apia	1983
5	G Sailosi	Papua New Guinea	Port Moresby	1969

MOST CONVERSIONS IN A MATCH

by the team

Cons	*Opponents*	*Venue*	*Year*
19	Papua New Guinea	Port Moresby	1969
18	Niue	Apia	1983
14	Papua New Guinea	Port Moresby	1969
11	Papua New Guinea	Port Moresby	1969
11	Solomons	Apia	1983
10	Belgium	Liege	1989
8	Namibia	Beziers	1999

by a player

Cons	*Player*	*Opponents*	*Venue*	*Year*
18	S Koroduadua	Niue	Apia	1983
12	S Sikivou	Solomons	Port Moresby	1969
11	I Musunamasi	Solomons	Apia	1983
10	S Koroduadua	Belgium	Liege	1989

MOST PENALTIES IN A MATCH

by the team

Penalties	*Opponents*	*Venue*	*Year*
7	Samoa	Toyo	2001
6	Tonga	Nuku'alofa	2001
6	Tonga	Nuku'alofa	2000
6	Hong Kong	Aberdeen	1996
6	Tonga	Nuku'alofa	1967

by a player

Penalties	*Player*	*Opponents*	*Venue*	*Year*
7	N Little	Samoa	Tokyo	2001
6	I Tabualevu	Tonga	Nuku'alofa	1967
6	N Little	Hong Kong	Aberdeen	1996
6	N Little	Tonga	Nuku'alofa	2000
6	N Little	Tonga	Nuku'alofa	2001

MOST DROPPED GOALS IN A MATCH

by the team

Drops	Opponents	Venue	Year
3	Romania	Brive	1991
3	W Samoa	Nadi	1994

by a player

Drops	Player	Opponents	Venue	Year
3	O Turuva	W Samoa	Nadi	1994
2	T Rabaka	Romania	Brive	1991

Career Records

MOST CAPPED PLAYERS

Caps	Player	Career Span
49	N Little	1996 to 2003
47	E Katalau	1995 to 2003
44	J Veitayaki	1994 to 2003
43	J Rauluni	1995 to 2003
42	I Tawake	1986 to 1999
40	G Smith	1995 to 2003
39	S Raiwalui	1997 to 2002
37	W Serevi	1989 to 2003
37	A Mocelutu	1993 to 2003
36	I Savai	1984 to 1995
35	I Rasila	1992 to 2003

MOST POINTS IN TESTS

Points	Player	Tests	Career
529	N Little	49	1996 to 2003
250	S Koroduadua	27	1982 to 1991
216	W Serevi	37	1989 to 2003
80	S Laulau	32	1985 to 1991
80	V Satala	27	1999 to 2002
80	F Lasagavibau	23	1997 to 2002

MOST TRIES IN TESTS

Tries	Player	Tests	Career
20	S Laulau	32	1980 to 1985
16	V Satala	27	1999 to 2002
16	F Lasagavibau	23	1997 to 2002
12	M Bari	18	1995 to 1999
11	W Serevi	37	1989 to 2003
11	K Salusalu	15	1982 to 1990

MOST CONVERSIONS IN TESTS

Cons	Player	Tests	Career
93	N Little	49	1996 to 2003
56	S Koroduadua	27	1982 to 1991
39	W Serevi	37	1989 to 2003
16	S Sikivou	6	1969 to 1973

MOST PENALTY GOALS IN TESTS

Penalties	Player	Tests	Career
109	N Little	49	1996 to 2003
41	S Koroduadua	27	1982 to 1991
26	W Serevi	37	1989 to 2003
10	I Batibasaga	13	1970 to 1979
9	E Rokowailoa	17	1982 to 1993

MOST DROPPED GOALS IN TESTS

Drops	Player	Tests	Career
6	O Turuva	11	1990 to 1999
5	S Koroduadua	27	1982 to 1991
3	W Serevi	37	1989 to 2003

Career Records of Fiji International Players
(up to 30 September 2003)

PLAYER	Debut	Caps	T	C	P	D	Pts
Backs:							
S Baikeinuku	2000 v J	11	2	0	0	0	10
R Caucaunibuca	2003 v Arg	2	5	0	0	0	25
V Delasau	2000 v US	13	8	0	0	0	40
F Lasagavibau	1997 v NZ	23	16	0	0	0	80
N Little	1996 v SA	49	2	93	109	2	529
N Ligairi	2000 v Tg	20	9	0	0	0	45
S Leawere	2003 v Tg	3	1	0	0	0	5
I Mow	2002 v Sm	5	2	0	0	0	10
A Nariva	2002 v S	3	0	0	0	0	0

J Narruhn	2002 v Sm	8	3	3	6	0	39
E Ruivadra	2002 v Tg	5	1	0	0	0	5
J Rauluni	1995 v C	43	6	0	0	0	30
M Rauluni	1996 v M	18	3	0	0	0	15
S Rokini	2000 v J	11	1	0	0	0	5
S Rabaka	1992 v W	31	3	0	0	0	14
S Rabeni	2000 v J	11	1	0	0	0	5
V Satala	1999 v C	27	16	0	0	0	80
W Serevi	1989 v Be	37	11	39	26	3	216
A Tuilevu	1996 v SA	14	10	0	0	0	50
A Uluinayau	1996 v SA	34	6	1	0	0	32
M Vunibaka	1999 v C	14	7	0	0	0	35
Forwards:							
P Biutanaseva	1999 v Sp	14	0	0	0	0	0
A Doviverata	1999 v Sp	24	4	0	0	0	20
I Domolailai	2001 v I	2	0	0	0	0	0
M Davu	2000 v I	2	0	0	0	0	0
V Gadolo	2000 v J	7	0	0	0	0	0
E Katalau	1995 v C	47	6	0	0	0	30
S Koyamaibole	2001 v Sm	19	1	0	0	0	5
K Leawere	2002 v S	5	0	0	0	0	0
V Maimuri	2003 v Arg	1	0	0	0	0	0
A Mocelutu	1993 v S	37	4	0	0	0	20
A Naevo	1996 v M	32	4	0	0	0	20
R Nyholt	2001 v F	11	0	0	0	0	0
H Qiodravu	2000 v US	11	0	0	0	0	0
S Raiwalui	1997 v NZ	39	3	0	0	0	15
I Rasila	1992 v WS	35	4	0	0	0	20
I Rawaqa	2002 v Sm	8	1	0	0	0	5
K Salawa	2003 v Tg	4	0	0	0	0	0
N Seru	2003 v Arg	2	0	0	0	0	0
K Sewabu	1999 v C	21	3	0	0	0	15
G Smith	1995 v W	40	1	0	0	0	5
S Tawake	1992 v WS	31	1	0	0	0	5
J Veitayaki	1994 v M	44	3	0	0	0	15

WOMEN'S TEST SEASON REVIEW 2002-03

A Year of Transition across the Globe

Nicola Goodwin

The 2002-03 season was one of great transition for women's rugby across the globe. After the success of the 2002 World Cup in Barcelona, where New Zealand emphasised their continued dominance, this season saw the major nations bring in new players and coaching personnel while the smaller nations benefited from a more relaxed and flexible international schedule.

The highlight of the past year has been the emergence of new names into the international women's scene. South Africa benefited from increased support from their governing bodies by forming their inaugural international squad for the visit of an England Development Squad in May and June. The South African President's XV went down 45-0 against England in Pongola, but it was a very proud moment for all involved in bringing to game to clubs and on to the international scene. The extensive tour also gave England the opportunity of taking on Natal and Pretoria and introducing both the South African public and club players to the women's game. South Africa has now been firmly established on the touring map and English Premiership side Richmond visited the nation in September, taking on the current champions, the Goodwood Gazelles, and Western Province.

Australia continued to strengthen and expand their domestic game with the Women's Invitational Tournament being staged at the Sydney Academy of Sport in July. Sydney Gold were crowned champions, but organisers were boosted by the representatives from Western Australia, Northern Territory and Australian Services. The three-day tournament also featured the newly formed Tasmanian Women's Rugby Union, a representative side who look set to have a long future in the game.

The Canada Cup returned this year with America and England competing against the home nation. For the first time the women's tournament was held alongside the men's competition for the Churchill Cup, which boosted the crowds, publicity and general awareness of the games. England were crowned women's champions and consolidated their second-placed international ranking after defeating Canada and America, now working with former women's international and Berkeley coach Kathy Flores, in the round-robin stage.

Canada's 18-13 defeat of old rivals the United States in the round-robin of the Churchill Cup gave a boost to the women's game across the Big Country and they went on to give England a stern test in the competition's grand final. England had to rely on a pushover try by Georgia Stevens in the fifth minute of added time for their 21-18 victory. Canada are following the example of the European nations by forming Youth Under 23 and Under 19 squads who will be attending regular training camps to boost the level of emerging rugby.

The Six Nations Championship started in style as England's women played as an international side at Twickenham for the first time. Their 57-0 victory over the 2002 champions France also emphasised their determination to take the crown, and they maintained their dominance throughout the tournament. Scotland were delighted with a second-place finish, the improved domestic structure, new coaching panel and closer links to the SRU paying dividends.

Ireland's victory against Spain was one of the shocks of the tournament. They were delighted to finally avoid the wooden spoon and they have undoubtedly started to see the results of an improved and increased provincial structure which has brought the exile players back home throughout the season. Spain were expected to have repeated the benefits from the excellent organisation and popularity of the World Cup, but this was not reflected in performance or results. However, playing numbers continue to increase amongst the club structure and they are certain to return as a dominant force.

Elsewhere in Europe, the strength of domestic rugby continues to increase in Holland and Sweden. In the Women's European Nations' Cup, Holland beat near neighbours Germany by 19-12 and the Dutch clubs continue to be popular touring destinations for teams from across Europe. A number of new European nations are continuing to work on introducing women's rugby with Poland, Portugal and Switzerland all introducing club rugby and women's workshops. Hungary is enjoying a surge in junior women's rugby and Bulgaria, Belgium, Norway and Denmark are all registering more than 200 women's players apiece. Kazakhstan have been a major force in the women's game for many years boosted by the popularity of the sport amongst their army personnel, but Russia is one nation experiencing a continued interest in rugby with more than 500 female players now registered.

The New Zealand Maori side proved unbeatable at the Hong Kong Sevens and, despite the outbreak of the SARS virus, the tournament once again gave women's rugby the chance to shine on the global stage. The Maoris beat England 27-0 in the final, and gave an outstanding display of fast and skilful sevens in front of a packed crowd and the world's media. The tournament continues to be the highlight of many players' international careers and gives nations such as Fiji, America, Kazakhstan and the Arabian Gulf the chance to come face to face in competitive rugby.

The future growth of women's rugby across the globe looks set to be centred on the Indian, South American and African continents. Amazing numbers of new female players are being registered by governing bodies and they look set to follow the pattern of progression highlighted by South Africa if they can gain similar assistance from the established nations through twinning schemes and international and domestic tours. Brazil, Chile, Venezuela and Argentina now have almost 200 female players each, and Zimbabwe and Madagascar are recording numbers of more than 500

England full-back Chris Diver swerves past France's Catherine Devillers during the Women's Six Nations match at Twickenham in February. England won the match 57-0 on their way to the Grand Slam.

women playing the game. The long history of rugby's popularity amongst the ex-pat populations is also boosting the fairer game, with the Arabian Gulf and Israel also finding that more and more women are attracted to the sport. The nations to watch in the future are undoubtedly India, Trinidad & Tobago and Fiji with 900, 600 and 800 registered players respectively. The Fijian women have followed their male counterparts by establishing a reputation as decent sevens players but they are also proving extremely adept at the traditional form.

New Zealand retain their top ranking in the international women's rugby world and finished the 2002-03 season as world champions, number one in the world rankings and Hong Kong Sevens Champions. In October they will face a World Women's XV in two NPC curtain raiser matches in Auckland and Whangerei. This will be a first for the international game and a perfect indicator of the continued progression of women's rugby.

Six Nations Results 2003

15 February: Wales 34, Spain 0; Scotland 25, Ireland 0; England 57, France 0; **21 February:** Wales 7, England 69; **22 February:** France 14, Scotland 19; Spain 0, Ireland 16; **8 March:** Ireland 0, France 20; **9 March:** England 74, Spain 0; Scotland 9, Wales 8; **21 March:** Wales 12, Ireland 0; **22 March:** England 31, Scotland 0; Spain 7, France 27; **28 March:** France 34, Wales 7; Ireland 3, England 47; **29 March:** Scotland 48, Spain 7

Six Nations 2003: Final Table

	P	*W*	*D*	*L*	*F*	*A*	*Pts*
England	5	5	0	0	278	10	10
Scotland	5	4	0	1	101	60	8
France	5	3	0	2	95	90	6
Wales	5	2	0	3	68	112	4
Ireland	5	1	0	4	19	104	2
Spain	5	0	0	5	14	199	0

Churchill Cup 2003

14 June: Canada 5, England 10; **18 June:** United States 8, England 15; **21 June:** Canada 18, United States 13

Churchill Cup 2003: Final Table

	P	*W*	*D*	*L*	*F*	*A*	*Pts*
England	2	2	0	0	25	13	4
Canada	2	1	0	1	23	23	0
United States	2	0	0	2	21	33	2

Churchill Cup Final 2003

28 June at Thunderbird Stadium, Vancouver: England 21, Canada 18

INTERNATIONAL RECORDS

Results of International Matches
(up to 30 September 2003)

Cap matches involving senior executive council member unions only.
Years for International Championship matches are for the second half of the season: eg 1972 means season 1971-72. Years for matches against touring teams from the Southern Hemisphere refer to the actual year of the match.
Points-scoring was first introduced in 1886, when an International Board was formed by Scotland, Ireland and Wales. Points values varied between countries until 1890, when England agreed to join the Board, and uniform values were adopted.

Northern Hemisphere seasons	*Try*	*Conversion*	*Penalty goal*	*Dropped goal*	*Goal from mark*
1890-91	1	2	2	3	3
1891-92 to 1892-93	2	3	3	4	4
1893-94 to 1904-05	3	2	3	4	4
1905-06 to 1947-48	3	2	3	4	3
1948-49 to 1970-71	3	2	3	3	3
1971-72 to 1991-92	4	2	3	3	3*
1992-93 onwards	5	2	3	3	–

**The goal from mark ceased to exist when the free-kick clause was introduced, 1977-78.*
WC indicates a fixture played during the Rugby World Cup finals. LC indicates a fixture played in the Latin Cup. TN indicates a fixture played in the Tri Nations.

ENGLAND v SCOTLAND

Played 120 England won 63, Scotland won 40, Drawn 17
Highest scores England 43-3 in 2001, Scotland 33-6 in 1986
Biggest wins England 43-3 in 2001, Scotland 33-6 in 1986

1871 Raeburn Place (Edinburgh) **Scotland** 1G 1T to 1T
1872 The Oval (London) **England** 1G 1DG 2T to 1DG
1873 Glasgow **Drawn** no score
1874 The Oval **England** 1DG to 1T
1875 Raeburn Place **Drawn** no score
1876 The Oval **England** 1G 1T to 0
1877 Raeburn Place **Scotland** 1 DG to 0
1878 The Oval **Drawn** no score
1879 Raeburn Place **Drawn** Scotland 1DG England 1G
1880 Manchester **England** 2G 3T to 1G
1881 Raeburn Place **Drawn** Scotland 1G 1T England 1DG 1T
1882 Manchester **Scotland** 2T to 0
1883 Raeburn Place **England** 2T to 1T
1884 Blackheath (London) **England** 1G to 1T
1885 No Match
1886 Raeburn Place **Drawn** no score
1887 Manchester **Drawn** 1T each
1888 No Match
1889 No Match
1890 Raeburn Place **England** 1G 1T to 0
1891 Richmond (London) **Scotland** 9-3
1892 Raeburn Place **England** 5-0
1893 Leeds **Scotland** 8-0
1894 Raeburn Place **Scotland** 6-0
1895 Richmond **Scotland** 6-3
1896 Glasgow **Scotland** 11-0
1897 Manchester **England** 12-3
1898 Powderhall (Edinburgh) **Drawn** 3-3
1899 Blackheath **Scotland** 5-0
1900 Inverleith (Edinburgh) **Drawn** 0-0
1901 Blackheath **Scotland** 18-3
1902 Inverleith **England** 6-3
1903 Richmond **Scotland** 10-6
1904 Inverleith **Scotland** 6-3
1905 Richmond **Scotland** 8-0
1906 Inverleith **England** 9-3
1907 Blackheath **Scotland** 8-3
1908 Inverleith **Scotland** 16-10
1909 Richmond **Scotland** 18-8
1910 Inverleith **England** 14-5

1911 Twickenham **England** 13-8
1912 Inverleith **Scotland** 8-3
1913 Twickenham **England** 3-0
1914 Inverleith **England** 16-15
1920 Twickenham **England** 13-4
1921 Inverleith **England** 18-0
1922 Twickenham **England** 11-5
1923 Inverleith **England** 8-6
1924 Twickenham **England** 19-0
1925 Murrayfield **Scotland** 14-11
1926 Twickenham **Scotland** 17-9
1927 Murrayfield **Scotland** 21-13
1928 Twickenham **England** 6-0
1929 Murrayfield **Scotland** 12-6
1930 Twickenham **Drawn** 0-0
1931 Murrayfield **Scotland** 28-19
1932 Twickenham **England** 16-3
1933 Murrayfield **Scotland** 3-0
1934 Twickenham **England** 6-3
1935 Murrayfield **Scotland** 10-7
1936 Twickenham **England** 9-8
1937 Murrayfield **England** 6-3
1938 Twickenham **Scotland** 21-16
1939 Murrayfield **England** 9-6
1947 Twickenham **England** 24-5
1948 Murrayfield **Scotland** 6-3
1949 Twickenham **England** 19-3
1950 Murrayfield **Scotland** 13-11
1951 Twickenham **England** 5-3
1952 Murrayfield **England** 19-3
1953 Twickenham **England** 26-8
1954 Murrayfield **England** 13-3
1955 Twickenham **England** 9-6
1956 Murrayfield **England** 11-6
1957 Twickenham **England** 16-3
1958 Murrayfield **Drawn** 3-3
1959 Twickenham **Drawn** 3-3
1960 Murrayfield **England** 21-12
1961 Twickenham **England** 6-0
1962 Murrayfield **Drawn** 3-3
1963 Twickenham **England** 10-8
1964 Murrayfield **Scotland** 15-6
1965 Twickenham **Drawn** 3-3
1966 Murrayfield **Scotland** 6-3
1967 Twickenham **England** 27-14
1968 Murrayfield **England** 8-6
1969 Twickenham **England** 8-3
1970 Murrayfield **Scotland** 14-5
1971 Twickenham **Scotland** 16-15
1971 Murrayfield **Scotland** 26-6
Special centenary match – non-championship
1972 Murrayfield **Scotland** 23-9
1973 Twickenham **England** 20-13
1974 Murrayfield **Scotland** 16-14
1975 Twickenham **England** 7-6
1976 Murrayfield **Scotland** 22-12
1977 Twickenham **England** 26-6
1978 Murrayfield **England** 15-0
1979 Twickenham **Drawn** 7-7
1980 Murrayfield **England** 30-18
1981 Twickenham **England** 23-17
1982 Murrayfield **Drawn** 9-9
1983 Twickenham **Scotland** 22-12
1984 Murrayfield **Scotland** 18-6
1985 Twickenham **England** 10-7
1986 Murrayfield **Scotland** 33-6
1987 Twickenham **England** 21-12
1988 Murrayfield **England** 9-6
1989 Twickenham **Drawn** 12-12
1990 Murrayfield **Scotland** 13-7
1991 Twickenham **England** 21-12
1991 Murrayfield *WC* **England** 9-6
1992 Murrayfield **England** 25-7
1993 Twickenham **England** 26-12
1994 Murrayfield **England** 15-14
1995 Twickenham **England** 24-12
1996 Murrayfield **England** 18-9
1997 Twickenham **England** 41-13
1998 Murrayfield **England** 34-20
1999 Twickenham **England** 24-21
2000 Murrayfield **Scotland** 19-13
2001 Twickenham **England** 43-3
2002 Murrayfield **England** 29-3
2003 Twickenham **England** 40-9

ENGLAND v IRELAND

Played 116 England won 69, Ireland won 39, Drawn 8
Highest scores England 50-18 in 2000, Ireland 26-21 in 1974
Biggest wins England 46-6 in 1997, Ireland 22-0 in 1947

1875 The Oval (London) **England** 1G 1DG 1T to 0
1876 Dublin **England** 1G 1T to 0
1877 The Oval **England** 2G 2T to 0
1878 Dublin **England** 2G 1T to 0
1879 The Oval **England** 2G 1DG 2T to 0
1880 Dublin **England** 1G 1T to 1T
1881 Manchester **England** 2G 2T to 0
1882 Dublin **Drawn** 2T each
1883 Manchester **England** 1G 3T to 1T
1884 Dublin **England** 1G to 0
1885 Manchester **England** 2T to 1T
1886 Dublin **England** 1T to 0
1887 Dublin **Ireland** 2G to 0
1888 No Match
1889 No Match
1890 Blackheath (London) **England** 3T to 0
1891 Dublin **England** 9-0
1892 Manchester **England** 7-0
1893 Dublin **England** 4-0
1894 Blackheath **Ireland** 7-5
1895 Dublin **England** 6-3
1896 Leeds **Ireland** 10-4
1897 Dublin **Ireland** 13-9
1898 Richmond (London) **Ireland** 9-6
1899 Dublin **Ireland** 6-0

1900 Richmond **England** 15-4
1901 Dublin **Ireland** 10-6
1902 Leicester **England** 6-3
1903 Dublin **Ireland** 6-0
1904 Blackheath **England** 19-0
1905 Cork **Ireland** 17-3
1906 Leicester **Ireland** 16-6
1907 Dublin **Ireland** 17-9
1908 Richmond **England** 13-3
1909 Dublin **England** 11-5
1910 Twickenham **Drawn** 0-0
1911 Dublin **Ireland** 3-0
1912 Twickenham **England** 15-0
1913 Dublin **England** 15-4
1914 Twickenham **England** 17-12
1920 Dublin **England** 14-11
1921 Twickenham **England** 15-0
1922 Dublin **England** 12-3
1923 Leicester **England** 23-5
1924 Belfast **England** 14-3
1925 Twickenham **Drawn** 6-6
1926 Dublin **Ireland** 19-15
1927 Twickenham **England** 8-6
1928 Dublin **England** 7-6
1929 Twickenham **Ireland** 6-5
1930 Dublin **Ireland** 4-3
1931 Twickenham **Ireland** 6-5
1932 Dublin **England** 11-8
1933 Twickenham **England** 17-6
1934 Dublin **England** 13-3
1935 Twickenham **England** 14-3
1936 Dublin **Ireland** 6-3
1937 Twickenham **England** 9-8
1938 Dublin **England** 36-14
1939 Twickenham **Ireland** 5-0
1947 Dublin **Ireland** 22-0
1948 Twickenham **Ireland** 11-10
1949 Dublin **Ireland** 14-5
1950 Twickenham **England** 3-0
1951 Dublin **Ireland** 3-0
1952 Twickenham **England** 3-0
1953 Dublin **Drawn** 9-9
1954 Twickenham **England** 14-3
1955 Dublin **Drawn** 6-6
1956 Twickenham **England** 20-0
1957 Dublin **England** 6-0
1958 Twickenham **England** 6-0
1959 Dublin **England** 3-0
1960 Twickenham **England** 8-5
1961 Dublin **Ireland** 11-8
1962 Twickenham **England** 16-0
1963 Dublin **Drawn** 0-0
1964 Twickenham **Ireland** 18-5
1965 Dublin **Ireland** 5-0
1966 Twickenham **Drawn** 6-6
1967 Dublin **England** 8-3
1968 Twickenham **Drawn** 9-9
1969 Dublin **Ireland** 17-15
1970 Twickenham **England** 9-3
1971 Dublin **England** 9-6
1972 Twickenham **Ireland** 16-12
1973 Dublin **Ireland** 18-9
1974 Twickenham **Ireland** 26-21
1975 Dublin **Ireland** 12-9
1976 Twickenham **Ireland** 13-12
1977 Dublin **England** 4-0
1978 Twickenham **England** 15-9
1979 Dublin **Ireland** 12-7
1980 Twickenham **England** 24-9
1981 Dublin **England** 10-6
1982 Twickenham **Ireland** 16-15
1983 Dublin **Ireland** 25-15
1984 Twickenham **England** 12-9
1985 Dublin **Ireland** 13-10
1986 Twickenham **England** 25-20
1987 Dublin **Ireland** 17-0
1988 Twickenham **England** 35-3
1988 Dublin **England** 21-10
Non-championship match
1989 Dublin **England** 16-3
1990 Twickenham **England** 23-0
1991 Dublin **England** 16-7
1992 Twickenham **England** 38-9
1993 Dublin **Ireland** 17-3
1994 Twickenham **Ireland** 13-12
1995 Dublin **England** 20-8
1996 Twickenham **England** 28-15
1997 Dublin **England** 46-6
1998 Twickenham **England** 35-17
1999 Dublin **England** 27-15
2000 Twickenham **England** 50-18
2001 Dublin **Ireland** 20-14
2002 Twickenham **England** 45-11
2003 Dublin **England** 42-6

ENGLAND v WALES

Played 110 England won 49, Wales won 49, Drawn 12
Highest scores England 60-26 in 1998, Wales 34-21 in 1967
Biggest wins England 50-10 in 2002, 46-12 in 2000, Wales 25-0 in 1905

1881 Blackheath (London) **England** 7G 1DG 6T to 0
1882 No Match
1883 Swansea **England** 2G 4T to 0
1884 Leeds **England** 1G 2T to 1G
1885 Swansea **England** 1G 4T to 1G 1T
1886 Blackheath **England** 1GM 2T to 1G
1887 Llanelli **Drawn** no score
1888 No Match
1889 No Match
1890 Dewsbury **Wales** 1T to 0
1891 Newport **England** 7-3
1892 Blackheath **England** 17-0
1893 Cardiff **Wales** 12-11

1894 Birkenhead **England** 24-3
1895 Swansea **England** 14-6
1896 Blackheath **England** 25-0
1897 Newport **Wales** 11-0
1898 Blackheath **England** 14-7
1899 Swansea **Wales** 26-3
1900 Gloucester **Wales** 13-3
1901 Cardiff **Wales** 13-0
1902 Blackheath **Wales** 9-8
1903 Swansea **Wales** 21-5
1904 Leicester **Drawn** 14-14
1905 Cardiff **Wales** 25-0
1906 Richmond (London) **Wales** 16-3
1907 Swansea **Wales** 22-0
1908 Bristol **Wales** 28-18
1909 Cardiff **Wales** 8-0
1910 Twickenham **England** 11-6
1911 Swansea **Wales** 15-11
1912 Twickenham **England** 8-0
1913 Cardiff **England** 12-0
1914 Twickenham **England** 10-9
1920 Swansea **Wales** 19-5
1921 Twickenham **England** 18-3
1922 Cardiff **Wales** 28-6
1923 Twickenham **England** 7-3
1924 Swansea **England** 17-9
1925 Twickenham **England** 12-6
1926 Cardiff **Drawn** 3-3
1927 Twickenham **England** 11-9
1928 Swansea **England** 10-8
1929 Twickenham **England** 8-3
1930 Cardiff **England** 11-3
1931 Twickenham **Drawn** 11-11
1932 Swansea **Wales** 12-5
1933 Twickenham **Wales** 7-3
1934 Cardiff **England** 9-0
1935 Twickenham **Drawn** 3-3
1936 Swansea **Drawn** 0-0
1937 Twickenham **England** 4-3
1938 Cardiff **Wales** 14-8
1939 Twickenham **England** 3-0
1947 Cardiff **England** 9-6
1948 Twickenham **Drawn** 3-3
1949 Cardiff **Wales** 9-3
1950 Twickenham **Wales** 11-5
1951 Swansea **Wales** 23-5
1952 Twickenham **Wales** 8-6
1953 Cardiff **England** 8-3
1954 Twickenham **England** 9-6
1955 Cardiff **Wales** 3-0
1956 Twickenham **Wales** 8-3
1957 Cardiff **England** 3-0
1958 Twickenham **Drawn** 3-3
1959 Cardiff **Wales** 5-0
1960 Twickenham **England** 14-6
1961 Cardiff **Wales** 6-3
1962 Twickenham **Drawn** 0-0
1963 Cardiff **England** 13-6
1964 Twickenham **Drawn** 6-6
1965 Cardiff **Wales** 14-3
1966 Twickenham **Wales** 11-6
1967 Cardiff **Wales** 34-21
1968 Twickenham **Drawn** 11-11
1969 Cardiff **Wales** 30-9
1970 Twickenham **Wales** 17-13
1971 Cardiff **Wales** 22-6
1972 Twickenham **Wales** 12-3
1973 Cardiff **Wales** 25-9
1974 Twickenham **England** 16-12
1975 Cardiff **Wales** 20-4
1976 Twickenham **Wales** 21-9
1977 Cardiff **Wales** 14-9
1978 Twickenham **Wales** 9-6
1979 Cardiff **Wales** 27-3
1980 Twickenham **England** 9-8
1981 Cardiff **Wales** 21-19
1982 Twickenham **England** 17-7
1983 Cardiff **Drawn** 13-13
1984 Twickenham **Wales** 24-15
1985 Cardiff **Wales** 24-15
1986 Twickenham **England** 21-18
1987 Cardiff **Wales** 19-12
1987 Brisbane *WC* **Wales** 16-3
1988 Twickenham **Wales** 11-3
1989 Cardiff **Wales** 12-9
1990 Twickenham **England** 34-6
1991 Cardiff **England** 25-6
1992 Twickenham **England** 24-0
1993 Cardiff **Wales** 10-9
1994 Twickenham **England** 15-8
1995 Cardiff **England** 23-9
1996 Twickenham **England** 21-15
1997 Cardiff **England** 34-13
1998 Twickenham **England** 60-26
1999 Wembley **Wales** 32-31
2000 Twickenham **England** 46-12
2001 Cardiff **England** 44-15
2002 Twickenham **England** 50-10
2003 Cardiff **England** 26-9
2003 Cardiff **England** 43-9

ENGLAND v FRANCE

Played 82 England won 45, France won 30, Drawn 7
Highest scores England 48-19 in 2001, France 37-12 in 1972
Biggest wins England 37-0 in 1911, France 37-12 in 1972

1906 Paris **England** 35-8
1907 Richmond (London) **England** 41-13
1908 Paris **England** 19-0
1909 Leicester **England** 22-0

1910 Paris **England** 11-3
1911 Twickenham **England** 37-0
1912 Paris **England** 18-8
1913 Twickenham **England** 20-0
1914 Paris **England** 39-13
1920 Twickenham **England** 8-3
1921 Paris **England** 10-6
1922 Twickenham **Drawn** 11-11
1923 Paris **England** 12-3
1924 Twickenham **England** 19-7
1925 Paris **England** 13-11
1926 Twickenham **England** 11-0
1927 Paris **France** 3-0
1928 Twickenham **England** 18-8
1929 Paris **England** 16-6
1930 Twickenham **England** 11-5
1931 Paris **France** 14-13
1947 Twickenham **England** 6-3
1948 Paris **France** 15-0
1949 Twickenham **England** 8-3
1950 Paris **France** 6-3
1951 Twickenham **France** 11-3
1952 Paris **England** 6-3
1953 Twickenham **England** 11-0
1954 Paris **France** 11-3
1955 Twickenham **France** 16-9
1956 Paris **France** 14-9
1957 Twickenham **England** 9-5
1958 Paris **England** 14-0
1959 Twickenham **Drawn** 3-3
1960 Paris **Drawn** 3-3
1961 Twickenham **Drawn** 5-5
1962 Paris **France** 13-0
1963 Twickenham **England** 6-5
1964 Paris **England** 6-3
1965 Twickenham **England** 9-6
1966 Paris **France** 13-0
1967 Twickenham **France** 16-12
1968 Paris **France** 14-9
1969 Twickenham **England** 22-8
1970 Paris **France** 35-13
1971 Twickenham **Drawn** 14-14
1972 Paris **France** 37-12
1973 Twickenham **England** 14-6
1974 Paris **Drawn** 12-12
1975 Twickenham **France** 27-20
1976 Paris **France** 30-9
1977 Twickenham **France** 4-3
1978 Paris **France** 15-6
1979 Twickenham **England** 7-6
1980 Paris **England** 17-13
1981 Twickenham **France** 16-12
1982 Paris **England** 27-15
1983 Twickenham **France** 19-15
1984 Paris **France** 32-18
1985 Twickenham **Drawn** 9-9
1986 Paris **France** 29-10
1987 Twickenham **France** 19-15
1988 Paris **France** 10-9
1989 Twickenham **England** 11-0
1990 Paris **England** 26-7
1991 Twickenham **England** 21-19
1991 Paris *WC* **England** 19-10
1992 Paris **England** 31-13
1993 Twickenham **England** 16-15
1994 Paris **England** 18-14
1995 Twickenham **England** 31-10
1995 Pretoria *WC* **France** 19-9
1996 Paris **France** 15-12
1997 Twickenham **France** 23-20
1998 Paris **France** 24-17
1999 Twickenham **England** 21-10
2000 Paris **England** 15-9
2001 Twickenham **England** 48-19
2002 Paris **France** 20-15
2003 Twickenham **England** 25-17
2003 Marseilles **France** 17-16
2003 Twickenham **England** 45-14

ENGLAND v NEW ZEALAND

Played 25 England won 6, New Zealand won 18, Drawn 1
Highest scores England 31-28 in 2002, New Zealand 64-22 in 1998
Biggest wins England 13-0 in 1936, New Zealand 64-22 in 1998

1905 Crystal Palace (London) **New Zealand** 15-0
1925 Twickenham **New Zealand** 17-11
1936 Twickenham **England** 13-0
1954 Twickenham **New Zealand** 5-0
1963 *1* Auckland **New Zealand** 21-11
2 Christchurch **New Zealand** 9-6
New Zealand won series 2-0
1964 Twickenham **New Zealand** 14-0
1967 Twickenham **New Zealand** 23-11
1973 Twickenham **New Zealand** 9-0
1973 Auckland **England** 16-10
1978 Twickenham **New Zealand** 16-6
1979 Twickenham **New Zealand** 10-9
1983 Twickenham **England** 15-9
1985 *1* Christchurch **New Zealand** 18-13
2 Wellington **New Zealand** 42-15
New Zealand won series 2-0
1991 Twickenham *WC* **New Zealand** 18-12
1993 Twickenham **England** 15-9
1995 Cape Town *WC* **New Zealand** 45-29
1997 *1* Manchester **New Zealand** 25-8
2 Twickenham **Drawn** 26-26
New Zealand won series 1-0, with 1 draw
1998 *1* Dunedin **New Zealand** 64-22

2 Auckland **New Zealand** 40-10
New Zealand won series 2-0
1999 Twickenham *WC* **New Zealand** 30-16
2002 Twickenham **England** 31-28
2003 Wellington **England** 15-13

ENGLAND v SOUTH AFRICA

Played 22 England won 9, South Africa won 12, Drawn 1
Highest scores England 53-3 in 2002, South Africa 44-21 in 1999
Biggest wins England 53-3 in 2002, South Africa 35-9 in 1984

1906 Crystal Palace (London) **Drawn** 3-3
1913 Twickenham **South Africa** 9-3
1932 Twickenham **South Africa** 7-0
1952 Twickenham **South Africa** 8-3
1961 Twickenham **South Africa** 5-0
1969 Twickenham **England** 11-8
1972 Johannesburg **England** 18-9
1984 *1* Port Elizabeth **South Africa** 33-15
2 Johannesburg **South Africa** 35-9
South Africa won series 2-0
1992 Twickenham **England** 33-16
1994 *1* Pretoria **England** 32-15
2 Cape Town **South Africa** 27-9
Series drawn 1-1
1995 Twickenham **South Africa** 24-14
1997 Twickenham **South Africa** 29-11
1998 Cape Town **South Africa** 18-0
1998 Twickenham **England** 13-7
1999 Paris *WC* **South Africa** 44-21
2000 *1* Pretoria **South Africa** 18-13
2 Bloemfontein **England** 27-22
Series drawn 1-1
2000 Twickenham **England** 25-17
2001 Twickenham **England** 29-9
2002 Twickenham **England** 53-3

ENGLAND v AUSTRALIA

Played 28 England won 11, Australia won 16, Drawn 1
Highest scores England 32-31 in 2002, Australia 76-0 in 1998
Biggest wins England 20-3 in 1973 & 23-6 in 1976, Australia 76-0 in 1998

1909 Blackheath (London) **Australia** 9-3
1928 Twickenham **England** 18-11
1948 Twickenham **Australia** 11-0
1958 Twickenham **England** 9-6
1963 Sydney **Australia** 18-9
1967 Twickenham **Australia** 23-11
1973 Twickenham **England** 20-3
1975 *1* Sydney **Australia** 16-9
2 Brisbane **Australia** 30-21
Australia won series 2-0
1976 Twickenham **England** 23-6
1982 Twickenham **England** 15-11
1984 Twickenham **Australia** 19-3
1987 Sydney *WC* **Australia** 19-6
1988 *1* Brisbane **Australia** 22-16
2 Sydney **Australia** 28-8
Australia won series 2-0
1988 Twickenham **England** 28-19
1991 Sydney **Australia** 40-15
1991 Twickenham *WC* **Australia** 12-6
1995 Cape Town *WC* **England** 25-22
1997 *1* Sydney **Australia** 25-6
2 Twickenham **Drawn** 15-15
Australia won series 1-0, with 1 draw
1998 *1* Brisbane **Australia** 76-0
2 Twickenham **Australia** 12-11
Australia won series 2-0
1999 Sydney **Australia** 22-15
2000 Twickenham **England** 22-19
2001 Twickenham **England** 21-15
2002 Twickenham **England** 32-31
2003 Melbourne **England** 25-14

ENGLAND v NEW ZEALAND NATIVES

Played 1 England won 1
Highest score England 7-0 in 1889, NZ Natives 0-7 in 1889
Biggest win England 7-0 in 1889, NZ Natives no win

1889 Blackheath **England** 1G 4T to 0

ENGLAND v RFU PRESIDENT'S XV

Played 1 President's XV won 1
Highest score England 11-28 in 1971, RFU President's XV 28-11 in 1971
Biggest win RFU President's XV 28-11 in 1971

1971 Twickenham **President's XV** 28-11

ENGLAND v ARGENTINA

Played 11 England won 8, Argentina won 2, Drawn 1
Highest scores England 51-0 in 1990, Argentina 33-13 in 1997
Biggest wins England 51-0 in 1990, Argentina 33-13 in 1997

1981 *1* Buenos Aires **Drawn** 19-19
2 Buenos Aires **England** 12-6
England won series 1-0 with 1 draw
1990 *1* Buenos Aires **England** 25-12
2 Buenos Aires **Argentina** 15-13
Series drawn 1-1
1990 Twickenham **England** 51-0
1995 Durban *WC* **England** 24-18
1996 Twickenham **England** 20-18
1997 *1* Buenos Aires **England** 46-20
2 Buenos Aires **Argentina** 33-13
Series drawn 1-1
2000 Twickenham **England** 19-0
2002 Buenos Aires **England** 26-18

ENGLAND v ROMANIA

Played 4 England won 4
Highest scores England 134-0 in 2001, Romania 15-22 in 1985
Biggest win England 134-0 in 2001, Romania no win

1985 Twickenham **England** 22-15
1989 Bucharest **England** 58-3
1994 Twickenham **England** 54-3
2001 Twickenham **England** 134-0

ENGLAND v JAPAN

Played 1 England won 1
Highest score England 60-7 in 1987, Japan 7-60 in 1987
Biggest win England 60-7 in 1987, Japan no win

1987 Sydney *WC* **England** 60-7

ENGLAND v UNITED STATES

Played 4 England won 4
Highest scores England 106-8 in 1999, United States 19-48 in 2001
Biggest win England 106-8 in 1999, United States no win

1987 Sydney *WC* **England** 34-6
1991 Twickenham *WC* **England** 37-9
1999 Twickenham **England** 106-8
2001 San Francisco **England** 48-19

ENGLAND v FIJI

Played 4 England won 4
Highest scores England 58-23 in 1989, Fiji 24-45 in 1999
Biggest win England 58-23 in 1989, Fiji no win

1988 Suva **England** 25-12
1989 Twickenham **England** 58-23
1991 Suva **England** 28-12
1999 Twickenham *WC* **England** 45-24

ENGLAND v ITALY

Played 9 England won 9
Highest scores England 80-23 in 2001, Italy 23-80 in 2001
Biggest win England 67-7 in 1999, Italy no win

1991 Twickenham *WC* **England** 36-6
1995 Durban *WC* **England** 27-20
1996 Twickenham **England** 54-21
1998 Huddersfield **England** 23-15
1999 Twickenham *WC* **England** 67-7
2000 Rome **England** 59-12
2001 Twickenham **England** 80-23
2002 Rome **England** 45-9
2003 Twickenham **England** 40-5

ENGLAND v CANADA

Played 5 England won 5
Highest scores England 60-19 in 1994, Canada 20-59 in 2001
Biggest win England 60-19 in 1994, Canada no win

1992 Wembley **England** 26-13
1994 Twickenham **England** 60-19
1999 Twickenham **England** 36-11
2001 *1* Markham **England** 22-10
2 Burnaby **England** 59-20
England won series 2-0

ENGLAND v SAMOA

Played 2 England won 2
Highest scores England 44-22 in 1995, Samoa 22-44 in 1995
Biggest win England 44-22 in 1995, Samoa no win

1995 Durban *WC* **England** 44-22
1995 Twickenham **England** 27-9

ENGLAND v THE NETHERLANDS

Played 1 England won 1
Highest scores England 110-0 in 1998, The Netherlands 0-110 in 1998
Biggest win England 110-0 in 1998, The Netherlands no win

1998 Huddersfield **England** 110-0

ENGLAND v TONGA

Played 1 England won 1
Highest scores England 101-10 in 1999, Tonga 10-101 in 1999
Biggest win England 101-10 in 1999, Tonga no win

1999 Twickenham *WC* **England** 101-10

SCOTLAND v IRELAND

Played 116 Scotland won 61, Ireland won 49, Drawn 5, Abandoned 1
Highest scores Scotland 38-10 in 1997, Ireland 44-22 in 2000
Biggest wins Scotland 38-10 in 1997, Ireland 36-6 in 2003

1877 Belfast **Scotland** 4G 2DG 2T to 0
1878 No Match
1879 Belfast **Scotland** 1G 1DG 1T to 0
1880 Glasgow **Scotland** 1G 2DG 2T to 0
1881 Belfast **Ireland** 1DG to 1T
1882 Glasgow **Scotland** 2T to 0
1883 Belfast **Scotland** 1G 1T to 0
1884 Raeburn Place (Edinburgh) **Scotland** 2G 2T to 1T
1885 Belfast **Abandoned** Ireland 0 Scotland 1T
1885 Raeburn Place **Scotland** 1G 2T to 0
1886 Raeburn Place **Scotland** 3G 1DG 2T to 0
1887 Belfast **Scotland** 1G 1GM 2T to 0
1888 Raeburn Place **Scotland** 1G to 0
1889 Belfast **Scotland** 1DG to 0
1890 Raeburn Place **Scotland** 1DG 1T to 0
1891 Belfast **Scotland** 14-0

1892 Raeburn Place **Scotland** 2-0
1893 Belfast **Drawn** 0-0
1894 Dublin **Ireland** 5-0
1895 Raeburn Place **Scotland** 6-0
1896 Dublin **Drawn** 0-0
1897 Powderhall (Edinburgh) **Scotland** 8-3
1898 Belfast **Scotland** 8-0
1899 Inverleith (Edinburgh) **Ireland** 9-3
1900 Dublin **Drawn** 0-0
1901 Inverleith **Scotland** 9-5
1902 Belfast **Ireland** 5-0
1903 Inverleith **Scotland** 3-0
1904 Dublin **Scotland** 19-3
1905 Inverleith **Ireland** 11-5
1906 Dublin **Scotland** 13-6
1907 Inverleith **Scotland** 15-3
1908 Dublin **Ireland** 16-11
1909 Inverleith **Scotland** 9-3
1910 Belfast **Scotland** 14-0
1911 Inverleith **Ireland** 16-10
1912 Dublin **Ireland** 10-8
1913 Inverleith **Scotland** 29-14
1914 Dublin **Ireland** 6-0
1920 Inverleith **Scotland** 19-0
1921 Dublin **Ireland** 9-8
1922 Inverleith **Scotland** 6-3
1923 Dublin **Scotland** 13-3
1924 Inverleith **Scotland** 13-8
1925 Dublin **Scotland** 14-8
1926 Murrayfield **Ireland** 3-0
1927 Dublin **Ireland** 6-0
1928 Murrayfield **Ireland** 13-5
1929 Dublin **Scotland** 16-7
1930 Murrayfield **Ireland** 14-11
1931 Dublin **Ireland** 8-5
1932 Murrayfield **Ireland** 20-8
1933 Dublin **Scotland** 8-6
1934 Murrayfield **Scotland** 16-9
1935 Dublin **Ireland** 12-5
1936 Murrayfield **Ireland** 10-4
1937 Dublin **Ireland** 11-4
1938 Murrayfield **Scotland** 23-14
1939 Dublin **Ireland** 12-3
1947 Murrayfield **Ireland** 3-0
1948 Dublin **Ireland** 6-0
1949 Murrayfield **Ireland** 13-3
1950 Dublin **Ireland** 21-0
1951 Murrayfield **Ireland** 6-5
1952 Dublin **Ireland** 12-8
1953 Murrayfield **Ireland** 26-8
1954 Belfast **Ireland** 6-0
1955 Murrayfield **Scotland** 12-3
1956 Dublin **Ireland** 14-10
1957 Murrayfield **Ireland** 5-3
1958 Dublin **Ireland** 12-6
1959 Murrayfield **Ireland** 8-3
1960 Dublin **Scotland** 6-5
1961 Murrayfield **Scotland** 16-8
1962 Dublin **Scotland** 20-6
1963 Murrayfield **Scotland** 3-0
1964 Dublin **Scotland** 6-3
1965 Murrayfield **Ireland** 16-6
1966 Dublin **Scotland** 11-3
1967 Murrayfield **Ireland** 5-3
1968 Dublin **Ireland** 14-6
1969 Murrayfield **Ireland** 16-0
1970 Dublin **Ireland** 16-11
1971 Murrayfield **Ireland** 17-5
1972 No Match
1973 Murrayfield **Scotland** 19-14
1974 Dublin **Ireland** 9-6
1975 Murrayfield **Scotland** 20-13
1976 Dublin **Scotland** 15-6
1977 Murrayfield **Scotland** 21-18
1978 Dublin **Ireland** 12-9
1979 Murrayfield **Drawn** 11-11
1980 Dublin **Ireland** 22-15
1981 Murrayfield **Scotland** 10-9
1982 Dublin **Ireland** 21-12
1983 Murrayfield **Ireland** 15-13
1984 Dublin **Scotland** 32-9
1985 Murrayfield **Ireland** 18-15
1986 Dublin **Scotland** 10-9
1987 Murrayfield **Scotland** 16-12
1988 Dublin **Ireland** 22-18
1989 Murrayfield **Scotland** 37-21
1990 Dublin **Scotland** 13-10
1991 Murrayfield **Scotland** 28-25
1991 Murrayfield *WC* **Scotland** 24-15
1992 Dublin **Scotland** 18-10
1993 Murrayfield **Scotland** 15-3
1994 Dublin **Drawn** 6-6
1995 Murrayfield **Scotland** 26-13
1996 Dublin **Scotland** 16-10
1997 Murrayfield **Scotland** 38-10
1998 Dublin **Scotland** 17-16
1999 Murrayfield **Scotland** 30-13
2000 Dublin **Ireland** 44-22
2001 Murrayfield **Scotland** 32-10
2002 Dublin **Ireland** 43-22
2003 Murrayfield **Ireland** 36-6
2003 Murrayfield **Ireland** 29-10

SCOTLAND v WALES

Played 108 Scotland won 47, Wales won 58, Drawn 3
Highest scores Scotland 35-10 in 1924, Wales 35-12 in 1972
Biggest wins Scotland 35-10 in 1924, Wales 35-12 in 1972 & 29-6 in 1994

1883 Raeburn Place (Edinburgh) **Scotland** 3G to 1G
1884 Newport **Scotland** 1DG 1T to 0
1885 Glasgow **Drawn** no score
1886 Cardiff **Scotland** 2G 1T to 0
1887 Raeburn Place **Scotland** 4G 8T to 0

1888 Newport **Wales** 1T to 0
1889 Raeburn Place **Scotland** 2T to 0
1890 Cardiff **Scotland** 1G 2T to 1T
1891 Raeburn Place **Scotland** 15-0
1892 Swansea **Scotland** 7-2
1893 Raeburn Place **Wales** 9-0
1894 Newport **Wales** 7-0
1895 Raeburn Place **Scotland** 5-4
1896 Cardiff **Wales** 6-0
1897 No Match
1898 No Match
1899 Inverleith (Edinburgh) **Scotland** 21-10
1900 Swansea **Wales** 12-3
1901 Inverleith **Scotland** 18-8
1902 Cardiff **Wales** 14-5
1903 Inverleith **Scotland** 6-0
1904 Swansea **Wales** 21-3
1905 Inverleith **Wales** 6-3
1906 Cardiff **Wales** 9-3
1907 Inverleith **Scotland** 6-3
1908 Swansea **Wales** 6-5
1909 Inverleith **Wales** 5-3
1910 Cardiff **Wales** 14-0
1911 Inverleith **Wales** 32-10
1912 Swansea **Wales** 21-6
1913 Inverleith **Wales** 8-0
1914 Cardiff **Wales** 24-5
1920 Inverleith **Scotland** 9-5
1921 Swansea **Scotland** 14-8
1922 Inverleith **Drawn** 9-9
1923 Cardiff **Scotland** 11-8
1924 Inverleith **Scotland** 35-10
1925 Swansea **Scotland** 24-14
1926 Murrayfield **Scotland** 8-5
1927 Cardiff **Scotland** 5-0
1928 Murrayfield **Wales** 13-0
1929 Swansea **Wales** 14-7
1930 Murrayfield **Scotland** 12-9
1931 Cardiff **Wales** 13-8
1932 Murrayfield **Wales** 6-0
1933 Swansea **Scotland** 11-3
1934 Murrayfield **Wales** 13-6
1935 Cardiff **Wales** 10-6
1936 Murrayfield **Wales** 13-3
1937 Swansea **Scotland** 13-6
1938 Murrayfield **Scotland** 8-6
1939 Cardiff **Wales** 11-3
1947 Murrayfield **Wales** 22-8
1948 Cardiff **Wales** 14-0
1949 Murrayfield **Scotland** 6-5
1950 Swansea **Wales** 12-0
1951 Murrayfield **Scotland** 19-0
1952 Cardiff **Wales** 11-0
1953 Murrayfield **Wales** 12-0
1954 Swansea **Wales** 15-3
1955 Murrayfield **Scotland** 14-8
1956 Cardiff **Wales** 9-3
1957 Murrayfield **Scotland** 9-6
1958 Cardiff **Wales** 8-3
1959 Murrayfield **Scotland** 6-5
1960 Cardiff **Wales** 8-0
1961 Murrayfield **Scotland** 3-0
1962 Cardiff **Scotland** 8-3
1963 Murrayfield **Wales** 6-0
1964 Cardiff **Wales** 11-3
1965 Murrayfield **Wales** 14-12
1966 Cardiff **Wales** 8-3
1967 Murrayfield **Scotland** 11-5
1968 Cardiff **Wales** 5-0
1969 Murrayfield **Wales** 17-3
1970 Cardiff **Wales** 18-9
1971 Murrayfield **Wales** 19-18
1972 Cardiff **Wales** 35-12
1973 Murrayfield **Scotland** 10-9
1974 Cardiff **Wales** 6-0
1975 Murrayfield **Scotland** 12-10
1976 Cardiff **Wales** 28-6
1977 Murrayfield **Wales** 18-9
1978 Cardiff **Wales** 22-14
1979 Murrayfield **Wales** 19-13
1980 Cardiff **Wales** 17-6
1981 Murrayfield **Scotland** 15-6
1982 Cardiff **Scotland** 34-18
1983 Murrayfield **Wales** 19-15
1984 Cardiff **Scotland** 15-9
1985 Murrayfield **Wales** 25-21
1986 Cardiff **Wales** 22-15
1987 Murrayfield **Scotland** 21-15
1988 Cardiff **Wales** 25-20
1989 Murrayfield **Scotland** 23-7
1990 Cardiff **Scotland** 13-9
1991 Murrayfield **Scotland** 32-12
1992 Cardiff **Wales** 15-12
1993 Murrayfield **Scotland** 20-0
1994 Cardiff **Wales** 29-6
1995 Murrayfield **Scotland** 26-13
1996 Cardiff **Scotland** 16-14
1997 Murrayfield **Wales** 34-19
1998 Wembley **Wales** 19-13
1999 Murrayfield **Scotland** 33-20
2000 Cardiff **Wales** 26-18
2001 Murrayfield **Drawn** 28-28
2002 Cardiff **Scotland** 27-22
2003 Murrayfield **Scotland** 30-22
2003 Cardiff **Wales** 23-9

SCOTLAND v FRANCE

Played 75 Scotland won 33, France won 39, Drawn 3
Highest scores Scotland 36-22 in 1999, France 51-16 in 1998
Biggest wins Scotland 31-3 in 1912, France 51-16 in 1998 and 38-3 in 2003

1910 Inverleith (Edinburgh) **Scotland** 27-0
1911 Paris **France** 16-15

1912 Inverleith **Scotland** 31-3
1913 Paris **Scotland** 21-3
1914 No Match
1920 Paris **Scotland** 5-0
1921 Inverleith **France** 3-0
1922 Paris **Drawn** 3-3
1923 Inverleith **Scotland** 16-3
1924 Paris **France** 12-10
1925 Inverleith **Scotland** 25-4
1926 Paris **Scotland** 20-6
1927 Murrayfield **Scotland** 23-6
1928 Paris **Scotland** 15-6
1929 Murrayfield **Scotland** 6-3
1930 Paris **France** 7-3
1931 Murrayfield **Scotland** 6-4
1947 Paris **France** 8-3
1948 Murrayfield **Scotland** 9-8
1949 Paris **Scotland** 8-0
1950 Murrayfield **Scotland** 8-5
1951 Paris **France** 14-12
1952 Murrayfield **France** 13-11
1953 Paris **France** 11-5
1954 Murrayfield **France** 3-0
1955 Paris **France** 15-0
1956 Murrayfield **Scotland** 12-0
1957 Paris **Scotland** 6-0
1958 Murrayfield **Scotland** 11-9
1959 Paris **France** 9-0
1960 Murrayfield **France** 13-11
1961 Paris **France** 11-0
1962 Murrayfield **France** 11-3
1963 Paris **Scotland** 11-6
1964 Murrayfield **Scotland** 10-0
1965 Paris **France** 16-8
1966 Murrayfield **Drawn** 3-3
1967 Paris **Scotland** 9-8
1968 Murrayfield **France** 8-6
1969 Paris **Scotland** 6-3
1970 Murrayfield **France** 11-9
1971 Paris **France** 13-8
1972 Murrayfield **Scotland** 20-9
1973 Paris **France** 16-13
1974 Murrayfield **Scotland** 19-6
1975 Paris **France** 10-9
1976 Murrayfield **France** 13-6
1977 Paris **France** 23-3
1978 Murrayfield **France** 19-16
1979 Paris **France** 21-17
1980 Murrayfield **Scotland** 22-14
1981 Paris **France** 16-9
1982 Murrayfield **Scotland** 16-7
1983 Paris **France** 19-15
1984 Murrayfield **Scotland** 21-12
1985 Paris **France** 11-3
1986 Murrayfield **Scotland** 18-17
1987 Paris **France** 28-22
1987 Christchurch *WC* **Drawn** 20-20
1988 Murrayfield **Scotland** 23-12
1989 Paris **France** 19-3
1990 Murrayfield **Scotland** 21-0
1991 Paris **France** 15-9
1992 Murrayfield **Scotland** 10-6
1993 Paris **France** 11-3
1994 Murrayfield **France** 20-12
1995 Paris **Scotland** 23-21
1995 Pretoria *WC* **France** 22-19
1996 Murrayfield **Scotland** 19-14
1997 Paris **France** 47-20
1998 Murrayfield **France** 51-16
1999 Paris **Scotland** 36-22
2000 Murrayfield **France** 28-16
2001 Paris **France** 16-6
2002 Murrayfield **France** 22-10
2003 Paris **France** 38-3

SCOTLAND v NEW ZEALAND

Played 24 Scotland won 0, New Zealand won 22, Drawn 2
Highest scores Scotland 31-62 in 1996, New Zealand 69-20 in 2000
Biggest wins Scotland no win, New Zealand 69-20 in 2000

1905 Inverleith (Edinburgh) **New Zealand** 12-7
1935 Murrayfield **New Zealand** 18-8
1954 Murrayfield **New Zealand** 3-0
1964 Murrayfield **Drawn** 0-0
1967 Murrayfield **New Zealand** 14-3
1972 Murrayfield **New Zealand** 14-9
1975 Auckland **New Zealand** 24-0
1978 Murrayfield **New Zealand** 18-9
1979 Murrayfield **New Zealand** 20-6
1981 *1* Dunedin **New Zealand** 11-4
2 Auckland **New Zealand** 40-15
New Zealand won series 2-0
1983 Murrayfield **Drawn** 25-25
1987 Christchurch *WC* **New Zealand** 30-3
1990 *1* Dunedin **New Zealand** 31-16
2 Auckland **New Zealand** 21-18
New Zealand won series 2-0
1991 Cardiff *WC* **New Zealand** 13-6
1993 Murrayfield **New Zealand** 51-15
1995 Pretoria *WC* **New Zealand** 48-30
1996 *1* Dunedin **New Zealand** 62-31
2 Auckland **New Zealand** 36-12
New Zealand won series 2-0
1999 Murrayfield *WC* **New Zealand** 30-18
2000 *1* Dunedin **New Zealand** 69-20
2 Auckland **New Zealand** 48-14
New Zealand won series 2-0
2001 Murrayfield **New Zealand** 37-6

SCOTLAND v SOUTH AFRICA

Played 15 Scotland won 4, South Africa won 11, Drawn 0
Highest scores Scotland 29-46 in 1999, South Africa 68-10 in 1997
Biggest wins Scotland 21-6 in 2002, South Africa 68-10 in 1997

1906 Glasgow **Scotland** 6-0
1912 Inverleith **South Africa** 16-0
1932 Murrayfield **South Africa** 6-3
1951 Murrayfield **South Africa** 44-0
1960 Port Elizabeth **South Africa** 18-10
1961 Murrayfield **South Africa** 12-5
1965 Murrayfield **Scotland** 8-5
1969 Murrayfield **Scotland** 6-3
1994 Murrayfield **South Africa** 34-10
1997 Murrayfield **South Africa** 68-10
1998 Murrayfield **South Africa** 35-10
1999 Murrayfield *WC* **South Africa** 46-29
2002 Murrayfield **Scotland** 21-6
2003 *1* Durban **South Africa** 29-25
2 Johannesburg **South Africa** 28-19
South Africa won series 2-0

SCOTLAND v AUSTRALIA

Played 19 Scotland won 7, Australia won 12, Drawn 0
Highest scores Scotland 24-15 in 1981, Australia 45-3 in 1998
Biggest wins Scotland 24-15 in 1981, Australia 45-3 in 1998

1927 Murrayfield **Scotland** 10-8
1947 Murrayfield **Australia** 16-7
1958 Murrayfield **Scotland** 12-8
1966 Murrayfield **Scotland** 11-5
1968 Murrayfield **Scotland** 9-3
1970 Sydney **Australia** 23-3
1975 Murrayfield **Scotland** 10-3
1981 Murrayfield **Scotland** 24-15
1982 *1* Brisbane **Scotland** 12-7
2 Sydney **Australia** 33-9
Series drawn 1-1
1984 Murrayfield **Australia** 37-12
1988 Murrayfield **Australia** 32-13
1992 *1* Sydney **Australia** 27-12
2 Brisbane **Australia** 37-13
Australia won series 2-0
1996 Murrayfield **Australia** 29-19
1997 Murrayfield **Australia** 37-8
1998 *1* Sydney **Australia** 45-3
2 Brisbane **Australia** 33-11
Australia won series 2-0
2000 Murrayfield **Australia** 30-9

SCOTLAND v SRU PRESIDENT'S XV

Played 1 Scotland won 1
Highest scores Scotland 27-16 in 1972, SRU President's XV 16-27 in 1973
Biggest win Scotland 27-16 in 1973, SRU President's XV no win

1973 Murrayfield **Scotland** 27-16

SCOTLAND v ROMANIA

Played 9 Scotland won 7, Romania won 2, Drawn 0
Highest scores Scotland 60-19 in 1999, Romania 28-55 in 1987 & 28-22 in 1984
Biggest wins Scotland 60-19 in 1999, Romania 28-22 in 1984 & 18-12 in 1991

1981 Murrayfield **Scotland** 12-6
1984 Bucharest **Romania** 28-22
1986 Bucharest **Scotland** 33-18
1987 Dunedin *WC* **Scotland** 55-28
1989 Murrayfield **Scotland** 32-0
1991 Bucharest **Romania** 18-12
1995 Murrayfield **Scotland** 49-16
1999 Glasgow **Scotland** 60-19
2002 Murrayfield **Scotland** 37-10

SCOTLAND v ZIMBABWE

Played 2 Scotland won 2
Highest scores Scotland 60-21 in 1987, Zimbabwe 21-60 in 1987
Biggest win Scotland 60-21 in 1987 & 51-12 in 1991, Zimbabwe no win

1987 Wellington *WC* **Scotland** 60-21
1991 Murrayfield *WC* **Scotland** 51-12

SCOTLAND v FIJI

Played 3 Scotland won 2, Fiji won 1
Highest scores Scotland 38-17 in 1989, Fiji 51-26 in 1998
Biggest win Scotland 38-17 in 1989, Fiji 51-26 in 1998

1989 Murrayfield **Scotland** 38-17
1998 Suva **Fiji** 51-26
2002 Murrayfield **Scotland** 36-22

SCOTLAND v ARGENTINA

Played 5 Scotland won 1, Argentina won 4, Drawn 0
Highest scores Scotland 49-3 in 1990, Argentina 31-22 in 1999
Biggest wins Scotland 49-3 in 1990, Argentina 31-22 in 1999 and 25-16 in 2001

1990 Murrayfield **Scotland** 49-3
1994 *1* Buenos Aires **Argentina** 16-15
2 Buenos Aires **Argentina** 19-17
Argentina won series 2-0
1999 Murrayfield **Argentina** 31-22
2001 Murrayfield **Argentina** 25-16

SCOTLAND v JAPAN

Played 1 Scotland won 1
Highest scores Scotland 47-9 in 1991, Japan 9-47 in 1991
Biggest win Scotland 47-9 in 1991, Japan no win

1991 Murrayfield *WC* **Scotland** 47-9

SCOTLAND v SAMOA

Played 4 Scotland won 3, Drawn 1
Highest scores Scotland 35-20 in 1999, Samoa 20-35 in 1999
Biggest win Scotland 31-8 in 2000, Samoa no win

1991 Murrayfield *WC* **Scotland** 28-6
1995 Murrayfield **Drawn** 15-15
1999 Murrayfield *WC* **Scotland** 35-20
2000 Murrayfield **Scotland** 31-8

SCOTLAND v CANADA

Played 2 Scotland won 1, Canada won 1
Highest scores Scotland 23-26 in 2002, Canada 26-23 in 2002
Biggest win Scotland 22-6 in 1995, Canada 26-23 in 2002

1995 Murrayfield **Scotland** 22-6
2002 Vancouver **Canada** 26-23

SCOTLAND v IVORY COAST

Played 1 Scotland won 1
Highest scores Scotland 89-0 in 1995, Ivory Coast 0-89 in 1995
Biggest win Scotland 89-0 in 1995, Ivory Coast no win

1995 Rustenburg *WC* **Scotland** 89-0

SCOTLAND v TONGA

Played 2 Scotland won 2
Highest scores Scotland 43-20 in 2001, Tonga 20-43 in 2001
Biggest win Scotland 41-5 in 1995, Tonga no win

1995 Pretoria *WC* **Scotland** 41-5
2001 Murrayfield **Scotland** 43-20

SCOTLAND v ITALY

Played 8 Scotland won 6, Italy won 2
Highest scores Scotland 47-15 in 2003, Italy 34-20 in 2000
Biggest wins Scotland 47-15 in 2003, Italy 34-20 in 2000

1996 Murrayfield **Scotland** 29-22
1998 Treviso **Italy** 25-21
1999 Murrayfield **Scotland** 30-12
2000 Rome **Italy** 34-20
2001 Murrayfield **Scotland** 23-19
2002 Rome **Scotland** 29-12
2003 Murrayfield **Scotland** 33-25
2003 Murrayfield **Scotland** 47-15

SCOTLAND v URUGUAY

Played 1 Scotland won 1
Highest scores Scotland 43-12 in 1999, Uruguay 12-43 in 1999
Biggest win Scotland 43-12 in 1999, Uruguay no win

1999 Murrayfield *WC* **Scotland** 43-12

SCOTLAND v SPAIN

Played 1 Scotland won 1
Highest scores Scotland 48-0 in 1999, Spain 0-48 in 1999
Biggest win Scotland 48-0 in 1999, Spain no win

1999 Murrayfield *WC* **Scotland** 48-0

SCOTLAND v UNITED STATES

Played 2 Scotland won 2
Highest scores Scotland 65-23 in 2002, United States 23-65 in 2002
Biggest win Scotland 53-6 in 2000, United States no win

2000 Murrayfield **Scotland** 53-6
2002 San Francisco **Scotland** 65-23

IRELAND v WALES

Played 108 Ireland won 42, Wales won 60, Drawn 6
Highest scores Ireland 54-10 in 2002, Wales 34-9 in 1976
Biggest wins Ireland 54-10 in 2002, Wales 29-0 in 1907

1882 Dublin **Wales** 2G 2T to 0
1883 No Match
1884 Cardiff **Wales** 1DG 2T to 0
1885 No Match
1886 No Match
1887 Birkenhead **Wales** 1DG 1T to 3T
1888 Dublin **Ireland** 1G 1DG 1T to 0
1889 Swansea **Ireland** 2T to 0
1890 Dublin **Drawn** 1G each
1891 Llanelli **Wales** 6-4
1892 Dublin **Ireland** 9-0
1893 Llanelli **Wales** 2-0
1894 Belfast **Ireland** 3-0
1895 Cardiff **Wales** 5-3
1896 Dublin **Ireland** 8-4
1897 No Match
1898 Limerick **Wales** 11-3
1899 Cardiff **Ireland** 3-0
1900 Belfast **Wales** 3-0
1901 Swansea **Wales** 10-9
1902 Dublin **Wales** 15-0
1903 Cardiff **Wales** 18-0

1904 Belfast **Ireland** 14-12
1905 Swansea **Wales** 10-3
1906 Belfast **Ireland** 11-6
1907 Cardiff **Wales** 29-0
1908 Belfast **Wales** 11-5
1909 Swansea **Wales** 18-5
1910 Dublin **Wales** 19-3
1911 Cardiff **Wales** 16-0
1912 Belfast **Ireland** 12-5
1913 Swansea **Wales** 16-13
1914 Belfast **Wales** 11-3
1920 Cardiff **Wales** 28-4
1921 Belfast **Wales** 6-0
1922 Swansea **Wales** 11-5
1923 Dublin **Ireland** 5-4
1924 Cardiff **Ireland** 13-10
1925 Belfast **Ireland** 19-3
1926 Swansea **Wales** 11-8
1927 Dublin **Ireland** 19-9
1928 Cardiff **Ireland** 13-10
1929 Belfast **Drawn** 5-5
1930 Swansea **Wales** 12-7
1931 Belfast **Wales** 15-3
1932 Cardiff **Ireland** 12-10
1933 Belfast **Ireland** 10-5
1934 Swansea **Wales** 13-0
1935 Belfast **Ireland** 9-3
1936 Cardiff **Wales** 3-0
1937 Belfast **Ireland** 5-3
1938 Swansea **Wales** 11-5
1939 Belfast **Wales** 7-0
1947 Swansea **Wales** 6-0
1948 Belfast **Ireland** 6-3
1949 Swansea **Ireland** 5-0
1950 Belfast **Wales** 6-3
1951 Cardiff **Drawn** 3-3
1952 Dublin **Wales** 14-3
1953 Swansea **Wales** 5-3
1954 Dublin **Wales** 12-9
1955 Cardiff **Wales** 21-3
1956 Dublin **Ireland** 11-3
1957 Cardiff **Wales** 6-5
1958 Dublin **Wales** 9-6
1959 Cardiff **Wales** 8-6
1960 Dublin **Wales** 10-9
1961 Cardiff **Wales** 9-0
1962 Dublin **Drawn** 3-3
1963 Cardiff **Ireland** 14-6
1964 Dublin **Wales** 15-6
1965 Cardiff **Wales** 14-8
1966 Dublin **Ireland** 9-6
1967 Cardiff **Ireland** 3-0
1968 Dublin **Ireland** 9-6
1969 Cardiff **Wales** 24-11
1970 Dublin **Ireland** 14-0
1971 Cardiff **Wales** 23-9
1972 No Match
1973 Cardiff **Wales** 16-12
1974 Dublin **Drawn** 9-9
1975 Cardiff **Wales** 32-4
1976 Dublin **Wales** 34-9
1977 Cardiff **Wales** 25-9
1978 Dublin **Wales** 20-16
1979 Cardiff **Wales** 24-21
1980 Dublin **Ireland** 21-7
1981 Cardiff **Wales** 9-8
1982 Dublin **Ireland** 20-12
1983 Cardiff **Wales** 23-9
1984 Dublin **Wales** 18-9
1985 Cardiff **Ireland** 21-9
1986 Dublin **Wales** 19-12
1987 Cardiff **Ireland** 15-11
1987 Wellington *WC* **Wales** 13-6
1988 Dublin **Wales** 12-9
1989 Cardiff **Ireland** 19-13
1990 Dublin **Ireland** 14-8
1991 Cardiff **Drawn** 21-21
1992 Dublin **Wales** 16-15
1993 Cardiff **Ireland** 19-14
1994 Dublin **Wales** 17-15
1995 Cardiff **Ireland** 16-12
1995 Johannesburg *WC* **Ireland** 24-23
1996 Dublin **Ireland** 30-17
1997 Cardiff **Ireland** 26-25
1998 Dublin **Wales** 30-21
1999 Wembley **Ireland** 29-23
2000 Dublin **Wales** 23-19
2001 Cardiff **Ireland** 36-6
2002 Dublin **Ireland** 54-10
2003 Cardiff **Ireland** 25-24
2003 Dublin **Ireland** 35-12

IRELAND v FRANCE

Played 77 Ireland won 28, France won 44, Drawn 5
Highest scores Ireland 27-25 in 2000, France 45-10 in 1996
Biggest wins Ireland 24-0 in 1913, France 44-5 in 2002

1909 Dublin **Ireland** 19-8
1910 Paris **Ireland** 8-3
1911 Cork **Ireland** 25-5
1912 Paris **Ireland** 11-6
1913 Cork **Ireland** 24-0
1914 Paris **Ireland** 8-6
1920 Dublin **France** 15-7
1921 Paris **France** 20-10
1922 Dublin **Ireland** 8-3
1923 Paris **France** 14-8
1924 Dublin **Ireland** 6-0
1925 Paris **Ireland** 9-3
1926 Belfast **Ireland** 11-0
1927 Paris **Ireland** 8-3
1928 Belfast **Ireland** 12-8
1929 Paris **Ireland** 6-0
1930 Belfast **France** 5-0
1931 Paris **France** 3-0

1947 Dublin **France** 12-8
1948 Paris **Ireland** 13-6
1949 Dublin **France** 16-9
1950 Paris **Drawn** 3-3
1951 Dublin **Ireland** 9-8
1952 Paris **Ireland** 11-8
1953 Belfast **Ireland** 16-3
1954 Paris **France** 8-0
1955 Dublin **France** 5-3
1956 Paris **France** 14-8
1957 Dublin **Ireland** 11-6
1958 Paris **France** 11-6
1959 Dublin **Ireland** 9-5
1960 Paris **France** 23-6
1961 Dublin **France** 15-3
1962 Paris **France** 11-0
1963 Dublin **France** 24-5
1964 Paris **France** 27-6
1965 Dublin **Drawn** 3-3
1966 Paris **France** 11-6
1967 Dublin **France** 11-6
1968 Paris **France** 16-6
1969 Dublin **Ireland** 17-9
1970 Paris **France** 8-0
1971 Dublin **Drawn** 9-9
1972 Paris **Ireland** 14-9
1972 Dublin **Ireland** 24-14
Non-championship match
1973 Dublin **Ireland** 6-4
1974 Paris **France** 9-6
1975 Dublin **Ireland** 25-6
1976 Paris **France** 26-3
1977 Dublin **France** 15-6
1978 Paris **France** 10-9
1979 Dublin **Drawn** 9-9
1980 Paris **France** 19-18
1981 Dublin **France** 19-13
1982 Paris **France** 22-9
1983 Dublin **Ireland** 22-16
1984 Paris **France** 25-12
1985 Dublin **Drawn** 15-15
1986 Paris **France** 29-9
1987 Dublin **France** 19-13
1988 Paris **France** 25-6
1989 Dublin **France** 26-21
1990 Paris **France** 31-12
1991 Dublin **France** 21-13
1992 Paris **France** 44-12
1993 Dublin **France** 21-6
1994 Paris **France** 35-15
1995 Dublin **France** 25-7
1995 Durban *WC* **France** 36-12
1996 Paris **France** 45-10
1997 Dublin **France** 32-15
1998 Paris **France** 18-16
1999 Dublin **France** 10-9
2000 Paris **Ireland** 27-25
2001 Dublin **Ireland** 22-15
2002 Paris **France** 44-5
2003 Dublin **Ireland** 15-12

IRELAND v NEW ZEALAND

Played 17 Ireland won 0, New Zealand won 16, Drawn 1
Highest scores Ireland 29-40 in 2001, New Zealand 63-15 in 1997
Biggest win Ireland no win, New Zealand 59-6 in 1992

1905 Dublin **New Zealand** 15-0
1924 Dublin **New Zealand** 6-0
1935 Dublin **New Zealand** 17-9
1954 Dublin **New Zealand** 14-3
1963 Dublin **New Zealand** 6-5
1973 Dublin **Drawn** 10-10
1974 Dublin **New Zealand** 15-6
1976 Wellington **New Zealand** 11-3
1978 Dublin **New Zealand** 10-6
1989 Dublin **New Zealand** 23-6
1992 *1* Dunedin **New Zealand** 24-21
2 Wellington **New Zealand** 59-6
New Zealand won series 2-0
1995 Johannesburg *WC* **New Zealand** 43-19
1997 Dublin **New Zealand** 63-15
2001 Dublin **New Zealand** 40-29
2002 *1* Dunedin **New Zealand** 15-6
2 Auckland **New Zealand** 40-8
New Zealand won series 2-0

IRELAND v SOUTH AFRICA

Played 14 Ireland won 1, South Africa won 12, Drawn 1
Highest scores Ireland 18-28 in 2000, South Africa 38-0 in 1912
Biggest wins Ireland 9-6 in 1965, South Africa 38-0 in 1912

1906 Belfast **South Africa** 15-12
1912 Dublin **South Africa** 38-0
1931 Dublin **South Africa** 8-3
1951 Dublin **South Africa** 17-5
1960 Dublin **South Africa** 8-3
1961 Cape Town **South Africa** 24-8
1965 Dublin **Ireland** 9-6
1970 Dublin **Drawn** 8-8
1981 *1* Cape Town **South Africa** 23-15
2 Durban **South Africa** 12-10
South Africa won series 2-0
1998 *1* Bloemfontein **South Africa** 37-13
2 Pretoria **South Africa** 33-0
South Africa won series 2-0

1998 Dublin **South Africa** 27-13
2000 Dublin **South Africa** 28-18

IRELAND v AUSTRALIA

Played 22 Ireland won 7, Australia won 15, Drawn 0
Highest scores Ireland 27-12 in 1979, Australia 46-10 in 1999
Biggest wins Ireland 27-12 in 1979, Australia 46-10 in 1999

1927 Dublin **Australia** 5-3
1947 Dublin **Australia** 16-3
1958 Dublin **Ireland** 9-6
1967 Dublin **Ireland** 15-8
1967 Sydney **Ireland** 11-5
1968 Dublin **Ireland** 10-3
1976 Dublin **Australia** 20-10
1979 *1* Brisbane **Ireland** 27-12
2 Sydney **Ireland** 9-3
Ireland won series 2-0
1981 Dublin **Australia** 16-12
1984 Dublin **Australia** 16-9
1987 Sydney *WC* **Australia** 33-15
1991 Dublin *WC* **Australia** 19-18
1992 Dublin **Australia** 42-17
1994 *1* Brisbane **Australia** 33-13
2 Sydney **Australia** 32-18
Australia won series 2-0
1996 Dublin **Australia** 22-12
1999 *1* Brisbane **Australia** 46-10
2 Perth **Australia** 32-26
Australia won series 2-0
1999 Dublin *WC* **Australia** 23-3
2002 Dublin **Ireland** 18-9
2003 Perth **Australia** 45-16

IRELAND v NEW ZEALAND NATIVES

Played 1 New Zealand Natives won 1
Highest scores Ireland 4-13 in 1888, Zew Zealand Natives 13-4 in 1888
Biggest win Ireland no win, New Zealand Natives 13-4 in 1888

1888 Dublin **New Zealand Natives**
4G 1T to 1G 1T

IRELAND v IRU PRESIDENT'S XV

Played 1 Drawn 1
Highest scores Ireland 18-18 in 1974, IRFU President's XV 18-18 in 1974

1974 Dublin **Drawn** 18-18

IRELAND v ROMANIA

Played 6 Ireland won 6
Highest scores Ireland 60-0 in 1986, Romania 35-53 in 1998
Biggest win Ireland 60-0 in 1986, Romania no win

1986 Dublin **Ireland** 60-0
1993 Dublin **Ireland** 25-3
1998 Dublin **Ireland** 53-35
1999 Dublin *WC* **Ireland** 44-14
2001 Bucharest **Ireland** 37-3
2002 Limerick **Ireland** 39-8

IRELAND v CANADA

Played 3 Ireland won 2 Drawn 1
Highest scores Ireland 46-19 in 1987, Canada 27-27 in 2000
Biggest win Ireland 46-19 in 1987, Canada no win

1987 Dunedin *WC* **Ireland** 46-19
1997 Dublin **Ireland** 33-11
2000 Markham **Drawn** 27-27

IRELAND v TONGA

Played 2 Ireland won 2
Highest scores Ireland 40-19 in 2003, Tonga 19-40 in 2003
Biggest win Ireland 32-9 in 1987, Tonga no win

1987 Brisbane *WC* **Ireland** 32-9
2003 Nuku'alofa **Ireland** 40-19

IRELAND v SAMOA

Played 4 Ireland won 3, Samoa won 1, Drawn 0
Highest scores Ireland 49-22 in 1988, Samoa 40-25 in 1996
Biggest wins Ireland 49-22 in 1988 and 35-8 in 2001, Samoa 40-25 in 1996

1988 Dublin **Ireland** 49-22
1996 Dublin **Samoa** 40-25
2001 Dublin **Ireland** 35-8
2003 Apia **Ireland** 40-14

IRELAND v ITALY

Played 10 Ireland won 7, Italy won 3, Drawn 0
Highest scores Ireland 61-6 in 2003, Italy 37-29 in 1997 & 37-22 in 1997
Biggest wins Ireland 61-6 in 2003, Italy 37-22 in 1997

1988 Dublin **Ireland** 31-15
1995 Treviso **Italy** 22-12
1997 Dublin **Italy** 37-29
1997 Bologna **Italy** 37-22
1999 Dublin **Ireland** 39-30
2000 Dublin **Ireland** 60-13
2001 Rome **Ireland** 41-22
2002 Dublin **Ireland** 32-17
2003 Rome **Ireland** 37-13
2003 Limerick **Ireland** 61-6

IRELAND v ARGENTINA

Played 5 Ireland won 3 Argentina won 2
Highest scores Ireland 32-24 in 1999, Argentina 34-23 in 2000
Biggest win Ireland 32-24 in 1999, Argentina 34-23 in 2000

1990 Dublin **Ireland** 20-18
1999 Dublin **Ireland** 32-24
1999 Lens *WC* **Argentina** 28-24
2000 Buenos Aires **Argentina** 34-23
2002 Dublin **Ireland** 16-7

IRELAND v NAMIBIA

Played 2 Namibia won 2
Highest scores Ireland 15-26 in 1991, Namibia 26-15 in 1991
Biggest win Ireland no win, Namibia 26-15 in 1991

1991 *1* Windhoek **Namibia** 15-6
2 Windhoek **Namibia** 26-15
Namibia won series 2-0

IRELAND v ZIMBABWE

Played 1 Ireland won 1
Highest scores Ireland 55-11 in 1991, Zimbabwe 11-55 in 1991
Biggest win Ireland 55-11 in 1991, Zimbabwe no win

1991 Dublin *WC* **Ireland** 55-11

IRELAND v JAPAN

Played 3 Ireland won 3
Highest scores Ireland 78-9 in 2000, Japan 28-50 in 1995
Biggest win Ireland 78-9 in 2000, Japan no win

1991 Dublin *WC* **Ireland** 32-16
1995 Bloemfontein *WC* **Ireland** 50-28
2000 Dublin **Ireland** 78-9

IRELAND v UNITED STATES

Played 4 Ireland won 4
Highest scores Ireland 83-3 in 2000, United States 18-25 in 1996
Biggest win Ireland 83-3 in 2000, United States no win

1994 Dublin **Ireland** 26-15
1996 Atlanta **Ireland** 25-18
1999 Dublin *WC* **Ireland** 53-8
2000 Manchester (NH) **Ireland** 83-3

IRELAND v FIJI

Played 2 Ireland won 2
Highest scores Ireland 64-17 in 2002, Fiji 17-64 in 2002
Biggest win Ireland 64-17 in 2002, Fiji no win

1995 Dublin **Ireland** 44-8
2002 Dublin **Ireland** 64-17

IRELAND v GEORGIA

Played 2 Ireland won 2
Highest scores Ireland 70-0 in 1998, Georgia 14-63 in 2002
Biggest win Ireland 70-0 in 1998, Georgia no win

1998 Dublin **Ireland** 70-0
2002 Dublin **Ireland** 63-14

IRELAND v RUSSIA

Played 1 Ireland won 1
Highest scores Ireland 35-3 in 2002, Russia 3-35 in 2002
Biggest win Ireland 35-3 in 2002, Russia no win

2002 Krasnoyarsk **Ireland** 35-3

WALES v FRANCE

Played 79 Wales won 41, France won 35, Drawn 3
Highest scores Wales 49-14 in 1910, France 51-0 in 1998
Biggest wins Wales 47-5 in 1909, France 51-0 in 1998

1908 Cardiff **Wales** 36-4
1909 Paris **Wales** 47-5
1910 Swansea **Wales** 49-14
1911 Paris **Wales** 15-0
1912 Newport **Wales** 14-8
1913 Paris **Wales** 11-8
1914 Swansea **Wales** 31-0
1920 Paris **Wales** 6-5
1921 Cardiff **Wales** 12-4
1922 Paris **Wales** 11-3
1923 Swansea **Wales** 16-8
1924 Paris **Wales** 10-6
1925 Cardiff **Wales** 11-5
1926 Paris **Wales** 7-5
1927 Swansea **Wales** 25-7
1928 Paris **France** 8-3
1929 Cardiff **Wales** 8-3
1930 Paris **Wales** 11-0
1931 Swansea **Wales** 35-3
1947 Paris **Wales** 3-0
1948 Swansea **France** 11-3
1949 Paris **France** 5-3
1950 Cardiff **Wales** 21-0
1951 Paris **France** 8-3
1952 Swansea **Wales** 9-5
1953 Paris **Wales** 6-3

1954 Cardiff **Wales** 19-13
1955 Paris **Wales** 16-11
1956 Cardiff **Wales** 5-3
1957 Paris **Wales** 19-13
1958 Cardiff **France** 16-6
1959 Paris **France** 11-3
1960 Cardiff **France** 16-8
1961 Paris **France** 8-6
1962 Cardiff **Wales** 3-0
1963 Paris **France** 5-3
1964 Cardiff **Drawn** 11-11
1965 Paris **France** 22-13
1966 Cardiff **Wales** 9-8
1967 Paris **France** 20-14
1968 Cardiff **France** 14-9
1969 Paris **Drawn** 8-8
1970 Cardiff **Wales** 11-6
1971 Paris **Wales** 9-5
1972 Cardiff **Wales** 20-6
1973 Paris **France** 12-3
1974 Cardiff **Drawn** 16-16
1975 Paris **Wales** 25-10
1976 Cardiff **Wales** 19-13
1977 Paris **France** 16-9
1978 Cardiff **Wales** 16-7
1979 Paris **France** 14-13
1980 Cardiff **Wales** 18-9
1981 Paris **France** 19-15
1982 Cardiff **Wales** 22-12
1983 Paris **France** 16-9
1984 Cardiff **France** 21-16
1985 Paris **France** 14-3
1986 Cardiff **France** 23-15
1987 Paris **France** 16-9
1988 Cardiff **France** 10-9
1989 Paris **France** 31-12
1990 Cardiff **France** 29-19
1991 Paris **France** 36-3
1991 Cardiff **France** 22-9
Non-championship match
1992 Cardiff **France** 12-9
1993 Paris **France** 26-10
1994 Cardiff **Wales** 24-15
1995 Paris **France** 21-9
1996 Cardiff **Wales** 16-15
1996 Cardiff **France** 40-33
Non-championship match
1997 Paris **France** 27-22
1998 Wembley **France** 51-0
1999 Paris **Wales** 34-33
1999 Cardiff **Wales** 34-23
Non-championship match
2000 Cardiff **France** 36-3
2001 Paris **Wales** 43-35
2002 Cardiff **France** 37-33
2003 Paris **France** 33-5

WALES v NEW ZEALAND

Played 19 Wales won 3, New Zealand won 16, Drawn 0
Highest scores Wales 17-43 in 2002, New Zealand 55-3 in 2003
Biggest wins Wales 13-8 in 1953, New Zealand 55-3 in 2003

1905 Cardiff **Wales** 3-0
1924 Swansea **New Zealand** 19-0
1935 Cardiff **Wales** 13-12
1953 Cardiff **Wales** 13-8
1963 Cardiff **New Zealand** 6-0
1967 Cardiff **New Zealand** 13-6
1969 *1* Christchurch **New Zealand** 19-0
2 Auckland **New Zealand** 33-12
New Zealand won series 2-0
1972 Cardiff **New Zealand** 19-16
1978 Cardiff **New Zealand** 13-12
1980 Cardiff **New Zealand** 23-3
1987 Brisbane *WC* **New Zealand** 49-6
1988 *1* Christchurch **New Zealand** 52-3
2 Auckland **New Zealand** 54-9
New Zealand won series 2-0
1989 Cardiff **New Zealand** 34-9
1995 Johannesburg *WC* **New Zealand** 34-9
1997 Wembley **New Zealand** 42-7
2002 Cardiff **New Zealand** 43-17
2003 Hamilton **New Zealand** 55-3

WALES v SOUTH AFRICA

Played 16 Wales won 1, South Africa won 14, Drawn 1
Highest scores Wales 29-19 in 1999, South Africa 96-13 in 1998
Biggest win Wales 29-19 in 1999, South Africa 96-13 in 1998

1906 Swansea **South Africa** 11-0
1912 Cardiff **South Africa** 3-0
1931 Swansea **South Africa** 8-3
1951 Cardiff **South Africa** 6-3
1960 Cardiff **South Africa** 3-0
1964 Durban **South Africa** 24-3
1970 Cardiff **Drawn** 6-6
1994 Cardiff **South Africa** 20-12
1995 Johannesburg **South Africa** 40-11
1996 Cardiff **South Africa** 37-20
1998 Pretoria **South Africa** 96-13
1998 Wembley **South Africa** 28-20
1999 Cardiff **Wales** 29-19
2000 Cardiff **South Africa** 23-13
2002 *1* Bloemfontein **South Africa** 34-19

2 Cape Town **South Africa** 19-8
SA won series 2-0

WALES v AUSTRALIA

Played 22 Wales won 8, Australia won 14, Drawn 0
Highest scores Wales 28-3 in 1975, Australia 63-6 in 1991
Biggest wins Wales 28-3 in 1975, Australia 63-6 in 1991

1908 Cardiff **Wales** 9-6
1927 Cardiff **Australia** 18-8
1947 Cardiff **Wales** 6-0
1958 Cardiff **Wales** 9-3
1966 Cardiff **Australia** 14-11
1969 Sydney **Wales** 19-16
1973 Cardiff **Wales** 24-0
1975 Cardiff **Wales** 28-3
1978 *1* Brisbane **Australia** 18-8
2 Sydney **Australia** 19-17
Australia won series 2-0
1981 Cardiff **Wales** 18-13
1984 Cardiff **Australia** 28-9
1987 Rotorua *WC* **Wales** 22-21
1991 Brisbane **Australia** 63-6
1991 Cardiff *WC* **Australia** 38-3
1992 Cardiff **Australia** 23-6
1996 *1* Brisbane **Australia** 56-25
2 Sydney **Australia** 42-3
Australia won series 2-0
1996 Cardiff **Australia** 28-19
1999 Cardiff *WC* **Australia** 24-9
2001 Cardiff **Australia** 21-13
2003 Sydney **Australia** 30-10

WALES v NEW ZEALAND NATIVES

Played 1 Wales won 1
Highest scores Wales 5-0 in 1888, New Zealand Natives 0-5 in 1888
Biggest win Wales 5-0 in 1888, New Zealand Natives no win

1888 Swansea **Wales** 1G 2T to 0

WALES v NEW ZEALAND ARMY

Played 1 New Zealand Army won 1
Highest scores Wales 3-6 in 1919, New Zealand Army 6-3 in 1919
Biggest win Wales no win, New Zealand Army 6-3 in 1919

1919 Swansea **New Zealand Army** 6-3

WALES v ROMANIA

Played 7 Wales won 5, Romania won 2
Highest scores Wales 81-9 in 2001, Romania 24-6 in 1983
Biggest wins Wales 81-9 in 2001, Romania 24-6 in 1983

1983 Bucharest **Romania** 24-6
1988 Cardiff **Romania** 15-9
1994 Bucharest **Wales** 16-9
1997 Wrexham **Wales** 70-21
2001 Cardiff **Wales** 81-9
2002 Wrexham **Wales** 40-3
2003 Wrexham **Wales** 54-8

WALES v FIJI

Played 5 Wales won 5
Highest scores Wales 58-14 in 2002, Fiji 15-22 in 1986 & 15-19 in 1995
Biggest win Wales 58-14 in 2002, Fiji no win

1985 Cardiff **Wales** 40-3
1986 Suva **Wales** 22-15
1994 Suva **Wales** 23-8
1995 Cardiff **Wales** 19-15
2002 Cardiff **Wales** 58-14

WALES v TONGA

Played 5 Wales won 5
Highest scores Wales 51-7 in 2001, Tonga 16-29 in 1987
Biggest win Wales 51-7 in 2001, Tonga no win

1986 Nuku'Alofa **Wales** 15-7
1987 Palmerston North *WC* **Wales** 29-16
1994 Nuku'Alofa **Wales** 18-9
1997 Swansea **Wales** 46-12
2001 Cardiff **Wales** 51-7

WALES v SAMOA

Played 6 Wales won 3, Samoa won 3, Drawn 0
Highest scores Wales 50-6 in 2000, Samoa 38-31 in 1999
Biggest wins Wales 50-6 in 2000, Samoa 34-9 in 1994

1986 Apia **Wales** 32-14
1988 Cardiff **Wales** 28-6
1991 Cardiff *WC* **Samoa** 16-13
1994 Moamoa **Samoa** 34-9
1999 Cardiff *WC* **Samoa** 38-31
2000 Cardiff **Wales** 50-6

WALES v CANADA

Played 6 Wales won 5, Canada won 1, Drawn 0
Highest scores Wales 40-9 in 1987, Canada 26-24 in 1993
Biggest wins Wales 40-9 in 1987, Canada 26-24 in 1993

1987 Invercargill *WC* **Wales** 40-9
1993 Cardiff **Canada** 26-24
1994 Toronto **Wales** 33-15
1997 Toronto **Wales** 28-25
1999 Cardiff **Wales** 33-19
2002 Cardiff **Wales** 32-21

WALES v UNITED STATES

Played 5 Wales won 5
Highest scores Wales 46-0 in 1987, United States 23-28 in 1997
Biggest win Wales 46-0 in 1987, United States no win

1987 Cardiff **Wales** 46-0
1997 Cardiff **Wales** 34-14
1997 *1* Wilmington **Wales** 30-20
2 San Francisco **Wales** 28-23
Wales won series 2-0
2000 Cardiff **Wales** 42-11

WALES v NAMIBIA

Played 3 Wales won 3
Highest scores Wales 38-23 in 1993, Namibia 30-34 in 1990
Biggest win Wales 38-23 in 1993, Namibia no win

1990 *1* Windhoek **Wales** 18-9
2 Windhoek **Wales** 34-30
Wales won series 2-0
1993 Windhoek **Wales** 38-23

WALES v BARBARIANS

Played 2 Wales won 1, Barbarians won 1
Highest scores Wales 31-10 in 1996, Barbarians 31-24 in 1990
Biggest wins Wales 31-10 in 1996, Barbarians 31-24 in 1990

1990 Cardiff **Barbarians** 31-24
1996 Cardiff **Wales** 31-10

WALES v ARGENTINA

Played 6 Wales won 5, Argentina won 1
Highest scores Wales 43-30 in 1998, Argentina 30-43 in 1998 and 30-16 in 2001
Biggest win Wales 43-30 in 1998, Argentina 30-16 in 2001

1991 Cardiff *WC* **Wales** 16-7
1998 Llanelli **Wales** 43-30
1999 *1* Buenos Aires **Wales** 36-26
2 Buenos Aires **Wales** 23-16
Wales won series 2-0
1999 Cardiff *WC* **Wales** 23-18
2001 Cardiff **Argentina** 30-16

WALES v ZIMBABWE

Played 3 Wales won 3
Highest scores Wales 49-11 in 1998, Zimbabwe 14-35 in 1993
Biggest win Wales 49-11 in 1998, Zimbabwe no win

1993 *1* Bulawayo **Wales** 35-14
2 Harare **Wales** 42-13
Wales won series 2-0
1998 Harare **Wales** 49-11

WALES v JAPAN

Played 5 Wales won 5
Highest scores Wales 64-15 in 1999 & 64-10 in 2001, Japan 30-53 in 2001
Biggest win Wales 64-10 in 2001, Japan no win

1993 Cardiff **Wales** 55-5
1995 Bloemfontein *WC* **Wales** 57-10
1999 Cardiff *WC* **Wales** 64-15
2001 *1* Osaka **Wales** 64-10
2 Tokyo **Wales** 53-30
Wales won series 2-0

WALES v PORTUGAL

Played 1 Wales won 1
Highest scores Wales 102-11 in 1994, Portugal 11-102 in 1994
Biggest win Wales 102-11 in 1994, Portugal no win

1994 Lisbon **Wales** 102-11

WALES v SPAIN

Played 1 Wales won 1
Highest scores Wales 54-0 in 1994, Spain 0-54 in 1994
Bigegst win Wales 54-0 in 1994, Spain no win

1994 Madrid **Wales** 54-0

WALES v ITALY

Played 9 Wales won 8, Italy won 1
Highest scores Wales 60-21 in 1999, Italy 30-22 in 2003
Biggest win Wales 60-21 in 1999, Italy 30-22 in 2003

1994 Cardiff **Wales** 29-19
1996 Cardiff **Wales** 31-26
1996 Rome **Wales** 31-22
1998 Llanelli **Wales** 23-20
1999 Treviso **Wales** 60-21
2000 Cardiff **Wales** 47-16
2001 Rome **Wales** 33-23
2002 Cardiff **Wales** 44-20
2003 Rome **Italy** 30-22

BRITISH/IRISH ISLES v SOUTH AFRICA

Played 43 British/Irish won 16, South Africa won 21, Drawn 6
Highest scores: British/Irish 28–9 in 1974, South Africa 35–16 in 1997
Biggest wins: British/Irish 28–9 in 1974, South Africa 34–14 in 1962

1891 *1* Port Elizabeth **British/Irish** 4-0
2 Kimberley **British/Irish** 3-0
3 Cape Town **British/Irish** 4-0
British/Irish won series 3-0
1896 *1* Port Elizabeth **British/Irish** 8-0
2 Johannesburg **British/Irish** 17-8
3 Kimberley **British/Irish** 9-3
4 Cape Town **South Africa** 5-0
British/Irish won series 3-1
1903 *1* Johannesburg **Drawn** 10-10
2 Kimberley **Drawn** 0-0
3 Cape Town **South Africa** 8-0
South Africa won series 1-0 with two drawn
1910 *1* Johannesburg **South Africa** 14–10
2 Port Elizabeth **British/Irish** 8–3
3 Cape Town **South Africa** 21–5
South Africa won series 2-1
1924 *1* Durban **South Africa** 7–3
2 Johannesburg **South Africa** 17–0
3 Port Elizabeth **Drawn** 3–3
4 Cape Town **South Africa** 16–9
South Africa won series 3-0, with 1 draw
1938 *1* Johannesburg **South Africa** 26–12
2 Port Elizabeth **South Africa** 19–3
3 Cape Town **British/Irish** 21–16
South Africa won series 2-1
1955 *1* Johannesburg **British/Irish** 23–22
2 Cape Town **South Africa** 25–9
3 Pretoria **British/Irish** 9–6
4 Port Elizabeth **South Africa** 22–8
Series drawn 2-2
1962 *1* Johannesburg **Drawn** 3–3
2 Durban **South Africa** 3–0
3 Cape Town **South Africa** 8–3
4 Bloemfontein **South Africa** 34–14
South Africa won series 3-0, with 1 draw
1968 *1* Pretoria **South Africa** 25–20
2 Port Elizabeth **Drawn** 6–6
3 Cape Town **South Africa** 11–6
4 Johannesburg **South Africa** 19–6
South Africa won series 3-0, with 1 draw
1974 *1* Cape Town **British/Irish** 12–3
2 Pretoria **British/Irish** 28–9
3 Port Elizabeth **British/Irish** 26–9
4 Johannesburg **Drawn** 13–13
British/Irish won series 3-0, with 1 draw
1980 *1* Cape Town **South Africa** 26–22
2 Bloemfontein **South Africa** 26–19
3 Port Elizabeth **South Africa** 12–10
4 Pretoria **British/Irish** 17–13
South Africa won series 3-1
1997 *1* Cape Town **British/Irish** 25-16
2 Durban **British/Irish** 18-15
3 Johannesburg **South Africa** 35-16
British/Irish won series 2-1

BRITISH/IRISH ISLES v NEW ZEALAND

Played 32 British/Irish won 6, New Zealand won 24, Drawn 2
Highest scores: British/Irish 20–7 in 1993, New Zealand 38–6 in 1983
Biggest wins: British/Irish 20–7 in 1993, New Zealand 38–6 in 1983

1904 Wellington **New Zealand** 9-3
1930 *1* Dunedin **British/Irish** 6–3
2 Christchurch **New Zealand** 13–10
3 Auckland **New Zealand** 15–10
4 Wellington **New Zealand** 22–8
New Zealand won series 3-1
1950 *1* Dunedin **Drawn** 9–9
2 Christchurch **New Zealand** 8–0
3 Wellington **New Zealand** 6–3
4 Auckland **New Zealand** 11–8
New Zealand won series 3-0, with 1 draw
1959 *1* Dunedin **New Zealand** 18–17
2 Wellington **New Zealand** 11–8
3 Christchurch **New Zealand** 22–8
4 Auckland **British/Irish** 9–6
New Zealand won series 3-1
1966 *1* Dunedin **New Zealand** 20–3
2 Wellington **New Zealand** 16–12
3 Christchurch **New Zealand** 19–6
4 Auckland **New Zealand** 24–11
New Zealand won series 4-0
1971 *1* Dunedin **British/Irish** 9–3
2 Christchurch **New Zealand** 22–12
3 Wellington **British/Irish** 13–3
4 Auckland **Drawn** 14–14
British/Irish won series 2-1, with 1 draw
1977 *1* Wellington **New Zealand** 16–12
2 Christchurch **British/Irish** 13–9
3 Dunedin **New Zealand** 19–7
4 Auckland **New Zealand** 10–9
New Zealand won series 3-1
1983 *1* Christchurch **New Zealand** 16–12
2 Wellington **New Zealand** 9–0
3 Dunedin **New Zealand** 15–8
4 Auckland **New Zealand** 38–6
New Zealand won series 4-0
1993 *1* Christchurch **New Zealand** 20–18
2 Wellington **British/Irish** 20–7
3 Auckland **New Zealand** 30–13
New Zealand won series 2-1

ANGLO-WELSH v NEW ZEALAND

Played 3 New Zealand won 2, Drawn 1
Highest scores Anglo Welsh 5-32 in 1908, New Zealand 32-5 in 1908
Biggest win Anglo Welsh no win, New Zealand 29-0 in 1908

1908 *1* Dunedin **New Zealand** 32-5
2 Wellington **Drawn** 3-3
3 Auckland **New Zealand** 29-0
New Zealand won series 2-0 with one drawn

BRITISH/IRISH ISLES v AUSTRALIA

Played 20 British/Irish won 15, Australia won 5, Drawn 0
Highest scores: British/Irish 31–0 in 1966, Australia 35–14 in 2001
Biggest wins: British/Irish 31–0 in 1966, Australia 35–14 in 2001

1899 *1* Sydney **Australia** 13-3
2 Brisbane **British/Irish** 11-0
3 Sydney **British/Irish** 11-10
4 Sydney **British/Irish** 13-0
British/Irish won series 3-1
1904 *1* Sydney **British/Irish** 17-0
2 Brisbane **British/Irish** 17-3
3 Sydney **British/Irish** 16-0
British/Irish won series 3-0
1930 Sydney **Australia** 6–5
1950 *1* Brisbane **British/Irish** 19–6
2 Sydney **British/Irish** 24–3
British/Irish won series 2-0
1959 *1* Brisbane **British/Irish** 17–6
2 Sydney **British/Irish** 24–3
British/Irish won series 2-0
1966 *1* Sydney **British/Irish** 11–8
2 Brisbane **British/Irish** 31–0
British/Irish won series 2-0
1989 *1* Sydney **Australia** 30–12
2 Brisbane **British/Irish** 19–12
3 Sydney **British/Irish** 19–18
British/Irish won series 2-1
2001 *1* Brisbane **British/Irish** 29-13
2 Melbourne **Australia** 35-14
3 Sydney **Australia** 29-23
Australia won series 2-1

FRANCE v NEW ZEALAND

Played 39 France won 10, New Zealand won 28, Drawn 1
Highest scores France 43-31 in 1999, New Zealand 54-7 in 1999
Biggest wins France 22-8 in 1994, New Zealand 54-7 in 1999

1906 Paris **New Zealand** 38-8
1925 Toulouse **New Zealand** 30-6
1954 Paris **France** 3-0
1961 *1* Auckland **New Zealand** 13-6
2 Wellington **New Zealand** 5-3
3 Christchurch **New Zealand** 32-3
New Zealand won series 3-0
1964 Paris **New Zealand** 12-3
1967 Paris **New Zealand** 21-15
1968 *1* Christchurch **New Zealand** 12-9
2 Wellington **New Zealand** 9-3
3 Auckland **New Zealand** 19-12
New Zealand won series 3-0
1973 Paris **France** 13-6
1977 *1* Toulouse **France** 18-13
2 Paris **New Zealand** 15-3
Series drawn 1-1
1979 *1* Christchurch **New Zealand** 23-9
2 Auckland **France** 24-19
Series drawn 1-1
1981 *1* Toulouse **New Zealand** 13-9
2 Paris **New Zealand** 18-6
New Zealand won series 2-0
1984 *1* Christchurch **New Zealand** 10-9
2 Auckland **New Zealand** 31-18
New Zealand won series 2-0
1986 Christchurch **New Zealand** 18-9
1986 *1* Toulouse **New Zealand** 19-7
2 Nantes **France** 16-3
Series drawn 1-1
1987 Auckland *WC* **New Zealand** 29-9
1989 *1* Christchurch **New Zealand** 25-17
2 Auckland **New Zealand** 34-20
New Zealand won series 2-0
1990 *1* Nantes **New Zealand** 24-3
2 Paris **New Zealand** 30-12
New Zealand won series 2-0
1994 *1* Christchurch **France** 22-8
2 Auckland **France** 23-20
France won series 2-0
1995 *1* Toulouse **France** 22-15
2 Paris **New Zealand** 37-12
Series drawn 1-1
1999 Wellington **New Zealand** 54-7
1999 Twickenham *WC* **France** 43-31
2000 *1* Paris **New Zealand** 39-26
2 Marseilles **France** 42-33
Series drawn 1-1
2001 Wellington **New Zealand** 37-12
2002 Paris **Drawn** 20-20
2003 Christchurch **New Zealand** 31-23

FRANCE v SOUTH AFRICA

Played 32 France won 8, South Africa won 19, Drawn 5
Highest scores France 32-36 in 1997 & 32-23 in 2001, South Africa 52-10 in 1997
Biggest wins France 30-10 in 2002, South Africa 52-10 in 1997

1913 Bordeaux **South Africa** 38-5
1952 Paris **South Africa** 25-3
1958 *1* Cape Town **Drawn** 3-3
2 Johannesburg **France** 9-5
France won series 1-0, with 1 draw
1961 Paris **Drawn** 0-0
1964 Springs (SA) **France** 8-6
1967 *1* Durban **South Africa** 26-3
2 Bloemfontein **South Africa** 16-3
3 Johannesburg **France** 19-14
4 Cape Town **Drawn** 6-6
South Africa won series 2-1, with 1 draw
1968 *1* Bordeaux **South Africa** 12-9
2 Paris **South Africa** 16-11
South Africa won series 2-0
1971 *1* Bloemfontein **South Africa** 22-9
2 Durban **Drawn** 8-8
South Africa won series 1-0, with 1 draw
1974 *1* Toulouse **South Africa** 13-4
2 Paris **South Africa** 10-8
South Africa won series 2-0
1975 *1* Bloemfontein **South Africa** 38-25
2 Pretoria **South Africa** 33-18
South Africa won series 2-0
1980 Pretoria **South Africa** 37-15
1992 *1* Lyons **South Africa** 20-15
2 Paris **France** 29-16
Series drawn 1-1
1993 *1* Durban **Drawn** 20-20
2 Johannesburg **France** 18-17
France won series 1-0, with 1 draw
1995 Durban *WC* **South Africa** 19-15
1996 *1* Bordeaux **South Africa** 22-12
2 Paris **South Africa** 13-12
South Africa won series 2-0
1997 *1* Lyons **South Africa** 36-32
2 Paris **South Africa** 52-10
South Africa won series 2-0
2001 *1* Johannesburg **France** 32-23
2 Durban **South Africa** 20-15
Series drawn 1-1
2001 Paris **France** 20-10
2002 Marseilles **France** 30-10

FRANCE v AUSTRALIA

Played 33 France won 14, Australia won 17, Drawn 2
Highest scores France 34-6 in 1976, Australia 48-31 in 1990
Biggest wins France 34-6 in 1976, Australia 35-12 in 1999

1928 Paris **Australia** 11-8
1948 Paris **France** 13-6
1958 Paris **France** 19-0
1961 Sydney **France** 15-8
1967 Paris **France** 20-14
1968 Sydney **Australia** 11-10
1971 *1* Toulouse **Australia** 13-11
2 Paris **France** 18-9
Series drawn 1-1
1972 *1* Sydney **Drawn** 14-14
2 Brisbane **France** 16-15
France won series 1-0, with 1 draw
1976 *1* Bordeaux **France** 18-15
2 Paris **France** 34-6
France won series 2-0
1981 *1* Brisbane **Australia** 17-15
2 Sydney **Australia** 24-14
Australia won series 2-0
1983 *1* Clermont-Ferrand **Drawn** 15-15
2 Paris **France** 15-6
France won series 1-0, with 1 draw
1986 Sydney **Australia** 27-14
1987 Sydney *WC* **France** 30-24
1989 *1* Strasbourg **Australia** 32-15
2 Lille **France** 25-19
Series drawn 1-1
1990 *1* Sydney **Australia** 21-9
2 Brisbane **Australia** 48-31
3 Sydney **France** 28-19
Australia won series 2-1
1993 *1* Bordeaux **France** 16-13
2 Paris **Australia** 24-3
Series drawn 1-1
1997 *1* Sydney **Australia** 29-15
2 Brisbane **Australia** 26-19
Australia won series 2-0
1998 Paris **Australia** 32-21
1999 Cardiff *WC* **Australia** 35-12
2000 Paris **Australia** 18-13
2001 Marseilles **France** 14-13
2002 *1* Melbourne **Australia** 29-17
2 Sydney **Australia** 31-25
Australia won series 2-0

FRANCE v UNITED STATES

Played 5 France won 4, United States won 1, Drawn 0
Highest scores France 41-9 in 1991, United States 17-3 in 1924
Biggest wins France 41-9 in 1991, United States 17-3 in 1924

1920 Paris **France** 14-5
1924 Paris **United States** 17-3
1976 Chicago **France** 33-14
1991 *1* Denver **France** 41-9
2 Colorado Springs **France** 10-3*
**Abandoned after 43 mins*
France won series 2-0

FRANCE v ROMANIA

Played 48 France won 38, Romania won 8, Drawn 2
Highest scores France 67-20 in 2000, Romania 21-33 in 1991
Biggest wins France 59-3 in 1924, Romania 15-0 in 1980

1924 Paris **France** 59-3
1938 Bucharest **France** 11-8
1957 Bucharest **France** 18-15
1957 Bordeaux **France** 39-0
1960 Bucharest **Romania** 11-5
1961 Bayonne **Drawn** 5-5
1962 Bucharest **Romania** 3-0
1963 Toulouse **Drawn** 6-6
1964 Bucharest **France** 9-6
1965 Lyons **France** 8-3
1966 Bucharest **France** 9-3
1967 Nantes **France** 11-3
1968 Bucharest **Romania** 15-14
1969 Tarbes **France** 14-9
1970 Bucharest **France** 14-3
1971 Béziers **France** 31-12
1972 Constanza **France** 15-6
1973 Valence **France** 7-6
1974 Bucharest **Romania** 15-10
1975 Bordeaux **France** 36-12
1976 Bucharest **Romania** 15-12
1977 Clermont-Ferrand **France** 9-6
1978 Bucharest **France** 9-6
1979 Montauban **France** 30-12
1980 Bucharest **Romania** 15-0
1981 Narbonne **France** 17-9
1982 Bucharest **Romania** 13-9
1983 Toulouse **France** 26-15
1984 Bucharest **France** 18-3
1986 Lille **France** 25-13
1986 Bucharest **France** 20-3
1987 Wellington *WC* **France** 55-12
1987 Agen **France** 49-3
1988 Bucharest **France** 16-12
1990 Auch **Romania** 12-6
1991 Bucharest **France** 33-21
1991 Béziers *WC* **France** 30-3
1992 Le Havre **France** 25-6
1993 Bucharest **France** 37-20
1993 Brive **France** 51-0
1995 Bucharest **France** 24-15
1995 Tucumán *LC* **France** 52-8
1996 Aurillac **France** 64-12
1997 Bucharest **France** 51-20
1997 Lourdes *LC* **France** 39-3
1999 Castres **France** 62-8
2000 Bucharest **France** 67-20
2003 Lens **France** 56-8

FRANCE v NEW ZEALAND MAORIS

Played 1 New Zealand Maoris won 1
Highest scores France 3-12 in 1926, New Zealand Maoris 12-3 in 1926
Biggest win France no win, New Zealand Maoris 12-3 in 1926

1926 Paris **New Zealand Maoris** 12-3

FRANCE v GERMANY

Played 15 France won 13, Germany won 2, Drawn 0
Highest scores France 38-17 in 1933, Germany 17-16 in 1927 & 17-38 in 1933
Biggest wins France 34-0 in 1931, Germany 3-0 in 1938

1927 Paris **France** 30-5
1927 Frankfurt **Germany** 17-16
1928 Hanover **France** 14-3
1929 Paris **France** 24-0
1930 Berlin **France** 31-0
1931 Paris **France** 34-0
1932 Frankfurt **France** 20-4
1933 Paris **France** 38-17
1934 Hanover **France** 13-9
1935 Paris **France** 18-3

1936 *1* Berlin **France** 19-14
2 Hanover **France** 6-3
France won series 2-0

1937 Paris **France** 27-6
1938 Frankfurt **Germany** 3-0
1938 Bucharest **France** 8-5

FRANCE v ITALY

Played 24 France won 23, Italy won 1, Drawn 0
Highest scores France 60-13 in 1967, Italy 40-32 in 1997
Biggest wins France 60-13 in 1967, Italy 40-32 in 1997

1937 Paris **France** 43-5
1952 Milan **France** 17-8
1953 Lyons **France** 22-8
1954 Rome **France** 39-12
1955 Grenoble **France** 24-0
1956 Padua **France** 16-3
1957 Agen **France** 38-6
1958 Naples **France** 11-3
1959 Nantes **France** 22-0
1960 Treviso **France** 26-0
1961 Chambéry **France** 17-0
1962 Brescia **France** 6-3
1963 Grenoble **France** 14-12
1964 Parma **France** 12-3
1965 Pau **France** 21-0
1966 Naples **France** 21-0
1967 Toulon **France** 60-13
1995 Buenos Aires *LC* **France** 34-22
1997 Grenoble **Italy** 40-32
1997 Auch *LC* **France** 30-19
2000 Paris **France** 42-31
2001 Rome **France** 30-19
2002 Paris **France** 33-12
2003 Rome **France** 53-27

FRANCE v BRITISH XVs

Played 5 France won 2, British XVs won 3, Drawn 0
Highest scores France 27-29 in 1989, British XV 36-3 in 1940
Biggest wins France 21-9 in 1945, British XV 36-3 in 1940

1940 Paris **British XV** 36-3
1945 Paris **France** 21-9
1945 Richmond **British XV** 27-6
1946 Paris **France** 10-0
1989 Paris **British XV** 29-27

FRANCE v WALES XVs

Played 2 France won 1, Wales XV won 1
Highest scores France 12-0 in 1946, Wales XV 8-0 in 1945
Biggest win France 12-0 in 1946, Wales XV 8-0 in 1945

1945 Swansea **Wales XV** 8-0
1946 Paris **France** 12-0

FRANCE v IRELAND XVs

Played 1 France won 1
Highest scores France 4-3 in 1946, Ireland XV 3-4 in 1946
Biggest win France 4-3 in 1946, Ireland XV no win

1946 Dublin **France** 4-3

FRANCE v NEW ZEALAND ARMY

Played 1 New Zealand Army won 1
Highest scores France 9-14 in 1946, New Zealand Army 14-9 in 1946
Biggest win France no win, New Zealand Army 14-9 in 1946

1946 Paris **New Zealand Army** 14-9

FRANCE v ARGENTINA

Played 37 France won 29, Argentina won 7, Drawn 1
Highest scores France 47-12 in 1995 & 47-26 in 1999, Argentina 33-32 in 2003
Biggest wins France 47-12 in 1995, Argentina 18-6 in 1988

1949 *1* Buenos Aires **France** 5-0
2 Buenos Aires **France** 12-3
France won series 2-0
1954 *1* Buenos Aires **France** 22-8
2 Buenos Aires **France** 30-3
France won series 2-0
1960 *1* Buenos Aires **France** 37-3
2 Buenos Aires **France** 12-3
3 Buenos Aires **France** 29-6
France won series 3-0
1974 *1* Buenos Aires **France** 20-15
2 Buenos Aires **France** 31-27
France won series 2-0
1975 *1* Lyons **France** 29-6
2 Paris **France** 36-21
France won series 2-0
1977 *1* Buenos Aires **France** 26-3
2 Buenos Aires **Drawn** 18-18
France won series 1-0, with 1 draw
1982 *1* Toulouse **France** 25-12
2 Paris **France** 13-6
France won series 2-0
1985 *1* Buenos Aires **Argentina** 24-16
2 Buenos Aires **France** 23-15
Series drawn 1-1
1986 *1* Buenos Aires **Argentina** 15-13
2 Buenos Aires **France** 22-9
Series drawn 1-1
1988 *1* Buenos Aires **France** 18-15
2 Buenos Aires **Argentina** 18-6
Series drawn 1-1
1988 *1* Nantes **France** 29-9
2 Lille **France** 28-18
France won series 2-0
1992 *1* Buenos Aires **France** 27-12
2 Buenos Aires **France** 33-9
France won series 2-0
1992 Nantes **Argentina** 24-20
1995 Buenos Aires *LC* **France** 47-12
1996 *1* Buenos Aires **France** 34-27
2 Buenos Aires **France** 34-15
France won series 2-0
1997 Tarbes *LC* **France** 32-27
1998 *1* Buenos Aires **France** 35-18
2 Buenos Aires **France** 37-12
France won series 2-0
1998 Nantes **France** 34-14
1999 Dublin *WC* **France** 47-26
2002 Buenos Aires **Argentina** 28-27
2003 *1* Buenos Aires **Argentina** 10-6
2 Buenos Aires **Argentina** 33-32
Argentina won series 2-0

FRANCE v CZECHOSLOVAKIA

Played 2 France won 2
Highest scores France 28-3 in 1956, Czechoslovakia 6-19 in 1968
Biggest win France 28-3 in 1956, Czechoslovakia no win

1956 Toulouse **France** 28-3
1968 Prague **France** 19-6

FRANCE v FIJI

Played 6 France won 6
Highest scores France 77-10 in 2001, Fiji 19-28 in 1999
Biggest win France 77-10 in 2001, Fiji no win

1964 Paris **France** 21-3
1987 Auckland *WC* **France** 31-16
1991 Grenoble *WC* **France** 33-9
1998 Suva **France** 34-9
1999 Toulouse *WC* **France** 28-19
2001 Saint Etienne **France** 77-10

FRANCE v JAPAN

Played 1 France won 1
Highest scores France 30-18 in 1973, Japan 18-30 in 1973
Biggest win France 30-18 in 1973, Japan no win

1973 Bordeaux **France** 30-18

FRANCE v ZIMBABWE

Played 1 France won 1
Highest scores France 70-12 in 1987, Zimbabwe 12-70 in 1987
Biggest win France 70-12 in 1987, Zimbabwe no win

1987 Auckland *WC* **France** 70-12

FRANCE v CANADA

Played 5 France won 4, Canada won 1, Drawn 0
Highest scores France 35-3 in 2002, Canada 20-33 in 1999
Biggest wins France 35-3 in 2002, Canada 18-16 in 1994

1991 Agen *WC* **France** 19-13
1994 Nepean **Canada** 18-16
1994 Besançon **France** 28-9
1999 Béziers *WC* **France** 33-20
2002 Paris **France** 35-3

FRANCE v TONGA

Played 2 France won 1, Tonga won 1
Highest scores France 38-10 in 1995, Tonga 20-16 in 1999
Biggest win France 38-10 in 1995, Tonga 20-16 in 1999

1995 Pretoria *WC* **France** 38-10
1999 Nuku'alofa **Tonga** 20-16

FRANCE v IVORY COAST

Played 1 France won 1
Highest scores France 54-18 in 1995, Ivory Coast 18-54 in 1995
Biggest win France 54-18 in 1995, Ivory Coast no win

1995 Rustenburg *WC* **France** 54-18

FRANCE v SAMOA

Played 1 France won 1
Highest scores France 39-22 in 1999, Samoa 22-39 in 1999
Biggest win France 39-22 in 1999, Samoa no win

1999 Apia **France** 39-22

FRANCE v NAMIBIA

Played 1 France won 1
Highest scores France 47-13 in 1999, Namibia 13-47 in 1999
Biggest win France 47-13 in 1999, Namibia no win

1999 Bordeaux *WC* **France** 47-13

SOUTH AFRICA v NEW ZEALAND

Played 62 New Zealand won 33, South Africa won 26, Drawn 3
Highest scores New Zealand 55-35 in 1997, South Africa 46-40 in 2000
Biggest wins New Zealand 52-16 in 2003, South Africa 17-0 in 1928

1921 *1* Dunedin **New Zealand** 13-5
2 Auckland **South Africa** 9-5
3 Wellington **Drawn** 0-0
Series drawn 1-1, with 1 draw

1928 *1* Durban **South Africa** 17-0
2 Johannesburg **New Zealand** 7-6
3 Port Elizabeth **South Africa** 11-6

4 Cape Town **New Zealand** 13-5
Series drawn 2-2
1937 *1* Wellington **New Zealand** 13-7
2 Christchurch **South Africa** 13-6
3 Auckland **South Africa** 17-6
South Africa won series 2-1
1949 *1* Cape Town **South Africa** 15-11
2 Johannesburg **South Africa** 12-6
3 Durban **South Africa** 9-3
4 Port Elizabeth **South Africa** 11-8
South Africa won series 4-0
1956 *1* Dunedin **New Zealand** 10-6
2 Wellington **South Africa** 8-3
3 Christchurch **New Zealand** 17-10
4 Auckland **New Zealand** 11-5
New Zealand won series 3-1
1960 *1* Johannesburg **South Africa** 13-0
2 Cape Town **New Zealand** 11-3
3 Bloemfontein **Drawn** 11-11
4 Port Elizabeth **South Africa** 8-3
South Africa won series 2-1, with 1 draw
1965 *1* Wellington **New Zealand** 6-3
2 Dunedin **New Zealand** 13-0
3 Christchurch **South Africa** 19-16
4 Auckland **New Zealand** 20-3
New Zealand won series 3-1
1970 *1* Pretoria **South Africa** 17-6
2 Cape Town **New Zealand** 9-8
3 Port Elizabeth **South Africa** 14-3
4 Johannesburg **South Africa** 20-17
South Africa won series 3-1
1976 *1* Durban **South Africa** 16-7
2 Bloemfontein **New Zealand** 15-9
3 Cape Town **South Africa** 15-10
4 Johannesburg **South Africa** 15-14
South Africa won series 3-1
1981 *1* Christchurch **New Zealand** 14-9
2 Wellington **South Africa** 24-12
3 Auckland **New Zealand** 25-22
New Zealand won series 2-1
1992 Johannesburg **New Zealand** 27-24
1994 *1* Dunedin **New Zealand** 22-14
2 Wellington **New Zealand** 13-9
3 Auckland **Drawn** 18-18
New Zealand won series 2-0, with 1 draw
1995 Johannesburg *WC* **South Africa** 15-12 (*aet*)
1996 Christchurch *TN* **New Zealand** 15-11
1996 Cape Town *TN* **New Zealand** 29-18
1996 *1* Durban **New Zealand** 23-19
2 Pretoria **New Zealand** 33-26
3 Johannesburg **South Africa** 32-22
New Zealand won series 2-1
1997 Johannesburg *TN* **New Zealand** 35-32
1997 Auckland *TN* **New Zealand** 55-35
1998 Wellington *TN* **South Africa** 13-3
1998 Durban *TN* **South Africa** 24-23
1999 Dunedin *TN* **New Zealand** 28-0
1999 Pretoria *TN* **New Zealand** 34-18
1999 Cardiff *WC* **South Africa** 22-18
2000 Christchurch *TN* **New Zealand** 25-12
2000 Johannesburg *TN* **South Africa** 46-40
2001 Cape Town *TN* **New Zealand** 12-3
2001 Auckland *TN* **New Zealand** 26-15
2002 Wellington *TN* **New Zealand** 41-20
2002 Durban *TN* **New Zealand** 30-23
2003 Pretoria *TN* **New Zealand** 52-16
2003 Dunedin *TN* **New Zealand** 19-11

SOUTH AFRICA v AUSTRALIA

Played 51 South Africa won 31, Australia won 19, Drawn 1
Highest scores South Africa 61-22 in 1997, Australia 44-23 in 2000
Biggest wins South Africa 61-22 in 1997, Australia 32-6 in 1999

1933 *1* Cape Town **South Africa** 17-3
2 Durban **Australia** 21-6
3 Johannesburg **South Africa** 12-3
4 Port Elizabeth **South Africa** 11-0
5 Bloemfontein **Australia** 15-4
South Africa won series 3-2
1937 *1* Sydney **South Africa** 9-5
2 Sydney **South Africa** 26-17
South Africa won series 2-0
1953 *1* Johannesburg **South Africa** 25-3
2 Cape Town **Australia** 18-14
3 Durban **South Africa** 18-8
4 Port Elizabeth **South Africa** 22-9
South Africa won series 3-1
1956 *1* Sydney **South Africa** 9-0
2 Brisbane **South Africa** 9-0
South Africa won series 2-0
1961 *1* Johannesburg **South Africa** 28-3
2 Port Elizabeth **South Africa** 23-11
South Africa won series 2-0
1963 *1* Pretoria **South Africa** 14-3
2 Cape Town **Australia** 9-5
3 Johannesburg **Australia** 11-9
4 Port Elizabeth **South Africa** 22-6
Series drawn 2-2
1965 *1* Sydney **Australia** 18-11
2 Brisbane **Australia** 12-8
Australia won series 2-0
1969 *1* Johannesburg **South Africa** 30-11
2 Durban **South Africa** 16-9
3 Cape Town **South Africa** 11-3
4 Bloemfontein **South Africa** 19-8
South Africa won series 4-0
1971 *1* Sydney **South Africa** 19-11
2 Brisbane **South Africa** 14-6
3 Sydney **South Africa** 18-6
South Africa won series 3-0
1992 Cape Town **Australia** 26-3
1993 *1* Sydney **South Africa** 19-12
2 Brisbane **Australia** 28-20
3 Sydney **Australia** 19-12
Australia won series 2-1

1995 Cape Town *WC* **South Africa** 27-18
1996 Sydney *TN* **Australia** 21-16
1996 Bloemfontein *TN* **South Africa** 25-19
1997 Brisbane *TN* **Australia** 32-20
1997 Pretoria *TN* **South Africa** 61-22
1998 Perth *TN* **South Africa** 14-13
1998 Johannesburg *TN* **South Africa** 29-15
1999 Brisbane *TN* **Australia** 32-6
1999 Cape Town *TN* **South Africa** 10-9
1999 Twickenham *WC* **Australia** 27-21
2000 Melbourne **Australia** 44-23
2000 Sydney *TN* **Australia** 26-6
2000 Durban *TN* **Australia** 19-18
2001 Pretoria *TN* **South Africa** 20-15
2001 Perth *TN* **Drawn** 14-14
2002 Brisbane *TN* **Australia** 38-27
2002 Johannesburg *TN* **South Africa** 33-31
2003 Cape Town *TN* **South Africa** 26-22
2003 Brisbane *TN* **Australia** 29-9

SOUTH AFRICA v WORLD XVs

Played 3 South Africa won 3
Highest scores South Africa 45-24 in 1977, World XV 24-45 in 1977
Biggest win South Africa 45-24 in 1977, World XV no win

1977 Pretoria **South Africa** 45-24
1989 *1* Cape Town **South Africa** 20-19
2 Johannesburg **South Africa** 22-16
South Africa won series 2-0

SOUTH AFRICA v SOUTH AMERICA

Played 8 South Africa won 7, South America won 1, Drawn 0
Highest scores South Africa 50-18 in 1982, South America 21-12 in 1982
Biggest wins South Africa 50-18 in 1982, South America 21-12 in 1982

1980 *1* Johannesburg **South Africa** 24-9
2 Durban **South Africa** 18-9
South Africa won series 2-0
1980 *1* Montevideo **South Africa** 22-13
2 Santiago **South Africa** 30-16
South Africa won series 2-0
1982 *1* Pretoria **South Africa** 50-18
2 Bloemfontein **South America** 21-12
Series drawn 1-1
1984 *1* Pretoria **South Africa** 32-15
2 Cape Town **South Africa** 22-13
South Africa won series 2-0

SOUTH AFRICA v UNITED STATES

Played 2 South Africa won 2
Highest scores South Africa 43-20 in 2001, United States 20-43 in 2001
Biggest win South Africa 38-7 in 1981, United States no win

1981 Glenville **South Africa** 38-7
2001 Houston **South Africa** 43-20

SOUTH AFRICA v NEW ZEALAND CAVALIERS

Played 4 South Africa won 3, New Zealand Cavaliers won 1, Drawn 0
Highest scores South Africa 33-18 in 1986, New Zealand Cavaliers 19-18 in 1986
Biggest wins South Africa 33-18 in 1986, New Zealand Cavaliers 19-18 in 1986

1986 *1* Cape Town **South Africa** 21-15
2 Durban **New Zealand Cavaliers** 19-18
3 Pretoria **South Africa** 33-18
4 Johannesburg **South Africa** 24-10
South Africa won series 3-1

SOUTH AFRICA v ARGENTINA

Played 9 South Africa won 9
Highest scores South Africa 52-23 in 1993, Argentina 33-37 in 2000
Biggest wins South Africa 46-15 in 1996, Argentina no win

1993 *1* Buenos Aires **South Africa** 29-26
2 Buenos Aires **South Africa** 52-23
South Africa won series 2-0
1994 *1* Port Elizabeth **South Africa** 42-22
2 Johannesburg **South Africa** 46-26
South Africa won series 2-0

1996 *1* Buenos Aires **South Africa** 46-15
2 Buenos Aires **South Africa** 44-21
South Africa win series 2-0
2000 Buenos Aires **South Africa** 37-33
2002 Springs **South Africa** 49-29
2003 Port Elizabeth **South Africa** 26-25

SOUTH AFRICA v SAMOA

Played 3 South Africa won 3
Highest scores South Africa 60-8 in 1995 and 60-18 in 2002, Samoa 18-60 in 2002
Biggest win South Africa 60-8 in 1995, Samoa no win

1995 Johannesburg **South Africa** 60-8
1995 Johannesburg *WC* **South Africa** 42-14
2002 Pretoria **South Africa** 60-18

SOUTH AFRICA v ROMANIA

Played 1 South Africa won 1
Highest score South Africa 21-8 in 1995, Romania 8-21 in 1995
Biggest win South Africa 21-8 in 1995, Romania no win

1995 Cape Town *WC* **South Africa** 21-8

SOUTH AFRICA v CANADA

Played 2 South Africa won 2
Highest scores South Africa 51-18 in 2000, Canada 18-51 in 2000
Biggest win South Africa 51-18 in 2000, Canada no win

1995 Port Elizabeth *WC* **South Africa** 20-0
2000 East London **South Africa** 51-18

SOUTH AFRICA v ITALY

Played 6 South Africa won 6
Highest scores South Africa 101-0 in 1999, Italy 31-62 in 1997
Biggest win South Africa 101-0 in 1999, Italy no win

1995 Rome **South Africa** 40-21
1997 Bologna **South Africa** 62-31
1999 *1* Port Elizabeth **South Africa** 74-3
2 Durban **South Africa** 101-0
South Africa won series 2-0
2001 Port Elizabeth **South Africa** 60-14
2001 Genoa **South Africa** 54-26

SOUTH AFRICA v FIJI

Played 1 South Africa won 1
Highest scores South Africa 43-18 in 1996, Fiji 18-43 in 1996
Biggest win South Africa 43-18 in 1996, Fiji no win

1996 Pretoria **South Africa** 43-18

SOUTH AFRICA v TONGA

Played 1 South Africa won 1
Higest scores South Africa 74-10 in 1997, Tonga 10-74 in 1997
Biggest win South Africa 74-10 in 1997, Tonga no win

1997 Cape Town **South Africa** 74-10

SOUTH AFRICA v SPAIN

Played 1 South Africa won 1
Highest scores South Africa 47-3, Spain 3-47 in 1999
Biggest win South Africa 47-3 in 1999, Spain no win

1999 Murrayfield *WC* **South Africa** 47-3

SOUTH AFRICA v URUGUAY

Played 1 South Africa won 1
Highest scores South Africa 39-3 in 1999, Uruguay 3-39 in 1999
Biggest win South Africa 39-3 in 1999, Uruguay no win

1999 Glasgow *WC* **South Africa** 39-3

NEW ZEALAND v AUSTRALIA

Played 118 New Zealand won 78, Australia won 35, Drawn 5
Highest scores New Zealand 50-21 in 2003, Australia 35-39 in 2000
Biggest wins New Zealand 43-6 in 1996, Australia 28-7 in 1999

1903 Sydney **New Zealand** 22-3
1905 Dunedin **New Zealand** 14-3
1907 *1* Sydney **New Zealand** 26-6
2 Brisbane **New Zealand** 14-5
3 Sydney **Drawn** 5-5
New Zealand won series 2-0, with 1 draw
1910 *1* Sydney **New Zealand** 6-0
2 Sydney **Australia** 11-0
3 Sydney **New Zealand** 28-13
New Zealand won series 2-1
1913 *1* Wellington **New Zealand** 30-5
2 Dunedin **New Zealand** 25-13
3 Christchurch **Australia** 16-5
New Zealand won series 2-1
1914 *1* Sydney **New Zealand** 5-0
2 Brisbane **New Zealand** 17-0
3 Sydney **New Zealand** 22-7
New Zealand won series 3-0
1929 *1* Sydney **Australia** 9-8
2 Brisbane **Australia** 17-9
3 Sydney **Australia** 15-13
Australia won series 3-0
1931 Auckland **New Zealand** 20-13
1932 *1* Sydney **Australia** 22-17
2 Brisbane **New Zealand** 21-3
3 Sydney **New Zealand** 21-13
New Zealand won series 2-1
1934 *1* Sydney **Australia** 25-11
2 Sydney **Drawn** 3-3
Australia won series 1-0, with 1 draw
1936 *1* Wellington **New Zealand** 11-6
2 Dunedin **New Zealand** 38-13
New Zealand won series 2-0
1938 *1* Sydney **New Zealand** 24-9
2 Brisbane **New Zealand** 20-14
3 Sydney **New Zealand** 14-6
New Zealand won series 3-0
1946 *1* Dunedin **New Zealand** 31-8
2 Auckland **New Zealand** 14-10
New Zealand won series 2-0
1947 *1* Brisbane **New Zealand** 13-5
2 Sydney **New Zealand** 27-14
New Zealand won series 2-0
1949 *1* Wellington **Australia** 11-6
2 Auckland **Australia** 16-9
Australia won series 2-0
1951 *1* Sydney **New Zealand** 8-0
2 Sydney **New Zealand** 17-11
3 Brisbane **New Zealand** 16-6
New Zealand won series 3-0
1952 *1* Christchurch **Australia** 14-9
2 Wellington **New Zealand** 15-8
Series drawn 1-1
1955 *1* Wellington **New Zealand** 16-8
2 Dunedin **New Zealand** 8-0
3 Auckland **Australia** 8-3
New Zealand won series 2-1
1957 *1* Sydney **New Zealand** 25-11
2 Brisbane **New Zealand** 22-9
New Zealand won series 2-0
1958 *1* Wellington **New Zealand** 25-3
2 Christchurch **Australia** 6-3
3 Auckland **New Zealand** 17-8
New Zealand won series 2-1
1962 *1* Brisbane **New Zealand** 20-6
2 Sydney **New Zealand** 14-5
New Zealand won series 2-0
1962 *1* Wellington **Drawn** 9-9
2 Dunedin **New Zealand** 3-0
3 Auckland **New Zealand** 16-8
New Zealand won series 2-0, with1 draw
1964 *1* Dunedin **New Zealand** 14-9
2 Christchurch **New Zealand** 18-3
3 Wellington **Australia** 20-5
New Zealand won series 2-1
1967 Wellington **New Zealand** 29-9
1968 *1* Sydney **New Zealand** 27-11
2 Brisbane **New Zealand** 19-18
New Zealand won series 2-0
1972 *1* Wellington **New Zealand** 29-6
2 Christchurch **New Zealand** 30-17
3 Auckland **New Zealand** 38-3
New Zealand won series 3-0

1974 *1* Sydney **New Zealand** 11-6
2 Brisbane **Drawn** 16-16
3 Sydney **New Zealand** 16-6
New Zealand won series 2-0, with 1 draw
1978 *1* Wellington **New Zealand** 13-12
2 Christchurch **New Zealand** 22-6
3 Auckland **Australia** 30-16
New Zealand won series 2-1
1979 Sydney **Australia** 12-6
1980 *1* Sydney **Australia** 13-9
2 Brisbane **New Zealand** 12-9
3 Sydney **Australia** 26-10
Australia won series 2-1
1982 *1* Christchurch **New Zealand** 23-16
2 Wellington **Australia** 19-16
3 Auckland **New Zealand** 33-18
New Zealand won series 2-1
1983 Sydney **New Zealand** 18-8
1984 *1* Sydney **Australia** 16-9
2 Brisbane **New Zealand** 19-15
3 Sydney **New Zealand** 25-24
New Zealand won series 2-1
1985 Auckland **New Zealand** 10-9
1986 *1* Wellington **Australia** 13-12
2 Dunedin **New Zealand** 13-12
3 Auckland **Australia** 22-9
Australia won series 2-1
1987 Sydney **New Zealand** 30-16
1988 *1* Sydney **New Zealand** 32-7
2 Brisbane **Drawn** 19-19
3 Sydney **New Zealand** 30-9
New Zealand won series 2-0, with 1 draw
1989 Auckland **New Zealand** 24-12
1990 *1* Christchurch **New Zealand** 21-6
2 Auckland **New Zealand** 27-17
3 Wellington **Australia** 21-9
New Zealand won series 2-1
1991 *1* Sydney **Australia** 21-12
2 Auckland **New Zealand** 6-3
1991 Dublin *WC* **Australia** 16-6
1992 *1* Sydney **Australia** 16-15
2 Brisbane **Australia** 19-17
3 Sydney **New Zealand** 26-23
Australia won series 2-1
1993 Dunedin **New Zealand** 25-10
1994 Sydney **Australia** 20-16
1995 Auckland **New Zealand** 28-16
1995 Sydney **New Zealand** 34-23
1996 Wellington *TN* **New Zealand** 43-6
1996 Brisbane *TN* **New Zealand** 32-25
New Zealand won series 2-0
1997 Christchurch **New Zealand** 30-13
1997 Melbourne *TN* **New Zealand** 33-18
1997 Dunedin *TN* **New Zealand** 36-24
New Zealand won series 3-0
1998 Melbourne *TN* **Australia** 24-16
1998 Christchurch *TN* **Australia** 27-23
1998 Sydney **Australia** 19-14
Australia won series 3-0
1999 Auckland *TN* **New Zealand** 34-15
1999 Sydney *TN* **Australia** 28-7
Series drawn 1-1
2000 Sydney *TN* **New Zealand** 39-35
2000 Wellington *TN* **Australia** 24-23
Series drawn 1-1
2001 Dunedin *TN* **Australia** 23-15
2001 Sydney *TN* **Australia** 29-26
Australia won series 2-0
2002 Christchurch *TN* **New Zealand** 12-6
2002 Sydney *TN* **Australia** 16-14
Series drawn 1-1
2003 Sydney *TN* **New Zealand** 50-21
2003 Auckland **TN New Zealand** 21-17
New Zealand won series 2-0

NEW ZEALAND v UNITED STATES

Played 2 New Zealand won 2
Highest scores New Zealand 51-3 in 1913, United States 6-46 in 1991
Biggest win New Zealand 51-3 in 1913, United States no win

1913 Berkeley **New Zealand** 51-3
1991 Gloucester *WC* **New Zealand** 46-6

NEW ZEALAND v ROMANIA

Played 1 New Zealand won 1
Highest score New Zealand 14-6 in 1981, Romania 6-14 in 1981
Biggest win New Zealand 14-6 in 1981, Romania no win

1981 Bucharest **New Zealand** 14-6

NEW ZEALAND v ARGENTINA

Played 11 New Zealand won 10, Drawn 1
Highest scores New Zealand 93-8 in 1997, Argentina 21-21 in 1985
Biggest win New Zealand 93-8 in 1997, Argentina no win

1985 *1* Buenos Aires **New Zealand** 33-20
2 Buenos Aires **Drawn** 21-21
New Zealand won series 1-0, with 1 draw
1987 Wellington *WC* **New Zealand** 46-15
1989 *1* Dunedin **New Zealand** 60-9

2 Wellington **New Zealand** 49-12
New Zealand won series 2-0
1991 *1* Buenos Aires **New Zealand** 28-14
2 Buenos Aires **New Zealand** 36-6
New Zealand won series 2-0
1997 *1* Wellington **New Zealand** 93-8
2 Hamilton **New Zealand** 62-10
New Zealand won series 2-0
2001 Christchurch **New Zealand** 67-19
2001 Buenos Aires **New Zealand** 24-20

NEW ZEALAND v ITALY

Played 6 New Zealand won 6
Highest scores New Zealand 101-3 in 1999, Italy 21-31 in 1991
Biggest win New Zealand 101-3 in 1999, Italy no win

1987 Auckland *WC* **New Zealand** 70-6
1991 Leicester *WC* **New Zealand** 31-21
1995 Bologna **New Zealand** 70-6
1999 Huddersfield *WC* **New Zealand** 101-3
2000 Genoa **New Zealand** 56-19
2002 Hamilton **New Zealand** 64-10

NEW ZEALAND v FIJI

Played 3 New Zealand won 3
Highest scores New Zealand 74-13 in 1987, Fiji 18-68 in 2002
Biggest win New Zealand 71-5 in 1997, Fiji no win

1987 Christchurch *WC* **New Zealand** 74-13
1997 Albany **New Zealand** 71-5
2002 Wellington **New Zealand** 68-18

NEW ZEALAND v CANADA

Played 2 New Zealand won 2
Highest scores New Zealand 73-7 in 1995, Canada 13-29 in 1991
Biggest win New Zealand 73-7 in 1995, Canada no win

1991 Lille *WC* **New Zealand** 29-13
1995 Auckland **New Zealand** 73-7

NEW ZEALAND v WORLD XVs

Played 3 New Zealand won 2, World XV won 1, Drawn 0
Highest scores New Zealand 54-26 in 1992, World XV 28-14 in 1992
Biggest wins New Zealand 54-26 in 1992, World XV 28-14 in 1992

1992 *1* Christchurch **World XV** 28-14
2 Wellington **New Zealand** 54-26
3 Auckland **New Zealand** 26-15
New Zealand won series 2-1

NEW ZEALAND v SAMOA

Played 4 New Zealand won 4
Highest scores New Zealand 71-13 in 1999, Samoa 13-35 in 1993 & 13-71 in 1999
Biggest win New Zealand 71-13 in 1999, Samoa no win

1993 Auckland **New Zealand** 35-13
1996 Napier **New Zealand** 51-10
1999 Albany **New Zealand** 71-13
2001 Albany **New Zealand** 50-6

NEW ZEALAND v JAPAN

Played 1 New Zealand won 1
Highest scores New Zealand 145-17 in 1995, Japan 17-145 in 1995
Biggest win New Zealand 145-17 in 1995, Japan no win

1995 Bloemfontein *WC* **New Zealand** 145-17

NEW ZEALAND v TONGA

Played 2 New Zealand won 2
Highest scores New Zealand 102-0 in 2000, Tonga 9-45 in 1999
Biggest win New Zealand 102-0 in 2000, Tonga no win

1999 Bristol *WC* **New Zealand** 45-9
2000 Albany **New Zealand** 102-0

AUSTRALIA v UNITED STATES

Played 6 Australia won 6
Highest scores Australia 67-9 in 1990, United States 19-55 in 1999
Biggest win Australia 67-9 in 1990, United States no win

1912 Berkeley **Australia** 12-8
1976 Los Angeles **Australia** 24-12
1983 Sydney **Australia** 49-3
1987 Brisbane *WC* **Australia** 47-12
1990 Brisbane **Australia** 67-9
1999 Limerick *WC* **Australia** 55-19

AUSTRALIA v NEW ZEALAND XVs

Played 24 Australia won 6, New Zealand XVs won 18, Drawn 0
Highest scores Australia 26-20 in 1926, New Zealand XV 38-11 in 1923 and 38-8 in 1924
Biggest win Australia 17-0 in 1921, New Zealand XV 38-8 in 1924

1920 *1* Sydney **New Zealand XV** 26-15
2 Sydney **New Zealand XV** 14-6
3 Sydney **New Zealand XV** 24-13
New Zealand XV won series 3-0
1921 Christchurch **Australia** 17-0
1922 *1* Sydney **New Zealand XV** 26-19
2 Sydney **Australia** 14-8
3 Sydney **Australia** 8-6
Australia won series 2-1
1923 *1* Dunedin **New Zealand XV** 19-9
2 Christchurch **New Zealand XV** 34-6
3 Wellington **New Zealand XV** 38-11
New Zealand XV won series 3-0
1924 *1* Sydney **Australia** 20-16
2 Sydney **New Zealand XV** 21-5
3 Sydney **New Zealand XV** 38-8
New Zealand XV won series 2-1
1925 *1* Sydney **New Zealand XV** 26-3
2 Sydney **New Zealand XV** 4-0
3 Sydney **New Zealand XV** 11-3
New Zealand XV won series 3-0
1925 Auckland **New Zealand XV** 36-10
1926 *1* Sydney **Australia** 26-20
2 Sydney **New Zealand XV** 11-6
3 Sydney **New Zealand XV** 14-0
4 Sydney **New Zealand XV** 28-21
New Zealand XV won series 3-1
1928 *1* Wellington **New Zealand XV** 15-12
2 Dunedin **New Zealand XV** 16-14
3 Christchurch **Australia** 11-8
New Zealand XV won series 2-1

AUSTRALIA v SOUTH AFRICA XVs

Played 3 South Africa XVs won 3
Highest scores Australia 11-16 in 1921, South Africa XV 28-9 in 1921
Biggest win Australia no win, South Africa XV 28-9 in 1921

1921 *1* Sydney **South Africa XV** 25-10
2 Sydney **South Africa XV** 16-11
3 Sydney **South Africa XV** 28-9
South Africa XV won series 3-0

AUSTRALIA v NEW ZEALAND MAORIS

Played 16 Australia won 8, New Zealand Maoris won 6, Drawn 2
Highest scores Australia 31-6 in 1936, New Zealand Maoris 25-22 in 1922
Biggest wins Australia 31-6 in 1936, New Zealand Maoris 20-0 in 1946

1922 *1* Sydney **New Zealand Maoris** 25-22
2 Sydney **Australia** 28-13
3 Sydney **New Zealand Maoris** 23-22
New Zealand Maoris won series 2-1
1923 *1* Sydney **Australia** 27-23
2 Sydney **Australia** 21-16
3 Sydney **Australia** 14-12
Australia won series 3-0

1928 Wellington **New Zealand Maoris** 9-8
1931 Palmerston North **Australia** 14-3
1936 Palmerston North **Australia** 31-6
1946 Hamilton **New Zealand Maoris** 20-0
1949 *1* Sydney **New Zealand Maoris** 12-3
2 Brisbane **Drawn** 8-8
3 Sydney **Australia** 18-3
Series drawn 1-1, with 1 draw
1958 *1* Brisbane **Australia** 15-14
2 Sydney **Drawn** 3-3
3 Melbourne **New Zealand Maoris** 13-6
Series drawn 1-1, with 1 draw

AUSTRALIA v FIJI

Played 16 Australia won 13, Fiji won 2, Drawn 1
Highest scores Australia 66-20 in 1998, Fiji 28-52 in 1985
Biggest wins Australia 66-20 in 1998, Fiji 17-15 in 1952 & 18-16 in 1954

1952 *1* Sydney **Australia** 15-9
2 Sydney **Fiji** 17-15
Series drawn 1-1
1954 *1* Brisbane **Australia** 22-19
2 Sydney **Fiji** 18-16
Series drawn 1-1
1961 *1* Brisbane **Australia** 24-6
2 Sydney **Australia** 20-14
3 Melbourne **Drawn** 3-3
Australia won series 2-0, with 1 draw
1972 Suva **Australia** 21-19
1976 *1* Sydney **Australia** 22-6
2 Brisbane **Australia** 21-9
3 Sydney **Australia** 27-17
Australia won series 3-0
1980 Suva **Australia** 22-9
1984 Suva **Australia** 16-3
1985 *1* Brisbane **Australia** 52-28
2 Sydney **Australia** 31-9
Australia won series 2-0
1998 Sydney **Australia** 66-20

AUSTRALIA v TONGA

Played 4 Australia won 3, Tonga won 1, Drawn 0
Highest scores Australia 74-0 in 1998, Tonga 16-11 in 1973
Biggest wins Australia 74-0 in 1998, Tonga 16-11 in 1973

1973 *1* Sydney **Australia** 30-12
2 Brisbane **Tonga** 16-11
Series drawn 1-1
1993 Brisbane **Australia** 52-14
1998 Canberra **Australia** 74-0

AUSTRALIA v JAPAN

Played 3 Australia won 3
Highest scores Australia 50-25 in 1975, Japan 25-50 in 1973
Biggest win Australia 50-25 in 1975, Japan no win

1975 *1* Sydney **Australia** 37-7
2 Brisbane **Australia** 50-25
Australia won series 2-0
1987 Sydney *WC* **Australia** 42-23

AUSTRALIA v ARGENTINA

Played 16 Australia won 11, Argentina won 4, Drawn 1
Highest scores Australia 53-7 in 1995 & 53-6 in 2000, Argentina 27-19 in 1987
Biggest wins Australia 53-6 in 2000, Argentina 18-3 in 1983

1979 *1* Buenos Aires **Argentina** 24-13
2 Buenos Aires **Australia** 17-12
Series drawn 1-1
1983 *1* Brisbane **Argentina** 18-3
2 Sydney **Australia** 29-13
Series drawn 1-1
1986 *1* Brisbane **Australia** 39-19
2 Sydney **Australia** 26-0
Australia won series 2-0
1987 *1* Buenos Aires **Drawn** 19-19
2 Buenos Aires **Argentina** 27-19
Argentina won series 1-0, with 1 draw
1991 Llanelli *WC* **Australia** 32-19
1995 *1* Brisbane **Australia** 53-7
2 Sydney **Australia** 30-13
Australia won series 2-0
1997 *1* Buenos Aires **Australia** 23-15

2 Buenos Aires **Argentina** 18-16
Series drawn 1-1
2000 *1* Brisbane **Australia** 53-6
2 Canberra **Australia** 32-25
Australia won series 2-0
2002 Buenos Aires **Australia** 17-6

AUSTRALIA v SAMOA

Played 3 Australia won 3
Highest scores Australia 73-3 in 1994, Samoa 13-25 in 1998
Biggest win Australia 73-3 in 1994, Samoa no win

1991 Pontypool *WC* **Australia** 9-3
1994 Sydney **Australia** 73-3
1998 Brisbane **Australia** 25-13

AUSTRALIA v ITALY

Played 7 Australia won 7
Highest scores Australia 55-6 in 1988, Italy 20-23 in 1994
Biggest win Australia 55-6 in 1988, Italy no win

1983 Rovigo **Australia** 29-7
1986 Brisbane **Australia** 39-18
1988 Rome **Australia** 55-6
1994 *1* Brisbane **Australia** 23-20
2 Melbourne **Australia** 20-7
Australia won series 2-0
1996 Padua **Australia** 40-18
2002 Genoa **Australia** 34-3

AUSTRALIA v CANADA

Played 5 Australia won 5
Highest scores Australia 74-9 in 1996, Canada 16-43 in 1993
Biggest win Australia 74-9 in 1996, Canada no win

1985 *1* Sydney **Australia** 59-3
2 Brisbane **Australia** 43-15
Australia won series 2-0
1993 Calgary **Australia** 43-16
1995 Port Elizabeth *WC* **Australia** 27-11
1996 Brisbane **Australia** 74-9

AUSTRALIA v KOREA

Played 1 Australia won 1
Highest scores Australia 65-18 in 1987, Korea 18-65 in 1987
Biggest win Australia 65-18 in 1987, Korea no win

1987 Brisbane **Australia** 65-18

AUSTRALIA v ROMANIA

Played 2 Australia won 2
Highest scores Australia 57-9 in 1999, Romania 9-57 in 1999
Biggest win Australia 57-9 in 1999, Romania no win

1995 Stellenbosch *WC* **Australia** 42-3
1999 Belfast *WC* **Australia** 57-9

AUSTRALIA v SPAIN

Played 1 Australia won 1
Highest scores Australia 92-10 in 2001, Spain 10-92 in 2001
Biggest win Australia 92-10 in 2001, Spain no win

2001 Madrid **Australia** 92-10

WORLD INTERNATIONAL RECORDS

The match and career records cover official cap matches *played by the dozen Executive Council Member Unions of the International Board (England, Scotland, Ireland, Wales, France, Italy, South Africa, New Zealand, Australia, Argentina, Canada and Japan) from 1871 up to 30 September 2003. Figures include Test performances for the (British/Irish Isles) Lions and (South American) Jaguars (shown in brackets). Where a world record has been set in a cap match played by another nation in membership of the IRB, this is shown as a footnote to the relevant table.*

MATCH RECORDS

MOST CONSECUTIVE TEST WINS

17 by N Zealand 1965 *SA* 4, 1966 *BI* 1,2,3,4, 1967 *A, E, W, F, S,* 1968 *A* 1,2, *F* 1,2,3, 1969 *W* 1,2

17 by S Africa 1997 *A* 2, *It, F* 1,2, *E, S,* 1998 *I* 1,2, *W* 1, *E* 1, *A* 1, *NZ* 1,2, *A* 2, *W* 2, *S, I* 3

MOST CONSECUTIVE TESTS WITHOUT DEFEAT

Matches	*Wins*	*Draws*	*Period*
23 by N Zealand	22	1	1987 to 1990
17 by N Zealand	15	2	1961 to 1964
17 by N Zealand	17	0	1965 to 1969
17 by S Africa	17	0	1997 to 1998

MOST POINTS IN A MATCH

by a team

Pts	*Opponents*	*Venue*	*Year*
155 by Japan	Chinese Taipei	Tokyo	2002
152 by Argentina	Paraguay	Mendoza	2002
145 by N Zealand	Japan	Bloemfontein	1995
144 by Argentina	Paraguay	Montevideo	2003
134 by Japan	Chinese Taipei	Singapore	1998
134 by England	Romania	Twickenham	2001
120 by Japan	Chinese Taipei	Tainan	2002

Hong Kong scored 164 points against Singapore at Kuala Lumpur in 1994

by a player

Pts	*Player*	*Opponents*	*Venue*	*Year*
60 for Japan	T Kurihara	Ch Taipei	Tainan	2002
50 for Argentina	E Morgan	Paraguay	San Pablo	1973
45 for N Zealand	S D Culhane	Japan	Bloemfontein	1995
45 for Argentina	J-M Nuñez-Piossek	Paraguay	Montevideo	2003
44 for Scotland	A G Hastings	Ivory Coast	Rustenburg	1995
44 for England	C Hodgson	Romania	Twickenham	2001
40 for Argentina	G M Jorge	Brazil	Sao Paulo	1993
40 for Japan	D Ohata	Ch Taipei	Tokyo	2002
39 for Australia	M C Burke	Canada	Brisbane	1996

MOST TRIES IN A MATCH

by the team

Tries	*Opponents*	*Venue*	*Year*
24 by Argentina	Paraguay	Mendoza	2002
24 by Argentina	Paraguay	Montevideo	2003
23 by Japan	Chinese Taipei	Tokyo	2002
21 by N Zealand	Japan	Bloemfontein	1995
20 by Japan	Ch Taipei	Singapore	1998
20 by England	Romania	Twickenham	2001
19 by Argentina	Brazil	Santiago	1979
19 by Argentina	Paraguay	Asuncion	1985

Hong Kong scored 26 tries against Singapore at Kuala Lumpur in 1994

by a player

Tries	*Player*	*Opponents*	*Venue*	*Year*
9 for Argentina	J-M Nuñez-Piossek	Paraguay	Montevideo	2003
8 for Argentina	G M Jorge	Brazil	Sao Paulo	1993
8 for Japan	D Ohata	Ch Taipei	Tokyo	2002
6 for Argentina	E Morgan	Paraguay	San Pablo	1973
6 for Argentina	G M Jorge	Brazil	Montevideo	1989
6 for N Zealand	M C G Ellis	Japan	Bloemfontein	1995
6 for Japan	T Kurihara	Ch Taipei	Tainan	2002
5 for Scotland	G C Lindsay	Wales	Raeburn Place	1887
5 for England	D Lambert	France	Richmond	1907
5 for Argentina	H Goti	Brazil	Montevideo	1961
5 for Argentina	M R Jurado	Brazil	Montevideo	1971
5 for England	R Underwood	Fiji	Twickenham	1989
5 for N Zealand	J W Wilson	Fiji	Albany	1997
5 for Japan	T Masuho	Ch Taipei	Singapore	1998
5 for Argentina	P Grande	Paraguay	Asuncion	1998
5 for S Africa	C S Terblanche	Italy	Durban	1999

10 tries were scored for Hong Kong by A Billington against Singapore at Kuala Lumpur in 1994

MOST CONVERSIONS IN A MATCH

by the team

Cons	Opponents	Venue	Year
20 by N Zealand	Japan	Bloemfontein	1995
20 by Japan	Chinese Taipei	Tokyo	2002
17 by Japan	Chinese Taipei	Singapore	1998
16 by Argentina	Paraguay	Mendoza	2002
15 by Argentina	Brazil	Santiago	1979
15 by England	Holland	Huddersfield	1998
15 by Japan	Chinese Taipei	Tainan	2002

by a player

Cons	Player	Opponents	Venue	Year
20 for N Zealand	S D Culhane	Japan	Bloemfontein	1995
16 for Argentina	J-L Cilley	Paraguay	Mendoza	2002
15 for England	P J Grayson	Holland	Huddersfield	1998
15 for Japan	T Kurihara	Ch Taipei	Tainan	2002

MOST PENALTIES IN A MATCH

by the team

Penalties	Opponents	Venue	Year
9 by Japan	Tonga	Tokyo	1999
9 by N Zealand	Australia	Auckland	1999
9 by Wales	France	Cardiff	1999
9 by N Zealand	France	Paris	2000

Portugal scored nine penalties against Georgia at Lisbon in 2000

by a player

Penalties	Player	Opponents	Venue	Year
9 for Japan	K Hirose	Tonga	Tokyo	1999
9 for N Zealand	A P Mehrtens	Australia	Auckland	1999
9 for Wales	N R Jenkins	France	Cardiff	1999
9 for N Zealand	A P Mehrtens	France	Paris	2000

Nine penalties were scored for Portugal by T Teixeira against Georgia at Lisbon in 2000

MOST DROPPED GOALS IN A MATCH

by the team

Drops	Opponents	Venue	Year
5 by South Africa	England	Paris	1999
3 by several nations			

by a player

Drops	Player	Opponents	Venue	Year
5 for S Africa	J H de Beer	England	Paris	1999
3 for several nations				

CAREER RECORDS

MOST CAPPED PLAYERS

Caps	Player	Career Span
111	P Sella (France)	1982 to 1995
111 (5)	J Leonard (England/Lions)	1990 to 2003
101	D I Campese (Australia)	1982 to 1996
93	S Blanco (France)	1980 to 1991
92	S B T Fitzpatrick (N Zealand)	1986 to 1997
91 (6)	R Underwood (England/Lions)	1984 to 1996
91 (4)	N R Jenkins (Wales/Lions)	1991 to 2002

MOST CONSECUTIVE TESTS

Tests	Player	Career Span
63	S B T Fitzpatrick (N Zealand)	1986 to 1995
62	J W Roff (Australia)	1996 to 2001
53	G O Edwards (Wales)	1967 to 1978
52	W J McBride (Ireland)	1964 to 1975
51	C M Cullen (N Zealand)	1996 to 2000

MOST TESTS AS CAPTAIN

Tests	Captain	Career Span
59	W D C Carling (England)	1988 to 1996
55	J A Eales (Australia)	1996 to 2001
51	S B T Fitzpatrick (N Zealand)	1992 to 1997
46 (8)	H Porta (Argentina/Jaguars)	1971 to 1990
41	L Arbizu (Argentina)	1992 to 2002
37	M Giovanelli (Italy)	1992 to 1999
36	N C Farr-Jones (Australia)	1988 to 1992
36	G H Teichmann (S Africa)	1996 to 1999

MOST TESTS IN INDIVIDUAL POSITIONS

Position	Player	Tests	Career Span
Full-back	S Blanco (France)	81	1980 to 1991
Wing	R Underwood (England/Lions)	91 (6)	1984 to 1996
Centre	P Sella (France)	104	1982 to 1995
Fly-half	C R Andrew (England/Lions)	75 (5)	1985 to 1997
Scrum-half	G M Gregan (Australia)	89	1994 to 2003
Prop	J Leonard (England/Lions)	111 (5)	1990 to 2003
Hooker	S B T Fitzpatrick (N Zealand)	92	1986 to 1997
Lock	M O Johnson (England/Lions)	85 (8)	1993 to 2003
Flanker	D J Wilson (Australia)	79	1992 to 2000
No 8	R S T Kefu (Australia)	58	1998 to 2003

Blanco, Sella, Andrew and Kefu were capped in other positions

MOST POINTS IN TESTS

Points	Player	Tests	Career Span
1090 (41)	N R Jenkins (Wales/Lions))	91 (4)	1991 to 2002
1010 (27)	D Dominguez (Italy/Argentina)	76 (2)	1989 to 2003
932	A P Mehrtens (N Zealand)	66	1995 to 2002
911	M P Lynagh (Australia)	72	1984 to 1995
851	M C Burke (Australia)	72	1993 to 2003
740 (36)	J P Wilkinson (England/Lions)	49 (3)	1998 to 2003
733 (66)	A G Hastings (Scotland/Lions)	67 (6)	1986 to 1995

MOST TRIES IN TESTS

Tries	Player	Tests	Career Span
64	D I Campese (Australia)	101	1982 to 1996
50 (1)	R Underwood (England/Lions)	91 (6)	1984 to 1996
46	C M Cullen (N Zealand)	58	1996 to 2002
44	J W Wilson (N Zealand)	60	1993 to 2001
38	S Blanco (France)	93	1980 to 1991
38	D Ohata (Japan)	36	1996 to 2003
37	J T Lomu (N Zealand)	63	1994 to 2002
35	J J Kirwan (N Zealand)	63	1984 to 1994
35	J H van der Westhuizen (S Africa)	85	1993 to 2003
34 (1)	I C Evans (Wales/Lions)	79 (7)	1987 to 1998

MOST CONVERSIONS IN TESTS

Cons	Player	Tests	Career Span
162	A P Mehrtens (N Zealand)	66	1995 to 2002
140	M P Lynagh (Australia)	72	1984 to 1995
133 (6)	D Dominguez (Italy/Argentina)	76 (2)	1989 to 2003
131 (1)	N R Jenkins (Wales/Lions))	91 (4)	1991 to 2002
118	G J Fox (N Zealand)	46	1985 to 1993
118 (5)	J P Wilkinson (England/Lions)	49 (3)	1998 to 2003

MOST PENALTY GOALS IN TESTS

Penalties	Player	Tests	Career Span
248 (13)	N R Jenkins (Wales/Lions)	91 (4)	1991 to 2002
214 (5)	D Dominguez (Italy/Argentina)	76 (2)	1989 to 2003
181	A P Mehrtens (N Zealand)	66	1995 to 2002
177	M P Lynagh (Australia)	72	1984 to 1995
172	M C Burke (Australia)	72	1993 to 2003
160 (20)	A G Hastings (Scotland/Lions)	67 (6)	1986 to 1995

MOST DROPPED GOALS IN TESTS

Drops	Player	Tests	Career Span
28 (2)	H Porta (Argentina/Jaguars)	66 (8)	1971 to 1990
23 (2)	C R Andrew (England/Lions)	76 (5)	1985 to 1997
19 (0)	D Dominguez (Italy/Argentina)	76 (2)	1989 to 2003
18	H E Botha (S Africa)	28	1980 to 1992
17	S Bettarello (Italy)	55	1979 to 1988
15	J-P Lescarboura (France)	28	1982 to 1990

PARTNERSHIP RECORDS

Position	Holders	Detail	Career Span
Centre threequarters	W D C Carling & J C Guscott	45 (1) for England/Lions	1989 to 1996
Half backs	D Dominguez & A Troncon	52 for Italy	1994 to 2003
Front row	A J Daly, P N Kearns & E J A McKenzie	37 for Australia	1990 to 1995
Second row	I D Jones & R M Brooke	49 for N Zealand	1992 to 1999
Back row	R A Hill, L B N Dallaglio & N A Back	38 for England	1997 to 2003

INTERNATIONAL REFEREES

Leading Referees

Up to 30 September 2003 in major international matches. These include all matches for which the eight senior members of the International Board have awarded caps, and also all matches played in the World Cup final stages.

W D Bevan	Wales	43
J M Fleming	Scotland	39
E F Morrison	England	30
D T M McHugh	Ireland	26
C Norling	Wales	25
D J Bishop	New Zealand	24
K D Kelleher	Ireland	23
D G Walters	Wales	23
M Joseph	Wales	22
C J Hawke	New Zealand	22
J Dumé	France	22
A J Watson	South Africa	22
R C Williams	Ireland	21
K V J Fitzgerald	Australia	21
P D O'Brien	New Zealand	21
F A Howard	England	20
W J Erickson	Australia	20

Major international match appearances 2002-03

Matches controlled up to 30 September 2003

2002	
I v R	**G de Santis** (Italy)
Ru v I	**J Jutge** (France)
I v Gg	**N Williams** (Wales)
W v R	**J Jutge** (France)
Arg v A	**K M Deaker** (New Zealand)
E v NZ	**J I Kaplan** (South Africa)
I v A	**S R Walsh** (New Zealand)
S v R	**A D Turner** (South Africa)
W v Fj	**S Dickinson** (Australia)
F v SA	**A C Rolland** (Ireland)
E v A	**P G Honiss** (New Zealand)
S v SA	**N Williams** (Wales)
W v C	**G de Santis** (Italy)
F v NZ	**S Young** (Australia)
I v Fj	**A J Spreadbury** (England)
E v SA	**P D O'Brien** (New Zealand)
W v NZ	**W T S Henning** (South Africa)
I v Arg	**C White** (England)
It v A	**P C Deluca** (Argentina)
F v C	**D T M McHugh** (Ireland)
S v Fj	**S M Lawrence** (South Africa)
2003	
It v W	**J Jutge** (France)
E v F	**P G Honiss** (New Zealand)
S v I	**A Cole** (Australia)
It v I	**A J Spreadbury** (England)
W v E	**S R Walsh** (New Zealand)
F v S	**P Marshall** (Australia)
I v F	**A J Watson** (South Africa)
S v W	**P C Deluca** (Argentina) rep by **A J Spreadbury** (England)
E v It	**A C Rolland** (Ireland)
W v I	**S J Lander** (England)
E v S	**A Lewis** (Ireland)
It v F	**N Williams** (Wales)
F v W	**P D O'Brien** (New Zealand)
S v It	**D T M McHugh** (Ireland)
I v E	**J I Kaplan** (South Africa)
A v I	**N Williams** (Wales)
SA v S	**J Jutge** (France)
NZ v E	**S J Dickinson** (Australia)
A v W	**S M Lawrence** (South Africa)
SA v S	**S Young** (Australia)
Tg v I	**S R Walsh** (New Zealand)
Arg v F	**S J Lander** (England)
Arg v F	**A Cole** (Australia)
Sm v I	**P G Honiss** (New Zealand)
NZ v W	**A Lewis** (Ireland)
A v E	**D T M McHugh** (Ireland)
NZ v F	**A J Watson** (South Africa)
SA v Arg	**N Williams** (Wales)
SA v A	**S R Walsh** (New Zealand)
SA v NZ	**A C Rolland** (Ireland)
A v NZ	**A J Spreadbury** (England)
A v SA	**P D O'Brien** (New Zealand)
NZ v SA	**P Marshall** (Australia)
NZ v A	**J I Kaplan** (South Africa)
I v W	**J Dumé** (France)
F v R	**G de Santis** (Italy)
W v E	**P C Deluca** (Argentina)

S v It	**D Courtney** (Ireland)	F v E	**S M Lawrence** (South Africa)
W v R	**A D Turner** (South Africa)	S v I	**N Whitehouse** (Wales)
W v S	**C White** (England)	E v F	**N Williams** (Wales)
I v It	**S J Lander** (England)		

Replacement referees in major internationals

F Gardiner (Ireland)	replaced	**J Tulloch** (Scotland)	**I v SA 1912**
B Marie (France)	replaced	**R W Gilliland** (Ireland)	**F v W 1965**
A R Taylor (N Zealand)	replaced	**J P Murphy** (N Zealand)	**NZ v SA 1965**
R F Johnson (England)	replaced	**R Calmet** (France)	**E v W 1970**
F Palmade (France)	replaced	**K A Pattinson** (England)	**F v S 1973**
J M Fleming (Scotland)	replaced	**J B Anderson** (Scotland)	**Arg v WS *1991**
J M Fleming (Scotland)	replaced	**C J Hawke** (N Zealand)	**E v F 1999**
D T M McHugh (Ireland)	replaced	**W T S Henning** (S Africa)	**E v F 2001**
D T M McHugh (Ireland)	replaced	**S J Dickinson** (Australia)	**E v SA 2001**
C White (England)	replaced	**D T M McHugh** (Ireland)	**SA v NZ 2002**
A J Spreadbury (England)	replaced	**P C Deluca** (Argentina)	**S v W 2003**

Dismissals in major international matches

A E Freethy	sent off	C J Brownlie (NZ)	E v NZ	1925
K D Kelleher	sent off	C E Meads (NZ)	S v NZ	1967
R T Burnett	sent off	M A Burton (E)	A v E	1975
W M Cooney	sent off	J Sovau (Fj)	A v Fj	1976
N R Sanson	sent off	G A D Wheel (W)	W v I	1977
N R Sanson	sent off	W P Duggan (I)	W v I	1977
D I H Burnett	sent off	P Ringer (W)	E v W	1980
C Norling	sent off	J-P Garuet (F)	F v I	1984
K V J Fitzgerald	sent off	H D Richards (W)	NZ v W	*1987
F A Howard	sent off	D Codey (A)	A v W	*1987
K V J Fitzgerald	sent off	M Taga (Fj)	Fj v E	1988
O E Doyle	sent off	A Lorieux (F)	Arg v F	1988
B W Stirling	sent off	T Vonolagi (Fj)	E v Fj	1989
B W Stirling	sent off	N Nadruku (Fj)	E v Fj	1989
F A Howard	sent off	K Moseley (W)	W v F	1990
F A Howard	sent off	A Carminati (F)	S v F	1990
F A Howard	sent off	A Stoop (Nm)	Nm v W	1990
A J Spreadbury	sent off	A Benazzi (F)	A v F	1990
C Norling	sent off	P Gallart (F)	A v F	1990
C J Hawke	sent off	F E Mendez (Arg)	E v Arg	1990
E F Morrison	sent off	C Cojocariu (R)	R v F	1991
J M Fleming	sent off	P L Sporleder (Arg)	WS v Arg	*1991
J M Fleming	sent off	M G Keenan (WS)	WS v Arg	*1991
S R Hilditch	sent off	G Lascubé (F)	F v E	1992
S R Hilditch	sent off	V Moscato (F)	F v E	1992
D J Bishop	sent off	O Roumat (Wld)	NZ v Wld	1992
E F Morrison	sent off	J T Small (SA)	A v SA	1993
I Rogers	sent off	M E Cardinal (C)	C v F	1994
I Rogers	sent off	P Sella (F)	C v F	1994
D Mené	sent off	J D Davies (W)	W v E	1995
S Lander	sent off	F Mahoni (Tg)	F v Tg	*1995
D T M McHugh	sent off	J Dalton (SA)	SA v C	*1995
D T M McHugh	sent off	R G A Snow (C)	SA v C	*1995

D T M McHugh	sent off	G L Rees (C)	SA v C	*1995
J Dumé	sent off	G R Jenkins (W)	SA v W	1995
W J Erickson	sent off	V B Cavubati (Fj)	NZ v Fj	1997
W D Bevan	sent off	A G Venter (SA)	NZ v SA	1997
C Giacomel	sent off	R Travaglini (Arg)	F v Arg	1997
W J Erickson	sent off	D J Grewcock (E)	NZ v E	1998
S R Walsh	sent off	J Sitoa (Tg)	A v Tg	1998
R G Davies	sent off	M Giovanelli (It)	S v It	1999
C Thomas	sent off	T Leota (Sm)	Sm v F	1999
C Thomas	sent off	G Leaupepe (Sm)	Sm v F	1999
S Dickinson	sent off	J-J Crenca (F)	NZ v F	1999
E F Morrison	sent off	M Vunibaka (Fj)	Fj v C	*1999
A Cole	sent off	D R Baugh (C)	C v Nm	*1999
W J Erickson	sent off	N Ta'ufo'ou (Tg)	E v Tg	*1999
P Marshall	sent off	B D Venter (SA)	SA v U	*1999
P C Deluca	sent off	W Cristofoletto (It)	F v It	2000
J I Kaplan	sent off	A Troncon (It)	It v I	2001
R Dickson	sent off	G Leger (Tg)	W v Tg	2001
P C Deluca	sent off	N J Hines (S)	US v S	2002
P D O'Brien	sent off	M C Joubert (SA)	SA v A	2002
P D O'Brien	sent off	J J Labuschagne (SA)	E v SA	2002
S R Walsh	sent off	V Ma'asi (Tg)	Tg v I	2003

** Matches in World Cup final stages*

HEINEKEN CUP 2002-03

French with and without Tears

Mick Cleary

It seemed a good idea at the time. However, as the nightmare scenario began to unfold one Sunday afternoon in late April, fingers began to twitch and heads began to be scratched. Was it such a clever ploy after all to commit so early in the tournament to a Dublin final come what may? The decision had been made before the competition even began with a fanfare of self-belief as well as, perhaps, of self-aggrandisement.

'In confirming the venue before the Pool stages begin it means that everyone knows where European club rugby's showpiece occasion will be staged. From today all roads lead to the Irish capital,' said European Rugby Cup (ERC) chairman Jean-Pierre Lux at the launch of the eighth Heineken Cup.

And so it was that for the first time in the competition's history two teams from the same country fought their way through to contest the final. It might have been an all-Ireland final, for Munster and Leinster made it to the semi-final. But it was not to be. Toulouse proved too strong for Munster on their own patch at the Stadium Municipal while Leinster blew a golden opportunity in front of their own fans when losing out to Perpignan at Lansdowne Road. If the local shindig had come to pass, we would probably have been hailing the final as one of those memorable days of sport – a local gig with universal appeal. As it was, the backdrop, although bright and brash, was not quite the real deal. There were great tracts of Lansdowne Road unoccupied, even though the crowd of 28,600 did their level best to fill the available space and provide a suitable backing track.

But it didn't feel right and it didn't look right. ERC were caught between a rock and a hard place. If they had left it until the later stages to decide on a venue, then they would have been charged with dithering. By going early, they stand accused of over-reaching themselves, of having an inflated notion of the competition's true worth. It was not an easy call either way.

In hindsight, that welcoming refuge of Yearbook editors, it would have been sensible to have had a back-up plan. There were calls for the final to be staged in Marseilles or even Barcelona once it was known that two French sides might make it through. There was never any attempt to follow through the feasibility of these suggestions. If the logistics had proved unworkable, or simply too damn costly, then so be it. As it was, there was a sense that not every option had been explored. An opportunity was missed.

The French public, taking their lead from the French clubs themselves, have always had an ambivalent view of the Heineken Cup. Their own domestic championship has far more appeal. It's no wonder. It has a century of tradition behind it. And so, to stage the first ever all-French final in front of a capacity 60,000 at the Stade Vélodrome in Marseilles would have been a wonderful marketing strategy, a visible, vibrant wooing of the sceptics. And if not that, then why not take the Heineken Cup to Barcelona – a new venture and a new chapter in an evolving tournament.

Of course, it's right also to argue that ERC stood its ground because it was – and is – confident of its status. It believes that the brand is strong. It's a fair argument, endorsed by the decision of the sponsors, Heineken, to commit for a further two years at a cost of some £14 million. However, it has to be pointed out that the attendance for the final was the lowest since the first year of the competition in 1995/6, when 21,800 turned up at the Arms Park to see Toulouse beat Cardiff 21-18 after extra-time. Those numbers tell a tale.

Toulouse cared little for the arguments. Most of them would have been happy playing on Margate Sands. 'It's good that the final is being played in Dublin,' was the opinion of young Toulouse wing, Vincent Clerc. 'It puts the game in a European context whereas if it were in France, it would be too much like the French championship.'

So much for the pros and cons. What was not in dispute is that Toulouse deserved to come through to match Leicester's record of winning the Heineken Cup twice. Even though the French side never really hit their straps, there was always a sense that they had both the class and the clout to see off all challenges. They were helped to a large degree by having effective home advantage through the knockout stages. Both games, the quarter-final against Northampton and semi-final against Munster, were played at the Stadium Municipal, supposedly a neutral venue for the semi-final. Leinster were supposedly also favoured by being able to stage their semi-final at Lansdowne Road. Neutral should mean neutral, not a stone's throw from the normal home ground.

Perpignan proudly flew the flag for Catalonia through the tournament and deservedly won through to their first ever Heineken final. They may not have had the biggest names on their roster but few players could match the resolve and raw-boned ability of the likes of prop Renaud Peillard (now bound for Northampton) or Canadian No 8 Phil Murphy (heading to London Irish), or his mates alongside in the back-row, Grégory Le Corvec and captain, Bernard Goutta. Good men and fine players.

Perpignan did it the hard way. They survived the toughest of all the pools, Pool 2 where they qualified along with Munster, Gloucester being the unlucky loser. All three clubs finished with the same number of pool points – eight from four victories – but Gloucester missed out because of the results among those three teams.

Perpignan, so impressive at their imposing Stade Aimé-Giral, had to prove themselves on the road after faltering during the pool stages. They did that with away victories in the knockout stages at Llanelli and Leinster.

Pool 2 threw up perhaps the tournament's most dramatic match, Munster beating Gloucester 33-6 in the final group game to sneak through. It had looked an impossible task. They needed to win by 27 points and score four tries to qualify. That concrete slab of dreams, Limerick's Thomond Park, did not disappoint, Ronan O'Gara landing the conversion of John Kelly's last-minute try to make the mathematics work. O'Gara was not even aware of the significance of the kick.

Munster made the most of their escape. They travelled to Welford Road for the quarter-final and utterly demolished the double Heineken Cup champions. It was a seminal moment. Leicester had never been so ruthlessly humiliated on their own patch. The Munster players and fans danced and sang on the Leicester turf long after the final whistle had sounded.

Elsewhere the pool stages were rather disappointing. Even though five of the eight quarter-final places were still up for grabs on the final weekend – ironically only Leicester, Leinster and Toulouse were assured of progressing – not many of the pools were truly competitive. The Welsh clubs, with the notable exception of Llanelli and, to a lesser extent, Neath, fell away badly. Cardiff didn't win a game while Swansea and Newport only managed three victories between them. Once again a Scottish side failed to reach the knockout stages. That matter needs urgent address for next season. Wales and Scotland need to make a final, wherever it might be held.

Pool Results

Pool One

Amatori & Calvisano 16, Béziers 32; Neath 16, Leicester 16; Béziers 21, Neath 16; Leicester 63, Amatori & Calvisano 0; Amatori & Calvisano 38, Neath 29; Béziers 12, Leicester 24; Leicester 53, Béziers 10; Neath 56, Amatori & Calvisano 10; Neath 23, Béziers 18; Amatori & Calvisano 22, Leicester 40; Béziers 16, Amatori & Calvisano 19; Leicester 36, Neath 11

Pool One Final Table

	P	*W*	*D*	*L*	*For*	*Against*	*Tries*	*Pts*
Leicester	6	5	1	0	232	71	31	11
Neath	6	2	1	3	151	137	18	5
Amatori & Calvisano	6	2	0	4	105	236	10	4
Béziers	6	2	0	4	107	151	8	4

Pool Two

Gloucester 35, Munster 16; Perpignan 46, Viadana 27; Munster 30, Perpignan 21; Viadana 28, Gloucester 80; Gloucester 33, Perpignan 16; Munster 64, Viadana 0; Perpignan 31, Gloucester 23; Viadana 22, Munster 55; Perpignan 23, Munster 8; Gloucester 64, Viadana 16; Viadana 35, Perpignan 39; Munster 33, Gloucester 6

Pool Two Final Table

	P	W	D	L	For	Against	Tries	Pts
Perpignan	6	4	0	2	176	156	23	8
Munster	6	4	0	2	206	107	27	8
Gloucester	6	4	0	2	241	140	31	8
Viadana	6	0	0	6	128	348	15	0

Pool Three

Llanelli 45, Glasgow 15; Sale 18, Bourgoin 24; Bourgoin 54, Llanelli 38; Glasgow 26, Sale 14; Bourgoin 35, Glasgow 21; Sale 19, Llanelli 30; Glasgow 13, Bourgoin 12; Llanelli 17, Sale 12; Sale 45, Glasgow 3; Llanelli 37, Bourgoin 22; Bourgoin 43, Sale 15; Glasgow 8, Llanelli 34

Pool Three Final Table

	P	W	D	L	For	Against	Tries	Pts
Llanelli	6	5	0	1	201	130	22	10
Bourgoin	6	4	0	2	190	142	21	8
Glasgow	6	2	0	4	86	185	9	4
Sale	6	1	0	5	123	143	16	2

Pool Four

Montferrand 47, Swansea 12; Leinster 29, Bristol 23; Bristol 24, Montferrand 19; Swansea 10, Leinster 51; Montferrand 20, Leinster 23; Swansea 26, Bristol 19; Leinster 12, Montferrand 9; Bristol 41, Swansea 23; Leinster 48, Swansea 19; Montferrand 22, Bristol 30; Bristol 12, Leinster 25; Swansea 19, Montferrand 24

Pool Four Final Table

	P	W	D	L	For	Against	Tries	Pts
Leinster	6	6	0	0	188	93	22	12
Bristol	6	3	0	3	149	144	15	6
Montferrand	6	2	0	4	141	120	15	4
Swansea	6	1	0	5	109	230	8	2

Pool Five

Toulouse 28, London Irish 23; Edinburgh 27, Newport 17; London Irish 24, Edinburgh 8; Newport 19, Toulouse 34; Newport 16, London Irish 12; Edinburgh 9, Toulouse 30; London Irish 42, Newport 5; Toulouse 50, Edinburgh 17; Toulouse 70, Newport 18; Edinburgh 32, London Irish 25; Newport 42, Edinburgh 32; London Irish 32, Toulouse 29

Pool Five Final Table

	P	W	D	L	For	Against	Tries	Pts
Toulouse	6	5	0	1	241	118	29	10
London Irish	6	3	0	3	158	118	12	6
Edinburgh	6	2	0	4	125	188	15	4
Newport	6	2	0	4	117	217	11	4

Pool Six

Cardiff 15, Biarritz Olympique 26; Northampton 32, Ulster 9; Biarritz Olympique 23, Northampton 20; Ulster 25, Cardiff 6; Ulster 13, Biarritz Olympique 9; Northampton 25, Cardiff 11; Biarritz Olympique 25, Ulster 20; Cardiff 0, Northampton 31; Northampton 17, Biarritz Olympique 14; Cardiff 21, Ulster 33; Biarritz Olympique 75, Cardiff 25; Ulster 16, Northampton 13

Pool Six Final Table

	P	*W*	*D*	*L*	*For*	*Against*	*Tries*	*Pts*
Northampton	6	4	0	2	138	73	14	8
Biarritz Olympique	6	4	0	2	172	110	21	8
Ulster	6	4	0	2	116	106	8	8
Cardiff	6	0	0	6	78	215	6	0

The Quarter-Finals

11 April, Stradey Park, Llanelli
Llanelli 19 (1G 4PG) **Perpignan 26** (2G 2PG 2DG)

The famous European battlers inflicted a grievous wound on themselves when flanker Dafydd Jones was sent off for stamping in the 10th minute. Not even the passionate support of the Stradey faithful could compensate for such a loss, although it took some stern rearguard action by the Catalans to keep out the late Llanelli charge. Perpignan also had a level head and accurate boot in the form of Australian fly-half Manny Edmonds. They did not venture that often into Llanelli territory in the second-half, but when they did Edmonds made it count. The former Waratah finished with 16 points from two penalties, two dropped goals and the conversions of the two tries that Perpignan scored in the first half.

For all their troubles, Llanelli only trailed by a point, 14-13, at the interval. But the early effort to make up lost ground took its toll. They were also badly served by their line-out.

Perpignan were quickly into their stride, Jean-Marc Souverbie's chip ahead in the second minute causing Guy Easterby to obstruct the full-back and so concede a penalty try. Eight minutes later referee Tony Spreadbury had no hesitation in reaching for the red card when Jones was seen stamping on scrum-half Ludovic Loustau.

Llanelli stirred themselves into legitimate action, Stephen Jones's break setting up prop Martyn Madden for a try. Phil Murphy's try for Perpignan late in the first half helped give his side a narrow advantage. Edmonds didn't waste it.

Llanelli: B Davies; G Evans, M Watkins, L Davies (*captain*), S Finau; S Jones, D Peel; I Thomas, R McBryde, M Madden, V Cooper, C Wyatt, D Jones, S Quinnell, S Easterby *Substitutions:* G Easterby for Peel (67 mins); M Jones for Finau (77 mins)

Scorers *Try:* Madden *Conversion:* S Jones *Penalty Goals*: S Jones (4)

Perpignan: J-M Souverbie; P Bomati, P Giordani, C Manas, F Cermeno; M Edmonds, L Loustau; R Peillard, M Konieckiewicz, N Mas, J Thion, R Alvarez-Kairelis, G le Corvec, P Murphy, B Goutta (*captain*) *Substitutes:* C Porcu for Murphy (66 mins); M dal Maso for Konieckiewicz (66 mins); L Mallier for Goutta (77 mins)

Scorers *Tries:* Murphy, penalty try *Conversions:* Edmonds (2) *Penalty Goals:* Edmonds (2) *Drop Goals:* Edmonds (2)

Referee A Spreadbury (England)

12 April, Stadium Municipal, Toulouse
Toulouse 32 (2G 6PG) **Northampton 16** (1G 3PG)

Toulouse did not have to go through all the gears in order to reach their semi-final destination, which just happened to be exactly the same stadium in which they played this game. The home run is a favourable route and an ecstatic crowd rose to salute their local heroes at the end of a hard-fought contest. For all the clunking and spluttering there was never any real doubt that Toulouse would prevail. Northampton, who had lost the Powergen Cup final to Gloucester only seven days earlier, rallied briefly and courageously midway through the second-half but could not muster enough firepower to seriously trouble their opponents. It would have helped if they had been able to put together a decent line-out, but that was beyond them.

The game turned on an incident just before half-time involving Ben Cohen. The England and Saints wing was bundled into touch and as he fell appeared to swing out with his leg and arm. The upshot was that wing Vincent Clerc had to leave the field to have a few stitches inserted above his eye. He was not a happy man. Nor were his team-mates. Toulouse kicked for touch from the resultant penalty. From there they drove hard at the Northampton line, first through exiled Irish flanker Trevor Brennan and finally through No 8 Christian Labit, who scored.

Frédéric Michalak and Yann Delaigue kicked four penalties between them in the first half. All Northampton could muster were two long-range efforts from Paul Grayson.

The Saints' purple patch came when Cédric Desbrosse was in the sin-bin. Matt Dawson and Andrew Blowers conspired to move the ball to the left wing where a neat pass from Tom Smith sent Jon Sleightholme to the line. Cédric Heymans later swooped on to a fumbled ball from James Brooks and hacked downfield to score.

Toulouse: C Poitrenaud; E Ntamack, C Desbrosse, X Garbajosa, V Clerc; Y Delaigue, F Michalak; P Collazo, Y Bru, J-B Poux, D Gerard, F Pelous (*captain*), J Bouilhou, C Labit, T Brennan *Substitutions:* C Heymans for Clerc (temp 36 to 41 mins) and for Ntamack (64 mins); F Maka for Brennan (55 mins); W Servat for Labit (68 mins); B Lecouls for Collazo (71 mins); Y Jauzion for Desbrosse (74 mins); G Lamboley for Gerard (78 mins)

Scorers *Tries:* Labit, Heymans *Conversions:* Delaigue (2) *Penalty Goals:* Delaigue (4), Michalak (2)

Northampton: N Beal; J Brooks, B Reihana, C Hyndman, B Cohen; P Grayson, M Dawson; T Smith, S Thompson, M Stewart, M Lord, J Phillips, M Connors, A Blowers, A Pountney (*captain*) *Substitutions:* M Tucker for Hyndman (37 mins); C Budgen for Stewart (46 mins); J Sleightholme for Beal (54 mins); R Hunter for Phillips (61 mins); M Stewart for Budgen (74 mins); M Soden for Connors (temp 33 mins to 40 mins) and for Lord (77 mins)

Scorers *Try :* Sleightholme *Conversion:* Grayson *Penalty Goals:* Grayson (3)

Referee A Lewis (Ireland)

12 April, Lansdowne Road, Dublin
Leinster 18 (1G 2PG 1T) **Biarritz 13** (1G 2PG)

A great crowd descended on Lansdowne Road for this quarter-final and had a rare old afternoon. Until the final seconds, that is, when the stadium almost succumbed to a collective coronary. Leinster had led 18-6 with the clock ticking down. Little did the crowd realise that injuries would add almost ten minutes to normal time. Still, no need to panic.

Then Biarritz managed to rouse themselves, scoring a converted try through Thomas Lièvremont. Almost over now. Not quite. One last break-out from the French side saw Marc Stcherbina hack the ball downfield and chase it like fury. The vast acres of Lansdowne Road lay before him. Stcherbina looked to be in the clear. Girvan Dempsey had other ideas, the Leinster full-back timing his claw-back tackle to perfection. Referee Chris White confirmed afterwards that had Dempsey hit a split-second earlier then it would have been a penalty try.

Leinster had seemingly done all that was necessary in the first half, with flanker Keith Gleeson scoring a well-crafted try and Brian O'Meara adding the kicks with a conversion and two penalties. Leinster sat pretty at the break, 13-0 ahead. Even though Dimitri Yachvili got his side on the board with a penalty early in the second half, Leinster looked to have done enough when they scored a second try through Victor Costello. Things did not turn out to be quite so straightforward.

Leinster: G Dempsey; D Hickie, B O'Driscoll (*captain*), D Quinlan, G D'Arcy; C Warner, B O'Meara; P Coyle, S Byrne, E Byrne, L Cullen, M O'Kelly, E Miller, V Costello, K Gleeson *Substitutions:* N Treston for Coyle (40 mins); A Kearney for Costello (68 mins); G Hickie for Byrne (76 mins)

Scorers *Tries:* Gleeson, Costello *Conversion:* O'Meara *Penalty Goals:* O'Meara (2)

Biarritz Olympique: N Brusque; P Bernat-Salles, M Stcherbina, J Isaac, P Bidabe; J Peyrelongue, D Yachvili; M Fitzgerald, J-M Gonzalez (*captain*), D Avril, D Couzinet, O Roumat, S Betsen, T Lièvremont, C Milhères *Substitutes:* G Bousses for Isaac (20 mins); O Tonita for Milhères (47 mins); O Nauroy for Roumat (65 mins); M Etcheverria for Bidabe (temp 71 mins to 79 mins) and for Bousses (79 mins)

Scorers *Try*: Lièvremont *Conversion:* Yachvili *Penalty Goals:* Yachvili (2)

Referee S Lander (England)

13 April, 2003 Welford Road, Leicester
Leicester 7 (1G) **Munster 20** (2G 2PG)

The Welford Road fortress had taken a few hits down the years and survived most all of them. But this was an invasion of an entirely different order. The sight and sound of thousands of red-clad Munster fans and players cavorting all over the pitch long after the final whistle is an image that will be etched on the minds of proud Leicester men who will strive to ensure that such happenings do not pass their way for a very long time again. It was humiliation on a grand scale for the double Heineken Cup winners.

If the game itself was error-strewn and disjointed, it was never less than utterly compelling. Munster faced down everything that Leicester had to offer. They gave not an inch in the forward battle and, although their strategy was to play the corners through the teasing kicks of Peter Stringer and Ronan O'Gara, their back-line did also manage to fashion what little slick and creative action there was on show.

The final moments proved symbolic. From a line-out the Munster pack marched their opponents 45 metres downfield. So frustrated had Martin Johnson become that he swung a punch. Even that had no effect. Leicester were impotent on all fronts.

The big boot of Tim Stimpson has so often managed to get them out of tight corners. Not so here. Four chances went begging.

The game swung decisively Munster's way in the 67th minute when a midfield collision between Leon Lloyd and Austin Healey led to a Munster scrum. Jim Williams and Anthony Foley headed straight towards a groggy Healey. From the confusion, O'Gara was able to reach over for the touchdown.

The tide was turning. Eight minutes earlier Leicester had taken the lead, Steve Booth latching on to Geordan Murphy's pass to score.

Munster were on the move. Their late superiority showed as they swept 60 metres to the Leicester try-line, Stringer rounding off a sequence that featured O'Gara, Rob Henderson, Mike Mullins and Alan Quinlan. The Midlands belonged to Munster.

Leicester: T Stimpson; G Murphy, L Lloyd, F Tuilagi, S Booth; A Healey, T Tierney; P Freshwater, D West, D Garforth, M Johnson (*captain*), B Kay, M Corry, W Johnson, N Back *Substitutions:* A Balding for W Johnson (47 mins); H Ellis for Tierney (58 mins); J Kronfeld for Kay (61 mins); S Vesty for Healey (68 mins); G Gelderbloom for Tuilagi (79 mins); G Chuter for West (79 mins)

Scorers *Try:* Booth *Conversion:* Stimpson

Munster: J Staunton; J Kelly, M Mullins, R Henderson, A Horgan; R O'Gara, P Stringer; M Horan, F Sheahan, J Hayes, D O'Callaghan, P O'Connell, R Williams (*captain*), A Foley, A Quinlan *Substitutions:* J Holland for Henderson (79 mins); M O'Driscoll for O'Connell (79 mins)

Scorers *Tries:* O'Gara, Stringer *Conversions:* O'Gara (2) *Penalty Goals:* O'Gara (2)

Referee N Williams (Wales)

The Semi-Finals

26 April, Stadium Municipal, Toulouse
Toulouse 13 (1G 2PG) **Munster 12** (2PG 2DG)

Another Munster cliff-hanger? Not really. Despite the closeness of the scoreline, Toulouse were markedly the better side. Munster offered what Munster are famed for offering – endeavour, commitment and cussedness. They refused to bow to the evident superiority of the Toulouse back line who threatened to cut loose on several occasions. The Munster line-out had yet another impressive afternoon, while the tight maul set Toulouse on to the back foot. That the game remained close also owed a fair amount to the conditions. Heavy rain teemed from the grey skies for an hour, dampening the efficiency of both teams but failing to dampen the enthusiasm of a full house of 36,500. The shared colours of the teams made for a vivid red backdrop.

Toulouse were guilty of trying to force the game too much in the early stages, often losing control of the ball in the tackle owing to the greasy surface. Once the rain eased, so too did their anxiety. They also made a significant tactical switch, moving Frédéric Michalak from scrum-half to fly-half. Only a despairing tackle by Peter Stringer prevented Xavier Garbajosa from scoring in the 64th minute, the Munster scrum-half dislodging the ball as the Toulouse centre went over the line. Ten minutes later the dam was breached, Michalak scoring wide out after a lovely low pick-up from Jean-Baptiste Elissalde. Munster still raged against the dying of the European light, two late, long-distance drop goal attempts from Ronan O'Gara going just wide.

Toulouse: C Poitrenaud; E Ntamack, Y Jauzion, X Garbajosa, V Clerc; Y Delaigue, F Michalak; P Collazo, Y Bru, J-B Poux, D Gerard, F Pelous (*captain*), J Bouilhou, C Labit, T Brennan *Substitutions:* F Maka for Bouilhou (temp 3 mins to 13 mins) and for Labit (84 mins); J-B Elissalde for Delaigue (53 mins); C Heymans for Ntamack (58 mins); B Lecouls for Collazo (62 mins); W Servat for Bru (70 mins); G Lamboley for Gerard (80 mins)

Scorers *Try:* Michalak *Conversion:* Elissalde *Penalty Goals:* Delaigue, Elissalde

Munster: J Staunton; J Kelly, M Mullins, R Henderson, A Horgan; R O'Gara, P Stringer; M Horan, F Sheahan, J Hayes, D O'Callaghan, P O'Connell, R Williams (*captain*), A Foley, A Quinlan *Substitutions:* J Holland for Henderson (77 mins)

Scorer *Penalty Goals:* O'Gara (2) *Drop Goals:* O'Gara (2)

Referee C White (England)

27 April, Lansdowne Road, Dublin
Leinster 14 (3PG 1T) **Perpignan 21** (1G 1PG 2DG 1T)

The nightmare scenario took on its alarming shape from early in this match. The prospect of an all-French final in the home of Irish rugby was not good box-office. No-one, though, could deny Perpignan their right to go through to their first ever Heineken final. They were sharper in thought and deed than their opponents, much to the disappointment of the thousands who had flocked to Lansdowne Road in expectation of Leinster crowning a fine season.

Instead, the 'home side' were jittery and lacklustre. Their scrummage was under constant pressure, even though for some strange reason referee Nigel Williams chose to find fault with the Perpignan front-row. In fact the Catalans overcame a massive imbalance in the penalty count – 23-8 against them – and also survived the sin-binning of two players.

It was a fractured game. The only score in a scratchy first-half came from the boot of Brian O'Meara, who succeeded with one penalty but missed several others. Leinster hopes briefly flared when, after an exchange of goals, they put themselves in the lead with a try from Gordon D'Arcy after good work from Denis Hickie. Thereafter, the game belonged to Perpignan who scored tries through Pascal Bomati and Marc dal Maso.

Leinster: G Dempsey; D Hickie, B O'Driscoll, D Quinlan, G D'Arcy; C Warner, B O'Meara; R Corrigan (*captain*), S Byrne, E Byrne, L Cullen, M O'Kelly, E Miller, V Costello, K Gleeson *Substitutions:* N Spooner for O'Driscoll (66 mins); A McCullen for Miller (66 mins); B O'Riordan for O'Meara (73 mins)

Scorers *Try*: D'Arcy *Penalty Goals*: O'Meara (2), Spooner

Perpignan: J-M Souverbie; P Bomati, P Giordani, C Manas, F Cermeno; M Edmonds, L Loustau; N Mas, M Konieckiewicz, S de Besombes, J Thion, R Alvarez Kairelis, G Le Corvec, P Murphy, B Goutta (*captain*) *Substitutions:* M dal Maso for Konieckiewicz (56 mins); J Basset for Loustau (66 mins); J Daniell for Murphy (66 mins); L Mallier for Le Corvec (73 mins); C Porcu for Daniell (79 mins); A Moreno for De Besombes (80 mins)

Scorers *Tries:* Bomati, Dal Maso *Conversion:* Edmonds *Penalty Goal:* Edmonds *Drop Goals:* Cermeno, Edmonds

Referee N Williams (Wales)

Heineken Cup Final

24 May, Lansdowne Road, Dublin
Toulouse 22 (1G 5PG) **Perpignan 17** (4PG 1T)

It was not a day for glory or for great drama – merely the playing-out of the eighth Heineken Cup final in a half-empty stadium. That was not to say that we did not have endeavour, or skill or even noise, for we did. Both teams went at each other with real sporting venom, crunching into each other with fearsome relish. And the side doing most of the crunching were Toulouse, the aristocrats of French rugby indulging their love of the artisans' work. They kept their line intact until the very end when a wonderfully disguised slice-kick by Manny Edmonds *a la* Carlos Spencer produced a try for Pascal Bomati. It took that little bit of magic to unlock the Toulouse defence, proof that the iron fist is a comfortable fit in the velvet glove.

Perpignan had their share of enforcers. It's a pity, however, that they couldn't find a line-out. The co-ordination between hooker Michel Konieckiewicz and his throwers was abysmal. Without the security of that platform, Perpignan were always chasing the game. They trailed 19-0 at the break and even though the elements were with them in the second-half, the force was not. They did manage to chip away at Toulouse's lead through four penalties from fly-half Manny Edmonds but the cause was already lost.

Edmonds gathered himself well after a dreadful opening. His kicking from hand was off-key, so too his tackling. He was hopelessly adrift on the half-hour when Toulouse snaffled yet more possession from a Perpignan throw. The ball was shifted infield to Yannick Jauzion who headed straight at Edmonds. A jolting hand-off by the Toulouse centre left the Australian on his backside and staring at the sight of his tormentor sending Vincent Clerc to the try-line.

Toulouse were efficient throughout that first half. They made sure that every time they reached Perpignan territory, they scored. Yann Delaigue knocked over four penalties and also converted the try. The Toulouse fly-half was also on hand to quell jitters late in the second-half with another penalty as Perpignan closed the gap.

Beleaguered English referee Chris White was forced to retire after 15 minutes with a hamstring problem to be replaced by Tony Spreadbury.

Perpignan may look back with regret on their first appearance in the Heineken Final. Their failings were primarily those of nerve and steadiness. Their fans, along with those of Toulouse, provided a vivid backdrop of noise and colour among the crowd of 28,600. At the final whistle, they saluted their fallen heroes while Toulouse, player and spectator alike, made the most of a cherished moment.

Toulouse: C Poitrenaud; E Ntamack, X Garbajosa, Y Jauzion, V Clerc; Y Delaigue, F Michalak; B Lecouls, Y Bru, J-B Poux, D Gerard, F Pelous (*captain*), T Brennan, C Labit, J Bouilhou *Substitutions:* W Servat for Bru (14 mins); F Maka for Brennan (65 mins); C Soulette for Poux (73 mins)

Scorers *Try:* Clerc *Conversion:* Delaigue *Penalty Goals:* Delaigue (5)

Perpignan: J-M Souverbie; P Bomati, P Giordani, C Manas, F Cermeno; M Edmonds, L Loustau; R Peillard, M Konieckiewicz, N Mas, J Thion, R Alvarez Kairelis, G le Corvec, P Murphy, B Goutta (*captain*) *Substitutions:* M dal Maso for Konieckiewicz (58 mins); S de Besombes for Mas (60 mins); L Mallier for Murphy (65 mins)

Scorers *Try:* Bomati *Penalty Goals:* Edmonds (4)

Referee C White (England) replaced by A Spreadbury (England) (16 mins)

Previous Heineken Cup Finals: 1996 Toulouse 21, Cardiff 18 (Cardiff); 1997 Brive 28, Leicester 9 (Cardiff); 1998 Bath 19, Brive 18 (Bordeaux); 1999 Ulster 21, Colomiers 6 (Dublin); 2000 Northampton 9, Munster 8 (Twickenham); 2001 Leicester 34, Stade Francais 30 (Paris); 2002 Leicester 15, Munster 9 (Cardiff); 2003 Toulouse 22, Perpignan 17 (Dublin)

HEINEKEN CUP RECORDS 1995-2003

Record	*Detail*		*Set*
Most team points in season	379 by Stade Français	in 9 matches	2000-2001
Highest team score	108 by Toulouse	108-16 v Ebbw Vale	1998-1999
Biggest team win	92 by Toulouse	108-16 v Ebbw Vale	1998-1999
Most team tries in match	16 by Toulouse	v Ebbw Vale	1998-1999
Most appearances	52 for Munster	A G Foley	1995-2003
Most points in matches	552 for Milan/Stade Français	D Dominguez	1995-2002
Most points in season	188 for Stade Français	D Dominguez	2000-2001
Most points in match	37 for Ulster	D G Humphreys v Wasps	2001-2002
Most tries in matches	24 for Toulouse	M Marfaing	1996-2002
Most tries in season	9 for Swansea	M F D Robinson	2000-2001
Most tries in match	5 for Gloucester	T D Beim v Roma	2000-2001
	5 for Llanelli	M D Cardey v Amatori & Calvisano	2001-2002
Most cons in match	12 for Stade Français	D Dominguez v L'Aquila	2000-2001
Most pens in match	9 for Stade Français	D Dominguez v Leicester	2000-2001
Most drops in match	4 for Ulster	D G Humphreys v Wasps	2001-2002

PARKER PEN CHALLENGE CUP 2002-03

Wasps Head English Clubs' Challenge in New Format Competition

David Llewellyn

This competition had the lot, from a suspected defection, to a suspension; from fine play to fines; from the Can-can to bans. There were matches of high quality and even higher scores; records and rows. But above all, thanks to its new format, it was crammed with excitement and meaningful matches.

There were shock results from the first round to the final as the tournament emerged from the round-robin format to a two-leg knock-out system for the early stages, a change which had a double effect: cutting the costs of travel for the clubs and the sponsors and heightening the drama and the tension.

One club which throughout seemed to be at the centre of much of the action was Saracens. They opened their campaign in Bucharest with a resounding 87-0 victory against Dinamo, the highest score of the first leg. However, they went a quantum leap better in the second leg. Their embarrassingly one-sided 151-0 win over the hapless Romanians was the highest score in the history of the competition beating the previous mark set by Saracens unsurprisingly against Bologna the season before.

The winning margin was a 41-point improvement on the old mark, while Sarries' 23 touchdowns beat their own record try count by six.

But defeat was only the third of it for the luckless Romanians. They not only lost the second leg but the evening before they also lost their No 8 Florin Pradais, last seen at London's Victoria Station.

The humiliation was completed when the Romanian Rugby Board decided that for bringing disgrace on the whole nation they should be banned from all international competition for two years. Their poor coach Mircea Paraschiv was fined five million lei, which sounds a lot but which was equivalent to about £100, and the players three million lei each. Fortunately the ban did not prevent Dinamo from taking part in the Parker Pen Shield, the secondary competition set up for the first round losers.

And among those were Castres. The previous season the French club had reached the semi-finals of the Heineken Cup, this year they crashed out to Treviso in one of the shocks of the tournament. Another French club Pau, found themselves on the wrong end of the score-line against Bridgend and they too joined Castres in the Shield.

Harlequins copped a bad 'un in the second round, drawing Stade Français. The first leg was a disaster. Perhaps greeting the French team as they ran out on to the pitch with a rendition of the 'Can-Can' was not such a great idea. The French club promptly showed they can twice, winning both legs. Leeds also went out, to Pontypridd, but the other Welsh club Bridgend succumbed to Bath after giving the West Country giants a torrid first leg, beating them by two points. Scottish Borders battled well at Montauban staying within three points but they just could not turn it around at home.

Saracens and Wasps had few problems with Colomiers and Bordeaux-Bègles, but there was another shock, if not quite as high on the Richter scale as Castres or Pau, when Connacht, the unfancied Irish Province, pipped Narbonne by a point on aggregate.

The Irish side then proceeded to make life tough for Pontypridd in the quarters, the Welsh side eventually stealing in by a dozen points, and Bath did magnificently after losing by three points in Montauban but scraping through thanks to a six-point margin on The Recreation Ground.

The price of Saracens' triumph over Newcastle came fairly high, though. Their state of the art under-soil heating failed to kick in at the start of a cold snap on the eve of their quarter-final first leg tie against Newcastle. The breakdown was apparently spotted by ground-staff around 8am but, confident that the Vicarage Road pitch would thaw in time, no-one told Newcastle, who consequently made the journey South. The overnight frost was as nothing compared with the icy atmosphere between the two clubs. Rob Andrew, the Newcastle director of rugby, wanted the tie played at nearby Wycombe straight after the Wasps match, but traffic problems, policing and stewarding logistics precluded that. The game was therefore rescheduled for the following evening, a match comfortably won by the home team. But three months later an independently appointed ERC disciplinary panel found Saracens guilty of not taking adequate precautions to protect their playing surface for the game on 12 January and failing to have an alternative venue available. The club was fined €10,000, ordered to pay compensation of €2,000 to ERC and was responsible for finding one-third of the costs of the hearing. The return leg was won by Newcastle, but not by enough.

Wasps meanwhile beat Stade Français at Adams Park while Newcastle and Saracens were kicking their heels just around the M25, then pulled off a convincing victory in Paris. Thus for the second season running (and the second time in the history of the competition) there was no French representation in the semi-finals.

As with the previous rounds the two-leg format was adopted for the last four. One tie proved rather one-sided, Pontypridd battling well but ultimately unable to keep out a rampant Wasps side at home and leaving themselves far too much to do at Sardis Road, where sadly they lost again. The other tie between Saracens and Bath though was a far tighter affair. The Watford-based team allowed Bath to claw their way to within eight points in the first leg, and oddly that was the gap separating the two of them in the second leg, thanks to an injury time try by Tom Voyce. And that try proved crucial, because it was the sixth one that Bath had scored over the two legs, compared with Saracens' five, so the West Country club squeezed into the final on the 'tries scored' rule.

Results

First round: Grenoble 12, Newcastle 19; Newcastle 33, Grenoble 17; (Newcastle won 52-29 on aggregate); Treviso 22, Castres 9; Castres 17, Treviso 33; (Treviso won 55-26 on aggregate); L'Aquila 14, Colomiers 58; Colomiers 75, L'Aquila 5 (Colomiers won 133-19 on aggregate); Dinamo Bucharest 11, Saracens 87; Saracens 151, Dinamo Bucharest 0; (Saracens won 238-11 on aggregate); Ebbw Vale 20, Montauban 16; Montauban 29, Ebbw Vale 16; (Montauban won 45-36 on aggregate); Madrid 22, Borders 73; Borders 77, Madrid 15; (Borders won 150-37 on aggregate); GR A N Parma 3, Bath 40; Bath 57, GR A N Parma 19; (Bath won 97-22 on aggregate); Pau 18, Bridgend 6; Bridgend 27, Pau 9; (Bridgend won 33-27 on aggregate); Rugby Parma 24, Wasps 40; Wasps 42, Rugby Parma 0; (Wasps won 82-24 on aggregate); La Moraleja 31, Bordeaux-Bègles 37; Bordeaux-Bègles 33, La Moraleja 15; (Bordeaux-Bègles won 70-46 on aggregate); Caerphilly 20, Harlequins 73; Harlequins 31, Caerphilly 27; (Harlequins won 104-47 on aggregate); Rovigo 6, Stade Français 64; Stade Français 81, Rovigo 20; (Stade Français won 145-26 on aggregate); Rugby Silea 23, Narbonne 34; Narbonne 41, Rugby Silea 14; (Narbonne won 75-37 on aggregate); Mont-de-Marsan 12, Connacht 26; Connacht 47, Mont-de-Marsan 29; (Connacht won 73-41 on aggregate); Padova 23, Leeds 29; Leeds 52, Padova 13; (Leeds won 81-36 on aggregate); Rugby Roma 18, Pontypridd 60; Pontypridd 83, Rugby Roma 8; (Pontypridd won 143-26 on aggregate)

Second round: Treviso 27, Newcastle 8; Newcastle 35, Treviso 5; (Newcastle won 43-32 on aggregate); Saracens 16, Colomiers 6; Colomiers 19, Saracens 30; (Saracens won 46-25 on aggregate); Montauban 19, Borders 16; Borders 6, Montauban 12; (Montauban won 31-22 on aggregate); Bridgend 28, Bath 26; Bath 38, Bridgend 10; (Bath won 64-38 on aggregate); Wasps 43, Bordeaux-Bègles 6; Bordeaux-Bègles 23, Wasps 29; (Wasps won 72-29 on aggregate); Harlequins 0, Stade Français 26; Stade Français 29, Harlequins 12; (Stade Français won 55-12 on aggregate); Narbonne 42, Connacht 27; Connacht 23, Narbonne 7; (Connacht won 50-49 on aggregate); Pontypridd 37, Leeds 23; Leeds 19, Pontypridd 19; (Pontypridd won 56-42 on aggregate)

Quarter Finals: Saracens 31, Newcastle 10; Newcastle 31, Saracens 29; (Saracens won 60-41 on aggregate); Montauban 27, Bath 24; Bath 24, Montauban 18; (Bath won 48-45 on aggregate); Wasps 35, Stade Français 22; Stade Français 12, Wasps 27; (Wasps won 62-34 on aggregate); Connacht 30, Pontypridd 35; Pontypridd 12, Connacht 9; (Pontypridd won 47-39 on aggregate)

Semi Finals: Saracens 38, Bath 30; Bath 27, Saracens 19; (Bath won 6-5 on tries after drawing 57-57 on aggregate); Wasps 34, Pontypridd 19; Pontypridd 17, Wasps 27; (Wasps won 61-36 on aggregate)

Parker Pen Challenge Cup Final

25 May, 2003, Madejski Stadium, Reading
Wasps 48 (6G 2PG) Bath 30 (2G 2PG 2T)

A feisty finale to an excellent competition culminated in the sending-off and subsequent suspension of Bath captain Danny Grewcock, found guilty of punching his England colleague and Wasps counterpart Lawrence Dallaglio.

The ban which ran for 14 days from 1 June meant Grewcock missed England's first two tour matches against New Zealand Maori and the All Blacks and after initially making it into the England tour party the player and management mutually agreed that he should stay at home.

Grewcock departed in the 61st minute after taking the law into his own hands by aiming punches at Dallaglio, who appeared to be killing the ball at a ruck on the Wasps line. It was not the first such infringement by a Wasp. Craig Dowd had committed a similar offence in the first half and should have gone to the sin bin.

One person who did receive a yellow card was Bath and Ireland centre Kevin Maggs after he was spotted stamping on Dallaglio, an action that came just moments after Bath's Gavin Thomas was apparently stamped on by an unidentified Wasps boot.

In Maggs's absence Wasps were able to take advantage of the gap he left in midfield and ran in 17 unopposed points, Alex King landing a penalty and converting tries by Josh Lewsey and Fraser Waters. Then Phil Greening, intercepting a pass from Olly Barkley, ran 50 metres to score shortly after Maggs's return to help Wasps into a 24-3 lead after only 25 minutes. Victory was deserved, despite the fact that Bath battled themselves to a standstill. Barkley brightened up Bath's day with a try before the interval to add to his two penalties, and his perfectly-judged cross-kick set-up a try for Mike Tindall.

The six tries in total merely served to underline the fact that Wasps had been the form side as the going got tougher after Christmas. Their victory meant that for the third year running the main Parker Pen Trophy remained in England following the successes of Sale the previous season and Harlequins the year before that.

Wasps: M van Gisbergen; J Lewsey, F Waters, S Abbott, J Rudd; A King, M Wood; C Dowd, P Greening, W Green, S Shaw, R Birkett, J Worsley, L Dallaglio (*captain*), P Volley *Substitutions:* K Logan for Rudd (32 mins); A McKenzie for Dowd (temp 37 to 40 mins and 59 mins); T Leota for Greening (59 mins); A Erinle for Abbott (65 mins); M Lock for Volley (65 mins); P Scrivener for Dallaglio (65 mins); R Howley for Wood (76 mins)

Scorers *Tries:* Lewsey, Waters, Greening, Wood, Logan, Leota *Conversions:* King (6) *Penalty Goals:* King (2)

Bath: I Balshaw; T Voyce, K Maggs, M Tindall, E Seveali'i; O Barkley, G Cooper; D Barnes, J Humphreys, J Mallett, S Borthwick, D Grewcock (*captain*), G Thomas, D Lyle, A Beattie *Substitutions:* G Delve for Lyle (temp 9 to 11 mins and 61 mins); L Mears for Humphreys (23 mins); J Scaysbrook for Thomas (44 mins); M Stevens for Mallett (53 mins); M Catt for Voyce (57 mins); M Perry for Seveali'i (74 mins); R Blake for Cooper (76 mins)

Scorers *Tries:* Barkley, Scaysbrook, Tindall, Balshaw *Conversions:* Barkley, Balshaw *Penalty Goals:* Barkley (2)

Referee N Williams (Wales)

Previous Parker Pen Finals (*including Shield finals to 2002)*: 1997 Bourgoin 18, Castres 9 (Béziers); 1998 Colomiers 43, Agen 5 (Toulouse); 1999 Montferrand 35, Bourgoin 16 (Lyons); 2000 Pau 34, Castres 21 (Toulouse); 2001 Harlequins 42, Narbonne 33 (Reading); 2002 Sale 25, Pontypridd 22 (Oxford); 2003 Wasps 48, Bath 30 (Reading)

PARKER PEN RECORDS 1996-2003
(INCORPORATING SHIELD TOURNAMENTS TO 2002)

Record	*Detail*		*Set*
Most team points in season	450 by Saracens	in seven matches	2001-02
Highest team score	151 by Saracens	151-0 v Dinamo Bucharest	2002-03
Biggest team win	151 by Saracens	151-0 v Dinamo Bucharest	2002-03
Most team tries in match	23 by Saracens	151-0 v Dinamo Bucharest	2002-03
Most points in matches	395 for Connacht	E P Elwood	1996-2003
Most points in match	35 for Colomiers	D Skrela v Petraraca	2001-02
Most tries in match	6 for Bordeaux-Bègles	A Bouyssie v Bologna	2001-02
Most cons in match	13 for Saracens	J H de Beer v Bologna	2001-02
Most pens in match	9 for Ebbw Vale	J Strange v Toulon	1999-2000
	9 for Bristol	S Vile v Mont-de-Marsan	2000-01
	9 for Narbonne	C Rosalen v Perpignan	2000-01
	9 for Bridgend	C Warlow v Pau	2002-03
Most drops in a match	4 for Dax	S Fauque v London Irish	2001-02

PARKER PEN SHIELD 2002-03

Castres Win Inaugural Competition for Challenge Cup Losers

David Llewellyn

Dinamo Bucharest must have wished the two-year ban from international competition slapped on them after their humiliating exit from the Parker Pen Challenge Cup had come into force straightaway. It didn't though, so they had to undergo a Groundhog Day in the Parker Pen Shield, the new secondary competition for the first round losers in the Challenge Cup.

There was not a whiff of trouble in the first round of the Shield when the Romanians disposed of Italian side L'Aquila. But the quarter-final draw threw them to the wolves of Castres and the nightmare was revisited. Owing to the severe weather in Romania, each of Dinamo's ties had to be played on French soil. Castres were not quite as effective as Saracens had been, but they still managed to stick 123 points on Dinamo in the second leg to bring the aggregate to a double century.

As against Saracens, the Romanians, in the face of well-organised defence and ruthless finishing, were unable to score. Considering that Castres had only just wriggled through to the last eight after scraping past Grenoble by two points on aggregate, their subsequent performances were quite remarkable.

In the semi-finals the previous season's Heineken Cup semi-finalists disposed of more French opposition in the shape of Pau. In the other half of the draw Welsh side Caerphilly were drawn against Italian opponents in every round up to and including the semi-finals, including Petrarca Padova, quarter-final conquerors of French club Mont-de-Marsan.

Caerphilly, though, proved to be a mountain for Padova. It was a different matter, however, for Caerphilly's compatriots Ebbw Vale. They had strolled past Madrid in the first round but found Pau too tough in the quarters.

Results

First round: Castres 14, Grenoble 13; Grenoble 30, Castres 31; (Castres won 45-43 on aggregate); L'Aquila 24, Dinamo Bucharest 27; Dinamo Bucharest 26, L'Aquila 24; (Dinamo Bucharest won 53-48 on aggregate); Ebbw Vale 37, Madrid 16; Madrid 16, Ebbw Vale 38; (Ebbw Vale won 75-32 on aggregate); GR A N Parma 21, Pau 16; Pau 32, GR A N Parma 20; (Pau won 48-41 on aggregate); La Moraleja 26, Rugby Parma 19; Rugby Parma 26, La Moraleja 13; (Rugby Parma won 45-39 on aggregate); Rovigo 26, Caerphilly 22; Caerphilly 58, Rovigo 17; (Caerphilly won 80-43 on aggregate); Mont-de-Marsan 17, Rugby Silea 7; Rugby Silea 17, Mont-de-Marsan 32; (Mont-de-Marsan won 49-24 on aggregate); Rugby Roma 18, Padova 38; Padova 14, Rugby Roma 14; (Padova won 52-32 on aggregate)

Quarter Finals: Dinamo Bucharest 0, Castres 88; Castres 123, Dinamo Bucharest 0; (Castres won 211-0 on aggregate); Ebbw Vale 29, Pau 3; Pau 63, Ebbw Vale 17; (Pau won 66-46 on aggregate); Caerphilly 41, Rugby Parma 28; Rugby Parma 15, Caerphilly 10; (Caerphilly won 51-43 on aggregate); Padova 15, Mont-de-Marsan 16; Mont-de-Marsan 16, Padova 30; (Padova won 45-32 on aggregate)

Semi Finals: Castres 54, Pau 25; Pau 26, Castres 24; (Castres won 78-51 on aggregate); Padova 10, Caerphilly 28; Caerphilly 26, Padova 33; (Caerphilly won 54-43 on aggregate)

Parker Pen Shield Cup Final

25 May, 2003, Madejski Stadium, Reading
Castres 40 (3G 3PG 2T) **Caerphilly 12** (1G 1T)

The part-timers of Caerphilly were proud in defeat, having given a good account of themselves against a slick and highly motivated Castres. And at least Caerphilly came away from Reading's Madejski Stadium with one record – when prop Rob Bilton trotted on as a 39th-minute replacement he became the oldest player to appear in a European final. The Caerphilly web-site gives Bilton's date of birth as March 1961, but the rumour-mill reckoned he was 44.

The Welsh semi-professional outfit had no answer to the power of the Castres pack, which eventually dominated the set-piece. And the French side's back row, most notably Romain Froment, who scored two of his team's five tries, was too slick and streetwise for the Welshmen.

At least Caerphilly scored the first try, a gem from centre Roddy Boobyer who early on jinked and stepped his way through a clutch of tackles before touching down near the posts. But another Romain, the Castres fly-half Romain Teulet, kept his side in touch and eventually thumped them into a 13-7 half-time lead. He had opened the scoring with a penalty goal, added his second after Boobyer's try and converted a try from Sebastien Roque when the game was in its second quarter.

After the interval Castres went into overdrive and put Caerphilly to the sword. The Frenchmen crossed for four more tries while Caerphilly could muster only a try by energetic back-rower Joe El-Abd.

Chief coach Mark Ring, the former Cardiff, Pontypool and Wales centre, was happy with his side's performance. 'It's a very proud day for Caerphilly Rugby Club,' he said. The club's chairman Phil Williams was impressed by the support for the side. 'You've all done the club proud turning out in your droves to support your team. It was a great sight to see all the green-and-white shirts throughout the ground,' he said.

Caerphilly: S Tuipulotu; R Howells, J Murphy, R Boobyer, T Taufahema; J Thomas, A Chilten; L Manning, C Ferris (*captain*), D Sweet, D Davies, P Jones, G Jones, M Workman, J El-Abd *Substitutions:* R Bilton for Manning (39 mins); L Richards for Boobyer (61 mins); G Liddon for Bilton (65 mins)

Scorers *Tries:* Boobyer, El-Abd *Conversion:* J Thomas

Castres: L Marticorena; U Mola, S Roque, C Stoica, L Arbo; R Teulet, A Albouy; M Reggiardo, R Vigneaux, J Garcia, D Barrier (*captain*), N Spanghero, R Froment, G Taussac, R Capo Ortega *Substitutions:* M Sans for Teulet (72 mins); S Sparks for Reggiardo (61 mins); N Nadau for Marticorena (53 mins); N Raffault for Stoica (61 mins); D Narjissi for Vigneaux (77 mins)

Scorers *Tries:* Froment (2), Roque, Spanghero, Arbo *Conversions:* Teulet (3) *Penalty Goals:* Teulet (3)

Referee D Courtney (Ireland)

Previous Parker Pen Shield Cup Finals: 2003 Castres 40, Caerphilly 12 (Reading)

PARKER PEN SHIELD RECORDS 2003

Record	*Detail*		*Set*
Most team points in season	374 by Castres	in seven matches	2002-03
Highest team score	123 by Castres	123-0 v Dinamo Bucharest	2002-03
Biggest team win	123 by Castres	123-0 v Dinamo Bucharest	2002-03
Most team tries in match	19 by Castres	123-0 v Dinamo Bucharest	2002-03

THE CELTIC LEAGUE 2002-03

Munster maintain Irish Supremacy

John Billot

Although Neath audaciously infiltrated Irish domination of the Celtic League for a well deserved place in the final at Cardiff Arms Park's Millennium Stadium in February 2003, Munster comprehensively saw them off with a stimulating performance of forward power, adventurous running and tactical acumen. It made satisfying amends for Munster's defeat by 24-20 against Leinster in the Dublin final of the previous season. Irish influence again proved a significant factor during the competition's second season. Although Leinster, the cup-holders, failed to reach the quarter-finals, Munster, Ulster and Connacht were all there.

Those who step out on to the Gnoll challenge a fate that is all-too-often inevitable. Neath had every appearance of being scornful of struggling Cardiff's resistance in the semi-final and the Black furies prospered mightily in front of 7,000 onlookers to build a 17-0 lead by the halfway mark. When Neath make an explosive start generally there is no way back for hapless visitors: that was the scenario on 4 January. The fact that Cardiff had proved successful during 11 of their previous 12 Premier Division meetings with the sinister wearers of the Maltese Cross appeared, if anything, to ignite the home men's performance. For a brief period early in the second half, Cardiff entered the fray with a try by Richard Smith from a kick-and-chase to the corner. Iestyn Harris converted and added a penalty goal.

But Neath's avalanche had been only temporarily halted. Their foundation, laid as Lee Jarvis fired over a penalty shot and converted tries by driving No 8 Nathan Bonnor-Evans and Dave Tiueti, was impressively embellished. First, Jarvis feinted to drop a goal and unexpectedly darted some 10 metres for a cheeky try; a little gem, right out of Hatton Garden. He converted and added a penalty goal for a haul of 17 points. To round off a remarkable victory by 32-10, Gareth Morris went over on an outflanking run.

The other semi-final was a similar rout. There were five Munster tries at Thomond Park as they hustled Ulster away by 40-10 watched by 12,000. The early dismissal of prop Justin Fitzpatrick for a spot of pugilism unsettled Ulster and their only points came from David Humphreys with a try, conversion and penalty goal. Munster, swinging their attacks wide and menacingly, crossed through John Kelly, Michael Mullins, John Hayes, Alan Quinlan and Mick Galwey. The ever-reliable Ronan O'Gara found the target with three conversions and three penalty shots. Most critics unhesitatingly nominated Munster as favourites for the cup.

The quarter-finals saw Munster dispatch Connacht by 33-3 at Musgrave Park with tries from Mullins (2) and Mossie Lawlor, plus a penalty try and 13 O'Gara goal points. Ulster's compelling fightback produced victory by 20-17 at Hughenden after Glasgow had appeared in control as Tommy Hayes found the target with four superbly judged penalty kicks and there was a try from Jon Steel. However, the 1999 European champions ensured their progress as Humphreys fired in a second long-range penalty shot after Jon Bell and Andy Ward had crossed. Humphreys converted both tries.

Neath became the first winners in a competitive fixture at Sardis Road to end Pontypridd's sequence of eight victories. It proved a colourless slog. Neil Jenkins landed four penalty goals, but he missed two kickable attempts and Ceri Sweeney replaced him for the closing stages. Neath sent on former Ponty favourite Lee Jarvis after 54 minutes and he guided in his second and decisive penalty five minutes from the end. Shaun Connor converted the controversial Neath penalty try when Iain Ramage decided the home side had pulled down a maul close to the goal-line.

Edinburgh's fast-raiding forwards sent Cardiff reeling initially at Meadowbank in their thrilling quarter to establish a 19-6 advantage by the interval. The home pack stormed like Dervishes into rucks and mauls with insatiable appetite for the work and Cardiff's forwards gave every indication of being overawed. Edinburgh, twice winners in previous encounters with the Welsh club, were on the verge of a place in the semi-finals. Scott Murray had heaved his way across and then full-back Derrick Lee sidled past an indecisive Iestyn Harris and slipped from Emyr Lewis's grasp for the second try. Brendan Laney's three penalty goals added to the visitors' discomfort.

Cardiff's response was far from convincing with two successful penalty attempts by Harris. An urgent clarion call, however, revitalised the Welsh for the second half and Rhys Williams and Ryan Powell obtained opportunist tries. Harris converted both and added two further penalty goals to complete a remarkable recovery and a tense victory by 26-22. Laney provided the home points in the second half with a penalty kick; another attempt bounced off the top of the post and went wide. Cardiff quite remarkably had survived. Nothing, however, would save them at the Gnoll.

Pool Results

Pool A

Neath 25, Caerphilly 6; Edinburgh 30, Swansea 20; Ebbw Vale 0, Ulster 19; Llanelli 13, Munster 20; Ulster 18, Edinburgh 19; Munster 48, Ebbw Vale 23; Swansea 16, Neath 20; Caerphilly 34, Llanelli 43; Edinburgh 21, Munster 28; Ebbw Vale 38, Caerphilly 25; Swansea 38, Ulster 10; Neath 29, Llanelli 13; Ulster 17, Neath 13; Munster 38, Swansea 27; Caerphilly 32, Edinburgh 66; Llanelli 37, Ebbw Vale 25; Edinburgh 38, Llanelli 14; Neath 34, Ebbw Vale 7; Ulster 26, Munster 17; Swansea 37, Caerphilly 32; Llanelli 62, Swansea 6; Ebbw Vale 20, Edinburgh 30; Caerphilly 15, Ulster 67; Neath 19, Munster 35; Munster 41, Caerphilly 0; Ulster 16, Llanelli 9; Edinburgh 27, Neath 13; Swansea 33, Ebbw Vale 20

Pool A Final Table

	P	*W*	*D*	*L*	*For*	*Against*	*Tries*	*BP*	*P/D*	*Pts*
Munster	7	6	0	1	227	129	25	4	+98	28
Edinburgh	7	6	0	1	231	145	24	3	+86	27
Ulster	7	5	0	2	173	111	15	2	+62	22
Neath	7	4	0	3	153	121	15	2	+32	18
Llanelli	7	3	0	4	191	168	23	5	+23	17
Swansea	7	3	0	4	177	212	18	4	–35	16
Ebbw Vale	7	1	0	6	140	226	16	1	–86	5
Caerphilly	7	0	0	7	144	324	17	3	–180	3

Pool B

Newport 5, Bridgend 13; Borders 27, Connacht 28; Leinster 31, Pontypridd 18; Cardiff 35, Glasgow 44; Bridgend 41, Borders 9; Connacht 23, Cardiff 22; Pontypridd 21, Newport 16; Glasgow 25, Leinster 21; Bridgend 9, Pontypridd 26; Borders 15, Cardiff 18; Leinster 23, Connacht 26; Newport 25, Glasgow 31; Connacht 18, Newport 12; Pontypridd 28, Borders 27; Glasgow 47, Bridgend 11; Cardiff 30, Leinster 17; Borders 23, Leinster 18; Pontypridd 34, Glasgow 28; Newport 25, Cardiff 27; Bridgend 23, Connacht 24; Borders 33, Glasgow 12; Leinster 42, Newport 14; Cardiff 37, Bridgend 12; Connacht 0, Pontypridd 40; Pontypridd 15, Cardiff 9; Bridgend 18, Leinster 39; Newport 24, Borders 8; Glasgow 29, Connacht 7

Pool B Final Table

	P	*W*	*D*	*L*	*For*	*Against*	*Tries*	*BP*	*P/D*	*Pts*
Pontypridd	7	6	0	1	182	120	15	2	+62	26
Glasgow	7	5	0	2	216	166	22	3	+50	23
Cardiff	7	4	0	3	178	151	17	4	+27	20
Connacht	7	5	0	2	126	176	11	0	–50	20
Leinster	7	3	0	4	191	154	22	6	+37	18
Borders	7	2	0	5	142	169	15	4	–27	12
Bridgend	7	2	0	5	127	187	11	2	–60	10
Newport	7	1	0	6	121	160	9	4	–39	8

Points: win 4; draw 2; one bonus point for any team scoring four or more tries in a game; one bonus point for a team who are within seven points when losing a game

Quarter Finals:

Munster 33 (*T:* Mullins 2, Lawlor, penalty try *C:* O'Gara 2 *PG:* O'Gara 3), **Connacht 3** (*PG:* McHugh); **Glasgow 17** (*T:* Steel *PG:* Hayes 4), **Ulster 20** (*T:* Bell, A Ward *C:* Humphreys 2 *PG:* Humphreys 2); **Pontypridd 12** (*PG:* N Jenkins 4), **Neath 13** (*T:* penalty try *C:* Connor *PG:* Jarvis 2); **Edinburgh 22** (*T:* Murray, Lee *PG:* Laney 4), **Cardiff 26** (*T:* R Williams, Powell *C:* Harris 2 *PG:* Harris 4).

Semi-Finals:

Munster 40 (*T:* Kelly, Mullins, Hayes, Quinlan, Galwey *C:* O'Gara 3 *PG:* O'Gara 3), **Ulster 10** (*T:* Humphreys *C:* Humphreys *PG:* Humphreys); **Neath 32** (*T:* Bonnor-Evans, Tiueti, Jarvis, Morris *C:* Jarvis 3 *PG:* Jarvis 2), **Cardiff 10** (*T:* Smith *C:* Harris *PG:* Harris).

Celtic League Final

1 February, Millennium Stadium, Cardiff Arms Park
Munster 37 (2G 6PG IT) **Neath 17** (3PG 1DG 1T)

Province versus club. And, as so often in this situation, the Welsh club came off second best. The result served to fuel the internecine warfare in Wales as the debate raged over the introduction of regional teams. At the time of this final, the position had not been resolved; but Neath's dramatic demise undoubtedly was another peg on which the regional lobby could hang their argument. Neath were hardly fancied to inflict real damage on a Munster side that had already registered a significant success by 35-19 at the Gnoll during the zonal qualifiers.

Munster, already Heineken Cup quarter-finalists for a fifth consecutive season, outclassed the Welsh. Ronan O'Gara's precision kicking hoisted the Reds into a 12-3 lead before Brett Sinkinson used the outside-half's ankle as a stepping-stone and O'Gara retired for repairs. Sinkinson was cited and banned for six matches. Jeremy Staunton proved a confident deputy when he switched from full-back to assume kicking duties with two penalty shots and a couple of conversions. Munster's outrage at O'Gara's injury was translated into devastating attack and three tries. Alan Quinlan, the game's outstanding forward, raced 40 metres following a charged kick for the first try; Marcus Horan touched down when a maul trundled Neath back helplessly; and then Rob Henderson, on as replacement, shook his tail at defenders and weaved his wicked way to score a memorable solo try.

Neath could not penetrate an unwavering defence until Adam Jones pounced from close up in the third minute of stoppage time. Lee Jarvis provided the other Welsh points with a dropped goal and three penalty shots. Attendance: 30,076.

Munster: J W Staunton; J P Kelly, M J Mullins, J Holland, M Lawlor; R J R O'Gara, P A Stringer; M J Horan, F J Sheahan, J J Hayes, M R O'Driscoll, D O'Callaghan, R W Williams (*captain*), A G Foley, A Quinlan *Substitutions:* K Keane for Holland (79 mins); M Prendergast for Lawlor (70 mins); R A J Henderson for O'Gara (25 mins); M Cahill for Horan (78 mins); J Blaney for Sheahan (78 mins); M J Galwey for O'Driscoll (76 mins); D Leamy for Quinlan (78 mins)

Scorers *Tries:* Quinlan, Horan, Henderson *Conversions:* Staunton (2) *Penalty Goals:* O'Gara (4), Staunton (2)

Neath: A P R Durston; G Morris, J Storey, D Tiueti, S M Williams; L Jarvis, A P Moore; D Jones, B H Williams, A Jones, G O Llewellyn (*captain*), A Newman, A Mocelutu, N Bonnor-Evans, B D Sinkinson *Substitutions:* A Matthews for B Williams (16 mins); S Tandy for Mocelutu (61 mins); S Connor for Jarvis (76 mins); R Phillips for Sinkinson (81 mins); A G Bateman for Moore (81 mins)

Scorers *Try*: A Jones *Penalty Goals*: Jarvis (3) *Dropped Goal*: Jarvis

Referee C White (England)

Previous Celtic Finals: 2002 Leinster 24, Munster 20 (Dublin); 2003 Munster 37, Neath 17 (Cardiff)

SUPER TWELVE SERIES 2003

Blues' Turn to Sing

Paul Dobson

At last the Crusaders lost a Super 12 Final. Not long ago the Blues looked invincible. Their two-year hegemony came to an abrupt end when the Crusaders beat them in 1998. For four of the next five years the Super 12 was the property of the Crusaders. Their Jerusalem fell at Eden Park this year. It was the Blues' turn to sing.

The best teams reached the final of the Super 12 – the Blues and the Crusaders. Of the two, the Blues were the ones who gave the 2003 Super 12 its exuberance. If the Super 12 were a band, Carlos Spencer was the bandleader. If it were a circus, Spencer was the ringmaster. And the leading players were all Blues.

It was a younger Super 12 than usual. Many of the hardened players were missing as the shadow of the World Cup loomed and many older players went into rehab and made arrangements for their lump-sum pension pay-out from European rugby. There was one 'veteran' who played and was the maestro of the Super 12 – Carlos Spencer, the Blues' fly-half, who conducted the Blues from one thrilling crescendo to the next. He made the Super 12 with his dashing creativity – he and the new rising star, Rupeni Caucaunibuca, the young Fijian who flashed into the Super 12's firmament like the Jonah Lomu of 1995. His genius was somewhat blighted by injury and a tug-of-war between Fiji and New Zealand about his World Cup availability, an impasse broken by the IRB's decision that he was a Fijian player.

The young rising stars of this year's Super 12 included Sam Tuitupou, Joe Rokocoko, Angus Macdonald and Daniel Braid of the Blues, Daniel Carter of the Crusaders, Ma'a Nonu of the Hurricanes, Matt Giteau, Mark Gerrard, Scott Fava and Tamaiti Horua of the Brumbies, Josh Valentine of the Reds, Morgan Turinui of the Waratahs, Enrico Januarie and Juan Smith of the Cats, Paul Williams of the Highlanders till he suffered severe injury, Luke Watson and Gary Botha of the Sharks and Dewey Swartbooi and the Cronjé brothers, Jacques and Geo of the Voortrekker looks, of the Bulls.

The Blues were simply the most exciting side that the Super 12 have seen with Doug Howlett, Joe Rokocoko, Mils Muliaina and Rupeni Caucaunibuca and Spencer to set them running from all parts of the field. Some of their tries were breath-taking miracles of delight. They suffered one defeat – when the Highlanders throttled them in Dunedin.

In the midst of their exciting ability to attack it may be possible to overlook their defence. Rugby is about attack and defence. The bubbling Blues scored the most points on attack – 393 in their 11 matches. They also had the fewest scored against them – 185, 61 fewer than the Highlanders.

The Crusaders were not the invincible unit of 2002 but when they got a sniff of the semi-final they ploughed forward to it with unsmiling efficiency. They had the ability to blot out opposition and score whatever points were on offer – and they did this almost completely without Andrew Mehrtens who spent most of the Super 12 on the bench or injured as Daniel Carter became the new star. The Crusaders' major asset was that grinding back division, whereas the Blues' major asset had been the flying backs.

The charge for semi-final spots was dramatic, as the Blues, the Crusaders and the Hurricanes sat back on the last weekend of round robin to see who was to join them. The Brumbies seemed to have eliminated themselves but then the Highlanders failed, then the Waratahs, and the Bulls could not muster victory by sufficient points to get in the backdoor – and so that brought the Brumbies back in after their disappointing defeat by the Crusaders on the Friday night.

The Hurricanes had some special moments – a team whose strike-force revolved around Tana Umaga and Ma'a Nonu in the centre with Christian Cullen, striving for form, behind them and was built on the powerful loose forward play of Jerry Collins and Rodney So'oialo. They made a semi-final for the first time since 1997, but the Crusaders smothered their hopes of a first final.

The Brumbies, plagued by injury, as most teams were, lacked their smooth consistency of the past. For a team whose handling and precision was a benchmark for the rest of the rugby world they now became wobbly and were wiped out by the Blues in the semi-final. They were at their best against the Bulls and the Waratahs.

The Highlanders had an erratic season, which ended in acrimony as strong accusations were made against retiring coach Laurie Mains, which he met with threats of court action.

The Waratahs were also an erratic team and their seasoned coach, Bob Dwyer, also handed in a prompt resignation at the end of the season. The Waratahs' best feat was probably beating the Highlanders in Dunedin. They just could not finish the business. They led 19-0 against a dilapidated Stormers side in Sydney and lost. They had to score four tries against the Chiefs in their last match to go into the semis and scored only three.

The Chiefs were the 'almost' team. They almost beat the Sharks, the Stormers, the Crusaders, the Blues, the Bulls and the Highlanders. In the end they beat only the Reds and the Cats but ended with most bonus points of all Super 12 sides.

The Reds finished strongly and delighted themselves by beating the Waratahs in Sydney and then thwarting the Highlanders in Brisbane.

The Bulls, for so long the whipping boys, were the big improvers of and during the Super 12. They began with a steady base and built each week on that foundation till they were playing balanced and exciting rugby. They deprived themselves of a semi-final spot by contriving to lose to the Stormers in a match they should have won.

The Sharks deserved better than their second last position, especially as they needed only a modicum of luck to come home from their four-match Australasian tour with more than just victory over the Chiefs.

The other two South African teams, both battered by injuries, played below their potential and actually deteriorated during the competition.

The Stormers had one glorious moment – in Sydney when, even more under the injury whip, they came back from 19-0 down to win 39-29. Otherwise they suffered from second-half insomnia and could not even cope with a 14-man Reds side at Newlands where the attendance dropped dramatically as the Super 12 wore on.

The Cats ended bottom for the second time in their Super 12 history, largely because they found tackling a chore beneath them.

2003 Round Robin Results

21 Feb: Chiefs 16, Highlanders 29 (Hamilton); Waratahs 18, Blues 31 (Sydney); Cats 26, Bulls 34 (Bloemfontein); Stormers 40, Sharks 18 (Cape Town)

22 Feb: Crusaders 37, Hurricanes 21 (Christchurch); Reds 19, Brumbies 22 (Brisbane)

28 Feb: Chiefs 27, Blues 30 (Hamilton)

1 Mar: Highlanders 41, Stormers 17 (Dunedin); Hurricanes 34, Bulls 46 (Napier); Crusaders 34, Reds 6 (Christchurch); Sharks 25, Brumbies 17 (Durban); Cats 36, Waratahs 48 (Bloemfontein)

7 Mar: Highlanders 29, Bulls 22 (Invercargill); Hurricanes 33, Stormers 18 (Wellington) Cats 34, Brumbies 32 (Johannesburg)

8 Mar: Chiefs 43, Reds 27 (Hamilton); Blues 39, Crusaders 5 (Albany); Sharks 36, Waratahs 49 (Durban)

14 Mar: Crusaders 36, Chiefs 29 (Christchurch); Brumbies 37, Stormers 22 (Canberra); Sharks 20, Hurricanes 35 (Durban)

15 Mar: Waratahs 26, Bulls 16 (Sydney); Cats 33, Highlanders 21 (Johannesburg)

21 Mar: Blues 62, Reds 20 (Whangarei); Waratahs 29, Stormers 39 (Sydney); Sharks 19, Highlanders 23 (Durban)

22 Mar: Brumbies 64, Bulls 26 (Canberra); Cats 21, Hurricanes 28 (Bloemfontein)

28 Mar: Blues 41, Brumbies 15 (Auckland)

29 Mar: Highlanders 16, Crusaders 17 (Dunedin); Hurricanes 24, Chiefs 14 (Wellington); Waratahs 23, Reds 35 (Sydney); Cats 23, Sharks 29 (Johannesburg)

4 Apr: Highlanders 22, Blues 11 (Dunedin); Reds 23, Hurricanes 26 (Brisbane)

5 Apr: Waratahs 34, Crusaders 31 (Sydney); Bulls 24, Stormers 27 (Pretoria);

6 Apr: Brumbies 55, Chiefs 31 (Canberra)

11 Apr: Hurricanes 42, Waratahs 26 (Wellington)

12 Apr: Chiefs 25, Sharks 31 (Hamilton); Crusaders 65, Cats 34 (Christchurch); Bulls 28, Blues 56 (Pretoria); Stormers 20, Reds 41 (Cape Town)

18 Apr: Crusaders 23, Sharks 18 (Christchurch); Brumbies 41, Waratahs 15 (Canberra)

19 Apr: Chiefs 40, Cats 9 (Rotorua); Hurricanes 37, Highlanders 15 (New Plymouth); Stormers 8, Blues 36 (Cape Town); Bulls 39, Reds 19 (Pretoria)

25 Apr: Highlanders 45, Brumbies 19 (Dunedin)

26 Apr: Blues 25, Sharks 16 (Auckland); Reds 41, Cats 13 (Brisbane); Bulls 32, Crusaders 31 (Pretoria); Stormers 24, Chiefs 23 (Cape Town)

2 May: Stormers 13, Crusaders 51 (Cape Town); Blues 33, Cats 9 (Auckland)

3 May: Highlanders 23, Waratahs 27 (Dunedin); Hurricanes 27, Brumbies 35 (Wellington); Reds 22, Sharks 13 (Brisbane); Bulls 29, Chiefs 26 (Pretoria)

9 May: Blues 29, Hurricanes 17 (Auckland); Brumbies 21, Crusaders 28 (Canberra)

10 May: Reds 28, Highlanders 23 (Brisbane); Waratahs 25, Chiefs 14 (Sydney); Sharks 16, Bulls 24 (Durban); Stormers 27, Cats 21 (Cape Town)

Super Twelve 2003: Round Robin Table

	P	*W*	*L*	*For*	*Against*	*Bonus Points*	*Pts*
Blues	11	10	1	393	185	9	49
Crusaders	11	8	3	358	263	8	40
Hurricanes	11	7	4	324	284	7	35
Brumbies	11	6	5	358	313	7	31
Waratahs	11	6	5	320	344	7	31
Bulls	11	6	5	320	354	6	30
Highlanders	11	6	5	287	246	5	29
Reds	11	5	6	281	318	6	26
Stormers	11	5	6	255	354	3	23
Chiefs	11	2	9	288	319	10	18
Sharks	11	3	8	241	306	5	17
Cats	11	2	9	259	398	5	13

Points: win 4; draw 2; four or more tries, or defeat by seven or fewer points 1

First semi-final 16 May Jade Stadium, Lancaster Park, Christchurch
Crusaders 39 (3G 5PG 1DG) Hurricanes 16 (1G 3PG)

Crusaders: L R MacDonald; M Vunibaka, C S Ralph, D W Carter, J Maddock; A J D Mauger, J W Marshall; D N Hewett, M G Hammett, G M Somerville, C R Jack, N M C Maxwell, R D Thorne (*captain*), S R Broomhall, R H McCaw *Substitutions:* B C Thorn for Maxwell (5 mins); S M Robertson for Broomhall (50 mins); A P Mehrtens for Mauger (70 mins); G E Feek for Hewett (70 mins); B C Hurst for Marshall (75 mins); S McFarland for Hammett (75 mins); S E Hamilton for MacDonald (75 mins)

Scorers *Tries:* Robertson, McCaw, Broomhall *Conversions:* Carter (3) *Penalty Goals:* Carter (5) *Dropped Goal:* Mauger

Hurricanes: C M Cullen; L M Fa'atau, M Nonu, J F Umaga (*captain*), B J Ward; D E Holwell, J E Spice; A W Penn, D A Smith, T J Fairbrother, K M T Ormsby, P D Tito, J Collins, R So'oialo, O K Vanisi *Substitutions:* R J Flutey for Holwell (58 mins); J Ward for Smith (64 mins); B R Thompson for Vanisi (70 mins);

B D T Haami for Spice (70 mins); R A Kennedy for Tito (75 mins); K T Tuirirangi for Penn (75 mins); N W Brew for Fa'atau (75 mins)

Scorers *Try:* B Ward *Conversion:* Holwell *Penalty Goals:* Holwell (3)

Referee P L Marshall (Australia)

Second semi-final 17 May Eden Park, Auckland
Blues 42 (3G 2PG 3T) **Brumbies 21** (3G)

Blues: D C Howlett; R L Gear, M Muliaina, S Tuitupou, J Rokocoko; C J Spencer, S J Devine; D T Manu, K F Mealamu, K J Meeuws, A J Williams, A J Macdonald, J A Collins, X J Rush (*captain*), D J Braid *Substitutions:* T D Woodcock for Manu (67 mins); D J C Witcombe for Mealamu (71 mins); B M Mika for Macdonald (76 mins); D B Gibson for Devine (80 mins); M Tuiali'i for Collins (80 mins); L Stensness for Tuitupou (80 mins)

Scorers *Tries:* Rokocoko (2), Devine, Meeuws, Muliaina, Howlett *Conversions:* Spencer (3) *Penalty Goals:* Spencer (2)

Brumbies: J W C Roff; D McInally, J Wilson, P W Howard, M Gerrard; M A Bartholomeusz, G M Gregan (*captain*); W K Young, J A Paul, B J Darwin, D T Giffin, D J Vickerman, T W Horua, S G Fava, G B Smith *Substitutions:* O D A Finegan for Horua (temp 40 mins to 51 mins and from 55 mins); J B G Harrison for Giffin (59 mins); D Beaumont for Paul (59 mins); L Beckett for Howard (67 mins); D Fitter for Darwin (75 mins)

Scorers *Tries:* Finegan, Wilson, Bartholomeusz *Conversions:* Roff (3)

Referee J I Kaplan (South Africa)

Final

24 May Eden Park, Auckland
Blues 21 (1G 3PG 1T) **Crusaders 17** (1G 2T)

The Blues ended singing; the Crusaders with their swords broken. From habitual champions the men from the South Island had tumbled to defeat. For the North Islanders it was a return to the glories of yesteryear.

The result was a just one as the Blues had been the team that made the 2003 Super 12 with their thrilling play. This was an absorbing match but not a fluent one. The intensity was too great, the scrums too messy, the line-outs too unpredictable and the tackling too meaty for smooth flow in the game.

After a rainy week in New Zealand, most of the final was played in good conditions. After a nervous week in Auckland and Christchurch, the match started nervously and neither side settled long in any pattern. It was a hard, close, tense contest from jerky start to frenetic finish.

At the start it seemed that the Crusaders would do what they were expected to do – strangle the Blues at source, dominating their forwards and destroying them at scrum-half. Then they kicked low and hard towards touch to control territory. The Blues did not do what was expected. Time and again fly-half Carlos Spencer, the greatest of runners, kicked high. In a reversal of rôles, the Crusaders became the counter-attackers. More and more they pressured the Blues.

The Crusaders were first to score when Scott Robertson peeled towards the front of the line-out and sent Mark Hammett trundling to the Blues' line. Over he went as Kees Meeuws and Joe Rokocoko tried to stop him. Daniel Carter missed the conversion and the Crusaders led 5-0 after 20 minutes.

Missed kicks proved expensive for the Crusaders. Carter fluffed a penalty and a conversion, Mehrtens one conversion and a penalty goal which bounced back off the upright.

The first penalty of the match came immediately after the restart. The Crusaders were penalised at the tackle, and Spencer made it 5-3. Later in the half Chris Jack conceded a penalty and Spencer gave his team a 6-5 lead.

It seemed a brittle lead when the Crusaders got their second try from the kick-off. David Gibson, in the side at scrum-half for injured Steve Devine, collected the deep kick-off and passed infield to Spencer who dropped the ball. Grateful Hammett seized it and drove over the line for his second try.

By this stage Andrew Mehrtens was on for a limping Marika Vunibaka. As a result Aaron Mauger went to outside centre and Caleb Ralph to the wing, a happier place for him than centre.

Mehrtens missed the conversion and at half-time the Crusaders led 10-6, two tries to nil.

Gibson, battered so often at scrum-half, shrugged off his rickety start and broke sharply in midfield and fed Mils Muliaina. The centre gave to Rico Gear who had Doug Howlett dashing up on his outside. Gear gave to Howlett who surged over, dangerously close to the dead-ball line. The Blues led 11-10.

The Blues had a sustained period of pressure. On one occasion, as he was about to be tackled deep in his in-goal Mehrtens managed a pass back to Ralph, who cleared. Gibson broke sharply and the Crusaders scampered in defence. Marshall grabbed Howlett's jersey before the ball could get to him and Spencer goaled the subsequent penalty. 14-10.

The major substitutions happened afterwards in a match that was too close and too tense to allow the luxury of fiddling with the team. Sam Broomhall came on for Scott Robertson and the Blues brought on two fresh front-row players – Derren Witcombe and Tony Woodcock.

Throughout the match the Blues' pack had stood up well. They created the next score. From a five-metre line-out, the Blues grouped around tall Ali Williams, one of the outstanding players of the Super 12. They got their maul going, it gathered impetus and it carried Daniel Braid over the line for a vital score, which Spencer converted. This took the Blues to 21-10, out of one-score range of the Crusaders.

Not that the Crusaders yielded softly. They came hammering back at the Blues, but found scant reward against the most parsimonious defence in the Super 12. In these last dozen or so minutes of the match the Blues' defence won the cup.

Daniel Carter was close but the television match official, in a microscopic call, ruled that he had lost the ball at the line as Braid tackled him. Then Howlett's diving tackle from behind dislodged the ball from Leon Macdonald's grasp as he dived for the corner.

The Crusaders attacked. The Blues defended and conceded penalties. The fifth penalty in quick succession became a tap kick and Ralph scored. Mehrtens converted. 21-17 with five minutes to play.

Guileful Carlos Spencer did not let the Crusaders play. He kicked them into their own territory and the pressure in this final period came from the Blues. They won a scrum in midfield as the siren signifying the end of the match sounded. Gibson gave to Spencer who ran half the width of the field with the ball to get it safely over the touch-line. Then the final whistle blew.

Both captains thanked everybody and praised their own teams and the opposition. But then it was a gentlemanly final, again well managed by referee André Watson in his fourth final.

Blues: D C Howlett; R L Gear, M Muliaina, S Tuitupou, J Rokocoko; C J Spencer, D B Gibson; D T Manu, K F Mealamu, K J Meeuws, A J Williams, A J Macdonald, J A Collins, X J Rush (*captain*), D J Braid *Substitutions:* T D Woodcock for Manu (64 mins); D J C Witcombe for Mealamu (64 mins); B M Mika for Macdonald (78 mins)

Scorers *Tries:* Howlett, Braid *Conversion:* Spencer *Penalty Goals:* Spencer (3)

Crusaders: L R MacDonald; M Vunibaka, C S Ralph, D W Carter, J Maddock; A J D Mauger, J W Marshall; D N Hewett, M G Hammett, G M Somerville, B C Thorn, C R Jack, R D Thorne (*captain*), S M Robertson, R H McCaw *Substitutions:* A P Mehrtens for Vunibaka (36 mins); S R Broomhall for Robertson (57 mins); S E Hamilton for MacDonald (71 mins); J J W Leo'o for Broomhall (temp 71 mins to 74 mins)

Scorers *Tries:* Hammett (2), Ralph *Conversion:* Mehrtens

Referee A J Watson (South Africa)

Previous Super Twelve Finals: 1996 Blues 45, Sharks 21 (Auckland); 1997 Blues 23, Brumbies 7 (Auckland); 1998 Crusaders 20, Blues 13 (Auckland); 1999 Crusaders 24, Highlanders 19 (Dunedin); 2000 Crusaders 20, Brumbies 19 (Canberra); 2001 Brumbies 36, Sharks 6 (Canberra); 2002 Crusaders 31, Brumbies 13 (Christchurch); 2003 Blues 21, Crusaders 17 (Auckland)

SUPER TWELVE RECORDS 1996-2003

Record	*Detail*		*Set*
Most team points in season	534 by Crusaders	in 13 matches	2002
Most team tries in season	70 by Blues	in 13 matches	1996
Highest team score	96 by Crusaders	96-19 v Waratahs	2002
Biggest team win	77 by Crusaders	96-19 v Waratahs	2002
Most team tries in match	14 by Crusaders	v Waratahs	2002
Most appearances	91 for Brumbies	G M Gregan	1996-2002
Most points in matches	926 for Crusaders	A P Mehrtens	1997-2003
Most points in season	206 for Crusaders	A P Mehrtens	1998

Most points in match	50 for Sharks	G Lawless v Highlanders	1997
Most tries in matches	56 for Hurricanes	C M Cullen	1996-2003
Most tries in season	15 for Brumbies	J W Roff	1997
Most tries in match	4 for Brumbies	J W Roff v Sharks	1997
	4 for Sharks	G Lawless v Highlanders	1997
	4 for Sharks	C S Terblanche v Chiefs	1998
	4 for Blues	J Vidiri v Bulls	2000
	4 for Blues	D C Howlett v Hurricanes	2002
	4 for Blues	M Muliaina v Bulls	2002
	4 for Crusaders	C S Ralph v Waratahs	2002
Most cons in matches	148 for Waratahs	M C Burke	1996-2003
Most cons in season	39 for Brumbies	S A Mortlock	2000
Most cons in match	13 for Crusaders	A P Mehrtens v Waratahs	2002
Most pens in matches	195 for Crusaders	A P Mehrtens	1997-2003
Most pens in season	43 for Crusaders	A P Mehrtens	1999
Most pens in match	8 for Bulls	J Kruger v Highlanders	1997
	8 for Highlanders	W J Walker v Chiefs	2003
Most drops in matches	17 for Crusaders	A P Mehrtens	1997-2003
Most drops in season	7 for Bulls	L J Koen	2003
Most drops in match	3 for Crusaders	A P Mehrtens v Highlanders	1998
	3 for Bulls	L J Koen v Cats	2003

DOMESTIC RUGBY IN ENGLAND 2002-03

Wasps Provide a Sting in the Tale of the Championship: The Zurich Premiership

Mick Cleary

Gloucester had a terrific Premiership record for eight months and 30 days of the season. And then a complete stinker on the final day. Fair? Probably not. But it's there in the record books. Wasps are the Zurich champions by dint of beating Gloucester, 39-3, in the winner-takes-all finale. Wasps came away with the trophy while Gloucester came away with red, tear-streaked faces and absolutely nothing to show for their dominance of the domestic season apart from a few sympathetic mumbles in the media.

You didn't have to look too hard to detect the source of the sour grapes. The Gloucester management and players did manage to keep a tin lid on their own emotions, gut-wrenching as the day had been. But to all neutral observers there was something flawed about a system that saw Gloucester win the normal league programme by 15 points, chalk up four more victories than second-placed Wasps, and yet officially be considered runners-up due to a bad day at the Twickenham office on 31 May. The marathon came down to a short, sharp sprint and Wasps were the side out of the blocks and heading towards the finishing tape before Gloucester had even laced their spikes.

The new format – with Wasps first playing off against third-placed Northampton – was a change from the much-criticised set-up of the previous years when the top eight teams battled it out for the play-off crown. In those days, though, there was also a trophy to mark the winning of the league, the status symbol that was coveted by all teams. That was all changed. This year there would be just three clubs involved. It was seen as an advantage that the league winners would have a bye straight to the final and the supposed benefit of a three-week rest between the last round of league games and the final. In fact, Gloucester had tailed off before then, actually claiming the league title on 27 April when beating Harlequins, 29-11.

The lay-off had a seriously detrimental effect on them. They had switched off in the head after a gruelling campaign and were never able to summon up the reserves of punishing forward play allied to fleet-footed finishing behind the scrum that had characterised their regular season. Wasps, meanwhile, had timed their run-in to perfection. They won 16 of their last 18 games in all competitions and were sharp, mean and hungry on the day that mattered.

'Wasps have been playing week-in, week-out,' said Gloucester director of rugby, Nigel Melville. 'We played as if it were pre-season, not the end of the season. It hurts, although Wasps were the better side on the day. We did not perform. We were a shambles and, as far as I am concerned, a disgrace. We can't complain about the format because we knew what it was before the start and we came here to play a final.'

In name, perhaps; in spirit, not so. Wasps had no such mental tussles going on inside their heads. 'We wanted to show people how much we have improved in the second half of the season,' said Wasps' director of rugby, Warren Gatland. 'People are making a big issue of the 15-point margin but we all knew the rules to start with. We would have pursued Gloucester more aggressively in the final part of the season if the rules had been different. Instead we shuffled our team selections in order to rest players. It was all about finishing in the top three and going from there.'

The credibility issue at the top end of the league was matched by a mix of feelings at the bottom end. Fear, anxiety, desperation, joy and relief – they were all there at some time or other. Only one point separated the bottom six sides as the league season entered its final month. On the final day, only points difference divided those old west-country rivals, Bath and Bristol, both of whom finished on 36 points with seven Premiership victories. It was that close, that nail-biting and, for a while, that disturbing.

The drama of the closing weeks had been undermined by fevered talk of a merger between Bath and Bristol. The two clubs finally had to admit that some exploratory discussions were taking place as various investors and backers looked to offset the financial hammering that comes with relegation. It was an unsettling time for the players, always last in the line when it comes to dispensing information.

'There is so much rubbish going on we don't know where the hell we are,' said Bristol coach Peter Thorburn just a few weeks before the last rites were read on his club's Premiership tenure. 'There are 80-plus people whose futures are up in the air. It's pretty cruel.'

And so it was. The uplift given by a dramatic 30-20 victory over Bath on the penultimate weekend in front of a Premiership record crowd of 20,793 at Ashton Gate proved to be short-lived. The following week Bath secured their own Premiership status by beating Newcastle 24-12 at the Rec while Bristol's hopes quickly slumped as they were turned over 41-21 by London Irish at the Madejski.

Newcastle themselves had been very much in the firing line. They were six points adrift at the turn of the year and only some frantic and inspired use of the chequebook by Rob Andrew managed to turn things round. The Newcastle director of rugby did a complete about-turn, moving away from his policy of grooming young English players and buying in foreign imports such as former internationals Mark Andrews from South Africa and Mark Mayerhofler from New Zealand. Andrews had a massive impact as Newcastle took 24 points from their final eight games to finish tenth. 'We should never have got ourselves into that hole,' said Andrew.

Leicester hit the doldrums after four years of smooth sailing. They lost three of their first five games, as well as four of their last five Premiership matches to end up in mid-table. Not surprisingly the Tigers surrendered their proud home league record, Northampton's 25-12 victory there in November the first time that Leicester had been beaten in the league in nigh on five years. London Irish were also to win at Welford Road before the season's end.

Sale tailed off after a bright opening while Northampton came through with typical cussedness to claim third spot, winning six of their last seven games. Saracens spluttered yet somehow managed to make the Heineken Cup wildcard play-offs. Harlequins improved marginally on the previous year's effort although their season had a huge pall hanging over it after the death of scrum-half Nick Duncombe. In a season typical of so many across the sporting landscape with its share of triumphs and mishaps, such news truly was a tragedy.

Final Zurich Premiership Table 2002-03

	P	*W*	*D*	*L*	*For*	*Against*	*Bonus*	*Pts*
Gloucester	22	17	2	3	617	396	10	82
Wasps	22	13	2	7	553	460	11	67
Northampton	22	13	0	9	512	376	10	62
Sale	22	12	2	8	556	470	10	62
Leeds	22	12	2	8	478	435	6	58
Leicester	22	12	0	10	448	396	7	55
Harlequins	22	9	0	13	461	560	8	44
Saracens	22	8	0	14	499	587	10	42
London Irish	22	8	1	13	432	485	6	40
Newcastle	22	8	0	14	388	545	8	40
Bath	22	7	2	13	385	490	4	36
Bristol	22	7	1	14	504	633	6	36

Points: win four; draw two; four or more tries, or defeat by seven or fewer points one

Zurich Championship Grand Final

31 May, 2003, Twickenham
Wasps 39 (3G 4PG 2DG) **Gloucester 3** (1PG)

We came expecting a fierce confrontation between the top two sides in the county. Instead we got a one-sided exhibition of power rugby. Fair play to Wasps. Whatever reservations there might be about the concept's legitimacy, the final did show us the best that the Premiership can offer. Or it did from one side.

Wasps were everything that Gloucester were not – assured, purposeful and murderously accurate. They played the game a good yard faster than their opponents; first to the breakdown and sharp both in thought and execution. There was a Man-of-the-Match performance from fly-half Alex King who ran the show, playing with both devil and composure. He deservedly won the inaugural Peter Deakin Memorial Medal, struck in honour of that great entrepreneurial trouper of the game who passed away in mid-season.

King had a lot to work with. The Wasps pack, in which lock Simon Shaw and flanker Paul Volley were outstanding, sent back first-rate ball. King mixed his options well. He used his centres Stuart Abbott or Fraser Waters to cut back through the traffic or sent it wide to where the irrepressible Josh Lewsey was looking to create mischief.

Wasps led 23-3 at the break and it was something of a miracle that Gloucester had even managed to get that close. They were leaden in body and mind. They simply were not at the races. They may well have pledged their support to the play-off format but their actions told another story. Not even captain Phil Vickery could rouse his men. Gloucester missed the speed and imagination of the injured young flyer James Forrester in the back-row.

The die was cast within two minutes. A Wasps drive from a line-out was checked but when the ball came into the midfield, Abbott carved a huge opening from where he was able to hand on to Lewsey to finish off. Ludovic Mercier managed a long-range penalty for Gloucester but King replied with two penalties and a drop goal.

The Gloucester defence was breached again just before half-time when good build-up work by Volley and King teed up Lewsey once again.

King put the game way beyond Gloucester in the opening stages of the second-half as he landed two penalties and a drop goal. A bungled Gloucester break-out ten minutes from time turned the ball over to Wasps. Joe Worsley accepted the offering to score.

Wasps: M van Gisbergen; O J Lewsey, F H H Waters, S Abbott, K M Logan; A D King, R Howley; C W Dowd, T Leota, W R Green, S D Shaw, R Birkett, J P R Worsley, P Volley, L B N Dallaglio (*captain*) *Substitutions* P B T Greening for Leota (62 mins); M Denney for Abbott (69 mins); M B Wood for Howley (71 mins); M Lock for Volley (72 mins); P Scrivener for Shaw (74 mins); A McKenzie for Dowd (75 mins); A Erinle for Waters (temp 28 to 35 mins), for King (temp 39 to 43 mins) and for Van Gisbergen (76 mins)

Scorers *Tries:* Lewsey (2), Worsley *Conversions:* King (3) *Penalty Goals:* King (4) *Drop Goals:* King (2)

Gloucester: G M Delport; M Garvey, T L Fanolua, H Paul, J Simpson-Daniel; L Mercier, A C T Gomarsall; R Roncero, O Azam, P J Vickery (*captain*), A Eustace, M Cornwell, J Boer, A Hazell, P J Paramore *Substitutions:* R J Fidler for Cornwell (40mins); P Buxton for Paramore (56mins); R Todd for Fanolua (62mins); S Amor for Mercier (69 mins); C Stuart-Smith for Garvey (76 mins)

Scorer *Penalty Goal:* Mercier

Referee A J Spreadbury (RFU)

Previous English Club Champions: 1987-88 Leicester; 1988-89 Bath; 1989-90 Wasps; 1990-91 Bath; 1991-92 Bath; 1992-93 Bath; 1993-94 Bath; 1994-95 Leicester; 1995-96 Bath; 1996-97 Wasps; 1997-98 Newcastle; 1998-99 Leicester; 1999-2000 Leicester; 2000-01 Leicester; 2001-02 Leicester; 2002-03 Wasps

(League winners 1988 to 2002; winners of the Grand Final in 2003)

ZURICH PREMIERSHIP CLUB DIRECTORY

Bath

Year of formation 1865
Ground Recreation Ground, London Road, Bath BA2 4BQ
Contacts Web: www.bathrugby.com Tel: Bath (01225) 325200
Colours Blue, white and black shirts; royal blue shorts
Captain 2002-03 Danny Grewcock
Zurich Premiership League 2002-03 11th
Powergen Cup 2002-03 Lost 29-30 to Northampton (quarter-final)

Competition Record 2002-03

Date	*Venue*	*Comp*	*Opponents*	*Result*	*Scorers*
1 Sep	A	ZP	London Irish	24-22	*PG:* Barkley 7 *DG:* Malone
8 Sep	A	ZP	Saracens	3-28	*PG:* Barkley
14 Sep	H	ZP	Wasps	27-27	*T:* Tindall, Lyle *C:* Malone *PG:* Malone 5
21 Sep	A	ZP	Northampton	3-24	*PG:* Barkley
28 Sep	H	ZP	Gloucester	21-21	*PG:* Barkley 6 *DG:* Malone
5 Oct	A	ZP	Leicester	20-22	*T:* Tindall, Maggs *C:* Barkley 2 *PG:* Barkley 2
11 Oct	A	PPC1	GRAN Parma	40-3	*T:* Lloyd, Beattie, Scaysbrook, N Thomas, Perry, Barkley *C:* Barkley 5
19 Oct	H	PPC1	GRAN Parma	57-19	*T:* Crockett 2, Maggs 2, G Thomas, N Thomas, Malone, Danielli, Barkley *C:* Barkley 6
26 Oct	H	ZP	Leeds	20-22	*T:* Perry, Barkley, Danielli *C:* Barkley *PG:* Barkley
2 Nov	A	ZP	Harlequins	9-18	*PG:* Barkley 3
10 Nov	H	ZP	Sale	24-18	*T:* Voyce, pen try *C:* Barkley *PG:* Barkley 3 *DG:* Malone
17 Nov	A	ZP	Newcastle	24-20	*T:* Voyce, A Williams *C:* Malone *PG:* Malone 2, Perry 2
24 Nov	H	ZP	Bristol	19-30	*T:* pen try *C:* Malone *PG:* Malone 4
29 Nov	A	ZP	Sale	18-36	*T:* Scaysbrook, Danielli *C:* Barkley *PG:* Barkley 2
6 Dec	A	PPC2	Bridgend	26-28	*T:* Balshaw, A Williams *C:* Malone 2 *PG:* Malone 4
14 Dec	H	PPC2	Bridgend	38-10	*T:* Balshaw 2, Crockett, Maggs *C:* Barkley 3 *PG:* Barkley 4
21 Dec	A	PC6	Wasps	20-17	*T:* Balshaw, Malone *C:* Barkley 2 *PG:* Barkley 2
28 Dec	H	ZP	Harlequins	23-9	*T:* Tindall, Maggs *C:* Barkley 2 *PG:* Barkley 3
3 Jan	A	ZP	Leeds	7-20	*T:* Cooper *C:* Barkley
11 Jan	A	PPCQF	Montauban	24-27	*T:* Tindall, Danielli *C:* Barkley *PG:* Barkley 4
18 Jan	H	PPCQF	Montauban	24-18	*T:* Catt, N Thomas *C:* Barkley *PG:* Barkley 4
25 Jan	H	PCQF	Northampton	29-30	*T:* Cooper, Barnes *C:* Barkley 2 *PG:* Barkley 5
1 Feb	H	ZP	Leicester	8-15	*T:* Danielli *PG:* Barkley
8 Feb	A	ZP	Gloucester	16-29	*T:* Borthwick *C:* Barkley *PG:* Barkley *DG:* Catt 2

1 Mar	H	ZP	Saracens	30-9	*T:* Danielli 2, Maggs, Seveali'i *C:* Malone 2 *PG:* Malone 2
15 Mar	H	ZP	Northampton	10-27	*T:* Voyce *C:* Barkley *PG:* Barkley
6 Apr	A	ZP	Wasps	17-36	*T:* Danielli, Cooper *C:* Barkley 2 *PG:* Barkley
10 Apr	H	ZP	London Irish	18-15	*T:* Borthwick, Seveali'i *C:* Barkley *PG:* Barkley 2
13 Apr	A	PPCSF	Saracens	30-38	*T:* Seveali'i 2, Voyce *C:* Barkley 3 *PG:* Barkley 3
26 Apr	H	PPCSF	Saracens	27-19	*T:* Seveali'i, Grewcock, Voyce *C:* Barkley 3 *PG:* Barkley 2
4 May	A	ZP	Bristol	20-30	*T:* G Thomas, Maggs *C:* Barkley 2 *PG:* Barkley 3
10 May	H	ZP	Newcastle	24-12	*T:* Balshaw, N Thomas, Voyce *C:* Barkley 3 *PG:* Barkley
25 May	–	PPCF	Wasps	30-48	*T:* Balshaw, Scaysbrook, Tindall, Barkley *C:* Barkley, Balshaw *PG:* Barkley 2

Bristol

Year of formation 1888
Ground Memorial Stadium, Filton Avenue, Horfield, Bristol, BS7 0AQ
Contacts Web: www.bristolshoguns.co.uk Tel: Bristol (0117) 3111461
Colours Navy blue and white
Captain 2002-03 Ross Beattie
Zurich Premiership League 2002-03 12th *-relegated*
Powergen Cup 2002-03 Lost 19-24 to Rotherham (6th round)

Competition Record 2002-03

Date	*Venue*	*Comp*	*Opponents*	*Result*	*Scorers*
1 Sep	H	ZP	Saracens	30-45	*T:* Rees, Contepomi *C:* Drahm *PG:* Drahm 5 *DG:* Contepomi
8 Sep	A	ZP	Wasps	35-38	*T:* Best, Contepomi *C:* Contepomi 2 *PG:* Contepomi 7
15 Sep	H	ZP	Northampton	28-36	*T:* Archer, Contepomi, Daniel *C:* Contepomi 2 *PG:* Contepomi 3
21 Sep	A	ZP	Gloucester	18-45	*T:* Archer, Daniel *C:* Contepomi *PG:* Contepomi 2
29 Sep	H	ZP	Leicester	25-20	*T:* Christophers *C:* Contepomi *PG:* Contepomi 6
6 Oct	A	ZP	Leeds	13-25	*T:* Brown *C:* Contepomi *PG:* Contepomi 2
11 Oct	A	HC	Leinster	23-29	*T:* Gibson, Contepomi *C:* Contepomi 2 *PG:* Contepomi 3
19 Oct	H	HC	Montferrand	24-19	*T:* Drahm, Contepomi *C:* Contepomi *PG:* Contepomi 4
1 Nov	A	ZP	Sale	14-28	*T:* Richards *PG:* Drahm 3
10 Nov	H	ZP	Newcastle	38-10	*T:* Higgins 2, Christophers 2, Contepomi, Daniel *C:* Contepomi 4
17 Nov	H	ZP	London Irish	32-32	*T:* Daniel, pen try, Drahm, Nelson *C:* Drahm 3 *PG:* Drahm 2
24 Nov	A	ZP	Bath	30-19	*T:* Best, Johnstone, Higgins *C:* Drahm 3 *PG:* Drahm 3
1 Dec	A	ZP	Newcastle	20-12	*T:* Daniel 3 *C:* Contepomi *PG:* Contepomi
7 Dec	A	HC	Swansea	19-26	*T:* Contepomi *C:* Contepomi *PG:* Contepomi 4
15 Dec	H	HC	Swansea	41-23	*T:* Gibson 3, Pichot, Higgins *C:* Drahm 2 *PG:* Drahm 4

22 Dec	H	PC6	Rotherham	19-24	*T:* Higgins *C:* Drahm *PG:* Drahm 4
29 Dec	H	ZP	Sale	18-6	*PG:* Contepomi 6
4 Jan	A	ZP	Harlequins	17-26	*T:* Rees 2, Gibson *C:* Contepomi
12 Jan	A	HC	Montferrand	30-22	*T:* Daniel 2, J Williams *C:* Contepomi 3 *PG:* Contepomi 3
19 Jan	H	HC	Leinster	12-25	*T:* Christophers, Rees *C:* Contepomi
2 Feb	H	ZP	Leeds	12-17	*PG:* Contepomi 4
8 Feb	A	ZP	Leicester	6-40	*PG:* Contepomi 2
2 Mar	H	ZP	Harlequins	48-41	*T:* Gibson 2, Pichot 2, Nelson, A Brown *C:* Contepomi 3 *PG:* Contepomi 4
16 Mar	H	ZP	Gloucester	21-38	*T:* Christophers, Drahm *C:* Contepomi *PG:* Contepomi 2, Drahm
16 Apr	A	ZP	Northampton	13-43	*T:* Archer *C:* Drahm *PG:* Drahm 2
20 Apr	H	ZP	Wasps	19-34	*T:* Daniel *C:* Drahm *PG:* Drahm 4
29 Apr	A	ZP	Saracens	16-17	*T:* Sheridan *C:* Drahm *PG:* Drahm 3
4 May	H	ZP	Bath	30-20	*T:* Contepomi 2, Gibson *C:* Drahm 3 *PG:* Drahm 2 *DG:* Drahm
10 May	A	ZP	London Irish	21-41	*T:* Short 2 *C:* Drahm *PG:* Drahm 3

Gloucester

Year of formation 1873
Ground Kingsholm, Kingsholm Road, Gloucester, GL1 3AX
Contacts Web: www.gloucesterrugbyclub.com Tel: Gloucester (01452) 422422
Colours Cherry and white
Captain 2002-03 Phil Vickery
Zurich Premiership League 2002-03 Winners
Zurich Premiership Finals 2002-03 Lost 3-39 to Wasps (FINAL)
Powergen Cup 2002-03 Winners Won 40-22 against Northampton (FINAL)

Competition Record 2002-03

Date	*Venue*	*Comp*	*Opponents*	*Result*	*Scorers*
31 Aug	A	ZP	Harlequins	25-19	*T:* Paramore, Garvey, Woodman *C:* Mercier, Paul *PG:* Paul 2
7 Sep	H	ZP	Sale	44-8	*T:* Forrester 2, Boer, Paul, Beim, Delport *C:* Mercier 4 *PG:* Mercier 2
15 Sep	A	ZP	Newcastle	22-19	*T:* Paramore *C:* Mercier *PG:* Paul 3, Mercier 2
21 Sep	H	ZP	Bristol	45-18	*T:* Garvey 3, Paramore, Boer, Mercier *C:* Mercier 3 *PG:* Mercier 3
28 Sep	A	ZP	Bath	21-21	*T:* Forrester, Paul *C:* Paul *PG:* Mercier 2, Paul
5 Oct	H	ZP	Saracens	44-14	*T:* Azam 2, Fanolua, Boer, Mercier *C:* Mercier 5 *PG:* Mercier 3
12 Oct	H	HC	Munster	35-16	*T:* Boer 2, Mercier, Garvey *C:* Mercier 3 *PG:* Mercier 3
18 Oct	A	HC	Viadana	80-28	*T:* Fanolua 3, Simpson-Daniel 3, Paul 2, Garvey, Roncero, Boer, Forrester *C:* Mercier 10
26 Oct	A	ZP	Wasps	16-23	*T:* Fanolua *C:* Mercier *PG:* Mercier 2, Paul
2 Nov	H	ZP	Northampton	18-9	*PG:* Mercier 5 *DG:* Gomarsall
10 Nov	A	ZP	London Irish	40-19	*T:* Eustace, Paramore, Forrester, Boer, Roncero *C:* Mercier 3 *PG:* Mercier 3
15 Nov	A	ZP	Leicester	15-20	*T:* Fanolua, Boer *C:* Paul *PG:* Paul
24 Nov	H	ZP	Leeds	28-10	*T:* Paramore, Todd, Boer *C:* Mercier 2 *PG:* Mercier 3
30 Nov	H	ZP	London Irish	25-20	*T:* Paramore, pen try, Boer *C:* Mercier 2 *PG:* Mercier 2

8 Dec	H	HC	Perpignan	33-16	*T:* Garvey 2, Mercier *C:* Mercier 3 *PG:* Mercier 4
14 Dec	A	HC	Perpignan	23-31	*T:* Mercier, Boer *C:* Mercier 2 *PG:* Mercier 3
21 Dec	H	PC6	Exeter	35-6	*T:* Catling 2, Boer, Buxton, O'Leary *C:* Paul 5
28 Dec	A	ZP	Northampton	16-13	*T:* Azam *C:* Mercier *PG:* Mercier 2 *DG:* Mercier
4 Jan	H	ZP	Wasps	24-17	*T:* Cornwell 2, Paul *PG:* Paul 2, Mercier
11 Jan	H	HC	Viadana	64-16	*T:* Paramore 2, Todd 2, Garvey, Forrester, Beim, Azam, Simpson-Daniel, Collins *C:* Mercier 7
18 Jan	A	HC	Munster	6-33	*PG:* Mercier 2
25 Jan	H	PCQF	Saracens	51-20	*T:* Forrester 2, Delport 2, Fanolua, Gomarsall, Roncero, Eustace *C:* Mercier 3, Paul *PG:* Mercier
2 Feb	A	ZP	Saracens	29-22	*T:* Fanolua, Mercier *C:* Mercier 2 *PG:* Mercier 4 *DG:* Mercier
8 Feb	H	ZP	Bath	29-16	*T:* Azam, Garvey *C:* Mercier 2 *PG:* Mercier 5
1 Mar	–	PCSF	Leicester	16-11	*T:* Garvey, Delport *PG:* Mercier 2
16 Mar	A	ZP	Bristol	38-21	*T:* Forrester 3, Hazell, Mercier, Garvey *C:* Mercier 4
5 Apr	–	PCF	Northampton	40-22	*T:* Simpson-Daniel 2, Forrester, Garvey *C:* Mercier 4 *PG:* Mercier 3 *DG:* Mercier
12 Apr	H	ZP	Newcastle	25-23	*T:* Woodman, Hazell, Delport *C:* Mercier 2 *PG:* Mercier 2
18 Apr	A	ZP	Sale	30-30	*T:* Mercier, Fanolua, Boer *C:* Mercier 2, Paul *PG:* Mercier 3
26 Apr	H	ZP	Harlequins	29-11	*T:* Mercier, Simpson-Daniel, Boer, Paul *C:* Mercier 3 *PG:* Paul
4 May	A	ZP	Leeds	23-30	*T:* O'Leary, Beim *C:* Paul 2 *PG:* Amor 3
10 May	H	ZP	Leicester	31-13	*T:* Beim, Gomarsall, Fanolua, Delport *C:* Mercier 4 *PG:* Mercier
31 May	–	ZPF	Wasps	3-39	*PG:* Mercier

Harlequins

Year of formation 1866
Ground Stoop Memorial Ground, Langhorn Drive, Twickenham, Middlesex, TW2 7SX
Contacts Web: www.quins.co.uk Tel: 0208 410 6000
Colours Light blue, magenta, chocolate, French grey, black and light green; white shorts
Captain 2002-03 Jason Leonard
Zurich Premiership League 2002-03 7th
Zurich Wildcard Finals 2002-03 Lost 39-51 (aggreg) to Leicester (semi-final)
Powergen Cup 2002-03 Lost 12-19 to Leicester (quarter-final)

Competition Record 2002-03

Date	*Venue*	*Comp*	*Opponents*	*Result*	*Scorers*
31 Aug	H	ZP	Gloucester	19-25	*T:* Moore *C:* Burke *PG:* Burke 3 *DG:* Burke
7 Sep	A	ZP	Leicester	6-30	*PG:* Slemen 2
14 Sep	H	ZP	Leeds	23-33	*T:* Satala, Greenwood *C:* Burke 2 *PG:* Burke 2 *DG:* Burke
21 Sep	H	ZP	London Irish	29-19	*T:* Moore, Gollings, Greenstock *C:* Slemen *PG:* Burke 3 *DG:* Slemen
27 Sep	A	ZP	Sale	16-20	*T:* Sanderson, Sherriff *PG:* Slemen *DG:* Williams

5 Oct	H	ZP	Newcastle	47-23	*T:* Sanderson, Gomez, Diprose, Greenwood, Duncombe, Fuga *C:* Williams 2, Slemen, Gollings *PG:* Slemen 3
12 Oct	A	PPC1	Caerphilly	73-20	*T:* Moore 2, Duncombe 2, Williams, Jewell, Sherriff, Evans, Gollings, pen try, Rudzki *C:* Williams 9
19 Oct	H	PPC1	Caerphilly	31-27	*T:* Gollings 2, Fitzgerald, Evans *C:* Williams 4 *PG:* Williams
2 Nov	H	ZP	Bath	18-9	*T:* Greenwood, Moore *C:* Williams *PG:* Williams 2
10 Nov	A	ZP	Saracens	30-36	*T:* Moore 2, Vos, Duncombe *C:* Williams 2 *PG:* Williams 2
17 Nov	H	ZP	Wasps	27-14	*T:* Greenstock, Burke *C:* Burke *PG:* Burke 4 *DG:* Burke
23 Nov	A	ZP	Northampton	7-35	*T:* Diprose *C:* Burke
30 Nov	H	ZP	Saracens	36-32	*T:* Fuga, Williams, Moore *C:* Burke 3 *PG:* Burke 5
7 Dec	H	PPC2	Stade Français	0-26	
14 Dec	A	PPC2	Stade Français	12-29	*PG:* Burke 4
21 Dec	H	PC6	Leeds	17-13	*T:* Gollings *PG:* Burke 4
28 Dec	A	ZP	Bath	9-23	*PG:* Burke 3
4 Jan	H	ZP	Bristol	26-17	*T:* Gollings, Greenwood *C:* Burke 2 *PG:* Burke 4
25 Jan	H	PCQF	Leicester	12-19	*PG:* Burke 4
1 Feb	A	ZP	Newcastle	17-32	*T:* Fuga 2 *C:* Burke, Williams *PG:* Burke
8 Feb	H	ZP	Sale	0-45	
2 Mar	A	ZP	Bristol	41-48	*T:* Gollings, Greenwood, Williams, Luger, Diprose *C:* Burke 5 *PG:* Burke 2
16 Mar	A	ZP	London Irish	16-6	*T:* Greenwood *C:* Burke *PG:* Williams 3
4 Apr	A	ZP	Leeds	22-23	*T:* Luger *C:* Burke *PG:* Burke 4 *DG:* Burke
19 Apr	H	ZP	Leicester	17-9	*T:* Gollings *PG:* Burke 3 *DG:* Burke
26 Apr	A	ZP	Gloucester	11-29	*T:* Fuga *PG:* Burke 2
2 May	H	ZP	Northampton	19-31	*T:* pen try *C:* Burke *PG:* Burke 3 *DG:* Burke
10 May	A	ZP	Wasps	25-21	*T:* Monye 2, M Powell *C:* Burke 2 *PG:* Burke *DG:* Burke
14 May	H	ZWSF	Leicester	26-23	*T:* Fuga, Deane *C:* Burke 2 *PG:* Burke 3 *DG:* Burke
18 May	A	ZWSF	Leicester	13-28	*T:* Monye *C:* Burke *PG:* Burke 2

Leeds

Year of formation 1991
Ground Headingley Stadium, St Michael's Lane, Headingley, Leeds, LS6 3BR
Contacts Web: www.leedsrugby.com Tel: 01132 786181
Colours White and blue
Captain 2002-03 Mike Shelley
Zurich Premiership League 2002-03 5th
Zurich Wildcard Finals 2002-03 Lost 48-70 (aggreg) to Saracens (semi-final)
Powergen Cup 2002-03 Lost 13-17 to Harlequins (6th round)

Competition Record 2002-03

Date	*Venue*	*Comp*	*Opponents*	*Result*	*Scorers*
31 Aug	H	ZP	Leicester	26-13	*T:* Scarbrough 2 *C:* Van Straaten, Ross *PG:* Ross 4
8 Sep	H	ZP	London Irish	41-16	*T:* Hyde, Ross *C:* Van Straaten 2 *PG:* Van Straaten 9

14 Sep	A	ZP	Harlequins	33-23	*T:* Scarbrough 2, Mather *C:* Van Straaten 3 *PG:* Van Straaten 4
20 Sep	H	ZP	Sale	29-29	*T:* Murphy, Mather *C:* Van Straaten 2 *PG:* Van Straaten 5
29 Sep	A	ZP	Newcastle	20-27	*T:* Scarbrough, Harder *C:* Van Straaten 2 *PG:* Van Straaten 2
6 Oct	H	ZP	Bristol	25-13	*T:* Scarbrough, Feaunati *PG:* Van Straaten 4 *DG:* Ross
12 Oct	A	PPC1	Petrarca	29-23	*T:* Hall 3, Mather *C:* Ross 3 *PG:* Ross
20 Oct	H	PPC1	Petrarca	52-13	*T:* Dickens 2, Emmerson 2, Davies, Ponton, Senillosa *C:* Ross 7 *PG:* Ross
26 Oct	A	ZP	Bath	22-20	*T:* Palmer *C:* Van Straaten *PG:* Van Straaten 5
3 Nov	H	ZP	Saracens	27-18	*T:* Ross, Hall *C:* Van Straaten *PG:* Van Straaten 4 *DG:* Ross
10 Nov	A	ZP	Wasps	27-27	*T:* Regan, Scarbrough *C:* Van Straaten *PG:* Van Straaten 5
17 Nov	H	ZP	Northampton	26-19	*T:* Harder, Emmerson, Scarbrough *C:* Van Straaten *PG:* Van Straaten 3
24 Nov	A	ZP	Gloucester	10-28	*T:* Emmerson *C:* Van Straaten *PG:* Van Straaten
1 Dec	H	ZP	Wasps	15-18	*PG:* Van Straaten 5
7 Dec	A	PPC2	Pontypridd	23-37	*T:* Feaunati 2 *C:* Van Straaten, Ross *PG:* Van Straaten 2, Ross
14 Dec	H	PPC2	Pontypridd	19-19	*T:* Dickens *C:* Van Straaten *PG:* Van Straaten 4
21 Dec	A	PC6	Harlequins	13-17	*T:* Scarbrough *C:* Van Straaten *PG:* Van Straaten 2
29 Dec	A	ZP	Saracens	6-11	*PG:* Van Straaten 2
3 Jan	H	ZP	Bath	20-7	*T:* Palmer, Hyde *C:* Van Straaten 2 *PG:* Van Straaten 2
2 Feb	A	ZP	Bristol	17-12	*T:* Feaunati, pen try *C:* Van Straaten 2 *DG:* Ross
7 Feb	H	ZP	Newcastle	12-17	*PG:* Van Straaten 4
15 Mar	A	ZP	Sale	20-32	*T:* Feaunati, Mather, Stanley *C:* Van Straaten *PG:* Van Straaten
4 Apr	H	ZP	Harlequins	23-22	*T:* Hall, Albanese *C:* Van Straaten 2 *PG:* Van Straaten 3
20 Apr	A	ZP	London Irish	26-14	*T:* Dickens, Murphy *C:* Ross 2 *PG:* Ross 2, Van Straaten *DG:* Ross
26 Apr	A	ZP	Leicester	17-18	*T:* Harder *PG:* Van Straaten 4
4 May	H	ZP	Gloucester	30-23	*T:* Stanley 2, Popham, Ross *C:* Van Straaten 2 *PG:* Van Straaten 2
10 May	A	ZP	Northampton	6-28	*PG:* Van Straaten 2
14 May	A	ZWSF	Saracens	21-57	*T:* Stanley 2, Hall *C:* Ross 3
18 May	H	ZWSF	Saracens	27-13	*T:* Mather, Murphy, Popham, Scarbrough *C:* Ross 2 *PG:* Ross

Leicester

Year of formation 1880
Ground Welford Stadium, Aylestone Road, Leicester, LE2 7TR
Contacts Web: www.tigers.co.uk Tel: Leicester (0116) 254 1607
Colours Scarlet, green and white shirts; white shorts
Captain 2002-03 Martin Johnson
Zurich Premiership League 2002-03 6th
Zurich Wildcard Finals 2002-03 Winners Won 27-20 against Saracens (FINAL)
Powergen Cup 2002-03 Lost 11-16 to Gloucester (semi-final)

Competition Record 2002-03

Date	*Venue*	*Comp*	*Opponents*	*Result*	*Scorers*
31 Aug	A	ZP	Leeds	13-26	*T:* Healey *C:* Stimpson *PG:* Stimpson 2
7 Sep	H	ZP	Harlequins	30-6	*T:* Back, Booth, J Hamilton, Stimpson *C:* Stimpson 2 *PG:* Stimpson 2
13 Sep	A	ZP	Sale	16-29	*T:* Ellis *C:* Stimpson *PG:* Stimpson 2 *DG:* Healey
21 Sep	H	ZP	Newcastle	52-9	*T:* Back, Kafer, Smith, Rowntree *C:* Stimpson 4 *PG:* Stimpson 7 *DG:* Stimpson
29 Sep	A	ZP	Bristol	20-25	*T:* Kafer, Ellis *C:* Stimpson 2 *PG:* Stimpson 2
5 Oct	H	ZP	Bath	22-20	*T:* Back, West, Corry *C:* Stimpson 2 *PG:* Stimpson
11 Oct	A	HC	Neath	16-16	*T:* Healey *C:* Stimpson *PG:* Stimpson 3
19 Oct	H	HC	Calvisano	63-0	*T:* Booth 3, Back 2, Murphy 2, Tierney, Corry, Freshwater *C:* Stimpson 3, Healey, Murphy *PG:* Healey
27 Oct	A	ZP	Saracens	26-18	*T:* Booth, Murphy *C:* Stimpson 2 *PG:* Stimpson 3 *DG:* Murphy
2 Nov	H	ZP	Wasps	9-6	*PG:* Stimpson 3
9 Nov	A	ZP	Northampton	16-3	*T:* Kronfeld *C:* Murphy *PG:* Murphy 3
15 Nov	H	ZP	Gloucester	20-15	*T:* Kronfeld 2, Lloyd *C:* Vesty *PG:* Vesty
24 Nov	A	ZP	London Irish	7-27	*T:* Smith *C:* Booth
30 Nov	H	ZP	Northampton	12-25	*PG:* Stimpson 4
8 Dec	A	HC	Béziers	24-12	*T:* Smith, Lloyd *C:* Murphy *PG:* Murphy 3 *DG:* Kafer
14 Dec	H	HC	Béziers	53-10	*T:* Tuilagi 3, Deacon, West, Kafer, Murphy, Vesty *C:* Murphy 5 *PG:* Murphy
21 Dec	H	PC6	Worcester	36-9	*T:* Lloyd, Chuter, Smith, Short, Balding *C:* Vesty 4 *PG:* Vesty
27 Dec	A	ZP	Wasps	13-26	*T:* Ellis *C:* Stimpson *PG:* Stimpson 2
4 Jan	H	ZP	Saracens	23-18	*T:* Kronfeld, Smith, Lloyd *C:* Murphy *PG:* Murphy 2
11 Jan	A	HC	Calvisano	40-22	*T:* Ellis 2, Chuter, Stimpson, Booth, Tournaire *C:* Stimpson 5
18 Jan	H	HC	Neath	36-11	*T:* Murphy, Hamilton, Kay, Kronfeld *C:* Stimpson 2 *PG:* Stimpson 4
25 Jan	A	PCQF	Harlequins	19-12	*T:* Stimpson, Moody *PG:* Stimpson 3
1 Feb	A	ZP	Bath	15-8	*T:* Murphy, Kay *C:* Murphy *PG:* Vesty
8 Feb	H	ZP	Bristol	40-6	*T:* Murphy 2, Kronfeld, Smith, Kafer, Booth *C:* Murphy 2, Stimpson 3
1 Mar	–	PCSF	Gloucester	11-16	*T:* Kronfeld *PG:* Stimpson 2
16 Mar	A	ZP	Newcastle	22-24	*T:* West 2, Booth *C:* McMullen, Booth *PG:* Booth
6 Apr	H	ZP	Sale	33-20	*T:* Murphy, Healey, Lloyd, Tuilagi *C:* Stimpson 2 *PG:* Stimpson 3
13 Apr	H	HCQF	Munster	7-20	*T:* Booth *C:* Stimpson
19 Apr	A	ZP	Harlequins	9-17	*PG:* Stimpson 3
26 Apr	H	ZP	Leeds	18-17	*PG:* Booth 5, McMullen
3 May	H	ZP	London Irish	19-20	*T:* Stimpson, Holtby *PG:* Stimpson 2 *DG:* Murphy
10 May	A	ZP	Gloucester	13-31	*T:* Tuilagi *C:* Murphy *PG:* Murphy 2
14 May	A	ZWSF	Harlequins	23-26	*T:* Murphy, Corry *C:* Stimpson 2 *PG:* Stimpson 3
18 May	H	ZWSF	Harlequins	28-13	*T:* Back, Gelderbloom, Skinner *C:* Stimpson 2 *PG:* Stimpson 3
31 May	–	ZWF	Saracens	27-20	*T:* Back, West *C:* Stimpson *PG:* Stimpson 4 *DG:* McMullen

London Irish

Year of formation 1898
Ground Madejski Stadium, Reading, RG2 0FL
Contacts Web: www.london-irish.com Tel: Reading (0118) 968 1000
Colours Green and black
Captain 2002-03 Ryan Strudwick
Zurich Premiership League 2002-03 9th
Powergen Cup 2002-03 Lost 9-38 to Northampton (semi-final)

Competition Record 2002-03

Date	*Venue*	*Comp*	*Opponents*	*Result*	*Scorers*
1 Sep	H	ZP	Bath	22-24	*T:* pen try *C:* Everitt *PG:* Everitt 4 *DG:* Everitt
8 Sep	A	ZP	Leeds	16-41	*T:* Horak *C:* Everitt *PG:* Everitt 3
15 Sep	H	ZP	Saracens	32-10	*T:* Everitt, Sackey, Strudwick, Dawson *C:* Everitt 3 *PG:* Everitt 2
21 Sep	A	ZP	Harlequins	19-29	*T:* Rossouw *C:* Everitt *PG:* Everitt 4
29 Sep	H	ZP	Wasps	21-31	*T:* Danaher 2, Worslet *C:* Everitt 3
5 Oct	A	ZP	Sale	14-36	*T:* Sackey *PG:* Everitt, Mapletoft *DG:* Everitt
12 Oct	A	HC	Toulouse	23-28	*T:* Burrows *PG:* Everitt 4 *DG:* Everitt 2
20 Oct	H	HC	Edinburgh	24-8	*T:* Edwards, Horak *C:* Everitt *PG:* Everitt 3 *DG:* Everitt
27 Oct	H	ZP	Northampton	12-14	*PG:* Everitt 4
3 Nov	A	ZP	Newcastle	24-16	*PG:* Everitt 6 *DG:* Everitt 2
10 Nov	H	ZP	Gloucester	19-40	*T:* pen try *C:* Everitt *PG:* Everitt 4
17 Nov	A	ZP	Bristol	32-32	*T:* Burrows, Danaher *C:* Everitt 2 *PG:* Everitt 6
24 Nov	H	ZP	Leicester	27-7	*T:* Horak, Everitt *C:* Everitt *PG:* Everitt 4 *DG:* Everitt
30 Nov	A	ZP	Gloucester	20-25	*T:* Sackey 2 *C:* Everitt 2 *PG:* Everitt 2
7 Dec	A	HC	Newport	12-16	*PG:* Everitt 4
15 Dec	H	HC	Newport	42-5	*T:* Horak, Everitt, Bishop, Venter, Mapletoft *C:* Everitt 4 *PG:* Everitt 3
22 Dec	A	PC6	Newcastle	17-16	*T:* Worsley, Hatley, Halford *C:* Mapletoft
29 Dec	H	ZP	Newcastle	20-0	*T:* Everitt, Burrows, Sackey *C:* Everitt *PG:* Everitt
4 Jan	A	ZP	Northampton	22-10	*T:* Horak *C:* Everitt *PG:* Everitt 5
10 Jan	A	HC	Edinburgh	25-32	*T:* Sheasby *C:* Mapletoft *PG:* Mapletoft 6
19 Jan	H	HC	Toulouse	32-29	*T:* Sackey 2, Worsley *C:* Everitt *PG:* Everitt 5
26 Jan	H	PCQF	Rotherham	30-11	*T:* Sackey, Drotské, Horak, Martens *C:* Everitt 2 *PG:* Everitt *DG:* Everitt
2 Feb	H	ZP	Sale	11-23	*T:* Horak *PG:* Mapletoft 2
9 Feb	A	ZP	Wasps	11-35	*T:* Sackey *PG:* Everitt 2
2 Mar	–	PCSF	Northampton	9-38	*PG:* Everitt 3
16 Mar	H	ZP	Harlequins	6-16	*PG:* Everitt, Mapletoft
6 Apr	A	ZP	Saracens	14-12	*T:* Horak *PG:* Everitt 2 *DG:* Everitt
10 Apr	A	ZP	Bath	15-18	*PG:* Everitt 4 *DG:* Everitt
20 Apr	H	ZP	Leeds	14-26	*T:* Sackey *PG:* Mapletoft 2, Everitt
3 May	A	ZP	Leicester	20-19	*T:* Worsley *PG:* Mapletoft 5
10 May	H	ZP	Bristol	41-21	*T:* Sackey, Horak, Hoadley, Appleford, Drotské *C:* Mapletoft 5 *PG:* Mapletoft 2

Newcastle

Year of formation 1877, reformed in 1995
Ground Kingston Park, Brunton Road, Kenton Bank Foot, Newcastle upon Tyne NE13 8AF
Contacts Web: www.newcastle-falcons.co.uk Tel: Newcastle (0191) 214 5588
Colours Black
Captain 2002-03 Jonny Wilkinson
Zurich Premiership League 2002-03 10th
Powergen Cup 2002-03 Lost 16-17 to London Irish (6th round)

Competition Record 2002-03

Date	*Venue*	*Comp*	*Opponents*	*Result*	*Scorers*
1 Sep	H	ZP	Wasps	24-17	*PG:* J Wilkinson 8
7 Sep	A	ZP	Northampton	13-31	*T:* Grimes *C:* J Wilkinson *PG:* J Wilkinson 2
15 Sep	H	ZP	Gloucester	19-22	*T:* Taione *C:* J Wilkinson *PG:* J Wilkinson 4
21 Sep	A	ZP	Leicester	9-52	*PG:* J Wilkinson 3
29 Sep	H	ZP	Leeds	27-20	*T:* Grimes, Charlton, Noon *C:* J Wilkinson 3 *PG:* J Wilkinson 2
5 Oct	A	ZP	Harlequins	23-47	*T:* J Wilkinson, Noon *C:* J Wilkinson 2 *PG:* J Wilkinson 3
12 Oct	A	PPC1	Grenoble	19-12	*T:* Hurter *C:* J Wilkinson *PG:* J Wilkinson 4
20 Oct	H	PPC1	Grenoble	33-17	*T:* Stephenson 3 *C:* J Wilkinson 3 *PG:* J Wilkinson 4
27 Oct	H	ZP	Sale	31-20	*T:* Dunbar, Noon, Charlton, Peel *C:* J Wilkinson 4 *PG:* J Wilkinson
3 Nov	H	ZP	London Irish	16-24	*T:* Noon *C:* J Wilkinson *PG:* J Wilkinson 3
10 Nov	A	ZP	Bristol	10-38	*T:* Taione *C:* Botham *PG:* Va'a
17 Nov	H	ZP	Bath	20-24	*T:* Shaw *PG:* Va'a 4 *DG:* May
24 Nov	A	ZP	Saracens	13-17	*T:* Taione *C:* Va'a *PG:* Va'a, Botham
1 Dec	H	ZP	Bristol	12-20	*PG:* Botham 4
7 Dec	A	PPC2	Treviso	8-27	*T:* Botham *PG:* Botham
15 Dec	H	PPC2	Treviso	35-5	*T:* Peel 2, Vyvyan 2, Godman *C:* Botham 5
22 Dec	H	PC6	London Irish	16-17	*T:* May *C:* Botham *PG:* Botham 3
29 Dec	A	ZP	London Irish	0-20	
3 Jan	A	ZP	Sale	3-38	*PG:* Botham
13 Jan	A	PPCQF	Saracens	10-31	*T:* Dowson *C:* J Wilkinson *PG:* J Wilkinson
19 Jan	H	PPCQF	Saracens	31-29	*T:* Thompson, Botham, Peel, Vyvyan *C:* J Wilkinson 4 *PG:* J Wilkinson
1 Feb	H	ZP	Harlequins	32-17	*T:* Grimes, Noon, Stephenson, Vyvyan *C:* J Wilkinson 3 *PG:* J Wilkinson 2
7 Feb	A	ZP	Leeds	17-12	*T:* J Wilkinson, Charlton *C:* J Wilkinson 2 *PG:* J Wilkinson
1 Mar	A	ZP	Wasps	12-13	*PG:* J Wilkinson 3 *DG:* J Wilkinson
16 Mar	H	ZP	Leicester	24-22	*T:* Noon, Stephenson *C:* J Wilkinson *PG:* J Wilkinson 3 *DG:* J Wilkinson
12 Apr	A	ZP	Gloucester	23-25	*T:* Shaw, Grindal, Mayerhofler *C:* J Wilkinson *PG:* J Wilkinson 2
20 Apr	H	ZP	Northampton	22-20	*T:* Vyvyan *C:* J Wilkinson *PG:* J Wilkinson 5
4 May	H	ZP	Saracens	26-22	*T:* J Wilkinson, Noon, pen try, Stephenson *C:* J Wilkinson 3
10 May	A	ZP	Bath	12-24	*PG:* J Wilkinson 2 *DG:* J Wilkinson 2

Northampton

Year of formation 1880
Ground Franklins Gardens, Weedon Road, St James, Northampton, NN5 5BG
Contacts Web: www.northamptonsaints.co.uk Tel: Northampton (01604) 751543
Colours Black, green and gold
Captains 2002-03 Budge Pountney/John Leslie
Zurich Premiership League 2002-03 3rd
Zurich Premiership Finals 2002-03 Lost 10-19 to Wasps (semi-final)
Powergen Cup 2002-03 Lost 22-40 to Gloucester (FINAL)

Competition Record 2002-03

Date	*Venue*	*Comp*	*Opponents*	*Result*	*Scorers*
30 Aug	A	ZP	Sale	21-24	*T:* Cohen, Ripol *C:* Grayson *PG:* Grayson 3
7 Sep	H	ZP	Newcastle	31-13	*T:* Cohen, Sleightholme, Grayson *C:* Grayson 2 *PG:* Grayson 4
15 Sep	A	ZP	Bristol	36-28	*T:* Cohen, Leslie, Pountney *C:* Grayson 3 *PG:* Grayson 5
21 Sep	H	ZP	Bath	24-3	*T:* Jorgensen 2, Cohen, Ripol *C:* Grayson 2
28 Sep	A	ZP	Saracens	19-31	*T:* Beal *C:* Grayson *PG:* Grayson 3 *DG:* Grayson
5 Oct	H	ZP	Wasps	34-20	*T:* Connors, Sleightholme, Williams *C:* Grayson 2 *PG:* Grayson 5
13 Oct	H	HC	Ulster	32-9	*T:* Dawson, Leslie *C:* Grayson 2 *PG:* Grayson 6
19 Oct	A	HC	Biarritz	20-23	*T:* Connors, Beal *C:* Grayson 2 *PG:* Grayson 2
27 Oct	A	ZP	London Irish	14-12	*T:* Cohen *PG:* Grayson 3
2 Nov	A	ZP	Gloucester	9-18	*PG:* Grayson 2, Dawson
9 Nov	H	ZP	Leicester	3-16	*PG:* Grayson
17 Nov	A	ZP	Leeds	19-26	*T:* Hunter *C:* Grayson *PG:* Grayson 4
23 Nov	H	ZP	Harlequins	35-7	*T:* Beal 2, Reihana, Sturgess *C:* Grayson 3 *PG:* Grayson 3
30 Nov	A	ZP	Leicester	25-12	*T:* Pountney, Vass, Hyndman *C:* Grayson 2 *PG:* Grayson 2
7 Dec	H	HC	Cardiff	25-11	*T:* Soden, Vass, Cohen *C:* Grayson 2 *PG:* Grayson 2
15 Dec	A	HC	Cardiff	31-0	*T:* Smith, Blowers, Budgen, Cohen *C:* Grayson 4 *PG:* Grayson
21 Dec	A	PC6	Orrell	55-44	*T:* Jorgensen 3, Vass 2, Reihana, Richmond, Brooks *C:* Grayson 3, Reihana 3 *PG:* Grayson
28 Dec	H	ZP	Gloucester	13-16	*T:* Leslie *C:* Grayson *PG:* Grayson 2
4 Jan	H	ZP	London Irish	10-22	*T:* Thompson *C:* Grayson *PG:* Grayson
11 Jan	H	HC	Biarritz	17-14	*T:* Thompson, Jorgensen *C:* Grayson, Dawson *PG:* Grayson
17 Jan	A	HC	Ulster	13-16	*T:* Cohen *C:* Grayson *PG:* Grayson 2
25 Jan	A	PCQF	Bath	30-29	*T:* Cohen 2, Jorgensen *C:* Grayson 3 *PG:* Grayson 3
2 Feb	A	ZP	Wasps	9-16	*PG:* Grayson 3
8 Feb	H	ZP	Saracens	34-25	*T:* Cohen, Dawson, Smith, Seely *C:* Grayson 4 *PG:* Grayson 2
2 Mar	–	PCSF	London Irish	38-9	*T:* Williams, Pountney, Connors, Jorgensen, Fox *C:* Grayson 5 *PG:* Grayson
15 Mar	A	ZP	Bath	27-10	*T:* Jorgensen 2 *C:* Grayson *PG:* Grayson 5
5 Apr	–	PCF	Gloucester	22-40	*T:* Beal *C:* Grayson *PG:* Grayson 5
12 Apr	A	HCQF	Toulouse	16-32	*T:* Sleightholme *C:* Grayson *PG:* Grayson 3

16 Apr	H	ZP	Bristol	43-13	*T:* Fox 2, Reihana, Tucker, Ripol, Sleightholme *C:* Reihana 5 *PG:* Reihana
20 Apr	A	ZP	Newcastle	20-22	*T:* Dawson 2, Lord *C:* Grayson *PG:* Grayson
26 Apr	H	ZP	Sale	27-17	*T:* Leslie 2, Cohen *C:* Reihana 3 *PG:* Reihana, Dawson
2 May	A	ZP	Harlequins	31-19	*T:* Sturgess, Beal, Tucker, pen try *C:* Dawson 3, Grayson *PG:* Grayson
10 May	H	ZP	Leeds	28-6	*T:* Jorgensen, Thompson, Ripol *C:* Reihana, Jorgensen *PG:* Reihana 2 *DG:* Grayson
17 May	A	ZPSF	Wasps	10-19	*T:* Cohen *C:* Reihana *PG:* Reihana

Sale

Year of formation 1861
Ground Heywood Road, Brooklands, Sale, Cheshire, M33 3WB
Contacts Web: www.salesharks.com Tel: 0161 283 1861
Colours Royal blue
Captain 2002-03 Bryan Redpath
Zurich Premiership League 2002-03 4th
Powergen Cup 2002-03 Lost 20-26 to Saracens (6th round)

Competition Record 2002-03

Date	*Venue*	*Comp*	*Opponents*	*Result*	*Scorers*
30 Aug	H	ZP	Northampton	24-21	*PG:* Hodgson 6 *DG:* Baxendell, Hodgson
7 Sep	A	ZP	Gloucester	8-44	*T:* Cueto *PG:* Hodgson
13 Sep	H	ZP	Leicester	29-16	*T:* Walshe, Jones *C:* Hodgson 2 *PG:* Hodgson 5
20 Sep	A	ZP	Leeds	29-29	*T:* Cueto, Hanley *C:* Hodgson 2 *PG:* Hodgson 4 *DG:* Hodgson
27 Sep	H	ZP	Harlequins	20-16	*T:* Cueto, Sanderson *C:* Hodgson 2 *PG:* Hodgson *DG:* Hodgson
5 Oct	H	ZP	London Irish	36-14	*T:* Cueto, Deane, Jones, Hanley *C:* Hodgson 2 *PG:* Hodgson 3 *DG:* Hodgson
11 Oct	H	HC	Bourgoin	18-24	*T:* Robinson, Hanley *C:* Walshe *PG:* Walshe 2
18 Oct	A	HC	Glasgow	14-26	*T:* Pinkerton *PG:* Walshe 3
27 Oct	A	ZP	Newcastle	20-31	*T:* Hanley, Walshe *C:* Walshe 2 *PG:* Walshe 2
1 Nov	H	ZP	Bristol	28-14	*T:* Cueto, Bond, Robinson *C:* Walshe 2 *PG:* Walshe 2 *DG:* Bond
10 Nov	A	ZP	Bath	18-24	*T:* Hanley, Bond *C:* Walshe *PG:* Walshe 2
15 Nov	H	ZP	Saracens	37-26	*T:* Hanley 2, Harris, Going, Pinkerton *C:* Walshe 3 *PG:* Walshe 2
24 Nov	A	ZP	Wasps	32-25	*T:* Hanley, Schofield, Jones, Cueto *C:* Walshe 3 *PG:* Walshe 2
29 Nov	H	ZP	Bath	36-18	*T:* Hanley 2, Pinkerton, Schofield, Cueto *C:* Baxendell *PG:* Baxendell 2 *DG:* Baxendell
6 Dec	H	HC	Llanelli	19-30	*T:* Thorp, Going, Cueto *C:* Baxendell 2
13 Dec	A	HC	Llanelli	12-17	*T:* Perelini, Bond *C:* Walshe
22 Dec	A	PC6	Saracens	20-26	*T:* Davies, Hodgson *C:* Hodgson 2 *PG:* Hodgson 2
29 Dec	A	ZP	Bristol	6-18	*PG:* Hodgson 2
3 Jan	H	ZP	Newcastle	38-3	*T:* Cueto 2, Robinson, Harris, Hanley *C:* Hodgson 2 *PG:* Hodgson 3

10 Jan	H	HC	Glasgow	45-3	*T:* Cueto, Robinson, Hodgson, Hanley, Titterall, Going *C:* Hodgson 6 *PG:* Hodgson
18 Jan	A	HC	Bourgoin	15-43	*T:* Perelini, Wilks *C:* Wigglesworth *DG:* Hodgson
2 Feb	A	ZP	London Irish	23-11	*T:* Fullarton, Titterall, Hanley *C:* Hodgson *PG:* Hodgson 2
8 Feb	A	ZP	Harlequins	45-0	*T:* Cueto, Hodgson, Hanley, Bond, Jones *C:* Hodgson 3, Walshe *PG:* Hodgson 4
15 Mar	H	ZP	Leeds	32-20	*T:* Robinson 2, Hanley, Harris, Titterell *C:* Baxendell 2 *PG:* Baxendell
6 Apr	A	ZP	Leicester	20-33	*T:* Bond, Schofield *C:* Baxendell 2 *PG:* Baxendell 2
18 Apr	H	ZP	Gloucester	30-30	*T:* Anglesea, Hanley, Robinson, Cueto *C:* Baxendell 2 *PG:* Baxendell 2
26 Apr	A	ZP	Northampton	17-27	*T:* Bond, Titterell *C:* Baxendell 2 *PG:* Baxendell
3 May	H	ZP	Wasps	9-16	*PG:* Baxendell 3
10 May	A	ZP	Saracens	19-34	*T:* Robinson 2, Schofield *C:* Walshe 2

Saracens

Year of formation 1876
Ground Vicarage Road Stadium, Watford, Hertfordshire, WD17 8ER
Contacts Web: www.saracens.com Tel: Watford (01923) 475222
Colours Black and red
Captain 2002-03 Kyran Bracken
Zurich Premiership League 2002-03 8th
Zurich Wildcard Finals 2002-03 Lost 20-27 to Leicester (FINAL)
Powergen Cup 2002-03 Lost 20-51 to Gloucester (quarter-final)

Competition Record 2002-03

Date	*Venue*	*Comp*	*Opponents*	*Result*	*Scorers*
1 Sep	A	ZP	Bristol	45-30	*T:* Shanklin, Goode, Castaignède, Horan, O'Mahony *C:* Goode 3, Castaignède *PG:* Goode 2, Castaignède *DG:* Goode
8 Sep	H	ZP	Bath	28-3	*T:* B Russell, Castaignède, Ross *C:* Goode, Little *PG:* Goode 3
15 Sep	A	ZP	London Irish	10-32	*T:* Sorrell *C:* Goode *PG:* Little
22 Sep	A	ZP	Wasps	23-51	*T:* Sorrell, Hooper *C:* Goode 2 *PG:* Goode 3
28 Sep	H	ZP	Northampton	31-19	*T:* Hooper *C:* Goode *PG:* Goode 6 *DG:* Goode 2
5 Oct	A	ZP	Gloucester	14-44	*T:* Johnston *PG:* Goode 2, Little
12 Oct	A	PPC1	Dinamo Bucharest	87-11	*T:* Shanklin 5, Chesney 2, Haughton 2, Castaignède, Horan, Winnan *C:* Little 10, Castaignède, Winnan *PG:* Little
20 Oct	H	PPC1	Dinamo Bucharest	151-0	*T:* Horan 4, Cairns 3, Croall 2, Chesney 2, Johnson 2, O'Mahony 2, Shanklin, Califano, Quinnell, Haughton, Castaignède, Winnan, Roques, B Russell *C:* Little 8, Winnan 8, Cairns, Horan
27 Oct	H	ZP	Leicester	18-26	*T:* Shanklin, Castaignède *C:* Goode *PG:* Goode 2
3 Nov	A	ZP	Leeds	18-27	*T:* Hall, Califano *C:* Goode *PG:* Goode 2
10 Nov	H	ZP	Harlequins	36-30	*T:* Haughton, Horan, Bracken, Kershaw *C:* Goode 2 *PG:* Goode 4
15 Nov	A	ZP	Sale	26-37	*T:* Haughton, Johnston, Califano *C:* Winnan *PG:* Goode 2 *DG:* Horan
24 Nov	H	ZP	Newcastle	17-13	*T:* Cairns *PG:* Goode 2 *DG:* Goode 2

30 Nov	A	ZP	Harlequins	32-36	*T:* Goode 2, Parkes, Chesney *C:* Goode 3 *PG:* Goode 2
8 Dec	H	PPC2	Colomiers	16-6	*T:* O'Mahony *C:* Castaignède *PG:* Winnan 2, Castaignède
14 Dec	A	PPC2	Colomiers	30-19	*T:* O'Mahony, Parkes *C:* Winnan *PG:* Castaignède 5 *DG:* Castaignède
22 Dec	H	PC6	Sale	26-20	*T:* Shanklin, Masters *C:* Castaignède 2 *PG:* Castaignède 2, Winnan *DG:* Castaignède
29 Dec	H	ZP	Leeds	11-6	*T:* Hill *PG:* Goode, Winnan
4 Jan	A	ZP	Leicester	18-23	*T:* Horan, Winnan *C:* Goode *PG:* Winnan 2
13 Jan	H	PPCQF	Newcastle	31-10	*T:* Yandell, Hill, Califano *C:* Goode 2 *PG:* Goode 4
19 Jan	A	PPCQF	Newcastle	29-31	*T:* Russell, Johnston, Cairns, Shanklin *C:* Goode 3 *PG:* Goode
25 Jan	A	PCQF	Gloucester	20-51	*T:* Shanklin, Winnan, Haughton *C:* Little *PG:* Little
2 Feb	H	ZP	Gloucester	22-29	*T:* Hill *C:* Little *PG:* Little 5
8 Feb	A	ZP	Northampton	25-34	*T:* Chesney, Goode, Castaignède *C:* Goode 2 *PG:* Goode 2
1 Mar	A	ZP	Bath	9-30	*PG:* Goode 3
16 Mar	H	ZP	Wasps	31-42	*T:* Hill, Horan, Haughton, Castaignède *C:* Little 4 *PG:* Little
6 Apr	H	ZP	London Irish	12-14	*PG:* Little 4
13 Apr	H	PPCSF	Bath	38-30	*T:* Haughton, Johnston, Sparg, Shanklin *C:* Little 3 *PG:* Little 3, Goode
26 Apr	A	PPCSF	Bath	19-27	*T:* O'Mahony *C:* Little *PG:* Goode 2, Little *DG:* Goode
29 Apr	H	ZP	Bristol	17-16	*T:* Haughton, O'Mahony *C:* Goode 2 *DG:* Goode
4 May	A	ZP	Newcastle	22-26	*T:* Horan, Storey, Russell *C:* Goode 2 *PG:* Goode
10 May	H	ZP	Sale	34-19	*T:* Haughton, O'Mahony, Benazzi, Ross *C:* Goode 4 *PG:* Goode *DG:* Horan
14 May	H	ZWSF	Leeds	57-21	*T:* Johnston, Shanklin, Chesney, O'Mahony, Sorrell, Horan *C:* Goode 6 *PG:* Goode 5
18 May	A	ZWSF	Leeds	13-27	*T:* Cairns *C:* Goode *PG:* Goode 2
31 May	–	ZWF	Leicester	20-27	*T:* Hill, Haughton *C:* Goode 2 *PG:* Goode 2

Wasps

Year of formation 1867
Ground Adams Park, Hillbottom Road, Sands, High Wycombe, Buckinghamshire HP12 4HJ
Contacts Web: www.wasps.co.uk Tel: 01494 769471
Colours Black and gold
Captain 2002-03 Lawrence Dallaglio
Zurich Premiership League 2002-03 2nd
Zurich Premiership Finals 2002-03 Winners Won 39-3 against Gloucester (FINAL)
Powergen Cup 2002-03 Lost 17-20 to Bath (6th round)

Competition Record 2002-03

Date	*Venue*	*Comp*	*Opponents*	*Result*	*Scorers*
1 Sep	A	ZP	Newcastle	17-24	*T:* Lewsey, Denney *C:* A King 2 *PG:* A King
8 Sep	H	ZP	Bristol	38-35	*T:* Leota, Abbott, Dallaglio, pen try *C:* A King 3 *PG:* A King 4
14 Sep	A	ZP	Bath	27-27	*T:* Lewsey 2, pen try *C:* A King 3 *PG:* A King *DG:* A King

22 Sep	H	ZP	Saracens	51-23	*T:* Dowd 2, Lewsey, Rudd, Dallaglio *C:* Van Gisbergen 2, A King, Logan *PG:* A King 5, Logan
29 Sep	A	ZP	London Irish	31-21	*T:* Sampson, Howley, Roiser, Dowd *C:* A King 4 *PG:* A King
5 Oct	A	ZP	Northampton	20-34	*T:* Lewsey, Logan *C:* A King 2 *PG:* A King 2
12 Oct	A	PPC1	Overmach Parma	40-24	*T:* Rudd 3, Van Gisbergen *C:* Van Gisbergen 4 *PG:* Van Gisbergen 4
20 Oct	H	PPC1	Overmach Parma	42-0	*T:* Dallaglio 2, Volley, Abbott, Roiser, Beardshaw, W Green *C:* A King 2 *PG:* A King
26 Oct	H	ZP	Gloucester	23-16	*T:* Van Gisbergen, Lewsey, Shaw *C:* Logan *PG:* A King, Logan
2 Nov	A	ZP	Leicester	6-9	*PG:* Van Gisbergen 2
10 Nov	H	ZP	Leeds	27-27	*T:* Volley, Roiser *C:* A King *PG:* A King 4, Logan
17 Nov	A	ZP	Harlequins	14-27	*T:* Greening *PG:* A King 3
24 Nov	H	ZP	Sale	25-32	*T:* Roiser *C:* A King *PG:* Van Gisbergen 4, A King 2
1 Dec	A	ZP	Leeds	18-15	*T:* Lewsey, A King *C:* A King *PG:* A King 2
8 Dec	H	PPC2	Bègles-Bordeaux	43-6	*T:* Van Gisbergen, Dowd, Dallaglio, Shaw, pen try, Abbott *C:* A King 5 *PG:* A King
14 Dec	A	PPC2	Bègles-Bordeaux	29-23	*T:* Erinle, Volley, Leota *C:* A King *PG:* A King 4
21 Dec	H	PC6	Bath	17-20	*T:* pen try, Leota *C:* A King 2 *PG:* A King
27 Dec	H	ZP	Leicester	26-13	*T:* Lewsey, Howley *C:* A King 2 *PG:* A King 3 *DG:* A King
4 Jan	A	ZP	Gloucester	17-24	*T:* Waters *PG:* A King 4
12 Jan	H	PPCQF	Stade Français	35-22	*T:* Rudd, Abbott, Dallaglio, Waters *C:* A King 3 *PG:* A King 2, Logan
18 Jan	A	PPCQF	Stade Français	27-12	*T:* Logan, Waters *C:* A King *PG:* A King 4, Logan
2 Feb	H	ZP	Northampton	16-9	*T:* Leota *C:* A King *PG:* A King 2 *DG:* King
9 Feb	H	ZP	London Irish	35-11	*T:* Lewsey, Van Gisbergen, Dowd, Waters *C:* A King 3 *PG:* A King 3
1 Mar	H	ZP	Newcastle	13-12	*T:* Rudd *C:* A King *PG:* A King 2
16 Mar	A	ZP	Saracens	42-31	*T:* Shaw 3, Kershaw, Volley *C:* A King 4 *PG:* A King 3
6 Apr	H	ZP	Bath	36-17	*T:* Worsley, Abbott, Rudd *C:* A King 2, Van Gisbergen *PG:* A King 3 *DG:* A King 2
12 Apr	H	PPCSF	Pontypridd	34-19	*T:* Dowd 2, pen try, Rudd *C:* A King 4 *PG:* A King 2
20 Apr	A	ZP	Bristol	34-19	*T:* Worsley, Van Gisbergen, Lewsey, Abbott, Volley, Erinle *C:* A King 2,
25 Apr	A	PPCSF	Pontypridd	27-17	*T:* Lewsey, Shaw, Worsley *C:* A King 3 *PG:* A King 2
3 May	A	ZP	Sale	16-9	*T:* Howley *C:* A King *PG:* A King 3
10 May	H	ZP	Harlequins	21-25	*T:* Dowd, Logan *C:* A King *PG:* A King 3
17 May	H	ZPSF	Northampton	19-10	*T:* Waters *C:* A King *PG:* A King 3 *DG:* A King
25 May	–	PPCF	Bath	48-30	*T:* Lewsey, Waters, Greening, Leota, Logan, Wood *C:* A King 6 *PG:* A King 2
31 May	–	ZPF	Wasps	39-3	*T:* Lewsey 2, Worsley *C:* A King 3 *PG:* A King 4 *DG:* A King 2

BRIGHT SPARKS ILLUMINATE POWERGEN FINALE: THE POWERGEN CUP

Mick Cleary

5 April 2003, Twickenham
Gloucester 40 (4G 3PG 1DG) **Northampton 22** (1G 5PG)

It was a good week for English rugby, with the national side's Grand Slam book-ended by a wonderfully upbeat cup final watched in bright sunshine by a full house of 75,000. For those present, it was a privilege to bask in the feel-good atmosphere. In a tiny corner of their souls, even the Northampton fans might have been able to appreciate the upbeat mood.

True, they had seen their side lose their third cup final in four years and are still in search of that elusive pot. Unlike the previous season, however, when the Saints could be accused of barely bothering to turn up so comprehensive was their defeat by London Irish, they played a full part in a rousing contest.

Gloucester, winning the cup for the fourth time, came through strongly in the second-half after trailing 22-20 at the break. There was that bit more snap in their play, more all-round edge and devil as shown most thrillingly by the contributions of two of their young England hopefuls, wing James Simpson-Daniel and flanker James Forrester. They scored three of their side's four tries. Simpson-Daniel already has a clutch of England caps. It will surely not be long before Forrester joins him in that elite gathering.

It was Forrester's surge and dummy that teed up Marcel Garvey's try towards the end of the first half. Just after the half-time interval, Forrester did the damage himself when he strode over following a poor Northampton scrum. Video replays suggested that Forrester had not grounded the ball properly, but as Saints' coach Wayne Smith graciously pointed out his team deserved to concede a try through their sloppiness.

Northampton's big guns spluttered on the day, a mis-firing that was to prove the difference between the teams. Small wonder that only six days after the Lansdowne Road Grand Slam experience, the likes of Matt Dawson, Steve Thompson and Ben Cohen should appear muted.

Dawson, so sharp and influential for England, never enjoyed such mastery here. In fact he directly contributed to two Gloucester tries. Early in the game a pass intended for Thompson only found the Twickenham turf from were Simpson-Daniel was able to pick it up and stroll over.

Late in the game, and striving to make up an 11-point deficit, a Dawson pass was intercepted by Ludovic Mercier who galloped to the half-way line before unloading to Simpson-Daniel who completed the job.

By then, Northampton were resigned to furiously chasing the game. In the first half they had played a full part in the two sides chasing each other across the scoreboard. The lead changed hand six times as the heavyweights of the English game traded blows. Paul Grayson was a key figure, scoring

17 points himself in that first half and making the break past his opposite number, Mercier, that set up Nick Beal for the Saints' try.

Things looked set fair at half-time. Gloucester, though, were not in fair-minded mood. They had had enough of an equal contest and ran out comfortable and deserved winners. Long-serving prop, Andy Deacon, 37, collected the Powergen Cup. He was the oldest player ever to appear in a cup final. It was a day he, and many others, will remember fondly.

Gloucester: G M Delport; M Garvey, T L Fanolua, H Paul, J Simpson-Daniel; L Mercier, A C T Gomarsall; T J Woodman, O Azam, A Deacon, R J Fidler, A Eustace, J Boer (*captain*), A Hazell, J Forrester *Substitutions:* P J Paramore for Boer (temp 25 mins to 38 mins) and for Hazell (61 mins); R Todd for Paul (75 mins); E Pearce for Paramore (75 mins)

Scorers *Tries:* Simpson-Daniel (2), Garvey, Forrester *Conversions:* Mercier (4) *Penalty Goals:* Mercier (3) *Dropped Goal:* Mercier

Northampton: N D Beal; B Reihana, P K Jorgensen, J A Leslie (*Co-captain*), B C Cohen; P J Grayson, M J S Dawson; T J Smith, S Thompson, R Morris, M Lord, S M Williams, M R Connors, A F Blowers, A C Pountney (*Co-captain*) *Substitutions:* M J Stewart for Morris (54 mins); C Hyndman for Jorgensen (63 mins); D Fox for Williams (77 mins)

Scorers *Try:* Beal *Conversion:* Grayson *Penalty Goals:* Grayson (5)

Referee A J Spreadbury (RFU)

Earlier Rounds

When is a scrum not a scrum? The answer to that little poser almost cost Gloucester their place in the final. Leicester had cause for grievance after the final stages of their Franklin's Gardens semi-final were marred by debate as to whether front-row replacements were fit to scrummage or not. Referee Steve Lander adjudged that the trio that Gloucester had on the field at the time – Trevor Woodman, Chris Fortey and Olivier Azam – were not capable of safely handling a scrum and so ordered that the last two scrums of the game should be uncontested. Gloucester were leading 16-11, Leicester were pressing, the try-line was in sight. Cue furore.

Azam, the Gloucester hooker, had moved across to the tight-head to allow Fortey to come on to replace injured prop Rodrigo Roncero. Azam, in fact, has propped for France A, but Gloucester insisted that he was now to be considered only as a hooker.

By the strict letter of the law, Gloucester were liable to forfeit the tie as the regulations state that: 'if on the second occasion a front-row player and his team cannot provide a replacement or other player capable of playing in the front-row, the referee will order uncontested scrums and the team will have been deemed to have lost the match.'

Gloucester had gone into the game with prop Andy Deacon struggling with a knee injury. He was replaced by Roncero after 67 minutes. The Argentinian then damaged his ankle. Gloucester only had two front-row replacements on the bench.

No-one was disputing Gloucester's 16-11 victory in itself for the Cherry and Whites had dominated the game. However they did seem to have taken a risk with the make-up of their replacement bench. Three days later an RFU panel gave them the all-clear for the final, although it did recommend an urgent review of the regulations. Leicester accepted the verdict with good grace.

'Under no circumstances would we have been happy winning this match by default,' said Leicester chairman, Peter Tom.

There was no disputing the right of Northampton to take their place in the final for the second year running. They gained a small measure of revenge for the drubbing handed out to them in the previous year's final by London Irish, when beating the Exiles 38-9 at Oxford's Kassam Stadium. Never mind uncontested scrums. There were times when this tie was close to an uncontested match.

Northampton had their fair share of drama en route to the final. They were involved in one of the most astonishing cup-ties ever staged in the sixth round. They beat Orrell of National League One 55-44 after extra-time. The scoreline alone is enough to conjure up images of thrust and counter-thrust, of scoreboard operators at Edge Hall Road working overtime. So it proved. Orrell, who lost their place in the top flight in 1997, actually had a ten-point lead eight minutes into extra-time, leading 44-34. Then the Saints, staring ignominy in the face, stirred themselves, scoring three tries, two from Ian Vass and one from Jorgensen to complete his hat-trick.

Northampton had another close call in the quarter-final when only a late rally took them past Bath, 30-29, at the Rec. It was a lively game, featuring a classy return to action for Mike Catt, a brace of tries for Ben Cohen and a dust-up between Bath lock Danny Grewcock and his opposite number, Australian Mark Connors whose transfer to Bath had fallen through only at the last minute that summer.

Gloucester's progress to the final was more orderly. They saw off Exeter, captained by former Kingsholm favourite, Dave Sims, 35-6 before clicking into top gear to beat Saracens 51-20 in the quarter-final.

Results

Fourth round: Birmingham-Solihull 44, Fylde 14; Henley 6, Exeter 37; London Welsh 52, Nottingham 7; Orrell 47, North Walsham 12; Otley 25, Plymouth Albion 37; Rosslyn Park 7, Rotherham 83; Waterloo 36, Halifax 38; Worcester 73, Manchester 12

Fifth round: Rotherham 41, Birmingham-Solihull 10, Halifax 12, Worcester 13; London Welsh 13, Exeter 36; Plymouth Albion 3, Orrell 8

Sixth round: Bristol 19, Rotherham 24; Gloucester 35, Exeter 6; Harlequins 17, Leeds 13; Orrell 44, Northampton 55 (aet); Leicester 36, Worcester 9; Newcastle 16, London Irish 17; Saracens 26, Sale 20; Wasps 17, Bath 20

Quarter-finals: Bath 29, Northampton 30; Gloucester 51, Saracens 20; Harlequins 12, Leicester 19; London Irish 30, Rotherham 11

Semi-finals: (at Franklin's Gardens) Leicester 11, Gloucester 16; (at Kassam Stadium) London Irish 9, Northampton 38

FINAL: (at Twickenham) Gloucester 40, Northampton 22

Previous RFU Cup Finals: 1972 Gloucester 17, Moseley 6; 1973 Coventry 27, Bristol 15; 1974 Coventry 26, London Scottish 6; 1975 Bedford 28, Rosslyn Park 12; 1976 Gosforth 23, Rosslyn Park 14; 1977 Gosforth 27, Waterloo 11; 1978 Gloucester 6, Leicester 3; 1979 Leicester 15, Moseley 12; 1980 Leicester 21, London Irish 9; 1981 Leicester 22, Gosforth 15; 1982 Gloucester 12, Moseley 12 (trophy shared); 1983 Bristol 28, Leicester 22; 1984 Bath 10, Bristol 9; 1985 Bath 24, London Welsh 15; 1986 Bath 25, Wasps 17; 1987 Bath 19, Wasps 12; 1988 Harlequins 28, Bristol 22; 1989 Bath 10, Leicester 6; 1990 Bath 48, Gloucester 6; 1991 Harlequins 25, Northampton 13; 1992 Bath 15, Harlequins 12; 1993 Leicester 23, Harlequins 16; 1994 Bath 21, Leicester 9; 1995 Bath 36, Wasps 16; 1996 Bath 16, Leicester 15; 1997 Leicester 9, Sale 3; 1998 Saracens 48, Wasps 18; 1999 Wasps 29, Newcastle 19; 2000 Wasps 31, Northampton 23; 2001 Newcastle 30, Harlequins 27; 2002 London Irish 38, Northampton 7; 2003 Gloucester 40, Northampton 22
All played at Twickenham

DOMESTIC RUGBY IN SCOTLAND 2002-03

Edinburgh Rule the Roost: The Scottish Professional Teams

Bill McMurtrie

Edinburgh were comfortably at the head of the league in Scottish professional rugby's domestic competition, winning the Bank of Scotland Pro Cup by a wide margin from The Borders. Over the whole season, too, Edinburgh had the best record of the three Scottish teams.

Yet again, however, none of the Scottish teams made a mark in European rugby. Edinburgh and Glasgow each won only two of their six matches in the Heineken Cup. The former beat Newport and London Irish, both at home at Meadowbank, but lost heavily on successive weekends against Toulouse, the eventual cup-winners. Glasgow did manage to keep alive hopes of qualifying for the knockout stages a little longer with Hughenden victories against Sale Sharks and Bourgoin. A late penalty goal by Calvin Howarth earned Glasgow the 13-12 home result against Bourgoin, a remarkable turn-round after a 21-35 defeat in France six days earlier. A month later, however, Glasgow's hopes were finally blown away in a 45-3 defeat at Sale.

The Borders, newcomers to the Scottish professional ranks, made a good start to their European campaign, knocking up more than 70 points in each of their two Parker Pen Challenge Cup games against Madrid. Nikki Walker scored seven tries over those two games, a prelude to the 20-year-old wing's international debut against Romania the following month. But The Borders then succumbed twice to Montauban, albeit by narrow margins – 16-19 in France and 6-12 on home ground at Netherdale.

In the Celtic League, similarly, the Scottish teams disappointed. Edinburgh and Glasgow went only as far as the last eight. In Glasgow's case that was one step less than they had achieved the previous season.

Yet Glasgow had opened their Celtic campaign in startling form, with four successive wins, including two away against Cardiff and Newport. To win the Rodney Parade game by 31-25 they overturned a 16-point deficit with three tries (by Tommy Hayes, Stuart Moffat, and Gordon Simpson) inside 10 minutes.

Not even away defeats by Pontypridd and The Borders could deny Glasgow a home quarter-final against Ulster. However, despite a furious finale, Glasgow succumbed by 17-20.

Edinburgh, too, had a home quarter-final after winning six of their seven pool games. Their one defeat was ironically at home, 21-28 against Munster, and, like Glasgow, they lost narrowly in the quarter-final, 22-26 against Cardiff.

As a harsh introduction to the professional game, The Borders lost their first four Celtic League matches, though three of them were agonisingly close – 27-28 against both Connacht and Pontypridd, and 15-18 against Cardiff. The newcomers were out of the running by the time they settled with a 23-18 home win against Leinster, and they followed up by upsetting Glasgow with a 33-12 win at Netherdale.

Scottish rugby's new domestic competition, the Bank of Scotland Pro Rugby Cup, was drawn out over six months from November to May, though it started as it was to finish, with Edinburgh setting the pace with a 29-13 victory over Glasgow at Meadowbank. Edinburgh so dominated that competition that they had qualified for the next season's Heineken Cup with three games in hand, and they followed up by winning the trophy with an emphatic home victory against The Borders by 44-7 (7-1 in tries). The Borders also tied up the other Heineken place with three games left.

However, it was not all roses for Edinburgh. At the end of the season they parted company with their team manager, Ian Rankin. Glasgow had management changes even before the end of the season, with the departure of two New Zealand coaches, Kiwi Searancke and Gordon Macpherson. Richie Dixon returned as caretaker coach, and Glasgow won their last two Hughenden games, 45-33 against Edinburgh and 23-10 against The Borders.

Bank of Scotland Pro Rugby Cup Final Table:

	P	*W*	*D*	*L*	*F*	*A*	*Bonus*	*Pts*
Edinburgh	8	5	1	2	266	140	6	28
The Borders	8	4	0	4	164	224	2	18
Glasgow	8	2	1	5	144	210	1	11

Points: win 4; draw 2; four or more tries or defeat by seven points or fewer 1

Bank of Scotland Pro Rugby Cup Results

Edinburgh 29, Glasgow 13; Glasgow 10, Edinburgh 10; Borders 21, Glasgow 6; Edinburgh 46, Borders 13; Edinburgh 37, Glasgow 9; Glasgow 19, Borders 42; Borders 23, Edinburgh 54; Glasgow 45, Edinburgh 33; Borders 28, Glasgow 19; Edinburgh 44, Borders 7; Glasgow 23, Borders 10; Borders 20, Edinburgh 13

SCOTTISH PRO-TEAM DIRECTORY

The Borders

Year of formation 2002
Ground Netherdale, Galashiels
Contacts Web: www.theborders.net Tel: Galashiels (01896) 750045
Colours Red and white
Captain 2002-03 Gary Armstrong

Competition Record 2002-03

Date	*Venue*	*Comp*	*Opponents*	*Result*	*Scorers*
30 Aug	H	CL	Connacht	27-28	*T:* Murray 2 *C:* Utterson *PG:* Utterson 5
7 Sep	A	CL	Bridgend	9-41	*PG:* Utterson 3
13 Sep	H	CL	Cardiff	15-18	*T:* Paterson, N Walker *C:* Townsend *PG:* Utterson
20 Sep	A	CL	Pontypridd	27-28	*T:* Feather, Townsend, Moir *C:* Utterson 3 *PG:* Utterson 2
27 Sep	H	CL	Leinster	23-18	*T:* Utterson, Sititi *C:* Utterson 2 *PG:* Utterson 3
4 Oct	H	CL	Glasgow	33-12	*T:* Utterson, N Walker, Paterson, Sititi, Cranston *C:* Vili 2, Utterson 2
12 Oct	A	PPC1	Madrid	73-22	*T:* N Walker 4, Paterson 2, Vili, Stuart, Morton, Fairley, Metcalfe *C:* Vili 9
18 Oct	H	PPC1	Madrid	77-15	*T:* N Walker 3, Paterson, Vili, Stewart, Utterson, Fairley, Weir, Laidlaw, Sititi, Moir, Morton *C:* Vili 2, Utterson 2, Laidlaw 2
26 Oct	A	CL	Newport	8-24	*T:* N Walker *PG:* Utterson
7 Dec	A	PPC2	Montauban	16-19	*T:* Paterson, Stuart *PG:* Utterson 2
13 Dec	H	PPC2	Montauban	6-12	*PG:* Utterson, Vili
31 Dec	H	SPC	Glasgow	21-6	*T:* Cranston, Townsend *C:* Utterson *PG:* Utterson 3
3 Jan	A	SPC	Edinburgh	13-46	*T:* Utterson *C:* Utterson *PG:* Utterson 2
31 Jan	A	SPC	Glasgow	42-19	*T:* Morton 2, N Walker, Sititi, Scott *C:* Vili 4 *PG:* Vili 3
7 Feb	H	SPC	Edinburgh	23-54	*T:* Townsend, Feather *C:* Vili 2 *PG:* Vili 3
11 Apr	H	SPC	Glasgow	28-19	*T:* Morton, Douglas, Feather, N Walker *C:* Vili *PG:* Vili 2
18 Apr	A	SPC	Edinburgh	7-44	*T:* Moir *C:* Morton
25 Apr	A	SPC	Glasgow	10-23	*T:* Morton *C:* Thomson *PG:* Thomson
2 May	H	SPC	Edinburgh	20-13	*T:* Feather, Fairley, Sititi *C:* Morton *PG:* Morton

Edinburgh Rugby

Year of formation 1998
Ground Meadowbank, Edinburgh
Contacts Web: www.edinburghrugby.com Tel: Edinburgh (0131) 346 5252
Colours Black and red
Captain 2002-03 Todd Blackadder

Competition Record 2002-03

Date	*Venue*	*Comp*	*Opponents*	*Result*	*Scorers*
30 Aug	H	CL	Swansea	30-20	*T:* Paterson, Hogg *C:* Laney *PG:* Laney 6
6 Sep	A	CL	Ulster	19-18	*T:* Laney *C:* Laney *PG:* Laney 3 *DG: Hodge*

13 Sep	H	CL	Munster	21-28	*T:* Paterson, Lee *C:* Laney *PG:* Laney 2 *DG: Hodge*
21 Sep	A	CL	Caerphilly	66-32	*T:* Laney 2, Lee 2, Dickson, Paterson, Blair, Smith, Brannigan *C:* Laney 9 *PG:* Laney
27 Sep	H	CL	Llanelli	38-14	*T:* Webster 2, Leslie, Joiner *C:* Laney 3 *PG:* Laney 4
5 Oct	A	CL	Ebbw Vale	30-20	*T:* Webster, Taylor, Blair *C:* Laney 3 *PG:* Laney 3
11 Oct	H	HC	Newport	27-17	*T:* Laney, Leslie *C:* Laney *PG:* Laney 4, Hodge
20 Oct	A	HC	London Irish	8-24	*T:* Jacobsen *PG:* Hodge
25 Oct	H	CL	Neath	27-13	*T:* Laney, Lee, Joiner *C:* Laney 3 *PG:* Laney *DG:* Laney
1 Nov	H	SPC	Glasgow	29-13	*T:* Jacobsen 2 *C:* Laney 2 *PG:* Laney 4, Hodge
30 Nov	H	CL¼	Cardiff	22-26	*T:* Lee, Murray *PG:* Laney 4
7 Dec	H	HC	Toulouse	9-30	*PG:* Laney 3
15 Dec	A	HC	Toulouse	17-50	*T:* Laney, Taylor *C:* Laney 2 *PG:* Laney
26 Dec	A	SPC	Glasgow	10-10	*T:* Laney *C:* Laney *PG:* Laney
3 Jan	H	SPC	Borders	46-13	*T:* Sharman 2, Paterson 2, Blair, Hogg, Dall *C:* Laney 4 *PG:* Laney
10 Jan	H	HC	London Irish	32-25	*T:* Blackadder 2, Taylor, Sharman, Laney *C:* Laney, Paterson *PG:* Laney
18 Jan	A	HC	Newport	32-42	*T:* Philip, Hogg, Smith, Sharman, Laney *C:* Paterson 2 *PG:* Paterson
24 Jan	H	SPC	Glasgow	37-9	*T:* Laney 2, pen try, Smith *C:* Laney 3, Paterson *PG:* Laney 3
7 Feb	A	SPC	Borders	54-23	*T:* Lee 2, Webster, Laney, Hall, Blair, Paterson, Jacobsen *C:* Laney 5, Hodge 2
4 Apr	A	SPC	Glasgow	33-45	*T:* Philip 2, Hall, Murray *C:* Hodge 2 *PG:* Hodge 3
18 Apr	H	SPC	Borders	44-7	*T:* Blair 2, Sharman 2, Laney, Taylor, Paterson *C:* Hodge 2, Paterson *PG:* Hodge
2 May	A	SPC	Borders	13-20	*T:* Sharman *C:* Warnock *PG:* Warnock 2

Glasgow Rugby

Year of formation 1998
Ground Hughenden, Glasgow
Contacts Web: www.glasgowrugby.com Tel: Glasgow (0141) 353 3468
Colours Dark blue and light blue
Captain 2002-03 Andy Nicol

Competition Record 2002-03

Date	*Venue*	*Comp*	*Opponents*	*Result*	*Scorers*
30 Aug	A	CL	Cardiff	44-35	*T:* Bartlett 2, A Bulloch, Simpson, Macfadyen *C:* Hayes 3, Howarth 2 *PG:* Hayes 2, Howarth
6 Sep	H	CL	Leinster	25-21	*T:* Moffat, Steel, Hayes *C:* Howarth 2 *PG:* Hayes 2
14 Sep	A	CL	Newport	31-25	*T:* Moffat, Simpson, Hayes *C:* Hayes, Howarth *PG:* Hayes 4
20 Sep	H	CL	Bridgend	47-11	*T:* A Bulloch 2, Metcalfe, Simpson, Beveridge *C:* Hayes 5 *PG:* Hayes 4
28 Sep	A	CL	Pontypridd	28-34	*T:* A Bulloch, Moffat, Wilson *C:* Hayes 2 *PG:* Hayes 3
4 Oct	A	CL	Borders	12-33	*PG:* Hayes 4

12 Oct	A	HC	Llanelli	15-45	*T:* White, Macfadyen *C:* Hayes *PG:* Hayes
18 Oct	H	HC	Sale	26-14	*T:* White, Petrie *C:* Hayes 2 *PG:* Hayes 4
25 Oct	H	CL	Connacht	29-7	*T:* Moffat, Howarth, Macfadyen *C:* Howarth *PG:* Howarth 4
1 Nov	A	SPC	Edinburgh	13-28	*T:* Petrie *C:* Howarth *PG:* Howarth 2
30 Nov	H	CL¼	Ulster	17-20	*T:* Steel *PG:* Hayes 4
7 Dec	A	HC	Bourgoin	21-35	*T:* Simpson, Howarth, Ross *C:* Howarth 3
13 Dec	H	HC	Bourgoin	13-12	*T:* Metcalfe *C:* Hayes *PG:* Hayes, Howarth
26 Dec	H	SPC	Edinburgh	10-10	*T:* Naufahu, Reid
31 Dec	A	SPC	Borders	6-21	*PG:* Howarth 2
10 Jan	A	HC	Sale	3-45	*PG:* Hayes
17 Jan	H	HC	Llanelli	8-34	*T:* Steel *PG:* Hayes
24 Jan	A	SPC	Edinburgh	9-37	*PG:* Howarth 3
31 Jan	H	SPC	Borders	19-42	*T:* Metcalfe, Wilson, Ross *C:* Howarth 2
4 Apr	H	SPC	Edinburgh	45-33	*T:* Metcalfe 2, Howarth 2, Kerr, Naufahu *C:* Howarth 3 *PG:* Howarth 3
11 Apr	A	SPC	Borders	19-28	*T:* Henderson *C:* Howarth *PG:* Howarth 4
25 Apr	H	SPC	Borders	23-10	*T:* Kerr, Beveridge *C:* Irving 2 *PG:* Irving 3

BOROUGHMUIR BACK AT THE TOP: BT PREMIERSHIP

Bill McMurtrie

Four years after suffering the ignominy of relegation, Boroughmuir were back at the top of Scottish club rugby. They were easily the most consistent of the BT Premiership Division 1 clubs in season 2002-03, and the final margin of seven points between the winners and second-placed Heriot's would have been greater if they had not been penalised for fielding an ineligible player.

Boroughmuir lost only three of their 18 matches and drew two games in winning the championship for the first time since 1991, but the last of those defeats – at home at Meggetland against Jed-Forest – was in their final game after the title and trophy had been secured. Both drawn matches were against Glasgow Hawks, who finished the championship in third place.

Two former Scotland caps, Iain Paxton and Sean Lineen, were the architects of Boroughmuir's success. The coaching duo had steered the Meggetland club through an immediate return from the second division in 2000, and after two near misses, third in 2001 and second in 2002, they struck gold at the third attempt.

Lineen's ability was recognised by the national hierarchy when he was enlisted to coach the Scotland Under-21 backs in 2003. His success also led to his departure from Boroughmuir into the professional ranks as he has taken over as Glasgow's backs coach. Another former cap, Shade Munro, who guided Hawks to third place in the league, has also joined the Glasgow coaching team.

Similarly, Ally Warnock, the Scotland Under-21 stand-off who played in all 18 of Boroughmuir's league matches, has gone professional with Edinburgh. Another two of his club colleagues have joined professional teams – Tom McGee with Edinburgh and Chris Cusiter with The Borders. In addition, Stuart Reid, the former Scotland No 8, has retired. So Boroughmuir will have a much-changed look as they defend the championship this season.

Warnock was Boroughmuir's top scorer in the league with 224 points plus 56 in the BT Cup competition. Malcolm Clapperton led the club's championship try-scorers with 11, his talent recognised by selection in Scotland's seven-a-side squad.

Boroughmuir set off at a cracking pace in their championship campaign, scoring six tries in each of their first three matches with wins against Aberdeen Grammar, Stirling County, and Peebles. Then followed the first of the drawn games against Hawks, when the Glasgow visitors snatched a share of the points thanks to Craig Hodgkinson's touchline conversion of Graeme Morrison's injury-time try.

That, however, was only a minor aberration by Boroughmuir. Successive victories followed against Currie, Heriot's, Jed-Forest, and Melrose. Against Heriot's in windy conditions at Meggetland, Boroughmuir needed six penalty goals by Warnock to counter the visitors' 3-1 try-count advantage for a 25-23 win. But in their next home game, two weeks later, Boroughmuir notched up what was to be their best championship victory of the season, beating Melrose 58-8 (8-1 in tries).

By then the Meggetland club were well ahead in the league table. Not even a 22-26 defeat at Hawick the following week could remove Boroughmuir from the top. Gavin Douglas dropped four goals for the Borderers in that match.

On the way to winning the championship Boroughmuir stumbled only twice more – a draw with Hawks at Old Anniesland and an 8-10 defeat at the Greenyards. That latter result was a sharp turn-round after the mauling Melrose had suffered at Meggetland three months earlier. Boroughmuir led 8-7 at the interval in the January game, but a Scott Ruthven penalty goal for Melrose was the only score of the second half.

Before the Christmas/New Year break Boroughmuir held a 13-point lead over Heriot's, but after the defeat at the Greenyards the margin was hauled back to just five. The four-point penalty had been imposed in the interim.

Boroughmuir, however, kept on course with revenge over Hawick in a 48-12 win at Meggetland. The home team scored eight tries in that match, two each by Rory Couper and Ben Fisher, and after nearly three months away from league duty, mainly because of the Six Nations Championship, the league title was settled when Boroughmuir scored three tries to nil in a 27-12 victory against Heriot's at Goldenacre.

Heriot's had handicapped themselves in the title challenge by losing four of their first eight matches, but they pulled themselves back into contention with an unbeaten six-match run, the winning sequence interrupted only by a 20-all draw at Hawick. That unbeaten run ended with a 13-19 defeat by Hawks in Glasgow, Kenny Sinclair snatching the winning injury-time try for the home team.

Hawks' challenge stumbled in mid-season, with four defeats in six games, but they picked themselves up after the second drawn match with Boroughmuir. Successive wins against Stirling, Currie, and Heriot's plus a draw with Peebles eased the Glasgow club into third place, a position that they held on to despite a last-match defeat by Aberdeen Grammar at Anniesland.

Hawick, champions for the two previous seasons, slipped into seventh place. Like Boroughmuir, they were deducted four points for fielding an ineligible player.

Because of league reorganisation, with the Premiership divisions increased from 10 to 12 clubs each, only Jed-Forest were relegated whereas Watsonians, Glasgow Hutchesons' Aloysians, and Ayr were promoted.

Watsonians were runaway champions in Division 2, but it was a much closer finish for the third-division title, Dundee High School FP securing it with a 35-15 win at home in a winner-take-all contest with West of Scotland.

Final BT Premiership League Table 2002-2003

	P	*W*	*D*	*L*	*F*	*A*	*Bonus*	*Pts*
Boroughmuir*	18	13	2	3	507	274	10	62
Heriot's FP	18	10	1	7	512	368	13	55
Glasgow Hawks	18	9	3	6	377	374	7	49
Aberdeen GSFP	18	9	1	8	436	401	10	48
Melrose	18	11	0	7	392	423	4	48
Currie	18	7	1	10	359	390	9	39
Hawick*	18	8	2	8	375	405	3	35
Stirling County	18	5	1	12	385	454	12	34
Peebles	18	6	1	11	308	400	6	32
Jed-Forest	18	6	0	12	295	457	6	30

Points: win 4; draw 2; four or more tries or defeat by seven points or fewer 1 (* Boroughmuir and Hawick each had 4 points deducted for fielding an ineligible player)

Previous Scottish League Champions: 1973-74 Hawick; 1974-75 Hawick; 1975-76 Hawick; 1976-77 Hawick; 1977-78 Hawick; 1978-79 Heriot's FP; 1979-80 Gala; 1980-81 Gala; 1981-82 Hawick; 1982-83 Gala; 1983-84 Hawick; 1984-85 Hawick; 1985-86 Hawick; 1986-87 Hawick; 1987-88 Kelso; 1988-89 Kelso; 1989-90 Melrose; 1990-91 Boroughmuir; 1991-92 Melrose; 1992-93 Melrose; 1993-94 Melrose; 1994-95 Stirling County; 1995-96 Melrose; 1996-97 Melrose; 1997-98 Watsonians; 1998-99 Heriot's FP; 1999-2000 Heriot's FP; 2000-01 Hawick; 2001-02 Hawick; 2002-03 Boroughmuir

HERIOT'S WIN ALL-EDINBURGH FINAL: THE BT CUP

Bill McMurtrie

26 April 2003, Murrayfield
Heriot's FP 25 (5PG 2T) **Watsonians 13** (1G 2PG)

Heriot's, making their debut in the final, won the BT Cup with a Murrayfield victory that was far more decisive than the actual margin against their Edinburgh rivals, Watsonians, suggested. Rarely did the Goldenacre club look anything less than a team destined for victory.

Afterwards, the Heriot's coach Phil Smith commented that he 'never really felt threatened even when we were under pressure.' Yet the try-count was only 2-1 to Heriot's. That, though, was a reflection on how low-key the final was. No one could deny that, not even the cup-winners.

It looked as though the final would spring to life when Hugh Gilmour popped up on his wrong wing to accept a Rory Lawson pass for the opening try. That put Heriot's 11-3 up after 28 minutes, but almost immediately James Easton blocked an attempted clearance by Ander Monro for a swift-response try. Bernard Hennessey added the conversion, cutting Heriot's back to a one-point lead. Heriot's then quickly replied when Craig Harrison scored after supporting a run by Gilmour.

Such work by Harrison earned him the man-of-the-match award, but his efforts were not enough to lift the game. Those three scores, packed into little more than five minutes' play, were the only tries of the match, a disappointment for the crowd of 14,246.

Watsonians' other scores were two penalty goals by Hennessey, one in each half. Monro kicked five, three of them in the second half as Heriot's eased away from 16-13.

Lawson, who led Heriot's to victory, is the son of Alan, the former Scotland scrum half, and grandson of Bill McLaren, the Voice of Rugby who retired from TV commentating in 2002. The winning captain's half-back partner, Monro, is the grandson of Lord Monro of Langholm, a past president of the Scottish Rugby Union.

In the subsidiary competitions' finals, played before the main event, Dundee High School FP won the Plate, and Annan lifted the Bowl. Dundee won against Preston Lodge 27-13, and Annan beat Irvine 23-13 in a match that was the best contest of the three.

Heriot's FP: G Lawrie; M Teague, N Armstrong, M Dey, H Gilmour; A Monro, R Lawson (*captain*); G Talac, S Mustard, G Cross, R Barrie, A McIntosh, T McVie, C Harrison, J White *Substitutions*: M Welch for Cross (79 mins); J Osbourne for Barrie (79 mins)

Scorers *Tries:* Gilmour, Harrison *Penalty Goals:* Monro (5)

Watsonians: C Gregor; G Haley (*captain*), J Easton, J Mayer, A Turnbull; B Hennessey, D Symmons; K Coertze, G Dickson, A Welsh, B King, C Houston, N Jackson, I Dryburgh, G Brown *Substitutions*: W Scott for Coertze (49 mins); S Tomes for King (49 mins); P McKee for Symmonds (78 mins);

Scorers *Try:* Easton *Conversion:* Hennessey *Penalty Goals:* Hennessey (2)

Referee G Davies (SRU)

Earlier rounds

Heriot's racked up two centuries on the way to the final, both at home – 115-6 against the islanders from Orkney, and 103-0 against West of Scotland. To reach the final Heriot's scored a 22-11 semi-final victory against Boroughmuir away at Meggetland.

Watsonians had the benefit of five successive home matches before the final, and they had piled up more than 200 points in three ties before they took the first of their Division 1 scalps in beating Peebles 26-22. Then followed a 23-10 win against Melrose at the semi-final stage, but in the final the second-division club could not claim a treble.

Hawick, the 2002 cup-winners, fell in the fifth round. Though playing at home at Mansfield Park, they were well beaten by Glasgow Hawks by 31-14 in a rematch of the previous year's final.

Hawks then slipped out of the competition with a quarter-final defeat at Meggetland. Boroughmuir won that tie by just 32-31, though Hawks scored five tries to four.

BT Cup Results

Third round: Aberdeen GSFP 93, Langholm 0; Aberdeenshire 9, East Kilbride 18; Allan Glen's 5, Gala 55; Berwick 66, GHK 20; Biggar 43, Preston Lodge FP 13; Boroughmuir 76, Linlithgow 3; Cartha Queen's Park 13, Dundee HSFP 10; Caithness 7, Peebles 42; Corstorphine 5, Kilmarnock 18; Dalziel 38, Ross High 15; Dunbar 15, Edinburgh Academicals 29; Duns 3, Grangemouth 15; Falkirk 0, Haddington 41; Glasgow Hutchesons' Aloysians 22, Livingston 9; Hamilton 13, Stirling County 49; Hawick 79, Lenzie 0; Hawick Trades 5, Kelso 59; Helensburgh 3, Glasgow Hawks 58; Heriot's FP 115, Orkney 6; Hillfoots 17, Stewart's Melville FP 42; Hillhead/Jordanhill 53, Forrester FP 5; Howe of Fife 10, Dunfermline 12; Jed-Forest 104, Gordonians 5; Kirkcaldy 59, Highland 0; Melrose 81, Perthshire 0; Murrayfield Wanderers 40, Ardrossan Academicals 22; Musselburgh 30, Edinburgh University 15; Selkirk 28, Ellon 14; St Boswells 7, Currie 93; Strathmore 7, West of Scotland 13; Trinity Academicals 12, Ayr 67; Watsonians 105, Cambuslang 3.

Fourth round: Aberdeen GSFP 29, Kirkcaldy 7; Ayr 10, Stirling County 18; Biggar 3, Peebles 17; Cartha Queen's Park 13, Jed-Forest 32; Dalziel 8, Melrose 59; Edinburgh Academicals 7, Heriot's FP 50; Glasgow Hawks 30, Currie 25; Glasgow Hutchesons' Aloysians 30, Stewart's Melville FP 29; Haddington 18, East Kilbride 10; Hawick 22, Kelso 0; Hillhead/Jordanhill 21, Grangemouth 6; Kilmarnock 24, West of Scotland 35; Murrayfield Wanderers 50, Berwick 0;

Musselburgh 13, Gala 37; Selkirk 0, Boroughmuir 10; Watsonians 64, Dunfermline 12.

Fifth round: Aberdeen GSFP 22, Peebles 39; Boroughmuir 42, Stirling County 17; Hawick 14, Glasgow Hawks 31; Heriot's FP 34, Jed-Forest 6; Hillhead/Jordanhill 15, Murrayfield Wanderers 24; Melrose 23, Gala 19; Watsonians 36, Glasgow Hutchesons' Aloysians 3; West of Scotland 21, Haddington 18.

Quarter-finals: Boroughmuir 32, Glasgow Hawks 31; Heriot's FP 103, West of Scotland 0; Murrayfield Wanderers 9, Melrose 30; Watsonians 26, Peebles 22.

Semi-finals: Boroughmuir 11, Heriot's FP 22; Watsonians 23, Melrose 10.

FINAL: (at Murrayfield) Heriot's FP 25, Watsonians 13.

Previous SRU Cup Finals (all at Murrayfield): 1996 Hawick 17, Watsonians 15; 1997 Melrose 31, Boroughmuir 23; 1998 Glasgow Hawks 36, Kelso 14; 1999 Gala 8, Kelso 3; 2000 Boroughmuir 35, Glasgow Hawks 10; 2001 Boroughmuir 39, Melrose 15; 2002 Hawick 20, Glasgow Hawks 17 (after extra time); 2003 Heriot's FP 25, Watsonians 13

DOMESTIC RUGBY IN IRELAND 2002-03

Progress for the Four Proud Provinces of Ireland

Jonathan McConnell

'Our country's call . . . From the four proud provinces of Ireland' shouts Ireland's rugby anthem, but there was a danger part-way through the 2002-03 season that Phil Coulter would have to re-work the lyrics of *Ireland's Call* before the World Cup came along.

Potential financial shortfalls at the IRFU led to rumblings that the axe would have to fall on the traditional 'Cinderella' province, Connacht. The suggestion met with staunch opposition not only in the West but also from supporters and players throughout the country. Ironically the threat came as the Province was enjoying its best competitive season for many years. South African Steph Nel had assembled a strong, youthful side that reached the knockout stages of both the Celtic League and the Parker Pen Shield.

They opened their campaign with five consecutive Celtic League wins, including a first ever away win over reining Celtic champions Leinster to secure a quarter-final berth. But at that stage, and with the controversy over their future in full swing, they went down to eventual champions Munster. In the European competition they were first-round winners over Mont-de-Marsan and then, by an aggregate 50-49, over Narbonne in the second round before falling to Pontypridd in the quarter-final. Happily the threat to their future never materialised, and with Nel retuning to South Africa it will be down to former Irish scrum-half Michael Bradley to continue the good work this season.

A second province to see a change at the helm for the new season is Leinster. Australian Gary Ella will be taking over from his fellow countryman Matt Williams, who has become Scotland's national coach. Williams had moulded Leinster into a very able and exciting side to watch and he will be sorely missed. Although they failed to qualify for the knockout stages of the Celtic League, which they had won the previous year, Leinster were a force to be reckoned with in the European Cup. With a strong defensive ethos and fine quality attacking players like Brian O'Driscoll and Denis Hickie, they flew through their group unbeaten and accounted for Biarritz in the quarter-finals. The prospect of a home semi-final against Perpignan, and with the final scheduled for Lansdowne Road, saw them installed as competition favourites. They failed, however, to adapt to the challenge offered by the French and crashed out 21-14.

Despite the vast disappointment, the stellar improvement in Leinster's fortunes under Williams has been clear to see. Nowadays there is a dramatic increase in the interest shown by the Dublin public in the province's games –

match days at Donnybrook now rival the atmosphere generated at Ravenhill when Ulster are at home – and Ella will have a firm footing on which to build.

In contrast Ulster failed to build on their past achievements on either the domestic or European fronts. Although South African Alan Solomons beefed up the physical presence in the pack with the likes of Robbie Kempson and Matt Sexton, he did not turn his back on local talent with Neil McMillan, Scott Young and Simon Best all making an impact. Ulster reached the semi-finals of the Celtic League after finishing third in their group. Their high point was a win at home against the eventual champions Munster by 26-17, and there were other wins over Llanelli, Caerphilly, Ebbw Vale and the eventual losing finalists Neath. They crashed out to Munster at the semi-final stage when, reduced to 14 men after Justin Fitzpatrick had been sent off, they went down by 42-10. Although they finished equal on points with Northampton in their European Cup group, they failed to go through to the knockout stage. Three home wins and a victory in Cardiff were not enough and the heavy loss on the opening weekend of fixtures at Northampton was the critical result.

Throughout the season Munster produced some excellent rugby. They were crowned as Celtic League champions and defeated Gloucester and Leicester away. Ultimately, though, their campaign was judged a disappointment. They failed to make their third European Cup final in four years when a one-point defeat by Toulouse in the semi-final put paid to their hopes. They have now lost two European semi-finals and two finals by an aggregate total of only nine points. They had topped their Celtic League group with only that one defeat against Ulster and were in top gear as they easily passed Connacht before exacting their revenge on the Northern Province on the way to the final against Neath in Cardiff. There they produced a first-class all-round performance to leave the Welsh in their wake and take the title with a 37-17 victory. This left them in good spirit for the assault on Europe where, in the toughest of the qualifying groups, they won at home against eventual champions Perpignan and secured their progress to the knockout stages with a memorable 27-point win against Gloucester at home. A quarter-final visit to Leicester gave them the chance of revenge for their defeat in the previous year's final – which they took in style, despatching the holders 20-7 to set up the semi-final in Toulouse.

This season Alan Gaffney will hope that the signing of New Zealander Christian Cullen will help as his side look to make the final step up to European success.

With Ireland playing three Tests in September 2002 – a warm-up match against Romania and two Rugby World Cup qualifiers – the subsequent demands of the Celtic and European competitions meant that there was no place in the busy representative schedule for the Interprovincial Championship.

IRISH PROVINCES DIRECTORY

Connacht

Year of formation 1884
Ground The Sports Ground, Galway, Republic of Ireland
Contacts Web: www.irfu.ie/connacht/connacht.asp Tel: 00353 91 770236
Colours Green, white and black
Captain 2002-03 Shane Moore

Competition Record 2002-03

Date	*Venue*	*Comp*	*Opponents*	*Result*	*Scorers*
30 Aug	A	CL	Borders	28-27	*T:* McFarland *C:* Elwood *PG:* Elwood 4, McHugh 2 *DG:* McHugh
6 Sep	H	CL	Cardiff	23-22	*T:* Uijs, Neville *C:* Elwood 2 *PG:* Elwood 3
13 Sep	A	CL	Leinster	26-23	*T:* Munn, Keane *C:* Elwood 2 *PG:* Elwood 3 *DG:* McHugh
20 Sep	H	CL	Newport	18-12	*T:* Munn, Norton *C:* Elwood *PG:* Elwood 2
28 Sep	A	CL	Bridgend	24-23	*T:* Munn, McHugh, Yapp *PG:* Elwood 2, McHugh
5 Oct	H	CL	Pontypridd	0-40	
12 Oct	A	PPC1	Mont-de-Marsan	26-12	*T:* Munn, Reddan *C:* Elwood 2 *PG:* Elwood 4
19 Oct	H	PPC1	Mont-de-Marsan	47-29	*T:* Uijs 2, McHugh, Moore, Rigney *C:* Elwood 4, McHugh *PG:* Elwood 2, McHugh 2
25 Oct	A	CL	Glasgow	7-29	*T:* McFarland *C:* McHugh
29 Nov	A	CL¼	Munster	3-33	*PG:* McHugh
7 Dec	A	PPC2	Narbonne	27-42	*T:* Munn 2, McHugh *C:* Elwood 3 *PG:* Elwood 2
15 Dec	H	PPC2	Narbonne	23-7	*T:* Yapp, Uijs *C:* Elwood 2 *PG:* Elwood 3
11 Jan	H	PPC¼	Pontypridd	30-35	*T:* Munn 2, Rigney, Frost *C:* Elwood 2 *PG:* Elwood 2
18 Jan	A	PPC¼	Pontypridd	9-12	*PG:* Elwood 3

Leinster

Year of formation 1879
Ground Donnybrook, Dublin 4, Republic of Ireland
Contacts Web: www.leinster-rugby.com Tel: 003531 6689599
Colours Blue, white and yellow
Captain 2002-03 Reggie Corrigan

Competition Record 2002-03

Date	*Venue*	*Comp*	*Opponents*	*Result*	*Scorers*
30 Aug	H	CL	Pontypridd	31-18	*T:* O'Driscoll 2, Hickie 2, O'Kelly *C:* Dunne 3
6 Sep	A	CL	Glasgow	21-25	*T:* Lewis, Gissing *C:* O'Meara *PG:* O'Meara 3
13 Sep	H	CL	Connacht	23-26	*T:* Gleeson 2 *C:* O'Meara 2 *PG:* O'Meara 3
21 Sep	A	CL	Cardiff	17-30	*T:* Kearney, Dillon *C:* O'Meara, Dunne *PG:* Dunne
27 Sep	A	CL	Borders	18-23	*T:* McWeeney, Gissing *C:* O'Meara *PG:* O'Meara 2

4 Oct	H	CL	Newport	42-14	*T:* Hickie, Horgan, Cullen, O'Kelly *C:* O'Meara 2 *PG:* O'Meara 6
11 Oct	H	HC	Bristol	29-23	*T:* Hickie, Costello *C:* O'Meara 2 *PG:* O'Meara 4, D'Arcy
19 Oct	A	HC	Swansea	51-10	*T:* D'Arcy 3, O'Driscoll 2, McCullen *C:* O'Meara 2, D'Arcy *PG:* O'Meara 4 *DG:* Warner
26 Oct	A	CL	Bridgend	39-18	*T:* Hickie 2, O'Kelly, O'Driscoll, Horgan *C:* O'Meara 4 *PG:* O'Meara 2
7 Dec	A	HC	Montferrand	23-20	*T:* Hickie, D'Arcy *C:* O'Meara 2 *PG:* O'Meara 3
13 Dec	H	HC	Montferrand	12-9	*PG:* O'Meara 4
10 Jan	H	HC	Swansea	48-19	*T:* Hickie 3, Costello, Gleeson, McCullen, Dillon, D'Arcy *C:* O'Meara *PG:* O'Meara 2
19 Jan	A	HC	Bristol	25-12	*T:* McCullen 2, Horgan, O'Driscoll *C:* O'Meara *PG:* O'Meara
12 Apr	H	HCQF	Biarritz	18-13	*T:* Gleeson, Costello *C:* O'Meara *PG:* O'Meara 2
27 Apr	-	HCSF	Perpignan	14-21	*T:* D'Arcy *PG:* O'Meara 2, Spooner

Munster

Year of formation 1879
Ground Musgrave Park, Pearse Road, Cork, Ireland/Thomond Park, Limerick, Republic of Ireland
Contacts Web: www.munsterrugby.ie Tel: 00353 21 4323563
Colours Red, navy and white
Captain 2002-03 Jim Williams

Competition Record 2002-03

Date	*Venue*	*Comp*	*Opponents*	*Result*	*Scorers*
31 Aug	A	CL	Llanelli	20-13	*T:* Lawlor *PG:* O'Gara 5
6 Sep	H	CL	Ebbw Vale	48-23	*T:* Mullins 2, J O'Neill, Holland, Lawlor, Quinlan, Williams *C:* Staunton 5 *PG:* Staunton
13 Sep	A	CL	Edinburgh	28-21	*T:* Henderson *C:* Staunton *PG:* Staunton 7
20 Sep	H	CL	Swansea	38-27	*T:* Crotty 2, Lawlor, Prendergast *C:* Staunton 3 *PG:* Staunton 4
27 Sep	A	CL	Ulster	17-26	*T:* Lawlor *PG:* Staunton 2 *DG:* Staunton, Holland
5 Oct	A	CL	Neath	35-19	*T:* Lawlor, O'Gara, Sheahan, Williams *C:* O'Gara 3 *PG:* O'Gara 3
12 Oct	A	HC	Gloucester	16-35	*T:* Stringer *C:* O'Gara *PG:* O'Gara 3
19 Oct	H	HC	Perpignan	30-21	*T:* Quinlan, Kelly, Hayes *C:* O'Gara 3 *PG:* O'Gara 3
25 Oct	H	CL	Caerphilly	41-0	*T:* Quinlan, Crotty, Mullins, Horan, Sheahan, Galwey, O'Driscoll *C:* O'Gara 3
29 Nov	H	CL¼	Connacht	33-3	*T:* Mullins 2, Lawlor, pen try *C:* O'Gara 2 *PG:* O'Gara 3
6 Dec	H	HC	Viadana	64-0	*T:* Foley 2, Horan, Sheahan, O'Connell, O'Gara, pen try, Holland, Prendergast *C:* O'Gara 8 *PG:* O'Gara
14 Dec	A	HC	Viadana	55-22	*T:* Holland 2, Quinlan 2, Sheahan 2, Foley, Kelly, Mullins *C:* O'Gara 5
3 Jan	H	CL½	Ulster	42-10	*T:* Quinlan, Hayes, Kelly, Mullins, Galwey *C:* O'Gara 3, Keane *PG:* O'Gara 3
11 Jan	A	HC	Perpignan	8-23	*T:* Foley, *PG:* O'Gara

18 Jan	H	HC	Gloucester	33-6	*T:* Kelly 2, Lawlor, O'Driscoll *C:* O'Gara 2 *PG:* O'Gara 3
1 Feb	-	CLF	Neath	37-17	*T:* Quinlan, Horan, Henderson *C:* Staunton 2 *PG:* O'Gara 4, Staunton 2
13 Apr	A	HCQF	Leicester	20-7	*T:* Stringer, O'Gara *C:* O'Gara 2 *PG:* O'Gara 2
26 Apr	-	HCSF	Toulouse	12-13	*PG:* O'Gara 2 *DG:* O'Gara 2

Ulster

Year of formation 1880
Ground Ravenhill Grounds, 85 Ravenhill Park, Belfast BT6 0DG, Northern Ireland
Contacts Web: www.ulsterrugby.com Tel: 02890 649141
Colours White
Captain 2002-03 David Humphreys

Competition Record 2002-03

Date	*Venue*	*Comp*	*Opponents*	*Result*	*Scorers*
30 Aug	A	CL	Ebbw Vale	19-0	*T:* Wallace *C:* Humphreys *PG:* Humphreys 4
6 Sep	H	CL	Edinburgh	18-19	*PG:* Wallace 6
14 Sep	A	CL	Swansea	10-38	*T:* Howe *C:* Humphreys *PG:* Humphreys
20 Sep	H	CL	Neath	17-10	*T:* Howe, Cunningham *C:* Doak 2 *PG:* Doak
27 Sep	H	CL	Munster	26-17	*T:* Doak 2 *C:* Doak 2 *PG:* Doak 4
5 Oct	A	CL	Caerphilly	67-15	*T:* N Best 2, Brosnihan, J Bell, Sexton, Howe, McWhirter, Stewart *C:* Humphreys 6 *PG:* Humphreys 5
13 Oct	A	HC	Northampton	9-32	*PG:* Humphreys 2, Doak
18 Oct	H	HC	Cardiff	25-6	*T:* Young *C:* Humphreys *PG:* Humphreys 5 *DG:* Humphreys
25 Oct	H	CL	Llanelli	16-9	*T:* Doak *C:* Humphreys *PG:* Humphreys 2 *DG:* Humphreys
30 Oct	A	CL¼	Glasgow	20-17	*T:* Bell, Ward *C:* Humphreys 2 *PG:* Humphreys 2
6 Dec	H	HC	Biarritz	13-9	*T:* Topping *C:* Humphreys *PG:* Humphreys 2
14 Dec	A	HC	Biarritz	20-25	*T:* Cunningham, Ward *C:* Doak 2 *PG:* Doak 2
3 Jan	A	CL½	Munster	10-42	*T:* Humphreys *C:* Humphreys *PG:* Humphreys
11 Jan	A	HC	Cardiff	33-21	*T:* McMillan 2, pen try *C:* Humphreys 3 *PG:* Humphreys 3 *DG:* Cunningham
17 Jan	H	HC	Northampton	16-13	*T:* McMillan *C:* Humphreys *PG:* Humphreys *DG:* Humphreys 2

Post-War Irish Interprovincial Champions: 1946-47 Ulster; 1947-48 Munster; 1948-49 Leinster; 1949-50 Leinster; 1950-51 Ulster; 1951-52 Ulster; 1952-53 Ulster & Munster (Shared); 1953-54 Ulster; 1954-55 Munster & Leinster (Shared); 1955-56 Ulster & Connacht (Shared); 1956-57 Ulster & Leinster & Connacht (Shared); 1957-58 Munster; 1958-59 Leinster; 1959-60 Munster; 1960-61 Leinster; 1961-62 Leinster; 1962-63 Munster; 1963-64 Leinster; 1964-65 Leinster; 1965-66 Munster; 1966-67 Ulster & Munster (Shared); 1967-68 Ulster; 1968-69 Munster; 1969-70 Ulster; 1970-71 Ulster; 1971-72 Leinster; 1972-73 Leinster & Ulster & Munster (Shared); 1973-74 Munster; 1974-75 Ulster; 1975-76 Leinster & Ulster & Munster (Shared); 1976-77 Ulster; 1977-78 Leinster & Ulster & Munster (Shared); 1978-79 Munster; 1979-80 Leinster; 1980-81Leinster; 1981-82 Leinster; 1982-83 Leinster & Ulster & Munster (Shared); 1983-84 Leinster; 1984-85 Ulster; 1985-86 Ulster; 1986-87 Ulster; 1987-88 Ulster; 1988-89 Ulster; 1989-90 Ulster; 1990-91 Ulster; 1991-92 Ulster; 1992-93 Ulster; 1993-94 Leinster & Ulster & Munster (Shared); 1994-95 Munster; 1995-96 Leinster; 1996-97 Munster; 1997-98 Leinster; 1998-99 Munster; 1999-2000 Munster; 2000-01 Munster; 2001-02 Leinster; 2002-03 Not staged

BALLYMENA TAKE THE TITLE: AIB CHAMPIONSHIP

Jonathan McConnell

The increasing demands by the Provinces on their contracted players may have gone someway to diminishing the allure of the AIB All Ireland League, but the contest continued to produce some fine rugby and, with the 'big names' absent for a large part of the season, it offered the opportunity for a much greater array of clubs to challenge for places in the end of season play-offs.

The 2002-03 campaign saw Dublin side Clontarf finish top of the round-robin phase, with Lansdowne, Ballymena and Buccaneers joining them in the semi-finals. Last season's champions Shannon finished just outside the play-off reckoning while at the other end of the table Terenure, who collected only seven points from their 15 games, and UL Bohemians were relegated to Division Two.

Clontarf, under coach Phil Werahiko, were considered the team to watch at the beginning of the campaign – and they certainly lived up to that billing, moving to the top of the table in the last week of December. They had suffered an opening day defeat at Ballymena but went on to collect a league record of twelve consecutive wins. Despite ultimately losing the play-off final – and hence the title – they were named as the Irish Rugby Writers' team of the year and produced some magnificent performances throughout the season.

One side that was more disappointed than most with their final league placing was Blackrock College. Heading the table before Christmas the Stradbrook side looked set for a top-four finish, but the wheels came off in the New Year with a thumping 37-14 defeat at home by Lansdowne the catalyst for a string of defeats that saw them finish in only eleventh place.

Lansdowne, who had finished two places clear of relegation last season, produced some fine results at crucial times to ensure their place in the knockout stages, most noticeably when they came from 0-11 behind to collect their first ever league win at Cork Constitution by 27-17. Cork Con, however, were unable to produce anything like the form which saw them reach the previous year's final and ended the season ninth.

Ballymena, under Australian coach Tony D'Arcy, were early-season pacesetters and emphasised their position as the leading side in Ulster, although Belfast Harlequins enjoyed a strong campaign and were, along with Ballymena, the only other side to beat Clontarf.

The final play-off place went to a young Buccaneers squad who had posted their intentions for the season with an opening week win over

Garryowen. A draw with Ballymena on the final day of the league phase helped them finish five points clear of Shannon and Harlequins.

Although Terenure's fate at the other end of the table was sealed long before the end of the campaign, it was only a final week win for Carlow over Bohemians that enabled Carlow to survive and consign Bohs to a drop to Division Two.

In the semi-finals Ballymena's pack produced a fine second-half display to overturn Lansdowne, who had home advantage, while Buccaneers were punished for indiscipline which resulted in the loss of two players to the sin bin in the second period. Clontarf ruthlessly exploited the advantage to win 20-6.

AIB All Ireland League Final Table

	P	*W*	*D*	*L*	*F*	*A*	*Bonus*	*Pts*
Clontarf	15	13	0	2	447	235	9	61
Lansdowne	15	12	0	3	442	277	10	58
Ballymena	15	11	1	3	458	239	8	54
Buccaneers	15	10	1	4	323	244	4	46
Shannon	15	8	1	6	365	261	7	41
Belfast Harlequins	15	9	0	6	305	255	5	41
Galwegians	15	8	0	7	346	349	9	41
Garryowen	15	6	2	7	295	282	8	36
Cork Constitution	15	7	0	8	372	382	8	36
St. Mary's College	15	6	1	8	344	386	7	33
Blackrock College	15	5	0	10	341	377	10	30
Dungannon	15	6	0	9	278	332	6	30
Co Carlow	15	6	0	9	289	383	5	29
UCD	15	5	0	10	327	443	6	26
UL Bohemians	15	4	0	11	272	444	6	22
Terenure College	15	1	0	14	193	508	3	7

Points: Win 4; draw 2; four or more tries, or defeat by seven or fewer points 1
Play-Offs Semi Finals: Clontarf 20, Buccaneers 6; Lansdowne 3, Ballymena 10

AIB All Ireland League Final

10 May 2003, Lansdowne Road Dublin
Ballymena 28 (2G 2PG 1DG 1T) **Clontarf 18** (1G 2PG 1T)

Despite finishing top of the league table seven points clear of third-placed Ballymena, Clontarf were denied their first All Ireland League title by an impressive second-half performance that was capped by an excellent individual try from Test wing James Topping.

The Dubliners had taken an early advantage through a second-minute Darragh O'Shea penalty, but after Paddy Wallace levelled the scores the Ulster side's pack, who dominated long passages of the game, nearly produced the opening try when a rolling maul allowed Paul Shields to break free on the bind-side, only to be brought down at the corner flag by the last-gasp covering tackle of Ollie Winchester.

This set the tone for the remainder of the first period as Clontarf produced an excellent defensive performance and looked capable of frustrating the well-organised Ballymena outfit. Although they failed to produce the flowing open rugby which had characterised their season, they did score the game's first try with their first real foray into opposition territory when O'Shea was on hand to complete a memorable team effort.

Wallace then narrowed the gap with his second penalty, but Clontarf came close to extending their lead just before the break when O'Shea was able to scythe through the Ballymena defence before a try-scoring pass was fumbled.

Despite the 10-6 deficit at half time – and the loss of Test lock Gary Longwell to the sin bin for a deliberate knock-on in the dying moments of the first period – Ballymena turned the screw after the restart with man-of-the-match Neil McMillan producing some fine work on the ground before Adam Larkin took his side into the lead with the first of his two tries.

This signalled a period of dominance for the Ulster side with Larkin's excellent kicking and some superb driving play from his pack keeping Clontarf on the back foot. It was after a 25-metre drive from a line-out and dextrous handling from Scott Young that Larkin went over for his second try, and barely three minutes later came the move of the game when Topping collected the ball in midfield on half-way and left the Clontarf defence flapping in his wake as he touched down in the corner to create a 25-13 lead.

Clontarf, however, refused to sit down and when Ollie Winchester crashed over in the corner with six minutes remaining Ballymena were forced to produce some stout defending. Clontarf No 8 Dave Moore drove over under the posts, but was penalised for a double movement before Ballymena made the title safe with a Larkin drop goal in injury time. For only the second time the title went north to Ulster.

Clontarf: D Hewitt; N O'Brien, D O'Shea, J Downey, O Winchester; A Dunne, M Walls; W O'Kelly, B Jackman, A Clarke, B Gissing, A Wood, D Quinn, D Moore, S O'Donnell *Substitutions:* D Higgins for O'Brien (60 mins); J Wickham for O'Kelly (80 mins)

Scorers *Tries*: O'Shea, Winchester *Conversion:* O'Shea *Penalty Goals:* O'Shea (2)

Ballymena: P Wallace; J Topping, M Waterhouse, H Jones, S Young; A Larkin, P Spence; S McConnell, P Shields, B Young, M Blair, G Longwell, M McCullough, R Nelson, N McMillan *Substitutions:* A Maxwell for Jones (40 mins); N McKenna for McConnell (40 mins)

Scorers *Tries*: Larkin (2), Topping *Conversions:* Wallace (2) *Penalty Goals:* Wallace (2) *Drop Goal:* Larkin

Referee A C Rolland (IRFU)

Previous All Ireland Champions: 1990-91 Cork Constitution: 1991-92 Garryowen; 1992-93 Young Munster; 1993-94 Garryowen; 1994-95 Shannon; 1995-96 Shannon; 1996-97 Shannon; 1997-98 Shannon; 1998-99 Cork Constitution: 1999-2000 St Mary's; 2000-01 Dungannon; 2001-02 Shannon; 2002-03 Ballymena

DOMESTIC RUGBY IN WALES 2002-03

Bridgend's First Big Prize for 20 Years: The Welsh Premiership

John Billot

An overlong season, irritating restrictions on leading players by the Wales team management and financial problems among a number of leading clubs. It was hardly harmonious. Especially for Swansea. The woebegone Whites endured a pretty desperate time on and off the field. They were successful in just one of their Heineken Cup qualifiers and lost 10 of their 16 Welsh Premier Division fixtures. But a worse fate awaited them.

On 10 March, 2003, Swansea RFC announced they had applied for temporary voluntary administration for six months to protect themselves from incurring heavy debts. This involved players having their wages trimmed by up to 70%. Colin Charvis, Ben Evans and Darren Morris were released with immediate effect. Swansea chairman Roger Blyth explained, 'With a guaranteed income of only £50,000 from the WRU next season, we would be acting unlawfully to continue to trade in our position. This is the most responsible action. The WRU stated it is up to clubs to handle their liabilities.'

Swansea director of rugby, former Wales captain Richard Moriarty, who made a record 424 appearances for the club, stated, 'Professionalism has ruined Swansea and left the club where we are today. I played in the amateur and pro eras and the amateur game was much better. Everyone enjoyed the game more.' Before the season started, the WRU gave Ebbw Vale an advance on their £600,000-plus funding for the season to solve a serious financial crisis. Severe cutbacks were necessary after director of rugby Ray Harris warned that the club could fold.

Events proved more cheerful for Bridgend. Inspiringly led by Gareth Thomas, they won the Premier Division title for the first time. In fact, it was their first major trophy for more than 20 years and their playing record was a huge improvement from the previous year, when they finished third from bottom. Although Neath stopped their headlong unbeaten sequence by 32-24 at the Gnoll in May (during which month Bridgend played seven League fixtures), the Brewery Field men took the return meeting by 22-13 and that ended Neath's threatening challenge. The only other defeat for Bridgend was in their final fixture by 27-13 in Cardiff.

After two seasons involved with Scottish Districts sides Edinburgh and Glasgow, the Welsh League reverted to a domestic structure; but standards had declined markedly. However, there are always exceptions to the rule and Bridgend proved this by their consistency. Allan Lewis coached them perceptively to produce an exciting blend of tactical awareness and combined attack. Tongan scrum-half Sililo Martens was recruited from Swansea to share the duties with experienced Huw Harries while Gareth Cull arrived as an important goal-kicker from Ebbw Vale. Victory by 41-20 at Stradey Park was Bridgend's record all-time score against Llanelli and there were certainly more bright moments than bleak for the Brewery boys. Surprisingly, the crowds that once thronged the ground were sparse. Bridgend deserved far more enthusiastic support.

Second-placed Neath were led by Gareth Llewellyn, Wales's most-capped forward, now aged 34 and still leaping like a gaffed salmon in the line-out. Only Pontypridd stole victory at the Gnoll (by 29-20), but successive failures at Llanelli and Bridgend spoilt their title chance. The Blacks were always vibrant attackers and none more so than Shane Williams, who possessed the elusive skill of legendary Barry John to be in two places at the same time; an enchanting deceiver on the wing. Coach Lyn Jones unfailingly brought the best out of his side and his abrasive pack regularly turned over opponents in the manner of days or yore at the Gnoll. To be startled by a Neath pack is no disgrace and there can't be a team, from the New Zealand All Blacks down, who have missed the experience!

Cardiff, undefeated at home in the Premier Division, suffered from lack of an authoritative pack. At times the Blue-and-Blacks were the despair of their supporters. After bombing out of the Heineken Cup qualifying stage, losing all six games, they were blasted by 44-10 as Llanelli hustled them out of the Principality Cup semi-final. Dai Young, former Wales prop with 51 caps, was the new coach while Martyn Williams, outstanding for Wales, assumed the captaincy. Neil Jenkins returned to Pontypridd after three years' exile from Sardis Road, and Rob Howley joined Wasps. The loss of their experience was difficult to overcome. Jonathan Humphreys left for Bath after 13 years at the Arms Park and Wales had to recall him as captain to inject new spirit in a team of strugglers.

Ben Evans was recruited from Swansea in April and other newcomers included Eastern Province lock Heino Senekal, who won 25 caps with Namibia, Jim Brownrigg (Bristol), scrum-half Richard Smith (Worcester) and Western Province full-back Donavan van Vuuren. Cardiff also bought back Craig Quinnell from Worcester for the current season.

Fijian lock Simon Raiwalui captained Newport again and they thundered their way to the Principality Cup final through the endeavours of a forceful pack and the superb goal-kicking of Percy Montgomery, a classy Springbok with 50 caps. They were blitzed in Toulouse by 70-18 in the Heineken Cup qualifying stage, but their forward strength was such that they could afford to lose such notable back-row men as Peter Buxton (Gloucester) and Alix Popham (Leeds). Unfortunately, their runners lacked cutting edge and rhythm and Newport had to look to Raiwalui's 'roughnecks' to do the job.

Llanelli, led by new skipper Leigh Davies, captured the Principality Cup for a record 12th time as some consolation for a mainly average season. Though they won five of their six Heineken Cup qualifying matches, the quarter-final was a disaster of seismic proportions. No French club had won at Stradey in the tourney, but Perpignan went on to the final after Llanelli flanker Dafydd Jones had been dismissed for stamping in the 10th minute. The Stradey faithful were stunned.

The Scarlets shocked rampant Neath by 27-25 in a vastly entertaining Stradey clash, but lost five of their closing six League matches. Matthew J Watkins proved their most successful signing. His switch from Newport to play in the centre brought him into prominence as a menacing attacker with a whole catalogue of unexpected angles. Someone at Newport slipped up!

Pontypridd were overjoyed at the return of Neil Jenkins, but after knee surgery he missed many games and it was a poor season by Ponty standards. Hooker Mefin Davies, the new captain, fired his pack tirelessly, especially with their driving line-out mauls. Tricky Ceri Sweeney continued to develop at outside-half while Gareth Baber made an invaluable deputy for injured Paul John. Robert Sidoli excelled for Wales and ruled the line-out while Richard Parks proved a dynamic flanker.

Caerphilly and Ebbw Vale finished at the foot of the table, but there was a high spot for Caerphilly in reaching the final of the Parker Pen Shield. It was too much to expect the part-timers to shock the Castres professionals, but Chris Ferris's men gave a determined account of themselves before losing by 40-12. They were only the third Welsh club to reach a European final, following Cardiff in the 1996 Heineken Cup (which Toulouse won by 21-18 in extra time) and Pontypridd in the 2002 Parker Pen Shield (won by Sale by 25-22). Caerphilly surprised Llanelli by 30-20 at Virginia Park and Swansea by 42-31 at St Helen's. Coach Terry Holmes and forwards coach Tony Faulkner, both former Wales stalwarts, left before the season began and Mark Ring took up the coaching challenge.

Final Welsh Premiership Table 2002-03

Team	*P*	*W*	*D*	*L*	*For*	*Against*	*Tries*	*Pts*
Bridgend	16	14	0	2	529	256	64	42
Neath	16	11	1	4	539	363	66	34
Cardiff	16	10	1	5	449	365	56	31
Newport	16	9	0	7	533	393	59	27
Llanelli	16	6	1	9	414	414	54	19
Pontypridd	16	6	1	9	370	390	37	19
Swansea	16	6	0	10	402	539	46	18
Caerphilly	16	4	0	12	299	683	33	12
Ebbw Vale	16	4	0	12	269	401	28	12

Three points awarded for a win; one for a draw and none for a defeat.

Previous Welsh Champions: 1990-91 Neath; 1991-92 Swansea; 1992-93 Llanelli; 1993-94 Swansea; 1994-95 Cardiff; 1995-96 Neath; 1996-97 Pontypridd; 1997-98 Swansea; 1998-99 Llanelli; 1999-2000 Cardiff; 2000-01 Swansea; 2001-02 Llanelli; 2002-03 Bridgend

WELSH CLUB DIRECTORY

Bridgend

Year of formation 1878
Ground Brewery Field, Tondu Road, Bridgend, Mid Glamorgan, CF31 4JE, Wales
Contacts Web: www.bridgendrfc.com Tel: Bridgend (01656) 652707
Colours Blue and white hoops
Captain 2002-03 Gareth Thomas
Welsh Premier 2002-03 Winners
Principality Cup 2002-03 Lost 23-27 to Newport (semi-final)

Competition Record 2002-03

Date	*Venue*	*Comp*	*Opponents*	*Result*	*Scorers*
30 Aug	A	CL	Newport	13-5	*T:* D Jones *C:* Warlow *PG:* Warlow 2
7 Sep	H	CL	Borders	41-9	*T:* Harris, Mustoe, Molitika, Horsman, G Thomas *C:* Warlow 5 *PG:* Warlow 2
13 Sep	H	CL	Pontypridd	9-26	*PG:* Warlow 3
20 Sep	A	CL	Glasgow	11-47	*T:* G Williams *PG:* Warlow 2
28 Sep	H	CL	Connacht	23-24	*T:* D James, Mafi *C:* Warlow 2 *PG:* Warlow 3
5 Oct	A	CL	Cardiff	12-37	*PG:* Warlow 4
12 Oct	A	PPC1	Pau	6-18	*PG:* Warlow 2
19 Oct	H	PPC1	Pau	27-9	*PG:* Warlow 9
26 Oct	H	CL	Leinster	18-39	*T:* D James 2 *C:* Warlow *PG:* Warlow 2
2 Nov	A	WP	Ebbw Vale	7-6	*T:* D James *C:* Warlow
6 Dec	H	PPC2	Bath	28-26	*T:* G Thomas 2, Loader *C:* Warlow 2 *PG:* Warlow 3
14 Dec	A	PPC2	Bath	10-38	*T:* G Thomas *C:* Carter *PG:* Warlow
20 Dec	A	WP	Newport	13-12	*T:* Havili *C:* Cull *PG:* Cull 2
26 Dec	H	WP	Caerphilly	48-3	*T:* Havili 2, pen try, Cull, Bishop, Horsman, Molitika *C:* Cull 5 *PG:* Cull
30 Dec	A	WP	Swansea	16-9	*T:* Horsman *C:* Cull *PG:* Cull 3
25 Jan	H	WP	Llanelli	19-5	*T:* Bishop *C:* Cull *PG:* Cull 4
8 Feb	A	PC7	Newbridge	39-8	*T:* Molitika 2, Harris, B Phillips *C:* Warlow 2 *PG:* Warlow 5
15 Mar	H	WP	Ebbw Vale	42-22	*T:* Havili 2, Taumalolo, Mustoe, Horsman, Harris *C:* Cull 3 *PG:* Cull 2
5 Apr	H	PCQF	Swansea	48-25	*T:* Joy, Budgett, Havili, Mustoe, Molitika, G Thomas *C:* Cull 3 *PG:* Cull 4
12 Apr	H	WP	Newport	56-30	*T:* Warlow 2, D James, Budgett, Molitika, Horsman *C:* Cull 4 *PG:* Cull 6
19 Apr	-	PCSF	Newport	23-27	*T:* Warlow, G Thomas *C:* Cull 2 *PG:* Cull 3
23 Apr	A	WP	Caerphilly	78-5	*T:* M James 3, P Jones 2, C Richards 2, Bishop 2, Mannix, Lloyd, Van Rensburg *C:* Mannix 6, P Jones, Bishop, C Richards
26 Apr	H	WP	Swansea	49-21	*T:* pen tries 2, Mustoe, Bishop, G Thomas, Horsman, M James *C:* Warlow 7
2 May	A	WP	Pontypridd	33-7	*T:* Richards, P Jones, Booth, Cull, Powell *C:* Cull 4
6 May	A	WP	Llanelli	41-20	*T:* Van Rensburg 2, G Thomas, Molitika, Horsman *C:* Cull 5 *PG:* Cull 2
9 May	A	WP	Neath	24-32	*T:* Harris, R Jones, Horsman *C:* Cull 3 *PG:* Cull

16 May	H	WP	Cardiff	35-12	*T:* Van Rensburg 2, Carter, Horsman *C:* Cull 3 *PG:* Cull 3
20 May	H	WP	Neath	22-13	*T:* Martens, Thiel, Cull *C:* Cull 2 *DG:* Cull
24 May	H	WP	Pontypridd	33-32	*T:* Bishop, B Phillips, Thiel, C Harris *C:* Cull, Warlow *PG:* Cull 2, Warlow
27 May	A	WP	Cardiff	13-27	*T:* Owen *C:* Cull *PG:* Cull 2

Caerphilly

Year of formation 1886
Ground Virginia Park, Pontygwindy Road, Caerphilly, CF83 3JA, Wales
Contacts Web: www.caerphillyrfc.co.uk Tel: Caerphilly (02920) 865077
Colours Green and white
Captain 2002-03 Christian Ferris
Welsh Premier 2002-03 8th
Principality Cup 2002-03 Lost 21-46 to Swansea (7th round)

Competition Record 2002-03

Date	*Venue*	*Comp*	*Opponents*	*Result*	*Scorers*
30 Aug	A	CL	Neath	6-25	*PG:* Richards 2
7 Sep	H	CL	Llanelli	34-43	*T:* P Jones, Workman, G Jones, Taufahema, Tuipulotu *C:* Richards 3 *PG:* Richards
14 Sep	A	CL	Ebbw Vale	25-45	*T:* Ashman, A Williams, Tuipulotu *C:* Richards 2 *PG:* Richards *DG:* Richards
21 Sep	H	CL	Edinburgh	32-66	*T:* Ashman, G Jones, Tuipulotu, Skuse, Boobyer *C:* Richards, McLoughlin *PG:* Richards
28 Sep	A	CL	Swansea	32-37	*T:* Lewis, Chilten *C:* Richards 2 *PG:* Richards 6
5 Oct	H	CL	Ulster	15-67	*T:* Chilten 2 *C:* McLoughlin *PG:* McLoughlin
12 Oct	H	PPC1	Harlequins	20-73	*T:* Lewis, Howell *C:* Richards 2 *PG:* Richards 2
20 Oct	A	PPC1	Harlequins	27-31	*T:* G Jones 2, Rouse, Williams, Vunipola *C:* Chilten
25 Oct	A	CL	Munster	0-41	
29 Oct	A	WP	Newport	10-36	*T:* Cox, Howell
2 Nov	H	WP	Neath	23-41	*T:* Taufahema, Hocking, Boobyer *C:* J Thomas *PG:* Tuipulotu 2
7 Dec	A	PPS1	Rovigo	22-26	*T:* Howell 2, Cox, Bressington *C:* Ashman
14 Dec	H	PPS1	Rovigo	58-17	*T:* Howell 2, Cox, G Lewis, R Boobyer, Tuipulotu, El Abd, pen try, A Williams *C:* J Thomas, McLoughlin *PG:* J Thomas 3
21 Dec	H	WP	Swansea	19-20	*T:* El Abd *C:* J Thomas *PG:* J Thomas 4
26 Dec	A	WP	Bridgend	3-48	*PG:* J Thomas
11 Jan	H	PPSQF	Parma	41-28	*T:* Taufahema 3, G Jones 2, P Jones *C:* J Thomas *PG:* J Thomas 3
18 Jan	A	PPSQF	Parma	10-15	*T:* Taufahema *C:* J Thomas *PG:* J Thomas
7 Feb	H	PC7	Swansea	21-46	*T:* Taufahema, Tuipulotu, G Jones *PG:* J Thomas 2
14 Feb	H	WP	Ebbw Vale	31-28	*T:* Taufahema 2, Boobyer, Howell *C:* J Thomas 4 *PG:* J Thomas
21 Feb	A	WP	Pontypridd	8-47	*T:* Tuipulotu *PG:* J Thomas
7 Mar	H	WP	Llanelli	33-20	*T:* G Lewis 2,Tuipulotu, Ashman *C:* Richards 2 *PG:* Richards 3
15 Mar	A	WP	Neath	14-67	*T:* Tuipulotu 2 *C:* J Thomas 2

20 Mar	H	WP	Newport	19-65	*T:* Murphy *C:* J Thomas *PG:* J Thomas 3 *DG:* J Thomas
25 Mar	A	WP	Llanelli	13-77	*T:* J Thomas *C:* Richards *PG:* Richards 2
12 Apr	A	PPSSF	Petrarca	28-10	*T:* G Lewis, A Williams, J Thomas *C:* J Thomas 2 *PG:* J Thomas 3
23 Apr	H	WP	Bridgend	5-78	*T:* Kestell
26 Apr	H	PPSSF	Petrarca	26-33	*T:* G Lewis 2, Ashman *C:* J Thomas *PG:* J Thomas 3
2 May	A	WP	Cardiff	8-38	*T:* R Boobyer *PG:* J Thomas
6 May	A	WP	Swansea	42-31	*T:* El-Abd 2, Howell 2, Tuipulotu *C:* Richards 4 *PG:* Richards 3
10 May	H	WP	Cardiff	32-48	*T:* Howell, D Davies *C:* Richards 2 *PG:* Richards 6
13 May	A	WP	Ebbw Vale	24-22	*T:* R Boobyer, Taufahema, Chilten *C:* Richards 2, J Thomas *DG:* J Murphy
17 May	H	WP	Pontypridd	15-17	*T:* Howell, D Davies *C:* J Thomas *PG:* J Thomas
25 May	-	PPSF	Castres	12-40	*T:* R Boobyer, El Abd *C:* J Thomas

Cardiff

Year of formation 1876
Ground Cardiff Arms Park, Westgate Street, Cardiff CF10 1JA, Wales
Contacts Web: www.cardiffrfc.co.uk Tel: Cardiff (02920) 302000
Colours Cambridge blue and black
Captain 2002-03 Martyn Williams
Welsh Premier 2002-03 3rd
Principality Cup 2002-03 Lost 10-44 to Llanelli (semi-final)

Competition Record 2002-03

Date	*Venue*	*Comp*	*Opponents*	*Result*	*Scorers*
31 Aug	H	CL	Glasgow	35-44	*T:* R Williams, Allen, R Powell, M Williams *C:* Harris 3 *PG:* Harris 3
6 Sep	A	CL	Connacht	22-23	*T:* Morgan 2, N Robinson *C:* N Robinson 2 *PG:* N Robinson
13 Sep	A	CL	Borders	18-15	*PG:* Harris 6
21 Sep	H	CL	Leinster	30-17	*T:* M Williams, Sullivan *C:* Harris *PG:* Harris 6
28 Sep	A	CL	Newport	27-25	*T:* Morgan 3 *C:* Harris 3 *PG:* Harris 2
5 Oct	H	CL	Bridgend	37-12	*T:* Allen 2, Tait, M Williams, C Morgan *C:* N Robinson 3 *PG:* N Robinson *DG:* N Robinson
12 Oct	H	HC	Biarritz	15-26	*PG:* Harris 5
18 Oct	A	HC	Ulster	6-25	*PG:* Harris 2
26 Oct	A	CL	Pontypridd	9-15	*PG:* Harris 3
30 Nov	A	CLQF	Edinburgh	26-22	*T:* R Williams, Powell *C:* Harris 2 *PG:* Harris 4
7 Dec	A	HC	Northampton	11-25	*T:* R Williams *PG:* Harris 2
15 Dec	H	HC	Northampton	0-31	
21 Dec	A	WP	Pontypridd	10-12	*T:* R Williams *C:* Harris *PG:* Harris
26 Dec	H	WP	Ebbw Vale	34-6	*T:* Walne 2, M Williams, Dewdney *C:* N Robinson 4 *PG:* N Robinson 2
1 Jan	A	WP	Newport	3-31	*PG:* N Robinson
4 Jan	A	CLSF	Neath	10-32	*T:* Smith *C:* Harris *PG:* Harris
11 Jan	H	HC	Ulster	21-33	*T:* Walne, Allen *C:* N Robinson *PG:* N Robinson 3
18 Jan	A	HC	Biarritz	25-75	*T:* C Morgan, Powell, Dewdney *C:* N Robinson 2 *PG:* N Robinson 2

24 Jan	A	WP	Swansea	32-19	*T:* C Morgan, Senekal, R Smith, Walne *C:* Harris 3 *PG:* Harris 2
4 Feb	A	WP	Llanelli	26-39	*T:* R Williams 2 *C:* Harris 2 *PG:* Harris 4
8 Feb	A	PC7	Bonymaen	41-16	*T:* McShane 2, Sullivan, Baugh *C:* N Robinson 3 *PG:* N Robinson 5
28 Feb	H	WP	Neath	20-20	*T:* C Morgan, Sullivan, Dewdney *C:* Harris *PG:* Harris
12 Mar	A	WP	Neath	24-39	*T:* N Robinson, Powell, Tait *C:* N Robinson 3 *PG:* N Robinson
4 Apr	H	PCQF	Pontypridd	20-18	*T:* J Robinson, M Williams, R Williams *C:* Harris *PG:* Harris
12 Apr	H	WP	Swansea	44-22	*T:* Smith 2, J Robinson, C Morgan, Van Vuuren, Powell, Tait *C:* N Robinson 3 *PG:* N Robinson
19 Apr	-	PCSF	Llanelli	10-44	*T:* Muller, R Williams
22 Apr	A	WP	Ebbw Vale	34-24	*T:* Dewdney 2, Brownrigg, Rogers *C:* N Robinson 4 *PG:* N Robinson 2
25 Apr	H	WP	Newport	39-17	*T:* R Williams 4, Brownrigg *C:* Harris 4 *PG:* Harris 2
2 May	H	WP	Caerphilly	38-8	*T:* Walne 2, Brownrigg, Smith, N Robinson *C:* N Robinson 5 *PG:* N Robinson
10 May	A	WP	Caerphilly	48-32	*T:* Dewdney, R Williams, Harris, A Jones, Van Vuuren, Powell *C:* Harris 6 *PG:* Harris 2
16 May	A	WP	Bridgend	12-35	*T:* Walne, Muller *C:* N Robinson
23 May	H	WP	Llanelli	28-27	*T:* Muller 2, Walne *C:* N Robinson, Macleod *PG:* N Robinson 3
27 May	H	WP	Bridgend	27-13	*T:* Abdul 2, Brownrigg, Dewdney *C:* N Robinson 2 *PG:* N Robinson
30 May	H	WP	Pontypridd	30-21	*T:* Dewdney, Smith, N Robinson *C:* N Robinson 3 *PG:* N Robinson 2 *DG:* Macleod

Ebbw Vale

Year of formation 1880
Ground Eugene Cross Park, Ebbw Vale, Gwent, NP23 5AZ, Wales
Contacts Web: www.ebbwvalerfc.co.uk Tel: Ebbw Vale (01495) 302995
Colours Red, white and green
Captain 2002-03 Chay Billen
Welsh Premier 2002-03 9th
Principality Cup 2002-03 Lost 20-41 to Newport (quarter-final)

Competition Record 2002-03

Date	*Venue*	*Comp*	*Opponents*	*Result*	*Scorers*
30 Aug	H	CL	Ulster	0-19	
6 Sep	A	CL	Munster	23-48	*T:* pen try, Morris *C:* Meenan 2 *PG:* Meenan *DG:* Meenan 2
14 Sep	H	CL	Caerphilly	45-25	*T:* Shorney 3, J Evans, Wakely *C:* Meenan 4 *PG:* Meenan 4
21 Sep	A	CL	Llanelli	25-37	*T:* R Davies, Shelbourne, N Edwards *C:* Shelbourne 2 *PG:* Shelbourne 2
27 Sep	A	CL	Neath	7-34	*T:* R Davies *C:* Meenan
5 Oct	H	CL	Edinburgh	20-30	*T:* Meenan, Mitchell *C:* Meenan 2 *PG:* Meenan 2
11 Oct	H	PPC1	Montauban	20-16	*T:* Ridley, Takarangi *C:* Meenan 2 *PG:* Meenan 2
19 Oct	A	PPC1	Montauban	16-29	*T:* R Davies, Tuipulotu *PG:* Meenan 2

26 Oct	A	CL	Swansea	20-33	*T:* R Davies, Wakely, Takarangi *C:* Mitchell *PG:* Mitchell
29 Oct	H	WP	Swansea	16-13	*T:* Wakely *C:* Meenan *PG:* Meenan 3
2 Nov	H	WP	Bridgend	6-7	*PG:* Meenan *DG:* Meenan
15 Nov	A	WP	Neath	12-34	*T:* Shorney, Tuipulotu *C:* Meenan
7 Dec	H	PPS1	Madrid 2012	37-16	*T:* Mitchell 2, Bevan 2, Tuipulotu 2 *C:* Shelbourne 2 *PG:* Shelbourne
14 Dec	A	PPS1	Madrid 2012	38-16	*T:* Bevan 3, Black, R Davies, Shorney *C:* Shelbourne 3, Shorney
21 Dec	H	WP	Llanelli	20-8	*T:* R Davies *PG:* Shelbourne 5
26 Dec	A	WP	Cardiff	6-34	*PG:* Shelbourne 2
4 Jan	A	WP	Pontypridd	10-6	*T:* Mitchell *C:* Shelbourne *PG:* Shelbourne
13 Jan	H	PPSQF	Pau	29-3	*T:* Tuipulotu, L Phillips *C:* Shelbourne 2 *PG:* Shelbourne 5
18 Jan	A	PPQF	Pau	17-63	*T:* R Davies, Bevan, Shelbourne *C:* Shelbourne
25 Jan	H	WP	Neath	26-27	*T:* Shelbourne, Takarangi, Black *C:* Shelbourne *PG:* Shelbourne 3
1 Feb	H	WP	Newport	15-37	*T:* pen try, Morris *C:* Shelbourne *PG:* Shelbourne
8 Feb	A	PC7	Carmarthen Q	13-8	*T:* P Williams, Tuipulotu *PG:* Shelbourne
14 Feb	A	WP	Caerphilly	28-31	*T:* R Davies, Penisini, Meenan *C:* Shelbourne 2 *PG:* Shelbourne 3
1 Mar	A	WP	Swansea	17-21	*T:* Tuipulotu, Shorney, Mitchell *C:* Shelbourne
15 Mar	A	WP	Bridgend	22-42	*T:* Shorney, Tuipulotu, Wakely *C:* Meenan 2 *PG:* Meenan
21 Mar	A	WP	Llanelli	11-16	*T:* Shorney *PG:* Shelbourne 2
5 Apr	H	PCQF	Newport	20-41	*T:* Meenan, Shelbourne *C:* Shelbourne 2 *PG:* Shelbourne *DG:* Shelbourne
22 Apr	H	WP	Cardiff	24-34	*T:* Shorney, Bevan, Tuipulotu *C:* Mitchell 2, Hayward *PG:* Hayward
9 May	H	WP	Pontypridd	25-6	*T:* Shorney, Matthews, Billen *C:* Hayward 2 *PG:* Hayward 2
13 May	H	WP	Caerphilly	22-24	*T:* Meenan, Mitchell, W Thomas *C:* Mitchell 2 *PG:* Mitchell
17 May	A	WP	Newport	9-61	*PG:* Hayward 3

Llanelli

Year of formation 1872
Ground Stradey Park, Llanelli, Dyfed SA15 4BT, Wales
Contacts Web: www.scarlets.co.uk Tel: Llanelli (01554) 783900
Colours Scarlet
Captain 2002-03 Leigh Davies
Welsh Premier 2002-03 5th
Principality Cup 2002-03 Winners Won 32-9 against Newport (FINAL)

Competition Record 2002-03

Date	*Venue*	*Comp*	*Opponents*	*Result*	*Scorers*
31 Aug	H	CL	Munster	13-20	*T:* M Jones *C:* S Jones *PG:* S Jones 2
7 Sep	A	CL	Caerphilly	43-34	*T:* M Jones 2, S Jones, D Jones, Bowen, I Boobyer *C:* S Jones 2 *PG:* Bowen 3
14 Sep	A	CL	Neath	13-29	*T:* I Thomas *C:* S Jones *PG:* S Jones 2
21 Sep	H	CL	Ebbw Vale	37-25	*T:* Watkins 2, M Jones, D Jones, Finau *C:* Bowen 3 *PG:* Bowen 2
27 Sep	A	CL	Edinburgh	14-38	*T:* L Davies, Madden *C:* S Jones 2

4 Oct	H	CL	Swansea	62-6	*T:* S Jones 2, G Evans, L Davies, Watkins, Selley, I Boobyer, Wyatt *C:* S Jones 5 *PG:* S Jones 4
12 Oct	H	HC	Glasgow	45-15	*T:* Peel 2, G Evans, I Boobyer, Madden *C:* S Jones 4 *PG:* S Jones 3, Bowen
18 Oct	A	HC	Bourgoin	38-54	*T:* pen try, Madden *C:* S Jones 2 *PG:* S Jones 8
25 Oct	A	CL	Ulster	9-16	*PG:* S Jones 3
6 Dec	A	HC	Sale	30-19	*T:* McBryde, G Evans, Quinnell, Madden *C:* S Jones 2 *PG:* S Jones 2
13 Dec	H	HC	Sale	17-12	*T:* Hodges *PG:* S Jones 4
21 Dec	A	WP	Ebbw Vale	8-20	*T:* B Davies *PG:* Bowen
26 Dec	H	WP	Newport	23-13	*T:* M Jones, G Evans *C:* S Jones 2 *PG:* S Jones 3
3 Jan	H	WP	Swansea	45-23	*T:* B Davies, Watkins, D Jones, G Evans, G Easterby, S Easterby *C:* S Jones 5, Bowen *PG:* S Jones
10 Jan	H	HC	Bourgoin	37-22	*T:* G Evans 2, Quinnell, Peel *C:* S Jones 4 *PG:* S Jones 2 *DG:* S Jones
17 Jan	A	HC	Glasgow	34-8	*T:* G Evans 3, B Davies, Madden, S Jones *C:* S Jones 2
25 Jan	A	WP	Bridgend	5-19	*T:* B Davies
4 Feb	H	WP	Cardiff	39-26	*T:* M Jones 2, Quinnell, D Jones, L Davies *C:* Bowen *PG:* S Jones 3 *DG:* S Jones
8 Feb	A	PC7	Pontypool	30-22	*T:* M Thomas 2, Selley, Hodges *C:* Bowen 2 *PG:* Bowen 2
14 Feb	A	WP	Neath	7-25	*T:* Walters *C:* B Davies
7 Mar	A	WP	Caerphilly	20-33	*T:* N Boobyer, M Jones L Davies *C:* B Davies *PG:* B Davies
21 Mar	H	WP	Ebbw Vale	16-11	*T:* Selley 2 *PG:* B Davies 2
25 Mar	H	WP	Caerphilly	77-13	*T:* G Evans 3, Cardey 2, L Davies 2, Proctor 2, Finau, Quinnell, B Davies, J Davies *C:* Bowen 3, N Boobyer 3
28 Mar	H	WP	Pontypridd	23-23	*T:* Finau, M Thomas *C:* Bowen 2 *PG:* Bowen 3
5 Apr	H	PCQF	Neath	49-17	*T:* D Jones 2, Watkins 2, B Davies, G Evans *C:* S Jones 5 *PG:* S Jones 3
11 Apr	H	HCQF	Perpignan	19-26	*T:* Madden *C:* S Jones *PG:* S Jones 4
19 Apr	-	PCSF	Cardiff	44-10	*T:* M Jones, Watkins, B Davies, G Evans, S Jones, L Davies *C:* S Jones 4 *PG:* S Jones 2
22 Apr	A	WP	Newport	13-33	*T:* pen try *C:* Bowen *PG:* Bowen *DG:* M Phillips
4 May	-	PCF	Newport	32-9	*T:* M Jones 2, L Davies, Finau *C:* S Jones 3 *PG:* S Jones 2
6 May	H	WP	Bridgend	20-41	*T:* Peel, Clapham *C:* Bowen 2 *PG:* Bowen 2
10 May	A	WP	Swansea	40-52	*T:* M Phillips, Bowen, Finau, Selley, Gross, Yelland *C:* Bowen 5
17 May	H	WP	Neath	27-25	*T:* Wyatt, Madden, Selley, Proctor *C:* Bowen 2 *PG:* Bowen
21 May	A	WP	Pontypridd	24-29	*T:* Selley 2, Wyatt, Bowen *C:* N Boobyer, C Thomas
23 May	A	WP	Cardiff	27-28	*T:* Selley, pen try, J Davies *C:* Bowen 2, C Thomas *PG:* Bowen, C Thomas

Neath

Year of formation 1871
Ground The Gnoll, Gnoll Park Road, Neath, West Glamorgan SA11 3BU, Wales

Contacts Web: www.neathrfc.co.uk Tel: Neath (01639) 769660
Colours All black with white Maltese cross
Captain 2002-03 Gareth Llewellyn
Welsh Premier 2002-03 Runners-up
Principality Cup 2002-03 Lost 17-49 to Llanelli (quarter-final)

Competition Record 2002-03

Date	*Venue*	*Comp*	*Opponents*	*Result*	*Scorers*
30 Aug	H	CL	Caerphilly	25-6	*T:* Durston, S Williams, K James *C:* Connor 2 *PG:* Jarvis, Connor
6 Sep	A	CL	Swansea	20-16	*T:* S Williams, A Moore *C:* Jarvis 2 *PG:* Connor *DG:* Connor
14 Sep	H	CL	Llanelli	29-13	*T:* Marsden, H Jenkins *C:* Jarvis 2 *PG:* Jarvis 5
20 Sep	A	CL	Ulster	13-17	*T:* S Williams *C:* Jarvis *PG:* Jarvis 2
27 Sep	H	CL	Ebbw Vale	34-7	*T:* G Morris 3, Jarvis, Tandy *C:* Jarvis 3 *PG:* Jarvis
5 Oct	H	CL	Munster	19-35	*T:* S Jones *C:* Connor *PG:* Jarvis 4
11 Oct	H	HC	Leicester	16-16	*T:* Tiueti *C:* Jarvis *PG:* Jarvis 3
19 Oct	A	HC	Béziers	16-21	*T:* Mocelutu *C:* Connor *PG:* Connor 3
25 Oct	A	CL	Edinburgh	13-27	*T:* D Jones *C:* M Jones *PG:* Connor 2
2 Nov	A	WP	Caerphilly	41-23	*T:* Durston, Marsden, pen try, Tiueti, S Williams *C:* Connor 3, Jarvis 2 *PG:* Jarvis, Connor
15 Nov	H	WP	Ebbw Vale	34-12	*T:* Morris 2, Marsden, Jenkins, Millward *C:* Connor 3 *PG:* Connor
29 Nov	A	CLQF	Pontypridd	13-12	*T:* pen try *C:* Connor *PG:* Jarvis 2
7 Dec	A	HC	Calvisano	29-38	*T:* Storey, pen try, R Phillips, B Williams *C:* Jarvis 3 *PG:* Jarvis
14 Dec	H	HC	Calvisano	56-10	*T:* Tandy 3, K James 2, pen try, Connor, Durston, S Jones *C:* Jarvis 4 *PG:* Jarvis
27 Dec	A	WP	Swansea	14-23	*T:* S Williams *PG:* Connor 3
30 Dec	H	WP	Pontypridd	20-29	*T:* Mocelutu, K James *C:* Connor 2 *PG:* Connor 2
4 Jan	H	CLSF	Cardiff	32-10	*T:* G Morris, Tiueti, Jarvis, Bonner-Evans *C:* Jarvis 3 *PG:* Jarvis 2
13 Jan	H	HC	Béziers	23-18	*T:* G Morris, Newman *C:* Jarvis 2 *PG:* Jarvis 3
18 Jan	A	HC	Leicester	11-36	*T:* S Williams *PG:* Connor *DG:* Connor
25 Jan	A	WP	Ebbw Vale	27-26	*T:* R Richards 2, R Phillips *C:* Connor 3 *PG:* Connor 2
1 Feb	-	CLF	Munster	17-37	*T:* A Jones *PG:* Jarvis 3 *DG:* Jarvis
5 Feb	A	WP	Newport	27-25	*T:* S Williams, R Phillips, Ringer *C:* Connor 3 *PG:* Jarvis, Connor
8 Feb	A	PC7	Glamorgan W	76-12	*T:* S Williams 4, R Phillips 2, K James 2, P James, Connor, A Jones, Tandy *C:* Connor 8
14 Feb	H	WP	Llanelli	25-7	*T:* Connor, S Williams, Tandy *C:* Connor 2 *PG:* Connor 2
28 Feb	A	WP	Cardiff	20-20	*T:* K James *PG:* Connor 5
12 Mar	H	WP	Cardiff	39-24	*T:* S Williams, Bateman, G Morris, Ringer, Connor, A Jones *C:* Connor 3 *PG:* Connor
15 Mar	H	WP	Caerphilly	67-14	*T:* Tiueti 2, S Williams, Durston, G Morris, Storey, Tandy, K James, Marsden *C:* Connor 4, Durston 4 *PG:* Connor *DG:* Connor
5 Apr	A	PCQF	Llanelli	17-49	*T:* Tiueti, G Morris *C:* Connor 2 *PG:* Connor

22 Apr	H	WP	Swansea	56-29	*T:* B Williams 2, Tiueti, Durston, K James, Connor, Horgan, M Jones *C:* Connor 5, M Jones 3
9 May	H	WP	Bridgend	32-24	*T:* S Williams 2 *C:* Connor 2 *PG:* Connor 6
13 May	A	WP	Pontypridd	47-23	*T:* Connor 2, Storey, P James, S Jones, Sinkinson, Mocelutu *C:* Connor 6
17 May	A	WP	Llanelli	25-27	*T:* Jarvis, Marsden, S Williams *C:* Jarvis, Connor *PG:* Jarvis 2
20 May	A	WP	Bridgend	13-22	*T:* S Williams *C:* Connor *PG:* Connor 2
23 May	H	WP	Newport	52-35	*T:* Carter 2, Connor, Durston, S Williams, B Williams, Peters, R Phillips *C:* Connor 6

Newport

Year of formation 1874
Ground Rodney Parade, Newport, Gwent NP9 0UU, Wales
Contacts Web: www blackandambers.net Tel: Newport (01633) 670690
Colours Black and amber stripes
Captain 2002-03 Simon Raiwalui
Welsh Premier 2002-03 4th
Principality Cup 2002-03 Lost 9-32 to Llanelli (FINAL)

Competition Record 2002-03

Date	*Venue*	*Comp*	*Opponents*	*Result*	*Scorers*
30 Aug	H	CL	Bridgend	5-13	*T:* Forster
7 Sep	A	CL	Pontypridd	16-21	*T:* Palmer *C:* Strange *PG:* Strange 2 *DG:* Strange
14 Sep	H	CL	Glasgow	25-31	*T:* Powell, Forster, Snow *C:* Strange 2 *PG:* Strange 2
20 Sep	A	CL	Connacht	12-18	*PG:* Howarth 4
28 Sep	H	CL	Cardiff	25-27	*T:* Pini *C:* Howarth *PG:* Howarth 5 *DG:* Tonu'u
4 Oct	A	CL	Leinster	14-42	*T:* Young *PG:* Strange 3
11 Oct	A	HC	Edinburgh	17-27	*T:* Tonu'u *PG:* Strange 4
18 Oct	H	HC	Toulouse	19-34	*T:* Forster *C:* Strange *PG:* Strange 4
26 Oct	H	CL	Borders	24-8	*T:* Luscombe, Ojomoh *C:* Howarth *PG:* Strange 4
29 Oct	H	WP	Caerphilly	36-10	*T:* Forster, pen try, Howarth, Gravell, Garvey *C:* Strange 4 *PG:* Strange
7 Dec	H	HC	London Irish	16-12	*T:* Forster *C:* Strange *PG:* Strange 3
15 Dec	A	HC	London Irish	5-41	*T:* Jones-Hughes
20 Dec	H	WP	Bridgend	12-13	*PG:* Strange 3, Howarth
26 Dec	A	WP	Llanelli	13-23	*T:* Snow *C:* Strange *PG:* Strange 2
1 Jan	H	WP	Cardiff	31-3	*T:* Forster, Voyle, Pritchard, Tonu'u *C:* Strange 4 *PG:* Strange
11 Jan	A	HC	Toulouse	18-70	*T:* Forster, Tonu'u *C:* Strange *PG:* Strange 2
18 Jan	H	HC	Edinburgh	42-32	*T:* Forster 2, Snow, Strange, Tonu'u *C:* Strange 4 *PG:* Strange 3
25 Jan	H	WP	Pontypridd	32-20	*T:* Mostyn 2, Tonu'u *C:* Montgomery *PG:* Montgomery 4 *DG:* Montgomery
1 Feb	A	WP	Ebbw Vale	37-15	*T:* Montgomery, Cadwallader, Tonu'u *C:* Montgomery 2 *PG:* Montgomery 5 *DG:* Montgomery
5 Feb	H	WP	Neath	25-27	*T:* Montgomery, Mostyn, Young *C:* Montgomery 2 *PG:* Montgomery 2
8 Feb	A	PC7	Bedwas	27-10	*T:* Mostyn, Jones-Hughes, pen try, Voyle *C:* Strange 2 *PG:* Strange

15 Mar	H	WP	Swansea	43-27	*T:* Montgomery 2, Jones-Hughes, Tonu'u, Raiwalui *C:* Strange 3 *PG:* Strange 3 *DG:* Strange
20 Mar	A	WP	Caerphilly	65-19	*T:* Forster 2, Mostyn 2, pen tries 2, Cadwallader, Veater *C:* Strange 4, Montgomery 4 *PG:* Strange 2, Montgomery
5 Apr	A	PCQF	Ebbw Vale	41-20	*T:* Nabaro 3, Forster 2, Snow *C:* Montgomery 4 *PG:* Montgomery
12 Apr	A	WP	Bridgend	30-56	*T:* Montgomery, Lane, Pritchard *C:* Montgomery 3 *PG:* Montgomery 3
19 Apr	-	PCSF	Bridgend	27-23	*PG:* Montgomery 9
22 Apr	H	WP	Llanelli	33-13	*T:* Cadwallader, Tonu'u, Raiwalui, S Williams *C:* Montgomery 2 *PG:* Montgomery 3
25 Apr	A	WP	Cardiff	17-39	*T:* Mostyn, Brew *C:* Strange 2 *PG:* Strange
4 May	-	PCF	Cardiff	9-32	*PG:* Montgomery 2 *DG:* Montgomery
6 May	A	WP	Pontypridd	30-25	*T:* Cadwallader, Marinos, Breeze *C:* Montgomery 3 *PG:* Montgomery 2, Strange
13 May	A	WP	Swansea	33-42	*T:* Jones-Hughes, Howarth, Breeze, Tonu'u, R Thomas *C:* Montgomery 3, Strange
17 May	H	WP	Ebbw Vale	61-9	*T:* Montgomery 2, Gravell 2, Mostyn, Cadwallader, Tonu'u, Snow *C:* Montgomery 5, Raiwalui *PG:* Montgomery 3
23 May	A	WP	Neath	35-52	*T:* Cadwallader, S Williams, Nabaro, Powell, Gravell *C:* Hook 3, Tonu'u 2

Pontypridd

Year of formation 1876
Ground Sardis Road Ground, Pwllgwaun, Pontypridd, CF37 1HA, Wales
Contacts Web: www.pontypriddrfc.co.uk Tel: Pontypridd (01443) 405006
Colours Black and white hoops
Captain 2002-03 Mefin Davies
Welsh Premier 2002-03 6th
Principality Cup 2002-03 Lost 18-20 to Cardiff (quarter-final)

Competition Record 2002-03

Date	*Venue*	*Comp*	*Opponents*	*Result*	*Scorers*
30 Aug	A	CL	Leinster	18-31	*T:* Bell, Kelly *C:* Davey *PG:* Davey 2
7 Sep	H	CL	Newport	21-16	*T:* Bryant, C Sweeney *C:* Davey *PG:* Davey 3
13 Sep	A	CL	Bridgend	26-9	*T:* Parks *PG:* N Jenkins 7
20 Sep	H	CL	Borders	28-27	*T:* Owen *C:* N Jenkins *PG:* N Jenkins 6 *DG:* N Jenkins
28 Sep	H	CL	Glasgow	34-28	*T:* Parker, C Sweeney, M Rees, Owen *C:* Davey 4 *PG:* Davey 2
5 Oct	A	CL	Connacht	40-0	*T:* Wyatt 2, E Lewis, Sidoli, Bryant *C:* N Jenkins 3 *PG:* N Jenkins 2 *DG:* Davies
12 Oct	A	PPC1	Roma	60-18	*T:* E Lewis 2, McIntosh 2, Parker 2, N Jenkins, G Lewis *C:* N Jenkins 7 *PG:* N Jenkins 2
19 Oct	H	PPC1	Roma	83-8	*T:* Wyatt 4, G Lewis 3, E Lewis 2, Nuthall, C Sweeney, Owen, S James *C:* C Sweeney 8, Wyatt
26 Oct	H	CL	Cardiff	15-9	*PG:* Davey 5
29 Nov	H	CLQF	Neath	12-13	*PG:* N Jenkins 4

7 Dec	H	PPC2	Leeds	37-23	*T:* Parker 2, Wyatt, Parks *C:* Davey *PG:* Davey 4 *DG:* C Sweeney
14 Dec	A	PPC2	Leeds	19-19	*T:* Davey *C:* Davey *PG:* Davey 4
21 Dec	H	WP	Cardiff	12-10	*PG:* N Jenkins 4
30 Dec	A	WP	Neath	29-20	*T:* Wyatt 2, Davey, Baber *C:* N Jenkins 3 *DG:* Davey
4 Jan	H	WP	Ebbw Vale	6-10	*PG:* Davey 2
11 Jan	A	PPCQF	Connacht	35-30	*T:* E Lewis, S James, G Lewis, Wyatt *C:* N Jenkins 2, Davey *PG:* N Jenkins 3
18 Jan	H	PPCQF	Connacht	12-9	*PG:* N Jenkins 4
25 Jan	A	WP	Newport	20-32	*T:* C Sweeney, Bell *C:* C Sweeney 2 *PG:* C Sweeney 2
8 Feb	A	PC7	Cross Keys	49-16	*T:* Wyatt 2, Davey, E Lewis, Baber, M Rees, McIntosh *C:* Davey 4 *PG:* Davey 2
21 Feb	H	WP	Caerphilly	47-8	*T:* Wyatt, Davey, John, James, Johnson *C:* Davey 4, John *PG:* Davey 4
28 Mar	A	WP	Llanelli	23-23	*T:* Parker, Baber *C:* N Jenkins 2 *PG:* N Jenkins 3
4 Apr	A	PCQF	Cardiff	18-20	*T:* M Owen, Baber *C:* Davey *PG:* N Jenkins 2
12 Apr	A	PPCSF	Wasps	19-34	*T:* C Sweeney *C:* Davey *PG:* Davey 4
19 Apr	A	WP	Swansea	31-36	*T:* Parks, Baber, Davey, M Davies *C:* N Jenkins 2, C Sweeney 2 *PG:* C Sweeney
25 Apr	H	PPCSF	Wasps	17-27	*T:* C Sweeney, Wyatt *C:* Davey 2 *PG:* Davey
29 Apr	H	WP	Swansea	42-14	*T:* Nuthall 2, S James 2, Parks, M Lewis *C:* N Jenkins 6
2 May	H	WP	Bridgend	7-33	*T:* Bryant *C:* Davey
6 May	H	WP	Newport	25-30	*T:* G Lewis, pen try, Davies *C:* N Jenkins 2 *PG:* N Jenkins 2
9 May	A	WP	Ebbw Vale	6-25	*PG:* C Sweeney *DG:* C Sweeney
13 May	H	WP	Neath	23-47	*T:* Wyatt, Fussell *C:* N Jenkins 2 *PG:* N Jenkins 3
17 May	A	WP	Caerphilly	17-15	*T:* John, M Rees *C:* N Jenkins 2 *PG:* N Jenkins
21 May	H	WP	Llanelli	29-24	*T:* S James, Fussell *C:* N Jenkins 2 *PG:* N Jenkins 4 *DG:* N Jenkins
24 May	A	WP	Bridgend	32-33	*T:* Bell, Fussell *C:* N Jenkins 2 *PG:* N Jenkins 6
30 May	A	WP	Cardiff	21-30	*T:* Davey, S James, Fussell *C:* N Jenkins 3

Swansea

Year of formation 1873
Ground St Helen's Ground, Bryn Road, Swansea, West Glamorgan SA2 0AR, Wales
Contacts Web: www.swansearfc.co.uk Tel: Swansea (01792) 424242
Colours All white
Captain 2002-03 Scott Gibbs/Darren Morris
Welsh Premier 2002-03 7th
Principality Cup 2002-03 Lost 25-48 to Bridgend (quarter-final)

Competition Record 2002-03

Date	*Venue*	*Comp*	*Opponents*	*Result*	*Scorers*
30 Aug	A	CL	Edinburgh	20-30	*T:* K Morgan, Payne *C:* Henson, A Thomas *PG:* A Thomas 2
6 Sep	H	CL	Neath	16-20	*T:* Winn *C:* A Thomas *PG:* Henson 3
14 Sep	H	CL	Ulster	38-10	*T:* K Morgan, Payne, Gibbs, M Robinson *C:* A Thomas 3 *PG:* A Thomas 4

20 Sep	A	CL	Munster	27-38	*T:* Winn, A Thomas, Charvis, Henson *C:* A Thomas 2 *DG:* A Thomas
28 Sep	H	CL	Caerphilly	37-32	*T:* Payne 2, A Thomas, Cordingley *C:* A Thomas 4 *PG:* A Thomas 3
4 Oct	A	CL	Llanelli	6-62	*PG:* A Thomas 2
12 Oct	A	HC	Montferrand	12-47	*PG:* Henson 4
19 Oct	H	HC	Leinster	10-51	*T:* Winn *C:* A Thomas *PG:* A Thomas
26 Oct	H	CL	Ebbw Vale	33-20	*T:* Vaughan, Brayley, Farley *C:* A Thomas 3 *PG:* A Thomas 2 *DG:* A Thomas 2
29 Oct	A	WP	Ebbw Vale	13-16	*T:* R Jenkins *C:* A Thomas *PG:* A Thomas 2
7 Dec	H	HC	Bristol	26-19	*T:* Charvis, M Robinson *C:* A Thomas 2 *PG:* Henson 2, A Thomas *DG:* Henson
15 Dec	A	HC	Bristol	23-41	*T:* Henson, Farley, A Thomas *C:* A Thomas *PG:* Henson, A Thomas
21 Dec	A	WP	Caerphilly	20-19	*T:* Gibbs, A Thomas *C:* A Thomas 2 *PG:* A Thomas 2
27 Dec	H	WP	Neath	23-14	*T:* Evans, Henson *C:* A Thomas, Henson *PG:* A Thomas *DG:* Henson 2
30 Dec	H	WP	Bridgend	9-16	*PG:* Henson 3
3 Jan	A	WP	Llanelli	23-45	*T:* Taylor, Robinson *C:* Henson 2 *PG:* Henson 3
10 Jan	A	HC	Leinster	19-48	*T:* Henson *C:* Henson *PG:* Henson 3 *DG:* Henson
18 Jan	H	HC	Montferrand	19-24	*T:* Winn *C:* A Thomas *PG:* A Thomas 4
24 Jan	H	WP	Cardiff	19-32	*T:* Henson *C:* Henson *PG:* A Thomas 4
7 Feb	A	PC7	Caerphilly	46-21	*T:* Vaughton, Gibbs, Payne, A Thomas, R Jenkins *C:* Henson 2, A Thomas *PG:* Henson 5
1 Mar	H	WP	Ebbw Vale	21-17	*T:* R Jones, Winn *C:* Henson *PG:* Henson 3
15 Mar	A	WP	Newport	27-43	*T:* M Robinson, Payne, Dorsey, Cordingley *C:* A Thomas 2 *PG:* A Thomas
5 Apr	A	PCQF	Bridgend	25-48	*T:* Swales, Payne, Winn *C:* Henson 2 *PG:* Henson 2
12 Apr	A	WP	Cardiff	22-44	*T:* Pugh 2, Swales *C:* Swales 2 *PG:* Swales
19 Apr	H	WP	Pontypridd	36-31	*T:* Pugh 2, Swales, Taylor, J Griffiths *C:* Henson 4 *PG:* Henson
22 Apr	A	WP	Neath	29-56	*T:* A Thomas 2, R Rees, Swales *C:* A Thomas 3 *PG:* A Thomas
26 Apr	A	WP	Bridgend	21-49	*T:* A Thomas, Winn *C:* A Thomas *PG:* A Thomas 3
29 Apr	A	WP	Pontypridd	14-42	*T:* R Sweeney 2 *C:* R Sweeney 2
6 May	H	WP	Caerphilly	31-42	*T:* Mackey, Wright, T Evans, Brayley *C:* A Thomas 4 *PG:* A Thomas
10 May	H	WP	Llanelli	52-40	*T:* R Sweeney 3, Payne 2, Swales *C:* R Sweeney 5 *PG:* R Sweeney 3, A Thomas
13 May	H	WP	Newport	42-33	*T:* R Sweeney, Swales, Farley, T Evans, G Evans, Balshen *C:* R Sweeney 6

FLAGSHIP LLANELLI MAKE IT CUP NO 12: THE PRINCIPALITY CUP

John Billot

3 May 2003, Millennium Stadium, Cardiff Arms Park
Llanelli 32 (3G 2PG 1T) **Newport 9** (2PG 1DG)

It was never going to be a memorable final. No-one gave Newport a chance against Llanelli, the flagship club of Welsh rugby and, sure enough, a second half broadside of three tries doomed the Black-and-Ambers. The Stradey men completed their record 12th WRU Cup triumph in their 17th final, but it was a wearing exercise before they imposed their will against a pugnacious pack who employed muscle and bustle with grim intent.

The Newport backs had been criticised caustically after their semi-final success by nine penalty goals and not a try in sight against Ebbw Vale. Coach Leigh Jones, resentful of the acerbic comments, doggedly defended his side. Alas, their performance in the final served only to vindicate the critics: Newport again failed to produce a try and only the classy Percy Montgomery looked the part. He hit all their points once more with a superb drop-shot and two penalty goals. In medieval times, Percy would have been Lord of the Manor, riding his warhorse to battle ahead of his serfs!

Gareth Jenkins, the Llanelli coach, admitted his team found it extremely difficult to break the stranglehold as their opponents dominated the lineout and generally caused innumerable problems. 'It was a difficult first 65 minutes,' he recalled. But Newport blunders enabled the Scarlets to shake off the chains.

The Rodney Parade team were leading 9-3 when Shane Howarth's inside pass to Montgomery was intercepted by David Hodges, who sent Mark Jones pelting some 70 metres. Stephen Jones converted and his team led 10-9 with no way back for Newport. Salesi Finau stampeded past Howarth's intended tackle and put Mark Jones across again. Then Leigh Davies's hint of a dummy opened the way for his try before impact replacement Finau powered over for the fourth. Stephen Jones finished with three conversions and a couple of penalty goals and 27,000 watchers accepted the inevitable. Fittingly, the Scarlets, acknowledged as kings of the Cup, won it for the last time by the leading Welsh professional clubs, who figure in a new structure in 2003-04.

Llanelli: B Davies; M Jones, M Watkins, L Davies (*captain*), G Evans; S Jones, G Easterby; I Thomas, R McBryde, J Davies, V Cooper, C Wyatt, D Hodges, S Quinnell, S Easterby *Substitutions:* L Gross for Wyatt (temp 52 to 59 mins); I Boobyer for Cooper (temp 58 to 59 mins) and for S Easterby (83 mins); M Madden for J Davies (61 mins); S Finau for B Davies (61 mins); D Peel for G Easterby (80 mins)

Scorers *Tries:* M Jones (2), L Davies, Finau *Conversions:* S Jones (3) *Penalty Goals:* S Jones (2)

Newport: P Montgomery; M Mostyn, J Jones-Hughes, J Pritchard, A Cadwallader; S Howarth, O Tonu'u; R Snow, P Young, C Anthony, S Raiwalui (*captain*), M Voyle, I Gough, S Ojomoh, J Forster *Substitutions:* J Richards for Young (temp 43-54 mins and 80 mins); A Garvey for Anthony (63 mins); N Brew for Jones-Hughes (68 mins); M Veater for Voyle (70 mins); J Strange for Howarth (73 mins); D Llewellyn for Tonu'u (80 mins); R Jones for Ojomoh (80 mins)
Scorer *Penalty Goals:* Montgomery (2) *Dropped Goal:* Montgomery
Referee N Williams (WRU)

Earlier rounds

Llanelli's route to the final began worryingly at Pontypool when the Premier Division clubs entered the fray in the seventh round. All the major clubs had compulsory away ties and the perils of Pontypool Park were all too evident. The home side were undefeated on their patch and had lost only two of 23 Cup and League fixtures. So the Scarlets had drawn the short straw and other clubs breathed cumulative sighs of relief that the task had not befallen them. Wales coach Steve Hansen compounded Llanelli's concern when he insisted none of his national squad would be released for Cup duty. Coach Gareth Jenkins was outraged. England and Ireland did not impose such restrictions on their clubs and Jenkins would be without 13 of his best players, including injury victims. He furiously denounced the decision.

'Not to be able to select the players we want will be devastating,' he grumbled. 'We all know what happened to Swansea up there last year [Pontypool dispatched the visitors by 16-14]. I believe Premier Division clubs need to be able to select the side they feel appropriate for Cup games.' Later, having expressed his extreme displeasure, Jenkins reluctantly agreed to Hansen's demands. The Llanelli coach saw his team forge away in the second half to win by 30-22. Hooker Marcus Thomas unzipped from a close-up maul to register the Scarlets' fourth, and his second, try to ensure the anxiety factor was overcome. However, Jenkins stressed that future ties be arranged with more awareness of mutual requirements.

Next up were Neath in the quarter-final at Stradey, success by an impressive 49-17 margin and a wolfish appetite to swallow Cardiff in very short order in the semi-final. Cardiff's abysmal season included this grisly fate as one of its lowest points: Llanelli inflicted their rivals' heaviest ever Cup reverse by 44-10. Pieter Müller and Rhys Williams produced attractive tries; but Llanelli swamped them with six: Barry Davies, Stephen Jones, Garan Evans, Mark Jones, Leigh Davies and Matthew J Watkins. Stephen Jones added 14 goal points.

The other semi-final (they were both played at the Millennium Stadium) had little to recommend it as a vehicle for entertainment. Percy Montgomery, the former Springbok, fired over nine penalty goals in nine attempts and Newport, showing neither a cutting edge nor vision, were winners by 27-23 after the lead had changed seven times. Bridgend scored the tries: smartly-crafted attacks saw Craig Warlow and captain Gareth Thomas cross; Gareth Cull converted both tries and hit three penalty shots. Ironically, Bridgend had seen off the Black-and-Ambers in three previous meetings during the season, including a swingeing verdict by 56-30 a week earlier at the Brewery Field. Sharing Cardiff's distress, captain Gareth Thomas lamented, 'We did not perform. We are a much better team than that.'

Pontypridd, the holders, were fancied to squeeze through with their pugnacious pack in the quarter-final at Cardiff because the home team's forward fragility always made them vulnerable. Five players served time in the sin-bin with Cardiff directing a 13-man operation for a while. Brett Davey, offered a last-gasp penalty chance to steal the game from some optimistic 60 metres, missed and Cardiff went through by 20-18. A try hat-trick by Hong Kong international Luke Nabaro, on the wing, enabled Newport to triumph 41-20 in their quarter at Ebbw Vale while Bridgend's six tries pounded desperate Swansea by 48-25.

It was too close for comfort for Ebbw Vale at Carmarthen Quins before they scraped through their quarter by 13-8 after Bryan Shelbourne's 40 metres penalty goal compelled extra time; whereupon flanker Paul Williams peeled from a rolling maul for the decisive try. Shane Williams went in for four tries in trademark electric fashion as Neath accounted for Glamorgan Wanderers by 76-12 in their quarter tie.

The sixth round conjured up a fright for Pontypool at Maesteg as the Old Parish outscored Pooler by 4-2 on tries until the visitors stole the decision by 23-22; and Carmarthen Quins ended the hopes of high-riding Aberavon by 13-12 to put a smart stopper on the Wizards' sequence of 13 successes. Shocks and sensations are the very essence of Cup competitions and long may they continue.

Results

Fifth round: Aberavon 93, Abertillery 0; Beddau 9, Merthyr 6; Blackwood 13, Cross Keys 15; Bonymaen 39, Llangennech 5; Carmarthen Quins w/o Brynmawr; Hirwaun 9, Maesteg 18; Llandovery 54, Pill Harriers 6; Llanharan 17, Tondu 15; Nantymoel 12, Taffs Well 8; Newbridge 54, Rumney 5; Penygraig 17, Narberth 26; Pontypool 66, Cwmavon 16; Tredegar 8, Bedwas 23; Treorchy 7, Glamorgan Wanderers 41; Whitland 14, Banwen 7.

Sixth round: Bedwas 33, Nantymoel 12; Bonymaen 22, Beddau 8; Carmarthen Quins 13, Aberavon 12; Cross Keys 25, Whitland 18; Glamorgan Wanderers 28, Llanharan 10; Llandovery 22, Caerphilly 35; Maesteg 22, Pontypool 23; Narberth 15, Newbridge 34.

Seventh round: Bedwas 10, Newport 27; Bonymaen 16, Cardiff 41; Caerphilly 21, Swansea 46; Carmarthen Quins 8, Ebbw Vale 13 (*aet*); Cross Keys 16, Pontypridd 49; Glamorgan Wanderers 12, Neath 76; Newbridge 8, Bridgend 39; Pontypool 22, Llanelli 30.

Quarter-finals: Bridgend 48, Swansea 25; Cardiff 20, Pontypridd 18; Ebbw Vale 20, Newport 41; Llanelli 49, Neath 17.

Semi-finals: (at the Millennium Stadium) Llanelli 44, Cardiff 10; Newport 27, Bridgend 23.

FINAL: (at Millennium Stadium) Llanelli 32, Newport 9.

Previous WRU Cup Finals: 1972 Neath 15, Llanelli 9; 1973 Llanelli 30, Cardiff 7; 1974 Llanelli 12, Aberavon 10; 1975 Llanelli 15, Aberavon 6; 1976 Llanelli 16, Swansea 4; 1977 Newport 16, Cardiff 15; 1978 Swansea 13, Newport 9; 1979 Bridgend 18, Pontypridd 12; 1980 Bridgend 15, Swansea 9; 1981 Cardiff 14, Bridgend 6; 1982 Cardiff 12, Bridgend 12 (Cardiff won on most tries rule); 1983 Pontypool 18, Swansea 6; 1984 Cardiff 24, Neath 19; 1985 Llanelli 15, Cardiff 14; 1986 Cardiff 28, Newport 21; 1987 Cardiff 16, Swansea 15; 1988 Llanelli 28, Neath 13; 1989 Neath 14, Llanelli 13; 1990 Neath 16, Bridgend 10; 1991 Llanelli 24, Pontypool 9; 1992 Llanelli 16, Swansea 7; 1993 Llanelli 21, Neath 18; 1994 Cardiff 15, Llanelli 8; 1995 Swansea 17, Pontypridd 12; 1996 Pontypridd 29, Neath 22; 1997 Cardiff 33, Swansea 26; 1998 Llanelli 19, Ebbw Vale 12; 1999 Swansea 37, Llanelli 10; 2000 Llanelli 22, Swansea 12; 2001 Newport 13, Neath 8; 2002 Pontypridd 20, Llanelli 17; 2003 Llanelli 32, Newport 9.

Played at Cardiff Arms Park 1972-1997; at Ashton Gate, Bristol 1998; at Ninian Park, Cardiff 1999; at the Millennium Stadium since 2000.

DOMESTIC RUGBY IN FRANCE 2002-03

Fairy-tale end for Galthié

Ian Borthwick

7 June 2003, Stade de France, Paris
Stade Français 32 (2G 6PG) **Stade Toulousain 18** (6PG)

With the French capital in the grips of political turmoil, general strikes and a heat-wave, more than ever this final between the two 'Stades' became a symbol, redolent of French rugby's historic anti-establishment, anti-conformist, anti-Paris heritage. Billed as a contest between Paris and 'la Province', between the aristocrats from rugby's heartland and the up-starts from the capital, between a club which this season broke all French records for attendance in both championship and European Cup games, and the ambitious Parisians who, despite all the glitz and the innovative marketing by their president Max Guazzini, continually struggle to attract spectators to their modest ground at the Porte d'Auteuil, it was all of that.

But it was also, and above all, a fairy-tale ending to a long and sometimes chequered career for the Stade Français scrum-half, and current French captain, Fabien Galthié. At 34 years of age, and after 17 seasons of First Division rugby, Galthié was playing his first championship final. And his last club game ever. 'I have never touched the Bouclier de Brennus, never even been anywhere near it,' he said, dewy-eyed, in the build-up.

As it turned out, Galthié not only touched the mythical Brennus shield for the first time, brandishing it in triumph before 75,000 people at Stade de France, but he was also the most influential player on the field. He scored a nifty individual try, figured several times in Ignacio Corleto's superb try which took the score to 26-15 twelve minutes into the second half, and continually marshalled his players, directing the game with consummate artistry.

Despite Diego Dominguez's opening penalty for Paris after only two minutes, Toulouse dominated the tense opening exchanges, playing percentage rugby and relying on their kickers, especially Frédéric Michalak who slotted two penalties from over 50 metres, to keep the score ticking over. Toulouse went out to a 15-6 lead after 33 minutes, but Dominguez added a third penalty (15-9), before Galthié's try, slicing through the defence from a ruck close to the line, gave Paris the lead (16-15) just before half-time.

In the second half, Toulouse clearly started to fade as the accumulated fatigue of their victory in the European Cup final two weeks earlier, followed by the gruelling semi-final against Agen played in 35 degree heat in Montpellier, began to take its toll. The Parisians on the other hand, encouraged by the success of their impenetrable defence, moved into top gear.

Brian Liebenberg, the South African centre, kicked a monster penalty from 58 metres to increase the lead, before sparking a scintillating Parisian attack in the 52nd minute. Liebenberg chipped over the Toulouse defence, regathered the ball and passed inside to prop Sylvain Marconnet who then fed Stéphane Glas on the outside. Christophe Dominici chimed in, then fed Canadian lock Mike James thundering up-field like a winger before cutting inside and running into the defence. From the ensuing ruck, Galthié had another dab, Dominguez carried on the movement, then Galthié fired a long cut-out pass to Argentinean full-back Ignacio Corleto who beat three defenders to score. Dominguez converted to put the Parisians 26-15 ahead, and for the first time the ubiquitous Toulouse drums were drowned out by the chants of 'Paris! Paris!' from the other end of the ground.

Paris, determined to see their scrum-half and sometime captain Galthié bow out in a blaze of glory, now held a vice grip on the match. The control, discipline and pragmatism drilled into them by their coach, South African Nick Mallett, took over and while Toulouse threw everything into the final minutes, Paris kept their cool, Dominguez adding two further penalties to one from Michalak from close range, for a final score of 32-18. Former Springbok coach Mallett, whose language skills were a definite plus after the unsuccessful experiment with John Connolly, thus became the first 'foreign' coach to win a French championship. But it was Galthié's night and the tearful French captain ended the evening by exhorting the Parisian crowd to come and support Stade Français next year. 'We need you,' he announced on the PA system. 'Because we are going to turn this into a great club, and we are going to give the kids in Paris something to dream about!'

For the Parisians it was their third championship title in the club's spectacular return to the top flight of French rugby in the late 1990s. Toulouse, meanwhile, have now featured in eight of the past 13 finals.

Stade Français: I Corleto; C Dominici, S Glas, B Liebenberg, T Lombard; D Dominguez, F Galthié (*captain*); S Marconnet, B August, P de Villiers, D Auradou, M James, R Jéchoux, P Tabacco, P Rabadan *Substitutions:* R Martin for Jéchoux (46 mins); M Blin for August (46 mins); P Lemoine for Marconnet (62 mins); C Mytton for Glas (79 mins); A Gomès for Lombard (82 mins); J Fillol for Galthié (82 mins); L Marchois for James (82 mins)

Scorers *Tries:* Galthié, Corleto *Conversions:* Dominguez (2) *Penalty Goals:* Dominguez (5), Liebenberg

Toulouse: C Poitrenaud; E Ntamack (*captain*), X Garbajosa, Y Jauzion, V Clerc; Y Delaigue, F Michalak; P Collazo, Y Bru, B Lecouls, D Gérard, F Pelous, T Brennan, C Labit, J Bouilhou *Substitutions:* J-B Poux for Collazo (41 mins); J-B Elissalde for Delaigue (55 mins); G Lamboley for Gérard (55 mins); W Servat for Bru (55 mins); C Heymans for Ntamack (64 mins); F Maka for Brennan (66 mins); C Desbrosse for Jauzion (75 mins)

Scorers *Penalty Goals:* Michalak (4), Delaigue (2)

Referee J Dumé (FFR)

French Championship Round-Up

The obstacle course that is the French Championship, nowadays known as 'le Top 16', once again proved to be a gruelling test of endurance for France's major clubs in 2002-03, and while Stade Français and Stade Toulousain battled their way through to the final, a number of other contenders fell by the way-side. One of the principal victims was the high-profile Montferrand club, stacked full of internationals such as Olivier Magne, Olivier Brouzet, Aurélien Rougerie, Tony Marsh, David Bory, and Gérald Merceron, plus former Wallaby Troy Jaques and Englishman Richard Cockerill. Despite this impressive line-up and no expense being spared by the sponsors-cum-owners, tyre giants Michelin, Montferrand had the misfortune of losing the second game of the season at home to Biarritz, a set-back from which they never recovered.

The formula of the Top-16 means that to have a chance of qualifying for 'les Play-Offs', teams have to win all their home games, plus try and win the odd one 'à l'exterieur'. Montferrand, however, then went on to lose at Castres, and draw at Bègles, but the final straw was when they lost the final round at home to minnows Grenoble. Finalists in 1999 and 2001, Montferrand failed to make the cut, and with the team despatched to the relegation pool ('les Play Down'), the club was thrown into turmoil: long-time director of rugby Christophe Mombet was sacked, along with Aussie coach Scott Wiesmantel, while star player Olivier Magne was suspended for careless use of the tongue, after openly criticising the club's officials on TV.

Biarritz and Agen became the first clubs qualified for the next season's European (Heineken) Cup when they finished first of their respective pools in the first phase of the championship, while Toulouse and Stade Français came in at second place. Perpignan also had a successful season, finishing third in their pool, but despite making it through to the European Cup final (or more likely, because of it), the Catalans failed to make an impact in the final phases of the domestic championship.

Meanwhile, the fortunes of Colomiers, club finalists in 2000 and European Cup finalists in 1999, continued to decline, and like Castres, they narrowly missed being relegated to the Second Division for 2003-04.

There was good news, however, for former European champions Brive who, after playing two Heineken Cup finals in 1997 and 1998, had just spent two seasons in the Second Division. With veteran fly-half Alain Penaud still at the helm, however, the men from the Correze clawed their way back into the Top 16, being promoted from the Second Division along with newcomers Montpellier.

They take the place of the two clubs relegated from the Top-16, both of which have a proud history in French rugby: Mont-de-Marsan, the club which produced André Boniface, Christian Darrouy and Thomas Castaignède, and Béziers, the giant who dominated French rugby in the 1970s.

French Championship: Le Top 16 2002-03 First Phase

Pool 1

	P	*W*	*D*	*L*	*For*	*Against*	*Pts*
1 Biarritz	14	10	0	4	347	273	34
2 Stade Français	14	9	1	4	306	241	33
3 Bourgoin	14	7	1	6	314	290	29
4 Grenoble	14	7	0	7	305	266	28
5 Montferrand	14	6	1	7	279	238	27
6 Bordeaux-Bègles	14	5	1	8	273	317	25
7 Castres	14	4	2	8	303	372	24
8 Montauban	14	4	2	8	228	358	24

Pool 2

	P	*W*	*D*	*L*	*For*	*Against*	*Pts*
1 Agen	14	12	0	2	359	198	38
2 Toulouse	14	11	1	2	402	236	37
3 Perpignan	14	8	0	6	326	208	30
4 Pau	14	6	2	6	307	317	28
5 Narbonne	14	6	1	7	282	330	27
6 Colomiers	14	5	0	9	227	345	24
7 Béziers	14	3	1	10	281	351	21
8 Mont-de-Marsan	14	2	1	11	208	407	19

French Championship: Le Top 16 2002-03 Second Phase – Les Play-Offs

POOL A

POOL A	*P*	*W*	*D*	*L*	*For*	*Against*	*Pts*
1 Biarritz	6	4	0	2	157	132	14
2 Toulouse	6	4	0	2	218	199	14
3 Bourgoin	6	3	0	3	195	141	12
4 Pau	6	1	0	5	149	247	8

POOL B

POOL B	*P*	*W*	*D*	*L*	*For*	*Against*	*Pts*
1 Stade Français	6	5	0	1	167	111	16
2 Agen	6	4	0	2	142	121	14
3 Perpignan	6	2	0	4	119	136	10
4 Grenoble	6	1	0	5	127	187	8

French Championship: Le Top 16 2002-03 Second Phase - Les Play-Downs

	P	*W*	*D*	*L*	*For*	*Against*	*Pts*
1 Montferrand	22	10	3	9	521	404	45
2 Narbonne	22	10	1	11	494	575	43
3 Montauban	22	9	2	11	440	544	42
4 Castres	22	8	2	12	545	579	40
5 Bordeaux-Bègles	22	8	1	13	516	522	39
6 Colomiers	22	8	1	13	404	573	39
7 Béziers	22	7	1	14	471	574	37
8 Mont-de-Marsan	22	5	2	15	393	650	34

Points: 3 for a win; 2 for a draw; 1 for a defeat

Results

Semi-finals: Stade Français 32, Biarritz 9; Toulouse 22, Agen 16

FINAL: (at Stade de France, Paris) Stade Français 32, Toulouse 18

Relegated To Pro D2 for 2003-04

Béziers, Mont-de-Marsan

Promoted For 2003-2004

Brive; Montpellier

Recent French Championship Finals: 1972 Béziers 9, Brive 0; 1973 Tarbes 18, Dax 12; 1974 Béziers16, Narbonne 14; 1975 Béziers 13, Brive 12; 1976 Agen 13, Béziers10; 1977 Béziers 12, Perpignan 4; 1978 Béziers 31, Montferrand 9; 1979 Narbonne 10, Bagnères 0; 1980 Béziers 10, Toulouse 6; 1981 Béziers 22, Bagnères 13; 1982 Agen 18, Bayonne 9; 1983 Béziers 14, Nice 6; 1984 Béziers 21, Agen 21; 1985 Toulouse 36, Toulon 22; 1986 Toulouse 16, Agen 6; 1987 Toulon 15, RCF 12; 1988 Agen 9, Tarbes 3; 1989 Toulouse 18, Toulon 12; 1990 RCF 22, Agen 12; 1991 Bègles-Bordeaux 19, Toulouse 10; 1992 Toulon 19, Biarritz 14; 1993 Castres 14, Grenoble 11; 1994 Toulouse 22, Montferrand 16; 1995 Toulouse 31, Castres 16; 1996 Toulouse 20, Brive 13; 1997 Toulouse 12, Bourgoin-Jallieu 6; 1998 Stade Français 34, Perpignan 7; 1999 Toulouse 15, Montferrand 11; 2000 Stade Français 28, Colomiers 23; 2001 Toulouse 34, Montferrand 22; 2002 Biarritz 25, Agen 22; 2003 Stade Français 32, Toulouse 18

DOMESTIC RUGBY IN ITALY 2002-03

Calvisano and Treviso Head the Italian Club Scene

Giampaolo Tassinari

For the first time since the introduction of the play-off system in 1988, Benetton Treviso were not favourites to win the title. Instead, it was predicted to be Calvisano's year. During the pre-season, the Lombard club had shown its hand with a summer of shrewd signings which saw the arrival of several key players. These included Nanni Raineri at centre, the South Africans Chean Roux and Wayne Boardman, and the mercurial outside-half Gerard Fraser from New Zealand. With a new coach in the Frenchman Gilbert Doucet, the hopes of the club were running high.

The first part of the Super Ten league featured twelve rounds before there was a two-month break for the Six Nations Tournament. In these opening rounds Calvisano confirmed all the predictions by winning their matches handsomely and scoring plenty of tries thanks to a much improved pack led by Italy's Giampiero de Carli and supported by fellow front-rankers Leandro Castrogiovanni and Andrea Moretti.

Only Benetton Treviso could keep pace with Calvisano, despite the former having many internationals involved in the autumn's Tests. However, the great revelation was Gr A N Parma, brilliantly coached by the former Italian prop Stefano Romagnoli. The club plays in the small village of Noceto and is the lesser known of the two Parma clubs, but they surprised many opponents with a very strong pack that was backed by the superb kicking game of South African Rouan Nel.

This was in contrast to the disappointing performances of Petrarca Padova and Parma FC. Petrarca Padova had many internal problems with players which led the coach Giuseppe Artuso to resign at the end of 2002 after a heavy defeat by Gr A N Parma. He was replaced by the Argentine-born Rodolfo Ambrosio. Parma FC, who were being coached for the second year running by former Springbok Dawie Snyman, featured in several disappointing matches despite an influx of new faces during the summer. This led to great disillusion among their supporters and administrators.

At the beginning of April, the League resumed its final six rounds and matters changed dramatically. Petrarca Padova began a relentless race to achieve the seemingly impossible task of taking the fourth and last place for the play-offs behind Calvisano, Benetton and Viadana.

The long break worked against Gr A N Parma, who lost their earlier confidence as the round-robin stage reached its conclusion. Although Petrarca Padova lost to Rovigo in the penultimate round, they still had a point more than each of the Parma clubs before the last round of League matches. Then, in front of their supporters at the Stadio Plebiscito, Petrarca Padova defeated Gr A N Parma to qualify for the play-offs.

Super 10 Standings

	P	*W*	*D*	*L*	*For*	*Against*	*Bonus*	*Pts*
Amatori & Calvisano	18	16	0	2	635	311	11	75
Benetton Treviso	18	15	0	3	710	322	13	73
Viadana	18	12	0	6	560	409	12	60
Petrarca Padova	18	9	1	8	485	406	10	48
Rugby Parma FC	18	9	1	8	429	440	5	43
Gr A N Parma	18	9	0	9	435	367	7	43
Rovigo	18	6	0	12	356	455	7	31
L'Aquila	18	5	1	12	349	571	6	28
Rugby Roma	18	4	0	14	304	747	4	20
Silea	18	3	1	14	302	537	5	19

Points: Win 4; draw 2; four or more tries, or defeat by seven or fewer points 1

Knockout stages

Calvisano and Benetton easily won their respective semi-finals to reach the final. The Lombard XV, having won both ties against Petrarca Padova in the round-robin, had to work much harder to win the first leg in Padua.

Their opponents' strong defence contained Calvisano's expansive tactics, but in the final quarter the visitors were well ahead by 16-3 thanks to Fraser's three penalties and a try scored by Raineri which Fraser converted. Only a penalty by the Samoan Ngapaku Ngapaku and a try by former Puma wing Facundo Soler in the dying minutes gave more respectability to the home team's score. But in the second leg, the black and yellows outplayed and out-muscled Petrarca Padova's forwards, scoring three tries as well as missing many others.

In the other semi-final, Benetton suffered a controversial loss at Viadana in the first leg despite dominating for most of the game. However at Monigo in the return tie, Benetton made sure of their place in the final thanks to former NSW Waratahs full-back Brendan Williams, who scored four tries in a match that Viadana hardly contested.

Play-off semi-finals:

First legs (17 May)

Petrarca Padova 13 (*Try:* Soler *Conversion:* Ngapaku *Penalty Goals:* Ngapaku 2), **Amatori & Calvisano 16** (*Try:* Raineri *Conversion:* Fraser *Penalty Goals:* Fraser 3)

Viadana 28 (*Tries:* Benatti, Phillips, Denhardt *Conversions:* Steyn 2 *Penalty Goals:* Steyn 3), **Benetton Treviso 26** (*Tries:* Williams, Palmer *Conversions:* Mason 2 *Penalty Goals:* Mason 4)

Second legs (24 May)

Amatori & Calvisano 31 (*Tries:* Raineri, Fraser, De Rossi *Conversions:* Fraser 2 *Penalty Goals:* Fraser 4), **Petrarca Padova 10** (*Try:* Ngapaku *Conversion:* Ngapaku *Penalty Goal:* Ngapaku); **Benetton Treviso 40** (*Tries:* Williams 4, Smith *Conversions:* Mason 3 *Penalty Goals:* Mason 3), **Viadana 15** (*Tries:* Jimenez, Persico *Conversion:* Goosen *Penalty Goal:* Goosen)

Championship Final

31 May, 2003, Stadio del Plebiscito, Padua
Benetton Treviso 34 (1G 4PG 3T) **Amatori & Calvisano 12** (4PG)

In the week leading up to the final, the question everyone was asking was would Benetton Treviso be able to halt the triumphant march of Calvisano towards their first and historic Scudetto? All the omens and predictions indicated that the title would go to Gilbert Doucet's men.

Indeed, in the first quarter of the match, played in front of 9,100 spectators, all went well. Yellow-and-black jerseys were regularly on the attack, putting plenty of pressure on the outsiders from Treviso. Calvisano opened a 6-0 lead in the first ten minutes with two successful penalties from the golden boot of Gerard Fraser and created several scoring opportunities, but Treviso showed their steely character to withstand the early onslaught.

The white-and-green hooped jerseys were prepared to put their bodies on the line in defence and Calvisano were unable to convert their pressure into points. The interval score was still in Calvisano's favour, but only by a three-point margin at 9-6: Fraser, Simon Mason and Franco Smith (who took over kicking duties when Mason retired hurt) having landed penalty goals.

Before half-time the match was marred by an awkward foul by Calvisano's wing Apenisa Tuta Vodo on Benetton's full-back Mason, who had to be replaced immediately. This rather tarnished a contest which had been played fiercely but fairly until that incident.

After the interval Benetton's approach radically changed. The momentum swung Treviso's way and with only eight minutes gone Kiwi-born Scott Palmer scored a pushover try to put his side ahead for the first time in the match. Calvisano disputed the try and their scrum-half Paul Griffen decided to make his thoughts known to referee Giulio de Santis who immediately issued the player with his marching orders.

Reduced to fourteen men for the remainder of the final, Calvisano were no longer serious contenders, although the score remained 9-11 with more than thirty minutes to play. They became nervous and irritable whereas Treviso grew in courage, inner calm and strength. Two more Franco Smith penalties stretched Benetton's lead to 17-9 before the only points scored by Calvisano in the second half materialised from a penalty by Fraser on the hour mark.

From that moment on it was one-way traffic. Benetton's forwards were driving at will, launching attacks whenever they wished. Half-back duo Alessandro Troncon and former Springbok Franco Smith called the shots almost free of pressure, and in the last quarter three more tries gave Treviso their tenth national title. Two were scored by centre Manuel Dallan with remarkable runs that stunned their discouraged opponents. The last try was scored by young No 8 Sergio Parisse in injury time with a burst from a ruck that took him over the line.

Experience, nerves of steel and patience were the key factors for this Benetton victory. Calvisano lacked character and never imposed their tactics as they had in their previous 20 matches. Their president Alessandro Manzoni resigned after the final, protesting against Griffen's dismissal by referee Giulio de Santis. 'After all those sacrifices in the last three years,' he said, 'we cannot lose a match through a bad refereeing decision against us.'

For Treviso it was a deserved win, although star Mauro Bergamasco was used only in the final quarter. It was also Alessandro Moscardi's last match, for after a brief stint in South African rugby, he finally drew the line under his distinguished playing career.

Benetton Treviso: S Mason; D Dallan, T Visentin, M Dallan, B Williams; F Smith, A Troncon; P Ribbens, A Moscardi (*captain*), F Properzi-Curti, C Checchinato, S Dellapé, S Garozzo, S Parisse, S Palmer *Substitutions:* E Pavanello for Checchinato (32 mins); F Mazzariol for D Dallan (temp 24 to 31 mins) and for Mason (38 mins); R Martinez Frugoni for Properzi-Curti (48 mins); M Bergamasco for Dellapé (61 mins); F Ongaro for Moscardi (71 mins); S Costanzo for Ribbens (76 mins); S Picone for M Dallam (79 mins)

Scorers *Tries:* M Dallan (2), Parisse, Palmer *Conversion:* Williams *Penalty Goals:* Smith (3), Mason

Amatori & Calvisano: M Ravazzolo; P Vaccari, G Raineri, C Zanoletti, A Vodo; G Fraser, P Griffen; G de Carli (*captain*), A Moretti, S Perugini, W Boardman, J Purll, A de Rossi, C Roux, C Mayerhofler *Substitutions:* E Trecate for Purll (58 mins); M Merli for Vaccari (66 mins); L Castrogiovanni for Perugini (71 mins); L Mastrodomenico for Boardman (71 mins); G Bocca for De Carli (83 mins); G Intoppa for Moretti (84 mins)

Scorer *Penalty Goals:* Fraser (4)

Referee G de Santis (FIR)

Previous Italian Championship Finals: 1988 Rovigo 9, Treviso 7 (Rome); 1989 Treviso 20, Rovigo 9 (Bologna); 1990 Rovigo 18, Treviso 9 (Brescia); 1991 Milan 37, Treviso 18 (Parma); 1992 Treviso 27, Rovigo 18 (Padua); 1993 Milan 41, Treviso 15 (Padua); 1994 L'Aquila 23, Milan 14 (Padua); 1995 Milan 27, Treviso 15 (Padua); 1996 Milan 23, Treviso 17 (Rovigo); 1997 Treviso 34, Milan 29 (Verona); 1998 Treviso 9, Padua 3 (Bologna); 1999 Treviso 23, Padua 14 (Rovigo); 2000 Rome 35, L'Aquila 17 (Rome); 2001 Treviso 33, Calvisano 13 (Bologna); 2002 Viadana 19, Amatori & Calvisano 12 (Rovigo); 2003 Benetton Treviso 34, Amatori & Calvisano 12 (Padua)

DOMESTIC RUGBY IN SOUTH AFRICA 2002

Blues Bull Run Raises their Stock: Bankfin Currie Cup

Dan Retief

If, at the beginning of the South African domestic season, you had suggested that the golden Currie Cup might be won by the Blue Bulls you would have been laughed out of court. The team who are the modern incarnation of the old Northern Transvaal had finished a lowly seventh the year before and as the master province of the Bulls in the Super Twelve they had propped up the log.

The Bulls did not have many stars, with the exception of a strapped-together Joost van der Westhuizen and Springbok lock Victor Matfield, and their opening salvos were off-target; a fact which tended to disguise that coach Heyneke Meyer had at his disposal some of the most formidable heavy artillery in the competition.

The fancied teams continued to be Western Province, Natal, the Lions (Transvaal) and the Cheetahs (Free State) and Meyer's key deployments went almost unnoticed – but then that is the way with fairy tales.

Midway through the campaign the coach decided to settle on a new young fly-half in Derick Hougaard, moved Jaco van der Westhuyzen to full-back and introduced a pattern based on the power of his pack.

In an instant the Bulls started to resemble the great Pretoria teams of the past. Their fortunes started to improve and press dispatches were talking of Hougaard as the reincarnation of Naas Botha.

The Bulls embarked on a run that took them to a 19th Currie Cup success and one that was particularly sweet for coach Meyer, who earlier in the season had faced an insidious campaign to have him removed as coach.

The Bulls had reached the final thanks to Hougaard kicking a last-minute penalty in Durban to shade Natal 22-19; a result that spoilt what was meant to be Mark Andrews's farewell parade. The great old warhorse of Natal and South African rugby had announced his intention to join Newcastle but, as has so often been the case in South Africa with significant farewells, his team were unable to secure his exit in a final.

The same was true of another great stalwart, André Venter. South Africa's second most-capped forward – after Andrews with 77 and 66 caps respectively – was hoping to inspire his beloved Free State Cheetahs to what would have been only their second Cup success, but it all went awry in the semi-final against the Lions.

A see-sawing match in Bloemfontein went into the final five minutes with the score locked at 29-all before Jaque Fourie made the decisive score as he beat Rassie Erasmus to his own kick ahead and then John Daniels intercepted and sprinted 70 metres to give the Lions a somewhat flattering 43-29 victory.

Decimated by injuries Western Province were unable to live up to the expectations that had seen them installed as favourites. A 50-13 defeat (five tries to one) by the Lions on the final weekend of Top Eight league play was a particularly bitter pill to swallow.

In the secondary Bankfin Cup competition – for teams dropping out of the top eight of the Currie Cup – the Eagles (South Western Districts) beat the Bulldogs (Border) 29-20 at their Outeniqua home-ground in George, while the drawing of the curtain on yet another season was yet again accompanied symbolically by the departure of top-class players to play for pounds in Britain. Percy Montgomery headed for Newport, Thinus Delport to Gloucester and Pieter Rossouw to London Irish.

Currie Cup Round-Robins

Section X

	P	*W*	*D*	*L*	*For*	*Against*	*Bonus*	*Pts*
Western Province	6	5	0	1	253	113	5	25
Cheetahs	6	5	0	1	239	122	5	25
Falcons	6	3	0	3	195	154	4	16
Griquas	6	3	0	3	207	228	3	15
Bulldogs	6	3	0	3	136	155	2	14
Boland Cavaliers	6	2	0	4	136	194	2	10
Griffons	6	0	0	6	107	307	0	0

Section Y

	P	*W*	*D*	*L*	*For*	*Against*	*Bonus*	*Pts*
Natal	6	4	1	1	267	135	4	22
Blue Bulls	6	4	1	1	185	125	4	22
Lions	6	4	0	2	227	189	5	21
Pumas	6	2	0	4	189	220	7	15
Eagles	6	3	0	3	152	194	3	15
Leopards	6	2	0	4	131	216	3	11
Mighty Elephants	6	1	0	5	158	230	4	8

Top Eight

	P	*W*	*D*	*L*	*For*	*Against*	*Bonus*	*Pts*
Natal	7	5	1	1	324	160	6	28
Cheetahs	7	6	0	1	273	181	3	27
Lions	7	5	0	2	250	184	6	26
Blue Bulls	7	5	1	1	225	136	3	25
Western Province	7	3	0	4	228	239	4	16
Pumas	7	2	0	5	213	298	6	14

Griquas	7	1	0	6	134	316	3	7
Falcons	7	0	0	7	146	279	4	4

Bankfin Cup

	P	*W*	*D*	*L*	*For*	*Against*	*Bonus*	*Pts*
Eagles	5	4	0	1	235	123	4	20
Bulldogs	5	3	0	2	139	112	6	18
Mighty Elephants	5	3	0	2	195	149	5	17
Leopards	5	3	0	2	112	132	4	16
Boland Cavaliers	5	1	0	4	161	187	6	10
Griffons	5	1	0	4	97	236	0	4

Points: Win 4; draw 2; four or more tries, or defeat by seven or fewer points 1
Relevant points from the sectional round-robins are carried forward into the Top Eight and Bankfin Cup

Bankfin Currie Cup Final

26 October 2002 Ellis Park, Johannesburg
Lions 7 (1G) **Blue Bulls 31** (5PG 2PG 2T)

The 19-year-old Blue Bulls' fly-half Derick Hougaard, who a year before had still been at school, was certainly the talk of the competition with one match-winning performance after another, but he saved his best for the Currie Cup Final.

Hougaard, a product of the Boland Agricultural High School, set a points record of 26, surpassing the 24 of Botha and Braam van Straaten, as the Blue Bulls pounded the Lions into submission to the tune of 31-7. His tally included a pair of dropped goals and a sharply-taken try and his fly-half generalship was such that there was great surprise when he was not included in the Springbok touring side later that evening.

Hougaard it was who attracted the plaudits, but the real heroes were the Bulls' forwards who threw up an impenetrable blue wall in front of their young fly-half.

Victor Matfield gave an immense performance in the line-outs and in the end the Lions were simply blown off the park and were, but for André Pretorius's try, never able to bring to bear the skills and pace of their back division.

While the Bulls' pattern might have been described as old fashioned there was no denying its effectiveness, especially from the moment in the season Hougaard was installed at fly-half and he started to keep the ball ahead of the fierce blue pack while complementing their efforts by putting points on the board.

In the final the subdue-and-penetrate formula worked to perfection against a disappointing and seemingly dispirited Lions outfit led by André Vos. The Blue Bull forwards gained the ascendancy in the set pieces, and in the loose they relentlessly put their bodies on the line to keep the ball safe and secure. And when the ball did emerge Hougaard kept it up in the Lions' half or the chunky centres Tiaan Joubert and Dries Scholtz drove it up powerfully.

So while Hougaard could deservedly celebrate an amazing odyssey that had taken him from the school benches in Paarl in 2001 to the man-of-the-match in the Currie Cup Final in 2002, the likes of Anton Leonard, Johann Wasserman, Pedrie Wannenburg, Matfield, Bakkies Botha, Richard Bands, Danie Coetzee and Wessel Roux deserved a deep swig of champagne from the old Cup.

In the first half the Lions must have wondered whether there was a ball on the field so superior was the Bulls' retention, and the pressure they were under forced them to constantly put the ball into touch – only to play into the hands of the towering Matfield.

The tall Springbok showed no signs of the ankle injury that had been troubling him and added to the strain being brought to bear on the Lions by disrupting their line-out by poaching a number of balls on Delarey du Preez's throw.

After turning 0-15 down the Lions made the ideal start to the second half to get André Pretorius over for a converted try but the Bulls, exhorted by that ultimate match-winner Joost van der Westhuizen, simply stuck to their blueprint and won a succession of vital turnovers to take the game away from the Lions.

Pressure on Pretorius resulted in a poor clearance that gave Pedrie Wannenburg his try in the 59th minute, increasing the Bulls' lead to 20-7, and when the Lions took what appeared to be a gamble by removing skipper André Vos to make way for Joe van Niekerk the Cup was Pretoria-bound.

The Lions, notably scrum-half Bennie Nortjé and full-back Jaque Fourie, another 19-year-old who had made great strides during the season, were feeling the pressure and making mistakes when it fell to Hougaard, drifting off Jaco van der Westhuyzen who was up from full-back, to score the try that sealed the Bulls' victory.

At 25-7 there was no way back for the Lions and all that remained was for Hougaard to kick his second drop and fifth penalty to claim the record for the most points by an individual in a Currie Cup Final and leave the Lions with the unenviable record of never having defeated the Bulls in a final.

Lions: J Fourie; J J Daniels, G Esterhuizen, G P Müller, J Booysen; A S Pretorius, B D Nortjé; L D Sephaka, G J D du Preez, W Meyer, J A Tromp, J J Labuschagne, A N Vos (*captain*), R G Winter, J L van Heerden *Substitutions:* J C van Niekerk for Vos (temp 2 to 4 mins and 65 mins); W Stoltz for Labuschagne (temp 14 to 16 min and 66 to 69 mins); P van Niekerk for Sephaka (55 mins); D de Kock for Nortjé (67 mins); J C Pretorius for Müller (86 mins)

Scorers *Try:* Pretorius *Conversion:* Pretorius

Blue Bulls: J N B van der Westhuyzen; W A Human, A W Scholtz, C H B Joubert, G A Passens; D J Hougaard, J H van der Westhuizen (*captain*); W G Roux, D Coetzee, R E Bands, J P Botha, V Matfield, P J Wannenburg, A Leonard, J G Wasserman *Substitutions:* I J Wagner for Bands (57 mins);

G Cronjé for Botha (temp 42 to 51 mins and 60 mins); G van G Botha for Coetzee (temp 66 to 75 mins) and for Roux (78 mins); R Vermeulen for Wannenburg (69 mins); J P Nel for Joubert (83 mins); N Jordaan for Van der Westhuizen (90 mins)

Scorers *Tries:* Wannenburg, Hougaard *Penalty Goals:* Hougaard (5) *Dropped Goals:* Hougaard (2)

Referee J I Kaplan (SARFU)

Results

Semi-finals: Natal 18 Blue Bulls 22 (Absa Stadium, King's Park, Durban); Cheetahs 29 Lions 43 (Vodacom Park, Bloemfontein)

Final: Lions 7, Blue Bulls 31 (Ellis Park, Johannesburg)

Recent Currie Cup Finals: 1990 N Transvaal 12, Natal 18 (Pretoria); 1991 N Transvaal 27 Transvaal 15 (Pretoria); 1992 Transvaal 13, Natal 14 (Johannesburg); 1993 Natal 15, Transvaal 21 (Durban); 1994 Orange Free State 33, Transvaal 56 (Bloemfontein); 1995 Natal 25, Western Province 17 (Durban); 1996 Transvaal 15, Natal 33 (Johannesburg); 1997 Western Province 14, Free State 12 (Cape Town); 1998 Blue Bulls 24, Western Province 20 (Pretoria); 1999 Natal Sharks 9, Golden Lions 32 (Durban); 2000 Natal Sharks 15, Western Province 25 (Durban); 2001 Western Province 29, Natal 24 (Cape Town); 2002 Lions 7, Blue Bulls 31 (Johannesburg)

DOMESTIC RUGBY IN NEW ZEALAND

All Change on the Provincial Front

Don Cameron

The 2002-03 period in New Zealand rugby will in years to come be known as the time the people at provincial rugby's grassroots demanded a stronger hand in the running of their national sport – and got it.

When the careless actions of senior members of the New Zealand Rugby Union board caused the loss in late 2002 of New Zealand's part-hosting of the 2003 World Cup, the initial NZRU action suggested small change at the top. The grassroots thought differently. They demanded complete, rather than partial, change. So the whole NZRU board was dismantled, and re-assembled by a special general meeting with Jock Hobbs, the former New Zealand captain and the white knight who averted the loss of the All Blacks to foreign promoters in 1996, taking over as chairman of a completely new board.

This contained other prominent ex-players in Graham Mourie, Paul Quinn and John Lindsay. Chris Moller, a new chief executive, completed the coup. The grassroots then told the new NZRU board that the cash poured into professional rugby would have to be spread more heavily among the 27 domestic unions where, apart from those five unions which were Super Twelve bases, financing domestic rugby was a growing mountain they could not climb. The NZRU obliged by lifting the basic provincial union grants a little to NZ$ 7.8 million.

While the game was struggling to adjust to post-revolutionary organisation, the players at National Provincial Championship level gave everyone new heart with encouraging class in all three divisions. In 2001, the national championship showed heavy South Island strength among the three divisions, with Canterbury still lording it as holder of the Ranfurly Shield, the Super Twelve title (in the name of the Crusaders) and the first division championship.

The Crusaders again won the Super Twelve in 2002, but Auckland and Waikato dominated the first division, with Auckland taking the final at Hamilton after a brilliant late winning run. Hawke's Bay were the dominant second division side, but fell just short of winning the promotion-relegation match against Bay of Plenty.

The only South Island success in the NPC came from North Otago, one of the great battlers in New Zealand rugby for all of their 75 years. After being near, or at the bottom of the third division since the start of the NPC in 1976, North Otago followed the example of another third division struggler, East Coast, and went looking for players.

The East Coast iwi or tribe is Ngati Porou, so they sent out the message to tribe-members throughout New Zealand to rally round their traditional home – and in no time at all East Coast had won the third division and been promoted to the second. Sadly, this do-it-yourself initiative may be at risk. The lawmakers will allow only so many Ngati Porou imports, but most of the team must be resident in the East Coast area.

North Otago looked to Fiji and the Pacific Islands for men to work on the local farms, and to stiffen the playing ranks. North Otago's success was just as spectacular as East Coast's, except that they were unsuccessful finalists for two seasons before gaining the title, and second-division status, by beating Horowhenua-Kapiti at the end of the 2002 campaign.

Auckland, a beaten semi-finalist in 2001, gave little hint of title-winning promise when they lost – at home on Eden Park – to Taranaki, a middle-of-the-order side, in the first round of first division matches. Waikato grew in stature, and when Auckland lost successive matches to those two sides, the odds were that Canterbury and Waikato would reach the final. However, Auckland found new strength and confidence, qualified third, upset Canterbury in a semi-final at Jade Stadium (Waikato eliminated Otago in a 41-37 cliffhanger) and then outclassed Waikato 40-28 at Hamilton's dazzling new stadium.

However, the good news about Auckland, Hawke's Bay and North Otago as division winners had to be measured against the fact that the gaps between the divisions – especially between the first and second – are growing wider. Counties-Manukau, for many years a formidable side with a dazzling playing style, were relegated to the second division, and remained there after losing the final to Hawke's Bay.

Now even more under the shade of the Auckland Super Twelve franchise, Counties-Manukau have a large playing population, but is finding that its best players are being enticed to first division unions. This is one daunting impact of professional rugby, and the fact that the five Super Twelve-based unions, Auckland, Waikato, Wellington, Canterbury and Otago, grow financially stronger each year means that strong areas such as Hawke's Bay and Counties-Manukau are finding it harder and harder to maintain their playing and financial strength.

There is another worrying aspect of this poor-getting-poorer provincial rugby syndrome. One of the catchy television commercials provided by sponsors Air New Zealand urges rugby people in the hinterland to support their home side, to 'Show Your True Colours.' It is cleverly and colourfully contrived, and suggests that everyone is face-painting with their local colours and hustling along to watch the games. Just how long this appeal lasts is questionable. Unions are allowed to sign up players from other unions who have completed their club commitments and are not further required by their home unions. Now there is a growing drift, especially toward the third division unions, of players who will be under convenient new 'colours.'

In the 2002 season 152 players were signed up by other unions. These were: Third division (73 transfers) – Wairarapa-Bush, North Otago and Horowhenua-Patiki had 10 imports, Buller, Wanganui and West Coast nine, King Country eight, South Canterbury six, Poverty Bay two; Second division (57) – East Coast, Thames Valley 10, Marlborough, Mid-Canterbury eight, Counties-Manukau, Hawke's Bay six, Manawatu five, Nelson Bays four; and First division (22) – Bay of Plenty 10, Southland six, North Harbour and Northland two, and Auckland and Taranaki one each.

Such hirings are a mixed blessing. They may give temporary strength to the weaker union (at the expense of home-grown players), but if the itinerant players show any improvement they are less likely to return to low-status sides the following year.

There is a danger, too, that that grand old trophy, the Ranfurly Shield, is losing some of its impact. Canterbury held the shield against seven challengers, with scores ranging from 78-10 to 48-27 before Otago gave the holders a fright, losing 13-16 in the final challenge of the year. Otago hustled and bustled Canterbury during the rain showers in the first half, and led 13-6 with Blair Feeney lining up a penalty goal attempt. The kick missed leaving Canterbury to show their traditional last-quarter skill with a try by Justin Marshall which Andrew Mehrtens converted.

Some years ago Mehrtens foiled a boisterous Otago shield bid with a last-minute penalty goal, and this time Mehrtens repeated the dose to give Canterbury their narrow win. Canterbury have now put together 16 defences over three seasons, but without arousing the crowd appeal that the shield used to create among the fanatical red-and-black supporters.

Final Air New Zealand NPC Round-Robin Table 2002

	P	*W*	*D*	*L*	*Bonus*	*For*	*Against*	*Pts*
Waikato	9	8	0	1	7	365	231	39
Canterbury	9	7	0	2	6	337	215	34
Auckland	9	6	0	3	8	325	167	32
Otago	9	6	0	3	5	237	215	29
Wellington	9	5	0	4	7	325	235	27
Taranaki	9	5	0	4	3	238	260	23
North Harbour	9	3	0	6	5	197	259	17
Northland	9	2	0	7	3	187	335	11
Southland	9	2	0	7	2	160	265	10
Bay of Plenty	9	1	0	8	5	203	392	9

Air New Zealand NPC Grand Final

26 October 2002, Waikato Stadium, Hamilton
Auckland 40 (2G 2PG 4T) **Waikato 28** (2G 3PG 1T)

Graham Henry may have been asked to leave his work as coach of Wales before he could fulfil his billing as the Great Redeemer, but Auckland were delighted to welcome back Henry, their outstanding coach during the 1990s, as the Great Defender.

By the end of the 2001 season Auckland were beginning to show the solidity that their coach Wayne Pivac (after outstanding club and representative coaching in North Harbour and Northland) and his assistant Bruce Robertson, the celebrated All Black centre, had demanded. They gained the fourth and last position in the semi-finals, but went down heavily 22-55 to Canterbury, conceding seven tries.

In the preliminary rounds Auckland's try ratio was 36-20, whereas Canterbury rated 52-17. So Henry was welcomed back to the Auckland team management, not as chief coach, but as the analyst who examined the opposition methods and planned defensive moves to counter them.

Auckland also encouraged youth, through Sam Tuitupou, Mils Muliaina and Steve Devine in the backs and Daniel Braid, Ali Williams, Brad Mika, Keven Mealamu and Angus Macdonald in the pack. At first this seemed an error, when on their home ground Auckland were outplayed and outpointed by Taranaki. But the planners stuck to their blueprints, recovered after mid-term losses to Waikato and Canterbury, and all the planning resulted in a splendid run of wins over Otago, Wellington and Canterbury (semi-final) in the run to the final.

Waikato had been the outstanding first division side from the start. They had found a brilliant midfield pairing in Keith Lowen with the light-footed Regan King, and a new and classy five-eighths in Derek Maisey, while the arrival of Stephen Bates, an Auckland flanker, and Keith Robinson, a heavy-duty lock, added strength to the pack. Bruce Reihana, as goal-kicker, and Roger Randle, the try-scoring wing, joined No 8 Deon Muir as leaders of the side.

Waikato won their first five games, lost 20-36 away to Otago, then marched to the final with another four wins. For many years before and after the Second World War the Auckland-Waikato fixture was the early-June start to the representative season, always played at Hamilton as Auckland's big-brother gesture – the 'gate' kept Waikato solvent for the rest of the season. Waikato repaid Auckland by fielding tough country forwards and smart backs. They were fired by Don Clarke's goal-kicking, clever Dick Everest coaching and, occasionally, by referees quite in tune with the attitude of the home-town crowds.

In those days the senior Auckland players did not spend too much time introducing themselves to the newcomers before the Waikato match. Auckland very often lost, the Auckland selectors sharpened their axe, and there would be another group of new players in the team for the second match.

There was some of this graveyard humour as Auckland went to play the final at Hamilton's handsome new stadium, and the fervent home crowd greeted the Aucklanders with the usual cacophony of cow-bell music. But this time the detailed Auckland pre-game planning, especially Henry's detailed defensive schemes, gave the Aucklanders a steady start built from defensive armour much thicker than usual.

After an exchange of penalty goals, Auckland hit their best attacking form which brought three tries and had Waikato reeling at 3-20. The home side fought back with King's 14th try of the season, and two Reihana penalty goals had Waikato in touch 16-20 after playing the first half with the help of a brisk breeze.

Auckland picked up two quick tries after half-time for a 32-16 cushion, Waikato fought back with a try by Greg Smith, Auckland replied with a penalty goal and Doug Howlett's second try – and a try by Lowen just before the end came too late to threaten the Auckland lead.

Ian Foster, the Waikato coach, bemoaned the fact that Waikato had let in six tries, and could only score three themselves. The triumphant Pivac had the answer: 'Graham Henry has done a fantastic job formulating how we will defend against opposition attacks . . . he has done a superb job and the guys have responded really well.'

The proof came in the statistics. Auckland conceded only 16 tries during the round-robin, and Canterbury were second with 26.

Auckland: B J Ward; D C Howlett, M Muliaina, S Tuitupou, B A C Atiga; C J Spencer, S J Devine; S K L Palmer, K F Mealamu, K J Meeuws, B M Mika, A J Williams, D J Braid, X J Rush (*captain*), J A Collins *Substitutions*: I Tanivula for Atiga; L Stensness for Tuitupou; D B Gibson for Devine; A J Macdonald for Braid; J F Afoa for Meeuws

Scorers *Tries:* Howlett (2), Muliaina, Spencer, Mealamu, Rush *Conversions*: Spencer (2) *Penalty Goals:* Spencer (2)

Waikato: T J Miller; R Q Randle,R M King, K R Lowen, B T Reihana; D J Maisey, R J L Duggan; M J Collins, G J Smith, D T Manu, K J Robinson, S D Hohneck, J B Gibbs, D D Muir (*captain*), M R Holah *Substitutions:* R M Ranby for Miller; L Crichton for Maisey; I J Boss for Duggan; S P Bates for Hohneck; S R Linklater for Smith; D J Briggs for Collins

Scorers *Tries:* King, Smith, Lowen *Conversions:* Reihana (2) *Penalty Goals:* Reihana (3)

Referee P D O'Brien (NZRU).

Results

Semi-finals: Auckland 29, Canterbury 23 (Jade Stadium, Christchurch); Waikato 41, Otago 37 (Waikato Stadium, Hamilton)

Final: Auckland 40, Waikato 28 (Waikato Stadium, Hamilton)

Previous NPC Grand Finals: 1992 Waikato 40, Otago 5 (Hamilton); 1993 Auckland 27, Otago 18 (Auckland); 1994 Auckland 22, North Harbour 16 (Takapuna); 1995 Auckland 23, Otago 19 (Auckland); 1996 Auckland 46, Counties-Manukau 15 (Auckland); 1997 Canterbury 44, Counties-Manukau 13 (Christchurch); 1998 Otago 49, Waikato 20 (Dunedin); 1999 Auckland 24, Wellington 18 (Auckland); 2000 Wellington 34, Canterbury 29 (Christchurch); 2001 Canterbury 30, Otago 19 (Christchurch); 2002 Auckland 40, Waikato 28 (Hamilton)

DOMESTIC RUGBY IN AUSTRALIA 2002

League Converts and World Cup Announcements Raise Game's Profile

Peter Jenkins

The 2002 season started with the fairytale the converts had craved. Wendell Sailor and Mat Rogers, lured across from rugby league on their massive salaries, were paraded in the season-opening World Series Sevens tournament in Brisbane. Australia won the final 28-0, beating New Zealand in the decider to claim their only Sevens trophy of the circuit, and Sailor and Rogers were instant heroes.

The season was young. It was 3 February when the Sevens took place. There were another three weeks to the Super Twelve kick-off. But the fast-tracking of the two league defectors had already started. When the southern hemisphere provincial series eventually got underway, Rogers would make an immediate impact.

Playing full-back for the NSW Waratahs, his deceptive running from the back field made him a constant threat to unsuspecting defences. Sailor, on the wing for Queensland, was less impressive. He lacked the instinctive rugby sense Rogers possessed; that intuition for the game partly developed during school days. Rogers possessed the natural fluency some players of flair are able to transport from one code to the next – the footwork to beat a defence, whether it be in the 13-or 15-man game, and the positional sense to provide most value in support.

Rogers was a standout as the Waratahs reached the Super Twelve semi-finals for the first time. The perennial under-achievers finally managed the breakthrough the talent at their disposal had always demanded. Coach Bob Dwyer, in his second season at the helm after returning from stints at various clubs in Europe, was delighted and outspoken early in the season when the Waratahs beat the Brumbies 19-11 at the Sydney Football Stadium. The match attracted a record Australian Super Twelve crowd of 41,645 and was sold out two weeks prior to the match.

What followed was also worthy of headlines. Dwyer, taking a dislike to the on-field attitude of Brumbies and Wallabies captain George Gregan, slammed the ACT No 9 as arrogant. He claimed Australian rugby did not need the kind of in-your-face and better-than-thou air that he claimed Gregan brought to the scene. The slur triggered not only ill-feeling between the two franchises, but a slanging match between Dwyer and Brumbies coach David Nucifora.

But there was a sting in the tail to be delivered. NSW headed into the final round of the Super Twelve preliminaries already assured of a home semi-final. Dwyer decided to rest key players and give several young fringe dwellers the chance to gain game time against defending champions the Canterbury Crusaders.

The move backfired with dire consequences. NSW was beaten 96-19, the worst-ever thrashing for the state in a history stretching back more than 125 years. The Crusaders were sublime in Christchurch, but after a promising start the Waratahs were little better than ridiculous. A week later, the Waratahs were at home to the ACT Brumbies in the semi-finals. Their confidence knocked around by the slaying in New Zealand, the Waratahs wilted further. The Brumbies, with Gregan wearing a look of contentment at the final whistle, crushed NSW 51-10. The hammering in back-to-back debacles ended what had been their most successful Super Twelve season, but as half-back Chris Whitaker lamented: 'People will remember this season for all the wrong reasons.'

The Brumbies, like the Waratahs, would find the Crusaders a class above and went down 31-13 in the Super Twelve final in Christchurch. The Crusaders had won all 11 matches of the round-robin, NSW had finished second on the table with eight wins from their 11, while the Brumbies were third qualifier into the knockout stages with seven victories. It had been a good season for the Australian sides. Queensland, like the Brumbies, had won seven of 11, but failed to accrue enough bonus points to reach the play-offs. The Reds finished fifth, four points behind the fourth-placed Otago Highlanders.

A highlight for Queensland came early in the 2002 season when long-serving No 8 Toutai Kefu equalled Todd Blackadder's record for most Super Twelve matches when he played his 71st against the Auckland Blues on 2 March. The following month, Matthew Burke became the most-capped NSW Waratahs player in history when he made his 92nd appearance. He passed the mark previously set by half-back Sam Payne. But the standout Australian player of the Super Twelve series would be ACT Brumbies centre Stirling Mortlock, a runaway winner of the annual award.

On the second tier of provincial rugby was the Bundaberg Rum Australian Rugby Shield, the annual competition for non-Super Twelve states and territories. A dropped goal in injury time by full-back Nathan Croft lifted NSW Country to a 25-24 win over Perth Gold in the final.

On the club front, a new Premier Rugby concept was introduced in both Sydney and Brisbane. A preliminary club competition was played parallel to Super Twelve before the Premier Rugby championships kicked off, allowing clubs to field the representative players they usually spend half a season without. The abridged competition in Sydney was deemed an enormous success with Eastwood taking out the title. In Brisbane, the Canberra Vikings completed back-to-back titles, downing Easts in the grand final.

Associates won the Perth competition, while Moorabbin defeated Northcote to win the Primus Cup in Victoria's Premier Division. The champion club in South Australia was Port Adelaide, the Darwin Dragons took out the premiership in the Northern Territory and the Tasmanian winners were Glenorchy.

In the background, too, there were promising signs for Australian rugby. The announcement in March that Australia would be sole hosts of the 2003 World Cup continued to lift the profile of the code and, by the end of 2002, most states had announced a significant increase in playing numbers. In NSW, senior registrations jumped 14% from 17,655 to 20,172 while juniors were up 15% from 13,257 to 15,299. NSW also continued its dominance at schoolboy level. NSW I defeated NSW II by 38-22 in the national championship final, and the NSW juniors won the Australian under 16 title, downing Queensland in the decider.

FIXTURES 2003-2004

Venues and fixtures are subject to alteration. At the time of going to press, only the weekends *for which Heineken Cup, Celtic League and European Shield matches had been scheduled were known. See press for further details.*

Friday, 10 October

RWC Pool A
AUSTRALIA v ARGENTINA (Sydney)

RFU/Zurich Premiership
Sale v Wasps

Fri, Sat 10/11 October

Celtic Leagues
Bridgend/Pontypridd v Neath/Swansea
Cardiff v Leinster
Connacht v The Borders
Edinburgh v Llanelli
Gwent Dragons v Glasgow
Munster v Ulster

Saturday, 11 October

RWC Pool A
IRELAND v ROMANIA (Gosford)
RWC Pool B
FRANCE v FIJI (Brisbane)
RWC Pool C
SOUTH AFRICA v URUGUAY (Perth)
RWC Pool D
NEW ZEALAND v ITALY (Melbourne)

RFU/Zurich Premiership
Bath v Rotherham
Gloucester v Leicester
Harlequins v Newcastle
Northampton v London Irish

Sunday, 12 October

RWC Pool B
SCOTLAND v JAPAN (Townsville)
RWC Pool C
ENGLAND v GEORGIA (Perth)
RWC Pool D
WALES v CANADA (Melbourne)

RFU/Zurich Premiership
Leeds v Saracens

Tuesday, 14 October

RWC Pool A
ARGENTINA v NAMIBIA (Gosford)

Wednesday, 15 October

RWC Pool B
FIJI v UNITED STATES (Brisbane)

RWC Pool C
SAMOA v URUGUAY (Perth)

RWC Pool D
ITALY v TONGA (Canberra)

Friday, 17 October

RWC Pool D
NEW ZEALAND v CANADA (Melbourne)

Fri, Sat 17/18 October

Celtic Leagues
Glasgow v The Borders
Gwent Dragons v Munster
Leinster v Connacht
Llanelli v Cardiff
Neath/Swansea v Edinburgh
Ulster v Bridgend/Pontypridd

Saturday, 18 October

RWC Pool A
AUSTRALIA v ROMANIA (Brisbane)
RWC Pool B
FRANCE v JAPAN (Townsville)
RWC Pool C

SOUTH AFRICA v ENGLAND
(Perth)

RFU/Zurich Premiership
Harlequins v Gloucester
Northampton v Newcastle
Rotherham v Sale

Sunday, 19 October

RWC Pool A
IRELAND v NAMIBIA (Sydney)

RWC Pool C
GEORGIA v SAMOA (Perth)

RWC Pool D
WALES v TONGA (Canberra)

RFU/Zurich Premiership
Bath v Saracens
Leeds v Leicester
Wasps v London Irish

Monday, 20 October

RWC Pool B
SCOTLAND v UNITED STATES
(Brisbane)

Tuesday, 21 October

RWC Pool D
ITALY v CANADA (Canberra)

Wednesday, 22 October

RWC Pool A
ARGENTINA v ROMANIA (Sydney)

Thursday, 23 October

RWC Pool B
FIJI v JAPAN (Townsville)

Friday, 24 October

RWC Pool C
SOUTH AFRICA v GEORGIA
(Sydney)

RWC Pool D
NEW ZEALAND v TONGA
(Brisbane)

Fri, Sat 24/25 October

Celtic Leagues
The Borders v Leinster
Bridgend/Pontypridd v Gwent Dragons
Cardiff v Neath/Swansea
Connacht v Llanelli
Edinburgh v Ulster
Munster v Glasgow

Saturday, 25 October

RWC Pool A
AUSTRALIA v NAMIBIA (Adelaide)

RWC Pool B
FRANCE v SCOTLAND (Sydney)

RWC Pool D
ITALY v WALES (Canberra)

RFU/Zurich Premiership
Gloucester v Leeds
Harlequins v Sale
Leicester v Northampton
Newcastle v Bath

Sunday, 26 October

RWC Pool A
ARGENTINA v IRELAND (Adelaide)

RWC Pool C
ENGLAND v SAMOA (Melbourne)

RFU/Zurich Premiership
London Irish v Rotherham
Saracens v Wasps

Monday, 27 October

RWC Pool B
JAPAN v UNITED STATES
(Gosford)

Tuesday, 28 October

RWC Pool C
GEORGIA v URUGUAY (Sydney)

Wednesday, 29 October

RWC Pool D
CANADA v TONGA (Wollongong)

Thursday, 30 October

RWC Pool A
NAMIBIA v ROMANIA (Launceston)

Friday, 31 October

RWC Pool B
FRANCE v UNITED STATES (Wollongong)

RFU/Zurich Premiership
Leeds v Harlequins
Sale v London Irish

Fri, Sat 31/1 Oct/Nov

Celtic Leagues
Gwent Dragons v Edinburgh
Glasgow v Leinster
Llanelli v The Borders
Munster v Bridgend/Pontypridd
Neath/Swansea v Connacht
Ulster v Cardiff

Saturday, 1 November

RWC Pool A
AUSTRALIA v IRELAND (Melbourne)

RWC Pool B
SCOTLAND v FIJI (Sydney)

RWC Pool C
SOUTH AFRICA v SAMOA (Brisbane)

RFU/Zurich Premiership
Bath v Leicester
Northampton v Gloucester
Rotherham v Saracens

Sunday, 2 November

RWC Pool C
ENGLAND v URUGUAY (Brisbane)

RWC Pool D
NEW ZEALAND v WALES (Sydney)
RFU/Zurich Premiership
Wasps v Newcastle

Fri, Sat 7/8 November

Celtic Leagues
The Borders v Neath/Swansea
Bridgend/Pontypridd v Glasgow
Cardiff v Gwent Dragons
Connacht v Ulster
Edinburgh v Munster
Leinster v Llanelli

Saturday, 8 November

RWC Quarter-Finals
WINNERS POOL D v RUNNERS-UP POOL C (Melbourne)
WINNERS POOL A v RUNNERS-UP POOL B (Brisbane)

RFU/Zurich Premiership
Gloucester v Bath
Harlequins v Northampton
Leeds v Sale
Leicester v Wasps

Sunday, 9 November

RWC Quarter-Finals
WINNERS POOL B v RUNNERS-UP POOL A (Melbourne)
WINNERS POOL C v RUNNERS-UP POOL D (Brisbane)

RFU/Zurich Premiership
Newcastle v Rotherham
Saracens v London Irish

Fri/Sat/Sun, 14/15/16 November

Celtic Cup Semi-Finals

Saturday, 15 November

RWC Semi-Finals
WINNERS QUARTER-FINAL 1 v WINNERS QUARTER-FINAL 2 (Sydney)

RFU Powergen Cup *Sixth round*

Sunday, 16 November

RWC Semi-Finals
WINNERS QUARTER-FINAL 3 v WINNERS QUARTER-FINAL 4 (Sydney)

Thursday, 20 November

RWC Third/Fourth Place Play-Off
LOSERS SEMI-FINAL 1 v LOSERS SEMI-FINAL 2 (Sydney)

Friday, 21 November

RFU/Zurich Premiership
Sale v Saracens
Wasps v Gloucester

Saturday, 22 November

RWC FINAL (Sydney)

RFU/Zurich Premiership
Bath v Harlequins
Northampton v Leeds
Rotherham v Leicester

Sunday, 23 November

RFU/Zurich Premiership
London Irish v Newcastle

Fri, Sat 28/29 November

Celtic Leagues
Bridgend/Pontypridd v Edinburgh
Glasgow v Llanelli
Gwent Dragons v Connacht
Munster v Cardiff
Neath/Swansea v Leinster
Ulster v The Borders

Saturday, 29 November

RFU/Zurich Premiership
Gloucester v Northampton
Harlequins v Leeds
Leicester v Bath
Newcastle v Wasps

Sunday, 30 November

RFU/Zurich Premiership
London Irish v Sale
Saracens v Rotherham

Fri, Sat, Sun, 5/6/7 December

Heineken Cup *First round*
Agen v The Borders
Bourgoin v Munster
Celtic Warriors v Calvisano
Edinburgh v Toulouse
Gwent Dragons v Ulster
Leeds v Neath/Swansea
Leinster v Biarritz
Llanelli v Northampton
Sale v Cardiff
Stade Francais v Leicester
Treviso v Gloucester
Wasps v Perpignan

European Challenge Cup *First round, first legs*

Fri, Sat, Sun, 12/13/14 December

Heineken Cup *Second round*
Biarritz v Sale
The Borders v Llanelli
Calvisano v Wasps
Cardiff v Leinster
Gloucester v Bourgoin
Leicester v Gwent Dragons
Munster v Treviso
Neath/Swansea v Edinburgh
Northampton v Agen
Perpignan v Celtic Warriors
Toulouse v Leeds
Ulster v Stade Francais

European Challenge Cup *First round, second legs*

Friday, 19 December

RFU/Zurich Premiership
Sale v Harlequins

Saturday, 20 December

Celtic Cup *FINAL*

RFU/Zurich Premiership
Bath v Newcastle
Northampton v Leicester
Rotherham v London Irish

Sunday, 21 December

RFU/Zurich Premiership
Leeds v Gloucester
Wasps v Saracens

Fri, Sat 26/27 December

Celtic Leagues
Cardiff v Bridgend/Pontypridd

Glasgow v Edinburgh
Llanelli v Neath/Swansea

Saturday, 27 December

RFU/Zurich Premiership
Gloucester v Harlequins
Leicester v Leeds
London Irish v Wasps
Sale v Rotherham
Saracens v Bath

Sunday, 28 December

RFU/Zurich Premiership
Newcastle v Northampton

Fri, Sat 2/3 January

Celtic Leagues
The Borders v Gwent Dragons
Connacht v Munster
Leinster v Ulster

Saturday, 3 January

RFU/Zurich Premiership
Leicester v Gloucester
Rotherham v Bath

Sunday, 4 January

RFU/Zurich Premiership
London Irish v Northampton
Newcastle v Harlequins
Saracens v Leeds
Wasps v Sale

Fri, Sat, Sun, 9/10/11 January

Heineken Cup *Third round*
Biarritz v Cardiff
Edinburgh v Leeds
Gloucester v Munster
Gwent Dragons v Stade Francais
Leinster v Sale
Llanelli v Agen
Northampton v The Borders
Perpignan v Calvisano
Toulouse v Neath/Swansea
Treviso v Bourgoin
Ulster v Leicester
Wasps v Celtic Warriors

Fri, Sat, Sun, 16/17/18 January

Heineken Cup *Fourth round*
Agen v Llanelli
The Borders v Northampton
Bourgoin v Treviso
Calvisano v Perpignan
Cardiff v Biarritz
Celtic Warriors v Wasps
Leeds v Edinburgh
Leicester v Ulster
Munster v Gloucester
Neath/Swansea v Toulouse
Sale v Leinster
Stade Francais v Gwent Dragons

Fri, Sat, Sun, 23/24/25 January

Heineken Cup *Fifth round*
Agen v Northampton
Bourgoin v Gloucester
Celtic Warriors v Perpignan
Edinburgh v Neath/Swansea
Gwent Dragons v Leicester
Leeds v Toulouse
Leinster v Cardiff
Llanelli v The Borders
Sale v Biarritz
Stade Francais v Ulster
Treviso v Munster
Wasps v Calvisano

Fri, Sat, Sun, 30/31/1 Jan/Feb

Heineken Cup *Sixth round*
Biarritz v Leinster
The Borders v Agen
Calvisano v Celtic Warriors
Cardiff v Sale
Gloucester v Treviso
Leicester v Stade Francais
Munster v Bourgoin
Neath/Swansea v Leeds
Northampton v Llanelli
Perpignan v Wasps
Toulouse v Edinburgh
Ulster v Gwent Dragons

Friday, 6 February

RFU/Zurich Premiership
Leeds v London Irish
Sale v Leicester

Fri, Sat 6/7 February

Celtic Leagues
Bridgend/Pontypridd v Connacht

Edinburgh v Cardiff
Gwent Dragons v Leinster
Munster v The Borders
Neath/Swansea v Glasgow
Ulster v Llanelli

Saturday, 7 February

RFU/Zurich Premiership
Bath v Wasps
Gloucester v Newcastle
Harlequins v Saracens
Northampton v Rotherham

Fri, Sat 13/14 February

Celtic Leagues
Bridgend/Pontypridd v The Borders
Cardiff v Glasgow
Edinburgh v Connacht
Gwent Dragons v Llanelli
Munster v Leinster
Ulster v Neath/Swansea

Saturday, 14 February

The Six Nations Championship
WALES v SCOTLAND (Cardiff)
FRANCE v IRELAND (Paris)

The European Nations Cup
ROMANIA v CZECH REPUBLIC
GEORGIA v PORTUGAL
RUSSIA v SPAIN

RFU/Zurich Premiership
Gloucester v Sale
Leicester v Harlequins
Rotherham v Wasps

Sunday, 15 February

The Six Nations Championship
ITALY v ENGLAND (Rome)

RFU/Zurich Premiership
London Irish v Bath
Newcastle v Leeds
Saracens v Northampton

Fri, Sat 20/21 February

Celtic Leagues
The Borders v Edinburgh
Connacht v Cardiff
Glasgow v Ulster
Leinster v Bridgend/Pontypridd
Llanelli v Munster
Neath/Swansea v Gwent Dragons

Saturday, 21 February

The Six Nations Championship
SCOTLAND v ENGLAND
(Murrayfield)
FRANCE v ITALY (Paris)

The European Nations Cup
RUSSIA v CZECH REPUBLIC
ROMANIA v PORTUGAL
SPAIN v GEORGIA

RFU/Zurich Premiership
Bath v Leeds
Northampton v Sale

Sunday, 22 February

The Six Nations Championship
IRELAND v WALES (Dublin)

RFU/Zurich Premiership
London Irish v Leicester
Rotherham v Gloucester
Saracens v Newcastle
Wasps v Harlequins

Fri, Sat 27/28 February

Celtic Leagues
Bridgend/Pontypridd v Llanelli
Cardiff v The Borders
Connacht v Glasgow
Edinburgh v Leinster
Gwent Dragons v Ulster
Munster v Neath/Swansea

Saturday, 28 February

RFU Powergen Cup *Quarter-finals*

Fri, Sat 5/6 March

Celtic Leagues
The Borders v Connacht
Glasgow v Gwent Dragons
Leinster v Cardiff
Llanelli v Edinburgh
Neath/Swansea v Bridgend/Pontypridd
Ulster v Munster

Saturday, 6 March

The Six Nations Championship
ENGLAND v IRELAND (Twickenham)
ITALY v SCOTLAND (Rome)

The European Nations Cup
ROMANIA v SPAIN
CZECH REPUBLIC v PORTUGAL
GEORGIA v RUSSIA

Sunday, 7 March

The Six Nations Championship
WALES v FRANCE (Cardiff)

Fri, Sat 12/13 March

Celtic Leagues
The Borders v Glasgow
Bridgend/Pontypridd v Ulster
Cardiff v Llanelli
Connacht v Leinster
Edinburgh v Neath/Swansea
Munster v Gwent Dragons

Saturday, 13 March

RFU Powergen Cup *Semi-finals*

Saturday, 20 March

The Six Nations Championship
ENGLAND v WALES (Twickenham)
IRELAND v ITALY (Lansdowne Road)

The European Nations Cup
RUSSIA v ROMANIA
SPAIN v PORTUGAL
GEORGIA v CZECH REPUBLIC

Sunday, 21 March

The Six Nations Championship
SCOTLAND v FRANCE (Murrayfield)

Friday, 26 March

RFU/Zurich Premiership
Sale v Gloucester

Fri, Sat 26/27 March

Celtic Leagues
Gwent Dragons v Bridgend/Pontypridd
Glasgow v Munster
Leinster v The Borders
Llanelli v Connacht
Neath/Swansea v Cardiff
Ulster v Edinburgh

Saturday, 27 March

The Six Nations Championship
IRELAND v SCOTLAND (Dublin)
WALES v ITALY (Cardiff)
FRANCE v ENGLAND (Paris)

The European Nations Cup
PORTUGAL v RUSSIA
CZECH REPUBLIC v SPAIN
ROMANIA v GEORGIA

RFU/Zurich Premiership
Bath v London Irish
Harlequins v Leicester
Northampton v Saracens

Sunday, 28 March

RFU/Zurich Premiership
Leeds v Newcastle
Wasps v Rotherham

Friday, 2 April

RFU/Zurich Premiership
Rotherham v Leeds

Fri, Sat 2/3 April

Celtic Leagues
The Borders v Llanelli
Bridgend/Pontypridd v Munster
Cardiff v Ulster
Connacht v Neath/Swansea
Edinburgh v Gwent Dragons
Leinster v Glasgow

Saturday, 3 April

RFU/Zurich Premiership
Bath v Sale

Sunday, 4 April

RFU/Zurich Premiership
London Irish v Harlequins
Newcastle v Leicester
Saracens v Gloucester
Wasps v Northampton

Fri, Sat, Sun, 9/10/11 April

Heineken Cup *Quarter-Finals*

Friday, 16 April

RFU/Zurich Premiership
Leeds v Wasps
Leicester v Saracens
Northampton v Bath
Sale v Newcastle

Fri, Sat 16/17 April

Celtic Leagues
Gwent Dragons v Cardiff
Glasgow v Bridgend/Pontypridd
Llanelli v Leinster
Munster v Edinburgh
Neath/Swansea v The Borders
Ulster v Connacht

Saturday, 17 April

RFU Powergen Cup *FINAL*
(Twickenham)

Sunday, 18 April

RFU/Zurich Premiership
Gloucester v London Irish
Harlequins v Rotherham

Sat, Sun, 24/25 April

Heineken Cup *Semi-Finals*

Fri, Sat 30/1 Apr/May

Celtic Leagues
The Borders v Ulster
Cardiff v Munster
Connacht v Gwent Dragons
Edinburgh v Bridgend/Pontypridd
Leinster v Neath/Swansea
Llanelli v Glasgow

Saturday, 1 May

RFU/Zurich Premiership
Gloucester v Wasps
Harlequins v Bath
Leicester v Rotherham

Sunday, 2 May

RFU/Zurich Premiership
Leeds v Northampton
Newcastle v London Irish
Saracens v Sale

Fri, Sat 7/8 May

Celtic Leagues
Bridgend/Pontypridd v Cardiff
Edinburgh v Glasgow
Gwent Dragons v The Borders
Munster v Connacht
Neath/Swansea v Llanelli
Ulster v Leinster

Saturday, 8 May

RFU/Zurich Premiership
Bath v Gloucester
London Irish v Saracens
Northampton v Harlequins
Rotherham v Newcastle
Sale v Leeds
Wasps v Leicester

Fri, Sat 14/15 May

Celtic Leagues
The Borders v Munster
Cardiff v Edinburgh
Connacht v Bridgend/Pontypridd
Glasgow v Neath/Swansea
Leinster v Gwent Dragons
Llanelli v Ulster

Saturday, 15 May

RFU/Zurich Premiership *Semi-finals*

RFU/Zurich Wildcard *Semi-finals*

Sat, Sun, 22/23 May

Heineken Cup *Final*

European Challenge Cup *Final*

Saturday, 29 May

RFU/Zurich Premiership *Final*
(Twickenham)

RFU/Zurich Wildcard *Final*

MEMBER UNIONS OF THE IRB

IRB MEMBER UNIONS

Andorra

Name: FEDERACIO ANDORRANA DE RUGBY
Address: Baixada del Moli, No.31 Casal de L'Esport del MICG, Andorra La Vella, ANDORRA
Tel: +37 682 12232
Fax: +37 686 4564
Email: jbeal@far.ad
Website: www.vpcrugby.org
Chairman: Josep Arasanz Serra
Official Kit: Yellow/Blue/Red
Clubs: 3
Coaches: 16
Referees: 8
Secretary: Carles Font
Players: 188
Founded: 1986
IRB Affiliation: 1991
Office Contact: Tom Kambfraat

Arabian Gulf Emirates

Name: ARABIAN GULF R.F.U.
Address: PO Box 65785, Dubai, UNITED ARAB EMIRATES
Tel: +971 434 52677
Fax: +971 434 52688
Email: agrugby@emirates.net.ae
Website: www.agrfu.com
Chairman: George Grant
Development Officer: Darryl Weir
Email: d.weir@agrfu.com
Treasurer: Peter Bray
Email: p.bray@agrfu.com
Official Kit: White/maroon/black/green
Clubs: 27
Coaches: 80
Referees: 30
Secretary: John Griffiths
Players: 2289
Founded: 1984
IRB Affiliation: 1990

Argentina

Name: UNION ARGENTINA DE RUGBY
Address: Avda Rivadavia 1227, entre piso, (1033) Capital Federal, ARGENTINA
Tel: +541 1 4383 2211
Fax: +541 1 4383 2570
Email: uarugby@uar.com.ar
Website: www.uar.com.ar
Official Kit: Sky blue/White
Clubs: 317
Coaches: 1603
Referees: 800
Secretary: Federico Fleitas
Players: 50180
Founded: 1899
IRB Affiliation: 1987

Australia

Name: AUSTRALIA R.U.
Address: Level 7, Rugby House, 181 Miller Street, North Sydney, NSW 2060, AUSTRALIA
Tel: +61 2 9955 3466
Fax: +61 2 99 55 3574
Email: maeve.moriarty@rugby.com.au
Email 2: strath.gordon@rugby.com.au
Website: www.rugby.com.au
Chairman: Bob Tuckey
CEO: John O'Neill
Official Kit: Green/Gold hoop
Clubs: 752
Coaches: 4282
Referees: 7000
Secretary: Ashley Selwood
Players: 139660
Founded: 1949
IRB Affiliation: 1949
Office Contact: Maeve Moriarty

Austria

Name: AUSTRIA R.U.
Address: Mr Paul Duteil, C/o Schneiders Vienna, Koppstrabe 27/29, A-1160 Vienna, AUSTRIA
Tel: +43-1-492-58 21 27
Fax: 0043-1-492-5826
Email: k.duteil@schneiders-vienna.at
Email 2: Christopher.Jones@osce.org
Email 3: cjones@osce.org
Website: www.rugby-austria.com
Chairman: Paul Duteil
Official Kit: Black/White hoops
Clubs: 9
Coaches: 27
Referees: 11
Secretary: Wolfgang Rohrer
Players: 540
Founded: 1990
IRB Affiliation: 1992
Vice President: Craig Morgan
Email: craig.morgan@gmx.at
Treasurer: Andreas Schwab

Email: andreas.schwab@rugby.at

Bahamas

Name: BAHAMAS R.F.U.
Address: PO Box N-7213, Nassau, BAHAMAS
Tel: +1242 323 2165
Fax: +1242 322 8185
Email: stephen@bahamasferries.com
Chairman: Alan Wilson
Official Kit: Gold/Black – Aqua marine
Clubs: 4
Referees: 5
Secretary: Stephen Thompson
Players: 270
Founded: 1973
IRB Affiliation: 1996

Barbados

Name: BARBADOS R.F.U.
Address: The Plantation Complex, St Laurence, Main Road, Christ Church, BARBADOS
Tel: +1 246 437 3836
Fax: +1 246 437 3838
Email: brewer@sunbeach.net
Website: www.rugbybds.com
Chairman: Joe Whipple
Official Kit: Royal Blue/Yellow
Clubs: 5
Referees: 4
Secretary: Jason Brewer
Players: 613
Founded: 1965
IRB Affiliation: 1995

Belguim

Name: FEDERATION BELGE DE RUGBY
Address: Avenue de Marathon 135C, 1020 Brussels, BELGIUM
Tel: +32 2 479 9332
Fax: +32 2 476 22 82
Email: fbrb@rugby.be
Website: www.rugby.be
Chairman: Philipe Damas
Official Kit: Black/Yellow/Red
Clubs: 48
Coaches: 170
Referees: 84
Secretary: Danny Brunet
Players: 4968
Founded: 1931
IRB Affiliation: 1988

Bermuda

Name: BERMUDA R.F.U.
Address: P.O Box HM 1909, Hamilton, HM BX, BERMUDA
Tel: +1 441 236 8442
Fax: +1 441 292 4649
Email: dfw@rcm.bm
Email 2: d.cherry@ibl.bm
Chairman: David Worsfold
Official Kit: Sky blue/Black collar
Clubs: 6
Secretary: Jonathan Cassidy
Players: 285
Founded: 1964
IRB Affiliation: 1992

Bosnia & Herzegovina

Name: RAGBI SAVEZ BOSNE I HERCEGOVINE
Address: Bulevar Kralja Tvrtka 1, br 5, 72000 Zenica, BOSNIA & HERZEGOVINA
Tel: +387 32 41 6323
Fax: +387 32 41 6323
Email: rugbybih@bih.net.ba
Official Kit: Sky Blue
Clubs: 7
Coaches: 25
Referees: 37
Secretary: Mirza Kapic
Players: 732
Founded: 1992
IRB Affiliation: 1996

Botswana

Name: BOTSWANA R.U.
Address: P.O Box 1920, Gaborone, BOTSWANA
Tel: +267 395 1008
Fax: +267 397 2362
Email: botsrugby@botsnet.bw
Official Kit: Black
Clubs: 8
Referees: 12
Secretary: Bob Lekan
Players: 947
Founded: 1992
IRB Affiliation: 1994

Brazil

A B R

Name: BRAZILIAN RUGBY ASSOCIATION
Address: R. Da Germaine Burchard, 451 – s.53 – Agua Branca, 05002-62, Sao Paulo – SP, BRAZIL
Email: rugbybrasil@uol.com.br, abr@rugbynews.com.br
Tel: +55 11 3864 1336
Fax: +55 11 3868 1703
Email: office@brasilrugby.com.br
Email 2: joaonogueira@brasilrugby.com.br
Chairman: Jean Francois Teisseire
Official Kit: Yellow/Green
Clubs: 5
Secretary: Joao M Nogueira

Players: 1879
Founded: 1972
IRB Affiliation: 1995

British Virgin Islands

Name: BRITISH VIRGIN ISLANDS R.U.
Address: C/o Smith-Hughes Raworth and McKenzin, Box 173, Road Town, Tortola, BRITISH VIRGIN ISLANDS
Tel: 1 284 494 3384
Fax: 1 284 494 4643
Email: bmitchell@s-hrm.com
Chairman: Barry Mitchell
Official Kit: Green & White
Clubs: 2
Coaches: 2
Referees: 3
Secretary: Mike Pringle
Players: 90
Founded: 1965
IRB Affiliation: 2001 Assoc Membership

Bulgaria

Name: BULGARIAN RUGBY FEDERATION
Address: 75 Vassil Levski Blvd, 1040 Sofia, BULGARIA
Tel: +359 2 958 5847
Fax: +359 2 958 0137
Email: pmomchilova@yahoo.com
Official Kit: Red
Referees: 4
Secretary: George Marinkin
Players: 1720
Founded: 1962
IRB Affiliation: 1992

Cameroon

Name: Federation Camerounaise de Rugby
Address: PO Box 316, Yaounde, **Cameroon**
Tel: +237 230 5392
Fax: +237 230 5392
Email: biotech@iccnet.cm
Email 2: theophiletiekm@hotmail.com
Chairman: Simon Mamba A Nyam
Official Kit: Green
Clubs: 24
Referees: 35
Secretary: Theophile Tiek Mambo
Players: 1085
Founded: 1997
IRB Affiliation: 1999

Canada

Name: RUGBY CANADA
Address: Toronto Office, 40 Vogell Road, Suite 26, Richmond Hill, Ontario, L4B 3N6 CANADA
Tel: +1 905 780 8998
Fax: + 1 416 352 1243
Email: info@rugbycanada.ca
Website: www.rugbycanada.ca
Official Kit: Red/Black Red & White Stripe
Clubs: 9
Referees: 20
Players: 50200
Founded: 1965
IRB Affiliation: 1987

Cayman

Name: CAYMAN R.F.U.
Address: PO Box 1161, Georgetown, CAYMAN ISLANDS, B.W.I
Tel: +1 345 949 7960
Fax: +1 345 946 5786
Email: techdir@candw.ky
Website: www.caymanrugby.com
Chairman: Derek Haines
Official Kit: Red/White/Blue
Clubs: 430
Referees: 200
Secretary: Greg Link
Players: 1133
Founded: 1971
IRB Affiliation: 1977

Chile

Name: FEDERACION DE RUGBY DE CHILE
Address: Av. Larrain 11. 095, La Reina, Santiago, CHILE
Tel: +562 275 9314
Fax: +562 275 1248
Email: feruchi@ctcinternet.cl
Email 2: mujicac@directo.cl
Website: www.feruchi.cl
Chairman: Miguel A Mujica
Official Kit: Red
Clubs: 5
Referees: 6
Secretary: Bernard Santillan
Players: 13515
Founded: 1935
IRB Affiliation: 1991

Colombia

Name: UNION COLOMBIAN DE RUGBY
Address: Transversal 15 # 126a – 81, Apto 102, La Carolina, Bogota, COLOMBIA
Tel: +571 520 5236
Fax: +571 520 5235
Email: rianovic@col.net.co
Website: scorpions.simplement.com/columbia.htm
Chairman: William Nelson Paul
Official Kit: Yellow
Clubs: 15
Players: 588
IRB Affiliation: 1999

Cook Islands

Name: COOK ISLANDS R.F.U.
Address: P.O. Box 898, Rarotonga, COOK ISLANDS
Tel: +682 25854
Fax: +682 25853
Email: cirugby@rugby.co.ck
Website: www.rugby.co.ck
Official Kit: White/Gold/Green
Clubs: 18
Referees: 8
Secretary: Anthony Turua
Players: 1000
Founded: 1989
IRB Affiliation: 1995

Côte d'Ivoire

Name: FEDERATION IVOIRIENNE DE RUGBY
Address: 1 BP 2357 Abidjan, 1 CÔTE D'IVORIE
Tel: +225 2021 2083
Fax: +225 20347 107
Email: anomacamille@hotmail.com
Email 2: zmarcellin@yahoo.fr
Official Kit: Orange
Clubs: 10
Referees: 30
Secretary: Camille Anoma
Players: 5134
Founded: 1961
IRB Affiliation: 1988

Croatia

Name: HRVATSKI RAGBI SAVEZ
Address: Trg Sportova 11, 10000, Zagreb, CROATIA
Tel: +385 1 365 0250
Fax: +385 130 92921
Email: cro.rugby@zg.hinet.hr
Website: www.rugbyunion.cz
Chairman: Ivo Jurisic
Official Kit: Red & White
Clubs: 14
Coaches: 31
Referees: 15
Secretary: Velimir Juricko
Players: 1294
Founded: 1962
IRB Affiliation: 1992

Czech Rupublic

Name: CESKA RUGBYOVA UNIE
Address: Mezi Stadiony PS 40, 160 17 Praha 6, CZECH REPUBLIC
Tel: +42 02 33351 341
Fax: +42 02 33351 341
Email: rugby@cstv.cz
Website: www.rugbyunion.cz
Vice President: Jaroslav Micke
Official Kit: Red/White & Blue stripes
Clubs: 19
Referees: 56
Secretary: Juraj Razga
Players: 2564
Founded: 1926
IRB Affiliation: 1988

Denmark

Name: DANSK R.U.
Address: Idraettens Hus, Brondby Stadion, 20 DK-2605 Broendby, DENMARK
Tel: +4543262800
Fax: +4543262801
Email: info@rugby.dk
Website: www.rugby.dk
Chairman: Ole Nielsen
Official Kit: Red
Clubs: 30
Coaches: 139
Referees: 68
Secretary: Inger Marie Godvin
Players: 2357
Founded: 1950
IRB Affiliation: 1988

England

Name: THE R.F.U.
Address: Council Services Department, Rugby House, Rugby Road, Twickenham, TW1 1DS, ENGLAND
Tel: +44 208 892 2000
Fax: +44 208 892 9816
Email: reception@rfu.com
Website: www.rfu.com
Chairman: Graeme Cattermole
Official Kit: White/Red contrast
Clubs: 1900
Coaches: 6669
Referees: 8469
CEO: Francis Baron
Players: 626987
Founded: 1871
IRB Affiliation: 1890

Fiji

Name: FIJI R.U.
Address: 35 Gordon Street, PO Box 1234, Suva, FIJI
Tel: +679 3302 787
Fax: +679 3300 936
Email: fijirugby@connect.com.fj
Website: www.teivovo.com
Chairman: Keni Dakuidreketi
Official Kit: White/Black
Clubs: 1800
Referees: 4000
Players: 151839
Founded: 1913

IRB Affiliation: 1987

Finland

Name: FINNISH RUGBY FEDERATION
Address: Tommilantie 3B-15, Kangasala 36270, FINLAND
Tel: 0033 235 60 60 40
Email: christophecroze@yahoo.fr
Website: www.rugbyfinland.com
Chairman: Esa Launis
Vice Chairman: Jaako Vilen
Treasurer: Scott Fraser
Official Kit: Light Blue
Clubs: 7
Coaches: 17
Referees: 12
Secretary: Mikko Johannsson
Players: 148
Founded: 1968
IRB Affiliation: 2001

France

Name: FEDERATION FRANCISE DE RUGBY
Address: 9 Rue de Liege, 75009 Paris, FRANCE
Tel: 331 5321 1515
Fax: 331 4491 9109
Email: MDUHART@ffr.fr
Website: www.ffr.fr
Chairman: Bernard Lapasset
Official Kit: Blue
Clubs: 1720
Coaches: 14424
Referees: 2650
Secretary: Alain Doucet
Players: 222609
Founded: 1919
IRB Affiliation: 1978

Georgia

Name: GEORGIA R.U.
Address: 49A, Chavchavadze Ave, Sports Department, Tbilisi 62, GEORGIA
Tel: 995 32 29 47 54
Fax: 995 32 29 47 63
Email: gru@gol.ge
Email 2: choconap@wanadoo.fr
Official Kit: Black/Bordo/Grey
Clubs: 25
Referees: 20
Secretary: Michael Bourdzgla
Players: 2336
Founded: 1964
IRB Affiliation: 1992

Germany

Name: DEUTSCHER RUGBY VERBAND
Address: Postfach 1566, D-30015 Hannover, GERMANY
Tel: +49 511 14763
Fax: +49 511 1610206
Email: office@rugby-verband.de
Website: www.rugby.de
Chairman: Ian Rawcliffe
Official Kit: White/Black/Red/Yes
Clubs: 102
Coaches: 277
Referees: 117
Secretary: Volker Himmer
Players: 4200
Founded: 1900
IRB Affiliation: 1988

Guam

Name: GUAM R.F.U.
Address: PO Box 7246, Tamuning, GUAM, USA 96931
Tel: +1 671 477 7250
Fax: +1 671 472 1264
Email: guamrfu@ambyth.guam.net
Website: www.rugbyonguam.com
Chairman: Greg David
Treasurer: Stephen Grantham
Official Kit: White/Black/Yellow
Clubs: 102
Referees: 145
Secretary: Andrew Miller
Players: 71
Founded: 1997
IRB Affiliation: 1998

Guyana

Name: GUYANA R.F.U.
Address: P.O. Box 101730, Georgetown, REPUBLIC OF GUYANA
Tel: +592 623-8186
Fax: +592 226 0240
Email: guyanarugby@yahoo.com
Treasurer: Leonardo Butcher
Official Kit: Green & Gold
Clubs: 2
Referees: 6
Secretary: Terrence B Grant
Players: 290
Founded: 1920
IRB Affiliation: 1995

Hong Kong

Name: HONG KONG R.F.U.
Address: Rooms 2001, Sports House, 1 Stadium Path, So Kon Po, Causeway Bay, HONG KONG
Tel: +852 2504 8311

Fax: +852 2576 7237
Email: info@hkrugby.com
Website: www.hkrugby.com
Chairman: John Molloy
Executive Director: Allan Payne
Official Kit: Red/White/Blue stripes
Clubs: 4
Referees: 5
Secretary: Trevor Gregory
Players: 3565
Founded: 1953
IRB Affiliation: 1988

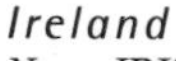

Hungary

Name: MAGYAR ROGBI SZOVETSEG
Address: Dozsa Gyorgy ut 1-3, H – 1143 Budapest 70.Pf.116, HUNGARY
Tel: +361 251 1222 ext. 1297
Fax: 00 36 1 471 43 35
Email: mrgsz@mrgsz.hu
Website: www.mrgsz.hu
Chairman: Tamas Fehervari
Official Kit: Red/Blue
Clubs: 15
Coaches: 31
Referees: 18
Secretary: Ria Ispanne
Players: 1549
Founded: 1990
IRB Affiliation: 1991

India

Name: INDIAN R.F.U.
Address: Nawab House, 2nd Flr, M. Karve 63 M K Road – Marine Lines, Mumbai, 400002, INDIA
Tel: +9122 2209 6357
Fax: +9122 2209 1822
Email: irfu_india@hotmail.com
Email 2: juzar.burmawala@irfu.org
Website: www.irfu.org
Treasurer: Maneck Unwala maneck.umwala@irfu.org
Chief Operating Officer: Juzar Burmwala juzar.burmawala@irfu.org
Official Kit: Light Blue & White
Clubs: 15
Referees: 25
Secretary: Chaitanya Sinh
Players: 5650
Founded: 1968
IRB Affiliation: 2001

Ireland

Name: IRISH R.F.U.
Address: 62 Lansdowne Road, Ballsbridge, Dublin 4, IRELAND
Tel: +353 1 647 3800
Fax: +353 1 647 3801
Email: info@irfu.ie
Website: www.irishrugby.ie
Chairman: John Hussey
Official Kit: Green & White
Clubs: 177
Referees: 970
Secretary: N/A
Total number female Players: 4500
Total number male Players: 47500
Founded: 1874
IRB Affiliation: 1886

Israel

Name: ISRAEL R.F.U.
Address: PO Box 560, Raanana 43104, ISRAEL
Tel: +972 9 7422 062
Fax: +972 9 7422062
Email: rugby@netvision.net.il
Official Kit: Blue & White
Clubs: 20
Coaches: 30
Referees: 18
Secretary: Cyril Morris
Players: 1290
Founded: 1971
IRB Affiliation: 1988

Italy

Name: FEDERAZIONE ITALIANA RUGBY
Address: Stadio Olimpico, Curva Nord, Foro Italico, 00194 Roma, ITALY
Tel: +39 06 36857 845
Fax: +39 06 36857 853
Email: federugby@atleticom.it
Website: www.rugbyitalia.com
Official Kit: Sky Blue
Clubs: 532
Coaches: 896
Referees: 527
Secretary: Guiliano Spingardi
Players: 38185
Founded: 1928
IRB Affiliation: 1987

Jamaica

Name: JAMAICA R.F.U.
Address: PO Box 144, Kingston 5, JAMICA
Tel: +1 876 925 6703
Fax: +1 876 931 1743
Email: thompson@n5.com.jm
Website: www.jru.org.jm
Chairman: Jacob Thompson
Official Kit: Gold/Black/Green

Clubs: 10
Secretary: Rohan Stewart
Players: 4495
Founded: 1946
IRB Affiliation: 1996

Japan

Name: JAPAN R.F.U.
Address: 8-35 Kitaaoyama, 2 Chome, Minatoku, Tokyo 107-0061, JAPAN
Tel: +813 3401 3323
Fax: +813 5410 5523
Email: jrfu@rugby-japan.or.jp
Email 2: tokumasu@rugby-japan.or.jp
Website: www.rugby-japan.or.jp
Chairman: Nobby Mashimo
Official Kit: White & Red stripes
Clubs: 4050
Secretary: Koji Tokumasu
Players: 130476
Founded: 1926
IRB Affiliation: 1987

Kazakhstan

Name: KAZAKHSTAN R.F.U.
Address: Apt. 4, 7 Kashgarskaya Street, 480091 Almaty, KAZAKHSTAN
Tel: +7 327 2 32 75 39
Fax: +7 327 2 32 7539
Email: kaz_rugby@nursat.kz
Chairman: Stanislav Knorr
Official Kit: Yellow
Clubs: 14
Players: 5860
Founded: 1993
IRB Affiliation: 1997

Kenya

Name: KENYA RFU
Address: Ngong Road, P.O. Box 48322, 00100, Nairobi, KENYA
Tel: + 254 2 562065/574425
Fax: + 254 2 574425
Email: krfu@iconnect.co.ke
Website: www.kenyarfu.com
Official Kit: Black/Red/Green
Clubs: 18
Secretary: Aggrey Chabeda
Players: 6990
Founded: 1923
IRB Affiliation: 1990

Korea

Name: KOREA R.U.
Address: Olympic Building, 88 Oryun-Dong, Songpa-Gu, Seoul, KOREA
Tel: +822 420 4244
Fax: +822 420 4246
Email: rugby@sports.or.kr
Executive Director: Won Jong-Chun
Official Kit: Red&Blue stripes/White
Clubs: 65
Secretary: Kim Jae-Taek
Players: 1672
Founded: 1945
IRB Affiliation: 1988

Latvia

Name: LATVIAN RUGBY FEDERATION
Address: Pulkv.Brieza Str.19/1, RIGA, LV-1010, LATVIA
Tel: +371 722 0320
Fax: +371 732 0180
Email: andrisd@mail.bkc.lv
Email 2: pasts.bbl@delfi.lv
Chairman: Andris Dennis
Official Kit: Dark Red
Clubs: 7
Coaches: 15
Referees: 15
Secretary: Gunars Perlbahs
Players: 489
Founded: 1960
IRB Affiliation: 1991

Lithuania

Name: FEDERATION LITHUANIENNE DE RUGBY
Address: 6 rue Zemaites, Vilnius 2600, LITHUANIA
Tel: +37 02 335 474/429036
Fax: +37 02 335 474
Email: litrugby@takas.lt
Chairman: Aleksandras Makarenka
Official Kit: Green
Clubs: 14
Coaches: 24
Referees: 21
Secretary: Alfonsas A Grumbinas
Players: 1560
Founded: 1961
IRB Affiliation: 1992

Luxembourg

Name: FEDERATION LUXEMBOURGEOISE DE RUGBY
Address: 14 Avenue de la Gare, Boite Postale 1965, L-1410 LUXEMBOURG
Tel: +352 29 7598
Fax: +352 29 7598
Email: moitilu@pt.lu
Website: www.rugby.lu
Vice President: Bernard Jargeac
Treasurer: John Watson
Official Kit: Sky Blue & white horozontal stripes
Clubs: 3
Coaches: 35

Referees: 3
Secretary: Luis Moitinho
Players: 518
Founded: 1974
IRB Affiliation: 1991

Madagascar

Name: FEDERATION MALGACHE DE RUGBY
Address: 12, Avenue Lenine, Lot 1VD 26 Ambatomitsangaria, Antananarivo, MADAGASCAR
Tel: +261 20 22 625 60
Fax: +261 20 22 623 73
Email: fmr-rugby@dts.mg
Email 2: ratsara@dts.mg
Official Kit: White/Green/Red
Clubs: 198
Secretary: Samuel Rakotomamonjy
Players: 11000
Founded: 1963
IRB Affiliation: 1998

Malaysia

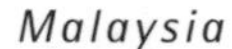

Name: MALAYSIAN R.U.
Address: Suite 1.12, Wisma OCM, Hang Jebat Road, 50150 Kuala Lumpar, MALAYSIA
Tel: +603 2078 8335
Fax: +603 2078 8336
Email: mru1985@yahoo.com
Official Kit: Blue/Yellow/Red
Clubs: 185
Referees: 230
Secretary: Msuhaimi Zainuddin
Players: 17280
Founded: 1927
IRB Affiliation: 1988

Malta

Name: MALTA R.F.U.
Address: 76A Gorg Borg Olivier Street, St Julian's STJ 08, MALTA
Tel: +356 21 380 440
Fax: +356 21 380 446
Email: secretary@mrfu.org
Email 2: president@mrfu.org
Website: www.maltarugby.com
Treasurer: Gordon Craig
Official Kit: Black/White/Red
Clubs: 185
Secretary: Christopher Martin
Players: 1411
Founded: 1991
IRB Affiliation: 2000

Moldova

Name: RUGBY FEDERATION OF MOLDOVA
Address: Str Columna 106, Chisinau, REPUBLICA MOLDOVA, MD 2012
Tel: +3 73 222 674
Fax: +3 73 222 674
Email: rugbymold@yahoo.com
Official Kit: Red
Clubs: 4
Coaches: 46
Referees: 4
Secretary: Oleg Sadovici
Total number female Players: 60
Total number male Players: 1190
Founded: 1992
IRB Affiliation: 1994

Monaco

Name: FEDERATION MONEGASQUE DE RUGBY
Address: 5, Ruelle St Jean, MC-98000 PRINCIPAUTE DE MONACO
Tel: +377 97 77 1568
Fax: 377 9325 7557
Email: fmr@monaco-rugby.com
Email 2: carine.impellizzeri@mimonaco.mc
Website: www.monacorugby.com
Chairman: Cedric Nardi
Official Kit: White & Red
Clubs: 1
Coaches: 10
Referees: 2
Secretary: Carine Impellizzeri
Players: 241
Founded: 1996
IRB Affiliation: 1998

Morocco

Name: FEDERATION ROYALE MAROCAINE DE RUGBY
Address: Complexe Sportif Mohamed V, Porte 9, Casablanca, MOROCCO
Tel: +212 22 94 82 47
Fax: +212 22 36 90 60
Email: frmr@menara.ma
Official Kit: Red/Green
Clubs: 24
Referees: 120
Secretary: Chougred Mohamed
Players: 8650
Founded: 1956
IRB Affiliation: 1988

Namibia

Name: NAMIBIA R.U.
Address: Lichtenstein Street, Olympia, Windhoek, NAMIBIA
Tel: +264 61251 775
Fax: +264 61 251 028
Email: nru@cyberhost.com.na
Website: www.geocities.com/VNamRugby
Vice President: Mr. Brian Stiger
Official Kit: Royal Blue/Red & White Stripes
Clubs: 19
Referees: 25
Secretary: Paulina Gideon
Players: 11675
Founded: 1990
IRB Affiliation: 1990

Netherlands

Name: NETHERLANDS RUGBY BOND
Address: National Rugby Stadium Amsterdam, Sportpark de Eedracht, PO Bix 8811, Amsterdam, 1006 JA NETHERLANDS
Tel: +31 20 4808100
Fax: +31 20 4808101
Email: info@rugby.nl
Website: www.rugby.nl
Chairman: Ab Ekels
Director: Joap Van Ommeren
Office Manager: Joyce van Eck
Official Kit: Orange
Clubs: 87
Coaches: 30
Referees: 83
Secretary: Anton Nuyten
Players: 7425
Founded: 1932
IRB Affiliation: 1988

New Zealand

Name: New Zealand R. F. U.
Address: New Zealand, 1 Hinemoa Street, CentrePort, P.O Box 2172, Wellington, New Zealand
Tel: +644 499 4995
Fax: +644 499 4224
Email: info@nzrugby.co.nz
Email 2: cath.ingram@nzrugby.co.nz
Website: www.nzrugby.com
Chairman: Jock Hobbs
Official Kit: Black
Clubs: 520
Referees: 2384
Players: 120069
Founded: 1892
IRB Affiliation: 1949

Nigeria

Name: NIGERIA RUGBY FOOTBALL ASSOCIATION
Address: National Stadium, PO Box 1381 Marina, Lagos, NIGERIA
Tel: +234 01 585 0529
Fax: 234 01 585 0530
Email: nigeriarugby@yahoo.com
Email 2: nrfa1998@yahoo.com
Email 3: ntiensewills@yahoo.com
Treasurer: Mrs. Alawiyeda
Chairman: Joshua Madaki RTD
Official Kit: Green
Clubs: 16
Referees: 8
Secretary: Adeniyi Beyioku
Players: 2720
Founded: 1998
IRB Affiliation: 2001

Niue Island

Name: NIUE R.F.U.
Address: PO Box 11, Alofi, NIUE ISLAND
Tel: +683 4153
Fax: +683 4322
Email: tokes@niue.nu
Website: nru.virtualave.net/
Official Kit: Gold & Navy Blue Stripes
Clubs: 11
Secretary: Norman Mitimeti
Players: 440
Founded: 1952
IRB Affiliation: 1999

Norway

Name: NORWEGIAN R.U.
Address: Serviceboks 1 Ullevaal stadion, N-0840 Oslo, NORWAY
Tel: +47 21 02 98 45
Fax: +47 21 02 98 46
Email: rugby@nif.idrett.no
Website: www.rugby.no
Official Kit: Red/White/light & Navy Blue
Clubs: 22
Coaches: 29
Referees: 18
Secretary: Kim J More Eriksen
Players: 750
Founded: 1982
IRB Affiliation: 1993

Papua New Guinea

Name: PAPUA NEW GUINEA R.F.U.
Address: Shop Front 2, Gateway Hotel, Morea-Tobo Road, P.O. Box 864, Port Moresby, PAPUA NEW GUINEA

Tel: +675 323 4212
Fax: +675 323 4211
Email: rugbypng@global.net.pg
Email 2: rugbypng@datec.com.pg
Official Kit: Black/Red/Yellow
Clubs: 57
Coaches: 30
Referees: 40
Secretary: Tony Francis
Players: 3100
Founded: 1963
IRB Affiliation: 1993

Paraguay

Name: UNION DE RUGBY DEL PARAGUAY
Address: Independencia Nacional 250 casi Palma 1er Piso Asuncion, PARAGUAY
Tel: +595 21 496 390
Fax: +595 21 496 390
Email: urprugby@pla.net.py
Official Kit: Red & White Stripes
Referees: 11
Secretary: Jorge Benitez
Players: 1975
Founded: 1970
IRB Affiliation: 1989

People's Republic of China

Name: CHINESE RUGBY FOOTBALL ASSOCIATON
Address: 5 Tiyuguan Road,Beijing 100763, PEOPLE'S REPUBLIC OF CHINA
Tel: +86 10 8582 6002
Fax: +86 10 8582 5994
Email: cga_cra@263.net
Official Kit: Red & Yellow Stripes
Clubs: 144
Referees: 80
Secretary: Li Gaochao
Players: 4330
Founded: 1996
IRB Affiliation: 1997

Peru

Name: UNION PERUANA DE RUGBY
Address: Malecón Cisneros 580, Lima 18, PERU
Tel: +51 1 241 2349
Fax: +51 1 241 3846
Email: mreyes@wayna.rcp.net.pe
Official Kit: White & Red Collar
Referees: 8
Secretary: Carlos Hamann
Players: 722
Founded: 1997
IRB Affiliation: 1999

Poland

POLSKI ZWIAZEK RUGBY

Name: POLSKI ZWIAZEK RUGBY
Address: Marymoncka 34, 01-813 Warszawa, POLAND
Tel: 48 22 835 3587
Fax: 48 22 835 3587
Email: pzrugby@onet.pl
Email 2: jga@interia.pl
Website: www.pzrugby.republika.pl
Clubs: 26
Coaches: 79
Referees: 33
Secretary: Grzergorz Borkowski
Players: 2350
IRB Affiliation: 1988

Portugal

FPR

Name: FEDERACAO PORTUGUESA DE RUGBY
Address: Rua Julieta Ferarao 12-3, Sala 303, 1600-131 Lisboa, PORTUGAL
Tel: +351 21 799 1690
Fax: +351 21 793 6135
Email: geral@fpr.pt
Website: www.fpr.pt
Treasurer: Jose Luis Silveira Botelho
Development Officer: Olgario Borges
Official Kit: Red & White
Clubs: 57
Coaches: 44
Referees: 49
Secretary: Delfim Barriera
Players: 3615
Founded: 1926
IRB Affiliation: 1988

Romania

Name: FEDERATIA ROMANA DE RUGBY
Address:, Bd. Marasti, No. 18-20, Sector 1, Bucaresti, ROMANIA
Tel: +40 2 1 224 26 28
Fax: +40 2 1224 54 81
Email: frr@frr.ro
Website: www.frr.ro
Official Kit: Yellow/Blue/Red
Clubs: 52
Referees: 102
Secretary: Silvia Theodorescu
Players: 3923
Founded: 1931
IRB Affiliation: 1997

Russia

Name: R.U. OF RUSSIA
Address:, 24 Lenina Street, Krasnoyarsk, 660049, RUSSIA
Tel: 7 3912 224 303
Fax: 7 3912 279 760
Email: info@rugby.ru
Email 2: secretar@rugby.ru
Website: www.rugby.ru
Official Kit: White/Blue/Red
Referees: 40
Secretary: Dmitri Morozov
Players: 9660
Founded: 1936
IRB Affiliation: 1990

Samoa

Name: SAMOA R.F.U.
Address: Cross Island Road, Malifa, P.O. Box 618, Apia, SAMOA
Tel: 685 26 792
Fax: 685 25 009
Email: srfu@samoa.ws
Email 2: saipele@samoa.ws
Email 3: ManuSamoa@xtra.co.nz
Chairman: Tuileapa Sailele Malielegaoi
Official Kit: Royal Blue & White
Secretary: Tauiliili Hary Schuster
Players: 16376
Founded: 1924
IRB Affiliation: 1988

Scotland

SCOTTISH RUGBY UNION

Name: SCOTLAND R.U.
Address: FAO Bill Hogg, Secretary, Murrayfield, Edinburgh EH12 5PJ, SCOTLAND
Tel: 44 131 346 5000
Fax: 44 131 346 5001
Email: Bill.Hogg@sru.org.uk
Email 2: feedback@sru.org.uk
Website: www.sru.org.uk
Chairman: Ken C Scobie
Official Kit: Marine Blue & Purple Stripe
Clubs: 242
Coaches: 330
Referees: 320
Secretary: IAL Hogg
Players: 78580
Founded: 1873
IRB Affiliation: 1886

Senegal

Name: FEDERATION SENEGALAISE DE RUGBY
Address: 73 rue Amadou Ndoye Dakar, SENEGAL
Tel: 221 821 5858
Fax: 221 821 8651
Email: guedel.ndiaye@sentoo.sn
Official Kit: Green
Secretary: Kebe Biram
Players: 510
Founded: 1960
IRB Affiliation: 1999

Serbia and Montenegro

Name: R.U. OF SERBIA AND MONTENEGRO
Address: Terazije 35/111, PO Box 1013, 11000 Belgrade, YUGOSLAVIA
Tel: +381 11 324 5743
Fax: +381 11 324 5743
Email: rugbyoffice@ptt.yu
Email 2: rugbyoffice@ptt.yu
Official Kit: Blue/Black/Green
Clubs: 15
Coaches: 60
Referees: 16
Secretary: Bijlana Milosevic
Total number male Players: 4800
Founded: 1954
IRB Affiliation: 1988

Singapore

Name: SINGAPORE R.U.
Address: Tao Payoh Swimming Complex, #02-04,301 Tao Payoh Lor.6, Singapore 319 392, SINGAPORE
Tel: 65 467 4038/6469 5955
Fax: 65 467 0283
Email: sru@pacific.net.sg
Email 2: keith.martin@amec.com
Website: www.sru.org.sg
General Manager: Ridzal Saat (gm.sru@pacific.net.sg
Official Kit: Red/White
Secretary: Tay Huai Eng
Players: 6680
Founded: 1948
IRB Affiliation: 1989

Slovenia

Name: RUGBY ZVEZA SLOVENIJE
Address: Pod hribom 55, 1000 Ljubljana, SLOVENIJA
Tel: +386 1 5076 377
Fax: +386 1 5076 377
Email: nikola.popadic@email.si
Website: www.rugby-zvenza-sovenije.si
Chairman: Mitja Rezar
Official Kit: Blue
Clubs: 7
Coaches: 25
Referees: 14
Secretary: Nikola Popadic
Players: 715
Founded: 1989
IRB Affiliation: 1996

Solomon Islands

Name: SOLOMON ISLANDS R.U. FEDERATION
Address: PO Box 642, Honaria, SOLOMON ISLANDS
Tel: 677 21595
Fax: 677 21596
Email: dbsi@welkam.solomon.com.sb
Official Kit: Royal Blue, Gold & Green stripes
Secretary: Jay Kabei
Players: 820
Founded: 1963
IRB Affiliation: 1999

South Africa

Name: SOUTH AFRICAN R.F.U.
Address: Boundary Road, PO Box, 99, Newlands 7725, Cape Town, SOUTH AFRICA
Tel: 2721 659 6900
Fax: 2721 685 6771
Email: sarfu@icon.co.za
Website: www.sarugby.net
Chairman: Silas Nkanunu
SA RUGBY: Rian Oberholzer
Official Kit: Green & Gold
Players: 582635
Founded: 1889
IRB Affiliation: 1949

Spain

Name: FEDERACION ESPANOLA DE RUGBY
Address: Ferraz 16-4, 28008 Madrid, SPAIN
Tel: 34 91 5414978
Fax: 34 91 5590986
Email: secretaria@ferugby.com
Email 2: prensa@ferugby.com
Email 3: tesoreria@ferugby.com
Website: www.ferugby.com
Chairman: Alfonso Mandalo Vasquez
Official Kit: Red/Yellow/Blue
Clubs: 179
Coaches: 446
Referees: 187
Secretary: Jose M Moreno
Players: 15468
Founded: 1923
IRB Affiliation: 1988

Sri Lanka

Name: SRI LANKA R.F.U.
Address: 7 A Reid Avenue, Colombo 07, SRI LANKA
Tel: +941 66 73 21
Fax: +941 66 73 20
Email: slrfu@dyna.web.lk
Treasurer: Shantha Kurumbalapitiya
Vice President: Priyantha Ekanayaka
Official Kit: Green
Clubs: 30
Referees: 175
Secretary: Group Captain Nalin de Silva
Players: 94525
Founded: 1908
IRB Affiliation: 1988

St. Lucia

Name: ST. LUCIA R.F.U.
Address: Union Hill Top, Castries, ST. LUCIA
Tel: 1 758 45 03896
Fax: 1 758 45 24728
Email: scolvis@hotmail.com
Official Kit: Blue/White/Yellow
Secretary: Christopher Wyatt
Players: 157
Founded: 1996
IRB Affiliation: 1996

St. Vincent &The Grenadines

Name: ST. VINCENT & THE GRENADINES R.U.F.C.
Address: PO Box 1034, Kingstown, ST. VINCENT & THE GRENADINES
Tel: 1 784 457 5135
Fax: 1 784 457 4396
Email: peakcons@caribsurf.com
Website: www.svrugby.islandmix.com
Chairman: Kelly Glass
Official Kit: Olive Green/Blue quarters
Secretary: Jacquie De Freitas
Players: 380
Founded: 1998
IRB Affiliation: 2003

Swaziland

Name: SWAZILAND R.U.
Address: c/o Homecentre 8 Mhlakuvane Street, Manzini, SWAZILAND
Tel: +268 40 40 740
Fax: +268 505 2886
Email: swazirugby@africaonline.co.sz
Email 2: lindac@africaonline.co.sz
Official Kit: White/Blue, red, yellow stripes
Secretary: Linda Collinson
Players: 633
Founded: 1995
IRB Affiliation: 1998

Sweden

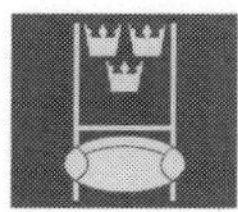

Name: SVENSKA RUGBY FORBUNDET
Address: Idrottens Hus, S-123 87 Farsta, SWEDEN
Tel: 468 605 6524
Fax: 468 605 6527

Email: gs@rugby.rf.se
Website: www.rugby.se
Chairman: Lars Ohlsson
Official Kit: Yellow/Blue
Clubs: 48
Coaches: 45
Referees: 25
Secretary: Torbjorn Johannson
Players: 2920
Founded: 1932
IRB Affiliation: 1988

Switzerland

Name: SWISS R.U.
Address: General Secretary, Pavillonweg 3, CH 3012 Bern, SWITZERLAND
Tel: 41 31 301 23 88
Fax: 41 31 301 23 88
Email: fsr@rugby.ch
Website: www.rugby.ch
Chairman: Luc Baatard
Official Kit: White
Clubs: 20
Coaches: 125
Referees: 25
Secretary: Norbert Li Marchetti
Players: 1870
Founded: 1972
IRB Affiliation: 1988

Tahiti

Name: FEDERATION TAHITIENNE DE RUGBY DE POLYNESIE FRANCAISE
Address: B.P. 650 Papeete, 98714 Papeete, TAHITI (FRENCH POLYNESIA)
Tel: 689 48 12 28/689 42 04 10
Fax: 689 48 12 28/589 42 3131
Email: tahitirugby@mail.pf
Official Kit: Red
Players: 632
Founded: 1989
IRB Affiliation: 1994

Tapei Chinese

Name: CHINESE TAIPEI R.F.U.
Address: Room 808, 8F N020, Chu Lun Street, Taipei 104, TAIWAN, REPUBLIC OF CHINA
Tel: +886 2877 22 159/167
Fax: +886 2877 22 171
Email: rocrugby@ms37.hinet.net
Chairman: Tsai Cheng Wei
Official Kit: Blue/White
Clubs: 30
Secretary: Lin Ching Chung
Players: 1600
Founded: 1946
IRB Affiliation: 1986

Thailand

Name: THAI R.U.
Address: National Stadium, Rama 1 Rd., BKK 10330, THAILAND
Tel: 662 215 3839
Fax: 662 214 17 12
Email: info@thairugby.com
Website: www.thairugby.com
President: Manessilpa Pong
Official Kit: Yellow/Royal Blue
Secretary: Thean-anant Somchai
Players: 3350
Founded: 1938
IRB Affiliation: 1989

Tonga

Name: TONGA R.F.U.
Address: P.O. Box 369, Nuku'alofa, KINGDOM OF TONGA
Tel: 676 26 045
Fax: 676 26 044
Email: tongarfu@kalianet.to
Chairman: Hon Tuivanuavou Vaca
Official Kit: Red and White Collar
Players: 5271
Founded: 1923
IRB Affiliation: 1987

Trinidad and Tobago

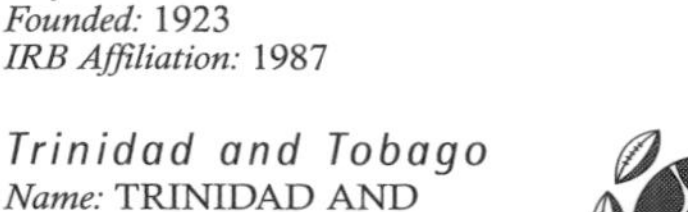

Name: TRINIDAD AND TOBAGO R.F.U.
Address: PO Box 5090, TT Post, Wrighton Road, Port of Spain, Trinidad 75009, TRINIDAD AND TOBAGO
Tel: 1 868 628 9048
Fax: 1 868 628 9049
Email: contact@ttrfu.com
Website: www.ttrfu.com
Vice President: Anthony Loregnard
Official Kit: Red/Black/White
Secretary: Brian Lewis
Players: 3070
Founded: 1928
IRB Affiliation: 1992

Tunisia

Name: FEDERATION TUNISIENNE DE RUGBY
Address: Boite Postale 318 – 1004, El Menzah, Tunis, TUNISIA
Tel: 216 7175 5066
Fax: 216 71 751 737
Email: ftrfhachicha@gnet.tn
Email 2: fethach@planet.tn
Official Kit: White & Red high neck and sleeves
Secretary: Nejib Boukottaya
Players: 2882
Founded: 1972

IRB Affiliation: 1988

Uganda

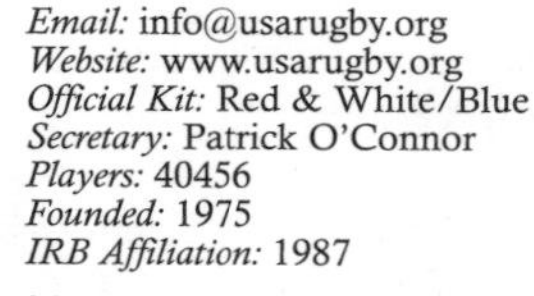

Name: UGANDA R.U.
Address: PO Box 22108, Kampala, UGANDA
Tel: +256 41 259 280
Fax: +256 41 259 290
Email: urfu@africaonline.co.ug
Website: www.urfu.org
Treasurer: Umah Tete Patrick
Chairman: Paul Wanyama Sigombe
Official Kit: Sky Blue/Yellow Stripes
Secretary: Stephen Paul Ojambo
Players: 2700
Founded: 1955
IRB Affiliation: 1977

Ukraine

Name: NATIONAL RUGBY FEDERATION OF UKRAINE
Address: 01023, Kyiv, 42, rue Esplanadna, UKRAINE
Tel: +380 44 220 6748
Fax: +380 44 246 4365
Email: igtko@yahoo.com
Email 2: malyuga@noc-ukr.org
Website: www.rugby.ua
Official Kit: Sky blue/Yellow Stripes
Secretary: Mykhailo Kyslyak
Players: 2050
Founded: 1991
IRB Affiliation: 1992

Uruguay

Name: UNION DE RUGBY DEL URUGUAY
Address: Bulevard Artigas 420, Montevideo, URUGUAY
Tel: +5982 712 3826/3648
Fax: +5982 712 916 6081
Email: uru@uru.org.uy
Website: www.uru.org.uy
Official Kit: Sky Blue
Secretary: Juan Minut
Players: 3960
Founded: 1951
IRB Affiliation: 1989

USA

Name: USA R.F.U.
Address: Suite M – 2, 3595 E. Fountain Boulevard, Colorado Springs, Colorado 80910, USA, (or) USA National Rugby Team, 2802 10th Street, Berkeley, CA 94710
USA Rugby Team Director: Scott Compton
Vice President: Bob Latham
Tel: +1 719 637 1022
Fax: +1 719 637 1315
Email: info@usarugby.org
Website: www.usarugby.org
Official Kit: Red & White/Blue
Secretary: Patrick O'Connor
Players: 40456
Founded: 1975
IRB Affiliation: 1987

Vanuatu

Name: VANUATU R.F.U.
Address: PO Box 284/1584, Port Vila, VANUATU
Tel: +678 424 93
Fax: +678 235 29
Email: vanuaturugby@vanuatu.com.vu
Email 2: mdunn@vanuatu.com
Vice President: Virasen Bakokoto
fficial Kit: Green/Yellow/Red & Black
Secretary: Brian Fong
Players: 1500
Founded: 1980
IRB Affiliation: 1999

Venezuela

Name: FEDERACION VENEZOLANA DE RUGBY AMATEUR
Address: AV Las Terrazas, Quinta la Quintana, Urb Santa Ines, #85, Caracas, VENEZUELA
Tel: +582 12 9791650
Fax: +582 12 256 1550
Email: rugbyven@hotmail.com
Email 2: bermudej@helios.com.ve
Email 3: rugbyven@hotmail.com
Chairman: Jorge Pesantes Y
Vice President: Mauricio Arevalo marevalo@telcel.net.ve
Official Kit: Red Wine
Secretary: Jorge Lobo
Players: 970
Founded: 1991
IRB Affiliation: 1998

Wales

Name: WELSH R.U.
Address: 1st Floor Golate House, 101 St. Mary's Street, Cardiff CF10 1GE, WALES
Tel: +44 2920 822 000
Fax: +44 2920 822 474
Email: info@wru.co.uk
Email 2: info@cardiff-stadium.co.uk
Website: www.wru.co.uk
Chairman: David Pickering
CEO: David Moffett
Official Kit: Red
Clubs: 239
Coaches: 8000
Referees: 180
Players: 55500
Founded: 1881
IRB Affiliation: 1886

Zambia

Name: ZAMBIA R.F.U.
Address: Room 116, 1st Floor Sanlam Building, Oxford venue, PO Box 21797, Kitwe, ZAMBIA
Tel: +260 2 23 1604
Fax: +260 2 23 1861
Email: zrfu@coppernet.zm
Official Kit: Green/Black Red & Gold Stripes
Secretary: Chibuye Rodgers
Players: 4800
Founded: 1975
IRB Affiliation: 1995

Zimbabwe

Name: ZIMBABWE R.F.U.
Address: Harare Sports Club, PO Box 1129, Harare, ZIMBABWE
Tel: +263 4 251 886/7/8
Fax: +263 4 790 914
Email: janice@rugby.co.zw
Website: www.zimrugby.com
National Development Manager: E Zigarwe
Vice President: Byrn Williams
Official Kit: Green & White Hoops
Secretary: Janice Johnny
Players: 35159
Founded: 1895
IRB Affiliation: 1987